Communities Directory

A Guide to Intentional Communities
and Cooperative Living

Communities Directory

A Guide to Intentional Communities and Cooperative Living

ⓑ

2000 Edition

Published by
Fellowship for Intentional Community
Rutledge, Missouri

ISBN 0-9602714-8-1

Third Edition, First Printing, March 2000

Printed by Sheridan Group, Ann Arbor, Michigan, on 30 percent post-consumer recycled paper with soy-based inks.

Article copyright information:

"Spiritual Community of Many Faiths: The Challenge Is to Love", by Stevie Abbot-Richards
 An older version of this article was originally printed in the Lama Foundation newsletter,
 Fall 1998 issue, "Lama Alive." It was updated and printed with permission.

"The Desire for Diversity: A Cohousing Perspective", by Zev Paiss
 Originally printed in *Communities* magazine, issue number 85, this was updated and printed with permission.

"Six Ingredients for Forming Communities (That Help Reduce Conflict Down the Road)",
 by Diana Leafe Christian, © Diana Leafe Christian, written for the *Directory*.

"In Community, Intentionally", by Geoph Kozeny, © Geoph Kozeny, written for the *Directory*.

Front cover and spine photos courtesy of (and © copyright): Jillian Downey, Elph Morgan, Barry Munger (4th column, 1st photo),
 and the Twin Oaks archives (4th column, 3rd photo)

Back cover photos courtesy of (and © copyright): Jillian Downey, Jesse Moorman (2nd photo),
 and the Dancing Rabbit archives (5th photo)

Cover design and layout: Heidi Dailey

Layout design: Jillian Downey and Elph Morgan

How to Use This Directory

Looking for Information (or Insights) on Community?
Enjoy the broad spectrum of information in the Articles section. Be sure to use the Article Index in the Appendix if you're looking for information on a specific concept.

Looking for Books on Community?
See the annotated Recommended Reading List, organized by subject category for ease of use.

Looking for a Resource Organization or Network?
See the community Resources section. The resources are organized alphabetically and by subject area.

Looking for a Community?
The most direct path to choose in using this directory will depend on:
• what you already know about (or seek in) a community,
• whether you're looking for a specific group (one you already know something about), or
• if you're interested in any group that satisfies a number of characteristics.

Do You Know the Name?
Look for a description in the Community Listings, and in the Cross-Reference Chart (sorted alphabetically by community name).

Do You Know the Geographic Region?
Look at the Maps (p. 148) to locate the North American groups in this directory. For all communities worldwide you can check the Key to Communities by Country/State/Province (p. 160).

Do You Know Some Defining Characteristics?
Examine the Cross-Reference Chart (p. 163). Hopefully, the specific characteristics you're seeking are among those reviewed in the chart. If a desired characteristic does not appear in the chart, try locating relevant keywords in the Community Listings Keyword Index (p. 435), in the Appendix.

Still Can't Find It?
If you followed the steps outlined above and were not successful, we suggest you write or call the Fellowship for Intentional Community (FIC), publishers of this directory, with your specific request. The FIC's database of intentional communities is quite extensive—not all choose to list in the *Directory*. Plus, The FIC has file cabinets full of resource information. Instructions on contacting the FIC for further information or services are provided in the Appendix (p. 455).

Want to Keep Your *Directory* Information Current?
In addition to the *Directory*, the FIC publishes *Communities* magazine. A regular feature of this quarterly is a "Directory Update" section, where we include all the new and revised listings that we collect over the three months between issues. See the colored tear-out cards at the back for subscription information.

Another choice is to purchase annual supplements to the *Directory*. For a one-time fee of $5, we'll send you annual compilations of all the new and revised community listings, for as long as this edition lasts. See the colored tear-out card at the back of the book.

Finally—you may have information about a group that we don't know about. If so, please let us know! We'd like to invite their participation in future printings. Please use the form on the last page of the book to share any new leads you have, or email us at directory@ic.org. Thanks!

☙ **Planning to visit some communities?**
Be sure to read the article "Red Carpets and Slammed Doors," by Geoph Kozeny, in the first section, for information on how to go about it.

☙ **Looking for more information about a specific community than what is available in the *Directory*?**
The FIC, the publishers of the *Directory*, may have more information to share; see the Feedback page in the Appendix to find out how to check.

☙ **Already visited some communities, and have some feedback about them to share with the FIC?**
Whether the information you have is glowing or critical, the FIC would like to hear from you—see the Feedback page in the Appendix and it will tell you how.

Table of Contents

State of the Communities Movement

Good Things Come in Threes

by Laird Schaub
Executive Secretary, Fellowship for Intentional Community

*I*F THREE IS YOUR NUMBER, this may be your lucky book. Welcome to the Fellowship for Intentional Community's third edition of the *Communities Directory*. Each of the prior two editions sold out three printings, and this fresh version arrives in the third month of the third millennium after Christ (whose early disciples were committed communitarians—check out Acts 2:44–45). Whether you've seen all three books or this is your first peek, it's an exciting time to be looking at community.

Separating the Forest From the Threes

Interest in community living comes in waves, and we've been recording high tides all through the 1990s. While no decade is devoid of community building (this *Directory* lists at least one community starting in every decade of the last century and one in every year going back to 1960), some stand out as more potent than others. Prior to the current surge, the surf was last up in the late '60s and early '70s, with the advent of the Flower Children. Before that it was the student co-ops and pacifists of the '30s and '40s.

At every point in time, the attrition has been high. Most communities fail before their fifth birthday. Rebellious youth get older, have kids, and set aside their dreams of a cooperative future. Actually *living* cooperatively turns out to be a great deal more challenging than naming what you didn't like about the mainstream. There are still dishes to wash, diapers to change, and money to be earned. Unresolved conflicts erode idealism and many groups dissolve.

Still, some survive their naive, idealistic beginnings and become an inspiration for the next generation of pioneers. Through a combination of stubbornness, deep pockets, and plain old luck, groups get the hang of listening to each other and working through differences to find common ground. They start learning how to make decisions that pull people together instead of apart.

Seeing this work, it was only natural that some would want to extend cooperation *within* communities to cooperation *among* communities ... and life was breathed into the Fellowship in 1986, to create a forum for exploring common issues and act as a clearinghouse for information about community options.

Always, there are new starts. Some blaze new ground; others search for what has gone before, to serve as a blueprint for what might work today. Immersed in the Information Age, it has never been easier to access the nuggets of wisdom mined by other groups—something the Fellowship has played no small part in abetting.

Today, whether you're a seeker, a reporter, a researcher, or a concerned parent, if you have a question about intentional communities, there's an FIC number you can call, a Web site to visit, and a thick, user-friendly directory to consult. Fifteen years ago, those didn't exist.

Movement Trends

Ten years into the current wave, intentional communities appear to be keeping abreast with demand through new starts and new buildings. While growth is not strong everywhere, many segments of the movement are recording high water marks: student co-ops are on the rise, the Federation of Egalitarian Communities (FEC) has more affiliated groups than ever, and the cohousing movement continues its steady growth (with 42 communities built as of fall 1999, and over 160 in planning or construction). It seems that the largest unmet demand is with ecovillages, around which there is much buzz, but not yet many buildings.

Even as the growth in *intentional* communities is being accommodated, the flood of community interest is spreading to the mainstream culture. As social animals, humans have a biological hunger for connection and there is widespread dissatisfaction with the deterioration of neighborhoods and the increase in alienation. More and more people are looking for community in their lives and intentional communities are poised to speak to this need.

There is a growing respect for what we are pioneering about inclusive decision making, low-impact resource use, and how to build a culture that integrates values into everyday living. The media has picked up on this, and there has been a sharp increase in coverage the last few years, reporting on how the learnings from our laboratories of cooperation can apply to the wider culture.

For our part, the FIC started offering semi-annual conferences called Art of Community weekends in 1997, tapping into this desire to learn about community in all its forms. We bring together an array of presenters who collectively offer nuts and bolts information about building intentional communities *and* workshops on how to create more community wherever you are.

Last time we checked in (when we released the 1995 edition) we noted a spate of spin-off communities. While this trend has slowed, there is still interest in locating new groups near existing ones for a source of local inspiration, an easier entrée into the local culture (the neighbors having greased the skids), an enhanced social pool (more folks for dances), and a more robust lending library of books, tools, and expertise.

Communities are still struggling with how to meet the needs of members suffering from multiple chemical sensitivity or from mental/emotional disabilities, and we are not reporting the discovery of any magic potion capable of dissolving the cycle of debilitation. By the time it is evident that someone is suffering from either of these illnesses, they are often too confused or disheartened to conduct their own search for help, or contribute a full share to a community that might have them. In this era of government deregulation, there is an increased need for communities and other private sector groups to step forward with ideas and energy to meet these challenges.

Start-Ups Are Easier … and Harder

In listening to the founding stories of groups which started in the 1960s and '70s, it is remarkable how few relied on the experience of others to find their way. Today the story is reversed; few groups try to go it alone. When you reflect on how often help at a critical juncture is crucial to a group's survival, it is heartening how much more help is available—and how much more it is being asked for.

At the same time, the road to utopia is more uphill in other respects. There is less and less land untouched by zoning laws, and this is hard on groups excited about innovative construction and resource management. Because zoning tends to be highly conservative (created mainly to protect property values), communities typically need to run a gauntlet of expensive and time consuming waivers, variances, and public hearings to gain approval for things like straw bale construction and greywater recycling.

In addition, land prices—even when adjusted for inflation—are spiraling ever higher. Just as traditional single-family housing is now out of reach for most Americans, buying even unimproved property is prohibitively expensive for many would-be communities.

Fortunately, the effect of higher prices is somewhat offset by an increased flow of financing for communities—both from within the movement and from supportive outsiders. Perhaps nothing signals the movement's emerging financial maturity better than the 1997 arrival of the Sunrise Credit Union, headquartered in the Colorado community of Sunrise Ranch. Any FIC member is automatically eligible to join this credit union, where your deposits help the movement help itself (see their ad on page 343 for details).

The bottom line: money *is* available if you have a solid vision and a solid business plan, even though today's start-up budgets are 10 times more expensive than in the boom days of the 1960s. Some of the larger projects, like cohousing developments, have budgets in the millions and are gaining the confidence of traditional lending institutions. It's turning out that building community is good business all around.

The Web Grows Stronger

Since the FIC launched its Web site, http://www.ic.org/ in 1994, we've been off and running on the electron highway. We're constantly adding links to new community Web sites and resources, and improving our services. The site traffic increases steadily every month. Hundreds of communities now have a Web presence, and the pace of the exchange of community information on the Web is always rising.

Already, our Web site brings in a majority of our retail publication sales, and we plan to launch an intentional communities e-commerce system in 2000. Starting off with Community Bookshelf, a mail-order bookstore, we hope to soon be offering community products and services worldwide.

Third Time's the Charm

This edition of *Communities Directory* is clearly the best of the three we've produced, and arguably the best published in the last millennium. However, this is not an ending. Demand for community information remains robust, and this won't be our last edition. With that in mind, we want your thoughts about this book—what works and what can be enhanced. We can't promise to do everything you ask, but we can try. If there is anything we've learned from cooperative living, it's the importance of keeping the door open to new ideas, finding ways to do things better the next time around, and not taking yourself too seriously.

Just remember, the truth (plus this book and community) shall make you three.

A Bit of the Directory Story, and Acknowledgments

by Jillian Downey and Elph Morgan
Managing Editors

THERE IS ALWAYS A HISTORY behind any project and the *Directory* is no exception. The sheer size of the task of creating a reference book such as this and the number of people necessary to complete it can be awe-inspiring. Both of us had been involved near the end of the process of making the 1995 *Directory*, which took three and a half years to complete. In 1997, when the Fellowship for Intentional Community (FIC) began talking about the 2000 edition, we were the only ones from the previous staff that were excited at the prospect. Work on this edition of the *Directory* essentially started back in January of 1998, when the two of us labored for a hundred or more hours, holed up in HeiWa House (the co-op we were part of in Ann Arbor, Michigan), creating the business plan. Neither of us had ever written one before, so that required some reading up and trial and error. In hindsight, we did pretty well with it. The *Directory* costs $125,000 dollars to produce and involves three or four dozen people, with many thousands of person hours involved. The official start date was October of 1998. In May, we both quit our jobs and took the summer off to travel and relax, knowing that, once we started, we would be pushing the limit to complete the book in our planned year and a half. We bought a small old RV, named it Ben Bulben (after a mountain in the west of Ireland), and spent four months on the road together that summer, visiting friends and interesting places before we settled down in October.

Our travels were not over, however. We would be hosted by a handful of communities during the course of producing the book, for two to three months at a time. In this manner, we could manage to live economically, involve people and communities from across the country in the *Directory* process, and also not be too much of a burden on any one community. We would donate 10 hours of work a week to our host. All this, and we got to spend time in some wonderful communities with some good friends! By the third move, we were experts at packing up our office into the RV and could rumble off to our next host in no time.

Twin Oaks was where we started the project, and when we were nearly done we came back to finish it there and complete the circle. During our first time there we were focused on getting the various parts figured out and rolling, including: article acquisition, photo gathering, database cleaning, survey design and mailing, and more mailing—we mailed several thousand surveys out around the world. Stuffing envelopes is more fun when done with company; we had a number of multi-day bulk mailing parties. During that winter the engine on our RV gave up the ghost, but thanks to the well-equipped garage and skilled hands of Tony at Acorn community we were able to continue our tour of duty.

We crossed the country from Virginia to Oregon, descended into the mossy rainforest of Alpha Farm, and arrived with lots of time to witness the end of the rainy season. The questionnaires were still returning in large batches and were piling up around us, we were still mailing new ones out, and the articles were in the middle of the editing process. The project was in full swing. Near the end of our stay at Alpha our good friend Amy Nesbitt paid a visit and noticed the considerable strain we were under. Within two weeks she left her job and home in San

Elph Morgan and Jillian Downey, Managing Editors of this edition.

Francisco to come and help us.

It was at our next host, HeiWa House cooperative, during the late summer and fall, that Amy joined up with us and took on the role of Production Associate, accomplishing a range of tasks from research to correspondence to calling hundreds of communities about their surveys to polishing the Resources and Reading List to marketing to layout. Her help on location with us was invaluable. There were many tasks that we couldn't spin off to folks who weren't there in the eye of the storm.

Having our work and our home in the same place meant that it was sometimes hard to stop working, and remember to do things like eat, sleep, exercise, and socialize. HeiWa House was where we did the best at remembering these little details.

Our next to last host was Hawk Circle cooperative in Iowa, where the three of us stayed for the fall. It was there that the many pieces of the project started coming together and threatened to become a book. We had finished with contacting communities and were trying to close the door on new entries and new advertisements. We had whipped together a beautiful brochure to let people know about the *Directory*, the Articles were finished, data entry was close to done, and the Recommended Reading List and Resources were cleaned and made ready for layout. At the end of our stay in Iowa, Amy headed back to San Francisco and we made our way back to Twin Oaks.

Once back at Twin Oaks at the beginning of December, we set a deadline for ourselves to get the pages to the printer by the winter solstice. All of the work at this point was in layout. We had Twin Oaks Indexing do our indexes and we pulled the information from our databases to create the Maps, Charts, Listings, Resources, and Recommended Reading List. As we moved from the longest night of the year into the dawn of the winter solstice, we finished up the pages.

While we waited the two months for the book to return from the printer, we kept busy with marketing, Web site design, returning photos and materials, closing up the financial books, archiving information, checking printer proofs, and documenting our process for the next team to learn from.

Personal Acknowledgements

First and foremost we would like to thank our community hosts, specifically: Twin Oaks community in Virginia, Alpha Farm in Oregon, HeiWa House cooperative in Michigan, and Hawk Circle cooperative in Iowa. They all graciously opened their homes to us, and provided us the support and infrastructure we needed as we worked. Their donation to the project was huge and very much appreciated. To name some of the very helpful folks at these communities would inevitably leave someone out, but we'll try anyway: Twin Oaks—Keenan, McCune,

Valerie, Scott, Alex, Kristen, Felix, Lynn, Pam, Bonnie, Dianne, Marione, Paxus, Hawina, Carrol, Doug, Gordon, Grá, Ione, River, Elliot, Heather, Hildegard, Inge, Ira, Jake, Rollie, Kat, Louis, Mara, Melissa, Nexus, Shakti, Shal, Tom, Val; Alpha Farm—Caroline, Jim, Dave, Lysbeth, Andrew, Leif, Russ; HeiWa House—Gaia, Beth, Tom, Kirk, Liz, Brian, Emily; Hawk Circle—Mary, Mark, Tom, Rollie, JoshAnn, Camerick.

Barbara Anderson and David Lam at the Population Studies Center at the University of Michigan very kindly gave us office space while we were hosted at HeiWa House.

If it weren't for a dedicated staff, there was no way we could have pulled this off in a year and a half's time.

Rajal Cohen and Melissa Wender were the Article Acquiring editors (along with Jillian who finished up after Melissa was no longer available). They picked up a huge piece of this project and ran with it, in a thorough, conscientious, and dedicated way. It was a tough job, and their patience and perseverance were much appreciated.

The FIC's Editorial Review Board (Betty Didcoct, Paul DeLapa, and Laird Schaub) spent many hours thoroughly reviewing the articles, and went above and beyond the call of duty.

Terry O'Keefe was our Advertising Manager, who brought his experience, good cheer, persistence, and care for details to bear on his work of acquiring some great ads.

Jenny Upton was our Photo Editor (as she was for the previous edition as well), she collected photos from various sources, and carefully selected images for the articles.

David Sower took hold of the task of making an annotated Recommended Reading List. He was willing to move into new territory on this one—since this was a brand new section of the *Directory* we had no easy model to point him to.

Jacob Stevens created the Resources section—contacting organizations, verifying their purposes and contact information, and carefully compiling the information.

Amy Nesbitt came in at a time when we really needed her help. Her upbeat nature, ability to tackle any project, and willingness to persevere in the trenches with us really saved our lives.

Heidi Dailey's talent and patience as the cover designer were much appreciated. She may not have known what she was getting in to when she started, but she came through with a beautiful product.

Velma Kahn did an enormous amount of work for the project in a very condensed time period, in the form of cleanup of the communities database. Her skilled help was essential.

McCune Renwick-Porter was a constant source of helpful information for us in the early stages and his bulk mailing expertise is unparalleled. McCune also served as our dedicated mail forwarder—sending us weekly packets of mail, no matter where we were, throughout the project.

Hilke Kuhlman gave us a German translation of our questionnaire and mailed it in Germany. Giovanni Ciarlo provided us with a Spanish translation and Muriel Delmas was kind enough to provide a French translation. All three were great at answering random translation questions.

The article process had a large number of people involved, and we would especially like to thank all the authors who took the time to write (and sometimes rewrite) for us. We think you will enjoy the results.

We had several copyeditors, working with the articles to polish them into finished pieces. Many thanks, to Pam Kasey, Rebecca L'Abbe, Mara Rockliff, and Lisa Cigliana.

And thanks as well to the excellent photographers and illustrators who donated their work for the article section and the cover.

Valerie Renwick-Porter and Ira Wallace helped brainstorm and gather the materials necessary to get a system rolling for calling and reminding communities about their surveys. Grá Darjeeling also pitched in helping organize some phone calling at Twin Oaks. Deborah Bors and Geoph Kozeny did some phone calling as well. Karen Edwards took on calling all the recalcitrant communities in Washington state and did a top notch job of getting their information. Amy Nesbitt spent countless hours on the phone with communities around the country.

Creating this book involved sending out many pieces of paper, all over the world. Folks who helped us with at least one of those many bulk-mailing parties we had included: Valerie Renwick-Porter, Ira Wallace, Alex McGee, Grá Darjeeling, Jackie McMillan, Caroline and Jim Estes, Russ Reina, Daria Mark, Dennis Brady, Megan Hoxeng, Betty Jane VanDenAkker, Yolanda Travers, Karl Reis, Adam Grandin, Katie O'Connor, Beth Davis, Jesse Davis, Rabbit Ewing, and Rich Linville.

Once the surveys were in hand, next they needed to be data entered, and then proofread. A host of folks helped with this. Gayla Groom took on the lion's share. Others included: Anne Zondlo, Grá Darjeeling, Jackie McMillan, Charlotte Morgan, Rachel Frankel, Karl Reis, Katie O'Connor, Eric Nusbaum, Nadine Geils, Amy Nesbitt, Teresa Smart, and Carol Eilers. We would have been buried under a sea of data entry without them!

Listings copyediting was done by Andrea Olson; her meticulous care was again much appreciated. (She did this for the previous edition as well.)

Rachel Sythe, Clarissa Kensho Fetrow, and Jake Kawatski were our sharp-eyed proofreaders.

Maps were worked on by Amy Nesbitt (and finished off by Elph Morgan).

Jake Kawatski of Twin Oaks Indexing indexed the articles and the community listings for us. His thorough product makes the *Directory* an even more useful tool.

Marty Klaif, Laird Schaub, Terry O'Keefe, McCune Renwick-Porter, and Russ Reina worked with us discussing presales issues, advertising, and marketing.

Geoph Kozeny was also a helpful source of advice; he went through all this for the last edition so he had some good perspectives to share.

Tony Sirna and Laird Schaub helped us dig out the numbers we needed to create the business plan that got the project rolling, in winter of 1998.

Many thanks to Meg Brier, the customer service representative at our printer, Sheridan Group, in Ann Arbor, Michigan. She cheerfully and patiently fielded what must have seemed like endless questions.

Last, we would like to thank BloomWhite Real Wealth Investing, LLC. They had the faith in us to loan FIC the capital to produce this book. Their vision and trust enabled this project to happen.

Colophon

Typefaces: Janson Text, Optima, Wake 'n Bake, Poetica SuppOrnamental, Nuptial Script, Kinesis

"Although designed by the Hungarian Nicholas Kis in about 1690, the model for Janson Text was mistakenly attributed to the Dutch printer Anton Janson. Kis' original matrices were found in Germany and acquired by the Stempel foundry in 1919. This version of Janson comes from the Stempel foundry and was designed from the original type; it was issued by Linotype in digital form in 1985. In the 1930s, Janson Text replaced Caslon as the face of choice for fine bookmaking." —Adobe

Equipment: Apple Macintosh Powerbook G3, Powerbook 2400, iMac, US Robotics 56K Cellular Modem PC Card, HP 4000N Laser Printer, Umax Astra 1220U Scanner, Asante FriendlyNet 8-port Ethernet Hub, APS HyperDATII DDS-2 Tape Backup, Zip

Software: Quark XPress 4, Filemaker Pro 4, BBEdit 5.1, Retrospect, GeoQuery 4, Freehand 8, Photoshop 5, Eudora Pro 4, GraphicConverter, Consultant, Anarchie, IPNetRouter, Virex

Telephony: Nokia 5120 Cell phone with ATT One-Rate service, Voicenet calling cards, JFax internet voicemail and fax service.

Music: Greg Brown, Ani DiFranco, Rebecca Riots, Nancy Griffith, Solas, Patty Larkin, Cheryl Wheeler, Moxy Früvous, Dar Williams, Loreena McKennitt, Susan Werner, Willy Porter, Tom Waits, Karen Casey

Reading Material: Tricycle, Sun, MacAddict, Path Without Destination—Satish Kumar, Communities magazine, Cohousing Journal, my.yahoo.com, Elements of Typographic Style—Robert Bringhurst, Divine Secrets of the Ya-Ya Sisterhood—Rebecca Wells, Living Lightly, Travels in Post-Consumer Society—Walter and Dorothy Schwarz, The Quest for Utopia in Twentieth Century America: 1900-1960—Tim Miller, Attacks—Erwin Rommel

Snack food: Mocha Frappuccinos, popcorn with nutritional yeast and parmesan cheese, Sun Chips, fried tempeh with garlic and cayenne, kalamata olives, anything from Zingerman's Deli

What This Directory Is, and Isn't

THIS DIRECTORY INCLUDES HUNDREDS OF intentional communities, from North America and overseas, who filled out a detailed survey and wrote their own description. These communities are, for the most part, willing to be contacted by other communities or by people interested in community. Some are looking for new members, others wish to make contact with other communities, and some are just willing to share their example—to be a source of information or inspiration to other communities. The *Directory* staff worked to invite as many communities to participate as possible.

Who Qualifies for Listing as an "Intentional Community"?

There are as many definitions of community as there are communities themselves, it seems. (An article from the previous edition of this directory covered definitions. That article is available on the Intentional Communities Web site, at http://www.ic.org/fic/cdir/art/05quest.html). Because of this ambiguity around definitions, the FIC chooses to let communities define themselves, and each participating community wrote their own description of themselves for the Community Listings section.

This means that the FIC didn't arbitrarily exclude communities through a too-narrow definition, but it also means that any group of two or more adults that considered itself a community was welcome to participate, or even one adult with a vision for starting a community, so long as they met the two basic screens that the FIC has used for all three editions of this book.

The FIC asked communities to participate only if they do not advocate violent practices or do not interfere with their members' freedom to leave their group at any time.

To the extent possible, no communities were listed that don't meet those two basic principles. However, readers should also be aware that the FIC certainly does not have the staff or the time to check each community first-hand—the *FIC has made no attempt to independently assess the accuracy of community statements and representations.*

What Is the FICs Definition of When a Community Is Categorized as "Forming"?

As mentioned earlier, a community with as few as one or two adults still qualifies for listing. However, that community will show up with a "forming" label in our listings. Listing forming communities is an important service, as it helps those communities find the new members they need. It's a bit tricky for a printed book, in that forming communities have a much greater tendency to change in a short period of time, causing the information here to quickly become out of date. However, we feel the benefits to the communities outweigh that cost. Deciding who gets a "forming" label is also tricky. The policy that the FIC has been using for a number of years now is as follows:

1. any community that labels itself as such,
2. any community with fewer than four adult members, or
3. any group that has not lived together for at least a year.

"Forming" communities are often, but are not always, brand new—some older existing communities go through periods of reorganization or upheaval where their population drops; others have held steady with a small number of members for a while.

Warning for Readers

Communities are often inspiring and wonderful places to live, and, because they are inhabited by humans, they are not perfect. As said earlier, each community writes their own description, and of course groups want to describe themselves at their best, en-route to fulfilling their vision of what they want their community to be. Readers need to know that communities sometimes have the same human failings as everywhere in the world, such as power struggles, miscommunication, and unrealistic expectations. So, it's up to each reader to assess the information that describes each group, and to try to identify what statements are part of the "grand plan," and which ones reflect the day-to-day reality.

How Does the FIC Handle Complaints About Listed Communities?

So, what does the FIC do when someone visits a community, and finds something quite different from what was written in this book? Based on experience with the previous two editions of the book, users were overwhelmingly pleased with what they found. However, very occasionally there is a complaint that a community has misrepresented itself in the *Directory*. In response to this, the FIC will make an effort to open constructive dialog between the community and the person with the complaint, to see what kind of understanding can be reached. If no resolution is found, the FIC will bring into play its system called "Feedback Files." All points of view in the disagreement will be written up and placed in a Feedback File on that community. These files are kept in the FIC office. The contents of the files can be summarized upon request, with a processing fee of $1 per community to compensate for the time. Please see the Feedback piece in the Appendix for information on where to send feedback or how to request information from Feedback Files.

Reasons Why You Might Not Find a Community Listed Here

Readers should be aware that there are hundreds, if not thousands, of communities that are not listed in this directory, for reasons including the following.

1. We know there are communities out there that the FIC has not heard about yet.
2. There are language barriers that get in the way of communicating with many international communities (although email has made communication around the world much easier as far as cost and speed, and we did provide questionnaires in Spanish, French and German).
3. Some communities receive our survey but choose not to list. Their reasoning for this choice might be one of the following:
   (a) they're worried that listing would attract attention they don't want;
   (b) networking within the communities movement does not appeal to them;
   (c) they don't want any new members and also don't wish to deal with visitors or inquiries;
   (d) they're looking for a very specific type of membership and this directory has a broader readership base; or
   (e) they prefer to attract visitors to their community through word of mouth.
4. Communities move and we aren't able to discover their new location to get them a survey.

Some communities didn't get their survey back in time to list in this edition, and their listing will be printed in the *Directory Updates* and in later editions of the book.

More Than the Community Listings

Before you dive into searching through the Community Listings, take some time to read through the Articles. They will round out your perspective on community living. They are all new for this edition, on a wide range of subjects. Brand new for this edition is an annotated Recommended Reading List. And, the Resources section is included again in this edition, slimmed down to point to the major resource organizations within interest areas—organizations who make it their business to compile information about their niche and will know the best, most up-to-date resources to refer people to.

Planning on Visiting Some Communities?

First, please read "Red Carpets and Slammed Doors: Visiting Communities," by Geoph Kozeny, in the first section of the Articles. He's been visiting communities for more than 12 years, and has packed this piece full of helpful advice. Enjoy!

When Did They Start?
A Few Facts About
the Communities Listed in This Book

When answering their surveys, 600 communities (out of the 728 communities that chose to be listed in the *Directory*) told us what year they were "formed." As it turned out, 255 were formed in the 1990s. And, you can look at any year back to 1960 and find at least one community listed that formed in that year. Additionally, you can find at least one listed in every decade back to the 1890s. Here's the decade breakdown:

1990s	255	1930s	18
1980s	133	1920s	2
1970s	164	1910s	1
1960s	46	1900s	1
1950s	9	1890s	1
1940s	16		

Jillian Downey

Intentional Community
What Is It All About?

This first section of the articles provides a broad overview of the communities movement, introducing some of the basic concepts of intentional community, some of the issues surrounding it, and the ideas and accomplishments of a few communities and individual community members. Those considering intentional community for themselves won't want to miss the practical advice about visiting and evaluating communities offered here. Last is an introduction to the nonprofit organization that publishes the *Directory*—how and when it came about, and what is its focus.

In Community, Intentionally

by Geoph Kozeny

"I WANT MORE OF A SENSE OF COMMUNITY in my life." If I had a dollar for every time I've heard someone utter that phrase, I could invest the funds, retire to my favorite rural community, and live off the interest.

What's remarkable is that this inspiration is not coming only from folks that might be called "alternative"—I hear it from people representing a wide spectrum of values, ideals, and lifestyles.

Because mainstream media fails to understand the phenomenon, very few people realize that the hippie communes of the '60s were collectively just one small blip in history's timeline of intentional communities (see footer starting on the following page). Efforts to create new lifestyles based on lofty ideals have been happening since our ancestors abandoned their caves.

Pursuing Dreams

What all intentional communities have in common is idealism—each one was founded on a vision of living in a better way, usually in response to something perceived as lacking or missing in the broader culture. Most communities aspire to provide a supportive environment for the development of members' awareness, abilities, and spiritual growth. Most seek to create a life that will satisfy the basic human cravings: security, family, relationship, fellowship, mutual cooperation, creativity and self-expression, a sense of place, a sense of belonging.

An Intentional Community ...

"is a group of people who have chosen to live or work together in pursuit of a common ideal or vision. Most, though not all, share land or housing. Intentional communities come in all shapes and sizes, and display an amazing diversity in their common values, which may be social, economic, spiritual, political, and/or ecological. Some are rural; some urban. Some live all in a single residence; some in separate households. Some raise children; some don't. Some are secular, some are spiritually based, and others are both. For all their variety though, the communities featured in our magazine hold a common commitment to living cooperatively, to solving problems nonviolently, and to sharing their experience with others."

—*Communities* magazine

Typically, today's intentional communities are melting pots of ideals and issues that have been in the public spotlight over the decades: equality and civil rights, women's liberation, antiwar efforts, ecology and conservation, alternative energy, sustainable agriculture, co-ops, worker-owned businesses, personal growth work, spirituality. Some groups focus on only one or a few of these areas, while oth-

---

Geoph Kozeny has lived in various kinds of communities for 27 years, and has been on the road for the past 12 years—visiting, studying, facilitating, and consulting for intentional communities scattered all across North America. He asks about their visions and realities, takes photos, and gives slide shows about the diversity and vitality of the communities movement. He was a core staff member for the first edition of the *Communities Directory*, and is a regular columnist for *Communities* magazine. Presently, he is completing production of a full-length video documentary on intentional communities, due for release in the spring of 2000. He can be reached via Community Catalyst Project, c/o 1531 Fulton Street, San Francisco CA 94117, USA.

ers try to integrate them all into a coherent whole. (For the groups listed in this directory, you can get a good overview of how broadly or narrowly they're focused by using the cross-reference charts that precede the listings.)

Although intentional communities are usually on the fringes of mainstream culture, the everyday values and priorities of community members are surprisingly compatible with the values and priorities of their less adventurous counterparts. Both tend to assign value to providing a stable home and good education for their children, finding meaningful and satisfying work, living in a safe neighborhood and an unpolluted environment, and participating in local organizations and activities. For many, finding a spiritual path is also important for providing a context for the other goals, and a basis for making decisions in times of uncertainty. The big difference is that the community members are not satisfied with the status quo. They want to do all those things *better* than in the past— better than their parents did them, and better than the generations before that. Intentional communities are testing grounds for new ideas about how to live more satisfying lives that enable us to actualize more of our untapped potential.

Jillian Downey

"What works for communities is whatever the members wholeheartedly believe in."

Time Is Not Standing Still

Most communities sound very clear and confident when describing their values and goals and practices, but such things inevitably evolve over time. When you come across a documentary or a directory listing that profiles a community, I suggest thinking of the description as a snapshot in their family scrapbook. Most of the images—the people, the buildings, the activities, the priorities, even the

---

Timeline: Intentional Communities Through the Ages

You thought communities were a fad that originated in the '60s and faded in the '70's? Think again. What follows (along the bottom of this article) is a very abbreviated overview that highlights only a few notable examples from each decade and shows the trend has existed at least two millennia. There is no indication that it's slowing down. (The FIC's database of intentional communities, for example, has 1,980 new entries since the release of the previous edition of this directory in 1995, charting the comings and goings of an active movement.)

6th Century BCE	**2nd Century BCE**	**1st Century CE**	**4th Century CE**	**1527**	**1540s**	**1620**	**1649**
Buddha's followers rejected wealth, turned to meditation, and joined together in ashrams to model an orderly, productive, and spiritual way to live.	Essene communities flourished, based on Old Testament law. Their *Dead Sea Scrolls* likely provided a matrix for early Christian monastics.	Early Christians banded together in "communities of goods" (described in Acts 2:44-45).	The first Christian monastic communities were established, with vows of poverty, chastity, and obedience, and a life of religious seclusion from the world.	Hutterian Brethren were founded— Anabaptists practicing common ownership.	Mennonites, a sect of radical Anabaptists, began living in community, using the Bible as the only rule.	Puritans founded Plymouth Colony based on simplicity.	The Diggers— common folks who revolted against the British nobility—communally occupied Crown lands.

visions—are subject to change over time.

I'm amazed at the number of times I've heard someone say "I couldn't live in a community without this," or "I could never live in a community that did that"—only to interview them several years later and discover that they were happily living without the former and with the latter. I suspect this lack of wisdom about what we really need and want is due in part to the fact that society does not adequately teach us to explore this type of question, and because people's needs change over time. On an individual level, needs can change as a person matures, while on a societal level cultural values and norms shift.

Major changes do happen overnight in communities occasionally. However, it is far more common for large shifts to happen over time. For example, I've visited at least a dozen communities that were radical and political in their early years (usually with a population of members mostly in their twenties). Within 20 years the members (now in their forties) had shifted their focus to improving the quality of their kids' schools, worrying about health concerns, and making plans for their old age.

A Unique Experience

Another scrapbook quality is, contrary to popular stereotypes, that every branch of the family is unique—no two brothers, sisters, aunts, uncles, or cousins lead identical lives—and so it is with communities. In the Catholic Worker network, for example, all the houses are based on a core philosophy that was articulated in the 1930s, yet no two are the same. Each community varies according to the number and ages of members, the projects emphasized, local laws and customs, and the cultural backgrounds and personalities of their members.

Likewise, the level of affluence in intentional communities runs the gamut from urban poor, to suburban and rural middle class, to quite well-heeled. Not surprisingly, there is a prevalence of nuclear families, single-parent families, and singles ... roughly proportionate to what

you'd find in the mainstream.

Although there's a full range of ages among the people living in communities—from newborns to those well into their 90s—that diversity does not reflect the demographics of the mainstream. Instead, there is a disproportionate representation of people in the 25- to 50-year-old age range, with the balance skewed toward the older end (the boomers). Likewise, many cultures and ethnic groups are represented in North American intentional communities, but the well-educated white middle class is represented in proportions greater than in the mainstream.

> Hippie communes of the '60s were just one small blip in history's timeline of intentional communities.

What Works

After living in six communities over 15 years, I thought I knew what worked best—wrong! Since then I've visited over 300 communities to talk with members and ex-members about their experiences, and to observe what seemed to work and not work. My new revised opinion about which structures and decision-making processes work best: whatever the members wholeheartedly believe in.

I've seen reasonably well-functioning examples of communities using consensus, majority voting, inspired anarchy, and benevolent dictatorships. I've also seen examples of each of those styles that seemed dysfunctional and disempowering. Sometimes the same community covered both ends of the spectrum, depending on the issue at hand and what side of the bed community members got up on that day. No amount of theory, dogma, and peer pressure can eliminate the need for clarity of vision, open mindedness, personal integrity, good communication, compassion, the spirit of cooperation, and common sense.

The structure a group uses is merely a tool; how it's applied is what's important. Strong leadership can prove to be inspirational and empowering, or it can prove to be dogmatic and repressive—and the same is true of decentralized individualism. What counts most is the resulting collective sense of well-being, empowerment, and community.

1698	1774	1825	1825	1841	1848	1855	1889
The Amish (founded by Jacob Ammon) created communities, and insisted on strict interpretation of the Mennonite principles.	The Shakers (founded by Mother Ann Lee) pursued spirituality, dancing, singing, celibacy, inventions, and handcrafts.	New Harmony was founded by Robert Owen as a nonreligious experimental "village of unity and cooperation."	Nashoba was founded by Frances Wright, to "train Negroes for freedom" and help them earn their own sale price.	Brook Farm was started, "an experiment in humane living to be achieved through education and discussion." It drew intellectuals such as Ralph Waldo Emerson and Nathaniel Hawthorne.	Oneida community was founded by John Humphrey Noyes, based on the practice of "complex marriage."	The Amana Colonies were established in Iowa by German Protestants seeking Christian community.	Hull House was founded in Chicago by Jane Addams, to "create a human community offering protection against the anonymous city."

The more egalitarian the group's vision, the more likely that there will be subtle internal power dynamics that go unnoticed, unacknowledged, or outright denied. This observation does not imply hierarchies have no inherent problems, including power dynamics, rather the way they describe their own decision-making process is normally closer to the truth than for those groups who aspire to equality. (See Joreen Freeman's article, "The Tyranny of Structurelessness," in the prior edition of the *Communities Directory* for a more detailed exploration of this tendency.[1])

While a sense of unity is typically one of the fundamental goals of intentional communities, it is a quality often lacking, sometimes existing only in theory, or deferred as a long-range goal that will be achieved only when the community becomes more "evolved." Unfortunately, we are quite capable of imagining a glorious utopian future without having developed many of the skills required to live up to our own high expectations.

Intentional community and mainstream culture share many values and priorities, such as meaningful work, safe neighborhoods, and good education for our children.

Novelty and Neighbors

One of the problems of pushing the envelope of mainstream society is running up against laws and regulations that make innovation either illegal, or full of bureaucratic hoops to jump through. Innovative construction styles such as strawbale, cobb, and earthships, as well as greywater systems, composting toilets, and organic farming technologies, have until recently been so far outside the norm that local inspectors rarely have a clue what the technologies are about. As a result, government officials regularly erect hurdles and walls in the path of such alternatives. Fortunately, the innovators have persisted, and local and national codes are slowly embracing the alternative technologies.

Zoning regulations have also proved challenging at times. Numerous cities have laws that prohibit more than three (or in some cases, up to five) unrelated adults from living together in one household. Although such laws were ostensibly instituted to protect neighborhoods from an excess of noise and cars, frequently they are enforced to protect against neighbors displaying nontraditional values and lifestyles. Some of these laws have been overturned in court, but many such laws still exist, and mostly don't draw much attention because enforcement is often very lax or nonexistent.

Another set of legal obstacles surfaces around the ownership and financing of commonly held property. Many communities seek to place ownership of their property into a land trust for reasons of affordability, equality, and land stewardship. Land trust philosophy has come a long way over recent decades, but much work has yet to be done before it'll be an easily available option in a culture

1900	**1910**	**1913**	**1920**	**1924**	**1933**	**1937**	**1939**
Arden was founded in Delaware, based on the Single Tax Theory proposed by economist Henry George.	Degania was founded in Israel, the first of 269 kibbutzim (Jewish communal societies), with a mixed agricultural and industrial economic base.	Gould Farm was founded to provide a community environment for the psychiatric treatment and rehabilitation of emotionally exhausted and disturbed people.	Darvell, the first community of the Bruderhof network, was founded, based on a life of Christian brotherhood.	Krotona Institute was established as a center of Theosophy, a philosophy that brings together science and religion, East and West.	The Catholic Workers movement was founded by Dorothy Day and Peter Maurin, to raise socio/economic consciousness through political agitation, nonviolent resistance, and voluntary poverty.	The first co-op house was started in what became the Inter-Cooperative Council (ICC), a network of 19 student housing co-ops in Ann Arbor, Michigan.	Several greenbelt "new towns" were created, as part of the US government's "New Deal" program.

Intentional Community: What Is It All About?

Community aspires to provide a supportive environment for the development of members' awareness, abilities, and spiritual growth.

geared to the sanctity of the individual.

This is also true with funding. It is rare to find a banker that understands and appreciates cooperation and shared ownership, and that makes financing community-held property difficult. For example, a lack of interim construction financing delayed the start of the cohousing movement by several years. It is much easier to secure such funding now that there are nearly five dozen existing prototypes to point to.

Further, because social innovations are often more threatening than technological and economic innovations, relations to the neighbors are often hugely challenging. The way the neighbors perceive the community —and more importantly, how they interact with it—can run the gamut from generic mistrust and violent hostility to hearty appreciation and mutual cooperation.

When there is a media "cult" scare in the news, some communities, most notably the secretive or isolated groups, experience unfavorable rumors and critical scrutiny from their neighbors. On the other hand, those deeply involved in local activities (thus having regular face-to-face encounters with folks living nearby) typically experience very little change in their neighborly interactions and the degree of acceptance locally.

This variance reflects the tendency in our culture to mistrust strangers and anyone "different from us." Thus when a community settles into a new area, the usual default mode is that the locals will eye the newcomers with suspicion until the newcomers have "proven themselves."

This "guilty until proven innocent" mentality has been fed by the media since the inception of the tabloid, and probably longer. The prevailing attitude among mainstream publishers is simple: sensational news is what sells newspapers and magazines. Yet, for some reason it seems that most readers fail to take that—and the cultural biases automatically built into so-called "objective" reporting—into account when assessing what of the coverage to believe.

So, it is the communities that are on familiar and friendly terms with their neighbors that fare the best during times of widespread paranoia. When facts are scarce, the tendency is to fill the gaps with imagination. Unfortunately, these projections do not often give newcomers the benefit of the doubt.

Reinventing Wheels

Most of these "unique new ideas" are neither new, nor unique. They seem so to us only because they're not commonly discussed or covered in standard history texts or the daily news. People all over the globe have been trying out similar, if not identical, ideas over many centuries,

---

1942
Koinonia was founded in Georgia by preacher Clarence Jordan, to promote racial reconciliation, in response to violence by whites toward blacks.

1946
Sunrise Ranch was established, the first community in the international "Emissaries" network.

1948
The FIC (originally named the "Fellowship of Intentional Communities") was established to provide connections and support among existing communities.

1955
The Ananda Marga network was founded by Shrii Anandamurti, to bring about a universal society based on love and Cosmic Brotherhood.

1956
Mitraniketan was founded—a nonpolitical, nonsectarian rural educational community that encouraged people to "think globally and act locally" and to develop the whole individual.

1957
Reba Place Fellowship was founded—an ecumenical lay community with a common purse.

1958
Yamagishism Life, large-scale agricultural cooperative communities, were founded in Japan.

often bucking resistance and persecution.

Many community groups are unaware of this history and end up starting the community-building process from scratch. There is also a tendency to resist advice from outside experts, usually because of a mistrust of outsiders, or a diehard sense that "We need to be able to do this for ourselves if our model is to be self-sufficient and sustainable." The reality is that the insights of an outsider—someone experienced with the issues at hand but not caught up in the internal dynamics of the community—can often provide the exact piece of information or insight needed to break through an impasse and move the community toward a constructive resolution.

One way around this tendency toward isolation is to develop sister communities and networks built around common ideals and interests (the *raison d'être* for the FIC and this directory). Communities in close association with one another can share ideas, resources, and mutual support and thereby benefit from each other's assets and experience. In addition, community networks can create common funds to do outreach, develop community-based business ventures, and cover medical emergencies (in lieu of expensive insurance policies that drain working capital out of the movement).

It Ain't Easy

Over the centuries well-intentioned attempts to live in community have generated a huge list of casualties. Countless thousands of folks have been inspired by a vision of a better world, and eventually ended up completely frustrated by the discrepancy between the vision and the reality.

At first glance this might seem peculiar, but it's exactly what should be expected, as most of us are products of an imperfect, overly competitive, alienating society. Although we tend to be aware of some of our negative conditioning, most of it is beyond the grasp of our limited worldview. If we're serious about creating a better world, we need to start with ourselves.

If you should happen to hear a glowing report about the perfect community somewhere, one with no rough edges, presume you're not getting the whole story. There's probably a shadow side somewhere that's unexplored and needs to be acknowledged before the members will be able to work through, rather than avoid, the underlying issues.

Conflict is inevitable, and traditionally it is handled so poorly that many of us have learned to dread it and avoid it. However, conflict is a useful indicator of points of non-alignment. Working creatively with these points usually results in tremendous positive growth spurts for everyone involved, both individually and collectively. The key to using conflict constructively is to get the affected parties to believe that a solution is possible, and to commit their best effort to finding a solution that works for all.

Every one of us brings along our own baggage wherever we go, and a supportive cooperative environment is the best possible place for us to explore our personal growing edge. It will prove to be the most challenging and frustrating inner work we've ever attempted, but if we pick the right people to work with, and approach it with the right attitude, it's entirely worth it—it's the best path available for actualizing our full potential.

> If you ... hear a glowing report about the perfect community somewhere, ... presume you're not getting the whole story.

Endnotes

1. Joreen Freeman's article from the previous edition of the *Communities Directory*, "The Tyranny of Structurelessness," is also available on the Web, at http://www.ic.org/fic/cdir/art/23joreen.html

1962	1964	1967	1970s	1972	1986	1992
Findhorn was established in rural Scotland, as a "center of light" in harmony with nature's intelligence.	L'Arche communities were founded by Jean Vanier, for developmentally disabled and those wanting to share their lives.	The "Summer of Love" gave rise to thousands of hippie communes, and also to the first wave of the contemporary "egalitarian" communities (including Twin Oaks).	The FIC database has many hundreds of listings for communities that were started throughout the '70s —a prolific time for community in the United States.	A Danish architect gathered a group of friends to discuss housing options, which resulted in the creation of a new form of community now called "cohousing."	N-Street, an urban retrofit, was the first cohousing community established in North America. Since then, 42 more have been completed, and 160 communities are in the construction or planning phases (as of fall 1999).	Ecovillages were founded in Ithaca, New York; Los Angeles, California; and St. Petersburg, Russia; marking the start of another new community model.

Why Choose Community?
Offering Service and Hope to the World

by Caroline Estes

*(Originally given as a speech to the 1993 Celebration
of Community, Olympia, Washington)*

I THINK THE WORLD TODAY is falling over the brink of disaster, that we are in a chaotic period. And I think a sense of community may be one of the ropes that pull us back, but only if we lead. It is not going to happen just on its own. It is going to take all of us who are committed to such things as cooperation, nonviolence, simple living, respect for Mother Earth, and all those things that we have come to realize are the only way this particular species can continue to exist. Not only that we can continue, but that all those other species that we are killing can survive. And so it is a tremendous responsibility that we have.

We cannot just go hide in our communities. We must make them strong; we must tackle all those horrible issues that come up in community that you'd like to kind of sweep under the rug, so we have some experience to give to the rest of the world on how to live in harmony. We can take our anger and our conflicts and work with them, and resolve them. The responsibility that the communities movement has today is enormous, and we are not all that large. But we each can make a difference, if we are out there saying, "We have another way." We do not need to go down the road of taking, always taking, and not returning.

Recently we had a visitor at Alpha Farm who had just come back from Bosnia. He's a photojournalist, and he's been in all of the horrible situations in the world. One of the most humble men I've ever met. And he said to me, because we were discussing this exact situation, "You know, it's no longer how much you can give back, it's can you just stop taking?" And we thought about that and talked about it a long time. It seems to me that one of the communities movement's possibilities is to learn how to

not take, and if we're really lucky, we get to give back some. This is very hard. Many of us use resources every day that we can't return to the Earth. However, there are other ones that we can return. We can return our love, our concern, our caring, we can do all those things which we in community know are necessary in order to make this world a paradise.

It's hard. Living in community is not the simple way out. But it is one way that offers hope, and the world is desperate for hope. The despair we see around us, the apathy, the giving up, is very, very potent. And we have some of the answers—not all, we still are working with many of them; however, we have a lot of them. And it isn't fair for us to sit and be content. We should be very discontented. I know this doesn't always sit well with people, because I've had some of these conversations before; however, I feel very strongly that we are one of the true answers to the problems of our species. And when we can get ourselves together into a group, our strength can spread.

I want to take Alpha Farm as a very tiny example, since it's my experience. We live in a very isolated section of Oregon in the Coast Range, in a little valley. No one could ever find us, and yet Alpha is now known around the world: just by being there and doing what we think is the right thing to do, so people can see that there is another way. We don't have to be giving our definition of value a dollar sign. Values of peace and cooperation, of harmony, can be lived in this world. And if some place as tiny and as far removed as Alpha Farm can be in *Life* magazine, anybody can.

So I know we have the opportunity in front of us to go out and be of help and service: service, a very old word that is somewhat out of mode right now. We need to take it back again and be of service to others as well as ourselves.

Caroline Estes, a founding member of Alpha Farm community in Oregon, is a trainer and consultant on consensus decision making and former FIC board member.

Jillian Downey

Caroline Estes and husband, Jim, enjoy living and giving service at Alpha Farm in Oregon.

So let me expand just a little bit on what I mean by cooperation and simple living. Does cooperation mean that you're never angry, that you're never frustrated, that all of those things never happen in community? In fact we live with them all the time, right? Because we are products of our own society. And so we have to keep struggling with the things that we grew up with, or in the case of some, are still growing up with. However, we have ways, which you will find in workshops and which you have found in your own communities, of how to work with them. How to turn anger into understanding, how to turn frustration into activity that removes it. We've all had those experiences. We need to share them, so that others who get angry and frustrated with this insane world find ways of dealing with them other than destruction. We have some of those ideas and techniques; we need to be sharing them.

What do we mean by simple living? Do we mean living at the level of Third World countries? Some people think so, and do. For others, if we had just half what we now have, we might start to get close to simple living. Well, that's a lot. As a bioregionalist, if all the things we served to eat at Alpha Farm were grown in our bioregion,

we'd have trouble with coffee and bananas and some of our spices; however, we'd eat very well, and we'd be much more in line with where we live. It's a hard way. Do we give up cars? Well, they may give us up pretty soon, because we may not have oil. Do we examine our lives, each of us in our community, to see what we don't need to take but can do without? Recently we looked at our standard of living at Alpha, and realized we're still pretty middle-class, even though our average per capita expenditure per month is somewhere between $200 and $250. That's below the poverty line, but we still live awfully well, and consume much too much. It's a constant struggle to get back in balance with where we really belong on this planet.

How can we be nonviolent in such a violent world? How can we maintain it, teach it, practice it, be it? How can we make it so that people who will help others are not labeled "leader," but rather, "servant"? How can we in the communities movement serve the world? I offer to you the challenge that we are the servants of this planet, and we need to give that service.

Making Magic
Ecological Community in an Urban Neighborhood

by Daniel Bartsch, Robin Bayer, Hilary Hug,
David Schrom, and Joan Schwan

A HANDFUL OF TWENTY-SOMETHINGS with dreams of a back-to-the-land ecological community rented a post office box in Palo Alto, California in 1972. We called ourselves Magic.

Like many of our peers in that era, we envisioned carving a little niche of sanity into what we considered an increasingly insane society. We wanted sustained, loving friendships. We wanted to earn livelihood by addressing fundamental human concerns. We wanted to discover how we might more fully apply ecology to live and die well.

Over the past 30 years we've realized or surpassed many of our early aspirations. Though we initially planned to gather friends, save money, buy country land, and move onto it ASAP, we've—to our amazement—stayed in the same urban Palo Alto neighborhood.

Our aim here is to share some of our experiences of the past three decades. We want to give you concrete examples of what's possible in your own neighborhood, and encourage you to go ahead and create community, right where you are.

Magic Today, an Overview

Five Magicians who have lived and worked together closely for periods ranging from 10 to more than 20 years, plus two infants, occupy two small adjacent homes. We typically share these with three to five interns whose tenures may vary from days to years.

Four resident Magicians generate livelihood by operating a nonprofit public service organization called Magic, where they demonstrate ways to apply ecology to further common good. Former residents and other long-term partners, most of whom live within easy walking or bicy-cling distance, also play key roles in this venture, and thousands of people who have supported the nonprofit organization form an extended public service community.

Residence, Then and Now

Some of us began living together in 1972. We jointly purchased a house in 1976. Between two and 12 of us have resided at Magic for nearly 25 years. During the 1990s, we've consistently been six or more.

At first we shared a home primarily to conserve resources and to enjoy the company of others similarly concerned about personal health, social justice, and environmental quality. Within a few years we realized much of what we wanted to remedy in the world around us was a mirror of our own beings, and we began to look inward more often.

Living and working in close quarters, we reveal a great deal. As we grow more appreciative of others' love and intelligence, we talk and listen more openly. With practice, we're becoming more adept at seeing self and others more accurately, and at assisting each other in doing so. Most of us now view this as a principal benefit of living as we do.

Consensual Livelihood

We incorporated the nonprofit Magic in 1979, and since then have served more than 20,000 people directly, and many more indirectly. From its inception we've used ecology, broadly defined, as a foundation and framework. In our programs we interweave four themes—health, cooperation, stewardship, and values inquiry. We perceive these to be fundamental issues of near-universal concern, and we aim to further common interest by addressing them.

Daniel Bartsch, Robin Bayer, Hilary Hug, David Schrom, and Joan Schwan have lived and worked at Magic for periods ranging from 10 to more than 25 years.

Nonresident associates who offer programs through Magic may draw personal compensation equal to the median wage in the locale where they reside. Magic residents who volunteer full-time for the nonprofit organization receive support similar to that offered by the US Peace Corps. We're fed and sheltered; our incidental expenses are paid. We cobble together medical care with a mixture of individual and institutional resources.

Ecological Service Community

As we live, laugh, labor, learn, and love together, we're shaping a dynamic service community with fluid boundaries. This informal partnership includes residents, associates, volunteers, donors, clients, and others who interact in Magic's name to demonstrate how people may learn to more consistently apply ecology to further common good.

Hundreds of people visit Magic for classes, workshops, mentoring, mediation, meetings, and parties each year. On a typical day, five to 10 visitors join us for lunch or supper. Magic residents and associates also deliver services off-site to school, government, business, nonprofit, and individual clients.

With this combination of unusually intimate and extensive public interaction we afford diverse opportunities to give to, receive from, and better understand Magic.

How "We" Do I Want to Be?

Magicians and those whom we serve benefit from synergies among residential, livelihood, and service communities. At the same time, residents especially walk a fine line to match engagement in each community to our individual tastes.

Some have felt too exposed in a home where guests or other program participants are ever present. Others have pursued livelihood outside Magic and felt less connected to those who serve full-time through the nonprofit.

Similarly, if we put too much emphasis upon readily measurable public service outcomes—youths mentored, disputes mediated, trees planted, or classes taught—we become strangers at home. If we dwell excessively upon relationships among residents, we sacrifice opportunities to interact with, and contribute to, others.

We see repeatedly how any of us can shift patterns of personal participation and send ripples of disturbance through others' lives. And we're also discovering that as we become

Magicians after a weekly community meeting, August 1999.

more practiced, we're better able to anticipate disequilibria, and restore balance before they become too large.

"Radical" Means "Root"

Some who become interested in Magic press for details about a specific project, or about how we structure and operate our residential community or nonprofit organization. Though we're pleased to talk about programs and policies, we think we risk misleading if we respond to inquiries about these without also mentioning our philosophy and practices.

We perceive the essence of Magic to be a commitment to practice ecology. When we said this in the early '70s, we meant the application of a set of principles such as recycling and conservation. Now we mean more consistently employing in everyday living the same method by which principles like recycling and conservation were discovered. This method includes holding ideas open to question, and using our senses and other faculties to test them. By questioning and testing our ideas, we discover which we can use to successfully (i.e., with better than random results) predict outcomes, and which will be a basis for disappointment.

Using this method, we're re-examining the underpinnings for our lives, our responses to the questions, "What do I want?" and "How can I get what I want?" By such inquiry we're probing toward the roots of our being—instructions coded in genes or training we received early in life about survival, reproduction, and meaning. We're shedding illusion, and learning to more often get what we want and want what we've got.

Intentional Community: What Is It All About?

Joel Simon

Neighbors brought together by Magic enjoy the fruits of cooperation.

What's the Deal?

Magicians concur that community entails evolving contracts, however informal. We're continuously probing those "deals," to make them more explicit and to assess, "Is this what I want to ask and offer?"

We lack sufficient resources to realize everyone's wildest dreams, so we've made trade-offs. We've foregone what we consider unnecessary, even burdensome, material trappings so that we may enjoy greater freedom.

In 1989, Daniel became suddenly ill and was hospitalized for 10 days. During that period, someone from Magic was with him around the clock, and members of the extended Magic service community beat a path to his door. A hospital administrator who volunteers with us reported that nurses on Daniel's unit were puzzled. "What's the deal?" they wanted to know. "Who's this moneyless, jobless, childless, unmarried, thirty-something that so many people care about so much?"

Some call us ascetics. We think we're hedonists. As we live more toward common good—with each other, and with the world beyond—we're enjoying life more. By demonstrating underacknowledged connections between pleasure and more consistent attention to common interests, we're prompting others to rethink and restructure their social contracts.

Begin Where You Are

Thirty years ago, Magicians thought of Palo Alto as a way station, a place to collect people and resources in anticipation of relocating to a more rural setting. Part of our strategy was to begin immediately to develop additional skills for creating and sustaining cooperative community

in our next location.

One sunny June Saturday in 1976, as we wrapped up a satisfying morning of gardening and gathered for lunch in the dining room of our newly purchased home, a driver careened his car around the corner and a passenger fired a bottle into the curb. As pieces of broken glass ricocheted onto our laboriously double-dug and freshly planted raised beds, Michael asked, "Is this why we moved here?"

Fifteen years, 7,000 hours of Magician life, thousands of hours of life from hundreds of other people, dozens of public meetings, more than 100 hours of public testimony, two lawsuits, one city-wide ballot measure, and who knows how many hundreds of thousands of dollars of city staff salaries later, we'd converted six through streets to cul-de-sacs. Daily vehicle entries and exits to our neighborhood had dropped from 13,000 to 3,000. Residents knew each other better and appreciated each other more. Magicians had evolved vision and selves to take giant strides toward ecological community right where we were.

Find Opportunity in Threat

In 1979, we received an ominous-looking registered letter from the Palo Alto City Attorney. Yep, we'd violated the law—by planting trees! He ordered us to remove the spindly saplings, which we'd put in a barren space between sidewalk and street outside our home, and he threatened enforcement proceedings if we failed to comply.

In the 20 years since, we've spearheaded two mayor-appointed tree task forces, successfully lobbied for major revision of local, state, and national government tree policies, and spurred the creation of tree advocacy organizations in Palo Alto and more than a dozen other Bay Area cities and towns. We've organized more than 10,000 residents to plant and maintain nearly 30,000 trees along streets, in parks, on open-space lands, on school grounds, and in residential and commercial landscapes. We've written and distributed software enabling people to better foresee consequences of different municipal tree management policies, published in the *Journal of Forestry*, presented papers at national and international conferences, been featured on network television, and taught many thousands of people about the needs and benefits of trees.

How did we do it? In a nutshell, through an ecological approach to community. With the sum of all the one-on-one relationships among Magicians and others with whom we've interacted toward the achievements listed above, we've created a community of tree advocates. Again and again we've asked, "Who else cares or might care about trees?" "What common ground can we establish with them?" "How can we together further our shared goals?"

Almost everyone we've encountered wants the same things. We're all to some extent mistaken about how to get them. Once people take an ecological approach, admitting to uncertainty, observing and reasoning and imagining together, we're much better able to surrender prejudice and misconception, find common goals, and reach agreement about how to move toward them. We have yet to find a better way to build community.

Listen to Others

In the early years of Magic's street redesign and tree programs, long-term residents around us frequently lamented the neighborhood's status as a forgotten corner of the city. Sympathetic elected officials advised us to gain political clout by creating a formal association. Though we were still planning to leave town in short order and had little desire to take on this task, we heeded what those around us were saying.

In the summer of 1980, Magicians organized a picnic attended by more than 100 residents to launch the Evergreen Park Neighborhood Association (EPNA). For a decade plus we shouldered a lion's share of responsibility, periodically sustaining the association when others flagged.

Since the early 1990s, young families have flooded into Evergreen Park. From their ranks Hilary has recruited and trained a new generation of EPNA leaders. Now others publish the newsletter, organize the annual picnic, and actively pursue issues ranging from school quality, to park maintenance, to emergency preparedness. A community rebirth is under way.

Through EPNA we've drawn neighbors together and given government officials reason to take us seriously. We know hundreds of neighbors by name, and Magicians are honored and respected as "people who made the neighborhood better for everyone."

The rewards of our leading role in EPNA extend far beyond neighborhood affairs. Elected officials—some of whom now occupy county, state, and even national office—and city staff we've met in our capacity as EPNA leaders have joined us in making Magic by facilitating permit processes for expansions and renovations, and by assisting with service projects.

Remember to Dance

Anarchist Emma Goldman is reported to have told some of her more somber colleagues, "If I can't dance, you can have your revolution!" Every Saturday evening 10 or 20

of us honor Emma with a couple hours of dancing and music-making, followed by a potluck supper. These events afford regular opportunities for participants in the extended Magic community to play together.

When Magicians make music and dance we're especially present, and especially grateful. Those of us who've lived and worked closely for many years evidence in our celebrating the richness of these shared pasts. Guests join us in exploring how to be more caring, genuine, and reassuring in such settings.

> Almost everyone we've encountered wants the same things. We're all to some extent mistaken about how to get them.

Stay Open

In February of 1992, we'd just stood up from a Sunday residents' meeting when the phone rang. A former client was calling from one of his neighbors' homes. In the yard outside, more than 100 people had gathered to protest a street closure on the line between their neighborhood and an adjoining town. An angry contingent of several dozen people were threatening to march across the border and vandalize property. The caller wondered if a Magician might come directly and explain how we'd used street closures to improve life in our area.

David hopped on a bike. Twenty minutes later he was standing before an agitated crowd. After he described the Evergreen Park experience, some listeners requested ongoing assistance. Eventually, with the endorsement of all parties, the legislators in the two local governments whose constituents were affected contracted Magic to conduct a public education program.

We soon heard ourselves being called mediators, a word with which we were only vaguely familiar, even though mediation turned out to be how we'd routinely resolved conflicts at Magic from day one. With generous guidance from professionals, training sponsored by a local foundation, and experience gained in two decades of living and working cooperatively, we were able to contribute to a resolution supported by the residents of 80 percent of the approximately 1,000 directly affected households. After reading extensive newspaper coverage of the conflict and its outcome, prospective clients were soon ringing our phone off the hook.

Since then we've mediated hundreds of disputes, and taught conflict resolution skills to couples, families, employee groups, and school children. We've generated substantial income for Magic, won a national award, earned a new identity, and drawn diverse new participants into the Magic service community.

Stand for Common Good

By publicly standing for broad interests of humankind, and backing words with deeds, Magicians provide a rally-

Intentional Community: What Is It All About?

Jennifer Brito

Robin discusses development of the Palo Alto Comprehensive Plan over tea at Magic with a fellow mayoral task force member.

ing point for other thoughtful, good-hearted individuals. We've discovered in our locale a large population of such folks, hungering for partners in a carefully considered approach to public service.

One way we stand is by challenging fundamental ideas long and widely supported by the powerful. During 1993–96 Palo Alto General Plan revisions, Robin served on a mayor-appointed advisory committee. The sole voice advocating strict limits to building and paving, she drew dozens of people to city hall to testify, broadened the public discourse, and prodded the consciences of those—including quite a few of her fellow committee members—who privately conceded that they shared her views but were unwilling to risk standing with her publicly. Individuals who respected our stand during the general plan review process have since supported Magic in other ways, or taken bolder stands in other land use controversies.

Ben Franklin wrote, "The best sermon is a good example." As Magicians learn to better align word and action, others are inspired to stand with us. We bike or walk wherever we go. Even Daniel manages by attaching a "handcycle" to his wheelchair. One day a fellow cyclist pulled up beside Joan and said, "After seeing you arrive on your bike to give that talk to our Rotary, I started commuting by bike. I'm in better shape than I've been since I played college baseball. Our family has saved more than $5,000 by selling our second car."

Integrate

Since the mid-1980s, we've engaged in youth mentoring.

Initially we worked through court referral programs or other agencies. In 1989 we began Magic Mentors. Using volunteer mentors, we've provided services for a fee to affluent families, and without charge to those with less money. Often we'll mentor someone continuously from middle school through high school.

The nominal objective of the mentoring relationship is usually improved academic performance, but our over-arching purpose is to model an ecological approach and to motivate youths to test it. This strategy has paid handsome returns. Mentees have turned failure to success at school, at home, at work, and in other forums. Some have developed talents for writing, music, or sports. Others have found a cause and worked diligently for it. Many have evidenced a newfound love of learning and sense of self-determination.

Through Magic Mentors we transfer wealth from those with surplus to those with little. We provide youths an integrated learning opportunity from a role model only a few years their senior. We assist them in adapting to the environments—school, work, family, larger society—in which they are embedded. And we elicit support for other Magic activities from those able and wanting to provide it. The program might "succeed" without our being attentive to one or several of these outcomes, but we make it much stronger by integrating as we do, and all of them contribute to the evolution of the Magic communities.

Organic Means More Than "Pesticide-Free"

Magic is organic. We grow toward opportunity. David broke a foot in the early 1970s. Previously a dedicated runner, and suddenly unable to run or even to bicycle vigorously, he learned to swim. In the process, he gained insights about how adults learn, and about how to swim farther, faster, with less strain.

Years later, Corinne was offering "lifestyle tune-ups" to people who wanted guidance in change. In 1980 one of her clients, a physician, introduced David to a cardiologist colleague who had injured a shoulder swimming. David suggested stroke technique adjustments. The pain disappeared. With the cardiologist's sponsorship, Magic initiated a swim program for Stanford University faculty and staff.

Over the next few years, we taught several hundred Stanford affiliates. Two of them, a planner and a grounds manager, became interested in a study of native California oaks on campus lands that Erica, a Magic resident intern, was performing. In 1985, they retained Magic to implement an oak regeneration program which continues as we write.

Other swim students included urban planning and civil engineering faculty. They provided expert testimony and research guidance for Magic's neighborhood street redesign and land planning projects. Still others were psychologists, psychiatrists, and anthropologists. They've counseled and advised us as we've explored our individual personalities and group dynamics.

Now, after Magic has been located for decades in the same neighborhood, and has established a reputation for excellence in diverse programs, such fortuitous connections are common. We're routinely presented with more opportunities to grow and develop than we can comfortably accept.

To make the best of these, we aim to remain unencumbered by rigid ideas about who we will be or what we will do in the future. We perceive that the less we insist upon, the freer we are to adapt. By taking an ecological—inherently a questioning—approach, we continuously transform Magic and ourselves.

Too Good to Be True?

All these satisfying tales of success and achievement are only part of our story. We have another side, one in which we've heaped disappointments high.

Within Magic we've been deceitful, rash, indecisive, insensitive, ill-humored, angry, reckless, narrow-minded, thoughtless, lazy, incompetent, fearful, and more. We've worked ineffectively, lived half-heartedly, and felt crummy. At one point in the late 1980s, we abandoned shared vision for individual, and dwindled in just a few months from eight residents to two.

We've sometimes been at odds with the world beyond Magic as well. We've made poor investments, had our property vandalized, been investigated by agencies ranging from the local building department to the US Postal Service, and endured anonymous threatening calls in the middle of the night, obscenities shouted at us on the streets, and malicious rumors.

We've been denied access to facilities, had courses and speaking engagements canceled, seen elected officials manipulate public hearings to limit our testimony, and been stonewalled by government employees. We've lost thousands of trees to drought, rodents, and vandals, mediated disputes without visible positive effect, and watched people we mentored go to jail or even kill themselves.

So yes, we've stumbled, and we've fallen. We have come of age in an era of alienation. We've come together ill-practiced in the arts of community. Like many who stood for common good before us, we've been opposed by those who fear loss of privilege. Like many others who innovate, we've been resisted by those who benefit from adherence to current ways. We're a learning community. So long as we keep learning, failure is impossible. We can only quit or persist.

Yes, We Can!

How many times have you exclaimed or heard someone else protest, "Somebody ought to do something about that!" and then go on to explain, "but I'm too … [tired, busy, powerless, ill-informed …]"? We've made Magic in

The next generation of Magicians learns to care for trees.

large part by seizing these opportunities. Sure, we care about big issues—human numbers, environmental quality, peace, justice, and sound information by which to address all of these. We show that we care by our everyday actions in Palo Alto. Six billion people living day-to-day have arrived at this moment and together we are all, as we write and you read, shaping the next.

29

"Cults" and Intentional Communities
Working Through Some Complicated Issues

by Tim Miller

A FAIR NUMBER OF PEOPLE TODAY believe that our society is swarming with dangerous "cults," religious (and sometimes political or social) organizations that are terribly destructive to their members and a real danger to society at large. For better or worse, intentional communities are often drawn into the "cult" controversy. Communities, after all, in many cases do have features about them that many consider "cultic." Individual will is sometimes suppressed for the good of the group; some communities have strong-minded leaders; commitment to the group can run high; and so forth. Community-minded people, therefore, cannot escape the "great American cult controversy."

While off-course groups and dysfunctional—or even outright evil—individuals certainly do exist, my own conclusion is that the "cult" scare is, by and large, seriously overblown. To say the least, many of the most frequent allegations about the "cult menace" don't hold up under scrutiny. Groups that represent a real threat to the public do not number many thousands, nor do their members number hundreds of thousands, or even millions, as some anticult activists assert—unless one considers every Hindu temple and Muslim mosque and intentional community in the land a dangerous "cult," a patently preposterous proposition. Nor is the "cult menace" growing; religions with unconventional appeal have been around as long as civilization, and the fear of the different is just as ancient as alternative pathways themselves are. While not all traditions and groups and persons are wholesome, most are relatively innocuous. One wishes that the anticult denunciations that are so easy to throw around in generalities would be based on real case-by-case evidence, not the sort of spectral hysteria that fueled the Salem witch trials.

If I could choose just one step forward in the "cult" controversy, it would consist of the abandonment of the term "cult" itself. As Catherine Wessinger once wrote in *Communities* magazine, "The word 'cult,' which formerly referred to an organized system of worship, is now a term that slanders any religion that you don't know about and don't like." The term has come to do for religion what "nigger" has done for race relations. And that does matter; when a society tolerates pejorative language, it announces that some people are marginal, even subhuman. Hate thought, we have painfully learned, can lead to hateful acts. The widespread belief that destructive "cults" are proliferating and posing a grave danger to society can lead to terrible acts. Many who have studied the Waco siege and fire believe that the federal agents at the scene badly overestimated the danger that the Branch Davidians posed to society, never tried to understand just who the Davidians were and what they believed, and as a result set up a situation in which several dozens of innocent persons (many of them children) were killed.

People who see "cults" as a major social menace often draw up lists of generalizations by which a savvy observer should be able to identify evil groups. The problem is that the items on those lists almost always apply just as fully to good, healthy groups as to problematic ones. Consider these items from the typical cult-hazard list:

• "A 'cult' has a strong, powerful, dominant leader." But that doesn't identify inherently dangerous situations. Alan Greenspan, the head of the Federal Reserve System, is

---

Tim Miller teaches in the Department of Religious Studies at the University of Kansas, where he specializes in alternative religions and intentional communities. He is the editor of *America's Alternative Religions* and author of *The Quest for Utopia in Twentieth-Century America*, a multivolume history of intentional communities over the last century. He may be reached at the Department of Religious Studies, University of Kansas, Lawrence KS 66045, USA. Email: tim@ic.org.

enormously powerful and makes decisions that deeply affect the lives of all of us, so is he automatically a "cult leader"?

- "A 'cult' works extremely zealously to attract new members." But missionary zeal is a crucial element of Christianity, Islam, and other religions the world over. Most religions are always very happy to receive new members. You can believe that you know the ultimate truth and work hard to get others to accept your version of truth without deserving to be considered a social menace.

- "A 'cult' is preoccupied with getting money." A lot of groups sure do want your money. In fact I don't think I've ever seen a religion that *wasn't* preoccupied with money. Moneytheism is probably the true American religion. It may be sad that our social institutions seem so uniformly thirsty for cash, but that situation is definitely not unique to "cults."

- "'Cults' suppress questioning and doubt." Most religions believe that they embody the truth, and urge followers to promulgate that truth, not question it. The Pope endlessly tells his flock to *follow* his teaching on birth control and quit questioning it. That hasn't worked too well for him, just as it hasn't worked too well for most leaders, "cultic" or otherwise.

- "Indoctrination techniques help keep people involved in the group." Most groups have rituals and practices that push members to stay involved. It's possible (at a stretch) to see things like meditation and chanting and speaking in tongues and group yoga as manipulative, but they don't cause otherwise sane people to lose their free will.

- "A 'cult' imposes major lifestyle restrictions on members, sometimes telling them what clothes to wear, how to raise their children, and even whom to marry." Most groups are not all that restrictive, but a few, indeed, are. Hardly any, however, are more restrictive than a Catholic religious community that tells its members they can't have sex, can't have much money, and must do as they're told. Most persons wouldn't like that, but those who voluntarily choose a restricted, guided lifestyle often find it empowering. Ask any nun about that.

- "'Cult' members often cut off ties with their birth families and old friends in favor of total dedication to the 'cult'." Actually, that's just what Jesus advised his followers to do; see Matthew 19:29 and Luke 14:26.

- "'Cult' members are asked to give huge amounts of their time to the group." All religions and most social groups urge their members to be highly dedicated to group purposes. Hard workers are prized. And what's so bad about

Mansion house of the historic and controversial Oneida community, 1848 to 1881.

Jillian Downey

working hard for a cause in which one believes? Building community isn't easy, and the most dedicated persons are the ones who make it happen.

All of that is not to say that abuses don't occur, that people don't get hurt. People *do* get exploited, and bad people take advantage of good people in every corner of our society—in child care, in schools, in religious organizations, in offices and businesses, in intentional communities, and everywhere else. What's unfair is singling out small religious organizations and intentional communities for special persecution just because they happen to fit someone's preconceptions about "cults." People have the right to basic freedoms as long as they're not hurting others, and they should be regarded as innocent until proven guilty. When truly abusive situations do occur, call the police. Short of that, friendly dialogue is usually possible if you don't come on like a mortal enemy.

The average person encounters thousands of individuals, groups, and communities in a lifetime, and inescapably has to work through a never-ending process of making judgments about them. If you encounter an intentional community or a religious group you need to evaluate, I would suggest keeping precepts like these in mind:

- Different is not always pathological, and "normal" is not always safe. Some groups can be wildly unconventional yet utterly harmless; others can look very normal, superficially, and still be deeply flawed.

- People have different needs. One person's great communitarian or religious experience can be another's worst nightmare.

- Double standards are unfair. Small, offbeat groups should have the same rights and privileges as large, well-established ones. Lots of groups of all sizes and types are eagerly looking for new members, for example, and it is not any more wrong for a small, unconventional community to urge you to join than it is for the biggest church or social club in town to do so.

- One should take responsibility for one's own actions. One of the most frequent allegations against "cults" is that they engage in brainwashing of prospective members. Actually, intelligent brains are next to impossible to wash. Most people are well capable of making decisions that are right for them and usually have mainly themselves to blame when they make bad ones. Our society seems to encourage people to blame others for their bad decisions, and that misses the real problem.

- The nature of personal relations is subtle and never the same twice. One individual may encounter a given group and find it the best thing that ever happened to him or her; another person may find the same group disgusting. People need to find their own congenial relationships. Joining a group is rather like romance—the chemistry that makes it magical is different in every case.

⑥

… religions with unconventional appeal have been around as long as civilization, and the fear of the different is just as ancient as alternative pathways themselves are.

Behaviors often criticized as signs of abusive situations do not necessarily identify a dysfunctional religious group or community. What, then, should a prospective communitarian do to avoid falling in with a bad crowd?

The basic answer is eternal vigilance. One should be on the lookout all the time—and probably more so in regular, daily life than in a communal situation. Keep both eyes open, and don't let emotion get in the way of common sense. Be wary of persons who are both authoritarian and convinced that they have all the answers. Most communities are wonderful, uplifting places that provide their members with good, meaningful lives, but a few fall short of the mark. If you'll indulge me in one last list, here are a few final tips on staying centered in life:

- Trust your instincts. If you don't feel good about a person or situation, remain skeptical until your doubts have been resolved.
- Don't give your money away unless you are willing to let it go unconditionally and never see it again.
- Remember that things are not always what they initially seem; keep your options open even as you begin to take steps toward serious commitment.
- Question authority.
- Stay away from people who have guns.
- Remember that life goes on; if you make a mistake, extract yourself from it and get on with things.

Communities, on the whole, are the greatest! With a bit of prudent common sense, living in the company of others can be the best experience life has to offer.

Resources/Notes

Many calm and reflective books on nonmainstream religions provide a useful counterpoint to the rather sensational array of popular volumes that have contributed so heavily to the widespread public fear of the influence and growth of "cults."

All of the works of the British sociologist of religion Eileen Barker offer useful insights; perhaps the most direct is *New Religious Movements: A Practical Introduction* (Unipub, London, 1989).

John A. Saliba, a Jesuit priest, knows a lot about disciplined community living; his books, especially *Understanding New Religious Movements* (Grand Rapids, Michigan, 1995), are fair, measured, and quietly rational.

Mariana Caplan, who lives in the Hohm Community in Arizona, offers solid personal insights into the stresses that occur in families when children make religious or personal choices not pleasing to their parents in her book *When Sons and Daughters Choose Alternative Lifestyles* (Hohm Press, Prescott, Arizona, 1996), and offers practical suggestions for getting beyond hostility and stereotyping in the generational conflict.

My own perspectives on "cult" issues are elaborated at greater length in a theme section on "Intentional Communities and 'Cults'" that I edited for *Communities* magazine, No. 88, Fall 1995.

Why I Joined a "Cult," Why I Left, and What I Learned
by Mark Schonbeck

In the following paragraphs, I will describe my experiences with a group that our society has labeled a "cult." The process of learning about, joining, participating in, then leaving this group taught me the value of thinking and observing for myself, and of respecting others' freedom to do so.

As a full time biology graduate student in the 1970s, I became convinced that biochemistry and other sciences would soon explain and "solve" every mystery, from why I was depressed and lonely, to what creates beauty in the world. Since I found the Christian version of God scary and oppressive, I initially took comfort in this rationalistic paradigm. But after a while, life began to seem pointless and meaningless.

Enter Scientology, the religious philosophy and self-help system developed by L. Ron Hubbard. My elder brother found some of its concepts helpful, and he introduced me and our parents to it. I began to read some of Ron Hubbard's basic books. Although I found them simplistic and a little condescending, I was struck by his basic tenet that each of us humans is a spiritual being who is "basically good." He also asserted that all the pain and distress in our lives is just "stuff" that can be removed by Scientology counseling and training. I took a couple of basic courses and played with the concepts in philosophical discussions with friends. Then, when my parents dramatically improved their marriage after doing some Scientology counseling, I became convinced that it really had something to offer.

In 1978, I received some Scientology counseling. It was very expensive, but it was one of the best decisions I ever made. My counselor was wonderful, and I broke through to a sense of hope that I had never before experienced. Spirit and purpose became real to me for the first time. During the next year, I was continually overjoyed by two simple facts: I was no longer depressed, and I could make *friends!* Within six months of starting a new job over 1,000 miles from my previous home, I had about a dozen good, trusted, enjoyable friends, and I was beginning to excel at work.

Scientology has a spiritual hierarchy, which they call The Bridge, that promises far higher levels of spiritual well-being than my new-found happiness. I had visions of climbing up The Bridge and then helping others to do so as well.

The Church of Scientology is quite a missionary movement, trying to bring as many people into its fold as possible, and promising salvation from the hell of one's past hurts and misdeeds (what we might call karma). Since the counseling had turned my life around, I felt ready to commit myself to this world-saving effort, and I began to invite work associates to explore Scientology (albeit without success). When newspapers and magazines published articles calling Scientology a "dangerous cult," I replied with a strongly worded letter in defense of Scientology. I found attempts by so-called "deprogrammers" to forcibly extricate young adults from Scientology and other "cults" particularly offensive, as they violated self determinism and freedom of religion.

In the early 1980s, when I began Scientology training on weekends in San Francisco, the glow began to wear off. I again had some problems coping with day to day life, and I took several steps up The Bridge without finding the solutions I sought. Meanwhile, I became increasingly disturbed by the soaring prices charged for Scientology services, the Church's high-pressure evangelizing approach to acquiring new members, and the authoritarian tone of Ron Hubbard's writings and directives. These factors made it harder for me to talk to my non-Scientology friends about my spiritual path.

The more I read and observed, the narrower the Scientology path seemed. Hubbard scorned other spiritual practices, medicine, psychiatry, and much of mainstream society, and forbade Scientology students and clients to engage in any other spiritual or self-help practice. The idea that Scientology could answer *all* questions and solve *all* personal and planetary problems, and that all other paths were therefore irrelevant, began to give me the same empty, meaningless feeling that I had experienced in my atheist/materialist phase.

In 1983, officials from Flag, the worldwide center of Scientology, came to San Francisco to blow the whistle on several small businesses run by Scientologists who had allegedly "altered or misused

(Continued on following page)

(Continued from previous page)

Scientology methods." Students who had patronized any of these businesses, including myself, were asked to go to Flag for a four-day minicourse on the evils of straying from the straight-and-narrow. Since Flag officials made it clear that we would not be allowed to continue our regular courses or counseling until we completed this minicourse, I chose to comply.

The Flag experience itself was mixed. I was energized by the shared belief that we were doing very important, world-saving work. However, I found Flag instructors and staff very controlling, and I observed that individual differences of opinion were suppressed.

Over the next 18 months, several of my closest friends left the Church of Scientology and joined an independent group of scientology practitioners offering affordable services in a less rigid manner. The Church condemned the independent group and insisted that I and other Church students cut off all communications with friends who had "deserted." However, when my own mother left the Church, I worked up the courage to visit the independent group so I could draw my own conclusions. What I saw was a benevolent, caring group of people offering counseling and courses in a relaxed, friendly atmosphere. I also saw a young woman who had been in my class at the Church a few months earlier, and she now looked as if a huge weight had been lifted from her shoulders.

My liberation began at that moment. After thinking it all over for a few weeks, I left the Church of Scientology in January 1985. "Now," I thought, "I'm free!" But that was just the beginning of a long learning. I still believed that scientology (with a small "s") was the best path to psycho-spiritual health, so I did counseling and training with the independent group. A year later, I felt that I was making little progress on my spiritual path. At first, I was quite dismayed, but then I found satisfaction in other aspects of life. I started a new relationship, spent more time on hobbies, and donated time to a peace group.

Later that year, I left my position with an agricultural chemical company, moved across the country, and joined New Alchemy Institute, a small alternative agriculture and technology research institute. Then a whole new world opened up to me. I met strong, compassionate, deep-thinking people on all kinds of spiritual paths—Sufi, new age, Hindu, Jewish, liberal Christian, pagan. Slowly, I realized that there could be many ways to "truth" and healing, and all of them could be valid. I listened as travelers of different paths engaged in friendly (and highly fascinating) dialogue. Gradually, I outgrew my fear that I would be forever lost if I strayed from "*the* path"—whatever that was.

In fall of 1988, I went to a weekend pagan spirituality workshop led by Starhawk, and I found my spiritual home. Here was a belief system that revered the Earth as much as the Heaven; celebrated male and female equally; encouraged song and dance, fun and laughter and creativity; and sought to heal both person and planet. Above all, there was no straight and narrow, only a rich polytheistic culture that honored a diversity of rituals, deities, personal lifestyles, and practices, and *encouraged me to think and feel as an independent adult person.* Much of what I had sought at the end of a long, costly Scientology Bridge, I could now find in a circle of equals.

In 1991, I joined a small intentional community of which I am still a member. Some of our basic tenets are to respect the diversity of members' choices in lifestyle and spirituality, and to honor the unique value of each individual, as well as the welfare of the group. In this context, I feel free to find my own path, and I am reminded to respect others' self determinism and religious freedom.

Reflecting on my story, I see that some Church of Scientology officials, as well as anticult "deprogrammers," lacked this respect for others. Did Scientology tromp on my self determinism, or did I *allow* it to do some of my thinking for me? Perhaps a little of both. In any case, my Scientology experience taught me valuable lessons: that mine is *not* the only path, that one can outgrow one system and move on to another practice, and that the multitude of spiritual paths enriches the lives of all.

Mark Schonbeck has been a member of Tekiah community (now merged with Abundant Dawn community) in Floyd, Virginia for eight years. He is an agricultural researcher, organic vegetable gardener, and technical writer. He is also learning to weave hemp hammocks as part of an on-site community business.

Red Carpets and Slammed Doors
Visiting Communities

by Geoph Kozeny

Hoping to visit a community? The good news is that most communities welcome visitors, and a majority of those are open to new members. The bad news? Because so many community seekers are wanting to visit, many communities are facing visitor overload and are feeling burned out from the seemingly never-ending flow of strangers. The best news: if you're considerate and persistent, the odds are good that you'll be able to arrange a visit and have a great experience.

An essential element of planning a satisfying visit is to get really clear about what it is, exactly, that you want from a community—what is the purpose of your visit? Further, you'll save considerable time and effort if you learn to intuit how well any given community's reality will match up with the picture you've envisioned. There's definitely an art to this prescreening process, as it's based solely on information from written materials, letters, phone calls, and perhaps a Web site—nothing physical that you can actually see, touch, smell, or taste.

While you're exploring communities from a distance, it also pays to sort through, point by point, all the different features and characteristics that you think you'll want. Ask yourself which attributes are mandatory for you, which are strong preferences, and which would be nice but you could live without? This directory is probably the best resource you'll find for helping you wrap your mind around the possibilities. Carefully study each group's entry in the cross-reference chart and its written description (in the Listings section)—with practice you can learn to use

that information to spot potential incompatibilities in visions, values, and social norms. And please, don't assume that the community welcomes visitors just because they're listed in this book. Be sure to check out the "Do you welcome visitors?" column in the charts.

Even under stress, many overloaded communities will agree to the idea of hosting more visitors, usually due to a sense of mission or obligation, but beware: often it is only the visitor coordinator and a few others who are enthusiastic about the idea. Some community members, typically acting from instinct rather than clarity, will go about their daily lives while keeping a low profile and acting distant in a weary, mostly subconscious attempt to minimize interactions with the newest batch of "tourists"—which might turn out to be you. Try not to take it personally.

Introductions and First Impressions

Usually the best line of first contact is through a friend who knows the community and is willing to give you a personal referral. If you don't have a friend with direct connections, friends-of-friends can prove just as effective.

Use your network of friends and acquaintances creatively—let it be known that you're interested in visiting certain communities, and ask your friends if they, or anyone they know, has a connection to those groups. If through correspondence, or especially through a visit, you make a good connection with a member of one community, ask that person if they can recommend an especially good contact at the other communities you hope to visit.

Geoph Kozeny has lived in various kinds of communities for 27 years, and has been on the road for the past 12 years—visiting, studying, facilitating, and consulting for intentional communities scattered all across North America. He asks about their visions and realities, takes photos, and gives slide shows about the diversity and vitality of the communities movement. He was a core staff member for the first edition of the *Communities Directory*, and is a regular columnist for *Communities* magazine. Presently, he is completing production of a full-length video documentary on intentional communities, due for release in the spring of 2000. He can be reached via Community Catalyst Project, c/o 1531 Fulton Street, San Francisco CA 94117, USA.

Remember: the community you are visiting is also someone's home.

If your feelers yield a connection, be sure to open your introductory letter or phone call by saying that "So-and-so over at Community 'x' referred me." On the other hand, avoid giving the impression that you're a name-dropper, or that you're trying to do an end-run around their official channels—alienating the community's designated visitor coordinator is a lousy way to start a visit.

If no leads materialize, there's still a reasonably good chance of making a fruitful connection through a self-introduction. Avoid sending a letter that poses a long list of questions about the community, but which provides little or no information about who you are and what you're seeking. Although there's a wide range of styles that can work well in a letter of inquiry, a good general formula is to give approximately equal emphasis to (1) describing what you're looking for, how you heard about them, and why they interest you; (2) telling about your history, skills, and special needs; and (3) posing questions about their community and their visiting protocols.

Your letter should be short, to the point, and engaging—if you send a long letter, you run the risk of overwhelming them right off the bat, or of having your letter shunted to the needs-to-be-answered-but-requires-a-lot-of-time-and-energy-to-deal-with pile. Such letters, unfortunately, only occasionally make it back to the top of the priority pile. Usually a one-page letter is best, and two pages should be the absolute maximum—anything

longer than that reduces your chances of getting a prompt response. If you want to be remembered, enclose a photo, art work, doodles, an interesting article, or something else eye-catching to make your letter stand out in the crowd (but please—no confetti, glitter, or other mess-making surprises). And be sure to include a self-addressed stamped envelope (SASE).

Another helpful hunting hint is to consider first visiting one or more groups located in your region, even if they are not a likely candidate for where you'll finally want to settle, so you can hone your visitor skills. The fact that they're relatively easy to get to means you can get some visiting experience under your belt without a large investment of your time or resources. It can be pretty devastating to use up all your precious vacation traveling cross-continent to visit your dream community, only to discover that it's not at all what you had in mind (which is fairly common, by the way). Instead, go through the steps face-to-face with real people, and get comfortable doing the interviews, the work, and the socializing.

Following Up

The sad truth is that many groups don't respond to letters in a timely fashion, in spite of good intentions (that's why the listings in this directory include the group's answer to the question "Can you commit to responding promptly?"). The reality is that living in community can be very demanding—there's always so much to be done—and answering a stack of correspondence doesn't usually rank as high on the chore list as milking the cows, supervising the kids, taking out the recycling, or building the new community center.

If your letter has received no response after three to four weeks, a short phone call is probably in order. Try to pick a time when folks are likely to be around and not otherwise busy. Often early evenings, or right before or after a meal, are good times to call. If you reach an answering machine, identify yourself, leave your number, and ask them to call you back at their convenience. Suggest times when you're most reachable, and explain that when they do get through, you'll be happy to hang up and call them right back on your dime.

When you finally reach a live person, first introduce yourself, mentioning your referral if you have one, and explain that you're interested in visiting. Be sure to note that you've already sent a letter. Ask whoever answers if they're a good person to talk with about visiting and arrangements, and verify that this is a good time to talk. If the time's not right, make a date to call back at a better time. If they suggest you talk with someone else, note the new name and ask for suggestions about how and when to reach the identified contact person. When you do finally connect with your contact person, be sure to verify up front all the details related to visiting (see sidebar on the following page).

If you wrote and got no response, it's usually far better to call first rather than show up unannounced. However, if they have no phone listing in the *Directory*, or if their line's always busy (fairly common these days with modems, fax machines, and teenagers), or if their published number has been disconnected and the community has no listing in Directory Assistance, then an exploratory "Hello" might be in order. If you've tried well in advance to reach a community but received no reply, it may work to "drop by" for a few minutes to introduce yourself—but be sensitive to their energy levels. Be prepared to find accommodations elsewhere, and arrange to come back when it's convenient for them. A 10- or 15-minute visit may be all that's appropriate if you catch them in the middle of something—but if your timing's good, you might get the deluxe two-hour tour right on the spot, plus get invited to dinner. Be flexible.

Drop-in visitors can be especially awkward for groups that are far off the beaten path, but in most cases you can locate a park or a campground within commuting distance. If they remember your letter, they'll know you made a bona fide effort to set up a visit and that they were the ones to drop the ball by not responding—so make your letter memorable.

Fitting In

Always remember: the community you want to visit is also somebody's home, so plan on using the same standards you'd use if you were visiting a hometown friend or relatives you see only occasionally.

Often it's helpful to figure out why they're open to visitors in the first place. They may be:
• seeking new members
• needing help with the work
• wanting the stimulation of meeting new people
• spreading their vision (e.g., egalitarianism, ecovillages) or religion (including the promotion of "community")

What will they gain from your stay? There are infinite ways to plug in and make yourself useful. Pitch in with everyday chores such as gardening, farm work, construction projects, bulk mailings, cooking, cleaning, dishes, childcare. You may gain "Much Appreciated Guest" status if you have special skills to offer: layout or graphic design (newsletters), computer skills, meeting facilitation, storytelling, music, massage. One fellow I met is a chiropractor who plies his trade, for free, at each community he visits. A woman therapist offers private counseling and

Get Things Clear Up Front

• Confirm that the community allows visitors, and that you'll be welcome to visit.
• Do they have particular times when visitors are welcome, regular visitor days, or a visitor program? Plan to be flexible to accommodate their scheduling needs.
• Do they have written Visitors' Guidelines that they could send you? Do they have policies or agreements about smoking, drugs, alcohol, diet, kids, pets, nudity, celibacy, quiet hours, etc. that you need to know about in advance?
• Usually it's best to leave pets at home.
• Do they have any literature about themselves that you can read in the meantime? Brochures? Copies of articles written about them? A Web site?
• Are there any costs involved (visitor fees, utilities, food)?
• Verify length of stay, and any work that will be expected of you. If no work is expected, ask if you'll be able to help them with their work projects. (This is one of the best ways to get to know individual members as well as to learn about the community's daily life.)
• Confirm what you will need to bring: bedding, towels, shampoo, rain gear, work clothes and gloves, special foods, etc. Inform them of any unusual needs you may have (diet, allergies, medications). To the extent possible, plan to cover for yourself so that meeting your special needs doesn't become a burden on the community.
• Let them know if you can provide your own accommodation, such as a tent, RV, or a van to sleep in. Sometimes, if they're feeling overwhelmed with visitors, being self-sufficient in that way will increase your chances of getting invited.
• If you are traveling by public transportation and need to be picked up, try to arrange a convenient time and place of arrival. If a special trip is required to pick you up, reimburse the community for their travel costs.
• Even if a community requires no visitor fees, offer to pitch in a few bucks for food and utility costs. Especially when visiting small communities, I like to bring a special treat for the members—a bag of fruit, almonds, gourmet coffee, ice cream (or rice dream for the vegans).
• If you need to alter your dates or cancel the visit, please inform the community immediately. They may have turned away other visitors in order to make room for you.

group sessions to community members. Another fellow built a solar oven at each community he visited. Alternative building technologies, permaculture, and composting toilet expertise are all skills generally in high demand. Often, however, the most appreciated contribution is your willingness to pitch in to help with whatever boring chore needs doing at the moment.

Some groups are not organized in a way that lets them take advantage of visitor labor, and your desire to pitch in can actually become more of a headache for them than a help. Use your intuition in such situations. Make suggestions, but be open— offer, but don't push too hard. If they aren't able to involve you in the work and don't have much time to spend with you, be prepared to entertain yourself: bring books, tapes, musical instruments, etc.

Some groups use a buddy system for orienting visitors, pairing each visitor with a community member who can serve as a guide and a liaison. Having an identified support person to turn to is often helpful, and if the community doesn't use such a system, you might look around for someone willing to fill that role.

It's important to be clear about your underlying motives so that both your expectations and the community's are realistic. Are you seeking a community to join, or gathering ideas about how groups deal with various issues so you can start your own, or perhaps just curious about shared living options and open to being inspired? Perhaps you're looking for a love affair or relationship? That may, in fact, be a possibility, but usually you'll alienate community members who sense you're on the prowl for romance rather than looking for community. What you're most likely to get in those situations is the hot seat, the cold shoulder, an invitation to leave, or some unpleasant combination of the three.

Sometimes awkward situations will come up, and it can take fairly sophisticated interpersonal skills to set things straight with your hosts. After all, many people have been conditioned to be stoic, and your hosts may be reluctant to say anything "impolite" about something you're doing that's bothering them. In those cases it's up to you to initiate the process of exploring any concerns or annoyances that they're sitting on, and it's much better to get those things out in the open early in your visit, before unexpressed resentments fester. Gracefully facing awkward issues head-on will give you the option to work on them and to develop a rapport with your hosts. Ignoring the tension will usually feed the sense of alienation or mistrust, and prompt your hosts to close up a bit more with every interaction.

It's a warm and wonderful feeling to be included by the group and to experience a sense of "being in community"

⑥

No two communities are identical and, in fact, no community is the same today as it was five years ago—nor will it be the same five years hence.

during your first visit, but don't count on it. Deep connections often take time, and sometimes come only after mutual trust and friendship have been solidly established.

Beyond First Impressions

"Being human" implies that we all bring along some baggage from our conditioning, and that we are seldom capable of living up to our own high standards. The discrepancy between our visions of an ideal world and the reality of our daily lives is probably the most common catalyst underlying the creation of new intentional communities. As a result, what we *say* we're going to do, both as individuals and as communities, is usually a lot more grandiose than what we actually accomplish. Keeping that perspective in mind while visiting communities can help keep your expectations in line with probabilities, and may ultimately help you avoid setting yourself up for a lot of unnecessary disappointment.

Visiting communities is much like dating—people have a tendency to put their best foot forward and try to hide what they consider to be weaknesses. It's helpful to fine tune your eyes and ears to pick up pieces of the hidden story, and to sensitize yourself to what kinds of conversations and interactions will give you an accurate sense of the underlying day-to-day realities. Remember, undesirable habits are easily obscured when members are on their best behavior. If you visit at least a handful of communities, you can compare and contrast their strengths and weaknesses. There's no better way than visiting to learn what to look for and where to find it.

To dig deeper, learn how to ask friendly but penetrating questions. After you've gotten to know a new group well enough to get more personal, try posing such open-ended queries as:

• What are some of the things you like best about living here? The least?
• What's the most difficult issue your community has had to deal with in the last year, or in the last five years?
• How many members have left in the past year or two, and why did they leave?
• How has the community changed over the years? What changes would you like to see in the future?
• What are some of the big challenges your community is facing now?
• How has living here contributed to your personal growth and happiness?

If the community members perceive you as being sincere, interested, and open minded, most will be willing to engage with you in a thoughtful dialogue. However, if they sense that you've already made up your mind about what's right—and are likely to pass judgment on them when they fall short of your expectations—not much information will be forthcoming.

Avoid stereotypes of how you think communities "should" be. If you assume they will have any particular standard or feature you associate with "communities"— things like art facilities, organic gardens, health food, homeschooling, sexual openness—you're asking for disappointment. Many will have at least a few of those features, but few will have them all. Being outspoken or opinionated about the "shoulds" is an easy way to wear out your welcome fast (or to not get invited in the first place, if it shows up during the introductory phase). If something you value highly seems to be missing, ask them about it. Would they be open to it in the future? Would there be room and support for you to introduce it? Present your concern as "Is it likely the group would be open to this?" rather than "I couldn't live here unless...."

While probing for deeper understanding, be sensitive to members' needs for privacy and quiet time, and to what kind of energy you're putting out. If you make a good personal connection, chances are good that they'll be happy to offer you hospitality; otherwise, hosting you tends to become a chore for them, or worse, an annoyance.

What's Really Important?

Having talked to thousands of community seekers over several decades, I am convinced that most of us do not truly know what would make us happy, nor do we see how habits we've developed over the decades stand in the way of our accomplishing the things we say we want. It's only after we've tried something a time or two that we really understand how important, or not, that thing is to our happiness. For example, I've witnessed dozens of back-to-the-land dreamers who moved to the country to do gardening, raise livestock, chop wood, and carry water ... only to discover that those things are hard work that cause calluses, sunburn, mosquito bites, sore backs, and are subject to the harsh unpredictabilities of nature. Many of those dreamers adapt to the reality and subsequently thrive in that environment, but nearly as many decide to move back to a more urban, less physically demanding lifestyle.

Real-life experience can be similarly eye-opening for folks with visions of a community based on shared ownership, cooperative businesses, and consensus decision making. Living that way can certainly be inspiring and fulfilling, but because most of us have grown up in a society that emphasizes individualism and competition, we are often surprised by how challenging and frustrating the cooperative life can be. Often we fail to see how our attitudes and actions are contributing to the problems rather than generating solutions.

One problem stems from the fact that we do mostly mental research and don't get nearly enough hands-on

Visiting communities can teach you what to look for and where to find it.

Jillian Downey

experience. The best way to learn about yourself, and about the communities themselves, is to visit. In that context you can experiment with balancing work involvement with social involvement, and experience how easy (or not) it is for you to adapt to a new culture.

Love at First Sight?

Investigating communities that are based on the idea of creating a better life can be very refreshing. However, be warned: there is a tendency to fall in love with the first group visited. It usually pays to check out a few more anyway. Your first impression may be based on the excitement of discovering the many ways the group's vision matches your own, but be sure that you also look for the differences. For a good match, both you and the community need to be able to tolerate each other's rough edges.

There may have been some common interactions that you missed. Did you get to see the group go through a meeting process? Did you watch them deal with a challenging issue? People's rough edges are most likely to show up when they're under heavy stress, so unless you saw them under pressure, you'll probably leave with an incomplete picture of how well they fare when dealing with interpersonal tensions. If you do witness them working on a conflict, try to hear both sides and watch to see if they approach differences with an open mind.

If you develop a closeness with folks in one subgroup, you will most likely see and hear an incomplete picture of the issues and norms in question. Seek out members holding an opposing point of view, and see if you can understand their side of the issue. It's also possible that a few influential members are away on trips, and the vibe at the community may be very different when they're home—more supportive if it's a primary nurturer/diplomat who's absent, or more strained if it's the chief skeptic/troublemaker who's gone. Additionally, there may be other visitors present whose issues or energy affect the dynamics.

You can learn a lot from other visitors, and from folks living in other communities. Both groups have a perspective that's somewhat detached from the hubbub of the everyday reality, and it's quite possible that they've witnessed the group under stress. Ex-members are also a great source of perspective on what tensions might be lurking below the surface, and how deep they're submerged.

It's usually a good idea to let your first impressions percolate before deciding to make a commitment to join a community. After a first visit, spend some time away from the group to see how well your initial impression holds up when you're no longer being influenced by their energy and enthusiasm. It's especially interesting and informative to listen to yourself handle questions about the community posed by your pre-community friends and acquaintances.

A Never-Ending Quest

No two communities are identical and, in fact, no community is the same today as it was five years ago—nor will it be the same five years hence. Visions change, priorities change, the cast of characters will change, people will get older, the weather will get colder. This ever-evolving nature makes the search for a community to join both interesting and challenging. What you experience during a first visit is unlikely to remain static, yet you must decide based on that initial impression. And you must be prepared to adapt to the shifts in values and priorities that will inevitably come with the passing of time.

With that in mind, pay careful attention to the ideas and interactions that feel best to you, noting whether it's the philosophy, the lifestyle, the place, or the people that

ⓖ

... there is a tendency to fall in love with the first group visited. It usually pays to check out a few more anyway.

touch you at the deepest level. If you feel yourself drawn most energetically to a group whose stated philosophy isn't very well aligned with your own, it'll probably not work out for you to be there for the long haul. However, if they're open to it, consider spending more time with them in order to explore what makes it work for you on the energetic level. Similarly, for a community with ideals matching yours but a shortage of group chemistry, try spending enough time with them to learn about what's either lacking or overdone—what's getting in the way of the synergy?

Sorting through all the complexities can be overwhelming, and the best thing you can do to gain perspective and solace is to connect with others who can relate to what you're going through. If you know of friends who are also on a community quest, consider creating a support group to share experiences, insights, and leads. Scan the ads in the alternative press and on the bulletin boards of nearby co-ops and health food stores, looking for announcements of support groups and networking opportunities. Check out the Intentional Communities Web site, http://www.ic.org/, and follow the links from there. Or participate in one of FIC's semiannual Art of Community conferences, a veritable cornucopia of seekers, networkers, and communitarians coming together to share information on the hows, whys, and wheres of shared living—it's a special opportunity to learn a lot in a few days about a number of communities, from a wealth of experienced communitarians, and in an atmosphere of community.

Living in intentional community is a lot of hard work, but it's a noble undertaking that offers great rewards for those with enough vision and perseverance to stick with it. The first step in that process is finding a group compatible with your vision of a better world, and the rest of the work—for the rest of your life—will require an open mind, creativity, flexibility, commitment, integrity, common sense, and a lot of heart. Daunting? Yes, but worth it. Happy hunting.

An Introduction to the Fellowship for Intentional Community

by the FIC Editorial Review Board

FORMED AS A REGIONAL NETWORK IN 1948, the Fellowship for Intentional Community (FIC) shifted to a continent-wide focus in 1986. We began holding semiannual organizational meetings in 1987, and set about identifying the intentional community movement's needs and selecting projects to meet those needs.

The Fellowship's work is based on four common values: cooperation, nonviolence, inclusivity, and unrestricted freedom to leave a group at any time.

To promote these values, the Fellowship has pursued four main goals:

• To act as a clearinghouse for up-to-date information about intentional communities, including referrals to match groups seeking new members with people in search of a group. This work occasionally leads to receiving critical feedback. When it does, we try to promote dialog and resolution between communities and dissatisfied members or visitors.

• To build familiarity and trust among communities by encouraging communication, contact, and joint activities.

• To facilitate exchange of skills, technical information, and practical experience among communities—both those that are well established and those newly forming.

• To broaden the wider culture's awareness of cooperative alternatives and the practical value of the structures and "tools" developed by intentional communities. We regularly explain the reality and potential of community choices to the press.

How do we accomplish these goals?

Publications

The Fellowship's first major project was creating the 1990 *Directory of Intentional Communities*, which took more than two years to compile. We sold out three printings and 18,000 copies of this highly successful book, and then repeated that performance with the second edition, released in 1995. Over the last decade the *Directory* has become the benchmark reference for options in intentional community living.

Encouraged by the popularity of the *Directory*, the Fellowship decided to revive a companion publication, *Communities* magazine. Launched in 1972, the magazine had been in decline in the mid-80s, and we breathed new life into it after becoming the publisher in 1992. Today it's a vibrant 80-page quarterly that complements the *Directory* with regular features like the "Directory Update" column and Reach ads, listing the latest news in what individuals and groups are looking for in each other.

In November 1994 a group coalesced at an FIC organizational meeting that went on to create the Intentional Communities Web site, http://www.ic.org/. The FIC portion of that site, http://www.ic.org/fic/, has up-to-date information about our activities, and select content of our publications available online.

In 1999 FIC took over Community Bookshelf, a 20-year-old mail order business specializing in titles on cooperative living. Our catalog is available both in print and online, at http://bookshelf.ic.org/.

The Editorial Review Board (ERB) of the FIC has responsibility for ensuring the quality of Fellowship publications with respect to organizational values and mission. This calls for balancing authors' freedom of individual expression with subject matter relevant to our publications and our audience's ability to understand and work constructively with the style and content of the writing. Our goal always is promoting dialog which enhances cooperation and community. FIC publications include *Communities Directory*, *Communities* magazine, the Fellowship Newsletter, and our Web site at http://www.ic.org/. Current members of the ERB are Betty Didcoct, Paul DeLapa, and Laird Schaub.

Intentional Community: What Is It All About?

FIC organizational meeting, November 1996, at The Farm community in Tennessee.

Fellowship Organizational Meetings

The Fellowship is administered by a board of directors, which gathers together with as much of the staff as can come, twice yearly for four-day meetings, hosted each time by a different community or support organization. In an attempt to make meetings accessible to participants from all corners of the continent, the location is rotated from region to region across North America. While the board sessions focus on values and policy questions, committee meetings are happening all around the edges, providing a rich foment for brainstorming and program development. Organizational meetings are open to all, and are operated by consensus in a way that encourages input from all who attend. There is no better way to meet the folks who make the FIC go, to find out what's going on, and to find a spot where your energy might fit in.

As we work together, understanding deepens, trust builds, and Fellowship meetings and projects become important personal experiences—much more than just occasions for doing business. As a decentralized organization, different tasks are managed from different sites, and it's not uncommon for a project team to be scattered across the continent.

Each gathering is a time to meet new people and renew established friendships—expanding the personal connections that are the ultimate wealth of our organization. Fellowship members receive copies of the periodic newsletter, and notice of all meetings. In addition, board meeting invitations are sent to everyone on our mailing list who lives within a day's drive of the meeting site.

FIC Events

In 1993, the Fellowship created the Celebration of Community. With 1,000 attending all or part of the event, it was the largest community-focused event ever held. There were more than 200 workshops spread out over six days. On the seventh day, as far as we know, everyone rested.

Since 1997, the Fellowship has put on regional Art of Community conferences at least twice a year, often in conjunction with our organizational meetings. Participants attend nuts and bolts workshops on practical topics like decision making, conflict resolution, sustainable building, community financing and fundraising, and also enjoy the excellent opportunities for face-to-face contact with other community-minded people from the area.

Revolving Loan Fund

The Fellowship assumed management of a long-established community loan fund when the Community Educational Services Council (CESCI) dissolved in the summer of 1994. Since 1952 this fund has loaned out over $200,000—in amounts up to $5,000—to help intentional community businesses with start-ups or expansions.

Who Joins the Fellowship?

Anyone who wants to be part of the fun! Anyone interested in supporting the intentional communities movement and the vision of the Fellowship. A member community may be of any form: an ecovillage, a cohousing group, a residential cooperative, a hippie farm, a monastery. Individual members may live in a cooperative situation, or may be completely unaffiliated. Alternative businesses and networking organizations can join as nonresidential affiliates (see the membership card at the back of the book for details).

A Dream in Progress

For many of us, the Fellowship is the realization of a long-sought vision: a continental association dedicated to nurturing and promoting a greater sense of community in lives everywhere, and to helping people find the right home in community for themselves and their families. This dream can grow only as fast as people feel the call to come together and do the work. If you're inspired to participate in the flowering of the intentional communities movement, please get in touch. We'd love to hear from you.

Fellowship Headquarters
RR 1 Box 156
Rutledge MO 63563, USA
Tel/Fax: 660-883-5545
Email: fic@ic.org
http://www.ic.org/fic/

Sandhill Farm

The Many Flavors of Community

Every community is unique, and yet, some of them share certain obvious characteristics, or choose to define themselves as specific types of community—including cohousing developments, ecovillages, student co-ops, communes, land trusts, ashrams, monasteries, urban collectives, housing co-ops, and more. These articles are meant to be a brief introduction to some of these types of communities, and are a good place to start. Reading the Community Listings section will fill in the rest of the picture of the wide spectrum of communities that make up the communities movement.

What is Ecovillage?

by Tony Sirna

ECOVILLAGE IS A VISION. ECOVILLAGE IS A GOAL. ECOVILLAGE IS AN IDEAL.

Around the world, many people are starting to use the term "ecovillage" to describe their communities, projects, and other endeavors. What do people mean by "ecovillage"? What do these projects share in common, and how are they diverse?

First, ecovillage is a vision, an ideal, a goal. Except for some aboriginal villages that have retained their ancient sustainable cultures, there are no examples of fully realized ecovillages as of this writing. Those using the term are describing a commitment or intent to live more sustainably, reintegrating their lives with ecology.

But what do people mean by "sustainability"? There is really no simple, clearly agreed-upon definition of sustainability. Some would try to define it in scientific terms: carrying capacity, energy flows, ecological systems, design strategies. Others would talk about the social factors: humans' relationship to nature, spirituality, wisdom, equality, decision-making processes, holism, a sense of place. Often people talk about looking ahead seven generations or creating systems that can be continued into the indefinite future. Of course, even if people agree on the definition, they will incorporate these ideals into their daily lives in very different ways and at different levels.

Beyond a shared commitment to sustainability, ecovillages are diverse in many ways. They exist in rural, urban, and suburban areas and in all parts of the world, among a variety of cultures. They can be embedded in a larger human settlement, such as a neighborhood in a large city. They can be newly formed projects just under way, or older groups redefining themselves or hanging a new term on what they've been doing all along.

In general, ecovillage is used to describe places that are aiming for a village-like quality. A village is more than just a place to live. A village is also a place for work and play, birth and death, trading of goods and services, celebrations, and all aspects of healthy lives. Equally important is being "human scale," meaning a population where it's still possible for people to know each other as people and not as anonymous masses.

As you are looking at ecovillages, remember to ask what folks really envision for their project when it comes to such things as size, scope, social structure, and ecology. Also ask where they are in the here and now. Ecovillage is a process as well as a vision, and we are all somewhere on a long path.

Resources

Ecovillage Network of the Americas (ENA), contact person: Albert Bates, PO Box 90, Summertown TN 38483, USA. Tel: 931-964-3992, fax: 931-964-2200. Email: ecovillage@thefarm.org, http://ena.ecovillage.org/

Global Ecovillage Network (GEN), contact person: Philip Snyder, Gaia Villages, Skodsborgvej 189, Nærum 2850, Denmark. Tel: +45 45 56 01 30, fax: +45 45 56 60 30. http://www.gaia.org/

Ecobalance Mailing List. This is a discussion group dedicated to the creation and maintenance of self-sufficient, sustainable communities, in which people live in harmony with each other and with nature. See http://www.ic.org/in/emailgrps.html for information on how to subscribe. Searchable archives are online at http://csf.colorado.edu/mail/ecobalance/

Tony Sirna is a member of Dancing Rabbit, an aspiring ecovillage in northeast Missouri. He lives there in a house of straw as part of an egalitarian income-sharing group called Skyhouse, and works with both the FIC and FEC. He can be reached at 1 Dancing Rabbit Lane, Rutledge MO 63563, USA, or via email at tony@ic.org.

Cohousing

by Don Lindemann

COHOUSING, A TYPE OF COMMUNITY that took root in North America in the 1990s, represents a new attempt to bridge the gap between two concepts: home as private sanctuary from the outside world versus home as a place rooted in a comforting web of relationships in a place-based community. Both concepts have a strong basis in the history and culture of the United States, but cohousing has emerged as a response to the overwhelming emphasis on home as private retreat and sanctuary that has dominated the thinking of conventional builders, especially since World War II.

The number of completed cohousing communities in North America has grown from just one in 1991 and only three in 1992 to more than 40 in 1999—with dozens of others in the planning or construction stages. They are located all over the United States, with the greatest concentration in the northwest, northern California, and Colorado, and several have now been completed in British Columbia as well. The projects range from around a dozen to 40 or more homes, and they are located about equally in urban, suburban, and rural settings. The architectural styles run the gamut from detached homes, to rows of townhouses framing a "pedestrian street," to apartment buildings.

It is difficult to attach a precise definition to cohousing, but we can start with a classic definition offered by Kathryn McCamant and Charles Durrett in their book, *Cohousing*, which has inspired thousands of people since its original publication back in 1988. Cohousing, they say, is characterized by resident involvement in the design process, a site plan that encourages interaction, a "common house" that provides a place for varied resident activities, and an emphasis on resident self-management. Frequent shared meals in the common house are also a prominent feature of cohousing, though not always mentioned in definitions of the concept. In addition to a

Sunward Cohousing of Ann Arbor, under construction, spring 1998.

Don Lindemann is editor of *CoHousing*, the journal of The Cohousing Network, and a resident of Berkeley Cohousing in Berkeley, California.

Elph Morgan

"Cohousing ... is characterized by ... a 'common house' that provides a place for varied resident activities ..."

ments, residents live in small, tightly clustered homes, enjoy well-attended dinners with neighbors up to five times a week, and bump into each other constantly on compact sites where the common house is a focus of daily life. But there are other projects—consciously developed on the cohousing model—where residents live in large detached houses on private lots and shared meals are less frequent. This is cohousing as well, and the residents may be perfectly happy with their living situations.

In any case, most cohousing communities have a look, feel, and social ambience that is quite a marked contrast from most housing projects built by conventional developers. When a core group of people gets involved in the planning of something so important as the physical space they will share as neighbors, when they learn to dream together and then fashion these dreams into reality, they learn a lasting lesson about the power of people, working collectively, to shape their environment and create a better life for all.

Resources

The CoHousing Network: http://www.cohousing.org/
Rob Sandelin's resources for cohousing:
   http://www.infoteam.com/nonprofit/nica/cohores.htm
Intentional Communities Web site page of links to cohousing groups: http://www.ic.org/iclist.coho.html
CoHousing-L email discussion group—several hundred messages a month; a lively discussion on creating and living in cohousing. See http://www.cohousing.org/ for instructions on how to join.
CoHousing: The Journal of The Cohousing Network. Quarterly. The CoHousing Network, PO Box 2584, Berkeley CA 94702, USA. Tel: 510-486-2656. Email: cohomag@aol.com.

Books

McCamant, Kathryn and Charles Durrett, with Ellen Hertzmann. *Cohousing: A Contemporary Approach to Housing Ourselves*, Second Edition. Berkeley, CA: Ten Speed Press, 1994.

Hanson, Chris. *The CoHousing Handbook: Building a Place for Community*. Point Roberts, WA: Hartley & Marks Pub. Inc., 1996.

kitchen and dining area large enough for most of the residents to eat together at one time, the common house often includes a sitting area/lounge, one or more playrooms for kids, laundry facilities, one or more guest rooms, and perhaps other spaces desired and planned by residents.

In many cases, cohousing projects have been conceived and carried out by groups of people with little or no real estate experience, though today many groups employ development consultants or enter into some kind of partnership with a seasoned developer. Also, some projects have been jump-started by developers (either nonprofit or for-profit) who are starting to perceive cohousing as a new market niche.

According to McCamant and Durrett, cohousing is "based on democratic principles, that espouse no ideology other than the desire for a more practical and social home environment." Such statements help to allay the fears of many people who are just beginning to tentatively explore alternatives to the isolation of conventional housing, but they also obscure the reality that cohousing does contain explicit or implicit values and goals.

The cohousing development process and the design of communities emphasize the values of participation, cooperation, sharing, and just plain intermingling of neighbors. Then, too, many cohousers—especially those who catalyze cohousing projects and those who join in the early stages—are ecologically aware people who want to minimize the environmental impacts of home construction and daily life thereafter.

At the same time, the lack of a formal cohousing philosophy, and the looseness of the cohousing definition, have resulted in projects that display a great range in terms of "sense of community." In some cohousing develop-

"My Other Car Isn't Mine Either"

Bumper Sticker for an Income-Sharing Community

by Valerie Renwick-Porter

INCOME-SHARING COMMUNITIES have one of the longest and richest histories that we know of in the communities movement. From tribal life, to the early days of convents and monasteries, to Oneida community in the 1800s, our roots are deep.

Current income-sharing groups may vary widely in their lifestyles and values, but all share a central economic practice. Some groups live a spiritual life focusing on the word of God, such as the Twelve Tribes communities, the Bruderhof, and many religious fellowships. Others, like those in the Federation of Egalitarian Communities (FEC), define themselves as secular and focus on aspects of shared decision making and ecological sustainability.

An income-sharing community is an economic unit unto itself. Income produced by members, either in a community-owned business or outside work, goes directly to the community. In exchange, the community provides for all the basic needs of its members, including housing, food, and health care. Individual groups may define "basic" needs somewhat differently. There is also collective ownership of community resources, such as land, buildings, and vehicles. In many cases, neither money nor particular skills are required to become a member; simply a willingness to wholeheartedly join the community in its purpose is sufficient. This opens membership to a wide range of people.

One of the most attractive features of this type of living is the interdependence and the level of engagement we share with each other. There is a high level of involvement in each other's daily lives. Our work opportunities tend to be concentrated in home businesses, so we often don't need to leave our home to earn money. Our coworkers are our extended family, and we come to know each other holistically. Members also have access to a variety of resources they might not otherwise have. For example, the community may provide a professional-quality woodworking shop for member use, or an outdoor hot tub, musical instruments, or free classes by a skilled member.

What else does it mean to live in this type of community? Living so interdependently often means members need to possess fairly well-developed social skills. The ability to cooperate with others, to keep agreements, and to resolve difficult interpersonal situations can go a long way in dealing with the conflicts that naturally arise out of such close living. A flexible attitude can help members respond to living with less personal financial autonomy than they may be used to. Most people who live with their own income are used to making decisions themselves about what quality of housing to live in, what style of car to drive, what type of food to buy, and how much to spend on favorite leisure activities. It can be challenging to make the same decisions with a group of people whose tastes, values, and class backgrounds may be radically different from one's own.

Income-sharing is definitely on one end of the spectrum of what it means to live communally. This type of community has never been a majority in the communities movement, and yet we have always been a strong presence. Much of this is due to our ability to focus resources, which in turn makes more time available to members to do networking and organizing.

Income-sharing is not for everyone, but those who choose to live this life find it a source of endless riches. It is a life full of unity and diversity, struggle and growth, and ultimately, deep community.

Valerie Renwick-Porter has lived at Twin Oaks for over nine years. She serves on the Executive Committee of the Federation of Egalitarian Communities (FEC) and coordinates the Twin Oaks Communities Conference. She works in her community's forestry program, and her passions include feminist utopias, chocolate, and soaking in hot tubs.

The Student Co-op Movement

by Megan Lindsey Case

THE STUDENT HOUSING COOPERATIVE movement serves more than 10,000 students across Canada and the United States. Student housing co-ops provide an alternative to living in dormitories, apartments, or fraternities and sororities, usually on a nonprofit, least-cost basis. They range in size from single houses with fewer than 10 members to multi-house systems with over a thousand.

Community

Many students originally choose co-ops as an inexpensive housing alternative, but they stay because of the community ties that form there. Co-ops provide a social living environment, often with shared meals, work holidays, and regular house meetings. Student co-opers play Scrabble and plant gardens together, and sometimes generate local community activism.

Cooperatives that bring people together around a theme often exhibit the strongest community bonds. Many student co-ops are vegetarian or vegan houses; others are kosher, women-only, gay and lesbian, students of color, or substance-free. Upon graduation, many student co-opers find themselves looking for a community to move into more permanently. If their co-op allows non-students, members may remain and strengthen the community that exists there.

Principles

Co-ops are guided by a set of economic, social, and philosophical principles. The Statement of Cooperative Identity reaffirmed by the International Cooperative Alliance in 1995 defines a cooperative as "an autonomous association of persons united voluntarily to meet their common economic, social, and cultural needs and aspirations through a jointly-owned and democratically controlled enterprise.

Jillian Downey

"Many students originally choose co-ops as an inexpensive housing alternative, but they stay because of the community ties that form there."

Megan Case has been involved in the co-op movement since 1996. She has worked for the North American Students of Cooperation (NASCO), and the National Association of Housing Cooperatives. She earned a master's degree from the University of Chicago, for which her thesis was a sociological study of student housing cooperatives. She has lived in and been a board member of housing co-ops in Chicago, Illinois and Ann Arbor, Michigan. She currently lives in the Lamont Street Collective in Washington, DC.

Cooperatives are based on the values of democracy, solidarity, self-help, and self-responsibility. In the tradition of their founders, cooperative members believe in the ethical values of honesty, openness, social responsibility, and caring for others."

The basic tenets, known as the Rochdale Principles, are as follows:
1 voluntary and open membership;
2 democratic member control;
3 member economic participation;
4 autonomy and independence;
5 cooperation among cooperatives; and
6 concern for community.

History

These principles have their roots in the mid-1800s in Rochdale, England. In 1844, a group of weavers opened a general store there to provide low-cost basic foods to their members. The statutes that they wrote are the basis of modern-day cooperation.

In 1882, North America's first student cooperative, The Harvard Cooperative Society, was formed. The co-op originally sold textbooks and firewood; it is now a "collegiate department store." The oldest North American student housing co-ops still in existence got their start half a century later, in the 1930s. Students during the depression found it difficult to pay for college; living and eating in co-ops allowed many to finance their educations. The co-ops at Berkeley, Ann Arbor, and Toronto got their start during this period. After a wartime decline, student co-ops resumed growth in the late 1940s, when co-ops began buying their houses and legally incorporating. The movement picked up steam again in the 1960s, as more people sought an alternative to mainstream ways of living. In 1968, the North American Students of Cooperation (NASCO) formed to join supporters and members of student co-ops, and has expanded to provide management assistance to new and ailing student cooperatives.

With college tuition rising through the 1990s, the need for affordable student housing has grown dramatically. Established student cooperatives are seeing low vacancy rates and are working with NASCO to assist new co-ops in meeting the great demand.

Resources

North American Students of Cooperation is the organized voice of the student co-op movement, providing education, training, networking, and development assistance to new and existing student housing cooperatives. More

Vail House, one of the 19 student co-op houses that make up the Inter-Cooperative Council (ICC) in Ann Arbor, Michigan.

Jillian Downey

information about student housing co-ops can be found on NASCO's Web page at http://www.umich.edu/~nasco/, or by calling NASCO's main office at 734-663-0889.

Books

Thompson, David J. *Weavers of Dreams*. University of California, 1994.

Jones, James R. *History of Student Cooperatives in North America*. Unpublished.

The Kibbutz Movement

by Wendy Weiss Simon

KIBBUTZ IS AN INTENTIONAL community. The pioneers of kibbutz came to pre-state Israel from eastern Europe at the height of the socialist ideal, to create communities where each would give according to his or her ability and take according to his or her need. The small groups of settlers to the malaria- and famine-stricken Palestine of the early- to mid-20th century were idealistic, educated, bourgeois Jewish youth searching for answers.

These young adults lived together, slept together, ate together, and used any income to provide for the group, equally and totally. Women and men alike worked the fields or built roads, cooked, and cleaned. Stories abound about these socialist settlers in Palestine. How group meetings of the early days lasted through the night, ceasing only with the rising sun and the need to work the fields. How a young couple wanted a tent of their own, and how another young couple did not like the name that the general meeting chose for their baby. There were those who talked of members having teakettles in their rooms: "… why would you come to the dining room if you could make tea in the room?" This obviously would bring about the fall of kibbutz!

And there is the story that I grew up with, of a childhood friend of my mother, who left the United States for Israel in the early '50s. When his mother received a photograph of him in the winter without a coat, she wrote and asked him where was his coat. His reply: "I hang it on the hook in the dining room and if someone needs a coat they take a coat. Some days I get that coat, some days another, and on some days, no coat." This for me was the epitome of kibbutz. "To each according to need, from each according to ability."

Three kibbutz movements exist in Israel. The largest and most loosely connected is the United Kibbutz Move-

Elph Morgan

Wendy Weiss Simon is a member of Kibbutz Lotan, a 16-year-old settlement in the southernmost area of Israel. A native New Yorker, 15 years in Israel, she has a degree in Human Resources from SUNY, with a background in business. Wendy has worked in many branches of the kibbutz ranging from coordinating building construction to teaching high school English. She lives on Lotan with her husband and two daughters.

ment (UKM), for many years connected with the political Labor party. The Kibbutz HaArtzi Movement, politically farther left and more socialist, was the last to give up collective child rearing. They are traditionally antireligious, whereas the UKM is a-religious. The smallest of the three is the Religious Kibbutz Movement, which combines the ideals of kibbutz with an Orthodox Jewish lifestyle.

Approximately 270 kibbutzim house fewer than two percent of the population of Israel. In the heyday of kibbutz, we never had more than three percent of the population, but the effect on society was far greater than our numbers: from the 1950s through the early 1980s, kibbutzim produced the bulk of Israel's agricultural produce, and turned out the elite in the army units, universities, and government.

Since the late 1980s, the level of "collectiveness" on kibbutz has dropped. Most of these changes came about as a result of economic realities. Some came about because the "chaver" (member/friend) wanted more freedom and choice. In "the olden days," the kibbutznik used to have only a small amount of pocket money. Everyone used the same type of toothbrush, one brand of shampoo, the same clothes. Little by little, things changed. More and more money was set aside for the individual member.

In recent years, a number of kibbutzim no longer have collective dining rooms, and some even pay salaries according to members' actual incomes: a teacher or nurse receives less than the computer programmer, once unheard of. Many kibbutzim have sold off property that was once agricultural for development into housing or shopping malls. Even more are renting houses to non-member families looking for comfortable settings with manicured lawns, swimming pools, and daycare. These changes have produced a new generation of kibbutzim and kibbutznikim.

But there are still kibbutzim striving to maintain the good things, as they see it. "Kibbutz Tamid" (Kibbutz Forever), a quasi-movement within a movement, came out of the desire of some kibbutzim to remain connected to the democratic socialism ideology of kibbutz. These kibbutzim work at keeping members coming to the dining room, and they find ways to give members what they need while looking out for the community as a whole. Some of these kibbutzim have stable incomes and factories that have become national or international concerns.

Kibbutz Lotan, our kibbutz, is one of those who see the future with direct connection to the past. Lotan is representative of struggling young kibbutzim. We were established in 1983, just as major economic and political upheavals were taking place in Israel, so we grew up with the understanding that not necessarily everyone believes in the idea of kibbutz. We attract newcomers who are interested in emotional commitment to others in the community and living within the community's means. Although we never have enough hands to do all that has to be done, people here find ways to do the things that are important to

Many communitarians have the opportunity to create the balance of indoor and outdoor work that suits their needs.

them. We are slowly becoming more "green," through construction of a bird reserve, organic gardens, an educational seminar center, and a complementary medical center. Kibbutz Lotan is in the minority in Israel with respect to our Judaism: we are Reform, liberal, progressive, egalitarian, and committed.

Kibbutz, "the experiment that didn't fail," has changed greatly since its inception, and will continue to do so.

Resources

The Green Kibbutz movement, contact Jan Martin Bang, email: ecowork@gezernet.co.il
Yad Tabenkin Institute, email: YadTab@actcom.co.il

Books

Kerem, Moshe. *Life in a Kibbutz*. 1955.
Spiro, M.E. *Kibbutz, Venture in Utopia*. 1955.
Leon, Dan. *The Kibbutz*. 1964.

L'Arche International Federation
Communities for the Mentally Handicapped

by Marty O'Malley and Lisa Cigliana

There is a facet of the intentional communities movement that serves people with mental or physical disabilities. Two international networks of such communities are the Camphill communities and the L'Arche International Federation. There are also communities for the disabled that are not part of a specific network, such as Innisfree community in Virginia. (See resources on the following page.) This article focuses on one of the L'Arche communities, in Mobile, Alabama. L'Arche is French for "the Ark," meaning a place of refuge. Marty O'Malley, the executive director of L'Arche Mobile, spoke with copy editor Lisa Cigliana about his community.

L'ARCHE IS A CLOSE-KNIT CHRISTIAN community in which people with mental handicaps live with nonhandicapped people in a family-like environment. We are part of the L'Arche International Federation, in which there are 110 communities in 27 countries.

We see our mission as: (1) creating a home where faithful relationships based on forgiveness and celebration are nurtured; (2) revealing the unique values and vocation of each person; and (3) changing society by choosing to live in community as a sign of hope and love.

In Mobile, we've welcomed 19 people with handicaps, and most have multiple handicaps. For example, some have mental retardation and seizure disorders, or they might be blind and can't walk. In addition, 17 have come from state institutions and there is little or no family con-

tact, so we quite literally become family. We try to live like brothers and sisters.

Nonhandicapped people (assistants) are an integral part of the team at L'Arche. They can be more-or-less permanent residents, and are often people who have had

Working together can give community members a strong feeling of connection and of belonging.

Marty O'Malley has been involved in L'Arche since 1976, serving as executive director of L'Arche Mobile since 1985. Prior to coming to L'Arche, he worked in the criminal justice to divert people with handicaps—particularly with mental illness—away from the criminal justice system and into community-based

treatment programs.

Lisa Cigliana lived in the Bright Morning Star community in Seattle, Washington in the mid-1990s. She is currently studying video production and filmmaking.

some sort of career and want a lifestyle change. We've had a chemist, a lawyer, a teacher, and nurses. Here in Mobile, 10 of us have been here over five years. Another group of people that we attract are those who stay from one to three years, and they are usually recent college graduates who want to live in our community before getting into a career. Finally, we attract people who are either in school or haven't yet started school. They want to stay a year or less, similar to an internship or a summer program.

In terms of administration, our board of directors takes care of the policies and procedures. The community council is responsible for the quality of life of the community. Donations make up about a third of our operating expenses. Not all L'Arche communities are that way; some are government-funded.

L'Arche Mobile is a part of the L'Arche International Federation. On an international level, the federation addresses issues such as our spirituality, retaining assistants long term, looking at issues that affect L'Arche globally as well as health insurance and recruitment. Within the United States, we are linked to communities in Jacksonville, Florida; Kansas City, Kansas; and Clinton, Iowa. These communities sponsor retreats for people with handicaps and also offer orientations in the L'Arche philosophy to assistants.

For those interested in learning more about L'Arche, our founder, Jean Vanier, has written numerous books; his most sought-after title, which we view almost as a "bible" of living in community, is *Community and Growth*. The late author Fr. Henri Nouwen lived in a L'Arche community for several years, and his book *The Road to Daybreak* tells of his experiences.

A store owned by Innisfree, another residential community for adults with mental disabilities. It is not part of the L'Arche or Camphill networks.

Resources

L'Arche Mobile, 151 South Ann St, Mobile AL 36604, USA. Email: larchmob@acan.net
http://www2.acan.net/~larchmob/
L'Arche Canada
http://www.larchecanada.org/
Camphill Association of North America, 224 Nantmeal Rd, Glenmoore PA 19343, USA. Tel: 610-469-6162. Email: information@camphillassociation.org
http://www.camphillassociation.org/
Camphill Communities, Britain and Ireland, http://www.camphill.org.uk/
Innisfree Village, 5505 Walnut Level Rd, Crozet VA 22932, USA. Tel: 804-823-5400.
Email: innisfree@cwixmail.com
http://monticello.avenue.gen.va.us/innisfree/

Books

Vanier, Jean. *Community and Growth*. Richmond Hill, Ontario: Daybreak Publications.
Email pubs@larchedaybreak.com

Publisher's note: This directory has a trio of articles about spiritual communities: one on groups that exist to rigorously follow a specific spiritual discipline by Mariana Caplan; one on eclectic spirituality by Stevie Abbott-Richards of the Lama Foundation; and one by Joe V. Peterson outlining what's offered by Christian communities. They all explore different senses of "spiritual community" and are included to offer as full a picture of the spectrum as possible. The Fellowship for Intentional Community does not endorse one definition or type of spiritual community over another. Rather, we celebrate the extraordinary diversity among groups that identify themselves as "spiritual," and we encourage readers to explore all the possibilities and aspects that feel right to them.

Spiritual Communities
There's More to Them Than Meets the Third-Eye

by Mariana Caplan

MANY COMMUNITIES IDENTIFY WITH the word "spiritual," and they do so for many reasons: to follow the golden rule, or because they believe in the power of meditation, for example. However, the word "spiritual" has an ancient, sacred meaning, and I use it to refer to a community that exists for the sole purpose of furthering the spiritual development of its members.

Spiritual communities are not like ordinary communities. Even communities with a spiritual bent to them—communities that give workshops, meditate, and do circle dances together—are not necessarily spiritual communities. Ecovillages are not spiritual communities. Cohousing communities are not spiritual communities. Any number of deeply spiritual people may live in these places, but there are important distinctions between spiritual and other communities. Spiritual communities are comprised of spiritual practitioners who have come together in community to share in the study, practice, and expression of their common spiritual values and traditions.

For Spiritual Seekers, Community Is a Means, Not an End

Although the form may be familiar, the context and intention of spiritual communities are distinct from the majority of communities. In spiritual communities, the "community," even the joyous functioning community, is the vehicle, but it is not the destination.

Community is an effective and beneficial lifestyle for many spiritual practitioners for a number of reasons. One reason is that "spiritual friendship" is an essential source of inspiration and sustenance for spiritual practitioners. It is so valuable that the Buddha considered the community of like-minded practitioners to be one of the "three jewels" of Buddhism, along with the other two jewels of the Teacher and the Teaching. The spiritual path can be a rough road, and support is needed to sustain the given discipline and get through the rough spots. For this reason, monasteries, nunneries, convents, yeshivas, and similar communities are found in the spiritual traditions of every culture.

A less recognized value of community to spiritual work is the transformational possibility the stress of community provides. The process of spiritual transformation, or alchemy, requires tremendous energy, or "heat." The clashing of personalities and the struggles that inevitably and frequently arises in all communities creates this heat, and the advanced spiritual student can learn to use this for their own spiritual transformation. Even shy of this alchemical possibility, the continuous contact with others that occurs in community serves to expose the ego. In community one is continuously getting feedback about what they are "up to," if only through watching how oth-

Mariana Caplan is a psychologist, author, and lecturer. Her books include: *When Sons and Daughters Choose Alternative Lifestyles* (Hohm Press,1996), *When Holidays are Hell! A Guide to Surviving Family Gatherings* (Hohm Press, 1997), *Untouched: the Need for Genuine Affection in an Impersonal World* (Hohm Press, 1998), and *Halfway Up the Mountain: The Error of Premature Claims to Enlightenment* (Hohm Press, 1999).

ers respond to them. It takes a lot of individual and collective denial for the ego to hide out in community, and rarely does it succeed.

Jakusho Kwong Roshi, founder of the Sonoma Mountain Zen Center, said that the most difficult years of his life have been the 25 years since he was given the transmission to teach by Suzuki Roshi. Already sanctioned a Zen master upon the completion of many years of Zen practice, he went "to the mountain" to create spiritual community. In an interview quoted in the book *Halfway Up the Mountain* he explains: "The metaphor for the sangha (spiritual community) is like rocks. You put all the rocks together, you shake the bucket, and the rocks rub

Jillian Downey

"… monasteries, nunneries, convents, yeshivas, and similar communities are found in the spiritual traditions of every culture."

each other and become smooth. You won't become smooth without being rubbed. I started spiritual life when I was 25 years old. I'll be 63. It's still a very short period. I've been here running our center for 25 years and this has probably been the hardest time of my sadhana (spiritual practice). I raised four sons here. The rocks rub. I didn't expect that. Even after you're a teacher, the rocks rub."[1]

The Need for Discernment

One must cultivate and exercise a refined level of discernment when discriminating between the various spiritual communities available. The current craze and popularity of spirituality has done an enormous disservice in terms of understanding what real spiritual discipline is about. Whenever anything becomes as popular as "enlightenment" and "spiritual development" has become today, it must lose the essence of its meaning, because true spiritual principles cannot be communicated in mass form. Therefore, those who seek community in order to live a life of spiritual practice and devotion can never assume that every community that labels itself as spiritual will be able to offer them what they seek.

Spiritual principles can also go against the grain of what some people imagine communities to be. Spiritual communities are often not egalitarian or democratic. Financial responsibilities are not shared equally. There is often a hierarchy, and as things would have it, a man sits at the top of the ladder more often than a woman. The guru, teacher, or founder of the community may indeed

have the final say in all matters, and disciples or community members to some degree feel the effect of this. For these and other reasons, spiritual communities receive a lot of flak.

The obvious danger of spiritual communities is the capacity for blind following, for charismatic but self-deluded leaders, for corruption in the hierarchy of the system. The media has detailed many accounts of this phenomenon. It is important for the community seeker considering a spiritual community to use careful discernment regarding this issue.

Lee Lozowick offers three basic criteria for considering a spiritual teacher and their community:

1. If you aren't very serious about your desire to progress on the path, don't look for a teacher in the first place.
2. Don't be impulsive in signing up.
3. Study the teacher's body of students. How are the students, and how is the teacher with the students?[2]

It is also useful to look at how long a group has been in existence, and to engage long-term members of the community regarding your questions and concerns. If you are to truly benefit from a lengthy involvement with a community, particularly with a spiritual teacher, you will need to trust him or her. There is no other way. Therefore, there is no need to rush in.

There is no definitive method for discernment. "Following one's heart" is not necessarily reliable, as what one perceives as the "heart" is often instead the ego in disguise. Similarly, following one's mind can be equally hazardous, for the mind is renowned for its tricks of perception.

Therefore, one watches out for the ever-present possibility of self-deception, and proceeds with their decisions to the best of their abilities.

Involvement in spiritual life will always be a risk: only high stakes yield high payoff. Of course it is always better to avoid an unproductive situation from the outset, but important lessons can be learned even from seeming mistakes. When one finds oneself in an unproductive situation, the best thing to do is to leave the situation as gracefully as possible.

Spiritual communities often receive media attention when they appear to go out of control, while those spiritual communities that are functioning long-term, quietly, soundly, and do not encourage guests or advertise community are overlooked. Even these communities are often criticized for being aloof and separatist, and in these cases I would suggest that much of the bias against gurus, teachers, authoritarian structures, and spiritual hierarchies may reflect the self-preserving ego that fears the loss of autonomy and of a life controlled by a force greater than itself.

Spiritual Communities Are Not for Everyone

Spiritual communities are very attractive to people who are looking for community. The authentic spiritual community is comprised of a body of dedicated practitioners, and spiritual practice creates a brightness and radiance that is very compelling. Therefore, community seekers are drawn to what they see in spiritual communities, often mistaking the brightness to be a product of community instead of recognizing that it is the result of decades of disciplined practice.

Spiritual communities are not for everyone. In fact, I do not recommend that anyone who feels that they have any other choice but to live in one seek out such a lifestyle. Real spiritual life is often a circumstance of "love in hell." It's a bitch. Spiritual life is the ceaseless wearing down of the egoic system of defenses, a process that often involves tremendous discomfort, disillusionment, and frustration. When spiritual life is undertaken in community, this defense structure is ceaselessly grated upon. As the ancient Sufis said, "The ego does not go with laughter and caresses. It must be chased with sorrow and drowned in tears."

Spiritual life is something that you give your body, mind, soul, guts, psyche, energy to—something you give your very life force to. And that can be different from community. Most people who are interested in community are interested in sharing resources, living off the land, growing food, raising children consciously. They may not be interested in pursuing an intense regime of discipline,

in abiding under the teacher's authority. They prefer to learn to follow their own inner guidance, to dissipate stress and tension, not to make use of it. And who could blame them?

While I discourage spiritual community for those for whom it is not an imperative, and perhaps create a somewhat daunting overall picture of this lifestyle, I suggest if one indeed has no other choice, there is no greater option. There is a type of bonding that occurs among people when their relationships are based on a mutual pursuit of God or Truth that is a rare and sublime type of friendship. There is profound joy in knowing that your fellow practitioners intend to hold the highest possibility of your life for you, and that an important aspect of their life is to serve your spiritual development, and vice versa. It is tremendously satisfying to know you are attempting to live in a way that teaches and serves others, and that you will be reeled in when you get too far away from yourself or become lost in self-deception. It is a source of profound gratification to live together knowing that, although you are unquestionably passengers on a "ship of fools," at least you are all in it together. There is a love among fools that is not based upon personal likes or dislikes, but instead upon a shared intention and devotion.

> There is profound joy in knowing that your fellow practitioners intend to hold the highest possibility of your life for you ...

Resources—Books

Feuerstein, Georg. *Holy Madness*. New York: Paragon House, 1990.

Rawlinson, Andrew. *The Book of Enlightened Masters*. Chicago, IL: Open Court, 1997.

Trungpa, Chogyam. *Cutting Through Spiritual Materialism*. Boston: Shambhala, 1973.

Tweedie, Irina. *Chasm of Fire*. Inverness, CA: The Golden Sufi Center, 1986.

Endnotes

1. Caplan, Mariana. *Halfway Up the Mountain: The Error of Premature Claims for Enlightenment*. Prescott, AZ: Hohm Press, 1999, p. 332.
2. Ibid., p. 416.

Spiritual Community of Many Faiths
The Challenge Is to Love

by Stevie Abbott-Richards

"*L*AMA FOUNDATION? *What, like in Dalai Lama?*" "*New Mexico? Do they only speak Spanish there?*" "*A whole year? What will you do there anyway?*" "*What will your kids (ages 20 and 22) do?*" "*Isn't this just opting out of life?*"

Questions, questions, questions! I carried on packing. I couldn't answer them anyway. A lone Aussie woman, I was about to set off half-way round the world to find the answers. I spent a year at the Lama foundation—a spiritual community perched high in the mountains of New Mexico where all faiths are honored and the main language is love. Its arms reach out and gently enfold you, until your heart of stone becomes a heart of flesh.

The Lama Foundation is one of a family of spiritual communities where many faiths are followed and honored. Lama has friendly interchanges with these other communities, including Findhorn community in Scotland, Ojai Foundation in California, and Sirius Community in Massachusetts. Lama also has relations with single-path spiritual communities and spiritual retreats.

Lama gives pilgrims of any faith a space to explore their own spiritual faith, and the chance to learn about that of others. It is not a school in the accredited sense of the word, but it is a place of learning. Being there was the most intensive course of study that I had ever enrolled for. Despite years in the tertiary sector of education, my learning curve at Lama was the steepest it's ever been. The potential for personal and spiritual growth is tremendous.

At 50, I suppose one would be tempted to call my sojourn there a midlife crisis. I prefer to think of it as starting out on the second half of my life. After many years of single parenting, working full-time as a high-school teacher and counselor and simultaneously completing a Masters and writing four books, I was very ready to start over and give myself an easier run this time. As an enthusiastic prison visitor, I felt that using my skills behind bars might be the next direction for me, but I needed to get off the carousel for long enough to consider if I was well enough equipped to do this—both professionally, but, more importantly, within myself.

The problem was that I never had the time to consider anything in depth. Life was running me instead of the other way around. I'm sure you recognize the row of hats slipped on and off throughout the week with the speed and alacrity normally only accredited to jugglers. At that moment of finale when all the hats sit neatly back on their pegs, thoughts of one's life path, of one's soul journey, one's self-actualization become very hazy and "following one's bliss" usually means taking a hot bath and a cup of tea in bed!

> "The purpose of Lama Foundation is to be a sustainable spiritual community and educational center dedicated to the awakening of consciousness, spiritual practice in all traditions, service, and stewardship of the land."
> —Statement of purpose, adopted June 1998

Ms. Stevie Abbott-Richards is a teacher, counselor, and writer. She emigrated to the Adelaide Hills in Australia 17 years ago from Yorkshire in England. Since her return from Lama she has begun studies which will lead to ordination as a prison chaplain. She is also writing her fifth book, entitled *One Flew Over the Empty Nest*, which deals with the problems encountered by parents when their children leave home. She has two grown children and is a committed Christian who honors all faiths as paths to God.

Mary Pat Waldron

Shabbat at Lama.

So, I gave my career hat away, hung a "for sale" sign on the nest and took a flight to New Mexico.

Did I opt out of life? Was it escapesville? Yes.

And then again, no.

At first I thought I had left challenges behind. At Lama, the plumber did not turn up late and then charge me an outrageous fee. There, I never ran the gauntlet of the local supermarket and wondered if I'd be able to cover the check. There, I never had to decide what to have for dinner, buy the ingredients, and then cook it. There, my laundry disappeared each week and then magically reappeared clean and dry on the same day. There, I was not a taxi service, a bank loan service, the emotionally starved owner of a house where people drop in to change their socks. There, I never saw TV or got bills or did ironing or worked to a frantic deadline. I didn't even buy clothes—I changed them every couple of weeks in the free second-hand store known as the "Gypsy."

Now don't get the wrong idea. We certainly worked hard, sometimes 16 hours a day, but every day was different and I could choose to make it so. On a Monday I may have worked in the garden, digging and weeding or best of all picking the homegrown produce. Tuesday I may have prepared the new and exquisite hermitage for a grateful visitor and Wednesday maybe I'd have helped create a path in delicate mosaic. I may have been welcoming and serving retreatants and their teachers on Thursday and on Friday I may have gotten the chance to participate in part of that retreat. Saturday might have been my free day and on Sunday I might have been writing an article like this.

Evenings had a variety of practices—Sufi dancing, Dhikr (Zikr), Kirtan, prayer and meditation, Hakomi, Heart Club, Temple worship, Native American ceremonies, yoga, herb walks, hikes, Reiki, Buddhist dharma talks, clowning, trust circles, Shabbat celebrations, juggling, Feldenkreis. It made my former Australian schedule look dull to say the least. Who would guess that an isolated small community would give me more of a social life than a big city?

So, how did I do without all those former challenges? I mean isn't life all about challenges and aims and goals? Did I turn into a mental jellyfish, sloshed about by the daily tide?

Well no, absolutely not!

There, I met daily challenges that made the supermarket look like Disneyland. There, I met myself. At home, if I don't like the "look" of myself, I can take in a movie, catch a concert, turn on the TV, check in with my long-term support group of friends who know all my "stuff" and graciously refrain from pushing any of my buttons. At home I can go and buy myself a treat, have a meal out, down a couple of glasses of wine, take the edge off my pain so that I can push it back down and not have to look at it.

At Lama there was nowhere to go to get away from me. Like a constantly playing video, my pain was being viewed and reviewed with love and compassion for the one who is myself, who has been buffeted about by life's storms. Like the jogger who must break through the pain barrier to reach a new level of victory, the only way forward was through it.

I am a Christian, and another challenge for me was

that for the year I was there, there were no other Christian members. The time I spent at Lama confirmed that I was following the appropriate faith for me, the one I just happened to have been born into and brought up in. I could see that being in an eclectic community could result in a change of faith, and that some people might see that as a "risk" one would have to take. I found myself more deeply committed and confirmed in my faith, and chastened—I was very impressed by the time and commitment invested by community members in their faiths and realized to my shame how little time I actually gave to God in the course of my daily life. I adopted many practices into my own faith, to consciously and purposefully make time for God every day, instead of once a week: lighting of incense; making an altar in my house; lighting candles; singing chants; dancing; bowing; prostrating; meditating; reading.

I also made a point of learning about other faiths so that I had more than a vague idea of what they were about, and I discovered that in their purest form, all faiths are about love, mercy, and compassion and all are paths to God. Now I revere and honor other faiths and any fear I might have had has gone.

Lama is a place of learning, with an unusual and challenging curriculum.

• Class one is *surrender*. The ego has no place there. Can you live for a bigger cause than just little you? Can you stop talking and start listening?

• Class two is *honesty*. There they try to relate on a level that is honest and that is not always pretty. The class assignment is to be real with each other.

• Class three is *humility*. There is a book called *Being Nobody, Going Nowhere*. That's pretty much the role you will be called upon to play there. No-one is interested in your past or your future, for that matter. Your status, experience, qualifications don't count for much. The only matter of interest is did you graduate from the class of love?

• Class four is *vulnerability*. At Lama they relate through the heart. This means you have to open yours. For those who have long ago closed the doors to their heart, this can feel like walking naked down main street. And once your heart is open, be prepared to feel other people's pain too. Sounds hard, but this will lead you to success in class five.

• Class five is *tolerance*. Look for the similarities, stay away from the differences and you will see that we are all the same at the core. We all want love, acceptance, praise, nurturing, encouragement. People's faults are just an expression of their wounds.

How big a challenge can you take? Can you open your arms to everyone—old and young, male and female, rich and poor, of all ethnicities—and hug them warmly with love? Can you share with 40-plus brothers and sisters your kitchen, your dining table, your relaxation space, your bathroom? Can you share their sadnesses, their moods, their celebrations, their commiserations?

Lama Foundation

Dancing in the Lama tipi circle.

Can you listen from your heartspace when people talk about the path of Allah, Sufism, Judaism, Christianity, Bhakti Yoga, and just accept that these are all paths to God? Can you hold your own particular spiritual space without wanting to impose it on anyone else? Can you let the nationalities, backgrounds, appearances, behaviors, and ages go and just relate to the God within all with unconditional love and acceptance? Can you "Let go and let God"?

These are the challenges of a multi-faith spiritual community. If you think you could even try to meet them, the community at Lama will meet you more than halfway. It's all very simple. The Lama challenge is to *love*.

Reprinted (with some changes) with permission from the Lama Foundation newsletter, Fall 1998 issue, "Lama Alive."

What You Should Know About Christian Communities

by Joe V. Peterson

And all that believed were together, and had all things in common …
—Acts of the Apostles, chapter 2, verse 44
New Testament, King James Version

THUS IS DESCRIBED THE FIRST intentional Christian community, which existed around 2,000 years ago. It is perhaps the best known community quote for the many thousands who have lived in Christian communities over the centuries. The Book of Acts is about the followers of Jesus of Nazareth, known to the Christians as the Lord Jesus Christ, and certain activities, or "acts," that occurred in that first-generation Christian community.

Most of the people described above had been living together in Jerusalem for several weeks as a rather *un*intentional community. A few had been together as a community for three years or so. In order to survive all that had happened to them as a result of the torture and execution of Jesus, their founder and leader, they were huddled together in Jerusalem, waiting. They were wanted by the Roman civil authorities as well as by the Jewish religious authorities, both of whom had hoped that this recent new messianic religious movement was over. But about 50 days after the execution and resurrection of Jesus, his followers were creating community. Intentional Christian communities have been with us ever since.

Three years prior to these startling events, at the outset of Jesus' journey to initiate his movement, Jesus had gathered his earliest community members. At the River Jordan, just upstream from the Dead Sea, crowds had gathered to listen to the radical wilderness "social justice prophet" John the Baptist. He was proclaiming that something new and revolutionary was about to happen. Two of John the Baptist's disciples saw Jesus coming through the crowd. John the Baptist said, "Behold the Lamb of God." The two disciples took note and followed Jesus. Jesus turned and asked them, "What are you looking for?" Their surprising reply was "Show us where you live." Jesus simply said, "Come and see." So they went with Jesus, and the community grew. It's interesting to note that those two were not searching for intellectual answers or even for good preaching and church services. Rather, they wanted to know about the community Jesus had. Little did they know where that would take them or how that community would change the world.

In the ensuing 2,000 years, many thousands would "come and see" what Christian communities have to offer. Christian communities have become numerous and diverse and can be found just about everywhere in one form or another. Many books and articles have appeared on the subject over the centuries. *Communities* magazine has featured a number of Christian community articles over the years (see "Christian Communities, Then and Now," No. 92, Fall 1996). My effort here at describing Christian community is not intended to be exhaustive, nor is it an endorsement or a critique. Rather, this is a brief and simple general explanation of a very old and diverse social and religious movement with roots stretching back a long, long way.

People of Diversity: Divisions and Growth

Christian communities are not all the same and certainly do not participate in a unified network. Churches have always been a rich source for intentional community to spawn. It is not uncommon to find communities that have

Joe V. Peterson has been involved in both secular and religious intentional communities since 1964, and has served on the boards of the Fellowship for Intentional Community (FIC) and the Communal Studies Association (CSA), and as an advisor to the World Council of Churches. Presently he teaches college courses in Sociology and Human Behavior and is the director of "Making Sense of Existence," an educational, counseling, and consulting service at PO Box 44981, Tacoma WA 98444, USA. Tel: 253-536-9080.

Lindsey Jones

Eating meals together is an important "glue" that strengthens all types of communities, spiritual and secular.

divided from more traditional or historic churches or even from other communities over differences about specific teachings or beliefs. Likewise, churches have had their origins within communities, splitting off and going their own ways to practice their beliefs, just as they did in the first millennium.

It is not uncommon to find a Christian community founded on a particular interpretation of the Bible. Many Christian communities have little contact with each other, even though from an outsider's view they appear to be doing the same things. Only a handful of networks of intentional Christian communities exist—and most of those share the same theological roots, practices, and, sometimes, leaders. This competition of ideas, doctrines, lifestyles, leadership, and so on stimulates the growth of Christian communities. This is more true for the non-Catholic communities. The Catholics have long made room for the "fanatics," keeping them in the fold by permitting religious orders, such as monasteries, for the enthusiasts and deep seekers to join, whereas the Protestant/reformers have usually kicked the "fanatics" out, in which case they usually form their own efforts: a new community or church.

The focus on "right belief" and doctrine especially affects the contact between non-Christian and Christian

communities. Some intentional Christian communities are opposed to being listed in this directory, and may even harbor suspicion toward *any* other communities. Others are simply uninterested, seeing their own efforts and goals as different from secular communities. While these folks certainly live a community lifestyle, they identify far more strongly with the rightness of their beliefs and mission than with being an intentional community as such.

Christian communities are not only competitive with their ideas and teachings, but some compete for members as well. "Make disciples" is an instruction Jesus himself left with his followers, and it is often fervently obeyed. The rapid proliferation of intentional Christian communities during the late 1960s and 1970s was fostered by intense recruitment activities across the country. One community I became part of had started over 175 "houses," or communal centers, in its first decade, 1968–78. The largest intentional Christian community network in the world today is in North America, with over 45,000 members, the Hutterites. In the case of the Hutterites' large numbers, it has mostly happened through procreation, generation after generation!

Much of Christian teaching and thinking is an effort at discovering what is "true" and who is "real" and living "right," and intentional communities are often the prov-

Learning opportunities are rarely lacking in community.

Geoph Kozeny

tion of tribes and communities, imagined and actual. Cover to cover, the Bible is about people pursuing a vision and the resulting rewards, conflicts, and disasters. And it is about the God of these people and that relationship and what the outcome of that is to be. Some Christian communities believe that outcome is living in community.

Some believe strongly that in order to be a real Christian, one absolutely must live in an intentional Christian community, as they do, and usually in their community. For some, "having all things in common" (Acts 2) is the primary evidence of the outcome of true faith. I have been to Christian communities that were amazed to learn there were other Christian communities besides their own. Sometimes they were apprehensive about those possibilities, if not outright suspicious! In addition, there are those communities that do use Jesus and the Bible to some extent but that do not call themselves "Christian." Perhaps that's in order to separate themselves from some of the more historic, traditional, theological, or enthusiastic Christian communities.

If it's so biblical, why aren't all Christians living in an intentional community like those in Acts 2? One reason is that it is easier to believe in Jesus than it is to believe Jesus. And, over the centuries, options have diversified and expanded. Not many Christians today see Acts 2 as a prescription for Christian living in the modern world, but rather read it as a description of something that occurred in early Christianity. Therefore, community references in the Bible become "history" and not "orthodoxy." And then there are the dualities: If you want to be really "holy" or "spiritual," go live in a community or monastery, but since not everyone can do that—somebody has to procreate the species, defend our freedoms, and collect those taxes—the rest can go to church on Sunday or engage in some "lesser" expectation. Finally, there are those Christians who see the Acts 2 community event as a mistake for which the early church later suffered. Not all intentional Christian communities see the Acts 2 events as significant for their own existence as a community. There is diversity in how one gets direction out of the Bible.

ing grounds of those discoveries. Consequently, it is not uncommon when visiting Christian communities to face some examination, to see if you are a Christian or even the right kind of Christian. Even Jesus was cross-examined by the "set-apart community of Bible believers" of his day, the Jewish Pharisees. Truth and faith are at stake, and are taken very seriously, usually more seriously than being a community. If you are drawn to intentional Christian community, you probably should be prepared to take Jesus and the Bible seriously. That's what most are looking for: serious followers of Jesus and the Bible.

People of the Bible: Community by the Book

So, what is a Christian community? What's the common denominator? Essentially, a Christian community is one that draws some or all of its emphasis for existing from Jesus Christ in the New Testament of the Holy Bible, be it historic, recent, Protestant, Orthodox, Catholic, Mormon, or some other adjustment and interpretation. The Bible is the seed of faith from which these many communities spring. Not many ancient sacred documents are as potent as the Bible at impregnating people with the concept of community. It is the number one guide for a Christian community, regardless of how it's interpreted. The seeking for and believing in something in the Bible is the fertilizer for the germination and growth of community.

That's because the Bible is rich in the images and language of tribe and community. It is a history and descrip-

The "Church Versus Community" Debate

The first-century Greek word for community used by the writers of the New Testament is "koinonia," and is translated in English as "fellowship," "sharing," or "community." It means something like "participation in common." Our English word "church" comes from "kirk," the old middle English word that can mean something like a decision-making group or a "parliament" of sorts. "Church" is a very "community" word in spite of its present use to indicate a building for a religious service or the people who occasionally meet in such a building.

The "church versus community" debate is perpetual in Christianity and can stir consternation among the believers. Some intentional Christian communities face this debate and struggle as they grow. There is more than one community that began in a church, yet, after a generation or two as an intentional community, returned to being just a church with little resemblance to its days as a community. In spite of apparent longevity and history, some intentional Christian communities are very fluid, changing and reemerging in a variety of forms. Faithfulness to the call of community and right belief may be much stronger than longevity to a particular configuration of people in a geographical location.

The debate among Christians might be more about what "church" is rather than what being in an "intentional community" means, and this debate is embodied in Christianity's most fundamental words. The world "church" is translated from the New Testament Greek word "ἐκκλησία," loosely meaning "to be called out." Not a religious term, as such, to the first-century people, but rather a term signifying "called to a community decision-making meeting" or a "town hall meeting." Jesus only used the word when he referred to decision-making activities of the members of the "believers' community" (e.g., Matthew 18:17).

People of Spirit: Charisma and Leadership

Possession of "The Book" is not always enough to create community. In the first few chapters of the book of Acts, there is recorded a particular phenomenon resulting in individuals possessing special spiritual gifts or *charisma* to make things happen, inspire others, heal the sick, or receive crucial guidance. *Charisma* is the New Testament Greek word for spiritual gifts given by God. The Book and this special spirit together make things happen.

People with these spiritual gifts or *charisma* call others to "be intentional," and they usually lead the group. Sometimes this is self-evident—the individual just has it direct from God with no other human intervention or permission. Sometimes it is bestowed by other humans equally gifted to recognize the calling to leadership. This all usually works when it is recognized, welcomed, and tolerated.

Some Christian communities are apprehensive about this leadership and charisma issue, and others are exuberant about it and about their leaders. Some are constantly at issue with the subject and with the charismatic personalities involved. And the issue often troubles outsiders, too. However, it is intrinsic to the history of Christianity because it is a major element in The Book: the question of who has legitimate authorized power and the right to control.

⑥

Many Christian communities have little contact with each other, even though from an outsider's view they appear to be doing the same things.

People of Vision: Being Mission-Oriented

"For lack of vision the people perish." So says the sage in the Proverbs of the Old Testament. Leaders are often good at articulating the visions others believe and pursue. No charisma, no leaders. No leaders, no vision. No vision, no followers. No followers, no community.

And what do believers follow? More often than not, they follow the teachings and deeds of Jesus Christ and other significant founders and leaders, either historic or contemporary. Be it healing the sick, fighting oppression, converting lost souls, feeding the hungry, making disciples, being closer to Jesus, waiting for the second coming—the return of Jesus—or getting "church" or "community" down right, they are on a mission for God.

Thus, when you have the combination of:
Bible • Jesus • Spirit • Leaders • Vision • Followers • Mission
all in the same place with the same people responding, you have the makings for an intentional Christian community. Hallelujah!

Life in a Resistance Community

by Sue Frankel-Streit

There are people all over the world, in and out of community, who work within "the system" for political change. They keep up with issues important to them and write letters to the editors of their local papers; they attend city council, town planner, or county commissioner meetings; they work on political campaigns and lobby their elected representatives. Other activists prefer to work outside the system, engaging in civil disobedience and "direct action." By focusing on the latter type of activism in this article, the Directory publishers do not mean to imply that this is the only sort of political activism, or necessarily the best.

I T'S A COLD BUT SUNNY MORNING at Little Flower Catholic Worker community. I am washing the breakfast dishes when there's a lull in the kids' playful yells and I hear the radio reporter announce that US warplanes have fired again at an Iraqi site, killing and wounding civilians. We have a full day of farm work ahead, and yet the words of the newscast haunt me as I finish the dishes and change Gabriella's diaper. "Scores of civilians injured." I feel the same anger and despair I've felt so often in these dozen years of life in an activist community: "Why is this happening? How can these lives seem expendable? What can I do?"

As other community members feed the animals and fold newsletters, I check in with them. In half an hour we've decided to spend the noon hour demonstrating at the Federal Building in Richmond to show our dismay over the continued bombing. We make a few phone calls, help the kids draw some posters, put together a quick leaflet and head out.

This is a scene that's repeated many, many times in different forms in communities all over the country, from weekly morning demonstrations at the Pentagon to hammering on Trident submarines, from taking food to squatters to organizing boycotts, from sleeping in city parks in solidarity with the homeless to taking medicines to Iraq in violation of the sanctions. This is activism—actively seeking justice. There are many forms of activism. To me, as a Christian pacifist, activism means nonviolent action directed at creating a more just and peaceful world. For me, especially as a parent, community is essential for healthy activism.

Entering into intentional community—intentionally putting your life together with the lives of others who share a vision, letting go of your personal agenda, sharing resources—all of this is a bit counter-cultural and pulls us toward the margin of American society. Once there, it is hard to ignore those who also inhabit this space (not by their own choice)—the poor, the homeless, minorities … much of the world, in fact. Once we step out of mainstream America, we begin to see the injustice around us, to hear the violence of so much of our country's politics.

Once we put our lives together in community, we become free to devote time and energy to the active pursuit of justice. When a group of people share one or more resources, such as income, childcare, or living quarters, the economic needs of an individual or family are not dependent on one person. Communal work and childcare can free up community members to spend time organizing, traveling to action sites, and doing support work. In addition, living with others who share a vision strengthens the activist's resolve; when you're discouraged, you can draw strength from others. When you cannot be as

---

Sue Frankel-Streit, her husband, and three children live at the Little Flower Catholic Worker farm in Goochland, Virginia, where they live in community; farm; organize and participate in actions for peace; and try to be of service to the poor. Before moving to Virginia, Sue and Bill spent over 10 years at the Catholic Worker in Washington, DC.

"Communal ... childcare can free up community members to spend time organizing, traveling to action sites, and doing support work."

active, you can support the activism of other community members. In community, activists can process the outcome of their actions—successes, failures, physical or emotional injuries, jail time. Massive support or unexpected repercussions can be dealt with together, which helps prevent burnout and blind spots.

Activist communities, or resistance communities, as we call them (since acting for justice inevitably involves resisting the current systems) take many forms and are active on many fronts. The history of resistance communities may go back to the first organized societies; certainly the existence of such communities was recorded in Biblical times. The Israelites organized themselves to resist the oppression of the Egyptians. The disciples of Jesus lived together, held all things in common, proclaimed a different way of life, and were jailed and killed for their beliefs. Gandhi's ashrams were certainly examples of activist communities, as were the "base communities" started in many oppressed regions of Latin America as part of the praxis of liberation theology in the 1970s. There are many other historical examples of communities who shared a vision and acted on it—from the communes that supported World War II resisters in the United States to groups like the "White Rose," students in Nazi Germany who were beheaded for distributing leaflets against fascism.

In many countries, the penalty for activism is death,

torture, or life in prison. In such circumstances, community is essential for activists' survival. I once heard Constancio Pinto speak. He is an East Timorese activist who fled Indonesian death squads after organizing nonviolent demonstrations for East Timorese independence. He described how he had hidden in the homes of members of the community, how he later hid in a cave and was fed by other friends, and how he was eventually smuggled out of the country by still others. Without the support of many activists, he would surely be dead.

The communities I know from experience include Community for Creative Non-Violence and several Catholic Workers communities (all residential). I am also familiar with the Atlantic Life Community (ALC), an intentional community of folks who don't live together, but who share a common activist vision and have challenged and supported one another in fulfilling that vision for over 20 years.

The ALC draws "resisters" from Maine to North Carolina to organize, engage in, and support each other in direct, nonviolent action against militarism, and in exploring a life of active resistance. It is primarily a faith-based group, including Christians, Buddhists, and others whose religions inspire them to action, as well as nonreligious people.

The ALC formed in 1974, inspired the by Pacific Life

65

Community, a group of nonviolent activists from the Bay area, Seattle, and British Columbia who were meeting on a regular basis to plan demonstrations against the then under-construction Trident submarine base in Puget Sound. Activists and supporters on the East Coast felt the need for a similar community to continue to act, reflect, and support each other.

When I joined the Dorothy Day Catholic Worker almost a dozen years ago, the biannual ALC gatherings were part of the calendar. I attended several, driving as far as New York or Massachusetts to spend three days meeting, talking, praying, planning actions, and discussing the life of resistance with up to 200 like-minded folks (including lots of children) from homes and intentional communities up and down the East Coast. I met many inspiring people, learned a lot, and participated in some powerful actions, but it wasn't until after I, myself, took part in a serious nonviolent action and served some jail time that I realized the importance of the ALC.

On January 1, 1991, 15 days before the Gulf War, my (now) husband Bill, Ciaron O'Reilly, Moana Cole, and myself, calling ourselves the ANZUS Plowshares, entered Griffiss Air Force Base and hammered and poured blood on a B-52 warplane. We served two months in jail before our trial, and shortly after our release on personal recognizance, we showed up at the Mother's Day ALC Retreat. I'll never forget the feeling of homecoming I experienced as the four of us were welcomed and embraced by so many of the people who'd inspired us to act, by people we'd come to know through their steadfast jail support, by people I may have only met once or twice, but whose vision was so similar that we were already community.

It was these people from the ALC who continued to support us through our trial, sentencing, and year imprisonment. And it has been these people who have become family in the ensuing eight years, as community members, including ourselves, came and went from the Dorothy Day House, as we attempt to raise children in community, and as we continue to struggle with the meaning of the call to be an active seeker of peace and justice in our violent world. Though the members of the ALC don't live together, they share a vision of a just, weapons-free world. Just knowing other members of the community exist gives us all strength. In winter 1999, when a few of us gathered again in front of the Richmond Federal Building to protest the bombing of Yugoslavia, it was a comfort to know that like-minded friends in Ithaca, New York; New York City; Baltimore, Maryland; Washington, DC; and Raleigh, North Carolina were doing the same thing.

During my years at the Dorothy Day House, I got to know several other Washington, DC-based activist communities whose activism came out of their love for the poor and homeless. One community we worked with in my early years at the Catholic Worker was the Community for Creative Non-Violence (CCNV), a massive 1400 bed shelter near the center of the city. For almost 30 years, CCNV has been a home for an eclectic collection of seekers who have sought creative, nonviolent solutions to the plague of homelessness that's grown steadily worse in the District of Columbia.

My own activism has also been nurtured and challenged over the years by the example of Dorothy Day, cofounder of the Catholic Worker Movement, and by countless Catholic Workers past and present. Whether serving soup to the poor or walking a picket line, Dorothy's life was bound up with the deep quest to live out God's love for all of humanity. There are over 150 Catholic Worker houses in the United States today; in each one a small group of people struggle to form community in solidarity with the poor, to live in voluntary poverty, to perform works of mercy, and to resist war and the causes of war. At the heart of the Catholic Worker philosophy is personalism—the belief that each person is sacred, and that each of us must take personal responsibility for what goes on around us. Personalism leads us into activism as we try to take seriously our responsibilities; it leads us into community as we look for ways to know each other as sacred. Personalism is really about love—love for humanity as a whole, love for the particular people who come into our lives, and especially love for those the world finds hardest to love.

Dorothy Day liked to quote Dostoyevski to define the life she attempted to lead: "Love in dreams is easy, love in reality is a harsh and dreadful thing." It is only that harsh and dreadful love, in fact, that will sustain both community and activism, and it is perhaps this common root that keeps the two intertwined. When we bind together community and activism with love, the universe bends a little closer to justice.

> ❧
>
> At the heart of the Catholic Worker philosophy is personalism—the belief that each person is sacred, and that each of us must take personal responsibility for what goes on around us.

Resources—Books

McAlister, Elizabeth and Phil Berrigan. *The Times Discipline.*

Vanier, Jean. *Community and Growth.* Richmond Hill, Ontario: Daybreak Publications. Email pubs@larchedaybreak.com

Lesbian Intentional Community

"Yer not from around here, are ya?"

by Kate Ellison

I AM ONE URBAN DYKE transplanted to the wilds of Kentucky who has received the honor of writing about the movement of which I am a part. There is no "typical" representative of us, so I write from my experience and knowledge, having lived in a rural lesbian community for over ten years. In this article you will see the words "wimmin" for "women" and "womyn" for "woman." Not a typo, it is common among some feminists and lesbians to use a word that does not make females derivative of males or men. Wimmin are not the outgrowth of Adam's rib, and many of us have created alternative spellings for our gender such as womon, womoon, and wems.

Since OWL (Oregon Women's Land) farm was established in 1975, there has been a small but growing number of intentional communities formed specifically for lesbians in North America. After OWL's pioneering efforts, so many settlements started up in Oregon that the roads leading to them have been loosely named "the Amazon Trail." Lesbian land also exists in New Mexico, Arizona, Louisiana, Florida, Quebec, British Columbia, Kentucky, Mississippi, California, Virginia, Wisconsin, Kansas—just about everywhere!

Lesbian land ranges from one or two wimmin who welcome female travelers to their home to well-established groups of a dozen residents. It may consist of a one-acre lot at the edge of town, a 700-acre rural tract of land, or anything in between. The focus of a land group may be on farming and self-sufficiency, art and culture, politics, or simple survival, to name a few.

One of the more famous efforts at establishing new ways of living for wimmin is Seneca Peace Camp in Seneca, New York. A political antimilitary action group,

Being in a wimmin's community can have familiar frustrations and misunderstandings, yet the work and play inspire many who choose to engage.

Kate Ellison has lived for 10 years at Spiral Wimmin's Land Trust in Kentucky. (See their listing in this directory.) She can be reached at Spiral's address, or email katespiral@juno.com.

"Lesbian land gives wimmin the chance to build our own homes, barns, studios, outhouses."

Seneca is a small farm bordered on one side by an Amish family and on the back by a military compound. It has been a staging ground for many peace actions, as well as home to numerous wimmin who are dedicated to the peace movement. The core group lives there year round and governs itself by consensus.

During Seneca's heyday, when actions were planned, acres of tents would appear and organization was crucial. The "affinity group" method allowed for consensus among each small group of wimmin who traveled and worked together, with representatives from each group participating in consensus decision making for the whole. One example of their activities was a nonviolent attempt to block the entrance to the military base when it was discovered that nuclear missiles were being transported in trucks labeled as if they were carrying food or auto parts. While the military's attention was on the gates, several wimmin sneaked in the back and then telephoned the front gate guards to let them know they'd been invaded.

One of the military's responses to the camp's presence was continual helicopter surveillance. One summer some wimmin climbed on the farmhouse roof and painted a huge spider web surrounded by the words "You can't kill the spirit!" which was a popular slogan and song.

The form of the peace movement has changed, but Seneca Peace Camp remains a source of education on a smaller scale, hosting lesbian-feminist conferences and retreats.

The "back to the land" movement by lesbians is part of the overall lesbian feminist focus on the Earth as female, the creatrix who birthed us all. We are an extremely diverse bunch; the term "eco-feminist" might just be the only label that fits everyone. A concern for the preservation of the natural environment and a search for an unpolluted place to live motivate many to live simply, in a place where food comes from gardens on the land and where everyone knows what happens to their sewage.

The ecology motive is familiar to all who seek rural community living. The lesbian feminist part is unique to our movement. Almost all those who seek wimmin-only space have been touched by the joy of recognizing the power in each of us to create lives that suit us, rather than lives handed down from patriarchal institutions.

Each settlement is different in size, shape, rules, and traditions. Most wimmin's land is populated by lesbians, not straight or bisexual wimmin. However, in my community, Spiral Land Trust for Wimmin, we choose to create community with wimmin, not specifically lesbians. Some wimmin who do not identify as lesbian have considered living here, but not very often. Their male partners and boy children could not move here, although male relatives and friends can and do visit. There are many opinions about our wimmin-only policy, but the bottom line to us is that a community of wimmin is not a community that includes male energy. This is difficult for wimmin with sons, but there are other wimmin's communities that do accept boy children.

We maintain good relations with our neighbors, people who may not ever have left the county. When I first moved to Spiral, I found myself having many more conversations with neighbors, especially men, than I had ever had in the city. They almost always observed, "Yer not from around here, are ya?" My explanation, that I was from Tennessee, seemed to satisfy them, even though we live only 25 miles from that state. Our peace and security rest in the fact that we are considered "good neighbors," allies who look out for each other and band together in emergencies.

Why do wimmin seek to establish a separate place for ourselves? Some would say it just makes sense to them. I have come up with a western, herstorical (that's female for *his*tory, folks) answer. Wimmin have lived for thousands of years in our fathers' houses, then our husbands'. At times we have been actual slaves owned by men, at times it was figurative. Even escaping to a nunnery meant being a bride of Christ, obedient to the priest and pope. The modern city womyn usually works for "the man," just like everybody else.

Lesbians have always been around, surviving as best we could and slowly developing a culture based on our own experiences, separate from the dominant culture. Now we have the chance to create culture deliberately, as we listen to each other in growing numbers, as we each speak our hearts. Wimmin-only space is the only place that is not run by men at all, and it feels very different.

Lesbian land gives wimmin the chance to build our own homes, barns, studios, outhouses. For many, the creative direction and implementation of a project, a home for herself or her friends, is profoundly life-changing. Female conditioning has led most of us to be comfortable assisting, not taking charge. Or we give directions but rely on a man's expertise and strength to get the job done. Now, even when there is a project leader, we share skills and create together.

Lia, who recently moved to Spiral, told me, "I feel a sense of empowerment I never had before. I am respected and taken seriously in a way that never really happened before moving here. I have a grown son that I dearly love; I certainly don't hate men. However, men live and take for granted a kind of entitlement, it's in their bones, and they don't necessarily mean to treat you different, but they do. It's a rare man that can treat everyone equal, and I'm tired of looking for him."

Another new resident of Spiral used to have her own farm a few hours from here. Gina says, "As a womyn, you can't get any help on the farm. You can't go down to the corner store and hang out with the guys, then ask some of them to come over and help with the fencing. When other farmers did help me, it was like the help they give a womyn—someone that's looked down on, or a possible opportunity for sex. And of course they never want me to help them, because I was just a womyn. Wimmin don't do that kind of work, none of their wimmin do. Besides, I like being around other wimmin, having a social life, being myself. In community with wimmin, I feel safe. I no longer have to look over my shoulder."

Everyday living has its frustrations and misunderstandings, no matter where you hang your hat. Yet sometimes I feel inspired by the work and the play that we engage each other in. It gives my life meaning the way nothing else ever has. Perhaps you feel that way about your community. I am grateful that we have enough freedom and sense of adventure to make these choices.

I appreciate the opportunity to learn from other wimmin in an environment of respect. We may have different backgrounds, but our commonalities as wimmin, and especially as lesbians, help me feel that I'm working with my own group. The support, understanding, and shared experiences make it easier. The only way to really know the difference is to experience it yourself.

Resources

The following addresses are given to help lesbians reading this article connect with the wider community of rural lesbians and wimmin's land. Please respect our intent.

Lesbian Natural Resources (LNR), a networking source for lesbian communities, was established over nine years ago to be a resource for community-owned (not-for-profit) lesbian lands and rural lesbians in Canada, Mexico, and the United States. LNR has a program for sharing rural living skills through its apprenticeship program. It does not maintain a contact list of rural communities to visit. For more information, write LNR at PO Box 8742, Minneapolis MN 55408, USA.

Shewolf publishes a 64-page directory containing "the philosophies and contacts for over 75 wimmin's settlements in the United States and Canada." To order, contact: Royal T., 2013 Rue Royal, New Orleans LA 70116, USA. Email: Wimminland@aol.com
http://members.aol.com/shewolfww/fave/index.htm

Recruiting Queer Communards!
Homophobia, Sexuality, and Community Living

by Sandorfag

Throughout this article the author makes use of expressions and stereotypes which have been used to describe homosexuals in a derogatory way: "queer," "fag," "dyke," "twisted," "freak," etc. Though the publishers of this directory are not altogether comfortable with these terms, the author chooses them consciously, believing that playing with stereotypes without shame subverts their power and transforms them from forces of hurtful oppression into tools of freedom and liberation.

PROBABLY MOST INTENTIONAL communities, like most schools, churches, workplaces, and families, have homosexual members. We are everywhere, after all. But we are most definitely not a visible presence everywhere. Many queers living in community suffer from homophobia, pressures to conform to heterosexual community norms, isolation, and invisibility.

Though I had fantasized since childhood of living in a commune in the country, it had never occurred to me that I could live in rural community and in the midst of thriving queer culture. The gay and lesbian community I was part of in New York was comprised of many folks who had fled the isolation of being queer in rural areas, small towns, suburbs, and smaller cities. Queer culture and country living seemed mutually exclusive. That is, until I met the radical faeries—outrageous playful subversive queers with city circles and rural communes. They magically enticed me to Short Mountain Sanctuary, which has been my home ever since.

The radical faerie "movement" is diverse and decentralized. It includes communities like Wolf Creek, which offer "faggot-only space," and communities like IDA, Pumpkin Hollow, Short Mountain Sanctuary, and Zuni Mountain Sanctuary, which define "faerie" much more broadly.

Short Mountain, like many other radical faerie communities, is first and foremost a queer space. That is the organizing principle that binds us together and draws into our ever-expanding circle a constant flow of queer folks with communitarian aspirations. Beyond that our shared ideology is hard to pin down. Part of our group identity is our indefinability. We are faeries, creatures of magic, myth, and mischief. It is not just the sexuality of gay men that we honor. This is a world for free/fluid/evolving/experimental/spiritual/political sexual expression, including gay, lesbian, bisexual, and polyamorous people, pagan monks, naturalists, and fetishists of many flavors. Often our community includes women. Sometimes the gay men and lesbian women end up becoming lovers. (Go figure.) We also attract a broad spectrum of people who are transgendered: female-to-male and male-to-female transsexuals, folks somewhere in the midst of their transformation (including some who elected to stop it somewhere in between), drag queens, and butch dykes. Almost all of us enjoy playing with our gender identity, doing things like wearing exotic lingerie while sporting a full beard. We call this "genderfuck." Once, a straight guy who stayed with us for a while took "Breeder" as his name. Queer culture, in my opinion, does not thrive by gay men cloistering themselves away from everybody else. It flourishes when we celebrate sexuality in all its kinky quirky variations.

Three of my fellow communards lived in predominantly straight intentional communities prior to moving to Short Mountain. *(Editor's note: Interested readers can contact the author for additional information about any of these experiences.)*

Sandorfag has lived at Short Mountain community in Tennessee since 1993, at 247 Sanctuary Lane, Liberty TN 37095, USA.

Weeder

In 1972, Weeder was part of a community and sexually active with other men when he was told, "If you want to stay in this community then you can't be homosexual." Forced to choose, he recalls 27 years later, "I wanted to be in community more than I wanted to pursue homosexuality." Weeder then spent eight years at The Farm, succumbing to the pressures of "hippie family values" to marry and have kids. *(Editor's note: We asked several current and former members of The Farm to verify this. The general consensus seemed to be that, while Weeder accurately reflects the atmosphere at The Farm at the time he was living there, attitudes have since shifted to be much more supportive of homosexuality.)*

Eventually he found himself having sex with men again, seeking work assignments that would bring him into proximity of gay cruising spots and creating elaborate alibis. "Repressing my sexuality wasn't working," he says in retrospect. "The lies were driving me crazy. One of the major appeals of community living was that I wanted to live a life where I could be truthful with people." Weeder left the community, split up with his wife, and lived in urban gay scenes in the southeast until he met some faeries at a Christmas potluck who attracted him to Short Mountain. His now grown daughters visit periodically.

Delilah

Half a world away, Delilah became involved in the Israeli kibbutz youth movement in his early teens, embracing a vision of transforming culture and society through collective living. After high school and mandatory military service, he went to live on a kibbutz. Although he had had sexual experiences with other young men, he was still in a state of denial about his homosexual desires. At the kibbutz he experienced a feeling of support and belonging that enabled him to open up to his sexuality for the first time. "It was the moment when my sexuality couldn't be split off from the rest of me anymore." At this critical juncture in his life, several gay and lesbian people from the United States came to live at the kibbutz and inquired about the kibbutz's policy toward gays and lesbians. The kibbutz didn't have one and had never before had occasion to consider one.

"That was a horrible time," groans Delilah. "Half the people were cool, half were homophobic, people threatened to leave and the kibbutz almost split." The community spent months processing the conflict, brought in

Breaking out of narrowly defined gender roles is an option that some people embrace in the communities movement.

outside facilitators, and ended up agreeing to disagree in a "don't ask, don't tell," neither yes nor no compromise on the homosexual question. "I got to the point where I needed to come out," Delilah says. He moved to New York, where he lived for several years before coming to live here. Although coming out resulted in his leaving the kibbutz, Delilah believes that the encouragement he felt there was what enabled him to do it. "My life here is completely consistent with a path I've been on for 20 years," the Israeli dissident says.

Ocea

Ocea sought refuge in his first community after his parents' hostile response to his coming out to them as a teenager in 1981. He was attracted to that community by its social critique and the promise of creating a new society that it offered. Ocea characterizes the community's attitude toward his homosexuality when he first joined as, "We accept you, and you should be working toward overcoming your neurosis and becoming heterosexual."

Ocea stayed there for 10 years. Occasionally he would have sex with other men who lived there, but mostly they were as uncomfortable as he was about homosexuality. As he "came out" more, the attitudes there toward his homosexuality became more and more hostile. Here is a brief excerpt from a lengthy missive issued by the community's founder: "The truth is that no matter how much you enema with perfume douches or coyly call it 'the chocolate canal' it wasn't made for that…. Nature will damn you, or any of us for any unnatural inorganic preference…. You're just a spoiled petulant neurotic trying to make a life-style out of a fetish."

By the time he learned of the existence of Short

Short Mountain

Queer communities parading at Nashville's Gay Pride celebration.

Mountain from an earlier edition of this directory, Ocea was desperate to explore his queer identity. In his letters to us he wrote, "I am being forced into a mold I can't/won't accept. I have to take control of my life…. I really long for, corny as it sounds, my long lost sisters and brothers." Ocea arrived six years ago and has lived at Short Mountain ever since.

Some people imagine a bunch of queers living together as a nonstop orgiastic pleasurefest. Well, we also decorate, dress up a lot, make gorgeous floral arrangements with the flowers we grow, cook gourmet cuisine, sew, knit, crochet, and embroider, dish each other endlessly, dance, and party. We practice the butch arts required to maintain our twisted lifestyle in this woodsy faerieland: we grow food and build buildings, raise goats and chickens, harness electricity from the sun, and cut firewood. We also process conflict as it arises.

Even in our out loud and proud queer community we face visibility issues. Last year Mish and Kasha had plans to go into town together to do errands. Kasha showed up dressed as he usually is, wearing a skirt over leggings, fingernail polish, jewelry and big hair, ready to go. "Being himself" is being a freak, and he thinks nothing of it. Mish, a community elder who has his own eccentric outfits and likes to shock and turn heads in a more anonymous context, felt that for Kasha to go into town dressed like that was disrespectful and could potentially endanger our community. Another time, two long-term visitors to our community (both men) ended up drunkenly making out at a big local event with thousands of people. They were harshly criticized by members of Short Mountain for engaging in behavior some judged to be reckless. Visibility can be complex and scary. We do live with a palpable sense of vulnerability as queers living in a conservative Christian rural area, but we are all out of the closet and none of us tailor our behavior to accepted local norms. As our extended community grows, we become bolder all the time.

The Faerie Gatherings that various faerie communities put on every year are an opportunity for attendees (women/men/kids/other) to explore their own queerness and experience a powerful sense of community. The magical freedom embodied in the queerness of faerie gatherings resonates for free-thinkers and nonconformists of diverse description. Breaking out of narrowly defined gender roles is a goal for many people in the communities movement. The faeries offer fertile ground for exploring those possibilities.

Radical faeries have established communities in Tennessee, New Mexico, Oregon, and Pennsylvania, and faerie groups have bought land in Minnesota, Ontario, and Vermont, where they gather and camp and plan someday to establish communities. Faeries are coming together in Europe and Australia as well, envisioning future communities.

Of course, there are many other paths for queers interested in living in community. Join a community. Revolutionize a community. Start a community. Be visible as queer in the community you are already part of. Encourage other queers into your community. Encourage other members of your community into their queerness. Only we can create queer visibility and presence in the communities movement.

Resources

See community listings for Ida, Pumpkin Hollow, Short Mountain Sanctuary, Sun Valley, Wolf Creek Sanctuary, and Zuni Mountain Sanctuary.

Rural Gay Web site: http://www.ruralgay.com/

RFD: A Country Journal for Queer Folks Everywhere. PO Box 68, Liberty TN 37095, USA. Short Mountain publishes this magazine, which includes faerie contacts around the globe, contact letters, and regular updates and articles on queer communities. http://www.rfdmag.org/

Queer in Community (QIC) network, c/o Mahantongo Spirit Garden, RD 1 Box 149, Pitman PA 17964, USA. Email: qic@ic.org, http://www.ic.org/qic/

Queer in Community
Another Perspective

by Rajal Cohen

O F THE GAY, LESBIAN AND BISEXUAL people who choose to live in intentional community, many—if not most—of us choose to live in integrated communities, where heterosexuals are the majority, as they are in the wider society.

Why is this? Well, many of us prefer the diversity. Just because I choose someone from one gender as a romantic partner doesn't mean I want to exclude folks of other genders and choices from my life. Also, deciding on a queer-only community limits your options in a lot of other aspects of community. If you want to live in a certain region of the country, or to live in a community with a certain focus or lifestyle, you have many more choices if you consider mixed communities.

Some strands of the communities web abound with members who are "straight but not narrow." They may be people who never really felt that they fit into mainstream society and the rigid roles it offers to men and women. They may know what it is like to have made important choices in their lives which their parents did not support. They may be dissatisfied with the isolation of the nuclear family. They may be people who always wanted to be physically affectionate with their friends, but were prevented by pervasive homophobia. They may understand that the "traditional family values" backlash is as much an attack on the communities movement as it is on gays and lesbians. People with these backgrounds and perspectives tend to be natural allies of queer folk, and often make good friends, too!

Even if having a bunch of other queer people around is a high priority for you, a mixed community may be a good choice. They are often quite a bit larger than queer-only

Mixed communities can offer more options and a broader experience than queer-only communities.

Eesha Williams

Rajal Cohen lived at Twin Oaks from 1990–94. She left to found Abundant Dawn community with a group of other experienced communitarians. She now lives at Dayspring Circle, at Abundant Dawn community (see the Community Listings). She can be reached via email: rajal@ic.org.

communities, and they may actually include more queers (especially those of the bisexual variety) among their numbers than a small lesbian or faery community does.

If you are queer and looking for community, here are a few suggestions:

• Don't assume that going to live with a group of other dykes or faeries will necessarily be simple and nurturing. People are people, and you may or may not have enough in common with any particular group to make living together feasible and rewarding. Even if you are well aligned with people, group living requires certain skills that take time to develop.

• Don't assume that you will or won't feel welcome in a mixed community. Every community is different, and they change from year to year, depending on who is living there. There are queer-friendly communities among rural communes, cohousing settlements, ecovillages, urban cooperative houses, activist collectives—just about any type of community out there. Out of the 278 communities who chose to answer questions about sexuality in this directory's survey, only six percent indicated that they have restrictions against nonheterosexual relationships.

• In your letter of introduction, it is probably a good idea to mention your sexual orientation, without making a big deal of it. There are communities that are not open to queer members, and you'll want to know this right away. On the other hand, many communities really do value diversity. They may be genuinely pleased at your potential contribution to their demographic. They may pass your letter on to a queer member of their community to answer, or give you useful information about local queer culture (or lack thereof).

• If your letter doesn't get answered right away, or you get a cool reply, don't assume it's because you are gay. We letter-answerers tend to be a little overworked, and, alas, we are not always as responsive as one might hope.

• Join QIC (see below) to find out the insiders' scoop on many communities!

Resources

Queer in Community: the intentional community network for lesbians, gays, bisexuals, transgendereds, queers, faeries, dykes, and the people who love them. Sponsors fun gatherings and maintains a database of queer and queer-friendly communities. QIC, c/o Mahantongo Spirit Garden, RD 1 Box 149, Pitman PA 17964, USA. Email: qic@ic.org, http://www.ic.org/qic/

Tony Sirna

There are queer-friendly communities throughout the movement.

Jillian Downey

Starting From Scratch (but Not Without Help)

This section provides nuts and bolts information about forming new communities: from legal issues to financial necessities, from decision-making processes to land-use design, from vision statements to qualifying for bank loans. The practical tips here are meant to save new communities time and energy, in effect to keep them from having to reinvent the wheel in some areas where there is now a large storehouse of experience from previous community founders. Existing communities may find some of these articles quite valuable, as well.

Six Ingredients for Forming Communities
(That Help Reduce Conflict Down the Road)

by Diana Leafe Christian

"I FOUND THE LAND!" JACK EXCLAIMED over the phone. As the originator of Skydance Farm, a small forming community in northern Colorado, he had been searching for just the right community land for years, long before he and a circle of acquaintances had begun meeting weekly to create community. He was so sure it was *the* land, he said, that he'd plunked down $10,000 of his own savings as an option fee to take it off the market long enough for us to decide.

I had joined the group several weeks earlier. I knew nothing about intentional communities at the time. However, it had seemed in their meetings that something was missing.

"What's the purpose of your community?" I had finally asked. "What's your vision for it?" No one could really answer.

That Saturday we all drove out to the land to check it out.

And promptly fell apart. Confronting the reality of buying land, no one wanted to commit. Frankly, there was nothing to commit *to*. No common purpose or vision, no organizational structure, no budget, no agreements. In fact we hadn't made decisions at all, but had simply talked about how wonderful community life would be. Although Jack tried mightily to persuade us to go in with him on the land, there were no takers, and he barely got his money out before the option deadline.

I became intensely curious about what it would take for a newly forming community to succeed. So over the next seven years, first as publisher of a newsletter about forming communities and then as editor of *Communities* magazine, I interviewed dozens of people involved in communities forming in the '90s as well as founders of long-established ones. I wanted to know what worked, what didn't work, how not to reinvent the wheel.

I learned that no matter how inspired and visionary the community founders, only about one out of 10 new communities actually seemed to get built. The other 90 percent seemed to go nowhere, occasionally because of lack of money or the right land, but mostly because of ... conflict.

And usually, conflict accompanied by heartbreak, and often, lawsuits. Many of these community break-ups resulted from what I call "structural conflict"—problems that arose when founders didn't explicitly take care of certain important issues at the outset, creating one or more flaws in their organizational structure. Several weeks, months, or even years later, the group ran into major problems that could have been largely prevented if they had handled these issues early on. Naturally, a great deal of interpersonal conflict arose at the same time, making the initial conflict much worse. I've seen forming communities founder and sink on such issues as:

- *"But our main purpose is* not *to run a retreat center; that's just a business. We can't spend money on that until we take care of our needs first!"*
- *"What? I have to cough up $10,000 more for 'land development'?"*
- *"My brother can't live here? But he's* my *brother. I didn't agree to this!"*
- *"What do you* mean *I can't get my money out again when I leave?!"*
- *"Maybe you* think *it's important to stay in the room and 'resolve the conflict' but I'm outta here! Have your 'conflict resolution' session without me!"*

Diana Leafe Christian has studied intentional communities since 1992, and edited *Communities* magazine since 1993. She is author of *Forming an Intentional Community: What Works, What Doesn't Work, How Not to Reinvent the Wheel,* and offers introductory and weekend workshops on this topic. She is cofounder of a small community in North Carolina. Email: diana@ic.org.

• *"Ever since Carl joined we've been dealing with his hurt feelings. It's exhaust-
ing. How did we let this happen?"*

You get the picture. While interpersonal conflict is normal and
expected, I believe that much of the
structural conflict in these communities could have been prevented, or
at least greatly reduced, if the
founders had paid attention to six
"ingredients":

1 Choosing a fair, participatory decision-making process that is appropriate for the group. And if it's consensus, getting trained in it.

2 Identifying their vision and creating
a vision statement.

3 Learning what resources, information, skills, and tasks they would
need, and then either learning or
hiring them.

4 Drawing up clear agreements, in
writing.

5 Learning good communication skills, and making clear
communication a priority, including ways of reducing
conflict.

6 Selecting cofounders and new members for emotional
well-being.

Communities need to make communication skills a priority.

To be fair, a number of well-established North American communities never included many of these structural
ingredients at their origin. In the '60s, '70s, or '80s, people usually just bought land and moved on. Some of these
communities are with us today, and proud of it.

Nonetheless, I recommend these "ingredients" for
communities forming now. Why? Because establishing a
new community is not easy. Since the mid '80s through
the early '90s, the cost of land and housing has skyrock-
eted, relative to people's assets and earning power. Zoning
regulations and building codes are considerably more
restrictive than in earlier decades. And because of the
media coverage that highlights any violent or extreme
practices of a group, the "cult" stereotype is still in public
consciousness, and may affect how potential neighbors
feel about *your* group moving into their neighborhood.

The challenges facing new communities today have
convinced me that nowadays community founders must
be more organized and purposeful—not to mention better capitalized—than their counterparts of earlier years.

1. Fair, Participatory Decision Making

It's probably pretty obvious that a great deal of conflict
would arise if people didn't feel that they had enough say
in community decisions, unless the community has explicitly created a structure in which members are not expecting to participate in decisions, such as one where a leader

or small group of members make decisions, as is sometimes the case in spiritual communities. So, one of the
first things I believe a forming community not structured
this way should do is to choose a fair, participatory form
of decision making.

Most communities I've observed use consensus. However, herein also lies a source of potential conflict. First,
the group needs to know that consensus is right for them,
which presumes that everyone has equal access to power.
It may not work out if one person is the landowner and
the rest tenants, for example.

Second, the group needs to get trained, and, ideally, have
a consensus facilitator for meetings. Consensus does not
mean, as many mistakenly assume, "We'll just keep talking
about a proposal for hours and hours until we all agree." It's
far more complex and subtle than that. (See the article that
immediately follows, called "Consensus Basics.") Unlike
majority-rule voting, in which people argue for or against a
proposal and it either passes or not, in consensus the proposal itself is modified as people express their concerns
about it. If everyone can support a final revision of the proposal, it passes; if even one person blocks the proposal, it
doesn't. Consensus therefore only allows decisions that
the whole group can live with and implement without
resentment. The process should *not* take hours and hours.
If it does, it means the group is not well-facilitated. A
good facilitator schedules breaks, suggests issues be tabled
for later discussion, or suggests certain items be sent to
committee. Blocking is used rarely, and only when someone, after long and heartfelt soul-searching, feels that the
proposal would harm the group in the long run—morally,
ethically, financially, legally, or in some other way.

Unfortunately, many well-meaning but untrained

Commitment to a viable decision-making process is a necessary ingredient to forming a community.

example using consensus for most decisions and an alternate method such as 90 percent voting for decisions affecting property value and only among members with equity in the land.

On the other hand, other experienced communitarians caution against using two methods. They assert that consensus is not a method but a philosophy of inclusion, and when people are less able to influence decisions while using a faster method it breaks down the trust and the cohesion of the group.

I believe that the decision-making method best for you depends on whether your group is together primarily to build the physical infrastructure of a community (regardless of what members you may lose due to a faster decision-making process), or for your connection and friendship (regardless of the great land deals you may lose due to a slower, more inclusive process).

Whatever method or methods your forming community chooses, if one of them involves consensus, *please* get good training in it first!

2. Vision and Vision Statement: "What We Are About"

Your vision is a compelling idea or image that inspires and motivates your members to keep on creating community, to persevere through the rough times, to remember why you're there, and to help guide your decisions. This is not necessarily verbal, but can be a feeling, or an energy presence. It gives voice to your group's deeply held values and intuitions. It is your picture or "feel" of the kind of life you'd like to lead together.

The vision is often described or otherwise implied in your collection of written expressions—your agreements, flyer, brochure, and/or Web site. These documents often include a paragraph or two describing what your community will be like, a list of shared values, a list of goals, often a "how we'll do it" mission statement, and … the vision statement.

The vision statement is a condensed version of your vision. The vision statement is a clear, compelling expression of your group's overall purpose and goals. Each of you can identify with it. It helps to unify your effort; it helps focus everyone's energy like a lens. Because it reveals and announces your group's core values, it gives you a reference point to return to in decisions or during confusion or disagreement. It keeps you all inspired, as it is a shorthand reminder of why you're forming community. When times get tough, the vision statement helps awaken your vision as an energetic presence. Ideally it is memorized, and everyone can state it.

groups fall into using what I call "pseudo-consensus":
• *"Everything we decide on must be decided by consensus! It 'betrays' consensus to use any other method."*
• *"Everyone in the group must be involved in every decision, no matter how small."*
• *"We'll stay in this room until we make a decision—no matter how long it takes!"*
• *"I block! This proposal just won't work for me."*
• *"I plan to block the proposal we're going to discuss today. So, since I'm already against it and plan to stop it, there's no need to even bring it up!"*

Consensus is like a chain saw. Consensus can chop a lot of wood; "pseudo-consensus" can chop your leg. While majority-rule voting can trigger conflict because up to 49 percent of the people can be unhappy with a decision, poorly understood and improperly practiced consensus can generate every bit as much conflict.

In the consensus process, deciding on a proposal usually takes more time than with majority rule voting. However, implementing a proposal once it's agreed upon usually takes far less time, since everybody is behind it. Nevertheless, because of the time factor, some community veterans recommend having two, or more, participatory decision-making methods, for example, consensus and one other "agreement-seeking" method, such as 70 percent voting, 80 percent voting, 90 percent voting, consensus-minus-two, or consensus-minus-one, etc. Some cohousing groups have an alternative method in place for when they need to make exceptionally fast decisions, such as when they have a narrow window of opportunity to tie up a parcel of sought-after land, or when they make decisions involving some but not all the members. And some communities may split up the kind of decisions made, for

The vision statement also communicates your group's core purpose to others and to potential new members quickly: "*This* is what we're about; *this* is what we hope to accomplish." It allows you to be specific about what you are—and are not. Some recommend that the vision statement express the "who," the "what," and the "why" of your forming community (and leave the "where," "when," and "how" for the mission statement or strategic plan). I think it's more potent if it's short, about 20–40 words.

⑥

We have joined together to create a center for renewal, education, and service, dedicated to the positive transformation of our world.
    —*Shenoa Retreat and Learning Center, Philo, California*

We are creating a cooperative neighborhood of diverse individuals sharing human resources within an ecologically responsible community setting.
    —*Harmony Village Cohousing, Golden, Colorado*

We are a neotribal permaculture village, actively engaged in building sacred community, supporting personal empowerment, and catalyzing cultural transformation.... We share a commitment to a vital, diversified spirituality; healthy social relations; sustainable ecological systems; and a low-maintenance/high-satisfaction lifestyle.
    —*Earthaven Community, Black Mountain, North Carolina*

While these vision statements leave plenty of room for interpretation, they are considerably more concrete and grounded than many I've seen. Some newly forming communities represent themselves with flowery, overly vague, or just plain pretentious vision statements, and … these are often the first to go bust. It seems that communities with vision statements that are more focused, specific, and grounded are often the ones that actually get built.

It is quite possible that people in a forming group have more than one vision among them—which means that the individuals present may represent more than one potential community. It's crucial to find this out early—*before* the group buys land together.

Imagine founders of a community with no common vision who buy land, move on, put up a few buildings—and begin to run out of money. Now they must decide how they'll spend their remaining funds. But they can't agree on priorities. Some want to finish the community building because they believe that creating a sense of community is the primary reason they're together, and know that having a community building will help focus their community spirit. Others want to finish the garden and irrigation system because they see their primary purpose as becoming

I learned that no matter how inspired and visionary the community founders, only about one out of 10 new communities actually seemed to get built.

self-reliant homesteaders. Different members have different visions, which they incorrectly assume everyone shares. By this time the members are arguing mightily most of the time, but the core of their problem is structural; it's *built into* the system. This a "time-bomb" kind of conflict, with members unable to see it's not that "John's being unreasonable" or "Sue's irresponsible," but that each member is operating from a different assumption about why they're there in the first place. So what now? Which members get to stay on the land and which ones must either live with a vision that doesn't fit them or move out?

Identifying a vision and crafting a vision statement is an enormous task, often requiring plenty of discussion, meditation, spiritual guidance, and "sleeping on it," through a series of meetings over many weeks.

Many community veterans believe that consensus is the appropriate process for this critical decision. As Betty Didcoct of TIES consulting says, "the consensus process itself fosters an attitude that can help forge a bond and build trust in your group. When the input of everyone is honored, who knows what might surface—a strong single vision that draws everyone, or multiple visions that suggest the presence of more than one potential forming community."

Other community activists, such as Rob Sandelin of Northwest Intentional Communities Association, suggest *not* using consensus to determine your vision and vision statement. It's a catch-22: for consensus to work well your group must have a common purpose, and at this point, it doesn't. A group needs a method, he says, (such as 90 percent voting, for example) in which some people can diverge radically from others about what they want in the community without bringing the whole process to a crushing halt. I personally agree with this view, although there are groups out there who employed consensus for the vision statement process and it worked just fine.

It is best if a strong, mutually reinforcing relationship exists between your community's values, goals, and vision and the legal structure or structures with which it will one day own or manage its land and assets. (See the article on legal structures, later in this section.) Identify your forming community's values, goals, and vision early in the formation process, and let these determine your legal structures—not the other way around!

3. Know What You Need to Know

Forming a new community, like simultaneously starting up a new business and beginning a marriage, can be a complex, time-consuming process requiring both business skills and interpersonal communication skills. Founders of successful new communities seem to know this. And those that get mired in severe problems have usually leapt in without a clue. These well-meaning folks didn't *know* what they didn't know.

This seems particularly true of spiritual communities. I've often seen founders with spiritual ideals and compelling visions flounder and sink because they had no idea how to conduct a land search or negotiate a bank loan. I've also seen people with plenty of technical or business savvy—folks able to build a nifty composting toilet or craft a solid strategic plan—who didn't know the first thing about how to communicate with people. And I've seen sensitive spiritual folks as well as get-the-job-done types crash and burn the first time they encountered any real conflict.

Consider the story of Sharon, who bought and attempted to develop land for a spiritual community. At first it looked promising. Sharon had received zoning approval for an innovative clustered-housing site plan. She met regularly with a group of friends and supporters to envision and meditate. But over the next 18 months this and a subsequent forming community group fell apart, disappointed and often bitter. Sharon struggled with money issues, land-development issues, interpersonal issues. After two years she said she was no longer attempting community, in fact loathed the idea of community, and didn't even want to hear the "C" word.

What had Sharon not known?

- How much money it would take to complete the land development process before she could legally transfer title to a buyer.
- How much each lot would eventually cost.
- That she shouldn't foster hope in those who could never afford to buy in.
- That she'd need adequate legal documents and financial data to secure private financing.
- That she should make it clear to everyone at the outset that as well as having a vision she was also serving as land developer.
- That she needed to explain that she fully intended to reimburse her land-purchase and development costs and make a profit to compensate her time and entrepreneurial risk.
- That she needed to tell people that, as the developer, she would make all land-development decisions.
- That a process was needed for who was in the group and who wasn't, and for what kinds of decisions the group would make and which Sharon alone would make.
- That consensus was the wrong decision-making option for a group with one landowner and others with no financial risk.
- That they weren't in fact practicing consensus at all, but some vaguely conceived idea of it.

> ...communities with vision statements that are more focused, specific, and grounded are often the ones that actually get built.

I believe that community founders would experience much less conflict if they understood the need for both "heart" and "head" skills. The latter include drafting clear written agreements; creating budgets, a timeline, a strategic plan; choosing legal structure(s) for land ownership or any planned business or educational activities; learning local zoning or land-use laws; and understanding finance and real estate, site planning, and the land development process (roads, power, water, sewage, etc.).

Not everyone in your forming group needs to have all these skills—that's one reason you're a group! Nor must you possess all this skill and expertise among yourselves. Many successful groups have hired an accountant, lawyer, project manager, meeting facilitator, and so on.

Nowadays community founders must anticipate challenges not faced by communities formed in earlier times. First, "ideal" land isn't ideal if zoning regulations and building codes prevent your developing it the way you want to. Second, if your group wants rural land, a lack of decent-paying local jobs will affect your attractiveness to future members. Difficulty attracting members will affect your ability to recoup early land investment costs, so think about the site relative to available jobs *before* you buy the land. And third, keep in mind that the initial impression you make on potential neighbors will affect whether or not they will support you in getting a needed zoning variance. If you call your endeavor a community or an intentional community, people may only hear "hippie commie cult." Perhaps call it a center, a project, or even a household, but be cautious with the loaded term "community" until they have a chance to learn, over time, that you're in fact fine, upstanding neighbors.

Forming communities need enough time, money, and "community glue" to pull off a project of this magnitude. To start with, it takes a great deal of committed time and hard work. Even if you meet weekly, you'll often need people on various committees—gathering information, drafting proposals, and so on—in between regular meetings. In my experience, this amount of work is equivalent to one or more group members working part-time or even full time.

It also takes adequate capitalization, often several hundred thousand dollars—for land purchase, land development if needed, new construction or renovation, and myriad lesser costs. As soon as it's feasible, you'll need to know roughly how much money your project will cost. Some people raise the money from others; some fund the whole thing themselves. And please don't put every last cent down on the land. Keep enough available for land development, construction, etc., even if that means buying a more modest parcel.

Tess

Discover what creates the feeling of connection and a shared sense of "us."

Elana Kann and Bill Fleming of Neighborhood Design Build, former project managers of Westwood Cohousing in Asheville, North Carolina, recommend that forming community groups understand and accept the difference between what is and what is not in their control. They've observed that probably 95 percent of the major variables involving a forming community are *not* in a group's control. (Land criteria is in a group's control; land use may not be if local zoning requirements are in place.) The group would ideally have a mechanism for building on each decision and moving forward, rather than meandering or even backtracking, as many groups unfortunately do. They would learn what questions to ask, how to research answers, how to present information to the group, and how to base decisions on the best information available. And, recommend Elana and Bill, they would talk frankly about the required financial and work commitments, as well as other real-world constraints, from the start.

It takes a sense of connection, a shared sense of "us"— the community "glue." This is usually born of group experiences: potluck dinners, preparing meals together, weekend camping trips, solving problems together. Work parties are one of the best ways for people to get to know each other, and not incidentally, great ways to learn each other's approaches to responsibility and accountability. Storytelling evenings are great ways to get to know each other on deeper levels, especially if the topics are self-revealing and personal, such as family attitudes about religion, child raising, or money and social class. Such

sharing sessions also reveal issues relevant to community living and shared resources later on.

Gathering this range of skills and information in order to reduce future conflict is complex, time-consuming, and often overwhelming.

Can your forming community afford to do without it? I don't think so.

4. Clear Agreements, in Writing

Many forming communities flounder because they haven't written down their agreements, and when people try to conjure up what they thought they had agreed on months or years before, they remember things differently. Unfortunately even people with the greatest good will can recall a conversation or an agreement in such divergent ways that each may wonder if the other is trying to cheat or abuse or manipulate them! This is one of the greatest stumbling blocks in newly forming communities—and it's so easily prevented.

Many agreements are of course embedded in legal documents such as corporation bylaws, lease agreements, or private contracts. Others are simple agreements with no legal "teeth," but which help the participants stay on track with each other nevertheless. Write out your agreements, read them, and for good measure, *sign what you've agreed to*, whether or not they're formal legal documents. Keep your agreements in a safe place and refer to them as needed.

What do you need to agree on?

- Who your members are.
- Your qualifications to become a member and the process to do so.
- Whether new people need to attend a minimum number of meetings and be approved by others.
- How new members are brought up to speed.
- How decisions are made, and who gets to make them.
- How meetings are run.
- How records are kept.
- Who takes notes, how are they distributed, and to whom.
- Your group's record of decisions to show new members.
- How tasks are assigned to members, and how people are held accountable for them.
- Expected expenses, how they are to be paid, and what happens in case of cost overruns.
- Any dues structure. (Many groups have found that a nonrefundable investment of some minimal amount such as $100 differentiates those "just looking" from those willing to commit time and energy to the project.)
- Who keeps records of what has been paid.
- Whether such monies are refundable, and from what source.
- Your criteria for whether, and how, people may be asked to leave the group.

Having these and other issues in writing, along with proper legal documents for financial matters such as land purchase, can prevent some of the most heart-rending misunderstandings in the months ahead.

5. Good Communication Skills

Every community experiences conflict—including those which include all the above ingredients at their origin! Interpersonal conflict is a given; it will arise. I believe a community is healthy when it deals openly with conflict and doesn't pretend it isn't there. Healthy communities recognize that community offers living "mirrors" for each other, and an opportunity for faster-than-normal spiritual and emotional growth. Dealing with conflict is an opportunity, not a problem.

Some people are naturally skillful and effective communicators. Most of us, however, probably need to unlearn many of our habitual ways of communicating. Unfortunately, Western culture tends to systematically train people away from any tendencies toward cooperation and empathy. We're taught to be competitive and win at all costs, to see conflict in terms of what's wrong with someone else, and to decide things in terms of "us versus them."

I've usually seen conflicts arise because of a misunderstanding, or when someone wants something he or she is not getting, or wants something to stop, and there's emo-

> Forming communities need enough time, money, and "community glue" to pull off a project of this magnitude.

tional charge on the issue. Conflict is exacerbated when someone refuses to speak up about what they want or need, or asks for it in a way that alienates others. Unfortunately, most people's unskilled ways of communicating about the conflict generates even more conflict than was there in the first place.

Fortunately there are plenty of books, courses, and workshops on communication methods that reduce conflict rather than amplify it.

My personal favorite is Marshall Rosenberg's Nonviolent Communication model. He suggests that most of us respond to something we don't like with an attitude and language that subtly blames, threatens, judges, or criticizes others, even if that's not our intention. His process involves a perceptual shift and a four-step process that defuses the level of conflict. Many other good methods exist as well. (See the "Conflict" issue of *Communities* magazine, No. 104, Fall 1999.)

I believe that the higher the degree of communication skill a forming community has, the greater its chances of success. So I urge your group to develop such skills, including some form of conflict resolution—ideally learned with a trainer. And learn these skills early on, when there's little or no conflict, for the same reason schools practice fire drills when there's no fire. Learning such skills at the outset can help reduce the potential destructiveness of poorly handled interpersonal conflict later on.

6. Select for Emotional Well-Being

Some people believe it's not really "community" unless it's inclusive and open and anyone can join. Others believe a community should have membership criteria and a multistep process for assessing potential new members.

Some veteran communitarians point out that people will naturally mature in community because of the (hopefully) constructive feedback they'll receive and the natural tendency to learn from the (hopefully) good communication skills modeled by more experienced members. This happens naturally in community; I call it the "rocks in the rock polisher" effect—everyone's rough edges can be worn smoother by contact with everyone else. Many communitarians know people who were really tough to be around when they first arrived, but who were so motivated that they learned fast and became model community members.

My observation of "the successful 10 percent" taught me that it's all in the willingness of the potential new member or cofounder. If he or she has what I call "high woundedness" (hey, don't we all?), it seems to only work if the person simultaneously has "high willingness"—to grow and learn and change. I have seen several forming communities in recent years—even those with powerful vision statements, fine communication skills, and good consensus training—break apart in conflict and sometimes lawsuits because even just one member didn't have enough self-esteem to function well in a group. The person's "stuff came up"—as everyone's does in community—but theirs was too destructive for the community to absorb. When a person is wounded and having a difficult time in life, he or she can certainly benefit from living in community, and, ideally, can heal and grow because of the support and feedback offered by others. But a certain level of woundedness—without "high willingness"—appears to be too deep for many new communities to handle. I believe one deeply wounded person can affect a group far more than 10 healthy people, because of that person's potential destructiveness to the group. Such a person can repeatedly derail the community's agenda and drain its energy.

This seems especially true of a potential new member or cofounder who has been abused as a child and hasn't had much healing before walking into your meeting. The person may unconsciously be desperately seeking community as a safe haven that will finally make things right. Such a person usually feels needy, and tends to interpret other people's refusal to or inability to meet his or her needs as further abuse. The person usually (subconsciously) expects to be victimized, and tends to seek out, provoke, or project onto others annoyance or anger and then conclude, "See, I knew you'd abuse me."

Where should this person go, besides those communities that are explicitly set up as therapeutic settings? A large, old, and well-established community can often take on difficult and wounded people without damage to itself. A mature oak tree, after all, can handle being hit by a truck. But I don't recommend taking on this challenge if your group is small, or brand new. It's just a sapling, not an oak tree, and still too vulnerable.

How can you determine the level of emotional health and well-being in prospective members and cofounders? One way is through questionnaires and interviews. Let's say you're seeking someone who is fairly financially stable and emotionally secure, who has some experience living cooperatively and a willingness to persevere through the rough spots. Irwin Wolfe Zucker, a psychiatric social worker and former Findhorn member, suggested asking: "How have you supported yourself financially until now? Can you describe some of your long-term relationships? What was your experience in high school or college? If you chose to leave school, why was that? Have you pursued alternative educational or career paths such as internships, apprenticeships, or on-the-job trainings?

⑥

the higher the degree of communication skill a forming community has, the greater its chances of success.

Where, and for how long? Did you complete them?" ("Admissions Standards for Communities?" *Communities* magazine, No. 96, Fall 1997.)

You can also ask for references, from former partners, employers, landlords, housemates, and former traveling companions.

I suggest "long engagements"—extended guest visits or provisional memberships of six months to a year, so the group and the prospective member can continue to get to know each other. Sometimes it takes a year to find out what someone is really like when the stress gets high.

"If your community front door is difficult to enter," writes Zucker, "healthy people will strive to get in. If it's wide open, you'll tend to attract unhealthy people, well-versed in resentful silences, subterfuge, manipulation, and guilt trips." Once these people become members, he warns, the energy of the group may be tied up in getting them to leave again.

So the last ingredient is to choose people who've already demonstrated they can get along well with others.

Creating healthy, viable communities is one of the finest projects we can undertake. And we can learn to set systems in place—right from the beginning—that give us the best chance of success.

I know of a new community dedicated to teaching ecological living via a community demonstration model. Its founders mastered consensus and good group process skills and created a new-member outreach process through a newsletter and Web site. They set up telecommuting jobs so they could live anywhere. They conducted a national rural county search, and when they found the right county with no zoning regulations, they took a proactive approach to finding their ideal land. They raised the necessary land-purchase funds in loans from supporters, and drew up effective agreements, covenants, and nonprofit and lease documents. They set up an impressive internship program to help them build their physical infrastructure. Right now they're living in their new straw bale cabins, eating from their organic garden, and making their own biodiesel fuel. Their new community is thriving. And so can yours.

Consensus Basics

by Tree Bressen

THE CONSENSUS PROCESS IS A POWERFUL tool for bringing groups together to move forward with inspired and effective decisions. Like many tools, consensus requires a particular set of skills. Groups who try to use consensus without learning those skills often end up frustrated, when what's really needed is more training, knowledge, and practice.

Cooperation is the basis of community. Consensus is a thoroughly cooperative form of decision-making. While not appropriate for all situations—it's not generally recommended for a quick fix to a crisis or deciding what color to paint the barn—for groups that have a shared purpose, explicit values, some level of trust and openness to each other, and enough time to work with material in depth, the consensus process can be immensely rewarding. In contrast with the polarities experienced in majority voting, consensus bonds people together.

The search for consensus agreement relies on every person in the circle bringing their best self forward to seek unity. The group need not all think the same, have the same opinion, or support the same proposal in a unanimous vote. Rather, what is being earnestly sought is a "sense of the meeting." This is the essence of what the group agrees on, the common ground, the shared understanding or desire.

Typically, a member brings forward a topic for discussion. It may be in the form of a question, a statement of a problem, or a proposal for action. After the item is framed by the presenter, it is time for clarifying questions. Often people in a meeting start to evaluate and form responses to an idea before the sponsor is even half finished stating

it. Setting aside explicit time for questions allows everyone to understand the idea and its context before entering into a discussion.

The next phase is usually open discussion. The facilitator keeps track of time and calls on people in turn. Participants may ask more questions, pose hypothetical examples, list concerns, support an idea, or make suggestions. A natural, free-flowing discussion can build energy, but if the pace gets too fast less assertive members may feel excluded. The facilitator may suggest the group use alternative methods to general discussion, such as brainstorms or small groups. People need to monitor their pace and pay attention to each other's needs. Finding the balance comes with practice and feedback.

As the facilitator integrates the participants' comments, a sense of the group's direction emerges. When the facilitator attempts to identify the direction and reflect it back to the group, it also becomes clear where there is not yet alignment. This is the main challenge in using consensus. If an environment is created where everyone's piece of the truth is welcome, the inherent wisdom and creativity of the group comes through.

Once issues have been aired and every member has made a good faith effort to find solutions and common ground, there are three structural responses available to each participant: agreement, standing aside, or standing in the way.

While everyone likes to get their way, it is simply not possible for a group to fulfill every individual's desire on every issue. Therefore, agreement in consensus does not necessarily indicate high enthusiasm or that the proposal fulfills a personal preference. Rather, it means the member

---

Tree Bressen is a consensus facilitator and teacher living at the Du-má Community house in Eugene, Oregon. She lived at Acorn Community from 1994–99, and served as delegate to the Federation of Egalitarian Communities (FEC). She currently serves on the board of Fellowship for Intentional Community (FIC). Her favorite ways to spend time include walking on the beach, folk singing, making love, and playing frisbee.

sees how the proposal benefits the group and can live with it. However, if no one is excited about an idea, it will likely fall flat during the implementation stage. It's up to each group to determine how much energetic support is necessary to feel comfortable moving forward with a decision.

A person may choose to stand aside due to personal conscience or strongly differing individual opinion. Either way, the individual owes the group an explanation. In the Quaker tradition, standing aside means that the person would not be called upon to implement a decision, though they would still be bound by it. Even though a member may vehemently disagree, they honor the group's need or desire to move in that direction. If more than one or two people stand aside, it is a signal that the group is not yet in alignment.

Standing in the way of a decision is also known as blocking. The ability to prevent the will of the rest of the group is what gives consensus its special power—it's also what many people are most scared of. Blocking is never to be undertaken lightly. It is the responsibility of participants to bring up concerns as early in the process as possible, as the ideas and feelings of every member are naturally woven in as the discussion moves along. In a well-functioning consensus group, the frequency of blocks ranges from nonexistent to extremely rare.

However, occasionally it happens that a member perceives a proposal to represent a disastrous direction for the group. Not a big risk or a decision they personally don't like, but an action that contradicts the group's purpose, mission, or values, or would irrevocably injure the organization or its members. It takes significant ego to presume one has more wisdom than the rest of the group; yet paradoxically, one must never block from an egotistical place or from personal preference. When the alternative is catastrophe, it becomes a member's responsibility to serve the group by standing in the way. Anyone considering blocking a decision is obligated to thoroughly explain the reasons and make every effort to find a workable solution. Respected consensus teacher Caroline Estes says that if you have blocked an emerging consensus half a dozen times, you've used up your lifetime quota.

Making a Plan

I lived at Acorn Community in rural Virginia for over four years. In my early days there, the standard meeting procedure was to gather around the breakfast table, where we

"As the facilitator integrates the participants' comments, a sense of the group's direction emerges."

ate and chatted until someone picked up the clipboard with the list of meeting topics and suggested one as a starting point. When that topic was finished, we'd move on to another one, until at some point a gardener would complain that the day was moving on and it was time to get to work outside. We would wrap up discussion, perhaps by agreeing in a bit of a rush to whatever was proposed most insistently, and the clipboard would be hung on a hook until the next meeting.

Some months later, Formal Consensus teacher CT Butler came through and suggested we consider planning our meeting agendas in advance. "Huh?" "What's that?" "Wouldn't that take too much time?" He suggested our meetings would move along so much more efficiently that it would be worth the extra time.

We decided to try it as an experiment. Three of us formed a committee and drew up an agenda for each meeting. We worked out in advance which items would be discussed when. We clarified who would present each item, for how long, and who would facilitate the meeting. We tried to give difficult items to more experienced facilitators, and used team facilitation, pairing experienced facilitators with those just learning the skills. All the roles were rotated among willing volunteers, and we made sure no one tried to present an item at the same time as they facilitated or took notes. We reserved a few minutes at the end of every meeting for brief evaluations so we could give ourselves feedback on what worked well and what could be improved.

In order to deal with the concern of losing our precious meeting time, we added an "overflow" item to the plan. If we finished all the other items faster than expected, we'd be ready to go with something to fill in the rest of the time.

85

"When a committee is set up, it's important to be clear about the extent of its power. What is the purpose of the committee? Is it to do research only and report back?"

Once we saw how much more effective we could be, there was no turning back. Many factors influenced the agenda, including who was home that week to sponsor or participate in the discussion; urgency of action needed; the balance of heavy and light items at each meeting; and which items had been waiting longest for attention. The agenda planners posted ahead of time whether the item would be an introduction, discussion, or possible decision. In the beginning it could take our committee 40 minutes to work it all out. Later, as we became accustomed to juggling the different factors, one person could plan a week's agendas in about 20 minutes.

Delegate, Delegate

Acorn's approach to agenda planning illustrates an important principle for making the consensus process work. How many times have you seen a meeting bog down in details to the point of exhaustion? Learning to distinguish when an item is small enough to fit in the box of a committee or manager's domain can save everyone countless hours of frustration and boredom.

Committees fall into two categories: standing and ad hoc. Standing committees perform ongoing tasks for an organization. Typical examples of standing committees in a community might include membership, finance, or road maintenance. Ad hoc committees are formed for a one-time task, such as planning a party or doing legal research on land zoning.

When a committee is set up, it's important to be clear about the extent of its power. What is the purpose of the committee? Is it to do research only and report back? Make

recommendations for the larger group to implement? Make decisions and follow through itself? Committees need a mandate from the larger group and a timeline. Reporting back regularly keeps the committee and the larger group in touch with each other.

The most functional size for a committee is usually three to five people. A balanced committee includes representatives of the breadth of opinion on a subject, as well as depth of expertise. You probably need people who are energetic initiators, thorough on follow-up, skilled at writing, smooth interpersonal communicators, linear thinkers and gestalt thinkers—luckily each person does not need to have all of these qualities, so long as they are represented in the group! One person should be designated as the convenor to set up the first meeting.

If the committee is open to it, posting the time and place of its meetings so that others can observe can help defuse possible tensions. Once trust is built and the relationship is established, the larger group will naturally send items to the committee for seasoning and input. When the committee returns its ideas to the larger group for final decisions, a sense of wider ownership and participation is created.

Minutes

Have members of your group ever sat around arguing or scratching their heads, wondering just what it was you decided about that guideline eight months ago? Figuring it out can take 10 minutes, three hours, or be impossible. Minutes make all the difference. They serve as the memory of the group and create a common record that everyone can access.

The note taker's goal is not to record who said what when. The information readers will likely want to know is:
• date of the meeting
• who was present
• clear description of each item
• main points of discussion
  • questions answered
  • range of opinion
  • concerns raised
    • whether each concern was resolved or not
  • "sense of the meeting"
  • new ideas
• agreements and decisions
  • reasons and intentions for a decision
• name and reason of anyone standing aside
• next steps

"For every group, in every situation, there is common ground that can be discerned...."

If there is a proposal, and *especially* if there is a consensus decision, that needs to be stated clearly and explicitly in the minutes. During the meeting, if the group is nearing consensus, the facilitator should have the note taker read out the proposed minutes to ensure there is agreement.

Finally, minutes will be most useful when the information is clearly organized. Acorn found it useful to index them by both subject and date. If no one is enthused at the prospect of taking on this task, you may consider hiring the services of a professional indexer.

The Role of the Facilitator

As Caroline Estes wrote in a previous edition of the *Communities Directory*, the role of the facilitator cannot be overemphasized. The facilitator is responsible for keeping the meeting on track. Yet every member is also responsible for each other and the group. Every person present at the meeting can engage in facilitative behaviors such as soliciting input from quieter members, bringing the discussion back to the main topic, and summarizing what's been said.

Facilitation is both an art and a skill, a science and an intuition. Every facilitator has room for growth. If your group is inexperienced in facilitation, consider bringing in someone to give a workshop or sending a few people off for training, who can then teach others when they

return. There are also books and other resources listed at the end of this article.

Rotating everyone through the role of facilitator helps minimize power differences in the group. As the members with the least experience get more practice, the level of the whole group is brought up a notch. Being thrust into the facilitator role makes people better meeting participants too. However, it makes sense to call upon more skilled facilitators for more challenging or controversial topics.

The facilitator is the servant of the group. She or he must never push their own agenda. While everyone has biases, for the duration of the meeting it is the facilitator's job to leave their attachments aside in order to be a clear channel for what the group needs. Neutrality and an ability to see all points of view are essential. If you are serving as facilitator, a few minutes before the meeting starts clear your mind of worries and fatigue, breathe and center, ground. All your attention will be needed for the task at hand.

The facilitator carries an attitude of group success. For every group, in every situation, there is common ground that can be discerned—the job of the facilitator is to see that and reflect it back, over and over. As each person speaks, listen carefully and step in every few minutes to weave together what's been said. Look for the reasons behind the positions. When someone's contribution is

87

hard for others to take, search for what's underneath that others will be able to relate to and name it. If someone becomes frustrated, look for what's not being heard. Unity is present, waiting to be discovered. Have faith.

Energy, tone, and body language reveal at least as much as the words spoken. Don't be afraid to name openly what you see happening, yet be gentle and concentrate on the positive. Some groups employ a "vibes watcher" to pay special attention to this. The vibes watcher may suggest a break, or a moment of silence. Silence is a powerful tool. Sometimes a moment to think is all that's needed to break tension. Seek the path forward, but don't be afraid of conflict—it's a natural experience and it shows that people care. Highly skilled facilitators are able to take the energy generated by conflict and use it to help the group.

If someone proffers a premature block, the facilitator can either work with the substance of their objection in the moment, or acknowledge the seriousness of the concern and ask them to hold it and listen with an open mind to more discussion. If you come to a stuck point, remember you have options. An item can be laid over for future discussion. You or someone else can talk one-on-one with an individual during a break. Items can be sent to a committee for further consideration. The group can request help from an outside facilitator. With patience and effort, agreements can nearly always be reached.

Facilitator Paul DeLapa sees consensus as a creative route to collective discovery. More than a decision-making method, "Consensus is a process that leads to agreements that people are unified on," he says. "It requires a different mind-set ... to create and build out of what's present." All our lives we're taught that we'll be rewarded for delivering the "right" answer—suddenly there is no right answer. Instead, there is a cooperative search for elegant, creative solutions that meet everyone's needs.

In a culture where we're taught that every person must struggle for themselves and we can't get ahead without stepping on others, consensus is a radical, community-building alternative. Consensus teaches that no one can get ahead by themselves: our success with the method depends utterly on our ability to work with others. Competition is no longer the root of experience; instead, we honor and integrate the diverse life surrounding us. Consensus is interdependence made visible.

Resources

CANBRIDGE (Consensus And Network Building for Resolving Impasse and Developing Group Effectiveness) offers consultation and assistance with consensus facilitation and training. Contact Laird Schaub, tel: 660-883-5545. Email: laird@ic.org.

Institute for Cultural Affairs (ICA) offers training in facilitation techniques. See listing in the Resources section of this directory.

International Association of Facilitators (IAF) sponsors an annual conference, and publishes a journal. 7630 West 145th St, Suite 202, St Paul MN 55124, USA. Tel: 612-891-3541. Email: iafoffice@igc.apc.org, http://www.iaf-world.org/

Books

Auvine, Brian, et al. *A Manual for Group Facilitators.* Rutledge, MO: Fellowship for Intentional Community, 1978. Tel: 800-995-8342. Email: fic@ic.org.

Avery, Michel, et al. *A Handbook for Consensus Decision Making: Building United Judgment.* Rutledge, MO: Fellowship for Intentional Community, 1981. Tel: 800-995-8342. Email: fic@ic.org.

Butler, CT and Amy Rothstein. *On Conflict and Consensus: A Handbook on Formal Consensus.* Portland, ME: Food Not Bombs Publishing, 1987. Tel: 800-569-4054. Email: fnbp@consensus.net.

Kaner, Sam. *Facilitator's Guide to Participatory Decision-Making.* San Francisco: Community at Work, 1996. Tel: 415-641-9773.

Kelsey, Dee and Pam Plumb. *Great Meetings! How to Facilitate Like a Pro.* Portland, ME: Hanson Park Press, 1997. Tel: 888-767-6338. Email: hppress@aol.com.

Schwarz, Roger. (1994) *The Skilled Facilitator: Practical Wisdom for Developing Effective Groups.* San Francisco: Jossey-Bass Inc., 1994. Tel: 415-433-1740.

Acknowledgments

The author would like to thank Lysbeth Borie, Paul DeLapa, Betty Didcoct, and Caroline Estes for their contributions to this article.

Decision Making in Practice
Leadership Decisions and Majority-Rule Democracy

by Rebecca L'Abbe

*I*DEALLY, THE PROCESS USED FOR DECISION making in an intentional community is based on the values of the group. To that end, a number of values-defining questions need to be asked, when settling on which process to use. Does everyone who will be affected by a decision need to be involved in the decision-making process? If so, to what degree?

The quality of the decisions produced by the process also needs to be examined periodically. Are the decision makers and all those affected by the decisions satisfied with the results? If not, what are the possible consequences? Is the intent of the original proposals being accomplished? Are the underlying issues being addressed? Are resources being used appropriately?

There are three basic forms of decision-making processes (with many variations on each) used in intentional communities today: consensus, decisions by a leader or group of leaders (or elders), and majority-rule democracy. Any of these methods can get the job done, and the quality of the process has become increasingly important to groups. Most intentional communities want to create a sense of interconnectedness and well-being. This goal is either helped or hindered both by specific decisions and by the process of how decisions are made and implemented.

It takes specific skills to create a process that empowers members and helps them to do their best, no matter what decision-making model is used. Facilitation, communication, and conflict resolution skills are at the top of the list.

What follows is a brief exploration of two decision-making systems: decisions by leaders/elders and majority voting, as used by two specific communities. I will not be

covering consensus, as that was done in the article preceding this one, "Consensus Basics."

Decision Making by a Group of Leaders/Elders, at Padanaram Community

Decision making by a single leader or group of leaders is a system used by groups and cultures around the globe. Padanaram Settlement is a spiritually oriented income-sharing community located in rural Indiana. The community was founded by Daniel Wright in 1966. Daniel, 80 years old as of this writing, continues as the spiritual leader and remains active in Padanaram's many businesses. Although Daniel was initially the sole leader of the community, under his guidance and nurturing, others have grown into leadership areas.

The community does not take a formal approach to decision making; rather, it guides itself by the principle, "Wisdom is our leader; truth is our guide." At Padanaram, leaders are not chosen by vote or consensus. They evolve rather than are selected. The various concerns of the community—schools, work areas, kitchen, farm, and public relations, to name a few, are governed by those leaders who have the expertise and experience in the particular area. Those in leadership positions have a group working with them. The group works together as a "mindpool" to find answers. The leader within the group makes the ultimate decision after considering the input of other workers in the group.

The two weekly meetings are open to the entire village and attendance is not mandatory. The Sunday night meeting is for sharing spiritual experiences and insights. The Wednesday night discussion meeting is totally open to whatever topics come up. It is a public forum in which

---

Rebecca L'Abbe lives at Shannon Farm, a rural land-trust community at the base of the Blue Ridge mountains in Afton, Virginia, founded in 1974.

"Most intentional communities want to create a sense of interconnectedness and well-being."

every person has a voice and a right to speak. Typical subjects include economics, the growth of the school, the farm, religion, and philosophy. It is also a time when people bring up problem areas.

"Conflict resolution and [meeting] facilitation are not common words within Padanaram," says long-time community member Rachel Summerton. "It is not formal—it is a group of friends discussing family problems." The community uses five principles to guide its decision making process: "As one would that others do, do unto them." "Hold all things in common; count nothing one's own." "Distribution to each according to the need." "Of one who has much, much is required." And, "One that won't work shall not eat."

Decision Making by Majority-Rule Democracy, at Bryn Gweled Homesteads

Majority-rule democracy is a well-known system of governance in which decisions are made by voting. More than half of the participants must be in agreement for a motion to pass.

Bryn Gweled Homesteads is a community located in suburban Philadelphia that was established in 1940. Its goal from the beginning has been simple—to be a friendly suburban neighborhood.

Decisions are made at Bryn Gweled by voting. The community uses a modified version of Robert's Rules of Order to govern the process. If the majority is close to 50/50 or there is strong disagreement by even a small minority, the motion is likely to be either tabled or rejected after a motion to reconsider. Members then discuss the issue more thoroughly for a month to several months until they are ready to bring it to a vote again. Bryn Gweled uses the motion to reconsider often; in the words of community member Robert Ewbank, they do so in order to "... ensure a bare majority would not create a disgruntled minority."

Committees play an integral part in the organization of the Bryn Gweled. Of the 23 committees, three are elected—nominating, membership, and housing. Each committee is empowered to carry out its individual work; however, no major decision is made without the consent of the Bryn Gweled membership.

Bryn Gweled has an elected seven-member board of directors that serves to set the agenda and facilitate the monthly business meeting. Because attendance at meetings is usually below 80 percent, important issues are handled by written ballot. Amendments to bylaws require a two-thirds vote by written ballot. A written ballot is also used with very important or controversial issues. Almost all Bryn Gweled members vote on items requiring the use of written ballots.

Membership decisions are made by secret ballot. An applicant must first attend at least two business meetings, meet with the membership committee, and complete a written application. A Bryn Gweled member is then appointed to assist the applicant in visiting the 73 member families. This process takes at least three months, and can take as long as the applicant wishes. The applicant must receive affirmation by 80 percent of those voting. Long-time community member John Ewbank considers both the deliberate thoroughness and the personal connections made during the membership application process to be the major reasons why the community has been able to function as satisfactorily as it has for 60 years.

Legal Structures for Intentional Communities in the United States

by Dave Henson
with Albert Bates, Allen Butcher, and Diana Leafe Christian

ANY OF US INVOLVED IN intentional communities have an aversion to legal procedures, government regulation, and taxes. It is often the ugly side of the American fetish for private property, lawsuits, and the corporate form that inspires us to create grassroots democracy and trust-based intentional communities in the first place. However, forming an intentional community where the members seek to collectively own land and buildings, and possibly run a business together, requires that at least some of those involved become fluent in the relevant aspects of property, tax laws, and regulations.

Residents of the United States have inherited a relatively recent tradition of placing the highest value—and legal rights—on private property. The vast majority of cultures around the world for the past many millennia have organized the relationship between themselves and the land they inhabit as community property, or with a sense of stewardship rather than any sense of private property ownership. As we know, the private property model has led to a rule of law that protects private "rights" to exploit nature for private benefit. Growth is valued above the sustainable management of the "common wealth" of the natural world. Intentional communities are a return to a more traditional—and more ecologically sustainable—model of social organization. Because we are going against the grain, we will run into all sorts of legal barriers. Persevere! We are reclaiming the traditions of our ancestors, and modeling solutions for our children.

What follows are summaries of the options a group of individuals have for holding land and/or conducting business. While we will primarily be looking at legal forms for owning land, in many cases that same legal form can be used for operating businesses. At times in this article, we will be discussing simultaneously the land owning and business opportunities of a particular legal form.

Options for Community Legal Structures

There are many legal forms that allow an individual or a group of individuals to own real property (land and buildings). Before we examine each organizational form, let's look at some of the more important questions a community should consider while comparing each legal form:

- Does the form fit the values of our community?
- What are the group and individual tax consequences?
- What are the group and individual liability consequences?
- How would the form influence a lender in deciding whether or not to refinance a mortgage or give a loan?
- Does the form set requirements or restrictions for how the organization must divide the organization's profits or losses among the individuals members, partners, or shareholders?
- Do the individual members, partners, or shareholders have to pay taxes on the organization's profits (as well as receiving the tax benefits from losses)? Does the organizational form itself have to pay the taxes, and benefit from losses? Or do both have to pay taxes?
- Does the form allow the group to assign its own criteria for management and economic decision-making authority (e.g., only active members get to vote), or does it mandate specific rules for decision making within a group?
- How easy is the form to set up, and to manage over time? How vulnerable is it to changes in the law, to the Internal Revenue Service (IRS), or to other governmental scrutiny? How much are annual filing fees?
- Does the form limit the group's political activity (as does the 501(c)3 tax-exempt status)? Is that important to our group?

Please see the last page of this article for the author biographies.

• How easy is it to make changes in the controlling documents of the organizational form, or to manage people's joining with or departing from the community?

For the purposes of this article, I have divided the various methods of holding real property into three basic categories:

I. "Sole Proprietorship" (ownership by an individual),
II. "Co-ownership" (ownership by a group of individuals),
III. "Corporate Ownership" (ownership by an artificial legal entity).

In addition, essentially there is a fourth category, "Mixed Ownership," which is where you create a mix of two or more legal forms.

I. Sole Proprietorship—Individual Ownership

Here, an individual alone owns real property and/or a business. That individual enjoys and suffers all the rights, benefits, profits, responsibilities, taxes, and liabilities of such ownership. In a community context, this is one way for an individual community member to operate her/his own business at a community while limiting the impact on the larger community to the terms of any lease agreement she/he might create—say for use of one of the community buildings as a business shop or office.

One form that communities can take is to subdivide a property into individually owned lots and homes, then create an intentional community of neighbors. When the owner dies, the sole proprietorship terminates, and her/his property is passed on by will to her/his heirs.

The relative advantages of typical individual home owning apply, including that this model fits better into the way lenders think about mortgages and refinancing. There will likely be a higher resale value for each home (unencumbered by complex contractual obligations to a larger community). To add more intentionality and legally binding restrictions to the community, the group of individual owners could create a homeowners association (see the "nonprofit" section of this article). There are only nominal filing and licensing fees for a sole proprietorship.

However, this is certainly the least communal of all options, as the individual or single-family owners are not contractually bound to sharing property, expenses, liabilities, or maintenance and decision-making responsibilities. Further, each individual home owner could sell or lease his/her property without the consent of the community.

II. Co-ownership

This covers a variety of ways a group of people can legally organize to buy and own land and buildings, and to legally conduct for-profit economic activities. Many of these organizational forms differ significantly from state to state, so it is important that you do your own research in addition to the general descriptions you read in this or other books.

1. Joint Tenancy

Joint Tenancy is the joint ownership of a single property by two or more people, where all of the joint tenants have an equal interest and rights in the property.

Joint tenancy can be created several ways: (a) when someone wills or deeds property to more than one person; (b) when more than one person takes title to a property (as when a married couple buys property in California, the deed usually names them as joint tenants); or (c) when joint tenants transfer property to themselves and others (as a way to add more people to your joint tenancy community). All the joint tenants have equal rights to use of the joint property, and all share equally in liabilities and profits. This most often includes sharing all necessary maintenance costs, taxes, and work responsibilities. However, a tenant is solely responsible for the costs of improvements made without the consent of the other tenants.

An advantage of this form is the right of "survivorship," which means that a joint tenant cannot will her/his interest in the property, but rather upon that joint tenant's death, the title is automatically passed to the surviving joint tenants. The surviving joint tenants take the estate free from all creditor's claims or debts against the deceased tenant.

The disadvantages of this are significant for most communities, including that a joint tenant may sell or give his/her interest to another person without the approval of the other tenants. Such action causes a severance of the joint tenancy, and the arrangement reverts to Tenancy in Common (see below). Also, if one tenant goes into debt, the creditor seeking collection could force the sale of the property to access the cash value of the debtor tenant's share in the property.

2. Tenancy in Common

Tenancy in common is when two or more people have undivided interest in a property. If not otherwise specified, the presumption is that all the tenants in common share interests in the property equally. The tenants may, however, distribute interest in the ownership of the property at whatever fractions they wish. Taxes and mainte-

⟨♭⟩

Intentional communities are a return to a more traditional—and more ecologically sustainable—model of social organization. Because we are going against the grain, we will run into ... legal barriers.

nance expenses, profits, and the value of improvements on the property must be distributed in the same proportion as the fractional distribution of their shares of ownership.

A tenant in common may sell, mortgage or give his/her interest in the property as s/he wishes, and the new owner becomes a tenant in common with the other co-tenants. Unlike with joint tenancy, there is no right of survivorship—the property interest of a deceased tenant in common would pass to her/his heirs.

There are not many advantages to use this form for most communities. This is a lowest common denominator legal form, meaning that in lieu of the group creating a more sophisticated and intentional legal form or written agreement, people holding property together are considered tenants in common. The same basic disadvantages as for joint tenancy hold, with the addition that any one tenant in common can force a sale of the property to recover the value of her/his interest in the property.

3. Partnership

A partnership is an association of two or more people who carry on a for-profit business. It is the most common way several people can form a small business together. In the simplest form of a partnership, each partner makes equal contributions, shares equally profits and losses, and has equal share to rights, responsibilities, and liabilities. If that partnership owns property together, a "tenancy in partnership" exists.

To make the legal side of interstate business easier to negotiate, the Uniform Partnership Act has been adopted in 43 states. It defines a partnership as a for-profit business association where two or more persons are co-owners. The controlling document for a partnership is the "partnership agreement," which at a bare minimum needs to state the names and addresses of the partners, the name of the partnership, and be signed by all the partners. It needs to be filed with the county clerk.

Unless otherwise stated in the partnership agreement, every partner can act on behalf of the partnership—including signing contracts and borrowing money—and have that act be binding on the partnership as a whole. This has the potential to be a big problem in that one community member could suffer a lapse of group process and borrow money in the name of the partnership, or buy a boat with the community's partnership checkbook (with the money the community was saving to overhaul the septic system). All the partners are *jointly and severally liable*,

One of the hermitages at Lama Foundation, a nonprofit 501(c)3 spiritual community in the mountains of northern New Mexico.

meaning that the whole partnership *and each individual partner* are responsible for the full value of contracts signed by any one partner. This is typically avoided by putting specific language in the partnership agreement that says something like "purchases over $100 made on behalf of the partnership must require consensus by the partners at a regular partnership meeting," or "no individual partner can borrow money on behalf of the partnership."

A "general partnership" is when each partner has all rights of ownership, and each is liable for all the debts and liabilities of the partnership. A "limited partnership" allows for limited partners to invest, but only be liable for partnership debts and liabilities up to the amount of their share in the partnership. Limited partners have reduced decision-making authority and other rights regarding the partnership. In a limited partnership, at least one partner must be a general partner, and that person or persons are jointly and severally liable for all the partnership debts and liabilities.

There are some advantages to this form. In a partnership, a partner cannot sell or otherwise assign her/his rights in partnership property to another. Similarly, a creditor, wanting to collect a personal debt that an individual partner owes, cannot force a sale or lien on the partnership's property. If a partner dies, his/her rights in the partnership return to the partnership, but the heirs of the deceased partner are entitled to the value of that partner's interest in the partnership. Also, for a community, the partnership form offers maximum decision-making control of the organization—the partners can put into their agreement any decision-making or profit-sharing structure they choose, and, if desired, they can change it over time with minimum legal hassles.

Dancing Rabbit ecovillage in northeastern Missouri is a 501(c)3 with the land held by a 501(c)2 land trust. Also on site is a 501(d) income-sharing group.

The other major advantage of a partnership is that it has "pass-through tax status," meaning that, while the partners are taxed on the profits of the partnership, the partnership itself is not taxed. Similarly, the tax advantages of losses to the partnership are distributed directly to the partners.

However, as noted above, all general partners have unlimited liability, although a strong partnership agreement can help remedy this problem. There is also the disadvantage of the fact that it is cumbersome to add new partners or to have a partner leave. In both cases, the partnership agreement needs to be re-signed by the remaining partners, and filed again with the county clerk. Dissolving a partnership can also be difficult, again depending on the clarity of the partnership agreement. And, a partnership cannot hold accumulated earnings in the partnership, but must pass on the profits and losses each year to the partners.

III. Corporate Ownership

There are several corporate forms that should be considered by a group of individuals who want to hold real prop-

erty together and/or conduct for-profit or nonprofit business as a community.

1. Corporation

A corporation is a legal entity consisting of one or more shareholders, but having existence separate from the shareholders. Over the course of American history, the corporation has been ruled by courts to have the legal status of a "natural person," meaning that it has many of the constitutionally protected rights of we flesh-and-blood people, including free speech, rights to standing in federal courts, rights to due process, and extensive private property rights. In the eyes of many, this has led to corporations wielding too much power, to the detriment of the very foundation of our democratic society, and there is a growing anticorporation grassroots movement. That said, let's get back to business of creating alternatives to corporate control of the world: building intentional communities!

The basic corporate form is not the best legal form for a community. Compared to a limited liability company (LLC) or a partnership, the disadvantages outweigh the advantages.

A corporation is a common way to raise capital. It is familiar to investors, and legal precedence has been established for every possible sticky situation. Ownership is transferred easily, and the corporation lives forever: it continues until terminated, surviving the departures and deaths of the shareholders. The main advantage is limited liability. A corporation can often also accumulate earnings over the years and distribute them when the tax advantages are best for the shareholders.

However, profits are taxed twice—once as corporate taxes, then again as shareholder personal income. There is somewhat stringent government oversight, and there are many legal requirements (keeping records, holding meetings, keeping minutes, and filing reports). Incorporation costs, legal fees, and annual registration fees should be considered too.

2. Chapter S Corporation

This form is essentially like a corporation, but with the tax advantages of a partnership or an LLC. In fact, tax filing is based on partnership return. The tax implications of an S corporation are the most complex of any of the similar legal forms—one should consult a tax attorney or accountant about the specifics. I'm not aware of any reason to form an S corporation over an LLC.

An S corporation eliminates the double taxing of the corporation. It keeps the limited liability advantages of the corporation. It allows pass-through of losses to offset income from other sources and is a common way to raise capital. Ownership is transferred easily. Like a regular corporation, this entity continues until terminated, outliving its shareholders of any one time.

However, all profits must be distributed and taxed annually. You can't have over 35 stockholders. And, there are lots of rules—more than a regular corporation. Plus, there are specific limits on who can join as shareholder.

3. Limited Liability Company (LLC)

All 50 states have enacted LLC laws since 1988. There is a move in Congress to make a uniform LLC law so states can have common LLC rules. For many communities who are holding real property and are conducting any kind of for-profit business, this is likely the best legal form to use.

The initial filing fees and annual taxes vary from state to state. An LLC is controlled by an "operating agreement," and the participants are called "members." The LLC is similar to an S corporation, with its limited liability and pass-through taxation status, but the LLC has substantially fewer restrictions than an S corporation.

An LLC is treated as a partnership for tax purposes instead of as a corporation, if it lacks a majority of the following corporate characteristics: (1) limited liability, (2) continuity of life, (3) centralized management, and (4) free transfer of ownership. The LLC law in most states makes it pretty easy to comply with these restrictions.

Like a partnership or an S corporation, the LLC avoids double taxation of a corporation. Unlike an S corporation, there is no limit on the number of shareholders. Unlike a partnership, LLC members are not liable for LLC debts. Unlike a corporation, there is no statutory necessity to keep minutes, hold meetings, or make resolutions. The operating agreement can allocate different decision-making rights to different kinds of members (for example, the community could decide that LLC investors are limited to voting only on expenditures which exceed a certain dollar amount, keeping day-to-day decision making in the resident group). Admitting new members is easy, and any type of legal entity can join an LLC, including a person (US citizenship is not required), a partnership, a corporation, another LLC, and trusts. However, an LLC cannot accumulate earnings like a partnership can. It must distribute them the year the earnings are made. Also, annual fees are typically greater than for a corporation.

4. Nonprofit Corporation[1]

Nonprofits are primarily organized to serve some public benefit, and do not provide individual profit. Hence, a nonprofit may obtain IRS and state approval for special

> ⑥
>
> Residents of the United States have inherited a relatively recent tradition of placing the highest value—and legal rights— on private property.

tax exemption. Most intentional communities have elected to organize as nonprofit corporations and to apply for tax-exempt status.

As with for-profit corporations, a nonprofit corporation is created by registering with the state—filing a list of corporate officers and articles of incorporation. After receiving state approval, the organization may apply for a federal tax exemption with the IRS.

For those seeking to form tax-exempt corporations, there are many IRS tax exemptions to choose from: cooperative or mutual benefit corporations; 501(c)7 social and recreation clubs; 501(c)3 educational, charitable, or religious corporations; 501(c)2 title holding corporations; 501(d) religious and apostolic corporations; private land trusts; community land trusts; homeowners associations and condominium associations; and housing cooperatives. It is best to decide which category of tax exemption you are seeking before filing articles of incorporation, because the articles may have to conform to certain language that the IRS expects before it will grant a particular exemption. A short section on each of these nine categories follows.

a. Cooperative or Mutual Benefit Corporations

"Co-ops" are often used by consumer cooperatives (such as food-buying co-ops or credit unions), worker cooperatives, or producer cooperatives and are another legal option for communities with good state laws governing cooperative corporations. Co-ops are usually organized as nonprofit corporations; however, some states offer a special "cooperative corporation" category that is neither nonprofit or for-profit.

In either case, to qualify as a co-op, the articles of incorporation must usually provide for open membership, democratic control (one member, one vote), no political campaigning or endorsing, and no profit motive—that is, a limited return on any invested capital. A co-op also provides limited liability to its members. In some states, members get nontransferable membership shares (instead of shares of stock) with an exemption from federal and state securities regulations. Any members who also serve as employees get tax-deductible fringe benefits.

b. 501(c)7—"Social and Recreation Clubs"

Nonprofit mutual benefit corporations can use the IRS tax exemption 501(c)7, which was created for private recreational or other nonprofit organizations, where none of the net earnings goes to any member. This exemption can be used by a community with land which cannot legally be subdivided, yet whose members are required to put money into the community in order to live there, and who wish to recoup their equity if they leave. Members of a community organized this way "buy" a membership in a mutual benefit corporation. They can later sell their membership (possibly at a profit) to an incoming member.

The advantages are that, if organized properly, the community would not be subject to state and local subdivision requirements—because members wouldn't own specific plots of land or specific houses. Rather, in a strictly legal sense, they would simply have use rights to any plots or dwellings (although the members' internal arrangements could specify which plots or dwellings each would have preferred rights to use). In addition, members could pay for their membership with a down payment and installments rather than in one lump sum. They would be afforded some liability for the actions of the mutual benefit corporation. They would also have the right to choose who joined the community, which could be an advantage over other land-owning legal entities such as planned unit developments (PUDs) or other subdivisions, wherein the landowners would be subject to federal antidiscrimination regulations if they attempted to choose who bought into their community.

The disadvantages are that 501(c)7 nonprofits can be quite complicated to set up and may require a securities lawyer, as they are regulated by the Securities and Exchange Commission. As such, a 501(c)7 cannot advertise publicly for new members, who are legally "investors." Rather, existing members or staff may only approach people they know personally to join them. A 501(c)7 may have no more than 35 investor/members. No donations to such a community are tax-deductible. There are no dividends or depreciation tax write-offs; members are taxed on any profit if and when they sell.

c. 501(c)3—Educational, Charitable, or Religious Corporations

Nonprofit 501(c)3 corporations must provide educational services to the public, offer charitable services to an indefinite class of people (rather than to specific individuals), combat negative social conditions, or provide a religious service to its members and/or the public. (The IRS interprets "religious" very liberally; this can include self-described spiritual beliefs or practices.) 501(c)3 nonprofits may receive tax-deductible donations from corporations or individuals, and grants from government agencies or private foundations. They are eligible for lower bulk mailing rates, some government loans and benefits, and exemption from most forms of property tax. Religious orders that qualify under 501(c)3 may also be exempt

from Social Security, unemployment, and withholding taxes in some cases.

In order to qualify for recognition as a 501(c)3, an intentional community must meet two IRS tests. It must be organized, as well as operated, exclusively for one or more of the above tax-exempt purposes. To determine the organizational test, the IRS reviews the nonprofit's articles of incorporation and bylaws. To determine its operational test, the IRS conducts an audit of the nonprofit's activities in its first years of operation.

Many communities have difficulty passing the operational test because of the requirement that no part of the net earnings may benefit any individual (except as compensation for labor or as a bona fide beneficiary of the charitable purpose). If the primary activity of the organization is to operate businesses for the mutual benefit of the members, it fails this operational test.

Even if the community passes the operational test by virtue of other, more charitable, public benefits—running an educational center, providing an ambulance service, or making toys for handicapped children, for instance—it can still be taxed on the profits it makes apart from its strictly charitable activities.

This catch, called unrelated business taxable income, has been a source of disaster and dissolution for some nonprofits because of the associated back taxes and penalties, which can assume massive proportions in just a few years of unreported earnings. Unrelated business taxes prevent tax-exempt nonprofits from unfairly competing with taxable entities, such as for-profit corporations. The IRS determines a nonprofit's unrelated business trade income in two ways: the destination of the income and the source. If a community uses profits from bake sales to build a community fire station (presumably a one-time project related to the community's purpose), the IRS may consider that income "related" and not tax it. If, however, the bake sales expand the general operations of the community, or pay the electric bill, the IRS may consider that "unrelated" income, and tax it.

A 501(c)3 nonprofit may not receive more than 20 percent of the corporate income from passive sources, such as rents or investments. If they are educational in purpose, they may not discriminate on the basis of race and must state that in their organizing documents. 501(c)3 are not allowed to participate in politics—they can't back a political campaign, attempt to influence legislation (other than on issues related to the 501(c)3 category), or publish political "propaganda." If they disband, they may not distribute any residual assets to their members; after payment of debts, all remaining assets must pass intact to a tax-

---

⑥

Nonprofit 501(c)3s must provide educational services to the public, offer charitable services to an indefinite class of people ... combat negative social conditions, or provide a religious service...

exempt beneficiary—such as another 501(c)3.

d. 501(c)2—Title-Holding Corporations

This legal structure is a useful option for owning, controlling, and managing a nonprofit group's property. The 501(c)2 is designed to collect income from property—whether it is a land trust, a retail business, or a passive investment such as space rental. All income is turned over to a nonprofit tax-exempt parent corporation, which is usually a 501(c)3. The tax-exempt parent must exercise some control over the 501(c)2 holding company, such as owning a majority of its voting stock or appointing its directors. The two corporations file a consolidated tax return. Unlike a 501(c)3, a 501(c)2 may not actively engage in "doing business," except for certain excluded categories such as renting real estate or negotiating investments … and a 501(c)2 can receive more than 20 percent of the corporate income from rentals or investments.

The legal structures at Ecovillage at Ithaca include a 501(c)3 nonprofit educational organization, a cohousing cooperative of 30 clustered homes, and a second neighborhood that is currently organized as a joint venture.

Many nonprofit communities, especially community land trusts (see below), find that having both 501(c)3s and 501(c)2s provides a needed structure to both run businesses and manage land and housing. The 501(c)2 limits the community's exposure to conflicts with the IRS over questions of income and possible personal "inurement," or illegal benefits.

e. 501(d)—Religious and Apostolic Associations

If a nonprofit community has a spiritual focus and a common treasury, it may apply for this tax-exempt status. (Again, the IRS interprets "religious" and "apostolic" very liberally; this can include self-described spiritual beliefs or practices, or secular beliefs that are strongly, "religiously" held.)

In any case, the 501(d) is like a partnership or chapter S corporation, in that any net profits after expenses are divided among all members pro rata, to be reported on the member's individual tax forms. Unlike the 501(c)3, the 501(d) corporation cannot confer tax deductions for donations.

501(d) nonprofits make no distinction between related and unrelated income. All income from any source is related. However, if a substantial percentage of community income is in wages or salaries from "outside" work, the 501(d) classification may be denied. A 501(d) can engage in any kind of businesses it chooses, passive or active, religious or secular. The profits are taxed like those of a partnership or S corporation. But, a 501(d) doesn't have the restrictions of a partnership (it doesn't have to reform itself with each change of members), and it isn't limited to 35 shareholders like the chapter S corporations.

501(d) corporations have no restrictions on their political activity—they can lobby, support candidates, and publish political "propaganda." They may or may not elect to have a formal vow of poverty. Upon dissolution, the assets of the 501(d) nonprofit may be divided among the members as far as federal law is concerned. However, state law generally requires that any assets remaining after payment of liabilities should be given to another nonprofit corporation.

The substantial advantages of the 501(d) may be outweighed in communities that would prefer to hold property privately.

f. Private Land Trusts

A private land trust is a legal mechanism to protect a piece of land from various kinds of undesirable future uses, like being sold for speculative gain; or to preserve land for various specific purposes—public use as a wilderness area, as rural farmland, or for low-cost housing. A land trust can be set up by an intentional community that has a specific purpose for the land, or simply to preserve it for future generations.

There are three parties to a land trust: the donor(s), who gives the land to the trust for a specific purpose or mission; the board of trustees, who administer the land and protect its mission; and the beneficiaries, who use or otherwise benefit from the land. People or institutions on the board of trustees are selected for their alignment with the goals and mission of the trust and their pledge of support. The trustees represent three separate interest groups: the beneficiaries, people in the wider community, and the land itself. The beneficiaries can be people who visit a wilderness preserve or park, the farmers who farm the land, the owners or residents in low-cost housing on the property, or the members of an intentional community who live and work on the land. The donor, trustees, and beneficiaries can be the same people in a private land trust.

g. Community Land Trusts (CLTs)

A CLT is designed to establish a stronger and broader board of trustees than a private land trust. This is accomplished by creating a board with a majority of trustees that are not land users. Usually only one-third of the trustees can live on the land or benefit directly from it, while two-thirds must live elsewhere and receive no direct benefit from the land. This ensures that any donors or land-resident beneficiaries who are also trustees cannot change their minds about the purpose or mission of the trust, use the land for some other purpose, or sell it. The two-thirds of the board of trustees from the wider community serve to guarantee the mission of the trust since they are theoretically more objective, and will not be tempted by personal monetary gain.

Private land trusts can be revocable by the original donors; community land trusts are usually not revocable.

Private land trusts and community land trusts are set up as nonprofit corporations, sometimes with a 501(c)3 tax-exempt status. The trust holds actual title to the land, and grants the land residents long-term, renewable leases at reasonable fees.

The original owners of the land and assets cannot get their money out of a community land trust once they have made the donation. Also, once land is placed in a CLT it can be difficult to use the land as collateral for loans.

A CLT is an option for those who wish to ensure that the original purpose for their land and activities continues unchanged into future generations, and are not altered by subsequent requirements for quick cash, loss of commitment, or personality conflicts among the land residents.

h. Homeowners Associations, Condominium Associations

Some communities may choose to organize as a "planned community"—a real estate term, in which members individually own their own plots of ground and dwellings, and are each members of a nonprofit corporation—a "homeowners association." The association, rather than the individual members, owns any community buildings and all the common areas, including land other than the individual plots.

Or a community may organize as a "condominium," where the members each individually own the air space

within their dwellings, and—as members of a nonprofit corporation, or "condominium association"—they own an undivided interest in the common elements of the property. The common property includes the structural components of the individual dwellings (roof, walls, floors, foundation), as well as the common areas and community buildings.

Planned communities and condominiums aren't legal structures; they are simply methods of purchasing land. In a planned community, the homeowners association owns everything but the individual units, and it must manage and maintain everything. In a condominium, the condominium association owns nothing, but must manage and maintain everything. Both kinds of associations are often organized as nonprofits, under the Internal Revenue Code (IRC), Section 528.

Under Section 528, such an association is exempt from taxation in acquiring, constructing, managing, and maintaining any property used for mutual benefit. Such tax-exempt "association property" may even include property owned privately by members, such as a greenhouse, meeting house, or retreat. But to qualify, the private property must affect the overall appearance of the community, the owner must agree to maintain it to community standards, there must be an annual pro rata assessment of all members to maintain it, and it must be used only by association members and not rented out.

The association must also receive at least 60 percent of its gross income from membership dues, fees, or assessments. Also, at least 90 percent of its expenses must be for construction, management, maintenance, and care of association property.

i. Housing Cooperatives

This is a very specific kind of cooperative corporation, also called a mutual benefit corporation. Housing cooperative nonprofits vary slightly from state to state. In general, however, members own shares in the housing cooperative, which gives them the right to live in a particular dwelling. Although nonprofits don't usually allow shares of stock or stockholders, a housing cooperative does. The number of shares the members buy is based on the current market value of the dwelling in which they intend to live.

The members don't own their individual houses or apartments; the housing cooperative does. The members have simply bought the shares, which gives them the right to occupy the dwelling of their choice. They pay a monthly fee—a prorated share of the housing cooperative's mortgage payment and property taxes, combined with general main-

> ⑥
>
> This catch, called unrelated business taxable income, has been a source of disaster and dissolution for some nonprofits because of the associated back taxes and penalties....

tenance costs and repairs. The monthly fee is based on the number of shares each of the members holds, which is equivalent to the dollar value given to the member's individual dwelling.

Personal Versus Community Property

So far we've reviewed ways for a community to hold title to real property. There still remains the question of *personal property*. Some communities require that, as part of joining the community, some or all of the individual's personal property be transferred to the organization, whether it be a partnership, LLC, corporation, or other form. This might include money and bank accounts, cars, and any other private personal property. Some communities require a "vow of poverty," and the giving up of personal property to the organization. Others have certain personal property contribution requirements listed in their partnership agreement, bylaws, or operating agreement. Such agreements can also govern what personal property a departing member or partner may take with them from the organization.

Most typically, the community holds title to the land, and individual community members retain ownership of their personal property. As for the buildings, there are two typical ways many communities work this out.

One way is that a community will hold title to all the homes and shared buildings as community property through its partnership or LLC, for example. The homes and other buildings are then used by community members for as long as they are members of the community, probably for some monthly payment to that partnership or LLC. When someone leaves, there is no need to sell the individual home. This eliminates the problem of having a departing member decide who will take their place in the community, and largely does away with housing cost speculation on the houses in the community. There is most often, however, a need to reconcile that departing member's financial, material, and/or sweat equity in that home. Some communities don't place a value on this at all—when you leave, you leave without equity. Others put simple or complex formulas into their written agreements so that when a person leaves (and it should be expected that it may not always be on the best of terms), there is no question of how to figure what monetary compensation that departing member receives. It is absolutely critical to address this question in your agreements *before* someone leaves. Otherwise, the irreconcilable differences may force you all into court, to nobody's benefit.

The other way that communities manage the question of who holds title to the buildings, is to have each individ-

The Farm School, a 501(c)3, was built in 1976 with recycled materials and a passive solar design at The Farm community in Tennessee.

Jillian Downey

ual or family own their own home, the improvements on that home, and sometimes the land under and just around the home. The community owns the overall property around which the homes are situated, and manages all of the common lands and common buildings. Often county zoning regulations will not allow for this level of subdivision of ownership, but if it is legal, it lets individuals and families have maximum control over their own homes.

The problem here is when someone wants to leave the community, they have to sell their house. Who decides on the value of the home? This begs the question of who decides whether a community member can build onto their home, thus raising the price of their home if they eventually leave. Does the community set style guidelines? Who decides whether or not to accept a particular willing buyer? These are very difficult questions that need to be addressed in your written agreements.

Resources and Research

As your community meets to craft your legal and organizational structures, focus your discussions on making decisions! It is common to have a two-hour discussion on these topics where real progress and agreements are made, but leave the room without writing the exact decision down. It is impossible to structure the legal organization of your community in one or two meetings, so save the last 15 minutes of each meeting to get down in that special binder exactly what was agreed upon, what the nature of the questions are on the issues where no decision was reached, what was left to discuss, and what the next steps you all will take to continue to move the process along.

My best advice is for you to form a committee of a few people in your community to take on a research project.

Starting From Scratch (but Not Without Help)

After doing some work, have the committee present the best options for community legal structures to the whole community for extensive discussion. This may be the one area where your community needs to pay for some legal advice—but do it after your committee has become literate about the questions and options. Ask around for an attorney with experience in tax and real estate law. You want someone who will really understand the "alternative" nature of your endeavor. A certified public accountant (CPA) can often be very helpful on the tax questions. Remember, an attorney or CPA works for you—their advice on organizational questions is only as good as the community's clarity about what your economic and organizational goals are.

Try the legal clinic at a law school near you. They often offer legal advice inexpensively or for free, and may be able to hook you up with a law student looking for a research project.

The Web is an excellent place to get free legal advice. In doing research for this article, I found many sites with very clear and lengthy legal notes about the options discussed here, such as Rob Sandelin's resource site, at http://www.infoteam.com/nonprofit/nica/resource.html. Search for "Limited Liability Company," "Partnership," etc., and you will find more than you can read!

Nolo Press, in Berkeley, California, puts out some great self-help legal books, including step-by-step books on how to set-up a corporation, partnership, LLC, or nonprofit. Some come with the papers you need to file on a computer disk. Nolo Press, 950 Parker St, Berkeley CA 94710, USA. Tel: 510-549-1976, http://www.nolo.com/

The Institute for Community Economics (ICE) puts out the *Community Land Trust Handbook* and other resources on land trusts. ICE, 57 School St, Springfield MA 01105, USA. Tel: 413-746-8660.

Endnotes

1. The entire "nonprofit" section of this article (part III, section 4) is reprinted with slight revisions from a previous edition of this directory: Bates, Albert, Allen Butcher, and Diana Christian. "Legal Options for Intentional Communities," *Communities Directory: A Guide to Cooperative Living.* Rutledge, MO: Fellowship for Intentional Community, 1995.

Author Biographies

Dave Henson is the Director of the Occidental Arts and Ecology Center (OAEC), a 501(c)3 tax-exempt educational and rural retreat center near the coast in Sonoma County, California, USA. OAEC offers residential workshops and training programs on such topics as organic gardening, permaculture, seed saving, environmental and social justice organizing, landscape and studio painting, and establishing school garden programs. Dave is also a founding member (July 1994) of the Sowing Circle Partnership and intentional community that holds the title to an 80 acre property, including four acres of organic gardens and orchards and over 25 buildings. OAEC leases from Sowing Circle the use of most of the buildings, gardens and wildlands to operate the learning center. Dave also leads weekend workshops at OAEC called "Creating and Sustaining Intentional Communities," and is available for phone or in-person consultation with your community about legal and organizational structures, group process and facilitation, and setting up nonprofit educational centers. For consulting information, or to receive a catalog about the Occidental Arts and Ecology Center, call OAEC at 707-874-1557, write to OAEC, 15290 Coleman Valley Rd, Occidental CA 95465, USA, or visit http://www.oaec.org/

Albert Bates is a former environmental attorney and author of seven books on law, energy and environment, including *The Y2K Survival Guide* (1999) and *Climate in Crisis* (1990) with foreword by Albert Gore, Jr. He holds a number of design patents and was inventor of the concentrating photovoltaic arrays and solar-powered automobile displayed at the 1982 World's Fair. He currently serves as President of the Ecovillage Network of the Americas and directs the Ecovillage Training Center, which has helped bring sustainable technology, agriculture, and community to persons in more than 50 nations. He produces "Ecovillages," the online journal of sustainable community, at http://dx.gaia.org/

Allen Butcher first got involved with tax law in the early '80s as a board member of the New Destiny Food Cooperative Federation and New Life Farm. He was a board member of the Fellowship for Intentional Community during the period of expansion from regional to continental organizing. He served as Treasurer of the School of Living Community Land Trust. Allen lived at East Wind and Twin Oaks communities for 13 years, becoming a student of comparative economic systems in intentional communities. He has written a series of resource booklets for understanding and developing intentional community. While he was at East Wind, Allen conceived the forerunner of this article for the 1990 *Communities Directory*. He now lives in Denver, Colorado.

Diana Leafe Christian has studied intentional communities since 1992, and edited *Communities* magazine since 1993. She is author of *Forming an Intentional Community: What Works, What Doesn't Work, How Not to Reinvent the Wheel,* and offers introductory and weekend workshops on this topic. She is cofounder of a small community in North Carolina. Email: diana@ic.org.

Permaculture
A Brief Introduction

by Jillian Hovey

PEOPLE OFTEN THINK THAT permaculture is about gardening or farming. Indeed, healthy and sustainable food production systems are very important, but that is only one part of the complex whole of sustainable communities. In fact, the term "permaculture" is a contraction of the words "permanent agriculture" *and* "permanent culture." This sheds light on the fact that permaculture is not just about agricultural systems, but indeed is concerned with meeting *all* of society's needs in sustainable ways.

Permaculture is a philosophy that informs an approach to planning, designing, building, and maintaining sustainable systems, the ultimate expression of which would be sustainable communities. It focuses on efficiently satisfying *true human needs* (not to be confused with consumer-induced "wants") and nonhuman needs, through a co-creative process with nature and other people. Permaculture draws on the knowledge of natural systems, and attempts to emulate their diversity, resilience, stability, and abundance, through the application of six basic permaculture principles.

1. Use Nature as Your Model

• Natural, physical, and biological processes in individuals, populations, and communities are the model for permaculture design. Observe, intuit, and replicate natural patterns in human-constructed systems, working co-creatively with nature.
• Use biological resources to perform work, save energy, and produce needed materials. For example, you can use free-range chickens or ducks to control insects, fertilize soil, and produce food.
• Create diversity: maximize the "edges" in a system. The transitions between two types of terrain, such as where a forest meets a field or where the sides of a pond meet the land, are highly productive biological areas, called edges. To this end, use irregularly wavy edges, vertical planting, and create different habitat types in your landscape (grasslands, forests, wetlands, ponds, etc.).

2. Emphasize Connections and Create Redundancy

• Every component should perform multiple functions. Design so that each element you introduce has at least three uses. Examples include: (a) a hedge could serve as a windbreak, a visual barrier, a wildlife habitat, and a pro-

Jillian Hovey

Jillian Hovey is a facilitator of sustainable community planning and design and permaculture education. She is based in community in the Great Lakes bioregion, and consults and teaches across "Turtle Island." She is available to help you and your community become more sustainable in holistic ways: everything from community agreements and land trusts, to gray water systems and composting toilets, to natural building materials and renewable energy systems, and organic gardening and farming. Tel: 416-488-4425. Email: jillian@permaculture.net, http://www.permaculture.net/

ducer of human food; (b) a building used for human habitation could also have water collection off the roof and support vertical and rooftop gardens; and (c) chickens can be very helpful in producing heat and carbon dioxide in greenhouses, and they also provide human food, provide feathers, and eat insects (see diagram below).

- Design so that each function (such as heat, electricity, and water) is supported by many elements. Heat can be generated through burning biomass (for example, sustainably harvested wood) and also through passively captured solar energy; electricity can be provided through solar cells and through wind and water turbines; and water can be provided from a flowing stream, pumped from a well, or harvested from roofs.
- Recognize that it is the connections that matter. Set up working relationships among plants, animals, people, land, and structures so that the needs of one component are met by the yields of another component.

3. Plan for Relative Locations

- Place components of the design in relation to each other, to make useful connections.
- Use the principle of "zones." Permaculture divides space into zones based on human usage patterns. Place elements of your design according to how often you will use or need to visit them. For example, "zone 1" would be the area immediately surrounding a dwelling, which gets the most human traffic. That is where you would want elements that you use every day to be placed, such as the location of your herb bed and composter.
- Design small-scale, intensive systems.

- Start with your back door, and work outward.

4. Design for "Wild" Energies Coming Onto Site

- Design your site to work with the patterns and effects of incoming energies, such as sun, wind, precipitation, fire, noise, and smell.

5. Design for Energy Cycling

- Catch, store, use, and cycle energy at its highest point of potential energy on site. For example, place water catchment systems at the highest elevation possible; gravity will work for you and you will have the most opportunity to work with the water as it flows through the system.

6. Ethics

- Care of the Earth and its people are fundamental tenets of permaculture.
- Look to the distribution of surplus, with a distinction between needs and wants.

Permaculture can help to facilitate a transition to more sustainable communities by helping us to provide for our food, water, shelter, energy, and livelihood in an interconnected web of relationships. Permaculture is not only about the *process* of planning and designing, building and maintaining sustainable communities, permaculture *is* sustainable communities.

(Please see the "Sustainability and the Environment" section of the Recommended Reading List for books on permaculture.)

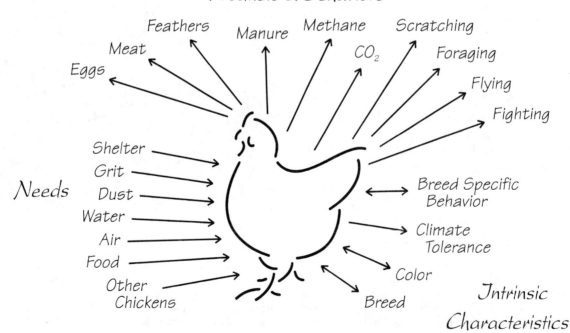

Products & Behaviors

Needs

Intrinsic Characteristics

Jason Bavington

An Introduction to
Financial Development of Communities

by Rob Sandelin and Lois Arkin

Although this article was initially written for cohousers intending to interact with mainstream financial institutions,[1] it has been revised so that much of the information applies across the board to any intentional community group seeking loan money. Nonetheless, if many long-standing intentional communities had to depend on commercial lending institutions, there might be fewer communities today with substantially less sustainability features. But until the intentional communities movement has developed its own financial institutions (and what are we waiting for, folks), communities need to be prepared to access conventional bank and lending institution dollars.

What is exciting about sharing this information with communitarians at this time is that some folks within mainstream financial institutions are beginning "to get it" about communities. That does not mean they are any less prudent in deciding whom to make loans to. But it does mean that there are increasing numbers of financial "insiders" who are potential advocates for lending to intentional communities of all kinds. (And if any of you "insiders" are reading this, please let the Fellowship for Intentional Community (FIC) know who you are.)

The quality of social entrepreneurship in many community founders generally leads them to develop, or find people with, the financial skills to get built what is needed in a way that is significantly sustainable. It's a direction that many communities strive for. With respect to finances, this means that it's not oriented toward debt or the "buy up" culture promoted by the home building and real estate industries. Each community has to critically evaluate what the most effective financial direction is for its members at

any given time. In some cases, conventional financing could deplete financial resources that might otherwise enable people to focus more on their relationships with one another, the broader society, and the Earth—what are called quality of life issues—rather than simply making a living, the primary purpose of which is to pay on a mortgage. Having explored a full range of options can help a group make a more informed decision.

The fact that intentional communities are even dealing with mainstream financial institutions says a lot about the broader culture, and the way in which social change is moving into the mainstream. What communitarians have and continue to achieve as a movement—including the cohousing and ecovillage movements—is increasingly attractive and desirable to many in the mainstream. Perhaps the ultimate institutional challenge for "communitizing" is the banking industry.

Sirius founders Gordon Davidson and Corinne McLaughlin in their classic book, *Builders of the Dawn*, said that today's communities can be seen as "blueprints for humanity's journey into the future … pioneering positive responses to global problems." Connections in which there are shared values between lenders and borrowers can give certain communities the freedom to more confidently carry on that research and development. But many times, the timing and resources are such that a group needs to just go get a bank loan! The information that follows can help.

The First Steps (Regardless of How You Are Going to Finance the Big Project)

As you define your community dreams, you will need to

Rob Sandelin lives at Sharingwood Community and is one of the founders of the Northwest Intentional Communities Association (NICA).

Lois Arkin is the founder of CRSP, a nonprofit resource center for small ecological cooperative communities, founded in 1998. CRSP is the sponsor of the Los Angeles Eco-Village where Lois lives and works doing public advocacy work for more sustainable urban neighborhoods.

investigate forms of ownership, and the financial requirements, for what you want to do. For example, if you want to buy an apartment building, you will need to know how much capital you can raise, what the lending options and requirements are, and how the ownership of the assets will be established. If you are creating a housing project from scratch, such as a cohousing development, you will find that banks generally do not loan money until a certain amount of development work has been done. You will find that long before you submit a loan application to a bank, you will need to spend money developing your project. Sometimes, lots of it, depending on the size of the project. You will be able to apply the money spent by members toward future down payments on mortgages, so keep track of every dime.

Funds for start-up costs can be generated in several ways. One is to charge a monthly assessment. Someone who is interested but not committed may not mind putting up 10 dollars a month for awhile. In almost every start-up group, the really committed people will put in large amounts of unsecured cash to cover the expenses. This may add up to thousands of dollars, especially when you start hiring architects, attorneys, and such. Once you get into it this far, you have enough capital commitment from members that they have enormous interest in seeing it through. The people with little investment are generally the ones that are most likely to leave the group.

Another way to generate money is to have a committed person or persons loan money to the group with payment based on future assessments of future members. Be sure to document any such agreements well. Misunderstandings about loans can cause problems later. Some forms of legal agreements allow for silent partners, who can contribute cash into the project but are not actually members. This is handy for borrowing money from relatives and friends of members, for example. But be sure you understand the securities laws in your state.

If you are creating a community as one large capital project that will be funded by future mortgages, such as a cohousing project, the development group will have to come up with enough money to:

- incorporate as a group and recruit a core group of members;
- provide group process training, parties, etc.;
- provide a down payment to secure the site;
- do feasibility studies on the site;
- provide costs related to any zoning changes;
- provide architectural and legal fees;
- provide permit fees; and
- provide a consultant fee to coordinate all of this in the event the group chooses not to take on this function itself.

Once you have an approved project, with engineered drawings more or less ready to go, and have a builder lined up, then the banks will talk about giving you a project loan. If your group is simply acquiring an already built property—a large house or apartment building or farm with structures on it—your prefinancing preparation work may be simpler.

Underwriting and Timelines

"Underwriting" is what lending institutions call the evaluation work they do on a loan application. The loan application can be two pages or 10 pages, but either number of pages might require backup data comprising hundreds more pages. The loan officer doing the underwriting checks it all out in a process that takes anywhere from one month to three or more months. If you have a tight timeline where time equals money, you may want to submit more than one loan application at the same time. This way if a lender ultimately rejects the loan at a critical time, you have another option. When you apply for a loan, you pay a loan fee that covers the cost of this underwriting. Often this loan fee is not refundable, even if you are turned down for a loan. Ask your potential lender about this. Some lenders do return some or all of the loan fees if you are not approved. This can sometimes be negotiated.

Lines of Credit

Some lenders will provide a line of credit to certain qualifying groups. A line of credit can cover many predevelopment expenses, also called soft expenses, such as architects, engineering, and legal and process training. There are a variety of methods for paying back the line of credit, depending on the lender. However, lines of credit may carry substantially higher interest rates than a long-term mortgage.

Cooperatives and Condominiums

The two most common types of legal entities for communities with respect to lending institutions are co-ops and condos. Banks first look at your legal ownership model (see the article on legal structures, earlier in this section). In general, cooperatives have a harder time finding bank loans than condominiums do, although this varies around the country so be sure to check your local banks. Banks understand and deal with condominiums on a regular basis, and the advantage to the bank is that each condominium has a single owner. Cooperatives hold a blanket mortgage on the whole project, but some cooperatives find that share loans, described below, are a handy thing to have once the community is settled in.

If condominiums are overbuilt in your area, or if there is a large vacancy rate in local condominium projects, you may have extra problems finding a lender.

When you approach banks, go to the main office first. Each bank usually has specialty people who have expertise in certain areas. Ask for the specialist who does condominium loans, or business venture loans, or construction loans.

Accessing Public Monies

Local, state, and federal housing programs and finance agencies can also provide financing for communities. In many cases, public monies can be used for alternative forms of ownership such as land trusts, limited equity co-ops, mutual housing associations, and certain types of nonprofit organizations serving persons with special needs or providing other public educational services.

As a rule of thumb, accessing public monies will require a significant percentage of the housing population served to have incomes under 80 percent of median household income for the area, according to the US Department of Housing and Urban Affairs standards. Many communitarians seeking to live more environmentally sensitive and less complex lives might qualify, even if their lower incomes are voluntary.

Programs using public monies are apt to have many strings attached. These strings are not very much of a barrier, but they can require considerably more paperwork and time, in some cases a year or more. Often, there are annual reporting requirements.

If you want your group to be considered for such financing, it is important to make an effort to get to know your elected officials, and local, state, or federal agency officials in the jurisdiction that has control of the money. They need to know and trust you. Also, since the legislation that makes the public monies available changes all the time, you need to keep track of that legislation. In some cases, you can help advocate for the legislation. In many areas, there are affordable housing advocacy groups that keep interested persons informed.

You may also want to hook up with an existing nonprofit housing developer with expertise in working with public agencies. Such an organization can act as your fiscal agent, package your loan documents, and provide the many services you will need whether you are creating a new development or acquiring an existing house, apartment building, ghost town, or farm. These organizations are prominent in both urban and rural areas, and often might be members of coalitions such as the Southern California Association of Non-Profit Housing. Check with your city or county's local community development or housing director to identify such organizations.

Because many communities live better for less, they are important to affordable housing officials. Qualifying groups can provide an important service by working with the public sector to demonstrate how higher quality community living can actually save taxpayer dollars.

"Often a substantial amount of infrastructure work is expected to be done before the construction loan is approved."

Community Lending

There are many nonprofit community lending institutions across the United States. They are part of the socially responsible community lending movement. Many such lenders are networked through the National Association of Community Development Loan Funds based in Philadelphia. They have an annual conference and a newsletter.

The underwriting criteria for some of these lenders can be more stringent than that of for-profit banks. Often, however, such lenders will provide a good deal of technical assistance not available from banks. The loans can be more flexible than banks, and community lenders always have socially and often environmentally responsible goals incorporated into their lending criteria.

Keeping Track of Unequal Monetary Contributions

The individual members of the core group do not necessarily have to contribute like amounts of money. However, be careful about documenting the disproportionate contributions of cash to the group. The group's partnership agreement, shareholder agreement, or other organizational documents should clearly provide that excess contributions be treated in one of the following ways:
- As a loan to the group, which accrues interest at some agreed upon rate, and which is payable to the contributor either on a certain date, upon the happening of a stated event (such as upon getting a bank loan), or upon demand;
- As a capital contribution to the group, which increases the contributor's capital account (or number of shares) in the venture, and providing that the capital be returned to the contributor in some manner out of proceeds from capital

Community groups are often disappointed by lenders who view nontraditional building materials as poor choices that can reduce resale value.

transactions (such as sale or refinancing of the assets/land owned by the group); or
• As a gift, in whole or in part, to the group.

Failure to address expressly these excess contributions in one of these ways is a formula for misunderstanding and conflict at a later date. At least one cohousing community failed to expressly address this issue and did not even realize until a few years after construction that the excess contributors had essentially made a gift to the community that they would never recover. That's fine, except it was not what the contributors intended and led to some upset on the part of these unwitting "donors."

Appealing to Secondary Loan Market

One key to finding bank support is to have a legal structure that is supported by the secondary loan market, Federal National Mortgage Association, fondly called Fannie Mae (FNMA). It is to your advantage to be as competitive as possible so you can shop around for the best deal. It makes resale much harder if you only have one bank you can get financing from. Banks, especially after all the savings and loan problems, are very reluctant to give loans that are not backed by FNMA. One major way banks make money is to sell batches of similar sizes and types of loans, usually in denominations of $500,000 to $1,000,000, to FNMA to free up capital to loan again. Small, unique loans, that are not underwritten by the secondary loan market, have to be held by the individual bank. Under federal regulations, banks are allowed to hold only a certain percentage of their total worth in these types of loans, and commercial banks do not want to be left holding loans they cannot sell. Banks or mortgage brokers can help you apply for FNMA approval.

Co-op Share Loans

If you can be defined as a cooperative, you may also want to be approved for FNMA share loans. This can be an important advantage for the co-op as well as for incoming and departing members. With share loans, a departing member can take out what they have paid into the co-op, the co-op does not have to come up with the money to pay out to the departing member, and a qualifying incoming member can get a share loan for their unit. Contact the National Cooperative Bank in Washington, DC, to determine what your group needs to do to be eligible for share loans.

Presale Advantages

If you can show a large number of the projected units in your development as being presold, it is a real bonus to your loan application. Having membership agreements, financial plans, and down payments already drawn up and ready to go can be a big help. The more you do to show that people are committed to carrying through the project financially, the better you look as a loan risk. Banks typically favor loans to projects that have presold 75 percent of the units.

Mortgagee Protection

Another factor in getting loan approval is the kind of protection offered to the lender, often called mortgagee protection. Lenders will examine your legal agreements for details on insurance, resale, condemnation of units, approvals of unit division, or anything that could devalue or make a mortgaged home hard to sell. Your loan application is evaluated with the assumption you will default on a mortgage and the lender will have to sell the property to get their loan money back. Anything you can do to make the resale of units simple and attractive makes your project a better risk to the bank.

Be sure any rules you put into your legal documents that define ownership will pass the scrutiny of the lenders. A good attorney usually passes such things for review by one or more financial institutions the attorney has a relationship with. Be sure to ask your attorney about this. It's really a problem to get this far into the process, and then have to redo everything because the lender won't approve the loan.

Some of the flags for lenders may include: restrictions on resale of units, building materials that are not standard, parking and vehicle access, sweat equity that is required prior to occupancy permits, garages, size of unit, and cost relative to cost of the lot.

The fact that some lenders will view these things as flags rather than the important public service that they often are can be very disappointing for many community groups. These groups have demonstrated commitments or plans to heal themselves and the planet by, among other things, caring about their neighbors, using alternative building materials, preserving land and open space, having fewer cars, reducing automobile dependency, and living in smaller, more compact spaces than the conventional consumerist American household.

There is an important public service that communitarians can provide by getting these mainstream loans, so make friends and build trust with the assorted lenders. If enough of us across the country get mainstream loans and prove our worth to lenders, local communities, and the public interest, over time the lending criteria will change.

Perhaps the ultimate institutional challenge for "communitizing" is the banking industry.

The Loan Process for Capital Projects

Once the developer has the approval of local government for the project, the lender gives an Acquisition and Development (A&D) loan which typically covers the cost of buying the land and development costs to date. This covers option money or a down payment on the land, feasibility study, architects fees, and permit fees. The A&D loan may also cover the costs of the commons, such as the common house.

In order to secure this first loan, the group must have a realistic budget, a high number of presold units (with owners prequalified for mortgages), and someone with recognized development expertise. In many cases, the group will have to come up with a percentage of the expected development costs, which may run several hundred thousand dollars. In most cases, the future owners have paid all the predevelopment costs and that money is credited toward the developer's portion of the A&D loan. It is crucial to keep accurate records and receipts of all money that goes into the project in order for it to be credited.

For the next step, the developer gets construction loans to cover the materials and labor of building the project. Often a substantial amount of infrastructure work is expected to be done before the construction loan is given. Usually each building gets a separate construction loan. Once the individual units are constructed and completely finished, the bank loans each prequalified owner a mortgage, based on a percentage of the appraised value, such as 90 percent of the appraised value. The funds generated by the mortgage pay off the construction loan and any other debts owed to contractors. In each step of the process, the banks will require lots and lots of different documents and often will ask for one set, then ask for something else, then yet another thing.

Loan Process for Build-As-You-Go Approach

If you are not doing a large capital project, but a gradual build-as-you-go approach, bank loans for intentional community projects can be more difficult than other sorts of similar developments. This is mainly due to the problems of clear title ownership of the mortgageable assets. As previously mentioned, banks evaluate your loan application with the assumption you will default on a mortgage and they will have to sell the property to make their loan money back. A single owner is much easier for the bank to deal with than a partnership or corporation, although this varies among lenders. Ask questions of local banks regarding their lending criteria. You can often find a local consultant or mortgage broker who knows the criteria for all the local lenders. One thing that makes it easier is if the group can show a substantial portion of investment, like 30–40 percent of the total costs.

Appraisals

Once the bank has tentatively accepted your project, they will do an appraisal of the project to determine how much money to loan. How much the lender will actually loan is called a loan-to-value ratio and is determined by the difference between the amount that the bank appraises units for and what they really cost. That difference has to be made up by the owner in terms of a down payment. For example, if a bank loans 90 percent (90 percent loan-to-value ratio) of the appraised value and they appraise a unit at $100,000 but the unit actually costs $125,000 to build, the bank will actually only give you a mortgage for $90,000 and the buyer will have to make up the extra $35,000.

Low appraisals can cause big problems, especially because they often come very late in the process. If an appraisal comes in unreasonably low, ask for a reappraisal. Having information about similar projects (condominium or co-op unit values) can help boost an appraisal. Be sure common elements are fairly evaluated in the appraisal.

If you are making an offer on a property, it is important to either get your own appraisal prior to making the offer or make the price you are offering subject to an appraisal that you will get before closing.

Getting Real About Financing: Screening Members for Financing

As the plans for the project are developed, the estimates for the costs begin to take shape. This is the place where many groups find that people drop out. The group needs to evaluate its individual and collective ability to qualify for bank loans. Depending on how you set up your loan, either the group or each individual will be responsible for coming up with a particular amount of money each month. This is a good time to closely evaluate personal finances. Check that each member has the ability to qualify for a loan. Banks typically look at some percentage of the individual's annual or monthly income as the amount they will loan. A common rule of thumb is that banks will loan 2.5 times your total annual income. In affordable housing circles, the rule of thumb is that the household pay no more than one-third of its monthly income toward its housing costs. Lenders also look for stable work history (two years at the same job). Independent business owners get a very critical and close scrutiny.

It is to your advantage to do this type of survey and evaluation as a group before the bank does. Having several people in the group not qualify for a loan is a major setback and this typically comes very late in the development process.

The "We Can Afford" Trap

Keep in mind that there are differences between what the bank will loan an individual and what the individual can really afford. In addition to the monthly mortgage payment, there are also taxes and insurance and perhaps monthly assessments for the community costs. It is common for people with a passion for community living to initially commit to making personal financial sacrifices in order to live in the community. These can be unrealistic commitments that they later are unable or don't want to keep, and this can put a financial strain on themselves and others. Encourage an honest appraisal of peoples' financial abilities before the loans are signed.

Setting Up a Community With No Banks Involved

If you are going to create a community with no mortgages or other encumbrances then you need:
- significant start-up capital to buy the land and other things you want; and
- a process for returning a person's investment when they leave or for returning loan monies to nonresident lenders.

One way communities often handle investments by members is to organize as a share co-op, with the clear understanding that the owner of shares is solely responsible for their purchase and sale, subject to approval and regulation by the group. For example, the group can set the share price at $5,000, restrict the transfer of the shares only to people approved by the group, and restrict the number of shares held by any individual. You can also tie share ownership to governance by allowing share holders one vote per share on particular matters such as financial

decisions. Some groups designate different types of shares, and restrict voting shares to one per household in order to ensure that their democracy is not tied to financial investment.

You should also have very clear written agreements about the assets a member brings and keeps. Do members retain personal ownership of their assets or do they assign them to the group? Certain assets, such as houses, property, or automobiles require title changes to document changes in ownership. If a member gives all their assets to the group, what exactly do they get, if anything, when they decide to leave the group? Document this clearly.

Many intentional communities have started, purchased land, and then gone broke and been forced to part with the land and buildings due to lack of funds. As you create your legal papers to define your community, be sure to put in a clause about dissolution of the community. Define who gets what and when they get it.

One way to avoid going broke is to not purchase land until you have a solid membership commitment. Define a minimum core group size that is elastic enough so that if a couple of people left, you would not go bankrupt right away. For example, if your core group is eight committed families, this gives you enough leeway so that if one leaves you can still make your payments while you recruit to fill their space. If you only have four families, and one leaves, this places a much larger financial strain on the remaining families to cover the payments.

Revolving Loan Fund

Revolving loan funds (RLFs) are generally associated with nonprofit community development activities, including many kinds of innovative affordable housing projects. RLFs bring together lenders, borrowers, and technical assistance providers for the purpose of providing access to development money that is not normally available through conventional channels, particularly for low income persons and groups. RLFs try to attract sufficiently large amounts of capital (from both loans and gifts) at low enough interest rates, in the case of loans, that the monies can be loaned or re-loaned out to development projects at high enough interest rates to support the administrative tasks of the funding organization. As monies are paid back to the fund, they can, in turn, be loaned out again for other projects, which is what gives the fund its "revolving" nature.

People interested in making socially and environmentally responsible investments are increasingly drawn to the good work being done by RLFs. In many cases, an RLF will pay a higher interest rate than can be obtained in con-

❧

If enough of us across the country get mainstream loans … over time the lending criteria will change.

ventional interest bearing accounts. But then, loans to RLFs are unsecured. Nonetheless, the RLF usually requires the monies it lends out to be secured. RLFs have excellent track records on both ends—paying back loans to their lenders, and having their borrowers make good on loans from the RLFs. Details on the performance of RLFs can be obtained from the National Association of Community Development Loan Funds in Philadelphia.

An RLF can be created as an arm of a nonprofit housing development organization or a local community development organization. More and more local government organizations and foundations committed to affordable housing are creating revolving loan funds.

Co-op Resources and Services Project (CRSP), the nonprofit umbrella organization of the Los Angeles Eco-Village, owns 48 units of housing in two adjacent central city apartment buildings (as of this writing) in one of the world's richest cities, and yet the organization has no bank loans. CRSP created its ecological revolving loan fund (ELF) in the mid 1980's, contributed about $20,000 of its money to it, and, over a period of four years in the 1990s, used money to leverage nearly $1 million for its acquisitions. People and organizations who know and trust CRSP's work over the years have loaned money to the ELF in sufficient quantities to enable them to purchase the properties without using banks or mortgages. Most of CRSP's loans are unsecured at both ends. It is one way they have been working toward demonstrating a sustainable economics system.

CRSP-ELF works exclusively in the Los Angeles Eco-Village neighborhood at this point, but most RLFs have a larger geographic area of service. The big challenge for a small RLF, such as CRSP-ELF with its single neighborhood focus, is to keep paying money back faster than it is borrowing. In this way the nonprofit sponsor is building equity in its buildings.

Although all groups would not necessarily qualify as state or federally exempt organizations, an RLF could be established by any group that collectively has the connections and the trust to generate a portfolio of loans sufficient to do its development. The National Association of Community Development Loan Funds holds an annual conference where people can learn more.

More Advice About Qualifying for a Bank Loan

• Learn from rejection. If the first bank turns you down, ask why. Then apply that knowledge on the next loan attempt.
• Don't be afraid to ask a loan officer about tips or help for

Jillian Downey

"Keep in mind that there are differences between what the bank will loan an individual and what the individual can really afford."

getting loans. They can offer some valuable insights on how to go about getting your loan. They want your money, so don't hesitate to ask lots of questions.
• If you're involved in a development project, it helps to have a contractor who has a good track record. Banks will require the financial statements of your contractor.
• Figure out early what financial resources your group really has. When applying for bank loans, do a pre-screening of the group to check qualifications for loans. Banks charge a loan application fee and making sure that everyone on the loan qualifies, especially if you need pre-sales in order to qualify for loans, can be crucial.
• Keep handy all your receipts and documents of money members have contributed. The bank will ask for them, perhaps several times, especially when you are signing off the mortgage. Don't pack your receipts away until you have signed your mortgage paperwork and own your home.
• Before you turn in your loan paperwork, make a copy of it and keep a copy of any paper you give the bank. Assume the bank is going to lose the most critical paperwork, so keep backups.
• Put someone in charge of keeping track of the loan paperwork. This person should collect all receipts and other proof of collections. Organize the paperwork into files, with one file for each unit or household.
• Banks will often look closely at the financial condition of your developer. Be sure the developer can stand that kind of scrutiny. Lenders look for a borrower who has enough financial reserve to cover the unknown.

One Last Word About the Funding Puzzle[2]

Whether a group is purchasing an existing home or building, or developing a new community, the most important thing to remember about financing is that it is like a jigsaw puzzle. It rarely comes from one source. Often you don't know how all the pieces are going to fit together. Initial financial commitments will leverage other financial commitments, and sometimes they won't. A group has to learn to live with that uncertainty. Commitments can be all lined up, then interest rates may plunge and a group may find itself wanting to start all over again. No matter how carefully developed the plans, a group should always be ready for a roller coaster ride. If it turns out that it was all easy—though there will always be much more paperwork than anyone wants to deal with—that will be frosting on the community cake.

Resources

Center for Community Change, 100 Wisconsin Ave NW, Washington DC 20007, USA. Tel: 202-342-0567, fax: 202-333-5462. Email: info@communitychange.org, http://www.communitychange.org/ Provides a range of technical assistance on affordable housing finance issues and sources.

US Department of Housing and Urban Development (HUD), Customer Service Center, Room B-100, 451 Seventh St SW, Washington DC 20410, USA. Tel: 800-767-7468, fax: 202-708-2313. Email: hudclips@aspensys.com, http://www.hudclips.org/ Access to all of HUD's handbooks, Federal Register notices, and more.

Institute for Community Economics, 57 School St, Springfield MA 01105, USA. Email: iceconomic@aol.com.

Land Trust Alliance, 1319 F St NW, Washington DC 20410, USA. Tel: 202-638-4725, fax: 202-638-4730. http://www.lta.org/ Offers detailed information as well as useful books on land trusts.

Local Initiative Support Corporation, http://www.liscnet.org/ This site is very detailed with listings and information on regional branches.

National Community Capital Association, 924 Cherry St, 2nd Floor, Philadelphia PA 19107, USA. Tel: 215-923-4754. http://www.communitycapital.org/

National Cooperative Bank, 1401 Eye St NW, Suite 700, Washington DC 20005, USA. Tel: 800-955-9622. http://www.ncb.com/

National Association of Housing Cooperatives, 1614 King St, Alexandria VA 22314, USA. Tel: 703-549-5201, fax: 703-549-5204. http://www.coophousing.org/

Northwest Intentional Communities Association (NICA), 22110 East Lost Lake Rd, Snohomish WA 98296, USA. Email: Floriferous@msn.com, http://www.infoteam.com/nonprofit/nica/

North American Students of Cooperation (NASCO), Campus Development Fund, PO Box 7715, Ann Arbor MI 48107, USA. Tel: 734-663-0889, fax: 734-663-5072. Email: NASCO@umich.edu, http://www.umich.edu/~nasco/

Rural Community Assistance Corporation, 2125 19th St, Suite 203, Sacramento CA 95818, USA. Tel: 916-447-2854, fax: 916-447-2878. Email: webmaster@rcac.org, http://www.rcac.org/

Southern California Association of Nonprofit Housing, 3345 Wilshire Blvd, Suite 1000, Los Angeles CA 90010, USA. Tel: 213-480-1249, fax: 213-480-1788. Email: hn1489@handsnet.org, http://www.cham.org/scanph.html

The Enterprise Foundation, 10227 Wincopin Circle, Suite 500, Columbia MD 21044, USA. Tel: 410-964-1230, fax: 410-964-1918. Email: mail@enterprisefoundation.org, http://www.enterprisefoundation.org/ Has an extensive library of online and software products for developing communities.

Also check with: The Commercial or Community Lending Departments of any major bank; city, county, and state housing and community development offices. Check the white pages of your phone book for the jurisdiction you are seeking.

Endnotes

1. Much of the information in this article came from the following: Sandelin, Rob. *Community Resource Guide*, 1997. Available on http://www.cohousing.org/

2. Cohen, Lottie and Lois Arkin. *Cooperative Housing Compendium: Resources for Collaborative Living*, Davis, CA: UC Davis Center for Cooperatives, 1993, p. 123. This paragraph is quoted with their permission.

Jillian Downey

Living It
Meeting the Needs of Your Members and Your Community

The joys and challenges that come with living in community create a rich mix of experience and learnings. Articles in this section share lessons that have been learned by seasoned communitarians, facing the complex issues that come up when people live closely with one another. How can communities successfully embrace the diversity of the people who wish to live together? How much diversity can communities really handle? What is the true nature of commitment? How can communities meet the needs and wants of their membership, while maintaining a fundamental integrity, stability, and solvency? How can we balance the needs of the old, the young, the sick, the well, the loud, and the quiet? This section aims to shed light on these questions.

Once More With Feeling

Conflict as an Opportunity for Harnessing Emotional Energy

by Laird Sandhill

WHILE THE DREAM OF COMMUNITY is living in harmony, the essential challenge of community is learning how to *dis*agree constructively.

No matter how careful we are about selecting community members who are aligned with common values, there will inevitably be disagreement, hopefully accompanied by occasional strong feelings (who wants to live in a community where the members lack passion?).

I define conflict as a situation with at least two different viewpoints and at least one emotional charge. I further assert that emotional charge about specific incidents is rooted in emotional distress, which depends on who we have come to be as a complex accumulation of inherent and learned responses. People have varying degrees of self-awareness about their emotional make-up and differing abilities and inclinations to separate charge in the moment from their general pattern. Also, individuals and groups have different commitments to exploring the connection between charge and distress.

For this article, when I talk about charge, upset, or distress, I am referring to whatever is accessible in the moment, whether it be direct and simple, or deep and complex. How far you take a particular examination will depend on the specifics of the situation. If the deeper distress is not triggered, fine. I'm focusing here on when it is, with the idea that the more complicated dynamic is the more challenging issue.

I view conflict as a naturally occurring phenomenon in any healthy group. As such, the problem with conflict is not so much that it occurs, but that we generally haven't learned to work with it well. Mostly we respond with attempts to coerce, intimidate, manipulate, outvote, submit, exit, or fight.

While there is quite a bit written about how to communicate in ways that reduce the risk of triggering emotional distress, I want to focus here on what happens when distress *is* triggered. It's good to know all you can about staying on the road, yet you won't be a complete driver until you also know how to get out of the ditch. (And it's my experience that fear of the ditch—emotional distress—can actually be worse than being in the ditch, and certainly makes travel more tense.)

There are good reasons for being nervous about emotional upset. It is typically commingled with aggression, and people often get hurt—at least psychologically, and possibly worse. You don't have to be caught too many times in the thunderstorms of distress before you start looking for protection as soon as storm clouds roll into the room. For the most part, if it's our distress, we either erupt or learn to stuff it. If we encounter it in others, we respond in kind or try to get safely out of the way. While some groups have the culture of embracing high-energy, spirited discourse in no-holds-barred free-for-alls, most prefer to ignore emotional surges, or, if they can't, to contain them, calling a break to let the belligerents cool down before re-engaging. I want to explore a counterintuitive approach—leaning into the emotional punch, with purpose. Not with the idea of promoting upset, but of working with the opportunities it presents.

Laird Sandhill has been living in the fire of intentional community since 1974, and active in intercommunity networking since 1979. He has been involved with the Fellowship for Intentional Community (FIC) since 1986 and been doing consulting work on group process since 1987. Excited about what community living has taught him and others about how to live cooperatively, today he is a principal in the CANBRIDGE process collective, making the learnings available to interested groups everywhere. He can be reached at RR 1 Box 156-D, Rutledge MO 63563, USA. Tel: 660-883-5545, email: laird@ic.org.

The first challenge is separating expression of feelings from abuse; emotions from aggression. I'm asking you to invite anger, while separating it from blame; to welcome tears, yet discourage guilt tripping; to make room for fear, yet expose paranoia.

Why Bother?

As you might imagine, it is easier to offer this guidance than to put it into practice, especially in the heat of the moment. With all the complications this entails, why do the work of sorting out emotions from aggression? I have two answers. First, emotions are part of who we are as human beings, and I find it crippling to not paint with a full palette. While the typical Western model of group interaction is based on the exchange of rational thought, what about feelings, intuition, kinesthetic knowledge, and spiritual truth? People take in, process, and share information in various ways. Rational discourse is only one. In an effort to open up other paths, I want to look expressly at emotional knowing.

Nonrational knowing can come in the form of strong feelings, and it can also be quiet. Have you ever been in a meeting where the discussion was proceeding steadily toward agreement when someone contributes, "I don't know, but there is something that just doesn't feel right"? Even in groups that try to make room for this kind of statement (meaning eyeballs don't start rolling immediately), the typical response is an inquiry into what that can mean, and then pressure mounts for the person with the uneasy feeling to either get articulate, or get some Alka-Seltzer and let the group move on.

If, instead, there is an attitude that feelings or intuitions can be just as valuable a path to insight as rational thought, you can get a different experience. For example, years ago I worked with a seven-person community about an issue they had with how group finances were handled. After only 15 minutes it was apparent that most group members preferred a switch to another method of recording and reporting expenditures. However, we didn't rest there because one person had an uneasy feeling about it—and that person was the finance manager.

I was there as an outside facilitator because the group had been at that juncture before and had repeatedly gotten stuck. What I did differently was assume that the uneasy feeling carried important information (even though this is not always the case—sometimes feelings are triggered by stimulation of unresolved past distresses that have nothing to do with the current issue, and until you look into it, you don't know the meaning of that uneasiness).

As facilitator, I created an environment of patient exploration (groups will let outside facilitators do almost anything once). I asked the finance manager if this feeling had come up before and went from there, never pushing. After an hour we'd discovered that the root worry had to do with fears that the proposed change would mask infor-

As an individual in conflict you can choose to disengage or see it as an opportunity to learn how to disagree constructively.

mation about how money was used, and the manager was afraid to disclose this interest because it might call into question their trust in the group. (There is great irony here in that the manager's lack of trust in the group's ability to talk constructively about trust led to the rest of the group not trusting the manager to implement agreements. It was quite a tangle.) Once we finally got that out in the open, it was relatively straightforward to get assurances from the group that the manager's interests were valid and could be met in more direct ways. This resolved the uneasy feeling and the proposed changes in accounting could finally go forward. For this issue, rational discourse alone was simply not getting the job done.

A second reason for welcoming strong feelings is that they are a source of energy. This is not so admired when the energy is wild and out of control like an untended fire hose randomly thrashing around the room. But what if we learned to harness that energy, and bring it to bear on our issues, instead of on our neighbor's head? Under control, we can direct that hose, and focus the powerful stream to quench hot issues. Have you ever noticed how people are more engaged when there is strong feeling in the room? Let's put that attention to work!

Living It: Meeting the Needs of Your Members and Your Community

What's at Stake?

Forcing people into the rational often prohibits people from working where they are most comfortable, and does not allow a full range of input. If you don't work with distress, you risk losing the contributions from and learnings for the people left unattended, plus it creates a background of tensions for those witnessing but not in the distress themselves. Can we afford this?

Working with distress in the dynamic moment allows the possibility of drawing out the poison and building creative, cross-viewpoint solutions which can have a dramatic impact on implementation.

I once worked with a multiracial, multiclass neighborhood association that was struggling to define its mission and just how much diversity it could bridge. In a pivotal meeting, one group member threatened to drop out, which would have left a segment of the neighborhood unrepresented on the council. Anxiety was high in the room, yet we stayed with the moment long enough to make a clear statement of intent to retain the dissenting member. When that person ultimately decided to leave, we worked immediately to access feelings of anger, fear, and guilt about the loss. Being clean and complete in its engagement with the dynamics, the council entered the most productive and cohesive two months of its existence.

This story illuminates two things. First, opening up emotional factors does not guarantee that everyone will like what's exposed or even remain in the group. Second, taking the time for in-depth emotional work often promotes group cohesion and sets the table for productive bursts.

Once you experience the positive results of welcoming emotions, you simultaneously reduce fear of emotions. And once you start expecting good results from meetings—any meetings—you are already half the way toward getting them.

How to Do It

While the range of human interactions is infinite, and there is no one-size-fits-all approach that guarantees success, here is an experience-tested four-step outline for productive engagement once conflict arises. While this model can be applied with any number of people, there is a strong tendency to process emotional distress alone or in pairs. Though much can be accomplished this way, there is a particular advantage to working with conflict in a group. It is more likely there will be neutral non-combatants present to ask questions and shepherd the process—whether this is being done by a designated facilitator or not. Questions posed by parties neutral to the conflict can elicit completely different responses than the same questions coming from the lips of protagonists. Thus, I suggest that this model may be most effective when neutral parties are available to actively facilitate.

A precondition for using this model effectively is gaining explicit agreement or permission from the group to do this. This model will

MEMBERS WERE ASKED : WHAT'S THE ONE THING THAT CAN ASSURE SINCERITY WILL THRIVE AS A UNIQUE COMMUNITY FOR ANOTHER 25 YEARS?

MORE COMPUTERS. / A TOTAL BAN ON COMPUTERS. / LESS RELIANCE ON ANIMAL AGRICULTURE. / MORE MEAT.

MORE TRADITIONAL MARRIAGES. / MORE GAY MEN. / MORE FACE-TO-FACE MEETINGS. / NO MORE DIPPY MEETINGS.

REPLACING OUR CARS WITH BIKES AND HORSES. / REPLACING OUR OLD CARS WITH NEWER CARS. / MORE PERSONAL SPACE + MONEY. / LESS PRIVATIZATION OF RESOURCES.

MORE POLICIES. / LESS RULES. / MORE COMMON GROUND. / MORE DIVERSITY.

only be effective if the group allows it to be. Please do not assume the mantle of divinely inspired conflict superhero who goes forth springing this process on the unsuspecting.

Step 1. Acknowledge the distress. Start anywhere and ask what's happening, making sure that everyone understands each person's story before moving on (understanding is different than agreeing). If there's a multicar wreck, attend to the most seriously injured first, staying on the job until everyone's wound has been (ad)dressed.

Step 2. After getting the important feelings named and acknowledged, you can move on to explore each person's version of how the accident happened. What are the perceptions of the "facts"? Sometimes providing an uninterrupted opportunity for each party to tell their story can lead to a breakthrough all by itself, where the principals can let go of attachment to history once they've been allowed to state it.

One pitfall here is the temptation to be the "truth police." What we're after is building relationship, not discovery of truth. With that in mind, you try to name the points in common and the points that differ, aiming for recognition, not reconciliation. Be prepared for stories to differ wildly—sometimes it's hard to credit that two people are talking about the same event. Each party can be laboring under the mistaken idea that there's a single objective reality (theirs), and these differences must be exposed and acknowledged before it's possible to build durable solutions.

Step 3. Ask each party what they want. What's the fullest expression of each person's views about this issue? Occasionally the strength of reaction in a conflict hinges around a gross misunderstanding about what others want. People in distress often make up stories about what's wanted by others, and forget to check it out. For this step, it isn't necessary that answers be bounded by what is reasonable or attainable. An answer can be modest or huge; it can be anything from second helpings of dessert to the Second Coming. As before, note the differences and similarities in responses, then go on.

Step 4. Finally, ask each what the person wants to do about it. (This is not "What do you want *others* to do about it?") Answers here should be concrete and measurable. In step (3), you might get "I want to be friends." To step (4), "I'm willing to meet for two hours every Thursday afternoon for the next two months to work on our relationship."

Having de-escalated the tension through steps (1) and (2), and established a common understanding of what's wanted in step (3), you finally begin problem solving, starting with what each can contribute. This sets the stage for creative exploration of new ways, or seeing old positions in a new light. It is important in this model to link the examination of hurts with active problem solving, taking advantage of openings in the former to forge agreements in the latter.

A common error in conflict resolution is people jumping to possible solutions (step (4)) as soon as tension surfaces, and before there's been a full expression or acknowledgment of the feelings and desires. Typically, these efforts fail to resolve the matter—even when the proposed action is no different than what evolves from following each step above. That's because buy-in is nearly impossible if one or more parties don't feel the other side has heard or understood their concerns.

What I'm proposing may sound like therapy, and there is certainly overlap with the skills of careful listening and reflecting. However, this is not therapy in any professional sense. It is peer counseling, which is equals trying to help each other out of the ditch. People who facilitate conflict in groups operate in a middle ground—somewhere in the wide terrain between traffic cop (deciding who gets to talk next) and psychologist (tell me all about it). It is crucial that the facilitator know what the group has agreed to undertake, so that there is a sense of boundaries and safety for the individual in the process. Everyone should know ahead of time what may occur among group members when probing conflict.

> ⑥
>
> Working with distress in the dynamic moment allows the possibility of drawing out the poison and building creative, cross-viewpoint solutions....

Choices in Distress

I want to end this article by looking at the healthy choices available for use once someone is in the ditch. I think there are four, all of which have their legitimate place … and all of which can be misused. Learning what they are and how to employ them in constructive combinations is a lot of what is meant by "emotional maturity." I think it's useful for groups to understand these choices, to help guide individuals once they are charged up.

1. Exit

This is disengaging and distancing yourself from the thing that's disturbing. It can be a minor shift or a major one: leave the topic; leave the room; leave the group.

2. Ignore

The fact is, there are too many irritating things out there to address them all. If we attempted to process every distress that came our way, we'd never do anything else. You have to pick your spots, choosing engagement where the

Jillian Downey

When conflict occurs, acknowledge the distress and take advantage of neutral parties' ability to facilitate clearly.

payoff is greatest (either in reduced anguish or improved happiness—and these, of course, are related). At the same time, the danger with making this choice is that people have a tendency to choose inappropriately. They hope that an upset will not hook into their distress, but sometimes it does. Once distress enters the picture, you only have two choices—pay now, or pay later. And the interest charged on deferred attention to emotional distress can really add up. In their determination to let go, people may hide the lingering distress (either consciously or unconsciously) and have it surface in surprising and unpleasant ways, such as distorted reactions in unrelated situations, loss of attentiveness, or even ill health.

If you're going to engage on the issue, that leaves only two options.

3. Request a Change

Ask the other person(s) to change their behavior. This, of course, tends to be everyone's favorite choice, and sometimes it works. When the other person has no attachment to the thing that was offending, or cares enough about relieving your distress relative to their inconvenience to make a change, you can get your wish.

However, that only works some of the time. When it doesn't, only one choice remains.

4. Change How You Feel About It

This option is the least frequently selected and the most commonly misunderstood, yet it has tremendous potential. Sometimes people insist that there be a reciprocal offering from the other person as a precondition for their own movement. While this occasionally works and there can be a feeling of power and a sense of balance in this approach, look again. By tying your relief to another's actions, you are accepting a disempowered position. Your experience of distress is held hostage to your demand for reciprocity.

While there is nothing wrong with reciprocity when you can get it, what can you do when that's not on the menu? Let's examine the power of unilateral work on one's feelings.

I am not suggesting something as simplistic as, "You're angry, get over it." I'm saying something much richer: first notice what your feelings are, and then do what you can to understand their roots. Ask the question, "Where does this reaction come from?" With the answer to that, ask yourself whether your reaction is appropriate to the current situation, or whether you are bringing an old pattern into play. If you decide your response is not apropos, do you want to work on changing your response? What's the payoff for staying in an old pattern? An answer might be to do some personal pruning to clear your psyche of dead wood, and bring your emotional reactions to present-day reality. I won't pretend this is easy; yet it's clearly your work and not the responsibility of the person whose actions triggered your emotional response.

If your feelings are appropriate to the situation, I suggest you work first to express your feelings and see that they are understood. (This is unrelated to a request for action; here you are just aiming for disclosure.) Next, ask, "What change can I effect?" Or, "What's possible?" The premise here is that feelings themselves are neither bad nor good; they are information and energy. What do you want to do with them? Even if you deem your response appropriate, you have the chance to assess the pros and cons of staying in that response. This examination can be done in a wide variety of ways: personal reflection, meditation, conversation with friends, peer counseling, therapy—use anything that helps!

The way I finally "got it" about the power of unilateral work was in relation to my father. He and I fought more or less continuously throughout my early adulthood. Part of my pattern in distress is to have imaginary conversations with my adversary (in which I invariably say witty, brave, and crushing things while the other observes meekly in clumsy humiliation), and I was having a lot of "talks" with dad during those years. Finally, after 15 years of rocky relations, I started reflecting on my part in why it wasn't working (instead of sustaining the charade that it was all his fault).

After months of agonizing, I wrote my father a letter. I called attention to my perception that despite deep caring for each other, we had a tough time doing anything other than fighting. I wrote that I felt we both played a part in why it didn't work. I told him a bunch of things I thought I was contributing to why it wasn't working, and invited his response. A few weeks later I got a letter … in which he told me some more things I'd been doing to make it not work. It was not to the response I was hoping for.

However, having finally started to look in the mirror, I was determined to not go back to pretending it was all his fault. I continued the work of examining my own role in the dynamic and was able to give up my feelings of anger toward my father for not respecting my life choices. I finally came to understand how I was a prisoner of my own anger. My father died three years after I wrote that letter and we never reconciled. I did, however, stop having imaginary conversations with him. I did finally look at the origins of my distress and made the choice to change my feelings. And that's how I came to know the possibility and power of unilateral emotional work. It took me 15

years, but I finally got it.

Thus, one reason for examining emotional distress is that once you begin to know yourself better, you might be able to eliminate barriers to hearing others more fully. Emotional distress can be thought of as a kind of psychic earwax; left unattended, it can permanently distort your hearing. Not working through distress is dangerous for another reason as well—you'll teach people around you not to give you information about their views and how you are perceived.

If you stay mired in your distress, people may find you unpleasant to be around. They may learn to avoid offering you information because they don't want to risk your reaction. If you have an aggressive response to distress, it is even worse. In its most straightforward application, people will learn to avoid offering feedback for fear it will trigger aggression that will be directed toward them (shooting the messenger).

My personal struggles with distress took a more subtle form. I didn't begin unraveling it until my mid-40s. I sabotaged the feedback loop not so much by fighting off the other person or their comments as by using the feedback to beat myself up. Witnessing my self-flagellation was so unpleasant that fellow community members hesitated to give feedback the next time, for fear I'd use it as a weapon against myself. While a person can hardly be held accountable for feedback they never received, it took me long years to understand that I was unwittingly discouraging the information from reaching me in the first place.

The good news is that this is reversible. If people see that you work constructively and creatively with emotional distress, they'll be encouraged to offer their perceptions. Since information about how we are perceived is crucial in assessing where we are in relation to where we want to be, it becomes essential to encourage the messengers, not shoo them (much less shoot them).

❦

> It is crucial that the facilitator know what the group has agreed to undertake, so that there is a sense of boundaries and safety for the individual in the process.

Disability and Ability: A Community Perspective

by Daniel Bartsch

I'm 48. I feel chronic pain. On a good day I walk maybe a hundred steps. Some days I venture out of bed for only an hour or so. Usually I sit in a wheelchair. Most people consider me disabled.

Each of us is a mix of disability and ability. Though I may be less able than many to independently satisfy material desires, I'm proving more able than many to empathize with others when they feel hardship, and to feel content myself.

I live and volunteer with Magic, a residential community, working partnership, and nonprofit organization (see article in the first section). Because Magicians aim for material simplicity and loving consciousness, I'm more valuable here than I've been in prior homes and workplaces.

For me, learning to see self and others more accurately is among the most difficult and rewarding aspects of life. I've been pleased with how much I can contribute to, and benefit from, this process at Magic.

For example, I'm hypersensitive to cold and drafts. Occasionally I still wait too long to ask for consideration, and then feel agitated when I do. Increasingly though, I remind people promptly and calmly, and they respond graciously. I'm also learning to use others' carelessness as a stimulus to be more considerate. When I concentrate on modeling the thoughtfulness

The author, 1999.

Magic community

I'm asking, I hurt less, others feel reassured, and all of us become more loving.

A few years ago I began growing carob and locust trees from seed. Though doing this "on my own time," and nominally "just for fun," I secretly wanted to develop it into a new Magic project. Soon I was importuning others for assistance, and cutting corners in fulfilling commitments to prepare meals, host guests, and mentor younger Magicians. I wanted to believe that I was able to initiate and establish "my own" project independently, but as others questioned and I listened to my own explanations, I realized that I was relying heavily on others and subverting our common agenda, so I wound down the venture.

Of course, in a healthful community environment each person strikes a beneficial balance between accepting others' views and advocating for her or his own. What we're learning at Magic, however, is that more often than we previously imagined we see each other more accurately than we see ourselves. We now think of stubborn refusal to acknowledge this pattern as one of the most common, crippling, and destructive "disabilities," and one of the least admitted.

Despite my own continuing—albeit waning—resistance, I've benefitted enormously from others' honest, loving assessments. I'm far more confident, articulate, poised, relaxed, knowledgeable, content—even healthier in some ways—than I was when I arrived at Magic 20 years ago. And I see how others have benefitted from my presence by becoming calmer, more loving, more peaceful, more grateful, and generally happier. I look backward with satisfaction and forward with enthusiasm.

Whatever your abilities and disabilities, there are opportunities for you in community. May you enjoy searching for and creating them!

All for One and One for All
Balancing Personal Needs With the Needs of Community

by Mitchel J. Slomiak

IN LATE 1981, A FEW MONTHS after I joined the Kerista community, I announced that my new-found art forms of song writing and documentary film making were so engaging and rewarding that I intended to cut back from a 30-hour work week to a 25-hour work week. After all, a utopian experiment certainly had room to support its budding artists.

After the uproar had subsided and the bemused refusal of my loving partners set in, I was left with lingering questions to ponder: Why was I the only Keristan who fully appreciated and supported my personal desires? Where was the loving, supportive "all for one" implied by the ideal of community?

I did learn that most of my peers preferred artistic play to the house-cleaning, gardening, and advertising sales work that occupied so many of our daylight hours. Yet they also valued paying the bills on time and steering clear of credit card debt. Indeed, during our original discussion of the matter there was puzzlement expressed that I was so far removed from the "one for all" concept embedded in our community.

As a recent college grad, it had simply not occurred to me that the community at large would have such significant concerns about making ends meet that it would interfere with my desires. I had framed the issue with the assumption that whatever resources I required, whether temporal or material, would be provided by my community. My community partners, in looking at me, were assuming that I would take on my fair share of support for the temporal and material requirements of the community.

This youthful incident provides a tiny peephole into

"When a group invites individuals to articulate their needs, all members must be prepared to create a safe environment for individual truths to be spoken."

Mitch Slomiak has lived in community his entire adult life: two years of shared housing in college, 11 years in the Kerista community, and three years with two other ex-Keristans. He now lives very happily with his three partners and four community cats in the San Francisco Bay Area. Mitch is actively involved with Bay Area men's communities, has recently begun playing guitar again, and loves communing with nature. Feel free to email him at mitchmjs@well.com.

"The needs of the individual and the needs of the community constantly press up against one another. Time and money emerge as finite resources."

type of activity (e.g., mostly emotional work with very little time left for fun and games or just hanging out), men simply stop showing up for monthly meetings and biannual retreats. Discontent sets in and passion deflates.

In this community, rotational leadership regulates the mixture of activities and group vision. Each change of leadership provides opportunity for a new orientation and fresh set of experiences. Elders help redirect grumbling and grousing toward a passion for leadership. Though some members lose interest and drop away, most step forward into leadership over time and offer their unique talents. Inevitably each new man in leadership alters the focus and mixture of activities to fit his vision. This leadership rotation revitalizes the community while providing powerful opportunities for individual development.

this enormous ongoing issue facing all communities and each individual in community. The needs of the individual and the needs of the community constantly press up against one another. Time and money emerge as finite resources. Individual and communal desires (leisure, travel, postgraduate work, restaurants, fashion, toys for the kids, new tools, rebuilding, more land, art projects) seem to be infinite. How is balance to be attained, and what is meant by "balance"?

Occasionally this balance feels like balancing a checkbook, a quantifiable situation that, with slight adjustments, locks into an objective steady state. When my Kerista partners and I wanted to distribute relatively undesirable tasks (cleanup of our messiest dwellings) we would often call a "cleaning bee" and agree that all of us would work the same number of hours at the same time. Conversely, when it came to desirable tasks (childcare, for example) or resources (barter with vacation resorts) we set up scheduling systems that allowed individuals to take turns and experience some of the pleasure without monopolizing the entire resource for themselves.

There are other situations in which balance feels like walking a tightrope. By subtle movements of musculature, a delicate toehold is sustained on a swaying gossamer line poised over an abyss. My men's community often faces this type of balance. We are a voluntary organization serving individuals who generally have very busy family and work lives within the teeming miasma of Silicon Valley. Members exhibit varying degrees of interest in a wide variety of activities: community service, emotional work, outdoor adventures, building and crafts, social events, spiritual retreats, and the like. If the balance sways too far toward any single

Sometimes balance takes the form of natural variation. Within my current four-adult home we often look toward complementary likes and dislikes to achieve balance. Some of us love to cook. Some enjoy the meditation of cleaning dishes. Two are outstanding organizers. One is an expansive visionary with a penchant for feng shui and another is a master gardener with a fondness for riotous color. The cooks prepare most meals, the meditative cleaners keep the kitchen in order, the planners figure out how to fit in vacations and social events and maintain the household finances, the interior decorating visionary is continually rearranging the furniture while the gardener rearranges plants.

Within our home, balance is at its most fluid in the area of conflict and emotional space. The four of us as individuals exhibit a broad spectrum of needs in this arena. These needs range from a desire to process all uncomfortable feelings in real-time to the inclination to sit out emotional storms and quietly contemplate them in privacy. Some have an easy time speaking difficult emotional truths and others struggle continually to let others in on personal upset. Factors such as workload, mood range, and physical health will affect how each of us relates to conflict and emotional work at any given time. Emotional balance is in place when we are all given the space we need for our inner work and the attention we need to resolve, or at least air, the feelings that emerge from within.

I have come to believe that the many forms of balance are most easily sustained (or regained) when a community understands the needs of its members. Though clairvoy-

When a group invites individuals to articulate their needs, all members must be prepared to create a safe environment for individual truths to be spoken. We may learn that Mitch wants more time to play with his new-found art forms, Debbie needs to visit her relatives twice a year, John needs more spiritual space and time, and Samantha needs her own room. It is vital to validate these needs, yet this act of listening does not mean that each of us gets what we need right now. It is our starting point, allowing us to construct a more comprehensive likeness that enlarges the community and reveals who the members are in the privacy of their desires.

"When all members experience dynamic balance the community becomes a place of great passion and deep contentment."

Jillian Downey

In order for the needs of the individual to be fulfilled, a second key dimension is required. Not only is it incumbent upon the community as a whole to make room for this articulation of need, the individual members of the community must actively assert their desires to the entire community. Hiding out or holding back can dilute and even poison the mutual trust and vulnerability that occurs within this dynamic process. If Susan does not tell us that she requires private time when she is emotionally upset I may focus group attention on her every foul mood and render it impossible for her to achieve equilibrium within the group.

Indeed, a profoundly authentic balance can occur when all the members grab hold of the community as their own and shape it in their own image. When my community becomes "Mitch Slomiak's community" I will repeatedly ask myself to describe what the Mitch Slomiak community looks like, feels like, acts like, plays like, worships like, works like, loves like. I will actively infuse my intention, vision, and spirit into the lifeblood of the community. As a matter of responsibility I will look around and try to determine the needs of my fellows and weave them into my tapestry of community.

There is subtlety to this mind-set. Rather than creating a personal fiefdom I will carefully weigh the needs of my partners as I prioritize my own needs. Why? Because I crave community and if I overlook or undervalue the needs of my community partners they may simply leave. If any community members regularly prioritize their own needs over those of the community, they may cause an imbalance that threatens the vitality of the entire community. This inner struggle for balance is an arena for my community heart to meet my independent spirit and find an inner voice that nurtures both. As I weave my heartfelt desires into community, I am weaving with each of my partners, as they, too, discover within themselves how to achieve their highest vision of community while making it work for themselves.

Whether gossamer thin or as solid as the base of the Great Pyramid, this balance I describe is a product of the attitudes and intentions of each member, flowing into action. While decisions continue to involve give-and-take, the presence of intention—the rock solid desire for all to achieve fulfillment in community—in the forefront of each member's heart and mind enables a perpetual balance to exist. When all members experience dynamic balance the community becomes a place of great passion and deep contentment.

Multiple Chemical Sensitivities

by Susan Molloy

The publishers of this directory recognize that a segment of the communities movement is concerned about multiple chemical sensitivities (MCS), and so asked Susan Molloy to write this short informational piece about it. In addition, please see the extensive resource list on the following page.

MULTIPLE CHEMICAL SENSITIVITIES (MCS) affect some individuals who are unable to withstand exposure to synthetic products common to our environment. MCS can result from a specific high-level chemical exposure, for example exposure to pest control chemicals, noxious smoke, or the wrong medication. It can also result from chronic, low-level exposure to chemicals. A percentage of the population is susceptible to MCS because of inborn genetic traits.

The diagnosis of MCS is still problematic within the medical and insurance industries for a number of reasons: MCS affects multiple organ systems; symptoms vary in type and severity from person to person; the precipitating toxic exposure cannot always be identified; and there is not yet a common, simple diagnostic protocol designed for profitable use by conventional physicians. As is the case with many autoimmune illnesses, women are somewhat more commonly affected than are men. Symptoms affect the brain, nervous system, and inflammatory processes, impairing endocrine, digestive, and respiratory function. Raging allergic-type reactions to formerly tolerated foods and natural substances are commonly triggered. People with MCS commonly have painful reactions to various electromagnetic and radio fields as well.

MCS symptoms range from annoying to extremely debilitating. If exposures cannot be controlled or avoided, for people with acute MCS the result is disability to the point of isolation and dependence on others for daily care. There exist no homeless or women's shelters, no nursing homes, no convalescent hospitals, and no accessible apartments in clean air that were constructed and maintained for people whose primary effective means of pain management is avoidance of modern synthetic products. So, people with MCS fortify their own homes themselves or find new places to live as best they can to meet their needs. It usually means a drastic lifestyle change. Contact with other people with MCS is a vital affirmation for many, and there are long distance communities of MCS people, linked by telephone, email, and support-group newsletters.

Once someone has MCS it is typically a lifelong disorder, but careful, diligent progress can lessen the severity. There are now helpful replacement products used by some people with MCS in lessening the effects within their own homes: fragrance-, chlorine-, and phenol-free cleaning and personal care products; organic or pressure-cooked cotton or silk clothing; and furniture of steel or even organic wood. Some people benefit from room or car air filters or charcoal-filled masks, and from use of some brands of industrial or military respirators to withstand brief exposures. Some therapies are designed to halt the current poisoning and rebuild the body's ability to process "ordinary" exposure to chemicals on its own. One is a program of vitamins, exercise, and saunas, although

---

Susan Molloy lives in the high desert east of Snowflake, Arizona, in a community of 10 households built by and for people with chemical- and electromagnetic-field–triggered disabilities. This remote, overgrazed former ranch land is affordable enough that each household secures between 20 and 80 acres, a barrier of space for protection from careless or casual use of common chemicals by "normal" people. She has a master's degree in Disability Policy from the Department of Public Administration, San Francisco State University, and works on state and national disability advocacy issues. Email her at susanm@cybertrails.com.

results vary. This treatment helps some people with MCS but can be very detrimental to others, so proceed cautiously, and only under careful supervision. The only surefire "therapy," for now, is identification of trigger exposures by each person, to clarify what materials, foods, electromagnetic fields, noises, or other stimuli must be minimized in their environment.

The number of people with MCS is growing, and public awareness is rising. The Chemical Manufacturers Association, pest control applicators, cosmetic companies, and Department of Defense wish people with MCS would "stop it" or at least be quiet, but this is impossible as the sensitized population inevitably grows more numerous. Exposure to synthetic chemical products, and coping with the disabling conditions caused by the exposures, are inescapable in the public, commercial, and military life of modern culture.

Resources

Organizations

American Environmental Health Foundation, a "nonprofit organization founded to provide research and education into chemical sensitivity." Dallas TX, USA. Tel: 214-361-9515, fax: 214-361-2534. Email: aehf@aehf.com, http://www.aehf.com/

California Council on Wireless Technology Impacts, 936-B 7th St #206, Novato CA 94945, USA. Tel: 415-892-1863.

Chemical Injury Information Network, a "nonprofit support and advocacy organization for people with MCS and other chemical injuries that provides medical, scientific, and government information to empower the chemically injured." Publishers of the monthly newsletter "Our Toxic Times." PO Box 301, White Sulphur Springs MT 59645, USA. Tel: 406-547-2255, fax: 406-547-2455. http://biz-comm.com/CIIN/

Chemical Sensitivities Disorders Association (CSDA). "CSDA was established to provide information and support to chemically sensitive people; to disseminate information to physicians, scientists and other interested persons; and to encourage research on chemical sensitivity disorders and minimizing hazards to human health." PO Box 24061, Arbutus MD 21227, USA. Tel: 703-560-6855.

Ecological Health Organization (ECHO). "Founded in 1992, ECHO is a statewide nonprofit, advocacy, support, education, and referral organization for people in Connecticut with MCS and those who care about its prevention." PO Box 0119, Hebron CT 06248, USA. Tel: 860-228-2693. Email: ECHOMCSCT@aol.com, http://members.aol.com/ECHOMCSCT/home.html

Electrical Sensitivity Network, PO Box 4146, Prescott AZ 86302, USA. Tel: 520-778-4637. http://www.northlink.com/~lgrant/

Environmental Health Association (EHA). "EHA is a nonprofit volunteer organization offering support, information, and advocacy for people who have been injured by chemicals in the environment. They also make referrals to health practitioners in southern California, and to the American Academy of Environmental Medicine nationwide." 1800 S Robertson Blvd, Suite 380, Los Angeles CA 90035, USA. Tel: 310-837-2048. Email: ehamcs@aol.com

Environmental Health Network of California, PO Box 1155, Larkspur CA 94977, USA. Tel: 415-541-5075. http://users.lanminds.com/~wilworks/ehnindex.htm

Human Ecology Action League, Inc. (HEAL), PO Box 29629, Atlanta GA 30359, USA. Tel: 404-248-1898, fax: 404-248-0162. http://members.aol.com/HEALNatnl/index.html

MCS: Health & Environment. "This group is organized to provide support, education, advocacy, and collaboration for the chemically sensitive. They publish a bimonthly newsletter, 'Canary News,' hold meetings, and have an extensive lending library of audiotapes, videotapes, and books." 1404 Judson Ave, Evanston IL 60201, USA. Tel: 847-866-9630, fax: 847-733-0665.

MCS Information Exchange, 2 Oakland St, Brunswick ME 04011, USA.

MCS Referral and Resources, Inc., c/o Support USA, 508 Westgate Rd, Baltimore MD 21229, USA. Tel: 410-362-6400. http://www.mcsrr.org/ and http://www.cosupport.org/

National Coalition for the Chemically Injured (NCCI). "A national coalition of support groups and nonprofit service and advocacy organizations that address the needs of people with chemical sensitivity disorders. NCCI's mission is to promote and facilitate efforts among these organizations to educate the public, media, elected officials, and medical professionals about the need for greater recognition, treatment, accommodation, research, and prevention of chemical injury and chemical sensitivity disorders, especially Multiple Chemicicl Sensitivity (MCS)." 2400 Virginia Ave NW, Suite C-501, Washington DC 20037, USA. Tel: 301-897-9614; 703-533-7864; 941-756-1606; 847-746-7792. http://ncchem.com/ncci.htm/

National Center for Environmental Health Strategies, Inc. (NCEHS). Publishers of "The Delicate Balance." Mary Lamielle, Executive Director, 1100 Rural Ave, Voorhees NJ 08043, USA. Tel: 609-429-5358. Email: wjrd37a@prodigy.com

North Carolina Chemical Injury Network (NCCIN), 6442 Hwy 42, Bear Creek NC 27207, USA. Tel: 336-581-3471. http://ncchem.com/

Rocky Mountain Environmental Health Association, PO Box 611, Indian Hills CO 80454, USA. Tel: 303-697-9346.

Rural Disabled Assistance Foundation, Inc. (RDAF). "RDAF is a nonprofit, tax-exempt, all-volunteer organization endeavoring to assist individuals who: (1) are seriously disabled and unable to work as determined by the Social Security Administration (other determination as needed); (2) receive very low (poverty-level) government income (or less); (3) live outside the city because their medical conditions are exacerbated by urban environmental pollution; (4) have used all other allowable financial resources available; and (5) have basic living expenses that still exceed their incomes." 1647 E Prince Rd, Tucson AZ 85719, USA. Tel: 520-795-3150. Email: rdaf@juno.com.

Safe Schools. "Irene Wilkenfeld, president, is a former high school teacher who was chemically injured in a contaminated classroom, and now works as an environmental health consultant to school districts." 205 Paddington Dr, Lafayette LA 70508, USA. Tel: 318-984-2766, fax: 318-984-3342. http://www.head-gear.com/SafeSchools/

Share, Care, and Prayer, Inc. "Serves 3,400 people with Multiple Chemical Sensitivity, Chronic Fatigue Syndrome, Fibromyalgia, and Gulf War Syndrome, with a 'newcomer packet' of basic information, occasional newsletters (Christian oriented), a tape and book library, a pen pal directory for interested members, the sponsorship of an international prayer day, and information packets for churches." PO Box 2080, Frazier Park CA 93225, USA. Fax: 661-245-6614. http://www.sharecareprayer.org/

Books

Ashford, A. and C. Miller. *Chemical Exposures: Low Levels and High Stakes.* Second Edition. New York: John Wiley and Sons, 1998.

Berkson, J.B. *A Canary's Tale.* Baltimore, MD: Jacob Berkson, 1996. (Available from PO Box 2041, Hagerstown MD 21742, USA.)

Colborn, T., Dumanoski, D., and J.P. Myers. *Our Stolen Future: Are We Threatening our Fertility, Intelligence, and Survival? A Scientific Detective Story.* NY: Penguin, 1997.

Duehring, C. and C. Wilson. *The Human Consequences of the Chemical Problem.* White Sulphur Springs, MT: TT Publishing, 1994. (Available from the Chemical Injury Information Network, PO Box 301, White Sulphur Springs MT 59645, USA. Tel: 406-547-2255.)

Gibson, P.R. *Multiple Chemical Sensitivity: A Survival Guide.* Oakland, CA: New Harbinger Publications, 1999.

Lawson, L. *Staying Well in a Toxic World: Understanding Environmental Illness, Multiple Chemical Sensitivity, Chemical Injury, and Sick Building Syndrome.* Chicago: Lynnword Press, 1993.

McCormick, G. *Living with Multiple Chemical Sensitivities: Narratives of Coping (working title).* Jefferson, NC: MacFarland & Co., 2000.

Randolph, T.G. and R.W. Moss. *An Alternative Approach to Allergies.* NY: Harper Collins, 1990.

Rogers, S.A. *The EI Syndrome: An Rx for Environmental Illness.* Syracuse, NY: Prestige Publishers, 1986.

Temple, T. *Healthier Hospitals: A Comprehensive Guide to Assist in the Medical Care of the Patient with Multiple Chemical Sensitivity.* Parma, OH: Toni Temple and the Ohio Network for the Chemically Injured (ONFCI), 1996. Available from PO Box 29290, Parma OH 44129, USA.

Westrom, Nancy. *The Safer Travel Directory: A Guide for the Chemically Sensitive Person.* Updated frequently, published by the author, 1501 Schooner Ln, Sebastian FL 32958, USA. Tel: 561-388-9042. Email: MCSTravel@aol.com.

Wilson, C. *Chemical Exposure and Human Health.* Jefferson, NC: MacFarland & Co., 1993.

Zwillinger, R. *The Dispossessed: Living with Multiple Chemical Sensitivities.* Paulden, AZ: The Dispossessed Project, 1997. Available from Rhonda Zwillinger, The Dispossessed Project, PO Box 402, Paulden AZ 86334, USA. Tel: 520-636-2802. Photographs with descriptive text.

Newsletters/Other

Molloy, Susan. "Best of the Reactor." A compilation culled from 11 years of the "Reactor" newsletter, of the best articles, bills, legislation, political efforts, and treatment protocols. Available as spiral bound or on disk, from the Environmental Health Network of California, PO Box 1155, Larkspur CA 94977, USA. Tel: 415-541-5075.

Montague, P. "Rachel's Environment and Health Weekly." Weekly environmental newsletter, available online at http://www.rachel.org/

Community and Old Age
Opportunities and Challenges for People Over 50

by Maria Brenton

BEING PART OF AN INTENTIONAL community in old age is a way to challenge the isolation and social exclusion that many older people experience in our youth-oriented western societies. Living in an intentional community is a way to maintain personal autonomy as well as add an active, vibrant, companionable dimension to one's later life. While group living is not everyone's cup of tea, if you are interested in it don't wait until you are really old to explore the available options. Anticipate and take action to join or start such communities while you have plenty of drive and energy for new opportunities, challenges, excitement, and personal growth. Don't wait for the future to be decided for you. Shape it for yourself. There are other people out there with whom you can share the experience.

Communities of Interest

For some people it is enough to belong to a supportive nonresidential community such as a club or network. For example, the Growing Old Disgracefully network was developed by older women specifically to address issues such as those outlined above. (This article will focus more on women than men, because women outnumber men by a ratio of three to one in extreme old age, women experience widowhood more often than men, and women are more likely than men to be poor and to be discriminated against.) In Britain, North America, Australia, and New Zealand this network offers a challenge to general expectations that older women will make a quiescent, retiring descent into old age—to be neither seen nor heard. It puts women into contact with each other to develop friendships, share ideas, time, social and recreational activities, and travel. For many women, this network offers a sufficient sense of a community for a certain phase of their lives. Groups such as Wise Old Women, a network of

Elph Morgan

"For people who plan to stay active and involved in older age, belonging to a group of people united by some common bond, ideology, or value base has much to recommend it."

Maria Brenton is a Senior Research Fellow at the University of Bristol, England, and a member of the British CoHousing Communities Foundation.

Jillian Downey

"My basic rule of thumb for defining community was: 'Is there mutual support? If you get sick or are in need, will someone notice and take care of you?'"

these are a specific type of intentional community that cater to women who want to settle temporarily between trips. I visited two of these parks while conducting research on older women's collaborative living arrangements in different countries.[2] My first question was: "Are they a community?" My basic rule of thumb for defining community was: "Is there mutual support? If you get sick or are in need, will someone notice and take care of you?" I found that alongside the many activities one would associate with mobile home or holiday park living, a strong supportive network exists. This is a real community, despite the fact that very few members live there all year round.

The relatively large traveling population of the RV parks offers scope for the formation of friendship networks and groupings based on particular interests from meditation to hiking to shooting pool. Over the years, women in these RV communities have cared for other women who are ill or dying. Members on the road have a strong sense that they are coming home to a place where they will be welcomed and drawn in. This transient community of "snowbirds" (who move south for the sun) manages to combine some of the benefits of a residential community with the attractions of a traveling way of life. It is an ideal arrangement for people over 50 who have the time and resources to live full or part-time in an RV, and who want both new challenges and support.

socially critical women aged 50+ in Amsterdam, and the Older Women's Networks in London, Toronto, and Sydney, offer stimulating involvement in public and political life in addition to support and social connections.

RV Communities

In North America, RV clubs offer a form of community that combines community of interest with transient forms of residence. These clubs are attractive to people over 50 who value adventure, self-reliance, and freedom. The RV, it should be explained for a European readership, is a recreational vehicle—the home on wheels for which North America's long tradition of covered wagons roaming wide open spaces offers such abundant scope. Dorothy and David Counts[1] estimate that there are some two million RVs traveling through North America at any one time. Touring by RV is an activity especially favored by older people who no longer have the ties of work, children, and schools. The bumper sticker, "We're Spending Our Children's Inheritance!" is a particularly gleeful reflection of the liberating effect of hitting the road in later life. RV clubs such as the Escapees, Slab City Singles, the Tin Can tourists, and RVing Women offer a sense of belonging to a specific community on the road, mutual assistance, and a social life.

A Transient Community

Through its networking activities, the RVing Women clubs founded a number of RV parks for its members. While there are thousands of RV parks in North America,

Intentional Residential Communities

Intentional residential communities are cooperative schemes purposefully set up to function as collaborative communities, rather than condominiums, which are basically a legal form underpinning a shared building. Resident control is an essential defining feature of community for the purposes of this article. Retirement homes, nursing homes, or sheltered housing for the old are often described as communities. While they may be companionable and supportive, they lack the key element of self-determination and governance that distinguishes them from intentional communities. Retirement and continuing care environments and retirement cities are an important resource base for those who choose or need to live in them, but they may or may not add up to community in a real sense. They are often the last recourse of the frail and they tend to concentrate too many people, who are united only by the fact of their aging and little else, in one place.

Utopian Communities

For people who plan to stay active and involved in older age, belonging to a group of people united by some common bond, ideology, or value base has much to recommend it. There are religious, utopian, and ecological communities both in North America and in Europe, where people grow old in a familiar environment with their own and other younger families around them. These communities are often only now, after 20 to 30 years of existence, coming to grips with the aging of their members and a new dimension of need for care and support. Where they have not been static but have bred or recruited new younger members over the years, they remain balanced and resilient. Preferable to the abrupt cessation of work enforced by many retirement systems, inter-generational communities can offer positive opportunities to stay involved and valued while gradually phasing out physical labor. However, where all have aged together and the common life of the group is based on physical labor, there is a need for such communities to take stock and make provision for the inevitable frailties of advanced age. People over 50 years of age joining or starting communities designed to be self-sufficient and labor intensive need to question how long they will be able to sustain the challenges this represents and make provision accordingly. This has been the experience of a number of groups in the Netherlands.

Cooperatives

In the less labor-intensive setting of an urban environment, there are a growing number of senior cooperatives described as "the fastest growing housing alternative in small town America."[3] As a member of an American senior cooperative commented, "Cooperative community is a lifestyle whose time has come. The elderly living out lonely years alone in a big house is no longer necessary. … I can enjoy as much or as little social life as I want but still feel secure in the knowledge that the community is always here. We do have concern for each other."[4] While it is a matter of taste whether one feels more at home in an intergenerational environment or with one's own age cohort in a senior cooperative, research into mixed age cooperatives in western Canada has found that older people in these cooperatives felt they had less say over decisions than their equivalents in seniors-only coops.[5] The voices of seniors tend to be drowned out by the demands

Jillian Downey

"… take action to join or start … communities while you have plenty of drive and energy for new opportunities, challenges, excitement, and personal growth."

of younger people. House sharing, where an older person shares his or her house with younger tenants in return for support and services, is widespread in North America. It has the advantage that the older person retains control, but it does not offer the scope and variety of social involvement found in a cooperative.

Canada has a strong tradition of housing cooperatives and some of them have been started by older people for older people. One such development in Vancouver was started by five university secretaries who were contemplating retirement and needed affordable housing. Now a flourishing cooperative in an award-winning building, this group of women and men have created a strong and challenging community where members feel a sense of responsibility for each other. A more recent development in Toronto is the OWN Co-operative developed by the Older Women's Network. It opened in 1997, after years of struggle against adverse political conditions. This 152-unit cooperative provides apartments for women and men over 45 years old and allocates a certain number of its units to disabled people and older women who have suffered abuse. The creation of this cooperative is a shining example of the energy and drive of older women. Its members are active, and live in a safe, congenial, and affordable environment.

Cohousing as Intentional Community

The cohousing movement, started in Denmark and imported to the United States by Kathryn McCamant and Charles Durrett,[6] has developed primarily through the efforts of younger families and single people, but also includes older members. Cohousing is a way of living for

Jillian Downey

People who prefer to live in intergenerational communities can grow old in an environment shared with young people and children.

tion, and for the ethos of mutual support to which members commit.

Most of these cohousing communities have not continued the cohousing tradition of eating together, although some groups do this periodically. Some of them started years ago with a collective farming model in mind, but have been unable to sustain this. Their social aim is to function as friendly neighbors and they recruit new members through a selection system based on readiness to share in the group's philosophy. There are cohousing developments in the Netherlands that cater to all ages. People who prefer this option can grow old in an environment shared with young people and children. Older people who form their own communities are making a definite choice to live with their own age-group. When I interviewed individual members and inquired into this preference, a typical response was, "We love our grandchildren but we are also glad when they go home." Many had come from environments where they felt isolated because their younger neighbors were out at work all day. It is also important for some people to share a common experience and understanding of aging. In cohousing communities with an age range of 55 to 90+ years, the groups that have been successful have taken care to spread their ages from the beginning so that they have a natural renewal process with younger recruits replacing older members who die or move on.

There is an extensive support and community education system in the Netherlands that assists older people to form these communities—including courses on group living and conflict resolution. This movement was built on the alternative culture of the 1960s and 1970s. As one cohousing member in her late seventies said, "We thought our children had had communes, so why not us? We had had enough of living in a family setup. And because the family is considered the most important cornerstone of society, the woman left on her own was threatened with no other role than that of a grandmother. Whoever didn't aspire to that quickly found herself a pitiful, isolated little old lady. And you picture yourself when you are 70 or 80, with your feminist ideas going into an ordinary old people's home!"[8]

There is a nascent cohousing group in Amsterdam of 50+ women who call themselves Now for Later. They are looking into the possibility of either converting an old warehouse or building from new to provide a mutually supportive living and working environment for lesbian women of different cultures in the city. Similarly, a group of women in London aged from their late forties to late seventies is meeting regularly to plan their own cohousing community in the capital. This will take some time to realize and they are, in the meantime, putting their efforts

those seeking to combine the privacy of their own dwellings with the advantages of shared facilities and community life in an environment that they and their companions design and control. Cooperatives may also share these characteristics, but they are frequently much larger, more physically scattered, and more oriented toward affordable accommodation. There are no cohousing communities exclusively for older people in the United States and only a few in Denmark, as far as this author knows. It is in the Netherlands where cohousing communities of older people, men and women ranging in age from 55 to 90+, have really taken off over the past 15 years. Some 200 of them are currently in existence or in the planning stage. I carried out a study of this movement in the Netherlands in 1998[7] and found their members valued them most for the "gezelligheid" (roughly translated as warmth and companionability) they provide, for the opportunities they offer for casual or regular social interac-

into community development and strengthening the bonds between their members. If they achieve their cohousing community, they will be the first such development by older people in the United Kingdom. As one member comments, "This sort of housing will break new ground. I need not be reduced to one of those sad characters that face you in old people's homes. I can grow old in good company and remain active, and when I heard of the cohousing movement, I thought—yes, I want to be part of that."[9] Only two housing cooperatives exist in Britain that have recruited older people, although there are also members of long-existing cooperatives who are aging. In the country that started the cooperative movement, the cooperative tradition does not have much of a hold and has been depressed by the rampant individualism of the past two decades. However, there are signs now of a surge of interest among older as well as younger Britons in cohousing, as a possible way of life for the future in a society that is planning to use up good land in building millions more individual houses for an ever-increasing population of singles.

Conclusion

While living in community offers many positive challenges and opportunities for people in the later years of their lives, it is not a problem-free experience. Where people share space there will always be personality conflicts, communication difficulties, and power struggles. None of the examples cited so far are exempt from this. In part, such struggles are integral to the endeavor—conflict can be dynamic and creative and should be viewed as such. Set against the difficulties of living completely alone, the potential for conflict or disagreement may be seen by many as a price worth paying for the chance of new friendships and wider interaction. Older people may also be able to bring the maturity of a lifetime of experience to the conflict resolution process. For some, this will be the wisdom distilled from having lived in communal settings in their youth. For others, it will be a new experience, but one for which they are prepared in part by living in and managing a family. The other side of the coin, however, is that many people, especially women, who are newly freed from the task of managing a family are keen to enjoy their newfound liberation and their personal space. Some of these people will face a conflict between their desire to avoid the responsibilities of a close domestic group and their need for the continuing intimacy they knew from family life.

This may be a very British perspective to end on, but the safeguarding of one's personal space and privacy is singularly important to most people over the age of 50 years, even where they are conscious of a need for community. Not only have they worked hard all their lives to create their own home, but, with the passing of years, they may have grown used to their own company and their own ter-

ritory. They are likely progressively to lose the flexibility, the ability to accept abrupt change, and the tolerance of discomfort they had in their youth. They are likely to be more set in their views and less ready to come to grips with a diversity of opinion. All these are factors that need to be considered in making choices for an alternative way of living late in life. The reality is, that for a minority of very old people who go into a form of residential care and for the very many who continue to live alone, the range of choice is extremely limited and far from comfortable. Making your own choice at a more vigorous stage of your life of a community where you are a voting shareholder is preferable to ending up with no choice. The best community for you is one where you feel you can make a real contribution, have a sense of shared control over decisions that affect you, and have a choice of compatible companions. It is where you can enjoy as much or as little social interaction as you determine, where you can have your own front door, and a sense of being in your own home. It is ideally an environment that is physically designed for you to grow older in so that you don't have to move out later. There are such communities. Where they don't exist, they can be developed. Go for it!

Endnotes

1. D. and D. Counts. *Over the Next Hill: an Ethnography of RVing seniors in North America.* Peterborough, Ontario, Canada: Broadview Press, 1996.

2. M. Brenton. *Choice, Autonomy and Mutual Support: Older Women's Collaborative Living Arrangements.* York, England: J. Rowntree Foundation and York Press, 1999.

3. Altus, Deborah. "Growing Older in Community," *Communities* magazine, No. 89, Winter 1995.

4. Carpenter, Bevelyn. "Growth and Well-Being in a Senior Co-op," *Communities* magazine, No. 89, Winter 1995.

5. Doyle, V. Unpublished Ph.D. Thesis. Vancouver, Canada: Simon Frazer University.

6. McCamant, K. and C. Durrett. *CoHousing: a Contemporary Approach to Housing Ourselves.* Berkeley, CA: Ten Speed Press, 1988.

7. Brenton, M. *"We're in Charge" CoHousing Communities of Older People in the Netherlands: Lessons for Britain?* Bristol, England: Policy Press, 1998.

8. Brenton, M. *Choice, Autonomy and Mutual Support: Older Women's Collaborative Living Arrangements.* York, England: J. Rowntree Foundation and York Publishing Services, 1999. (A quote from a member of Dutch cohousing group.)

9. Meredeen, Shirley. Growing Old Disgracefully Network, personal communication.

Children in Community
Fairyland or Fairy Tale?

by Daniel Greenberg

Come away, O human child!
To the waters and the wild
With a faery, hand in hand,
For the world's more full of weeping than
You can understand
—William Butler Yeats

SEVERAL YEARS AGO, I SET OFF on a journey to learn what has been tried, what works, and what does not work with respect to raising children in alternative communities. Though "community" takes many forms, I focused my attention on communal environments in which members live and work together. Along with an arsenal of notepads, audio tapes, survey instruments, and psychological assessments, I also brought with me my idealism, hope, and perhaps some naiveté. Looking back on it now, I realize I was really searching for utopia. What I actually found was quite a bit more complex, yet still very inspiring. In this article, I will focus on some of the benefits and challenges of child-adult friendships, shared parenting/childcare, and integration of children into community life. I hope that my observations will be relevant in a wide range of community settings and will encourage thought and discussion about this very personal and, at the same time, very public topic.

Child-Adult Friendships

Intentional communities are highly social places. Consequently, children living in these environments often form unusually independent friendships with adults who are neither their parents nor teachers. As one adult community member commented:

"When I was growing up, my parents' friends were never my friends.... There isn't that distinction, I would say, in our community.... I mean, we all know each other very well and the kids know everybody just as well as I know everybody."

"It is very important for adults in communities that share responsibilities for their children to discuss questions such as, ... what are considered appropriate and inappropriate behaviors for children?"

Dancing Rabbit

Daniel Greenberg collected material for his Ph.D. dissertation on children and education in communities by visiting and corresponding with over 200 intentional communities in the United States. He later spent a year working with children and families at the Findhorn Foundation in northern Scotland. Daniel currently lives at Sirius Ecovillage and directs college-level programs on sustainable community in the United States and abroad.

In community, such friendships do not exist solely because a child belongs to a family or attends school, but simply because two individuals enjoy spending time together. When children are able to experience adults as friends rather than caretakers, teachers, or other authority figures, the adult world becomes more demystified and real. Furthermore, children in community have access to a wide variety of role models and resource persons. They know whom to confide in, whom to ask for advice, and who will let them into the kitchen after hours:

"You know how little kids like to have books read to them. The way they learn is to have the same book read to them 15 or 20 times in a day. Usually a parent, or even two parents, can't deal with that, but here a kid can have it read to him 10 or 15 times a day—the same book over and over."

Adults, of course, also benefit from these relationships. In the larger culture, it is often difficult for childless adults to create meaningful relationships with children—unless they are teachers, or close to a relative or friend that has children. Adult friendships with children in communities tend to develop informally during mealtimes, planned events, and chance meetings around the community. The wide range of involvement available to childless adults lets them participate in the joy and the work involved in caring for children without having to assume the awesome responsibilities and obligations of becoming a parent. One nonparent went so far as to say:

"Living in community helped me make the decision not to have my own kids…. I enjoy knowing so many children so well. Today's teenagers, I knew as babies and they've always known me. It feels like I've had a small share in the raising of a big family."

There are drawbacks with communities being such social environments. For children, the omnipresence of social interactions may occasionally make it difficult for them to find time or space to be alone. Also, children are more often caught in the double bind of being told to do something by one adult, only to discover it has been forbidden by another. At other times, more than one adult may reprimand a child for the same violation of a rule or norm.

There also exists the potential for adults assuming a great deal of responsibility for, and emotional attachment to, other people's children. (One communal child calls such (male) adults "false daddies.") For the children, having an adult friend leave the community can be especially painful and confusing. This confusion was aptly described by an adult member of a group house:

Jillian Downey

"The wide range of involvement available to childless adults (in community) lets them participate in the joy and the work involved in caring for children…"

"Some of the people I'm very fond of, love dearly, and depend on for my support are mobile-type people. These people have the free choice to do what they need and wish. I may sort of see what sends them away or brings them back, but for the children its very much beyond their control, and I'm sure feels mystifying and, thus, very undependable…. I find that whenever the house becomes less stable in this way, the children relate and cling to me more and I necessarily feel more responsible for them."

The adult perspective is not dissimilar and carries its own emotional hardship. As one nonparent commented:

"Even though we pay a lot of lip service to shared child rearing, the fact is that all the parents here have legal custody over their children and it always boils down to that. Those are the people ultimately responsible for their kids; if they leave the community, the kids are going to leave with them."

While on the topic of child-adult relationships, it seems important to address, at least briefly, the issue of child abuse—physical, emotional, and sexual. While intentional communities by and large attract and screen for nonviolent members who tend to watch out for each other's welfare and safety, there is also the fact that—while this may be hard for some to accept—the same kinds of dysfunctional and dangerous behaviors we despise in the wider culture can and sometimes do happen within intentional communities. The power of denial works equally well in community, and members may be reluctant to pursue a suspicion of abuse, fearing that such a disclosure would rock the foundations of the community. It is easy to falsely believe that bad things just don't happen in community. That said, I want to iterate that the vast majority of communities, particularly those in rural environments, are exceptionally safe and may actually act as buffers between children and the violence within our broader society:

"Much of what children seem to desire most from others in their community is a sense of being included, ... of being acknowledged, ... and that their community is their home."

"This is a very safe place to raise children just as it is a very safe place to live…. When I lived in town, I was always having to be aware of where it was okay to walk after dark and where it wasn't. Or being in a laundromat late at night and having a man come in and feeling myself go all tense, you know. There's none of that here. On the property, there's a feeling of total safety and all that tension is gone. It's gone both for me personally and around my kids. If [my daughter] doesn't show up 'til half an hour after dinner starts, I'll figure she's off on a rock somewhere and forgot her watch. My first thought isn't, 'Who has accosted her on the street?' That's really nice."

Shared Parenting/Childcare

A wealth of wisdom is available to parents in most communities. Parents or childcare workers can receive helpful advice on everything from diapers to dating. As one mother stated:

"I started having them fairly young and I felt extremely isolated and like I didn't know what I was doing or how to take care of them. I didn't have a lot of people I could talk to about it. I really like sharing responsibility and decisions about the children in community."

As in extended families, those in community also benefit from sharing hand-me-downs and other resources:

"I needed new pants for my child and some Calamine lotion.

I put a note up and within 10 minutes, I had six pairs of pants, a bottle of cough syrup, and a brand new bottle of Calamine."

When communities share childcare and related tasks such as cooking, laundry, shopping, and cleaning, parents (most notably mothers) have greater freedom to pursue activities other than parenting and to be more fully engaged in work and social activities both in and out of the community. Perhaps most significantly, parents can choose to interact with children more often when they *want to* rather than when they *have to*, thus reducing burnout and enhancing the overall quality of parent-child relationships.

Similarly, the combined parental experience of multiple caregivers often facilitates more relaxed attitudes toward childhood conflicts. Consequently, overly intense parent/child relationships are often diffused that may otherwise lead to overdependency on one hand or to rebellion or even child abuse on the other. For example, one woman was really fixated on watching her child eat and telling her what to eat. The result was that the child was nervous at meals and hardly ate at all. From watching other adults and children, the mother realized that other people were not doing this to their children and they were eating more sensibly than her own child. Although she still was anxious about what her child ate, she was able to stop hounding her daughter about it and let her eat (or not eat) in peace.

The multitude of theories and practices about just about everything relating to children can occasionally turn parenting in community into a real circus. It is very important for adults in communities that share responsibilities for their children to discuss questions such as, how much authority are parents really willing to give up?; what are considered appropriate and inappropriate behaviors for children?; who disciplines children when they get out of line?; how does an adult handle a grievance with another person's child?; how much responsibility are community members *really* willing to share?

Integration Into Community

While few intentional communities have the resources to be able to offer formal schooling to their children, diverse informal learning experiences for children are ubiquitous. Children in community see adults building houses, building relationships, and building political structures. Children in community also see adult arguments, "process," and real tears. An acculturated parental "front" of omniscience and strength is difficult to maintain in such situations. Parents and other adults consequently become more human in the eyes of children. As one community member noted:

"Kids on the farm got to hear so many heavy life and death sort outs between adults, so many real-life situations, that it made them really good at understanding human nature and how to deal with it."

Practically, the range of experiences available to chil-

Jesse Moorman

"... children living in [intentional communities] often form unusually independent friendships with adults who are neither their parents nor teachers."

dren through casual participation in adult activities is astounding. Examples from a questionnaire about materials or areas used in the education of children included the following: woodworking shops, weaving studios, bike shops, indoor grolabs, organic gardens, dairy cattle, barns, house construction, kitchens, woods, streams, miles of trails for walking, and rocks for climbing.

Other respondents mentioned adult members, and also visitors, as invaluable resources for the education of children. Examples of adult activities available to children include gardening, seasonal ceremonies and rituals, recycling, spiritual practices and meditation, sweats, political activities such as rallies, tree planting, craft activities, cooking, and multitudes of formal and informal meetings and gatherings.

Furthermore, as most contemporary communities are concerned with developing a certain degree of self-sufficiency, other practical skills such as composting, food storage, incorporating solar energy into building designs, and other skills are commonly available learning experiences for these children. They have many opportunities to be included in community work projects and learn by doing.

So, with all of this social interaction, are children in community more socially and verbally mature than children living in mainstream society? I believe so. There are stories in almost every community about two and three year olds surprising adults with their social finesse and their accurate mirroring of adult behaviors.

"They, all of them, are very verbal. Boy, can they talk! They can think in the social sense. They have picked up social mores that just tickle me. I heard one of them the other day say, 'Oh you're not supposed to do that,' and an adult asked, 'Well, what should we do about it if he keeps doing that?' [He] thought about it and said, 'Well ... well, we should put up a note!' That's exactly what we do. We put up a note. Anyway, by and large the children are encouraged to develop their intelligence in a verbal way to a much greater degree than a child in [our surrounding] county would."

Despite the many and varied benefits of integrating children into the daily life of their community, few communities take full advantage of their situation. For many community members, the benefits of including children are simply not obvious or considered to be worth the trouble. Children get in the way, they slow things down, they're noisy, and they might get hurt. It takes patience, understanding, and commitment to involve children in adult-oriented activities and not all adults are interested in putting forth the required effort. One mother lamented:

"I guess the idea of children participating in the social and work activities of the community is just not as acceptable here as it could be. There are so many people who feel like they don't want to be around children. Or they want to be around them as long as they're being cute…. I think it's pretty normal in our society. We're not used to living with children any way except in families. As a society, we don't integrate children. Most of the work areas—even most living areas—aren't even safe for children. It's just not a child-friendly society out there—or here."

Without adequate social and physical support, families are likely to become dissatisfied and leave. This is especially true among communities that have a high turnover rate and/or few children. Adults who are uninterested in having children in their community, or communities struggling to survive, may well ask, "Why put all this effort into children when they end up leaving anyway?" Such "cost-benefit" analyses often lead to difficult decisions:

"Close friends of mine have come here and gotten pregnant and had to leave because they hadn't been here long enough. The community [didn't] want to support them because they [didn't] know if they [were] planning to stay or, … if they know them well enough, … to give that much support to them."

So, support of children and families within communities is not a simple matter. And yet, in many ways, the difference between a community that does not adequately support its children and one that does can be simply a matter of attitude. Much of what children seem to desire most from others in their community is a sense of being included, a sense of being acknowledged, a sense that their community is their home. It is perhaps at this basic level of acceptance that real change can happen.

Communities should, of course, realistically assess what resources (in terms of person power, money, training, and patience) they are willing to commit to children. But some of the most profound ways that they can support their children and families actually require little more than a conscious commitment and some creativity. Mutually discussed and agreed upon guidelines for children's and adults' behaviors, and a process to work with grievances and suspicions of abuse, can provide immense support to parents and increase the general awareness of children within communities. Another way to support children that requires few physical resources is to create rituals and celebrations that acknowledge and honor significant transitions within the community. A child is born, a toddler enters school, an adolescent becomes an active member, a teenager goes off to college—these are all events that have lasting meaning within a community. To honor them as such provides children and adults a sense of shared meaning and connection. And really, isn't that what community is all about?

The following guidelines are offered as a starting point for discussion about values and expectations regarding children in community.

Guidelines for Adults

If a child in our community behaves in my presence in a way that I perceive as inappropriate or dangerous, and I lovingly intervene, our community family is strengthened. I strive, therefore, to demonstrate personal responsibility for the children in my community by:
- being a positive example,
- upholding the following children's guidelines with justice and integrity,
- mindfully avoiding violence or verbal abuse,
- empowering others to do likewise.

In addition, I agree to supportively share with parents (and other individuals when appropriate) any disturbing (or inspiring) incident with a child of theirs that I have been involved in or have witnessed.

Guidelines for Children

Children are encouraged and expected to:
- abstain from intentional physical or emotional cruelty to others,
- respect others' property,
- be sensitive of their own and others' personal boundaries and safety.

Resources—Books

Faber, Adele, Elaine Mazlish, and Kimberly Ann Coe (Illustrator). *How to Talk So Kids Will Listen and Listen So Kids Will Talk*. New York: Avon Books, 1991.

Lamb, Michael E. (Editor). *Nontraditional and Traditionally Understudied Families: Parenting and Child Development*. Mahwah, NJ: Lawrence Erlbaum Assoc., 1998.

Mintz, Jerry (Editor). *National Coalition of Alternative Community Schools: The Almanac of Education Choices*. New York: Simon & Schuster, 1996.

Mental Illness in Community
What Can We Offer?

by Rajal Cohen

A STORY...

I was in college in Connecticut when I met Delancey: a strong, big-boned, graceful woman, with a proud and open carriage. When she left school to find work as an apprentice on an organic farm in Maine, I was inspired by her example. A semester later, I moved to Twin Oaks community in Louisa, Virginia. We stayed in touch, and Delancey visited and joined Twin Oaks the following fall.

Delancey suffered from bouts of severe depression. It is likely that, had the membership of Twin Oaks understood their full extent, she would not have been invited to join. Delancey had already tried to kill herself several times, but she convinced herself, and the membership team, that all that was behind her. Eventually, however, everyone knew that she was depressed and potentially suicidal.

When Delancey's condition became generally known, a number of people thought she should leave. Some were afraid they would be overwhelmed by her needs, and didn't want to risk getting emotionally attached to her. Others felt angry, and resented the phenomenon of the "sweet young thing" getting all the attention. Some declared that suicide is violence, she was potentially suicidal, and therefore she did not belong in a nonviolent community. Others were firmly convinced that we could not help Delancey and should not be trying—that only professionals stood a chance of helping her.

Still, there were many who wanted to help. We never thought of ourselves as "professionals"—she had those in town. We were her family. We formed a care group, composed of three (later four) core members and several more volunteers approved by Delancey. We had weekly lunch meetings at a picnic table slightly removed, but still visible, from the main eating area. During this time we set up a schedule of people to check in with Delancey.

These meetings were always an ordeal for her. There she was—the focus of attention as a person with special needs, in a community where she knew that many people believed that her needs were not appropriate. She told me that she often felt humiliated by her situation.

The care group took on the work of looking for other living situations. Where could Delancey go that would be more suitable? We discovered there was no place. The institutions that call themselves therapeutic communities tend to have a clear division between staff and patients, they are not democratic, and they are expensive. For $100 a day, we found a few places that just offer maintenance. Programs that include therapy cost at least $800/day. What we had was a highly intelligent and motivated adult, who functioned extremely well about half the time, and other times did not function at all. She needed to be someplace that could challenge and interest her when she was in her high-functioning mode, as well as nurture her through her hard times. She needed to be somewhere that she could make a meaningful contribution to the lives of others. Most importantly, it had to be affordable. Eventually the care group concluded that Twin Oaks was probably her best bet.

The core members of the care group also tried to act as an advocate for Delancey by negotiating through complicated community politics. We wrote reports and asked for feedback from the community. We tried to balance advocacy for Delancey with consideration for the needs of the community.

Rajal Cohen lived at Twin Oaks from 1990–94. She left to found Abundant Dawn community with a group of other experienced communitarians. She now lives at Dayspring Circle, at Abundant Dawn community (see the Community Listings). She can be reached via email: rajal@ic.org.

Delancey worked almost constantly on her own healing. She signed a contract with the health team in which she promised to continue to work toward wellness in specific ways. She participated in a sexual abuse survivors' support group in nearby Charlottesville. She saw both a therapist and a psychiatrist. She was on Prozac and Xanax. She tried to exercise regularly and eat well. When things got really bad, she checked herself into a mental hospital. Once, a few members of the care group went through extensive community process in order to receive permission to use some of their frozen prior assets (money outside the Twin Oaks style income-sharing) to send Delancey to an expensive special program for a week. Twin Oaks paid half the cost.

One doctor who worked with Delancey gave her a diagnosis of severe post-traumatic stress disorder. "Delancey's is a terminal case," she told the core group. "She will almost certainly die from it, unless she gets very expensive treatment, which you probably can't afford." The doctors at the special program had a more optimistic outlook. They diagnosed her with a dissociative disorder, and said she might eventually "grow out of it." Of course, we preferred the second prognosis.

Delancey loved Twin Oaks. She loved the land, and the people, and being able to make a difference in our little society. She toiled in the gardens in the hot summer sun, and in the forests making firewood in the winter. She milked cows in the early morning and did afternoon shifts at the sewage treatment plant. She played with the children, took food to the sick, and consoled the heartbroken. However, she fell behind in her labor contribution.

Delancey was hesitant about claiming sick hours for her depression, although often, when it was severe, she was unable to get out of bed. Even though she worked hard when she could, she was unable to meet her labor obligation to the community. After having been a member for a year, she reverted to provisional member status.

When this second provisional period was over, and she came up short again, standard community policy was followed. There was a confidential poll on whether to accept or reject her for full membership. In her words, she flunked it. Of the 90-some adult members at Twin Oaks, 19 voted to revoke her membership status. That was twice the number required, and a surprise to many of us.

At the time of the poll, I was the only core member of the care group who was home. I followed Twin Oaks' appeal policy through the regular channels. Both the membership team and the board of planners declined to take action, and my appeal ended up as an override petition on the bulletin board. If a majority of the full members signed it, Delancey would be reinstated as a member.

The petition was on the board a full week and was one name short of a majority, with several days to go. I

remember hearing rumors that this or that person was waiting until the last day to sign if nobody else did. There was a half-hearted attempt at a community meeting, but it was too late for simple conversation; everyone was waiting to see what would happen. The unusually hot July air was tense and still with the waiting.

Then one morning, Delancey didn't show up. Driving to the community's farm a few miles away, two friends and I found the orange pickup truck, still running. The auto shop exhaust hose was jammed into a fogged-up window, and the gap was stuffed with pillows. We found a bottle of prescription sleeping pills in the glove compartment, and a stiff, bloated body lying face down on the floor of the cab.

The community was torn apart: bitterly divided and churning with guilt, recriminations, anger, alienation, confusion, grief, and fear. People who had not signed the override petition were not speaking to those who had, and vice versa. Many members did not go to the funeral that we held at the Twin Oaks graveyard. Even first-time visitors to the community could feel the heaviness hanging in the air. It was terrible.

In the aftermath, which lasted a long time, there was more community process than there had been during Delancey's membership. There were separate meetings, each with an outside facilitator, for the signers of the override and the nonsigners. Each gathered as a group to vent and discuss the issue. There was a full community meeting to try to bridge the divide. There were meetings to try to change the anonymous polling system. There were discussions about whether to try harder not to accept high-risk members. Many people left the community. The impact continues, from policy changes to subtle attitude shifts to greater overall awareness, but not necessarily to answers.

Critical Factors

The Contract/Personal Responsibility

The contract Delancey signed with the health team was an important part of her continued membership at Twin Oaks. Her willingness to sign that contract, and the actions she took toward healing, demonstrated that she was willing to take responsibility for her own health. It is much harder to live with a mentally ill person who is not able to do that much.

There are, however, some problems with the contract idea. How would one determine compliance with a contract that includes such items as "Try to exercise every day," and, "Work as much as you can"? Would spending a day sick in bed be a violation of that contract? Some of the behaviors of people with mental illness seem clearly out of their control; others are less clear. Where is the

Every year more than five million Americans suffer acute episodes of mental illness.

line? How can we live in community with somebody (ill or not) who does not behave responsibly and keep commitments? In what circumstances are the standards different for the mentally ill? These are serious questions, to which I do not have the answers.

Another problem I see in the contract is an imbalance. Delancey promised to take care of herself, and the health team promised to offer limited financial support for therapy and transportation to support groups. However, there was an implication that they could have her expelled from the community if she failed to comply with the contract. There was no promise from them to officially intervene on her behalf if she was deemed to be in compliance with her contract.

"The community was torn apart: bitterly divided and churning with guilt, recriminations, anger, alienation, confusion, grief, and fear."

Discretion, Secrecy, and Sharing Information

It is hard to know how much intimate information to share in a large, nonintimate group, or how to do it appropriately. I have often wished the care group had been more discreet. On the other hand, we have been accused of having been too secretive. I think overhearing tense, low-toned conversations without knowing what was really going on was hard for many people. Some who had grown up in homes with a mentally ill family member were especially bothered.

The care group made many reports to the community, but we often heard little response. We got the sense that people hoped the issue would just go away. When the poll came, resentment and lack of information must have been widespread.

The confidentiality of the poll left Delancey's allies feeling helpless. Without knowing who wanted her to leave, or why, there was no way to have a productive conversation. Did people know how hard we had tried to find a more suitable home for Delancey? Did they have other concerns which could have been addressed if we had known about them? We will never know.

Dealing With Unusual Situations

While it is important for a community to establish policies, procedures, and precedents, it is dangerous to substitute those impersonal institutions for human caring and flexible thinking. Sometimes, going along with the regular procedure in an irregular situation has catastrophic results. The labor hole policy is designed to remove members who are lazy and don't care. Dealing with Delancey through that policy was inhumane. I wish that the care

group had been able to interrupt the institutional machinery that was treating Delancey's situation like a membership/labor problem rather than a mental illness problem. However, the culture at Twin Oaks is geared to operate in a certain way. Face to face dialogue and decision making are not expected; voting is.

The Power of Friendship

Many times, singly or together, Delancey's close friends were able to help her break through from the frozen numbness of extreme isolation to the warmth of human connection. The tools of supportive listening that some of us learned from co-counseling were of tremendous benefit to us in this. Co-counseling is a peer counseling system in which one learns to face and feel emotions such as despair or fear without giving in to them. Putting those ideas into practice with Delancey taught me what a profound difference love can make. This remains one of the most valuable lessons I have ever learned.

The Health Care System

Delancey's therapist was a caring and dedicated woman who gave Delancey her home number and allowed her to call when she was in crisis. I don't know much about her psychiatrist, but I assume he had all the requisite degrees. The mental hospital served as a last resort, a place where Delancey knew she could at least be prevented from killing herself. In the end, all these intelligent and highly trained professionals were no more able to "save" Delancey than we were.

I suppose it is possible that the most brilliant or lucky psychiatrist in the world, with all the information we could have provided, might have hit upon some magical combination of drugs that would have made the differ-

Jillian Downey

While all communities may not currently have members with disabilities, it is inevitable that this issue will come up over time. Planning ahead will help.

ence. It is just as possible, however, that there was no such miracle waiting to be found.

Acknowledging the Limits of What We Can Do

Every other time there was a death at Twin Oaks, the community members drew together to support each other in the aftermath. Delancey's death was different.

It is possible that Delancey would not have survived, no matter how much time, love, and support we gave her, and no matter how many different medications she tried. If we were to accept that her death was inevitable, then the most important question would be not, "How could we have saved her?" but rather, "How could we have kept the spirit of the community whole through the difficulties of her life and the tragedy of her death?"

What if we had treated Delancey like a person with a potentially terminal illness? Could we have graciously allowed her a few extra sick hours here and there, or a disability pension? Could the community have allowed those who loved her to give to her, without causing others to feel that justice was being violated? Could we somehow have responded to her needs as a united community, instead of a divided one?

Mental Illness in the World

Prevalence of Mental Illness

Are people with mental illness drawn to intentional community in numbers disproportionate to their prevalence in society at large? It is difficult to say. I have personally had more knowing contact with mental illness within the communities movement than outside of it, and I have heard others say the same thing. Many of us are motivated to look for another way of living partly from a feeling of not fitting in to mainstream culture. Surely that same feeling would tend to attract some people with mental illnesses. On the other hand, we get to know people more deeply when we live in community with them. It may be that we see more mental illness just because we are closer to people. Who knows how many depressed or medicated people we pass on a city street or interact with on a superficial level every day?

According to the National Alliance for the Mentally Ill (NAMI), mental illness affects 20 percent of all families in the United States. Schizophrenia and bipolar disorder affect one percent of the population each, and severe depression affects close to five percent. Alzheimer's disease affects as many as 10 percent of those over 65 years old, and as many as 50 percent of those over 85. Every year more than five million Americans suffer acute episodes of mental illness. Grouped together, mental illnesses are the number one reason for hospital admission, account for 20 percent of all hospital beds in the United States at any given time, and are responsible for more missed days of work than any single physical disorder. The mentally ill, according to various estimates, comprise from one-third to one-half of the US homeless population.

Mental Illness, Fear, and Irrationality

People don't think well when confronted with mental illness. It scares us, and we tend to want to distance ourselves from it. We have all been affected by the media portrayals of violent mentally ill people. In reality, very few mentally ill people are violent toward anyone but themselves.

Mental illness reminds us how fragile we all are. Each of us has our own carefully constructed view of the world as a stable and sensible place. To see somebody else lose that is terrifying. Many of us carry a secret fear that we, ourselves, could be crazy, and being around somebody in a psychotic state tends to intensify that fear.

Mental illness makes people angry. When we agree to live with someone, we believe that we are accepting a particular personality with which we have become somewhat familiar. When mental illness strikes, that personality may change radically, leaving us feeling cheated and betrayed.

Mental illness is bewildering. It is often hard to diagnose, and medical treatment is not always successful (as it is not always successful for other diseases, such as heart disease or cancer). It is easy to see mental illness as a murky whirlpool of confusion, endlessly sucking financial and emotional resources from the people around it. We do not want to wrestle with the difficult questions about how much we can afford to give, or when we should give up. It is easier to push the question away altogether and pretend it is not part of our world or our responsibility.

Cultural Context[1]

The amount of money spent researching mental illness lags far behind that spent on comparably devastating illness, such as cancer and heart disease. The degree to which severe mental illnesses are caused or influenced by genetics, brain injury, viral agents, early childhood abuse, life traumas, social isolation, or other factors is unknown.

Psychiatric medications have been described as a miracle of the late twentieth century. Indeed, they can enable many people with mental illness to function more or less normally. Some severely ill individuals may even get long-term benefit from carefully diagnosed medications combined with effective therapy and a healing environment. However, medications can also cause some highly unpleasant (and, in the case of antipsychotics, disfiguring) side effects. Also, they don't work for everybody, and there is evidence suggesting that certain medications may actually inhibit long-term healing processes for people with certain diagnoses.

Over the past few decades, mental institutions have been closing their doors at a rapid rate. Mental patients are stabilized on medications as quickly as possible, and then released "into the community," as hospital after hospital shuts down. Many of these people have nowhere to go, and approximately one-third of them end up in jails or on skid row. More than half are eventually readmitted to the hospital (often after a long wait), to repeat the cycle.

On the other hand, there is some anthropological evidence suggesting that people living in more tribal civilizations, where the word community has more meaning, have higher rates of spontaneous recovery from mental illness. People in nonindustrial societies who experience mental illness are generally not labeled, stigmatized, or isolated as they tend to be in our culture. They are more likely to receive the kind of nonjudgmental support from family and friends that facilitates rehabilitation. Can we, in the intentional communities movement, learn from these examples?

Worth It?

Supporting Delancey was hard work, and it was often emotionally draining. Many times over those years I, and

others who later joined Delancey's care group, set aside our day's plans in order to try to help Delancey. Often we felt that we were failing. It was a heavy burden to try to convince a person that life is worth living, but we took it up voluntarily—out of love and the sense of possibility, and because we believed it was the right thing for friends to do for each other.

Being with someone in an extreme state is tremendously informative about what it is to be human. Frightening and confusing, yes, but also deepening. Hard as it was, the whole experience was undeniably *real*. I learned about love and intimacy in a way I might never have known if I hadn't dared to get close to Delancey.

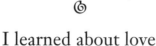

I learned about love and intimacy in a way I might never have known if I hadn't dared to get close to Delancey.

We have grown accustomed to shielding ourselves from sick people of all kinds, and even from normal aging. Finding Delancey's body stiffening in the cab of a truck on a sunny summer morning changed my understanding of life and death forever.

The only true guarantee that comes with human beings is death. All else is unknown. We cannot create utopia by throwing out the difficult surprises that people bring our way. If we were running a summer camp, we would send a sick person home. If we really want to create intentional community, however, we have to accept that we are home.

Advice for Communities

- Educate yourselves about mental illness. Pay attention to current medical research, as well as alternative theories. If you read pop psychology books, take them with a large dose of salt.

- If you or someone you know is seeking psychiatric treatment, be involved. Strongly consider taking NAMI's free 12-week program for family members of people with mental illness and subscribing to NARSAD's newsletter (see resources at the end of this article). Don't assume that a doctor or psychiatrist knows everything. Many of them do not have time to keep up with current research on everything in their fields. Find out all the names of all the medications prescribed, and do your own research.

- Talk in your community about how you would handle it if one of you developed a disability. Put this in a broad context: from Alzheimer's, AIDS, and arthritis ... through wheelchairs. What are your commitments to each other? What are the realistic limits of your resources? If members develop a serious disorder will they probably have to leave? If so, better to have it understood up front than to surprise someone with it in their time of greatest need. If a full member is forced to leave, can the community commit to helping them find another place? Encourage everyone to have a backup plan, in case it doesn't work out for them in the community. It's no good to feel trapped in a community.

- Discuss whether you want to try to screen potential members based on their risk of physical or mental illness. Realize that although you can try to manage your risks, you can't know the future. Attempts to screen out people who are potentially unstable are likely to deprive your community of some wonderful members, and some people who appear stable will develop a severe illness anyway.
- Discuss your community's attitude toward psychiatric medications and involuntary hospitalization. If a member is diagnosed with a mental illness, does taking a medication for that illness become a requirement for continued membership? If a member is acting peculiar and others are concerned or frightened, at what point will you involve the law?
- Recognize extraordinary circumstances. If you suspect that a problem with a member (such as causing disruption or failing to meet community obligations) might have a mental illness component to it, don't ignore that aspect. If your community operates by consensus of the full group, have an alternate plan for when quick response is necessary and everyone can't be gathered. Make sure that the people making the decision have as much information as possible.
- If you purchase health insurance, make sure major mental illness is covered. (Several states now have mental health care parity laws, thanks to the work of consumer advocacy groups like NAMI.)
- If you live most of your adult life in a situation in which you are not paying social security taxes, [working for room and board, or living in an income-sharing community with 501(d) tax status, for example] you may not ever qualify for social security benefits, including disability. Find out what your situation is. You may want to pay those taxes!
- Being compassionate does not require surrendering appropriate boundaries. Don't let your compassion and desire to help turn into codependence. It is not sustainable to always be willing to drop what you were planning to do in order to be with someone in crisis, especially if those crises occur frequently. It breeds resentment among the other people to whom you are responsible. Behaviors that endanger the community or other people should not be allowed.
- Create a structure that fosters trust and intimacy in your community. Set aside time and space for talking at a deeper level than is possible at the dinner table or during a business meeting. Share your stories, your fears, and your hurts, and listen to those of others. Stretch yourself a little. That way, when real crisis comes, you'll be better prepared to handle it together.

Resources

National Alliance for the Mentally Ill (NAMI) has chapters throughout the United States. They sponsor education programs, including a free 12-week course for family members of people with major mental illness, the Family to Family Education Program. Call or write to their central office for information about activities in your area. 200 North Glebe Rd, Suite 1015, Arlington VA 22203, USA. Tel: 800-950-6264. http://www.nami.org/

Global Alliance for Mental Illness Advocacy Networks (GAMIAN), c/o IDEA, Via Statuto 8, 20121 Milano, Italy. Tel: 39-02-65-3994. http://www.gamian-europe.com/

National Alliance for Research on Schizophrenia and Depression (NARSAD) provides major funding for research about depression, bipolar disorder, schizophrenia, autism, attention deficit disorder, obsessive-compulsive disorder, anorexia nervosa, drug addiction, etc. The NARSAD Research newsletter contains information on cutting-edge research. 60 Cutter Mill Rd, Suite 404, Great Neck NY 11021, USA. http://www.mhsource.com/NARSAD.html

National Institute for Mental Health (NIMH) is the US government agency responsible for researching mental illness and approving treatments. Public inquiries: 6001 Executive Blvd, Rm 8414, MSC 9663, Bethesda MD 20802, USA. Email: nimhinfo@nih.gov, http://www.nimh.nih.gov/

There are two major organizations that teach co-counseling. Both offer tools and a structure that people can use to give and receive emotional support. While their counseling techniques are similar, their organizations are quite different. Re-evaluation Counseling®: http://www.rc.org/ and Co-Counseling International: http://users.multipro.com/circle/index.html

The Process Work Center treats "extreme states" as part of a continuum on which we all exist. 2049 NW Hoyt St, Portland OR 87209, USA. Tel: 503-223-8188. http://www.processwork.org/training.htm

Books

Shorter, Edward. *A History of Psychiatry: From the Era of the Asylum to the Age of Prozac.* New York: John Wiley and Sons, Inc., 1997. (Not as well-balanced as the following reference, but easier to find.)

Warner, Richard. *Recovery from Schizophrenia: Psychiatry and Political Economy.* New York: Routledge, 1994. (Especially interesting are the chapters on schizophrenia in the third world and on antipsychotic drugs.)

Endnotes

1. Much of the information in this section came from the following: Warner, Richard. *Recovery from Schizophrenia.* New York: Routledge, 1994.

The Desire for Diversity
A Cohousing Perspective

by Zev Paiss

WHAT IS MEANT BY "DIVERSITY" can include a wide range of traits, including age, income, family structure, occupation, sexual orientation, ethnicity or race. Most cohousing communities have succeeded in attracting diversity of age, income, family structure, and occupation. Ethnic and racial diversity continues to elude these communities, even in locations where the general population is extremely diverse. Indeed, this is the case for most intentional communities in the United States, and not just cohousing communities, and as I speak about my cohousing experiences in this article, much of it can be extended to apply to the wider movement, as well.

Why We Currently Lack Ethnic and Racial Diversity in Cohousing

I believe there are basically four reasons why we are not seeing more ethnic and racial diversity within cohousing communities. The first reason may be the basic definition of what it means to be "diverse." When a new group, almost always composed of white, middle-aged professionals, sets a goal of an ethnically diverse community, they often set aside space for a "realistic" number of nonwhite households. At the Nyland community in Lafayette, Colorado, for example, the goal was to save five of our of 42 homes for nonwhite members. However, from the perspective of people of color, a diverse and thus "integrated" community may have been closer to 50 percent nonwhite.

A second, more subtle factor affecting the composition of a cohousing group is its mission statement or vision. The mere fact that a cohousing group values a certain location, shared resources, clustered dwellings, and consensus decision making, and its members have the time and ability to attend numerous lengthy meetings, greatly limits who wants to join. A cohousing group that values energy conservation and the environment assumes a range of philosophical beliefs that may not be a priority for a large portion of the wider population.

"… it is imperative for cohousing communities to focus on and celebrate the diversity that already exists within their membership."

Zev Paiss is a resident of the Nomad cohousing community in Boulder, Colorado, is the Executive Director of The Cohousing Network, and is busy along with his wife, raising their two infant daughters.

These larger principles are often apparent to newcomers considering joining a cohousing group. However, the more subtle values and lifestyle issues (including parenting and communication styles, daily schedules, eating habits, and a host of other personal preferences), can also lead to incompatibilities. Cohousing groups need to take time out to discuss these differences and how they might affect the evolution of the community, and who they might attract.

For example, Kevin Wolf, a member of the "N" Street cohousing community in Davis, California, explained in a *Denver Post* article that cohousing communities are like "native tribes, in which a clear cultural set of beliefs, philosophies, rituals, practices, and tenets become dominant, and are eventually imbued in the subconscious fiber of all who live there."

A third reason for the relative lack of diversity is that the vision being espoused by cohousing communities is in many ways contrary to the traditional, materialistic "American Dream." Owning a single-family detached house, a two-car garage, and a private yard is quite often contrary to the vision of many cohousing groups. The majority of cohousers have grown up living some version of that lifestyle and are now looking for a simpler, less materialistic, more sustainable way of life. It may be unrealistic to expect that nonwhite potential cohousing members, many of whom have grown up in limited material circumstances, are going to want to live simply if they have never had the opportunity to live out the "American Dream."

This view is reflected by an African-American member of the Tucson cohousing group, who says that most of her friends are still in the accumulation stage of their lives and are not interested in "living with less." This perspective needs to be acknowledged and the question asked: "If we truly want more diversity in our cohousing communities, are we also willing to allow a more materially accumulative value to be a part of our vision?"

I believe a fourth reason that cohousing communities are not attracting ethnic and racial minorities is because in considering the search for "community"—that longing to reconnect to family, friends, and neighbors—it is the *white* population that apparently has experienced the greatest loss of community. People of color often look at the white population in disbelief when they extol the benefits of community, because in many nonwhite communities, they've never lost it!

Suggestions for Forming Cohousing Groups

How could the perspective of ethnic and racial minorities be included in the ongoing discussions of a cohousing group? And what would it take to make cohousing communities more diverse?

Many cohousers assume that cohousing is filling an important need in the larger society. However, when approaching members of ethnic and racial minorities, it is critical to first *check* those assumptions. A short one-on-one conversation with a sympathetic person of color could save a cohousing group months of wasted effort.

Further, the initial marketing approach that a cohousing group uses can create a public image which, once established, can be very difficult to alter. I suggest that the tone of all informational materials about a particular cohousing group be targeted to the diverse populations desired for that community, whether they be single parents, families with small children, or people of color.

Established Groups: Focus on the Diversity Already Present

I believe it is imperative for cohousing communities to focus on and celebrate the diversity that already exists within their membership. Only after that has been accomplished will it be possible to take the next step. (I have seen cohousing groups struggle with much simpler aspects of diversity than ethnic or racial issues—including vegetarian and nonvegetarian, parents and nonparents, old and young, owners and renters, television watchers and book readers, A- and B-type personalities, etc.) The Nyland community, for example, was willing to address the differences of sexual preference among its members—exposing many members' beliefs, fears, and expectations—and this discussion considerably deepened and strengthened the community.

If cohousing communities can successfully establish processes to deal with and even encourage diversity within their members, they will have learned an important skill well worth sharing with the larger society.

Updated by the author and reprinted with permission from Communities *magazine, No. 85, Winter* 1994.

> People of color often look at the white population in disbelief when they extol the benefits of community, because in many nonwhite communities, they've never lost it!

Committing to Community for the Long Term

Do We Have What It Takes?

by Carolyn Shaffer

*(Adapted from the November 21, 1998 keynote address at the
FIC's Art of Community weekend conference, Willits, California)*

TWO YEARS AGO, I MADE A PERSONAL COVenant with a place and a group of people with whom I thought I would be involved for the rest of my life. At the very end of the 1996 annual fall retreat of the Shenoa Owners' Association, also known as the Shenoa Land Stewards, those of us who remained on-site conducted a personal recovenanting session. For my recovenanting, I used the traditional words of the marriage vows. I committed to Shenoa for better and for worse, for richer and for poorer, in illness and in health, until death do us part. Some of the others present made equally strong commitments. I was especially impressed with the choice of words of one man. He said, "I commit to Shenoa without reservation." Think about that—"without reservation." To me that means holding nothing back. Closing all the escape routes. And being fully there with your whole being.

I came away from this session—attended by less than half of the membership—happy, even though the earlier part of the retreat had been extremely difficult. Shenoa was facing difficulties, and conflicts, fear, distrust, and divisions were arising within our membership. But I was convinced that if even a handful of us were really committed wholeheartedly for the long term, we would find a way to survive and even thrive.

I was wrong. One year later, each of us who had been in that recovenanting session and every other co-owner in good standing voted unanimously to put our beloved 160 acres of Shenoa on the market. In essence, we decided officially to begin to end the dream that we call Shenoa, a

dream in which we had invested enormous amounts of time, energy, and money. People had stretched themselves, really stretched themselves. Financially, emotionally, and energetically, many of us, including some of the staff, went to the limit. Even with this level of commitment, we were not able to pull off the dream for more than 10 years.

We accomplished a lot in a decade. Shenoa developed a marvelous organic garden, a successful garden apprenticeship program, and a program that provided fresh, organic produce to food pantries in urban areas. In the movement toward sustainable, natural construction, Shenoa became a pioneer, building California's first code-approved, load-bearing straw bale building, enabling many others in the state to build with straw bales. Shenoa also developed and ran courses on sustainability and a thriving ElderHostel program.

Despite these accomplishments, the dream did not last. So, what does this sad story say about commitment? Does it mean you shouldn't get committed? "Better not get involved, it might end." Does it mean we Shenoans didn't have what it takes, or maybe we weren't committed enough or we weren't committed in the right way? Or perhaps other mysterious or not-so-mysterious factors led to our demise? I could go on for hours about what went wrong at Shenoa, but that's not what this piece is about. I would like to share what I learned about commitment from this Shenoa experience. The learning has been profound, and I'm not sure there was any other way I could have grasped these lessons.

Carolyn Shaffer is the coauthor of *Creating Community Anywhere* (Tarcher/Putnam, 1993), and has been involved in pioneering collaborative endeavors for 30 years. For 12 of these years she was active in the co-ownership and governance of Shenoa Retreat Center in northern California. Since 1987, she has also conducted a private practice in clinical hypnotherapy and has happily practiced the art of commitment with her husband, Sypko Andreae. Currently, Carolyn is writing a series of books about living with commitment. Contact her at: Growing Community Associates, PO Box 5415, Berkeley CA 94705, USA. Tel: 510-869-4878.

100 Mile House

"Making a full-out commitment to community is worth the effort, whether the form that emerges lasts two years or 200 years."

Forms Change Even When Commitment Remains Strong

The big insight I arrived at from my Shenoa experience is that commitment to a particular form—"until death do us part," to quote the traditional marriage vows—is a trap. It's an illusion. It's like trying to hold on to a wave in the ocean and get this wave to stand still for you so you can be comfortable and familiar with it. Forms change. They need to change, or else the organisms they embody become rigid and dead. I'll bet if you are a member of a long-term community—or if you ask any member who's been in community for 20, 30, or more years—you know that your community has died at least once or twice and been reborn, through a painful labor, into new form, even if your community has kept the same name and stayed in the same place for all these years.

One community that comes to mind is The Farm in Tennessee. I visited there in the early 1980s and thought: "This place is not going to make it." The Farm was going through especially difficult times. As I understand it, a core group of members took a hard look at The Farm's finances and structure and decided that, to survive, the community had to completely change its membership requirements. Members had to figure out ways to sustain themselves if they were going to live on the land—they couldn't just hang out at The Farm and let "mama community" sustain them. Evidently, a lot of people left. Those who stayed reworked the finances and structure, and developed fresh missions and new approaches to implementing these. From what I hear, The Farm is a stable community now, engaged in, among other things, exciting demonstrations of what an ecovillage looks like and can do.

Another example is Sirius community in Massachusetts. When Sirius was founded in the late 1970s, the community bound itself to a fairly strict ideology of communal living. Members pooled all their income and shared from a common pot. They generated a common vision and, to help implement this, they meditated regularly as a group, working on their personal and interpersonal issues, and doing their best to remove any obstacles to manifestation. Yet, in those early years, the members, collectively, were barely able to generate enough money for survival. They kept asking spirit, Why are we in this downward cycle of poverty? Why can we barely afford to buy coats for our children in winter? Finally, they realized that it may not be their attitude but their structure, especially the economic system they had developed. The members changed to a system that combined communal holding of properties with private enterprise. Within a couple of months, they experienced enormous surges of creativity and generated income much more easily, and their endeavor began thriving.

What I've learned through my experience at Shenoa and through these other examples of cooperative living is that it's not enough simply to be committed. We have to look at what we're committed to. If we're committed to a rigid form or a fixed ideology, we might be doing more harm than good to the whole endeavor. Or, we may be committed to a form that was effective for awhile but now needs to change.

Hospice Work for a Dying Organization—Another Form of Commitment

When I first joined in that vote to put the Shenoa property on the market, a part of me thought: "Oh my God, have I broken my commitment? Have I shattered those marriage vows I made only a year ago? How can I ever talk again about community and commitment? I've lost my credentials. I've blown it." Now I look at the situation differently. I realize that my experience with Shenoa, my going through almost the entire life cycle of this endeavor from birth to death, gave me insights about commitment that I would never have received if Shenoa were still growing and thriving. I was not breaking a commitment but keeping my commitment, "until death do us part," to Shenoa.

As financial and other problems arose, I began looking much more clearly at the structure as well as the essence of Shenoa. I began relating to Shenoa not just from the heart but also with my discerning head. Some had been doing this much longer than I. Over time, more and more of us came to see that the form was no longer working. I finally grasped that, if we continued on, trying to cobble things together and borrow more money—or whatever it took to keep the doors open—we would be hurting a lot of people. More and more of those invested in Shenoa, financially and emotionally, would no longer be able to afford the cost. I came to the decision that, to stay in integrity with myself, the others, and the land, I could no longer push the group to try to carry on in the face of impossible odds. Such behavior, at that point, would be neither courageous nor compassionate. I also came to see that I wasn't breaking my commitment to Shenoa by agreeing to sell the property. I was breaking through denial. And I was moving into a different phase of commitment. Finally, I was acknowledging that the organism I had vowed to stay with "in sickness and in health, until death do us part" had contracted a terminal illness. My commitment now called me to become a hospice worker for Shenoa. I and others who have chosen to stay involved during this terminal phase have the opportunity to show our love for the dream—and the form—by helping Shenoa die with as much grace and dignity as possible. Being a hospice worker for a dying organization is not a well-trod path. I certainly stumble now and then as I attempt to walk it. Yet any of you who have helped someone die know that hospice work can be a beautiful expression of commitment.

Not every participant in the Shenoa endeavor views the process as I do. Some, no doubt, believe that we should have begun the wind-down process earlier, while others feel passionately that we should have tried harder and carried on longer. A few might even consider the hospice-worker metaphor a delusion that helps some of us feel better about what we're doing. For me, the greatest challenge lies in acknowledging our differences of perspective, continually refining mine based on new information, and, in my mind, not turning those who view the situation differently into fools or monsters.

Ego-Death at Shenoa, or, the Spiritual Value of Adversity

In its dying, Shenoa has giving me a precious gift—a pearl beyond price. Acting as hospice worker for this beloved organism has opened my heart and cleared my mind to an extent I had not known before, while, at the same time, revealing how easily my heart returns to a closed position and my mind fogs over. Such positive outcomes have been hard won.

Letting go of the dream of Shenoa has been a gut-wrenching, heart-rending experience. It has called me to look at the darkest corners of my psyche, at my deepest shadow. I have been tempted to point fingers, and at times have. A part of me would love to find someone outside myself to blame. I've had to look at what my scapegoating tendency reveals about myself. I have had to watch one beautiful ego-illusion after another crumble.

I realized just how ego-attached I was to the form of Shenoa. Shenoa was my future. It was my demonstration model—the place where I would live out what I wrote in my first book on community and the place that would provide material for future books. In my heart, I had dedicated myself completely to Shenoa and soon planned to live and work there full-time. I believed that being involved with this visionary endeavor was my God-given destiny. Painfully during the dying process, I began to realize that my dedication to this vision was not as purely altruistic as I initially thought. A good part of my identification with and devotion to Shenoa was ego attachment. I wanted to make a name for myself and Shenoa. When I realized that Shenoa was coming to an end, I had to look at every one of the illusions my ego had constructed around this dream. I had to ask: "Who am I? What am I committed to now? What is commitment, really?" And I'll tell you, the freedom that came with facing these questions and shedding these illusions—as painful and humbling as the process was—is a pearl beyond price.

Community does this to you. If you want to be on a spiritual path, if you want to make great breakthroughs, stay in your community or join one or create one, because it will be a great teacher. It will be a stern teacher in many ways. Dedicating yourself to community—or to any collaborative endeavor—is a tremendous ego-breaker-downer in the best sense. If you let it, this commitment will open your heart, allow your mind to see clearly, and free you from illusion.

What Commitment Means—and Why Love Is Not Enough

Commitment is the willingness to be wholeheartedly engaged and fully honest with yourself and others for the long term. It means staying engaged and honest through good times and hard times, order and chaos, harmony and conflict. Commitment means using discernment: discernment about when telling a particular truth would be helpful and when it wouldn't, and then about when, by holding back certain things, you are hurting your soul in a way that isn't good for you and that won't be good for others. The only guide I've found to knowing when to speak up and when not to is personal integrity. When you sense you can stay in your integrity while not saying anything about a situation, you're probably being discerning and wise in holding back. But if you feel that you'd have a hard time living with yourself if you stayed quiet—that this would undermine your integrity—then the discerning thing to do is to speak up.

Commitment also means—and this is the piece that I've learned from the dying of Shenoa—being willing to disengage from a particular form when that form is no longer serving yourself, the others, or the larger whole. It means being willing to disengage when you can no longer stay in integrity with yourself while staying in that particular form. You may be able to make changes in the form so you can stay in integrity in it—or you may have to let the whole thing go.

The Buddhists say we need two wings, the wing of truth and the wing of love. Commitment has these two aspects: being wholeheartedly engaged and being fully honest. Some of us tend to be better at one than the other. The love part of commitment is about being present, giving, receiving, surrendering to the process, opening your heart, and experiencing oneness. But love alone is not enough—it must be joined by the discerning mind, by truth. The truth part of commitment requires taking a clear-eyed look at what's working and what's not working. It involves analyzing, structuring, experimenting with the structure, and restructuring when necessary. In my involvement with Shenoa, I didn't have a problem engaging wholeheartedly, but I did have difficulty seeing clearly. It took me a long time to grasp the consequences of certain aspects of the complicated structure that gave form to Shenoa. After thinking: "We have to be able to make this work, we have to, we have to," I finally got how many people it would hurt, including myself, my husband and our relationship, and many other people. When I got that, then I knew in integrity what I had to do.

What Commitment Does Not Mean

The notion of commitment is misunderstood in our culture. I'd like to break through a few stereotypes about it. First of all, commitment is not the same as duty. It's not gritting your teeth and bearing with a relationship when your heart is no longer in it—or when you're no longer able to tell the whole truth about yourself and the relationship. It's not about some "should." Commitment comes from within. It is a free choice of your heart. We've all seen marriages that last for 50 or 60 years in which the partners have hardly spoken to one another for the last two decades. That might be a long marriage in its legal form, but, to me, that's not an alive, authentic commitment.

Commitment is also not about sacrificing yourself in the sense of acting in self-destructive ways. It's not hanging in there until your health is depleted or your bank account is empty or you've lost most of your friends. It's not about burning yourself out. Commitment is to yourself and your own well-being as well as to the well-being of others and the whole. If you don't take care of yourself, you won't be in good enough shape to be available to others for the long term.

Commitment is not a trap. By its very nature, commitment is always a free and powerful choice. It's one that you review and renew regularly. It is not a one-time event. The vows I made to Shenoa two years ago in the recovenanting session were not cast in stone. Neither are the vows a husband and wife take on their wedding day, or community members make when initially forming their community. The stories above about The Farm and Sirius attest to this. The particular form a commitment takes needs to change over time to stay alive.

Commitment is also not for sissies. Commitment is not for those who hang in there only as long as it's nice and smooth and harmonious and who leave when it gets messy—or withdraw into themselves, or accommodate at all costs. It is not about always going along with others to keep things running smoothly. Authentic commitment requires standing up for your truth, but not in an aggressive or manipulative way. It's not about blaming others as soon as things go wrong or trying to take over control.

What Commitment Requires

Long-term commitment to community—or to a partner or friend—requires knowing yourself and the others, seeing yourself and them clearly and loving what you see. It's about acceptance and forgiveness; being open and vulnerable; generating trust and intimacy; and having firm, clear boundaries. The last two aspects may seem contradictory. You may wonder whether firm boundaries prevent intimacy. Actually, the opposite is true. People in a committed couple relationship or a committed community are like cells in an organ of the body. The cell requires a cell wall, a clear boundary, to perform its function in the organ. But that cell wall is smart; it's discerning. It knows what to let in and what to keep out to stay healthy and functioning. It demonstrates love and the truth working hand in hand.

Commitment also requires being courageous, being willing to stand up and speak your truth in integrity. It requires having patience and perseverance, and being there, fully engaged. Sometimes it also means not being there, knowing when you need time out for yourself and taking a personal retreat for renewal so that, when you return to your partner or your community, you can be fully engaged once again. Commitment is about finding balance. It's not about working all the time, just as it's not about playing all the time, either. It's about working, playing, and—to use a religious term—praying together. I use the word "praying" to indicate any kind of common practice that connects you with a larger whole. This might be a spiritual practice, or—for groups without an overt spiritual orientation—it could be a psychological practice, or an ecological practice. Finally, commitment involves doing all of these with joy and humor. It means lightening up at times.

Why Bother?

Building community, I believe, is one of the hardest things we can do today. It is also one of the most important. Without learning and practicing the art of living simply and sharing resources, we will not be able to reverse the ecological destruction that's going on. I don't think I have to say more about that, other than that sharing is hard. Agreeing on a common vision and mission is hard. Carrying it out is harder still. You have to deal with differences. Twenty-five years ago I decided to share my sweet little car, at that time a 1967 Volvo sedan, with a dear friend of mine. It was a disaster. She and I had totally different ideas about how to maintain a car and when to spend money on it. If we hadn't stopped sharing after a year or so, we probably wouldn't be friends today. At that time we weren't very good at working through our differences.

So it is darned hard to build community and practice sharing and work through differences. Any of you in community, even if you're sharing a house with just one other person, know how hard it is. This is where the commitment comes in: being willing to hang in there, to work through the differences, to listen to the other person's side, to share your own truth, to work it out. I had problems just sharing a car with a friend! Think about living in a residential community where you have a mortgage, buildings to take care of, childcare issues, food issues, where everyone has different child-rearing and food ideologies. Oy vey, the problems are legion!

What I can now say is that the payoffs are also legion. These can come in the form of simple pleasures: eating delicious meals together with produce from your garden; cultivating, planting, and weeding that garden as a team; sharing deeply from your heart in circles and councils. The payoffs can also come from the spiritual work of recognizing and shedding your ego-illusions. To reap these rewards you do need to engage fully. If I had not jumped into the Shenoa experience with both feet and with my heart on my sleeve, I wouldn't have gotten nearly as much out of it. If I had stood on the sidelines and kind of dipped my toe in now and then, Shenoa would have come and gone, and while other Shenoans were living fully, learning from their mistakes, and achieving breakthroughs, I would still be on the sidelines, safely and boringly the same as I had been 10 years before at the beginning. So I have no regrets about jumping in completely and engaging myself fully with Shenoa. If I had it to do over, I would engage even more fully. Next time I'd balance the business meetings with more time relating to the land and the people in non-task-oriented ways.

Making a full-out commitment to community is worth the effort, whether the form that emerges lasts two years or 200 years. Without engaging wholeheartedly and honestly for the long term, you're going to miss out on a lot. You'll learn and grow at a snail's pace. You'll miss out on the soul-satisfying experience of bonding with others in a healthy way, receiving their support and encouragement, and accomplishing together something challenging. Until

Growing your own food can be a deeply satisfying aspect of living in community.

Jillian Downey

you are committed, you are not going to generate the power for real social transformation. What you can do and be together, when aligned in love and truth, far surpasses anything you can do and be alone.

Resources

National organizations that offer workshops/trainings:
The Fellowship for Intentional Community (FIC), RR 1 Box 156, Rutledge MO 63563, USA. Tel: 660-883-5545. Email: fic@ic.org, http://www.ic.org/fic/
The Foundation for Community Encouragement (FCE), PO Box 17210, Seattle WA 98107, USA. Tel: 888-784-9001. FCE's workshops help you learn about community building through a group process based on the work of Dr. M. Scott Peck.

Books

McLaughlin, Corinne and Gordon Davidson. *Builders of the Dawn: Community Lifestyles in a Changing World.* Shutesbury, MA: Sirius Publishing, 1986.

Peck, M. Scott. *The Different Drum: Community-Making and Peace.* New York: Simon & Schuster, 1987.

Shaffer, Carolyn R. and Kristin Anundsen. *Creating Community Anywhere: Finding Support and Connection in a Fragmented World.* Tarcher/Putnam, 1993.

Corinna Bloom

About the Maps

This section contains maps showing community locations in North America. The United States maps are spread out over the next 10 pages. The maps of Canadian and Mexican communities are on page 159. Unfortunately, we were not able to include maps of any additional countries in this edition.

We have split the United States maps into regions based on some obvious groupings and on how well the various sections fit on a page. Some pages will seem somewhat sparse and others a bit crowded. We assigned each community an abbreviated name in the interest of saving space. The Chart section serves as a cross-reference for these short names. In addition to community names, the maps also show major cities, which we hope will be helpful.

The community locations are somewhat approximate. The placement is based on the postal zip code, so with rural locations the dot can be quite far removed—these maps are meant to be rough guides only. If you are going to visit some communities, please contact each community ahead of time for detailed directions.

What conclusions can be drawn from these maps? They do indicate where some of the concentrations of community activity are: the Colorado front range; San Francisco bay area; Seattle area; Asheville, North Carolina; Charlottesville and Floyd, Virginia; and others. They also seem to indicate areas that lack communities, such as the Plains states and provinces. What you should know, however, is that these maps don't show *all* the community activity—just the activity that had individual listings in this book. For example, in the northern Plains states, there are hundreds of long-standing Hutterite communities, which are all covered under only one listing. And, there are many communities that chose not to list, for reasons that we talked about in the article in the front, "What This Directory Is, and Isn't."

Finally, help keep us accurate—if you notice errors please email us at directory@ic.org.

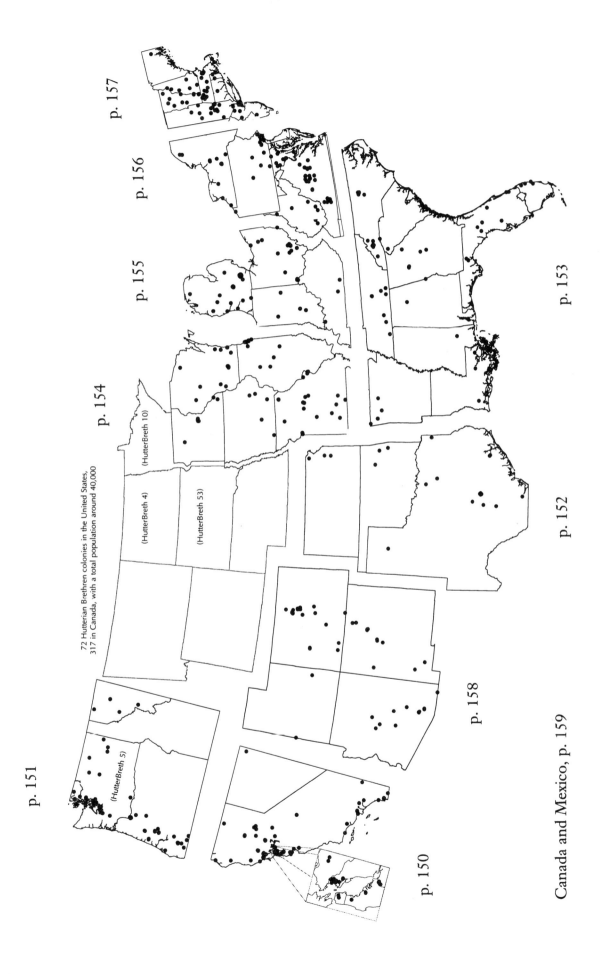

p. 157

p. 156

p. 155

p. 154

p. 153

p. 152

p. 151

p. 158

p. 150

Canada and Mexico, p. 159

(HutterBreth 10)

(HutterBreth 4)

(HutterBreth 53)

(HutterBreth 5)

72 Hutterian Brethren colonies in the United States,
317 in Canada, with a total population around 40,000

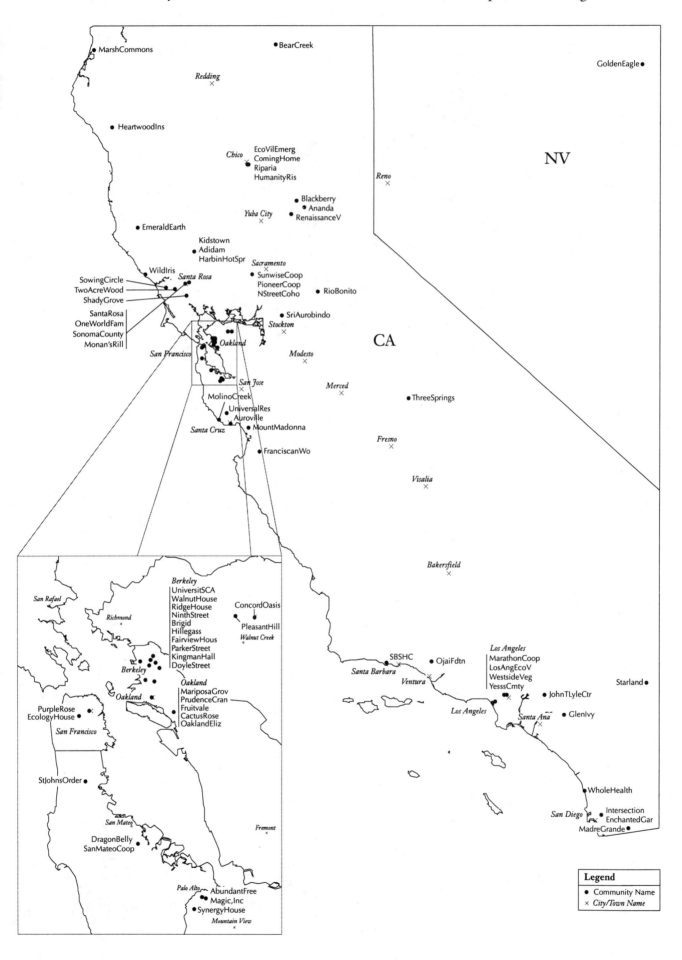

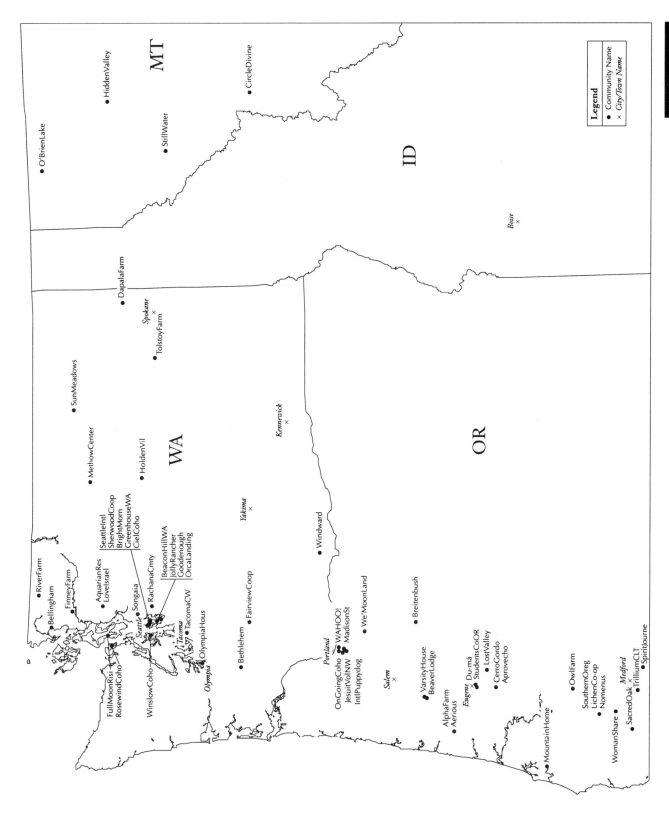

FunFamily ●

Kansas City

KS

Topeka
× *Lawrence*
RainbowHouse ●

WindWalker ●

Wichita
×

Tulsa
× ● PaganIsland

OK

SparrowHawk ●

Oklahoma City
×

ElohimCity ●

Amarillo ● PeaceFarm
×

Lawton
×

Wichita Falls
×

Lubbock
×

● RainbowValTX

MariposaGrp ●

Fort Worth *Dallas*
× × JonahHouse
●

Longview
×

Abilene
×

Odessa
×

TX

Waco
×

Temple
×

RainbowHeart ●

Austin ━━ ICC-Austin
● StudentHerit
Whitehall
Sunflower
SenecaFalls

● ChristHills

Houston
TomorrowsBrd ●
TeramoTexas ●

San Antonio
AlphaOmega ●

Legend
● Community Name
× *City/Town Name*

CorpusChrist ●

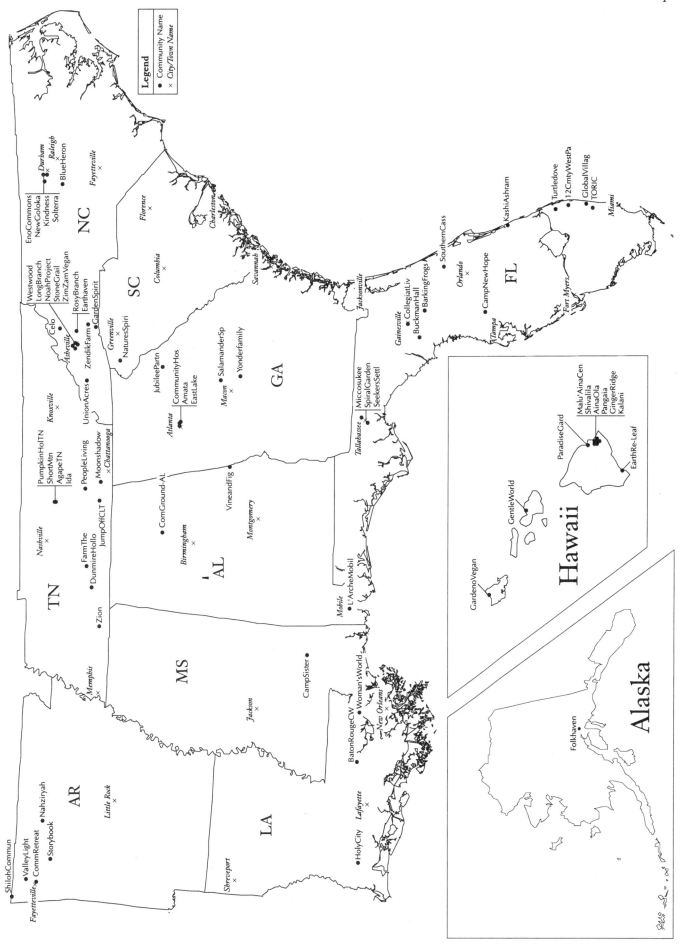

Legend
• Community Name
× City/Town Name

NC
EnoCommons
NewGoloka
Kindness
Solterra
Durham ×
Raleigh ×
BlueHeron
Fayetteville ×

Florence ×
Charleston

SC
Columbia ×

Westwood
LongBranch
NoahProject
StoneGrail
ZimZamVegan
RosyBranch
Earthaven
GardenSpirit
Celo
Asheville ×
ZendikFarm
Greenville ×
NaturesSpiri

Savannah

GA
JubileePartn
ComunityHos
Amata
EastLake
Macon ×
SalamanderSp
Yonderfamily
Atlanta ×

Knoxville ×
UnionAcres
PeopleLiving
Moonshadow
Chattanooga ×
Ida
AgapeTN
ShortMtn
PumpkinHolTN

TN
Nashville ×
FarmThe
DunmireHollo
JumpOffCLT
Zion

Birmingham ×

AL
ComGround-AL
VineandFig
Montgomery ×

L'ArcheMobil
Mobile ×

MS
Jackson ×
CampSister

Woman'sWorld
BatonRougeCW
New Orleans ×

AR
ShilohCommun
ValleyLight
Fayetteville ×
CommRetreat
Nahziryah
Storybook
Little Rock ×
Memphis ×

LA
HolyCity
Lafayette ×
Shreveport ×

Jacksonville

SouthernCass
Gainesville ×
CollegiatLiv
BuckmanHall
BarkingFrogs
Orlando ×
CampNewHope

FL
Tampa
Fort Myers
KashiAshram
Turtledove
12CmtyWestPa
GlobalVillag
TORIC
Miami

Hawaii
Malu'AinaCen
Shivalila
AinaOla
Pangaia
GingerRidge
Kalani
ParadiseGard
EarthRe-Leaf
GentleWorld
GardenoVegan

Alaska
Folkhaven

153

ChesterCreek

• Nishnajida

• CamphillMinn
Saint Cloud
×

MN

CommunityOne   *Minneapolis*
MontereyCoho
BoschCoop
DaytonHouse

• RiverHayven   *Wausau*
×
Eau Claire
×
• ChristineCtr

Green Bay

Appleton
×

WI

Rochester
×   WiscoyValley

ZephyrValley •   *La Crosse*
×

Sheboygan
HighWind •   ×

• DreamtimeVil

• Wellspring

• DancingWater

Madison   LothlorienWI   *Milwaukee*
MadisonCC   SummitAvenue   • CasaMariaCW
FairOaksCoho   OfekShalom   Sichlassenfa
PhoenixCoop   BlackWalnut
Martha'sHous   FriendsCo-op   • Watersmeet
EmmaGoldman
YaharaLinden

Waterloo   *Dubuque*
×   ×

Rockford
×

IA

Cedar Rapids
• HawkCircle

Chicago
AcmeArtists
StFranCW-IL
RebaPlace
JesusPeople
Chicago   StoneSoup
•   MaxWoodInst
YorkCenter •   Covenental
SuCasaCW
QumbyaCoop
VivekanandaV

Iowa City
• RiverCity

Des Moines   *Davenport*
×   ×

Joliet
×

• SkunkValley

• PlowCreek

• Maharishi

IL

Peoria
• WilliamStrCW

• StrangersCW

Bloomington
• ClareHouse

SandhillFarm • • DancingRabbt
Skyhouse

Champaign
• StJudeCW

• SaintsChrist

Springfield   *Decatur*
×   ×

Saint Joseph
×

MO

Kansas City
×   • Glendower
•   Hearthaven

EsseneSkoola

Columbia
CaveCreek •   × • ColumbiaCoHo
TerraNova   • Shepherdsfie

Saint Louis
VillageInThe
KarenHouseCW
CoLibriUrban

• Sunnyside

• 12CmtyLakeOz

• Nasalam
Springfield
×

Joplin
×   • Sweetwater

• EcoCityProj   • AnandaKanan

• EastWind

Legend
• Community Name
× *City/Town Name*

SongMorning

MI

MichiganWomy

MikecoRehtle

SylvironCoop   *Saginaw*
×

ICC-AnnArbor
KingHouse
MichiganSoc
VailHouse
Minnie'sCoop
JointHouse
LinderHouse
LesterHouse
OwenHouse
LutherBuchel
BlackElk
StevensHouse
O'KeefeCoop
RenaissanceC
DebsHouse
SojournerTru
Ruth'sHouse
Osterweil
Nakamura
GregoryHouse

SkyWoodsCos

Grand Rapids
GreenHouseCo

ElsworthCoop
FerencyCo-op
BealHouse
LivingROCK
BowerHouse
NewCommunity

LandSteward

Lansing
×

VivekanandaM

Kalamazoo
LakeVillage
×

Ann Arbor
×

Detroit
×

ElderWood

HeiWa
Henderson
SouthEMECO
SunwardCoho
ZenBuddhist

Heartlight

Toledo

Cleveland
CathWorkOH

Gary
×

Fort Wayne
×

IN

Akron
HouseofPeace

Canton
OhioBio-Envi
×

OH

Lafayette
GlenwoodCoop

OakwoodFarm

Homestead

Columbus
×

Indianapolis
×

Dayton   ValeThe
×

SharingCmty   Edges
Athens   FarValley
LocustGrove   CarpenterVil
SusanBAnthon

Bloomington
LothlorienIN

Cincinnati   CommunityHou
NewJerusalem
COMNGround

HillTopFarm

Padanaram

Louisville
×

Lexington
×

Evansville
ZionUCC

KY

CedarHollow

SpiralWimmin

Legend
● Community Name
× *City/Town Name*

155

Legend
• Community Name
× City/Town Name

Western NY

• Birdsfoot
• Ness

Rochester

Syracuse UnityKitchen
• RaphaCmty
NewEnviron

Buffalo ×

• AbbeyGenesee

• 12CmtyHambur

• CommonPlace

Ithaca Watermargin
• EcoVilCohoNY
StewartLittl

• Panterra

Erie L'ArcheErie

Binghamton × Zacchaeus

PA

• JulianWoods
State College ×

• Hermitage

Allentown ×

Pittsburgh ×

Philadelphia
CasaAmistad
Greenwood
LifeCenter
EternalCause
AdultFellow
YogodaCmty
FatherDivine

• GreeningLife *Harrisburg* ×

CamphillKimb
CamphillSolt
CamphillSpec

• BrynGwelec

Montclaire •

• NewVrindavan

TanguyHomest

Philadelphia

• Hundredfold

Wilmington

Cumberland *Hagerstown* × • Heathcote

• LibertyVil
• EcoVilLoudou *Baltimore*

• Wygelia

• BaltimorCoho

MD

CathWorkMD

Washington DC

DE

TakomaVil

DorothyDayCW
FamilyThe

• JupiterHollo

WV

VA

Charleston ×

• WoodburnHill

• Gesundheit!

• StFranCW-VA

Innisfree *Charlottesville*
× MaatDompin
ShannonFarm • CreeksideVA

TwinOaks
LearnersTrek

HorizonsEcoV
ComGround-VA NewLand • Springtree
NorthMount • Quarries

• AcornCmty
LittleFlower

• AshlandVine

• HighHorizons
• Sassafras

• LIFE • Yogaville

Richmond ×

Lynchburg ×

Roanoke ×

• NewRiverVal

PodofDolphin AbundantDawn
Floyd DayspringCir
• LightFreedom Tekiah
ZephyrFloyd
KynHeartH
HighFlowing

Norfolk

Downeast
SEADSofTruth
FormingCmty

ME

Bangor × ● Heartsong

12CmtyIsland ●
● EarthHeartCe
Burlington × ● GoodrichFarm ● 12CmtyLancas
● HuntingtnOWL ● BurchHouse

Eastern NY VT

QuarryHill ● ● BlueMoonCoop ● DancingBones
● 12CmtyRutlan NH

UnknownTruth ● ● NamastéGreen
● AtlantisRisi *Portland* ×

EarthSeed ● *Portsmouth* ×
12CmtyBellow ●
Adirondack ● ● 12CmtyCambr ●
Kanatsiohare ● LesbianGaySp *Manchester*
FaerieCamp ● × Monadnock
● RoweCamp MA ●
Albany ×
StarseedCmty ● ● HealingGrace
12CmtyOakHil ● PotashHill ● NewViewCoho ●
12CmtyCrox ● ● Sirius
CamphillTrif ● PioneerVal ● *Boston*
12CmtyPalen ● PumpkinHolNY ● *Amherst* × *Worcester* CambridgCoho
WiseWomanCtr ● ● CantineIsld CamphillUSA ● AgapeMA ● × SaintsFranci *Boston* CommonThread
CamphillNA ● *Springfield* × ShimGumDoZen
Turtlesisl ● 12CmtyBoston
Sivananda ● *Hartford*
Poughkeepsie × ● StMartinCW *Providence* ● BrownAssoc
CT × StJosephCW ●
RI *New Bedford* 12CmtyHyan ●
New Haven × *Groton* × AlchemyFarm ●
FellowshipCo ● *Bridgeport* ×

SphereLight ●
New York
TibetanBuddh ●
New York
MaYogaShakti
EmmausCmty
Women'sArt
FreetheLand
Ganas

Trenton × NJ

Meadowdance ●

Atlantic City ×

Legend
● Community Name
× *City/Town Name*

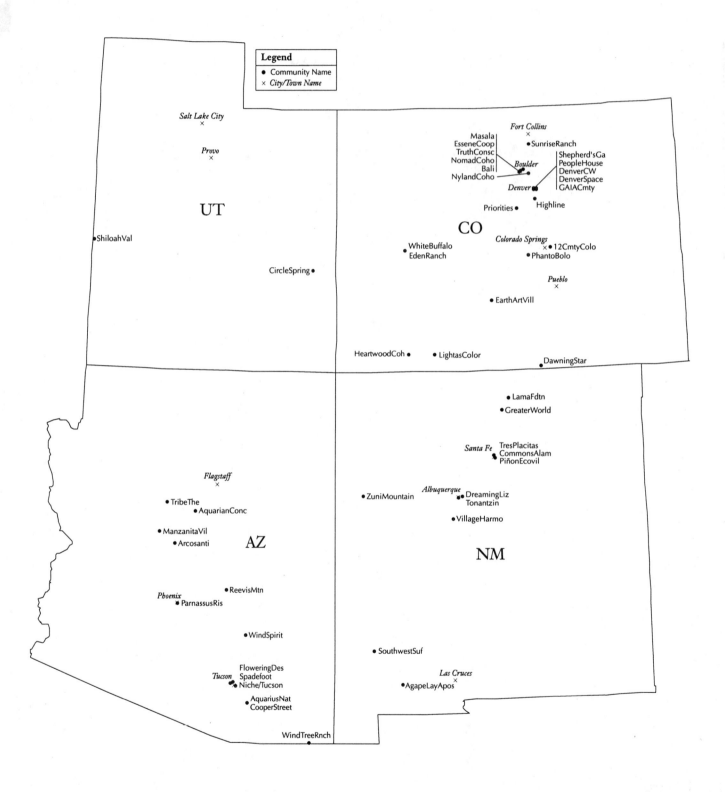

Legend
- Community Name
- × City/Town Name

Salt Lake City ×

Provo ×

UT

• ShiloahVal

CircleSpring •

Fort Collins ×

Masala
EsseneCoop
TruthConsc
NomadCoho
Bali
NylandCoho

Boulder •

• SunriseRanch

Shepherd'sGa
PeopleHouse
DenverCW
DenverSpace
GAIACmty

Denver •

Priorities •   • Highline

CO

WhiteBuffalo •
EdenRanch

Colorado Springs ×   × 12CmtyColo
• PhantoBolo

Pueblo ×

• EarthArtVill

HeartwoodCoh •   • LightasColor

• DawningStar

• LamaFdtn
• GreaterWorld

Santa Fe • TresPlacitas
CommonsAlam
PiñonEcovil

Flagstaff ×

• TribeThe
• AquarianConc

• ManzanitaVil   AZ
• Arcosanti

• ZuniMountain   Albuquerque • DreamingLiz
Tonantzin

• VillageHarmo

NM

Phoenix • ReevisMtn
• ParnassusRis

• WindSpirit

• SouthwestSuf

FloweringDes
Tucson Spadefoot
• Niche/Tucson

Las Cruces ×
• AgapeLayApos

• AquariusNat
CooperStreet

WindTreeRnch •

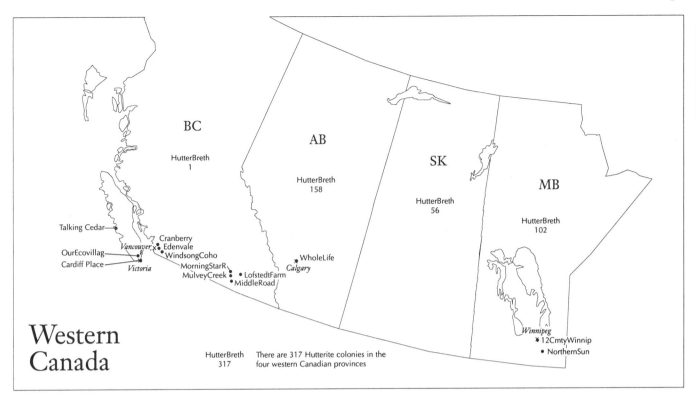

Western Canada

BC

HutterBreth
1

AB

HutterBreth
158

SK

HutterBreth
56

MB

HutterBreth
102

Talking Cedar
Cranberry
Edenvale
Vancouver
OurEcovillag
WindsongCoho
Cardiff Place
Victoria
MorningStarR
MulveyCreek
LofstedtFarm
MiddleRoad

WholeLife
Calgary

Winnipeg
12CmtyWinnip
NorthernSun

HutterBreth
317

There are 317 Hutterite colonies in the
four western Canadian provinces

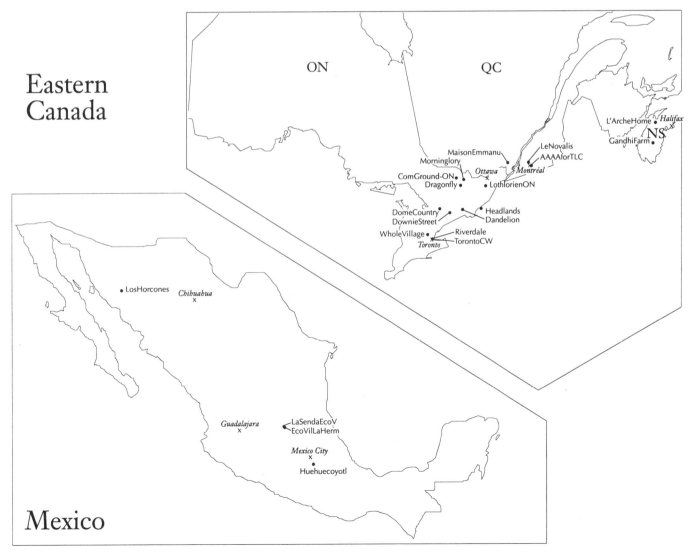

Eastern Canada

ON

QC

L'ArcheHome
Halifax
NS
GandhiFarm

LeNovalis
MaisonEmmanu
AAAAforTLC
Morninglory
Ottawa
Montréal
ComGround-ON
Dragonfly
LothlorienON

DomeCountry
DownieStreet
Headlands
Dandelion
WholeVillage
Riverdale
Toronto
TorontoCW

Mexico

LosHorcones
Chihuahua

Guadalajara
LaSendaEcoV
EcoVilLaHerm

Mexico City
Huehuecoyotl

Key to Communities by Country/State/Province

W HAT FOLLOWS is a list of the communities in this book alphabetized by state or province within each country. In addition to the United States, Canada, and Mexico there are 20 other countries represented. If you are interested in looking for communities within a particular state, begin your search here and then look up the communities in the Cross-Reference Chart (a highlighter pen is handy for this) or in the Community Listings section. There are 10 communities that chose not to list their location and are included at the end of this list. In addition, a number of communities chose not to list their city names, in which case we used a dash instead.

The abbreviated community names are used in the Maps, in the Index, and are also used on right-hand pages in the Cross-Reference Chart, where the left-hand page contains the full names.

For each entry in this list, the abbreviated community name is followed by a comma, and then the city/town associated with the community's mailing address.

United States

AK–Alaska
Folkhaven, Wasilla

AL–Alabama
ComGround-AL, Blountsville
L'ArcheMobil, Mobile
VineandFig, Lanett

AR–Arkansas
CommRetreat, Fayetteville
Nahziryah, Yellville
ShilohCommun, Sulphur Springs
Storybook, Pettigrew
ValleyLight, Deer

AZ–Arizona
AquarianConc, West Sedona
AquariusNat, Vail
Arcosanti, Mayer
CooperStreet, Vail
FloweringDes, Tucson
ManzanitaVil, Prescott
Niche/Tucson, Tucson
ParnassusRis, Phoenix
ReevisMtn, Roosevelt
SacredMtn, –
Spadefoot, Tucson
TribeThe, Paulden
WindSpirit, Winkelman
WindTreeRnch, Douglas

CA–California
AbundantFree, Palo Alto
Adidam, Middletown
Ananda, Nevada City
Auroville, Santa Cruz
BearCreek, Fall River Mills
Blackberry, North San Juan
Brigid, Berkeley
CactusRose, Oakland
ComingHome, Chico
ConcordOasis, Concord
DoyleStreet, Emeryville
DragonBelly, San Mateo
EastBayCoho, Oakland
EcologyHouse, San Francisco
EcoVilEmerg, Chico
EmeraldEarth, Boonville
EnchantedGar, San Diego
FairviewHous, Berkeley
FranciscanWo, Salinas
Fruitvale, Oakland
GlenIvy, Corona
HarbinHotSpr, Middletown
HeartwoodIns, Garberville
Hillegass, Berkeley

HumanityRis, Chico
Intersection, San Diego
JohnTLyleCtr, Pomona
Kidstown, Middletown
KingmanHall, Berkeley
LosAngEcoV, Los Angeles
MadreGrande, Dulzura
Magic,Inc, Stanford
MarathonCoop, Los Angeles
MariposaGrov, Oakland
MarshCommons, Arcata
MolinoCreek, Davenport
Monan'sRill, Santa Rosa
MountMadonna, Watsonville
NinthStreet, Berkeley
NStreetCoho, Davis
OaklandEliz, Oakland
OjaiFdtn, Ojai
OneWorldFam, Santa Rosa
ParkerStreet, Berkeley
PioneerCoop, Davis
PleasantHill, Pleasant Hill
PrudenceCran, Oakland
PurpleRose, San Francisco
RenaissanceV, Penn Valley
RidgeHouse, Berkeley
RioBonito, Sutter Creek
Riparia, Chico
SanMateoCoop, San Mateo
SantaRosa, Santa Rosa
SBSHC, Isla Vista
ShadyGrove, Penngrove
SonomaCounty, Santa Rosa
SowingCircle, Occidental
SriAurobindo, Lodi
Starland, Yucca Valley
StJohnsOrder, South San Francisco
SunwiseCoop, Davis
SynergyHouse, Stanford
ThreeSprings, North Fork
TwoAcreWood, Sebastopol
UniversalRes, Ben Lomond
UniversitSCA, Berkeley
WalnutHouse, Berkeley
WestsideVeg, Los Angeles
WholeHealth, Cardiff
WildIrisRnch, Jenner
YesssCmty, Venice
Yohana, –

CO–Colorado
12CmtyColo, Colorado Springs
Bali, Boulder
DawningStar, Weston
DenverCW, Denver
DenverSpace, Denver
EarthArtVill, Moffat

EdenRanch, Paonia
EsseneCoop, Boulder
GAIACmty, Denver
HeartwoodCoh, –
Highline, Littleton
LightasColor, Pagosa Springs
Masala, Boulder
NomadCoho, Boulder
NylandCoho, Lafayette
PeopleHouse, Denver
PhantoBolo, Cripple Creek
PhoenixCmty, –
Priorities, Pine
Shepherd'sGa, Denver
SunriseRanch, Loveland
TruthConsc, Boulder
WhiteBuffalo, Paonia

CT–Connecticut
StMartinCW, Hartford

DC–Washington DC
DorothyDayCW, Washington
FamilyThe, Washington

FL–Florida
12CmtyWestPa, West Palm Beach
BarkingFrogs, Sparr
BuckmanHall, Gainesville
CampNewHope, Zephyrhills
CollegiatLiv, Gainesville
GlobalVillag, Boca Raton
KashiAshram, Sebastian
Miccosukee, Tallahassee
SeekersSettl, Tallahassee
SouthernCass, Cassadaga
SpiralGarden, Tallahassee
TORIC, Margate
Turtledove, Jupiter

GA–Georgia
Amata, Atlanta
CommunityHos, Decatur
EastLake, Decatur
JubileePartn, Comer
SalamanderSp, Haddock
Yonderfamily, Jeffersonville

HI–Hawaii
AinaOla, Pahoa
EarthRe-Leaf, Naalehu
GardenoVegan, Hilo
GentleWorld, Paia
GingerRidge, Kapoho
Kalani, Pahoa
Malu'AinaCen, Kurtistown
Pangaia, Pahoa
ParadiseGard, Hilo
Shivalila, Pahoa

IA–Iowa
HawkCircle, Cedar Rapids
Maharishi, Fairfield
RiverCity, Iowa City
SkunkValley, Ackworth
StrangersCW, Maloy

IL–Illinois
AcmeArtists, Chicago
ClareHouse, Bloomington
Covenental, Chicago
EsseneSkoola, Golden Eagle
JesusPeople, Chicago
MaxWoodInst, Chicago
PlowCreek, Tiskilwa
QumbyaCoop, Chicago
RebaPlace, Evanston
StFranCW-IL, Chicago
StJudeCW, Champaign
StoneSoup, Chicago
SuCasaCW, Chicago
VivekanandaV, Chicago
WilliamStrCW, Peoria
YorkCenter, Lombard

IN–Indiana
GlenwoodCoop, W Lafayette
LothlorienIN, Bloomington
OakwoodFarm, Selma
Padanaram, Williams

KS–Kansas
FunFamily, Robinson
RainbowHouse, Lawrence
Windwalker, Ottawa

KY–Kentucky
CedarHollow, Edmonton
SpiralWimmin, Monticello
ZionUCC, Henderson

LA–Louisiana
BatonRougeCW, Baton Rouge
HolyCity, Lake Charles
Woman'sWorld, Madisonville

MA–Massachusetts
12CmtyBoston, Dorchester
12CmtyHyan, Hyannis
AgapeMA, Ware
AlchemyFarm, Hatchville
CambridgCoho, Cambridge
CommonThread, Somerville
HealingGrace, Shelburne Falls
NewViewCoho, Acton
PioneerVal, Amherst
PotashHill, Cummington
RoweCamp, Rowe
SaintsFranci, Worcester

ShimGumDoZen, Boston
Sirius, Shutesbury
StarseedCmty, Savoy

MD–Maryland
BaltimorCoho, Baltimore
CathWorkMD, Silver Spring
EcoVilLoudou, Frederick
Heathcote, Freeland
LibertyVil, Libertytown
TakomaVil, Bethesda
WoodburnHill, Mechanicsville
Wygelia, Adamstown

ME–Maine
Downeast, Bar Harbor
FormingCmty, Lubec
Heartsong, Orono
SEADSofTruth, Harrington

MI–Michigan
BealHouse, E Lansing
BlackElk, Ann Arbor
BowerHouse, E Lansing
DebsHouse, Ann Arbor
ElderWood, Manchester
ElsworthCoop, E Lansing
FerencyCo-op, E Lansing
GreenHouseCo, Grand Rapids
GregoryHouse, Ann Arbor
Heartlight, Sturgis
HeiWa, Ann Arbor
Henderson, Ann Arbor
ICC-AnnArbor, Ann Arbor
JointHouse, Ann Arbor
KingHouse, Ann Arbor
LakeVillage, Kalamazoo
LandSteward, Columbiaville
LesterHouse, Ann Arbor
LinderHouse, Ann Arbor
LivingROCK, E Lansing
LutherBuchel, Ann Arbor
MichiganSoc, Ann Arbor
MichiganWomy, Walhalla
MikecoRehtle, Big Rapids
Minnie'sCoop, Ann Arbor
Nakamura, Ann Arbor
NewCommunity, East Lansing
O'KeefeCoop, Ann Arbor
Osterweil, Ann Arbor
OwenHouse, Ann Arbor
RenaissanceC, Ann Arbor
Ruth'sHouse, Ann Arbor
SkyWoodsCos, Muskegon Heights
SojournerTru, Ann Arbor
SongMorning, Vanderbilt
SouthEMECO, Ann Arbor
StevensHouse, Ann Arbor
SunwardCoho, Ann Arbor
SylvironCoop, Blanchard
VailHouse, Ann Arbor
VivekanandaM, Fennville
ZenBuddhist, Ann Arbor

MN–Minnesota
BoschCoop, Minneapolis
CamphillMinn, Sauk Centre
ChesterCreek, Duluth
CommunityOne, Edina
DaytonHouse, Saint Paul
MontereyCoho, Saint Louis Park
WiscoyValley, Winona
ZephyrValley, Rushford

MO–Missouri
12CmtyLakeOz, Warsaw
AnandaKanan, Willow Springs
CaveCreek, Boonville
CoLibriUrban, Saint Louis
ColumbiaCoHo, Columbia
DancingRabbt, Rutledge
EastWind, Tecumseh

EcoCityProj, Reeds Spring
Glendower, Independence
Hearthaven, Kansas City
KarenHouseCW, Saint Louis
Nasalam, Fair Grove
SaintsChrist, Trenton
SandhillFarm, Rutledge
Shepherdsfie, Fulton
Skyhouse, Rutledge
Sunnyside, Mokane
Sweetwater, Mansfield
TerraNova, Columbia
VillageInThe, Saint Louis

MS–Mississippi
CampSister, Ovett

MT–Montana
CircleDivine, Stevensville
HiddenValley, Bigfork
O'BrienLake, Eureka
StillWater, Plains

NC–North Carolina
BlueHeron, Pittsboro
Celo, Burnsville
Earthaven, Black Mountain
EnoCommons, Durham
GardenSpirit, Tryon
Kindness, Durham
LongBranch, Leicester
NewGoloka, Hillsborough
NoahProject, Leicester
RosyBranch, Black Mountain
Solterra, Durham
StoneGrail, Alexander
UnionAcres, Whittier
Westwood, Asheville
ZendikFarm, Mill Spring
ZimZamVegan, Asheville

NH–New Hampshire
12CmtyLancas, Lancaster
AtlantisRisi, Bradford
BurchHouse, Bethlehem
DancingBones, Wentworth
Monadnock, Temple
NamastéGreen, Ctr Barnstead

NJ–New Jersey
Meadowdance, Cherry Hill
SphereLight, Morristown
TibetanBuddh, Washington

NM–New Mexico
AgapeLayApos, Deming
CommonsAlam, Santa Fe
DreamingLiz, Albuquerque
GreaterWorld, Taos
LamaFdtn, San Cristobal
PiñonEcovil, Santa Fe
Pro-Fem, –
SouthwestSuf, Silver City
Tonantzin, Albuquerque
TresPlacitas, Santa Fe
VillageHarmo, Bosque
ZuniMountain, Ramah

NV–Nevada
GoldenEagle, Carlin

NY–New York
12CmtyCambr, Cambridge
12CmtyCrox, Coxsackie
12CmtyHambur, Lake View
12CmtyOakHil, Oak Hill
12CmtyPalen, Palenville
AbbeyGenesee, Piffard
Adirondack, Galway
Birdsfoot, Canton
CamphillNA, Copake
CamphillTrif, Hudson
CamphillUSA, Copake

Cantinelsld, Saugerties
CommonPlace, Truxton
EcoVilCohoNY, Ithaca
EmmausCmty, New York
FellowshipCo, Spring Valley
FreetheLand, New York
Ganas, Staten Island
Kanatsiohare, Fonda
MaYogaShakti, New York
Ness, Hermon
NewEnviron, Syracuse
Panterra, Westfield
PumpkinHolNY, Craryville
RaphaCmty, Syracuse
SimeonCenter, –
Sivananda, Woodbourne
StewartLittl, Ithaca
TurtlesIsl, Stanfordville
UnityKitchen, Syracuse
UnknownTruth, Warrensburg
Watermargin, Ithaca
WiseWomanCtr, Woodstock
Women'sArt, Poughkeepsie
Zacchaeus, Binghampton

OH–Ohio
CarpenterVil, Athens
CathWorkOH, Cleveland
CommunityHou, Norwood
COMNGround, Cincinnati
Edges, Glouster
FarValley, Amesville
HillTopFarm, Vinton
Homestead, Granville
HouseofPeace, Akron
LocustGrove, Creola
NewJerusalem, Cincinnati
OhioBio-Envi, Canton
RavenRocks, –
SharingCmty, South Bloomingville
SusanBAnthon, Athens
ValeThe, Yellow Springs

OK–Oklahoma
ElohimCity, Muldrow
PaganIsland, Tulsa
SparrowHawk, Tahlequah

OR–Oregon
Aerious, Deadwood
AlphaFarm, Deadwood
Aprovecho, Cottage Grove
BeaverLodge, Corvallis
Breitenbush, Detroit
CerroGordo, Cottage Grove
Du-má, Eugene
IntlPuppydog, Portland
JesuitVolNW, Portland
LichenCo-op, Wolf Creek
LostValley, Dexter
MadisonSt, Portland
MountainHome, Coquille
Nomenus, Wolf Creek
OnGoingCoho, Portland
OwlFarm, Roseburg
SacredOak, Selma
SouthernOreg, Sunny Valley
SpiritJourne, Ashland
StudentsCoOR, Eugene
TrilliumCLT, Jacksonville
VarsityHouse, Corvallis
WAHOO!, Portland
We'MoonLand, Estacada
WomanShare, Grants Pass

PA–Pennsylvania
AdultFellow, Wayne
BrynGweled, Southampton
CamphillKimb, Kimberton
CamphillSolt, Glenmoore
CamphillSpec, Glenmoore
CasaAmistad, Philadelphia

EternalCause, Philadelphia
FatherDivine, Gladwyne
GreeningLife, Shermans Dale
Greenwood, Lansdowne
Hermitage, Pitman
Hundredfold, Orrtanna
JulianWoods, Julian
L'ArcheErie, Erie
LifeCenter, Philadelphia
Montclaire, Lancaster
TanguyHomest, Glen Mills
YogodaCmty, Philadelphia

RI–Rhode Island
BrownAssoc, Providence
StJosephCW, Foster

SC–South Carolina
NaturesSpiri, Salem

TN–Tennessee
AgapeTN, Liberty
DunmireHollo, Waynesboro
FarmThe, Summertown
Ida, Smithville
JumpOffCLT, Sewanee
Moonshadow, Whitwell
PeopleLiving, McMinnville
PumpkinHolTN, Liberty
ShortMtn, Liberty
Zion, Selmer

TX–Texas
AlphaOmega, San Antonio
ChristHills, Blanco
CorpusChrist, Sandia
ICC-Austin, Austin
JonahHouse, Garland
MariposaGrp, Bivins
PeaceFarm, Panhandle
RainbowHeart, Burnet
RainbowValTX, Sanger
SenecaFalls, Austin
StudentHerit, Austin
Sunflower, Austin
TeramoTexas, Houston
TomorrowsBrd, Houston
Whitehall, Austin

UT–Utah
CircleSpring, Moab
ShiloahVal, Eskdale

VA–Virginia
AbundantDawn, Floyd
AcornCmty, Mineral
AshlandVine, Ashland
ComGround-VA, Lexington
CreeksideVA, Charlottesville
DayspringCir, Floyd
HighFlowing, Floyd
HorizonsEcoV, Nellysford
Innisfree, Crozet
KynHeartH, Floyd
LearnersTrek, Louisa
LIFE, Gladstone
LightFreedom, Willis
LightMorning, –
LittleFlower, Goochland
MaatDompin, Charlottesville
NewLand, Faber
NewRiverVal, Blacksburg
NorthMount, Lexington
OakGroveFdtn, Round Hill
OneSpirit, Clifton
PodofDolphin, Check
Quarries, Schuyler
ShannonFarm, Afton
Springtree, Scottsville
StFranCW-VA, Spotsylvania
Tekiah, Floyd
TwinOaks, Louisa

Yogaville, Buckingham
ZephyrFloyd, Floyd

VT–Vermont

12CmtyBellow, Bellows Falls
12CmtyIsland, Island Pond
12CmtyRutlan, Rutland
BlueMoonCoop, White River Junction
EarthHeartCe, East Johnson
EarthSeed, Putney
FaerieCamp, Brattleboro
GoodrichFarm, Hardwick
HuntingtnOWL, Huntington
LesbianGaySp, Brattleboro
QuarryHill, Rochester

WA–Washington

AquarianRes, Arlington
BeaconHillWA, Seattle
Bellingham, Bellingham
Bethlehem, Chehalis
BrightMorn, Seattle
CielCoho, Seattle
DapalaFarm, Elk
FairviewCoop, Seattle
FinneyFarm, Sedro Woolley
FullMoonRisi, Freeland
Goodenough, Seattle
GreenhouseWA, Seattle
HoldenVil, Chelan
JollyRancher, Seattle
LoveIsrael, Arlington
MethowCenter, Twisp
OlympiaHous, Olympia
OrcaLanding, Seattle
RachanaCmty, Redmond
RiverFarm, Deming
RosewindCoho, Port Townsend
SaltCreek, Port Angeles
SeattleIntl, Seattle
Sharingwood, Snohomish
SherwoodCoop, Seattle
Songaia, Bothell
SpokaneHutt, Reardan
SunMeadows, Tonasket
TacomaCW, Tacoma
TolstoyFarm, Davenport
WalkerCreek, Mount Vernon
Windward, Klickitat
WinslowCoho, Bainbridge Island

WI–Wisconsin

BlackWalnut, Madison
CasaMariaCW, Milwaukee
ChristineCtr, Willard
DancingWater, Gays Mills
DreamtimeVil, La Farge
EmmaGoldman, Madison
FairOaksCoho, Madison
FriendsCo-op, Madison
HighWind, Plymouth
LothlorienWI, Madison
MadisonCC, Madison
Martha'sHous, Madison
Nishnajida, Three Lakes
OfekShalom, Madison
PhoenixCoop, Madison
RiverHayven, Colfax
Sichlassenfa, Milwaukee
SummitAvenue, Madison
Watersmeet, Mukwonago
Wellspring, Newburg
YaharaLinden, Madison

WV–West Virgnia

Gesundheit!, Hillsboro
HighHorizons, Alderson
JupiterHollo, Weston
NewVrindavan, Moundsville
Sassafras, Hinton

Argentina

12CmtyBuenos, Buenos Aires
ChacraMillal, El Bolson
ProyectoEcoV, Buenos Aires

Australia

12CmtySydney, Picton NSW
BackyardTech, Macleay Island QLD
CascadeCoho, South Hobart Tasmania
Cennednyss, Summertown SA
Co-ordCo-op, Near Nimbin NSW
CrossroadsMe, Yass NSW
CrystalWater, Maleny QLD
Gabalah, Chillingham NSW
JesusChrist, Sydney South NSW
MolloyAshram, Mt Molloy NQ
MtMurrindal, W Tree VIC
OshoMevlana, Myocum NSW
RosneathFarm, Dunsborough WA
Shamballa, Bellingen NSW
SunriseFarm, W Tree VIC

Austria

RatandTat, Frauendorf

Belgium

DeRegenboog, Brussels
LaVieilleVoi, Liège

Brazil

12CmtyLondri, Londrina, Paraná
12CmtyQuatro, Quatro Barras, Parana
LothlorienBR, Palmeiras, BA

Canada

AB–Alberta

WholeLife, Calgary

BC–British Colombia

CardiffPlace, Victoria
Cranberry, Burnaby
Edenvale, Abbotsford
LofstedtFarm, Kaslo
MiddleRoad, Nelson
MorningStarR, Winlaw
MulveyCreek, Slocan
OurEcovillag, Shawnigan Lake
TalkingCedar, Tofino
WindsongCoho, Langley

MB–Manitoba

NorthernSun, Sarto

NS–Nova Scotia

12CmtyWinnip, Winnipeg
GandhiFarm, Queens County

ON–Ontario

ComGround-ON, Killaloe
Dandelion, Enterprise
DomeCountry, Barrie
DownieStreet, Peterborough
Dragonfly, Lake Saint Peter
Headlands, Stella
L'ArcheHome, Wolfville
LothlorienON, Ompah
Morninglory, Killaloe
Riverdale, Toronto
TorontoCW, Toronto
WholeVillage, King

QC–Québec

AAAAforTLC, Montreal
LeNovalis, Auteuil, Laval
MaisonEmmanu, Val Morin

Colombia

Atlantis, Tolima

Denmark

Hertha, Galten
Hesbjerg, Blommenslyst
Mørdrupgård, Lynge
Svanholm, Skibby
Udgaarden, Sabro
Valsølillegå, Jystrup

France

12CmtydeSus, Sus-Navarenx
CommduPain, Valenciennes
CommdeLArche, Roqueredonde
TaizéCmty, Taizé

Germany

12CmtyOberbr, Stodtlen-Oberbronnen
12CmtyPennin, Osterholz-Scharmbeck
BreadandRose, Hamburg
DolphinCmty, Hausen im Wiesental
FreieChrist, Lüdenscheid
Kana-Gemeins, Dortmund
Lebensgarten, Steyerberg
Märchenzentr, Vlotho
Niederkaufun, Kaufungen
OekoLeA-Ulos, Klosterdorf
ProjektEulen, Wasserburg/Bodensee
ProWoKultA, Frankfurt
UFA-Fabrik, Berlin
ZEGG, Belz

Greece

NewHum, Kalamata

India

Atmasantulan, Maharashtra

Israel

KibbutzKetur, DN Eilot
KibbutzLotan, DN Chevel Eilot
KibbutzMvmt, Kibbutz Kfar Menachem
KibbutzNeotS, DN Eilot
KibbutzTamuz, Beit Shemesh
NeveShalom, DN Shimshon

Italy

Arcobaleno, Napoli
Damanhur, Baldissero Canavese TR
Hairakhandi, Pietralunga PG
Nomadelfia, Grosseto
OshoMiasto, Frosini Siena
Utopiaggia, Montegabbione TR

Japan

Ittoen, Kyoto
Yamagishi, Ayama-gun Mie

Mexico

EcoVilLaHerm, San Miguel de Allende
Huehuecoyotl, Morelos
LaSendaEcoV, San Miguel de Allende
LosHorcones, Hermosillo

Netherlands, The

DeHobbitstee, HW Wapserveen
EmmausHaarz, SJ Haarzuilens
Landelijke, HE Utrecht
WeystThe, SV Handel

New Zealand

AwaawaroaBay, Waiheke Island
CreeksideNZ, Christchurch
HeartwoodCom, Christchurch
OtamateaEcoV, Kaiwaka
RainbowValNZ, Takaka
Riverside, Nelson
TuiLandTrust, Takaka
WaitakereEco, Auckland

Nigeria

Palmgrove, Abak AKS

Northern Ireland

CamphillClan, Co Tyrone
CamphillMour, Co Down
Columbanus, Belfast

Poland

AssocEarth, Staroscin

Portugal

Tamera, Colos

Russia

Aleskam, Kamchatka

Spain

12CmtySanSeb, San Sebastian
ElBloque, La Nucia
ElSemillero, Madrid
Guayrapá, Montral (Tarragona)

Sweden

KadeshBiyqah, Arvika
Lindsbergs, Falun
Stiftelsen, Stjärnsund
Tullstugan, Stockholm
Wäxthuset, Väddö

Switzerland

MonteVuala, Walenstadtberg
ZentrumWalde, Wengen

United Kingdom

England

12CmtyStentw, Devon
AshramCmty, Sheffield
BarnThe, Devon
BeechHill, Devon
BirchwdHall, Worcs
CamphillPenn, W Yorkshire
CoraniHousin, Leicester
Cornerstone, W Yorkshire
Earthworm, Shropshire
Frankleigh, Wilts
GrailCmty, Middx
Grimstone, Devon
Gwerin, W Midlands
LeeAbbeyAsto, Birmingham
LittleGrove, Bucks
LosangDragpa, Todmorden
LowerShaw, Wilts
MonktonWyld, Dorset
NewCreation, Northampton
OthonaCmty, Essex
Pathfinder, London
PlantsFuture, Cornwall
SimonCmty, London
Skyros, London
SteppingSton, Yeovil
TownHead, Sheffield
TwoPiers, E Sussex

Scotland

CamphillNewt, Aberdeen
Findhorn, Forres
Iona, Argyll
IsleofErraid, Argyll
KitezhChildr, Forres
Laurieston, Castle Douglas

Wales

CentreforAlt, Powys
ChickenShack, Gwynecki
CwrtyCylchau, Lampeter
FoxHousing, Carmarthen Dyfed

No Location

12CmtyNet
BacktoLand
BeisAharon
DeltaInfinit
East-West
LakeClaire
RainbowPeace
SocietyCreat
TaoWorksVil
TenStones

Nathaniel White

About the Cross-Reference Chart

The first step in compiling the information necessary to make this book was to send out a questionnaire to every community we knew about. We printed them up and sent them out at the end of 1998 and throughout 1999, and did our best to remind communities about the *Directory* and encouraged them to participate. The widespread use of email, which is a big change since we did the last edition of the *Directory* in 1995, was helpful in that process.

We then compiled these charts from some of the questions on our eight-page questionnaire. Not all the questions from the survey are in the charts; we used the ones we thought were most relevant and useful to *Directory* readers.

For each entry, the date that the community submitted their questionnaire is indicated. Some information (such as total population) may be outdated quickly, while other figures (such as year founded) are stable. Other information (such as diet) can be misleading in its simplicity when the reality is usually very complex. As mentioned before, tbe FIC is not in a position to verify the data each community submitted about itself. We suggest using the data as a guide while keeping in mind that this is just a snapshot of how that community saw itself at the date listed.

The first column on the right-hand page is the community name abbreviation that we use on the Maps, the Key to Communities by State/Province/Country, and in the Index. The Chart serves as a cross-reference for the short names.

An empty space by a community name indicates that they did not fill out the data section of the questionnaire, and we only received a text description from them.

Communities Directory: A Guide to Intentional Communities and Cooperative Living

	State/Prov. or Country	Forming, Reforming	Year Formed	Year Purchased	Year Began Living	Open to More Adults?	Open to More Children?	Total Population	# Adults	# Children (<19yrs)	Percentage Women	Identified Leader	Leadership Core Group	How are Major Decisions Made?	Join Fee?	Income Shared/Indep.	Who Owns Land	Survey Date
Abbey of the Genesee	NY		1951	1951	1951	Y	n	40	40		0%	Y	Y	C L	N	S	cmty	Sep99
Abundant Dawn Community	VA		1994	1997	1995	Y	y	12	10	2	70%	N	N	C	N		cmty	Sep99
Abundant Freek	CA	F	Dec98			Y	y	2	2		0%	N	N	C	N			Dec98
Acme Artists Community	IL	F	1992	1996		Y	y	28	24	4		Y	Y	C	Y		n profit	Jan99
Acorn Community	VA		1993	1993	1993	Y	m	16	12	4	67%	N	N	C	N	S	cmty	Sep99
Adidam	CA		1972	1973	1973	Y	y	1085	1060	25	40%	Y	Y	C M L E	N		cmty	Sep99
Adirondack Herbs	NY		1990	1982		Y	y	6	6		33%	N	Y	O	N	I	other	Aug99
Adult Fellowship Condo Community	PA																	
Aerious / YewWood	OR										50%	Y	Y	E	N	I	indiv	Nov98
Agape	MA	RF	1982	1982	1982	Y		3	2	1	67%	Y	Y	C	N		indiv	Jan99
Agape Community	TN		1972	1972	1972	Y	y					Y		C	N		cmty	Sep99
Agape Lay Apostolate Community	NM		1972	1980	1972	Y	y	23	10	13	47%	Y	Y	E	N	I	cmty	Sep99
AinaOla	HI	F	Mar99	1998	Mar99	Y	y	3	3		33%	N	Y	C	N		mix	Aug99
Alchemy Farm Cohousing	MA	F	1991	1991	1996	Y	y	26	18	8	50%	N	N	C	N	I	other	Aug99
Aleskam	[ru]		1991			Y	y	94	48		47%	Y	Y	C	N	I		Apr99
Alpha Farm	OR		1972	1972	1972	Y	y	19	12	7	33%	N	Y	C	N	S	cmty	Aug99
Alpha Omega Christian Communities...	TX	F				Y	y					Y		M	Y	I		Jan99
Amata Community	GA		1976	1988		N	n	14	13	1	46%	N	Y	C E O	N	I	indiv	Aug99
Ananda	CA		1968	1968	1968	Y	y	263	193	70	51%	Y	Y	M E	N	I	cmty	Jan99
Ananda Kanan Ozark Retreat Center	MO		1984	1983	1984	Y	y	10	10		0%	Y	Y	L	N		cmty	Feb99
Aprovecho Research Center	OR		1976	1981	1981	M	m	15	14	1	43%	N	N	C	N	I	mix	Oct99
Aquarian Concepts	AZ		1989			Y	y	110	82	28	50%	Y	Y	L E O	Y		cmty	Mar99
Aquarian Research Foundation	WA	F	1969	1978		Y	y	3	2	1	50%	Y	Y	O	N	S I	other	Sep99
Aquarius Nature Retreat	AZ		1981			Y	y	9	9	0	25%	N	Y	C	Y		indiv	Nov98
Arcobaleno Fiammeggiante (Tribe)	[it]	F	1986	1986	1986	Y	y	8	8		50%		Y	C	Y	S		May99
Arcosanti	AZ	F	1970	1968	1970	Y	y	52	42	10	45%	Y	Y	C M L E O	Y		mix	Jan99
Ashland Vineyard Community	VA		1983	1979	1986	N	n	23	18	5	55%	N	N	C	N		indiv	Jan99
Ashram Community	[uk]		1967			Y		40	40		55%	Y	Y	C	N		cmty	Mar99
Association for the AAAC for TLC	QC	F	Oct98			Y	y	24			60%	Y	Y	C	Y	I	clt	Oct99
Association for the Earth	[pl]		1981			Y	y	99	55	44	49%			C	N		indiv	May99
Atlantis	[co]		1970			Y	y	25	13	12	47%	Y	Y	C M L E O	N	S	cmty	Mar99
Atlantis Rising, Inc.	NH		1973	1975	1975	Y	y	7	4	3	33%	N	N	M	Y		mix	Nov98
Atmasantulana Village	[in]		1980	1982	1983	Y	y	69	57	12	61%	Y	Y	C L E	Y		mix	Oct99
Auroville	in	F	1968	1968	1968	Y	y	1300	1124	176	46%	N	Y	C M O	Y	S I	other	Sep99
Awaawaroa Bay Eco-Village	[nz]		1994			Y	y		18	14	61%	N	N	C	Y	I		Jun99
Back to the Land Community	-		1979	1979	1979	Y	y	16	10	6	50%	N		C O		I	indiv	Jan99
Backyard Tech	[au]		1985			Y	n					Y	N	L O	Y	I	other	Mar99
Bali	CO	RF	1994	1996		Y	y	5			40%	Y		C	Y	I	cmty	Dec98
Baltimore Cohousing	MD	F	May99			Y	y				60%	N	N	C				Jul99
Barking Frogs Permaculture Center	FL	F	1997	1999	1988	Y	n	2	2		50%	N	Y	C O			indiv	Feb99
Barn, The	[uk]		1980		1983									C			n profit	May99
Baton Rouge Catholic Worker	LA	RF	1994	1994	1993	Y	n	11	11		0%	N	N	C	N	I	cmty	Jan99
Beacon Hill House	WA		1996	1996	1997	Y	y	8	7	1	43%	N	N	C	N	S	clt	Sep99
Beal House Co-op	MI					Y	n	7	7	0	43%	Y	Y	M	Y	I	cmty	Aug99
Bear Creek Farms	CA	F	1985	1985	1987	Y	y	4	4		50%	Y	N	C	Y	I	other	Nov98
Beaver Lodge Incorporated	OR		1940	1930	1940	Y	n	22	22	0	0%	Y	Y	M	N		other	May99
Beech Hill Community	[uk]		1994			Y	y		12	5	75%	N	N	C	N	I		Dec99
Beis Aharon Community	-		1994			Y	y		2	3	100%	N	Y	C E	N			Feb99
Bellingham Cohousing	WA	F	1995	1997	Mar00	Y	y	46	31	15	68%	N	N	C	Y	I		Aug99
Bethlehem Peace Farm Catholic Worker	WA	F	1991	1991	1998	Y	y	7	7		43%	N	Y	C	N		ldlord	Jul99
Birchwood Hall Community	[uk]		1970			Y	y		9	1	44%	N	N	C	N			Jan99
Birdsfoot Farm	NY		1972	1972	1972	Y	y	9	6	3	50%	N	N	C	N		cmty	Oct99

KEY Canadian Provinces: BC = British Columbia, MB = Manitoba, NS = Nova Scotia, ON = Ontario, SK = Saskatchewan.
Country: [ar] = Argentina, [au]= Australia, [at] = Austria, [be] = Belgium, [br] = Brazil, [co] = Colombia, [dk] = Denmark, [fr] = France, [de] = Germany, [gr] = Greece, [in] = India, [il] = Israel, [it] = Italy, [jp] = Japan, [mx] = Mexico, [nl] = The Netherlands, [nz] = New Zealand, [ng] = Nigeria, [uk] = United Kingdom, [uk*] = Northern Ireland.
Decisions: C = Consensus, M = Majority, L = Leader, G = Group of leaders or elders, O = Other.
Income: S = Members Share Income, I = Independently Handle Own Finances.
Who Owns Land: CLT = Community Land Trust, Cmty = Community, Indiv = Individual, Ldlord = Landlord, Subgrp = Subgroup of members.
Survey Date: Date shown is when survey questionnaire was completed or last updated by community.

Map / Index Name	Eat Together How Frequently?	What % of Own Food Is Grown?	Organic Food in Diet	Dietary Norms	Alcohol Use	Tobacco Use	# Homeschooled	Some Labor Expected	Rural, Urban, or Both	# of Buildings	Acres of Land	GLB Ok	Spiritual Path	Primary Purpose and/or Focus
AbbeyGenesee	Nearly all dinners	1-5%	some	no red	some	none			R				Y	Catholic Monastic Contemplative
AbundantDawn	2-5 times/week	6-20%	yes!	no red	some	ok		X	R	5	90	GLB	N	Loving and sustainable culture
AbundantFree			yes!	omni	some	some		X					N	Food, for Freeks, culturonomic change.
AcmeArtists		None							U	3		GLB	N	artists, craftsmen, and community activists
AcornCmty	Nearly all dinners	6-20%	often	omni	ok	ok	3	X	R	3	72	GLB	N	Egalitarianism, Process
Adidam	Nearly all dinners	6-20%	yes!	vgn	some	some		X	B		1000	GLB	Y	Devotees of Adi Da Samraj
Adirondack	2-5 times/week	6-20%	yes!	omni	ok	yes!		X	R	6	210	GLB	Y	Conservation, Tolerance
AdultFellow														
Aerious	1 time/week	6-20%	yes!	vgn	ok	ok		X	R	3	15	GLB	Y	hands-on spirit/earth connexion
AgapeMA	Nearly all meals	>50%	yes!	veg	some	none			R	2	32		Y	Prayer Poverty Nonviolence
AgapeTN	2-5 times/week	1-5%		omni			1		R	6	400		Y	
AgapeLayApos	2-5 times/week	None	some	omni	yes!	none		X	R	5	10		Y	Christian Families & Service to Poor
AinaOla	Nearly all dinners	21-50%	yes!	omni	none	none		X	R	7	3	GLB	N	(Attractively) Model sustainable living
AlchemyFarm	1 time/week	6-20%	yes!	omni	some	ok			B	6	16		N	Social Care, Ecological Design
Aleskam	Rarely	None	often	veg	ok				R				N	Sustainable Development
AlphaFarm	Nearly all dinners	21-50%	yes!	omni	some	ok		X	R	6	280	GLB	N	
AlphaOmega	Nearly all meals							X	R	64	1,384		Y	Christian MCS Healing
Amata	2-5 times/week	6-20%	yes!	omni	often	some		X	B	5	2.5		N	Community, Ecology, and Health
Ananda	1-3 times/month	1-5%	yes!	veg	none	ok	3	X	R	80	760		Y	Disciples of Paramhansa Yogananda
AnandaKanan	Nearly all meals	6-20%	yes!	veg	none	none		X	R	7	66		Y	spiritual elevation and service
Aprovecho	Nearly all dinners	21-50%	yes!	no red	some	ok		X	R	7	40	GLB	N	sustainable living education
AquarianConc	Nearly all dinners	6-20%	yes!	omni	none	none		X	B	23	25		Y	Spiritual Unity/Global Change
AquarianRes	2-5 times/week	6-20%	often		ok	none	1		R		320		Y	Positive Future w/o violence or sexual repression
AquariusNat	1-3 times/month	None	ok	vgn	ok	ok	0	X	R	4	25	GLB	N	live in communion with nature
Arcobaleno	2-5 times/week	None	yes!	veg	none	none		X	U	2			Y	beauty of unity in the diversity
Arcosanti	Nearly all meals	21-50%	yes!	omni	often	often			B	12	4000	GLB	N	Building Urban Prototype
AshlandVine	1 time/week	1-5%						X	R	6	40		Y	Quaker Oriented Family Community
AshramCmty	1-3 times/month		often	no red					U	4		GL	Y	
AAAAforTLC	2-5 times/week		yes!	vgn	ok	none		X	R			GLB	Y	love, spiritual, eco/alt-tech, healing, inner truth
AssocEarth		1-5%	yes!	omni	often	yes!			R	26	123.5		N	Contact with nature, alternative lifestyle
Atlantis	Nearly all meals	>50%		veg	none	none		X	R	5	175 ha		Y	organic self-sufficient ecology
AtlantisRisi	1 time/week	6-20%	some	omni	some	ok			R	3	220	GLB	N	Sustainable agri- silvaculture
Atmasantulan	Nearly all meals	6-20%	often	veg	none	none		X	R	30	14		Y	holistic healing community
Auroville	2-5 times/week	21-50%	yes!		none	none	3		B		2700		Y	Peace/An Effective Human Unity
AwaawaroaBay	1 time/week	21-50%			none	none	1	X	R	15	420		N	Restoration & Conservation of Land
BacktoLand		21-50%	yes!	omni	some	none	5	X	R	6	287		N	living simply and in harmony
BackyardTech	Nearly all dinners	>50%	yes!	omni	none	none		X	R	2			Y	Care & share, nature & neighbors
Bali	1 time/week	None	often	no red	some	none	0		R	0	176		N	Beautiful ecological neighborhood
BaltimorCoho		None					1		U				N	cohousing in Baltimore
BarkingFrogs	Nearly all dinners	6-20%	yes!	omni	some	none			R	1.5	16		Y	
BarnThe	Nearly all dinners	21-50%		veg					R		15		Y	
BatonRougeCW	Nearly all dinners	None	some	omni	none	yes!		X	U	1		G	N	Community of hospitality
BeaconHillWA	2-5 times/week	1-5%	yes!	veg	some	ok		X	U	1		GLB	N	Sustainable activist equality
BealHouse	2-5 times/week								U	1			N	Student Housing Community
BearCreek	Nearly all meals	6-20%	yes!	omni	none	none		X	R				N	Post Y2K Homeopath 16th Century
BeaverLodge	Nearly all meals	1-5%	some	omni	ok	ok			U	1			N	College Housing for Men
BeechHill	Nearly all dinners	21-50%	yes!	no red	often		0	X	R		7		N	environmentally sustainable
BeisAharon	Nearly all dinners	None	often	omni	some	none	3	X	U				Y	Orthodox Jewish Mussar Community
Bellingham	2-5 times/week	None	some				1		U				N	urban cohousing community
Bethlehem	Nearly all dinners	21-50%	often		some	some		X	R	6	44		N	doing the works of mercy
BirchwdHall	Nearly all dinners	6-20%	often	veg	ok	none		X	R	1	8		N	enjoy living together
Birdsfoot	Nearly all dinners	21-50%	yes!	veg	ok	ok		X	R	6	73	GLB	N	Learn/Grow good food and friends

KEY *Diet:* omni = includes red meat, no red = no red meat—includes fish or poultry and dairy, veg = vegetarian—no meat—includes dairy, vgn = vegan—no meat or dairy.
Diet note: Some communities list omni and provide vegan options, some list vegan yet allow personal food without restriction. Take the label as a rough guideline.
Rural, Urban or Both: Some communities used both (B) to indicate having both an urban and rural location or that the one property was both urban and rural, as suburban.
Acres of Land: Hectare is abbreviated ha and is approximately 2.5 acres.
Some Labor Expected: Members are expected to regularly contribute labor to the group.
GLB Ok: The community indicated that gay men (G) or lesbians (L) or bisexuals (B) are welcome as members.
Spiritual Path: The community indicated it has a primarily spiritual or religious focus.

Communities Directory: A Guide to Intentional Communities and Cooperative Living

Community	State/Prov. or Country	Forming, Reforming	Year Formed	Year Purchased	Year Began Living	Open to More Adults?	Open to More Children?	Total Population	# Adults	# Children (<19yrs)	Percentage Women	Identified Leader	Leadership Core Group	How are Major Decisions Made?	Join Fee	Income Shared/Indep.	Who Owns Land	Survey Date
Black Elk Co-op	MI				1986													Oct99
Black Walnut Cooperative	WI		1986	1986		Y	y	5	5		60%	N	N	C	N		cmty	Aug99
Blackberry	CA	RF	1988	1989	1988	Y	y	4	2	2	50%	N	N	C	N	S	indiv	Sep99
Blue Heron Farm	NC		1992	1994	1995	Y	y	18	11	7	45%	N	Y	C	Y	I	cmty	Jan99
Blue Moon Cooperative Community	VT		1983	1986	1985	N	n	17	10	7	50%	N	N	C	Y	I	cmty	Jan98
Bosch Co-op	MN		1982	1982	1982	Y	n	6	6		50%	N	N	C	N	I	cmty	Oct99
Bower House Cooperative	MI		1950			Y	m	17	17		59%	N	Y	M	Y		cmty	Jul99
Bread and Roses - Base Community	[de]		1994			Y	y		6	0	67%	N	N	C	N	S		Jan99
Breitenbush Hot Springs	OR		1977	1977	1977	Y	y	42	40	2	50%	N	Y	M	Y		cmty	Nov98
Bright Morning Star	WA		1979	1986	1979	N	n	8	7	1	71%	N	N	C	N		indiv	Jan99
Brigid Collective	CA		1985	1985	1985	N	n	8	8		71%	N	N	C	N	I	subgrp	Feb99
Brown Assoc. for Cooperative Housing	RI		1970		1970	Y	n	27	27		67%	Y	Y	C	N		cmty	Aug99
Bryn Gweled Homesteads	PA		1940	1940	1940	Y		124		43	53%	N	N	C M	Y	I	cmty	Nov98
Buckman Hall Co-op	FL		1973		1973	Y	n	122	84	38	57%	Y	Y	C	N	I	other	Jan99
Burch House	NH		1979			Y		9	9		67%	Y	Y		N	I	n profit	Feb99
Cactus Rose	CA					N		5	5		60%	N	N	C	N	I	cmty	Sep99
Cambridge Cohousing	MA		1995	1997	1998	N	n	96	80	16	56%	Y	Y	C	N	I	indiv	Jul99
Camp New Hope Community	FL	F	1997	1997	1997	Y	n	7	7		14%	N	N	O	N	I	mix	Nov98
Camp Sister Spirit Folk School	MS		1993	1993		Y	m	5	4	1	100%	Y	Y	C	O	N	I	other	Sep99
Camphill Assoc. of North America	NY		1960		1961													Jul99
Camphill Community Clanabogan	[uk*]		1984			Y	y	71	55	16	50%	N	Y	C	N	S	n profit	Feb99
Camphill Community Mourne Grange	[uk*]		1971	1971	1971	Y	y	131	106	25	59%	N	Y	C	N	S	cmty	Apr99
Camphill Community Pennine	[uk]		1977			Y	y		26	8		N	Y	C	E		S		Feb99
Camphill Community Triform	NY		1978	1979	1979	Y	m	62	49	13	45%	N	Y	E	N		cmty	Sep99
Camphill Soltane	PA		1988	1988	1988	Y	y	74	65	9	50%	Y	Y	C	N	S	cmty	Apr99
Camphill Special School	PA		1963	1963	1963	Y	y	75	51	24	49%	N	Y	C	N	S	cmty	Sep99
Camphill Village Kimberton Hills	PA		1972	1972	1972	Y	y	125	101	24	50%	N	N	C	N	S I	other	Nov98
Camphill Village Minnesota, Inc.	MN		1980	1980	1980	Y	y	57	46	11	40%	N	N	C	N		cmty	Nov98
Camphill Village Newton Dee	[uk]		1960			Y	y	200			50%	N	N	C	N	S	n profit	Jun99
Camphill Village U.S.A., Inc.	NY		1961	1961	1961	Y	y	230	230		50%	N	Y	C	N		cmty	Jan99
Cantine's Island Cohousing	NY		1990	1995	1997	Y	y	28	18	10	61%	N	N	C	Y	I	mix	Dec98
Cardiff Place Cohousing Community	BC		1992	1994	1994	Y	y	27				N	N	C	N	I	cmty	Sep99
Carpenter Village	OH	F		1992		Y						N	N	M	Y	I	mix	Aug99
Casa Amistad	PA	F	1996	1996	1996	Y	p	3	3		33%	N	Y	C	N	I	indiv	Sep99
Casa Maria Catholic Worker Community	WI		1966	1966	1967	Y	y	20	13	7	36%	N	N	C	N	I	mix	Nov98
Cascade Cohousing	[au]		1991						19	6	32%	N	N	C M	Y	I		Apr99
Catholic Worker Community of Cleveland	OH		1984	1986	1986	Y	m	14				N	Y	C			other	Dec98
Catholic Worker Pretrial House	MD	F				Y	y							C	N			Sep99
Cave Creek	MO	F	1997	1998	1997	Y	y	2	2		50%	N	N	C			cmty	Feb99
Cedar Hollow Community	KY		1983	1983	1983	Y	y	5			60%	N	N		Y		clt	Jul99
Celo Community	NC		1938	1938	1939			113	73	40	50%	N	N	C	N		cmty	Nov98
Cennednyss Community	[au]		1978						10	6	50%	N	N	C	O	N			Jul99
Centre for Alternative Technology	[uk]		1973	1973	1973	M	m	12	12		33%	N	N	C M	O	N	I	other	Nov98
Cerro Gordo Community	OR		1970	1973	1974	Y	y	48	39	9	50%	N	N	M	Y		mix	Nov99
Chacra Millalen	[ar]		1990	1983	1990	Y	y	6	5	1	40%	N	N	C	N		mix	Mar99
Chester Creek House	MN	RF	1971	1981	1981	Y	n	4	4	0	100%	N	Y	C	N	I	cmty	Aug99
Chicken Shack Housing Cooperative	[uk]		1992	1995	1995	N	n	7	6	1	33%	N	N	C	Y		cmty	Sep98
Christ of the Hills Monastery	TX		1968	1975	1969	Y	y	20	19	1	0%	Y	Y	E	N	S	cmty	Aug99
Christine Center for Unitive Spirituality	WI	RF	1980	1990	1980	Y	n	8	6	2	67%		Y	C	N	I	n profit	Jan99
Ciel Cohousing	WA	F	1996	1996		Y	y	27	20	7	65%	Y	Y	C	Y	I	cmty	Jul98
Circle of Divine Unity Foundation	MT	F	1992			Y		20	18	2	63%	Y	Y	C	L E	Y		clt	Sep98
Circle Springs	UT	RF	1993	1994		Y	y	8	7	1	25%	N	Y	C	Y	I	mix	Dec98

KEY *Canadian Provinces:* BC = British Columbia, MB = Manitoba, NS = Nova Scotia, ON = Ontario, SK = Saskatchewan.
Country: [ar] = Argentina, [au]= Australia, [at] = Austria, [be] = Belgium, [br] = Brazil, [co] = Colombia, [dk] = Denmark, [fr] = France, [de] = Germany, [gr] = Greece, [in] = India, [il] = Israel, [it] = Italy, [jp] = Japan, [mx] = Mexico, [nl] = The Netherlands, [nz] = New Zealand, [ng] = Nigeria, [uk] = United Kingdom, [uk*] = Northern Ireland.
Decisions: C = Consensus, M = Majority, L = Leader, G = Group of leaders or elders, O = Other.
Income: S = Members Share Income, I = Independently Handle Own Finances.
Who Owns Land: CLT = Community Land Trust, Cmty = Community, Indiv = Individual, Ldlord = Landlord, Subgrp = Subgroup of members.
Survey Date: Date shown is when survey questionnaire was completed or last updated by community.

Chart

Map / Index Name	Eat Together How Frequently?	What % of Own Food Is Grown?	Organic Food in Diet	Dietary Norms	Alcohol Use	Tobacco Use	# Homeschooled	Some Labor Expected	Rural, Urban, or Both	# of Buildings	Acres of Land	GLB Ok	Spiritual Path	Primary Purpose and/or Focus
BlackElk														
BlackWalnut	2-5 times/week	1-5%	yes!	veg	ok	ok		X	U	1		GLB	N	cooperative housing
Blackberry	Nearly all dinners	1-5%	yes!	no red	ok	ok	1	X	R	6	50	GLB	N	Ecology, homeschool, extended family
BlueHeron	1-3 times/month	6-20%	yes!	omni	some	ok	2	X	R	7	64	GLB	N	ecological & psychological sustainability
BlueMoonCoop	1-3 times/month	1-5%	yes!	no red	yes!			X	R	5	165		N	Cooperation and conviviality
BoschCoop	1 time/week	1-5%	yes!	veg	ok	none		X	U				N	cooperative community house
BowerHouse	Nearly all dinners	1-5%	yes!	veg	none		O	X	B	1		GLB		live cooperatively
BreadandRose	Nearly all meals	None	some	veg	ok	ok			U				Y	Community household with homeless refugees
Breitenbush	1 time/week	None	yes!	veg	ok	ok	2		R	22	86		N	Service Health Growth
BrightMorn	Nearly all dinners	1-5%	yes!	omni	some	ok			U	1		L	N	Supportive gay-friendly family
Brigid	2-5 times/week	None	yes!	no red	ok	none			U	1			N	communication support activism
BrownAssoc	Nearly all dinners	1-5%	yes!	veg	yes!	often		X	U	2			N	to live cooperatively
BrynGweled	1-3 times/month	1-5%							B	74	240	GLB	N	Cherish Diversity Neighborhood
BuckmanHall	Rarely	None	ok	vgn	ok	ok			U	1			N	Inexpensive living for students
BurchHouse	Nearly all dinners	6-20%	often	omni	none	none		X	R	1	13		N	Therapeutic residential community
CactusRose	Nearly all dinners	1-5%	yes!	no red	some	none		X	U	1		B	N	Social, progressive, and artsy
CambridgCoho	2-5 times/week	None	yes!	omni	often	none	O	X	U	41		GLB	N	
CampNewHope	Nearly all dinners	None							R	6	3		N	Recovery Home & SSI on disabilities/homeless
CampSister	Nearly all meals	None	ok	omni	none			X	R	6	120	GLB	N	Experiential learning, all volunteer, cmty-based
CamphillNA													Y	Spiritual Social Renewal Care
CamphillClan	Rarely	>50%	yes!	omni	none	ok			R	8	70		Y	living and working together
CamphillMour	Nearly all meals	21-50%	yes!	omni	none	ok		X	R	18	80		Y	Mentally and physically disadvantaged
CamphillPenn	Nearly all meals	>50%	yes!	omni	ok	ok		X	B		35		Y	Camphill Community - Anthroposophy
CamphillTrif	Nearly all meals	21-50%	yes!			some			R	7	125		Y	anthroposophy
CamphillSolt	Rarely	1-5%	yes!	omni	none	some	O		R	8	50	GLB	Y	for developmentally disabled young adults
CamphillSpec	Rarely	1-5%	yes!	omni	none	ok			R	11	70		Y	
CamphillKimb	Rarely	21-50%	yes!	omni	ok	ok		X	R	18	430	GLB	Y	Anthroposophy / Lifesharing
CamphillMinn	Rarely	>50%	yes!	omni	some	some	6	X	R	7	450		Y	Live with special needs adults
CamphillNewt	Nearly all meals	6-20%	yes!	omni	none			X	B	~25	170		Y	Anthroposophical community
CamphillUSA	Nearly all meals	21-50%	yes!	omni					R	20	750		Y	
Cantinelsld	2-5 times/week	1-5%	yes!	omni	often	none	2	X	U	12	8	L	N	Private homes and shared commons
CardiffPlace	2-5 times/week	None	some	omni	ok			X	U	2			N	creating community together
CarpenterVil									R		50		N	Ecovillage/permaculture/outreach
CasaAmistad	Nearly all meals	1-5%	often	omni	none	none		X	U			GLB	Y	God, community, transformation
CasaMariaCW	Rarely	1-5%	yes!	omni	none	some	4		U	5			Y	
CascadeCoho	2-5 times/week	1-5%	often				O	X			15		N	Cohousing to develop sense of community
CathWorkOH								X					Y	Faith based hospitality
CathWorkMD		None							U					
CaveCreek	Nearly all meals	21-50%	yes!	veg	none				R	1	45	GLB		ecological living/personal growth
CedarHollow	2-5 times/week	>50%	yes!	omni	some	ok		X	R	4	42.5	GLB	N	Personal and Planetary Healing
Celo	Rarely	1-5%	some	omni	some	some	2		R		1000	L	N	Social Responsibility
Cennednyss	1 time/week	21-50%	yes!	omni	ok	ok			R	5	16		N	mutual support
CentreforAlt	2-5 times/week	1-5%	yes!	omni	ok	ok		X	R	10	40		N	living sustainably
CerroGordo	Rarely	1-5%							R	12	1186		N	ecological community sustainable
ChacraMillal	Nearly all meals	21-50%	yes!	veg	ok	ok		X	R	4	30		N	Human relationships & ecology
ChesterCreek	2-5 times/week	1-5%	yes!	veg	ok	ok		X	B	1	<1	L	N	Lesbian Communal Household
ChickenShack	2-5 times/week	6-20%	yes!	omni	yes!	yes!		X	R	3	5		N	permaculture, & alternative technology
ChristHills	Nearly all meals	6-20%	yes!	no red	some	none	1	X	R	32	105		Y	We are here to seek God.
ChristineCtr	Nearly all meals	1-5%			some	none		X	R	13	145	GLB	Y	ecumenical eclectic
CielCoho	1-3 times/month		yes!	omni	some	none		X	U	23			N	Sharing Neighbors
CircleDivine	1-3 times/month	None	yes!	omni	some			X	R	20	760		Y	Enlightenment for All of Humanity
CircleSpring	1 time/week	6-20%	yes!	no red	some	some	1		R	3	124		N	Permaculture, natural building

KEY *Diet:* omni = includes red meat, no red = no red meat—includes fish or poultry and dairy, veg = vegetarian—no meat—includes dairy, vgn = vegan—no meat or dairy.
Diet note: Some communities list omni and provide vegan options, some list vegan yet allow personal food without restriction. Take the label as a rough guideline.
Rural, Urban or Both: Some communities used both (B) to indicate having both an urban and rural location or that the one property was both urban and rural, as suburban.
Acres of Land: Hectare is abbreviated ha and is approximately 2.5 acres.
Some Labor Expected: Members are expected to regularly contribute labor to the group.
GLB Ok: The community indicated that gay men (G) or lesbians (L) or bisexuals (B) are welcome as members.
Spiritual Path: The community indicated it has a primarily spiritual or religious focus.

	State/Prov. or Country	Forming, Reforming	Year Formed	Year Purchased	Year Began Living	Open to More Adults?	Open to More Children?	Total Population	# Adults	# Children (<19yrs)	Percentage Women	Identified Leader	Leadership Core Group	How are Major Decisions Made?	Join Fee?	Income Shared/Indep.	Who Owns Land	Survey Date
Clare House of Hospitality	IL	F	1977	1978	1978	Y	y	2	2	0	100%	Y		C	N		cmty	Aug99
Co-ordination Co-op	[au]		1973			Y	y	315			50%	N	Y	M O	Y	I	cmty	Jul99
CoLibri Urban Housing Collective	MO	F	1996	1998	1998	Y	y	12	12		58%	N	N	C	Y	I	cmty	Sep99
Collegiate Living Organization	FL		1931	1953		Y	n	72	72		36%	Y	Y	E				Aug99
Columbanus Cmty of Reconciliation	[uk*]	RF	1983	1983	1983	Y	n	4	4		100%	Y	Y	C O	N	I	other	Sep99
Columbia CoHousing Community Project	MO	F	1996			Y	y	25	14	11	62%	N	Y	C	N		other	Dec98
Coming Home Community	CA	F	1998			Y	y	4	4		25%	N	N	C	N		mix	Sep99
Common Ground Community	AL		1980	1975	1987	N	n	16	13	3	55%	N	N	O	N	I	other	Feb99
Common Ground (VA)	VA		1980	1980	1981	Y	y	12	12		58%	N	N	C	Y	I	mix	Sep99
Common Place Land Cooperative	NY		1980	1976	1976	Y	y	37	23	14	48%	N	N	C	Y	I	clt	Jan99
Common Threads	MA		1994	1995	1995	Y		8	6	2	50%		Y	C E	N	S	cmty	Jan99
CommonGround Community	ON	F	1996	1997	1996	Y	y	4	4		50%	N	N	C	N	I	indiv	Sep99
Commons on the Alameda, The	NM		1990	1991	1992	Y	y	65	57	8	62%	Y	Y	C	N	I	indiv	Jan99
Communauté de L'Arche	[fr]		1946			Y	y		25	13	56%	Y		C	N	S		May99
Communauté du Pain de Vie	[fr]		1976			Y	y		300	250	50%		Y	M O	N	S		May99
Community and Retreat for Mindful Living	AR	F	1997			Y	y	3	2	1	67%	N	N	C	Y		other	Sep99
Community House	OH	F	1997	1995	1995	Y	y	25	15	10	36%	Y	Y	C	N	S	mix	Dec98
Community of Hospitality	GA		1981	1981	1981	Y		5	5		60%	N	N	C	N		cmty	Mar99
Community of One - "Minnesota"	MN	RF	Oct98			Y	n	3	3		80%	Y	N	O	N		other	Nov98
COMN Ground	OH		1993	1995	1993	Y	y	8	4	4	50%	Y	Y	C	N	S	ldlord	Aug99
Concord Oasis EcoHousing	CA	RF	1995	1988	1996	Y	y	9	8	1	44%	Y		O	Y	I	indiv	Mar99
Cooper Street Household/Triangle F Ranch	AZ		1971	1969	1969	Y	y	5	5		50%	N	Y	C		I	indiv	Mar99
Corani Housing and Land Co-op	[uk]		1978			Y	y	9	7	2	57%	N	N	C	N	S	other	Mar99
Cornerstone Housing Co-operative	[uk]		1993			Y	y	10	10		50%	N	N	C M	Y	I		May99
Corpus Christi Abbey	TX		1927	1975	1927	Y	n	24	24		0%	Y	Y	M L	N	S	cmty	Mar99
Covenental Community	IL		1979	1979	1979	Y	y	57	39	18	67%	N	Y	M	Y	I	n profit	Dec98
Cranberry Commons Cohousing	BC	F	1992	May99		Y	y	25	17	8	50%	N	N	C	Y	I	cmty	Jun99
Creekside	[nz]		1972			N	n	16	12	4	58%	N	N	C	N		indiv	Sep99
Creekside Cohousing	VA		1994	Jan99				32	23	9	43%	N	N	C	Y	I	cmty	May99
Crossroads Medieval Village	[au]		1992			Y	y		50	30	40%	Y	Y	C M	Y			Apr99
Crystal Waters Permaculture Village	[au]		1985	1988	1988	Y	y	198	138	60	50%	N	Y	C M E	N			Dec98
Cwrt y Cylchau	[uk]		1998			Y	y	5	0		60%	N	N	C	Y			Jan99
Damanhur, Federation of	[it]		1977			Y	y		453	96	55%	Y	Y	C M L E	Y	S I		Feb99
Dancing Bones	NH	F	1997	1998	1998	Y	y	4	4		80%	N	N	C	N	I	clt	Sep99
Dancing Rabbit Ecovillage	MO		1993	1997	1995	Y	y	19	14	5	43%	N	N	C	N		clt	Apr99
Dancing Waters	WI		1982	1982	1983	N	n	13	11	2	64%	N	N	C	N		cmty	Dec98
Dandelion Community Co-op, Inc.	ON	RF	1974	1975	1975	Y	m	7	5	2	60%	N		C	N	S	cmty	Sep99
Dapala Farm	WA	F	1990	1990	1990	Y	y	7	6	1	50%	N	N	C	S	S	mix	Dec98
Dawning Star	CO	F	1998	1996	1997	Y		2	2		50%	Y		C	N	I	indiv	Feb99
Dayspring Circle	VA		1994	1997	1996	Y	y	5	5		80%	N	N	C	Y		cmty	Sep99
Dayton House	MN	F	Jun99		Jun99	Y	m	6	6		67%	N	Y	C	N		ldlord	Jun99
De Hobbitstee	[nl]	RF	1969			Y	y	7	6	1	67%	N	N	C	N	S	cmty	Aug99
De Regenboog (The Rainbow)	[be]		1974			Y	y		8		63%	N	N	C	N	I		May99
Debs House	MI		1967															Jan99
DeltaInfinity	-	F	Aug99			Y	y					N	N	O	Y	I	clt	Aug99
Denver Catholic Worker	CO			1978		N	n	5	5	0	60%	N	N	C	N		ldlord	Oct99
Denver Space Center	CO			1979	1977	Y		4	4		50%	Y		C	Y		indiv	Sep99
Dolphin Community (Ökodorf Delphin)	[de]		1995			Y	y		7	7	57%	N	Y	C E				Mar99
Dome Country	ON		1977	1975	1975	Y	y	6	6		50%	N	Y	C	Y	I	n profit	Jan99
Dorothy Day Catholic Worker	DC		1981	1981	1981	Y	y	8	8		38%	N	N	C	N		n profit	Jan99
Downeast Friends Community	ME	RF	1978	1978	1978	Y	y	12	10	2	50%	N	P	C	N	I	indiv	Feb99
Downie Street Collective	ON	RF	1996		1996	M	m	4	4		75%	N	N	C	N		ldlord	Aug99

KEY *Canadian Provinces:* BC = British Columbia, MB = Manitoba, NS = Nova Scotia, ON = Ontario, SK = Saskatchewan.
Country: [ar] = Argentina, [au]= Australia, [at] = Austria, [be] = Belgium, [br] = Brazil, [co] = Colombia, [dk] = Denmark, [fr] = France, [de] = Germany, [gr] = Greece, [in] = India, [il] = Israel, [it] = Italy, [jp] = Japan, [mx] = Mexico, [nl] = The Netherlands, [nz] = New Zealand, [ng] = Nigeria, [uk] = United Kingdom, [uk*] = Northern Ireland.
Decisions: C = Consensus, M = Majority, L = Leader, G = Group of leaders or elders, O = Other.
Income: S = Members Share Income, I = Independently Handle Own Finances.
Who Owns Land: CLT = Community Land Trust, Cmty = Community, Indiv = Individual, Ldlord = Landlord, Subgrp = Subgroup of members.
Survey Date: Date shown is when survey questionnaire was completed or last updated by community.

Map / Index Name	Eat Together How Frequently?	What % of Own Food Is Grown?	Organic Food in Diet	Dietary Norms	Alcohol Use	Tobacco Use	# Homeschooled	Some Labor Expected	Rural, Urban, or Both	# of Buildings	Acres of Land	GLB Ok	Spiritual Path	Primary Purpose and/or Focus
ClareHouse	Nearly all meals	6-20%	often	no red	some	none		X	U	1			Y	To serve those in need
Co-ordCo-op	Rarely		yes!	omni	some	yes!		X	R			GLB	N	Alternative Lifestyle Choices
CoLibriUrban	2-5 times/week	1-5%	yes!	veg	some	often		X	U	2		GLB	N	Affordable Environ. and Socially Responsible Living
CollegiatLiv	Nearly all meals	None					0						N	Housing for UF Students
Columbanus	Nearly all dinners	None	some	omni	some	none		X	U	2			Y	Reconciliation, education, unity
ColumbiaCoHo													N	Cohousing
ComingHome	Nearly all meals	>50%	yes!	veg	none	none		X				GLB	N	Eco-sustainable, Peer counsel
ComGround-AL	1-3 times/month	6-20%			some			X	R	7	80	GLB	N	Community ecology humor
ComGround-VA	2-5 times/week	>50%	yes!	omni	some	ok	1	X	R	8	80		N	Homestead/Group Process/Ecology
CommonPlace	1-3 times/month	6-20%	yes!	omni	some		9		R	13	432	GLB	N	Stewarding Trusterty Consensus
CommonThread	2-5 times/week	1-5%	yes!	veg	ok	none		X	U	1		GLB	Y	Social change/ Spirit diversity
ComGround-ON	Nearly all dinners	6-20%	often	no red	some	ok			R	1	115	GLB	N	Inspiring creative healing
CommonsAlam	2-5 times/week	6-20%	yes!	no red	ok	ok		X	U	28	5	LB	N	Enjoying our neighborhood
CommdeLArche		>50%	yes!	veg	some	ok	1	X	R	4	450		Y	nonviolence, work, sharing, spirituality
CommduPain	Nearly all dinners	21-50%	yes!	omni	none	some			B	60			Y	adoration and respect for poor people
CommRetreat	Nearly all meals	6-20%	yes!	veg	none	ok	1		B				Y	Awareness compassion service
CommunityHou	Nearly all dinners	None	often	omni	ok	ok	2	X	U		20		Y	Urban outreach
CommunityHos	2-5 times/week	1-5%	often	no red	ok	ok			R	1		GLB	Y	Volunteer with homeless people
CommunityOne	Nearly all meals	21-50%	often	no red	none	none	0		B	2	36	GLB	Y	Master all your abilities now & here
COMNGround	2-5 times/week	None	none	omni	none	none			U	1				family and community
ConcordOasis	Rarely	1-5%	yes!	no red	ok	none			B	4			N	ecological cohousing seed (resort?)
CooperStreet	1 time/week	None	some	omni	some	none		X	B	4	22	GLB	N	enriched life thru community
CoraniHousin	2-5 times/week	1-5%		omni				X	U				N	Cooperation Housing and Work
Cornerstone	Nearly all dinners	1-5%	yes!	vgn	ok	ok		X	U	2			N	Direct action & Mutual aid
CorpusChrist	Nearly all meals	1-5%	some	omni	some	some			R	6	40		Y	semi-Contemplative monks
Covenental	1 time/week	6-20%	often	omni	ok	ok		X	U	1		GLB	Y	Interracial / Intergenerational
Cranberry	1-3 times/month	None							U	22			N	To Build a CoHousing Community
CreeksideNZ	2-5 times/week	1-5%						X	U	5			N	Co-operative Living
CreeksideVA	2-5 times/week	None	yes!	omni	some	some		X	U	25			N	sharing resources
CrossroadsMe	Rarely	1-5%							R	0	453		N	Medieval and Permaculture
CrystalWater	Rarely	6-20%	yes!	omni	yes!	yes!		X	R	83	640	GLB	N	Permaculture, Educational Tourism, Ecovillage
CwrtyCylchau	Nearly all dinners	>50%	yes!	veg	some	none		X	R	4	5		Y	To manifest the group soul
Damanhur	Nearly all meals	21-50%	often	omni	often	none		X	B	85	250		Y	Human Being's reawakening
DancingBones	2-5 times/week	1-5%	yes!	no red	some	ok			R	3	40		N	Simple living, rural ecovillage
DancingRabbt	Nearly all dinners	>50%	yes!	omni	some	ok	2	X	R	3	280	GLB	N	ecologically sustainable town
DancingWater	1 time/week	21-50%	yes!	omni	some				R	4	130		N	Cooperative rural community
Dandelion	Nearly all dinners	21-50%	yes!	omni	ok	ok		X	R	3	50		N	
DapalaFarm	Nearly all meals	>50%	yes!	no red	none	none		X	R	2	16	GLB	N	Self-Reliant, Simplified Living
DawningStar	1 time/week	None	yes!	omni	ok	none			R	2	358	GLB	Y	Unfolding Lightbody
DayspringCir	2-5 times/week	6-20%	yes!	omni	ok	ok		X	R	3	90	GLB	N	Stewardship and friendship
DaytonHouse	Nearly all dinners	21-50%	yes!	omni	yes!	none		X	U	1			N	City folk, bloom where planted
DeHobbitstee	Nearly all dinners	21-50%	yes!	veg	ok	none			R	4	3,5		N	Pers-Spirituality - Non-violence, solidarity
DeRegenboog	Nearly all meals	None	yes!	no red	some			X	U				N	sharing life and justice and non-violence
DebsHouse														
DeltaInfinit		>50%	yes!	vgn	none	none			R			GLB		Anti- Authoritarian, Scientific, Probablism
DenverCW	Nearly all meals	1-5%	some	omni	none	ok		X	U	1		GLB	Y	Hospitality and simplicity
DenverSpace	1-3 times/month	1-5%						X	U	1			N	good friends, interesting company
DolphinCmty	1 time/week	1-5%	yes!	veg	none	none			R	1			Y	helping others finding God
DomeCountry	Nearly all dinners	>50%	yes!	veg	some	some			B	3-5	4-140		Y	hi-tech eco-village with domed houses
DorothyDayCW	Nearly all dinners	1-5%	often	omni	none	ok			U	1		GLB	Y	Hospitality and Resistance
Downeast	Nearly all dinners	1-5%	yes!	no red	ok	none		X	U	1			Y	Ecology environment art baking
DownieStreet	2-5 times/week	1-5%	yes!	no red	some	ok			U	1			N	sustainable housing/ local food

KEY *Diet:* omni = includes red meat, no red = no red meat—includes fish or poultry and dairy, veg = vegetarian—no meat—includes dairy, vgn = vegan—no meat or dairy.
Diet note: Some communities list omni and provide vegan options, some list vegan yet allow personal food without restriction. Take the label as a rough guideline.
Rural, Urban or Both: Some communities used both (B) to indicate having both an urban and rural location or that the one property was both urban and rural, as suburban.
Acres of Land: Hectare is abbreviated ha and is approximately 2.5 acres.
Some Labor Expected: Members are expected to regularly contribute labor to the group.
GLB Ok: The community indicated that gay men (G) or lesbians (L) or bisexuals (B) are welcome as members.
Spiritual Path: The community indicated it has a primarily spiritual or religious focus.

Chart

Community	State/Prov. or Country	Forming, Reforming	Year Formed	Year Purchased	Year Began Living	Open to More Adults?	Open to More Children?	Total Population	# Adults	# Children (<19yrs)	Percentage Women	Identified Leader	Leadership Core Group	How are Major Decisions Made?	Join Fee	Income Shared/Indep.	Who Owns Land	Survey Date
Doyle Street Cohousing	CA		1990	1990	1992			25	19	6				C		I	cmty	Sep99
Dragon Belly Farm	CA	RF		1991		Y	y	6	4	2							indiv	Sep99
Dragonfly Farm	ON		1978			N	n		4		25%	N	N	C	Y	I		May99
Dreaming Lizard Co-House	NM	F	1997	Jul99	Sep99	Y	y	5	3	2	67%	N	Y	C	N	I	subgrp	Aug99
Dreamtime Village	WI	RF	1991	1991	1991	Y	y	10	9	1	20%		Y	CM E O	N	I	mix	Aug99
Du-má	OR		1988	1990	1990	P	p	8	8		63%	N	N	C	Y	I	mix	Dec98
Dunmire Hollow	TN		1973	1974	1973	Y	y	14	12	2	50%	N		C	N		other	Sep99
Earth Heart Center	VT	F	1998	1991	1998	Y	y	3	3		0%	N	N				indiv	Aug99
Earth Re-Leaf	HI	RF	1982	1985	1985	Y	y	2	2	0	50%	N	Y	C	N	I	clt	Dec98
EarthArt Village (EAV)	CO	F	1998	1997		Y	y				50%	N	Y	C	Y	I	other	Sep99
Earthaven	NC		1990	1994	1998	Y	m	50	45	5		N	Y	C	Y	I	subgrp	Sep99
EarthSeed	VT		1994			Y	y					N	Y	C	N	I		Mar99
Earthworm Housing Co-op	[uk]		1989	1989	1989	Y	y	10	7	3	43%	N	N	C	N		cmty	Mar99
East Bay Cohousing	CA	F	Nov98	2000	2000	Y	y					N	Y	C	Y	I		Oct99
East Lake Commons	GA	F	1996	1996	1997	Y	y	74	52	22		N		C O	Y	I	mix	Sep99
East Wind Community	MO		1970	1974	1970	Y	y	75	64	11	38%	N	N	CM		N	S	cmty	Sep99
East-West Housing Cooperative	-		1957	1972	1957	Y	y	13	13		62%	N	N		Y	I	clt	Jul99
Eco-Village of La Hermita	[mx]		1998			Y	y		4	8	75%	N	Y	C	Y	I	indiv	Aug99
EcoCity Project	MO	F	1998			Y	y					Y	Y	C E	N	I		Mar99
Ecology House Two	CA																	Sep99
EcoVillage Cohousing Cooperative	NY		1992	1992	1996	Y	y	90	54	36	59%	N	N	C	Y		cmty	Dec98
EcoVillage Emerging	CA	F	1997			Y	y					N	N					Sep99
EcoVillage of Loudoun County	MD	F	1990	1997	Nov99			78	57	21	59%	Y	Y	O	Y	I	other	Jun99
Eden Ranch Community	CO	F		1995		Y	y	2	2		50%	Y	Y	C			I	indiv	Sep99
Edenvale	BC	RF	1973			Y	y	13	10	3	69%	N	N	C O	N	I	other	Dec98
Edges	OH		1992	1993	1994	Y	y	13	8	5	63%	N	N	C	Y	I	clt	Sep99
El Bloque	[es]		1980			Y	y	10	3		60%	Y	Y	C	N	S		May99
El Semillero	[es]	F	1993			Y	y	5	4	1	40%	N	Y	M	N	S	mix	Nov98
ElderWood	MI		1995	1993		Y	y	4	2	2	0%	N	Y	E		I	indiv	May99
Elohim City	OK			1972	1972	Y	y	100			60%	Y	Y	C E	N	I	cmty	Feb99
Elsworth Cooperative	MI		1940	1940	1940	Y	n	18	18		56%	Y	Y	M		N		clt	Feb99
Emerald Earth	CA	RF	1989	1989	1994	Y	y	9	8	1	50%	N	N	C		Y		n profit	Jun99
Emma Goldman Co-op	WI		1996	1996	1996	Y	y	18	13	5	50%	N	N	C		Y		cmty	Mar99
Emmaus Community/Harlem	NY		1965			Y		43	43		42%	Y	Y	C		N	S	mix	Jan99
Emmaus -- Haarzuilens	[nl]		1966	1966	1966	Y		12	12		50%	N	Y	M		N		ldlord	May99
Enchanted Garden Intentional Cmty	CA		1980		1989	Y		9	9		56%	Y	Y	O			I	mix	Aug99
Eno Commons CoHousing	NC		1992	1993	1998			53	34	19	58%	N	N	C O	N		other	Jan99
Essene Cooperative	CO	F	1994			Y	y	15	12	3			Y	C				indiv	Aug99
Essene Skoola Phish (ESP)	IL	F	1992			Y	y	5	3	2		N	N	C		N			Sep99
Eternal Cause Society	PA		1992	1994	1995	Y	n	14			29%			C L E	N	S	I	mix	Nov98
Faerie Camp Destiny	VT		1994			Y	y					Y	Y	C		N		cmty	Feb99
Fair Oaks Cohousing	WI																	May99
Fairview Cooperative	WA	F	Dec98	Dec98		Y	y	2	2		50%			C		N	I	indiv	Sep99
Fairview House	CA			1990		N	n	10	9	1	67%	N		C		Y	I	clt	Mar99
Family, The	DC	RF	1968		1968	Y	y	14	7	7	75%	N	Y	M		N	S	other	Nov98
Far Valley Farm, Inc.	OH		1980	1980	1977	Y	y	11	11	0	36%	N	N	C		Y	I	other	Oct99
Farm, The	TN		1970	1971	1971	Y	y	163	111	52	53%	N	Y	M		Y		clt	Feb99
Father Divine's Int'l Peace Mission Mvmt	PA		1932			Y	y					Y	Y	L O	N		other	Oct99
Fellowship Community	NY		1966	1966	1966	Y	y	124	100	24		N	Y	E		N		mix	Dec98
Ferency Co-op	MI		1964	1964	1964	Y	n	9	9		44%	Y	Y	M		Y		mix	Feb99
Findhorn Foundation Community	[uk]		1962			Y	y		128	33	67%	Y	Y	CM	O	Y			Mar99
Finney Farm	WA		1990	1990	1990	Y	y	7	6	1	50%	N	N	C		M	I	clt	Jan99

KEY *Canadian Provinces:* BC = British Columbia, MB = Manitoba, NS = Nova Scotia, ON = Ontario, SK = Saskatchewan.
Country: [ar] = Argentina, [au]= Australia, [at] = Austria, [be] = Belgium, [br] = Brazil, [co] = Colombia, [dk] = Denmark, [fr] = France, [de] = Germany, [gr] = Greece, [in] = India, [il] = Israel, [it] = Italy, [jp] = Japan, [mx] = Mexico, [nl] = The Netherlands, [nz] = New Zealand, [ng] = Nigeria, [uk] = United Kingdom, [uk*] = Northern Ireland.
Decisions: C = Consensus, M = Majority, L = Leader, G = Group of leaders or elders, O = Other.
Income: S = Members Share Income, I = Independently Handle Own Finances.
Who Owns Land: CLT = Community Land Trust, Cmty = Community, Indiv = Individual, Ldlord = Landlord, Subgrp = Subgroup of members.
Survey Date: Date shown is when survey questionnaire was completed or last updated by community.

Map / Index Name	Eat Together How Frequently?	What % of Own Food Is Grown?	Organic Food in Diet	Dietary Norms	Alcohol Use	Tobacco Use	# Homeschooled	Some Labor Expected	Rural, Urban, or Both	# of Buildings	Acres of Land	GLB Ok	Spiritual Path	Primary Purpose and/or Focus
DoyleStreet	2-5 times/week	None							U	1		LB	N	Cohousing Intentional Neighborhood
DragonBelly		21-50%	yes!	omni	some	some		X	R		39			
Dragonfly	Rarely	1-5%	often	omni	yes!	yes!			R	6	250		Y	enjoy life
DreamingLiz	1 time/week	1-5%	yes!	no red	ok	ok		X	U	3			Y	Cooperation, sustainability
DreamtimeVil	1-3 times/month	1-5%	yes!	omni	some	often	1	X	R	4	80	GLB	N	Permaculture Hypermedia
Du-má	Nearly all dinners	6-20%	yes!	veg	ok	none		X	U	1		GLB	N	intentional/urban
DunmireHollo	1 time/week							X	R	10	163		N	Small, rural, land stewardship
EarthHeartCe			yes!	no red	none				R	2	45			
EarthRe-Leaf	Rarely	>50%	yes!	vgn	none	none			R	4	3		Y	Consensus natural spiritual
EarthArtVill	2-5 times/week	21-50%	yes!	omni	some	some		X	R	1	480			wholistic sustainability
Earthaven	1-3 times/month	1-5%	yes!	no red	some	none		X	R	13	325		Y	A bridge to a new paradigm of sustainable culture
EarthSeed	1-3 times/month	1-5%	yes!						R			GLB	Y	space for healing/connection
Earthworm	Nearly all dinners	6-20%					2	X	R	3	7		N	practical ecological living
EastBayCoho						ok			U				N	Make/Find CoHo Berk/Oakland
EastLake	1-3 times/month	6-20%					2	X	U	67	20		N	Cohousing community; gardens
EastWind	Nearly all meals	>50%	yes!	omni	ok	ok	5		R	15	1045	GLB	N	Cooperation and Sharing
East-West	Nearly all dinners	1-5%	yes!	veg	none			X	U	1			S	low income collective living
EcoVilLaHerm	Rarely	None							R	4	28		N	Develop consciousness
EcoCityProj			yes!	vgn	none	none		X	B				N	sustainability, social change
EcologyHouse														
EcoVilCohoNY	2-5 times/week	6-20%	often	omni	ok	ok	5	X	B	16	35	GLB	N	Ecological Cohousing Village
EcoVilEmerg									R					ecosustainable cluster of I.C.
EcoVilLoudou	2-5 times/week		yes!	omni	some	ok		X	R	70	180		N	Environ.; cohousing; homeschooling; sharing
EdenRanch	Nearly all dinners	6-20%	yes!	veg	ok	none		X	R	1	65		N	Responsible Stewardship
Edenvale	1-3 times/month	1-5%	yes!	omni	yes!	some		X	R	4	118		Y	Spiritual regeneration of humanity
Edges	2-5 times/week	6-20%	yes!	omni	ok	none		X	R	4	94		N	permaculture alt energy balance
ElBloque	Nearly all meals	6-20%	yes!	veg	yes!	yes!		X	R	6	3 ha		N	building awareness
ElSemillero	Nearly all dinners	21-50%	yes!	no red	none	none		X	R	1	5	GLB	N	Sharing Simple Conscious
ElderWood	2-5 times/week	1-5%	yes!	no red	some	ok		X	R	1	35			Self Sustainability, high quality of life
ElohimCity	Rarely	21-50%	ok	vgn					R	22	400		Y	Pragmatic expression of Christian Faith
ElsworthCoop	Nearly all dinners	None	ok	omni	ok	some		X	U	1		GLB	N	very cheap student housing
EmeraldEarth	Nearly all meals	6-20%	yes!	veg	some	ok		X	R	3	189		N	getting in the mud
EmmaGoldman	Nearly all dinners	1-5%	yes!	veg	ok	ok		X	U	1		GLB	N	activist cooperative
EmmausCmty	Nearly all meals	None		no red	none	ok		X	U	2			Y	empowerment, healing, personal & social change
EmmausHaarz	Nearly all meals	None	ok	omni		yes!		X	B	1			N	
EnchantedGar	Rarely	1-5%			none	none		X	U		1/3	GLB	N	Seed Dreams Grow Here
EnoCommons	1 time/week	None	yes!	omni	yes!			X	B	22	11.2	GLB	N	Being a good neighbor
EsseneCoop		21-50%	yes!	veg	none	none		X						
EsseneSkoola		6-20%	some		some	none			R				Y	Make Heaven on Earth
EternalCause	Nearly all dinners	1-5%	some	no red	none	none		X	U	2		GLB	Y	Cosmic-Workers/Whole-Cause
FaerieCamp								X	R	0	150		Y	Providing sanctuary for radical faeries
FairOaksCoho														
FairviewCoop	2-5 times/week	1-5%		no red	none	none		X	R	3	20		N	Beauty, sustainability, growth
FairviewHous	2-5 times/week	1-5%	yes!	veg	ok	none		X	U	2		GLB	N	Food and Creative Love!
FamilyThe	Nearly all meals	None	often	omni	some	none		X	U	1			Y	non-conventional christians
FarValley	1-3 times/month	6-20%	yes!	veg	ok	ok			R	12	200+		N	
FarmThe	Rarely	1-5%	often	vgn	ok	ok	5		R		1750		Y	
FatherDivine	Nearly all meals		yes!	omni	none	none			B				Y	Practical Christianity
FellowshipCo	Nearly all meals	>50%	yes!		none	some			R					spiritual growth through service
FerencyCo-op	Nearly all dinners	None	yes!	omni	often	often		X	U	1			N	community housing
Findhorn	Nearly all meals	6-20%	often	no red	some	ok		X	R	50	30		Y	Love all, serve all
FinneyFarm	2-5 times/week	21-50%	yes!	omni	often	ok	1	X	R	2	105	GLB	N	Sustainable living

KEY *Diet:* omni = includes red meat, no red = no red meat—includes fish or poultry and dairy, veg = vegetarian—no meat—includes dairy, vgn = vegan—no meat or dairy.
Diet note: Some communities list omni and provide vegan options, some list vegan yet allow personal food without restriction. Take the label as a rough guideline.
Rural, Urban or Both: Some communities used both (B) to indicate having both an urban and rural location or that the one property was both urban and rural, as suburban.
Acres of Land: Hectare is abbreviated ha and is approximately 2.5 acres.
Some Labor Expected: Members are expected to regularly contribute labor to the group.
GLB Ok: The community indicated that gay men (G) or lesbians (L) or bisexuals (B) are welcome as members.
Spiritual Path: The community indicated it has a primarily spiritual or religious focus.

Community	State/Prov. or Country	Forming, Reforming	Year Formed	Year Purchased	Year Began Living	Open to More Adults?	Open to More Children?	Total Population	# Adults	# Children (<19yrs)	Percentage Women	Identified Leader	Leadership Core Group	How are Major Decisions Made?	Join Fee	Income Shared/Indep.	Who Owns Land	Survey Date
Flowering Desert Permaculture Center	AZ	F	1997	May99	1997	Y	n	4	4	0	50%	N	Y	O	N	I	indiv	Sep99
Folkhaven Community	AK	RF	Oct98	1996	Oct98	Y	y	3	3		0%	Y	Y	C	N	I	cmty	Feb99
Forming Community	ME	F												C				Dec98
Fox Housing Cooperative	[uk]	F	1998	Oct98	1998	Y	y	8	7	1	25%	N	Y	C	N	I	cmty	Apr99
Franciscan Workers of Junipero Serra	CA		1982			Y	y	16	15	1	88%	N	Y	C	N		cmty	Oct99
Frankleigh House	[uk]		1995			Y	y		13	15	54%	N	N	C O	Y	I		Jan99
Free-the-Land NYC Squatters Community	NY		1967	1967	1967	Y	y	142	102	40	35%	N	N	C	N		mix	Feb99
Freie Christliche Jugendgemeinschaft	[de]		1976			Y	y		250	100		Y	Y	E	N		other	Mar99
Friends Co-op	WI		1960	1960	1960	Y	y	12	11	1	50%	N	N	C	Y	I	other	Jan99
Fruitvale Housing Cooperative	CA																	Nov99
Full Moon Rising	WA	RF	1997	1997	1998	Y	y	9	4	5	50%	N	Y	C	Y	I	cmty	Jan99
Fun Family Farm	KS		1982					12	9	3	50%	N	Y	C	N	I	indiv	Aug99
Gabalah	[au]		1998			Y	y		3		33%	N	Y	C M	N			
GAIA Community	CO	F	1994	1995		Y	y	4	4			N	Y	C	N		other	Feb99
Ganas	NY		1978	1980	1978	Y	y	74	72	2	40%	N	Y	C	N		mix	Oct99
Gandhi Farm	NS					Y	y	7	7		57%	N	N	C	N	S	other	Oct99
Garden o' Vegan	HI	F	Jun99			Y	y	8	5	3	40%	N	N	C	N		subgrp	Oct99
GardenSpirit	NC	F	1998	Sep98	Oct98	Y	y	4	4		75%	N	N	C O	Y	I	mix	Sep99
Gentle World	HI	RF	1970		1974	Y	y	19	17	2	53%	Y	Y	C M L	Y		cmty	May99
Gesundheit! Institute	WV	RF	1972	1980	1972	N	n	9	9		44%	Y	Y	C L E O	N		cmty	Mar99
Ginger Ridge Farms	HI	F	Feb99	1980	Feb99			9	8	1		Y		C M L		S	indiv	Sep99
Glen Ivy	CA		1977	1977	1977	Y	y	25	24	1	60%	N		C	Y	I	cmty	Nov98
Glendower	MO	RF	1995	1995	1995	Y		2	2	0	50%	N	Y	C	N	I	other	Sep99
Glenwood Cooperative	IN		1939					34			100%		Y	M			n profit	Sep99
Global Village/School of the Americas	FL		1997			Y	y	17	14	3	43%	N	Y	M	Y		cmty	Oct99
Golden Eagle Traditional Indian Camp	NV	RF	1998	1976	1998	N	n	4	3	1	67%	Y	Y	C M L E	N	I	indiv	Nov98
Goodenough Community	WA		1969			Y	y	101	83	18	60%		Y	C	N		indiv	Sep99
Goodrich Farm Cooperative	VT	F	1967	1979	1997	Y	y	6	6		33%	Y		C M	N		indiv	Dec98
Grail Community, The	[uk]		1930			Y			16		100%	Y	Y	C M L	N	S		Apr99
Greater World Community	NM		1996	1996	1996	Y	y					Y	N		Y	I	other	Sep99
Green House Cooperative	MI	RF	1993	1993	1993	N	n	7	7	0	29%	N	Y	E	N	I	indiv	Dec98
Greenhouse	WA		1989	1993	1989	Y	n	4	4		100%	N	N	C	N	I	indiv	Oct99
Greening Life Community	PA		1972		1973	N	n	12	12		50%	Y	N	C	Y	I	cmty	Feb99
Greenwood	PA	F	1995	1987	1995	Y	y	4	4		50%	Y	Y	C M L E	N	S	other	Oct96
Gregory House	MI		1995	1995	1995	Y	n	30							Y	I	cmty	Jul99
Grimstone Community	[uk]		1990			Y	y		9	2	33%	N	N	C	Y	I		Apr99
Guayrapá	[es]		1992			Y	y		7	0	43%	Y	N	O	N			Jul99
Gwerin Housing Association	[uk]		1979			Y	y		21	1	48%	N	N	C				Mar99
Hairakhandi Love Hashram	[it]		1993	1988	1993	Y	y	7	4	3	43%	Y	N	L	N		cmty	Aug99
Harbin Hot Springs	CA		1972	1972	1972	Y	y	180	162	18	50%	Y	Y	C	Y	I		May99
Hawk Circle Cooperative	IA		1992		1993	Y	y	6	4	2	25%	N	N	C	N	I	subgrp	Oct99
Headlands	ON		1971	1971	1972	N	n	9	5	4	40%	N	N	M	N		other	Sep99
Healing Grace Sanctuary	MA	F		1981		Y	y	1	1	0	100%			C O	N			Jul99
Hearthaven	MO		1988	1988	1988	Y	n	6	6	0	33%	N	N	C			cmty	Sep99
Heartlight Center	MI		1987	1987	1987			16	15	1								Nov98
Heartsong	ME	F	1999			Y	y	6	6		33%	Y		L				Jul99
Heartwood Cohousing	CO	F	1994	1998	Dec99	N	n	65	43	22	53%	N	N	C	Y	I	mix	Sep99
Heartwood Community	[nz]		1970			Y	y	30	20	10	45%	Y	N	C M	Y	I		Apr99
Heartwood Institute	CA		1978	1982	1982	Y	n	96	91	5	61%	Y	Y	E	N		other	Sep99
Heathcote Community	MD					Y	y	16	11	5	45%	N	N	C	Y		mix	Oct99
Hei Wa House	MI		1985	1999	1985	Y	y	7	6	1	50%	N	N	C		I	subgrp	Sep99
Henderson Cooperative House	MI		1945		1945	Y	n	31	31	0	100%	Y	Y	C M L E	N	I	other	Aug99

KEY *Canadian Provinces:* BC = British Columbia, MB = Manitoba, NS = Nova Scotia, ON = Ontario, SK = Saskatchewan.
Country: [ar] = Argentina, [au]= Australia, [at] = Austria, [be] = Belgium, [br] = Brazil, [co] = Colombia, [dk] = Denmark, [fr] = France, [de] = Germany, [gr] = Greece, [in] = India, [il] = Israel, [it] = Italy, [jp] = Japan, [mx] = Mexico, [nl] = The Netherlands, [nz] = New Zealand, [ng] = Nigeria, [uk] = United Kingdom, [uk*] = Northern Ireland.
Decisions: C = Consensus, M = Majority, L = Leader, G = Group of leaders or elders, O = Other.
Income: S = Members Share Income, I = Independently Handle Own Finances.
Who Owns Land: CLT = Community Land Trust, Cmty = Community, Indiv = Individual, Ldlord = Landlord, Subgrp = Subgroup of members.
Survey Date: Date shown is when survey questionnaire was completed or last updated by community.

Map / Index Name	Eat Together How Frequently?	What % of Own Food Is Grown?	Organic Food in Diet	Dietary Norms	Alcohol Use	Tobacco Use	# Homeschooled	Some Labor Expected	Rural, Urban, or Both	# of Buildings	Acres of Land	GLB Ok	Spiritual Path	Primary Purpose and/or Focus
FloweringDes	Nearly all dinners	6-20%	some		some	none		X	R	2	2.27		N	permaculture, intimacy, education, fun
Folkhaven	Nearly all meals	6-20%	often	omni	ok	none		X	B	2	3		Y	kinsmen tribe and folk
FormingCmty									R		100			
FoxHousing	Nearly all dinners	6-20%	yes!	vgn	some	none	1	X	R	3	53		Y	ecological/social change
FranciscanWo	1 time/week	1-5%	yes!	veg	ok	ok			U	5			Y	
Frankleigh	1 time/week	1-5%	yes!	omni	some		5		R	9	17		N	respect each other's needs
FreetheLand	1 time/week	1-5%	yes!	omni	yes!	yes!	5	X	U	7			N	squatting, mutual aid, cooperation
FreieChrist	Nearly all meals	None			none	none			U				Y	Communal Living and Charitable work
FriendsCo-op	2-5 times/week	1-5%	yes!	veg	ok	ok		X	U	1		GLB	N	Consensus Decision-Making
Fruitvale														
FullMoonRisi	1 time/week	6-20%	yes!	omni	often	none		X	R	6	29		N	Creating community together
FunFamily	1 time/week	21-50%	often	omni	yes!	yes!		X	R	4	125		N	Intentional Neighborhood
Gabalah	Nearly all meals	21-50%	yes!	veg	some	some		X	R		128		Y	Green Consciousness Good Living
GAIACmty	Nearly all dinners	6-20%	yes!	omni	ok	ok			B	4	40	GLB	N	sustainable egalitarian cooperative
Ganas	Nearly All Dinners	1-5%	ok	omni	some	ok			B	8	70	GLB	N	love dialogue group wisdom
GandhiFarm	Nearly all dinners	21-50%	yes!	vgn	none	none		X	R		20	GLB	N	
GardenoVegan	Nearly all meals	>50%	yes!	vgn	none	none	2	X	R				N	Cruelty-free self-sufficiency
GardenSpirit	Nearly all dinners	6-20%	yes!	no red	ok	none		X	R	2	11		Y	self-reliant homesteading
GentleWorld	Nearly all dinners	6-20%	yes!	vgn	none	none			R				Y	vegan loving gentle sun
Gesundheit!	Nearly all dinners	1-5%	yes!	omni	ok	ok	0	X	R	3	310		N	Fun, Friendship, & The Joy of Service
GingerRidge	Nearly all meals	21-50%	yes!					X						common-unity
Glenlvy	Nearly all meals	1-5%	yes!	omni	ok	ok		X	R	19	70	G	Y	intentional spiritual community
Glendower	Nearly all dinners	None	ok	omni	none	none		X	U	2		LB	Y	polyamorous and neopagan family
GlenwoodCoop	Nearly all meals	None	often		ok	none			B					
GlobalVillag	Nearly all dinners	21-50%	yes!	omni	ok	none	1	X	B		10	GLB	Y	multicultural ecovillage
GoldenEagle	1 time/week	1-5%	yes!	omni	none	ok		X	R	6	262	GLB	Y	To practice our original ways.
Goodenough	1 time/week	1-5%	yes!	omni	some	some	4	X	B	6			Y	a demonstration of transformation
GoodrichFarm	2-5 times/week	21-50%	yes!						R	1			N	
GrailCmty	Nearly all meals	1-5%	some	omni	some	ok		X	B	2			Y	Creating a sacred place
GreaterWorld	1-3 times/month	1-5%								30			N	to build and inhabit earthships
GreenHouseCo	1-3 times/month	1-5%	yes!	veg	ok	ok			U	3		GL	Y	Simple living, green values
GreenhouseWA	1-3 times/month	6-20%	yes!	veg	some	none		X	U	1		LB	N	ecology feminist vegetarian
GreeningLife	1-3 times/month	6-20%	yes!	veg	ok	ok		X	R	8	136		N	Growth in spirit; balance
Greenwood	1 time/week	1-5%	yes!	vgn	ok	ok			R	1	1/8		N	Balance Self Sustaining Interdependent
GregoryHouse	Nearly all dinners	None			none	none		X	U	1			N	Student Cooperative Housing
Grimstone	Nearly all dinners	1-5%	yes!	no red	some	ok		X	R	2	27		Y	Personal and Planetary Transformation
Guayrapá	Nearly all meals	21-50%	yes!	no red	some				R	5	1h		N	conscience, good living together
Gwerin	Rarely	1-5%	some	omni	often	yes!	0		U	5			N	Mutual support by consent
Hairakhandi	Nearly all meals	None	yes!	veg		yes!			R	2		GLB	Y	Love Simplicity Truth Healing
HarbinHotSpr	1-3 times/month	6-20%					3		R	50	1160		Y	Heart Consciousness
HawkCircle	2-5 times/week	1-5%	often	omni	some	ok		X	B	1	3.2		N	Beneficial Cooperative Living
Headlands	Rarely	>50%	yes!	omni	yes!	ok			R	2	350		N	cooperative living
HealingGrace	Nearly all dinners	>50%	yes!	omni	none	none		X	R		85	GLB	Y	Spirit -led tribal village
Hearthaven													Y	
Heartlight														seek first the kingdom of god
Heartsong				vgn	none	none			R				Y	Optimal relationship/growth
HeartwoodCoh	2-5 times/week	6-20%	often	omni	often	ok	8	X	R	24	250+	GLB	N	Harmony with people and Nature
HeartwoodCom	Nearly all dinners	1-5%	yes!	omni	ok	ok		X	B	3	35		N	Enjoy Community Living
HeartwoodIns	Nearly all meals	6-20%	yes!	no red	ok	ok	2		R	30	240	GLB	N	education planetary healing
Heathcote	Nearly all dinners	6-20%	yes!	no red	ok	none	1	X	R	7	44	GLB	N	sustainable cooperative living
HeiWa	2-5 times/week	1-5%	yes!	veg	ok	none		X	U	1			N	affordable cooperative housing, sustainibility
Henderson	Nearly all meals	None	ok	omni	ok	none		X	U	1			N	Affordable housing for University women

KEY *Diet:* omni = includes red meat, no red = no red meat—includes fish or poultry and dairy, veg = vegetarian—no meat—includes dairy, vgn = vegan—no meat or dairy.
Diet note: Some communities list omni and provide vegan options, some list vegan yet allow personal food without restriction. Take the label as a rough guideline.
Rural, Urban or Both: Some communities used both (B) to indicate having both an urban and rural location or that the one property was both urban and rural, as suburban.
Acres of Land: Hectare is abbreviated ha and is approximately 2.5 acres.
Some Labor Expected: Members are expected to regularly contribute labor to the group.
GLB Ok: The community indicated that gay men (G) or lesbians (L) or bisexuals (B) are welcome as members.
Spiritual Path: The community indicated it has a primarily spiritual or religious focus.

Chart

Community	State/Prov. or Country	Forming, Reforming	Year Formed	Year Purchased	Year Began Living	Open to More Adults?	Open to More Children?	Total Population	# Adults	# Children (<19yrs)	Percentage Women	Identified Leader	Leadership Core Group	How are Major Decisions Made?	Join Fee	Income Shared/Indep.	Who Owns Land	Survey Date
Hermitage at Mahantongo Spirit Garden	PA	F	1987	1988	1988	Y	n	3	3		0%	Y	Y	O	N		I	cmty	Dec98
Hertha Community	[dk]	F	1993			Y	y	45	33	12	67%	N	Y	CM	N		I	mix	May99
Hesbjerg	[dk]		1958			Y	y		30	5	40%	N	P	CM	N		I		Jul99
Hidden Valley	MT	F																	May99
High Flowing	VA		1990	1988	1990	Y	y	8	7	1	50%	N	N	C	Y		I	indiv	Oct99
High Horizons	WV	F	1989			Y	y	4	3	1		Y	N	L	N		I	indiv	Nov99
High Wind Association	WI		1977		1981	P	p	17	13	4	62%	Y	Y	C L E O	N		I	mix	Oct98
Highline Crossing Cohousing	CO		1991	1993	1995	Y	y	83	64	19	61%	N	Y	C	Y		I	mix	Jan99
Hill Top Farm	OH	RF	1980	1980	1980	Y	y	12	6	6	33%	Y	Y	M L E O	Y		I	indiv	Nov98
Hillegass House	CA		1979			N	n	10	10		50%	N	N	C	N				May99
Holden Village	WA	RF	1963			Y	y	56	40	16	60%	Y	Y	C	N		I	other	Jan99
Holy City Community	LA	RF	1970	1971	1971	Y	y	33	14	19	50%	Y	Y	C E	N		I	cmty	Aug99
Homestead at Denison University, The	OH		1976	1977	1977	Y		12	12	0	38%	N	N	O	Y		I	n profit	Oct99
Horizons Eco Village	VA		1997	1997	1997	Y	y	52	35	17	57%	N		M	Y		I	mix	Sep99
House of Peace	OH	F	Sep98	Oct98	Nov98	Y	n	5	5		80%	N	Y	C	N		I	clt	Sep99
Huehuecoyotl	[mx]		1973		1973														
Humanity Rising	CA	F	1992			Y	y					Y	N	C L O					Aug99
Hundredfold Farm	PA	F	1998			Y	y	18	13	5	50%	N	N	C					Apr99
Huntington Open Womyns Land (HOWL)	VT	RF	1998	1984	1998	Y	y	4	3	1	100%	N	N	C	N		I	clt	Sep99
Hutterian Brethren	WA		1528			Y	y	40000				N	Y	M E	N	S		cmty	Jan99
Ida	TN		1993		1993	Y	y	8	8		13%	N	N	C	N			ldlord	Jan99
Innisfree Village	VA		1971		1971	Y	y	75	68	7	53%	Y	Y	C M L E	Y		I	other	Dec98
Inter-Cooperative Council, Ann Arbor	MI		1937	1944	1932	Y	m	600	600			Y	Y	C M	Y		I	cmty	Sep99
Inter-Cooperative Council, Austin	TX		1937	1970	1937	Y	m	166	166	0	50%	Y	Y	C M	Y		I	cmty	Feb99
International Puppydogs Movement	OR	F	1993			Y	m	4	4		0%	N	N	C	N		I		Jul99
Intersection House	CA	RF																	
Iona Community	[uk]		1938			Y	n		23		57%	Y	Y	C M L O	N		I		Jan99
Isle of Erraid	[uk]		1979			Y	y	11		2	64%	Y	Y	C	Y				Jun99
Ittoen Foundation	[jp]		1905	1929		Y	y	130			54%	Y	Y	L	N	S		cmty	May99
Jesuit Volunteer Corps: Northwest	OR		1950			Y	n				70%	Y		C L	N			nonprofit	Apr99
Jesus Christians	[au]		1980			Y	y	12		1	33%	Y	N	C M L E O	Y	S			Mar99
Jesus People USA Evangelical Covenant Church	IL		1968	1975	1972	Y	n	500	350	150	36%	N	Y	C E O	N	S		cmty	Oct98
John T Lyle Center for Regenerative Studies	CA	RF	1993	1992	1993	Y		18	16	2	50%	N	N	C	N		I	other	Sep99
Joint House	MI							42	42										Oct99
Jolly Ranchers	WA	RF	1994	1995	1995			5	5		40%	N	N	C	N		S	subgrp	Dec98
Jonah House	TX		1984	1986	1986							N	Y	C	N		I	subgrp	Mar99
Jubilee Partners	GA		1979	1979	1979	Y	m	26	14	12	50%	N	N	C L O	N	S		cmty	Dec98
Julian Woods Community	PA		1970	1974	1971	Y	y	21	14	7	47%	N	N	C	Y		I	other	Jan99
Jump Off Community Land Trust	TN		1990			Y	y	12	9	3	44%	N	N	C	Y		I	clt	Sep99
Jupiter Hollow	WV		1976	1976	1976	Y	y	11	8	3	50%	N	N	M	Y		I	cmty	Dec98
Kadesh-biyqah	[se]		1997			Y	y		7	5	57%	Y	Y	O	Y	S			May99
KALANI Oceanside Eco - Resort	HI		1973	1975	1975	Y	n	28	27	1	57%	Y	Y	M L E	Y			other	May99
Kana-Gemeinschaft (Cana Community)	[de]		1990	1993		Y	n	7	7		71%	N	Y	C M	N			other	Jan99
Kanatsiohareke (Gana jo haleke)	NY		1993																Oct99
Karen House Catholic Worker	MO				1977	Y	y	7	7		71%		Y	C	N			ldlord	Mar99
Kashi Ashram	FL		1976	1976	1974	N	n	165	121	44	55%	Y	Y	E	N		I	cmty	Oct99
Kibbutz Ketura	[il]		1973			Y	y	290	150	140	50%	Y	Y	M	N	S			Mar99
Kibbutz Lotan	[il]		1983			Y	y	125	80	45	55%	Y	Y	M	N	S		cmty	Dec98
Kibbutz Movement, The	[il]		1910			Y	y				50%	N	Y	M	N	S		other	May99
Kibbutz Neot Semadar	[il]		1979		1989	Y	y	158	96	62	58%	N	Y	O	N	S		other	Aug99
Kibbutz Tamuz	[il]		1987			Y	y		31	26	48%	N	N	C	N	S			May99
Kidstown	CA		1990	1990	1991	N	y	4	4		25%								Apr99

KEY *Canadian Provinces:* BC = British Columbia, MB = Manitoba, NS = Nova Scotia, ON = Ontario, SK = Saskatchewan.
Country: [ar] = Argentina, [au]= Australia, [at] = Austria, [be] = Belgium, [br] = Brazil, [co] = Colombia, [dk] = Denmark, [fr] = France, [de] = Germany, [gr] = Greece, [in] = India, [il] = Israel, [it] = Italy, [jp] = Japan, [mx] = Mexico, [nl] = The Netherlands, [nz] = New Zealand, [ng] = Nigeria, [uk] = United Kingdom, [uk*] = Northern Ireland.
Decisions: C = Consensus, M = Majority, L = Leader, G = Group of leaders or elders, O = Other.
Income: S = Members Share Income, I = Independently Handle Own Finances.
Who Owns Land: CLT = Community Land Trust, Cmty = Community, Indiv = Individual, Ldlord = Landlord, Subgrp = Subgroup of members.
Survey Date: Date shown is when survey questionnaire was completed or last updated by community.

Chart

Map / Index Name	Eat Together How Frequently?	What % of Own Food Is Grown?	Organic Food in Diet	Dietary Norms	Alcohol Use	Tobacco Use	# Homeschooled	Some Labor Expected	Rural, Urban, or Both	# of Buildings	Acres of Land	GLB Ok	Spiritual Path	Primary Purpose and/or Focus
Hermitage	2-5 times/week	6-20%		veg	ok	ok		X	R	7	63	GLB	Y	Queer Pantheist Hermitage
Hertha	1-3 times/month	21-50%							R	10	40			
Hesbjerg	1-3 times/month	21-50%	yes!	omni	often	often		X	R	20	100		N	Peace Ecology Art Hospitality
HiddenValley														
HighFlowing	2-5 times/week	21-50%	yes!	no red	none	none			R	9	100	GLB	Y	sustainable love spirit arts
HighHorizons	Nearly all dinners	1-5%			none	none		X	R	2	260			homestead seekers - beginners
HighWind	Rarely	>50%	ok	vgn	ok	ok	3	X	R		148		Y	Modeling Sustainable Community
Highline	2-5 times/week	1-5%						X	B	40	3.6		N	Learning to live as friends
HillTopFarm	2-5 times/week	6-20%	yes!	omni	none	yes!		X	R	3	20	B	Y	living an honest life
Hillegass	Nearly all dinners	1-5%	often	omni	ok	none		X	U	3			N	consensual group living, respect
HoldenVil	1 time/week	1-5%	some	omni	ok	ok		X	R	20			Y	Lutheran retreat/volunteer community
HolyCity	Rarely	1-5%						X	B	11	80		Y	Roman Catholic
Homestead	Nearly all dinners	6-20%	often	veg	ok	ok		X		3	10	GLB	N	
HorizonsEcoV	Rarely								R	40	500		N	Ecovillage sanctuary
HouseofPeace	Nearly all dinners	None	often	omni	none	none			U	1			Y	homeless shelter
Huehuecoyotl														
HumanityRis			yes!		none	none							Y	Manifest spiritual principles in daily life
Hundredfold									R					
HuntingtnOWL	1 time/week	6-20%	yes!	no red	none	ok		X	R	1	50		N	Womyns Access to Land
HutterBreth	Nearly all meals	>50%	ok	omni	some	none			R				Y	Christian Community
Ida	Nearly all meals	6-20%	yes!	veg				X	R	2	250	GLB	N	art, ecology, and queer revolution
Innisfree	2-5 times/week	1-5%	some	omni	some	some		X	R	12	600		N	
ICC-AnnArbor	Nearly all dinners	None							U				N	affordable quality housing and co-op services
ICC-Austin	Nearly all dinners	1-5%	often	omni	yes!	some		X	U	8			N	
IntlPuppydog	2-5 times/week	None	yes!		some				U			G	N	Extended intimate family
Intersection														
Iona	Nearly all meals	1-5%	some	omni	ok	ok			R	6			Y	sharing - common - life - integration
IsleofErraid	Nearly all dinners	>50%	yes!	omni	some	some			R	8			Y	spiritual-ecological-sustainable
Ittoen	Nearly all meals								B				Y	
JesuitVolNW	1 time/week	1-5%	some	no red	some	ok			B				Y	community spirituality justice
JesusChrist	Nearly all meals	None	some	omni	some	ok	1	X	U	3			Y	Faith, Love, Jesus, Sincerity
JesusPeople	Nearly all meals	None	ok	omni	none	none		X	U	2	740+		Y	Inner- City Christian Service
JohnTLyleCtr	Nearly all dinners	21-50%	yes!	omni	some	ok		X	B	2	16	GLB	N	Education, demonstration, research
JointHouse														
JollyRancher	2-5 times/week	1-5%	yes!	no red	some	ok			U	2		GLB	N	Self knowlede thru intimacy
JonahHouse	Rarely	1-5%	ok	veg	none	none			U	2			Y	
JubileePartn	Nearly all meals	21-50%	often	omni	ok	ok		X	R	7	258		Y	Christian Service Community
JulianWoods	Rarely	6-20%							R	9	140		N	
JumpOffCLT	1-3 times/month		yes!	omni	some	ok		X	R	5	1100			revere land; live in harmony
JupiterHollo	Rarely	1-5%						X	R	7	180	GLB	N	neighbors and friends
KadeshBiyqah	Nearly all meals	1-5%	yes!	omni	none	none	3	X	R	3	10		Y	Prophetic Patriarchal Christian
Kalani	Nearly all meals	1-5%	yes!	no red	ok	ok		X	R	23	113	GLB	N	Humanitarian compassionate consideration
Kana-Gemeins	2-5 times/week	None	some	omni	none	ok			U	3		GLB	Y	Christian solidarity with poor
Kanatsiohare														
KarenHouseCW	2-5 times/week	1-5%						X	U	3		GB	Y	Catholic Worker House
KashiAshram	Nearly all dinners	None	often	veg	none	none		X	B	5	80		Y	Spirituality, service, education
KibbutzKetur	Nearly all meals	1-5%	ok	omni	ok				R	194			Y	mutual responsibility
KibbutzLotan	Nearly all meals	6-20%	yes!	omni	ok	ok			R	54	143		Y	Judaism, ecology, equality, economic cooperation
KibbutzMvmt	Nearly all dinners	1-5%							R				Y	
KibbutzNeotS	Nearly all meals	21-50%	yes!	no red	some	yes!			R	100	400		N	Learning of man's condition
KibbutzTamuz	1 time/week	None	some	omni	some	ok			U	24			N	communal involved Socialist secular
Kidstown														

KEY *Diet:* omni = includes red meat, no red = no red meat—includes fish or poultry and dairy, veg = vegetarian—no meat—includes dairy, vgn = vegan—no meat or dairy.
Diet note: Some communities list omni and provide vegan options, some list vegan yet allow personal food without restriction. Take the label as a rough guideline.
Rural, Urban or Both: Some communities used both (B) to indicate having both an urban and rural location or that the one property was both urban and rural, as suburban.
Acres of Land: Hectare is abbreviated ha and is approximately 2.5 acres.
Some Labor Expected: Members are expected to regularly contribute labor to the group.
GLB Ok: The community indicated that gay men (G) or lesbians (L) or bisexuals (B) are welcome as members.
Spiritual Path: The community indicated it has a primarily spiritual or religious focus.

Name	State/Prov. or Country	Forming, Reforming	Year Formed	Year Purchased	Year Began Living	Open to More Adults?/Children?	Total Population	# Adults	# Children (<19yrs)	Percentage Women	Identified Leader	Leadership Core Group	How are Major Decisions Made?	Join Fee?	Income Shared/Indep.	Who Owns Land	Survey Date
Kindness House	NC		1993	1993	1994	Y m	7	7		57%	Y	Y		N		nonprofit	Feb99
King House	MI						8	8									Oct99
Kingman Hall	CA		1977	1977	1977	N	51	43	8	49%	N	Y	C M L O	Y	I	other	Feb99
Kitezh Children's Eco-Village Community	[uk]		1992			Y y		22	33	50%	Y	Y	C	N	S		May99
KynHearth	VA	RF	1994	1994	1995	Y y	3	3		67%	N		C O	N	S	indiv	Oct99
L.I.F.E.	VA		1991	1995	1996	N n	25	15	10				C	Y	I		Apr99
L'Arche Erie	PA	RF	1972	1972	1972	Y n	63	63		55%	Y	Y	E		I	cmty	Jul99
L'Arche - Homefires	NS	RF	1981			Y n					Y	Y	C		I		Jan99
L'Arche Mobile Inc	AL				1974	Y m	44	40	4	50%	Y	Y	E		I	cmty	Jan99
La Senda Ecovillage	[mx]		1997			Y n	7	0		71%	N	N	C M	Y	I		May99
La Vieille Voie Communauté	[be]		1988			Y		11	16	64%	Y	Y	C	N	I		May99
Lake Claire Cohousing	-		1994	1997	1997	N n	29	20	9	60%	N	N	C	N	I	mix	Sep99
Lake Village	MI		1965	1971	1966	Y y	42	32	10			Y	E		I	cmty	Nov98
Lama Foundation	NM	RF	1968	1967	1968	Y y	12	12	0	60%	N	Y	C E			nonprofit	Oct99
Land Stewardship Center, The	MI		1991	1970	1993	Y y	7	4	3	50%	N	N	C		I	mix	Aug99
Landelijke Vereniging Centraal Wonen	[nl]																
Laurieston Hall	[uk]		1972			Y y		24	9	46%	N	N	C	N	I		May99
Le Novalis	QC	F	1996			Y m					N	N	C				Jul99
Learners Trek	VA	F	1999														Sep99
Lebensgarten Steyerberg	[de]		1985			Y y		90	50	56%	N	Y	C	N	I		Mar99
Lee Abbey Aston Household Community	[uk]		1988	1988	1988	Y m	4	4		75%	Y	Y	C	N	S	other	Feb99
Lesbian and Gay Spiritual Community	VT	F				Y y	2	2		100%	N	Y	C M E		I	other	Sep99
Lester House	MI																Oct99
Liberty Village Cohousing	MD		1989	1996			42	28	14	54%	N	N	C				Oct99
Lichen Co-op	OR		1971			Y y	6	6	0	33%			C	Y		clt	Jan99
Life Center Association	PA		1973	1973	1973	Y y	36	32	4	44%	N	Y	C	N		clt	Jan99
Light as Color Foundation	CO	F	1997	1994	1997	Y y	8	8		50%	N	Y	C	N	I	indiv	Jan99
Light Morning	VA		1973	1973	1973	M m	18	13	5	38%	N	N	C	N	I	clt	Jan99
Light of Freedom, Inc	VA	F	1993	1996	Jan99	Y y	6	6		50%	N	N	C		I	mix	May99
Linder House	MI			1989	1989												Oct99
Lindsbergs Kursgård	[se]		1974			Y y		330			N	N	C	Y			May99
Little Flower Catholic Worker Farm, The	VA		1996	1996	1996	Y	10	4	6	50%	N	N	C	N	S	ldlord	Jun99
Little Grove	[uk]	RF	1981		1983	Y y	11	11		64%	N	N	C	N	I	cmty	Mar99
Living ROCK Christian Men's Co-op	MI		1942			Y n	10	10		0%	Y	Y	C M E	Y	I	clt	Aug99
Locust Grove Community, Inc.	OH		1995	1990	1996	Y y	4	4		25%		Y	E	N	S	cmty	Jan99
Lofstedt Farm Community	BC	F	1984			Y y	16	10	6	50%	Y	Y	L		I	indiv	Dec98
Long Branch Environmental Education Ctr	NC		1974	1974	1974	Y y	11	10	1	50%			M	Y	I	nonprofit	Sep99
Los Angeles Eco-Village	CA		1993		1994	Y y	29	17	12	50%	Y	Y	C L E O	Y	I	mix	Sep99
Los Horcones	[mx]	F	1973	1973	1973	Y y	24	19	5	32%	N	N	O	N	S	mix	Dec98
Losang Dragpa Buddhist Centre	[uk]		1985	1991	1991	Y y	29	28	1	41%	Y	Y	E		I	other	Jun99
Lost Valley Educational Center	OR		1988	1989	1989	Y y	23	15	8	47%	N	Y	C	Y	S I	nonprofit	Jan99
Lothlorien	IN		1983	1987	1987	Y y	500	460	40	50%	N	Y	E		I	mix	Sep99
Lothlorien - Centro de Cura e Crescimento	[br]		1984			Y y		8	4	50%	N	Y	C	N	S I		Feb99
Lothlorien Co-op	WI			1973	1973	Y y	33	32	1		N	N	C	N	I	nonprofit	Feb99
Lothlorien Farm	ON		1972	1972	1972	Y y	15	14	1	50%	N	S	C	Y	I	cmty	Feb99
Love Israel Family, The	WA		1968	1977	1968	Y y	60				Y	Y	C L E	N		indiv	Mar99
Lower Shaw Farm	[uk]	RF	1974	1974	1974	N n	5	2	3	50%	N	N	C	N	I	ldlord	Sep99
Luther Buchele House	MI																Oct99
Ma Yoga Shakti International Mission	NY		1979	1979	1979	Y p	420				Y		O			other	Feb99
Maat Dompin	VA	F	1992	1298		M					Y		O	N		cmty	Dec98
Madison Community Cooperatives (MCC)	WI		1968		1968	Y y	189	156	33	50%	N	Y	C M	Y	I	cmty	Jan99
Madison Street House	OR	F	Feb99	Nov98	Feb99	Y n	1	1		0%	N	N	C		I	indiv	Aug99

KEY *Canadian Provinces:* BC = British Columbia, MB = Manitoba, NS = Nova Scotia, ON = Ontario, SK = Saskatchewan.
Country: [ar] = Argentina, [au]= Australia, [at] = Austria, [be] = Belgium, [br] = Brazil, [co] = Colombia, [dk] = Denmark, [fr] = France, [de] = Germany, [gr] = Greece, [in] = India, [il] = Israel, [it] = Italy, [jp] = Japan, [mx] = Mexico, [nl] = The Netherlands, [nz] = New Zealand, [ng] = Nigeria, [uk] = United Kingdom, [uk*] = Northern Ireland.
Decisions: C = Consensus, M = Majority, L = Leader, G = Group of leaders or elders, O = Other.
Income: S = Members Share Income, I = Independently Handle Own Finances.
Who Owns Land: CLT = Community Land Trust, Cmty = Community, Indiv = Individual, Ldlord = Landlord, Subgrp = Subgroup of members.
Survey Date: Date shown is when survey questionnaire was completed or last updated by community.

Map / Index Name	Eat Together How Frequently?	What % of Own Food Is Grown?	Organic Food in Diet	Dietary Norms	Alcohol Use	Tobacco Use	# Homeschooled	Some Labor Expected	Rural, Urban, or Both	# of Buildings	Acres of Land	GLB Ok	Spiritual Path	Primary Purpose and/or Focus
Kindness	Nearly all meals	21-50%	yes!	veg	none	none		X	R	4	13	GLB	Y	Spiritual Practice and Service
KingHouse														
KingmanHall	Nearly all dinners	1-5%	yes!	omni	ok	ok		X	B	1	1-2	GLB	N	cooperative living
KitezhChildr	Nearly all meals	21-50%	yes!	omni	ok	ok			R	10	90		Y	partnership for orphans within an eco-village
KynHeartH	Nearly all dinners	1-5%	yes!	vgn	some	none		X	R	2	69	GLB	N	polyamorous, vegetarian, ecovillage
LIFE	1 time/week	1-5%	yes!				10		R				Y	christian community
L'ArcheErie	Rarely	None	none	omni	yes!	ok			U	7			Y	Disabled Individuals
L'ArcheHome	Nearly all meals	None							B	5			Y	
L'ArcheMobil	1-3 times/month	None		omni	ok	ok		X	U				Y	Christian Community for mentally handicapped
LaSendaEcoV	1-3 times/month	21-50%	yes!	no red	ok	none			R	4	19.2		Y	Healthy individual development
LaVieilleVoi	1 time/week	None							U				Y	Fraternal life, communal prayer
LakeClaire	2-5 times/week	1-5%	some	veg				X	U	12		GLB	N	Sharing, Resource Conservation
LakeVillage	Rarely							X	B	12	300+		N	Earth Oriented Sustainable Homestead
LamaFdtn	Nearly All Meals	1-5%	often	veg	ok	ok		X	R		105	GLB	Y	Spiriitual Community and School
LandSteward	1-3 times/month	21-50%	yes!						R	3	150		Y	Land Stewardship
Landelijke														
Laurieston	1-3 times/month	>50%	often	omni	ok	ok		X	R		150	N		collectivity
LeNovalis			yes!	veg	some	some			B			GLB	Y	Ecolo - arto - socio - philo R & D grp
LearnersTrek														
Lebensgarten	Rarely	1-5%	yes!	veg	some	some			R	50	4		N	
LeeAbbeyAsto	Nearly all meals	1-5%	some	omni	some	none			U	1			Y	Jesus Love of Neighbour Church
LesbianGaySp	Nearly all dinners	21-50%	yes!	veg	ok	none		X	R			GLB	Y	lesbian / gay spiritual rural
LesterHouse														
LibertyVil	2-5 times/week						2		R	36	23			A caring community
LichenCo-op	1-3 times/month	6-20%		veg	often	none		X	R	4+	140		Y	Environmental Interdependent
LifeCenter	Nearly all dinners	1-5%	yes!	veg	ok	ok		X	U	7			N	Co-op community land trust
LightasColor	Rarely	21-50%	yes!	no red	some	none			R	2	2	GLB	Y	Visual arts, nature, holism
LightMorning	Nearly all meals	21-50%	yes!	veg	ok	ok	5	X	R	5	150		Y	This place is a dream. (Rumi)
LightFreedom	2-5 times/week	6-20%	yes!	omni	yes!	yes!		X	R	2	40		Y	God Realized Oneness
LinderHouse														
Lindsbergs	Nearly all dinners	1-5%	yes!	veg	ok	ok		X	R	1	2 ha		N	solidarity, environmental consciousness
LittleFlower	Nearly all meals	6-20%	yes!	veg	some	ok	3	X	R	3	13	GLB	Y	Radical Christian non-violence
LittleGrove	2-5 times/week	None	some	omni	some	ok			R	2	5			
LivingROCK	Nearly all dinners	None	ok		ok	ok		X	U	1				spiritual growth for male collegiates
LocustGrove	Nearly all meals	>50%	yes!	omni	some	none		X	R	3	160		Y	Native style living and teaching
LofstedtFarm	Nearly all meals	>50%	yes!	omni	some	ok		X	R	5	60		Y	Biodynamic Agriculture
LongBranch	1-3 times/month	>50%	yes!	omni	ok	ok		X	R	9	1635	L	M	sustain conservation education
LosAngEcoV	1 time/week	1-5%	yes!	omni	some	none		X	U	48			N	cooperative and ecological
LosHorcones	Nearly all meals	21-50%	yes!	omni	some	none	3		R	12	240		N	
LosangDragpa	Nearly all dinners	None	yes!	veg	none	none			B	4	15		Y	
LostValley	Nearly all meals	6-20%	yes!	veg	none	none		X	R	13	87	GLB	N	Sustainability, ecology, growth
LothlorienIN	1-3 times/month	1-5%	ok	vgn	ok	ok			R	3	109		Y	creating / maintaining sanctuary
LothlorienBR	Nearly all meals	1-5%	often	veg	none	none	2	X	R	6	14 ha		Y	Nature, spirituality, ecology
LothlorienWI	2-5 times/week	1-5%	yes!	veg	ok	ok		X	U	1		GLB	N	vegetarian enviro & LGBT-friendly
LothlorienON	Rarely	6-20%	often	omni	often	some		X	R	4	700		N	land stewardship, friendship
LoveIsrael	Rarely	6-20%	often		ok	none	12	X	R	15	300		Y	Manifesting Love and Oneness
LowerShaw	Nearly all dinners	6-20%	yes!	omni	some	ok		X	B	4	3		N	To live together well
LutherBuchel														
MaYogaShakti														
MaatDompin			yes!	omni				X	R		134		N	Womyn of Color Projects
MadisonCC	Nearly all dinners	1-5%						X	U	10			N	Affordable cooperative housing - dining
MadisonSt	Rarely	1-5%	often	omni	some	none	0		U			GLB	N	Sharing Community

KEY *Diet:* omni = includes red meat, no red = no red meat—includes fish or poultry and dairy, veg = vegetarian—no meat—includes dairy, vgn = vegan—no meat or dairy.
Diet note: Some communities list omni and provide vegan options, some list vegan yet allow personal food without restriction. Take the label as a rough guideline.
Rural, Urban or Both: Some communities used both (B) to indicate having both an urban and rural location or that the one property was both urban and rural, as suburban.
Acres of Land: Hectare is abbreviated ha and is approximately 2.5 acres.
Some Labor Expected: Members are expected to regularly contribute labor to the group.
GLB Ok: The community indicated that gay men (G) or lesbians (L) or bisexuals (B) are welcome as members.
Spiritual Path: The community indicated it has a primarily spiritual or religious focus.

Community	State/Prov. or Country	Forming, Reforming	Year Formed	Year Purchased	Year Began Living	Open to More Adults?	Open to More Children?	Total Population	# Adults	# Children (<19yrs)	Percentage Women	Identified Leader	Leadership Core Group	How are Major Decisions Made?	Join Fee?	Income Shared/Indep.	Who Owns Land	Survey Date
Madre Grande Monastery	CA	RF	1975	1975	1975	Y	y	9	9		56%	N	Y	E	N	S I	nonprofit	May99
Magic, Inc.	CA		1972	1976	1972	Y	y	39	31	8	49%	Y	Y	C	N		nonprofit	Dec98
Maharishi University of Management	IA		1974	1974	1974	Y	y	4460	4100	360	50%	Y	Y	L E	N		nonprofit	Aug99
Maison Emmanuel	QC	RF	1983	1982	1983	Y	y	51	36	15	49%	N	Y	C	N	S	mix	Sep99
Malu 'Aina Ctr for Nonviolent Educ & Action	HI		1979	1980	1981	Y	n	4	4	0	50%	Y		C	N	·	cmty	Sep99
Manzanita Village of Prescott	AZ	F	1994	1997	1999	Y	y	24	18	6	50%	N	Y	C	Y	I	mix	May99
Marathon Cooperative	CA		1988			Y	y							M	Y	I	cmty	Feb99
Mariposa Group, The	TX	RF	1984	Nov98		Y	y	8	6	2	67%	Y	N	O		I	indiv	May99
Mariposa Grove	CA	F	Feb99	Jan99	Feb99	Y	y	5	5		60%	N	N	C		I	mix	Oct99
Marsh Commons Cohousing	CA		1990	1993	1998	Y	y	24	16	8	50%	N	N	C	N		indiv	Sep99
Martha's Housing Cooperative	WI		1969	1969	1970	N	y	37	27	10	59%	N	Y	O	Y		nonprofit	Dec98
MASALA Community Housing	CO	F	Aug99	Sep99	Sep99	Y		11	11		45%	N	N	C	Y	I	nonprofit	Oct99
Maxwood Institute	IL	RF	1983	1984	1988	Y	y	11			27%	N	Y	O	N	I	mix	Oct99
Meadowdance Community Group	NJ	F	1997	1999	Apr00	Y	y	12	8	4	50%	N	N	C	N		cmty	Apr99
Methow Center of Enlightenment	WA	F	1990	1990	1990	Y	y	1	1			Y		M				
Miccosukee Land Co-op	FL		1972	1973	1973	Y	y	163	124	39	53%	Y	Y	C	N	I	indiv	Sep99
Michigan Socialist House	MI		1932	1932	1932	Y		19					Y			I	cmty	Jul99
Michigan Womyn's Music Festival	MI		1976		1976	Y	y	800			100%	Y	Y	L E	Y	I	indiv	Oct99
Middle Road Cohousing	BC		1994			N	n		23	26	48%	N	N	C	N			Jun99
Mikeco Rehtle	MI	F				Y	y	2	1	1	0%	Y	Y	C	N		mix	Nov99
Minnie's Co-op	MI		1970	1970														Oct99
Molino Creek Farming Collective	CA		1982			N	n	20	14	6	46%	N	N	C		I	cmty	Feb99
Molloy Ashram Retreat	[au]		1979	1979		Y	n	4	3	1	33%			L			indiv	Mar99
Monadnock Geocommons Village	NH	F	1999			Y	y	20	16	4	50%	N	Y	C		I	indiv	Oct99
Monan's Rill	CA		1972	1973	1974	Y	y	30	22	8	55%	N	N	C	Y	I	cmty	Jan99
Monkton Wyld Court	[uk]		1982			Y	y		12	4	58%	N	Y	C M	N		mix	Mar99
Montclaire	PA	RF		1983									Y	C	Y	I	mix	Jul99
Monte Vuala	[ch]		1993			Y	n					N	Y	C M	N	S		May99
Monterey Cohousing Community	MN		1991	1992	1993	Y	y	33	24	9	54%	N	N	C	N		cmty	Jan99
Moonshadow	TN		1971	1965	1971	N	n	9	9	0	56%	N	Y	C	N		indiv	Sep99
Mørdrupgård	[dk]		1970			N	n	32	21	11	50%	N	N	C	N		cmty	May99
Morning Star Ridge Community	BC		1992	1992	1992	Y	y	16	13	3	55%	N	Y	C E O	Y	I	indiv	Dec98
Morninglory	ON		1969	1969	1969	Y	y	17	8	9	50%	N	N	C M E	Y	I	clt	Dec98
Mount Madonna Center	CA		1971	1977	1978	Y	y	96	80	16	56%	Y	Y	O	N		cmty	Jan99
Mountain Home	OR	RF	1989	1989	1989	Y	y	4	4		25%	Y	Y	O	N		indiv	Sep99
Mt. Murrindal Cooperative	[au]		1982	1983	1983	Y	y	20	20		55%	N	N	C	Y		other	Apr99
Mulvey Creek Land Co-operative	BC	RF	1991	1991	1991	Y	y	22	14	8	42%			O	Y		cmty	Feb99
"N" Street Co-housing	CA		1986		1986	Y	y	55	39	16	48%	N	N	C	N	I	mix	Sep99
Nahziryah Monastic Community	AR			1970	1970	Y	y					Y	Y	L	O	N S	cmty	Oct99
Nakamura Co-op	MI					Y	n	54			50%	N	Y	M	Y		cmty	Jan99
Namasté Green	NH	F				Y	y	3			33%	N	Y	C	Y		indiv	Dec98
Nasalam	MO		1984	1995	1995	Y		4			0%	Y	Y	E	N	S	nonprofit	Sep99
Nature's Spirit	SC		1996	1997	1997	Y	y	6	6		50%	N	N	C M	O N	I	cmty	Sep99
Ness	NY	F	1991	1987	1991	Y	y	4	4		25%	N	N	C	O M	I	indiv	Jan99
Neve Shalom	[il]		1972		1977													
New Community	MI			1969		N	n	15			40%	N	Y	C M	Y	I	cmty	Jan99
New Creation Christian Community	[uk]		1974			Y	y	680	520	160	50%	Y	Y	C M E	Y	S	mix	Jan99
New Environment Association	NY		1974															Jan99
New Goloka	NC		1982	1982	1982	Y	y	24	18	6	50%	Y		L E	N	S	mix	Sep99
New Humanity Centre	[gr]	F	1992			Y	y	25	25		48%	Y		C	Y	S I	clt	Mar99
New Jerusalem Community	OH		1971	1973		Y	y	110	65	45	58%	N	Y		Y	I	nonprofit	Jan99
New Land	VA		1979	1979	1979	Y	y	54	44	10		N	N	M	N	I	indiv	Nov98

KEY *Canadian Provinces:* BC = British Columbia, MB = Manitoba, NS = Nova Scotia, ON = Ontario, SK = Saskatchewan.
Country: [ar] = Argentina, [au]= Australia, [at] = Austria, [be] = Belgium, [br] = Brazil, [co] = Colombia, [dk] = Denmark, [fr] = France, [de] = Germany, [gr] = Greece, [in] = India, [il] = Israel, [it] = Italy, [jp] = Japan, [mx] = Mexico, [nl] = The Netherlands, [nz] = New Zealand, [ng] = Nigeria, [uk] = United Kingdom, [uk*] = Northern Ireland.
Decisions: C = Consensus, M = Majority, L = Leader, G = Group of leaders or elders, O = Other.
Income: S = Members Share Income, I = Independently Handle Own Finances.
Who Owns Land: CLT = Community Land Trust, Cmty = Community, Indiv = Individual, Ldlord = Landlord, Subgrp = Subgroup of members.
Survey Date: Date shown is when survey questionnaire was completed or last updated by community.

Map / Index Name	Eat Together How Frequently?	What % of Own Food Is Grown?	Organic Food in Diet	Dietary Norms	Alcohol Use	Tobacco Use	# Homeschooled	Some Labor Expected	Rural, Urban, or Both	# of Buildings	Acres of Land	GLB Ok	Spiritual Path	Primary Purpose and/or Focus
MadreGrande	Nearly all dinners	6-20%	yes!	veg	some	ok		X	R	10	264	GLB	Y	positive spiritual path
Magic,Inc	Nearly all dinners	1-5%	yes!	veg	none	none			U			GLB	Y	Ecological Approach to Value
Maharishi	2-5 times/week	21-50%	yes!	veg	none	none	60		B	50	1500		Y	T.M. Program & T.M Sidhis in Large Group
MaisonEmmanu	Nearly all meals	1-5%	yes!	omni	ok	ok			B	6	35		Y	Life - sharing Community
Malu'AinaCen	Nearly all dinners	>50%	yes!	omni	some	ok		X	R	4	22		Y	peace and justice
ManzanitaVil	2-5 times/week	6-20%	yes!	omni	often	ok		X	B	36	12.5		N	community
MarathonCoop	Rarely	None							U	66			N	We share our housing.
MariposaGrp									R		3			Happiness, freedom, responsibility
MariposaGrov	2-5 times/week	1-5%	yes!	veg	ok	none		X	U	3		GLB	N	Arts & Activism
MarshCommons	2-5 times/week	1-5%	yes!	omni	yes!			X	B	13	1.5	GLB	N	neighborliness/sustainable
Martha'sHous	Nearly all dinners	1-5%	yes!	veg	ok	ok		X	U	1			N	Housing, Food, Children-friendly
Masala	2-5 times/week	1-5%	yes!	veg	ok				U	1			N	environmental consensus driven housing co-op
MaxWoodInst	1 time/week	1-5%	often	omni				X	U	1			Y	conserve, reuse, reforest
Meadowdance	Nearly all meals	6-20%	yes!	omni				X	R				N	cooperative, ecology, children
MethowCenter		21-50%							R		88			provide community for all
Miccosukee	Rarely	1-5%							R				N	Building a caring cmty with respect for all life
MichiganSoc	Nearly all dinners	None						X	U	1			N	Student Cooperative Housing
MichiganWomy	Nearly all meals	None	yes!	veg	none	ok		X	R		650	LB	N	Womyn's Music and Culture
MiddleRoad	2-5 times/week	1-5%	some	no red	often		3		R	12	52		N	cooperative family friendly living
MikecoRehtle	Nearly all dinners	1-5%	yes!	vgn	none	none	1					GLB	Y	we are seekers
Minnie'sCoop														
MolinoCreek	Rarely	21-50%	yes!	omni	yes!				R	10			N	Organic farm collective & Home
MolloyAshram	1 time/week	None		veg	none	none			R	1	2.5		Y	spiritual yoga advaita vedanta
Monadnock			yes!	no red				X	R		40+	GLB	N	mindful sustainable living
Monan'sRill	1-3 times/month	1-5%	ok	vgn	ok	ok		X	R	13	460		N	shared land and values
MonktonWyld	Nearly all meals	6-20%	yes!	veg	ok	ok			R	4	11		N	Holistic Education
Montclaire	Nearly all dinners	>50%	yes!	no red	none	none		X	R		250		Y	to model peaceful lifestyles
MonteVuala	1 time/week	None	yes!	veg	some	ok		X	R	2			Y	to make a place/guesthouse for women
MontereyCoho	2-5 times/week	1-5%					2	X	U	2			N	A Cohousing Community
Moonshadow	Nearly all dinners	21-50%	yes!	no red	some	some		X	R	9	300	GLB	N	Eco Ed Activist Art Media Arch
Mørdrupgård	1 time/week	6-20%						X	B	5-6	100 ha		N	
MorningStarR	2-5 times/week	21-50%	yes!	vgn	ok	ok	3	X	R	7	160		Y	Loving & Serving Life & Spirit
Morninglory	1-3 times/month	21-50%	yes!	no red	some	some	3		R	9	100		N	Live simply, respect all Life
MountMadonna	Nearly all meals	21-50%	yes!	veg	none	none		X	B	30	355		Y	yoga and service
MountainHome	Nearly all meals	6-20%	yes!	omni	some	yes!		X	R	5	360		Y	Permaculture/Social Justice
MtMurrindal	1-3 times/month	6-20%	often	veg	ok	ok		X	R	6	120		N	personal and community growth
MulveyCreek	1-3 times/month	6-20%	yes!	vgn	ok	ok	2		R	7	35		N	
NStreetCoho	2-5 times/week	6-20%	yes!	omni	ok	ok			U	14			N	communally sharing resources
Nahziryah	Nearly all meals	21-50%	yes!	vgn	none	none		X	B		103		Y	service toward consciousness expansion
Nakamura	Nearly all dinners	None						X	U	2		GLB	N	A co-operatively run home
NamastéGreen	Rarely	6-20%	often	no red	ok	ok		X	R	1	49		Y	Family permacultural cooperative
Nasalam	Nearly all meals	6-20%	often	vgn	some	ok		X	R	1	21	LB	Y	Spritual growth
NaturesSpiri	Nearly all meals	6-20%	yes!	no red	some	none		X	R	3	210		Y	Spiritual growth and sustainable living
Ness	1-3 times/month	1-5%	yes!	omni	some	some			R	3	100		N	land stewardship/cooperation
NeveShalom														
NewCommunity	Rarely	None	ok	vgn	ok	ok	0	X	U	1		GLB	N	
NewCreation	Nearly all dinners	1-5%	some	omni	none	none			B	85	200		Y	Evangelical Christian
NewEnviron														
NewGoloka	Nearly all meals	1-5%	yes!	veg	none	none		X	R	2-4	16		Y	Please chant Hare Krishna.
NewHumanity	1-3 times/month	6-20%					5	X	B	2			Y	Pansophic/Holistic/Monastic
NewJerusalem	Rarely	None	yes!	omni	some	ok	5	X	U	0			Y	Catholic Eucharistic Lay Led
NewLand	Rarely	1-5%							R		200			develop our spiritual paths

KEY *Diet:* omni = includes red meat, no red = no red meat—includes fish or poultry and dairy, veg = vegetarian—no meat—includes dairy, vgn = vegan—no meat or dairy.
Diet note: Some communities list omni and provide vegan options, some list vegan yet allow personal food without restriction. Take the label as a rough guideline.
Rural, Urban or Both: Some communities used both (B) to indicate having both an urban and rural location or that the one property was both urban and rural, as suburban.
Acres of Land: Hectare is abbreviated ha and is approximately 2.5 acres.
Some Labor Expected: Members are expected to regularly contribute labor to the group.
GLB Ok: The community indicated that gay men (G) or lesbians (L) or bisexuals (B) are welcome as members.
Spiritual Path: The community indicated it has a primarily spiritual or religious focus.

Name	State/Prov. or Country	Forming, Reforming	Year Formed	Year Purchased	Year Began Living	Open to More Adults?	Open to More Children?	Total Population	# Adults	# Children (<19yrs)	Percentage Women	Identified Leader	Leadership Core Group	How are Major Decisions Made?	Join Fee	Income Shared/Indep.	Who Owns Land	Survey Date
New River Valley Cohousing	VA	F	1997	1999				23	17	6	53%	Y	Y	C	Y	I		Sep99
New View Cohousing	MA		1989	1994	1995	Y	y	83	46	37	59%	N	Y	C	N	I	cmty	May99
New Vrindavan	WV		1968	1968	1968	Y	y	230				N	Y	E	N		mix	
Niche / Tucson Community Land Trust	AZ							4	4			N	N	O			clt	Jan99
Niederkaufungen Kommune	[de]		1986			Y	y		55	18	45%	N	N	C	Y	S	cmty	Mar99
Ninth Street Associates	CA		1993	1986	1993	N	n	8	7	1	57%	N	Y	C O	Y	I	cmty	Mar99
Nishnajida	WI		1989	1990	1991	Y	y	7	6	1	33%	N	N	C O	N		other	Sep99
Noah Project Communities	NC	F	1998		1999			150						C	N		mix	Jan99
Nomad Cohousing	CO		1994	1996	1997			24	18	6	67%			C	Y	I	other	Oct99
Nomadelfia	[it]	F	1931	1949	1948	Y	y	330	185	145	51%	Y	Y	O	N	S	clt	Oct99
Nomenus Radical Faerie Sanctuary	OR		1984	1987	1989	Y	n	4	4		0%	N	N	C	N		nonprofit	Feb99
North Mountain Community Land Trust	VA	RF	1972	1972	1972	Y	y	5	3	2	67%			C	Y	I	clt	Dec98
Northern Sun Farm Co-op	MB		1984	1984	1984	Y	y	15	8	7	57%	N	N	C	Y	I	cmty	Jan99
Nyland Cohousing Community	CO		1990	1990	1993			140	100	40	65%	N	N	C	Y	I	other	Oct99
O'Brien Lake Homesteaders	MT		1976	1977	1980	N	n	12	9	3	44%	N	Y	CM	Y	I	mix	Feb99
O'Keefe Co-op	MI					Y	m	85	85						Y		cmty	Oct99
Oak Grove Foundation	VA	F	1993			Y	y	1	1		100%			C	P		indiv	Jan99
Oakland Elizabeth House	CA		1991		1993	Y	y	24	9	15	100%	Y	Y	C E	N	I	nonprofit	Apr99
Oakwood Farm	IN		1974	1974	1974	Y	y	16	15	1	50%	N	Y	E	N		cmty	Nov98
Ofek Shalom Co-op	WI			1991	1991	Y	y	13	11	2	46%	N	N	O	Y	I	other	Nov98
Ohio Bio-Enviro Settlements, Inc.	OH	F	May99			Y	y	138	95	43	59%	Y	Y	L E	Y	I	cmty	Aug99
Ojai Foundation, The	CA		1979					11	7	4		Y	Y	CM L E O	N		nonprofit	Nov98
ÖkoLeA - Klosterdorf	[de]		1992						19	11	58%	N	N	C	Y			May99
Olympia Housing Collective	WA	F	Jun99		Sep99	Y	y	25	25		60%	N	N	C	N	I	other	Oct99
One Spirit Free Catholic Community	VA		1998			Y	y	80	49	31	63%	Y	Y	E	N		other	Aug99
One World Family Commune	CA		1967		1967	N		9	8	1	25%	Y	Y	CM	N	S	ldlord	Dec98
OnGoing Cohousing Community	OR		1990	1991	1991	Y	y	19	15	4	53%	N	N	C	N	I	subgrp	Jul99
Orca Landing	WA		1990	1990	1990	Y	y	6	4	2	50%	N	N	C	N	I	indiv	Mar99
Osho Mevlana	[au]		1996			Y	y		15	4	53%	N	Y	CM E	Y	I		Dec98
Osho Miasto	[it]	F	1981	1991	1981	N	n	28	28		64%		Y	E	N		other	Jul99
Osterweil Cooperative	MI		1946	1946	1946	N	n	13	13	0	54%	Y	Y	C	Y		cmty	Jan99
Otamatea Eco-Village	[nz]	F	1995	1996	Jan99	Y	y	27	18	9	44%	N	N	C	Y		cmty	Sep99
Othona Community, The	[uk]			1946	1946	Y	y	600				Y	Y	O	N		cmty	Jan98
Our Ecovillage	BC	RF	1990	1990	1990	Y	y	10	4	6	60%	N	Y	C E	N	I	mix	Mar99
Owen House	MI																	Oct99
Owl Farm	OR																	
Padanaram Settlement	IN		1966	1966	1966	Y		200	120	80	45%	Y	Y	E	N	S	mix	Jan99
Pagan Island Community (PIC)	OK	F	1997			Y	y	36	21	15	48%	N	N	C	N		other	Sep99
Palmgrove Community Farms	[ng]		1987	1989	1990	Y		270				Y	Y	M	N	S	cmty	Jun99
Pangaia	HI	RF	1991	1990	1992	Y	y	5	4	1	60%	N	Y	C L O	N	S	indiv	Aug99
Panterra	NY	RF	1992	1992	1992	Y	y	2	2		50%	N	Y	C	N	I	subgrp	May99
Paradise Gardens	HI	F	1990	1999		Y	y	2	2		0%	Y	Y	C O	N	I	other	Oct99
Parker Street Cooperative, Inc.	CA		1987	1992	1987	N	n				50%	Y	Y	C	Y		cmty	Nov98
Parnassus Rising	AZ	F	1990	1943		Y	y	4	4		25%	Y	Y	M L E	N	S I	cmty	Jan99
Pathfinder Fellowship	[uk]		1922	1942		N	n	17	12	5	41%	Y	Y	L E	N	I	mix	Mar99
Peace Farm	TX	F	1986	1986	1986	Y	n	1	1		100%	Y		E	N	I	other	Nov98
People House	CO	RF	1974	1984		Y						Y	Y	E	N		cmty	Mar99
People of the Living God	TN		1935	1983	1935	Y	y	63	52	11	60%	Y	Y	L E	N	S	cmty	Jan99
Phanto Bolo	CO	F	1993	1993	1993	Y	y	8	6	2	50%	N	Y	C	N		indiv	Oct99
Phoenix Co-op, The	WI	F	1996	1970	1996	Y	n	25	25	0	44%	N	N	C	Y		clt	Jan99
Phoenix Community	CO	F	1982		1983	Y	n	3	3	0	67%	N	N	C	N		cmty	Oct99
Piñon Ecovillage	NM	F	Jun99	2000	Jun99	Y	y	2	2		50%	N	N	C	N	S	cmty	Oct99

KEY *Canadian Provinces:* BC = British Columbia, MB = Manitoba, NS = Nova Scotia, ON = Ontario, SK = Saskatchewan.
Country: [ar] = Argentina, [au]= Australia, [at] = Austria, [be] = Belgium, [br] = Brazil, [co] = Colombia, [dk] = Denmark, [fr] = France, [de] = Germany, [gr] = Greece, [in] = India, [il] = Israel, [it] = Italy, [jp] = Japan, [mx] = Mexico, [nl] = The Netherlands, [nz] = New Zealand, [ng] = Nigeria, [uk] = United Kingdom, [uk*] = Northern Ireland.
Decisions: C = Consensus, M = Majority, L = Leader, G = Group of leaders or elders, O = Other.
Income: S = Members Share Income, I = Independently Handle Own Finances.
Who Owns Land: CLT = Community Land Trust, Cmty = Community, Indiv = Individual, Ldlord = Landlord, Subgrp = Subgroup of members.
Survey Date: Date shown is when survey questionnaire was completed or last updated by community.

Chart

Map / Index Name	Eat Together How Frequently?	What % of Own Food Is Grown?	Organic Food in Diet	Dietary Norms	Alcohol Use	Tobacco Use	# Homeschooled	Some Labor Expected	Rural, Urban, or Both	# of Buildings	Acres of Land	GLB Ok	Spiritual Path	Primary Purpose and/or Focus
NewRiverVal							1		B				N	to live together in community
NewViewCoho	2-5 times/week	1-5%	yes!	omni	some	none	2	X	B	18	18	GLB	N	respect of the earth
NewVrindavan	1-3 times/month	6-20%	some	veg	none	none	3		R		3000		Y	Spiritual retreat yoga ashram
Niche/Tucson	2-5 times/week		yes!	vgn	ok	ok		X	U	2	2			
Niederkaufun		>50%	yes!	omni	some	yes!	4		B	7	7			changing society / alternative living
NinthStreet	Rarely	1-5%	yes!	omni	ok	ok		X	U	5		GLB	N	limited equity housing cooperative
Nishnajida	Nearly all dinners	None	often	omni	none	none		X	R	5	80	GLB	Y	Native-Earth balanced lifeway
NoahProject									R				Y	
NomadCoho	2-5 Times/week	1-5%							U	11			N	cohousing urban energy-efficient
Nomadelfia	Nearly all meals	>50%	yes!	omni	yes!	none	140	X	R	~120	800		Y	The brotherhood of the Gospel
Nomenus	Nearly all dinners	1-5%	some	omni	some	ok	0	X	R	4	80	GB	Y	Gay Spirituality & Community
NorthMount	1 time/week	6-20%	yes!	veg	none	none			R	3	130		N	steward the land together
NorthernSun	1-3 times/month	6-20%	yes!	omni	some	yes!	1	X	R	7	160	GLB	N	living lightly on the land
NylandCoho	2-5 Times/week	1-5%							R	43	42		N	
O'BrienLake	Rarely	6-20%	often	omni	some	some		X	R	5	160		N	a community of good neighbors
O'KeefeCoop									U					
OakGroveFdtn	Nearly all dinners	1-5%		no red					R	1	82		Y	earth peace spirit simplicity
OaklandEliz	2-5 times/week	1-5%	some	omni	some	yes!		X	U	1		LB	Y	Hospitality for Homeless
OakwoodFarm	Rarely	1-5%	often	omni	some	ok			R	9	326	GLB	Y	sacred space provider
OfekShalom	Nearly all dinners	1-5%	often	veg	ok	ok		X	U	1		GLB	Y	fun, friendly, articulate folk
OhioBio-Envi	1-3 times/month	>50%						X	R	125	22		Y	Pagan Bio-Community
OjaiFdtn	1 time/week	1-5%	often	veg	ok	ok			R	1	40	GLB	Y	the way of council
OekoLeA-Ulos	2-5 times/week	6-20%	yes!	omni	ok	ok	4	X	R	4	1 ha		N	
OlympiaHous	Nearly all dinners	None	yes!	veg	ok	ok		X	U	5			N	sustainable cooperative community
OneSpirit	1 time/week	None					0			0	0		Y	Liberal Catholic Christianity
OneWorldFam	Nearly all dinners	1-5%	yes!	vgn	some	none		X	U	2			Y	new world sharing demonstration
OnGoingCoho	2-5 times/week	6-20%	yes!	veg	ok				U	6		GLB	N	environment social justice art
OrcaLanding	2-5 times/week	1-5%	yes!	omni	often	none		X	U	1	0		N	
OshoMevlana	2-5 times/week	1-5%	yes!	veg	yes!	often			R	11	400		Y	Meditation, Celebration, Osho
OshoMiasto	Nearly all meals	1-5%		vgn				X	R	5	132		Y	Osho's Zorba the Buddha
Osterweil	Nearly all dinners	None	ok	omni	none	none		X	U	1			N	To live together cheaply
OtamateaEcoV	2-5 times/week	6-20%	yes!	omni	some	some		X	R		251	GLB	N	Permaculture eco-village
OthonaCmty	Nearly all meals	None	yes!	omni	yes!	yes!			R	10	410		Y	Christian, Ecumenical, Undogmatic
OurEcovillag	2-5 times/week	>50%	yes!	veg	some	ok	1		R	2	25	GLB	Y	Sustainability: all things connected
OwenHouse														
OwlFarm														
Padanaram	Nearly all meals	>50%	yes!	omni	ok	ok			R	50	3000		Y	Kingdomism Spiritual Selfsustaining
PaganIsland	2-5 times/week	>50%	yes!	no red	ok	none	15		R			GLB	Y	Tropical Pagan Eco-village
Palmgrove	Nearly all meals	>50%							B		12			sustainable human development settlement
Pangaia	2-5 times/week	>50%	yes!	omni	none	none		X	R	6	33	B	Y	raw foods, permaculture, service, love
Panterra	Nearly all dinners	None	yes!	veg	ok	none		X	R	3	36	GLB	Y	Personal enrichment
ParadiseGard	2-5 times/week	>50%		vgn	none	none		X	R	1		GLB	Y	Life in Paradise restored
ParkerStreet	1-3 times/month	1-5%	often	omni	ok	none			U	2			N	open voluntary diverse affordable
ParnassusRis	Rarely	None	yes!	no red	none	none		X	B		200	B	N	Communitarian, Matriarchal, Polyfidelitous
Pathfinder	Nearly all dinners	None	ok	omni	ok	ok		X	U	1		GL	Y	Christian
PeaceFarm	Rarely	None	often	veg	some	none		X	R	3	20		N	
PeopleHouse	Rarely	1-5%						X	U	1		GLB	Y	nonsectarian spiritual community
PeopleLiving	Nearly all meals	1-5%	some	omni	none	none		X	U	20	1500		Y	Obedience to words of Jesus Christ
PhantoBolo	1-3 times/month	None	often	no red	none	yes!			R	3	80	GLB	Y	Walking In Balance
PhoenixCoop	2-5 times/week	1-5%	yes!	omni	yes!	yes!		X	R	1	<1	GLB	N	Egalitarian Social Living
PhoenixCmty	Nearly all dinners	None	ok		ok	ok			U	1			Y	Lifelong Personal Development
PiñonEcovil	Nearly all dinners	6-20%	yes!	veg	ok	none		X	R			GLB	N	sustainable, egalitarian

KEY *Diet:* omni = includes red meat, no red = no red meat—includes fish or poultry and dairy, veg = vegetarian—no meat—includes dairy, vgn = vegan—no meat or dairy.
Diet note: Some communities list omni and provide vegan options, some list vegan yet allow personal food without restriction. Take the label as a rough guideline.
Rural, Urban or Both: Some communities used both (B) to indicate having both an urban and rural location or that the one property was both urban and rural, as suburban.
Acres of Land: Hectare is abbreviated ha and is approximately 2.5 acres.
Some Labor Expected: Members are expected to regularly contribute labor to the group.
GLB Ok: The community indicated that gay men (G) or lesbians (L) or bisexuals (B) are welcome as members.
Spiritual Path: The community indicated it has a primarily spiritual or religious focus.

	State/Prov. or Country	Forming, Reforming	Year Formed	Year Purchased	Year Began Living	Open to More Adults?	Open to More Children?	Total Population	# Adults	# Children (<19yrs)	Percentage Women	Identified Leader	Leadership Core Group	How are Major Decisions Made?	Join Fee?	Income Shared/Indep.	Who Owns Land	Survey Date
Pioneer Cooperative	CA	RF				Y	n	10	8	2	50%	Y	N	M L	N	I	other	Feb99
Pioneer Valley Cohousing	MA		1989	1993	1994	Y	y	90	55	35	50%	N	N	C		I	cmty	Aug99
Plants for a Future	[uk]		1986			Y	y	5	4	1	50%	N	N	C	N	I		Jan99
Pleasant Hill EZ Cohousing	CA	F	1997	Mar00	2001	Y	y					N	N	C		I	cmty	Sep99
Plow Creek Fellowship	IL	RF	1971	1971	1971	Y	n	36	28	18	50%	Y	Y	C	N	S	cmty	Sep99
Pod of Dolphins	VA	F	1996	1977	1996	Y	y	5	3	2	67%	N	Y	C	N		subgrp	Mar99
Potash Hill Community	MA		1994	1994	1995	Y	y	15	14	1	57%	N	N	C	N	I	mix	Oct99
Priorities Institute, The	CO	F	1979	1995	1998	Y	y	2	2		50%	N	N		Y	I	indiv	Aug99
Pro-Fem	NM	F	1999		1999	Y	y					Y	Y	E	N		indiv	Jul99
Projekt Eulenspiegel	[de]		1976			Y			6	1	50%	N		C O	N	I		Apr99
ProWoKultA	[de]		1995					27	25	2								Nov99
Proyecto Eco-Villas - Asociación GAIA	[ar]		1996			Y	y	5			40%	N	N	C M	Y	I		Feb99
Prudence Crandall House	CA		1972	1972	1972	S	s	8	8		100%	N	Y	C	N	I	indiv	Dec98
Pumpkin Hollow Community	TN	F	1996	1996	1996	Y	y	6	4	2	25%	N	N	C	N	I	subgrp	Feb99
Pumpkin Hollow Farm	NY		1937			Y	n		7	0	29%	N	Y	C E	N			Dec98
Purple Rose	CA		1978	1978	1978	N	n	10	10		50%	N	N	C	N	I	cmty	Jul99
Quarries, The	VA	F	1999	Apr99		Y	y	2	2					M	N		mix	Nov99
Quarry Hill	VT		1946		1960	Y	y					N	Y	C E O	N	I	other	Aug99
Qumbya Cooperative	IL		1991	1991	1991	Y	n	34	32	2	53%	Y	N	C	Y		nonprofit	Jan99
Rachana Community	WA		1996		1992	Y	n	6	6	0	50%	N	N	C			clt	Nov98
Rainbow Family Gatherings	-		1972			Y	y					N	N	C			other	Jan99
Rainbow Hearth Sanctuary	TX			1981		Y	y	6	6		50%	N	Y	E			other	Oct99
Rainbow House	KS		1977			Y	n	9	7	2	75%	N	N	C			ldlord	Nov98
Rainbow Peace Caravan	-		1996			Y	y		25	4	48%	N	Y	C O	Y			May99
Rainbow Valley	[nz]		1974			Y	y		14	8	57%	N	N	C M	Y	I		Oct99
Rainbow Valley Agricultural Cooperative	TX		1978	1990	1978	Y	y	32	21	11	45%	N	Y	M	Y	I	cmty	Feb99
Rapha Community	NY		1971			Y		38	29	9	55%	N	N	C	N		other	Oct99
Rat & Tat Familien-Gemeinschaft	[at]	F	1996			Y	y	13	6	7	67%	N	N	C	N	S	indiv	Mar99
Raven Rocks	OH		1970	1970	1970	Y	y	11	11	0				C	N		cmty	
Reba Place Fellowship	IL		1957		1957	Y	y	50	38	12		Y	Y	C	N	S	cmty	Aug99
Reevis Mountain School of Self-Reliance	AZ	RF	1979	1979	1980	Y	n	4			50%	Y	Y	E	Y		mix	Jan99
Renaissance Co-op	MI							66	66									Oct99
Renaissance Village	CA	F	Apr99	Feb99	Sep99	Y	y	2	2		100%	Y	Y	E	N		mix	Oct99
Ridge House Co-op	CA																	Jan98
Rio Bonito - Belize	CA	F	1982			Y	y	7	7		57%	N	N	C	N	I	indiv	Sep99
Riparia	CA		1987			N	n	25	14	11	62%	N	Y	C	Y	I	subgrp	Oct99
River City Housing Collective	IA		1977	1982	1977	Y	y	29	25	4	50%	N	Y	C M O	Y	I	cmty	Apr99
River Farm Community Land Trust	WA			1971		N	n	26	17	9	44%	N	N	C		I	clt	Jan99
River Hayven Eco-Village and Tubing Society	WI	RF	1992	1993		Y	y	11	6	5	50%	N	Y	O	Y	I	cmty	Aug99
Riverdale Cohousing	ON	F	1998	Jun99	Jun99	Y	y	60	41	19		N	Y	C	N		mix	Sep99
Riverside Community	[nz]		1941	1941	1941	Y	y	34	20	14	50%	N	N	C O	N	S	other	May99
Rosewind Cohousing	WA	F	1989	1992	1997	Y	y	40	35	5	51%	N	N	C	Y		cmty	Jan99
Rosneath Farm Eco-Village	[au]	F	1994			Y	y	6	6		50%	Y	Y	C M L E O	N	I	cmty	Nov98
Rosy Branch Farm	NC		1987	1987	1987	N	n	23	16	7		N	N	C	Y	I	other	Apr99
Rowe Camp & Conference Center	MA		1973	1973	1973	N	n	12	11	0	64%	Y	Y	M L O	N	I	nonprofit	Sep99
Ruth's House	MI			1993	1993	N		12	12		42%	Y	Y	C	Y	I	indiv	Jan99
Sacred Mountain Ranch	AZ	F		1997	Nov98	Y	y	4	4		40%			C L	N		other	Dec98
Sacred Oak Community, The	OR	F	Jun99		Jun99	Y	y	4				N	N		N		mix	Sep99
Saints' Christian Retreat, The	MO	RF	1995	1995	1996	Y	y	8	6	2	38%	N	Y	M E	N	I	indiv	Jan99
Saints' Francis & Therese Catholic Worker	MA		1986			Y	n	9	5	4	20%	N	Y	C	N	S	clt	Nov98
Salamander Springs	GA	F	1998	1995	1998	Y	p	7			40%	N	N	C	N	I	other	Dec98
Salt Creek Intentional Community	WA	F				Y	y	4	4		50%	N						Oct99

KEY *Canadian Provinces:* BC = British Columbia, MB = Manitoba, NS = Nova Scotia, ON = Ontario, SK = Saskatchewan.
Country: [ar] = Argentina, [au]= Australia, [at] = Austria, [be] = Belgium, [br] = Brazil, [co] = Colombia, [dk] = Denmark, [fr] = France, [de] = Germany, [gr] = Greece, [in] = India, [il] = Israel, [it] = Italy, [jp] = Japan, [mx] = Mexico, [nl] = The Netherlands, [nz] = New Zealand, [ng] = Nigeria, [uk] = United Kingdom, [uk*] = Northern Ireland.
Decisions: C = Consensus, M = Majority, L = Leader, G = Group of leaders or elders, O = Other.
Income: S = Members Share Income, I = Independently Handle Own Finances.
Who Owns Land: CLT = Community Land Trust, Cmty = Community, Indiv = Individual, Ldlord = Landlord, Subgrp = Subgroup of members.
Survey Date: Date shown is when survey questionnaire was completed or last updated by community.

Map / Index Name	Eat Together How Frequently?	What % of Own Food Is Grown?	Organic Food in Diet	Dietary Norms	Alcohol Use	Tobacco Use	# Homeschooled	Some Labor Expected	Rural, Urban, or Both	# of Buildings	Acres of Land	GLB Ok	Spiritual Path	Primary Purpose and/or Focus
PioneerCoop	2-5 times/week	None	some	omni	ok	ok	0		U	1	0	G	N	Cooperative Living
PioneerVal	2-5 times/week	1-5%							R	33	23		N	
PlantsFuture	1-3 times/month	21-50%	yes!	vgn	ok	ok		X	R	1	100		N	Vegan Organic Permaculture
PleasantHill	2-5 times/week								U	36			N	Intergenerational cohousing
PlowCreek	2-5 times/week	1-5%	often	omni	ok	none	5		R	9	189		Y	To be Faithful to Jesus
PodofDolphin	Nearly all dinners	1-5%	often	omni	ok	none		X	R	2	7.5	GLB	Y	polyfidelity extended family
PotashHill	1-3 times/month	1-5%					0	X	R	7	115		N	
Priorities	Nearly all meals	1-5%	often	omni	yes!	ok	0		R	1	11	GLB	Y	Intellectual stimulation/ creative endeavors
Pro-Fem		None	yes!	omni	ok	ok			R				Y	relationships, difference between men and women
ProjektEulen	2-5 times/week	None	yes!	omni					R	2	1330		N	Self-governed & ecologically oriented living
ProWoKultA									U	1				
ProyectoEcoV	Nearly all meals	21-50%	yes!	veg	none	ok		X	R	5	20		N	Education y Permacultura
PrudenceCran	2-5 times/week	6-20%	yes!	omni	some	none		X	U	2		GLB	N	To create community in the city
PumpkinHolTN	Nearly all dinners	1-5%	yes!	omni	ok	ok	2	X	R	3	120	GLB	N	
PumpkinHolNY	2-5 times/week	6-20%	often	veg	none	ok		X	R	3	130		Y	Theosophical community
PurpleRose	Nearly all dinners	1-5%	yes!	veg	some	none		X	U				N	Self managed housing
Quarries		1-5%							R		357	GLB		respect for the land and people
QuarryHill	1-3 times/month	1-5%	yes!					X	R	20+	150	GLB	N	Caring for Children, Creativity
QumbyaCoop	Nearly all dinners	None	yes!	veg	ok	ok		X	U	2			N	cheap rent and food, fun, tofu!
RachanaCmty	2-5 times/week	1-5%	often	no red	ok	ok		X	B	11	15	GLB	Y	Conscious Harmonious Win-Win
RainbowFam	Nearly all meals	None	yes!	veg	ok	yes!			R				Y	pray for world peace and celebrate life.
RainbowHeart	Nearly all dinners	6-20%	yes!	no red	ok	none		X	R	5	7	GLB		eco-spiritual health vitality
RainbowHouse	Rarely	1-5%	yes!	omni	some	yes!		X	U	1		B	N	To Facilitate a Healthy Environment
RainbowPeace	Nearly all meals	1-5%	yes!	no red	some	ok	4		B				N	Permaculture, arts, indigenous
RainbowValNZ	1-3 times/month	6-20%	yes!	omni	some	ok		X	R				N	extended family, love of land, peace
RainbowValTX	Rarely	6-20%	often	omni	often	often			R	14	210		N	ecology, stewardship, community
RaphaCmty	1-3 times/month	None	some		none	none		X	U	0			Y	family on a spiritual journey
RatandTat	Nearly all meals	>50%							B	4	6 ha		Y	Perhaps "Oneida III" led by the Holy Spirit
RavenRocks									R		1047			education, ecology, sharing
RebaPlace		1-5%					1		U	20			Y	Radical Discipleship, Service, Radical Reconciliation
ReevisMtn	Nearly all meals	>50%	yes!	omni	none	none		X	R	12	12		Y	Live what you love
RenaissanceC														
RenaissanceV	Nearly all meals	6-20%	yes!	veg	none	none	0	X	R		20		Y	Ecology, Spiritaulity, Service
RidgeHouse														
RioBonito	1-3 times/month	21-50%	yes!	no red	ok	none	1	X	R	2	25	GLB	N	organic, natural living
Riparia	1-3 times/month	21-50%	yes!	veg	ok	ok	2	X	R	8	12		N	peace and social justice issues
RiverCity	Nearly all dinners	1-5%	yes!	veg	ok	ok		X	U	2		GLB	N	Education Ecology Diversity
RiverFarm	1 time/week	21-50%	yes!	omni	some	some		X	R	7	80	GLB	N	land stewardship & consensus
RiverHayven	1 time/week	>50%	yes!	omni	some	ok	4	X	R	2	233	GLB	N	sacred honest ecological life
Riverdale	1-3 times/month	None	often	no red	some	none		X	U				Y	Diversity, community, caring, earth
Riverside	2-5 times/week		often	omni	ok	ok		X	R	20	500		N	Full community life
RosewindCoho	1 time/week	6-20%	yes!	omni	often	ok	1		U	19	9	GLB	N	Neighbors sharing time, projects, & support
RosneathFarm	Nearly all meals	>50%							U	70	365		N	Permaculture village and farm
RosyBranch	1-3 times/month	1-5%	some		some	some			R		50			modeling cooperative options
RoweCamp	Nearly all dinners	None	often	omni	often	often			R	4	45		N	Personal & Spiritual Growth
Ruth'sHouse	2-5 times/week	None	some	omni	ok	ok		X	U	1		GLB	N	To Provide cheap student housing
SacredMtn	2-5 times/week	21-50%	yes!	no red	ok	none		X			20			health/spiritual growth
SacredOak	Nearly all dinners	6-20%	yes!	veg	none	none		X	R	1	5	GLB	N	responsible freedom
SaintsChrist	1-3 times/month	1-5%	often	omni	often	none	1	X	R	5	80		Y	SOLD OUT FOR JESUS!
SaintsFranci	Nearly all dinners	1-5%	often	veg	none	none			U	1			Y	
SalamanderSp	Nearly all dinners	6-20%	yes!	no red	yes!	ok	2	X	R		50	GLB	S	sustainability; planetary healing
SaltCreek	2-5 times/week	1-5%							R	1	55			save land adaptable loving

KEY *Diet:* omni = includes red meat, no red = no red meat—includes fish or poultry and dairy, veg = vegetarian—no meat—includes dairy, vgn = vegan—no meat or dairy.
Diet note: Some communities list omni and provide vegan options, some list vegan yet allow personal food without restriction. Take the label as a rough guideline.
Rural, Urban or Both: Some communities used both (B) to indicate having both an urban and rural location or that the one property was both urban and rural, as suburban.
Acres of Land: Hectare is abbreviated ha and is approximately 2.5 acres.
Some Labor Expected: Members are expected to regularly contribute labor to the group.
GLB Ok: The community indicated that gay men (G) or lesbians (L) or bisexuals (B) are welcome as members.
Spiritual Path: The community indicated it has a primarily spiritual or religious focus.

Community	State/Prov. or Country	Forming, Reforming	Year Formed	Year Purchased	Year Began Living	Open to More Adults?	Open to More Children?	Total Population	# Adults	# Children (<19yrs)	Percentage Women	Identified Leader	Leadership Core Group	How are Major Decisions Made?	Join Fee?	Income Shared/Indep.	Who Owns Land	Survey Date
San Mateo Cooperative Community	CA	RF	1998	1998	1998	Y	y	9	9		56%				N		mix	Sep99
Sandhill Farm	MO		1973	1974	1974	Y	y	8	6	2	67%	N	N	C	N	S	cmty	Oct99
Santa Rosa Creek Commons	CA		1968	1978	1982	Y	y	39	33	6	67%	N	N	C	Y	I	cmty	Dec98
Sassafras Ridge Farm	WV		1972	1972	1972	N	n	28	14	14	33%	N	Y	C	N	I	mix	Nov98
SBSHC: Santa Barbara Student Housing Co-op	CA		1976	1977	1977	Y	n	71	71		48%	Y	Y	M	Y	I	cmty	Nov98
SEADS of Truth, Inc.	ME	F	1979	1980	1980	Y	y	3	2	1	0%	N	Y	C E	Y	I	mix	Dec98
Seattle's Intentional Community Program	WA		1992		1992	N	n	17	17	0	65%	Y	Y	C		I	ldlord	Oct99
Seekers and Settlers	FL	F	1990	1992	1998	Y	y	4	3	1	67%	Y	Y	C E			indiv	Aug99
Seneca Falls Co-op	TX																	Feb99
Shady Grove	CA		1995	1999	1996	P	n	8	8	0	50%	N	N	C	N	I	indiv	Oct99
Shamballa	[au]		1973			S	s		18	5	44%	N	N	C M O	Y	I		Mar99
Shannon Farm Community	VA		1972	1974	1973	Y	y	89	62	27	46%	N	N	C	N		clt	Sep99
Sharing Community	OH	F	1999	1993	1999	Y	y	4	4	0	50%	Y	Y	C	Y	I	other	Feb99
Sharingwood	WA		1984	1984	1990	N	n	85	50	35	50%	N	N	C	N	I	mix	Apr99
Shepherd's Gate Community	CO		1991			Y	y	9	6	3	50%	N	N	C	N	I	indiv	Mar99
Shepherdsfield	MO		1979	1979	1979	Y	y	29	29	0		Y	Y	C E	N	S	cmty	Jan99
Sherwood Co-op	WA		1946			Y		13	13		42%	N	N	C M	Y	I	ldlord	Oct99
Shiloah Valley Community	UT		1955	1955	1955	Y	y	59	34	25	56%	Y	Y	M E	N	S	cmty	Nov98
Shiloh Community	AR																	
Shim Gum Do Zen Sword Center	MA		1978	1981	1976	Y	y	106	80	26	20%	Y	Y	C M L E	Y		other	Jan99
Shivalila	HI		1994	1993	1994	Y	y	16	10	6	50%	N	N	C	Y	S	cmty	Aug99
Short Mountain Sanctuary, Inc.	TN		1979	1973	1980	M	m	18	18	0	6%	N	N	C	N	I	clt	Nov98
Sichlassenfallen	WI		1965	1965	1965	Y	n	6	6	0	33%	N	N	C		I	nonprofit	Dec98
Simeon Center	NY		1993	1999		Y	y				67%			C M	Y	I	clt	Jan99
Simon Community, The	[uk]		1963		1963	Y	n				40%			C L O	N			Jan99
Sirius	MA		1978	1978	1979	Y	y	38	30	8		N	Y	O	N	I	other	Nov98
Sivananda Ashram Yoga Ranch Colony	NY		1974	1974	1974	Y	y	11	11	0	36%	Y	Y	L	N	S	other	Oct99
Skunk Valley Community Farm	IA	F	1999					2	2		50%	Y	Y	C	N	I	other	Aug99
Sky Woods Cosynegal	MI	RF	1972	1977	1972	Y	y				50%	N		C	N	S	clt	Dec98
Skyhouse Community	MO		1996	1997	1995	Y	y	6	6		33%	N	N	C	N	S	clt	Apr99
Skyros Holistic Holidays	[uk]		1979	1978		Y	y				67%	Y		C	N		other	Mar98
Society for the Promotion of Creative Interchange	-	F	1987		1987	Y	n	2	2		50%	N	N	C	N	S		Aug99
Sojourner Truth House	MI					Y	n	50			34%	Y	Y	M	Y	I	cmty	Jan99
Solterra	NC		1993	1994	1998	Y	y	80	62	18	60%	Y	Y	C			mix	Sep99
Song of the Morning	MI		1969	1970	1971	Y	y	9	9	0	56%	Y	Y	O	N	I	other	Oct99
Songaia	WA		1987	1987	1987	Y	y	19	14	5	50%	Y	Y	C	Y	I	mix	Jan99
Sonoma County CoHousing	CA	F	1998			Y	y	15	10	5	50%	N		C	Y	i		May99
Southeastern Michigan Eco-Community	MI	F	1999															Aug99
Southern Cassadaga Spiritualist Camp	FL		1894	1894		Y	n				50%	N		M O	Y	I	cmty	Aug99
Southern Oregon Women's Network	OR	F	1972	1972		Y	y	72	68	4	100%	N	Y	O	N	I	mix	Jan99
Southwest Sufi Community (SSC)	NM		1993	1995		Y	y	75	69	6	48%	N	Y	O	Y	I	cmty	Sep99
Sowing Circle	CA		1994	1994	1994	N	n	19	17	2	41%	N	Y	C	Y		clt	Dec98
Spadefoot	AZ		1995		1995	Y	n	20	20		40%	N	N	C O	N	I	ldlord	Nov98
Sparrow Hawk Village	OK		1981	1981	1981	Y	y	81	68	13	68%	N	Y	O	N	I	mix	Sep99
Sphere of Light	NJ	F	1998		1998	Y	y	4	3	1		N	Y	C	N	S	cmty	Sep99
Spiral Garden	FL		1980			Y	y	35	25	10	48%	N		C	N	I	indiv	Aug99
Spiral Wimmin's Land Trust	KY		1979	1980		Y	y	8	8		100%	N	N	C	Y	I	clt	Sep99
Spirit Journey	OR	F	Nov99			Y	y	3			100%	Y	N	L	N	I	indiv	Oct99
Springtree Community	VA		1971	1971	1972	N	n	6	6		50%	N	N	C M	N	S	cmty	Nov98
Sri Aurobindo Sadhana Peetham	CA		1993	1989		Y	n	4	4		50%	N	Y	C E	N		cmty	Jan99
St Francis Catholic Worker	VA	F	1979	1993	1979	Y	m	2	2		50%	Y	Y	C	N		cmty	Feb99
St Francis Catholic Worker	IL		1974	1974	1974	Y	n	15	14	1	40%	N	Y	C	N	I	clt	Feb99

KEY *Canadian Provinces:* BC = British Columbia, MB = Manitoba, NS = Nova Scotia, ON = Ontario, SK = Saskatchewan.
Country: [ar] = Argentina, [au]= Australia, [at] = Austria, [be] = Belgium, [br] = Brazil, [co] = Colombia, [dk] = Denmark, [fr] = France, [de] = Germany, [gr] = Greece, [in] = India, [il] = Israel, [it] = Italy, [jp] = Japan, [mx] = Mexico, [nl] = The Netherlands, [nz] = New Zealand, [ng] = Nigeria, [uk] = United Kingdom, [uk*] = Northern Ireland.
Decisions: C = Consensus, M = Majority, L = Leader, G = Group of leaders or elders, O = Other.
Income: S = Members Share Income, I = Independently Handle Own Finances.
Who Owns Land: CLT = Community Land Trust, Cmty = Community, Indiv = Individual, Ldlord = Landlord, Subgrp = Subgroup of members.
Survey Date: Date shown is when survey questionnaire was completed or last updated by community.

Map / Index Name	Eat Together How Frequently?	What % of Own Food Is Grown?	Organic Food in Diet	Dietary Norms	Alcohol Use	Tobacco Use	# Homeschooled	Some Labor Expected	Rural, Urban, or Both	# of Buildings	Acres of Land	GLB Ok	Spiritual Path	Primary Purpose and/or Focus
SanMateoCoop	1 time/week	6-20%	yes!	omni	some	yes!		X	U	2		B	Y	sustainability and social change
SandhillFarm	Nearly all meals	>50%	yes!	omni	some	none			R	4	135	GLB	N	Organic, Equality, Dialog, Fun
SantaRosa	1-3 times/month	1-5%						X	U	27	2		N	urban housing co-op; consensus
Sassafras	Rarely	21-50%					5	X	R	10	400	GLB	Y	Cooperative Farm Neighborhood
SBSHC	2-5 times/week	1-5%	yes!	omni	some	ok		X	U	4		GLB	N	Co-op living for students
SEADSofTruth	Rarely	1-5%	often	omni	ok	none		X	R	3	60		N	Solar Environment Peace Education
SeattleIntl	2-5 times/week	None			none			X	U				Y	Christian urban ministry
SeekersSettl	1 time/week	6-20%	yes!	veg	ok	none		X	R	2	2.5			Help each one live a good life
SenecaFalls														
ShadyGrove	1-3 times/month	6-20%	yes!	omni	often	none		X	B	4	0	GLB	Y	Erotic Community Celebrating Nature
Shamballa	Rarely	1-5%							R	14	1 sq mile		N	to have quality life in the bush
ShannonFarm	1-3 times/month	6-20%	yes!	omni	some	some	4	X	R	33	520	GLB	N	Cooperative rural lifestyles
SharingCmty	2-5 times/week	21-50%	often		none				R		60		N	environ. stewardship, sustainable lifestyles
Sharingwood	2-5 times/week	1-5%	often	omni	yes!	ok	6	X	B	16	40		N	rural cohousing, large greenbelt
Shepherd'sGa	2-5 times/week	1-5%	often			none		X	U	1			Y	Mutual support and hospitality
Shepherdsfie	Nearly all meals	1-5%	often		ok	none			R		95.5			to follow the way of christ
SherwoodCoop	Nearly all dinners	1-5%	yes!	veg	ok	none		X	U	1		GLB	N	low cost student housing
ShiloahVal	Nearly all meals	21-50%	some	omni	none	none			R	18	4000		Y	Prepare for Christ's Return
ShilohCommun														
ShimGumDoZen	Nearly all dinners	1-5%	often	omni	ok			X	R	1			Y	Zen Buddhism / Martial Arts
Shivalila	Nearly all meals	21-50%	yes!	omni	some	none	4		R	3	47	B	N	Mothers, Babies and Nature
ShortMtn	Nearly all dinners	6-20%	yes!	omni	often	ok		X	R	9	200	GLB	N	Rural Queer Sanctuary
Sichlassenfa	1-3 times/month	1-5%	often	omni	some	none			U	1			N	Common Life Style
SimeonCenter	2-5 times/week	1-5%	often	omni	ok	ok	0	X	R	6	90			intergenerational cohousing
SimonCmty	Nearly all meals	None	ok	omni	none	yes!			B	6		GLB	N	Provision for street homeless
Sirius	Nearly all dinners	21-50%	yes!	veg	ok	ok	5	X	R	8	90		Y	Spiritual Educational Ecological
Sivananda	Nearly all meals	21-50%	yes!	veg	none	none		X	R	5	77		Y	practice & teach yoga & vedanta
SkunkValley		1-5%	yes!	vgn	ok	none			R			GLB	N	Retreat center, Preserve, and CSA
SkyWoodsCos	Nearly all meals	6-20%	often	omni	some	some		X	B	1	20			
Skyhouse	Nearly all dinners	>50%	yes!	veg	some	ok	0	X	R	3	1/280	GLB	N	social change ecology equality
Skyros	Nearly all meals	1-5%		no red				X	B					holistic holiday resort
SocietyCreat	Nearly all meals	None	often	vgn	none	none		X	U				Y	Promoting a particular social process
SojournerTru	Nearly all dinners	None	ok	omni	often	often		X	U	1		GLB	N	affordable student housing
Solterra	1 time/week	1-5%	often	omni	some	some	1	X	B	40	20	L	N	green, community meals peace making consensus
SongMorning	Nearly all dinners	1-5%	often	veg	none	none			R	5	800		Y	Realization of the self/meditation
Songaia	2-5 times/week	6-20%	yes!	no red	some	none		X	B	2	11		N	Earth-conscious cohousing
SonomaCounty	1-3 times/month											GLB	N	Cohousing Neighborhood Community
SouthEMECO														
SouthernCass	1-3 times/month	None							R		57		Y	Belief that life is continuous.
SouthernOreg	Rarely	6-20%	yes!	omni	none	none	2		B		100s	L	Y	Feminism/Ecology/Spiritual/Lesbian
SouthwestSuf	1-3 times/month	1-5%	often	veg	none	ok		X	R	2	1889		Y	spiritual center/nature preserve
SowingCircle	Nearly all dinners	21-50%	yes!	veg	ok	ok		X	R	12	80	GLB	N	Community, Ecology, Education
Spadefoot	Nearly all meals	1-5%	yes!	veg	ok	ok		X	U	1		GLB	N	Rochdale Based Consumers Union
SparrowHawk	1 time/week	1-5%	some		some	some	2		R	46	440	GLB	Y	
SphereLight	Nearly all dinners		yes!	vgn	none	none			B				Y	love yoga music consciousness
SpiralGarden	1-3 times/month	6-20%	yes!	omni	some	some				12			N	Enjoy Earth and One Another
SpiralWimmin	1 time/week	6-20%	yes!	omni	some	none		X	R	11	300	L	Y	Lesbian intentional community
SpiritJourne	1 time/week	21-50%	yes!	omni	some	ok		X	R	2	1.5	GLB	Y	music healing living simply
Springtree	Nearly all meals	21-50%	yes!	no red	yes!	ok		X	R	2	100		N	Sharing and cooperation
SriAurobindo	Nearly all dinners	1-5%	often	veg	none	none		X	R	2	3		Y	Ashram for Sri Aurobindo's Yoga
StFranCW-VA	Nearly all meals	None							R		10		Y	Christian - Retreat Ministry
StFranCW-IL	Nearly all dinners	1-5%	yes!	omni	ok	yes!		X	U	1		GLB	N	Simple living with homeless

KEY *Diet:* omni = includes red meat, no red = no red meat—includes fish or poultry and dairy, veg = vegetarian—no meat—includes dairy, vgn = vegan—no meat or dairy.
Diet note: Some communities list omni and provide vegan options, some list vegan yet allow personal food without restriction. Take the label as a rough guideline.
Rural, Urban or Both: Some communities used both (B) to indicate having both an urban and rural location or that the one property was both urban and rural, as suburban.
Acres of Land: Hectare is abbreviated ha and is approximately 2.5 acres.
Some Labor Expected: Members are expected to regularly contribute labor to the group.
GLB Ok: The community indicated that gay men (G) or lesbians (L) or bisexuals (B) are welcome as members.
Spiritual Path: The community indicated it has a primarily spiritual or religious focus.

Chart

Community	State/Prov. or Country	Forming, Reforming	Year Formed	Year Purchased	Year Began Living	Open to More Adults?	Open to More Children?	Total Population	# Adults	# Children (<19yrs)	Percentage Women	Identified Leader	Leadership Core Group	How are Major Decisions Made?	Join Fee	Income Shared/Indep.	Who Owns Land	Survey Date
St John's Order	CA	RF	1970			Y	y	4	4		75%	N	Y	E	N	S		ldlord	Feb99
St Joseph the Worker House and Farm	RI	F	1997	1997	1997	Y	y	3	2	1	50%	Y	N	C	N		other	Feb99
St Jude Catholic Worker House Community	IL	F	1980	1991	1980	Y	m	3	3			N	Y	C O	N		cmty	Sep99
St Martin de Porres Catholic Worker	CT		1992	1993	1993	Y	y	6	3	3	25%	N	N	C	N	S	other	Sep99
Starland	CA	F	1992	1997	1997	Y	n	6	6		0%	Y	Y	E	N	I	subgrp	Sep99
Starseed Community	MA	F	1987			Y	y	5	3	2	67%	Y	Y	C L	N		indiv	Sep99
Stepping Stones Housing Co-operative	[uk]	F	1997			N	n	20	11	9	55%	N	N	C	Y			Dec98
Stevens House	MI		1943	1943	1943	Y	m	20	11	9	50%	Y	Y	C	Y	I	nonprofit	Feb99
Stewart Little Co-op	NY		1978		1978	Y	n	14	14		50%	N	N	M	N	I	ldlord	Apr99
Stiftelsen Stjärnsund	[se]		1984			Y	y		25	4	60%	N	Y	C M				May99
Still Water Sabbatical	MT		1991	1994	1994	Y	y	15	11	4	36%	N	Y	C		I	ldlord	Oct99
Stone Grail Theatre Community	NC	F	1998			Y	y	12	9	3	58%	N	Y	C		I	cmty	Aug99
Stone Soup Co-op	IL		1997		1997	N	n	18	18		50%	N	N	C	Y		ldlord	Sep99
Storybook Glen	AR	F	1998	1978				8	8	0	38%	Y	Y	C	M		other	Aug99
Strangers & Guests Catholic Worker Cmty	IA		1986	1986		Y	y	4	2	2	50%			C O	N		indiv	Aug99
Student Heritage Houses	TX	RF	1936	Apr99	1936			196	196		90%	N	Y	C M				Nov99
Students Cooperative Association	OR		1937	1961	1937	Y		60	41	19	50%	N	Y	C	Y		cmty	Jan99
Su Casa Catholic Worker Community	IL		1990	1990	1990	Y		11	11		45%	Y	Y	C	N	S	cmty	Jan99
Summit Avenue Cooperative	WI		1970	1972	1970	Y	n	18	18		50%	N	N	C M O	Y		cmty	Mar99
Sun Meadows, Inc.	WA	RF	1974	1974	1973	Y	y	4	4		50%	N	N	M	N	I	cmty	Nov98
Sunflower Cooperative	TX		1980	1980	1980	Y		7	7		57%	N	Y	C	N		cmty	Aug99
Sunnyside Farm Christian Community	MO		1992	1992	1992	Y	y					Y	N	L	N		cmty	Jan99
Sunrise Farm Community	[au]		1978	1978	1978	Y	y	28	22	6	59%		Y	C M	Y		mix	Jan99
Sunrise Ranch	CO		1932	1945	1946	Y	y	98	83	15	53%			C O	Y		cmty	Mar99
Sunward Cohousing	MI		1994	1995	1998	Y	y	85	65	20	55%	N	Y	C	Y		cmty	Sep99
Sunwise Co-Op	CA		1978	1979		Y	n	9	9		56%	N	N	C	Y		cmty	Jan99
Susan B. Anthony Women's Land Trust	OH		1981	1979	1981	Y	m	6	5	1	100%	N	N	C	N		clt	Sep99
Svanholm	[dk]		1978			Y	y		70	40	60%	N	N	C	Y	S		Mar99
Sweetwater Community Land Trust	MO		1981	1981	1984	Y	y	19	12	7	50%	N		C	N	I	clt	Nov98
Sylviron Cooperative	MI	F	1995			Y	y	56				Y	Y	M O	Y		other	Sep99
Synergy House	CA	RF	1972	1972	1972	N	n	45	45		51%	M	M	C	N		other	Jan99
Tacoma Catholic Worker	WA		1989	1989	1989	M	m	12	11	1	33%	N	Y	C	N		cmty	Dec98
Taizé Community	[fr]		1940			Y	n		100		0%	Y	N		N	S		Mar99
Takoma Village Cohousing	MD	F	1998	1999	2000	Y	y	46	40	6	65%	N	N	C	Y		other	Oct99
Talking Cedars	BC	F		1988		Y	y					N	Y	O	Y		mix	Aug99
Tamera - Center for Humane Ecology	[pt]		1995			Y	y		30	5	53%	N	N	O	N			Oct99
Tanguy Homesteads	PA		1945	1945	1945	Y	y	93	67	26	54%	S	Y	C	Y		other	Jan99
TaoWorks Village	-		1996			Y	y					Y	Y	L E	N			Oct99
Tekiah Community	VA	RF	1991	1991	1991	Y	m	3	3	0	67%	N		C	Y	S	other	Sep99
Ten Stones Community	-		1989	1992	1994	N	n	44	28	16	57%	N	N	C	Y	I	mix	Nov98
Teramo Texas	TX	F	Jan99	Jan99	Jan99	Y	y	17	13	4	56%	N	Y	C	N		mix	Jan99
Terra Nova Community	MO		1995	1996	1995	Y	n	4	4		25%	N	N	C	N	S	mix	Sep99
Three Springs Community Land Trust	CA		1993	1992	1996	Y	y	7	7		57%	N	N	C	N	I	clt	Sep99
Tibetan Buddhist Learning Center	NJ		1958	1968														Aug99
Tolstoy Farm	WA		1963	1964	1963	N	n	48	33	15	48%	N	N	C O	N	I	mix	Feb99
Tomorrow's Bread Today	TX	F	1995	1998	1998	Y	y	8	5	3	60%	Y	Y	M	N	S	cmty	Jan99
Tonantzin Land Institute	NM		1982			Y	y		20	7	41%	Y	N	C E	Y			Jul99
TORIC	FL	F	1992			Y	y	3			67%	Y		O	N	I	cmty	Nov98
Toronto Catholic Worker	ON				1990	Y	y	18	16	2	44%	N	N		N	I	nonprofit	Feb99
Town Head Collective	[uk]		1994	1994	1994	N	n				40%		Y	O	N		ldlord	Feb99
Tres Placitas Del Rio	NM	F	1996	1996	1996	Y	y	16	11	5	55%	N	N	C O	Y		cmty	Jan99
Tribe, The	AZ		1993	1996	1993	Y	y	13	6	7	67%	S	S	C	M	I	indiv	Nov98

KEY *Canadian Provinces:* BC = British Columbia, MB = Manitoba, NS = Nova Scotia, ON = Ontario, SK = Saskatchewan.
Country: [ar] = Argentina, [au]= Australia, [at] = Austria, [be] = Belgium, [br] = Brazil, [co] = Colombia, [dk] = Denmark, [fr] = France, [de] = Germany, [gr] = Greece, [in] = India, [il] = Israel, [it] = Italy, [jp] = Japan, [mx] = Mexico, [nl] = The Netherlands, [nz] = New Zealand, [ng] = Nigeria, [uk] = United Kingdom, [uk*] = Northern Ireland.
Decisions: C = Consensus, M = Majority, L = Leader, G = Group of leaders or elders, O = Other.
Income: S = Members Share Income, I = Independently Handle Own Finances.
Who Owns Land: CLT = Community Land Trust, Cmty = Community, Indiv = Individual, Ldlord = Landlord, Subgrp = Subgroup of members.
Survey Date: Date shown is when survey questionnaire was completed or last updated by community.

Map / Index Name	Eat Together How Frequently?	What % of Own Food Is Grown?	Organic Food in Diet	Dietary Norms	Alcohol Use	Tobacco Use	# Homeschooled	Some Labor Expected	Rural, Urban, or Both	# of Buildings	Acres of Land	GLB Ok	Spiritual Path	Primary Purpose and/or Focus
StJohnsOrder	Nearly all meals	None	yes!	veg	none	none		X	U	1			Y	Divine Realization, Service
StJosephCW	Nearly all dinners	21-50%	often	omni	none				R	1	5		Y	
StJudeCW	Nearly all meals	1-5%			none				U	2		GLB	Y	works of mercy
StMartinCW	Nearly all dinners	1-5%	often	omni	often	none		X	U				Y	Poverty Relief Peacework
Starland	1 time/week	None	often	omni	none	none		X	B	3	11	GLB	Y	Retreats/erotic spirituality
StarseedCmty	Nearly all dinners	21-50%	yes!	veg	some	none		X	R	2	130		Y	Healing sanctuary retreat center
SteppingSton	2-5 times/week		yes!	vgn	often	ok	3	X	R	2-3	50	GLB	N	co-operative economics, green politics
StevensHouse	2-5 times/week	None	some	omni	some	some		X	U	1			N	low cost student housing
StewartLittl	Nearly all dinners	1-5%	yes!	veg	often	none		X	U	1		GLB	N	community, friendship, and fun
Stiftelsen		6-20%	yes!	no red	none	ok			R	6	1ha		Y	to live and work together in peace
StillWater	1-3 times/month	6-20%	yes!	omni	ok	ok	4	X	R	3	41		Y	Spiritual, mental, physical health
StoneGrail			yes!	no red	some	some		X	R			GLB	Y	Creative imagination spiritual
StoneSoup	2-5 times/week	1-5%	yes!	veg	ok	ok			U	1			N	Joy and Justice
Storybook	2-5 times/week	1-5%	yes!	no red	none	none	2	X	R	2	170		Y	Show a better way
StrangersCW	2-5 times/week	>50%	yes!	omni	some	none		X	R	1	4		Y	Rural Catholic Worker
StudentHerit	Nearly all dinners	None							U	9				
StudentsCoOR	Nearly all dinners	None	yes!	omni	yes!	yes!			U	2		GLB	N	Student democratic co-op
SuCasaCW	Nearly all dinners	1-5%	some	omni	none	ok		X	U	1		GLB	Y	Hospitality for homeless Latino families
SummitAvenue	Nearly all dinners	1-5%	often	no red	ok	ok		X	U	1		GLB	N	Residential housing and meals
SunMeadows	2-5 times/week	6-20%	yes!	no red	ok	ok		X	R	3	40	GLB	N	One earth one people
Sunflower	1 time/week	1-5%	yes!	veg					U	2			N	
Sunnyside	Nearly all meals		some	omni	none	none			R	1	10		Y	Christian Pentacostal
SunriseFarm	Rarely	6-20%	yes!	no red	ok	some	1		R	12	600		N	Sharing and caring for our land
SunriseRanch	Nearly all meals	21-50%	yes!	omni	ok	ok		X	R	35	360	G	Y	
SunwardCoho	2-5 times/week	1-5%	often		ok	ok	3	X	B	4	20	GLB	N	Cohousing, stewardship of land
SunwiseCoop	2-5 times/week	6-20%	yes!	veg	yes!	ok		X	U	1			N	
SusanBAnthon	1-3 times/month	6-20%	often	omni	some	some		X	R	3	150	L	N	
Svanholm	Nearly all meals	>50%	yes!	omni	ok	ok			R	12	1000		N	sharing and ecological living
Sweetwater	Rarely	6-20%	often	omni	ok	ok	5		R	5	480	B	N	Rural / land stewardship
SylvironCoop		21-50%	often		some	ok			R		77		N	cooperative, strong environmental concern
SynergyHouse	2-5 times/week	1-5%	yes!	vgn	often	often		X	U	1			N	College coop, veggie, ecology
TacomaCW	Nearly all dinners	1-5%	often	omni	none	ok			U	5	4		Y	Welcome homeless in community
TaizéCmty	Nearly all meals	1-5%					0		R				Y	Parable of Reconciliation
TakomaVil	1 time/week	1-5%					1		U	43			N	old fashioned community of the future
TalkingCedar									B	48	17		Y	community ecology spiritual
Tamera	Nearly all meals	1-5%	often	veg	ok	ok	3		R	8	330		Y	future community, free love, free sexuality
TanguyHomest	Rarely							X	R	38	100		N	Diverse cooperative community
TaoWorksVil	Rarely	None	often	omni									Y	Taoist internet community
Tekiah	Nearly all dinners	6-20%	yes!	omni	some	ok		X	R	1	90	GLB	N	Sustainable Loving Connections
TenStones	Rarely	6-20%	yes!	no red	ok	ok			R	13	88		N	Building caring relationships
TeramoTexas	Nearly all meals	1-5%	yes!	no red	none	none		X	B	4			N	learn, heal, have fun
TerraNova	Nearly all dinners	6-20%	yes!	omni	ok	none			U	2	1.5	GLB	N	Making town life sustainable
ThreeSprings	2-5 times/week	21-50%	yes!	veg	ok			X	R	5	160	GLB	N	Care of each other and the earth
TibetanBuddh														
TolstoyFarm			yes!	omni	some	some	5	X	R	27	200	GLB	N	Decentralized rural living
TomorrowsBrd	Nearly all meals	None	some	omni	ok	none			B	2	5		Y	Community with Surplus to Poor
Tonantzin	1 time/week	None						X	R				Y	Recobrar nuestras tradiciones y ceremonias ancestrales
TORIC	2-5 times/week	None							U	1		GLB	N	Mutual Trust Respect and Support
TorontoCW	1 time/week	1-5%	yes!	omni	none	ok			U	7		GLB	Y	Spirituality, justice, queer
TownHead	Nearly all dinners	1-5%	yes!	veg	yes!	yes!	7	X	R	19	2.5		N	environmental sustainability
TresPlacitas	1 time/week	1-5%	often	omni	some	none			B	4	2.5	GLB	N	Caring Home Creating Awareness
TribeThe	1-3 times/month	1-5%	yes!	no red	ok	ok	6	X	R		2.5		Y	New culture and evolution

KEY *Diet:* omni = includes red meat, no red = no red meat—includes fish or poultry and dairy, veg = vegetarian—no meat—includes dairy, vgn = vegan—no meat or dairy.
Diet note: Some communities list omni and provide vegan options, some list vegan yet allow personal food without restriction. Take the label as a rough guideline.
Rural, Urban or Both: Some communities used both (B) to indicate having both an urban and rural location or that the one property was both urban and rural, as suburban.
Acres of Land: Hectare is abbreviated ha and is approximately 2.5 acres.
Some Labor Expected: Members are expected to regularly contribute labor to the group.
GLB Ok: The community indicated that gay men (G) or lesbians (L) or bisexuals (B) are welcome as members.
Spiritual Path: The community indicated it has a primarily spiritual or religious focus.

Communities Directory: A Guide to Intentional Communities and Cooperative Living

Community	State/Prov. or Country	Forming, Reforming	Year Formed	Year Purchased	Year Began Living	Open to More Adults?/Children?	Total Population	# Adults	# Children (<19yrs)	Percentage Women	Identified Leader	Leadership Core Group	How are Major Decisions Made?	Join Fee	Income Shared/Indep.	Who Owns Land	Survey Date
Trillium Community Land Trust	OR	RF	1976			Y	2	2		50%	Y		C L		I	other	Sep99
Troubadour Märchenzentrum	[de]	F	1983			Y		10	10	70%	Y		C O		I	other	Sep99
Truth Consciousness Sacred Mountain Ashram	CO		1974	1974	1974	Y					Y		C L E			cmty	Jan99
Tui Land Trust	[nz]		1982	1984	1983	S s	47	28	18	50%	N N		C		Y	I	clt	Nov99
Tullstugan kollektivhus	[se]		1993			Y y	43	18		56%			M O	N	I		May99
Turtledove Pond	FL	F				Y y					Y N		C		I	ldlord	Aug99
Turtles Island	NY	RF	1964	1964	1964	Y y	6	6		50%	N Y		C	N	I	cmty	Jan99
Twelve Tribes Communauté de Sus	[fr]		1983			Y y	116			50%	N Y		E O	N	S	indiv	Feb99
Twelve Tribes Communidad de Quatro Barras	[br]		1997			Y y	40			50%	N Y		E O	N	S	indiv	Feb99
Twelve Tribes Communidad de San Sebastian	[es]		1994			Y y	71			50%	N Y		E O	N	S	indiv	Feb99
Twelve Tribes Communidad en Buenos Aires	[ar]		1997			Y y	22			50%	N Y		E O	N	S	indiv	Feb99
Twelve Tribes Communidade de Londrina	[br]		1992			Y y	44			50%	N Y		E O	N	S	indiv	Feb99
Twelve Tribes Community at Stentwood Farms	[uk]		1997			Y y	25			50%	N Y		E O	N	S	indiv	Feb99
Twelve Tribes Community in Bellows Falls	VT		1984			Y y	115			50%	N Y		E O	N	S	indiv	Feb99
Twelve Tribes Community in Boston	MA		1981			Y y	35			50%	N Y		E O	N	S	indiv	Feb99
Twelve Tribes Community in Cambridge	NY		1997			Y y	72			50%	N Y		E O	N	S	indiv	Feb99
Twelve Tribes Community in Colorado Springs	CO					Y y	20			50%	N Y		E O	N	S	indiv	Feb99
Twelve Tribes Community in Coxsackie	NY		1997			Y y	54			50%	N Y		E O	N	S	indiv	Feb99
Twelve Tribes Community in Hamburg	NY		1993			Y y	72			50%	N Y		E O	N	S	indiv	Feb99
Twelve Tribes Community in Hyannis	MA		1991			Y y	55			50%	N Y		E O	N	S	indiv	Feb99
Twelve Tribes Community in Island Pond	VT		1978		1978	Y y	51			50%	N Y		E O	N	S	indiv	Feb99
Twelve Tribes Community in Lancaster	NH		1988			Y y	35			50%	N Y		E O	N	S	indiv	Feb99
Twelve Tribes Community in Oak Hill	NY		1997			Y y	77			50%	N Y		E O	N	S	indiv	Feb99
Twelve Tribes Community in Palenville	NY		1996			Y y	88			50%	N Y		E O	N	S	indiv	Feb99
Twelve Tribes Community in Rutland	VT		1993			Y y	67			50%	N Y		E O	N	S	indiv	Feb99
Twelve Tribes Community in Sydney	[au]		1995			Y y	60			50%	N Y		E O	N	S	indiv	Feb99
Twelve Tribes Cmty Lake of the Ozarks	MO		1998			Y y	53			50%	N Y		E O	N	S	indiv	Feb99
Twelve Tribes Community in West Palm Beach	FL		1995			Y y	55			50%	N Y		E O	N	S	indiv	Feb99
Twelve Tribes Community in Winnipeg	MB		1983	1993		Y y	87			50%	N Y		E O	N	S	indiv	Feb99
Twelve Tribes Gemeinschaft in Oberbronnen	[de]		1995			Y y	40			50%	N Y		E O	N	S	indiv	Feb99
Twelve Tribes Gemeinschaft in Penningbuttel	[de]					Y y	36			50%	N Y		E O	N	S	indiv	Feb99
Twelve Tribes (Network)	-		1972			Y y					N Y		E O	N	S	indiv	Feb99
Twin Oaks Community	VA		1967	1967	1967	Y n	90	73	17	50%	N Y		O	N	S	cmty	Nov98
Two Acre Wood Cohousing	CA	F	1994	1996	May99	N n	35	25	10	60%	N Y		C O	Y	I	mix	Nov98
Two Piers Housing Co-operative	[uk]		1976			Y y		75	7	53%	N N		C	Y	I		Jan99
Udgaarden	[dk]		1985			Y y		27	28	52%	N N		C M	Y	I		May99
UFA-Fabrik Kommune	[de]		1976			Y y		30	10	50%	N		O	N			Mar99
Union Acres Intentional Community	NC	RF	1989	Dec89	Dec89	Y y	42	30	12	55%	N Y		C	N	I	mix	Sep99
Unity Kitchen Cmty of the Catholic Worker	NY		1970			Y n	4	4		50%	Y		C	N	I	other	Jan99
Universal RPCRMKSMKIND	CA	F	1984			Y y					Y Y		C M L E O				Apr99
University Students' Cooperative Association	CA		1933	1933	1933	Y n	1250	1250	0	50%	Y N		M	Y	I	mix	Nov98
Unknown Truth Fellowship Workers - Atlantis	NY	F	1943			Y y	1	1			Y Y		O	N		indiv	Nov98
Utopiaggia	[it]		1975	1975	1975	Y y	19	15	4	60%	N N		C	Y		cmty	May99
Vail House	MI		1960	1960													Oct99
Vale Inc, The	OH		1960		1950	N n	40	22	18	52%	N Y		C		I	clt	Nov98
Valley of Light	AR	RF				Y y	8	6	2	50%	N N		C M	Y	I	other	Jan99
Valsølillegård	[dk]		1982	1983		N n	36	21	15	47%	N N		M	Y		ldlord	May99
Varsity House	OR					Y n	49			0%	Y Y		M	N		other	May99
Village In The City	MO	F				Y y	15	15		60%	N Y		C O	Y	I	other	Sep99
Village of Harmony	NM	F	1993	1995	1995	Y y	8	6	2	50%	N N		C	N	I	mix	Sep99
Vine and Fig Tree	AL		1986		1986	Y y	8			50%	N N			N	I	indiv	Sep99
Vivekananda Monastery and Retreat Center	MI		1960		1960	Y	7	7		29%	Y Y		L	N	I	other	Nov98

KEY *Canadian Provinces:* BC = British Columbia, MB = Manitoba, NS = Nova Scotia, ON = Ontario, SK = Saskatchewan.
Country: [ar] = Argentina, [au]= Australia, [at] = Austria, [be] = Belgium, [br] = Brazil, [co] = Colombia, [dk] = Denmark, [fr] = France, [de] = Germany, [gr] = Greece, [in] = India, [il] = Israel, [it] = Italy, [jp] = Japan, [mx] = Mexico, [nl] = The Netherlands, [nz] = New Zealand, [ng] = Nigeria, [uk] = United Kingdom, [uk*] = Northern Ireland.
Decisions: C = Consensus, M = Majority, L = Leader, G = Group of leaders or elders, O = Other.
Income: S = Members Share Income, I = Independently Handle Own Finances.
Who Owns Land: CLT = Community Land Trust, Cmty = Community, Indiv = Individual, Ldlord = Landlord, Subgrp = Subgroup of members.
Survey Date: Date shown is when survey questionnaire was completed or last updated by community.

Map / Index Name	Eat Together How Frequently?	What % of Own Food Is Grown?	Organic Food in Diet	Dietary Norms	Alcohol Use	Tobacco Use	# Homeschooled	Some Labor Expected	Rural, Urban, or Both	# of Buildings	Acres of Land	GLB Ok	Spiritual Path	Primary Purpose and/or Focus
TrilliumCLT	2-5 times/week	6-20%	yes!					X	R	11	82		Y	Life
Märchenzentr	1-3 times/month	1-5%	often	veg	some	ok		X		3	5		Y	
TruthConsc	2-5 times/week	21-50%	yes!	veg					R				Y	Truth Consciousness
TuiLandTrust	Nearly all dinners	21-50%	yes!	veg	none	none		X	R	13	145		N	community
Tullstugan	Nearly all dinners	None		omni				X	U	25			N	basic sense of community, to simplify everyday life
Turtledove		None							R	2	2.5		Y	Peace - Music - Fun - Love
Turtleslsl	1 time/week	1-5%						X	B	8	70			Dedicated to ecological solutions
12CmtydeSus	Nearly all meals	6-20%	often	omni	none	none			R				Y	Establish the Twelve Tribes
12CmtyQuatro	Nearly all meals	6-20%	often	omni	none	none		X	R				Y	Establish the Twelve Tribes
12CmtySanSeb	Nearly all meals	1-5%	often	omni	none	none		X	U				Y	Establish the Twelve Tribes
12CmtyBuenos	Nearly all meals	1-5%	often	omni	none	none		X	R				Y	Establish the Twelve Tribes
12CmtyLondri	Nearly all meals	1-5%	often	omni	none	none		X	U				Y	Establish the Twelve Tribes
12CmtyStentw	Nearly all meals	1-5%	often	omni	none	none		X	U				Y	Establish the Twelve Tribes
12CmtyBellow	Nearly all meals	>50%	often	omni	none	none		X	B				Y	Establish the Twelve Tribes
12CmtyBoston	Nearly all meals	None	often	omni	none	none		X	U				Y	Establish the Twelve Tribes
12CmtyCambr	Nearly all meals	1-5%	often	omni	none	none		X	R				Y	Establish the Twelve Tribes
12CmtyColo	Nearly all meals	None	often	omni	none	none		X	U				Y	Establish the Twelve Tribes
12CmtyCrox	Nearly all meals	None	often	omni	none	none		X	U				Y	Establish the Twelve Tribes
12CmtyHambur	Nearly all meals	1-5%	often	omni	none	none		X	U				Y	Establish the Twelve Tribes
12CmtyHyan	Nearly all meals	1-5%	often	omni	none	none		X	U				Y	Establish the Twelve Tribes
12CmtyIsland	Nearly all meals	None	often	omni	none	none		X	U				Y	Establish the Twelve Tribes
12CmtyLancas	Nearly all meals	6-20%	often	omni	none	none		X	U				Y	Establish the Twelve Tribes
12CmtyOakHil	Nearly all meals	6-20%	often	omni	none	none		X	R				Y	Establish the Twelve Tribes
12CmtyPalen	Nearly all meals	None	often	omni	none	none		X	R				Y	Establish the Twelve Tribes
12CmtyRutlan	Nearly all meals	None	often	omni	none	none		X	U				Y	Establish the Twelve Tribes
12CmtySydney	Nearly all meals	6-20%	often	omni	none	none		X	U				Y	Establish the Twelve Tribes
12CmtyLakeOz	Nearly all meals	None	often	omni	none	none		X	U				Y	Establish the Twelve Tribes
12CmtyWestPa	Nearly all meals	6-20%	often	omni	none	none		X	U				Y	Establish the Twelve Tribes
12CmtyWinnip	Nearly all meals	None	often	omni	none	none		X	B				Y	Establish the Twelve Tribes
12CmtyOberbr	Nearly all meals	None	often	omni	none	none		X	U				Y	Establish the Twelve Tribes
12CmtyPennin	Nearly all meals	6-20%	often	omni	none	none		X	U				Y	Establish the Twelve Tribes
12CmtyNet	Nearly all meals		often	omni	none	none		X					Y	Establish the Twelve Tribes
TwinOaks	Nearly all dinners	>50%	yes!	omni	ok	ok	7	X	R	8	450	GLB	N	egalitarianism, income-sharing
TwoAcreWood	2-5 times/week	6-20%	yes!	omni	often	ok		X	U	14 u		GLB	N	community oriented lving
TwoPiers								X	U	7			N	Tenant Controlled Housing
Udgaarden	Nearly all dinners	>50%	yes!	omni	ok	ok		X	R	16	40		N	Environment Ecology Eco-energy
UFA-Fabrik	Nearly all dinners		often	omni	often	often			U	3				
UnionAcres	1-3 times/month	6-20%	yes!	veg	ok	none	4	X	R	12	80		Y	
UnityKitchen	2-5 times/week	None			none	none			U	1			Y	
UniversalRes			yes!	vgn	none	none								Sant Mat (Eternal Truth) !
UniversitSCA	Nearly all dinners	None	yes!	omni	ok	ok		X	U	21		GLB	N	student housing (university)
UnknownTruth		1-5%			none	none			R				Y	Believe Unknown Truth Now
Utopiaggia	Nearly all dinners	6-20%	often	omni	yes!	yes!		X	R	3	~200		N	Egalitarian, self-organized living close to nature
VailHouse														
ValeThe	1-3 times/month	6-20%		omni	some	none		X	R	11	40	GLB	N	Relieve lonliness
ValleyLight	2-5 times/week	None	yes!	veg	some	some			B	2	49	GLB		
Valsølillegå	1-3 times/month	21-50%	yes!	omni	often	often			R	3			N	Organical - recycle - green
VarsityHouse	Nearly all meals	None	ok	omni	none	none			U	2			N	Christian Cooperative Living
VillageInThe	2-5 times/week	None						X	U			GLB	N	Caring & Cooperative Neighbors
VillageHarmo	1-3 times/month	>50%	yes!	vgn	ok	ok	2		R	4	7		N	Simplicity, self-reliance, sustaining
VineandFig	2-5 times/week	21-50%	yes!	omni	yes!	ok			R	6	260	GLB	N	Living a good life
VivekanandaM	2-5 times/week	1-5%	yes!	veg	none	ok		X	R	12	105		Y	Spiritual Development

KEY *Diet:* omni = includes red meat, no red = no red meat—includes fish or poultry and dairy, veg = vegetarian—no meat—includes dairy, vgn = vegan—no meat or dairy.
Diet note: Some communities list omni and provide vegan options, some list vegan yet allow personal food without restriction. Take the label as a rough guideline.
Rural, Urban or Both: Some communities used both (B) to indicate having both an urban and rural location or that the one property was both urban and rural, as suburban.
Acres of Land: Hectare is abbreviated ha and is approximately 2.5 acres.
Some Labor Expected: Members are expected to regularly contribute labor to the group.
GLB Ok: The community indicated that gay men (G) or lesbians (L) or bisexuals (B) are welcome as members.
Spiritual Path: The community indicated it has a primarily spiritual or religious focus.

Community	State/Prov. or Country	Forming, Reforming	Year Formed	Year Purchased	Year Began Living	Open to More Adults?	Open to More Children?	Total Population	# Adults	# Children (<19yrs)	Percentage Women	Identified Leader	Leadership Core Group	How are Major Decisions Made?	Join Fee?	Income Shared/Indep.	Who Owns Land	Survey Date
Vivekananda Vedanta Society	IL		1930		1967	Y	n	11	11		27%	Y	Y	E	N		cmty	Nov98
WAHOO!	OR	F	1998			Y	y	9	8	1	50%	N	Y	C M	Y		cmty	May99
Waitakere Eco-Neighbourhood Cohousing	[nz]		1995			Y	y		25	12	64%	N	N	C	Y	I		Jan99
Walker Creek Farm	WA		1975	1975	1975	N		17	13	4	55%	N	N	C M	Y	I	other	Nov98
Walnut House Cooperative	CA		1981	1981	1981	N	n	25	24	1		Y	Y	C	Y	I	cmty	Jan99
Watermargin Cooperative	NY		1948		1948	N	n	23	18	5	67%	Y	Y	E	N	I	ldlord	Jan99
Watersmeet Homes	WI	F		1988		Y	y				50%	Y		L			indiv	Nov98
Wäxthuset Väddö	[se]		1979			Y	y	19	15	4	47%	Y	Y	C M L	N		mix	Jul99
We'Moon Land	OR	RF	1973	1973	1973	N	n	12	10	2	100%	N	Y	C	N	I	indiv	Dec98
Wellspring	WI		1982	1988	1988	Y	n	4	4		25%	Y	Y	C	N		other	Feb99
Westside Vegetarian Community	CA		1989	1990	1993	Y	n	8	8		63%	Y			Y	I	indiv	Nov98
Westwood Cohousing	NC		1992		1998						60%	N		C M		I		Dec98
Weyst, The	[nl]		1984	1984	1984	Y	y	5	2	3	50%	Y	Y		N	I	nonprofit	May99
White Buffalo Farm	CO		1975	1975	1975	Y	y	14	12	2	42%		Y	C M	N	I	indiv	Sep99
Whitehall Co-op	TX		1949		1949	N	n	13	13		54%	N	Y	C	N	I	cmty	Nov98
Whole Health Foundation	CA		1972	1973	1972	N	n	12	12		30%	Y	Y	C O	Y	I	indiv	Jan99
Whole Village King	ON	F	1995	Aug99		Y	y	82	48	34	56%	N	Y	C	Y	I	mix	Sep99
WholeLife Housing	AB	F	1995			Y	y	41	24	17	54%	N	N	C	Y		other	Sep99
Wild Iris Ranch	CA	F	1989	1990	1992	Y	y	4	4		50%		Y	C E	Y	I	cmty	Dec98
William Stringfellow Catholic Worker	IL	RF	1985	Nov98	Nov98	Y	n	3	3		33%			C		N		indiv	Mar99
Windsong Cohousing	BC																	
WindSpirit Community	AZ		1995	1996	1995	M	m	24	21	3	29%	N	N	C M	Y		cmty	Oct98
WindTree Ranch	AZ	F	1989	1996	1997	Y	y	12	12		45%		Y	E	N	I	nonprofit	Sep99
Windwalker Farm	KS	F	1994	1988	1994	Y	y	6	4	2	50%	N	N	C	N	I	indiv	Oct99
Windward	WA		1977	1987	1980	Y	y	12	10	2	60%	N	Y	E	N	I	nonprofit	Sep99
Winslow Cohousing	WA		1989	1989	1992	Y	y	81	50	28	54%	N	N	C	N	I	other	Sep99
Wiscoy Valley Land Cooperative	MN		1975	1973	1975	N	m	34	27	7	50%	N	N	C	Y	I	cmty	Mar99
Wise Woman Center / Laughing Rock Farm	NY	F	1982	1978	1984	Y	m	9	8	1	100%	Y		C L O	Y	I	indiv	Nov98
Woman's World	LA	F	1993	1990	1993	Y	y	3	3	0	100%	Y	Y	L	N	I	indiv	Jul99
WomanShare	OR																	
Women's Art Colony at Millett Farm	NY		1979	1978	1998	Y	n					Y	Y	C L	N	I	other	Jan99
Woodburn Hill Farm	MD		1975	1975	1975	Y	y	13	10	3	60%	N	Y	C	N	I	cmty	Nov98
Wygelia	MD	F	1985	1978	1985	Y	y	3			67%	N	N	C		S	indiv	Sep99
Yahara Linden Gathering	WI		1977	1977		N	n	6	6		50%	N	N	C	N	I	clt	Feb99
Yamagishi-kai	[jp]		1958	1958	1958	Y	y	4000	2000		50%	N	N	O	Y		cmty	May99
Yesss Community	CA	F	1991			Y	y	65	64	1	38%	Y	Y	C M L E	Y		other	Jan99
Yogaville - Satchidananda Ashram	VA		1966	1979	1980	Y	y	223	180	43	64%	Y	Y	O	N	I	nonprofit	May99
Yogoda Community Project	PA	F	Feb99			Y	y	2	2		50%	N	N	C	N		cmty	Mar99
Yohana	CA	F	1998			Y	y	3	3		67%	N	N	C	N	I	indiv	Oct99
Yonderfamily Housing and Land Trust Inc.	GA		1967	1987		Y	y					Y	Y	C L O	N	I	clt	Jan99
York Center Community Co-operative, Inc.	IL		1944	1945	1947			200				Y	Y	M	Y	I	mix	Sep99
Zacchaeus House	NY		1973			N	n	10	6	4		N	N	C M L E	N	S		Apr99
ZEGG - Ctr for Experimental Cultural Design	[de]		1978			Y	y	80	18		55%	N	Y	C	N	I		Jan99
Zen Buddhist Temple	MI		1970			Y	y	300				Y	Y	L	Y			Aug99
Zendik Farm Arts Foundation	NC		1969	1969	1969	S	n	60	53	7	47%	Y		O	Y	S	indiv	Oct99
Zentrum Waldegg	[ch]		1989			Y	y	24	2		50%	Y	N	C E O	Y	S I		May99
Zephyr	VA		1981					19	7	12	57%			C		Y	I clt	
Zephyr Valley Community Co-op	MN		1993	1994	1995	Y	y	21	11	10	55%	N	N	C	Y	I	cmty	Mar99
Zim Zam Vegan Community	NC	F	1996	1198		Y	y	2			50%	N	N	C	N	I	indiv	Dec98
Zion	TN		1989	1999	1996	Y	y	216	73	143	50%	Y	Y	O	N		indiv	Jul99
Zion UCC Intentional Community	KY	F	1871		1992	Y	y	60	60		58%	Y	Y	C	N		cmty	Feb99
Zuni Mountain Sanctuary	NM	F	1995	1996	1995	N	n	8	8		0%	N	N	C	N	S	cmty	Nov98

KEY *Canadian Provinces:* BC = British Columbia, MB = Manitoba, NS = Nova Scotia, ON = Ontario, SK = Saskatchewan.
Country: [ar] = Argentina, [au]= Australia, [at] = Austria, [be] = Belgium, [br] = Brazil, [co] = Colombia, [dk] = Denmark, [fr] = France, [de] = Germany, [gr] = Greece, [in] = India, [il] = Israel, [it] = Italy, [jp] = Japan, [mx] = Mexico, [nl] = The Netherlands, [nz] = New Zealand, [ng] = Nigeria, [uk] = United Kingdom, [uk*] = Northern Ireland.
Decisions: C = Consensus, M = Majority, L = Leader, G = Group of leaders or elders, O = Other.
Income: S = Members Share Income, I = Independently Handle Own Finances.
Who Owns Land: CLT = Community Land Trust, Cmty = Community, Indiv = Individual, Ldlord = Landlord, Subgrp = Subgroup of members.
Survey Date: Date shown is when survey questionnaire was completed or last updated by community.

Map / Index Name	Eat Together How Frequently?	What % of Own Food Is Grown?	Organic Food in Diet	Dietary Norms	Alcohol Use	Tobacco Use	# Homeschooled	Some Labor Expected	Rural, Urban, or Both	# of Buildings	Acres of Land	GLB Ok	Spiritual Path	Primary Purpose and/or Focus
VivekanandaV	Nearly all meals	None	some	veg	none	none		X	B	10	130		Y	
WAHOO!	1 time/week		yes!	omni	some	some		X					N	Love + Ecological Sustainability
WaitakereEco	1-3 times/month	None							U	25			N	Sustainable cohousing
WalkerCreek	1-3 times/month	>50%	yes!	omni	some	ok	1		R	8	20			
WalnutHouse	Rarely	None					1	X	U	1			N	
Watermargin	2-5 times/week	1-5%	some	omni	often	ok		X	B	1		GB	N	cooperative living
Watersmeet		21-50%							B	132	110		Y	Christian hearted community
Wäxthuset		1-5%	yes!	veg	none	none		X	R	10	138 ha		Y	
We'MoonLand	2-5 times/week	21-50%	yes!	veg	ok	ok	2	X	R	8	52	LB	Y	Providing rural womyn-only space
Wellspring	Nearly all meals	>50%	yes!	veg	none	none		X	R	3	31.5		Y	education gardening environment
WestsideVeg	1-3 times/month	None	yes!	veg	yes!	none			U				N	Ovo Lacto Vegetarian - Adult
Westwood	1-3 times/month	1-5%					1	X	U	24		GLB	N	
WeystThe	2-5 times/week	>50%						X	R		1		Y	
WhiteBuffalo	1-3 times/month	6-20%	yes!	omni	none	some		X	R	6	60	GLB	Y	Natural Mysticism/Pagansim
Whitehall	Nearly all dinners	None	yes!	veg	ok	none		X	U	1			N	independence within community
WholeHealth	1-3 times/month	21-50%	ok	veg	none	none			U	1			N	
WholeVillage	1 time/week	6-20%	yes!	omni	yes!	ok	6	X	R	30	300		N	CoHousing biodynamic Farm ecovillage
WholeLife		None						X	U	25			N	Affordable Sustainable Respect
WildIrisRnch	2-5 times/week	21-50%	yes!	veg	some	none	0	X	R	2	5	GLB	N	kinship with nature and humans
WilliamStrCW	1 time/week	None	often	vgn	ok	none		X	U	1		GLB	Y	Catholic Worker House
WindsongCoho														
WindSpirit	1 time/week	6-20%	yes!	veg	some	yes!	1	X	R	4		GLB	Y	Organic Permaculture God in All
WindTreeRnch	Nearly all meals	21-50%	yes!	vgn	none	none		X	R	5	1227		Y	"Walk'n R Talk" 4 Planet Earth
Windwalker	Nearly all dinners	6-20%	yes!	veg	often	none	1		R	2	100	GLB	N	Sustainable & Connected Living
Windward	Nearly all dinners	6-20%	often	omni	some	some	1	X	R	10	111		N	stewardship self-reliant
WinslowCoho	2-5 times/week	1-5%	yes!	omni	ok	none	3	X	B	22	6	GLB	N	Intentional village
WiscoyValley	1-3 times/month	21-50%							R	13	356		N	We have none.
WiseWomanCtr	Nearly all dinners	21-50%	yes!	omni	ok	ok		X	R	3	55	LB	Y	Woman spirit, Herbal medicine
Woman'sWorld	1 time/week	1-5%	often	veg	ok	ok	0		R	2	115	L		Lesbians Living Lightly on Land
WomanShare														
Women'sArt	Nearly all meals	6-20%	often	omni	often	often			R	4	85	GLB	N	Art colony for women
WoodburnHill	2-5 times/week	21-50%	yes!	omni	ok	ok	1	X	R	5	128		N	Earth Based
Wygelia	Nearly all meals	1-5%	some	omni	none	none		X	R	1	65	GLB	N	Empowerment of Creativity
YaharaLinden	1-3 times/month	1-5%	yes!	omni	ok	none			U	1		GLB	N	Co-operative Housing
Yamagishi	Nearly all meals	>50%	yes!	no red					B				N	income-sharing agrarian village
YesssCmty	Rarely	None	yes!	no red					U	3			Y	positive healthy living
Yogaville	2-5 times/week	1-5%	yes!	veg	none	none	3		R	50	1000	GL	Y	Spiritual vegetarian, yoga, and meditation
YogodaCmty	Nearly all meals	None	yes!	veg	none	none		X	R				Y	spiritual growth, Yogananda
Yohana	2-5 times/week	6-20%	yes!	vgn	none	none			B				M	Pursuit, Arts, Knowledge, Culture
Yonderfamily		6-20%	yes!	omni	yes!	yes!		X	R		100	GLB	Y	Forestry eco services housing
YorkCenter	Rarely							X		79	104			Living in a tranquil oasis
Zacchaeus	2-5 times/week		some	omni	ok	ok			B					social justice; resist militarianism; shelter
ZEGG	Nearly all meals	6-20%	yes!	veg	yes!	yes!			R	20	15		N	nonviolence, love without fear and jealousy
ZenBuddhist	Rarely	6-20%	yes!					X	U	2			Y	
ZendikFarm	Nearly all meals		yes!	omni	none	none		X	R		116		Y	
ZentrumWalde	2-5 times/week	1-5%		no red	ok	none		X		1			N	to live, love, learn together
ZephyrFloyd	1 time/week	21-50%							R		29			environmental consciousness
ZephyrValley	1 time/week	1-5%	yes!	omni	some	some			R	7	550		N	Rural residential community
ZimZamVegan	Nearly all dinners	1-5%	yes!	vgn	none	none		X	U	1	1	GLB	N	Eco, ForestGrdn, NO OwnedAnimals
Zion	Rarely	6-20%	some	omni	some	none			R		79		Y	Follow Christ, God's Son
ZionUCC	1 time/week	1-5%	yes!	omni	some	some			U	1			Y	Just-peace, inclusive, activist
ZuniMountain	Nearly all meals	1-5%	some	veg	some	yes!			R	2	315	GLB	Y	Rural Radical Faeries

KEY *Diet:* omni = includes red meat, no red = no red meat—includes fish or poultry and dairy, veg = vegetarian—no meat—includes dairy, vgn = vegan—no meat or dairy.
Diet note: Some communities list omni and provide vegan options, some list vegan yet allow personal food without restriction. Take the label as a rough guideline.
Rural, Urban or Both: Some communities used both (B) to indicate having both an urban and rural location or that the one property was both urban and rural, as suburban.
Acres of Land: Hectare is abbreviated ha and is approximately 2.5 acres.
Some Labor Expected: Members are expected to regularly contribute labor to the group.
GLB Ok: The community indicated that gay men (G) or lesbians (L) or bisexuals (B) are welcome as members.
Spiritual Path: The community indicated it has a primarily spiritual or religious focus.

THE ART OF COMMUNITY

Weekend events focused on cooperative living and creating more community in your life!

Meet intentional communities. Meet people exploring cooperative living.

Join the Fellowship for Intentional Community and hundreds of other community enthusiasts for presentations, workshops, slide shows, a community products store, information tables, and a joyful experience of community.

Workshops on the Nuts and Bolts of Building Community

- Community Businesses
- Facilitation
- Communication
- Forming Communities

- Community Visioning
- Sustainable Technology
- Consensus

- Cooperative Games
- Finding Your Community
- Conflict Resolution

There are multiple events each year, in various regions around the country. Contact us to find out where we'll be next. We'd love to see you there!

If you would like to offer a workshop, volunteer for the event, help us get the word out in your area, or offer your community as a host site, please get in touch.

 FIC Events • RR 1 Box 156 • Rutledge MO 63563 • USA
Tel/Fax: 660-883-5545 • Web: http://www.ic.org/ • Email: gathering@ic.org

Elph Morgan

About the Community Listings

The Community Listings contains descriptions of over 700 intentional communities around the world, with contact information for most of them (a few groups asked to be listed without any location information). Two-thirds of the communities have email or Web addresses this time around, in addition to postal address and telephone numbers.

At the beginning of each listing, we have included some helpful descriptive data from our questionnaire. The categories are as follows: year began, population, forming or reforming, dietary habits, urban/rural, and whether the community feels it has a primarily spiritual or religious focus.

A community's listing is where you'll get a sense of how the group sees itself—its vision, history, and daily life. Hopefully these descriptions will give you a feeling for each community, to complement the facts and figures listed in the Chart.

At the end of each listing we indicate whether the community felt they could commit (cc) to corresponding in a timely manner, requested or required a self-addressed stamped envelope (sase) to be included when writing for information, or preferred email as a method of correspondence.

A few general disclaimers: First, we can't guarantee that the information in the Chart and Community Listings is accurate—each community decided what to say about itself. We edited lightly, and only for length and clarity. We caution each reader to verify information before getting involved with any of the groups listed. Second, these listings should be viewed as a "snapshot" of how each community saw itself at the time when they wrote their listing. You may visit the community and view it differently. In addition, communities change. Information becomes outdated. Some groups wrote about their plans for the future, but others did not. Third, community descriptions may vary depending on who wrote the description; each person brings their own unique perspective.

ABBEY OF THE GENESEE

3258 River Rd
Piffard NY 14533

716-243-0660
abbeygen@frontiernet.net
http://web.lemoyne.edu/
~bucko/genesee.htm

Began 1951 | Pop. 40
Diet: No red meat | Rural | Spiritual

A Roman Catholic community of monks wholly ordered to contemplation belonging to the Cistercian Order of the Strict Observance, more commonly known as Trappists. The monks are dedicated to the worship of God in a hidden life within the monastery following the Rule of St. Benedict. They lead a life of solitude and silence, prayer and penance in a joyful spirit of faith. The monastic community supports itself by the common work of baking monks' bread. In addition, the brothers help out on the farm and with cooking, laundry, cleaning, hospitality, formation of new members, and care of the sick and elderly of the community. The community is cloistered and has no outside ministry. Guests are received for quiet, private retreats at the retreat house. The monastic day begins with vigils at 2:25 A.M. and ends with compline at 6:40 P.M. Throughout the day there is a good balance between prayer, reading, and work, all lived in fraternal love and support. Silence is practiced seriously. The brothers speak only when necessary and then as briefly as possible. Some of the brothers are priests; most are not. At the end of their formation pro-

gram candidates take the monastic vows and remain with the community for the rest of their lives. [Sep99]

ABUNDANT DAWN COMMUNITY

PO Box 433
Floyd VA 24091

540-745-5853
AbundantDawn@ic.org
http://www.abundantdawn.org/

Began 1995 | Pop. 12
Diet: No red meat | Rural

We are the stewards and human inhabitants of 90 acres of hilly and diverse land, nestled in a bend of a river in the Blue Ridge Mountains. We're 28 miles from a state university and an hour from a small city with an airport.

We envision a community of several mostly autonomous subcommunities, or "pods" (like the small groups dolphins travel in). Pods are small enough for all their members to sit together and make a decision. Each pod decides its own membership, financial, and housing arrangements, within the community's standards of ecologically sound practices and democratic decision making. We hope to keep a balance between income-sharing and independent-income groups.

Pods cluster their homes on one to three acres each, leaving much of the land habitable for wildlife.

We are living in (fairly civilized) temporary homes, finishing our land plan and environmental building guidelines, and preparing to build our dream.

Our adult members include single, partnered, and married people, with a diversity of sexual orientations. We've grown to be good at listening to each other and making decisions together. While we have no unified

spiritual path, we do make time regularly for sharing deeply with one another and for bringing interpersonal issues to light.

We share community expenses in several different ways, including as a fraction of income and per capita.

If you would like to visit, please write in advance. Families (all types) welcome. We are also open to the possibility of an already formed small group joining us as a new pod. This would require a substantial period of getting to know each other and an investment in Abundant Dawn.

Please see Tekiah and Dayspring Circle listings for descriptions of our first two pods. [Sep99, sase requested]

ABUNDANT FREEK

c/o Chris Balz
159 Melville Ave
Palo Alto CA 94301

650-324-0345
ChristopherBalz@yahoo.com
http://www.best.com/
~fmrfreek/AF.html

Began Dec98 | Pop. 2 | Forming
Diet: Omnivore

The Abundant Freek community-in-formation is specifically attuned to addressing the challenge of enabling a preexisting, substantial community of freaky people to build an economy that is semiseceded from the dominant global despoiler economy, also known as "Babylon."

The immediate, local segment of the preexisting community consists of 35 or so highly committed people who are now and have been in local residence for 5 years or more and who are more or less continually in residence. The related community consists of several hundred people who have spent 3–19 years in residence previously and who visit the family in its locality every few years or so. Abundant Freek will secure a minimum of 10 acres of good, flat farmland in the locality (i.e., in Orleans, Blue Lake, Dunsmuir, etc.) with ample art-barn and equipment-shop space, a main house, and associated small cabins. By effective tractor and hand cultivation of the land, we will be in a position to offer biodynamic bulk produce to the community in exchange for any hand weeding needed and the picking labor. By making equipment-shop facilities available to responsible parties, we will enable members of the community to own low-cost, functional trucks, etc. By keeping our

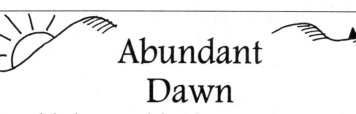

Abundant Dawn

Grounded, adventurous, dedicated, experienced pioneers looking for a few more! We value integrity, curiosity, flexibility and laughter, personal and environmental responsibility, and our beautiful mountain land. See listings for Abundant Dawn Community and our subcommunities, Dayspring Circle and Tekiah.

POB 433, Floyd, VA 24091.   SASE requested.   <abundantdawn@ic.org>

Key to bracketed text: cc = cannot commit to prompt correspondance, sase = self-addressed stamped envelope

land open to all enthusiastic people, we will enable people to find their own relationship to the land. By providing community facilities, we will enable people to find their own relationship to each other. By offering a very-low-cost but abundant lifestyle, we will enable people to find out what cultural-economic ("culturonomic") change is about. [Dec98, cc, sase required]

ACME ARTISTS COMMUNITY

2418 W Bloomindale
Chicago IL 60647

773-278-7677
nnwac@artswire.org
http://www.if.org/acme/

Began 1992 | Pop. 28 | Forming | Urban
Acme Artists Community is the result of artists, artisans, and cultural activists designing and building a community by sharing the power of creativity. Members are committed to the model of cooperative enterprise to create grassroots investment in an urban inner city. Located in a rehabbed warehouse, the 17 residential and 3 commercial units house artists and their families in an environment supportive of creative work and collaboration. The community is structured as a limited-equity condominium association; the Near NorthWest Arts Council is the nonprofit developer and a resident member. Training and technical assistance are provided by the Chicago Mutual Housing Network, also a residential member. Democratic control limits risk and insures member diversity and affordability. Common-area resources include the community room, lobby exhibits, kitchen, laundry, workshop, laundry, and roof deck garden. Cooperative enterprise includes an international artists exchange program, a bed-and-breakfast unit, and an Arts Resource Center. [Jan99, cc]

ACORN COMMUNITY

1259-CD0 Indian Creek Rd
Mineral VA 23117

540-894-0595, 540-894-0582
acorn@ic.org
http://www.ic.org/acorn/

Began 1993 | Pop. 16
Diet: Omnivore | Rural

Acorn is a young community seeking ways of living that are cooperative, caring, and ecologically sustainable. Our ideals embrace a diverse, egalitarian society that welcomes feminism, multiculturalism, varied sexual and relationship orientations, and personal growth. We value energy spent on improving interpersonal communication. We have a formal structure. Our decisions are made by consensus. We enjoy a close relationship with Twin Oaks Community, seven miles down the road.

We currently have about 20 members, and we would like to grow to at least 30 adults plus associated children. Our ages range from 6 to over 50. As of this writing we have 3 kids who are homeschooled and 2 at public school. We want children integrated into the life of the community, learning skills to contribute to the group.

Our beautiful 72 acres border on the South Anna River and include towering oaks, open hayfields, wildflowers, and berry bushes. Our two main residences are a white clapboard farmhouse built in 1908 and a new community center with a dozen bedrooms, built almost entirely by people living here.

Acorn's money and resources are held in common. Members work full-time in exchange for coverage of basic needs such as housing and food. We give "labor credit" for community work, such as building, gardening, cooking, cleaning, etc., whether or not it produces income. But we need everyone to pitch in for us to pay the bills.

Our main businesses at this time are tinnery crafts (made from recycled cans) and community-supported agriculture, where local folks buy weekly subscriptions to our organic gardens. Several of us earn money in Twin Oaks' established industries, including tofu, hammock pillows, book indexing, and a reading school. Other members take occasional jobs off the farm such as planting trees, practicing massage, teaching facilitation, and performing other "odd jobs."

Recreational activities come and go according to the interests and energy of those living here. Groups may gather for swimming in the river, folksinging, videos, dances, yoga class, poetry readings, birthdays, seasonal holidays, and many other occasions. We have a home-built hot tub in the woods that's been the highlight of many a party. In addition, many members take advantage of cultural opportunities at Twin Oaks, in the college town of Charlottesville, or in Washington, DC.

We are actively seeking new members. Please contact us for more information or check our Web site for more current information. [Sep99, sase requested]

ADIDAM

12040 N Seigler Spr Rd
Middletown CA 95461

707-928-1100
Outside the US call 707-928-4936
correspondence@adidam.org
http://www.adidam.org/

Began 1973 | Pop. 1085
Diet: Vegan | Rural/Urban | Spiritual

(Also known as Free Daist Communion, Johannine Daist Communion.) A life submitted to a fully enlightened teacher. Adi Da Samraj founded the Way of Adidam (or the way of the heart) in 1972. Its purpose is to realize God, to invoke God. Cooperative living is one of many disciplines we happily observe. One must be a formally acknowledged devotee of Adi Da Samraj in order to participate. For more information, read *The Promised God-Man Is Here* or *The Knee of Listening*. For a free brochure on the way of Adidam contact us.

We have communities around the world—northern California; southern

Additions and corrections: Email: directory@ic.org, Web: http://directory.ic.org/, Mail: RR 1 Box 156-D, Rutledge MO 63563, USA.

California; Seattle; Boston; Washington, DC; Chicago; Toronto; London; Amsterdam; Australia; New Zealand; Hawaii; and Fiji. [Sep99, cc, sase required]

ADIRONDACK HERBS

7295 Fishhouse Rd
Galway NY 12074

518-883-3453, 518-835-6887
herb@klink.net
http://www.kosovoforum.net/herbs/

Began 1990 | Pop. 6
Diet: Omnivore | Rural

Three farms 30 miles apart in the Adirondacks near Sacandaga Lake; 210 acres. We grow medicinal herbs, produce tea bags, sell to health-food stores, build wood-fired water heaters. Minimum 17 hours work/week; additional optional work counts toward land ownership; profit shares. Option to start your own business here.

We have a good library, a piano, sailboats, a Windsurfer, soon a hang glider or an ultralight. We are very interested in bees, flywheels, alternative-energy vehicles, small airships, steel-fiber-reinforced ferro-cement, aquaculture, winter ice refrigeration. We

---

HELP WANTED

We are searching for intelligent, enthusiastic, highly motivated, hard working people willing to dedicate their brilliant minds to challenging work in the space age setting of Adirondack Herbs. What follows are job descriptions for positions we must urgently fill. If you feel that you might qualify, please send us your resume.

A: Firewood Reader

B: "New Science" Officer—must be a person of Atlantian background, familiar with ancient technologies of free energy and perpetual motion

C: Multimedia Analyst—must be able to spend multi-hours(a minimum of 8) daily,analyzing television. Will submit detailed quarterly reports.

D: Curriculum Director—for our own Horizontally Challenged Studies Institute, dedicated to the study of afternoon sleep disorders.

E: Meteorological Officer—must observe work from a reclining position and promptly warn workers if it starts to rain.

F: Stove Leaner— consideration for this position will be given only to persons qualified to make split-second decisions, the briefest delay in distancing posterior from stove may have dire consequences.

G: Triage Specialist—scientifically determines which vehicle or piece of equipment ought to be decommissioned and promptly breaks it.

H: Slow Motion Researcher—must be qualified to move small objects very slowly from one place to another for no apparent reason.

Adirondack Herbs ～～～～～518-883-3453

---

prefer using dumped or surplus material, such as paper, envelopes, lumber, steel, bananas with brown spots. We'd rather pick firewood at the town dump than cut down trees. We respect all religions/spiritual paths, propose herbal medicine as an adjuvant rather than an alternative to modern medicine. We take very seriously environmental degradation, the destruction of indigenous cultures, cruelty against humans and animals, television, waste, war, peace, and science. We take a bit less seriously astrologers, therapists, political correctness, the New Age, disco, and the New World Order, by which we mean that astrologers, numerologists, iridologists, kinesiologists, and even phrenologists ought to expect some good-humored kidding if they come here. [Aug99, sase requested]

ADULT FELLOWSHIP CONDO COMMUNITY

48 Drummers Ln
Wayne PA 19087

610-964-8857, 610-964-8550 fax
idream@erols.com

A condo community offering fellowship with adult neighbors by breaking bread together five nights a week. Ideal for the busy person (or couple) with little spare time, who prefers to use that spare time to form meaningful friendships rather than perform domestic chores individually, while at the same time retaining a fully independent lifestyle and a sense of self-sufficiency. The community would consist of 29 or more individually owned townhouses, with one townhouse jointly owned that will serve as a Club House. In the Club House, dinner will be served all week nights. Residents will share tasks of maintaining the club house, any common grounds, and week-day dinners, which can all be fun if done collectively, with the option of hiring a cook and/or lawn mower if group prefers it. Beyond this, residents are free to associate with other members of the group as little or as much as they want. The Club House will offer spare bedrooms, open to guests of members, as well as a basement that can be used as an exercise room. Children would be most welcome as guests, but the purpose of this community is to find a comfortable, friendly nest for empty nesters that want to feel a part of a flock, as opposed to flying totally solo.

AERIOUS / YEWWOOD

93640 Deadwood Cr Rd
Deadwood OR 97430

541-964-5341
aerious@pioneer.net

Diet: Vegan | Rural | Spiritual

Located rurally to be closer to the earth, nature spirits, and our wonderful green world, YewWood is a retreat center for health and healing of mind/body/spirit. We accept visitors and apprentices by arrangement and host seasonal gatherings and workshops in a variety of growth-oriented healing arts and life skills, including homesteading and building and gardening/wildcrafting. Be prepared to look at your shadow if you come here and let go of all distractions that may be getting in your way.

We encourage visitors only in the warmer months, only by specific and advanced arrangement. We are small and fill easily. We also are not specifically an intentional community but a group of humyns seeking stewardship with the natural and devic realm. We are also off the grid and encourage nonelectric independence. Live your dreams, be it elsewhere, or here, if your dreams are compatible with ours. [Nov98, sase requested]

AGAPE

2062 Greenwich Rd
Ware MA 01082

413-967-9369

Began 1982 | Pop. 3 | Re-Forming
Diet: Vegetarian | Rural

Agape is a lay Catholic nonviolent community dedicated to prayer, poverty, and nonviolent education. We are ecumenical in practice and interfaith in orientation. We accept interns for stays of one year. We live on 32 acres of land in the Quabbin Reservoir in central Massachusetts. We grow our own food and have recently completed a straw-bale house with solar energy, compost toilet, and other ecological features. We support ourselves through a nonviolent education ministry that includes outreach to inner-city youths and adults and retreats and other programs at the community. We pray together, study Scripture, and witness out of this base against all forms of violence including war, abortion, capital punishment, and euthanasia. We have a youth coordinator–educator position open. We are interviewing for new interns and one

---

Key to bracketed text: cc = cannot commit to prompt correspondance, sase = self-addressed stamped envelope

member now. Person must have a yearning for a community life based on prayer, simplicity, and nonviolence. No TV or commercial radio but lots of music and a definite love of art in all its forms. [Jan99]

AGAPE COMMUNITY

1180 Orthodox Way
Liberty TN 37095

615-536-5239
agape@dekalb.net

Began 1972
Diet: Omnivore | Rural | Spiritual

Agape Community is a residential settlement of the Russian Orthodox Church outside of Russia. It is located in a remote rural area of mountain hollows some 60 miles southeast of Nashville. Permanent residence is open to those who share fully with the community in the faith, either as landholders purchasing neighboring property or as leaseholders on community-owned property (presently one family and visitors).

Temporary residence on community property is possible for those who seriously seek instruction in the faith. Visitors who seek information concerning the Orthodox Christian faith and an experience of a life centered therein are welcome for short periods of time by prior arrangement, but should be prepared for primitive living conditions and a diet and daily life conditioned by the discipline of the church.

The community operates a small religious press and publishes a bimonthly magazine, *Living Orthodoxy*, at $18/year (US). For fur-

ther written information and recent issue, send $5 to cover the cost of response. Our resources are severely limited. [Sep99, sase required]

AGAPE LAY APOSTOLATE COMMUNITY

1320 West Elm St
Deming NM 88030

505-546-0013
agape@zianet.com
http://www.zianet.com/agape/

Began 1972 | Pop. 23
Diet: Omnivore | Rural | Spiritual

The Agape Community is a small group of 7 adults and 14 children living on 10 acres in southwestern New Mexico.

Our Catholic background led us to serve the poor and needy by opening a St. Vincent de Paul Thrift Store that includes a soup kitchen and a homeless shelter. All members volunteer at the store and help clean the shelter.

The adult men and single woman in the community have jobs in Deming to support their families and the community. The women with children are stay-at-home moms. The community operates an apartment complex of 10 apartments. All members help clean each apartment and do groundskeeping around the complex.

The community meets on Wednesday evenings for dinner and a meeting to discuss the week's events and any decisions that need to be made.

On Saturday evenings, an "Agape

Service" is held in the members' homes. This fellowship includes the Sunday readings and a communion service. All faiths are invited. On the first Sunday of the month, Mass is attended in one of the local Catholic churches. On a regular basis, members also fellowship in other Christian services in town.

Interested people may visit the community and take part in the work at St. Vincent's and Wednesday dinner. Please write a letter of interest to: Agape Community, 1401 West Birch, Deming, NM 88030. [Sep99, sase requested]

AINAOLA

RR 2 Box 3344
Pahoa HI 96778

808-965-7704
ainaola@secalarm.com

Began Mar99 | Pop. 3 | Forming
Diet: Omnivore | Rural

AinaOla means "Land of Aliveness." We are located on the big island of Hawaii, and our vision is to create a sustainable, exclusively raw-food, tribal homestead. For us, this begins with actively growing our own organic, raw food using efficient permaculture systems. But that's just the start. The AinaOla vision also encompasses truly human sustainability through shared responsibility and ownership; consensus decision making; egalitarian, tribal social structure—including coparenting; open and honest communication with group dialogues; service and teaching in the greater community;

and real commitments to personal, family, and community growth and spiritual awakening. We're also exploring how to live our sexuality with freedom, responsibility, and sanity, such that it strengthens and enriches our community. And our vision is open to change and growth as new folks arrive.

So far, our greatest mastery has been in the homesteading and raw-food realms. Creating an intimate, stable, bonded core family is taking more time. We've definitely found that humans are the toughest crop of all, but we like 'em, so we're not giving up.

Is our vision compellingly attractive to you? Let's talk. (If you think you could live another way, we're probably not your community.)

Aloha, from AinaOla [Aug99, cc, sase required]

ALCHEMY FARM COHOUSING

233 Hatchville Rd
Hatchville MA 02536

508-563-3101, 508-564-4325
508-563-5955 fax
j.hackler@whrc.org

Began 1996 | Pop. 26 | Forming
Diet: Omnivore | Rural/Urban

Alchemy Farm Cohousing combines the social design of cohousing with ecological forms of housing and agricultural use of our common landscape. Our mission is "to create and nuture a Cohousing Community where individuals live in integrity and harmony with each other and with nature, using sustainable agriculture and energy-efficient methods to produce and provide food, energy, and shelter; and where community members are encouraged to grow to their greatest potential while living cooperatively."

Our large common house and pedestrian center are bordered by organic fields, gardens, and mature tree crops. New residents develop their own house design and personal landscape. Most recent new homes include photovoltaic electricity, radiant floor heat, waterless toilets, and modular construction.

Alchemy Farm occupies 16 acres of fields, gardens, play areas, and woodlands and is bordered by forested conservation land with a large lake. One-third of the land contains 13 private homesites in two clusters, and two-thirds is shared common land, common house, and social areas.

Our cohousing community is in the large community of Cape Cod, with nearby beaches, historic seaside towns, and the active scientific and cultural community of Woods Hole. [Aug99]

ALESKAM

Ludmila Ignatenko - Chief
60 let Oktyabrya Str 1 apt17
Razdolny settlement Elizovo region
Kamchatka 684020
RUSSIA

(8-231) 97-1-40, 415-31-93-5-13
415-31-97-1-40 fax
upik@elrus.kamchatka.su

Began 1991 | Diet: Vegetarian | Rural

(Also known as Ketkino-Pinachevo Territory Community.) Aleskam is a community uniting the aboriginal peoples of Kamchatka. Our mission combines three goals: to assure the ecological health of the region; to influence legislation in the defense of indigenous peoples; and to develop infrastructure for ethno-ecotourism.

Our community is located 45 kilometers from Kamchatka's only city, Petropavlovsk-

Kamchatksky, and includes representatives from the Aleut, Innuit, Itelmen, Kamchadal, Koryak, and even Chukchee peoples. Today we have 146 members. We have united in order to preserve and revive our traditional lifestyles, occupations, and handicrafts—such as hunting, fishing, gathering, and others—and to bring back our spiritual culture.

Our community was founded in 1993 when a large hatchery was being built along the shores of a wild-salmon-spawning river located on our land. We originally united to ensure the environmentally safe operation of the hatchery. Thanks to our efforts to raise the awareness of the environmental community, and the office of the public prosecutor, the community forced the builders of the plant to conduct an environmental-impact statement.

Since that event, we have begun to address a much wider scope of environmental issues. We have also begun efforts to preserve the cultural treasures of our people and to revive our traditional feasts. As an example, the International Assembly of Aboriginals of the World took place on our territory. This event gathered representatives from Alaska, Canada, Poland, the United Kingdom, and other nations and aimed to conserve our national identity in the contemporary world.

The south of Kamchatka has traditionally been inhabited by natives. Many of the native settlements in the north of Kamchatka were closed in the past, forcing many of the inhabitants from those areas to migrate south. Our members, whose people are originally from the north, still maintain close contact with their relatives and friends, and we often participate in conferences, feasts, and events organized there (in the north of Kamchatka).

Some of the environmental issues that we have tackled include: (1) protecting spawning grounds from wastes introduced by settlements; (2) ensuring that the national parks that have been established in Kamchatka do not jeopardize the traditional lifestyles of Kamchatka's indigenous peoples; and (3) fighting proposed gold mines that threaten healthy ecosystems. In addition, our community has a branch organization for youth called "EthnoInitiative." The organization carried out a monitoring program on the Avacha River, "Biogenic elements flowing into the Avacha River and their influence on the hydrochemical regime of the Avacha Bay."

Overall, influencing regional legislation is

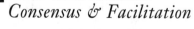
Key to bracketed text: cc = cannot commit to prompt correspondance, sase = self-addressed stamped envelope

among our most important activities. Members of our community have participated in the creation of legislation on communities; traditional land use in the Kamchatka region; youth politics in Kamchatka; priority territories in Kamchatka; and other issues.

We are now working to promote the concept of sustainable development in the south of Kamchatka based on the knowledge of Kamchatka's aboriginals (traditional knowledge). We have plans to create an ethnocultural center for the minorities of Kamchatka on our 10-hectare property, which we have leased out of an area totaling 64,000 hectares. This land is located not far from medicinal hot springs. The center will be a place for physical and spiritual healing and the revival of national and traditional occupations. Eventually, we would like to create an "ecovillage" on our land that will help us to develop some infrastructure for ethno-ecotourism.

We have received support in the past from the Russian Society of Nature Protection; the Kamchatka nongovernmental organization (NGO) "Harmony"; the NGO Kamchatka League of Independent Experts; and the Kamchatka NGO Sarana. Technical and financial support have come to us through the "Glocal Greengrants" program, the Pacific Environment and Resources Center, and the Sacred Earth Network, which provided us with the capacity for communication.

In 1998, the community received a grant for Internet access for the purpose of serving the aboriginals in our region. We are open for collaboration and new ideas. [Apr99]

ALPHA FARM

92819 Deadwood Cr Rd
Deadwood OR 97430

541-964-5102
alpha@pioneer.net
http://www.pioneer.net/~alpha/

Began 1972 | Pop. 19
Diet: Omnivore | Rural

Alpha Farm is an extended-family-style community on 280 acres in the Coast Range of Oregon. Consensus, our decision-making process, is also a metaphor for the ideal world we seek to create here—and so help create in the larger world. We seek to honor and respect the spirit in all people and in nature; to nurture harmony within our-

selves, among people, and with the Earth; and to integrate all of life into a balanced whole. We value service and work as love made visible. Group process is a strong point; we meet regularly for business and sharing.

Founded in 1972, we average 10–15 adults and 4–6 children. New people spend a year as residents (trial members) before becoming eligible for membership. Members and residents work primarily on the farm or in community-owned business (a cafe-bookstore-gift shop, contract mail delivery, and a consensus and facilitation training/consulting practice) or occasionally in paid work off the farm. All income and resources are held in common. We are experimenting with different housing patterns, particularly for families; individuals have private rooms, while other living space is common; evening meals are communal.

We are open to new residents; visitors are welcome for a three-day initial visit. Please call well ahead to arrange dates. [Aug99, sase requested]

ALPHA OMEGA CHRISTIAN COMMUNITIES FOR THE CHEMICALLY INJURED (AOCCCI)

PO Box 71
San Antonio TX 78291
ao_communities@yahoo.com
http://members.truepath.com/
aocommunities/

Forming | Rural | Spiritual

(Also known as Eagle Ranch.) We are a non-profit ministry and are looking for individuals who are committed to serving God by living in community and volunteering time toward the creation of larger communities for individuals who have multiple chemical sensitivity/environmental illness and related diseases. This first community will be located in the San Antonio, Texas, area. [Jan99, cc, sase requested]

AMATA COMMUNITY

317 Nelms Ave NE
Atlanta GA 30307

404-378-3954

Began 1988 | Pop. 14
Diet: Omnivore | Rural/Urban

We are in Atlanta's most vibrant neighborhood. Only four miles away is downtown;

one mile away is Atlanta's biggest alternative business district with a huge natural-foods co-op. Within one-half mile are a 50-acre city park, a two-mile-long off-road bike road, a subway station, and numerous bus stops. Two blocks away are shops and restaurants. Sidewalks, trees, and greenery are very abundant throughout the area. Next door to us is Lake Claire Cohousing Community.

Amata is on a gorgeous, hilly, 2-1/2-acre plot with organic gardens, fruit orchards, solar well, farm animals, ponds, sauna, fire circles, outhouses, playgrounds, picnic tables, and a playfield. We have two permanent common houses with a common kitchen, baths, five bedrooms, living rooms, and a 20 (35 foot indoor recreation/dance room. These common houses have been crafted to last centuries. We also have three less-permanent buildings with five bedrooms and a modest but well-stocked workshop. Tent living sites are available.

We have 4 core decision makers/owners and 10 residents with some decision power. Owner status is based on residency length and contribution. Land work, meeting attendance, and other requirements exist. Our rents are affordable, and numerous jobs are available in the surrounding area.

Amata's residents are varied in sex, religion, diet, color, career, education, etc. We are committed to community, ecology, and health and welcome others who share this commitment. [Aug99, sase requested, no openings]

ANANDA

14618 Tyler Foote Rd
Nevada City CA 95959

530-478-7500
http://www.ananda.org/

Began 1968 | Pop. 263
Diet: Vegetarian | Rural | Spiritual

(Also known as Ananda Church of Self-Realization, Ananda Village, Ananda World Brotherhood Village.) The Ananda Community is dedicated to the teachings of Paramhansa Yogananda, author of the spiritual classic *Autobiography of a Yogi*. Yogananda spoke of the need for a direct experience of God. Meditation, he said, is the missing ingredient in most religions. By sharing with countless Americans these life-transforming techniques of yoga and meditation, he opened the door to their own direct experience of the spiritual realities.

Ananda Village

Ananda Village offers a variety of opportunities for those who wish to experience life in a spiritual cooperative community.

Our guest yoga and meditation retreat facility, *The Expanding Light* (800-346-5350) offers a community tour every Sunday afternoon.

The community includes a private school for grades K-8; a high school; organic foods market; deli and bakery; holistic health center; publishing company; construction company; plus many other businesses.

The following books on intentional communities are available from Crystal Clarity Publishers (800-424-1055): *Intentional Communities: How to Start Them and Why* by J. Donald Walters ($7.95); *Cities of Light* by J. Donald Walters ($9.95); and *Reflections on Living 30 Years in a Spiritual Community* by Sara Cryer ($16.95).

Each summer the community offers a variety of summer internship and work exchange programs, a youth drama, art, and nature camp, family retreats and more.

Contact Us:
website, www.ananda.org,
e-mail: ananda@ananda.org
or write
Ananda Village
14618 Tyler Foote Rd.
Nevada City, CA 95959.

Ananda exists as a community of people dedicated to helping each other achieve this purpose.

Founded in 1968 by a small group inspired and guided by Yogananda's direct disciple, Kriyananda (J. Donald Walters), Ananda today is one of the largest intentional spiritual communities in the world. The main community, Ananda Village, is located near Nevada City, California, and for the last 30 years has been a living laboratory for the integration of Spirit into all aspects of life. Here 300 people apply the teachings of yoga creatively to marriage, child raising, leadership, business, healing, education, the arts, and recreation. The practice of meditation forms the heart of community life, together with a spirit of service to others.

Ananda operates on the free-enterprise system with a focus on cooperation. Members currently run many thriving businesses, including Nevada County's largest natural-foods market and vegetarian restaurant. Ananda Village is also home of the Expanding Light, a yoga education and retreat facility; the Education for Life Foundation, which provides training on Ananda's educational system and runs a private girls' high school; and the Ananda School, with over 50 students in grades K–9.

Each member pays monthly dues toward community maintenance and schools. Individuals are responsible for their own housing.

Ananda branch communities and teaching centers are to be found in Sacramento; Palo Alto; Portland; Seattle; Australia; and Assisi, Italy.

Many retreats, work-study, and internship programs are available year-round to support people in learning about yoga, education, and the dynamics of community living. Please visit our Web site. [Jan99]

ANANDA KANAN OZARK RETREAT CENTER

3157 County Rd 1670
Willow Springs MO 65793

417-469-4713, 417-469-3026
dadaik@anandakanan.com
http://www.anandakanan.com/

Began 1984 I Pop. 10
Diet: Vegetarian I Rural I Spiritual

Ananda Kanan is a spiritually oriented, self-sustaining rural-development project. It is owned and operated by Ananda Marga, a meditation/yoga/social-service organization. It serves both as a facility for group retreats and as a model for spiritually based community development. Currently there are only single men living on the property and working on gardening and other projects. These are all members of Ananda Marga, and all practice vegetarianism, yoga, and meditation. A monk of Ananda Marga is the project director. In the future family people may live on or close by the property as businesses are developed to support them. Future plans include a bakery, a school, a children's home, seed and plant distribution, beekeeping, etc. Classes in yoga and meditation are taught, and special events happen year-round—like alternative spring break and yogafest. Ananda Marga holds semi-annual retreats there, and other groups (Quakers, etc.) rent the facilities for their gatherings. Visitors are welcome to join in daily meditations in the beautiful sanctuary. There are a lake, a hiking trail, and acres of fields and woods of the Ozarks. We wish to help create a universal human family living in close cooperation with all of creation. "Anandakanan" means "garden of bliss." See our Web site for current events. [Feb99, sase requested]

APROVECHO RESEARCH CENTER

80574 Hazelton Rd
Cottage Grove OR 97424

541-942-8198, 541-942-0302 fax
apro@efn.org
http://www.efn.org/~apro/

Began 1981 I Pop. 15
Diet: No red meat I Rural

The mission that inspires our community is to provide a basis for scientific research on appropriate technologies and techniques for simple and cooperative living, and to serve an educational role in disseminating information on such technologies and techniques. Our initial mission has expanded somewhat, to emphasize sustainable forestry, food production, and related skills as well as appropriate technology, but the spirit of our work remains unchanged: to learn how to live together sustainably and ecologically and to help others to do the same, in this and other countries. Our sustainable forestry research focuses on selective thinning as an alternative to clear-cutting, low impact methods of timber removal (such as horse logging), planting, cultivation, and use of non-timber forest products. Our appropriate technology research concentrates on developing energy-efficient, nonpolluting, renewable technologies that reflect current research but which are designed to be made in most any country. Our designs use readily available materials, many of them considered trash, to create devices that can improve the quality of life while lessening environmental degradation. In our acre-plus organic garden, we grow the great majority of fresh produce we consume year round. [Oct99, sase requested]

AQUARIAN CONCEPTS

Aquarian Concepts
PO Box 3946
West Sedona AZ 86340

520-204-1206
aquarianconcepts@sedona.net
http://www.aquarianconcepts.com/

Began 1989 | Pop. 110
Diet: Omnivore | Rural/Urban | Spiritual

Aquarian Concepts, a multifaceted nonprofit organization in Sedona, Arizona, was founded by Gabriel of Sedona and Niann Emerson Chase, who share the Mandate of the Bright and Morning Star of Salvington. The guidelines for all facets of Aquarian Concepts are based on teachings found in Fifth Epochal Revelation (the *Urantia* book) and Continuing Fifth Epochal Revelation (the Cosmic Family volumes), with an emphasis on the life of Jesus of Nazareth, known as Christ Michael, Sovereign Creator Son of Nebadon.

Members of the religious order of Aquarian Concepts (the intentional community) are international, and so are the students of the Starseed and Urantian Schools of Melchizedek for children, teenagers, and adults. Classes on the *Urantia* book and Continuing Fifth Epochal Revelation are offered in Sedona for religious-order members and local residents; home-study courses are offered for others. Weekend seminars on Continuing Fifth Epochal Revelation are held at the end of every second month. Hundreds of others worldwide are affiliated in other ways.

The religious order has about 110 members, including children, with openings for new members. Living in divine pattern, service to others, and soul growth are emphasized. Healing incorporates the spiritual and scientific techniques of Reiki, Tron therapy (an advanced form of energy transference

from touch), personal transmissions (a unique source of information of past lives), and morontia counseling. Religious-order members gain experiential training in organic gardening and animal husbandry at Avalon Gardens and in landscaping, stone masonry, carpentry, plumbing, etc., by working in local outreach services offered through Planetary Family Services. Members expand their skills and talents continually by participating in other facets of Aquarian Concepts.

Future Studios, an affiliate of Aquarian Concepts, is the soundstage where Gabriel of Sedona and the Bright and Morning Star Band; the Bright and Morning Star Choir; the Starseed Acoustic Ensemble; and the drama troupe, Morontia Players, perform publicly. Aquarian Concepts also has a new-millennium store, a spiritual touring company, and a publishing company.

Visitors welcome by appointment. [Mar99, sase requested]

AQUARIAN RESEARCH FOUNDATION

14724 184th St NE
Arlington WA 98223

360-403-9533, 800-254-8291
messages
artr@juno.com
http://www.ic.org/aq/

Began 1969 | Pop. 3 | Forming
Diet: Vegetarian | Rural | Spiritual

After 20 years in the Bruderhof and in other communities, including group marriages, Art found a house in Philadelphia for a communal research center for a positive future. Aquarian Research, tax exempt since 1970, was never truly communal, but with a 1958 Cessna we visited many groups. In Germany ZEGG folks encouraged Art to start a similar group here. In 1998, Judy and Linda, Joel (14), and Art moved to the Love Israel Family in Arlington, Washington, to share a 24-foot yurt, finding ways to a positive future and dreaming of a community like ZEGG. Love Israel says Jesus wants us all to "love one another," so accepts the ZEGG ideal. Each household is independent. We can live as we wish in our own yurt and invite others also.

Our future search led to startling discoveries in physics by Dr. Randell Mills of Blacklight Power Company that can end pollution and fossil-fuel use in a few years. Right now we're working with Mills to cre-

ate a home heater needing only water. This sounds incredible but is solidly based on a whole new physics. We hope to sell such heaters before 2000 so all will know that a positive future is really coming. See our Web site for more on Aquarian and link to Mills in print and voice on Radio for Peace International. [Sep99, sase required]

AQUARIUS NATURE RETREAT

PO Box 69
Vail AZ 85641

520-449-3588

Began 1981 | Pop. 9 | Diet: Vegan | Rural

Aquarius is a textile-free ecovillage. Our life among wildlife offers a dramatic experience of contrast from urban environment, allows a real commune with nature. We preserve purity of our acreage, using natural rock blending into the mountain. There are no power lines to our dwellings, because we are striving for solar self-sufficiency. The next construction projects are a hot tub in a greenhouse, another rainwater-storage tank, a hydroponic garden. A seven-mile jeep trail leads to the interstate, and Tucson is an hour's drive to jobs. The serenity and safety are ideal for artists to create. Then the time comes to go to sell the product. Because of our remoteness we will not become overcrowded. We have more associates than full-time residents. The basic cost share is $50/month/person. On rotation basis you will have to supply Sunday supper for all present. At this time issues are discussed and resolved. There is always a vehicle going to town on Monday and back Friday night. Your supplies will be delivered weekly if you do not shop yourself. A variety of shelters is available at $1/square foot/month. You can reserve a location of your choice for next time it is available by placing a month's deposit. Try our unstructured, liberal life with few rules. You may become enchanted and spend a lifetime. [Nov98, sase required]

Listings

ARCOBALENO FIAMMEGGIANTE (TRIBE)

vicos. pietro a majella 6
Bioregione Partenopea
I-80138 Napoli
ITALY

0039 081 455026
0039 081 459021 fax

Began 1986 | Pop. 8 | Forming
Diet: Vegetarian | Urban | Spiritual

The "Arcobaleno Fiammeggiante" is a tribe in formation for the development of new conscience in harmony with nature and with spiritual interior guided (dharma) for the new age of Aquarius, a shining bridge between traditional and native cultures of East and West with new visions of new time. We mainly operate in the ancient city of Nepal, south Italy, the area around which has a strong millenary culture and is a meeting place for many diverse peoples. We manage a vegetarian/macrobiotic restaurant, an organic food store, and a specialized bookstore/library. We organize courses and seminars on integral yoga, natural nutrition, ayurvedic massage, tai chi chuan, and so on. We have as guests teachers and gurus of various spiritual traditions of the world. We have regular meditation meetings, fire ceremonies for the full moon, celebrations for equinox and solstice with music, dance, poetry, vegetarian food, and meditation. Our project and vision are to realize an ecological and spiritual village in a magic country of sirenes. The "Arcobaleno Fiammeggiante" is a point of meeting between the millenary mediterranean Pythagorean wisdom, the yogic one of vedas, and the shamanist one of Native Americans. The melting pot of Aquarius. Om Namo Narayanaya! That All Beings Be Happy! Om Shanty Shanty Shanty. [May99]

ARCOSANTI

HC 74 Box 4136
Mayer AZ 86333

520-632-7135, 520-632-6233
Terigrine@getnet.com
http://www.arcosanti.org/

Began 1970 | Pop. 52 | Forming
Diet: Omnivore | Rural/Urban

(Also known as Cosanti Foundation.) Arcosanti is an experimental architectural project of the Cosanti Foundation, a non-profit educational foundation. As a construction site our goal is to build a prototype

structure called an "Arcology." Arcology (architecture as ecology) is a concept developed by founder and chief architect Paolo Soleri. When complete Arcosanti will rise 25 stories on approximately 30 acres of land in a complex, three-dimensional, energy-efficient, pedestrian configuration of integrated living/working/social spaces for about 5,000 people of all ages.

As it is now we serve as a learning center, offering five-week workshops in which over 5,000 students and people of all interests have come to participate. All of our residents, volunteers, and interns come in through our five-week workshops. After completing the workshop, you have the option to become a resident or volunteer. We offer many areas of interest, including construction, planning, bronze foundry, woodworking, landscaping, and agriculture. We offer a gallery, bakery and cafe open to the public as well as guided tours from our gallery seven days a week from ten until four. We do welcome visitors and have overnight accommodations available. Closed Chistmas and Thanksgiving. Call for details. [Jan99]

ASHLAND VINEYARD COMMUNITY

Ashland Vineyard Ln
Ashland VA 23005

Began 1986 | Pop. 23 | Rural | Spiritual

Ashland Vineyard Community is an intentional community of six families sharing 40 acres of land, of which over 30 are held in common. We are a Quaker-oriented community, although not all of us are Quaker. Thus we make our decisions using consensus, and we incorporate the Friends' traditions of silence and attentiveness to the spirit in our routine business. Our purpose is to foster an environment where our families may live simply in an atmosphere that encourages personal growth, inward spiritual insight, and outward expression of commitment. We maintain separate family households, but we share meals, childcare, transportation, and equipment we use to maintain the gravel road, fields, pond, and woods. We have only one rule, the "no gossip rule." This means that "we aspire to speak of others without malice or self-serving interest and to speak directly and lovingly with each other about concerns." This rule has deeply enriched our lives together by building trust and safety. With the

knowledge that we always know when there is a problem and we always work it out, we have been able to form deeply satisfying relationships. The same six families have lived together on this land since 1986 and have no plans to ever leave. [Jan99, cc, sase required, no openings]

ASHRAM COMMUNITY

178 Abbeyfield Rd
Sheffield, 54 7AY, England
UNITED KINGDOM

0114-243-6688

Began 1967 | Pop. 40
Diet: No red meat | Urban | Spiritual

A relaxed community of individual radical Christians of all and no denominations who support each other in individual and corporate lifestyle issues, including joint projects and community houses.

Current projects include inner-city houses, a whole-foods shop–cooperative, homes with some income sharing. Publications include *Radical Theology, Lifestyle, Neighbourhood Community, Ecological Urban Living*. [Mar99, sase requested]

ASSOCIATION FOR THE ADVANCEMENT OF ABSOLUTE ALTRUISM COMMUNITY FOR TENDER LOVING CARE

PO Box 186
Succ Snowdon
Montreal Québec H3X 3T4
CANADA

514-342-9414, 514-342-9414 fax
nfinkelstein_tlc@hotmail.com
http://www.montrealsites.com/tlc/

Began Oct98 | Pop. 24 | Forming
Diet: Vegan | Rural | Spiritual

Shalom. Jewish universal spiritual intentional rural community is forming. One hour to Montreal/six years UN number one nation, at new center in an urban home for all Jews. Virgin land, hundreds to thousands of acres will include ecovillage single homes; cohousing; 24-hour: kitchen/grocery, library, gym/co-op sports, social, audio/visual, health center; small/large commerce/industry employee-owned ecobusiness; organic farm; preservation of some land; use of dowsing; use of sacred math/pyramidology, feng shui, etc. Energy will be 100 percent alternative self-reliant. The community will have only natural products; will fully recycle;

Key to bracketed text: cc = cannot commit to prompt correspondance, sase = self-addressed stamped envelope

will use no chemicals and no EMF/microwave; will be Gaia sensitive. Education will be local Montessori/Waldorf/Jewish. Diet is ecokosher organic vegan. The community will have Orthodox area and total openness and respect and will study all traditions. Consensus is to decide request to include non-Jews. Join via consensus, vision attuned to our concepts, possessing list factors. We go deep into Kabbala, psi, new/old sciences, healing frontiers via spiritual masters, doctors, scientists, Nobel laureates, applied uses. Wise seniors, mental/physical handicap, Isedaka/charity via nonprofit tax exempt are involved. The center has Friday Onegs, services, havdala/mela malka/parties—music, dance, creative to end Shabbat, Sunday business meals. Our focus is love/tender loving care/being childlike/altruism/play/laughter. Lehtraot/Good-bye. [Oct99, sase required]

ASSOCIATION FOR THE EARTH

Stowarzyszenie dla Ziemi
Bratnik 5 KamionKa
21-134
POLAND
0603912223
DLaZiemi@dlaziemi.most.org.pl
http://www.most.org.pl/las/

Began 1981 | Pop. 99
Diet: Omnivore | Rural

(Also known as Community of DabrowKa.) The association is a group of families, lots of artists, often craftspeople. Inside the association has around 15 members working for integration of the community itself and with the people around with which we have good contacts. That's important for us, that our community is itself inside of the community of our farmer's neighbors.

In the association we have the vision of a sustainable development of all our region, and we work with institutions (school culture house ...) and local government to achieve that. We are nonhermetic. [May99]

ATLANTIS

Icononzo
Tolima
COLOMBIA
SOUTH AMERICA

Began 1970 | Pop. 25
Diet: Vegetarian | Rural | Spiritual

(Also known as Caquetá Rainforest Campaign.) Atlantis is a gutsy tribe of three generations, mainly English, Irish, Colombian; 10 adults; 10 kids; hundreds of visitors. Dedicated to bypassing "civilization," 30 years old, we have lived on deserted islands and in mountain forests in Ireland and Colombia, developing creative ways of relating cooperatively with full self-expression.

Our kids are self-reliant, happy, hard-working, and talented, brought up with physical freedom but not allowed to piss the adults off! They have no formal education but masses of practical skills.

We're vegetarian, atheist, revolutionary politically. Own food organically grown. We began as a therapeutic community. Our free expression can shock some people. No drugs; alternative medicine; 100 percent ecological lifestyle; no electricity; we reject twentieth-century values. One hundred seventy-five hectares of forest, caves, streams, waterfalls; 5,000-foot mild climate. Hard physical work, lots of fun, theater, music; we write songs, plays, books; do psychic work, dancing, sports, yoga. We run a traveling "Green Theatre."

Nonsmoking visitors welcome any time; must have sense of humor and willingness to express feelings. We are not "politically correct"! Donations of seeds for our tree-saving, organic-farming campaign among Colombian peasants welcome. This is a guerilla area (calm). [Mar99]

ATLANTIS RISING, INC.

PO Box 154
Bradford NH 03221
603-938-2723

Began 1975 | Pop. 7
Diet: Omnivore | Rural

We are a small community in a very quiet, secluded, rural location. There are presently two member families. We have a mixture of community-owned and private lands totaling 220 acres. We adjoin the 1,760-acre Low State Forest. Our mission is to practice sustainable agriculture, agroforestry, and silviculture. There are presently two homes and one under construction on the land. A blacksmith shop is nearly complete. Future plans include selling hardwood lumber to cabinetmakers and building a woodworking shop. There is an established fruit and nut orchard. We may take on new members and purchase nearby lands. Long-term timber income is a community objective. Current member interests include Reiki, intuitive readings and healings, herbalism, organic grains, history, blacksmithing, sand and gravel pits, bioregional and watershed politics, libertarianism, community self-reliance, biodiversity preservation, solar energy, real estate, books and antiques, football, hiking, camping, moviemaking and movie watching, guitar, and traveling. Future plans include building a pond and sauna, large livestock, and possibly establishing a community branch in New Mexico. [Nov98, cc, sase required]

ATMASANTULANA VILLAGE

Nr MTDC Holiday Resort
Karla 410 405
INDIA
(+91) 2114-82261, (+91) 2114-82291

Began 1983 | Pop. 69
Diet: Vegetarian | Rural | Spiritual

Atmasantulana Village: a holistic living, healing, and learning community. An ancient university for modern times, Atmasantulana Village was founded and inspired by Shri Balaji Tambe, an Ayurvedic doctor. This community was created by and for members all over the world who could visualize the need for it and can accept a simple life with the principle of "service above self."

Atmasantulana Village is a space in nature surrounded by mountains, close to a beautiful river about 110 kilometers from Mumbai. It offers facilities for cultural and educational activities. Ayurveda is practiced—an ancient holistic healing system—including preventive medicine and alternative therapies for purification of body, mind, and soul. The healing work done in the village is an opportunity for the residents to offer their services.

Nature, fresh air, healing, music, devotion, pure food, and natural medicine are giving miraculous results. Courses are offered in art of living, yoga, meditation, massage, and Ayurveda. The Aum Temple, unique in the world, is the nucleus of the community, open to people of all religions and beliefs. The village is a model, and the members wish that such communities would develop all over the world, as they are the answer to the disintegration of modern life. [Oct99]

AUROVILLE

AVI-USA
PO Box 877
Santa Cruz CA 95061
also
Auroville-Secretariat
Bharat Nivas
Auroville 605101
Tamil Nadu
INDIA

831-425-5620
aviusa@aol.com
http://www.auroville-india.org/

Began 1968 | Pop. 1300 | Forming
Diet: Omnivore | Rural/Urban | Spiritual

Auroville wants to be a universal town where men and women of all countries are able to live in peace and progressive harmony above all creeds, all politics, and all nationalities. The purpose of Auroville is to realize human unity.

AUROVILLE CHARTER

(1) Auroville belongs to nobody in particular. Auroville belongs to humanity as a whole. But to live in Auroville one must be a willing servitor of the Divine Consciousness.

(2) Auroville will be the place of an unending education, of constant progress and a youth that never ages.

(3) Auroville wants to be the bridge between the past and the future. Taking advantage of all discoveries from without and from within, Auroville will boldly spring toward future realizations.

(4) Auroville will be a site of material and spiritual researches for a living embodiment of an actual human unity. [Sep99]

AWAAWAROA BAY ECO-VILLAGE

RD 1
Waiheke Island
NEW ZEALAND

64-9-372-8514, 64-9-372-6586
64-9-372-6586 fax
simon@sdg.pl.net
http://www.converge.org.nz/evcnz/

Began 1994 | Rural

Awaawaroa Bay Eco-Village owns 169 hectares (420 acres) of land consisting mainly of steep hill country that has been farmed pastorally for many years. There is also a large wetland and estuarine system that has been identified as a site of ecological significance. There are a number of large pockets of regenerating bush, and more than 50 percent of the bush will be covenanted in the near future.

The coastal area is a habitat for a variety of wading bird species. To protect the wildlife the goal is to have no cats or dogs on the property. Nontoxic and energy-efficient building materials and methods are encouraged with an internal building code in place. We are off the grid, so alternative energy sources are essential. Also alternative wastewater systems are required. We aim for a chemical-free environment with all land-use practices to be organic.

Our community vision statement is as follows:

"Awaawaroa will be a place where we live in harmony with the land, conserving and enhancing the land and its ecosystems. Our methods of working the land will be organic and sustainable, encouraging biodiversity. The community will be based on co-operation and honesty, respecting people's diversity, while striving for consensus. We will create a safe, nonviolent and caring environment, with hope for the future."

We are actively seeking foundation members. As of June 1999 the shares cost around $66,500, and there are 4 out of 15 still available. Purchasing a share entitles you to a 1-hectare allotment on which to live and work. All members are entitled to access all common land and community facilities as they are developed.

A tractor shed/barn will be built soon, and planning is under way for a multipurpose community facility that will be built once two further shares are sold. [Jun99]

BACK TO THE LAND COMMUNITY

100 miles from nowhere
c/o FIC Office
Rt 1 Box 156
Rutledge MO 63563
wildriver@saber.net

Began 1979 | Pop. 16
Diet: Omnivore | Rural

We are a remote back to the land community. In 1979, we got 80 acres of land on a beautiful river. It was undeveloped land so we worked hard to create a community where we could live simply in harmony with nature and each other. We're still learning—mixing primitive skills and appropriate technology, consensus process and anarchy. Currently we have 10 adults and six children. Most of us have lived here five years or longer. We homeschool our children, have large gardens, orchards, and vineyards. We have a 45-foot community lodge and nuclear

Key to bracketed text: cc = cannot commit to prompt correspondance, sase = self-addressed stamped envelope

family lodges. All of our houses are basically octagons of poles and boards. Two cob houses are being built this year. We have solar and hydro electricity and hot water from our wood stoves and solar hot water panels. There is a lot of flexibility in our community structure. Some years we eat together and council regularly and some years we live more village style. We all have a focus of personal growth and spirituality which we each do in our own way. Sometimes we share in sweat lodge ceremonies and fire circles. We support ourselves through several small craft businesses and a nonprofit environmental group. We enjoy a simple and remote lifestyle. [Jan99, cc]

BACKYARD TECH

Cone St
Macleay Island QLD 4186
AUSTRALIA

(07) 34095100

Began 1985
Diet: Omnivore | Rural | Spiritual

We show folk how to enjoyably and effortlessly thrive on less than $25 a week by first acquiring, inventing, or redesigning all 200+ life-support systems to ingeniously make this the country's most truly sustainable and loving solar open home—complete with edible tropical jungle and needing few external resources and plenty of varied lateral R& D practical projects. Bonus: appropriate library, workshop, and museum of the future.

Island natural living includes basic shops, pub, cheap ferry, beach, rain forest, wetlands, wildlife refuge, plenty of laughs, and friendly neighbors. Welcome over anytime, and may God bless. [Mar99, sase required]

BALI

4439 Driftwood Place
Boulder CO 80301
buzz@diac.com
http://www.diac.com/~geneva/

Began 1994 | Pop. 5 | Re-Forming
Diet: No red meat | Rural

(Also known as Geneva Community.) We own 176 gorgeous acres along the Little Thompson River in the foothills of the Rockies. Only 35 minutes from Boulder, our property combines the best of both worlds: quiet, peaceful, with a good growing cli-

mate, while near to the active social, recreational, and cultural town of Boulder.

We have final plat approval and are now selling lots. Due to the rural environment, only seven lots will be available, all clustered with the rest of the property on a conservation easement. Each resident will be the owner of one of the lots, which cost $70,000–$95,000. Each owner will build their custom home, guided by ecological and sustainable covenants.

Geneva community was going to be cohousing, but now Bali will be a great neighborhood of terrific individuals. We invite you to join us. [Dec98, sase requested]

BALTIMORE COHOUSING

1514 Medford Rd
Baltimore MD 21218

410-268-3346, 410-466-8372
paul_kilduff@hotmail.com
lhunt76949@aol.com

Began May99 | Forming | Urban

We are, in July 1999, attempting to establish a cohousing community in Baltimore, Maryland. We have two married couples, two single women, and one 12-year-old young woman. We hope to be able to walk to a grocery store, to have a waterfront connection, and to have a purchase price of less than $100,000. Rentals would be nice. [Jul99]

BARKING FROGS PERMACULTURE CENTER

PO Box 52
Sparr FL 32192
Permacltur@aol.com
YankeePerm@aol.com

Began 1988 | Pop. 2 | Forming
Diet: Omnivore | Rural

(Also known as Elfin or Yankee Permaculture.) The major thrust of Barking Frogs Permaculture Center is permaculture.

Permaculture design brings our lives back into participation with the Earth. Permaculturists and other environmentalists warn of global destruction unless we learn to live with the Earth rather than continuing to prey upon her. Permaculture trusts that the Earth shows us solutions to halt the destruction of the biosphere while sustaining ourselves in wholesome and fulfilling ways.

Permaculture design integrates people into nature's design for the bioregion as a whole so that it is respected, enhanced, and

strengthened. People receive shelter, energy, food, water, income, community, and aesthetic as well as spiritual fulfillment as part of the permaculture design, all within a balanced biological community. Permaculture-design students learn to make practical recommendations to develop the natural potential of a site. They also learn to identify the source and availability of every resource required to implement the permaculture design. A timetable for orchestrating the unfolding of the design and using each stage of implementation to prepare for the next helps to assure practical and efficient results. Thus the design integrates the goals of the Earth and the people in that place. [Feb99, cc, sase required]

BARN, THE

Lower Sharpham Barton
Ashprington
Totnes
Devon TQ9 7DX, England
UNITED KINGDOM

01803-732661

Began 1983
Diet: Vegetarian | Rural | Spiritual

The Barn is a rural retreat center offering an integrated lifestyle combining meditation practice, working on the land, and community living. Uniquely located, we overlook the beautiful River Dart. Accommodation is single, and there is guidance from experienced meditation teachers. Our aim is to live simply and be as self-sufficient as possible. We have extensive vegetable gardens, polytunnels, woodland, ducks, chickens, and geese. Please contact us for further information. [May99]

BATON ROUGE CATHOLIC WORKER

1275 Laurel St
Baton Rouge LA 70802

225-343-3045, 225-389-9572
timvining@mindspring.com

Began 1993 | Pop. 11 | Re-Forming
Diet: Omnivore | Urban

(Also known as Solidarity House.) We are a gospel-based multiracial and interfaith community. We offer hospitality and work at building a cooperative community of hope and resistance to economic and racial injustice. Most of us who live here would otherwise be called homeless. We are determined to, by the way we live, tear down barriers of race, class, sexual orientation, religion, and education. [Jan99]

BEACON HILL HOUSE

1309 13th Ave South
Seattle WA 98144

206-324-6822
bhhouse@yahoo.com

Began 1997 | Pop. 8
Diet: Vegetarian | Urban

Formed in 1996, the Beacon Hill House is an urban community located in the heart of Seattle. We inhabit a large Victorian house that we are renovating ourselves, located within a diverse neighborhood and walking distance from downtown. We currently have eight members ranging in age from 12 to 46, and we desire to grow to fill our 12 bedrooms.

Our core values are nonviolence, egalitarianism, environmental sustainability, social change, and community. These values inform all our agreements about how we live together. We share income and resources, vegetarian meals, and the use of our few cars. We make community decisions by con-

sensus at our weekly meetings. We are a member of the Federation of Egalitarian Communities and seek to promote peace, justice, and ecological responsibility in our endeavors.

Individual members choose for themselves a satisfying mix of income-generating and household work to fulfill our 36 hour/week work expectation. We tend to be involved with the wider world on a daily basis, in both our professional lives and our volunteer activities. We enjoy meeting others who are seeking to create a culture rich in compassion, cooperation, and peace. Please contact us if you would like more information or to arrange a visit. [Sep99, sase requested]

BEAL HOUSE CO-OP

525 Mac
E Lansing MI 48823

517-332-5555, 517-332-5556

Pop. 7 | Urban

Beal House is a student housing community looking for residents who attend college and plan on remaining for an extended period of time. Summer openings. Please call for details and room openings. [Aug99]

BEAR CREEK FARMS

Bear Creek Farms
PO Box 1049
Fall River Mills CA 96028

530-336-5414, 530-336-5509

Began 1987 | Pop. 4 | Forming
Diet: Omnivore | Rural

Focus: Sustainable agriculture/orchards, off electric grid, in mountain sanctuary.

Income: Health/books/thrift store and communal buildings in exchange for labors. Town apartments for store workers. Bring house trailer/converted bus to farm. Huge community structure half built.

Theme: Alternative health. Sober 100 percent. Second Amendment advocates. No guru. Individual spirituality. No racist.

Therapy: Laugh a lot. Inner tubing. Yoga. Martial arts. Bird-watching. Mountain biking. Sewing. Blacksmithing. Archery. Sprouting. Goats/mules/cat. Fishing. Art/craft classes. Rafting.

Eco: Million-acre private timber preserve; 5.7 average daily solar hrs. Post Y2K perfect at 70 miles off interstate highway; 350+ miles from nuclear power meltdown.

Primeval/pure. No poison oak! Mild four seasons???

Seek self-reliant couples seriously into nutrition and holistic remedies. Limited to core of 11 adults.

Caffeine addicts and overweight folks must stay on strict recovery diets. There is no hurry with our program!

Addicts must be three years free of pot/tobacco/cocktails/welfare schemes. Homophobics and religious dogma are outlawed in land-trust documents.

Visitors: Be ready to relocate! How will presence make post Y2K livable and fun at Bear Creek? Pretend this is *Atlas Shrugged*, of Ayn Rand fame. [Nov98, sase required]

BEAVER LODGE INCORPORATED

1360 NW Van Buren
Corvallis OR 97331

541-752-2013
huffh@ucs.orst.edu
http://www.orst.edu/groups/
beaverlodge/

Began 1940 | Pop. 23
Diet: Omnivore | Urban

(Also known as The Lodge.) We provide a close-community-living group for students at Oregon State University. By sharing work around the house, costs are kept to a minimum. We interact socially with other co-ops at the university and have a very close social group within the house. The house is run by the members. [May99, cc]

BEECH HILL COMMUNITY

Morchard Bishop
Crediton
Devon EX17 6RF, England
UNITED KINGDOM

01363-877228, 01363-877587

Began 1994 | Diet: No red meat | Rural

We live in a large country house in the rolling Devon Hills. Accommodation is both rented and leasehold, in converted outbuildings and in the main house. On our seven acres of land we grow organic fruit and vegetables. We have a paddock with three sheep and chickens, an orchard, a vineyard, a welled garden, a swimming pool, compost toilets, and a reed-bed sewage system. Together we run a course center and spend the income on community projects. We share responsibility for our home and the

Key to bracketed text: cc = cannot commit to prompt correspondance, sase = self-addressed stamped envelope

land on which we live. There is the choice of a shared meal each evening and at least 20 birthdays a year (cake, candles, and song). We participate in the wider community, promoting awareness of everyone's impact on the environment, through the local recycling scheme, community open days, and the parish GMO Concern Group. Individuals earn their income in the wider world in journalism, education, building, complementary health, editing, alternative ceremonies, and nursing; some work from home. We do not want our community to be a place of dogmatism, judgment, or preaching. We value our diversity and flexibility. We aim to care for one another and enjoy life as it happens. We welcome each other's differences and enjoy visitors and volunteers. [Dec99, sase requested]

BEIS AHARON COMMUNITY

c/o Friends of Beis Aharon
at erfr2@dirconcouk

(0)181 203 8793
erfr2@dircon.co.uk

Began 1994
Diet: Omnivore | Urban | Spiritual

Beis Aharon is a small, "intentional," orthodox Jewish community that began in London in the early 1990s. It consists of a core group of two single women who have experience of living in community in different contexts. One has several children, who are fully involved and at the heart of Beis Aharon. The larger of the two households is used for daily davenning (no minyan), shared meals, and the children's learning. The households are linked in care to those of their parents and grandparents, and with a wider circle of friends and inquirers this makes up the picture.

For the next two to three years we will be allowing the vision to mature and develop a formal structure. We are independent, and we belong to local shuls. The children grow up entirely in a frum environment and may only attend chareidi schools. While we anticipate very gradual growth, we are open to new members. These could be older couples, families, or those who have come to terms with singleness.

Members will be Jewish and will have in common a deep commitment to a Torah life, a sense of calling to live formally "in community," and a shared vision for Beis Aharon as primarily a "mussar community" but one

also looking toward a wider field of service. [Feb99]

BELLINGHAM COHOUSING

2614 Donovan Ave
Bellingham WA 98225

360-671-1086, 360-734-8325
nkaten947@aol.com
http://www.bellinghamcohousing.org/

Began Mar00 | Pop. 46 | Forming
Diet: Omnivore | Urban

The mission of Bellingham Cohousing is to work together to create a diverse multigenerational neighborhood of 33 homes on the historic Donovan Farm site. We intend to be supportive of one another, share resources, and strive to be stewards of the land. We aspire to collaborate with the larger Bellingham community to build housing for mixed-income households. [Aug99]

BETHLEHEM PEACE FARM CATHOLIC WORKER

508 Coal Creek Rd
Chehalis WA 98532

360-748-1236
gbrever@juno.com

Began 1998 | Pop. 7 | Forming
Diet: Omnivore | Rural

We are a forming Catholic Worker farm. [Jul99, sase requested]

BIRCHWOOD HALL COMMUNITY

Storridge Malvern
Worcestershire
WR13-5EZ, England
UNITED KINGDOM

Began 1970 | Diet: Vegetarian | Rural

Birchwood Hall is a housing co-op with two houses, set in eight acres of garden. Each house operates separately on a day-to-day basis with a shared budget for maintenance, etc.

The Main House is large and Victorian with lots of space. Individuals have their own rooms or share with a partner. Communal rooms include: kitchen, sitting room, TV room, etc. It is a difficult house to heat and be energy efficient but we're trying. Currently we are nine adults and one child, who has lived here all his life and goes to a local school. Some of us have grown-up

offspring who lived here and now visit. We'd very much like more people with children. Our joint politics are leftish, greenish, and feminist, with enough variation for some rowdy teatime arguments. We hope we're fun people to live with! We eat together in the evenings, and take turns cooking, trying to accommodate likes and dislikes. We're a mixture of vegetarians and meat eaters but eat mostly vegetarian with an occasional meat extravaganza! We take turns shopping for food. Estimating the amounts of silver-, red-, and blue-top milk we need each day is one of life's more difficult tasks! We do clean and maintain the house sometimes but we don't operate a three-line whip saying we must all clean toilets today. Meetings are once a week.

We don't have many defined expectations of each other but trust that everyone will add to the community and pull their own weight in some way.

The Coach House is divided into three living areas with a degree of communality. Currently there are five adults and one teenager in the house. [Jan99]

BIRDSFOOT FARM

1263 CR 25
Canton NY 13617

315-386-4852
molteng@northnet.org

Began 1972 | Pop. 9
Diet: Vegetarian | Rural

Birdsfoot Farm is a consensus-based agricultural community founded in 1972. Our farm is located where the St. Lawrence River Valley meets the foothills of the Adirondack Mountains. Though the area is quite rural, the presence of four colleges nearby brings a cultural diversity we appreciate. Currently we have 6 adult members and 2 kids. We welcome new members, including children and elders. Each growing season our population swells to 15–20 people—visitors and interns come to learn organic farming, experience community, and help create a more sustainable lifestyle.

Our 73-acre farm has fertile loam soil, woods, a stream, two barns, a large community house, a school building, three comfortable homes, and some funky seasonal housing. In order to grow we need to build new dwellings. The land and buildings are owned by the community.

Our vegetable business grows much of the community's food and sells locally. We are excited about the new elementary school on our land, Little River Community School. Each year the veggie business and school seek several interns. These projects provide income for some community members; others work off the farm.

Members share monthly living expenses, purchase equity in the property, and participate in community work projects. We care a lot about each other and find time for many kinds of sharing—such as communal meals, rituals, parties, etc. Each person follows their own spiritual path. Individuals are active in social and environmental issues. The new-member process includes a one-year trial period. For more information about our community, or internship programs, please send a letter. [Oct99, sase requested]

BLACK ELK CO-OP

902 Baldwin
Ann Arbor MI 48104
http://www.umich.edu/~umicc/

Began 1986

Black Elk Cooperative was founded in 1986 and continues to be a member of the Inter-Cooperative Council (ICC). Black Elk is named for the Oglala Sioux holy man Black Elk. The house has space for 11 men and 11 women. At Black Elk, house members jointly share responsibility for proper functioning of the house, i.e., cooking, cleaning, and maintenance. Furthermore, house members share in decisions related to budgeting expenses.

Throughout the years Black Elk has developed a strong commitment to maintaining a cooperative and social atmosphere. Black Elk has a VCR and monitor in our basement common area for watching movies as a group (but no television receiver). We also have a red-brick fireplace in the second-floor study area that draws people together during all hours of the day. But perhaps the most credible house trait is our long-running tradition for healthy vegetarian cuisine. Besides giving the house members a unified sense of purpose, regularly scheduled dinners offer all members a chance to share news and gossip and to keep track of each other's lives. Our members vary greatly in age and interests; we are a queer-friendly environment! [Oct99]

BLACK WALNUT COOPERATIVE

1353 Rutledge St
Madison WI 53703

608-257-5949

Began 1986 | Pop. 5
Diet: Vegetarian | Urban

Black Walnut is a small, independent cooperative made up of five individuals (and Monster the cat). We live together, eat together, work together, and play together, to create a saner life on the east side of Madison. [Aug99, cc]

BLACKBERRY

PO Box 208
North San Juan CA 95960
janiekess@hotmail.com

Began 1988 | Pop. 4 | Re-Forming
Diet: No red meat | Rural

(Also known as Community Evolving.) Blackberry is a close-knit intentional family committed to living, working, learning, and growing together in the Sierra Foothills north of Nevada City, California. We place much value on raising our children and ourselves in a nonviolent, healthy emotional and physical environment.

We are an income-sharing group, working to perfect our egalitarian, collective economics. All our decisions are made by consensus. In our daily lives we like to experiment with various forms and rituals gleaned from many sources. We share an Earth-based spirituality, celebrating the seasons together.

A main focus of our community is responsible stewardship of the Earth, starting with this piece of the forest. We intend to create an environmental-learning center here to help others to appreciate the integrity of the forest ecosystem.

We need to build a core of initiators for this project: people with experience in designing educational curriculum, permaculture, and nonprofits as well as building, gardening, and bookkeeping.

We see ourselves being active in local and global issues of health, peace, and the environment. Underlying all this is the desire to be deeply involved in each others' lives, to be sources of inspiration and learning, and to grow older and wiser together [Sep99, sase requested]

BLUE HERON FARM

117 Blue Heron Farm Rd
Pittsboro NC 27312

919-542-2151, 919-542-0140
919-489-3907 fax
barbara@emji.net
bhfarm@hotmail.com
http://come.to/blueheron/

Began 1995 | Pop. 18
Diet: Omnivore | Rural

We are a small rural community of individuals and families who support each other emotionally and physically while striving to live lightly on the land. We are a co-op where the members own all of the land and buildings together and each member owns shares in the co-op representing the amount of money they have spent building their house. We have a commitment to affordable housing, so there is a cap on profit from resale of members' homes to avoid gentrification. We make decisions by consensus. We work a lot together on community projects and on each other's homes. We share tools, childcare, food, ritual, games, music. Our houses are all either recycled, i.e., moved onto the farm from elsewhere, or owner built. We are looking to reclaim 20 acres of farmed-out soil to do organic farming but we need a farmer and we need to harvest our timber sustainably. We have been at it five years, growing slowly so that we stay solid. We have five or six more sites open for new members to build on, and while we're open to anyone, we do hope to attract more young families with children. All but one of us still works off the farm, but we are moving toward generating income from farm-based enterprises. Our politics are left-wing antimaterialist. [Jan99, sase required, email preferred]

BLUE MOON COOPERATIVE COMMUNITY

c/o Jim Schley
Chelsea Green Publishing Co
PO Box 428
White River Junction VT 05001

Began 1985 | Pop. 17
Diet: No red meat | Rural

(Also known as Golden Lotus, Inc..) This cooperative neighborhood on a gorgeous old farmstead in central Vermont was established by a group of friends who met in the early 1980s while working together in regional antinuclear, feminist, and disarma-

---

Key to bracketed text: cc = cannot commit to prompt correspondance, sase = self-addressed stamped envelope

ment coalitions. Initially we gathered as an informal study group to learn about land trusts and collective living. We spoke with people who had lived in communes and collectives and began to explore alternative legal and financial structures with a lawyer who specializes in cooperatives and worker-owned businesses. Our goal was simplicity, not to underestimate the importance of fairness and flexibility. Fortunately, it meanwhile took us more than two years to find land that we could afford, by which time we had a strong basis of understanding among our members (during those two years we met together at least monthly), as well as a solid set of bylaws. Being a cooperative instead of a land trust has been important to all of us; also important has been the fact that we "live off the grid"—our homes are powered by solar photoelectricity. Our present shared projects include maple sugaring, woodland stewardship, and building a community swimming pond. We're a musical, good-humored group, very tuned into our kids. [Jan98, cc, sase requested, no openings]

BOSCH CO-OP

1823 15th Ave S
Minneapolis MN 55404
612-871-2835, 612-871-4260
david@bitstream.net

Began 1982 | Pop. 6
Diet: Vegetarian | Urban

Bosch Co-op is an age/gender/orientation diverse community of six adults (age 20s–40s) living in an old Victorian house in an urban inner-city neighborhood of Minneapolis, MN. We are all left-oriented progressives with strong concerns for social and economic justice. We are queer friendly and very tolerant, inclusive, and affirming of each other's lifestyles. Living in an economically depressed and underserved neighborhood that faces many of the difficulties of urban blight, we have focused energy into community justice and revitalization issues. This has included organizing a block group and helping to develop a community garden. We share vegetarian and organic food and are active members of our local food co-op. We make decisions by consensus and all contribute our labor into keeping our house and our community going. We're all friendly, down-to-earth folks; feel free to contact or visit us. [Oct99]

BOWER HOUSE COOPERATIVE

127 Whitehills Dr
East Lansing MI 48823
517-351-4490

Began 1950 | Pop. 17
Diet: Vegetarian | Rural/Urban

Our house is a cooperative that is part of Student Housing Organization (12 houses total). We are the only vegetarian house, full of creativity, passion, and fire. We have a beautiful garden that we grow every summer, full of organic goodies. There are many activities that most members participate in together. These include camping, potlucks, initiatives, and many other things. Our house is full of love and happiness. [Jul99]

BREAD AND ROSES - BASE COMMUNITY

Fabriciusstrasse 56
D-22177 Hamburg
GERMANY
+49.040.69702085
+49.040.69702086 fax
jens.schild@weitblick.de
http://www.brot-und-rosen.de/

Began 1994
Diet: Vegetarian | Urban | Spiritual

(Also known as Brot und Rosen.) Bread and Roses is a Christian base community living in a rented 12-room building in Hamburg, Germany. We live together, share our house with homeless refugees, and share income and a lot of other resources. We are inspired by the Catholic Worker movement, other houses of hospitality, and Christian communities in the United States and Latin America. We have daily morning prayer and a biweekly worship and try to spread our social vision by inviting people to our house and by social action for marginalized people. We are pacifists and try to live simply to protect the environment. Although presently we live in the city, a move to the countryside or to a sister community in the countryside is not excluded. [Jan99]

Don't miss the FIC's **late-breaking news**— send away for your

Directory Updates!

Use the tear-out card at the back of the book.

BREITENBUSH HOT SPRINGS RETREAT & CONFERENCE CENTER

PO Box 578
Detroit OR 97342
503-854-3314
office@breitenbush.com
http://www.breitenbush.com/

Began 1977 | Pop. 42
Diet: Vegetarian | Rural

We are an intentional community and worker-owned cooperative that operates Breitenbush Hot Springs Retreat and Conference Center. Located 60 miles east of Salem, Oregon, Breitenbush sits on 80 acres surrounded by ancient forests of the Mount Jefferson wilderness on the west slope of the Cascades. Currently our community ranges from 45 to 70 adults and children. We honor all spiritual traditions and offer the services of the retreat center (yoga classes, meditation, ritual, healing arts) to staff at little or no charge. We are off the grid using hydroelectricity and geothermal heat and practice a low-impact approach to Earth stewardship.

From our credo: "Our primary service is to provide a healing retreat and conference center that promotes holistic health and spiritual growth, and facilitates the gathering of people in celebration of the experiences of life. Our community is supported by the services we provide. We are committed to the health and well-being of ourselves and our families, to live, to work, play, and grow together harmoniously. We mutually support and respect each person's dignity, and awaken to the Spirit within each of us that acknowledges we are all One."

Breitenbush Hot Springs is a rustic hot-springs resort that was built in the late 1920s and early 1930s. In 1977 our founder purchased the idle and deteriorating property and spent several years restoring the old resort and getting it ready for guests again. The members of the worker-owned cooperative participate in a profit-/loss-sharing program, make most of the major decisions about community and business affairs, and elect our board of directors. To be a worker-owner, a community member must be employed for one year, be a community member and employee in good standing, and purchase a membership share of $500.

The community lives across the river from the retreat and conference center in a villagelike setting. We have regular community sharings, and three times a year we

Additions and corrections: Email: directory@ic.org, Web: http://directory.ic.org/, Mail: RR 1 Box 156-D, Rutledge MO 63563, USA.

Listings

close our guest facilities for a four-day community renewal where we join together for training, fun, and community building.

As each year passes, more and more people come to Breitenbush. A whole book could be written about our adventures, explorations, and lessons learned over the 21 years. We live a rich, full life here. We delight in an abundance of diverse people, innovative ideas, healing practices, friendships, challenges, spirit, and nature. [Nov98]

BRIGHT MORNING STAR

302 NW 81st St
Seattle WA 98117

206-782-9305

Began 1979 | Pop. 8
Diet: Omnivore | Urban

Bright Morning Star is a small urban cooperative, formed to support our members in their social change and artistic pursuits. Located in Seattle, we enjoy many benefits of city living, including a wide range of friends and interests outside our home: Quaker meeting, opera, the Center for Spiritual Living, aikido, reevaluation counseling, and the Northwest Intentional Community Association, among others. We are especially proud to be gay and straight together. We share food, mostly vegetarian meals, and chores and meet regularly, making decisions by consensus. Our workdays honor the continued well-being of our home, and our celebrations recognize the Light within each of us. Occasionally one of us spontaneously bursts into song. We began in Philadelphia in 1979 via the Life Center as two couples (gay and straight) combining incomes and coparenting three children. In 1985 we moved to Seattle and eventually bought a large, airy house. Although members have come and gone over the years, we are still committed to maintaining a pleasant, cooperative, and nurturing environment for personal growth and social activism. Invited guests are welcome. Advance notice required. [Jan99, sase required, no openings]

Subscribe to
Communities Magazine
800-462-8240
order@ic.org • http://www.ic.org/
or use the tear-out card at the back.

BRIGID COLLECTIVE

2012 Tenth St
Berkeley CA 94710
frida_stein@hotmail.com

Began 1985 | Pop. 7
Diet: No red meat | Urban

Our lovely two-story home was purchased in 1985 by six individuals who lived collectively. The house was first occupied on the feast of Brigid, the goddess of healing, inspiration, and smithcraft. We have separate bedrooms, an assortment of common spaces, and a large yard with garden and hot tub.

Presently there remain two original members and five renters. New ownership structure is currently being discussed with an emphasis on community-oriented legal models.

Currently, we are two men and five women, ranging in age from 27 to 50. We are a combination of the following: feminists, artists, cooks, body workers, writers, teachers, social workers, world savers, and troublemakers. Our community is committed to keeping balance across gender, age, and sexual orientations. We are spiritually and politically diverse.

Brigid members meet weekly, purchase and cook mostly organic vegetarian foods, regularly maintain the house, and, most importantly, practice clear communication and consensus process. Because of environmental sensitivities, we discourage drug and alcohol abuse. Our collective spirit encourages our playful sides as well as nurtures our authentic selves in a group setting.

Occasional openings become available as members leave. Please write before visiting and please be patient for our reply. [Feb99, cc, sase required, no openings]

BROWN ASSOCIATION FOR COOPERATIVE HOUSING (BACH)

Box 2568
Eastside Post Office
Providence RI 02906

401-272-2391, 401-421-3270
Bach_Housing@brown.edu

Began 1970 | Pop. 27
Diet: Vegetarian | Urban

The Brown Association for Cooperative Housing (BACH) is a nonprofit student-run housing cooperative in Providence, Rhode Island. Since 1971 it has dedicated itself to providing affordable housing and a sense of

community to the students, faculty, administration, and employees of Brown University.

Each house runs its own food cooperative, allowing its members and others to discover the joys of bulk orders and cooking enough for 25 at a time. BACH is run entirely by its members. It is governed by a board of directors that takes responsibility for day-to-day operations as well as long-term projects of the corporation. There are currently two houses, Finlandia and Watermyn, housing a total of 27 people.

While every house makes its own rules, every BACH member is expected to behave and interact according to certain cooperative principles. Central to cooperative living is the idea of consensus that we use at the board and in the houses. [Aug99, sase required]

BRYN GWELED HOMESTEADS

1150 Woods Rd
Southampton PA 18966

215-357-3977
hmvl@libertynet.com

Began 1940 | Pop. 124 | Rural/Urban
Alumni will help celebrate the sixtieth reunion of Bryn Gweled (BG) Homesteads in August 2000. Insofar as known, no former owner of a BG home is disgruntled. Unexpected employment opportunities in faraway places, departure for retirement communities, and death account for substantially all departures. This intentional community was founded to provide merely a friendly neighborhood cherishing a diversity of wealth, religion, politics, aesthetics, race, etc. Notwithstanding a complete turnover of membership, the same values flourish, permitting family autonomy for nonconformists. About 100 acres of common land for soccer fields, tennis courts, swimming pool, garden, community center, etc., plus 74 homes on two-acre lots. About one mile north of Philadelphia. Two miles private roads. Applicants visit each member family, not more than three at a time, analogous to the bridegroom of Victorian era seeking permission from a prospective father-in-law. If 80 percent support an applicant on secret written ballot, then the applicant gains approved status, thus permitting (a) purchase of home from withdrawing member and leasing her relinquished lot; or (b) leasing vacant lot and building dream home. Many reject BG. BG rejects few. Successful voluntarism with zero threat of coercion for

---

Key to bracketed text: cc = cannot commit to prompt correspondance, sase = self-addressed stamped envelope

more than 58 years. About 20 active committees enhance neighborliness. [Nov98, cc, sase requested]

BUCKMAN HALL CO-OP

University of Florida
Buckman Drive
Gainesville FL 32612
http://www.geocities.com/
CollegePark/Stadium/9665/

Began 1973 | Pop. 122
Diet: Vegan | Urban

Buckman is an opportunity for students of the University of Florida to live on campus in less expensive housing and without the traditional freshman atmosphere. Our residents perform their own custodial duties to cut down on rent, and through time spent living in the community students can gain priority for single rooms and run for the elected area government offices. Buckman provides an environment conducive to studying by supplying a study room and a separate lounge for socializing.

The responsibilities of our residents include sharing bathroom and kitchen duties with those who share the facilities, cleaning our lounges one day a semester, and a special duty once a semester that is chosen by the resident as a permanent improvement for the building. Buckman has many programs for residents to meet one another and interact. Programs may bring faculty or educational speakers or may be only for their social aspects. For information please check our Web page or contact UF Division of Housing. [Jan99]

BURCH HOUSE

249 Main St
Bethlehem NH 03574

603-444-6804
info@Burchhouse.org
http://www.burchhouse.org/

Began 1979 | Pop. 9
Diet: Omnivore | Rural

Burch House is a residential community that serves people in emotional distress. People live here to do extensive psychotherapy. All community members share in the upkeep of the household, including preparing a communal dinner each evening.

Burch House offers one the time and place to explore and experience feelings that are part of traumatic stress, depression, anxi-

ety, panic, and spiritual crisis. Our goal is to encourage people to acknowledge where they have been and to develop a vision of where to go in the future. By offering a time for self-reflection, Burch House provides a place where one can come home to one's self and integrate one's experiences. Self-reflection occurs in group conversations, meditation, yoga, and groups of therapeutic art. [Feb99]

CACTUS ROSE

2187 38th Ave
Oakland CA 94601
alinaever@ibm.net

Pop. 5 | Diet: Omnivore | Urban

We are a collective house currently with five adult members. We share food, meals, chores, meetings, and gardening. We enjoy informal social hanging out with each other as well as events, rituals, parties, etc. Once a month we have a music night/song swap open to everyone. We all love music and the arts.

We own the house and enjoy its beauty and spaciousness. We love cooking and sharing meals with each other and inviting friends over on a regular basis. We live a block away from a sister collective and enjoy spending time with each other. We buy bulk food with the other collective. We grow some vegetables and hope to grow more.

We share values of compassionate communication, social justice, caring for the Earth, making connections with our neighbors and the neighborhood. We are feminist

and queer friendly. We are spiritual in individual ways. We try to create a toxin-free home environment. We have a smallish garden with veggie plots, fruit trees, lots of roses (hence our name), and a compost bin. [Sep99, cc, no openings]

CAMBRIDGE COHOUSING

175 Richdale Ave
Cambridge MA 02140

617-661-1682
cambridgecohousing@yahoo.com
http://www.cohousing.org/

Began 1998 | Pop. 96
Diet: Omnivore | Urban

We are a large urban cohousing community, 41 units on 1.5 acres. Our households are varied in size, age, background, abilities, professions, and lifestyles. Ages range from newborn to 80 years old. Sixteen families have children living at home, 13 are single, and there are 12 couples.

Our community includes townhouses and apartments ranging from studios to four bedrooms, play areas, gardens, a large common house, emphasis on energy conservation and environmentally sustainable practices.

All units were sold and occupied by October 1998.

Friend of Cambridge Cohousing, as a benefit of membership, may place their names on our housing list for notification when units become available.

For detailed description, see *Co Housing*, vol. 12, no. 1 (spring 1999), pp. 7–14: "A New Model for Urban Cohousing." [Jul99, sase requested, no openings]

Additions and corrections: Email: directory@ic.org, Web: http://directory.ic.org/, Mail: RR 1 Box 156-D, Rutledge MO 63563, USA.

CAMP NEW HOPE COMMUNITY

1910 Deer Ln
Zephyrhills FL 33540

813-783-3151, 813-782-2990

Began 1997 | Pop. 7 | Forming | Rural
(Also known as Crystal Springs Wilderness Retreat.) Recovery home. Private room, clean house, woodsy, pond, creek, quiet. Shared kitchen and daily 60-second communication circle at 6 p.m. followed by dinner. No drugs or alcohol. [Nov98]

CAMP SISTER SPIRIT FOLK SCHOOL

PO Box 12
Ovett MS 39464

601-344-1411
sisterspir@aol.com
http://members.aol.com/SisterSpir/

Began 1993 | Pop. 5
Diet: Omnivore | Rural

Internships available for three months with prior trial period. We operate a food bank, produce many festivals and events. We welcome group rental for retreat and gatherings. We have a women's bunkhouse and small cabins. We welcome visitors/volunteers for $10 to $20 per night, per-person sliding scale, meals included.

We produce the Lesbigaytrans and Allies Sober Spring Break. We produce the Gulf Coast Womyn's Festival. We host Spiritfest, a women's spirituality gathering. We have several ongoing projects: antipoverty, sharing resources and skills, educational program here and in Mexico.

We faced great opposition to our presence in this community but have worked hard to earn our rightful space here, and the opposition has been quiet since we won our lawsuit.

Men who are allies are welcome to visit this space. No pets, no s/m, no violence in word or deed, no illegal drugs or alcohol. Please, at least three days notice needed before you visit. You must preregister. We need self-motivated volunteers who are willing to learn and work. [Sep99, sase requested]

CAMPHILL ASSOCIATION OF NORTH AMERICA (CANA)

Camphill Recruitment Office
c/o Camphill Village
Copake NY 12516

518-329-7288, 518-329-2286
recruitcamphill@taconic.net
http://www.camphillassociation.org/

Began 1961 | Spiritual

The Camphill Recruitment Office is here to tell you about the wide range of opportunities offered by the Camphill Communities in North America (seven in the USA and two in Canada) for the following. 1. Learning: learn people skills, crafts, the arts, home-making, and biodynamic agriculture, among others. 2. Community Living: live with colleagues from a variety of cultural backgrounds, as well as children, adolescents, or adults with developmental disabilities. 3. Service: serve the needs of your fellow human beings and of the Earth. 4. Inner Growth: develop greater awareness of your spiritual nature and of your purpose and responsibilities on the Earth.

The Camphill Recruitment Office is a branch of the Camphill Association of North America. [Jul99]

CAMPHILL COMMUNITY CLANABOGAN

Drugeon Rd
Omagh
Co Tyrone BT78 1TY
NORTHERN IRELAND

01662-256100, 01662-256120

Began 1984 | Pop. 71
Diet: Omnivore | Rural | Spiritual

We have 70 acres in the beautiful rolling countryside of county Tyrone, Ireland, four miles from the town of Omagh. The community began in 1984, and now about 70 people live here in six households, some large, some small.

In this therapeutic community, adults who have difficulties arising from mental and emotional disability live and work together with coworkers and children.

Agriculture and horticulture are very important activities in the community and provide healthy and meaningful work as well as enhancing people's awareness of the environment, the seasons, and the land on which they live. Food production is done using biodynamic principles.

Coworkers join Clanabogan as volunteers and do not receive wages, their material needs being met from a common fund. In all aspects of life and work, mutual agreement is the basis of a committed and responsible involvement.

This is an attempt to live in a new kind of community life, to include people of many nationalities and people with different problems, strengths, and weaknesses. Most people, whether disadvantaged or not, find that as well as encountering struggles and challenges, they meet interesting and rewarding experiences, learn new skills, grow, and develop. [Feb99, sase requested]

CAMPHILL COMMUNITY MOURNE GRANGE

Kilkeel
Co Down BT34 4EX
NORTHERN IRELAND

016937.60108, 016937.60128

Began 1971 | Pop. 131
Diet: Omnivore | Rural | Spiritual

Mourne Grange is a village community of more than 130 people, where mainly mentally disadvantaged adults live and work together with coworkers and families. Nobody in the community receives wages, but the community provides for individual

Key to bracketed text: cc = cannot commit to prompt correspondance, sase = self-addressed stamped envelope

needs, which can vary from person to person. Volunteers staying for a year or less receive pocket money.

Life in the various households is like that of an extended family. The farm, vegetable gardens, and orchards, as well as village store, laundry, and bakery, all serve the needs of the community. There are craft workshops like weavery, basketry, pottery, and woodwork shop where products are made for sale in the community's craft shop and elsewhere.

The Christian festivals, along with the seasons and a rich cultural life, are celebrated together. The work of Rudolf Steiner, an Austrian philosopher, educator, and humanitarian (1861–1925) gave the underlying principles to the striving of this community. There is a foundation course in anthroposophy and social therapy on offer, and with a Waldorf Steiner kindergarten and school carried by the community the educational impulse is very much alive. Other initiatives embraced by the Community are div. therapies, biodynamic farming, and anthroposophical medicines. [Apr99]

CAMPHILL COMMUNITY PENNINE

**Boyne Hill
Chapelthorpe
Wakefield WF4 3JH, England
UNITED KINGDOM**

**01924 255281, 01924 254054
01924 240257 fax
enquiriew@pennine.org.uk
http://www.pennine.org.uk/**

Began 1977
Diet: Omnivore | Rural/Urban | Spiritual

Pennine is part of the Camphill movement. The Camphill movement creates community settings in which children, young people, and adults, many with learning difficulties, can live, work, and learn with others in healthy social relationships based on mutual care and respect. Pennine's main activities are supporting a college for those with learning difficulties.

Most coworkers live within the 35-acre site, working on a voluntary basis and receiving no wage or salary but with their daily needs being met by the community. There is always an international flavor to the community, with usually half the coworkers coming from other countries,

often as a gap year after or before college or university.

Our small farm and vegetable gardens are worked biodynamically and provide much of the community's needs. There are several craft workshops and a riding school run jointly with the Riding for Disabled Association.

We are always open to inquiries; our usual request is that a potential coworker has a year free of commitments and would be prepared to live, work, and learn alongside others in the community. Many people come to help at the Pennine Community for about a year at a time. There are often places available, so please get in touch. [Feb99]

CAMPHILL COMMUNITY TRIFORM

**20 Triform Rd
Hudson NY 12534**

**518-851-9320, 518-851-2864 fax
info@triformcamphill.org
http://triformcamphill.org/**

Began 1979 | Pop. 62 | Rural | Spiritual

Triform Camphill Community is a residential, therapeutic community, founded in 1979, that includes young adults with special needs. The mission of Triform is to build a vital community life that provides each person the possibility for healing, self-development, and fulfillment of potential.

Building community life means consciously making the effort to create a healthy social environment, rich in helpful human interactions, where the unique contribution of every person is recognized and appreciated.

Begun in 1940, the Camphill movement today comprises over 90 independent villages, schools, and training centers worldwide serving people of different ages and backgrounds. Camphill is based on the teachings of educator Rudolph Steiner and pediatrician Karl Koenig, and its hallmark is a genuine recognition of the spiritual integrity of the individual regardless of ability. Camphill places share a common goal of providing residents with dignified meaningful work, a supportive social atmosphere, and a vibrant cultural, artistic, and spiritual life. [Sep99]

CAMPHILL SOLTANE

**224 Nantmeal Rd
Glenmoore PA 19343**

**610-469-0933, 610-469-1054 fax
info@camphillsoltane.org
http://camphillsoltane.org/**

Began 1988 | Pop. 74
Diet: Omnivore | Rural | Spiritual

Camphill Sotane is a lifesharing intentional community based on Anthroposophy, as developed by the Austrian educator Rudolf Steiner. Soltane is part of the International Camphill movement, with 90 locations worldwide. Our work is with mentally retarded young adults, on 50 acres in a beautiful part of Pennsylvania, one hour northwest of Philadelphia. We have biodynamic orchards and gardens, weaving and pottery studios, and facilities for baking, painting, singing, drama, and many arts and crafts, which we employ in building community together with handicapped people. Ours is a spiritual and service community with a reverence for life, for cooperation, and for celebration.

We have approximately 62 people living and working together, including children. A Waldorf School is located nearby, as are

other communities with which we are closely associated. We welcome visitors, and have many. We usually request that people seeking long-term involvement make a one-year commitment to get to know us, our "students," and the many details, involvements, and activities of our life. Many people come from different countries, bringing a unique and lively atmosphere to Soltane. Altogether, this is a high energy, full, and busy life—especially the very rewarding but demanding work with our handicapped companions. See our Web site! Give us a call, write, or (best) visit! [Apr99]

CAMPHILL SPECIAL SCHOOL

1784 Fairview Rd
Glenmoore PA 19343

610-469-9236, 610-469-9758 fax
BvrRn@aol.com
http://www.beaverrun.org/

Began 1963 | Pop. 75
Diet: Omnivore | Rural | Spiritual

(Also known as Beaver Run.) Camphill Special Schools, Inc., is a residential community of 150 people; almost half are developmentally disabled children and adolescents living with trained curative educators and their families. Called "Beaver Run," this children's village is located on 77 woodland acres in Chester County, one hour west of Philadelphia, Pennsylvania. The campus includes 11 custom-built family homes for the special children and those who work with them; a schoolhouse; a cultural hall; space for group and individual therapeutic treatments; a medical care unit; a craft house with a store and workshop; a stable for therapeutic riding; and various auxiliary buildings.

Camphill's educational philosophy, called "Curative Education," is based on the social, educational, and spiritual insights of Rudolf Steiner, an Austrian scientist and philosopher, and aims for a more complete understanding and appreciation of man's spiritual nature and destiny. Camphill recognizes that the relationship between one person and another is the basis for all healing and social renewal and that in such relationships one receives as much as one gives. The school offers a three-year training for qualified adults in Curative Education that combines conceptual academic course work with hands-on practical experience. Life is intense and demanding here but very enriching.

Please contact us for further information. [Sep99]

CAMPHILL VILLAGE KIMBERTON HILLS

Box 155
Kimberton PA 19442

610-935-3963, 610-935-0300
mwild@camphillfdn.org

Began 1972 | Pop. 125
Diet: Omnivore | Rural | Spiritual

Camphill Village of Kimberton Hills is one of eight North American communities in the Camphill movement—each one unique, yet all with similar purposes. We seek to create a renewed village life and to establish healthy social forms of human interdependence. Our approach is a nondenominational Christian way of life based on the inspirations of Rudolf Steiner's anthroposophy, which allows each person to evolve to their potential as a respected individual.

Started in 1972, our 430-acre biodynamic farm is run by a community of 125 members, including some with developmental disabilities. We have 15 houses that shelter "extended families" who work the farm, gardens, orchard, bakery, cheese house, and coffee shop. We have a strong cultural life that involves many visitors and neighbors. Volunteers are welcome to share in the life and work here as space permits. Preference is given to those who can commit for a minimum of one year. We also have a small apprentice program in biodynamic agriculture for "on the job training." All visitors are welcome by appointment—and letters are preferred to phone calls. [Nov98, sase requested]

CAMPHILL VILLAGE MINNESOTA, INC.

Rt 3 Box 249
Sauk Centre MN 56378

320-732-6365

Began 1980 | Pop. 57
Diet: Omnivore | Rural | Spiritual

Camphill Minnesota is one of 70 Camphill communities around the world. 60 of us—children, adults, and adults with mental handicaps—live in extended families in seven houses on two adjoining farms totaling 400 acres.

We live together for a variety of reasons that all come together in the quest to bring

the needs of the land, people, and animals into harmony with the needs of the Spirit. All of our work is based on athroposophy (literally, "the wisdom of man"), which came about through Rudolf Steiner (1861–1925), an Austrian-born philosopher, artist, and scientist.

We farm and garden biodynamically—an approach that combines organics, the rhythms of the planets, and other factors. Through a creative approach that uses art to introduce subjects to the children, the goal of our home school is to bring the child's thinking, feelings, and will into harmony. In all that is done (including our houses, weavery, woodshop, and bakery) the dignity of humanity is enkindled collectively and individually. We are open to new members as space is available. Please inquire by letter or phone. [Nov98]

CAMPHILL VILLAGE NEWTON DEE

Bieldside
Aberdeen
AB15 9DX, Scotland
UNITED KINGDOM

01224-868701

Began 1960 | Pop. 200
Diet: Omnivore | Rural/Urban | Spiritual

Newton Dee Village is one of 70 Camphill communities around the world. We are a semirural community of around 200 people, 93 of whom are adults with learning disabilities. Our striving is based on anthroposophy, formulated by Rudolf Steiner. We work out of Christianity and celebrate the festivals of the year.

We live and work together in 21 households on a 170-acre estate. The products of our village workshops include dolls, toys, metalwork, batik, and bakery and confectionery goods. In addition, we have a cafe, laundry, gift shop, and grocery store and also two farms and gardens that are run using biodynamic methods.

We receive no salaries, and our needs are met by the community. Our workforce is based on volunteers, with young people (minimum age 19) from Britain and abroad joining us for a minimum of one year. We are open to new members as space is available. Please inquire by letter or phone to: The Reception Group, Newton Dee Village, Bieldside, Aberdeen AB15 9DX; telephone: 01224 868701. [Jun99]

CAMPHILL VILLAGE U.S.A., INC.

**Camphill Village
Copake NY 12516**

518-329-4851
cvvolunteer@taconic.net

Began 1961 | Pop. 230
Diet: Omnivore | Rural | Spiritual

Camphill Village USA, Inc., is one of eight Camphill centers in the United States, where approximately 220 people—108 developmentally disabled adults, 40 permanent volunteers, 40 short-term volunteers, and 35 children—live and work together in community.

Volunteers live in one of our 20 houses along with 6 to 8 developmentally disabled adults. Volunteers have their own room. Responsibilities vary, but generally a volunteer would be involved in meal preparation, physical care of disabled adults, housework, and social life. There is also work on the land—farming; estate work; gardening; or work in a shop, including weaving, bookbinding, candle dipping, woodworking, bakery, seeds, herbs, and glass shop. A volunteer's day begins about 6:30 a.m. and goes until evening. Free time is not formally scheduled but arranged by mutual awareness of the needs of and responsibility for one another. Life is intense and very rewarding. We welcome your interest. [Jan99]

CANTINE'S ISLAND COHOUSING

**Cantine's Island
Saugerties NY 12477**

914-246-0697

Began 1997 | Pop. 28
Diet: Omnivore | Urban

Recently completed cohousing community of 12 modest private houses and common house built on 1 1/2 acres of an 8-acre property, with one-quarter mile frontage on the Esopus, a deep- water creek, between the falls over Barclay's Dam and the Hudson River. Saugerties is a friendly provincial town, near Woodstock and the city of Kingston. Our uniquely lovely property is the largest in the village, offering the convenience of town living and a nice degree of privacy. We worked long and hard to achieve our success, and in so doing came to know each other as trusted partners. We're all delighted to be living here!

We are looking for two or three more households to join us, who will be able to engage in an abbreviated version of the development phase that we went through, building on lots contiguous to the main site and joining as equal partners in this warm, well-functioning community. We will offer support and guidance, but we can't do it for you, because the growth into community life comes with the commitment to do it! Cohousing embodies an ideology of sharing, balanced with respect for privacy. We are egalitarian, tolerant, open to alternative lifestyles. Only a few of us are vegetarians, but most of the food we serve in the common house is vegetarian or vegan. [Dec98]

CARDIFF PLACE COHOUSING COMMUNITY

**#404 - 1246 Fairfield Rd
Victoria BC V8V 3B5
CANADA**

250-480-5152, 250-920-7488
cp@ic.org
http://www.cohousing.ca/

Began 1994 | Pop. 27
Diet: Omnivore | Urban

Cardiff Place is an urban cohousing community of 17 households, each in its own condominium (most are owner occupied). At present, the ages of the 27 community members range over a broad spectrum.

Since moving in, during 1994, the community has continued to define itself and has begun a vision/mission process. The community is nonhierarchical, with decisions made at general meetings by consensus—supplemented by committees. Community life includes three common dinners a week, celebrations, general meetings every three weeks, special meetings as needed, and work bees. Outdoor common areas comprise grass, plant beds, patios, and a kids' play area. Common rooms include kitchen, dining, lounge, kids', guest, laundry, workshops, and bike storage.

Combinations of members have got together around shared interests such as childcare; reading; film-, lecture-, theater-, and museum-going; music; gardening; running; camping; skiing; picnics; personal support; and personal growth. Aside from one toddler, members are in school; part- or full-time work—mostly in caring fields such as medical, counseling, or teaching; self-employed or in a home-based business; unemployed by choice; or retired. [Sep99, cc]

CARPENTER VILLAGE

**Box 5802
Athens OH 45701**

740-593-6562
**http://www.carpenter-inn.com/
    carpentervillage/**

Forming | Rural

Carpenter Village is a new, affordable, permaculture-oriented community on 50 acres in southeast Ohio near Ohio University. Private 3+-acre tracts for diverse home-based workers. Housing choice, includes starter housing, subject to approval; 10-acre commons land. Precommunity questionnaire and weekend meetings to assemble people with shared concerns and work interests/skills to enhance cooperative and collaborative opportunities, such as brainstorming, share learning, cooperative workplaces. Anticipate permaculture outreach learning-center programs. A human-scale, caring, learning/doing environment that combines independent effort, small-group synergy, and a focus on furthering appropriate technologies in alternate energy,

Additions and corrections: Email: directory@ic.org, Web: http://directory.ic.org/, Mail: RR 1 Box 156-D, Rutledge MO 63563, USA.

housing, food production. For information and a questionnaire contact us. [Aug99]

CASA AMISTAD

2615 North 4th St
Philadelphia PA 19133

215-423-7465
AmigoJorge@aol.com
Cityquake@aol.com

Began 1996 | Pop. 3 | Forming
Diet: Omnivore | Urban | Spiritual

Casa Amistad/Friendship House is the center for a Friends' ministry in a multiracial, bilingual, inner-city neighborhood. It is a ministry of a loving, peaceful presence to a neighborhood known for violence, poverty, and drugs. Members of the ministry have helped the neighborhood reclaim a park from drug dealers and now are working with neighbors, school groups, city agencies, and organizations to make improvements in the park, sustain a community garden, create activities for local children, address neighborhood needs and crises, and build a supportive community. Our three-story row house is home to three adults and two children (part-time). We host regular neighborhood gatherings and have two weekly meetings for unprogrammed worship and prayer. Our community is also the home base for ministries to Quaker groups, a prison, AVP programs in Ecuador, and the wider world. Our life together provides both support and challenge to become more loving and authentic. We are attempting to live faithfully, prophetically, and with joy, testifying to the reality and power of God's active presence in the world and in our daily lives and at the same time calling/inviting others to transformed ways of thinking and living. [Sep99, sase requested]

CASA MARIA CATHOLIC WORKER COMMUNITY

1131 North 21st St
PO Box 05206
Milwaukee WI 53205

414-344-5745, 414-344-5585

Began 1967 | Pop. 20
Diet: Omnivore | Urban | Spiritual

We are a community of people dedicated to living out the Gospel values of loving our enemies and attempting to take personal responsibility for the needy sisters and brothers in our society. We follow the tradition of the Catholic Worker movement. We believe in nonviolence as a way of life, gentle personalism, and the practice of the spiritual and corporal works of mercy. We choose to live a life of voluntary poverty.

The Casa Maria Hospitality House gives hospitality to four homeless families and two single women at one time, and they stay with us until they find places of their own. We provide food, clothing, used furniture, etc., which are donated to us by the public, to help our guests and others in need of such. We also try to root out the causes of poverty and violence by nonviolently protesting and refusing to cooperate with the military and the US government. Pat's House provides hospitality to homeless women seeking to recover from addictions to drugs and/or alcohol. They stay with us until such a time as they receive counseling, find work, and find a suitable place to live. Mapendo House provide hospitality to homeless single women who have disabilities that make them unable to gain employment and are not receiving any aid. Women suffering from sexual abuse are also accepted. They stay with us until they are able to find some kind of assistance.

We have two community houses where many of our volunteers stay and live in common. Lazarus House and Harmony House both offer hospitality. Our community members do not receive compensation for working at our houses, and many of them have jobs on the outside to provide for their own personal needs and the needs of the houses. Anyone who wishes to live a life of voluntary poverty, to dedicate their life to the needy and oppressed, and to live a life of nonviolence and gentle personalism and who is willing to live in community is invited to join the Casa Maria Community. We accept volunteers of any race, religion, or nationality. [Nov98]

CASCADE COHOUSING

10 Saunders Cres
South Hobart 7004
Tasmania
AUSTRALIA

+61 3 6223 4405
+61 3 6234 1822 fax
ian@sonardata.com
mtb@netspace.net.au
http://www.verdant.com.au/
cascadecohousing/

Began 1991

Cascade Cohousing is a cohouse modeled on the Danish and US experiences described in the book *Cohousing* by McCammant and Durret.

We have a strong focus on the sharing of meals as a catalyst of "sense of community" and have three to four common meals per week available in our common house. The community has a concern to reduce environmental impact of our lifestyles, and this concern is discussed often, but generally individuals choose their own paths. We have a strong emphasis on both community and privacy. Half the group are vegetarian. We have common gardens, a workshop, children's areas, and the like. We enjoy working and playing together. We lack a common ideology other than wanting to live this type of lifestyle. Our children love living at Cascade Cohousing. [Apr99]

CATHOLIC WORKER COMMUNITY OF CLEVELAND

3601 Whitman Ave
Cleveland OH 44113

216-631-3059

Began 1986 | Pop. 14 | Spiritual

Deeply convinced of the radical truth of the Gospel, we strive to follow a Catholic Worker philosophy. We emphasize the corporal works of mercy—identifying with and ministering to the homeless, poor, sick, imprisoned—and radical action against the causes of poverty and oppression. We seek to be nonviolent and opposed to all war and to answer Jesus' call to be peacemakers. We recognize the continual need to clarify our thought through prayer, reflection, dialogue, and action.

We are forming a loving and caring resistance community with a strong spiritual base that will enable us to share our lives with those who are broken—not just for their

---

Key to bracketed text: cc = cannot commit to prompt correspondance, sase = self-addressed stamped envelope

sake but for ours as well, knowing that we are all sisters and brothers.

Come to Cleveland! We need new community members to live in our intentional community and to help in our work with the homeless on Cleveland's west side. Our ministry includes a cooperative community, a drop-in center, several small houses of hospitality, a newspaper, and efforts in resistance to violence and militarism. We invite those interested in this possibility to write us or call 216-631-3059 and ask for Joe. [Dec98]

CATHOLIC WORKER PRETRIAL HOUSE

15405 Short Ridge Ct
Silver Spring MD 20906

301-598-5427
TobyTerrar@aol.com
http://www.angelfire.com/
md/TobyTerrar/index.html

Forming | Urban

This seeks to be a Catholic Worker collective that will restore the pretrial house that existed in Washington, DC, from the 1960s to the 1980s. A pretrial house is a place where those in the criminal justice system who cannot make bond can await trial without being in jail. It allows them to keep or obtain jobs, family ties, and drug-treatment programs.

The house would also be available to homeless parolees, probationers, and ex-offenders and serve as a job training center. There are hundreds of abandoned buildings in DC, despite a large homeless population. Many involved in the criminal justice system are skilled in the building trades: masons, carpenters, painters, plumbers, electricians. The prison ministry already runs a program in this area. The pretrial house could contribute to it.

Finally the house would be available to temporarily house families that have become homeless because of the incarceration of a parent and that therefore risk having their children removed and placed in foster care. It would give them a chance to get on their feet.

It is easier to plan about getting a building than it is to get a building; that is why this project is still in the start-up stage. [Sep99]

CAVE CREEK

23780 Cave Creek Rd
Boonville MO 65233

660-841-5229

Began 1997 | Pop. 2 | Forming
Diet: Vegetarian | Rural

Border bioregion 30 miles west of Columbia, Missouri. We envision creating a community of six to eight adults plus children. Following permaculture and companion planting ideas, we cultivate beautiful gardens/orchards and will raise animals in our open land near Cave Creek. As of 2/99, we are living in and completing construction of a photovoltaic-powered, passive-solar, straw-bale/cob community center. Ecological living, personal growth, crafts, community outreach/environmental education, and consensus-based decision making are our main goals. We intend for our livelihood to thrive on the land. Gatherings for interpersonal growth, business, dinners, and other fun activities happen on a regular basis. We have exchanges with other intentional communities in the region to further our mutual learning and growth. We invite people to join us who are creative and energetic and can follow through with thought, action, and emotion. Apprenticeships possible. A letter or phone call required. [Feb99, sase required]

CEDAR HOLLOW COMMUNITY

590 Pleasant Ridge Church Rd
Edmonton KY 42129

Began 1983 | Pop. 5
Diet: Omnivore | Rural

The community of the Cedar Hollow Community, the Center for Ecological Design and Restoration (CEDAR), resides in a permaculture demonstration site and homestead. Established in 1983, CEDAR—part of a 43-acre land trust—emphasizes education and attunement by example of simple living, land restoration, and sustainable agricultural practices. Community members live off the grid and carry water by choice and creatively explore ways to heal themselves and the land. Contact information: CEDAR, 590 Pleasant Ridge Church Road, Edmonton, KY 52129-8802. [Jul99, sase requested]

CELO COMMUNITY

Corresponding Secretary
Ernest Morgan
1901 Hannah Branch Rd
Burnsville NC 28714

828-675-4361, 828-675-4012

Began 1939 | Pop. 113
Diet: Omnivore | Rural

Celo Community is a land trust with 1,200 acres occupied by some 40 households. Members do not own the land in fee simple but purchase "holdings" that carry most, but not all, the privileges of regular ownership. A holding may be sold only to another member or to the community. Plans for building houses, roads, or power lines must be submitted to the Property Committee for approval.

The community includes a few single people and unmarried couples but is made up predominantly of families. The member families live in separate homes and make their livings independently. They come together once a month for a meeting and function on a variety of committees. Now and then they have a "community workday" in which groups come together to carry out community projects or to assist a member family. Lifestyles are simple, and there is concern with ecology and social issues.

Families wishing to join Celo Community apply for trial membership, which runs for eight months if the family is housed in the community or one year if they are living nearby. At the end of the trial membership period the family and community decide whether the family should become accepted as a regular member.

At present there are about 30 families waiting to become trial members. Since only two trial members are accepted at a time a family applying now could expect to wait several years to become a member. Also, holding sites are limited, and that introduces an element of uncertainty.

I should mention, however, that it is a common practice for candidates to move nearby and take part in community activities while waiting. We sometimes refer to these folks as "our sane fringe." In fact, in most Celo Community activities the community members are outnumbered by the nonmembers. [Nov98]

Additions and corrections: Email: directory@ic.org, Web: http://directory.ic.org/, Mail: RR 1 Box 156-D, Rutledge MO 63563, USA.

CENNEDNYSS COMMUNITY

**PO Summertown
SA 5141
AUSTRALIA**

**0061 08 8390 3166
0061 08 8390 1203 fax
donestel@camtech.net.au**

Began 1978
Diet: Omnivore | Rural

We share concerns about our planetary and local environments, social justice and human rights, and gender and interpersonal issues at all levels. We practice organic farming and are committed to revegetation and conservation. We support each other in our outside work and activities for social change.

Legally we are an incorporated association that owns the land and houses, several motor vehicles, and farm equipment. We make loans to the association to enable capital purchases and developments, and each of us contributes an agreed percentage of our gross income to cover the costs of running the community. This includes house and car maintenance, insurance, rates, and telephones.

Our main object as a group is to provide mutual support, emotional and practical, and to develop and maintain the property that we share. We meet formally once a fortnight to discuss various issues, including child-related matters and the property, gardens, and orchards as well as finance and any issues related to our collective lives.

We eat one evening meal together each week, and once a week we share in a working bee and lunch or morning tea. Once every six weeks we have a "gathering" for social activities or to celebrate a birthday. At these and other opportunities informal discussions occur about our individual personal involvements and commitments and a range of community concerns.

Through all of these things, we all (children and adults—ages 7 to 75) have a very strong sense of belonging, which gives us strength in our various activities outside the community. [Jul99]

Trying to run a meeting?

FIC has some tools you need—the best books around on consensus facilitation.

http://consensusbooks.ic.org/

CENTRE FOR ALTERNATIVE TECHNOLOGY

**Centre for Alternative Technology
Machynlleth
Powys SY20 9AZ, Wales
UNITED KINGDOM**

**+44 (0) 1654 702400
+44 (0) 1654 702782 fax
info@catinfo.demon.co.uk
http://www.cat.org.uk/**

Began 1973 | Pop. 12
Diet: Omnivore | Rural

Back in the early 1970s a bunch of crazy young idealists set up a community in an abandoned slate quarry in mid-Wales. The aim was to find practical solutions to the problems of pollution and environmental damage and put into practice a way of living that was environmentally sustainable. This particularly incorporated environmental building, renewable energy, energy efficiency, alternative sewage/water treatment, and organic growing. So many people were interested and wanted to come and see what it was all about that it was decided to open to the public as an educational center, and so the Centre for Alternative Technology was born.

The community is still a strong part of the center and our belief in living and working with sustainable technologies. Living on-site each person has their own space—usually their own small cottage—many of them converted miner's cottages. There is also a community house where meals are shared during the week and people can socialize or watch TV. Sometimes everyone gets together to do communal chores such as wood chopping, and meetings happen every couple of months, usually over a few bottles of wine.

Membership of the community is only open to staff at the Centre for Alternative Technology or their partners/children. [Nov98, sase required]

CERRO GORDO COMMUNITY

**Dorena Lake Box 569
Cottage Grove OR 97424**

**541-942-7720
info@cerrogordo.net
http://www.cerrogordo.net/**

Began 1974 | Pop. 48 | Rural

Our goal is a symbiosis of village, farm, and forest for up to 2,500 people on 1,200 acres—a whole valley on the north shore of Dorena Lake, near Eugene, Oregon. Homes, businesses, and community facilities are being clustered in and near a pedestrian solar village, preserving over 1,000 acres of forest and meadow.

We're planning a self-supporting settlement, with organic agriculture, sustainable forestry, and a variety of small businesses on-site. While homes and businesses are privately owned, all residents are members of the nonprofit Cerro Gordo Cooperative, which owns community land and utilities and facilitates democratic self-government. We're seeking to create a life-enhancing community that reintegrates the human community and our inner selves with the larger community of the biosphere. We invite you to join our extended community of residents, future residents, and supporters who are working together to create Cerro Gordo as a prototype symbiotic community and to network with ecovillage and ecocity projects worldwide. Send for our introductory publications and visitor's guide (available for $5 from the Cerro Gordo Forum). [Nov99]

CHACRA MILLALEN

**Apartado 125
8430 El Bolson
ARGENTINA**

**54-2944-471569
charles@red42.com.ar
http://www.millalen.org/**

Began 1990 | Pop. 6
Diet: Vegetarian | Rural

Millalen is a learning center situated in southwest Argentina at the foot of the Andes. We are dedicated to promoting peace by learning to live together—with each other and with nature. In our experience, listening, communication, and mutual agreement provide a path toward healthy relationships. In the principles of ecology, we have found valid criteria for our relationship with nature. As a learning center, each year we offer a program of gatherings and retreats, which include personal-growth exercises, self-discovery games, circle dances, and meditation.

"Experience weeks" in the summer months include theoretical and practical teaching in organic gardening, home food preservation, bread making, and vegetarian cooking. We also receive visitors apart from these programs, who join in our daily life in a more informal way. For much of the year

---

Key to bracketed text: cc = cannot commit to prompt correspondance, sase = self-addressed stamped envelope

our work is centered in the practical tasks of caring for the land, maintaining and expanding the garden (using a biointensive method), construction projects, and the daily work in the kitchen and in maintenance. Spanish is our common language, but members of the group also read and write English, French, German, and Italian. Please feel welcome to contact us for more information. [Mar99, cc]

CHESTER CREEK HOUSE

c/o Dept of Wo St
UMD H485
Duluth MN 55812

218-728-5468, 218-724-4118
tritmees@ol.umn.edu

Began 1981 | Pop. 4 | Re-Forming
Diet: Vegetarian | Rural/Urban

Founded as a communal household in 1971, Chester Creek House became a lesbian community in 1981. We currently have four members and have one or two openings for long-term members. We live in a +100-year-old three-story Victorian home in the city of Duluth (population 83,000). We make decisions by consensus. The house is owned by current and past household members. Each member has her own room(s). First floor is communal space. Shared chores, upkeep, and food costs. We cook and eat together two to three times/week; meet weekly. Community-minded visitors are welcome. We are a gathering place for community events and parties. [Aug99, sase requested]

CHICKEN SHACK HOUSING COOPERATIVE

Brynllwyn
Rhoslefain, Tywyn
Gwynecki LL36 9NH, Wales
UNITED KINGDOM

01654.711655
permaculture.uk@btinternet.co.uk

Began 1995 | Pop. 7
Diet: Omnivore | Rural

Chicken Shack Housing Cooperative is born out of a need for affordable quality housing for people like ourselves on low incomes. We are all involved in working for some kind of positive social change and have a primary focus around issues relating to sustainability. We are slowly developing our home to be cheap, energy efficient, ecosensitive, and easy to run. We are also slowly developing the land to provide for some of our basic needs, and we invest any surpluses into furthering this process.

We have chosen to live in a beautiful, remote, impoverished, and depopulating area—partly for its beauty and partly for its potential. Our principal aim is to create a stable and loving home for ourselves and to inspire and support others with similar interests to do the same. [Sep98, sase requested, no openings]

CHRIST OF THE HILLS MONASTERY

Box 1049
Blanco TX 78606

830-833-5363, 830-833-5813
newsarov@moment.net
monks@newsarov.com
http://www.newsarov.com/

Began 1969 | Pop. 20
Diet: No red meat | Rural | Spiritual

(Also known as New Sarov.) This is deadly serious, hard, and the rewards are spiritual yet produce great peace. We are a loving, honest, and open family of monks who

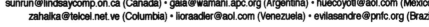
Additions and corrections: Email: directory@ic.org, Web: http://directory.ic.org/, Mail: RR 1 Box 156-D, Rutledge MO 63563, USA.

struggle to develop oneness of mind and heart. The life is rugged, but physical handicaps are not an impediment. [Aug99]

CHRISTINE CENTER FOR UNITIVE SPIRITUALITY, THE

W 8291 Mann Rd
Willard WI 54493

715-267-7507
weareone@Christinecenter.org
christinecenter@hotmail.com
http://www.christinecenter.org/

Began 1980 | Pop. 8 | Re-Forming
Rural | Spiritual

The Center for Unitive Spirituality is an educational not-for-profit corporation that embraces the wisdom and practices of all mystical traditions in the philosophy we call Unitive Spirituality. The mission of the center is the promotion of individual and global spiritual transformation. Toward this end the center is engaged in activities such as seminars, retreats, spiritual studies, and guidance. The center is located on 145 acres of tranquil forestland with abundant wildlife to nurture the re-creation of body, mind,

and spirit. As a community we support and share with each other a life of service, spiritual practice and celebration. This community, with people of diverse backgrounds and traditions, has a vision of a unitive presence that underlies all outer phenomena. The center began in 1980 as a place for solitude, meditation, and spiritual studies. [Jan99]

CIEL COHOUSING

525 N 62nd St
Seattle WA 98103

206-789-3574, 206-766-8911

Began 1996 | Pop. 27 | Forming
Diet: Omnivore | Urban

Ciel Cohousing is a new, urban cohousing community being built in west Seattle, about 10 minutes from downtown. Our membership, which will eventually reach 23 households, is filling quickly, and we plan to move into our new homes next year (1999). Our neighborhood will be made up of fully equipped duplex townhomes owned as condominiums and generous common facilities including large kitchen and dining spaces; two indoor and two outdoor child play

areas; a woodshop; a craft studio; a weight room; a laundry; an office; a sunroom/living room; sunny decks and patios; large playfields; an outdoor room; large areas of preserved vegetation; and several community gardens. Our homes line pedestrian pathways and courtyards that are all handicapped accessible. Our 2.7 acres of land are located in a multicultural neighborhood, and we are prioritizing including people of many cultures and races, as well as several other types of diversity in our community. Some of our values include working cooperatively with our surrounding neighbors, using consensus, sharing various activities, environmental preservation, and building support and neighborliness among ourselves. [Jul98]

CIRCLE OF DIVINE UNITY FOUNDATION/MONTANA CENTER, THE

341 Blue Grouse Ln
Stevensville MT 59870

406-777-6960, 406-777-6961
406-777-6961 fax

Began 1992 | Pop. 20 | Forming
Diet: Omnivore | Rural | Spiritual

The Montana Center of the Divine Unity Foundation is presently forming. We are a strongly spiritual group, with an equally strong dedication to full stewardship of the environment. We do a lot of silent meditation together, and we believe that everyone is best guided from within. So when there is conflict or uncertainty about what to do, we tend to meditate on it, or "vision" it, Our founder and leader is fully clairvoyant, but most of us are just beginning to open up to the subtler levels of consciousness. We've been doing a lot of visioning lately, to try to literally see how we are going to interact with the lovely piece of land we are buying to build our community on, here in the Bitterroot Valley of Western Montana. Some of us are better at visioning than others. Some of us are more verbal; we get our inner guidance as thoughts. We work together pretty well, and our various skills and abilities are quite synergistic. Our service, as a group, is to guide, teach, and heal anyone who comes to us, or that we extend ourselves to, with the overall goal of the full enlightenment of humanity and the release from suffering for all sentient beings. We welcome inquiries about this work. We would also like to hear from any one who has expertise on free-energy technologies. [Sep98, cc]

Key to bracketed text: cc = cannot commit to prompt correspondance, sase = self-addressed stamped envelope

CIRCLE SPRINGS

PO Box 1171
Moab UT 84532
wgaia@lasal.net
http://www.gj.net/~wgaia/
circlesprings/

Began 1993 | Pop. 8 | Re-Forming
Diet: No red meat | Rural

(Also known as Sky Ranch, Circle Op Springs.) Circle Springs is nestled at the base of high mountains, among streams, pinyon forest, and solitude, and surrounded by the spectacular canyon country.

Our Vision: A relationship with the land based on an awareness of its support of us, our effect on it, and our essential unity with the wild earth. This manifests as a commitment to conservation, energy efficiency, sustainable agriculture, and land restoration.

• To create bonds grounded in the shared practice of our everyday activities—gardening, meals, livelihood, play, and contemplation.

• To create a fluid balance between our personal and community lives, facilitating companionship without infringing on one's need for privacy.

• A rich exchange with the greater community; sharing ourselves, sharing knowledge, and demonstrating the potential of regenerative development.

• To have fun.

Currently we're building our straw-bale common house, running natural-building workshops and internships, installing a solar-power system, and doing stream restoration. Other community activities include shared meals, play at the river, and seasonal celebrations. We are looking forward to finishing initial development by the end of 1999, then building smaller residences, doing more workshops, and working with plants more. [Dec98, sase requested]

CLARE HOUSE OF HOSPITALITY

703 E Washington St
Bloomington IL 61701

309-828-4035

Began 1978 | Pop. 2
Diet: No red meat | Urban | Spiritual

Clare House is a Catholic Worker house that offers hospitality to homeless women and their children. We also have a food pantry at the house where we hand out approximately 150 bags of food a week. At a local church we operate a soup kitchen two days a week. The house was opened in 1978 and has a good support community. Live-in community receives room and board and a small stipend. [Aug99, cc]

CO-ORDINATION CO-OP

CMB Upper Tuntable Falls Rd
via Nimbin, NSW 2480
AUSTRALIA
66891005

Began 1973 | Pop. 315
Diet: Omnivore | Rural

(Also known as Tuntable Falls Co-op.) Tuntable Falls Community emerged from the Aquarius Festival 1973. The community has changed extensively since its formation, though some aspects can never change—the valley we live in is one unchanging aspect: nature is respected and assisted to reclaim its right to grow. There is a focus on preservation and protection of our rain-forest home with development as minimal impact. Members live separately from each other and, while adhering to our rules, may choose their own lifestyles. There are no enforced communal practices, though we encourage energy contributions toward projects like buildings, weed control, reafforestation, fire prevention, administration, and social support. All ages and all religious, political, and general views are represented in a spirit of tolerance and respect with monthly meetings providing a venue for decision making and discussion. While we may be granted the right to occupy a piece of land, we do not own it. We own only the materials of any buildings we may erect; all the lands remain in common ownership. We are discovering, learning, and perfecting modes of living; works of art; forms of communication; methods of awareness; and skills of communication, craft, and construction—sharing responsibility for the quality of all life. [Jul99]

COLIBRI URBAN HOUSING COLLECTIVE

2723 Ann
St Louis MO 63104

314-772-4743, 314-773-2842
slk1@gwbmail.wustl.edu
http://www.cyberstlouis.com/colibri/

Began 1998 | Pop. 12 | Forming
Diet: Vegetarian | Urban

Our mission is to provide an affordable opportunity for those who share our vision to live in a socially and ecologically responsible nonprofit housing cooperative. We intend for our cooperative-living project to be a step toward a society in which people manifest this respect through maintaining sustainable, ecologically aware lifestyles, becoming more self-sufficient so as to have more control over one's life, and solving problems together in order to satisfy the individual and the group. Our group reflects a wide array of interests, including international human rights, environmental concerns, feeding the poor, and supporting those who are disabled and other families in need. We are students and nonstudents and range in age from 23 to 59. We are currently renovating our living space and look forward to purchasing other buildings for renovation. While our individual lives are filled with many activities, we are bound by a common belief in sustainable living and developing more affordable housing opportunities. We gather each Sunday evening for a common meal and house meeting to discuss group activities and concerns. [Sep99, sase requested]

COLLEGIATE LIVING ORGANIZATION

117 NW 15th St
Gainesville FL 32603

352-338-8290
clo@grove.ufl.edu
http://grove.ufl.edu/~clo/

Began 1931 | Pop. 72

Providing inexpensive housing for University of Florida students since 1931, the Collegiate Living Organization, also known as CLO, is student run and offers a diverse and supportive environment for students. We elect our leaders from among our members to govern the corporation. Members also share in the work to keep CLO operating. [Aug99]

COLUMBANUS COMMUNITY OF RECONCILIATION

683 Antrim Rd
BT154EG Belfast
NORTHERN IRELAND

02890 778009
Columbanus@cinni.org

Began 1983 | Pop. 4 | Re-Forming
Diet: Omnivore | Urban | Spiritual

A small residential community of men and women from different Christian traditions, living, working, praying together. Committed to a ministry of reconciliation in all aspects of its life. It seeks to challenge visibly the unacceptable divisions, injustices, and inequalities in society and in the churches. It strives to develop ways of living out and sharing with others its commitment to Christian unity, to justice and peace as a witness to God's love for the world.

Columbanus Community of Reconciliation (CCR) implements its aims by affording Protestants and Catholics an opportunity to share and develop together their common faith in Jesus Christ (twice-daily prayer, regular eucharistic celebration, occasional Bible study); providing a setting that encourages simplicity, communal responsibility, and accountability (evening meal together, cooking, and jobs rota); providing a place of hospitality and accommodation; running educational programs for adults and children; offering a forum where all can be accepted; taking an active part in the religious, social, and political life of the wider community in northern Ireland. The Columbanus family of reconciliation, incorporating CCR, is a growing circle of

Christians who seek both to reconcile and to celebrate the diversity they represent

CCR seeks to be holistic in its approach—is planning to use its large garden, chapel, and library as resources for health and healing, wisdom, and inner growth. [Sep99, sase requested]

COLUMBIA COHOUSING COMMUNITY PROJECT

5316 Godas Circle
Columbia MO 65202

573-814-3632
http://cohousing.missouri.org/

Began 1996 | Pop. 25 | Forming

Columbia Cohousing is seeking balance between rural and urban, solitude and community, comfort and respect for the environment, work and play. We are working with the cohousing model of energy-efficient, private homes with shared land and common spaces. We plan to cluster buildings to leave lots of wild land.

We have been dreaming together, socializing, and celebrating life's events for two years. Now we are looking for land and a developer to build. We are looking for a site that feels rural but is within easy commuting distance of Columbia, a liberal university town of 70,000. We are planning a common house with meals together several times a week and possibly shared businesses, art studios, and gardens.

New members are very welcome. Please write for more information or see our Web site. Come grow with us! [Dec98, sase requested]

COMING HOME COMMUNITY

Shandin or Dale Rudesill
Valley Oaks Village
1962 Wild Oak Ln
Chico CA 95928

530-891-5059, 417-679-4682
417-679-4684 fax
home@ic.org

Began 1998 | Pop. 4 | Forming
Diet: Vegetarian

We are a small group looking to settle on land in northern California in a year. We intend to be a pod community in EcoVillage Emerging. We are members of the Fellowship for Intentional Community (FIC) and hope to join the Global Ecovillage Network (GEN) and Federation

of Egalitarian Communities (FEC). We plan to hold our resources in common and the use of land in a trust. We are working toward healthy relationships with ourselves, each other, the community, and our world. We use processes such as peer counseling (Satir's human validation model, reevaluation counseling), mediated conflict resolution, and formal consensus decision making. We have years of experience in community. We are egalitarian, practice nonviolence, support liberation for all, and appreciate freedom and diversity—though we do select for members who support our agreements. We plan to pursue ecological sustainability, assessing our progress using measures such as pollution levels. Our initial goal is to be at less than 50 percent of average US levels overall and decreasing each year. We have agreements such as growing organic and not buying old-growth timber. We see ourselves living rurally and simply and working toward self-sufficiency. We hope to grow to 8–16 people, with the age demographics of a stable zero- population-growth society. Write us for more information and please include postage to cover a 2-ounce reply. [Sep99, sase requested]

COMMON GROUND COMMUNITY

500 Red Maple Rd
Blountsville AL 35031
205-429-3088, 205-429-4120

Began 1987 | Pop. 16 | Rural

We are 11 like-spirited adults and 5 children. Our purpose includes harmony with our environment, nurturance, celebration of spiritual diversity, and social change. The community leases 80 acres of farmland from Gaia Land Trust, created in 1980, and members sublease holdings. The trust's purpose is to own and preserve land and improvements, promote community, honor ecosystems, and prevent abuse of resources. The community pays monthly rent to the trust. Community members pay dues and rent equally, and in-kind service is an option. Each member is economically independent. The trust pays taxes, fire protection, maintenance, etc. With no community members, the land would devolve to a party committed to preservation.

We gather monthly for a day of work, play, and business (using modified consensus). Working through difficult decisions and writing our guidelines have developed

---

Key to bracketed text: cc = cannot commit to prompt correspondance, sase = self-addressed stamped envelope

deep trust and extended family. In 17 years as a community, only one full member has left. We dream of all being on the land full-time, and most of us are now. We live in owner-built structures heated with wood and solar, passively cooled. Power varies from solar to conventional to mixed, but conservation is key in all. We enjoy visitors, but our membership is closed. Visitors must write in advance. [Feb99, cc, sase required, no openings]

COMMON GROUND (VA)

131 Brd Wing Trail
Lexington VA 24450
herb@s-o-l.org
http://www.s-o-l.org/

Began 1981 | Pop. 12
Diet: Omnivore | Rural

Common Ground, a homesteading intentional cooperative community, holds a perpetual lease on 77 acres of land owned by the School of Living—a regional community land trust. Members hold lifetime subleases. Each household has use rights to two acres. The community exists and operates for the mutual benefit of its members, to help one another become established on the land while conserving, protecting, and improving the environment and its resources.

Members follow their own spiritual and dietary leadings. Currently we have eight households. To date, all our children have been homeschooled. Members work together in our organic gardens, on community-building or maintenance projects. We build shared facilities, through group planning, joint and individual labor. We are now planning our new community center, which will help us realize a goal of becoming an educational center.

We celebrate birthdays, holidays, and special occasions. Intergenerational play includes softball, swimming in the pond, hiking, and drumming circles. Neighborhood events include sweat lodges, the Fourth of July, and the local ice cream social. Neighbors and area organizations use our land for approved activities.

Open monthly business meetings use consensus decision making. Monthly discussion evenings and periodic retreats focus on current interests and concerns. A yearly community budget is adopted; each household is assessed a monthly fee to cover operating expenses.

We seek members with homesteading skills, commitment to ecological land use, those of goodwill and initiative with good communication skills, and the ability to work cooperatively and to enthusiastically share their lives with others.

Our membership process is extensive, lasting from 6 to 21 months. Full membership is by consensus. The membership fee is $1,750. Members finance, own, and maintain their "improvements." Each household is responsible for their own income.

Visitors are welcome weekends upon pre-arrangement. Tenting, camping spaces, and a few rooms are available. Learn more about us at the School of Living Web site at http://www.s-o-l.org/. [Sep99, sase requested]

COMMON PLACE LAND COOPERATIVE

4211 State Rt 13
Truxton NY 13158

607-84-6799, 607-842-6801

Began 1976 | Pop. 37
Diet: Omnivore | Rural

Common Place Land Cooperative is a 432-acre rural land trust located in the rolling hills of central New York State. We are currently 18 adults and 14 children, and we are actively seeking new members. We expect to evolve into a small-scale community of 35–40 households, aiming at greater food and energy self-sufficiency. Twelve homesteads have been created on the land, and the farmhouse serves as transitional housing.

Over 20 years, we have come to agreement on 11 core ideals, which define and guide our community, including land stewardship and trust, economic self-reliance, diversity, consensus decision making, community participation, and voluntary simplicity. Members have diverse views and interests. As a community we are not affiliated with any political or religious organization. Our varied individual interests include organic gardening and homesteading, alternative energy, attachment parenting, homeschooling, the arts and music, Earth celebrations, natural healing, activism, spirituality, home birth, and writing.

Our decision-making process consists of two meetings per month. We are working to create a cohesive community that inhabits the land preserving its integrity and resources. For more information send a letter. [Jan99, sase requested]

COMMON THREADS

PO Box 441713
Somerville MA 02144

617-576-6878
commonthreads@ic.org
http://home.earthlink.net/~susnrose/

Began 1995 | Pop. 8
Diet: Vegetarian | Urban | Spiritual

A small urban community with a commitment to personal growth, social change, diverse spiritual practice, resource sharing, and communal living. We are creating a new kind of family. Nurturing close adult relationships and parenting are both important parts of our lives. We are a community-in-dialogue with the FEC and part of a larger group, Common Unity. We have a multi-level membership process. We are looking for others who share our values and desire long-term community. [Jan99, sase requested]

COMMONGROUND COMMUNITY

RR4
767 Stone Church Rd
Killaloe Ontario K0J 2A0
CANADA

613-757-0847, 613-757-2174
613-757-2174 fax
visionwk@web.net
healing@web.net

Began 1996 | Pop. 4 | Forming
Diet: No red meat | Rural

CommonGround is a small community in Killaloe, Ontario (formed in 1996), seeking new members to grow and realize our vision of a flourishing ecovillage. Our farm near Algonquin Park consists of 115 acres of clearings surrounded by forest and is ideal for the cohousing model of individual dwellings sharing land with communal spaces. Common areas include a four-bedroom restored log farmhouse with workshop space and spa, barns, organic garden, woods, fields, and ponds.

At present we are four adults living on the land, in various stages of engagement with the collective. As a group we share a commitment to inspiring creative healing and to fun, friendship, and sustaining joyful service. We offer workshops and retreats integrating natural medicine with Earth-based spirituality and creative expression. We also teach the fundamentals of community. We have built a spa/healing space with sauna, hot tub,

Additions and corrections: Email: directory@ic.org, Web: http://directory.ic.org/, Mail: RR 1 Box 156-D, Rutledge MO 63563, USA.

massage and meditation room for our use and for guests. We have plans to convert our largest barn into an art studio, dance space, and accommodation space.

Generally, prospective members begin with a three-month acquaintanceship, then spend a year here before joining. Members and prospective members share in cooking and chores, work in the garden, in the learning and retreat center, and in freelance professional work, contributing a certain amount of time and income to the community. We meet regularly for business and sharing; we make decisions by consensus and enjoy communal meals in the evening. We have a strong interest in sustainability, permaculture, alternative building technologies, and creative entrepreneurship. We are family, children, elder and queer friendly. Visitors are welcome to come for a two- to three-day stay, but arrangements must be made ahead of time. [Sep99, sase requested]

COMMONS ON THE ALAMEDA, THE

2300 West Alameda
Santa Fe NM 87501

Began 1992 | Pop. 65
Diet: No red meat | Urban

The Commons on the Alameda is an adobe-style cohousing community on five acres in the outskirts of Santa Fe. The last 2 houses were completed in 1997, and we are now landscaping the four placitas (courtyards) around which the 28 houses, many with rental casitas, cluster. The common house and home businesses surround the main plaza. We have communal organic meals Mondays and Thursdays with produce from the kitchen garden. Residents cook/clean for one meal per month and put the remaining

of their eight hour/month labor commitment into building and ground work.

Managers (kitchen, guest room, grounds, compost) orchestrate much of the nitty-gritty. We have two community meetings/month—one to discuss and make consensus-based decisions on business items and the other to consider "what's on your mind?" Issues we've been addressing: pets, home businesses, integrated pest management, conflict resolution, and Y2K preparedness. Every fall we celebrate our feast day with tree planting, horse rides, cider making, clown/jugglers, green chili stew, and dancing. As some members are moving on to new dreams, several 2,000- to 2,700-square-foot houses are for sale ($250–$375K). Contact the community for more information. [Jan99, cc]

COMMUNAUTÉ DE L'ARCHE

La Borie Noble
F-34650 Roqueredonde
FRANCE

Began 1946
Diet: Vegetarian | Rural | Spiritual

Families and single people share a fraternal life of work, service, and spiritual search. The communities follow a simple lifestyle, some choosing the rural life (respecting the environment as they work the land), others giving priority to hospitality and training.

The life of the community is built on the practice of nonviolence in daily life, the sharing of tasks and responsibilities, decision making, reconciliation. This daily existence is rooted and grounded in the life of prayer and silence, where each person is invited to deepen the practice of their own religion and to value that of others. The Companions are committed by vow to this

fraternal life while respecting each other's path. [May99]

COMMUNAUTÉ DU PAIN DE VIE

9 Place Verte
F-59300 Valenciennes
FRANCE

Began 1976
Diet: Omnivore | Rural/Urban | Spiritual

We live with the people, all together (families, celibates, priests) around the Eucharist, welcoming the poor. We live an evangelical life as radically as possible, in the poverty, obedience, and chastity that goes with our state. In all our houses on all continents, we live a life of work, prayer, and welcoming the poor. Our daily life resembles that of the people we live among. Our life is given its rhythm by prayer, work shared with poor people, and in service to poor people. Our primary vocation is to show the grace of God that removes the sin of the world and brings Peace. This is why perpetual adoration is central with us. [May99]

COMMUNITY AND RETREAT FOR MINDFUL LIVING

2304 Abbott Ln
Fayetteville AR 72703

501-973-9873
attentiveness@hotmail.com

Began 1997 | Pop. 3 | Forming
Diet: Vegetarian | Rural/Urban | Spiritual

The focus of the community is living mindfully and awakening in ourselves compassion for all beings. Daily silent periods, extended silent retreats, and living mindfully with others provide an environment for being still and dwelling in the present moment, in awareness, and extending this awareness into our everyday lives. We view our daily activities as opportunities to understand ourselves and express kindness and understanding. We see serving the world through the operation of a silent retreat, cooperative businesses, and nonviolent social action. We exercise our responsibility to the Earth by living simply, organic gardening, sustainable building, and appropriate technology, allowing our basic needs to be fulfilled in compassionate ways. We are currently looking for land. All are welcome to inquire. May you be happy and peaceful in this very moment. [Sep99]

Key to bracketed text: cc = cannot commit to prompt correspondance, sase = self-addressed stamped envelope

COMMUNITY HOUSE

1757 Mills Ave
Norwood OH 45212

513-396-7202 x201
djnixon@ix.netcom.com

Began 1995 | Pop. 25 | Forming
Diet: Omnivore | Urban | Spiritual

As a community we're learning to not take ourselves so seriously but God very seriously. An emerging focus among us is urban housing renewal. We've gained many valuable skills from our home renovation and maintenance business that we plan on using to acquire declining properties in economically depressed areas and convert them into low-rent, high-quality, professionally managed housing.

Another exciting, to us at least, project is also emerging at this time. Though we are a young community, we plan to launch a new community in another urban neighborhood close by. Ultimately we'd love to see community houses sprinkled throughout our city in many different neighborhoods.

Our daily life while certainly less exciting than the emerging projects is very rich in relationships, and we focus on following Christ's teachings as fully as we can. It's been fun trying to simplify our lives—less TV, more interaction. Being frugal has also been an adventure as we try to spend less on food costs, for example. We're close to our goal of spending only 50 cents per person per meal.

Cooperative living for us means exploring ways to live creatively and simply. All in all it's been great fun and full of meaning. We have some not so fun stories as well, but we'll share those over coffee when you visit. [Dec98]

COMMUNITY OF HOSPITALITY

305 Mead Rd
Decatur GA 30030

404-376-7840
http://samhouse.home.mindspring.com/cafevol.html

Began 1981 | Pop. 5
Diet: No red meat | Rural | Spiritual

Community of Hospitality is a faith-based intentional community providing full-time volunteer opportunities. Volunteer placements are available with Cafe 458, a restaurant serving meals to people without homes, and Georgia Justice Project, a legal nonprofit that provides criminal defense in conjunction with social and rehabilitative services to indigent individuals accused of crime. Volunteers share a house and community life with 5–7 people. Worship and fellowship also occur with a nonresidential community of 30–40 people.

Benefits: community life, room and board, transportation, health insurance, monthly stipend. Diversity in age and race is encouraged. [Mar99]

COMMUNITY OF ONE - "MINNESOTA"

PO Box 24125
Edina MN 55424

Began Oct98 | Pop. 3 | Re-Forming
Diet: No red meat | Rural/Urban | Spiritual

Change in everything we can be—the way we think—the way we go about our business—more especially what is best for ourselves and others around us. It appears nothing will come from above—in either government or God—it appears you and I will have to pull ourselves up by our bootstraps—it is possible—but only through change. The present system is taking us away from growth—for we have been given everything we need to do whatever we are supposed to do. All we have to do is remember or learn more about ourselves or who we are. We are spiritual beings having a human experience—nature-oriented people welcomed.

Master all your abilities now and here both known and unknown.

No money needed—the poorer the better; no education needed—the less the better; for maybe the less one has, the less one has to discard.

This may be your chance to excel. [Nov98]

COMN GROUND

1791 Westwood Ave
Cincinnati OH 45214

513-251-9147
Gaius@pol.com
PantherClan@pol.com
http://www.pol.com/people/COMN/

Began 1993 | Pop. 8
Diet: Omnivore | Urban

(Also known as Panther Clan.) We're currently a poly pagan family consisting of a group marriage of two women and two men, plus all our kids. Our dream is to live in a semirural commune in which we can expand our membership and host events for the pagan and alternative-lifestyle communities. [Aug99, cc, sase required]

CONCORD OASIS ECOHOUSING

994 A Oak Grove Rd
Concord CA 94518

925-687-2560, 925-687-8772
mdemaio@juno.com
http://members.tripod.com/~Oasis_Ecohousing/

Began 1996 | Pop. 9 | Re-Forming
Diet: No red meat | Rural/Urban

The purpose of Concord Oasis EcoHousing is to provide a mini-cohousing seed source for the creation of an environmentally responsible community-based housing entity within central Contra Costa County. We believe that infill establishment of cohousing communities along the organic-growth development model can eventually result in the creation of human and environmentally friendly ecovillages within existing neighborhoods.

Nestled on a quiet, courtlike, private

Additions and corrections: Email: directory@ic.org, Web: http://directory.ic.org/, Mail: RR 1 Box 156-D, Rutledge MO 63563, USA.

Listings

drive off Oak Grove Road near the Concord/Walnut Creek border (San Francisco Bay area, California), Concord Oasis EcoHousing is being developed as "retrofit/infill mini-cohousing" and is currently comprised of three "lots," with 2+ existing units and a research-quality straw-bale structure under construction. The straw-bale structure has been designed to provide common-house facilities and accommodate two to three households during the initial core-group-development/community-growth phase. One of the completed units is a unique flexible-floor-plan environmental home. This home, which has significant expansion potential and flexibility preengineered, has been awarded Real Goods Demonstration Home Program status. Plans to remodel the second existing home are being considered. [Mar99, cc, sase requested, email preferred]

COOPER STREET HOUSEHOLD/TRIANGLE F RANCH COOPERATIVE

PO Box 220
Vail AZ 85641

Began 1969 | Pop. 5
Diet: Omnivore | Rural/Urban

Cooper Street Household is a cooperative intentional household living in a suburban home in Tucson and on a 22-acre "ranch" in an isolated foothills canyon that has limited water. These two settings permit flexibility in responding to differing needs for togetherness.

We have been evolving over the last two years, with some change in membership. We are now five adults living within an organizational structure that is loose. There are few rules, but tolerance for the lifestyles of others is expected. Consensus is used for major decisions such as the acceptance of a new family member.

All members need to be self-supporting financially, as we have yet to establish a community business.

We feel that we can lead a better life together, living in community, than separately. Despite the diversity of our occupations, religious beliefs, cultural backgrounds, and belief systems, we have a common value system related to right treatment of ourselves, right treatment of others, and right treatment of the environment.

Visitors are welcome but should be pre-pared to camp if facilities are crowded. [Mar99, cc]

CORANI HOUSING AND LAND CO-OP

12 Bartholomew St
Leicester LE2 1FA, England
UNITED KINGDOM

0116-254-5436
ascltd@gn.apc.org

Began 1978 | Pop. 9
Diet: Omnivore | Urban

(Also known as Some People in Leicester.) There are two adjoining Corani houses in Leicester where six to eight of us live collectively and that act as a center for the other Some People in Leicester network activities. Housing is flexible and need not be collective. There are another Leicester house and one in Stafford. Homes are mostly urban terraces at present. We work large and small allotments, and we own one in Leicester that is becoming a forest garden. Capital is not essential to join, but those who have it are asked to deposit some with Corani. Income pooling is expected of members, and this grouping is spread equally between Leicester and the west Midlands—and includes non-Corani people. Two children have been coparented for 10 years since birth and attend school. Decision making is essentially pragmatic: by consensus where all are concerned and otherwise with sensitive autonomy. We welcome, by arrangement, visitors who will help out or participate while with us. We probably have one or two room spaces in Leicester and Stafford for new members. Alternatively, we have been known to accept people and their houses! Corani is a non-equity-sharing, fully mutual body IE commonwealth.

We are a city-based cooperative network with a variety of practical activities: cooperative work (electrical and building businesses); radical bookshop; vehicle pool; shared childcare; organic gardening; permaculture; income pooling; cooperative housing; capital pooling.

We feel it is vital that local groups do not exist in isolation but are involved in wider struggles and broader visions. Our aim is to change the world! We are active members of Radical Routes Secondary Co-op—a network of radical housing and worker co-ops. Some of us are also working for people power; overseas development; Nicaragua link group; UK direct democracy and regional autonomy; recovering our genuine histories and cultures. We welcome visitors by arrangement and are looking for more people to get involved. [Mar99, cc, sase requested]

CORNERSTONE HOUSING CO-OPERATIVE

16 Sholebroke Ave
Chapeltown, Leeds
W Yorkshire LS7 3HB, England
UNITED KINGDOM

+44 (0) 113 262 9365
cornerstone@gn.apc.org
http://www.sol.co.uk/ d/diffusion/cornerstone/

Began 1993 | Pop. 10
Diet: Vegan | Urban

(Also known as Rillbank Housing Co-operative.) Cornerstone Housing Co-op is a community of about 14 people (and several animals) living in two large Victorian houses in inner-city Leeds. It was set up to provide a base for green activists, and we are still nearly all full-time activists of one sort or another. We have many plans for improving the houses and large gardens, but only a few have been realized so far, due to lack of time and experience.

Most of us are involved in ecological or antimilitarist direct action, as well as being, variously, publishers, permaculture teachers, artists, students, and community activists. We run an office/resource center, which is used by many campaign groups (mainly ours), and a recent addition to no.16's basement is the rodent sanctuary, with nearly 30 animals at time of writing. Our other house is, however, animal free.

Our membership has been pretty transient but is beginning to settle down now, so we are on the lookout for long-term, cooperative-minded members who can teach us building skills or are very keen gardeners!

Cornerstone is a member of Radical Routes, the secondary co-op and ethical investment fund promoting cooperation and working for social change. [May99]

Key to bracketed text: cc = cannot commit to prompt correspondance, sase = self-addressed stamped envelope

CORPUS CHRISTI ABBEY

HC2 Box 6300
Sandia TX 78383

512-547-3257, 512-547-5765
louisdemontfort_98@yahoo.com

Began 1927 | Pop. 24
Diet: Omnivore | Rural | Spiritual

We are a group of semicontemplative monks in a rural area of south Texas. As monks we live a common life and share what we are and have for the common good. We come together daily to pray, eat, and work together. Our main purpose is to offer our lives to God. We pray for all people in the world. We try to live our lives in such a way that all can see that God fills all the longings of the human heart. We also run a retreat open to individuals and groups of all faiths to help them in their walk with God. Visitors are welcome to visit and pray with us if they would like to.

Members use their talents for the good of all. We currently have monks working here as cooks, bakers, auto mechanics, welders, groundskeepers, among many other things. We follow in the tradition of St. Benedict, who wrote a rule that has been adopted by all Roman Catholic monks from his time in the sixth century to today. [Mar99]

COVENENTAL COMMUNITY

c/o Judith Arleen Mitchell
Box 377530
Chicago IL 60633

773-493-9225

Began 1979 | Pop. 57
Diet: Omnivore | Urban | Spiritual

First, everyone is committed to some spiritual path that is shared with the group, but we are very open to learning about paths that are not part of the more commonly held radically liberal Protestant variety. Our sponsor is a local church of that variety. Second, we are interracial and intergenerational. Third, we are urban but ecologically committed, and many of us garden energetically. Group process is important to us, but we do not practice consensus. Every adult has their own career path or life path, supports themselves and dependents financially, and pays proportionally for their use of space. Adults must help maintain the building and its financial management with labor. Children are individually raised with much informal input from everyone else. Many of us are vegetarian, but it is not a policy. All

the arts are encouraged. The group process leads to lots of self-examination, but now that we have reached 20 years we are beginning to feel more self-confident. We have a covenant—each agrees to and does an annual recovenanting. Visitors and inquiries are welcome. Membership is always open, but housing is only irregularly available. [Dec98, cc, sase required]

CRANBERRY COMMONS COHOUSING

4274 Albert St
Burnaby BC V5C 2E8
CANADA

604-298-9220, 604-526-9924
604-526-9923 fax
walmsley@bc.sympatico.ca
ravens2@axionet.com
http://www.cohousing.ca/
cohsng4/cranberry/

Began 1992 | Pop. 25 | Forming | Urban

Cranberry Commons will be the third cohousing community in the Vancouver, Canada, area, with planned occupancy in mid-2000. We are presently in the design stage, envisioning a three-story building with ground-oriented townhouses and one-level flats with elevator access. Twenty-one units in different sizes are planned to suit needs of singles, couples, and families. The complex will include a common house with kitchen, dining area, kids' playroom, guest room, and boardroom; and a large courtyard with plenty of green space, gardens, and kid-friendly play areas.

Cranberry Commons will be in the heart of "the Heights," an established village-type enclave along Hastings Street in North Burnaby. Family-run businesses, bakeries, cappuccino bars, and delicatessens abound. There are numerous community amenities, including leisure pool and fitness center, seniors' center, library, and parkland all blocks away. Breathtaking views of mountains beckon. The neighborhood is established with a rich diversity of ethnic backgrounds and homeowners who have lived in and cherished the neighborhood for much of their lives.

As of June 1999, we have eight committed-member households, four associate-member households comprising three families, two retired singles, one retired couple, and three professional singles. We are looking for new members!

Please contact Ronaye Matthew at 604-

298-9220 (e-mail: walmsley@bc.sympatico.ca) or visit our Web site. [Jun99]

CREEKSIDE

119 Warrington St
Christ Church
NEW ZEALAND

3853646

Began 1972 | Pop. 16 | Urban

Creekside is made up of a group of people who think that living closely together for mutual support is a good thing to do. [Sep99, cc, sase requested, no openings]

CREEKSIDE COHOUSING

113 Elkhorn Rd
Charlottesville VA 22903

804-961-9402, 804-963-4688
gfifer@pen.k12.va.us

Began 1994 | Pop. 32
Diet: Omnivore | Urban

(Also known as Charlottesville Cohousing Association .) We are composed of individuals and families who meet together regularly to plan and develop this new neighborhood. All of the present members live and work in the Charlottesville/Albemarle area. Many of us have children; many are married; some are single. We come from a variety of backgrounds and beliefs, yet we hold in common certain values and goals for this neighborhood.

We plan to create housing that is designed to encourage community; has extensive common facilities shared by all; is composed of 25 units; has a range of unit sizes, from 800 square feet to 2,000 square feet; and is located within minutes of downtown Charlottesville.

We have a vision of a cohousing community that shares these values: openness to people of diverse ages, races, backgrounds, and lifestyles; interest in a greater sense of connection and belonging through respectful, supportive relationships; healthy balance of personal independence and community interdependence; involvement of group members in decision making through consensus process; opportunities to share resources and skills; cooperative problem solving and nonviolent conflict resolution; maintenance of a safe, supportive environment for children; aspiration toward living in ways that are positive and creative; and commitment to environmental responsibility.

Additions and corrections: Email: directory@ic.org, Web: http://directory.ic.org/, Mail: RR 1 Box 156-D, Rutledge MO 63563, USA.

Listings

Imagine your home in a community that has neighbors (singles, families, seniors) whom you know and trust; shared facilities such as a dining area, offices, workshops, laundry, gardens, and childcare; a variety of social and civic activities within steps of your door; individual input and participation in planning and decision making; and an environmentally sensitive design emphasizing pedestrian access and maintaining open space. [May99]

CROSSROADS MEDIEVAL VILLAGE

PO Box 505
Yass NSW 2582
AUSTRALIA

+612-6226-3737
+612-6226-3737 fax
crossroads@crossroads.org.au
rhys.howitt@aspect.com.au
http://www.crossroads.org.au/

Began 1992 | Rural

We're a group of (mainly) medievalists and permaculturists who formed a cooperative in 1992, with the objective of building a medieval village in which our members

could live and work. Our property is near Yass, just north of Canberra, Australia. We adjoin the Hume Freeway, the major road between Sydney and Melbourne.

Our residential area will be under community title, where you own your house lot and have a share in the common land. Houses will have to be medievally inspired and environmentally considerate. We're planning to use composting toilets, and we'll have reed beds for gray-water recycling. Our plans also include a camping area with some visitor cabins; these will be used for medieval events and at other times by community groups.

We're also planning a reproduction of a small, early-fifteenth-century French village, with a tavern, a great hall for feasts, a bakery, a teahouse and similar small shops. We'll use the village area for visiting school groups, for day visitors, and for craft workshops.

We anticipate that the village and camping ground will generate a certain amount of employment, to supplement primary production on site. We expect that many of our members will choose to work in Canberra, and with increasing telecommuting and a shared minibus we can reduce the environ-

mental impact for those not working locally. [Apr99]

CRYSTAL WATERS PERMACULTURE VILLAGE

Crystal Waters Community Co-op
Kilcoy Ln
Conondale QLD 4552
AUSTRALIA

+61 7 5494 4620, +61 7 5494 4741
+61 7 5494 4653 fax
cwcoop@ozemail.com.au
http://www.ecovillages.org/
australia/crystalwaters/

Began 1988 | Pop. 198
Diet: Omnivore | Rural

Crystal Waters has been designed from inception according to the principles of permaculture. A wildlife sanctuary where dogs and cats are banned and people really do try to live in harmony with nature. Eighty percent of the 640 acres are owned in common, and these are a mix of terrains: the clear waters of the Mary River, serene lakes, open grasslands, timbered hills and gullies, and increasingly, pockets of rain-forest trees planted as part of the community's passion

Key to bracketed text: cc = cannot commit to prompt correspondance, sase = self-addressed stamped envelope

for reforestation. The idea was that people should be able to operate from home, and many businesses operate from here, e.g., foresters; rammed-earth builders; mail-order businesses—books, organic gardening supplies; carpenters; builders; electricians; permaculture course providers and consultants; nurseries; caterers; craftspeople; architects; entertainers; bicycle hirer; bed-and-breakfast accommodation; furniture manufacturers; and also the base for the Oceania/Asia secretarist of the Global Ecovillage Network. Crystal Waters won an award in the 1996 World Habitat Awards and was a finalist in the 1998 Best Practices Awards. Many innovative ideas in building, wastewater, water, agriculture, and nature conservation are evident. The model has proved attractive to the relatively mainstream as well as an alternative market. A short video is available from the GEN Oceania/Asia office. [Dec98, cc, sase requested]

CWRT Y CYLCHAU

Llanfair Clydogau
Lampeter SA48 8LJ, Wales
UNITED KINGDOM

+44.01570.493688,
+44.01570.493526
+44.01570.493688 voice/fax
bristol.goodwill@ukonline.co.uk
http://web.ulkonlin.co.uk/
   bristol.goodwill/amadea/

Began 1998
Diet: Vegetarian | Rural | Spiritual

(Also known as Part of Amadea Cohousing Project.) We are a new cohousing/community project at an isolated rural setting in a scenic part of Wales. The number of permanent residents, currently five adults, will be unlikely to rise at any time much above seven due to planning constraints, but guests and visitors are encouraged to linger or stay and experience the profound healing energies of this special place.

We seek to develop and manifest our group soul. As individuals we are determined to overcome any obstacles or differences that may arise within or around us so that we may learn to love the group and fulfill that purpose which has drawn us to this unique position.

At a practical level we have a number of skills, ranging from complementary medicine to landscape gardening, plus many other useful additions gained over the years by the varied lifestyles of the residents. We

are keen to live lightly off the land and learn and implement as much as we can of positive environmental issues.

Caring for the land, trees, ponds, and the many species of birds and other wildlife in our small but beautiful five acres is an important part of our operation as is growing appropriate fruit and vegetables. We have our own water supply electrically pumped from a well quite close to a stream that marks part of our boundary.

A local farmer provides sheep to perform the task of "caring" for the meadows, and the previous owners, who had worked tirelessly to create this beautiful haven, recently planted about 1,000 trees as part of a woodland grant scheme. [Jan99]

DAMANHUR, FEDERATION OF

Via Pramarzo 3
I-10080 Baldissero Cse Torino
ITALY

+39 0124 5122239, +39 0124 512184
+39 0124 512184 fax
federation@damanhur.org
welcome@damanhur.org
http://www.damanhur.org/

Began 1977
Diet: Omnivore | Rural/Urban | Spiritual

Founded in 1977, Damanhur is an international spiritual center for research. Situated in Valchiusella Valley, in the Alpine foothills of northern Italy, Damanhur is a federation of communities with over 800 citizens, a social and political structure, a constitution, 40 economic activities, its own currency, schools, and a daily paper.

The federation now numbers over 450 full time citizens and 350 others who live nearby and take part in its activities. Damanhur offers different kinds of citizenship. It is possible to be a full-time resident or to live in other parts of the world and visit regularly.

The homes and the companies of the federation are scattered all over the Valchiusella Valley. They include approximately 200 hectares of woods, urban surface, and farmland and over 80 buildings, including private homes, studios, laboratories, and farms. Since the very first day of its foundation, Damanhur has been engaged in creating a

sustainable way of life. The federation has many centers in Italy and Europe and contact with spiritual groups worldwide. Our Temple of Mankind is a great underground building carved by hand out of the rock and decorated by Damanhur's citizens.

Damanhur consists of three "bodies." The first relates to content and memory, (the School of Meditation), the second relates to innovation and planning (The Game of Life), and the third relates to practical everyday life and organization (the social environment). [Feb99]

DANCING BONES

PO Box 232
Wentworth NH 03282

603-764-9844
dancingbones@eagle1st.com

Began 1998 | Pop. 4 | Forming
Diet: No red meat | Rural

We are cocreating a rural village of small cabins sharing life day to day. We advocate living simply and sustainably in full harmony with the Earth. "Sacred circle dance" celebrations are a weekly event along with rituals to mark

the seasons and life passages. A community land trust holds our land in perpetuity.

The proposed 22 cabins will be privately owned, most without commercial electricity or water. As an ecovillage, the amenities building will provide facilities for cooking, bath, laundry, and common space. Composting toilets prevail. Full consensus.

A rugged heavily wooded site of 40 acres on the edge of the White Mountain National Forest. Low-impact, low-cost living, mindfulness in nature. [Sep99, sase requested]

DANCING RABBIT ECOVILLAGE

1-2K Dancing Rabbit Ln
Rutledge MO 63563

660-883-5511, 660-883-5553
dancingrabbit@ic.org
http://www.dancingrabbit.org/

Began 1995 | Pop. 19
Diet: Omnivore | Rural

At Dancing Rabbit (DR), we understand how difficult it can be to live sustainably and responsibly while enmeshed within modern US culture. We believe that together we can break free and create our world as we want it to be. We are living our dream now, building an ecovillage where a diverse group of people can live in an ecologically sound way and show the world a real example of life in harmony with the Earth.

In 1997 our land trust purchased 280 acres of rolling hills in northeastern Missouri. We are now deep into a pioneering phase, putting up buildings while planning and developing community systems and structures. People's social and economic needs are met primarily on-site and locally, with an increasing emphasis on an internal economy, supporting barter and other forms of exchange. We hope that someday we will have up to 1,000 people living in our small ecotown with businesses and homes surrounding the village green.

As an ecovillage, ecological sustainability is a primary focus in our vision and throughout our daily lives. We build our homes using alternative techniques such as straw

bale and cob, powering them with renewable energy from the sun and wind. We are dedicated to eating local, organic, and in-season foods with vegetables grown primarily in our own gardens. Vehicles at DR are owned by a car cooperative and will be powered by biodiesel, an alternative fuel made from used vegetable oil.

We strive to be good stewards of our land with much of our acreage set aside as wildlife habitat. We have planted thousands of trees to both restore our land to its pre-settlement ecology and provide a sustainable source of wood for our community. In our grasslands we are reintroducing native prairie grasses to preserve our region's bio-diversity.

Diversity is important among our human population as well. Our village is comprised of individuals, family units, and an income-sharing community (see Skyhouse listing). We look forward to having other communities join us and encourage the development of cohousing and cooperatives. To allow for economic diversity and simple living, we have kept lease fees and membership dues low and have no fee to join DR.

In addition to being a wonderful home, Dancing Rabbit is a model for social change. Outreach and education are integral to our goals. Rather than isolating ourselves from the mainstream United States, we promote ourselves as a viable example of sustainable living and share our discoveries and ideas.

If you are interested in Dancing Rabbit, write us to arrange a visit or receive our newsletter. We have internships available, so write us for an application. We are actively seeking new members and are excited about our future; together we can build our dreams! [Apr99, sase requested]

DANCING WATERS

RR 2 Box 69
Gays Mills WI 54631

608-872-2295

Began 1983 | Pop. 13
Diet: Omnivore | Rural

(Also known as Permaculture Coop.) Dancing Waters Permaculture Co-op is on 130 acres in the beautiful hills and hollows of southwestern Wisconsin. We are 11 adults and 2 children owning land and buildings in common. Primary focuses include annual and perennial communal gardening, house building, and learning how to live in harmony long term with each other

and with the land. We use the ideas of permaculture in our building, gardens, hayfields, orchard, and woodlots.

We gather twice monthly for a potluck and meeting. Decisions are made by consensus. Individual and family housing units are clustered so we bump into each other as we go about our daily lives, sharing food, meals, work, childcare, song, and spirit on an informal basis.

Individuals follow a variety of spiritual paths and diets. Some individuals make their incomes at home. Some have jobs off the land. Income is not shared. Each adult pays a monthly fee for group expenses. We are surrounded by an extensive alternative community, including a food co-op, community building, and Waldorf school. This wider community helps us create a home that is more than a refuge from the mainstream. We are blessed with a stable membership but have occasional openings. Visitors are required to make advance arrangements. [Dec98, sase requested, no openings]

DANDELION COMMUNITY CO-OP, INC.

194 Jackson Rd
RR 1
Enterprise Ontario K0K 1Z0
CANADA

613-358-2304, 613-358-1204 fax
dlion@kingston.net

Began 1975 | Pop. 7 | Re-Forming
Diet: Omnivore | Rural

(Also known as Stonehedge.) Dandelion, formerly Dandelion AKA Stonehedge, is a small, rural, income-sharing community. For the past eight years we've operated as a resource-sharing cooperative using the name Stonehedge.

We, having come full circle, now share income, labor, meals, and other activities in common. Our hammock business provides most of our income. Organic gardens and livestock provide much of our food.

We are currently seeking members and welcome visitors most times of the year. A modest contribution to help defray costs is required. Visitors are welcome for one week with extension possible. [Sep99, sase requested]

Key to bracketed text: cc = cannot commit to prompt correspondance, sase = self-addressed stamped envelope

DAPALA FARM

E 15014 Laurel Rd
Elk WA 99009

509-292-0423
http://www.infoteam.com/
nonprofit/nica/dapl.htm

Began 1990 | Pop. 7 | Forming
Diet: No red meat | Rural

Our community is dedicated to teaching self-reliance, voluntary simplicity, and lifestyle solutions to unequitable/unsustainable socioeconomic systems. Proving new cultural paradigms that better the quality of life for all is our vocation. We embrace our interdependence, practice creative conflict resolutions, the "precautionary principle" to prevent unknown harm, and the "seventh-generation principle" when arriving at consensus. Our service projects are published in our Web site. Our cottage industries are our education center, produce sales, and soon a "community-supported agriculture." We also offer apprenticeships on which our Web site has details. We incorporate new members into our community, businesses, and land trust after a year trial, cautiously building an extended family of 12. We average 6 adults; our population grows each spring/summer as we host several apprentices. Housing is a three-bedroom home, a trailer, and a 20-foot tipi. A community center is under construction, having four more bedrooms. We will also build a few low-cost, energy-efficient shelters. We cocreate communal rituals, but each person follows their own path. We care about community and each other. For dialogue with us, please send us a long personal letter with photo. [Dec98, sase required]

DAWNING STAR

PO Box 38
Weston CO 81091

719-868-3620
dawnstar@ria.net
http://www.dawningstar.com/

Began 1997 | Pop. 2 | Forming
Diet: Omnivore | Rural | Spiritual

Dawning Star is a community dedicated to aligning individual consciousness with the unlimited transcendent self; and reflecting this unfolding awareness in the social, economic, and environmental life of the community. We see ourselves as one of the islands of light emerging around the Earth and dedicate our days to embodying more of this energy and presence. In this way we seek to create an increasingly transformative light field at Dawning Star as a gift to ourselves, to nature, to our guests, and to the Earth and humanity.

Our primary intention is to contribute to the human and earthly journey from ignorance and suffering to bliss, creativity, and wisdom. Situated on 358 spectacularly beautiful acres in the mountains of southern Colorado, it is as much our intention to deepen our experience and understanding of our greater physical body—the Earth—as to enhance awareness of our transcendent spirit, or Lightbody. We have a three-bedroom straw-bale guest house that is available for individual and guided retreats, as well as for private retreats. As a forming community, many aspects of community life are unstructured. We invite members dedicated to the adventure of Lightbody. [Feb99]

Additions and corrections: Email: directory@ic.org, Web: http://directory.ic.org/, Mail: RR 1 Box 156-D, Rutledge MO 63563, USA.

DAYSPRING CIRCLE

PO Box 433
Floyd VA 24091

540-745-5653
abundantdawn@ic.org
http://www.abundantdawn.org/

Began 1996 | Pop. 5
Diet: Omnivore | Rural

We are a subgroup (pod) of Abundant Dawn Community. We are committed to the vision of Abundant Dawn and to living thoughtfully—with beauty, economy, conviviality, and care.

We love this land where we live, and we try to treat it well. We study and practice environmentally sound building methods, use composting toilets, and are designing a constructed wetland for our gray-water treatment.

Our current members are all self-employed, range in age from 29 to 60, and include a diversity of spiritual beliefs, sexual orientations, and dietary preferences.

We eat together frequently, help each other out, and enjoy each other's company. When together, we tend to laugh a lot.

We envision our permanent home as a circle of five or six modest, well-built dwellings (possibly including a group house and/or common house), around a courtyard with flowers, fruit trees, vegetable gardens, picnic tables, and a solar-powered fountain.

We are open to new members, including single people, couples, or families with children. We expect to take some time to get to know potential members.

See also Abundant Dawn Community.
[Sep99, sase requested]

DAYTON HOUSE

1034 Dayton Ave
St Paul MN 55104

651-644-7439
ccrawford@isd.net

Began Jun99 | Pop. 6 | Forming
Diet: Omnivore | Urban

The Dayton House is a large Victorian house in the heart of St. Paul, Minnesota. It is conveniently located in a multicultural neighborhood close to bus lines, co-ops, the arts, and city life. There is room for communitarians who want to live together and share life's good times and tough times. Work on preparing for disasters together. We share meals, expenses, gardening, house maintenance, bartering, neighborhood projects, and pets.

We are looking for community-minded people who are willing to get out of yourself and think on a bigger scale. We love spirituality (all kinds), music, and dance. We require healthy-minded people who have no addictions. We study and live by the psychology of mind model (POM).

This is a busy household with working adults. Our daily lives have different schedules, but we always have time for kindness and thoughtfulness and an evening meal.

We are open to visitors and hostels.
[Jun99, sase required]

DE HOBBITSTEE

Van Zijlweg 3
NL-8351 HW Wapserveen
THE NETHERLANDS

0521-321328, 0521-321324
hobbitstee@wxs.nl

Began 1969 | Pop. 7 | Re-Forming
Diet: Vegetarian | Rural

Community De Hobbitstee, in the Netherlands, was founded in 1969, so it already has existed for 30 years. The desires to change society, to stimulate personal growth, to get rid of bourgeois mentality were important aims for the initiators in the late 1960s. Times change, just as people and their social environment change.

But the primal ideas of seeking love, harmony, simplicity are still the drives, the wells from which present inhabitants draw their energy to form and re-form daily community life and our relation toward society. Besides the promotion of organic/biological agriculture and the handicrafts candle factory, issues we embrace are nonviolent conflict resolution and the receiving of guests in various forms. A small-scale camping facility for nature-loving people is a new development, also providing some income. De Hobbitstee is small, and more and more it may become a kind of alternative-activity center, seeking and trying out new ways of personal and spiritual growth and social/political engagement.

That is what gives us a kind of right to exist. The hope or wish to become a larger community in this country of utmost individualism is no longer among us. And maybe it's better that way. We can still direct our energy, as a core group, toward the topics we find important. Together with short- or long-term guests, therapy groups, and environmental and peace organizations,

---

Key to bracketed text: cc = cannot commit to prompt correspondance, sase = self-addressed stamped envelope

we'll resist the worldwide devastating religion of the so-called free market.

The right to existence, that's what binds all groups and communities working for positive social change on the eve of the twenty-first century. [Aug99, sase requested]

DE REGENBOOG (THE RAINBOW)

Norbert Gillelaan 20
B-1070 Brussels
BELGIUM
02/520.65.86

Began 1974 | Diet: No red meat | Urban

De Regenboog has five purposes. (1) Community: sharing daily life, learning the conditions to and consequences of brother-sisterhood in practice. (2) Justice: more than economic justice; the organization of society so that every person (and nature) can really live in freedom and security, with guarantee for all rights. (3) Nonviolence: community life is a continuous exercise in nonviolent approach to differences and conflicts. (4) Deepening: against the superficiality in thinking and relations in society; study, sharing, prayer, liturgy for a realistic, sober, and liberating spirituality. (5) Utopia: a symbolic word to synthesize the whole of our life; the vision of another world in peace, love, and justice—not possible (u-topos) but now directly started in smaller unities, e.g., communities.

Our life is very simple and sober, supposing trust and friendship and openness to other people in search of security, friendship, etc. Since the death of the father of the family, we only participate in peace manifestations and other events; we no longer organize them. Living in the city and working outside (teaching or studying), we do not have much contact with our neighbors. We are part of the movement of basic Christian communities in the Flanders. The engaged members of the community are de facto Christians (this is not a condition); there also is no condition for the guests who participate in our life but do not have right of decision. We speak Dutch, also French, some of us also English or German. [May99]

DEBS HOUSE

909 E University
Ann Arbor MI 48104
http://www.umich.edu/~umicc/

Began 1967

Debs, a student co-op, was purchased by the Inter-Cooperative Council (ICC) in 1967 and has added richness to the lives of many wonderful people over the years. The house members themselves are our finest assets, encompassing people from diverse backgrounds who wish to create a mutual living environment of unique personality and interest. To characterize this atmosphere, Debs members have been exceptionally dedicated to the discussion of various political/social issues, to creating a tight-knit community within the house, and last but not least, to having great parties.

Housing 23 members in five singles and nine doubles, Debs was named for E.V. Debs, the renowned labor activist and socialist who won six percent of the popular vote while running for president on the Socialist Party ticket in 1916. After being imprisoned for his opposition to World War I, Debs ran for president from his jail cell; hence the slogan on our T-shirts, "Convict No. 9653 for President." Debs members eat their meals at other student co-ops within the ICC, either at Lester or Owen houses. [Jan99]

DELTAINFINITY

faed@deltainfinity.org
za_el@yahoo.com
http://www.deltainfinity.org/

Began Aug99 | Forming
Diet: Vegan | Rural

DeltaInfinity is an organization of true scientists whose primary goal is long-term survival via eternal cultural change. We seek to continuously reevaluate ourselves as individuals as well as the governing rules of our culture so that we can continually enhance our ability to survive. The culture of a people is likely the most powerful technology of those people, simply because culture lies at the base of almost everything they do as individuals. Hence, any other technology invented is used in accordance with the underlying message of the culture. If the individuals of a culture don't think critically about the impact of their actions upon the long-term survival of their children, then their chances of survival are likely minimal.

A caring culture with foresight would focus on the conservative use of finite resources, not shortsighted hedonistic squandering in the hope that somehow we will discover a means to magically create bountiful resources for the future. That type of attitude fosters further ignorance and generates only misery. A member of DeltaInfinity, a DeltaInfinite, works for their own sake by researching, studying, and meditating upon the problems of survival—to continuously work toward a better culture and thus a better future for their children. [Aug99, sase required]

DENVER CATHOLIC WORKER

2420 Welton St
Denver CO 80205
303-296-6390
denvercw@juno.com

Began 1978 | Pop. 5
Diet: Omnivore | Urban | Spiritual

We are a faith community committed to voluntary simplicity and hospitality. Our group is currently 5 members, and we live with temporary guests (numbering an average of 10–12) who join us based on their financial and housing needs. Food and household goods are received through donations, and our extended community joins our hospitality efforts. We welcome new members who are serious about living a lifestyle committed to service. If so, please write, e-mail, or call about arranging a trial visit. [Oct99, sase requested, no openings]

DENVER SPACE CENTER

NE Denver Colorado
303-296-8061
MQuesting@aol.com

Began 1977 | Pop. 4 | Urban

We are an urban cooperative household established in 1979—more intentional than a boarding house, less intense than a commune; more civilized than a fraternity, less crowded than a dormitory. We have relatively few rules, though relatively much experience in this lifestyle. We share the rent, the common spaces, the housework, a piano, and a big yard with gardens and make decisions by consensus when possible. We encourage friendships, good company, interesting conversations, aesthetic ruminations, and connections to a developing circle of friends. We have a nonbiological resemblance that eludes prosaic description. [Sep99, cc]

DOLPHIN COMMUNITY (ÖKODORF DELPHIN)

Bergwekstr 33
D-79688 Hausen im Wiesental
GERMANY

07622-671363, 07622-671322
07622-671322 fax
oekodorf@gemeinschaften.de
delphin@gemeinschaften.de
http://www.gemeinschaften.de/

Began 1995
Diet: Vegetarian | Rural | Spiritual

In Native American mythology, the dolphin represents the combination of heaven and Earth, spirituality and matter, vision and realization. In this sense, we are already living communally without having a communal home, through spiritual diversity (within the limits of the ancient rules of the great religions of the world), communal singing, eating, hiking, baby-sitting, decision making by consensus, solving conflicts. We are learning from the experiences of older communities and are passing on our own experiences through the Ökodorf Institute: consultations, festivals, a mail-order business, seminars on searching for and founding communities. Service to fellow human beings: at the moment we are supporting the establishment of free health care for poor people in India. We are friends with several dozen local residents and are in friendly contact with the others. Hausen considers itself something like a melting pot since southern and eastern Europeans have been working in the textile industry here for over 150 years. In the long run, we would like to establish a spiritual-ecological village in addition to being integrated in the existing village. This new village will probably be close by and will make it easier to become self-sufficient. We would like to build the village together with the regional network of friends of our community. As a first step in this direction, we have established a local labor-exchange system (Wiesentaler instead of Euro). We trust that God/inner voice will guide us in deciding what to do next, just as we have been guided so well since 1995. People interested in joining should first send us a few pages about themselves and their vision. We will then send more information about ourselves as well. [Mar99]

DOME COUNTRY

1786 Huronia Rd
Barrie Ontario L0L 1M0
CANADA

705-436-2408
captian1@bconnex.net
domecountry@hotmail.com

Began 1975 | Pop. 6
Diet: Vegetarian | Rural/Urban | Spiritual

To expand our existing ecovillage, we are buying more land, building more, and expanding existing organic gardens and Web businesses. [Jan99, sase requested]

DOROTHY DAY CATHOLIC WORKER

503 Rock Creek Church Rd NW
Washington DC 20010

202-882-9649

Began 1981 | Pop. 8
Diet: Omnivore | Urban | Spiritual

The Dorothy Day Catholic Worker is a house of hospitality and resistance. We are a seamless garment community. We try to live by the principles of nonviolence. The core community of singles, married couples, and families offers hospitality to five would-be homeless families. The house also serves as a place for people to drop in for a meal or drink or other needs. Once a week we serve a meal to 100 people on the streets of Washington, DC. We distribute scavenged food once a week to whoever might come to the door. The community also tries to address war and poverty by public witness and, sometimes, by acts of civil disobedience. We try to bring a voice for the voiceless to those in places of power. We work together and have a common purse. We are supported entirely by donations. [Jan99]

DOWNEAST FRIENDS COMMUNITY

122 Cottage St
Bar Harbor ME 04609

207-288-2152

Began 1978 | Pop. 12 | Re-Forming
Diet: No red meat | Urban | Spiritual

We envision a community that nurtures the individuality of each member. We envision a community that practices a way of living that is sustainable for generations to come, a way of living that defines by practice and direction the meaning of human ecology.

We envision a community that strives to work out our personal difficulties between members through its own ingenuity.

Established in 1978 as a collective working to create a whole-grain bakery, the community has evolved into a group of artists and human ecologists. Located in town, we have been a source of housing and support for College of the Atlantic people for 15 years. Some of our members are actively involved in protecting the environment of Maine through grassroots and legislative involvement.

In practice, we are economically independent with an individual contribution toward upkeep and taxes of the building, phone, electric, and recycled paper products. Physically, our community consists of one large commercial building, one large organic garden, and one large shed. We have a complete woodworking shop and dream of a pottery studio. [Feb99, sase requested]

DOWNIE STREET COLLECTIVE

459 Downie St
Peterborough Ontario K9H 4J6
CANADA

705-742-7621

Began 1996 | Pop. 4 | Re-Forming
Diet: No red meat | Urban

We are four individuals who don't want to be suffocated by the city. We try to eat together every day (vegetarian), communicate openly, and create a positive space to live in. Two of us are students, and two of us aren't. We are three women and one man from different backgrounds who get involved in all sorts of projects from guerilla seed planting to anticorporate activism to community gardens. Although we aren't currently seeking new members, we may be soon, and if you want to visit, please call in advance. [Aug99, cc, sase required]

DOYLE STREET COHOUSING

5514 Doyle St
Emeryville CA 94608

510-601-7781

Began 1992 | Pop. 25 | Urban

Small urban cohousing community, 12 units plus common house. All units (condominiums) currently owner occupied. Units recently sold at $160,000 to $319,000. Group formed in 1990. Project completed and first occupied in spring

---

Key to bracketed text: cc = cannot commit to prompt correspondance, sase = self-addressed stamped envelope

1992. Second cohousing project built in North America. Ask to be put on waiting list if you want to be notified when a unit is for sale. [Sep99, cc]

DRAGON BELLY FARM

Currently in California:
3329 Los Prados St
San Mateo CA 94403

360-732-4855, 650-574-7155
sanda@bigfoot.com
http://www.wordrunner.com/
sanda/dbf.htm

Pop. 6 | Re-Forming
Diet: Omnivore | Rural

We wish to build intentional community amid the greater community in Jefferson County on 39 acres, 17 miles south of Pt. Townsend, 30 miles and a ferry northwest of Seattle on the Olympic Peninsula. The land has a variety of ecosystems, about half forest, some of which are wetlands; a quarter meadow on glacial moraine; and a quarter pasture on wetter bottom land. There are two creeks and two ponds. We expect land owned in common with some form of private ownership of home and homesite. We prefer environmentally sensitive, ecologically sustainable building materials and design. Current growth limitations may require multifamily housing with shared kitchen.

Our values include sustainable organic agriculture, conscious eating of a natural-foods diet, a recognition of how dietary choices involve/affect planetary economics and the environment. We prefer open communication with regular community meetings and other shared rituals, shared activities, shared reality.

We still envision community on this land, but the form and timing have changed. Owners are currently living in California, building urban community, accumulating capital, seeking partners, and probably waiting until retirement to return full-time. There are caretakers on the land. [Sep99, sase required]

DRAGONFLY FARM

Gen Del
Lake St Peter Ontario K0L 2K0
CANADA

613-338-3316, 613-338-2709
yes@bancom.net

Began 1978
Diet: Omnivore | Rural | Spiritual

Situated just east of Algonquin Park amid the rolling, pre-Cambrian hills of the Canadian Shield is Dragonfly Farm. Our small collection of people persists on 250 acres of trees, marginal agricultural land, in a rather severe climate. Our seasonal businesses include a commercial greenhouse offering a plurality of flowers and organic vegetable and herb starts, a mobile sawmill that custom cuts local people's logs, and a wreathing co-op. There are also a horse, cow, chickens, cats, and dogs. Our gardens provide us joy and bounty.

Presently we are not seeking new permanent members. We welcome visitors, especially those from foreign lands who wish to experience rural Canada and need a place to stay. Accommodations are primitive. We

heat with wood, have electricity, and use an outhouse since there is no indoor running water. In the summer months camping is available (on the back 40). During winter we can always find a way to squeeze people into our homes. Donations of monies from visitors go toward taxes etc. A few hours of assisting in farm activities is welcomed.

Here at Dragonfly the "politics of anarchy" rule within a sense of "communal individualism." Communication is preferred before arrival. [May99, no openings]

DREAMING LIZARD CO-HOUSE

4507 Marble NE
Albuquerque NM 87110

505-266-7567

Began Sep99 | Pop. 5 | Forming
Diet: No red meat | Urban | Spiritual

This is an urban project in an established neighborhood, 1 1/2 miles from our local food cooperative and the vibrant university district. We own two large city lots with trees, gardens, porches, and a greenhouse. There is a main house with a garage apart-

ment, and there are two cottages in back. Common areas include all outdoor space, laundry room, and large living room (for dinners, meetings, etc.). We each pay our share of the mortgage based on the amount of square footage we occupy. Obligations are spelled out in our legal contract as tenants in common, with remaining decisions made by consensus.

We are musicians, dancers, activists, and anarchists who believe that doing the work of cooperating with others is practicing sustainability on an emotional level. [Aug99, sase required]

DREAMTIME VILLAGE

10375 City Hwy A
LaFarge WI 54639

608-625-4619, 608-625-2412
dtv@mwt.net

Began 1991 | Pop. 10 | Re-Forming
Diet: Omnivore | Rural

Dreamtime Village (DTV) is emerging as an experiment in ecovillage design whose mission is to create new planetary culture. By consciously drawing from the more biodiverse and imaginative resources of present-day and ancient cultures, we garden the complex interface between plant, animal, and human worlds. Our challenge is to design a landscape that is functional, alive, and phantasmagorical while simultaneously serving as an ecovillage demonstration and a hands-on learning environment for people of all ages. We delight in discovery, innovation, and experimentation.

We lean toward open systems and self-organization, allowing the ecovillage to grow as an organism. A diversity of DTV residents and visitors tends to create an eclectic mix; folks are drawn here through a broad variety of channels. Studios, woods, wetlands, gardens, orchards, a huge 1920 brick school building, five other buildings, and 80 acres of land form the facility for DTV workshops, gatherings, retreats, and more. Our focus is on permaculture and "hypermedia" (a term we use to expand on common notions of "art" and "media"). Dreamtimers past or present have been involved in pottery, yoga, musical improvisation and instrument making, wood turning, gourds, herbs, computers, natural building, bookmaking, etc. [Aug99, cc, sase requested]

DU-MÁ

2244 Alder St
Eugene OR 97405

541-343-5023
http://www.efn.org/~dlamp/

Began 1988 | Pop. 8
Diet: Vegetarian | Urban

We are a stable urban community that formed in 1988 based on five values—ecological responsibility, personal growth, diversity, equality, and community. Daily examples of our values include growing vegetables, recycling, looking at gender and class issues, cocounseling, naka ima, consensus decision making, and rituals.

Visitors remark that we are neat, well organized, and accountable to our values. We eat vegetarian meals together, nurture our relationships with one another, and share the joys and responsibilities of owning a home and yard large enough for eight people. We share expenses but not our incomes.

In 1998 we rekindled our mission "to be of service to others as an inspirational model of living and working together to create community and social change." We are in the early stages of making our mission a reality; how it unfolds will undoubtably be an ongoing journey.

We seek members who are compatible with us, have substantial energy to contribute, are emotionally and financially stable, feel settled in Eugene, and are looking for a close group of people to grow with. Membership process helps us determine who will thrive and be happy here. [Dec98, sase requested]

DUNMIRE HOLLOW

2017 Dunmire Hollow Rd
Waynesboro TN 38485

931-722-9201, 931-722-3078
harvey@ic.org

Began 1973 | Pop. 14 | Rural

Dunmire Hollow (est. 1973) is a community of about a dozen people sharing their lives and 163 acres in a magic hollow in Tennessee. We have fields, orchards, gardens, woods, springs, creeks, a community center, a woodshop, a sauna, a food co-op, family houses, etc. Each family is economically independent; we make/have made our livings in a variety of ways—teaching, construction, woodworking, nursing, doctoring, lawyering, auto repair, sewing, truck driving,

small-engine repair, crafts—and from providing for ourselves more directly through domestic economy and barter.

As individuals, we have a variety of enthusiasms that often involve us with the world and other people: organic gardening, music, crafts, environmentalism, peace work, sports, community networking, aquaculture, alternative energy, etc. Each resident adds to the diverse mix that makes up our community.

We are happy to communicate with people who are interested in rural-community living. We enjoy visitors; please write for more information or to arrange a visit. [Sep99, sase requested]

EARTH HEART CENTER

VT RT 100 C
RR 1 Box 1079
East Johnson VT 05656

802-635-2674
lgray@together.net
http://homepages.together.net/~lgray/

Began 1998 | Pop. 3 | Forming
Diet: No red meat | Rural

My vision is to find a handful of like-minded people to form a small intentional community with an Earth-centered focus on sustainable living, holistic healing, spirituality, and creativity. I value working collaboratively and consensually.

I live on approximately 45 acres of beautiful land in Johnson, Vermont. The land is mostly wooded and has a pond and a small brook with a waterfall. I have built a small house and shop, a small greenhouse with a massage/hot tub, a sauna, and a small hydroelectric generating plant. I have cleared and planted two garden plots and have started construction on a larger (32-foot by 48-foot) structure intended to be used for communal housing and a dance/movement and workshop space. There are also a sweat lodge by the brook and access to miles of cross-country skiing and hiking trails.

The land adjoins a farm owned by Johnson State College, a small state liberal-arts college. The town is also home of the Vermont Studio Center, where there is a colony of visual artists and writers.

I would love to connect with other dancers, healers, gardeners, parents, etc., to

Key to bracketed text: cc = cannot commit to prompt correspondance, sase = self-addressed stamped envelope

discuss these dreams and to explore possibilities. [Aug99, cc, sase requested]

EARTH RE-LEAF

Box 599
Naalehu HI 96772

808-929-8003
earthreleaf@hotmail.com
forest@wics.net

Began 1985 | Pop. 2 | Re-Forming
Diet: Omnivore | Rural | Spiritual

Earth Re-Leaf (continually refining) is a cooperative-consensus organic farm and nature sanctuary focusing on several areas including but not limited to: (1) refining consensus council; (2) evolving relationships; (3) responsible consensus childcare; (4) raw-foods vegan; (5) evolving life and language beyond polarity; (6) nonviolence; (7) self-sufficiency and co-op business; (8) land trust; (9) spiritual evolution. Our foundational council agreements are: (1) short silent period before speaking; (2) all get uninterrupted three-minute speaking rotations; (3) divisions into groups of 12 or less; (4) decisions and actions based on 100 percent agreement.

A permaculture orchard plus a few small private shelters and community buildings is situated on one acre of land at 800 feet. Another two acres near by at 5,000 feet. We seek to attract a core group of self-reliant, grounded, country-farmer spiritual pioneers that grows and divides into supportive splinter families. Our simple council guarantees freedom from control and domination. Call, e-mail, or write with questions. [Dec98, sase required]

EARTHART VILLAGE (EAV)

64001 County Rd DD
Moffat CO 81143

719-256-5003
linda@ecovillage.org

Began 1998 | Forming
Diet: Omnivore | Rural

EarthArt Village is a model, holistic, sustainable community—living harmoniously with the Earth, sharing resources and responsibilities, and balancing the common good of the group with the well-being of each member. The purposes of this cooperative association are to:

• Own, manage, and maintain land and facilities for the benefit, health, and well-being of the residential community and other members;

• Cultivate lifestyles demonstrating the learning and living of cooperation, simplicity, creative expression, and respect for one another and nature;

• Honor, steward, protect, and enhance the natural environment;

• Establish energy-efficient, ecologically sound living, learning, working, and playing environments, using sustainable design, methods, and materials;

• Research, develop, and maintain alternative, off-grid, sustainable infrastructure: common food, energy, water, and waste-management systems;

• Conduct community endeavors, such as member-managed agriculture and businesses, cooperative purchasing programs, publications, research projects, and artistic and cultural activities;

• Provide a living context and example for educational demonstration of sustainable community living—socially, spiritually, economically, and environmentally. [Sep99, cc]

EARTHAVEN

PO Box 1107
Black Mountain NC 28711

828-669-3937
info@earthaven.org
http://www.earthaven.org/

Began 1998 | Pop. 50
Diet: No red meat | Rural | Spiritual

Earthaven's vision of its role in bridging the way to sustainable, regenerative culture is of a small-scale village that encompasses the best we can bring from our past with the highest we can envision for our future, while remaining grounded in the present. Central to our purpose are the ongoing demonstration and teaching of those skills that make this vision possible.

Our first five years have brought us training and practice and considerable success in consensus governance, group-process work, permaculture fundamentals and village design, natural building, appropriate technology, and more.

As we approach the year 2000, we are putting our dreams and training to the test, developing extended functional family, building the homes and structures we will live and work in, and clearing forest to make way for agriculture.

We are challenged to shelter and feed ourselves as we gradually develop comfort and convenience on our 325 still primarily forested acres, while remembering and celebrating the primacy of our inner/spiritual being and the power of love, life, and laughter. As we grow and mature, we are learning to let go of unrealistic expectations and discover our real potential: "life is not a problem to be solved but a mystery to be explored." [Sep99, cc, sase requested]

EARTHSEED

PO Box 163
Putney VT 05346
earthseed@ic.org

Began 1994 | Rural | Spiritual

EarthSeed is a community of people living in and near southeastern Vermont, with an ongoing web of relationships and a strong commitment to healing and activism on behalf of all life.

We meet regularly for potlucks; business/council meetings; deep personal sharing circles; Earth-based healing rituals and seasonal celebrations; and occasional weekend gatherings. Food shared at EarthSeed gatherings is free of animal products.

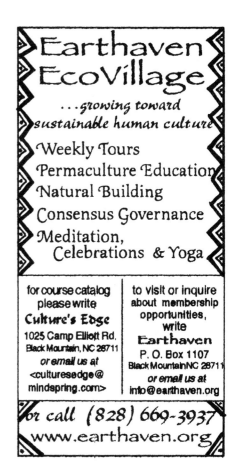

Additions and corrections: Email: directory@ic.org, Web: http://directory.ic.org/, Mail: RR 1 Box 156-D, Rutledge MO 63563, USA.

Listings

The consensus process is used to make decisions affecting the community.

We support each other in making and maintaining individual life choices based on self-responsibility, healing, and growth. We also support each person's lifework and creative activities.

The first EarthSeed meeting was held in October 1994, and then a meeting was held one weekend every one to two months. From September 1996 through April 1998 a group of us rented a house together in Athens, Vermont, and lived as a consensus-run household. There is currently no collective EarthSeed household.

Updates, with news of recent gatherings, meeting minutes, and announcements of upcoming events, are mailed and (preferably) e-mailed to people who request them. Donations toward the cost of mailing are welcomed.

Many of our gatherings are open to visitors, with advance notice. [Mar99, cc, sase requested]

EARTHWORM HOUSING CO-OP

Dark Ln
Leintwardine
Shropshire SY7 0LH, England
UNITED KINGDOM
01547-540461

Began 1989 | Pop. 10 | Rural
(Also known as Wheatstone.) An experienced housing co-op, we live and work communally at Wheatstone, where there are a large old house, outbuildings, and seven acres of land on the Welsh borders. We make decisions through regular meetings and on a day-to-day basis almost always by consensus. The group's membership and direction have undergone several changes since we arrived in 1989, but the same original principles and ideals remain, including an ecological focus, trying to be more kind to the Earth, limiting use of products that poison and pollute, and trying to be more ethical consumers.

We farm our land by vegan-organic methods, using permaculture and forest-garden techniques. We use composting toilets and have recently built a wetland reed-bed system to process wastewater from the house. We grow seasonal vegetables, herbs, and fruit in the gardens and two polytunnels. We don't keep food animals. All communal areas and meals are vegan,

but you do not have to be vegan or vegetarian to live here.

We host gatherings, courses, and camps. We are currently winning the battle to renovate our house, which was badly vandalized and neglected before we arrived. We supplement our income by selling garden produce and willow coppiced from our wetland system. [Mar99, sase requested]

EAST BAY COHOUSING

Greater Oakland CA
510-845-0481, 510-594-8551
info@ebcoho.org
http://www.ebcoho.org/

Began 2000 | Forming | Urban
(Also known as Berkeley/Oakland CoHousing.) A group of households and individuals working together to create a residential community in the urban East Bay region of the San Francisco Bay area.

The mission of East Bay Cohousing is to develop a cohousing community in the urban East Bay based upon the following shared values and goals: private unit ownership with shared, smoke-free common space and common meals; desire to live in an intentional community; consideration, kindness, and respect toward other community members; willingness to compromise, cooperate, share leadership, and make decisions by consensus; desire for an environmentally sustainable lifestyle.

East Bay Cohousing has been meeting since November 1998. Our membership is dynamic and committed to creating a warm, vibrant residential community within a few years. We are currently in the planning stage and meet for monthly general meetings/potlucks and regular committee meetings. Our committees include Development, Operations, and Membership/Process.

East Bay Cohousing is currently recruiting new members. Regularly scheduled orientations are available for interested households and individuals. [Oct99, cc, sase requested]

EAST LAKE COMMONS

Decatur GA 30032
404-377-5444, 404-377-5757
vmoreland@mindspring.com
http://www.eastlakecommons.org/

Began 1997 | Pop. 74 | Forming | Urban
East Lake Commons is a cohousing commu-

nity in Decatur, Georgia, six miles from downtown Atlanta. When completed it will include 67 townhomes and common-house facilities. Some homes are already occupied, and construction will continue into the year 2000. Approximately half of our 20-acre site is dedicated to an organic garden, a pond, green space, and wooded areas. Cars are kept to the periphery of the site, with townhomes clustered around pedestrian courtyards and walkways.

We seek to create a community that nurtures children with playmates; supports teenagers with mentors and role models; provides adults with a social network and seniors with a friendly supportive community. Our members represent a rich diversity of age; religion; lifestyle; racial, ethnic, and cultural background; differently abled; and economic status. Residents organize and participate in the planning, design, and management of the community. The consensus decision-making process assures that everyone is heard and all needs are understood. Critical community goals and values also include the preservation and enhancement of the natural environment and participation in the revitalization of our surrounding neighborhoods. [Sep99]

EAST WIND COMMUNITY

East Wind Community
Box CD-00
Tecumseh MO 65760
417-679-4682
visit@eastwind.org

Began 1970 | Pop. 75
Diet: Omnivore | Rural

We are a 75-member collective located on 1,045 acres of rural Ozark Hills in southern Missouri. We are a member of the Federation of Egalitarian Communities, and as such, we put great value in cooperation, nonviolence, and sharing. We also strive to practice sustainability and ecological consciousness. Our membership is very diverse, we have no central leadership, and we practice democracy. Our work lives are busy and varied, but we always find time to relax and enjoy community meals, music jams, and Ozark sunsets. Our land is one of a kind, very rural, and filled with all sorts of wildlife. We encourage individuality and diversity in our members. Prospective visitors are encouraged to contact someone on our Membership Team to arrange a visit, but please call or write first, as dropping in

Key to bracketed text: cc = cannot commit to prompt correspondance, sase = self-addressed stamped envelope

unannounced is an unwelcome strain on our resources [Sep99, sase requested]

EAST-WEST HOUSING COOPERATIVE

415-346-8066 fax
ewhouse@slip.net
greggjordan@hotmail.com

Began 1957 | Pop. 13
Diet: Vegetarian | Urban

East-West House has a long and rich history, and there have been many transitions and changes over the years. Presently, our focus is on sharing food, cooking, chores, decision making, and mutual support and friendship. Much of our time together is centered around the (almost) nightly dinners, although it is rare that all of us are present at one time. We do not have a stated philosophy. Following is a sampling of what some of our members are involved in: social activism, spiritual practices or paths, music or art, working 9–5, school, gardening.

In 1991–1992 a major renovation was done on our house, in which some loans and grants from the state and city were used. As a result of this, we have some income limits for people who want to live here. So, we now serve the additional purpose of providing low-income housing.

Our household is very quiet, you might say "mellow," with occasional bursts of zaniness, and for the past couple of years has been extremely harmonious. [Jul99, cc]

ECO-VILLAGE OF LA HERMITA

AP 555
San Miguel de Allende
GTO 37700
MEXICO

4-154-4580, 4-152-7372
4-152-60-61 fax
la_hermita@yahoo.com
http://www.infosma.com/lahermita/

Began 1998 | Rural

Our vision is to establish an alternative social system in which the development of consciousness and respect for nature is stressed. Living in harmony with all our relations is our goal. [Aug99]

ECOCITY PROJECT

The Center for Sustainable Living
c/o Chip Ballew
HC5 Box 587-1
Reeds Spring MO 65737

417-739-5718, 417-883-2915
vegman@hotmail.com

Began 1998 | Forming
Diet: Vegan | Rural/Urban

We are a nonprofit group working to create a "model" city and center for education/development of sustainable living practices: renewable energy, organic farming, plant-based diet, permaculture, "green" building, recycling, conservation, etc. Our goal is to "sell" sustainable living to the world and preserve our planet.

We feel, to be most effective, the city has to be big enough to attract attention from the media and draw a large number of visitors. It will be small for a city (10,000), yet have the vitality and amenities of larger cities, while retaining the best qualities of smaller communities. The design is compact to preserve land for wildlife, parks, and agriculture.

We will have affordable housing, cottage

Additions and corrections: Email: directory@ic.org, Web: http://directory.ic.org/, Mail: RR 1 Box 156-D, Rutledge MO 63563, USA.

industries, shops, restaurants, cooperatives, clinics, a health spa and conference/retreat center, schools, libraries, museums, and more. Our top priority will be to help residents have richer, more fulfilling lives with access to education, recreation, a variety of volunteer/work options, social activities and cultural pursuits, seminars, workshops, youth camps, concerts, festivals, etc. Our profits will go to support environmental/social causes, protect land and wildlife, fund similar projects. People needed! Write or call for a brochure or more information. [Mar99, sase requested]

ECOLOGY HOUSE TWO

537 Jones St
San Francisco CA 94118
jbarshak@hotmail.com

A new community forming in northern California for those with multiple chemical sensitivity (MCS). This will be the second apartment building in the United States constructed and maintained with materials that are safe for persons with MCS. [Sep99]

ECOVILLAGE COHOUSING COOPERATIVE

100 Rachel Carson Way
Ithaca NY 14850

607-255-8276, 607-273-5563
ecovillage@cornell.edu or
mnolan@ecovillage.ithaca.ny.us
http://www.cfe.cornell.edu/
ecovillage/

Began 1996 | Pop. 90
Diet: Omnivore | Rural/Urban

(Also known as EcoVillage at Ithaca.)
Located in the beautiful rolling hills of New York's Finger Lakes region, Ecovillage at Ithaca has a thriving 30-unit cohousing community and is actively seeking members for the second neighborhood. Both feature cooperative dining in the common house, swimming ponds, permaculture gardens, hiking trails, play spaces, and energy-efficient construction in a multigenerational community.

Our goal is to build a replicable model of a cooperative, environmentally sensitive community clustered in three or more neighborhoods of 25–30 clustered homes each. The design provides for a pedestrian village surrounded by orchards, woods, wetlands, and sustainable agriculture areas.

Ecovillage is located on 176 acres located 1 1/2 miles from downtown Ithaca and 3 1/2 miles from Cornell University and Ithaca College. Eighty percent of the land will be preserved as green space for organic agriculture and wildlife habitat. A 9-acre vegetable farm has been operating on the land for six years, and plans for an educational center have begun. We hope that you will join us! [Dec98, sase requested]

ECOVILLAGE EMERGING

c/o Dale Rudesill
1962 Wild Oak Ln
Chico CA 95928

530-891-5059 Dale
417-679-4682 Shandin
417-679-4684 fax Shandin
emerge@ic.org

Began 1997 | Forming | Rural

We are a network of people sharing ideas and working toward creating a cluster of intentional communities having a common goal of ecological sustainability. Beyond this and some other basic agreements, each pod community in the ecovillage will define itself. A pod community can be small enough to maintain a focus and for its members to know each other well, while having the advantages of the ecovillage scale: friendly neighboring communities to exchange resources and social life with, economic ability to buy more acres at fewer dollars/acre, and the knowledge that the area will be treated well. We are looking to settle in northern California or southern Oregon. More than 150 people have put themselves on the network contact list; about half of those have attended one of our meetings. One project is of a zine of our writings. To receive an issue or to put yourself on our contact/information list, please include postage to cover a 2-ounce reply and include US$1 to defray costs. Please submit material about your ideas for the ecovillage or a pod community to be included in future issues. As we share our thinking, our commonalities and differences will emerge; dialogues may be initiated and develop into pod communities. As pod communities and individuals come together, we can further define EcoVillage Emerging and move toward settling. [Sep99, sase required]

ECOVILLAGE OF LOUDOUN COUNTY

1726 Shookstown Rd
Frederick MD 21702

301-662-4646, 301-682-7932 fax
ECOVIL@aol.com
http://www.ecovil.com/

Began Nov99 | Pop. 78 | Forming
Diet: Omnivore | Rural

Mission: EcoVillage of Loudoun County combines the cohousing ideal of people living together in community with the ecovillage ideal of people living in harmony with Earth and its inhabitants. We aim to restore nature and expand human potential by creating a lifestyle that nurtures the human spirit and offers hope for future generations.
Values:
A simple lifestyle that incorporates respect, work, open communication, humor, free inquiry, fun, and creative expression nurtures the human spirit.
A wise and sustainable society restores biodiversity and integrates the community with nature.
Human health, community health, and the health of our planet are interconnected and interdependent.

Key to bracketed text: cc = cannot commit to prompt correspondance, sase = self-addressed stamped envelope

Every person has inherent dignity and worth regardless of age, sex, race, sexual orientation, abilities, financial resources, or spiritual or political beliefs.

Cooperation and teamwork are our model for interaction.

Collaboration is most likely to occur in an environment that respects individual rights to privacy.

Taking individual responsibility for our own needs and decisions as well as caring about the well-being of others supports community.

Our children deserve special attention, support, and nourishment.

Ecological Goal: Preserve and restore biodiversity, quality, and abundance of natural resources. Balance natural systems so that each generation acts to benefit future generations.

Social Goal: Maintain a community lifestyle that protects individual rights; fosters a spirit of community; and facilitates activities that benefit individuals, enrich the community, and promote positive relations with the larger world. [Jun99]

EDEN RANCH COMMUNITY

PO Box 520
Paonia CO 81428

970-835-8905, 970-835-8907
woodwetz@aol.com
http://www.edenranch.com/

Pop. 2 | Forming
Diet: Vegetarian | Rural

Forming community seeking members desiring rural, spiritual environment, sharing labor and resources on planned biodynamic, permaculture 65-acre farm operating under limited-liability company and bylaws. Ecovillage concepts leading toward ultimate self-sustainability.

Located on western Colorado mesa, wondrous 360 degree views. Bring your own business or work nearby. Future community business envisioned. Diversity in thought and age; consensus decision making results from mutual respect and trust.

Approximately $15,000 (flexible terms available) plus cost of Earth-friendly home of your choice; $2 for community plan and materials. [Sep99]

EDENVALE

4330 Bradner Rd
Abbotsford BC V4X 1S8
CANADA

604-856-3388
edenvale@imag.net

Began 1973 | Pop. 13 | Re-Forming
Diet: Omnivore | Rural | Spiritual

Edenvale was purchased in 1973 by the Emissaries of Divine Light as part of an international network of intentional, spiritual communities. It is located in the lush Fraser Valley near Vancouver, British Columbia.

This community was initiated primarily as an educational facility for Emissary classes in spiritual leadership and in attunement, a nontouch physical and spiritual alignment process. At that time, people from all over the world attended these classes and enjoyed the spirit of home here. The dedication of many volunteer hours has contributed to the building of the atmosphere of this place.

The 118-acre property includes self-contained apartments, single rooms, and shared facilities; a retreat and conference center; barns; forested areas; trails; and certified organic farmland. Also on the farm is a therapeutic program with animals designed primarily for people with disabilities.

Over the past few years, the experience in the Edenvale community has transitioned from a hierarchial style of leadership to a collective, consensus process of stewarding community affairs. Some of the 13 residents work in the retreat business, while others are employed in the larger community. Residents eat in their own homes or share a kitchen and occasionally have potluck dinners. We also volunteer our time in work parties on the property. We have a residents' committee, weekly community meetings, worship services, and a heart space time.

The people of this community are dedicated to actualizing the Emissary mission in everyday living, which is "to assist in carrying forth a work of the spiritual regeneration of humanity under the influence of the spirit of God." We know the challenges of living together and acknowledge the dark and light parts of ourselves. There is a strong commitment to personal and collective inner work and a diligence in creating clarity among ourselves, as we continue in the process of building true community.

If you would like to receive more information on this community or wish to arrange a visit, please contact the Residents'

Committee at edenvale@imag.net For further information on the Emissary organization: http://www.emissaries.org. [Dec98]

EDGES

10770 Hooper Ridge Rd
Glouster OH 45732

740-448-2403, 740-448-3006
juem@frognet.net

Began 1994 | Pop. 12
Diet: Omnivore | Rural

(Also known as Athens Land Coop.) Edges is nestled in the foothills of the Appalachian mountains near Athens, progressive home of Ohio University. Ninety-four acres of wooded and clear hills include many "edges," hence much diversity. Eight adults and five children, ages 2 to 57, work together to create a supportive environment, steward the land, and evolve sustainable livelihoods.

Sources we are developing are an alternative-energy and construction business, market gardening, a camp, and an education and retreat center. Many ideas have been discussed, and we are open to other interests.

We grow and put up a percentage of our own food from several gardens, have begun land restoration and a permaculture plan. We've held a variety of permaculture workshops and events such as cider pressing.

The land with an existing farmhouse was purchased in 1993. Our first cooperative effort was a community house operated by wind and solar power, which has six bedrooms. An outhouse will be replaced by an indoor compost toilet as in all our new houses. At present (1999), two women live in a log house with a greenhouse, hot tub, and solar and wind power; one family's house is nestled in the woods with a dance practice space; another woman and her two sons are starting their house on the ridge. It will be a small, simple house using lots of solar and passive solar. One member is considering building a straw-bale house, so we have lots of diversity.

We enjoy working, playing, meeting, and eating together as the ebb and flow of our busy lives allows, and we exercise our commitment to good group process and conflict resolution. Our vision of cooperation includes making decisions based on what will work best for each and the group as a whole. We use consensus for major decisions and rather than emphasizing rules, prefer living by guidelines and conscious-

Listings

ness. Flexibility allows for changes in the balance between individual and community needs. Everyone contributes time and money, working at projects we choose, from gardening, ordering community food, and outreach, to maintenance and construction projects. We are looking for responsible, positive people dedicated to intentional community life on a land trust. Write for information and include an introduction about yourself. [Sep99, sase requested]

EL BLOQUE

Apartado 51
ES-03530 La Nucia
SPAIN

00349 689 5551, 00349 587 0270 fax
elbloque@usa.net

Began 1980 | Diet: Vegetarian | Rural
(Also known as Evolutionary Centre.) In western civilization, a new awareness of spirituality is emerging. Many of us recognize an integrative and purposeful spirit as the force that moves us all and see all beings living on this planet as one family for which we are all responsible. This new awareness is evident in the revival of religious and spiritual traditions. It is also representing itself through other disciplines, such as science, art, psychology, and education. But most important of all, we can experience it in the process of our own daily life.

Discovering who we are, plus the still-hidden but ever-present possibilities within us, is the central theme of the workshops and seminars in El Bloque. These workshops and seminars are offered for those who are experiencing a growing capacity for change in themselves.

An essential part of El Bloque is the living-work community that supports and complements the workshop program. A small staff of dedicated people share the year-round community life and coordinate the daily work. Central to El Bloque's vision is the small scale. The entire community—including guests—does not exceed 35 in number. Thus everyone receives a quality experience, and everyone's gifts contribute uniquely to the little society. [May99]

EL SEMILLERO

La Cardosa 200
ES-28816 Valdeavero Madrid
SPAIN

341-886-4489
semillero@yahoo.com

Began 1993 | Pop. 5 | Forming
Diet: No red meat | Rural

We envision a community with people of all ages and diverse interests, races, and backgrounds. In common we are open minded, tolerant, environmentally conscious, and aware of all issues that endanger future human life and the Earth; we commit to our personal growth using all suitable tools and to learning how to work with others for the common good. Located in the countryside near Madrid, we care for an organic garden and for a few hens and serve organic food to visitors. All this, plus facilitating our space for courses and gatherings of all kinds, keeps us in touch with our fellow humans, so increasing the chances for others to follow. We strongly believe that the right education and childcare will make a difference in the future; we will be an educational community. Our simple lifestyle allows us to carry through a luxury life. Masters of our days, we use them to live mindfully, renouncing only all that we actually do not need. We have plenty of time for experimenting with alternate solutions in areas like health, relationships, construction, economy, and everything else. Our model communities are those that provide fertile space for many different people with diverse missions to accomplish their goals, while cooperating with all others; The Farm, Twin Oaks, Findhorn. [Nov98, sase required]

ELDERWOOD

15210 Schleweis Rd
Manchester MI 48158

734-428-0859
ferguson@wunderground.com

Began 1995 | Pop. 4
Diet: No red meat | Rural

ElderWood is located in rural southeast Michigan, 35 minutes west of Ann Arbor. Our summers are hot, and our winters are surprisingly mild. ElderWood is interested in creating a self-sustaining entity, complete with perennial flower gardens, berries, grapes, asparagus, and fruit trees. We are blessed with plenty of wooded areas for the harvest of fuel, and we enjoy our swimming

Key to bracketed text: cc = cannot commit to prompt correspondance, sase = self-addressed stamped envelope

hole in the summer sun. We understand respect to be at the center of human relationships, and individuality is praised. We don't offer much to "join," but instead we are open to the travelers among us willing to contribute time and energy. ElderWood is a rest stop on the road less traveled. [May99, cc, sase required]

ELOHIM CITY

Rt 3 Box 293
Elohim City
Muldrow OK 74948

918-427-1971

Began 1972 | Pop. 100
Diet: Vegan | Rural | Spiritual

(Also known as Bethel Christian.) Christ centered, ecology minded, nonexploitive, self-reliant, caring, rural. [Feb99, cc]

ELSWORTH COOPERATIVE

711 West Grand River Ave
East Lansing MI 48823

517-337-3236
http://www.msu.edu/user/coop/

Began 1940 | Pop. 18
Diet: Omnivore | Urban

(Also known as Elsworth House.) Elsworth Co-op is primarily directed toward students, but anyone is welcome to live here. Tenants are required to sign a lease through the end of the current school year. Rent is adjusted to make it as low as possible, because our main focus is on "housing for people—not for profit." Another requirement is that each tenant must work roughly five hours each week toward betterment of the house. Duties vary and include such things as cleaning, cooking, and general maintenance. We have a meal plan that caters to both vegetarians and meat eaters. [Feb99, sase requested]

EMERALD EARTH

PO Box 764
Boonville CA 95415

707-895-3302

Began 1994 | Pop. 9 | Re-Forming
Diet: Vegetarian | Rural

Emerald Earth is a re-forming intentional community in rural Mendocino County. We have 189 acres of mixed redwood and hardwood forest; open, south-facing meadows with majestic oaks; two springs; a pond; and

a seasonal creek. The land is held in trust by a 501(c)3 nonprofit corporation.

Our values include sustainable living, simplicity, social and environmental justice, and reverence for the Earth and all living things. Our mission is to develop and demonstrate a model of living in harmony with the land and with each other. The original founding group was and is committed to developing our spiritual connection to the Earth through ritual, song, and seasonal celebrations.

Currently we are four adults and one child on-site and four adults off-site. We are looking for more people. We are developing the infrastructure for 12 to 20 permanent residents plus guests, interns, and students. We envision a large central common house, tiny private cabins, orchards, gardens, and food forest.

For more information or to arrange a visit, please send a letter describing your background and interests. [Jun99, sase requested]

EMMA GOLDMAN CO-OP

625 North Frances St
Madison WI 53703

608-259-1976
**http://www.stdorg.wisc.edu/
mcc/home.html**

Began 1996 | Pop. 18
Diet: Vegetarian | Urban

Emma Goldman is the newest Madison Community Cooperatives (MCC) house, founded in 1996, located just half a block from beautiful Lake Mendota and two blocks from the UW-Madison campus. Our house is a "safe space" for anyone interested in a more socially just society, and we strongly encourage activist endeavors of all sorts. Like Emma herself, though, we also have lots of fun! ("If I can't dance, I don't want to be part of your revolution.")

We are a dog-friendly house, and all our meals are vegetarian with vegan option. Visitors are welcome for dinner or to stay overnight anytime—just drop by or call ahead! [Mar99]

EMMAUS COMMUNITY/HARLEM

Emmaus
PO Box 1177
New York NY 10035

212-410-6006

Began 1965 | Pop. 43
Diet: No red meat | Urban | Spiritual

Emmaus is a community of homeless people building new lives through work, supportive community, therapy, personal change, social change, education, etc., while serving others on the street: community kitchen, food pantry, outreach, AIDS education, hospitality, advocating for homeless and oppressed.

Emmaus communities of and for the poor are in 42 nations.

We seek to be economically self-sufficient.

We seek radical social change—through aggressive nonviolent action—to be a society where resources are more equally shared.

Others join the poor—bringing resources and skills the poor community needs.

We are mostly black, some Hispanics, and a few whites and Asians. We are open to all. [Jan99]

EMMAUS — HAARZUILENS

Eikstraat 14
NL-3455 SJ Haarzuilens
THE NETHERLANDS

030-677-1540
emmaus@emmaus.nl

Began 1966 | Pop. 12
Diet: Omnivore | Rural/Urban

The community engages itself in social action in favor of homeless people and projects in the Third World. [May99]

ENCHANTED GARDEN INTENTIONAL COMMUNITY

6008 Arosa St
San Diego CA 92115

619-582-9669, 619-583-2337 fax
EnGarden@aol.com

Began 1989 | Pop. 9 | Urban

The Enchanted Garden
Welcomes You!
Through flowers, live herbs,
and whole foods present
and circulating through
our daily lives, we can help
the world grow healthy
and beautiful from the ground up.

Additions and corrections: Email: directory@ic.org, Web: http://directory.ic.org/, Mail: RR 1 Box 156-D, Rutledge MO 63563, USA.

Listings

The Earth, through our own hands,
very close to home, beginning in our
own backyard, can become an
Enchanted Garden!
—Leslie Goldman, Enchanted Gardener

Eight of us live together on a 1/3-acre parcel surrounded by canyons in the state-college area of San Diego. The land exists as an oasis of green with many aromatic herbs and simple foods growing. The work that has gone into preserving this natural environment for more than 20 years is an inspiration to many. The land is rich in nature spirits and life energies drawn here through many hands working together.

We have a large library of books in the areas of natural food, gardening, Feng Shui, personal growth, and eclectic spiritual studies. The library houses books and materials created by Leslie Goldman, founder, and works by his mentors, Bernard Jensen, natural healing arts elder, and Edmond Bordeaux Szekely, modern Essene renaissance pioneer.

The community archives a rare Essene school of thought library of hours of audiotapes cocreated by Leslie Goldman and Kevin Ryerson. Kevin was featured in the *Out on a Limb* ABC miniseries, and book by Shirley Maclaine.

The property is in private ownership and is a house offering rental to those who would like to live as extended family and join together in house meetings and shared house duties. We live by basic agreements to keep the house orderly and maintain the property. Rentals occur from time to time. We maintain one room for paying guests, who come for miniretreats and visits. One space is available for work trade.

The Enchanted Garden is a name for the new Earth we can each grow one person at a time, one plant at a time, organically. Growing the Enchanted Garden is a by-product of our own human flowering, and reestablishing the bonds between our highest seed dreams and the Earth. An international network of friends spreads the message of the Enchanted Garden through joining the Enchanted Garden Club and signing a Declaration of Interdependence. Ongoing projects include support for local organic farming. We aspire to create more and more extended community around gardening together and shared rituals. Individuals who would like to live in this special environment while fulfilling their personal seed dreams and learning more about the Enchanted Garden are encouraged to be in touch. [Aug99, cc]

ENO COMMONS COHOUSING

3 Indigo Creek Trail
Durham NC 27712

919-406-8366 [406-8ENO], 919-382-9643, 382-9668
ncaidin@aol.com
robert_heinich@juno.com
http://www.employees.org/~enoweb/

Began 1998 | Pop. 53
Diet: Omnivore | Rural/Urban

Ours is a community of 22 households of folks who have chosen to live here because they want to know their neighbors and be involved. We have clustered our homes to free up more common spaces for play and mutual enjoyment. When our commons house is complete we plan to share three or four meals a week. We have a vegetable garden that we share as well. We care deeply about our children and want them to grow up in a friendly and stimulating environment. We have designed our community to facilitate spontaneous interactions. For example, cars are located near the edges of the property; the space inside is reserved for people. We believe in learning through the diversity of each other, although we did not attract as much ethnic and cultural diversity into our community as we had hoped.

We believe we are connected to the larger communities of our adjacent neighborhoods, our city, our county, our world. Hopefully we will make a difference in each other's lives and the life of our planet through work and play freely given. [Jan99, sase requested]

ESSENE COOPERATIVE

1705 14th St #408
Boulder CO 80302

541-963 2429
angelman24@excite.com
vegivic@aol.com
http://bcn.boulder.co.us/
community/essene/

Began 1994 | Pop. 15 | Forming
Diet: Vegetarian

Our community is still forming. We would like to be supportive of other groups in the community process and look forward to networking with other groups. Our philosophy is in our Web site, and we believe in being loving and supportive of people who are looking to live a spiritual life, sharing, growing, and, above all, in alternative energy and ecological, sustainable living and using herbs for healing. [Aug99, sase required]

ESSENE SKOOLA PHISH (ESP)

Route 1 Box 169
Golden Eagle IL 62036
lkindr@hotmail.com

Began 1992 | Pop. 5 | Forming
Rural | Spiritual

We have started farming organically. We are certified by OCLA. We may start an organic religion, if the USDA succeeds in gutting the organic movement, in order to maintain the right to use the word *organic* as it should be used. Members should be open to a higher power of good and prefer organic living. *Organic* means using foods grown without environmentally toxic substances or methods and with optimum nutrition. It also means peaceful and cheerful. Our area is rural with urban St. Louis 50 miles away. Tourists come to enjoy our scenery. We're looking into biodynamics. We seek others of like mind and those who'd like to help start a private skool of spiritual organic living (see SOOL at http://www.egroups.com). Students are welcome too. We're compatible with most religions but favor spiritual, not physical, reincarnation. Organic "preachers" are welcome and writers of organic religious literature, etc. Land trust, cohousing, psychic and spiritual development, free energy, etc., are some of our interests. Aloha! [Sep99, sase requested]

ETERNAL CAUSE SOCIETY

c/o Counsel for Progressive Action-CPAC
1652 Ridge Ave
Philadelphia PA 19130

Began 1995 | Pop. 14
Diet: No red meat | Urban | Spiritual

We call ourselves and the efforts of life that we commence the Eternal Cause Society or the Enlightenment Society of Eternal Cause. We are predominantly and primarily of a spiritual nature and orientation, even though there is a strong and practical planetary and progressive worldly side to our being here and our collective cause. Concerns about the state of self-sufficiency, social and productive ecology, progressive eclectivism, synchronized diversity, whole-cause perspective, harmony with all life, preservation of all life, divine justice and equality, cooperation, profound acknowledgment of and accord to the laws and standards of nature and reality, and the establishment and achievement of an advanced society and culture are very much

Key to bracketed text: cc = cannot commit to prompt correspondance, sase = self-addressed stamped envelope

in line with our perspective. Collectively, we follow a path of life and reality that is primarily very different from that of many other spiritual groups and efforts in that we focus and act on what we see and recognize as being our profound and divine celestial purpose and will of life and existence upon this world and even beyond this world. Because of this, we consider ourselves as being cosmic workers, destiny workers, profoundists, enlightened essentialists and existentialists, and celestial emissaries, all working together among the higher abodes of the divine direction and will toward the whole and entire cosmic plan that we see as being eternal cause. There are not many of us on this higher path and level of celestial cause and divine will of reality and life to be well applied to world-changing determination and consciousness. We respond to the innate calling of the cosmos toward our profound purpose and higher cause of life that we very well know and understand, and we seek very much to guide and teach other people who are ready to follow this quest through our lead and practice. There is still a lot of work in this world and cosmos that has to be done in direct relation to our highest destiny and mission of life, among the eternal will of all being. If you are seeking a path of higher cause and profound universal direction among our divine destiny of being toward a state of social and world enlightenment and embetterment upon this planet— then through the realization of eternal cause and coherences this can be prominently fulfilled. For more information on the Eternal Cause Society movement or becoming a member of its community and endeavors, please write us. [Nov98, sase required]

FAERIE CAMP DESTINY

**PO Box 1492
Bratteboro VT 05302**

**802-257 4871
jimjackson@mediaone.net
gabrielque@hotmail.com
http://www.FaerieCampDestiny.org/**

Began 1994 | Rural | Spiritual

Six years ago, a few Vermont faeries rented a large house at a former summer camp and began to host gatherings of northeast faeries. They raised money and defined a vision of community. When the house was sold, they had to move on, but the nonprofit corporation continued. In June 1997, with much fund-raising and excitement, 150 acres was purchased to become a faerie sanctuary in New England. Land once held as the property of King George III is now in the stewardship of faeries, and the stone-walled meadows are filled with maple and beech, hemlock and fern, deer, owls, a moose, and occasionally faeries.

Currently, we camp on the land, with temporary shelters, and are learning about the land. We have created trails from the stream on the bottom to the meadow at the top as well as a kitchen area and fire circle. A permit process is under way to build a gathering center with kitchen and bathing facility as a first step in meeting our mission. Eventually, we will establish a community of residents and a winter retreat space. Other visions include hospice care and a museum/archive of radical faerie history and culture. [Feb99]

FAIR OAKS COHOUSING

**3414 Dawes St
Madison WI 53714**

**608-243-7892, 608-249-3569
krwilson@bigfoot.com
lavendel@bigfoot.com
http://freenet.msp.mn.us/housing/
cohousing/retrofit/fairoaks.htm**

Fair Oaks Cohousing is an urban retrofit cohousing community located in Madison, Wisconsin.

Currently, we are six families (11 adults, 4 kids) in six units. We share a large organic garden, an orchard, and a child play area. In good weather we hold outdoor potlucks, campfires, and musical jam sessions. We do childcare exchange, share laundry facilities, and do food preserving together. We hold rotating dinners and will develop plans for common space over time. Behind our houses are an expansive city park and Starkweather Creek, with lots of birds and other wildlife to enjoy. Lake Monona and Olbrich Botanical Garden are less than three blocks away. A bus-transfer station is nearby, affording easy access to several bus lines. A bike path goes from our back door to downtown Madison.

We plan to continue to expand the community. Nearby homes (ranging from one bedroom on up) are regularly available for rent or sale, and we hope to gradually expand the community. We seek a diversity of members—singles, seniors, and families. [May99]

FAIRVIEW COOPERATIVE

**15630 Fairview Lake Rd SW
Port Orchard WA 98366
tomgaro@yahoo.com**

Began Dec98 | Pop. 2 | Forming
Diet: No red meat | Rural

Fairview Cooperative is a new community situated on 20 acres of gently rolling forest/meadow near Gig Harbor, Washington. Its purpose is to provide a cooperative, socially supportive lifestyle for those interested in the arts, sustainable-systems design, permaculture, and land preservation.

Co-op decisions are by consensus. Property is held individually. Our long-term goal is to replace our three mobile homes with four clustered homes and a common house.

Some of our values are nonviolence, land stewardship, personal growth, connecting with and serving the greater community, and appreciating our spiritual nature. We are open to prearranged visits from interested people. [Sep99, sase requested]

FAIRVIEW HOUSE

**1801 Fairview St
Berkeley CA 94703**

510-658-3899

Pop. 10 | Diet: Vegetarian | Urban

We are a 10-person, organically evolving, multigenerational household made up of educationalists, spiritual aspirants, activists, musicians, and artists. We range in age from 12 to 54. Our house is seven years old. We cook dinners (vegetarian/vegan) five days a week, meet bimonthly, and are intently fixing up our two houses that we proudly own. We have a beautiful flower garden, a small vegetable garden, a dog, three cats, two birds, and two mice.

Though we don't believe in a specific dogma or religion as a whole, we are all progressively minded and share an interest in political, social, environmental, and spiritual matters. We are generally committed to making our house an affordable, pleasant place to live. Implicitly, there is a commitment to open, loving communication with each other. We also strive to be emotionally responsible and work out personal issues as they arise. We are involved in our neighborhood, specifically in trying to get everyone in the area together to make our neck of south Berkeley a better place.

Mail and phone inquiries only. [Mar99, sase requested, no openings]

FAMILY, THE

2020 Pennsylvania Ave NW
Suite 102
Washington DC 20006

202-298-0838
familydc@juno.com
http://www.thefamily.org/

Began 1968 | Pop. 14 | Re-Forming
Diet: Omnivore | Urban | Spiritual

(Also known as Children of God.) The Family, formerly known as the Children of God, was founded in 1968 as a fundamentalist Christian movement. The Family has been operating as a communal society for 30 years, with nearly 800 communities in over 70 countries of the world and over 13,000 full-time and associate members.

The Family's founder, David Brandt Berg, pointed members to the Book of Acts in the Bible as a blueprint of how Christ's disciples should live; sharing their earthly goods and common potting finances, abilities, and resources.

The Family's primary mission is to "preach the Gospel to every creature" by every possible means, such as personal evangelization, humanitarian aid, and the distribution of Christian videotapes and audiotapes they produce. Two-thirds of their membership is second-generation members, most of whom are homeschooled.

The Family's nonconventional beliefs regarding sexuality have been greatly highlighted by the media. It is the Family's scriptural belief that God created human sexuality and that as such, when practiced as God ordained and intended between consenting persons of the opposite sex and of legal age with the consent of all parties concerned, it is a pure, needful, and beautiful creation of God. [Nov98]

FAR VALLEY FARM, INC.

12788 New England Rd
Amesville OH 45711

740-448-4894, 740-448-2039

Began 1977 | Pop. 11
Diet: Vegetarian | Rural

We are 10 adults and 7 children living in sub-Appalachia on 234 acres of open and wooded land in southeast Ohio (near Athens, the home of Ohio University). We incorporated with the state of Ohio in 1980 and eventually renamed ourselves "Far Valley Farm." We are multiskilled and are moving toward a goal of relative self-sufficiency. We regard ourselves as stewards of this land, sharing sort of an overall respect for life and the life force that includes self-respect, growth, and love. We have grown fairly organically, are pretty tolerant, and tend to be honest and up front with each other. We are presently full and are not accepting new membership applications at this time. Please, written inquiries only. [Oct99, sase requested]

FARM, THE

34 The Farm
Summertown TN 38483

931-964-3571
thefarm@usit.net
http://www.thefarm.org/

Began 1971 | Pop. 163
Diet: Vegan | Rural | Spiritual

The Farm is an intentional community of families and friends living on 1,750 acres in south-central Tennessee. Since its inception in 1971, the purpose of the Farm community has been to provide a secure, ecologically healthy, commonly held land base for its members and succeeding generations. It is a place where we can relate to each other and the natural environment in a sustainable way, draw upon the collective strength of the community, and contribute to the positive transformation of the world.

The Farm school offers alternative education to school-age students. The Farm midwives have delivered over 2,000 babies since 1970. We hold the sacrament of birth as an inherent right of all women, newborns, and families. Plenty International is an international aid and development nongovernmental organization (NGO) that benefits indigenous peoples and the environment. Its Kids To the Country project brings at-risk kids to the Farm to enjoy nature and study peace education. Ecovillage Training Center, another not-for-profit, is a member of the Global Ecovillage Network and offers conferences and seminars on organic gardening, permaculture, straw-bale construction, and sustainable technologies.

Approximately 170 residents and over 20 Farm businesses (including Farm Soy, the Farm Store, the Book Publishing Company, and the Farm Education/Conference Center) contribute to the maintenance of the community. We welcome scheduled visits and tours. Please write or call. [Feb99, sase requested]

FATHER DIVINE'S INTERNATIONAL PEACE MISSION MOVEMENT

1622 Spring Mill Rd
Gladwyne PA 19035

610-525-5598
fdipmm@libertynet.org
http://www.libertynet.org/fdipmm/

Began 1932
Diet: Omnivore | Rural/Urban | Spiritual

The followers of the Reverend Major J. Divine make up the interracial, international, interdenominational, peace-mission movement. By revelation we know Father Divine is God, Jesus Christ in the fathership degree. We live together as a holy spiritual family, knowing God is our father/mother and we are brothers and sisters. We cut all ties of blood relationships. We live as though we died and went to heaven. Heaven is a state of consciousness.

When we put off mortal thinking and living and conform to the Christ mind and spirit, our bodies can live on in youthfulness here on Earth. If one dies to self and all its connections, there is no need for propagation. God expresses his love for us in mental, spiritual, and material blessings. We express our love for God by working and serving, giving wholeheartedly our all to the cause of magnifying the actual presence of

From the Farm Community

The New Farm Vegetarian Cookbook—recipes developed by talented cooks from the *Farm*. Includes how to make tofu and soy milk at home.

In *Voices from The Farm* members past and present recount the trials and triumphs of building this enduring new age, intentional community.

To order call: 800-695-2241—$12.95 ea. ppd.

Key to bracketed text: cc = cannot commit to prompt correspondance, sase = self-addressed stamped envelope

God on the Earth. By serving our fellow man and lifting up a standard for the people, we make Christianity practical. We daily work together and praise God in song together. Our ongoing project is to bring the Christ to fruition individually and collectively, be a glorious church without a spot or wrinkle, living the brotherhood of man, depending on God alone for our sustenance. [Oct99]

FELLOWSHIP COMMUNITY

241 Hungry Hollow Rd
Spring Valley NY 10977

914-356-8494

Began 1966 | Pop. 124
Diet: Omnivore | Rural

(Also known as Rudolf Steiner Fellowship Foundation.) We are an intergenerational care community centered around the care of the elderly but taking up the care of handicapped young adults—children in need of special help and one another. Our care extends to the land, animals, and objects we are responsible for. We are very hardworking, seeking to incorporate ideas

from the spiritual world into our daily life rather than merely talking about them. Our impulses come from the work of Dr. Rudolf Steiner.

We live a rural-type existence in an urban setting and have a varied life. We support ourselves through social, therapeutic, and educational efforts such as our medical practice, biodynamic farming, metal shop, woodshop, candle shop, gift shop, print shop, weavery, and pottery as well as our care activities. We do most of our own small building and maintenance work. We have a children's garden for our preschoolers, and our children attend the local Waldorf school. We have a rich study and cultural life. Music and art are emphasized.

Our spiritual ideas permeate our community organization, economics, work activities, education, and cultural life. We are open to new coworkers who have at least an interest in learning more about Rudolf Steiner, who want a full and varied life, and who are unafraid of hard work—inner and outer—in the service of others. We welcome inquiries and prearranged work-along visits. [Dec98]

FERENCY CO-OP

146 Collingwood Av
East Lansing MI 48823

517-332-0846, 517-332-0847
coop@pilot.msu.edu
http://www.msu.edu/user/coop/

Began 1964 | Pop. 9
Diet: Omnivore | Urban

(Also known as Key Largo Co-op.) Ferency Co-op is located in East Lansing, Michigan, less than one block from the campus of Michigan State University and downtown East Lansing.

Ferency is a part of the Student Housing Corporation (SHC) (which owns and operates 12 houses in the area). It is situated between two other SHC co-ops, which makes for a happy community.

Ferency is a nonsmoking house and is in excellent condition. There is generally a house pet.

Ferency is mostly comprised of MSU students, though other residents are certainly welcome. Most residents are temporary, being students, but some residents stay a few years.

Stop by and see our house! [Feb99]

Listings

FINDHORN FOUNDATION COMMUNITY

The Park
Findhorn
Forres IV36 3TZ, Scotland
UNITED KINGDOM

+44 (0) 1309 690311
+44 (0) 1309 691301 fax
reception@findhorn.org
communications@findhorn.org
http://www.findhorn.org/

Began 1962
Diet: No red meat | Rural | Spiritual

The Findhorn Foundation Community has many aspects to its work, all motivated by the conviction that a joyful, loving, and sustainable future on Earth will require changes in the way that we as humans relate to ourselves, other people, the natural environment, and the spiritual dimension of life.

Ever since its founding in 1962, the community has been a place where ordinary life is transformed into a learning experience. This happens by living together and working together in the kitchen, gardens, or any area of the community with an attitude of service. Each person takes responsibility for their own spiritual focus, with an awareness that they are an integral part of the evolution of the whole community and of all of humanity.

When people come here, they can experience an expansion of consciousness and their heart opening to themselves, other people, the natural world, and spirit. Sharing this kind of education with the thousands of people who come here each year for Experience Weeks or other programs is a major means by which the community sustains itself. The community is also engaged in developing its built environment and creating an ecovillage as a natural continuation of its earlier work in cooperation and cocreation with nature. [Mar99]

FINNEY FARM

41638 South Skagit Hwy
Sedro Woolley WA 98284

360-826-4004
fstaub@earthlink.net

Began 1990 | Pop. 7
Diet: Omnivore | Rural

Our vision involves sustainable living—organic gardening, growing as much of our food as possible, producing as much of our power with as little pollution as we can, living lightly on the land. We live in an extremely fertile area where much of this can be achieved. Most of the land is being conserved as habitat. We are clustering houses toward the front clearing to minimize our impact and are building energy-efficient, small cabins. It is a place where we can raise our children to be as comfortable with nature as with people. Some of us will homeschool, hopefully cooperatively with others. It is a place without urban fears—no crime, clean air and water, etc. The farm nurtures us spiritually, emotionally, and physically as we nurture the land and each other.

We envision about five houses with several shared meals each week; common gardens and orchards; a communal laundry facility; a community well; land-based businesses. It is a place where we can be our word and practice what we preach (environmentalism); a place we each come to with different strengths and weaknesses and in which we can share them and learn from others' skills, problem solving, parenting, facilitating; a place where we and the land can grow together to become a whole. [Jan99, cc, sase required]

FLOWERING DESERT PERMACULTURE CENTER

PO Box 44110
Tucson AZ 85733

520-578-9557, 520-578-9564 fax
info@floweringdesert.com
http://www.floweringdesert.com/

Began 1997 | Pop. 4 | Forming
Diet: Omnivore | Rural

Flowering Desert is a two-year-old project originally inspired by the German ZEGG community. We have just recently moved from urban Tucson to our new rural desert site with four residents, and this site also serves as a meeting place for our larger circle. We are expanding our living spaces to accommodate more of us, but in the meantime we meet with the larger group several times a week to do projects and work parties on the land, as well as our group process, which is Marshall Rosenberg's Compassionate Communication process (from his book *Non-Violent Communication*). Since several of us are permaculture educators and workshop facilitators, this site will also be a workshop and seminar center, and indeed, even though we currently lack large facilities, we can't avoid doing such events already.

At Flowering Desert we are attempting to create a sustainable ecological environment but ecological in the broadest sense of the word, which includes using the principles of permaculture applied not only to our land, flora, and fauna but applied to, and including, human ecology as well.

So we ask the same questions as all permaculturists, questions like, "What environment does this plant like?" "What support systems allow it to flourish?" "What environmental conditions attract plant and animal life and allow them to see this place as home?" And then we go one step further and apply those same questions to ourselves as well, by asking, "In what environment does this person best thrive?" "What support systems and relationships will allow this person to be the happiest and flourish?" "What environments attract people and allow them to develop in the ways that are most valuable to them?" and "What allows and encourages this person to contribute to the growth and happiness of the community as a whole?" In other words, an expansion of the permaculture "zone-zero" concept.

Part of what we recognize is that an essential condition for human happiness is to be able to grow and learn, and we are

Key to bracketed text: cc = cannot commit to prompt correspondance, sase = self-addressed stamped envelope

crucially interested in what conditions promote that growth. This is one of the reasons we are developing our community as an adult educational center. We are trying to attract others who also have an excitement in adventure, growth, and learning and who want to help create a place where everything can be learned from practical permaculture gardening techniques, to body-work classes and conflict-resolution training, to tantra and sexual healing. Since we have developed a large network of friends around the United States and in Europe we hope to soon have enough guest space for them to visit and bring their skills and seminars to our community. So this also means we encourage a diversity of relationship styles.

For more information visit our constantly changing Web site. Those who wish to visit need to contact us first since we still have limited guest space. [Sep99, sase required]

FOLKHAVEN COMMUNITY

PO Box 878791
Wasílla AK 99687

907-376-7344

Began Oct98 | Pop. 3 | Re-Forming
Diet: Omnivore | Rural/Urban | Spiritual

As per our name, our primary concern is the welfare and survival of our folk. Environmental concern and our evolutionary ties to nature underlie our worldviews. Our core social values include kinship, cooperation, strength, courage, honor, joy in life, loyalty, vigor, freedom, and persistence. In sociobiology we seek to identify and utilize those aspects of human nature that promote cooperation, cohesion, and permanence in community.

Our social model is tribal. Our organizational model includes a network of small closely knit communities confederated into local, regional, national, and eventually international organizations.

We will create our own businesses, schools, and other institutions as needed. Vocationally and businesswise, we aspire to science, technology, and evolving professions on the cutting edge of Earth-friendly change. Believing that US society is unfixable, we choose a separate future. Although, of necessity, our first communities will maintain economic and other ties with the mainstream, those ties will not be social and will wither as the United States disintegrates and as our resources and numbers allow for greater autonomy and self-sufficiency.

We seek strong, vigorous members who wish to take their destiny in their own hands and build a worthwhile future for themselves, their descendants, and their folk. [Feb99]

FORMING COMMUNITY

c/o Paul Lauzier
RR 1 Box 5140
Lubec ME 04652

Forming | Rural

Have 100 acres to share with religious (spiritually oriented) homesteaders keen on handwork seeking to promote Gandhian "villagism" among ourselves and in the surrounding community primarily by practicing it.

Founder has been established for 13 years as a local woodenware peddler hoping to find other idealists committed to local self-reliance and voluntary poverty (limiting use of resources to basics necessary for a wholesome life; no power machinery, electricity, or telephone; no government welfare; learning to live without automobiles, etc.).

"Villagism" depicts a decentralized economic and social order based on universal religious principles that Mahatma Gandhi worked out for the revival and liberation of the villages undermined by an exploitive and corrupting economic system. It emphasizes small-scale production and local self-sufficiency especially in basic necessities and avoids trade merely for profit. It is a nonexploitative, ecologically sustainable system allowing for the greatest freedom and responsibility in cooperation, production, and spiritual growth for all members of the community. [Dec98]

FOX HOUSING COOPERATIVE

Werndolau
Golden Grove
Carmarthen Dyfed
SA32 8NE, Wales
UNITED KINGDOM

01558 668798

Began 1998 | Pop. 8 | Forming
Diet: Vegan | Rural | Spiritual

Our focus is to practically and effectively apply our values. These are broadly summarized by responsibility—to yourself, others, and the land. How we hope to live these values is complex. Living simply and lightly translates into everyday policies such as a carbon debt of one pound on cars visiting the site, making your own entertainment (no TV). All members have some form of meditative practice and are committed to spending one weekend in six with other co-op folk. Accepting responsibility for when we fall short of our values is an important aspect of life here.

We live on a 53-acre ex–dairy farm. We wish to provide space for members to pursue their vocations while sharing Werndolau with as many others as possible. Good design and clear structure are crucial to avoid these aims conflicting. We're involved in agroforestry, woodland planting, and three organic-vegetable deliveries run from the site. We also have cheap bunkhouse accommodation/camping for backpackers/visitors.

We've got a lot to do, a lot to learn, and we're going to make mistakes and have fun. We welcome offers of both long- and short-term help. If you'd like to visit, please contact us. [Apr99, sase requested]

FRANCISCAN WORKERS OF JUNIPERO SERRA

715 Jefferson St
Salinas CA 93905

831-757-3838, 831-757-5987
jesus@redshift.com

Began 1982 | Pop. 16
Diet: Vegetarian | Urban | Spiritual

The mission of the Franciscan workers community is to live and work together in harmony and serve the poor in the spirit of St. Francis, with respect and dignity for all. Through a daily rhythm of prayer and service, community is formed, and through the practice of creative love and beauty, hope is renewed. The Franciscan workers seek to be instruments of peace in the "ordinariness of life." We strive to follow the practices of voluntary simplicity, nonviolence, the works of mercy, contemplation, and community. Our projects include a hospitality center, a soup kitchen, a health clinic, a work co-op, a farmworker ministry, tutoring children, summer camps, work with the disabled, immersion experiences for youth, and roundtable discussions and education. We seek a transformation of culture that is nonviolent and personalist. A major focus of ours is the practice of reconciliation between religions. We dream of a rural community to focus on nurturing children, youth, and the disabled. To love without limits, to

Listings

receive the blessing of the poor, and to welcome children are our basic call. "Imagine paradise, practice beauty" is our sustaining vision. [Oct99]

FRANKLEIGH HOUSE

Bath Rd
Bradford on Avon
Wiltshire BA15 2PB, England
UNITED KINGDOM

+44 (0) 1225 867696
+44 (0) 1225 866467
+44 (0) 1225 864300 fax
david@ic.org
dmichael@compuserve.com
http://ourworld.compuserve.com/
   homepages/dmichael/

Began 1995 | Diet: Omnivore | Rural
Seven families share a massive Victorian mansion house; each family has its own large self- contained living unit. We have many communal areas, including a theater, pottery/art room, meeting room, dance room, tennis court, swimming pool, 17 acres, communal kitchen. We often come together to celebrate festivals, e.g., Chanukah, Divali, New Year for Trees, and our birthdays. We eat communally about once a week.

Decision making is by consensus or 80 percent. Personal conflicts are often not very well resolved. When it's good here it's wonderful. When it's bad it's hell. The swimming pool is very popular in the summer—the children play hide and seek with neighbors in the main house and run around. They form and break relationships and are better at working things out than the adults. We have a 300-yard flying fox/zipper from a tree house. Our vision is to get on with each other and accept each other as we are. [Jan99]

FREE-THE-LAND NYC SQUATTERS COMMUNITY

c/o Blackout Books
50 Ave B
New York NY 10009

212-777-1967
http://www.panix.com/
   ~blackout/squatters.html

Began 1967 | Pop. 142
Diet: Omnivore | Urban

(Also known as NYC Homesteaders.) Based on the concept that housing is a right for all; buildings that were abandoned were turned into homes. Each house has its own vision and eclectic bunch. The legal standing of each building also differs, but some have become legal. You may spend time out of each week renovating a space, attending house meetings, or eating a potluck meal. Winters can be hard; some use a wood stove for heat, other buildings have electricity, telephones, etc.

Some of these homesteaders have been living in these houses in the lower East Side and the Bronx for three generations. Current projects include community gardens, recycling centers, theater and performance spaces.

Groups or individuals are needed to contribute construction skills and debris removal and to reclaim additional buildings. The squatters of England, Spain, Berlin, etc., have demonstrated that squatting can be a viable, cooperative way of life. Survival without rent is a possibility and helps to renew burned-out urban areas. Equality, collective decision making, and anarchistic ideals are important to most community members, as well as acceptance of alternative lifestyles.

Join the fight! Free the land! [Feb99, sase required]

FREIE CHRISTLICHE JUGENDGEMEINSCHAFT (FREE CHRISTIAN YOUTH FELLOWSHIP)

Altenaer Strasse 45
D-58507 Lüdenscheid
GERMANY

0-23-51-35-80-39
0-23-51-2-13-87 fax
http://www.shineon.com/shine/fcjg/

Began 1976 | Urban | Spiritual
The Free Christian Youth Fellowship is a missionary movement founded in 1976 that is characterized by community life and a resulting missionary lifestyle as well as supporting the unity of the body of Christ. Among others the Freie Christliche Jugendgemeinschaft is putting a main emphasis on:

• Mercy ministries (i.e., drug rehabilitation and working with various fringe groups)
• Training programs (especially the School for Evangelism and World Mission, seminars, and congresses)
• Evangelistic Urban Mission (i.e.,

Key to bracketed text: cc = cannot commit to prompt correspondance, sase = self-addressed stamped envelope

teenagers' and children's ministry, looking after refugees)
• World Mission [Mar99]

FRIENDS CO-OP

437 W Johnson
Madison WI 53703

608-251-0156

Began 1960 | Pop. 12
Diet: Vegetarian | Urban

We are a co-op house in downtown Madison, near the university campus. We emphasize consensus decision making, by which each of our 12 members has equal say in what goes on in the house—though no one is expected to weigh in on or even care about every single issue. Members are required to attend house meetings, which happen every other week. They are an important tool for dealing with issues that come up and also draw us closer together as a community. We have dinner together four nights/week—we all take turns cooking. So there's great variety in our vegetarian meals. Though we're pretty diverse—undergraduates, graduates, folks with "real jobs"; Jewish, Buddhist, pagan, evangelical Protestants, atheist, agnostic, and fill-in-the-blank; and running the gamut in terms of sexuality and sexual orientation—we love being with each other. While we (or subsets of us) do things like go out to dance, swim in a nearby lake, or bar hop, we equally enjoy just sitting at home and talking or bonding as we take care of housework. Our organic garden and ongoing house-improvement projects are sources of joy (and a wee bit of pride, too). We work with other downtown housing co-ops, trading knowledge and offering mutual support. [Jan99, sase requested]

FRUITVALE HOUSING COOPERATIVE

2011 38th Ave
Oakland CA 94601

510-261-2268, 510-261-2267 fax
rebeccak@igc.org

The Fruitvale Housing Cooperative is an intentional community, collective household, in the Fruitvale neighborhood of Oakland, California. We strive toward ecological sustainability, social justice, and community mindedness. We share food and frequent dinners (mostly vegan). Decisions are made by consensus, and we have no official religious/spiritual orientation. We like to promote collective living, and help others to start similar households. [Nov99]

FULL MOON RISING

1668 East Dow Rd
Freeland WA 98249

360-331-4087, 360-331-4087 fax
smauk@sw.wednet.edu

Began 1998 | Pop. 9 | Re-Forming
Diet: Omnivore | Rural

Full Moon Rising, an intentional farm community, was started in 1997 on the historic Dow farm outside of Freeland, Washington. Founded on the principles of voluntary simplicity, ecological awareness, family, consensus, and community-created ritual, Full Moon Rising is a beacon illuminating ways of living a crative, spiritual, and cooperative lifestyle in an ever-changing world.

Located on South Whidbey Island in the heart of Puget Sound, Full Moon Rising has diverse coniferous forest and fertile pasture and is surrounded by hundreds more acres of forest between two bays. Local raptors such as owls and eagles, coyotes, and deer are among the wild residents. Intermittent streams and springs on the farm and lands on the same ridge feed the bays west and east. Full Moon Rising has the advantage of easy ferry access to the Olympic Peninsula and Cascades, the waters of Puget Sound, and the major cities on the I-5 corridor.

The Bioregional Center for Art and Ecology—Earth calls, art answers.

The Full Moon Rising Bioregional Center for Art and Ecology evolved in 1998 in response to a growing need for a local arts and education center based in the environment and the synergy of the creative talents in our community. The mission of the center is to model and teach sustainability and facilitate creativity and healing in the local environment. We believe that children and adults learn from direct experience with nature and that art and gardening support people's originality. Art provides access for adults to learn how children organize their experience and meaning; that's how we learn from them. The center will host intergenerational, creative, hands-on, educational programs integrating bioregionalism, art, organic gardening and permaculture, and wilderness-based education. [Jan99]

FUN FAMILY FARM

2127 205th St
Robinson KS 66532

Began 1982 | Pop. 12
Diet: Omnivore | Rural

The core group of three families lives on the farm and helps each other with daily living. The large group, the Wednesday Night Group, meets each week to exercise, eat dinner, talk, and play music. We publish a literary paper every week entitled the *Wednesday Night Exchange*. In it we publish original essays, poetry, short stories, a weekly cartoon, and excerpts from other sources. We recently published our 250th issue.

Besides our own intentional community, we try to build community in our small town. We organize and cook a monthly community dinner to raise funds to one day open a community store. We also publish a monthly newsletter entitled the *Robinson Voice*.

This year we began international activism by starting the People's Children's Project to raise money to build and fund an orphanage for disabled children in Haiti. [Aug99, cc]

GABALAH

Dead Gum Revival Inc
Hopkins Creek Rd
Chillingham NSW 2484
AUSTRALIA
stakiri@hotmail.com
http://www.maths.unsw.edu.au/
~brianj/gabalah.html

Began 1998
Diet: Vegetarian | Rural | Spiritual

(Also known as Dead Gum Revival.) We live close to the Earth with good spirit. We work the Earth and reap her fruits. A simple and honest life. As free as we can be! We are becoming self-sufficient and interdependent with local systems. We work with the seasons, sun, and moon. Our life here is goodness we hope leads to greatness with a big community family and lots of love and creation all around. Blessed be.

GANAS

135 Corson Ave.
Staten Island, NY 10301
(718) 720-5378
fax: 448-6842
email: ganas@well.com
web: www.ganas.org

**the residential facility
of the Foundation for Feedback Learning
A 20 year old NYC intentional community**

An experiment in open communication committed
to exploring applications of feedback to learning

G.R.O.W. II

548 Cooley Rd.
Parksville, NY 12768
For info: call, write
or email Ganas
or call (914) 295-0655

GROUP REALITIES OPEN WORKSHOPS

**a quaint country hotel,
conference center, workshop facility,
campground and concert area**

on 70 acres of woods, fields of wildflowers,
cool streams, and a spring-fed pond

Ganas' goals are to learn to focus attention, hear and respond. We want to bring reason and emotion together in daily dialogue, and to create our world, with love, the way we want it to be.

Ganas people dream of developing open minds with which to talk together and understand each other better. We want to learn how to give up competitive power plays and cooperate, care, and welcome anyone who wants to join us — with pleasure. Hopefully, if we succeed, whatever we create will be replicable.

The Foundation for Feedback Learning began in 1978. 6 of us started Ganas on Staten Is. in 1979, and we're all still here. Our population has grown from 6 to 75. Most of us are now a bonded, caring, hard working, fun loving, extended family.

People of many races, nationalities, religions, professions, and life views live together at Ganas in surprising harmony. Possibly that is because about half of us get together every day to talk about work, personal issues and anything else that comes up.

We share 9 large, mainly adjacent residences on Staten Island in a racially mixed, lower middle class, suburban neighborhood, a half-hour free ferry ride from downtown Manhattan. Many of us work in our 4 commercial buildings nearby. We renovated all of our buildings ourselves to suit our needs and our pleasure.

Most of the houses are connected by flower and vegetable gardens. We have many trees (some fruit bearing), berry bushes, a small swimming pool, a large deck, and pretty spots for hanging out. It feels rural, although we have views of the Manhattan skyline.

Living space is comfortable, attractive and very well maintained. The food is plentiful, meals are excellent and varied enough to suit most people, including a few vegans. Dinner is served at 7, but anyone who wants to can prepare meals for themselves in one of our 4 fully stocked, well-equipped community kitchens.

Cable TVs; VCRs; extensive video, music, audiotape and book libraries; an equipped exercise room, and 5 laundries are available. Biofeedback equipment, computers and software, good sound systems, slide show and projection equipment, copy facilities, and a carpentry workshop can be accessed by special arrangement.

What Ganas does and does not offer is sometimes unclear. *We are not a therapeutic community* and we don't give feedback to everyone. People have to be able to make good use of personal input before we offer it. But we do always try to help if we can.

G.R.O.W. II IS LOOKING FOR PEOPLE INTERESTED IN STARTING A NEW COMMUNITY IN OUR COUNTRY FACILITY.

We have land to garden or farm (if you like), and we will try to support whatever industry you develop if we can. If you want to start your own workshops, we will try to help, or you might partner in our conference center work.

Facilities include: cozy rooms & baths for up to 200 people (some in dorms), & space for 150 campers; a large concert area; an indoor and an outdoor stage; good dance floors & sound system; a disco; lots of good meeting, rehearsal, and workshop space, including two 40'x60' rooms; a large swimming pool; saunas; exercise equipment; a pool table; some sports equipment; games; and lots of comfortable indoor and shady outdoor lounging spots.

Affordable rates for groups: $55 a day for dble. room & bath.

Ganas people are still developing G.R.O.W. II: During the summers we host a large variety of interesting weekend events, and we work in the Ganas facility in New York City year round.

G.R.O.W. II needs competent help during the summer and responsible caretakers during the winter when we're away.

The people who form a new community at G.R.O.W. II will also be invited to participate in Ganas in NYC if they want to.

(Ganas continued)

Recycling is the community's business. Most of our work happens in 4 resale stores called Every Thing Goes. One refinishes and sells furniture; the second sells clothing. The third is a gallery. The original store sells everything else. The shops are all near our houses. They are well organized, efficiently run, and very attractive.

Visitors are welcome. If you want to work in the community, we'll discuss our needs and your skills when you get here. Approximately 40 people work in the businesses and the houses. Full time work is 40 hours a week. This pays all costs plus up to $300 per mo. and a share of the businesses' profits. Please bring money for your expenses in case you can't work with us.

If you decide to try living at Ganas for a while and don't work with us, all your expenses can be met with one fee of $500-650 a month. People staying for up to 6 nights are asked to pay $35 a day and help out some. Visitors coming for longer stays (but less than 1 mo.) can pay expenses at the rate of $200 a wk.

IF YOU WOULD LIKE TO LIVE, WORK & PLAY IN COMMUNITY WITH INTERESTING & INTERESTED PEOPLE,

If you care about good problem-solving dialogue based on truth and goodwill (and want to learn how to do it); If you have sought close relationship with varied people who hear, understand, and care about each other; If you want interesting, valuable work, and you enjoy working productively (or want to learn how to);

IF SUCH THINGS FEEL RIGHT FOR YOU ... YOU ARE INVITED TO VISIT AND PERHAPS TO LIVE & WORK WITH US

GAIA COMMUNITY

622 West 6th Ave
Denver CO 80204

303-501-9647
portlock@mscd.edu
http://clem.mscd.edu/~portlock/

Began 1994 | Pop. 4 | Forming
Diet: Omnivore | Rural/Urban

The GAIA Community is an egalitarian cooperative that is committed to establishing sustainable culture through environmental preservation, social integration, and economic stability. Our mission is to provide education and resources to individuals and groups to create and maintain sustainable communities. A formalized process of consensus decision making will be used by the GAIA Community in its every deliberation. Subcommittees will be formed to address specific needs of the community when appropriate. These committees will be chosen by and facilitated through consensus. [Feb99]

GANAS

135 Corson Ave
Staten Island NY 10301

718-720-5378
ganas@well.com
http://www.ganas.org/

Began 1978 | Pop. 74
Diet: Omnivore | Rural/Urban

(Also known as Foundation for Feedback Learning.) At Ganas, a very diverse group of about 75 people of all ages have learned how to live together harmoniously. Perhaps we get along so well because of our commitment to open dialogue. We meet daily to discuss community, work, and interpersonal issues.

We live in eight well-maintained two- or three-family buildings in a racially mixed, lower-middle-class neighborhood on Staten Island, about a half-hour free ferry ride from Manhattan. Joined backyards with many trees, berry bushes, andflower and vegetable gardens contribute to a surprisingly rural feeling.

We share excellent facilities. Food is plentiful, good, and varied. People can eat together or alone in one of several stocked, equipped kitchens.

Five commercial buildings nearby house four resale shops. We restore, repackage, and recycle furniture, artwork, clothing, household goods, and anything else we get.

In April of 1996 we bought a 54-room hotel with a lot of meeting space, an indoor stage and disco, a large campground, an outdoor concert area, a swimming pool, a pretty pond, and a charming stream, on 70 acres of woods and fields of wildflowers about 100 miles north of New York City in the Catskill Mountains.

The hotel, called G.R.O.W. II (Group Realities Open Workshops), hosts a range of workshops, conferences, and cultural or social events. We hope eventually to start a second community at G.R.O.W. II, and we're looking for people interested in this possibility.

Our purpose in both places is learning to express, hear, and understand every individual's emotional as well as conceptual truth. We value loving awareness of each other, respect for everyone's personal preferences, and above all, we highly value having a good time together. Feedback is important to us but rarely happens without specific consent. We try to offer anyone who speaks full attention and relevant response.

Ganas is populated by several separate but complementary groups. The core group serves as the board of directors. It consists of 13 people who share all their resources and do whatever needs to be done. Although application for membership in the core group is open to everyone, very few have applied, and even fewer have left.

An extended core group of 20–25 people do not have to share their resources, but they can do almost anything else the core group does, if they choose. These two groups make most of Ganas's decisions, either by consensus, majority vote, or delegated authority. Most of them work in the community and are highly motivated to do the daily job of helping to create a great place to live. Both groups are very stable, rarely leave, and have developed a lot of loving closeness over the years. The six Ganas founders are all still here.

Another approximately 35–40 people live in the Ganas housing. They generally feel they benefit a lot from the experience, but most are not much involved with Ganas's goals or activities. They tend to form subgroups with shared interests. Like everyone at Ganas, they are invited but not required to join whatever is going on. About 20–25 percent of this third group consists of short-term visitors from all over the world.

If you want to visit, you are welcome to come to dinner at no cost or to stay for a few days at $35 a day. If you choose to stay

longer, $200 a week or $500–$650 a month covers all your in-house costs. If you prefer, depending on our needs and your skills, we may be able to arrange for you to work with us for your expenses, plus up to $300 a month and a share of our profits. For more information, see our full-page ad. [Oct99]

GANDHI FARM

Brookfield Mines
Queens County Nova Scotia B0T 1X0
CANADA
http://members.rotfl.com/ gandhifarm/

Pop. 7 | Diet: Vegan | Rural

If you have interest in living a truly radical life that centers on building environmentally integrated community and works to free humanity from the bondage of our hierarchical capitalist industrial society, please consider joining us.

We live on 20 acres of rural Nova Scotia without electricity or running water. We use no fossil fuels, and heat and cook sparingly (about once a week in summer) using wood. We seek to grow all our own food for the year 2000 and beyond, thereby doing away with our need for money completely.

We presently focus on developing a no-till permaculture system of noninvasive agriculture using humanure, and natural vegan methods of increasing fertility.

We seek to minimize the agricultural workload to two hours per person per day for six months of the year, with the other six months left open for personal creativity. If this appeals to you please email or drop by any time. [Oct99, cc, sase requested]

GARDEN O' VEGAN

Garden o' Vegan
PO Box 1954
Hilo HI 96721
gardens@bigisland.net
muth@bigfoot.com
http://www.angelfire.com/ hi3/vegans/

Began Jun99 | Pop. 8 | Forming
Diet: Vegan | Rural

We started because of the apparent lack of vegan communities in good locations suitable for families with children. Our aim is for a community free of drugs, alcohol, smoke, dogma, cruelty of any form, or lifestyles not suited to family units. We are, nevertheless, open to single people.

Situated on large acreage on the big Island of Hawaii with its ideal growing conditions we expect to be almost completely self-sufficient in food and energy needs. We are totally vegan, with no animal products being permitted within community grounds. Pets are not desirable but will be considered on a case-by-case basis. Our aim of building ecofriendly homes is helped by widely available materials and by not requiring substantial structures in this climate.

Decisions will be made by full consensus until numbers make this impractical. Members are expected to contribute a combination of money or work suited to both themselves and the community.

Our vision for the future is a community almost completely nondependent on the outside world and in which its members may enjoy the simple art of living. [Oct99]

GARDENSPIRIT

290 McEntire Rd
Tryon NC 28782

828-863-4425, 828-863-2802
828-863-4425 fax
diana@ic.org
amina@teleplex.net
http://www.ic.org/gardenspirit/

Began Oct98 | Pop. 4 | Forming
Diet: No red meat | Rural | Spiritual

We're a small group of family and friends learning to live sustainably and self-reliantly on our land, as spiritual and emotional allies to one another. We live on 11 rural acres an hour south of Asheville. Many of our neighbors are homesteaders and organic gardeners. We have woods, pasture, a large organic garden, two houses (with room for people to bring or build their own dwellings), two wells, and off-grid power. One of our founders leads spiritual tours to Egypt; another is editor of *Communities* magazine. We anticipate growing to 8–10 people altogether.

Community values include supporting our various spiritual paths; living as self-reliantly as possible (organic food, solar energy, permaculture principles, bulk food, recycling wastes, alternative health care); honing our communication skills; dealing openly with conflict when it arises; having fair agreements regarding community tasks and legal and financial matters; keeping open books and having open contracts and agreements;

all members being responsible for personal finances and sharing in community expenses; honoring the financial/organizational contributions of founders as well as offering equity ownership, over time, to people who join us; and striking a balance between privacy and autonomy, on one hand, and interdependence, cooperation, and community on the other. [Sep99, sase requested]

GENTLE WORLD

PO Box 110
Paia HI 96779

808-878- 4008
gentle@alona.net
http://www.veganbooks-gentle.com/

Began 1974 | Pop. 19 | Re-Forming
Diet: Vegan | Rural | Spiritual

We are love-minded people who have joined forces to help build a better world. Together we strive to use the ideals of compassion, honesty, integrity, cleanliness, friendship, and *love* to help each other achieve our highest goals. Our foundation and common bond is veganism. Our belief is that compassion, as it is exemplified in veganism, is the next step for humanities evolution, a choice that every human being can make to help save the lives of the animals, plants, water, trees, and our own bodies and souls.

We like to live simply, in the country with lots of clean air, water, and sunshine. Sunsets and nature are a very important part of our daily lives. We have been living in Maui and are now looking to relocate to the big island, which is wonderful and less commercial. Another important aspect of our lives is the belief that the greatest tool we have to lift us from a limited world to a higher plane of unlimited possibilities is to be *in love*. Together we attempt to make a supportive environment that is conducive to making this ideal a reality . [May99, sase requested, sase required]

GESUNDHEIT! INSTITUTE

HC 64 Box 268
Hilsboro WV 24946
land@achooservice.com
http://www.patchadams.org/

Began 1972 | Pop. 9 | Re-Forming
Diet: Omnivore | Rural

Gesundheit Institute is a group of healers, visionaries, and clowns working to build a

healing community based on humor, compassion, generosity, and enthusiastic hard work.

Much more than a hospital, Gesundheit is and will further develop into a microcosm of vibrant life, integrating art, education, fun, and friendship with health care. Gesundheit's future home is on 310 acres of wooded land in West Virginia.

Together, we have created a four-level multipurpose building, a five-level staff dwelling with onion domes, a three-acre pond, and a ton of friendships since the land site was purchased in 1980. With the collaboration of people from all the healing arts, we are working to build an ecological, integrated community and a state-of-the-art facility. Our vision includes a 40-bed hospital where good health is a laughing matter, where "patients" and "caregivers" work and play together, and where the spirit of community is itself the most potent medicine.

Patch Adams, our founder, presently lectures and performs for caregivers around the world in order to raise awareness and money toward the design and building of the Gesundheit community. The land staff in West Virginia stewards the property and hosts a one- to two-week summer work camp. We invite our volunteers to participate in making community alive on a daily basis. How can you help? Please send a silly postcard and inquire about our volunteer program!

Wahoo! [Mar99, sase requested, no openings]

GINGER RIDGE FARMS

RR 2 Box 4051
Kapoho HI 96778

808-965-7622
hjames3432@aol.com

Began Feb99 | Pop. 9 | Forming

People already with practices (tai chi, yoga, etc.) and healthy diets in place who understand how to work with others and can contribute strength and clarity to building a bubble—a small part of this universe where the choice of "yes, I can" comes very easily. The format as it stands now is 15 acres that have been farmed organically for the past 10 years with the potential to acquire 35 more as a community land trust. A 4,000-square-foot building with three-phase electricity, plumbing, phone. Farm equipment, mechanic shop. Deep soil, 2,000-foot elevation—can be cool and rainy. Production has been ginger, beans, corn, and baby salad mix. We need people who enjoy working hard on the land, growing food, fixing machinery, building, marketing, preparing great food, exercising, meditating, massaging. A little, but not too much processing, of the emotional psychobabble. Can you clearly tell someone what to do if you're running a project? Can you follow directions simply and easily? Do you have any expertise? Do you have any money? This is real life—you want it to be special. Make it special except what's expectable. Do what's do-able! [Sep99, sase required]

GLEN IVY

25000 Glen Ivy Rd
Corona CA 92883

909-277-8711, 909-277-8701

Began 1977 | Pop. 25
Diet: Omnivore | Rural | Spiritual

The Glen Ivy Community thrives as a working example of the practical application of spiritual principles in everyday living. This necessitates an evolving design of community life that invites risk taking and creativity, as vision and operational practicalities come together. Community members accomplish this balance by working and learning together in an atmosphere of respect and open communication. The community values the uniqueness of each individual, recognizing that personal development is key if the collective is to flourish. Glen Ivy is also a gracious and love-filled home, both for its residents and for the many who come to visit. The activities of the Glen Ivy Community have emerged in service to its primary spiritual purpose—a collective revelation of the one spirit in form. The Glen Ivy Community was established in 1977 in accordance with the spiritual purposes of the International Emissary program: to assist in carrying forward a work of spiritual regeneration of humanity, under the inspiration of the spirit of God. [Nov98, cc]

Don't miss the FIC's **late-breaking news**— send away for your

Directory Updates!

Use the tear-out card at the back of the book.

GLENDOWER

PO Box 520291
Independence MO 64052

816-252-6023
Glendower@ic. org

Began 1995 | Pop. 3 | Re-Forming
Diet: Omnivore | Urban | Spiritual

Currently just a married couple hoping to achieve maximum ecological savings by expanding to a larger family. We want three to four more older adults to join with us and combine resources. We seek those who will be compatible with neopagan values and polyamory. We share common expenses and make decisions by consensus. New members will eventually be considered part of the family. We envision a six-month to one-year time period as necessary to become a primary member. "Open relationships" rather than monogamy require the ability to resist jealousy and possessiveness. Those with previous experience with nonmonogamous relationships, and those over the age of 40, have best potential to be part of our community. Singles, couples, Earth-centered should write us for more information. We are non-smokers, do not use alcohol, but have four cats. Glendower is Celtic for "Valley of Water." [Sep99, sase requested]

GLENWOOD COOPERATIVE

503 University St
W Lafayette IN 47906

765-743-3880

Began 1939 | Pop. 34
Diet: Omnivore | Rural/Urban

Glenwood Cooperative House is about 33 young women who live together in a system of 12 other male or female houses at Purdue University. Our house prides itself on academics, a sisterhood, friendship, athletics, community service, social functions, grand prix, leadership, and sisterly love. We have a house with 12 bedrooms, a kitchen where we all have kitchen duties, a formal living room, a TV room, and many other rooms for fun and socializing. Cooperative living provides the opportunity for women and men both to live and work together at college while providing a fun and friendly atmosphere.

Members go through an eight-week pledgeship and learn about the cooperative system and Glenwood. They also develop a special bond with their pledge sisters. Glenwood is a special place, and the memo-

ries last a lifetime. We get involved in community services such as visiting nursing homes, spring rally, and a football philanthropy. We also participate in intramurals as a house. Glenwood has a big winning tradition. We also got involved in the grand prix last year with our own kart, and we are very excited about the new Glenwood tradition. Glenwood is an exciting place with great traditions and a wonderful sisterhood. [Sep99]

GLOBAL VILLAGE/SCHOOL OF THE AMERICAS

21 Royal Palm Way Suite 202
Boca Raton FL 33432

561-368-2687
globalvillageschool.org@yahoo.com
joanna500@yahoo.com
http://geocities.com/
globalvillageschool/

Began 1997 | Pop. 17
Diet: Omnivore | Rural/Urban | Spiritual

The purpose of our community is to promote world peace and environmental stewardship through experiential education. Our core group is currently in south Florida and is planning to purchase property in Costa Rica by 2002. This learning center/community will have approximately 30 bedrooms (to start) and focuses primarily on Spanish, English, and environmental education. We're also getting equipment to run hiking, rafting, scuba, mountain biking, and horseback trips around Central and South America. Future plans include centers in an Arab-speaking area (probably Egypt) and a Mandarin-speaking area (either Taiwan or Singapore). Our centers are powered with solar, wind, and water; have organic garden, aqua, and poultry farms; are built with stone and natural woods; and have large outdoor living spaces. Most meals are communal, all with vegetarian options. We have a communal Sunday spiritual celebration ... and various workshops in world religions, philosophy, yoga, dance, art, and more. Most community members are educators or multimedia developers, several now with doctorates and master's degrees in languages, science, anthropology, world religions, communication technologies, distance learning (thru Internet), video production, software design, but there are "significant" others with outside jobs or who do construction, food prep, driving, marketing, accounting, etc. We'd like you to join us

Additions and corrections: Email: directory@ic.org, Web: http://directory.ic.org/, Mail: RR 1 Box 156-D, Rutledge MO 63563, USA.

Listings

here in Florida for our weekly Sunday celebration and potluck dinner! Overnight accommodations are possible. [Oct99, sase required]

GOLDEN EAGLE TRADITIONAL INDIAN CAMP

PO Box 700
Carlin NV 89822

Began 1998 | Pop. 4 | Re-Forming
Diet: Omnivore | Rural | Spiritual

(Also known as Meta Tantay.) We are a traditional Native American community. We live much the same way as our ancestors did as tribes and bands. We live in harmony with all nature. Respect for all things that have life is basic to our way of life. Because we are just reorganizing after many years of inactivity, we cannot accept new members at this time, but visitors are welcomed. Our future plans include a spiritual learning center that will house Rolling Thunder's videos, tapes, and writings and his large personal library. We strive for self-sufficiency through gardens, livestock, solar power, and wind power. We are not Christians or any other foreign religion. Our spiritual way of life is 24 hours a day. We perform the ceremonies of our ancestors as taught to us by Rolling Thunder. We are not following the ways of one particular tribe versus another,

as Rolling Thunder was an intertribal medicine man. We have been called political and activists as for us there are no separate categories. All things are related. Our task in this life we believe is to make things better for everyone: plants, animals, mountains, people, and Mother Earth as well as the entire cosmos. But too, we are not passive. We choose to live as free as possible under the yoke of the foreigners. [Nov98, sase required, no openings]

GOODENOUGH COMMUNITY

2007 - 33rd Ave So
Seattle WA 98144

206-323-4653, 206-322-3279
goodenuf@wolfenet.com
http://www.wolfenet.com/
~goodenuf/

Began 1969 | Pop. 101
Diet: Omnivore | Rural/Urban | Spiritual

(Also known as American Association for the Furtherance of Community.) The Goodenough Community may be thought of as a small town with a governing council, school, church, and small businesses with potential for growth. This is a town with a challenging invitation.

"Come, live here if you are interested in exploring your fullest potential as a human being while collaborating with others who

are so engaged. We offer a variety of programs and services designed to fit your needs for development and transformation. This isn't a place for folks who want quick and easy solutions to life's issues. This is a place where we intend to accomplish our individual growth through our collective ability to make life in this town the best living and learning environment for everyone, young and old."

A nonprofit educational organization, the Goodenough Community is better thought of as a core of committed friends who are organized by a selected council that is required to demonstrate the mission, goals, and current work plan—all of which express the values and priorities of our membership. While many of our programs are offered to the public, we seek persons who are interested in preparing themselves for living in community.

The mission of the community is demonstrated by the contribution it has made to many individuals who, having been healed and trained here, have made their way into other communities and creative social experiments. We have also demonstrated that a multiresidential community can create deep and lasting bonds while also encouraging individual freedom and creativity. This community has existed for 30 years, although its roots go back years before that into prior communities. Our legal name, the American

Key to bracketed text: cc = cannot commit to prompt correspondance, sase = self-addressed stamped envelope

Association for the Furtherance of Community, declares our real purpose. In the early 1980s, we formalized our relationship with each other through a covenant (see below), only to discover that most of us were unable to keep some specific promises of our covenant. Thus, we have come to offer a therapeutic and educational training program that enables people to feel empowered as individuals as well as feeling socially secure. A core of experienced trainers and mental-health practitioners consults within our community as well as being available to other organizations and communities.

Our covenant is as follows.

The purpose of the Goodenough Community is to create a way of life, a culture we share. By entering into this covenant we define our community and shape all our relationships. We agree to be accountable to each other for living this covenant.

As a member of the Goodenough Community, I commit to being the best version of myself:
• By entering fully into life's experiences,
• By giving myself fully to the process of transformation through the expression of love,
• By trusting the good intentions of each of us,
• By relating with respect and acceptance,
• By making and keeping my agreements with great care,
• By being constant through conflict,
• By honoring and respecting leadership in others as a method of developing the leader in myself,
• By taking responsibility for my unique and significant role in the Universe, and

• By acknowledging the inner and interconnectedness of all creation, thus making myself safe and at home in the Universe.
So be it! [Sep99]

GOODRICH FARM COOPERATIVE

RD 1 Box 934
Hardwick VT 05843

802-472-2242
Houriet@PlainField.bypass.com

Began 1997 | Pop. 6 | Forming | Rural
Goodrich Farm Cooperative aims to be a cooperative community based on agriculture with both common and separate houses: 55.5 acres; 25 years in organic-vegetable production. We had a bad fire last year and are rebuilding the main house this year. Looking for people with some experience and self-motivation. [Dec98, sase requested]

GRAIL COMMUNITY, THE

125 Waxwell Ln
Pinner
Middx HA5 3ER, England
UNITED KINGDOM

0181 866 2195, 0181 866 0505
0181 866 1408 fax
waxwell@compuserve.com
grailcentre@compuserve.com

Began 1930
Diet: Omnivore | Rural/Urban | Spiritual

Whatever work we undertake, we see it as a means of enabling people to grow toward

their full potential and of healing the relationship between ourselves and our environment. Our ministry is expressed in many ways: organizing and running seminars/workshops; counseling and stress management; helping people on their spiritual quest; caring for those who use our "poustinias"; cooking, cleaning, and gardening. We also run a small center with 10 acres of garden. We enjoy celebrating and taking every opportunity to mark events: liturgical celebrations, feasts, and stages within the life of the community and of individuals. [Apr99]

GREATER WORLD COMMUNITY

PO Box 1041
Taos NM 87571

505-751-0462
earthship@earthship.org
http://www.earthship.org/

Began 1996

The Greater World Community is Taos's first Earthship Community. Located 15 minutes from historic Taos, New Mexico, the Greater World Community is 634 acres of rolling mesa with great views of the Sangre de Cristo Mountains and the town of Taos. Two and a half miles of the community front New Mexico State Highway 64 W.

The Greater World Community is divided into four phases of development. This first phase, the Gravel Pit Reclamation Project, also called Lemuria, is located on

Additions and corrections: Email: directory@ic.org, Web: http://directory.ic.org/, Mail: RR 1 Box 156-D, Rutledge MO 63563, USA.

the northeast corner of the Greater World Subdivision. By combining the Earthship's innovative water-catch-and-reuse systems with permaculture techniques to trap and direct surface-water runoff, the Gravel Pit Reclamation Project will demonstrate how to rejuvenate and reclaim a formerly worthless piece of discarded land.

Residents of the Greater World will also enjoy access to 347 acres of community land, open green space with hiking, biking, and parks. There will be a community center in the gravel pit with a basketball court and amphitheater. Greater World members will have access to backup water from the solar-powered community well.

A major objective is to reduce the economic and institutional barriers between people and sustainable housing. [Sep99, cc, sase requested]

GREEN HOUSE COOPERATIVE

315 Eastern SE
Grand Rapids MI 49503

616-831-5987
akkerhug@hotmail.com
http://www.geocities.com/
RainForest/3421/

Began 1993 | Pop. 7 | Re-Forming
Diet: Vegetarian | Urban | Spiritual

We are a small housing cooperative, living simply with green values in communal anarchy. We do urban agriculture, housing rehab, political activism, and hospitality to the homeless. We are home to the Grand Rapids Area Greens and have been influenced by Quakerism and the Rainbow Family of Living Light. We are bicycle fanatics, mostly vegetarian, and have mixed sexual orientations. We like visitors but please call ahead. Floor space and camping available. [Dec98, no openings]

GREENHOUSE

716 N 63rd St
Seattle WA 98103

206-781-9110
joanhill@msn.com
lcanar@speakeasy.org

Began 1989 | Pop. 4
Diet: Vegetarian | Urban

We are a vegetarian, nonsmoking, cooperative household of four women. Our food and cooking arrangement is flexible. We recycle, compost, and choose various household products with ecological and political considerations. Some of our various current interests include backpacking; yoga; nutrition and natural health care; "exotic" vegetarian cooking; organic gardening; city and country exploration; rabble-rousing around various ecological, political, and feminist issues; and, lest we sound frightfully healthy, occasional ice cream and video nights. [Oct99, sase required]

GREENING LIFE COMMUNITY

Greening Life Ln
Shermansdale PA 17090

Began 1973 | Pop. 12
Diet: Vegetarian | Rural

Greening Life was established in 1972 on a 135-acre farm in south central Pennsylvania. We are a planned, intentional community. We built our own homes, roads, and water system. We follow organic-farming practices on our 50 acres of tillable land and in our 2-acre garden, which produces the majority of our vegetables. Our orchard is providing us with fruit.

The effort to create a balance of cooperative living, with time for individual and family has been a rewarding struggle. Growth in spirit, both individual and community, is an important part of our life together. We respect all persons and value their opinions as a voice to help guide us. We are open to share our spirit and resources with other individuals and groups. [Feb99, no openings]

GREENWOOD

258 West Greenwood Ave
Lansdowne PA 19050

610-623-5656

Began 1995 | Pop. 4 | Forming
Diet: Vegan

Greenwood is a small home in Lansdowne, Pennsylvania, a suburb just outside of Philadelphia. Greenwood is a house of transition—taking people who are interested in coming closer to nature without them moving directly to the woods. We feel places of transition like Greenwood in and around cities are important to us all.

We'd like to make Greenwood a model home (which it is now becoming) and a physical manifestation of permaculture projects, edible landscapes, condensed gardening, daily walks, yoga, mind-body work, projects using recycled materials, raw foods, community service, natural healing techniques, spiritual rituals, financial stability, and nonownership (land trust). In the future we hope to branch out to other like-minded groups and acquire more land for growing and to expand self-sufficiency.

We have an 80-page booklet that describes our values and our daily routines and contains pictures of completed projects and ideas for potential ones. Our next project is a steam room and after this a greenhouse. [Oct96, sase requested]

GREGORY HOUSE

1617 Washtenaw
Ann Arbor MI 48104

734-213-6816, 734-662-4414 Office

Began 1995 | Pop. 30 | Urban

Founded in 1995, Karl D. Gregory House is the newest addition to the ICC. Because our house is the only substance-free house in the ICC, we pride ourselves on a house culture quite unique from that of many other co-ops. We tend to attract friendly, slightly wacky housemates. Just because we're substance free doesn't mean we don't know how to have fun! Our house is usually quiet enough to get your work done, but there's just about always something going on, whether it be housemates goofing around in our large basement TV/recreation room, making up something tasty in our beautiful kitchen, or just hanging in our living room, enjoying a cozy fire or engaged in a death match of Twister or a philosophical discussion about the true meaning of *bologna*. We pride ourselves on being one of the cleanest houses in the ICC. Most of our rooms have original hardwood floors, and we have a large number of single rooms, although new members will probably spend their first year in a double. We have house meetings every two weeks and are one of the few houses to still run on a modified-consensus system for decision making; i.e., for an important house decision to be made, 85 percent of our members must agree. Call to arrange to join us for dinner and get to know the house and its members! Gregory House is a great place to live, filled with great people. It's nice to go home after class and actually have a *home* to go to. [Jul99, cc, sase required]

Key to bracketed text: cc = cannot commit to prompt correspondance, sase = self-addressed stamped envelope

GRIMSTONE COMMUNITY

Grimstone Manor
Yelverton
Devon PL20 7QY, England
UNITED KINGDOM

01822 854358, 01822 852318 fax
GrimstoneManor@compuserve.com

Began 1990
Diet: No red meat | Rural | Spiritual

Grimstone Community was originally formed in 1990 to buy and develop the existing successful workshop center at Grimstone Manor. A magical spot on the edge of Dartmoor, it is set in 27 acres of garden, pasture, and wilderness. Members make a financial investment in the property and join the business partnership. We are presently nine adults, two children, and three families who have joined as affiliate members, investing as nonresidential co-owners of the property. Our main focus as a community is to service the many varied self-development groups who come to work in, receive, and feed the special energies here. We meet once a week, alternating business and process meetings. All decisions are taken by consensus between equal partners. Members focalize different areas of work, but, generally, all work is shared and paid at the same hourly rate. Short-term volunteers work in return for their keep. We are moving toward building a sense of community on material, emotional, and spiritual levels. Together we eat daily, meditate weekly, laugh, work, and grow. There are local community links through circle dancing, chanting, and other events. We are open to new members with capital, flexibility, and enthusiasm. [Apr99]

GUAYRAPÁ

C/Estragón s/n
E-43364 Montral (Tarragona)
SPAIN

+34-977-846-887, +34-977-760-156
+34-977-846-887 fax
sarvam@teleline.es
guayrapa@teleline.es

Began 1992 | Diet: No red meat | Rural

Since the beginning in 1992 Guayrapá has been a private country house owned by a couple and their two young adult sons, with one hectare farmland and its own organic garden, vegetarian but not strictly so, with some yoga and therapeutic activities and no obligation or clear form of guidance in the

Spanish Tarragona Mountains at an 850-meter elevation with a view of the sea. The location and an interest in personal growth led to the idea of preparing the farm for holiday, weekend, and group visitors to gain daily sustenance and make the house run. Later, with several people in constant residence, the sense of community began. Our form of co-living is defined individually. Two persons are paid by the community for doing cleaning, cooking, and gardening. One earns his own money and contributes with it, receiving food and other services in exchange. The common base is the desire for a good and deep relationship between the members. The owners are the leaders, but nevertheless many decisions are arrived at and discussed in almost weekly meetings. Guayrapá is a really good place to live in the countryside, open to visitors (paying or working when there is need for it) or for long-term members with economic independence. [Jul99]

GWERIN HOUSING ASSOCIATION

Registered Office
121 Hagley Rd
Oldswinford Stourbridge
West Midlands DY8 1RD, England
UNITED KINGDOM

+44 (01384) 396 582
+44 (01384) 832 537
+44 (01384) 863 982 fax
gwerin@twonky.demon.co.uk
magick5@hotmail.com
http://www.twonky.demon.co.uk/
gwerin/

Began 1979 | Diet: Omnivore | Urban

Gwerin is a community of five houses, four of which are part of a Victorian terrace. These large houses are shared between members of the Association. Each house is run differently, according to the individuals who live there. We have weekly meetings where the membership comes together to discuss the running of the Association.

We are a mixture of individuals, and as a community have no particular ideological focus.

We operate on a small budget produced by rents, and the labor of all members in renovation of the properties and supporting the decisions of the weekly group meetings. Every aspect of the Association is open to scrutiny by all members who, in turn, volunteer their skills to ensure that the rules of

the constitution are tempered by the day-to-day reality of life in the community.

Gwerin also strives to support adults with special needs, in a community atmosphere, using our strong ties with Dudley Social Services.

The Coachouse Project offers various arts/crafts activities to the local community. It is a partnership with St. Mary's Church, and Gwerin's members living in the cottage next door help oversee the project. [Mar99]

HAIRAKHANDI LOVE HASHRAM

VOC/LO Villarosa 56
Corniole
I-06026 Pietralunga (PG)
ITALY

075-933074

Began 1993 | Pop. 7
Diet: Vegetarian | Rural | Spiritual

Haidakandi Love is a center inspired by Baba JI where the primary focus is on faith, great cosmic energy (God), and spiritual and emotional work on oneself. Fundamental is the discovery of the void within, and devotion becomes the instrument that fills this void. The fire of devotion creates union between the people in their diversity. We work with energy, teach Reiki, and work on various aspects of the person—physical, emotional, and spiritual. Healing and devotion form the basis of the center. All the cultures of the Earth are invited to offer their teachings. We are preparing to be self-sufficient in electricity, water, and fruit and vegetables. We hope to have another family living and working with us in the near future to create total self-sufficiency. [Aug99]

HARBIN HOT SPRINGS

PO Box 782
Middletown CA 95461

707-987-2477, 707-987-0616 fax
comments@harbin.org
http://www.harbin.org/

Began 1972 | Pop. 180 | Rural | Spiritual

(Also known as Heart Consciousness Church.) Harbin Hot Springs is a nonprofit retreat center owned by Heart

---

Additions and corrections: Email: directory@ic.org, Web: http://directory.ic.org/, Mail: RR 1 Box 156-D, Rutledge MO 63563, USA.

Consciousness Church. It is operated and maintained by more than 150 members of the Religious Order of Heart Consciousness. We welcome guests from around the world who travel here to soak in our natural-spring pools, bask on our clothing-optional sun decks, receive massages from our certified therapists, attend workshops, hike our 1,160 acres, or otherwise simply relax. [May99]

HAWK CIRCLE COOPERATIVE

**4681 Lincoln Heights Dr
Cedar Rapids IA 52403**

319-247-0952

Began 1993 | Pop. 6
Diet: Omnivore | Rural/Urban

The Hawk Circle Cooperative was formed for the purpose of providing the benefits of cooperative living to our members. We believe that cooperative living has something to offer every member of the wider culture and provides a response to the environment and economic issues that we all face. We also prefer to focus on the things that people have in common rather than only on what divides them.

Our group currently consists of four adults and two teenagers. We use consensus decision making. We try to practice clear communications skills in every day life. We do not practice a particular brand of politics, religion, or diet at Hawk Circle. We believe that there is value in all perspectives, and we choose to try and honor these and make room for each other's beliefs.

We have commitment to recycling, and we are active in energy conservation. We are an expense-sharing group rather than an income-sharing group. This means that we set a monthly budget and share these expenses together. However, we all have our own sources of income. We value service to the wider society and encourage activities that serve a variety of causes.

Hawk Circle is located on the outskirts of Cedar Rapids, Iowa. We have a newly remodeled seven-bedroom house on a three-acre hillside surrounded by trees. Our members enjoy gardening, cooking, brewing, movies, paintball, and poultry raising as well as computers and Web-site design. We also have members interested in alternative building design. [Oct99, cc]

HEADLANDS

**14775 Front Rd
Stella Ontario K0H 250
CANADA**

**613-389-3444
headlands@sympatico.ca**

Began 1971 | Pop. 9
Diet: Omnivore | Rural

Headlands was founded in 1971 by 5 people on Amherst Island, Ontario. The commune dissolved amicably in 1975. Three communal members and a friend bought the farming assets and most of the land from the other 12 members.

We are now 5 adults and 4 teens living cooperatively. The adults are equal shareholders in Topsy Farms, which owns the real estate and a sheep flock of over 1,000 ewes.

Headlands rents two homes from Topsy and charges each adult a levy for room and board. Each adult member is responsible for their monthly headlands' payment. We support each other's income work.

Each house is private; those living there decide how things are done. We cooperate with each other in a spirit of mutual self-interest enriched by feelings of family and friendship. The sharing of resources and abilities allows each of us more personal freedom than we would have in more traditional living and working arrangements.

We find our land on the shores of Lake Ontario to be very beautiful. Each of us is active in the island community (400 people): fire department; publishing a newsletter; volunteer teaching. Three of the teen-agers are in two rock bands that practice here. [Sep99, sase required, no openings]

HEALING GRACE SANCTUARY

Shelburne Falls MA 01370

413-625-9386

Pop. 1 | Forming
Diet: Omnivore | Rural | Spiritual

*The "First World" lives as if
nature has it all wrong. Creating
Dead World, all institutionalized
de-natured.* COME BACK TO LIFE! *Come home
Reclaim
the Healing Grace Sanctuary
living within you, and all.*

So far Healing Grace is ... *a place:* an 85-acre nature sanctuary and quiet retreat embraced in a magical river bend. Tipis, wigwam, and old barn. We're unplugged and drug free, guided by voluntary simplic-ity, voluntary service, and the voice of spirit. Our beliefs: *the* most simple optimistic empowering we can possibly imagine.

A dream: We envision a tribal village ... a small family-centered clan of gentle souls living together and keenly devoted to ultra-wholesome choices in all realms: patterned after natural systems and truly sustainable ways, living outdoors as much as possible. Warm, loving relationships; money and rank get no say in who we honor, help, or invite into our midst. Trusting spirit for guidance, savoring life and each other, all ages inter-mixed. To us, *a seamless web of connection* with nature, spirit, kin is birthright, lifeblood.

Potential: Focalizers are welcome for permaculture garden, indigenous structures and skills, native music and crafts, rituals and celebrations, group process, re-evolutionary education, innovative community service, social transmutation. Top priorities:
- Y2K balms
- Empower youth
- Boost powers of mind (prayer works; thought creates)
- Defuse blind spots/divisiveness/one-right-way codes and the monoculture, separation, and abuse they spawn
- Social change via *personal change* ... 180 degree turns in attitude and focus, beliefs, connectedness. Boosting our *social* immune system via inner filters regained. (The microcosm *is* the macrocosm.)
- *We aim to look in the mirror often:* via an enthused, open forum ... avoiding the pitfalls many groups succumb to. Sharing needs, offerings, bold dreams, loyal dissent, change. Unveiling blind spots.
- Are we nurturing all facets of what it means to be human?
- What do and don't we like and why? Do *we* do that?
- Who practices what we preach? Do we notice, welcome, and embrace them?
- Who is *not* among us and why? Are they excluded by money? Age? Rank? Need? By our failure to see their gifts? Does their absence benefit or diminish us?
- Do we own up to and, with the group's support, heal our woundedness and our hunger for touch and tender loving care? *Let's detox from divisive social conditioning,* living into and popularizing alternative ways. Becoming awesome gardeners of heart and spirit ... dissolving elitism and external authority ... replacing all monoculture, oppression, double-talk with ultrahumaneness, win-win, and "How can we do better still?"

Key to bracketed text: cc = cannot commit to prompt correspondance, sase = self-addressed stamped envelope

Is this your heart song? *Call us!* (Or write with your enthusiasms and hugs, phone number, and best time to call.) Then come intern with us in:

• Innovative service
• Rustic indigenous ways
• Paradigm shift *now* ... reLanguaging dominion to communion, judge and blame to acceptance, love.

(Freewill donations warmly welcome.) Strong medicine/bright tomorrows. ImPossible dreams. Shall we dance? Hugs abounding and Namasté. [Jul99, cc, sase required]

HEARTHAVEN

3728 Tracy
Kansas City MO 64109
816-531-8164, 816-561-0531
maril@prodigy.net

Began 1988 | Pop. 6 | Spiritual

We are an urban community of six members who seek to model a way of living from the heart that involves living responsibly, nonviolently, and ecologically. We put a high value on the practice of hospitality to all beings and on living life out of love rather than fear. We are open to being joined by one or two individuals at a time who wish to live in and contribute to the healing ways of our household. We are also open to visitors depending on schedules and needs. [Sep99, sase requested]

HEARTLIGHT CENTER

67138 Shimmel Rd
Sturgis MI 49091
616-651-2234

Began 1987 | Pop. 16

Heartlight Center is a spiritual center dedicated to seeking first the kingdom of God. It is available to help provide a way for those of us who truly wish to love God our Heavenly Father with all our hearts, our minds, and our souls; to break free from the bondage of our ego world; to discover the will of God within our lives; and to finally move out of illusion into reality. Although there is a community of people living at Heartlight Center, this is not the primary focus of the center. We have come together with a deep commitment to love God so wholly that we entrust our entire self into his hands. There is a daily program of meditation, selfless service, reflection, reading,

and vegetarian meals, as well as weekly classes and a Sunday inspirational service. Heartlight uses both Eastern and Western sacred texts, and extensive study is made of the life and writings of Francis of Assisi. There is also a nongraded elementary school designed to help children and adult volunteers to learn that we are all children of the universe, learning to love God and each other with no limitation. We do welcome serious inquiries. So, if your heart resonates to this simple, yet intensive, way of life, you can call to arrange for a visit. If you would like to know about other ways to get involved in what is happening at Heartlight Center, please feel free to call or write. [Nov98]

HEARTSONG

P O Box 227
Orono ME 04473

Began 1999 | Pop. 6 | Forming
Diet: Vegan | Rural | Spiritual

We have developed a truly close, and caring, sense of community, or synergistic relational we- ness, grounded in a new understanding of optimal relationship/communication and personal growth, in which hearts, minds, and spirits are deeply empathically connected in a state of nondualistic communion, or harmonious attunement. Through this, as well as other means, we help our members awaken to their unique heartsong—i.e., their inherent archetypal life theme; basic life function; or most attractive life dream, vision, mission, or destiny—that provides them with an optimal sense of caring and joyful, regenerative, life-energy flow. This produces healings of all kinds, as well as the optimal actualization of their highest natural real-life potentials. Their unique individual heartsong is gradually integrated into our community heartsong, and each serves to mutually enhance the other. Relatedly, we have developed innovative programs in transformative education, arts, mentoring, holistic healing, and optimal creativity. We are seeking new members who are predominantly relationship oriented and tend to be open, honest, warmhearted, and sincerely caring, as well as cooperative, rather than habitually conflictual, in their relationship with others. [Jul99, sase requested]

HEARTWOOD COHOUSING

800 Heartwood Ln
Bayfield CO 81122

970-884-2196
ganesh@rmi.net
http://www.heartwoodcohousing.com/

Began Dec99 | Pop. 65 | Forming
Diet: Omnivore | Rural

(Also known as San Juan Cohousing.) Imagine a cohousing neighborhood with a deep sense of community nestled gently on just a few acres within 250 acres of pine forest and pastureland. Now imagine that community located in southwest Colorado where the biggest mountains in the state are just minutes away and the red-rock canyons of the Colorado Plateau are close enough for a day hike. That's Heartwood Cohousing. [Sep99, no openings]

HEARTWOOD COMMUNITY INCORPORATED TE NGAKAU O TE RAKAU

51 Browns Rd
Christchurch 8001
NEW ZEALAND

NZ 03-355-4746 (city)
NZ 03-312-3058 (rural)
NZ 03-355-4794 fax
katet@ihug.co.nz
http://www.converge.org.nz/evcnz/

Began 1970 | Pop. 30
Diet: Omnivore | Rural/Urban

(Also known as Community Assistance Incorporated (1970-97), Chippenham, Mansfield, Gricklegrass Community.) Heartwood Community was founded in 1970 on the alternative-society visions of that era. In 1971 a large gabled mansion, Chippenham, was purchased for communal living; in 1972 an adjoining property, Mansfield, was added; in 1973 a small farm, Gricklegrass, and a small bakery were purchased, and the bakery was run as a cooperative for some years. Each house is shared by 8–12 people, sharing meals, work, and renovation tasks but with individuals retaining their own income and independent lifestyles and varying beliefs. The houses are owned by the community, a nonprofit society, and residents do not need to invest money—just commit to community goals and pay a weekly rental. Each of the three properties runs more or less as an autonomous community, but they work together as one society. Chippenham and Mansfield share common grounds (especially the kids!), a beautiful enclave not far from the center of Christchurch City (population 320,000). Gricklegrass, with 30 acres, mainly in pasture, some organic crops, is near Oxford nearly 30 miles away. Visitors and guests (small charge), especially from other communities, are welcome; prior contact preferable. Heartwood also publishes a small newsletter, *Chip n Away*, for its own members and sharing news between 30 communities around New Zealand. [Apr99]

HEARTWOOD INSTITUTE

220 Harmony Ln
Garberville CA 95542

707-923-5000
hello@heartwoodinstitute.com
http://www.heartwoodinstitute.com/Community.html

Began 1982 | Pop. 96
Diet: No red meat | Rural

We are a unique and healing vocational school that provides a supportive community environment for staff, faculty, students, and work-exchange participants. We are a teaching community of dedicated individuals who care how men and women live in balance with Mother Earth, who care about the truth of our experience with one another. Basing our lives on the principles of integrity, authenticity, and truth, we see ourselves as a role model for human relationships, self-actualization, and stewardship of our planet.

As an organization, Heartwood is in action, playing an important role as a catalyst for planetary healing through personal transformation. Vocational training in the natural healing arts, workshops, and experience in community living are our vehicle. We share three vegetarian meals a day. The resident staff members get room, board, and a stipend. Participants in the work-exchange program pay a small fee and get meals and classes. Work-exchange participants camp in dry months and share small rooms in the wet months. Our land is 240 acres of mountains, meadows, and forests in the rural mountains of northern California. [Sep99, sase requested]

HEATHCOTE COMMUNITY

21300 Heathcote Rd
Freeland MD 21053

410-343-3478
heathcote@s-o-l.org
http://www.s-o-l.org/heathcote/heathcote.html

Pop. 16
Diet: No red meat | Rural

Heathcote is a small nurturing group of adults and children who welcome and honor diversity in a context of healthy, loving, and sustainable living. We are located on 44 acres of wooded stream valley that is part of the School of Living community land trust. We believe that we have a responsibility to care for the land and each other, treating the Earth and one another with dignity and respect.

In community we support one another in living a life that we love, which includes sharing food, work, play, monthly sing-alongs, meditation, and celebration. We make decisions by consensus and foster deeper relationships through weekly meetings, informal gatherings, and quarterly retreats.

We strive to discover, practice, and share ever-more-sustainable ways of living. Our

Key to bracketed text: cc = cannot commit to prompt correspondance, sase = self-addressed stamped envelope

current projects focus on creating a living demonstration of permaculture principles and ecological sustainability, including the expansion of our organic gardens and orchards and the renovation of existing structures.

We sponsor an annual permaculture design course, hands-on workshops, and other educational events at our conference center, located in a 150-year-old grist mill. Our vision includes building new Earth-friendly community residences, developing community businesses on-site, and expanding our educational program.

We offer full and associate membership options and welcome inquiries from people who share our passion for creating a better world. We hope to see you at one of our monthly visitor weekends. [Oct99, sase requested]

HEI WA HOUSE

**530 Miller Ave
Ann Arbor MI 48103**

**734-994-4937
heiwa@umich.edu
http://www.ic.org/heiwa/**

Began 1985 | Pop. 6
Diet: Vegetarian | Urban

HeiWa was founded in 1985. Our current membership capacity is six members. We are a vegetarian household, and our membership tends to be environmentally conscious, politically active, lesbian/gay/bisexual/transgender celebratory, and musically inclined. Our home has often served as a meeting space for political and social-justice organizations, personal-growth groups, and community-strengthening gatherings.

In June 1999, we purchased our house, realizing a 14-year dream of establishing a permanent location for HeiWa. We continue to dream about expanding to include other houses on our block, creating a cooperative neighborhood in northwest Ann Arbor.

HeiWa's mission statement is as follows: to provide affordable cooperative housing for a diverse membership through cooperatively owned property, communal living, and resource sharing, while upholding principles of sustainability, peace, economic justice, lifelong cooperative living, and involvement in local community. [Sep99, cc, sase requested]

HENDERSON COOPERATIVE HOUSE

**1330 Hill St
Ann Arbor MI 48104
http://www.housing.umich.edu/
reshals/hh.html**

Began 1945 | Pop. 31
Diet: Omnivore | Urban

Henderson provides a less-expensive alternative to both residence-hall and private-apartment living. Developed for women attending the University of Michigan, Henderson is helping many women attend college who might otherwise be unable to attend due to financial constraints. [Aug99, cc]

HERMITAGE AT MAHANTONGO SPIRIT GARDEN, THE

**Attn: Bro Johannes
Pitman PA 17964**

**717-425-2548 (winter only)
BroJoh@yahoo.com**

Began 1988 | Pop. 3
Diet: Vegetarian | Rural | Spiritual

(Also known as Christiansbrunn Brotherhood, Mahantongo Spirit Garden, Christiansbrunn Kloster.) The Hermitage at Mahantongo Spirit Garden is a queer intentional community open to men and women of diverse sexualities seeking a spiritual life based on stewardship to the Earth and her creatures. As Pantheists, we believe everything is both alive and spirit. As caretakers of the garden, we nurture ourselves, each other, and the animals and plants we live among. As hermits, we each inhabit our own house as well as sharing the historic log-and-timber-frame communal buildings. As a working farm, we raise hay, corn, soybeans, flax, and a variety of livestock.

We also make crafts, give demonstrations in historic craft processes, and offer workshops and retreats. We are affiliated with the Queer Friendly Communities Network. Some people come here to heal themselves and to seek personal wholeness. Others want to engage with the plants and animals of the garden, as well as with other hermits here. Each is free to choose their own spiritual path. The Hermitage is a nonprofit, tax-exempt organization operated by a board of caretakers who voluntarily assume a higher level of stewardship under the leadership of an abbot. Free sample copies of our newsletter are available as are associate memberships. Visitors welcome. [Dec98]

HERTHA COMMUNITY

**Landsbyvenget 12
Herskind
DK-8464 Galten
DENMARK**

86954620, 40890383

Began 1993 | Pop. 45 | Forming | Rural

Forty-five people of all ages. Practicing reverse integration with young developmentally delayed people (13 persons) on an anthroposophical basis (undogmatic). Intention is a village with about 200 persons where people help and support each other and live in a sustainable way. [May99]

HESBJERG

**Hesbjergvej 50
DK-5491 Blommenslys
DENMARK**

**+45 6596 7505, +45 2121 4533
+45 6596 7490 fax
hesbjerg@post5.tele.dk
andpa@post5.tele.dk**

Began 1958 | Diet: Omnivore | Rural

Hesbjerg was born of the monastic idea, generated by personal youthful experience of Benedictine monasteries in Europe and Africa. Project "Modern Monastery" defined 1950 (= Def. I).—Successive peak events, discoveries: 40 hectares appropriate property, castle, buildings, acquired.— Pedagogical experiments started; students working four hours daily for stay, no cash. University entrance exam in one year (= Def. II).—Peace research introduced to Denmark by us (= Def. III).—Buddhist-Christian compatibility discovered, accepted, combining East and West (= Def. IV).—Artists´invasion, recognition of "Beauty will save the world" (Dostoyevsky).—Ecology finally conquered our agriculture, our minds, as a common ideological denominator (= Def. V).—Now we are preparing for twin monastery, Buddhist and Christian, and building guest house for monastic aspirants.—We believe five rock definitions above (not forgetting Dostoyevsky) are essential for saving the world: Monasticism (discipline perseverance prayer) + Work real work, everyman´s opportunity—and duty + Ecological principle: global sustainability + Peace research

Additions and corrections: Email: directory@ic.org, Web: http://directory.ic.org/, Mail: RR 1 Box 156-D, Rutledge MO 63563, USA.

leading to world order world peace + Buddhism and Christianity cooperating, strengthening each other.—It is not enough to save yourself! You have to save the world. [Jul99]

HIDDEN VALLEY

PO Box 572
Bigfork MT 59911

406-837-2511

Forming

Our vision of "Hidden Valley": An ecologically self-sufficient multicultural mountain intentional community held in a land trust. There would be shared income; experiential homeschooling; community cooperative work with current interests in watershed rehab, stream site hatchery, organic gardening, alternative-energy healing and research, inventions, music, art, writing, theater, draft-horse selective logging, botany, herbology, wildlife, and education.

The community of approximately 12–14 adults and beginning with 6–8 children would enjoy healthy fresh air. Meals home cooked by community members in the large community lodge. There would be separate living spaces for individuals, couples, families, or roommates.

Decision making would be by timed consensus, then majority rule by rotating councils, and there would be clear rules for dealing with conflict resolution that involve Re-evaluation Counseling (RC).

Earth-centered spirituality—create our own ceremonies. Inquire and/or join us if you are respectful; team worker; optimistic; industrious; monogamous—bi, straight, or gay; encourage parent(s) who want to raise their kids in a creative, respectful, noncompetitive, healthy home. When writing include why you desire to live in community. [May99, sase required]

HIGH FLOWING

PO Box 496
Floyd VA 24091

540-763-2651
highflow@usit.net

Began 1990 | Pop. 8
Diet: No red meat | Rural | Spiritual

Our membership is growing toward about 20 shareholders collectively owning the High Flowing self-sufficient ecovillage. We envision a strong tribal family meeting regularly in general consensus decision making and enlightened relationships.

In our daily circles we open up to peaceful solutions and truth of our hearts and honor the spirit of all is one. We define ourselves as a "Love and Light, New Time, Ecovillage, Permaculture, Art and Music, Healing, Spiritual Community." The Mayan calendar of galactic synchronization brings us into universal timing and opens gateways to the past and Universe.

We are an intentional community focusing on sustainable agriculture, spiritual development, and art with an emphasis on Mayan and shamanic influence.

At the time of this writing we are developing policies to safeguard shareholders' investment. Our goal for the garden is to grow most of our own food. We are mostly vegetarian. There are several musicians and painters here. The foundation for a complete music studio is done; this is our first straw-bale building. Our future structures will be sustainable and Earth congruent. A greenhouse of windows will soon be ready for greens. [Oct99, sase requested]

HIGH HORIZONS

RR 2 Box 63E
Alderson WV 24910

304-392-6222

Began 1989 | Pop. 4 | Forming | Rural

I have 260 acres of mountain land. Because I follow "Spirit" guidance it is difficult to know in advance just what is shaping up. Apparently a place where folks can come to learn and save money to purchase their own homestead. Then we would act as a community networking/cooperating for the benefit of all.

No alcohol, tobacco, or drugs here. Serious-minded ambitious folks are welcomed. No cash rent needed thus far, but you must help out some. If freeloaders come it will all go down the drain. Financial situation to be determined when there are others here to share the basic setup. The property is paid for. I am not in this to make money but to serve those who qualify. Hangups are burdensome. Many possibilities. Have large garden/orchard, barn with loft, and a new root cellar. Also 3,000-gallon gravity-flow water supply, septic, electric, and phone. Land is 1.1 mile off hard-top road. Lane is pretty good. Earth friendly, natural health, organic gardening, permaculture, etc. Hope to put it all together. [Nov99, sase required]

Key to bracketed text: cc = cannot commit to prompt correspondance, sase = self-addressed stamped envelope

HIGH WIND ASSOCIATION

W7136 County Rd U
Plymouth WI 53073

920-528-8488, 920-528-8488
paulson@danet.net

Began 1981 | Pop. 17
Diet: Vegan | Rural | Spiritual

(Also known as Plymouth Institute.) High Wind began in 1977 as a nonprofit whose vision is: "To walk gently on the earth, to know the spirit within, to hear our fellow beings, to invoke the light of wisdom, and to build the future now." We were drawn to technologies modeling sustainable living and to becoming a conference and retreat center exploring higher consciousness. Those attracted to this agenda came to live on our 148 rural acres, creating demonstrations of renewable energy and sharing ideas through workshops, seminars, tours. Visitors discover the peaceful, healing qualities of our rolling meadows, woods, and wetlands. With up to 22 members we continued for 12 years as an intentional community, then opted for less structure and more individual autonomy as an econeighborhood. Over the years members have initiated private enterprises: a community-supported agriculture (CSA) on 20 acres feeding 375 families, a piano school, desktop publishing, and furniture making. A small ecosettlement is now being developed to implement more Earth-friendly features. High Wind's priority is education—collaborating with universities and organizing gatherings—focusing on viable futures, applying inner awareness and values, designing solar homes, hands-on experiences. Partnerships with a city school district introduce central-city youth to thinking about building a sustainable world.

Contact us to see if there are any home-sites remaining in our forming ecovillage. [Oct98, sase required]

HIGHLINE CROSSING COHOUSING

1620 West Canal Court
Littleton CO 80120

303-347-8351, 303-798-0477 fax
rod_champney@hp.com
debbeh@auto-trol.com
http://denver.neighborhoodlink.com/

Began 1995 | Pop. 83 | Rural/Urban

We've been forming since mid-1991. The energy-efficient, community-designed buildings were completed in stages between 1995

and 1997. Since then, we've been learning more about how to be with each other, give each other space and respect, and learn and grow together. The main challenge we confront regularly is balancing individual needs with community needs. We're an eclectic group including counselors, mediators, computer pros, lawyers, full-time parents, retirees, defense-industry workers, technical salespeople, teachers (including a nationally honored teacher), construction workers, oriental-medicine practitioners, graphic artists, corporate educators, business owners, inventors, architects, bankers, and more.

Recent events have included a Super Bowl party (Go Broncos!), a presentation and dinner with Tom Sutherland (former hostage), and our regular fall gathering (2 1/2 days of looking at ourselves as a community). Regular events include community meals, potlucks, parent-kid tea times, individual garden plots, and workdays.

Amenities include a community garden and immediate access to the Highline Canal Trail system (over 70 miles of foot/bike/horse trails, just across a footbridge). There is a wide variety of cultural and sporting activities locally. [Jan99, cc, sase required]

HILL TOP FARM

908 Gravel Valley Rd
PO Box 129
Vinton OH 45686

740-388-8966

Began 1980 | Pop. 12 | Re-Forming
Diet: Omnivore | Rural | Spiritual

(Also known as Our Kibbutz.) Welcome to Hill Top Farm. We are a small group located in southern Ohio. Our goals are to set up a small, safe community. We seek to

do the following: use and promote animal and human power; use alternative technology; promote low Earth impact and conservation of natural resources; use farm businesses to help support our group; build a safe community for our group and a safe environment for our children in a nonviolent atmosphere. These are our goals. We believe in plural marriage, i.e., one man and two or more wives, and encourage polygamist families to join us, as well as ladies who wish to know more. All skills are needed, so all who may be interested please contact us.

Donations of how-to books, cash, or labor are needed. We need seeds, plants, canning supplies, and tack. We are building a new life. We are open to all races and to all religions. We need heirloom seeds and information on all old-fashioned equipment and skills from horseshoeing to old-fashioned recipes, etc. Help us reach our goals. Write if you wish to contribute cash for more information. We need help. We also need members—ladies are needed. So please contact us. We hope to hear from you soon. We need those who know how and those who wish to learn. We work hard, expect the same. [Nov98, sase required]

HILLEGASS HOUSE

3056 Hillegass
Berkeley CA 94705

510-848-3022

Began 1979 | Pop. 10
Diet: Omnivore | Urban

Hillegass House is an 11-member 20-year-old collective in Berkeley. We began as a (mostly) single-parent house made up of 6 adults who wanted to share the burdens (and joys) of parenting. The age spread of the current membership runs from the early 30s

Additions and corrections: Email: directory@ic.org, Web: http://directory.ic.org/, Mail: RR 1 Box 156-D, Rutledge MO 63563, USA.

to mid-60s, with the median age being mid-30s to mid-40s.

Our group is relatively stable—we've had only one opening within the last couple of years, and one of our original members still lives in the house.

We are an exceptionally diverse group in most regards (i.e., interests, diet, spirituality, sexuality, employment, etc.), and we think that's important. We blend together so well because we balance a strong commitment to group living and a real enjoyment of group dynamics on the one hand with a healthy respect for one another's privacy because we realize having time to one's self is absolutely vital.

Other factors of our success? Well, it helps that we live in a lovely house that can accommodate our number pretty graciously. Even more significantly, dinners are shared, and we all perform at least honorably in the kitchen (and we have several outstanding cooks). Written inquiries only. (We're sometimes slow in answering.) [May99, sase required, no openings]

HOLDEN VILLAGE

HC00 - Stop 2
Chelan WA 98816

509-687-3644

Began 1963 | Pop. 56 | Re-Forming
Diet: Omnivore | Rural | Spiritual

Holden Village Mission Statement

Holden Village, an ecumenical community rooted in the Lutheran tradition, is organized to provide healing, renewal, and refreshment of people through worship, intercession, study, hilarity, work, recreation, and conversation in a climate of mutual acceptance under the lordship of Jesus Christ.

The purpose of this community is to participate in the renewal of the church and the world by proclaiming the Gospel of God's unconditional love in Jesus Christ; challenging and equipping people for ministry in the world; lifting up a vision of God's kingdom of peace, justice, and wholeness; and celebrating the unity and the diversity of the church, all humanity, and all creation. [Jan99]

HOLY CITY COMMUNITY

5611 Welcome Rd
Lake Charles LA 70611
prolife@aol.com

Began 1971 | Pop. 33 | Re-Forming
Rural/Urban | Spiritual

(Also known as Open House Community). We are presently 33 people. We are making a directed effort to create a new society based on Gospel values. We support one another materially and prayerfully. We tithe, birth lots of babies, and celebrate the sacraments joyfully together. Our efforts are directed toward re-forming our personal and family lives, creating a new set of peer relationships, and growing in our lifetime commitments to one another. In all of this we purposely try to become detached from many old ways of being and acting.

The words of our covenant describe us and guide us on our journey to the New Jerusalem: "We are a Covenant Community in the Roman Catholic Tradition, subject to the authority of our Bishop and to our designated leadership. Our life is centered in God, the Father, the Son, and the Holy Spirit: our model of perfect Community. We understand ourselves to be in God's image most fully as a Community rather than as individual persons, and together we aspire to

a life of Gospel Poverty." [Aug99, cc, sase requested]

HOMESTEAD AT DENISON UNIVERSITY, THE

1385 North St
Granville OH 43023

740-587-5679
leareyf@denison.edu
http://www.denison.edu/homestead/

Began 1977 | Pop. 12 | Diet: Vegetarian

The Homestead is a community offering a living alternative for students at Denison University. Started as a short experiment in living simply off the land, the Homestead has outlived its expectations and is flourishing 20 years later.

A trio of cabins about a mile from Denison's campus can house 12 students who share space with cats, dogs. We are off the grid, utilizing solar energy to pump water and to power some appliances. Cooking and heating are accomplished with wood-burning stoves.

We are striving toward sustainability but must struggle with an ever-changing population and with the balance of academic work and homestead living. We attempt to integrate the two and utilize available resources and expertise from the university, and we presently have ambitious plans for increasing efficiency and capacity.

Important aspects of homesteading include the opportunity to take responsibility for our own lives; the empowerment of admitted interdependence; the intensity of living, working, and playing together; and the opportunity to integrate lifestyle with personal ideologies. The Homestead is an amazing opportunity for students to learn far more than we could ever learn in the classroom. [Oct99]

HORIZONS ECO VILLAGE

PO Box 310
Nellysford VA 22958

804-361-1212
ecovillage@mindspring.com
http://www.horizons-ecovillage.com/

Began 1997 | Pop. 52 | Rural

While Horizons EcoVillage recognizes that the inspiration for true respect for the Earth and all of its creatures can only come from within each individual, we feel that in order to preserve the vision that is the heart of this

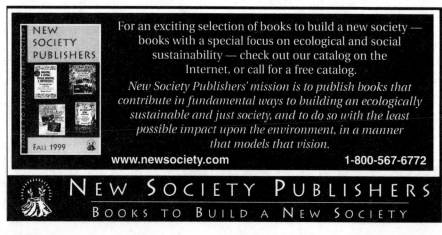
Key to bracketed text: cc = cannot commit to prompt correspondance, sase = self-addressed stamped envelope

Listings

project, we must make the protection of this land, its habitat, and its resources our primary priority.

We feel that by selling homesteads with protective covenants that are carefully considered to be for the benefit of the whole community (including its wildlife), now and for generations still to come, we will be creating a framework in which the spirit of cooperation and respect between neighbors, the security for our children, and a deep respect for the Earth will be fostered.

It is our intention that the covenants, which will run with the land (they will remain in effect if the land is sold), embody the common threads that will set this community development apart from a standard subdivision. These common threads can be summarized as three basic principles: respect for the Earth, respect for all of the Earth's life-forms, and respect for ourselves and for other people. [Sep99]

HOUSE OF PEACE

838 Princeton St
Akron OH 44311

330-438-1112
ab190@acorn.net, mayday@raex.com

Began Nov98 | Pop. 5 | Forming
Diet: Omnivore | Urban | Spiritual

(Also known as Akron Catholic Worker.) Extended Christian family offering shelter to the poor. Strong emphasis on social justice by civil disobedience, i.e., necessary nonviolence. [Sep99]

HUEHUECOYOTL

A P 111 Tepoztlán
62520 Morelos
MEXICO

52-739-52640
huehue@laneta.apc.org
http://members.aol.com/Huecoyotl/
Huehuepages.html

Began 1973

Huehuecoyotl is an ecovillage in the mountains of Tepoztlan, Mexico, founded by a group of adults and their children— artists, ecologists, artisans, and educators from seven different nationalities. The community has 26 years of existence and 18 years on the land. Over the years it has developed into an extended family; an experimental center; a model of rural, simple community living; and an important site where different traditions, cultures, and visions blend harmoniously with each other. There are low-cost guest facilities and extensive gardening as well as the use of organic materials and designs for construction and water management.

Ideal communities exist only in the imagination of visionaries, but real communities are a long daily process of understanding, hard work, patience, and love. Our village reflects both the frustrations of not being able to materialize our ideals and also achievements that are beyond description in terms of solidarity, cooperation, harmony in diversity, and an example of libertarian, eco-topian visions functioning since the early 1970s. We are now facing a new cycle of our growth, which implies moving into a more balanced relationship with our environment and with our collective cultural center, which is rapidly becoming an alternative educational center for new communities, the arts, networking, and information. We´try to bring together the best of all worlds, and we live a fairly happy life.

HUMANITY RISING

PO Box 528
Chico CA 95927

530-899-7719
jomaha@sunset.net

Began 1992 | Forming | Spiritual

We are a clean and sober community manifesting the 12-step principles of Humanity Rising in our daily lives. We are united by a common spirituality, a belief that the universe and everything in it are our Higher Power. We celebrate our at-oneness with the universe in the Great Mystery Lodge of Humanity Rising. Our spirituality brings together many disparate elements from the human experience, including shamanism, psychic practice, Taoism, Buddhism, psychology, cosmology, and more. Our goal is a fully realized life on a human scale. We believe we all live in both ordinary and nonordinary reality, whether we are aware of it or not. We are healers, working in both realities.

In our daily lives we live simply, organically, ecologically. Every act is a spiritual act. We strive for integrity and grace. Presently we support ourselves through counseling in recovery. One goal is to establish a rural recovery center to provide an income stream for the community. We want to be self-sustaining. For spiritual reasons, we have a bias against machines and only use them when absolutely necessary. We harmonize our lives psychologically through regular practice of group therapy.

If you want what we have to offer and are willing to go to any lengths to get it, contact us. [Aug99, cc, sase required]

HUNDREDFOLD FARM

181 Orrtanna Rd
Orrtanna PA 17353

717-334-4488
rhubarb@cvn.net

Began 1998 | Pop. 18 | Forming | Rural

We hope to combine a small cohousing community with an organic CSA (community supported agriculture). [Apr99]

HUNTINGTON OPEN WOMYNS LAND (HOWL)

PO Box 53
Huntington VT 05462

802-434-3953
wehowl@juno.com

Began 1998 | Pop. 4 | Re-Forming
Diet: Omnivore | Rural

(Also known as Vermont Women's Land Trust, Common Womon.) Huntington Open Womyns Land (HOWL) is a 50-acre land trust for womyn in northwestern Vermont. The land is fully paid for; we now only have to cover taxes quarterly. The monthly donation of the residents is enough to cover all necessary expenses, which relieves us of the pressure of fund-raising. We are newly defining ourself as intentional community and working to learn what that means and how we will play it out. The four who currently live here range in age from 10 to 59, and we would welcome new residents.

There is an old funky farmhouse with four bedrooms, kitchen, bath, and two large common spaces. There is also a barn that contains two apartments for Crones and space for more to be created. Several womyn's groups have their yearly gatherings here, and there is lots of camping space, both on the land and in the buildings. We also have a pond and a sauna, both of which were created with grants from Lesbian Natural Resources.

We love the land here and are dedicated to keeping it as a wildlife sanctuary and as a sanctuary for all womyn. [Sep99, sase requested]

HUTTERIAN BRETHREN

Contact: Philip J Gross
3610 N Wood Rd
Reardon WA 99029
philsjg@juno.com
http://www.hutterianbrethren.com/

Began 1528 | Pop. 40,000
Diet: Omnivore | Rural | Spiritual

The Hutterian Brethren originated in central Europe in 1528, after the Reformation. The Hutterites are a Christian church that advocates total community, spiritually and materially, which they believe fulfills the highest command of love, and they also believe that one must not only recognize Christ as Savior but also follow him. They use both the Old and New Testament in their worship services. Since they are of German descent, they still teach and use their native tongue at home and in church. Some of their history, which is preserved and published today, is already in English. Each community conducts its own youth work through Sunday school and other activities. They practice adult baptism upon confession of faith, are war resistors, refuse to participate in politics, dress differently, and operate their own schools, and the meals are all eaten together. The Hutterites are agriculturists by trade, some also engaged in manufacturing, and they use modern tools to carry out these endeavors. They distribute the work among the members wherever the need arises. There are 389 colonies with close to 40,000 members in North America.

The colonies (and the count) are located in Alberta (158), Manitoba (102), Saskatchewan (56), South Dakota (53), Minnesota (10), Washington (5), North Dakota (4), British Columbia (1). [Jan99, sase requested]

IDA

PO Box 874
Smithville TN 37166

615-597-4409
trayburn@dekalb.net

Began 1993 | Pop. 8
Diet: Vegetarian | Rural

We are Ida, the all-purpose queer arts com-

munity tucked away on 250 acres of nature-iffic loveliness in the backwoods of Tennessee. We are an ever-changing arrangement of wimmin, men, and kids trying to live an alternative to consumerist, corporate-controlled spirit-numbing culture. We grow lots of vegetables, build fancy outhouses, play music, dance in caves, produce plays, agitate, bitch, kvetch, hike, and sing. We go to Dairy Queen in tattered dresses. We don't cook animals in our kitchen. We're thankful for our sweet gushing spring, crashing waterfalls, and wild animals. We're hell on heels wielding chain saws for firewood. We have dozens of queer neighbors within biking distance. We are your cross-dressing, bread-baking sissy monks. We welcome visitors and are open to new members. [Jan99, sase requested]

INNISFREE VILLAGE

5505 Walnut Level Rd
Crozet VA 22932

804-823-5400, 804-823-5027 fax
innisfree@cwixmail.com
http://monticello.avenue.org/
**   innisfree/**

Began 1971 | Pop. 75
Diet: Omnivore | Rural

Nestled in the foothills of the Blue Ridge Mountains, Innisfree Village was founded in 1971 as a creative alternative for adults with mental disabilities (coworkers). We are a service-oriented community located on 550 acres about 20 miles from Charlottesville. Thirty-five adults with mental disabilities live in 10 village houses and 2 Charlottesville houses, along with about 25 full-time volunteers. The community members live together in family-style homes and work together in our workstations. The gardens, weavery, woodshop, kitchen, and bakery give meaning to our lives as therapeutic work, as well as practical, purposeful work.

Our volunteer "staff," many of whom come from overseas, work and live together with coworkers, helping with their personal care, running a household, and working in the workstations. We ask a one-year minimum commitment for volunteers and offer room, board, medical insurance, and a monthly stipend. For many the most substantial reward is the giving and receiving that come from living and working together in an atmosphere of mutual respect.

Innisfree is a registered nonprofit corporation, governed by a board of directors.

There are an executive director and assistant director. There are many decisions of daily life that are made by consensus, but there are also certain decisions made by the board or the director. We are not an egalitarian community. While self-sufficiency is one of our dreams, most of our energy is directed to creating and supporting a life of respect, empowerment, and creativity for persons with special needs.

If interested in becoming a volunteer, please write for more information. Visitors are welcome if arrangements are made in advance. [Dec98]

INTER-COOPERATIVE COUNCIL AT UNIVERSITY OF MICHIGAN

337 E William
Ann Arbor MI 48104

734-662-4415, 734-662-5870 fax
icc.info@umich.edu
http://www.icc.umich.org/

Began 1932 | Pop. 600 | Urban

(Also known as ICC-Ann Arbor.) Inter-Cooperative Council (ICC) was formed in 1937 by the housing co-ops on the University of Michigan campus in order to gain greater efficiency and economy in certain functions such as recruitment of new members, paying the taxes and mortgages, and overseeing large maintenance projects. In addition, ICC helps train new members and officers so that houses run more smoothly.

Our housing co-ops are owned and managed by the students who live in them. There are 18 group and 1 apartment house located on both central and north campus. The number of members in each house ranges from 13 to 150, with the average being about 33. The buildings range from wood frame to brick, from historic to modern. We have nonsmoking houses, coed houses, and houses that serve vegetarian meals. Most houses serve dinner daily, while breakfast and lunch are do it yourself.

Houses are run democratically, each member having an equal voice. At house meetings, students decide how much to spend on food, when quiet hours will be, what newspapers to subscribe to, what to do about a problem member, what work needs to be done, and so on. We rely on members to do all the work needed to run the houses (cooking, cleaning, planning, bookkeeping, etc.). Each member puts in four to six hours of work per week.

Key to bracketed text: cc = cannot commit to prompt correspondance, sase = self-addressed stamped envelope

Eating and working with the housemates, participating in group decision making, and sharing good times help our members develop close bonds. This strong sense of community combined with the knowledge of shared ownership is what turns co-op houses into homes. [Sep99]

INTER-COOPERATIVE COUNCIL (ICC-TEXAS)

**510 W 23rd St
Austin TX 78705**

**512-476-1957
iccmail@uts.cc.utexas.edu
http://www.utexas.edu/students/icc/**

Began 1937 | Pop. 166
Diet: Omnivore | Urban

(Also known as ICC-Austin.) Established in 1937 and incorporated in 1970, ICC is a student housing cooperative in Austin. Student members share the responsibility and benefits of operating our eight co-op houses, while our professional staff maintains a central office. Houses run democratically, and members do all the work to run our houses—cooking, cleaning, etc.—spending four to six hours per week on these tasks.

Our coed houses are walking distance to the University of Texas and house 12 to 32 students each. We offer several vegetarian and upper-division houses and theme houses as well. Our programs and services are aimed to increase access to college education, and we operate as a nonprofit.

Members enjoy being part of local co-op community, and we are active members of NASCO, the federation of student co-ops. [Feb99]

INTERNATIONAL PUPPYDOGS MOVEMENT

Portland Oregon

503-231-2512, 503-235-3374 fax

Began 1993 | Pop. 4 | Forming | Urban

Puppydogs are known for warmth, humanity, and profoundly social patterns of living. The name "International Puppydogs Movement" comes from the fact that residents like to lie (sometimes sleep) very close together, curled up like puppies in front of the fireplace. Over time we have come to call our basic family unit the "pile," a term that stems from a complex set of overlapping philosophies. There are at least as many philosophies about the group as there are members.

We are a small number of gay and bisexual men, geographically centered in Oregon. At present, most of us own our own homes; in the future we plan to live together cooperatively. We are people attempting to love each other—willingness to accept an atmosphere of heightened communication and intimacy is perhaps the most important qualification for joining us in this search. [Jul99]

INTERSECTION HOUSE

**6161 El Cajon Blvd #B-407
San Diego CA 92115**

**619-583-3088
intersectionhouse@juno.com
http://move.to/ICA/**

Re-Forming

Intersection House is beginning a new chapter in our history. As of spring 1999, the organization that had provided much of our

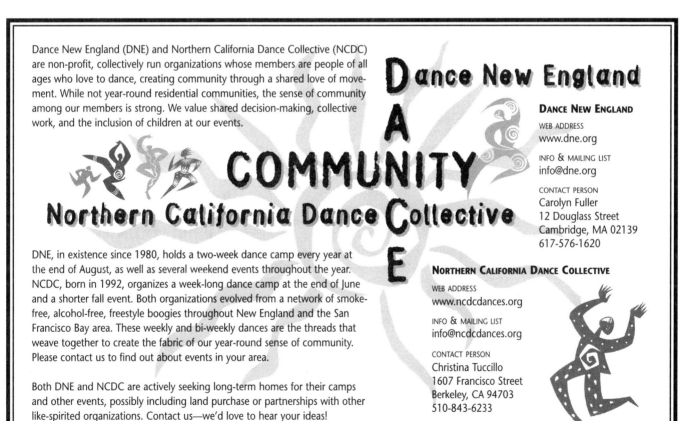
Listings

financial support decided to start a new program. Intersection's program is no longer in their budget, and we have vacated their property that was our lifelong location. Therefore, the Intersection Community Association (our new name as we no longer have the "House") has been compelled to reassess; to look at what we have been and what we want to become.

The Intersection House community is dedicated to practicing and modeling fellowship, respect, and healthy, ecologically sustainable living. We want to continue to provide this for our community. Our most pressing task for the immediate future is to relocate our program. We are looking for property to buy or rent so that we can continue to perform community service. Presently we are in promising discussions with the Unitarian Church, the Campus YMCA, and others about the possibility of being partners in a cooperative center. We are looking at our situation as a great opportunity to become an improved Intersection Community for the new millennium and to continue to pass on to future generations our spirit of activism.

IONA COMMUNITY

The Abbey
Isle of Iona
Argyll PA76 6SN, Scotland
UNITED KINGDOM

44141.445.4561, 44168.170.0404
44141.445.4295 fax
ionacomm@gla.iona.org.uk
ionacomm@iona.org.uk
http://www.iona.org.uk/

Began 1938
Diet: Omnivore | Rural | Spiritual

The Iona Community is a ecumenical Christian community seeking new ways of living out the Gospel in today's world. It comprises over 200 members, living throughout Britain and beyond, who are committed to a rule involving a spiritual and economic discipline, regular meeting together, and action for peace and justice in society.

The community's administrative base is in Glasgow, Scotland, where outreach workers in the fields of worship and youth and the publications department are located, together with general support staff.

The community runs three residential centers (the restored medieval Benedictine monastery and Macleod Centre on the island of Iona and Camas Adventure Camp nearby on Mull) where over 100 guests come for weeklong programs to share with the resident staff and volunteers in the building of community and the exploration of the relevance of faith and an integrated spirituality to contemporary issues. [Jan99]

ISLE OF ERRAID

Findhorn Foundation
Fionnphort, Isle of Mull
Argyll PA66 6BN, Scotland
UNITED KINGDOM

01681-700384, 01681-700660 fax
http://www.findhorn.org/erraid/

Began 1979
Diet: Omnivore | Rural | Spiritual

Erraid (one square mile) has been in the care of the Findhorn Foundation for nearly 20 years. A small, self-supporting community flourishes here, interpreting the same ideals and spirituality as the Foundation, in ways appropriate to the purpose and nature of the island.

Life on this wild and beautiful Hebridean island is down-to-earth, challenging, and inspiring. As our guest, you are invited to take part in our daily work, community life, meditations, and celebrations. Being here allows us, residents and guests alike, to connect with nature and the elements in a very immediate way, be it growing vegetables, caring for our animals, confronting tides and weather, or exploring the rugged landscape of Erraid itself.

The heart of the community is the garden and much of the work is outdoors, chopping wood or maintaining buildings for example, but you don't have to be a youthful, pioneer type to enjoy yourself! There is gentler work in the kitchen and candle studio, or other areas. The cottages are cosy, and as long as you are mobile and can cope with outside toilets, you'll manage fine. There is also plenty of room for personal time and reflection.

Erraid is ideal in its simplicity and groundedness, either before or after Experience Week, or other programs. Or visit us independently. We invite you to come for one or two weeks, or longer. Children are very welcome and usually love the adventure and freedom of Erraid. [Jun99]

ITTOEN FOUNDATION

8 Yanagiyama-cho Shinomiya
Yamashina Kyoto
JAPAN 607-8025

075-581-3136, 075-581-3139 fax

Began 1905 | Rural/Urban | Spiritual

Ittoen was founded by Rev. Tenko Nishida in 1905. It is a community of people who seek to live a life of having no possessions and giving service to others, in a spirit of penitence. At the foundation of this community is the faith that when human beings live in accordance with the ways of nature, we are enabled to live even without owning things and even without converting labor into money.

At Ittoen, all necessities for life that are provided through the blessing of Light (God, Buddha, Mother Nature) are entrusted to "Senkosha." "Senkosha," then, is an economic organ for managing goods in such a way that they serve people and do not become a source of social conflict. The physical and social community embodying the ideals of Ittoen exists as the village of Kosenrin in the Yamashina Ward of Kyoto. Kosenrin Village was established in its present location in 1928, and it was incorporated as a foundation in 1929. At present, there are about 70 structures spread over 33 hectares of land, and there are approximately 130 persons living in the community.

The permanent members (residents) are actively living and working in accordance with the way of Light as a big family. [May99]

JESUIT VOLUNTEER CORPS: NORTHWEST

PO Box 3928
Portland OR 97208

503-335-8202
jvcnw@JesuitVolunteers.org

Began 1950
Diet: No red meat | Rural/Urban | Spiritual

The Jesuit Volunteer Corps: Northwest offers women and men an opportunity to work full-time for justice and peace. Jesuit volunteers are called to the mission of serving the poor directly, working for structural change in the United States, and accompanying persons in developing countries.

The challenge to Jesuit volunteers is to integrate Christian faith by working and living among the poor and marginalized, by living simply and in community with other Jesuit volunteers in Alaska, Oregon, Washington, and Montana and by examining the causes of social injustice. [Apr99, sase required]

JESUS CHRISTIANS

Box A678
Sydney South NSW 1235
AUSTRALIA

02-49600393
fold@idl.net.au
xian6@md2.vsnl.net.in
http://www.fortunecity.com/
meltingpot/harrow/753/index.htm

Began 1980
Diet: Omnivore | Urban | Spiritual

(Also known as Christians, Christian Volunteers, The Australians, Gandhian Christians, Voices in the Wilderness.) We sometimes refer to the "larger community" in terms of society in general. However, living in community suggests a group held together by some common unity. It could be language, geographical location, etc. Because we believe that attitudes toward money are fundamental in all human relationship, "living in community" for us means "common ownership." [Mar99]

JESUS PEOPLE USA EVANGELICAL COVENANT CHURCH

920 W Wilson Ave
Chicago IL 60640

773-561-2450, 773-989-2076 fax
jpusa@jpusa.org
http://www.jpusa.org/

Began 1972 | Pop. 500
Diet: Omnivore | Urban | Spiritual

Jesus People USA (JPUSA) is a Christian community in the inner city of Chicago. We operate both as an intentional Christian community and as a worshiping church. The 500 people who live together at a single address on Chicago's north side hold all goods and property in a common fund, looking to the model of Christian community depicted in the New Testament (Acts 2:44–47, 4:32–35). Living communally and

pooling our resources in this way have enabled us to minister to one another and those outside the community in ways that might not have been otherwise possible. The outreach of the community is local, national, and international. Locally, JPUSA is best known for its social-service ministries, which include a transitional shelter for homeless families, a soup kitchen, a senior citizens' residence, and a women's warming center. *Cornerstone* is our journal of culture, arts, politics, and faith. The annual Cornerstone Music and Arts Festival gathers 20,000+ young Christians for five days of camping, concerts, and seminars. JPUSA's many and varied musical groups have made an impact worldwide. We have been privileged to function as a resource to the church, a haven for people in need, a learning experience for many whose journey has taken them in our doors and out to serve elsewhere. [Oct98]

JOHN T LYLE CENTER FOR REGENERATIVE STUDIES

4105 W University Dr
Cal Poly Pomona
Pomona CA 91768

909-869-5155 Office
909-869-5146 Commons
909-869-5188 fax
regenerative@earthlink.net
listserv@regen.org
http://www.regen.org/
http://www.csupomona.edu/~crs/

Began 1993 | Pop. 18 | Re-Forming
Diet: Omnivore | Rural/Urban

(Also known as Center for Regenerative Studies, Regens.) Students, staff, faculty, and volunteers live, work, and play in this high-

tech ecovillage on the campus of Cal Poly Pomona. Named for founder John T. Lyle, the facility provides modern human habitat with a reduced environmental footprint.

Residence is open to all Cal Poly students, personnel, and others by special arrangement. We plan to expand to a 90-person population.

Live the regenerative lifestyle: sustainable agri/aquaculture, pedestrian community, green architecture, solar power, in an ancient black-walnut woodland.

Explore the future of residential community firsthand while earning your college degree. [Sep99]

JOINT HOUSE

917 S Forest Ave
Ann Arbor MI 48104

Pop. 42

We are a student cooperative house with 23 rooms, housing 42 people. We have dinner every day but Saturday, and vegetarian option is always available. Amenities include TV, VCR, fish room, fireplace, pool table, and tire swing. [Oct99]

JOLLY RANCHERS

2711 S Elwood Pl
Seattle WA 98144

206-322-8071
jollyranchers@ic.org

Began 1995 | Pop. 5 | Re-Forming
Diet: No red meat | Urban

The Jolly Ranchers are a family-style commune in a diverse setting in Seattle, Washington. We own two houses on a corner lot that has garden space, a small green-

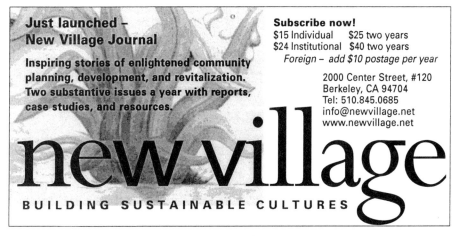

Additions and corrections: Email: directory@ic.org, Web: http://directory.ic.org/, Mail: RR 1 Box 156-D, Rutledge MO 63563, USA.

preparation for a probable move to a more rural area, which would allow for increased self-sufficiency and more potential for community growth. We are currently three members, several guests, and many pets. We have no children but would welcome them. We practice consensus in all matters concerning the group, eat vegetarian common meals, tend an organic garden, and work at jobs that reflect our values and that we think make a positive impact in our community. We believe that careful examination of words and actions in a compassionate environment results in more ethical behavior, deeper intimacy, and happier, healthier lives. We go pretty deep but don't take ourselves too seriously. The Jolly Ranchers are devoted to egalitarianism and, as such, are a money-sharing community. All earned income is deposited in a joint account held by members from which the mortgage, bills, and household expenses (including food) are paid. Members are paid discretionary money for their work at a common rate decided upon by consensus. We are excited about what we are doing and looking for new members. Visitors are welcome. [Dec98]

JONAH HOUSE

c/o Mike Kennedy
660A Castleglen Dr
Garland TX 75043, 972-240-1466

Began 1986
Diet: Vegetarian | Urban | Spiritual

(Also known as Dallas Catholic Worker.) Cohousing with immigrants to Dallas with an emphasis at looking at social conditions taking place in countries economically less well off than the United States.

Occasional bike repairs with children in the local neighborhood and other vocational-skills training, including garden and fowl raising.

Peace studies, contemplated mainly but not entirely from a religious perspective. [Mar99, cc]

JUBILEE PARTNERS

PO Box 68
Comer GA 30629
706-783-5131

Began 1979 | Pop. 26
Diet: Omnivore | Rural | Spiritual

Jubilee Partners is a Christian service community that was started in 1979 on 258 acres

of land in north Georgia. We seek to understand and live by the radical implications of following Jesus Christ and the biblical vision of "Jubilee." The community is comprised of approximately 25 adults and 10 children. About half of these folks are resident partners, and half are volunteers who come through an application process for periods of three to five months. Jubilee's ministries include resettling refugees from various countries; working to abolish the death penalty; peacemaking; and raising money to promote justice, peace, and healing in Nicaragua.

We try to live a compassionate lifestyle. We want our life together to reflect biblical values rather than cultural values of materialism, consumerism, and individualism. We are open to new members, but everyone interested in living here must come as a volunteer for the first year. [Dec98]

JULIAN WOODS COMMUNITY

225 Julian Woods Ln
Julian PA 16844
814-355-5755, 814-355-7801
cab21@psu.edu

Began 1971 | Pop. 21 | Rural
Julian Woods (established 1975) is a diverse group of 14 adults and 7 children on 140 acres held in common as part of a land trust. We are located 15 miles from Pennsylvania State University. Members may own or lease home lots after a capital investment. Families are autonomous, are financially independent, and own their own homes. Community decisions are made by consensus. We own and operate a pair of greenhouses that constitute our wastewater-treatment plant and offer some indoor growing space. We have lots of gardens (and lots of deer), a recreational pond, and an interest in finding others interested in working with us to continue to build our community. [Jan99, sase required]

JUMP OFF COMMUNITY LAND TRUST

1423 Tate Trail
Sewanee TN 37375
931-598-5942, 931-598-9146

Began 1990 | Pop. 12
Diet: Omnivore | Rural

(Also known as was Ecanachaca & Earth Star Community.) Our purpose is to pro-

mote and encourage environmental awareness by maintaining our land for wilderness, educational, and homestead uses; to demonstrate an ecologically sustainable lifestyle that includes affordable housing, energy efficiency, and sustainable agriculture within a cooperative community; and to host seminars, workshops, speakers, and research residencies in natural sciences, arts, spirituality, and related subjects.

We support each other in our livelihoods, spiritual growth, arts and crafts, and other projects. We are trying to become self-sufficient on the land and grow our own organic food. The land is owned in common, but we each have our own house, income, car, tools, etc.

We have 1,100 acres of land, 30 acres cleared, and the balance woodland that has been protected for over 50 years. We are splitting the price of the land. Each household's down payment is $2,000, and interest-free monthly payments of $100 are made until $20,000 is paid. A resident member may sell, bequeath, or rent their residence subject to approval of the other members. Alterations to the land such as building or tree cutting must be approved by all resident members. No firearms are permitted on the property. [Sep99]

JUPITER HOLLOW

Rt 1 Box 277
Weston WV 26452
304-269-4207, 304-269-4875
kimmel4875@aol.com

Began 1976 | Pop. 11 | Rural
We are a community in transition. Our land is currently commonly owned. We feel that we each "own" our homes, but on a strictly legal basis this is not the case. Our structure has worked for over 20 years, but we now feel a need to change it. Unfortunately, we are now split into two factions with very different views about what changes to make. We do expect to continue as a community, though possibly some members may leave.

Our focuses have been, and will probably continue to be, friendship, neighborliness, ecological awareness, and a desire for a simpler, less materialistic lifestyle than the standard US one. Beyond this, our lives are primarily individually or family focused, rather than community focused. What we share is 180 acres of beautiful wooded land and a sense of stewardship for it. The possibilities for this community's future lie in the

Key to bracketed text: cc = cannot commit to prompt correspondance, sase = self-addressed stamped envelope

visions of present and future participants. [Dec98, sase requested]

KADESH-BIYQAH

Box 120
S-671 23 Arvika
SWEDEN

00946-570-42001
Kadesh@nccg.org
cwarren@online.no
http://www.nccg.org/
FB-Col-HP.html

Began 1997
Diet: Omnivore | Rural | Spiritual

(Also known as Chavurah Bekorot.) An evangelical, patriarchal, prophetic Christian community aiming eventually to be self-sufficient in food, education, and spiritual life for the difficult times ahead but with strong spiritual links to urban and other rural church organizations. Though permanently settled by several core families we receive a constant stream of visitors from our own spiritual and other Christian communities for fellowship, education, and worship. We are attempting to build home industries, including publishing, which we have been doing for some time. Our goal is to establish a network with other international communities based on the same spiritual values. [May99]

KALANI OCEANSIDE ECO - RESORT

RR 2 Box 4500
Beach Rd
Pahoa HI 96778

808-965-7828, 800-800-6886
808-965-0527 fax
kalani@kalani.com
http://www.kalani.com/

Began 1975 | Pop. 28
Diet: No red meat | Rural

(Also known as Institute for Culture and Wellness.) Kalani is a community of long-term residents on a 113-acre coastal site, plus short-term (three-month) resident volunteers and others from the area, all of whom operate a not-for-profit educational conference center and retreat. Kalani provides on-site visitor experiences and out-reach programs that support the well-being of the local environment and communities.

Kalani is great for year-round personal getaways or group retreats (up to 100)! Hawaii's ecoresort, Kalani is the only coastal lodging facility within the Aloha State's largest conservation area.

Kalani treats you to delicious, wholesome cuisine; comfortable, affordable accommodation options; Olympic pool/spa; massage therapies; traditional culture; and a rainbow of seminars. Kalani-sponsored seminars usually are six nights, seven days, beginning with dinner, ending with lunch.

Nearby are thermal springs, a dolphin beach, orchid farms, snorkel tidal pools, steam bathing, waterfalls, botanical gardens, historic villages, and spectacular Volcanos National Park. [May99]

KANA-GEMEINSCHAFT (CANA COMMUNITY)

c/o Bernd Büscher
Mallinckrodtstr 108
D-44145 Dortmund
GERMANY

0231/839853

Began 1990 | Pop. 7
Diet: Omnivore | Urban | Spiritual

(Also known as Kana Soupkitchen.) The Kana Community is a Christian, ecumenical base community in solidarity with the poor. We are located in Dortmund, Germany. We run a soup kitchen for about 300 guests per meal four times a week and give out sleeping bags and blankets to the homeless. We are also speaking out politically for our guests (demonstrations, nonviolent direct actions).

The community consists of 7 core members, with about 70 volunteers helping in our projects. We have monthly worship services and roundtable discussions. We feel close to the Catholic Worker movement and organize regional network meetings of soup kitchens twice a year. [Jan99]

KANATSIOHAREKE (GANA JO HALEKE)

Place of the Clean Pot
4934 State Hwy #5
Fonda NY 12068

516-673-5692

Began 1993

We are a group of traditional Mohawk people who moved in 1993 from the Akwasasne Reservation back to our ancestral homeland in the Mohawk Valley. Our community is working to preserve our Native culture and language through outreach and education programs, and by creating a traditionally oriented village, farm, and conference center. We have 372 acres of woods and fertile fields on the Mohawk River with multiple buildings and barns and a beautiful spring.

Currently we have 10 adult members and four children, and a large community of Native and non-Native friends who regularly spend periods of time with us. We run a large, organic farm, raise horses and beef cattle, have a bed and breakfast and a Native craft shop, put on an annual Strawberry festival in late June, plus many educational programs, including the summer Immersion School for the Mohawk Language.

We welcome as members or interns all Native people who are mature, hardworking, and sincerely interested in preserving the traditional ways. On our land we have no gambling, alcohol, drugs, or weapons. We try to adopt a peaceful, wholistic, spiritual, and healing approach to everything we do, and make decisions by consensus.

We are open to visitors and working visitors (with advance notice) and are willing to share knowledge of Native traditions with everyone. [Oct99]

KAREN HOUSE CATHOLIC WORKER

1840 Hogan
St Louis MO 63106

314-621-4052

Began 1977 | Pop. 7 | Urban | Spiritual
(Also known as St. Louis Catholic Worker.) We are a Catholic Worker community established 22 years ago. Most members live together in an old convent in north St.

Louis where we provide hospitality in the form of shelter to homeless women and children. Some members live in apartments in the neighborhood. We have a small organic community garden on a nearby vacant lot.

Some members are activist in area issues such as Green Party, peace and justice, refugee-support work with people from Central America and Africa.

We share a daily contact with our guests, who are homeless women—our house is nonviolent, nonsmoking, culturally diverse. Some members have a vision for the future that would allow for a larger cohousing community to be built on vacant lots close to our house.

Roundtable is a three-times-yearly publication produced by our community.

Interested person(s) are urged to write a letter with as much information as possible. We would of course do our best to answer any of your questions and perhaps arrange a visit to Karen House. [Mar99, sase requested]

KASHI ASHRAM

11155 Roseland Rd
Sebastian FL 32958

561-589-1403 x100
kashinfo@kashi.org
http://kashi.org/

Began 1974 | Pop. 165
Diet: Vegetarian | Rural/Urban | Spiritual

(Also known as Neem Karoli Baba Kashi Ashram.) Kashi Ashram is an interfaith spiritual community founded in 1976 by Ma Jaya Sati Bhagavati, a US-born spiritual teacher. The community embraces the sacred practices of many traditions. The essence of the teaching is based upon loving kindness, compassion, and a commitment to the Truth through service to humanity and to oneself. Ma offers a spiritual path alive with color, creativity, love, service, and the rituals of many faiths.

The community stretches over 80 acres of woodlands with a number of shared residences. At the center of the ashram there is a large pond surrounded by temples and shrines to many of the world's religions. This pond symbolically represents the Ganges, the sacred river of India. The Ganga is an earthly manifestation of the Divine Mother, purifying the Earth and anyone who touches her waters.

Ma and her student, Dr. Thomas B.

Byrom, professor at Oxford and Harvard Universities, founded the River School in 1979. The River School weaves together hands-on service and awareness along with nonbigotry and nonviolence to provide quality education in an inspirational, creative, and thought-provoking environment. The school provides education from preschool through 12th grade.

Kashi is a community of service, taking care of people in need. The River Fund, established in 1990, is dedicating to providing loving, nurturing care for people with challenging illnesses, especially people with HIV and AIDS. In 1994, the River House was established as a residence for people facing life-threatening illnesses.

In addition to serving and educating, Kashi fosters spiritual growth. People come to Kashi seeking a deeper, more meaningful, and fulfilling life. Through the uniqueness of this community many lives have been transformed. The Kashi Center for Advanced Spiritual Studies offers workshops, retreats, and intensives. Residents teach meditation, yoga, and Kirtan and facilitate workshops and seminars. Visitors are welcome. [Oct99, no openings]

KIBBUTZ KETURA

IL-88840 Div Eilot
ISRAEL
ketura-secretary@ardom.co.il
http://www.ardom.co.il/
heilot/ketura/

Began 1973
Diet: Omnivore | Rural | Spiritual

Ketura is located 50 kilometers north of Eilat in the Arava rift, a uniquely tranquil region of Israel. The kibbutz itself is lush and green, situated against the stark desert landscape, which, in turn, is framed by two mountain walls. While the desert summers can be difficult, the Arava is renowned for its mild, sunny winters, and a wealth of desert fauna and flora awaits those who would seek it out.

Ketura was founded by a small group of young Americans, graduates of the Young Judaea Year-in-Israel Course, at the close of the Yom Kippur War in November 1973. The first years of the kibbutz were marked by great difficulties and frustrations, leading many of the founders to leave. In time, the core group of those who remained was joined by other Young Judaeans, a variety of

immigrants, and graduates of the Israeli Scout movement.

As Ketura grew, a more stable lifestyle was created, and the members began raising families in their new home. Today, Ketura has grown to be the second-largest settlement in the region, with 140 members and candidates and over 140 children. One-third of the members are native Israelis; the majority of the immigrants come from English-speaking countries with a smaller number from Europe and the former USSR. [Mar99]

KIBBUTZ LOTAN

IL-88855 DN Chevel Eilot
Israel

+972-7-6356888, +972-7-6356935
+972-7-6356827 fax
edt_lot@hotmail.com
http://www.kibbutzlotan.com/

Began 1983 | Pop. 125
Diet: Omnivore | Rural | Spiritual

Kibbutz Lotan: Our Path to the Fulfillment of Our Vision

We the members of Kibbutz Lotan, have chosen to establish here our home and our future. Through our commitment to Am Yisrael, Torat Yisrael, and the State of Israel, we are working together to create a community based on Reform Zionist Jewish values:

We the members of Kibbutz Lotan, have chosen to establish here our home and our future. Through our commitment to Am Yisrael, Torat Yisrael, and the State of Israel, we are working together to create a community based on Reform Zionist Jewish values:

• Jewish Renewal: We work toward creating a progressive expression of Jewish religion and culture in our rituals and day-to-day life, through Nitzvot in our relationship between each other and with God.

• Equality: Our belief in equality is expressed in direct democracy, equality in the workplace, gender equality, and mutual responsibility.

• Economic Cooperation: Together we are responsible for our livelihood and share our resources as an expression of our belief in the strength of communal action.

• Ecology: We strive to fulfill the biblical ideal to tell and preserve it in our homes, our region, the country, and the world. We are working to create ways to live in harmony with our desert environment.

• I-Thou: We aspire to meaningful relationships with one another of openness, communication, and mutual respect.

• Livelihood: We strive for economic independence and aim to support ourselves in ways that are in keeping with our values.

• Home and Community: Our commitment to our home and community is expressed through cooperative action in work, education, culture, health, and day-to-day life.

• Tikun Olam—Repairing the World: We work toward the betterment of ourselves, our people, and the world. Our home is a community of Shlichut. Our way of life constitutes a message we wish to impart to those that enter our gates and to the circles of society in which we are involved.

This declaration is a living document that requires of us ongoing involvement and action.

It is not for you to complete the work. Neither are you free to desist from it. Signed by the members of Kibbutz Lotan, 23 October 1997 [Dec98]

KIBBUTZ MOVEMENT, THE

Yoel Darom
Kibbutz Kfar Menachem
IL-79875
ISRAEL
08-8508422

Began 1910 | Rural | Spiritual

The Kibbutz movement is the largest communitarian movement in the world today. The first Kibbutz was founded in 1910; today (1999) there are 260 Kibbutzim with a population of about 123,000; most of them range between 150 and 700 adults and children.

Each Kibbutz is a socially and economically autonomous unit, but there are strong bonds of cooperation and mutual help between them. These bonds have been formalized and streamlined in national federations that coordinate activities of their member Kibbutzim and provide them with economic, social, cultural, and other services.

Each Kibbutz is a distinct socioeconomic entity, based on a common purse, with no (or nearly no) private property.

Economic operations are communally owned and run, making the Kibbutz the most complete example of worker ownership and management. Work is an important part of the Kibbutz way of life and is regarded as a vital means of personal

involvement in the life of the community. That is why even most of the older people choose to work a few hours a day. Teamwork is stressed in an atmosphere of informality. Advances in higher educational and professional training have encouraged more members to find satisfying work outside the Kibbutz.

All housing is provided by the Kibbutz. While consumption is in principle collective, the growing influence of consumerism (of the last 10 to 20 years) has led to a redistribution of resources, with more money allocated to personal budgets in order to allow for greater individual choice. Most needed services are provided by the Kibbutz, but increasingly family life becomes more central to members, and the collective often has to take second place. A few Kibbutzim have introduced "differential wages," and this step is seen by many as passing the border between Kibbutz and non-Kibbutz. However, the vast majority of the Kibbutzim keep up their initial principles of communal life, with changes in lifestyle and rules that modern times dictate.

The Kibbutz federation issues two weeklies and one magazine, *CALL*, that endeavors to contact and network all communes and communities in the world. [May99, cc]

KIBBUTZ NEOT SEMADAR

Kibbutz Neot Semadar
IL-88860 DN Eilot
ISRAEL
972-7-6358111, 972-7-6358168 fax

Began 1989 | Pop. 158
Diet: No red meat | Rural

Neot Semadar was founded in 1989 in the Negev Desert by a group of friends from Jerusalem. This step came about after years of self-inquiry and collective study of the problems all individuals face worldwide—alienation, prejudice, competition—all that which leads to a life devoid of true joy, depth, and creativity. Today we number 110 adults and 70 children, averaging in age 30–45 and professionally trained and educated in a large variety of fields, which has allowed us to branch out into many different areas simultaneously. It is through special projects that our common interest in forming this learning community gets truly expressed. A challenge to one's preconceived notions and fixed habits, these projects foster a conducive space for meeting the obstacles that get in the way of true cooperation

through self-observation, and they provide the community with an opportunity to experience the joy of being together. They have also become a source of steady income. We have invested most of our energy into organic agriculture and are building a small produce factory that will house our products: winery, olive-oil press, goat dairy, honey, and fruit jam. Other branches include a documentary film company, a construction company, a roadside tavern, and a souvenir shop. The Arts and Crafts Center is our main project that all members help to build. An experiment in desert architecture, it will provide an educational center for the kibbutz, for foreign and local students, for tourists and volunteers. Interested colearners can write us. [Aug99, sase requested]

KIBBUTZ TAMUZ

PO Box 4566
IL-99500 Bet Shemesh
ISRAEL
972 2 9918872, 972 2 9918872 fax
kibbutztamuz@geocities.com
http://www.tamuz.org.il/

Began 1987 | Diet: Omnivore | Urban

Kibbutz Tamuz is located in the city of Beit Shemesh, Israel, which is approximately 30 minutes west of Jerusalem. The kibbutz was founded in the summer of 1987 by nine people who had previously been active in the kibbutz movement on other kibbutzim but had been disillusioned with the traditional kibbutz. The kibbutz belongs to the United Kibbutz Movement and is one of three urban kibbutzim in the country.

Kibbutz Tamuz is an urban kibbutz, a small Jewish community, and like the traditional kibbutz, Tamuz is a collective. Its 33 members function as a single economic unit, expressing the socialist ideals of equality and cooperation, ideas and praxis. However, unlike the traditional kibbutz, we are located in an urban environment, keeping us in tune with what is happening in society around us.

Equality and collectivism, like in the traditional kibbutz, are expressed through financial, social, and culture cooperation. All salaries and incomes are given to the kibbutz, and the members receive a budget according to the size of their family. The kibbutz covers all housing, health, transportation, and joint cultural expenses, and the personal budget covers the rest (unlike on most traditional kibbutzim, food and utilities are paid for by the member's personal budget). Any jobs or activities that need to be done around the kibbutz are done by members volunteering at weekly general assembly meetings, which also deal with decisions that have to be made by the group. [May99]

KIDSTOWN

PO Box 826
Middletown CA 95461

707-987-0669

Began 1991 | Pop. 4

We presently parent and grandparent deprived neighborhood children, teaching them high principles and how to live a harmonious life within dysfunctional families and society. We have been trying to prepare our neighborhood, town, county, and neighboring counties for the Y2K debacle since 1998. Hopefully we'll continue with our highest priority, which is turning around tyrannical corporations and countries depriving people of their human rights and abuse and destruction of the environment.

We are evolving into a spiritual, activistic community, which may seem like an oxymoron but which is necessary for our own emotional, spiritual, and psychological health if we are to oppose the dark forces unleashed by uncontrollable and destructive corporate power.

We don't feel pets, alcohol, drugs, tobacco, and violence are necessary to achieve our ideals and goals.

Everything and everyone can and will be questioned for any reason.

Folks into green-business creation will be assisted as will children learning to be entrepreneurs. We are networking with other unlisted communities in our beautiful and healthful Lake County that are into organic gardening and permaculture. Real Goods is an hour away by auto. Call or write post Y2K. With love, Bob B. [Apr99, sase required, no openings]

KINDNESS HOUSE

Rt 1 Box 201-N
Durham NC 27705

919-304-2220
http://www.humankindness.org/

Began 1994 | Pop. 7
Diet: Vegetarian | Rural | Spiritual

(Also known as Human Kindness Fdtn/Prison-Ashram Project.) Kindness House is a rural interfaith spiritual community that revolves around service. Our main work is to run the Human Kindness Foundation and its long-standing Prison-Ashram Project, which keeps us in touch with tens of thousands of people around the world.

If you are familiar with Bo Lozoff's writings or talks, you already have some idea of our lifestyle: A threefold focus of simple living, committed spiritual practice, and a dedication to service. If you are not familiar with his work, you may visit our Web site or order materials from our catalog in order to get a basic feel for the views and evolution of our organization and community.

We believe that in order to be of service to others, we must always continue to deepen our own spiritual realization, and so our community life emphasizes work, practice, and study in a spirit of simple joy, mindfulness, and quietude, seeing every task equally as spiritual practice; every moment worthy of equal respect and attention.

There are several ways to join us in our work and community life—as a visitor, an intern, a parolee, or a member of our staff. If you wish to visit Kindness House, please contact us for information at least a month in advance, with your preferred dates clearly noted. [Feb99]

KING HOUSE

804 E Kingsley
Ann Arbor MI 48104

Pop. 8

King House is a nonsmoking apartment cooperative with six units.

Current ICC members have priority for signing contracts. King contracts are for 12 months, September 1–August 31. Apartments are not furnished. However, kitchen appliances, washer and dryer, and on-site parking are available. King is required to contribute to the ICC governance structure by electing a president to sit on the ICC board. King also encourages members to either sit on an ICC committee or provide ICC office labor. Other house jobs include yard maintenance, serving as maintenance manager, purchasing supplies, and acting as treasurer, among others. [Oct99]

KINGMAN HALL

1730 La Loma Ave
Berkeley CA 94709

510-841-6455

Began 1977 | Pop. 51
Diet: Omnivore | Rural/Urban

(Also known as The Living Love Center). Kingman is so funky, it would take a government crew eight weeks to remove all the funk.

The essence of our former identity, Living Love Center, permeates the wandering nooks and spaces in this house; be it in ephemeral murals found up here or behind there or within the constant flux of kindred spirits. Smile, smile, smile.

It's cool "cuz all my homies can kick it and it's all good ..."

Kingman has a giant amoeba-shaped dining room table that everyone can sit around and face each other while enjoying good food and gooder conversation.—Zak (English major)

It is a really social place here and great for networking.

It's superfly.

Kingman Hall is above all a home for 49 students who get to experience communal

Key to bracketed text: cc = cannot commit to prompt correspondance, sase = self-addressed stamped envelope

living with all its benefits and all its drawbacks.

Indeed, Kingman surpasses all expectations. —Half-Fish. [Feb99, no openings]

KITEZH CHILDREN'S ECO-VILLAGE COMMUNITY

Kaluzhuskaya oblast
Baryatino rayon
249650
RUSSIA
care of Ecologia Trust
The Park
Forres IV36 OTZ, Scotland
UNITED KINGDOM

+7-08454-23224
+7-095-969-2181 fax Marina Furta
kitezh@kaluga.ru
ecoliza@rmplc.co.uk
http://www.ecovillages.org/
russia/kitezh/

Began 1992
Diet: Omnivore | Rural | Spiritual

Kitezh is an exciting place, one of a kind in Russia, a community of happiness and joyful refuge for abandoned or orphaned Russian children. Kitezh is a new way of looking at life: it is a living, working community, a spiritual movement of people who build their lives on the principles of harmony, peace, and love. Kitezhans aim to live in harmony with nature. They are warm, open-hearted. By serving others, they serve themselves.

Since 1992 Kitezh has functioned as a community of foster families who offer secure homes and schooling for orphaned Russian children. At present seven families with 30 children live 300 kilometers south of Moscow in Kaluga region on 90 hectares of land, and Kitezh is growing fast. They have already built 10 houses, a school, a church, and an organic farm. The Kitezh school is recognized by the state.

Every summer volunteers and students from all over the world come to Kitezh to help: building, gardening, and working with the children. You're welcome!

The Kitezh way of fostering and educating children has already proved a real alternative to state orphanages. One day communities based on the Kitezh model will replace all orphanages in Russia. This is our dream, to give loving homes and a future to *all* orphan children. [May99]

KYNHEARTH

1398 Cox Store Rd SW
Floyd VA 24091
pat@swva.net
http://www.geocities.com/
RainForest/6956/

Began 1995 | Pop. 3 | Re-Forming
Diet: Vegan | Rural

(Also known as Access.) KynHearth is presently in the midst of re-forming. We are a polyamorous, inclusive, vegetarian ecovillage. We are living on 69 acres of wooded land in the beautiful Blue Ridge Mountains of southwestern Virginia. Solar-powered energy supply, fresh free-running springwater, two lively streams, a very small organic garden, and magical woodland spaces describe our home.

We are open to new "family" members to share our lives, home, and dreams. We are dedicated to interpersonal and environmental sustainability.

Current projects include monthly drum circles, biodiesel fuel production, building deconstruction, nontimber forest products, green building projects, polyamorous workshops, and innovative recycling concepts.

Our basic principles include honest communication, love, trust, respect, nonviolence (physical and emotional), hand tools or non–petrochemically powered tools, and as much fun as we can possibly create.

Write or e-mail for more information or to arrange a visit. [Oct99]

L.I.F.E.

111 Charity Ln
Gladstone VA 24553

Began 1996 | Pop. 25 | Rural

Land Investments for Edification (L.I.F.E.) is a partnership of nine families. We collectively own 135 acres in rural Virginia. We are building an intentional Christian community that can serve as a "retreat" environ-

Additions and corrections: Email: directory@ic.org, Web: http://directory.ic.org/, Mail: RR 1 Box 156-D, Rutledge MO 63563, USA.

Listings

ment as well as a stable, alternate lifestyle. An emphasis is placed on "old-fashioned" extended family, simplicity, mutual ministry, hospitality, consensus, and financial freedom and independence.

The concept for L.I.F.E. began in fall 1991, with official formation in spring 1993. Property was purchased in April 1995, and in January 1996 residents moved in.

We are associated with Grace Edification Ministries and produce a monthly Bible study entitled the *Bible Student's Notebook* and operate a mail-order book ministry, Grace Clearinghouse [Apr99, no openings]

L'ARCHE ERIE

1101 Peach St - 2FL
Erie PA 16501

814-452-2065, 814-452-4188 fax
L'ARCHE@velocity.net

Began 1972 | Pop. 63 | Re-Forming
Diet: Omnivore | Urban | Spiritual

(Also known as "The Hearth".) L'Arche Erie is a Christian community in which persons with developmental disabilities and those who help them live, work, and share their lives together in a home setting.

Our emphasis is on sharing our life together as we seek to build mutual relationships of respect, acceptance, and interdependence while encouraging a positive self-image for all persons. We believe that each person has unique gifts and encourage the growth of all individuals to their fullest potential.

Our community is inspired by a Gospel-based vision that unites all communities in the International Federation of L'Arche. [Jul99, cc]

L'ARCHE - HOMEFIRES

PO Box 1296
Wolfville Nova Scotia B4N 3R4
CANADA

902-542-3520

Began 1981 | Re-Forming
Rural/Urban | Spiritual

(Also known as Wolfville L'Arche Homefires Soc.) L'Arche Homefires is an ecumenical Christian community where people with developmental disabilities and those who choose to share life with them live together and build community. We are a member of the International Federation of L'Arche Communities. Our mission is: (a) to create

homes where faithful relationships based on forgiveness and celebration are nurtured; (b) to change society by choosing to live in community as a sign of hope and love.

Our community presently has five homes, a workshop, and a day program. We provide home/work for 17 people with disabilities. Our life is simple, centered around building relationships and celebrations. Assistants and persons with a disability live in the same home and build relationship through doing tasks together, cooking, prayer, cleaning, etc. We work together; sometimes the work is hard as we learn to serve each other. But there is much joy, and we discover that we often receive more than we give. [Jan99]

L'ARCHE MOBILE INC

151 S Ann
Mobile AL 36604

334-438-2094
larchmob@acan.net
http://www2.acan.net/archmob/

Began 1974 | Pop. 44
Diet: Omnivore | Urban | Spiritual

L'Arche Mobile is a Christian community that provides family-like homes for people with a mental handicap and assistants who chose to live in our community homes. Our life consists of creating authentic relationships with each as well as trying to meet the needs of each person who lives in our homes.

The fundamental aspects of L'Arche are as follows: (1) Recognition of the unique value of a person with a developmental disability to reveal that human suffering and joy can lead to growth, healing, and unity. (2) Life sharing, where persons with a developmental disability and those who assist them live, work, and pray together. (3) Relationships of mutuality in which people give and receive love. (4) Based on the Gospel and dependent on the spirit of God where faithful relationships, forgiveness, and celebration reveal God's personal presence and love.

Our mission is: (1) to create homes where faithful relationships based on forgiveness and celebration are nurtured; (2) to reveal the unique value and vocation of each person; 3. to change society by choosing to live relationships in community as a sign of hope and love. [Jan99]

LA SENDA ECOVILLAGE

APDO 595
San Miguel de Allende
GTO 37700
MEXICO

(52) 415-35161
rickwelland36@hotmail.com
juliettesanchez@hotmail.com

Began 1997
Diet: No red meat | Rural | Spiritual

Our vision—to make the most of our spiritual, mental, and physical capacities in a sustainable environment. Our location in Mexico provides us with mild year-round climate and food production; plenty of water; a beautiful canyon/river ambience. Living units are on a south-facing slope for passive-solar heating and cooling and are 850-square-foot two-bedroom accommodations with arched 14-foot brick ceilings providing beauty and insulation. Common area consists of learning/studio space, laundry, and two-person solar-heated Jacuzzi. All water is solar pumped to roof tanks, then recycled—gray to garden areas; black to a methane digester—then to constructed wetlands and our fruit trees. We have restructured an old river bed into large ponds for beauty and aquaculture.. With several artists living here we maintain a small gallery in the art-colony city of San Miquel de Allende 11 miles away. Lacking a handy dictator or guru our chosen path to harmony is consultation aimed at consensus after the facts are on the table. Comfortable self-subsistence is our aim—maintaining careful consumption levels. We try to be thankful for the clean *air*, beautiful *earth*, usable *water*, and *fire*—goodhearted indigenous families that provide us with the opportunity to reach out beyond ourselves. [May99]

LA VIEILLE VOIE COMMUNAUTÉ

Vieille Voie de Tongres 33
B-4000 Liège
BELGIUM

33 4 224 46 37, 33 4 226 45 75
j.defourny@ulg.ac.be

Began 1988 | Urban | Spiritual

(Also known as L'Habitat Groupé.) Our community was born in the context of a renewal of a local Catholic parish in the 1970s and 1980s. A large number of Christians then formed groups ("équipes de vie"), and one of them wanted to have a more intensive collective life and prayer. So we built six houses after having bought part of the priests' garden. We are still active members of this parish of which we are "a stone among many others."

The highest priority of the community is the autonomy of each family life, and we have in common

• a large meeting room and a room for visitors as well as a small "chapel";

• the garden;

• two funds to which each member contributes a small part of their income, one for collective material expenses, the other for spiritual activities or donations to other associations.

Our common life is mainly composed of

• a common meal each Saturday noon;

• a common prayer each night;

• regular meetings and an annual spiritual weekend. [May99]

LAKE CLAIRE COHOUSING

404-687-0179
greenelowe@mindspring.com

Began 1997 | Pop. 29
Diet: Vegetarian | Urban

(Also known as Arizona Avenue Commons.) We are an urban cohousing with 12 townhouses and a common house on one acre. About half the households have children, and these kids are like siblings to each other. The adults range in age from 30 to 50. We have common dinners twice a week and potlucks several times a month. Our common meals are vegetarian, but only half our members eat vegetarian in their own homes. On Sunday mornings, we gather at the common house for bagels and the *New York Times*. Some members practice yoga together; some watch videos together; some of us volunteer to help resettle refugees. Sometimes we have a bonfire in our courtyard, and sometimes we sit around one of our fountains. The architecture is beautiful and the gardens are lush, lending a European-village feeling to our small site. Our small size (30 adults) makes for an intimate group, but it's harder to get things done. We recycle, we compost, and we have a small organic garden. We are trying to do some ride sharing, but this is not an efficient system yet. We make decisions by consensus. Right now our community is doing pretty well, having completed some major landscaping projects and worked through some social problems.

It can be hard, but mostly wonderful. [Sep99, cc, no openings]

LAKE VILLAGE

7943 So 25th St
Kalamazoo MI 49001

616-327-0614, 616-323-3629

Began 1966 | Pop. 42 | Rural/Urban

The Lake Village farm was begun in 1971, dedicated to exploring a more sustainable environmental ethic. This extended-family commune occupies a mile and one-half of Long Lake's northeast shoreline, having grown to approximately 350 acres of forest, meadow, and farming space. Over the past 30 years there have been approximately 300 different people from all over the world who have participated in the Lake Village program. Today there are 50 members in all who are a part of this cooperative farm effort. Most members live on additional land purchased privately, bordering the Lake Village premises. Some members live off the farm while working there during the day. Others live on the commune and hold jobs in the greater Kalamazoo area as teachers, social workers, secretaries, waitstaff, plumbers, roofers, counselors, and, of course, as students in the various area schools.

We consider ourselves a large extended family and are very much a part of the greater Kalamazoo community, which we hope is likewise dedicated to promoting an ecological, sustainable lifestyle—so that our children's children may enjoy the future blessings of a healthy Mother Earth. Welcome to our home and yours. [Nov98]

LAMA FOUNDATION

PO Box 240
San Cristobal NM 87564

505-586-1269, 505-586-1964 fax
lama@compuserve.com
lama@newmex.com
http://www.taosnet.com/lama/

Began 1968 | Pop. 17 | Re-Forming
Diet: Vegetarian | Rural | Spiritual

Lama Foundation aims to serve as a sustainable spiritual community and educational center dedicated to the awakening of consciousness, service, spiritual practice with respect for all traditions, and stewardship of the land. Community life is viewed as a school of practical spirituality whose focus is individual and collective spiritual growth through service to others, simplicity of lifestyle, self-awareness, and commitment to daily spiritual practice in some form. Members learn mindfulness and responsible stewardship as well as skills such as gardening, cooking, carpentry, and silk-screen printing. Community-building skills are a continuing focus. The community works together as a circle in caring for the foundation, and we strive for consensus in decision making. Summers are an out breath with many visitors and a public program of spiritual workshops, retreats, and hermitage. We also operate a cottage industry for producing prayer flags and rubber stamps. Winters are an in breath where members continue to serve and can also take more time for intensive contemplative practice and study.

At this time, we are still in the process of rebuilding facilities destroyed in a 1996 fire. Life is rustic. The land and views are amazing. [Oct99, sase requested]

Additions and corrections: Email: directory@ic.org, Web: http://directory.ic.org/, Mail: RR 1 Box 156-D, Rutledge MO 63563, USA.

LAND STEWARDSHIP CENTER, THE

PO Box 225
Columbiaville MI 48421

810-793-5303, 810-793-7528
clark@booray.new-era.com

Began 1993 | Pop. 7 | Rural

The Land Stewardship Center in Columbiaville, Michigan, is a local, non-profit organization formed to help revitalize and maintain the Tibbits farm as a demonstration of good land stewardship practices. There are currently three households at the center that live and work cooperatively to demonstrate and promote good land stewardship practices. Our goal is to learn to live more in harmony with the rest of nature. Community activities include gardening, reforestation, wetland and animal habitat restoration, potluck meals, and having fun together. We welcome casual, day visitors as well as extended stays by apprentices, interns and other people who think they might be interested in working and living with us on a long-term basis. [Aug99, sase requested]

LANDELIJKE VERENIGING CENTRAAL WONEN

Grenadadreef 1-J
NL-3563 HE Utrecht
THE NETHERLANDS

030-2612585

National association of cohousing projects in Holland. Each household has its own house or apartment and one share in the common facilities, which typically include a fully equipped kitchen, play areas, and meeting rooms. Residents share cooking, cleaning, and gardening on a rotating basis. By working together and combining their resources, collaborative-housing residents can have the advantages of a private home and the convenience of shared services and amenities.

LAURIESTON HALL

Laurieston
Castle Douglas DG7 2NB, Scotland
UNITED KINGDOM

Began 1972 | Diet: Omnivore | Rural

Some of us live singly, some in families, and some in small living groups. There's a huge house, plus cottages and caravans, and about 135 acres of forest and grazing.

We don't income share, but we do all take a share of the work, which keeps everyone's living expenses fairly low; processing of wood for fuel, growing food, animal care, looking after the finances, maintenance of and improvements to the buildings and land.

Much of what we eat is home-produced—there are cows, calves, hens, bees, pigs, and a large fruit and vegetable garden—and we have a food co-op for brought-in food.

Our heating is all from woodstoves—all the adults go on a weekly wood-collecting trip into the forest—and we have a hydro-electric scheme.

Every year we have three "Maintenance Fortnights" when we all eat and work together. Visitors are welcome to stay with us at these times.

The *People Center* provides income-earning work for some of us; organizing and running events, courses, and workshops for groups of 15–75 people from spring to autumn. [May99]

LE NOVALIS

Frédéric Lemire
810 boul des Mille - îles
Auteuil Laval Québec H7L 1K5
CANADA

514-897-8266
flemire@cam.org
fredavatar@moncourrier.com
http://www.cam.org/
~flemire/novalis/fr/novalis.htm

Began 1996 | Forming
Diet: Vegetarian | Rural/Urban | Spiritual

Le Novalis is a forming community, possibly modular (i.e., disseminated), where we'll gather around projects of artistic/creative, social/ecological, and philosophical/spiritual scope, often using computers. Leisure won't be our last preoccupation. Each resident will have their own bedroom. Children won't be accepted as residents unless they are age seven and over and come voluntarily. There is a trial period for newcomers. Decisions will be taken by all members (resident or not) and by consensus. As much as possible, we will produce our own food and cook it ourselves. The community will also be an inn, an art gallery, and a restaurant for visitors. It will be vegetarian and will recycle as

Key to bracketed text: cc = cannot commit to prompt correspondance, sase = self-addressed stamped envelope

much as possible. It will be situated possibly in Quebec, possibly in or around Montreal, but possibly also elsewhere on the globe, in places where people speak French or English, ideally near a lake. The name of the community has been chosen after Novalis, a German romantic writer of the eighteenth century, who left us mystical poems and the fragments of a thought that was still dreaming (he died at the age of 29) of a reconciliation between science and poetry, music and mathematics, nature and metaphysics. Please surf our French Web page listed above. [Jul99, cc, sase requested]

LEARNERS TREK

138 Twin Oaks Rd
Louisa VA 23093

503-217-1368 fax
LearnersTrek@yahoo.com
http://www.twinoaks.org/
members/felix/learnerstrek.htm

Began 1999 | Forming
Learners Trek (LT): is a community forming based on the lifelong desire to learn, play, and teach. I would like to help create a community where the pursuit of knowledge, systems thinking, personal growth, health, and recreation are the main goals. I feel there is passion and synergy in proactive learning and play with others that satisfies my soul, matures my spirit, and frees my creative juices. I envision a community of people who wish to prioritize their time and resources to learn the knowledge and skills that empowers a human being personally and in our society at large.

The community would embrace the use of multimedia and the Internet to maximize learning, systems thinking, communicating, and teaching in and from the community. I imagine LT to use the Internet to support community administration and industries.

Aside from the main agenda of learning, I envision a mostly income-sharing system with the creation of and contribution to leaving/retirement accounts for every member so that they may have more options as they grow older or decide to leave the community. This I believe is fair and would allow people to feel more flexibility when committing to LT. [Sep99]

LEBENSGARTEN STEYERBERG

Ginsterweg 3
D-31595 Steyerberg
GERMANY

05764-2370, 05764-2578 fax
lebensgarten_eu@t-online.de
http://www.lebensgarten.de/

Began 1985 | Diet: Vegetarian | Rural
Fourteen years ago, the nonprofit organization Lebensgarten Inc. was founded. In 1985, the people who began to fill the settlement that was originally built in 1938 with new life wanted a lifestyle characterized by mutual respect, tolerance, affection, and love. They wanted to enable women, men, and children to develop, to foster their creativity, to support each other, and to discover or develop their own brand of spirituality. Equally important were and are cooperation with nature and living ecologically soundly from day to day. By now, 90 adults and 52 children are part of the project.

Everybody is responsible for their own finances. We do not have a guru. We are using a restricted system of consensus to make our decisions.

We have a large communal building at our disposal and a hall that can seat as many as 500 people during events and that we are currently renovating. Apart from running the seminar house and guest house and the office buildings, we built the school for communication and mediation; consulting rooms for nature-cure practitioners, ergotherapists, psychotherapists, and music therapists; goldsmith and jewelry workshops; a bookstore; a small riding stable; a shop selling ecological construction material; an office for consulting businesses in ecological questions; and an ecological architectural and planning office. We also have freelance artists and musicians who are enriching our life here. [Mar99]

LEE ABBEY ASTON HOUSEHOLD COMMUNITY

121 Albert Rd
Aston
Birmingham B65ND, England
UNITED KINGDOM

0121-326-8280

Began 1988 | Pop. 4
Diet: Omnivore | Urban | Spiritual
Our aim is to model the Jesus life in fellowship with local churches. To live simply, sharing all expenses, tasks. To have open house for local people, most of whom are from the Caribbean, India, Pakistan, or Bangladesh.

All members work locally to enable the house to function, and they belong to local churches and support action taken to benefit the neighborhood. We often have short-term visitors seeking help, counsel, or healing. Members agree to be honest with each other and seek to discover how to know Jesus better and how to do his will. [Feb99, sase requested]

LESBIAN AND GAY SPIRITUAL COMMUNITY

c/o Sabina Zeeb
1 Mountain Home Park
Brattleboro VT 05301

802-257-2734
sabinazeeb@yahoo.com

Pop. 2 | Forming
Diet: Vegetarian | Rural | Spiritual
The Lesbian and Gay Spiritual Community (temporary name) is in its formation stages.

Additions and corrections: Email: directory@ic.org, Web: http://directory.ic.org/, Mail: RR 1 Box 156-D, Rutledge MO 63563, USA.

We envision a land-based community in southeastern Vermont, with some 25 adults (and children?) who have a desire to live out their personal spiritual ideals through committed, harmonious relationships with each other and the planet. While there would be no specific spirituality, gays and lesbians (and allies) with developed spiritual practices can come together to share knowledge, support, and individual and group practices.

The community seeks to provide a queer-positive space for lesbians and gays who may have been marginalized in traditional spiritual communities, and to form committed, familial bonds among members. We hope for a diverse community; racial, socio-economic, age, ability, and lifestyle (individuals, couples, celibate or not, etc.). Contact with the broader gay/lesbian community, as well as personal political/social/ecological activism, would be encouraged.

Legal details, financial and governance structures, etc. will be worked out with a core group once it forms. Currently we are two lesbians (a couple) with over 20 years of community living experience and some 30 years of spiritual practice between us. Please write us. [Sep99, sase requested]

LESTER HOUSE

**900 Oakland
Ann Arbor MI 48104
http://www.umich.edu/~umicc/**

Lester is a cozy 15-person vegetarian co-op with a vegan option. As a smaller house, Lester definitely has a different feel than the other co-ops. When you move into Lester, you move into a home. That means that you know everyone in the house and it is noticeable when you aren't around. This is good and bad, depending on what you like. Because we are such a small house, our house meetings are run by consensus, so that everyone's voice is heard. Compromise and communication are paramount in Lester.

Lester is one of the older houses in the ICC and was originally an all-female house. Lester has an extensive progressive history. So, as you move into the "red barn" feel free to take on the forward-thinking attitude that helped create this house. [Oct99]

LIBERTY VILLAGE COHOUSING

**Liberty Village
Route 26 at Route 31
Libertytown MD**

**800-400-0621, 301-652-5946
info@libertyvillage.com
cstarke@mc.cc.md.us
http://www.libertyvillage.com/**

Began 1989 | Pop. 42 | Rural

Our vision: a community where every voice of every age is valued; a place where we can achieve more together than individually.

Some of us have known each other for a decade. Most of us have known each other for three or more years, attending biweekly business meetings and potluck dinners. Our members have been drawn mostly from the Frederick, Baltimore, and Washington, DC, areas.

When we get home in the evening, we can eat dinner together in the common house, talk about the day's activities, watch beautiful sunsets, go bike or hike, garden, play with the kids, watch TV, work on projects, yawn, and go home to bed.

The homes are mostly duplexes, clustered on 8 of the 23 acres around a green, pedestrian common area. All can walk to the community building in a minute or less. Six of the units, closest to the community building, are designed to be handicap/elderly friendly.

The remaining 15 acres will be a mix of fields, woods, gardens, orchards, and wetlands. We are fortunate to have a 105-acre public park next door that already has soccer and softball fields, tennis and basketball courts, a children's play area, hiking and biking trails, fields and woods. On another side is a horse farm and, on another, 5-acre farmettes. [Oct99]

LICHEN CO-OP

**PO Box 25
Wolf Creek OR 97497**

541-866-2665

Began 1971 | Pop. 6
Diet: Vegetarian | Rural | Spiritual

Lichen, established in 1971 as a cooperative, is a community of organisms, living and growing together for mutual benefit. Several years ago, we also became a land conservancy trust, with the trust owning the land. Our facilities include a community building, four satellite retreats, a lab, a shop, a small solar greenhouse, and a garden area. Most of our 140 acres are devoted to a wildlife

refuge and environmental sanctuary; as a result, we now prohibit domestic animals. Some regular monthly income is necessary, earned here or elsewhere, or previously (such as a pension check). Monthly expenses vary with seasons, tastes, and other factors, but about $250 a month would be a minimum. Environmentalism is our nearest approach to a community spirituality, and our philosophy of personal growth is based on the individual's development within a community context. This is not a putdown of individuals; rather, it emphasizes each as a part of an interdependent group. Visitors are welcome with advance arrangements. For more information, please write, including significant information about yourself. A dollar or two to help with various correspondence expenses would also be appreciated. [Jan99, sase required]

LIFE CENTER ASSOCIATION

**4722 Baltimore Ave
Philadelphia PA 19143**

Began 1973 | Pop. 36
Diet: Vegetarian | Urban

Originally formed as a support community for MNS (Movement for a New Society), the Life Center Association (LCA) is now a democratically structured organization created to develop and promote nonprofit cooperative ownership and management of property. The LCA owns and holds property in trust, keeping it affordable and well maintained for the long-term use of individuals and groups.

Six of our seven west Philadelphia properties are leased to communal houses of six or seven people each. The seventh property has two apartments, as well as offices for three nonprofit community organizations. Each household chooses its own members and is fairly autonomous. Many members are involved in community and political activities. Openings occur sporadically. [Jan99, sase required]

LIGHT AS COLOR FOUNDATION

**PO Box 2947
Pagosa Springs CO 81147**

970-264-6250

Began 1997 | Pop. 8 | Forming
Diet: No red meat | Rural | Spiritual

A spiritually conscious group of neighbors

Key to bracketed text: cc = cannot commit to prompt correspondance, sase = self-addressed stamped envelope

in south Colorado, attuned to nature, holism, and the visual arts. Modeled somewhat after Findhorn University of Light in Scotland. An educational retreat and conference center, small but networked. Pristine natural environment with gardens beside river and national forest. We have studios for multiple media: pottery, photography, stained glass, painting, weaving, dyeing, etc. Emphasis on freedom of creative flow through visual and tactile arts and the useful power of color to balance, heal, and uplift. We offer multitraditional shamanic journeys, spirit walks, and ceremonies. Apprentice programs in all the above. Organic process in new membership and a centering conduit for those who want to try living at 7,000-foot river valley. Our community of neighbors interacts with similar holistic focus. General ambience of peace and upliftment, natural serenity, and quiet industry. Individual development supported. Self-responsibility for livelihood. Focused organic process without rigid preconceptions for growth. Shop and mail order for products. Guests welcome with advance notice. Mature, responsible folks interested in both community and privacy most welcome. Excellent hot springs in town. [Jan99, sase requested]

LIGHT MORNING

Light Morning
Southwest Virginia

Began 1973 | Pop. 18
Diet: Vegetarian | Rural | Spiritual

Light Morning is a small community of diverse folks who share meals, work, and a common vision. Since our arrival here in 1974, we have been exploring the following possibilities—that good health and self-esteem deserve cultivation; that a simpler lifestyle will enable us to live closer to the Earth; that the Earth itself is a living creature; that we, as a species, are ripening into an awareness that we cocreate our personal and world circumstances; that a new kind of family can greatly assist in this ripening; and finally, that our daily life is the proving ground for such hypotheses.

Our experiments along these lines have resulted in varying degrees of success. What we have to offer are our lifestyle, our experience, and our tentative conclusions—as well as a good collection of unresolved issues and questions. We highly value our continuing exchanges with visitors, friends, and neighbors, many of whom are exploring similar growing edges. [Jan99, sase required]

LIGHT OF FREEDOM, INC

Rt 3 Box 185
Willis VA 24380

540-593-2169, 540-593-3053
lightoffreedom@usa.net
loftricia@aol.com, thaisbo@usa.net,
tommypancke@hotmail.com

Began Jan99 | Pop. 6 | Forming
Diet: Omnivore | Rural | Spiritual

Light of Freedom is located near the beautiful Blue Ridge Parkway in southern Virginia. We are a community dedicated to truth—all is one. In oneness we see our equality as God created us. Our relationships with each other, nature, and God are derived from the principles of *A Course in Miracles*, which we highly value as a guide for a happy life. Everyone has their own chosen work and interests including horticulture, art, crafts, architecture, aquaculture, and writing, on land owned by the community. Individuals live in a community house or build their own sustainable homestead. Alternative building methods are encouraged. We live off the grid, preferring to catch and use the sun, wind, water, and earth given us, returning them naturally to the life cycle. We maintain our quiet enjoyment of organic gardening, ponds, and

Additions and corrections: Email: directory@ic.org, Web: http://directory.ic.org/, Mail: RR 1 Box 156-D, Rutledge MO 63563, USA.

orchard with future vineyard plans. We give workshops on *A Course in Miracles* and alternative building methods. We meet as a community on a regular basis where decisions are made by consensus. Meetings begin with our acknowledgment of peace as our one goal, and in peace, understanding comes, allowing us to perceive solutions to community problems. We recognize we share one spirit and one life, and all decisions are given to spirit for guidance, directions, and resolution.

For our community, living by the "Golden Rule" is to perceive in others what you would have them perceive in you. Our vision at Light of Freedom is, and will be, a happy gathering of equals. We welcome visitors—call or write for directions and availability of accommodations. [May99, sase required]

LINDER HOUSE

**711 Catherine
Ann Arbor MI 48104
http://www.umich.edu/~umicc/**

The ICC bought Linder in 1989. The house itself has been around for a long time and has a lot of collective history in it, as it has been home to many organized groups.

The house was built in 1894 ... over 100 years old! Wow! Anyway ... it was inhabited by fraternity members back then, as it was the Phi Chi fraternity in 1896. In 1904 it became property of the New York State Club; then it turned over into the hands of the Keystone Club the next year; and by 1907 the Empire State Club owned it.

In the 1920s the McNaughton family bought the house, but by the 1960s it was a boardinghouse once again. In 1989 the ICC bought the house, and the first co-opers moved in. Check out our house portfolio/scrapbook to "meet" some of these folks!

My favorite part of Linder is the beautiful woodwork. The banisters and the window frames are especially beautifully carved, and the wooden floors in the common areas are wonderful. Our west-facing porch swing is great in the afternoon when it's sunny, and you can always go over to Ruth's House if you want to hang out on a porch with morning sunshine.

We have a working fireplace in our common area! It has been the site of many late-night games and discussions. We also have a pool table--it's a great way to pass the time.

There are 20 members of Linder. Ten of these folks live in singles, and 10 live in doubles. We all share a washer and dryer; a kitchen (not used for house dinners because it's too small); 3 1/2 bathrooms; a three-line phone system; a TV and VCR; a Macintosh computer, printer, and modem; and a fish tank. None of us smoke tobacco in the house, but you can smoke on the porch. [Oct99]

LINDSBERGS KURSGÅRD

**Lindsberg 10
S-79191 Falun
SWEDEN**

**+46(0)23-43030, +46(0)23-43084 fax
lindsberg@geocities.com
http://www.geocities.com/
    rainforest/3189/**

Began 1974 | Diet: Vegetarian | Rural

Lindsberg is an alternative course center situated in a big old house nearby Falun in the middle of Sweden. It was established in the early 1970s and originates from and is inspired by environmental and radical labor movements and solidarity organizations.

The building is from the turn of the century and is placed in a scenic neighborhood. Beautiful nature surrounds Lindsberg; an old oak gives us shelter when the sun is too hot in the summer. A short walk takes us to the lake where a sauna and a rowboat are available.

The course center is managed by a commune (Lindsbergskollektivet) who are trying to live by small resources by eating vegetarian food and growing vegetables and herbs in an ecological and self-sufficient way. Right now we're preparing the garden, planting seeds, and so on. We're also in the middle of restoring the house. [May99, email preferred]

LITTLE FLOWER CATHOLIC WORKER FARM, THE

**2780 Hadensville-Fife Rd
Goochland VA 23063**

804-457-2631

Began 1996 | Pop. 10
Diet: Vegetarian | Rural | Spiritual

Little Flower is a small Catholic Worker homestead/farm. We are committed to helping create a nonviolent, just world in harmony with the land. We share our lives and resources with each other and with those in need. We live as simply as we can; we organize and engage in nonviolent direct action against systemic violence; we try to enflesh the Gospel mandates to love God, one another, and our enemies.

Our daily life includes caring for six small children, our animals, and the gardens. We meet weekly as a community, share most meals, and have a liturgy together on Sundays. We also take a meal to folks on the street in Richmond on Sundays. We are exploring starting prison-support work at a nearby women's prison. We organize vigils, protests, and direct actions together with Catholic Worker houses in Washington, DC, and Norfolk and with other groups in the Richmond area. Some of our focus includes nuclear weapons, School of the Americas, and the Iraqi sanctions.

Some of us work part-time. We also receive some donations to support our work. [Jun99]

LITTLE GROVE

**Grove Ln
Chesham
Bucks HP5 3QQ, England
UNITED KINGDOM**

01494-778080

Began 1983 | Pop. 11 | Re-Forming
Diet: Omnivore | Rural

Little Grove is in a rural setting but close to London. It has several buildings; two have residential accommodation, and there are studios and office space. Some of us work from here, and others have outside jobs. We make our decisions at our house business meetings fortnightly. We have monthly meetings too to discuss the process of living together. Each member has one or more rooms of their own. We share bathrooms and kitchens, lounge, television room, and so on. We let out part of our space for courses. [Mar99, sase required]

LIVING ROCK CHRISTIAN MEN'S CO-OP

**803 East Grand River
East Lansing MI 48823**

517-332-1437

Began 1942 | Pop. 10 | Urban | Spiritual

(Also known as Bethel Manor.) We are a community of Christian college-age men who live near the campus of Michigan State University. Our goal as a community is to encourage one another to spiritual growth, then to send spiritually mature members out of our small community into the regular world to allow God to use them as "reapers" or gatherers of the non-Christian harvest into God's kingdom. Daily life here for most might include reading the Bible, going to class, studying for school, participating in house or campus spiritual activities, and eating dinners and cooking them together, as well as cleaning and maintaining the house together. Occasionally we meet for house decisions, and we meet weekly for all-house prayer, Bible teaching, and worshiping God. [Aug99]

LOCUST GROVE COMMUNITY, INC.

26328 Locust Grove Rd
Creola OH 45622

740-596-4379

Began 1996 | Pop. 4
Diet: Omnivore | Rural | Spiritual

Locust Grove Farm, southeast Ohio. Income-sharing "children of the Earth" community practicing Native American spirituality. Organic and Native American farming, free-range poultry, and publishing businesses. Provide staffing for Resilience Institute, a retreat center offering workshops on self-reliance, Native spirituality, and sustainable farming. Rustic woodworking business envisioned. Learning antique Native American ways of living in harmony with the Earth. Simple technology: nonelectric homes, wood heat, food self-sufficiency, no TV or radio. Electric, computers, and office technology in our business area. Community school planned. Omnivorous Native diet, no smoking.

160 beautiful acres, farmland and forest, in Ohio's least populated county. We share two low-technology houses; plan small nonelectric cottages. Farm with tractor; plan horse power for local trips and field work. If you have read Tom Brown, Jr., and Stalking Wolf, you know what we are about. If not, read *Grandfather*, *The Journey*, and *The Search*, available from most libraries. If you are willing to live extremely close to the land and are a dedicated "child of the Earth," send $2.00 for information packets. Singles, couples, families welcome. Locust Grove Community, 26328 Locust Grove Road, Creola, OH 45622. [Jan99]

LOFSTEDT FARM COMMUNITY

George and Bridget Baumann
PO Box 1270
Kaslo BC V0G 1M0
CANADA

250-353-7441, 250-353-7167
250-353-7441 fax
vanallen@netidea.com

Began 1984 | Pop. 16 | Forming
Diet: Omnivore | Rural | Spiritual

Sixty-acre biodynamic-farm-based community located in the forested mountainous Kootenays. Wet climate, mild summers, winter cold (approx 20 degrees cent. zone 5). Farm located five minutes south of Kaslo. Lofstedt Farm, Lofstedt Farm Community Supported Agriculture (CSA) Project, and Lofstedt Farm Forestry Society (LFFS) are the three main businesses. There are two other projects based on the farm, Kootenay Woodland Herbs and a small Waldorf farm school. We are a dedicated, hardworking community trying to create a diverse farm ecosystem using a variety of crops and farm animals. Many people volunteer on the farm to learn organic farming using the Demeter standards of biodynamic farming. The farm is owned by an elderly Swiss couple who are trying to turn the farm into a land trust in order to preserve the farm as an agricultural learning center. More people are needed to help with farming, gardening, teaching, carpentry, animal husbandry, beekeeping, horse farming, logging, etc. [Dec98, cc, sase required]

LONG BRANCH ENVIRONMENTAL EDUCATION CENTER

PO Box 369
Leicester NC 28748, 828-683-9211
fax
paulg@buncombe.main.nc.us
http://buncombe.main.nc.us/LBEEC/

Began 1974 | Pop. 11
Diet: Omnivore | Rural

We are a small group of people who are deeply concerned about the interwoven and accelerating problems of population growth, natural-resource depletion, and environmental degradation. We are individuals who have chosen to live cooperatively and steward this land ... caring for it in a way that it will be healthy and beautiful for our children's children.

We align ourselves with all the other

groups and centers across the country that are dedicated to helping heal the Earth. As our particular focus, we have chosen to demonstrate specific, practical strategies by which individuals can simplify their lifestyles and become more self-reliant—with organic gardening, ecological agriculture, solar energy, and appropriate technology.

Our 1,635 acres of land are managed as an ecological sanctuary and wildlife-habitat preserve, and we have developed a small, hands-on environmental-education center. We have staff, interns, and a volunteer program. We are open to the public every Saturday and frequently offer weekend workshops on a variety of topics, including permaculture design, organic gardening, low-cost building-system design with indigenous materials, solar-greenhouse design, country crafts, composting-toilet systems, and natural history. [Sep99, cc, sase required]

LOS ANGELES ECO-VILLAGE

3551 White House Pl
Los Angeles CA 90004

213-738-1254
laev@ic.org
http://www.ic.org/laev/

Began 1994 | Pop. 29
Diet: Omnivore | Urban

The Los Angeles Eco-Village (LAEV) was founded in 1993 in the two-block neighborhood of Bimini and White House Place in the centrally located Wilshire Center/Koreatown area of Los Angeles. It began as a project of CRSP (Cooperative Resources and Services Project; see Resource listing) after the 1992 civil uprisings. Its initial purpose was to demonstrate the processes of healing a sick neighborhood

deeply affected by the uprisings and to facilitate development of a sustainable community. The start-up of LAEV was the culmination of a 10-year planning process for a new-construction ecovillage seven miles away from the current location. The uprisings were a wake-up call for EV planners: we decided to heal our already existing built-out older neighborhood! We felt this was essential if there was to be any significant quality of life in the future of urban dwellers. We were also on a mission to influence city dwellers everywhere to establish more cooperative and ecologically sensitive living patterns.

We are still working toward a common vision among the very diverse intentional and preexisting neighbors who live here. Overall, the founding vision included demonstrating low-impact and high-quality living patterns among newly arriving Eco-Villagers and pre-existing neighbors drawn to that vision. We screen potential residents for an ecological and cooperative orientation, then try to balance our diversity in the following areas: income, ethnicity, generational, gender, and household composition. There are about 20 proactive neighbors out of approximately 500 residents in the two-block neighborhood, some who have come intentionally, others who were preexisting. Many neighbors who are not involved nonetheless appreciate the work that has been done to make Eco-Village a safer, more friendly neighborhood.

Over the past few years, CRSP has purchased several apartment buildings. We are eco-retrofitting the buildings and intend for them to become completely resident owned and controlled in a way that maintains permanent affordability of the units. Some units have been set aside as common units. A residents' building committee meets regularly and establishes priorities for the buildings. A number of organic gardens are contained within the two buildings and at other locations in the neighborhood. Regular community dinners open to any neighbors help glue the community together.

The neighborhood and surrounding areas are quite dense, with many public and private schools and colleges and universities. We are also rich in public transit, with many employment and green-business-development opportunities. Approximately a dozen intentional neighbors live and work in the neighborhood, though not all in community-controlled businesses. Many intentional neighbors are actively involved in social,

ecological, and planning issues in the city, e.g., bus-riders union, bicycle coalition, restoring the river, planning and advocacy for sustainable communities, school reform, urban food security, changing ecologically and socially destructive corporate practices, etc.

We are very child friendly, and there is a K–2 public school in the heart of Eco-Village and a middle school adjacent to us. We provide regular tours, urban-sustainable-community workshops, public talks on a variety of related topics, some internships, work, and vacation visits. [Sep99, cc, sase required]

LOS HORCONES

Apdo Postal #372
Hermosillo Sonora 83000
MEXICO

(52-62) 14-72-19
walden2@infosel.net.mx
http://www.LosHorcones.org.mx/

Began 1973 | Pop. 24 | Forming
Diet: Omnivore | Rural

Los Horcones began in 1973. It is located on 250 acres in Sonora Mexico, below Arizona. Since 1995 we have been planning a branch of Los Horcones in the United States. Our basic objectives are to design a society where people cooperate for a common good, share property, and reinforce egalitarian pro-ecological and pacifist behaviors.

Los Horcones is an ecological- and self-sufficient-oriented community. However, we devote most of our resources in the area of human behavior (education, human relationships, and behavioral research). We have orchards, organic gardens, and farm animals. We have communal child rearing. All members who participate in the care and education of children are trained to do so. We have our own school. Students learn personal and social behaviors (self-knowledge, interpersonal skills, etc.) as well as academics.

We have an experimental approach to the design of a community, basing our practices (education, economy, family, government) on scientific research, not on personal beliefs. We are deeply concerned with personal growth and interpersonal relationships, so our main focus is human behavior. We are a Walden Two community in the sense we apply behavioral principles in our daily life to learn communitarian behaviors.

Being a Walden Two does not mean we are inspired by or follow the novel *Walden Two* (Skinner) but rather that we apply the science of behavior on which Walden Two was based.

Los Horcones is an income-sharing community. We have many communal buildings (dining room, laundry, etc.) and private quarters. We organize our labor not only looking for efficiency but also for satisfaction and creativity.

Generally we work eight hours daily. Labor distribution is not based on gender. We earn income from various sources—selling natural food products, special education, summer camps, and consulting. We value the participation of all members in decision making. We call our organization "personocracy." We are open to new members or visitors. Please write or call in advance. [Dec98, cc, sase requested]

LOSANG DRAGPA BUDDHIST CENTRE

Dobroyd Castle
Pexwood Rd
Todmorden Lancashire
OL14 7JJ, England
UNITED KINGDOM

00 44 1706 812247, 00 44 1706 815236
LosangD@aol.com

Began 1991 | Pop. 29
Diet: Vegetarian | Rural/Urban | Spiritual

Losang Dragpa Centre is a residential Buddhist center, part of the new Kadampa tradition. It was founded in 1985 by Venerable Geshe Kelsang Gyatso. The purpose of the center is to provide a facility where people can learn about the Buddhist way of life. It offers the chance to experience the special quality of life found in a spiritual community.

There is an opportunity to live and work with people from all walks of life, from all over the world. Every day at the center there are teachings, meditations, and study programs as well as many opportunities to use your talents and skills in helping with the daily running of the center.

Surrounded by the rugged beauty of moors and crags and yet only 10 minutes walk from Todmorden Station, Dobroyd Castle is a perfect setting for a Buddhist center, combining accessibility with the peace and quiet of the countryside. The estate comprises the main building and sev-

---

Key to bracketed text: cc = cannot commit to prompt correspondance, sase = self-addressed stamped envelope

eral outbuildings and cottages set in 23 acres of grounds and woodland. Set on the hillside above the small Pennine town of Todmorden it overlooks the beautiful Calder Valley and is in the heart of the Pennine walking country. [Jun99, cc, sase requested]

LOST VALLEY EDUCATIONAL CENTER

**81868 Lost Valley Ln
Dexter OR 97431**

**541-937-3351
lvec@lostvalley.org
http://www.lostvalley.org/
http://www.talkingleaves.org/**

Began 1989 | Pop. 23
Diet: Vegetarian | Rural

Lost Valley Center has recently completed 10 years of experimentation and growth. We have 15 adults/9 children (from baby to 55) living and working together on our 87 beautiful acres of gardens, meadows, forests, and creek. We are located 18 miles southeast of Eugene, Oregon, between the forested Cascade Range and farmland of the Willamette Valley, and 1 1/2 hours from the coast.

We live in small cabins, yurts, and two apartments. We hope to build new community housing using alternative architecture and sustainable materials. We serve organic vegetarian meals partly grown in our three large gardens or purchased bioregionally. Although we hope to start our own school in the future, our children now attend public school or Waldorf classes or are taught at home.

Lost Valley Educational Center is also a nonprofit retreat and conference center with 150 beds plus camping. We also organize our own workshops in areas such as permaculture, naka ima (personal growth), and vision questing. We publish an internationally distributed magazine called *Talking Leaves: A Journal of Our Evolving Ecological Culture* ($18/year).

We offer longer-term experiences to learn, heal, and grow in community through our intern and apprentice programs. People wishing to apply for community membership generally begin with one of these options.

Adult members work between half- and full-time, sharing the responsibilities and the income from our various activities. Individuals and families keep their personal assets and pay their own bills, including a

monthly room-and-board fee. We live simply and well. We seek grants and encourage memberships ($35) and donations to support our educational work.

One of our unique gifts is to create and offer a balance between a strong ecological focus and a deep sharing of commitment to the functional extended family that we are cultivating. We strive to be creative, caring, embracing of change, eclectic in our approach, and open to diversities in age, race, spirituality, and sexuality.

For more information, visit us on the Web, e-mail, call, or write for our current visiting policy and tour dates. [Jan99, sase requested]

LOTHLORIEN

**ELF PO Box 1082
Bloomington IN 47402**

**812-275-0585
elf@kiva.net
http://www.elflore.org/**

Began 1987 | Pop. 500
Diet: Vegan | Rural | Spiritual

(Also known as Elf Lore Family.) We believe in elves and the reality of Faerie. We believe in nature and the elemental forces. We believe in willed evolution and the blending of art and science to make environment healing magic. We believe in music and throwing festivals to raise money to purchase land for nature sanctuaries. We believe in love, rock 'n' roll, and holding land in common. We believe in alternative energy, organic gardening, and being responsible personally for our relationship with nature. We are elves. We are good people who wish to network with other good people to find ways to establish more nature sanctuaries. We would love to connect with you. We have a campground. We throw public festivals. Please send $2 for our annual *Greenbook* so you know what the elves are up to now and next. Not only do we believe in alternative lifestyles, we believe in creating an alternative reality, fully grounded in fact and finances. Maybe you might wish to be a member too. We do not support freeloaders or feed people. We are looking for self-sufficient people. The Lothlorien nature is a great place to take a vacation. [Sep99]

LOTHLORIEN - CENTRO DE CURA E CRESCIMENTO

Caeté - Açu
46940-000 Palmeiras BA
BRAZIL

071-351-2008
miklos@bahianet.com.br
http://www.webserve.co.uk/
   lothlorien/

Began 1984
Diet: Vegetarian | Rural | Spiritual

Lothlorien is a community concerned with naturopathy and spirituality. Founded in 1984 on the model of the Findhorn Foundation in Scotland, we try experiencing and propagating alternative lifestyles, within a holistic approach. We are open to receive guests throughout the year, and we organize many therapeutic as well as educational events.

Lothlorien is located in a very beautiful valley in the Chapada Diamantina mountain range, called Vale do Capão, right in the center of the state of Bahia, 470 kilometers west of Salvador, the state capital city. The valley, at a height of 1,000 meters, is endowed with rich tropical vegetation and surrounded by mountains where many crystals are still found and where, up to 50 years ago, diamond mining was the major source of income for the whole region.

There are many options of walks to rivers and waterfalls, as well as trails through the mountains and plains of the area.

In order to get to Lothlorien, you should first get to the city of Salvador and then catch a bus in the local bus station (Rodoviaria), run by Real Expresso, to the city of Palmeiras. The journey takes approximately seven hours. Once in Palmeiras, take a local taxi to Vale do Capão—the drivers know how to get to Lothlorien. [Feb99]

LOTHLORIEN CO-OP

244 W Lakelawn Pl
Madison WI 53703

608-257-8540

Pop. 33 | Diet: Vegetarian | Urban

We are a community of 33 members striving for a feminist/queer-supportive egalitarian atmosphere. We work toward creating an environment that's an all-around good place to live for both students and nonstudents.

Our benefit concerts, coffeehouses, and vegetarian/vegan meals are wonderful social times. A lot of our food is locally grown. House decisions are made by consensus. We have a beautiful plant-filled living room, grand piano, fireplace, lakefront porch, terraced garden, dock, canoe, and a few cats. Soon we will also have a brand-new kitchen. Our location is great. We are right downtown, only a short walk from campus, State Street, and the state capitol. [Feb99]

LOTHLORIEN FARM

RR 1
Ompah Ontario K0H 2J0
CANADA

Began 1972 | Pop. 15
Diet: Omnivore | Rural

(Also known as Lothlorien Rural Co-op Inc.) Lothlorien Farm is a loose-knit land-based community in the forested lake country of the Canadian Shield. Since 1972 we have collectively held 700 acres in the Ottawa Valley watershed. Although we are not too far from more settled parts of Ontario, the country is bush—wild and peaceful.

We have individually owned houses and workshops, gardens, a small lake, a maple bush, and cross-country ski trails. On the

farm currently there are four households, with six adults and a teenager; the other seven members and their families live elsewhere but stay in touch. Membership is extremely stable.

Although there are relatively few communal activities or responsibilities, members share a lot informally, and residents are very involved in the surrounding community. Most residents are self-employed, while two commute to part-time jobs.

Group decisions are generally made by consensus. We have not been actively seeking new members, but we would welcome serious inquiries from Canadian residents who would have a way of earning a living here long term. We require at least six months' residency before joining. Members make a one-time nonrefundable "donation loan" to the co-op, based on ability to pay. Joining involves building a home, as there is no available housing. [Feb99, sase required]

LOVE ISRAEL FAMILY, THE

14724 184th St NE
Arlington WA 98223

360-435-8577
israelfamily@wa.freei.net

Began 1968 | Pop. 60
Diet: Omnivore | Rural | Spiritual

(Also known as Jordan Village.) Members of our family have all received visions, dreams, and revelations without which we would never have understood our purpose on this Earth or our relationship to one another. This divine intervention has given us a common understanding that has sustained us for more than 30 years. We know that we are one, that love is the answer, and that now is the time. We know that in the center of all people is the same *I am*—and this *I am* is the God we serve and worship. This is the God that introduced himself to Moses out of a burning bush, saying, "*I am* that *I am*."

We have been called together by a force that is greater than ourselves but as close and intimate as the "me" that resides in the center of each of us. And we have been given a purpose: to put our individual talents together into a more perfect whole—to assemble ourselves as the body of Jesus Christ and thereby to discover the unique and necessary role that each one of us has been created to fulfill.

Our eternal life begins when we accept the premise that our love can sustain our relationships forever—ultimately having the

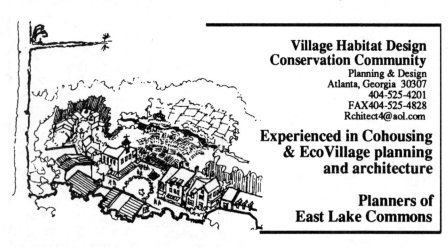

Key to bracketed text: cc = cannot commit to prompt correspondance, sase = self-addressed stamped envelope

power to overcome death itself. We are each other's reward. Our family is the gift that God gave us, rooted in a common revelation and nurtured by the total commitment that we have made to one another. Living together in community provides the context for the experience of lasting security and joy.

We are not here to perpetuate concepts of religion but to discover who we really are when we create together in service and love. [Mar99, cc]

LOWER SHAW FARM

Shaw
Swindon
Wiltshire SN5 9PJ, England
UNITED KINGDOM
01793 771080
enquiries@lsfarm.globalnet.co.uk

Began 1974 | Pop. 5 | Re-Forming
Diet: Omnivore | Rural/Urban

Though formerly a Wiltshire dairy farm, since 1976 Lower Shaw has been running short courses and events as well as hosting other groups and organizations. Both short- and long-term residents recognize that Lower Shaw's strength lies in the communal atmosphere it creates, a contribution to which is its natural environment, its ram-shackle but loved and cared for three acres with trees, ponds, animals, gardens, and out-buildings.

At present there is just one family living here, with regular volunteers and temporary residents. At the moment we are not actively looking for new permanent members, but for travelers or those looking for a shorter-term experience, we may be just the right place. We like to have links with people around the world. We also have many links with local people and organizations. The Swindon Literature Festival is organized here. [Sep99, sase requested, no openings]

LUTHER BUCHELE HOUSE

1510-1520 Hill St
Ann Arbor MI 48104
http://www.umich.edu/~umicc/

We are a student cooperative house. Meals are served every evening at 6:00. If you cannot be present for dinner and would like a dinner saved for you, sign up on the save-meal list posted on the refrigerator. Everyone is required to work approximately four hours every week performing various tasks to keep the house running. Members select jobs at the term's work holiday, a day of cleaning and maintenance that is rather fun and ends with pizza and sometimes beer. No matter what your schedule, there is a job for you. You can cook, perform mainte-nance, clean the kitchen, clean the bath-rooms, vacuum the hallways and stairs, etc. If you cannot complete your required work at the required time, you must find a replacement. You are responsible for making sure the job gets done. Everyone (officers too!) is also required to complete two dinner cleans each term, so that no one has to get stuck washing dishes every Friday or Saturday evening. [Oct99]

MA YOGA SHAKTI INTERNATIONAL MISSION

114-41 Lefferts Blvd
South Ozone Park
New York NY 11420

718-641-0402, 407-725-4024
yogashakti@aol.com
http://www.nirmand.com/
 mayogashakti/

Began 1979 | Pop. 420

The Yogashakti Mission was started by Maha Mandaleshwar Shakti Sant Shiromani Ma Yogashakti Saraswati to further the spiri-tual development of humankind through the practice of yoga based on the techniques of highest values and truth embodied in the Upanishads, Geeta, and other scriptures.

The Yogashakti Mission is an interna-tional family dedicated to serving God and humanity in order to bring about a revival of spirituality through yoga.

The registered office of the mission is at 11, Jaldarshan, Nepean Sea Road, Mumbai 400 026, India. The mission also has centers at Gondia (Nagpur), Calcutta, New Delhi, New York, and Florida (United States.) Regular yoga classes are conducted by trained disciples at these centers.

The mission publishes a brief monthly journal, in English and Hindi, keeping the devotees in touch with the activities of the mission. Mataji has also published several books on yoga and allied subjects in Hindi and English that are available from Yogashakti Mission. If you are interested in learning the higher values of life, keeping your body and mind healthy, assisting humanity toward spiritual growth, you are welcome to join the Ashram. Age, religion, caste, or creed are no barriers. [Feb99, sase required]

MAAT DOMPIN

Maat Dompin
PO Box 7724
Charlottesville VA 22906
540-992-0248

Began 1992 | Forming
Diet: Omnivore | Rural

Ecologically friendly opportunities for womyn of color, their friends, and their allies.

The seven years of looking for land and the 12 months it took to close the deal have generated a network that contains the nucleus of talents necessary to create a model Earth-friendly family-type farm that can offer a peaceful, supportive, natural environment. Initial stages on the land will provide skill-sharing opportunities in land management, site planning, and alternative construction. We hope to attract individuals experienced in new games and team build-ing. Some of us are considering fund-raising tours to invite input, answer questions, and raise money for building land payments, insurance, travel expenses for volunteers, etc. As facilities come into being, the farm will become a place of rest for wimmin who work for a better world and the ones they choose to work and rest with. [Dec98, cc, sase requested]

MADISON COMMUNITY COOPERATIVES (MCC)

306 N Brooks St
Madison WI 53715, 608-251-7748 fax
madicoop@aol.com,
 msncoop@macc.wise.edu

Began 1968 | Pop. 189 | Urban

Madison Community Cooperatives (MCC) is an ongoing experiment in housing that is radically different from the ordinary. Instead of an absentee or money-hungry landlord providing housing based on a profit motive, the houses of MCC exist for the people who live in them. Each house, as well as the fed-eration known as MCC, is controlled by its members. We keep ourselves informed and actively participate.

MCC's role is to provide stability and support self-management by the houses. MCC board, officers, and staff do this by training and working with house members so that each house has the needed skills.

Every month, each house adds money to the collective MCC purse, which is disbursed to pay our property taxes and mortgages, maintain an office with computers and copy machine, create and distribute housing brochures to attract members, and more, through the central MCC budget.

MCC is run by members of all the houses. Past MCC members decided that most MCC decisions should be made by a representative body, the board of directors. Every two weeks, houses send one representative for every 25 members (or any fraction thereof.) Yet, every single member of MCC is invited to general membership meetings three times a year, at which everyone gets a vote. [Jan99]

MADISON STREET HOUSE

8130 SE Madison St
Portland OR 97215

503-255-0139

Began Feb99 | Pop. 1 | Forming
Diet: Omnivore | Urban

New community forming with space for five to six adults in urban farmhouse with organic garden. Members will share vision, energy, meals, etc. Bring maturity, responsibility, compassion, and the ability to communicate. Make your dream reality. [Aug99]

MADRE GRANDE MONASTERY

18372 Highway 94
Dulzura CA 91917

619-468-3810, 619-468-3006
traceyd@madregrande.org
http://www.madregrande.org/

Began 1975 | Pop. 9 | Re-Forming
Diet: Vegetarian | Rural | Spiritual

As an eclectic monastery, we have monks who are men and women, of any spiritual persuasion, so long as they follow a positive path to spiritual perfection. Membership in the monastery is necessary for permanent residence. The members are monks who make all decisions and set community goals and who are highly skilled in their abilities. Leadership in the monastery is by annual

election among the monk community. Students are studying for friar or monk status in the Paracelsian order. Students and retreat guests take limited part in community functions according to their skills and conditions of residence. The ability to work cooperatively on group goals is valued above all else. Special skills are needed, especially organic gardening, vegetarian cooking, maintenance, and a willingness to do even the menial to manifest our goals. We are working to publish our journal, *The Philosopher's Stone*, on-line. For current and past issues and for further information please see our Web site. Call, write, or e-mail to make reservations for a visit. [May99, cc]

MAGIC, INC.

PO Box 5894
Stanford CA 94309

650-323-7333
magic@ecomagic.org
http://www.ecomagic.org/

Began 1972 | Pop. 39
Diet: Vegetarian | Urban | Spiritual

Residents of Magic operate a nonprofit, public-service organization with the same name, through which we demonstrate how people may live better by learning to see self and surroundings more accurately.

Core themes in our community life and in the programs we offer the general public are: (1) clarify values; (2) improve health; (3) increase cooperation; and (4) steward the environment.

Our activities include lectures and seminars about the nature of value; life-planning workshops; swimming, running, bicycling, and hatha yoga instruction; youth mentoring; mediation; community organizing; planting and caring for trees and other vegetation; water- and land-management planning; neighborhood design; and publishing. Several of our programs have been awarded national and international recognition for excellence.

We aim to strike a balance between utilizing the diverse resources of our Stanford University/Silicon Valley surroundings and maintaining contemplative, modest lives. We welcome opportunities to meet new people and to explore how we may interact to mutual benefit. When writing us we request $1 or more to defray costs. [Dec98, sase requested]

MAHARISHI UNIVERSITY OF MANAGEMENT

TM Center
1601 N 4th St
Fairfield IA 52556

515-472-4514, 515-472-6855 fax
tm@lisco.com
capt108@yahoo.com

Began 1974 | Pop. 4460
Diet: Vegetarian | Rural/Urban | Spiritual

(Also known as Maharishi International University.) We have a commitment to establish a permanent group of 7,000 people practicing the T. M. Sidhis program to establish world peace for the *world!* [Aug99]

MAISON EMMANUEL

1561 Chemin Beauline
Val-Morin Quebec J0T 2R0
CANADA

819-322-7014
m.emmanuel@polyinter.com
http://www.maisonemmanuel.com/

Began 1983 | Pop. 51 | Re-Forming
Diet: Omnivore | Rural/Urban | Spiritual

We are a life-sharing, therapeutic community for children, adolescents, and adults in need of special care. It is located in a beautiful, rural setting on 35 acres of land in the heart of the Laurentians, 100 kilometers north of Montreal.

Maison Emmanuel is modeled on the Camphill communities existing worldwide. The Camphill movement, which was founded in 1939, endeavors to create communities in which children and adults with special needs can live, learn, and work with others in healthy, social relationships based on mutual care and respect.

Camphill is inspired by Christian ideals as articulated by Rudolf Steiner and recognizes the spiritual uniqueness of each human being regardless of disability or religious or racial background. There are approximately 90 Camphill communities existing worldwide, which are recognized by the respective governments as viable alternatives to institutional care. [Sep99]

Key to bracketed text: cc = cannot commit to prompt correspondance, sase = self-addressed stamped envelope

MALU 'AINA CENTER FOR NONVIOLENT EDUCATION & ACTION

PO Box AB
Ola'a (Kurtistown) HI 96760

808-966-7622
JA@interpac.net

Began 1981 | Pop. 4
Diet: Omnivore | Rural | Spiritual

Malu 'Aina (Land of Peace) is the Hawaiian name given to the Center for Nonviolent Education and Action located 10 miles south of the city of Hilo on the island of Hawaii. We are a small-scale 22-acre agriculturally based spiritual community committed to justice, peace, and preserving the environment. Established as a nonprofit organization in 1979, permanent residency at Malu 'Aina Farm began in 1981. Our initial structures were tents. In fact, for more than five years, our kitchen remained a tent.

Malu 'Aina is located on the slopes of the world's most active volcano and in one of the most poverty-stricken areas in Hawaii. The climate is wet, averaging 175 inches of rain annually. Temperature is normally mild: 75–85° F daytime and 60–70° F nights, although some winter nights can be quite cool with temperatures dropping into the 50s.

Life on the farm involves physical labor and simple living. Our water supply is rain-catchment tanks. We have small-scale solar power and use a composting toilet.

At Malu 'Aina we try to live a life of community service by helping people in need of food and through our work for peace and justice. We are interested in people who want to make life changes for justice. [Sep99, sase requested]

MANZANITA VILLAGE OF PRESCOTT

PO Box 4412
Prescott AZ 86302

520-445-3015, 800-555-3810
520-445-4228 fax
zarch@primenet.com
ldeking@primenet.com
http://www.mwaz.com/cohousing/

Began 1999 | Pop. 24 | Forming
Diet: Omnivore | Rural/Urban

We are persons creating our own richly diverse community, balancing group harmony with individual growth and following the principles of ecological soundness, social awareness, and economic viability.

We seek to live in an environment that is mutually supportive; that fosters neighborliness while allowing privacy; and that encourages the interaction of people of all ages, beliefs, and backgrounds.

We are located in northern Arizona, at one mile above sea level, in Prescott. We own 12 1/2 acres of land that is across from a 79-acre city park. We are only one mile from the center of town and even closer to the national forest. We are currently (5/12/99) under construction and are looking for individuals and families to join us. We are the developers of our own community, and it has taken us five years of working together to create a pedestrian-oriented, energy-efficient, Earth-friendly community. Inquiries are encouraged. [May99]

MARATHON COOPERATIVE

732 Maltman Ave
Los Angeles CA 90026
OR
c/o Solari Enterprises Inc
1544 W Yale Ave
Orange CA 92867
apiser@earthlink.net

Began 1988 | Urban

We are a housing cooperative consisting of members of all ages, religious persuasions, and political beliefs. We have a seven-member board of directors serving alternate two-year terms. There are three committees: membership, building and grounds, and finance. [Feb99]

MARIPOSA GROUP, THE

PO Box 86
Bivins TX 75555

903-799-6161
903-799-6161 voice/fax
ericnb@gte.net

Began 1984 | Pop. 8 | Re-Forming | Rural

1. *Physical and financial security*—Our land is paid for. Houses will be. Develop ways in which time, personal energy, and financial resources can brought together so as to minimize the personal risk that any individual may experience in the areas of physical and financial security.

2. *Personal and interpersonal comfort and self-esteem*—Emphasize and practice methods of self-knowledge, friendship, intimacy, interpersonal communication, and interaction that promote respect, comfort, and trust between individuals, such that relationships have their basis in these qualities.

3. *Freedom for higher levels of personal development and expression*—Explore, develop, and promote ways of joyfully enhancing fully free personal development.

In short, to create a community space where there is more opportunity for people in a loving, supportive, free, and responsible environment to truly and fully enjoy life. [May99, sase required]

MARIPOSA GROVE

c/o Alan van Tress
PO Box 20427
Oakland, CA 94620

look in Oakland Phone Book

Began Feb99 | Pop. 5 | Forming
Diet: Vegetarian | Urban

Mariposa Grove is a newly forming activism and arts community in north Oakland. The three adjacent buildings contain apartments (mostly shared) as well as shared space (including a common "house") for many meals, creative pursuits and collaborations, office space, workshop, gardens, etc. We are rebuilding severely deteriorated houses into a place where creativity inspires social change, activism inspires creative collaboration, and everyone is actively engaged in the urban fabric we inhabit. We engage in mural painting, singing, and community organizing, sometimes together at home, sometimes separately with others in the broader community. We are also looking for a rural community in our region to build social and economic links with. [Oct99, cc, sase required]

Additions and corrections: Email: directory@ic.org, Web: http://directory.ic.org/, Mail: RR 1 Box 156-D, Rutledge MO 63563, USA.

Listings

MARSH COMMONS COHOUSING

**31 South U St
Arcata CA 95521**

**707-822-1860, 707-822-6609
joyce_plath@aol.com**

Began 1998 | Pop. 24
Diet: Omnivore | Rural/Urban

We are a cohousing community located in a university town in northern California. Arcata has active art, environmental, and spiritual communities, making it a socially rich place to live. We also have easy access to the redwood forest, beaches, mountains, and other natural wonders.

Marsh Commons site is a reused industrial property adjacent to a wildlife sanctuary and marsh with many miles of walking trails. We chose this site for its location close to the town plaza and a beautiful wild place.

Our houses and common house feature sustainable materials, including carpet from pop bottles, redwood from an old barn we tore down, reused lighting, flooring resawn from old mill buildings, recycled-newspaper insulation, sustainably harvested construction lumber, and recycled-plastic lumber for decking.

We eat together at least three times a week, share childcare, and look forward to putting in our garden this summer.

We do have a guest room for visitors if you are interested in visiting. This summer we will begin building our last four homes—they are still available. [Sep99]

MARTHA'S HOUSING COOPERATIVE

**225 E Lakelawn Place
Madison WI 53703**

608-256-8476

Began 1970 | Pop. 37
Diet: Vegetarian | Urban

Martha's is one of 10 houses in Madison Community Co-op. We are a community of workers, students, parents, and kids striving to be feminist oriented, antiracist, and lesbian/bisexual/gay affirming.

Our work-job system includes some childcare, and we offer rent subsidies to parents.

We have vegetarian/vegan meals every night and try to buy local, organic food. There is a food-co-op-only option, too.

We decide issues by a modified-consensus process. Any decision can be objected to if a member cannot live with it. Nonmembership objections can be overturned at the next meeting, however. [Dec98, sase requested, no openings]

MASALA COMMUNITY HOUSING

**744 Mavine St
Boulder CO 80302**

303-443-8178

Began Sep99 | Pop. 11 | Forming
Diet: Vegetarian | Urban

Masala Community Housing is a nonprofit, vegetarian, consensus-driven, environmentally focused housing cooperative. We are the first North American Students of Cooperation (NASCO) owned co-op in Colorado. The co-op is a mix of students and nonstudents, we purchase food cooperatively and eat five meals a week together. [Oct99]

MAXWOOD INSTITUTE

**Maxwood Institute
716 W Maxwell St
Chicago IL 60607**

**312-226-3248, 877-REFOREST
312-226-3274 fax**

Began 1988 | Pop. 11 | Re-Forming
Diet: Omnivore | Urban | Spiritual

(Also known as Maxworks Cooperative.) We are a semi-nonprofit workers' cooperative for environment, education, and art, based since 1984 in America's Favorite Endangered Neighborhood, with an office at 716 Maxwell Street. Our mission: to creatively/adaptively reuse/recycle "the stone the builders rejected" (Ps. 118:22)—lumber ("expand ... research in the use of recycled and waste timber product materials"—US Congress 1974), glass, metal, plastic, books, bikes, rugs, garments, and persons with previously "semi-dysfunctional" talents—plus 36 historic, reusable buildings!

Semi-volunteers and part-timers wanted to help operate Creative Reuse Carpentry Center at 729 W. O'Brien; repair endangered buildings and equip them for materi-

Key to bracketed text: cc = cannot commit to prompt correspondance, sase = self-addressed stamped envelope

als storage, workspace, marketing space (storefronts on Maxwell Street!), and personal loft space for the visiting and resident workers; repair and remarket pre-used goods; co-design eco-appropriate new products using materials from the waste stream and generate hundreds of fascinating handcraft jobs for toddlers, grayhairs, and between; publish and document inventions in *Recyclopedia*.

Help co-redesign a neighborhood in gentle transition. Set up food provisions, composting, landscaping, gardening, fence and wall beautification, etc.

We have joint ventures with the University of Illinois and other neighborhood institutions and operate Green Publishing (Chicago Greens Newsletter, Maxwood Newsletter). [Oct99]

MEADOWDANCE COMMUNITY GROUP

c/o Luc Reid
100 Park Blvd Apt 72-D
Cherry Hill NJ 08034

609-616-8340
info@meadowdance.org
http://www.meadowdance.org/

Began Apr00 | Pop. 12 | Forming
Diet: Omnivore | Rural

(Also known as New England Intentional Community Group, Vermont Intentional Community Group.) Meadowdance is a group in the process of building an intentional community near Brattleboro, Vermont, by spring of 2000. Our vision encompasses:

 • a supportive and socially cohesive environment;
 • ecological sustainability;
 • an unusual economic model that uses a base work requirement to secure the necessities of living for all members, while not restricting individuals' other financial activities;
 • financial stability;
 • working primarily within the community;
 • diversity of ages, ethnicities, religions, and lifestyles in an egalitarian community;
 • developing a rich, nurturing, challenging environment for children;
 • a secular community that is supportive of individuals' spiritualities;
 • music and fun in day-to-day life.
Housing options are based on individual preference. There are no fees or dues.

Investment is suggested where possible, but we have no minimum investment requirement. Investment is secured by the land, buildings, businesses, and other major assets of the community. Monetary investments carry no additional decision-making power.

We use formal consensus for decision making and are committed to egalitarian, participatory, respectful, and constructive governance. [Apr99]

METHOW CENTER OF ENLIGHTENMENT

PO Box 976
Twisp WA 98856

509-997-2620

Began 1990 | Pop. 1 | Rural

The Holy Wise Ones have designated Methow as a major spiritual center in development upon this planet. It is the responsibility of each spiritual group upstairs to position their ground ambassadors, aligning them with their spiritual center of choice. It is unfortunate that so few can actually align with these centers and ironic that the future of humankind lies in backcountry rural areas where natural, uncontaminated resources are plentiful. Our interdimensional celestial project in north-central Washington is designed to be a major communications command post and cultural-development learning and healing center for all who have access to it. Space people (UFO intelligences) from all dimensions will come and go freely from this celestial-city location.

We are reaching out to gather as many as divine guidance and time allow (Earth and economic changes); our goal is 2,000 settlers. At Methow there are no rules or regulations of any kind, since the whole valley is our spiritual center, including everybody in it. It is a clean, simple plan, approved by the Holy Wise Ones, and allows for every one to do their thing naturally, finding their way in their own time.

MICCOSUKEE LAND CO-OP

9601-23A Miccosukee Rd
Tallahassee FL 32308

Began 1973 | Pop. 163 | Rural

The Miccosukee Land Cooperative (MLC) is a community of 100 families and individuals who together own 279 acres situated nine miles east of Tallahassee. Co-op members privately own their own homesteads,

which range in size from 1 acre to several acres each. A total of 90 acres is preserved in its natural state as common land, owned collectively and enjoyed by the entire membership.

MLC members are drawn together by a common desire to live in a rural environment where the land is respected and interaction between neighbors is a sought-after experience. All activities (other than paying assessments for necessities such as taxes and insurance) are purely voluntary, allowing each person to choose the level of sharing and socializing they prefer. While we are a diverse group in age, occupation, and religious practice, many adults are in the prime years of their careers. Time to do all one would like is scarce. Despite this busy pace, we make time to celebrate the milestones of our lives and to support one another in times of sickness or tragedy. Many of us carry the vision of more time for shared meals and sitting on the porch shelling peas, gossiping, and singing. In the meantime we walk more separate paths but always give thanks for our land and precious neighbors. [Sep99, cc, sase requested]

MICHIGAN SOCIALIST HOUSE

315 North State St
Ann Arbor MI 48104

734-996-5952

Began 1932 | Pop. 19 | Urban

Michigan Co-op is the oldest house in the Inter-Cooperative Council (ICC). Founded in 1932, we have been feeding and housing people for 65 years now. There are 10 rooms in "Mich House"—one enormous triple, two singles, and seven doubles for a total of 19 people living in the house. We have a stereo complete with record collection, cable TV, a VCR, a Coke machine, a beer machine, and a porch where we typically spend many hours just enjoying the outdoors.

Some of our policies include no smoking in the house, food for various diets, five-minute seat reservation, and clothing is optional.

Each resident is required to do four hours, and each boarder (which includes folks from Minnie's house) is required to give about three hours of work a week to the house. Typical jobs include dinner cook; breakfast, lunch, dinner, or late-night dish cleans; bathroom cleans; hall, TV room, living room, pantry/laundry room clean; or various other odd jobs such as goodies cook or brunch cook. We must also give 8 percent of our labor credit hours to the ICC. At the beginning of each term, we hold "Work Holiday," which is when we spend all day cleaning, fixing, mopping, scrubbing, vaccuuming, partying, and painting to get our house all fixed up. [Jul99]

MICHIGAN WOMYN'S MUSIC FESTIVAL

WWTMC
P O Box 22
Walhalla MI 49458

231-757-4766
http://www.michfest.com/home.htm

Began 1976 | Pop. 800
Diet: Vegetarian | Rural

Michigan Womyn's Music Festival is a crucible for womyn's culture; a place to get your opinions stretched and your senses rocked. We build this community anew every year and take with us the inspiration, power, and hope that it ignites in each of us. The experience? Truly extraordinary ...

Situated on 650 acres of secluded forest and meadows, Michigan is home to 8,000 womyn from around the world. We are communally run by each woman who attends—all participate in two- to four-hour work shifts in addition to the efforts of hundreds of womyn who work to create and maintain the festival space.

Three meals a day are served of woodfire-cooked vegetarian specialties. There is a full peer-support system for all needs: medical, emotional, disability, sober support, and childcare.

There are over 300 other workshops offered and nightly screenings of womyn's film works. The massive and wonderful crafts bazaar features the work of over 130 craftswomyn.

And the music ... The multiple stages serve for both day and night shows, acoustic as well as loud and funky. The gathering of eclectic womyn's music spans the globe: rock, classical, percussion, folk, African, punk, a cappella, Latin, gospel, jazz, and pop—it's all here!

Please write, visit us on the Web, or call for more information. [Oct99, sase requested]

MIDDLE ROAD COHOUSING

RR1 Site 12 Comp 38
Nelson BC V1L 5P4
CANADA
ockenden@netidea.com
http://www.cohousing.ca/
   cohsng4/middle/

Began 1994 | Diet: No red meat | Rural

(Also known as The Heddle Road Community.) We are a community of 12 households on 52 acres. Each family owns its home and shares ownership of most of the land and converted barn/common house. We have meals together two or three times a week, celebrate festivals, garden together, and are finding more and more ways to be supportive of each other [Jun99, no openings]

MIKECO REHTLE

1127 Fuller Ave #9
Big Rapids MI 49307

231-592-0014, 231-768-4610
mikeco_35@hotmail.com
http://www.mikecorehtle.com/

Pop. 2 | Forming | Diet: VeganSpiritual
We are seekers.

We seek to be and to do those things that bring us into a state of full self-realization and humanness and to facilitate others, especially our children, to do the same. In the end, we wish to bring about a permanent state of happiness, joy, peace, and serenity for ourselves and others.

We seek to meet all of our healthy human needs and to help others to meet theirs.

We seek the humility to admit that we are ignorant of our journey and that we are limited: we can study "universal" laws, approximate them, and surrender to our lack of ultimate knowledge.

We create our own stories by our thoughts and actions. What we think and feel in our minds and hearts, we will produce in our experiences and lives. What we give, we get. As within, so without.

Life is a process, force, and flow that lives us. We do not live it. When we surrender to it, flow with its processes, and take responsibility for our participation in it, we become co-creators. We can then become free of our suffering that comes with our attachment to resisting flowing with our lives.

Inner peace and serenity is knowing, practicing, and being all of the above. We

ultimately discover that we are already and always serenity and with a higher power. [Nov99, sase requested]

MINNIE'S CO-OP

307 N State St
Ann Arbor MI 48104

Began 1970

Welcome to the Purple Palace of unearthly delights. Welcome to Minnie's Co-op. Minnie's is named for Minnie Wallace, who owned the house until 1970. Minnie, who was a spinster for most of her life, fell in love with and ran off with a man who was renting a room in the house. Her man was a nudist taxi driver named Bill Bixby. (We're not kidding!) Luckily, Minnie decided to sell us her house.

Minnie's has 24 members during the school year in 13 rooms (3 singles, 9 doubles, and 1 huge triple). All of the members of Minnie's board (take our meals) next door at Mich House (it's the house on the right). We do have our own small guff kitchen. There is no smoking allowed in Minnie's. [Oct99]

MOLINO CREEK FARMING COLLECTIVE

PO Box 69
Davenport CA 95017

Began 1982 | Pop. 20
Diet: Omnivore | Rural

Molino Creek Farming Collective has two major goals: to foster community through collective living and to operate an organic farm on our 137-acre parcel on the central California coast.

There are 10 separate households, comprised of one or two adults and their children. Some members work on the farm, and some work in nearby Santa Cruz in a variety of occupations.

Our group uses consensus to make all decisions. We meet regularly (once or twice a month) to discuss management of collective affairs.

The property is "off the grid" with no incoming utilities. Each household satisfies its power needs with photovoltaics/generators. Each member contributes money to maintain the five-mile road that connects us to the highway.

All residents at Molino Creek are shareholders; we do not have facilities for long-term guests. The cost of a share is in the $100,000 range. A share entitles a family to reside on the farm, participate in the consensus process, and be part of the farm operation. [Feb99, cc, sase requested, no openings]

MOLLOY ASHRAM RETREAT

Fraser Rd
Mount Molloy NQ 4871
AUSTRALIA

070.40.941168

Began 1979 | Pop. 4
Diet: Vegetarian | Rural | Spiritual

(Also known as Siuananda Ashram.) Molloy Ashram Retreat is a small spiritual community in a tiny village west of Cairns in the mountains. Vegetarian. No smoking, drugs, or alcohol permitted. Simple living and high thinking. The essence of all true religions with emphasis on yoga of synthesis and advaita vedanta as taught by Swami Sivananda of Rishikesh, India. Opportunity for learning, reading, meditation, and quiet relaxation. [Mar99, sase requested]

MONADNOCK GEOCOMMONS VILLAGE

Derbyshire Farm
Temple NH 03084

603-654-2523, 603-654-6705
goe@tellink.net
http://www.ic.org/geo/

Began 1999 | Pop. 10 | Forming
Diet: Omnivore | Rural

We are a new group (March '99) in the Monadnock Region of southern NH creating an ecovillage for mindful, sustainable living. Some of us have been exploring this vision for several years with the Geocommons College semesters at Findhorn, Plum Village, and Auroville. We are planning a cohousing model with an intentional focus on psychospiritual development and service to the Earth community. We want to grow in our capacities to live simply, happily, and ecologically, to practice love in our relationships, and enjoy the celebration and interbeing of life. We are evolving agreements for mindful, sustainable practices in community relations, business, construction, study, meditation, service work, meals, and child raising. We will share learnings with visitors and through educational programs.

Our proposed site is a beautiful 40-acre farm in southern NH, adjoining 200 protected acres used by Gaia Education Outreach Institute which border the Wapack National Wildlife Refuge. It is 1 1/2 hours from Boston. The first phase of construction may have 12 member-financed residences, separate and attached, with a common house that already exists, organic gardens, and alternative energy systems. Over years we envision a much larger ecovillage with cohousing clusters on adjoining lands, a farm, green businesses, and educational, cultural, and service projects. Members may become involved in the educational activities of the GEO Institute next door. We welcome inquiries. [Oct99, sase requested]

MONAN'S RILL

7899 St Helena Rd
Santa Rosa CA 95404

707-537-1198
psandfs@sonic.net

Began 1974 | Pop. 30
Diet: Vegan | Rural

The goal of Monan's Rill is having a balanced and diverse community reflecting a variety of ages, occupations, marital status, and family structure (some households have children; others do not). Our ages range from elementary-school-age children to the early eighties.

We work as teachers, psychotherapists, administrators, nurses, medical technologist, cabinet makers/contractors, artists, social activists, and parents. Our legal structure is a general partnership, and as such none of us hold individual title to the houses or land. Each member contributes an initial monetary investment and a monthly fee. Each family or individual lives in their own home.

Additionally, we share an organic garden and orchard, a large community center, a play area, a woodworking and maintenance shop, and a small barn and stables. Twice a month we gather for a community potluck dinner, business meeting (consensus decisions), and workday; however, informal smaller gatherings occur frequently. We try to recognize and cherish the different skills and insights of each individual and are committed to helping and encouraging one another. [Jan99]

MONKTON WYLD COURT

Charmouth Bridport
Dorset DT6 DQ, England
UNITED KINGDOM

01297 560342, 01297 560395 fax
monktonwyldcourt@btinternet.com
http://www.btinternet.com/
~monkton/

Began 1982 | Diet: Vegetarian | Rural

Since 1982 the community at Monkton Wyld Court has taken care of this center for holistic education. Why holistic education? Because we know that the quality of people's experience in the group, in the place, or with the facilitators is as important as the content of the course. We believe that the beauty of the environment, the organic food, the clean water, and the network of community support for each group help participants get the most out of—and put the most into—their time here.

Monkton is an educational charity overseen by a group of trustees. The community consists of a core group of members, longer-term volunteers, and a steady throughput of

short-term volunteers. The membership procedure is decided by the members.

The community has no one worldview, but many would resonate with the permaculture ethics of people and Earth care. We try to find the balance between a humane and supportive working environment and the necessities of the business. We seek to encourage both personal and collective responsibility.

We are always open to short-term volunteers, and this is the necessary first stage for anyone considering longer-term residence here. Contact us for more information. [Mar99]

MONTCLAIRE

**238 W Chestnut St
Lancaster PA 17603**

**717-394-6466, 717-394-6466 fax
juneo4@juno.com**

Re-Forming
Diet: No red meat I Rural I Spiritual
Seeking: individuals who envision a future

that integrates science and spirituality, art and nature. Who are *committed* to healing and health. Who know the *merit* in developing systems that take care of the basic needs for all members . Who are *aware* of important paradigm shifts for durable peace and prosperity. Who *believe* in the importance of a supportive and caring environment for the personal and spiritual growth of each individual. Who desire to live in *harmony* with the natural environment and ecosystem.

Attracting: those who wish to live and work for sustainability; *embracing* affirmative, joyful, and meaningful living models, *using* biodynamic and permaculture methods and concepts. Who want to *share* in developing an ecovillage, with simple, appropriate, and sustainable technology to build the infrastructure and develop income-generating microindustries. Who desire to *develop* and build affordable homes that are aesthetically pleasing, vitalizing, and nurturing. Who accept and *encourage* alternative collaborative leadership styles, decision making, and consensus building for self-reliance, independence, and interdependence. And

who wish to *explore* aspects of the Mondragon cooperatives models and to develop models for *positive* social change. [Jul99, cc, sase requested]

MONTE VUALA

**Monte Vuala Frauenhotel
CH-8881 Walenstadtberg
SWITZERLAND**

**0041-81-735-11-15
0041-81-735-11-15 fax**

Began 1993
Diet: Vegetarian I Rural I Spiritual

We feminist women have joined to realize a women-place/women-guesthouse in Switzerland. We opened May 1, 1993, an alternative hotel with 30 beds for women only. We offer massages, shiatsu, Qigong, rituals, and a large course program. Women can book holidays here, seminars, and cure. [May99]

MONTEREY COHOUSING COMMUNITY

**2925 Monterey Ave So
Saint Louis Park MN 55416
http://www.jimn.org/mococo/**

Began 1993 I Pop. 33 I Urban

(Also known as MoCoCo.) Monterey Cohousing Community has 15 households located just outside the city limits of Minneapolis, consisting of eight retrofit units in an Edwardian mansion and seven newly constructed townhouses, connected by tunnel for year-round convenience. The central courtyard and play area are separated from the driveway and the parking areas, as well as the front yard, which includes a community garden and picnic area. The entire grounds are lovingly landscaped.

The community is also blessed with an abundance of interior common space, including the original rich decor of the living room, library, and dining room, adjacent to the newly remodeled kitchen. Also included in the common space are an office, a large three-season porch, an elevator, three working fireplaces, a workshop, a laundry room, an "entertainment" room, and a children's playroom next to the dining room.

Each unit is a complete, privately owned living space, with members coming together in the common spaces for shared dinners and other community activities. Members

Key to bracketed text: cc = cannot commit to prompt correspondance, sase = self-addressed stamped envelope

have built a real sense of community that only comes from working together and shared community experiences. [Jan99]

MOONSHADOW

Rt 1 Box 304
Whitwell TN 37397
mediarights@bledsoe.net

Began 1971 | Pop. 9 | Diet: Vegan | Rural

(Also known as Sequatchie Valley Institute). Moonshadow is deeply integrated with the land, a forested Appalachian valley with caves, creeks, and bluffs. Our deliberate existence has a minimum impact on the forest ecosystem. We combine traditional knowledge with appropriate scientific methods to interact intelligently with nature. Our handcrafted buildings are made of natural materials. Our energy is from the sun and the forest. Trees and shrubs are integrated with food crops and herbs for self-sufficiency. We experiment with native and exotic plants for nutrition and medicine. Artistic expression fulfills personal, functional, and political needs. As organizers in the environmental and social-justice movements, we network with other groups and individuals.

We are striving to facilitate an evolutionary process that will radically change the system—the dominant paradigm—to ensure a sustainable future and equality for all life. We have created a solar-powered office space where *Media Rights*, an alternative nonprofit production company, is now based. Education is our major goal: to share our collectively gained wisdom through publication, video, radio, workshops, music, computer networking, and gatherings. We have nonprofit status (educational/scientific) for our community and are seeking outside sources of support. We hope that sharing our experience and vision will help people move more gently on the Earth. Ecology! [Sep99, sase required, no openings]

MØRDRUPGÅRD

Mørdrupvej 7
DK-3540 Lynge
DENMARK

0045-48187007

Began 1970 | Pop. 32 | Rural/Urban
Beautifully situated in the countryside 30 kilometers from Copenhagen. [May99, no openings]

MORNING STAR RIDGE COMMUNITY

G 4 C17 RR#1
Winlaw BC V0G 2J0
CANADA

250-355-2206, 250-355-2585
star@netidea.com
http://www.netidea.com/~jmerkel/

Began 1992 | Pop. 16
Diet: Vegan | Rural | Spiritual

Founded in 1992 as a spiritual community, our intention is to be grounded on *spirit*, *love*, and *service* with the goal of offering an example of a spiritual ecovillage. We are also fully embedded and actively engaged in cocreating a healthy greater community and bioregion. We live on 160 acres of land in the Selkirk mountain range of British Columbia. The community houses "Morning Star Center" and the "Global Living Project."

Morning Star Center focuses on (1) bringing sacredness into all relationships; (2) discovering and embodying the Christ within; (3) personal growth, self-knowledge, and wakeful awareness; (4) research, implementation, and sharing of sustainable living skills—all within a communal village context.

The Global Living Project researches the question, "Is it possible to live equitably and harmoniously within the means of nature in North America?" We seek the place where science and spirit meet and aim to value all life equally. We track our ecological footprint, recording our consumption, waste, and life quality. Each year we take our findings to universities, schools, and communities.

These two aspects of Morning Star Ridge Community complement each other, while providing and promoting unique and distinct ways of service to the world. [Dec98, sase requested]

MORNINGLORY

RR#4
Killaloe Ontario K0J 2A0
CANADA

613-757-3044, 613-757-3579
aa632@valleynet.on.ca

Began 1969 | Pop. 17
Diet: No red meat | Rural

We are a village of separate households scattered over 100 hilly acres, single people and families. We homestead in varying degrees,

use only solar electricity and wood heat, and grow organically most of our fruits and veggies. We've spent 30 years learning how to be good neighbors, which has been a worthwhile process.

Most of our children were home birthed; some are homeschooled; ages 10 to 18. Swimming and skating on our pond, trampolining, tobogganing, snowshoeing, full-moon drumming, and sing circles are some of the things we do for fun. We all share a love of nature and music making.

Guests are welcome if they arrange in advance and help out while they're here.

There may be space for new members.

May all people find harmony with Earth and each other! [Dec98, cc, sase required]

MOUNT MADONNA CENTER

445 Summit Rd
Watsonville CA 95076

408-847-0406, 408-847-2683 fax
programs@mountmadonna.org
http://www.mountmadonna.org/

Began 1978 | Pop. 96
Diet: Vegetarian | Rural/Urban | Spiritual

(Also known as Hanuman Fellowship.) We are a spiritual community, focused on yoga and service, with some 100 members living on 355 mountaintop acres, operating a conference center and a children's school. Our larger fellowship also operates a yoga and conference center in Santa Cruz, and a metaphysical bookstore. We share in work, meals (vegetarian), spiritual practices, rituals, and play, and strive to live by positive values. Our teacher, Baba Hari Dass, embodies and teaches the classical Ashtanga (eight-limbed) yoga, with all its vital relevance to our lives today. Our fellowship started in 1971, and our resident community in 1978. Primary criteria for membership are good work, positive attitude, and interest in spirituality. Our conference center hosts some 14,000 people each year, our children's school has some 160 students from preschool through high school, and our town center and bookstores are successful. Most work is done on a volunteer basis. Many members also hold outside jobs. Visit our Web site or send for information. [Jan99, sase requested]

MOUNTAIN HOME

HC 83 Box 402
Coquille OR 97423

Began 1989 | Pop. 4 | Re-Forming
Diet: Omnivore | Rural | Spiritual

Mountain Home is an off-grid ecovillage in the Oregon Coast Range. The 360 acres we are privileged to steward is part of a 10-square-mile roadless area of diverse wildlife and forests. Our sustainability vision is to restore the native ecology as we integrate human settlement: we garden, build with recycled and indigenous materials, use solar power, and are now developing our permaculture design. Our justice vision is social, economic, and legal justice for all. We publish *Justice Denied*, http://www.justicedenied.org/, a magazine exposing the plight of the wrongly convicted. We've provided homes for parolees and people with substance-abuse problems, believing that communities are more restorative than institutions.

We do not share income but are functionally communal and share time with each other in daily work, meals, town trips, and socializing. Visible love is more practiced than preached as we strive to be servants of each other. We are essentially Christian but are open to people of all faiths. We once had the ideal of a Christian community but slowly realized that in sharing land with others, a more fundamental requirement may be a common Earth ethic. Religious professions do not seem to be an accurate gauge of personal compatibility.

We have been greatly influenced by many other communities and homesteaders, especially Ianto Evans and Linda Smiley, formerly of Aprovecho Institute. As directors of Cob Cottage Company now, they are still our friends and mentors. We want to interact more with other communities in our bioregion—maybe through work trades, barter, and gatherings. [Sep99]

MT. MURRINDAL COOPERATIVE

W Tree via Buchan
Victoria 3885
AUSTRALIA

(03) 5155-0279

Began 1983 | Pop. 20
Diet: Vegetarian | Rural

We are a registered community settlement cooperative. We own, and live together on, a 40- hectare (120-acre) grazing property in the foothills of the Snowy Mountains in the southeast corner of mainland Australia. Our current resident population is nine adults. Other members and friends visit us from time to time.

We have six family-sized dwellings here, including a community house. We have a large organic vegetable garden, organic orchards, and a flock of free-range chickens. We are able to produce some of our own food. We manage community affairs by means of a monthly general meeting, and we hold a half-day working bee every weekend. As a group, we are not bound by any particular philosophy or belief system. Each person is free to do their own thing within the context of maintaining and developing community spirit. [Apr99]

MULVEY CREEK LAND CO-OPERATIVE

c/o Laara Kapel secretary
Box 218
Slocan BC V0G 2C0
CANADA

250-355-2393 #1433
gophertower@hotmail.com

Began 1991 | Pop. 22 | Re-Forming
Diet: Vegan | Rural

Our community tries to live harmoniously with nature; this includes each other as well as the animals and the land. We strive to be friendly neighbors, keeping our lines of communication open and clear. We try to support each other in our individual visions as well as any cooperative ventures. We strive for principles before personalities, and we support the "no leader" model of community. The community aims for maximum self-sufficiency in the long term, as well as simplicity. We are open to new people, children, and new ideas. [Feb99, sase requested]

"N" STREET CO-HOUSING

624 "N" St
Davis CA 95616

530-753-8075, 530-759-0121 fax
member3987@aol.com

Began 1986 | Pop. 55
Diet: Omnivore | Urban

"N" Street is a cohousing group that was started in 1986 when two tract homes built in the early 1950s took down their side fences. "N" Street continues to grow slowly, adding one house at a time. We currently have expanded to 12 houses, 7 homes on "N" Street that back up to 5 homes on the adjacent street. The removal of fences has created a beautiful open-space area that includes vegetable, flower, and water gardens; a play structure; a hot tub; a sauna; and a chicken coop.

We enjoy sharing community meals together about three times per week and work parties once a month. Informally, people get together to share dinners at home, a soak in the hot tub, a game of cards, or just a nice cup of tea. We are a tight-knit group of peole who enjoy living together and sharing resources. [Sep99, sase requested]

NAHZIRYAH MONASTIC COMMUNITY

Rev Nazirmoreh K B Kedem
P O Box 1280
Yellville AR 72687

870-449-4381, 504-945-1432
carrier@nmcnews.org
http://www.nmcnews.org/

Began 1970
Diet: Vegan | Rural/Urban | Spiritual

(Also known as The Purple People, Nazir Order of the Purple Veil.) Rev. Nazirmoreh, founder, director, and spiritual head of Nahziryah Monastic Community, is our spiritual teacher and guide. Rev. Nazirmoreh teaches that there are many paths—one goal, many names—*one divine creator*. The Nazir community is monastic, abiding by rules, order, and disciplines. The

Key to bracketed text: cc = cannot commit to prompt correspondance, sase = self-addressed stamped envelope

monastery includes men, women, and children. Resident members live a simple, monastic, communal life—we work hard, meditate, study, and strive daily to overcome the lower ego.

At the monastery, Nahziryah Monastic Community, Retreat for Meditation and Holistic Living, we do organic gardening to help sustain the community's dietary needs (vegan). To support the community and the effort toward consciousness expansion and further spiritual development, we make and sell art crafts, as well as metaphysical/esoteric/spiritual literature of all faiths, recordings, essential and fragrant oils, incense, and meditation supplies.

Nahziryah Monastic Community sustains itself through its own laborious efforts, except for the occasional donations given by the few who are sympathetic with the Nazir way of life and are willing and able to help, financially and otherwise, to support the service. The Nazir path is for those who hear the call and come to give their All in All... Behold the One in All. [Oct99, cc]

NAKAMURA CO-OP

807 Hill St
Ann Arbor MI 48104

734-996-9059

Pop. 54 | Urban

We provide an extremely friendly and memorable cooperative experience. Combining modern amenities such as a Macintosh computer, a TV/VCR/cable, a piano, and a new stereo system with a strong sense of tradition, a weird house culture, and fierce Nak pride, this co-op operates with abundant comfort and mirth. We provide a stable balance for students of all persuasions, including smokers/nonsmokers, cat lovers/haters, and vegetarians/carnivores. All your vices can be satisfied due to our prime location, proximate to campus (wake up five minutes before class), several eateries (fight the munchies), and three party stores (get your "pop and pretzels"). Our front porch, the best in all of Ann Arbor and the source of countless escapades, is marked by a beloved Pteranodon. Adept at throwing major parties as well as quieter social gatherings, Nakamura welcomes diverse students of all backgrounds. Stop by and check us out! We house 47 in 13 singles, 15 doubles, and 2 suites and seven more members in the Kagawa Annex. [Jan99, cc, sase required]

NAMASTÉ GREEN

373 Peacham Rd
Ctr Barnstead NH 03225

603-776-7776

Pop. 3 | Forming
Diet: No red meat | Rural | Spiritual

Namaste Green forming permaculture village (a local green group) is active politically and socially. We encourage cluster housing, pods, ecobusiness, nature sanctuary, activist retreat camping (the natural-way lifestyle)

We seek coparticipants, investors for ecovillage-/community-controlled land trust. Elders especially welcome.

Visits prearranged April to November.

Focused on loving cooperation, direct action, and a sustainable global future while blending with nature.

One-year prospective membership and a land investment after two-week visit. We envision many local green communes networked globally as catalyst for positive change. We must withdraw our energies from global transnationals to cocreate local self-reliance.

p.s.: We are currently promoting the idea of national referendum as the means of returning to "government by, for and to the people." [Dec98, sase required]

NASALAM

864 N Ranch Rd
Fair Grove MO 65648

417-759-7854
nasalam@aol.com
http://members.aol.com/nasalam/

Began 1995 | Pop. 4
Diet: Vegan | Rural | Spiritual

Nasalam is a tantric spiritual community dedicated to the spiritual unfoldment of humankind. Our lifestyle is designed to assist us in that goal by being gentle to the planet and all living things, made easier by living in the country on sacred land. We will develop a tribal lifestyle to provide the physical and emotional support needed by all humans. As a tantric community we believe in enjoying life to the fullest but within the context of spiritual growth. For that reason, we abstain from consuming animal protein and strive to be free of substances that pollute the body or enslave it through addiction. We employ daily practices to regulate the spiritual life of the community, and as we believe that sexual energy is a primary tool for realization of the divine we employ

erotic interaction as part of our spiritual practice. Because of our erotic orientation we are primarily interested in gay/lesbian/bisexual members.

The complete vision of Nasalam, its spiritual beliefs and social philosophy, can be found in the *Foundation for a New Age*, which can be obtained from the community. [Sep99, sase requested]

NATURE'S SPIRIT

455 Quail Ridge Rd
Salem SC 29676

864-944-6992
NaturesSpirit@worldnet.att.net
http://www.naturesspirit.org/

Began 1997 | Pop. 6
Diet: No red meat | Rural | Spiritual

Nature's Spirit is organized as a nonprofit organization with a central spiritual focus and values the diversity of all life and lives in the question, "How does one live in harmony with nature and spirit?" Nature's Spirit is intended to be a place that belongs to no one in particular but to humanity as a whole.

Nature's Spirit is situated on 210 acres of mostly forested land and a 10-acre lake. We currently have 6 resident members and expect to grow to about 50 people. We are dedicated to:
• caring for the land as stewards rather than "owners";
• creation of a spiritual center that will be a place of meditation and involve different means of spiritual expression, such as insight dialogue (based on Vipassana meditation) and synergic inquiry;
• growing our food organically, biointensively, and sustainably;
• using alternative sustainable methods of building and energy sources;
• initiating enterprises that are sustainable and assure economic viability;
• being the initiator and conduit for educational, leadership, intern, and exchange programs that will enable us to be of service to others, communicate and share our experiences, and link with similar local and global efforts.

People are welcome to visit or inquire about membership. Please call, e-mail, visit our Web site, or write for newsletter and information before coming for a visit. [Sep99, sase requested]

Additions and corrections: Email: directory@ic.org, Web: http://directory.ic.org/, Mail: RR 1 Box 156-D, Rutledge MO 63563, USA.

NESS

381 Hewlett Rd
Hermon NY 13652

Began 1991 | Pop. 4 | Forming
Diet: Omnivore | Rural

100 acres, mostly forested Adirondack foothills. We are three full members and one trial member in three households. Land stewardship and neighborly cooperation are guiding principles to date. Leaning toward land trust with private ownership of homes. Interests of current members include voluntary simplicity, homesteading, gardening, foraging, community organizing/activism (sustainable agriculture and energy, environment), home power, nonmotorized travel, footwear, carpentry/woodworking/timber framing, soccer, mead making, Russia, holistic health care, nonelectronic connectedness, etc.

We are an active part of a diverse "extended community" of friends and acquaintances, spread through the nearby towns and countryside (including Birdsfoot Farm, old-order Amish).

Ness is still forming and will likely evolve for some time. We hope that our willingness and ability to interact kindly with each other will reduce the need for formal rules and structure. Visitors and potential new members are welcome—prior arrangements preferred. Long-term guest space sometimes available. [Jan99]

NEVE SHALOM

IL-99761 Doar Na Shimshon
ISRAEL
pr@nswas.com
http://nswas.com/

Began 1977

Neve Shalom/Wahat al-Salam (pronounced nevey shalom/wahat as-salaam) is a cooperative village of Jews and Palestinian Arabs of Israeli citizenship. Situated equidistant from Jerusalem and Tel Aviv-Jaffa, Neve Shalom/Wahat al-Salam was founded in 1972 on 100 acres of land leased from the adjacent Latrun Monastery. In 1977, the first family came to reside here. By 1998, 30 families had settled in the village. The members of Neve Shalom/Wahat al-Salam are demonstrating the possibility of coexistence between Jews and Palestinians by developing a community based on mutual acceptance, respect, and cooperation. Democratically governed and owned by its members, the community is affiliated with no political party or movement. Neve Shalom/Wahat al-Salam gives practical expression to its vision through its various branches.

NEW COMMUNITY

425 Ann St
East Lansing MI 48823

517-351-3820

Pop. 15 | Diet: Vegan | Urban

Started in 1969 by a faction of Hedrick House members who wanted a less-structured living style, the group, which called themselves New Community, began renting different houses in the late 1960s and running them as sort of counterculture, utopian co-op experiments.

The Student Housing Corporation (SHC) rented a property at 437 Abbott, a location of several previous co-ops (such as Nexus and Phoenix), and it became New Community in 1979. With money from a HUD loan in 1980, SHC purchased properties 415 and 425 Ann to provide housing for New Community members. New Community did not last long as a two-house

Key to bracketed text: cc = cannot commit to prompt correspondance, sase = self-addressed stamped envelope

cooperative. In 1981, the properties split, and New Community became exclusively the property of 425 Ann. SHC operated 415 Ann Street as a rental property until 1995, when it became a brand-new five-member co-op, Toad Lane. Recently, New Community became a "theme house" for Honors College students. [Jan99, no openings]

NEW CREATION CHRISTIAN COMMUNITY

New Creation Farmhouse
Nether Heyford
Northhampton NN7 3LB, England
UNITED KINGDOM
+44.01327.349991, +44.07700.Jesus
+44.01327.349997 fax
nccc@jesus.org.uk
http://www.jesus.org.uk/nccc

Began 1974 | Pop. 680
Diet: Omnivore | Rural/Urban | Spiritual

The New Creation Christian Community is part of the Jesus Fellowship Church, which is also known as the Jesus Army. The fellowship is an evangelical Christian church with a contemporary charismatic emphasis. It is orthodox in doctrine, upholding the universally accepted Christian creeds.

The church numbers around 2,500, about 700 of whom live in Christian Community in 60 or so houses around the United Kingdom. Each community house consists of anything between 6 and 60 people, who live as a large "family."

The businesses, community houses, and other community assets are owned by the members and held in a legally constituted noncharitable Trust Fund. Within the community, each house has a "common-purse" arrangement, with members pooling their income to meet all personal and household expenses.

Community houses are open to receive visitors on a temporary basis for up to 6 months (which can be extended to up to 12 months). If visitors' stay is longer than a week, they pay a board-and-lodging charge, but the remainder of their income is at their disposal. [Jan99]

NEW ENVIRONMENT ASSOCIATION

270 Fenway Drive
Syracuse NY 13224
315-446-8009

Began 1974

The association, begun in 1974, provides a framework and process for people to come together in order to create a sustainable society—a "New Environment"—by raising their awareness, modifying their lifestyles, developing a sense of community, and taking part in cooperative activities. A wide range of topics gets addressed at our general meetings and study groups, from organic gardening and holistic health to new economics and alternative education.

Activities vary and depend on members' interests. Currently, we have established a community-supported agriculture (CSA) project in the Syracuse area, are publishing a new economic reader, and are also looking for land to create an educational center, possibly with a small community. The long-range goal is new communities that are humanly and environmentally sound. Members gather periodically for weekend retreats and pursue specific projects in small working groups. Our monthly newsletter reaches readers across the United States and in several other countries. Send for a free sample copy! [Jan99]

NEW GOLOKA

PO Box 897
Hillsborough NC 27278
919-732-6492
103336.145@compuserve.com
http://supersoul.com/

Began 1982 | Pop. 24
Diet: Vegetarian | Rural | Spiritual

(Also known as ISKCON of N.C..) New Goloka is a beautiful rural Radha-Krishna temple located 20 minutes from Chapel Hill, North Carolina. Our property is 16 acres that is surrounded by lush forest and large streams. The atmosphere is tranquil and spiritually uplifting. We have daily temple services and meditation. Our philosophy stresses that eating is a spiritual process, and so we cook and offer many sumptuous preparations daily.

We have flower and vegetable gardens that we use for temple worship and cooking.

We do have a guest facility, but one must make arrangements in advance and there is a screening process.

Our founder, His Divine Grace AC Bhaktivedanta Swami Prabhupada, said we should make a life of simple living and high thinking, so we hope to imbibe this mood here at New Goloka.

We daily study the Bhagavad-Gita as well as the Srimad Bhagavatam.

Please call for directions or visit any Sunday at 5:00 p.m. for open house. This open-house program is available worldwide in all of our 350 centers of the International Society for Krishna Consciousness. Thank you very much. [Sep99, sase requested]

NEW HUMANITY CENTRE

2001 Eleonon Rd
Akroyali
GR-24100 Kalamata
GREECE
721-58172, 721-58035 fax

Began 1992 | Pop. 25 | Forming
Rural/Urban | Spiritual

(Also known as Universal Alliance, Ensophion of Humanity and New Humanity Group.) The New Humanity Centre is a monastic-pluralistic nongovernmental organization that consists of the following world-service branches.

1. The Ensophion of Humanity is the new educational branch imparting Ensophia as a new Aquarian age philosophy of life. It also teaches Esperanto and promotes it as the one common transnational language of humanity.

2. The Universal Alliance is a world movement promoting the one familyhood of humanity and the establishment of a federated world panhumanity administration. It also promotes the use of Esperanto as the universal common language of humankind.

3. The New Humanity Group is a group working and co-working for the manifestation in nature of the Enhumanity new world according to the one life plan and purpose.

4. *Enhumanity* is a newsletter edited in Esperanto and in Greek, promoting the philosophy of the above-mentioned groups.

In addition, the New Humanity Centre acts as a spiritual service, as a retreat center for visitors, as an international conference hall, and as a self-enlightened center, through its 2,000-volume Esoteric Library, for Truth Seekers. [Mar99, sase required]

NEW JERUSALEM COMMUNITY

745 Derby Ave
Cincinnati OH 45232

513-541-4748, 513-541-4811 fax

Began 1971 | Pop. 110
Diet: Omnivore | Urban | Spiritual

New Jerusalem, established in 1971, is a lay Catholic community of approximately 60 families. Our community center brings our lives together in an integrated, working-class neighborhood in Cincinnati. Each Sunday we gather for worship. During the rest of the week we seek to live out the Gospel of Jesus as extended family to one another and to brothers and sisters down the street and around the globe. Monthly we gather for prayer and discussion about our community life together.

Some of our current involvements include the care of Central American refugees, with a special commitment to our sister community in Nicaragua; housing rehabilitation; and work to protect the environment. Ten percent of our annual income is given away to those in need and those working for change.

After our founding by a Franciscan priest, and his departure in 1985, we have struggled to give authority to one another, to rechoose the community for what it is, and to accept responsibility for our own lives. While maintaining a good relationship with the church and respecting the tradition, we are also listening to the Holy Spirit and honoring our own experience. Our life is rich, full, and challenging as we integrate our personal journeys, families, careers, and community. We are happy to welcome you and to serve you as God leads, trusting that God will continue to bless us all with more abundant life together. [Jan99, cc]

NEW LAND

184 Rainbow Ridge Rd
Faber VA 22938

Began 1979 | Pop. 54 | Rural

The New Land is an intentional community of individual homesites in a beautiful rural setting, with mountain views, access roads, and a lake—on land shared with the Monroe Institute, a research and educational organization dedicated to the study and development of human consciousness through the use of audiostimulated brain hemispheric synchronization and other scientific techniques. Residents and landholders who chose to join the New Land come mostly through experience with the institute.

Homes are privately owned, and most members are self-employed (in a wide range of professional fields) or retired. The only common land is at the nearby Monroe Institute. Personal freedom and evolving consciousness are shared values. Occupations, types of homes, and land use are a matter of individual choice (i.e., gardens, greenhouses, horses, llamas, etc.). Members get together as desired to share in special projects, social affairs, and spiritual growth. Some homesites are available. [Nov98]

NEW RIVER VALLEY COHOUSING

c/o 609 Rose Ave
Blacksburg VA 24060

540-951-0566
fmignone@usit.net
http://www.nrvcohousing.org/

Began 1997 | Pop. 23 | Forming
Rural/Urban

We are a group of New River Valley residents, including families and individuals of all ages, who have joined together to build a cohousing neighborhood. We envision a community of private dwellings together with a common house where meals and activities may be shared.

Guiding values include:
• a commitment to create and maintain a supportive and enriching community that fosters connection with each other, the larger community, and the Earth;
• living in harmony with ecological systems;
• selecting a location with natural beauty and open space close to Blacksburg;
• creating a balance between private life and community life;
• encouraging diversity in membership;
• working to create and maintain creative and positive relationships through consensus decision making, open dialogue, and creative conflict resolution.

Membership is based on self-selection. [Sep99, cc, sase requested]

NEW VIEW COHOUSING

c/o Novak
4 Half Moon Hill
Acton MA 01720

978-263-2997, 978-266-9409
carolnovak@bicnet.net
http://www.newview.org/

Began 1995 | Pop. 83
Diet: Omnivore | Rural/Urban

Suburban cohousing. Basically families and individuals who want to share meals, child rearing, joys and sorrows, taking care of the land, and creating beauty and who want a balance of privacy and community in their lives. [May99, cc]

NEW VRINDAVAN

RD 1 Box 319
Moundsville WV 26041

304-843-1600, 304-843-1409
nityodita@juno.com
http://www.newvrindavan.com/

Began 1968 | Pop. 230
Diet: Vegetarian | Rural | Spiritual

(Also known as City of God.) New Vrindavan, founded in 1968, is the oldest and largest Hare Krishna (2,000 acres) farm community in the West. The community serves as a place of pilgrimage for the Hindu/Vaisnava population and attracts many thousands of visitors. It is also the

Key to bracketed text: cc = cannot commit to prompt correspondance, sase = self-addressed stamped envelope

home of the Palace of Gold, one of the major tourist attractions in the state of West Virginia. A guest lodge and cabins, two gift shops, and a vegetarian restaurant operate seasonally. The community offers housing for families and an alternative school for their children. Those in the monastic order reside in the temple, where daily worship services and classes are held. New Vrindavan is based on the principles of Bhagavad Gita and the practice of Bhakti-yoga, devotion to Krishna, or God. The community grows a good portion of its food and protects over 200 cows. Many members are developing cottage industries, including a health-food store, to maintain their families. Throughout the year there are numerous festivals, gatherings, and retreats. Members conduct workshops on a variety of topics including the Bhagavad Gita and other scriptures of India, organic gardening, vegetarian cooking, mantra meditation, yoga, healing arts, and sacred storytelling. [sase requested]

NICHE / TUCSON COMMUNITY LAND TRUST

1050 S Verdugo
Tucson AZ 85745

Pop. 4 | Diet: Vegan | Urban

Niche is a cooperative house held in trust, located on two acres of floodplain near downtown Tucson. The fruit trees are happy and waiting for rain. "Women Build Houses," a group that teaches construction of various natural solar, etc., structures holds classes here. Don't move to Tucson to join Niche, but if you are already here, let's have dinner together. Se habla Espanol. [Jan99, cc, sase required]

NIEDERKAUFUNGEN KOMMUNE

Kirchweg 1
D-34260 Kaufungen
GERMANY

05605-80070, 05605-800740 fax
kommune@t-online.de
http://home.t-online.de/
home/kommune/

Began 1986
Diet: Omnivore | Rural/Urban

Kommune Niederkaufungen is Germany's largest secular income-sharing community and is located in a semiurban setting near the city of Kassel in central Germany. Founded in 1986 the commune presently (3/99) consists of 55 adult members and 18 children/teenagers. We are a community with a rather left-wing but undogmatic understanding of politics; as a group we are nonreligious and nonspiritual. The main focuses are a shared economy, consensus decision making, and an ecological approach to work and lifestyle. We run 11 community-owned businesses:

- carpentry shop;
- seminar center;
- construction company;
- kitchen/catering businesses;
- organic-vegetable business;
- cattle operation;
- leather workshop;
- architect's office;
- kindergarten and childcare center;
- metal workshop;
- administration/consulting business.

Some people work in external jobs. We presently live in 12 living groups, share all our meals, and have a general meeting once a week. Newcomers go through a three- to six-month trial period. We frequently offer orientation weekends and orientation weeks for interested people. Visitors have to make arrangements first. [Mar99]

NINTH STREET ASSOCIATES

1708 Ninth St
Berkeley CA 94710

Began 1993 | Pop. 8
Diet: Omnivore | Urban

(Also known as Ninth Street Coop.) Ninth Street Co-op is a limited-equity housing cooperative owned by the residents. The co-op consists of two duplexes and one cottage with a common area, four garages, fruit trees, and an organic garden. We are in an urban, working-class neighborhood that is ethnically diverse. Members are low to moderate income. All members serve on the board of directors that meets monthly to discuss co-op business. Members share maintenance tasks. Ninth Street Co-op is self-managed. The group became a co-op in 1993. [Mar99, cc, sase requested, no openings]

Additions and corrections: Email: directory@ic.org, Web: http://directory.ic.org/, Mail: RR 1 Box 156-D, Rutledge MO 63563, USA.

NISHNAJIDA

7124 Military Rd
Three Lakes WI 54562

715-546-2944
tdrums2@newnorth.net

Began 1991 | Pop. 7
Diet: Omnivore | Rural | Spiritual

(Also known as Teaching Drum Outdoor School.) We are a group of latter-day Natives returning to the old way. Dedicated to the healing of self and the Earth Mother, we are listening to the ancestral voices and relearning the skills of awareness, attunement, honor, and respect. The talking circle is our forum; the sweat lodge is our heart; the wild herbs are our healers.

On the shore of a quiet lake in the wilderness lies our camp—a cluster of five bark-and-thatch wigwams. We make some of our clothing from skins; fish and forage some of our food; make an array of craft items from dugout canoes and cradleboards to bows and bowls.

Our days vary with the seasons: In the spring are syruping and lodge construction and gathering fresh greens; in the summer are trail work, boat making, and hide tanning; autumn is time for cranberries and firewood; when the snows lie heavy we do craftwork and explore. About half of each day is spent on group endeavors and half on personal. We all enjoy swimming and canoeing and feasting.

We are a living-learning center, and others come to heal, intern, take classes. We offer Native-oriented relationship and emotional counseling and dream and spiritual guidance and give classes and living-history presentations at historical events and schools. [Sep99, sase required]

NOAH PROJECT COMMUNITIES

PO Box 1173
Leicester NC 28748

828-683-5739, 888-noah-316
noahproject@earthling.net
http://www.noahproject.com/

Began 1999 | Pop. 150 | Forming
Rural | Spiritual

The Noah Project Community is being designed and built at this time and will be dedicated to those planetary citizens who have given themselves permission to believe in the ancient prophecies or the teachings regarding the Hopi purification process currently in progress here on planet Earth. Each community will focus on or be centered around the underground home designed by the Noah Project of Asheville. This home has been designed to take anything that Mother Nature or Mother Earth wants to throw at it. It has also been designed to be as environmentally friendly, ergonomically sound, and as respectful of green space as is humanly possible. The main motivation of those becoming residents of the Noah Project Communities will be the survival of themselves and their families, so as to become the future architects and designers of the New World and the first recipients of the thousand years of peace promised to all who hear the calling. We are trying to create the place from which to begin the journey. It will then be up to those who reside in each of these communities to take them to the next level of becoming truly meaningful places to live and spiritually conscious homes for the soul to prosper and grow. [Jan99, sase required]

NOMAD COHOUSING

1460 Quince Ave #102
Boulder CO 80304

303-413-9227

Began 1997 | Pop. 24
Diet: Omnivore | Urban

Nomad Cohousing is an 11-unit urban community on one acre two miles from downtown Boulder. Our common dining area is attached to a 50-year-old community playhouse that we share with them where they hold opening-night receptions for their plays. We are adjacent to a small shopping center within a minute walk of the Boulder mountain open space. [Oct99]

NOMADELFIA

Nomadelfia 14
I-58100 Grosseto
ITALY

0039-0564-338243, 0039-0564-338244
nomadelfia@gol.grosseto.it
nomadelfia.scuola@gol.grosseto.it
http://www.gol.grosseto.it/
asso/nomadelfia/

Began 1948 | Pop. 330 | Forming
Diet: Omnivore | Rural | Spiritual

"Nomadelfia" is a name that is derived from Greek and means "the law of brotherhood." It is the name given to a community of Catholic volunteers whose common purpose is to build a new kind of society based on the teachings of the Gospel. Nomadelfia is neither an institute nor a "boys' town" even though it takes in the abandoned, particularly children.

The Founder: It was founded by Fr. Zeno Saltini (1900–1981), who, at the age of 20, decided to change society by first changing himself. After his ordination into priesthood in 1931, he adopted a young man who had been released from prison. Since then, more than 5,000 young people have been taken in by the families of Nomadelfia.

The People: Nomadelfia is made up of 320 people that in turn make up 50 families. They live on four square kilometers of land near Grosseto in Tuscany. The community is considered a parish by the church and a civil association by the state. Nomadelfia is structured as a democracy; it has its own constitution, and its values are inspired by the Gospel, while it resembles the democratic state law.

The Families: The families do not live in isolation from one another but rather in "family groups" consisting of four or five families.

Nomadelfia has no need for money, and it owns no property. No form of exploitation is allowed, and all goods are held in common, in accordance with Jesus' words at the Last Supper: "Father, all that is mine is yours, all that is yours is mine." [Oct99]

NOMENUS RADICAL FAERIE SANCTUARY

P O Box 312
Wolf Creek OR 97497

541-866-2678
nomenus@budget.net

Began 1989 | Pop. 4
Diet: Omnivore | Rural | Spiritual

The Wolf Creek Sanctuary is the manifestation of Nomenus's statement of purpose to "create, preserve, and manage places of cultural/spiritual sanctuary for Radical Faeries and their friends to gather in harmony with nature for renewal, growth, and shared learning." Nomenus is incorporated as a church under 501(C)3 of the tax code and is a resource for issues concerning the connections between gay men's sexuality and spirituality. The land is also available to outside groups as a rustic gathering/retreat center with primitive campsites and limited indoor lodging and supports a small group of residents who are members of, and in service to, Nomenus. [Feb99, cc, sase requested]

NORTH MOUNTAIN COMMUNITY LAND TRUST

154 Hayslette Rd
Lexington VA 24450

540-463-1760

Began 1972 | Pop. 5 | Re-Forming
Diet: Vegetarian | Rural

North Mountain began in 1972 as a rural commune. We have a beautiful piece of land—130 acres, mostly hilly woods, about 10 of it tillable. We are located in a valley encircled by the ancient Allegheny Mountains.

The commune continued with many comings and goings through the 1970s and into the mid-1980s. As our membership grew older and most began having families, the need for individual housing grew. In 1990 we changed our structure to that of a land trust.

The land is owned by the community with members having lifetime leases to individual 2-acre plots. Homes are owned by the members. There is a work commitment each month as well as a monetary one. We have meetings monthly, potlucks regularly, and labor exchanges among us.

We now consist of five members—two homes, three adults, two teens, various dogs, cats, chickens, a barn, a shop, and a granary. We do some gardens together, others individually. We have hopes to grow in the future but no desire to grow too quickly or too large, remaining at six to eight households at most.

If interested, please write to schedule a visit. We want to ensure that you know us and we know you and we all know what's involved when we join together in the dance of community living. Come dance with us at North Mountain Community. [Dec98, sase requested]

NORTHERN SUN FARM CO-OP

PO Box 71
Sarto Manitoba R0A 1X0
CANADA

204-434-6887, 204-434-6143

Began 1984 | Pop. 15
Diet: Omnivore | Rural

Northern Sun Farm Co-Op is a rural community with the land being cooperatively owned by all members. We have both resident and nonresident members. Our focus is on alternative energy, appropriate technology, simple lifestyles, and self-reliance. We live in family groups, and we promote individual responsibility for life choices. Northern Sun Farm is always open to visitors. [Jan99, cc]

NYLAND COHOUSING COMMUNITY

3518 Nyland Way
Lafayette CO 80026
klorenz@compuserve.com

Began 1993 | Pop. 140
Diet: Omnivore | Rural

The Nyland CoHousing Community is one of the first completed cohousing communities in the United States. Nyland began as Colorado CoHousing in 1988 after a few friends got together to talk about the new book *CoHousing* by McCamant and Durrett. In May of 1990 we optioned the land; in August 1992 we began moving in; and all residents were in by May of 1993.

Our community of 122 people includes 87 adults, 6 teens, and 29 kids—with an assortment of visiting children and friends of the community. We own 42 acres of land, annexed by the town of Lafayette, in a rural area just outside the city of Boulder. There are 42 homes, a 6,000-square-foot common house, a 860-square-foot shop building, and a 600-square-foot greenhouse. Houses are individually owned, and common properties are being held in unison through a homeowners association. All properties are maintained and managed by the residents of Nyland.

Our decision-making structure consists of committees and consensus. We meet two times a month in general gatherings, and smaller work groups handle the tasks of managing the land and community affairs. Day care is provided during the day, and we generally have shared meals four nights a week in the common house. Tours of the community are available at 11:00 a.m. the last Sunday of each month. [Oct99]

O'BRIEN LAKE HOMESTEADERS

PO Box 38
Eureka MT 59917

Began 1980 | Pop. 12
Diet: Omnivore | Rural

(Also known as The Quiet Place.) Our community has existed for over 20 years as a group of good neighbors who treasure our rural lifestyle and appreciate the grandeur of our surroundings. By owning expensive equipment as a group and cooperating in its use, we maintain comfortable access and enjoy affordable improvements. All our various lifestyles here are respected. [Feb99, cc, sase required, no openings]

O'KEEFE CO-OP

1500 Gilbert Ct
Ann Arbor MI 48105
http://www.umich.edu/~umicc/

Pop. 85 | Urban

O'Keeffe is a part of the larger North Campus Co-ops Building. Nestled in a quiet wooded area, we are a 10-minute walk from the University of Michigan (UM) north campus and just a few minutes from a UM bus stop (en route to central campus). Although the North Campus Co-ops are collectively the largest co-op in the ICC, the houses are divided into suites of 16 to 20 people, each with a TV lounge, a kitchen, and four individual bathrooms. These intimate arrangements facilitate social interactions and make the house feel smaller than it really is.

O'Keeffe is generally quiet and clean but certainly not sedate. We engage in lively conversation at dinner (prepared with the help of a professional chef) each evening. We have regular parties, and, depending on the mood and interests of the current members, we organize activities such as theater trips, skiing, white-water rafting, or camping.

The membership is comprised largely of graduate students, along with some upper-class undergraduates and nonstudents. We are an extremely diverse international crowd. On recent count, over 30 languages are spoken here! We actively share our

Listings

backgrounds via discussion, music, dance, movies, and cuisine. [Oct99]

OAK GROVE FOUNDATION

16170 Mountain Orchard Ln
Round Hill VA 20141
lellasmith@Juno.com

Began 1993 | Pop. 1 | Forming
Diet: No red meat | Rural | Spiritual

The Oak Grove Foundation, a Blue Ridge Mountain center/farm, emphasizes Earth mystery traditions, harmony and peace with the Earth, simplicity, and spiritual development—in workshops, seminars, research, and writing as well as in ceremonies/celebrations.

Established in 1993, it includes the Earthpeace Center for workshops; the beginnings of a small, model 8–12-house ecovillage—emphasizing simplicity, sustainability, and alternative living and building—and a fledgling press.

The 82-acre center in a low gap in the Blue Ridge (Vermont), 60 miles from Washington, DC, is traditionally viewed as a Native American "place of peace" and a ceremonial ground for Native Americans living at the foot of the ridge along the Shenandoah River. Numerous medicine people are attracted to the land to give ceremonies, workshops, and vision quests.

Part of the land is an ancient mountain farm with venerable trees, stone walls, and lanes; views over three states; an old mountain dancing ground; the mystery and beauty of the Blue Ridge—the world's oldest mountains; and many ley lines.

Currently, one writer (Quaker/Buddhist) lives in a passive solar house, while tipis and a trailer house participants and guests. At this early stage, the center can accommodate only experienced or semiprofessional organic farmers/gardeners and builders. [Jan99, sase required]

OAKLAND ELIZABETH HOUSE

PO Box 1175
Berkeley CA 94701

510-658-1380

Began 1993 | Pop. 24
Diet: Omnivore | Urban | Spiritual

We are a community of families and single women. Reopened in 1993, we serve low-income homeless and women in crisis by providing safe, affordable housing and good food. A core group of four live-in volunteers teaches and sustains a process of cooperative decision making that empowers the women living here to be independent and accountable for their successful reunification with their children and transition into permanent housing. We are based in the values of Dorothy Day and the Catholic Worker movement, living together with the poor in the spirit of love, peace, and compassion. [Apr99, sase requested]

OAKWOOD FARM

3801 SCR 575 E
Selma IN 47383

765-747-7027

Began 1974 | Pop. 16
Diet: Omnivore | Rural | Spiritual

Oakwood Farm is a 326-acre home and retreat center in central Indiana. It is an international Emissary community dedicated to spiritual regeneration, cocreation, and Earth stewardship. The current focus is the provision and creation of sacred space for healing and transformational work. [Nov98]

OFEK SHALOM CO-OP

12 N Butler St
Madison WI 53703

608-257-4768, 608-257-8754
http://mcc.studentorg.wisc.edu/ofek/

Pop. 13 | Diet: Vegetarian | Urban | Spiritual

Our co-op includes students, working people, and cats. We live in the center of downtown in a 1920s three-story house. Our recently remodeled kitchen is the hub of our vibrant community.

We are a Jewish house, but not all members are Jewish. We express our Jewishness in ways like creating new rituals and learning Jewish history. Every year we have at least one seder, and every Friday we welcome guests for a Shabbat meal, complete with fresh homemade challah.

Our work-job system tries to balance administrative and grunt work. We hold house meetings biweekly and use a modified-consensus process to create our own policies. We have an annual Purim masquerade party and a Scorpio drag party.

As one of Madison Community Cooperative's houses, we share its decision-making process and financial strength, as well as its parties, potlucks, and educational events.

We welcome new members to join us. Spaces open up August 15 and January 1. Please contact the membership coordinator if you'd like to check us out. Shalom! [Nov98, sase requested]

OHIO BIO-ENVIRO SETTLEMENTS, INC.

PO Box 35932
Canton OH 44718

330-454-1178, 330-454-2563 fax
obes@obes.itgo.com
http://www.obes.itgo.com/

Began May99 | Pop. 138 | Forming
Rural | Spiritual

(Also known as Unicorns Glen Eco-Community.) A 22-acre biological and environmental sanctuary, located in mideastern Ohio, one mile from New Athens. The sanctuary is 20 to 30 minutes from St. Clairsville, Ohio, and Wheeling, West Virginia; 1 hour from Columbus, Akron, Canton, and Youngstown, Ohio, and Pittsburgh, Pennsylvania. It's located on State Route 519 and accessible from Harrison County Road 41. The property was chosen because of its dead nature. Strip-mined 22 years ago, the land is home to scrub grass and is totally useless for farming or other horticultural activities. With our plans to totally "biologically as well as environmentally rehabilitate" the property, while we build the ecocommunity, it was a natural choice. Within 3 years we will prove that any land, even with limited or no natural resource, can be made beautiful, productive, and also biologically and ecologically sustainable once more. [Aug99]

OJAI FOUNDATION, THE

9739 Ojai-Santa Paula Rd
Ojai CA 93023

805-646-8343
ojaifdn@jetlink.net
http://www.ojaifoundation.org/

Began 1979 | Pop. 11
Diet: Vegetarian | Rural | Spiritual

Located on a 40-acre ridge of semi wilderness in Ojai, California, the Ojai Foundation is an educational retreat center for both youth and adults, a place of personal retreat, and a community dedicated to the way of council, honoring spiritual practice in all traditions, service to others, and stewardship of the land.

Key to bracketed text: cc = cannot commit to prompt correspondance, sase = self-addressed stamped envelope

Our adult programs include training in the council process, which involves speaking and listening "from the heart"; storytelling; mindfulness in a variety of traditional and contemporary settings; permaculture; and relationship intensives. We serve individuals, schools, and business organizations interested in community building, spirit in business, and the exploration of sacred arts. Wilderness rites of passage and a ropes adventure course are available for all ages.

The community is an essential part of this work: staff, guests, teachers, and students all create and explore how to learn and live together. Our common practices include daily morning meditation, council, mindful work, and service to the foundation's vision and the land we steward. We have nine residential staff positions and offer work retreat to four individuals each month. Core staff positions usually arise from the pool of work retreatants.

Our work-retreat program is for those interested in exploring the relationship between mindful work, spiritual practice, and community experience. The work is 25 hours a week to help maintain the center and support the foundation programs with time left for personal retreat. A 24-hour solo in nature is offered at the end of each month's stay. There are biweekly councils, and there are weekly teachings by our retreat coordinator. To apply, contact us by phone or letter. Please include the dates you wish to come, the skills you offer, and the intentions you have for your time here. Cost is $25/week. We encourage people to come for a full month; a week's stay is minimum.

For work retreatants, foundation programs are available at a reduced price. Please call or write for our brochure and program schedule. [Nov98, cc]

ÖKOLEA - KLOSTERDORF

**Hohensteinc Weg 3
D-15345 Klosterdorf
GERMANY**

**03341-35-939-30, 03341-35-939-0
03341-309998 fax
oekolea@miregal.berlinet.de**

Began 1992 | Diet: Omnivore | Rural

In March 1993, we founded the nonprofit association OekoLeA Klosterdorf Inc. and began to settle on an old local farm.

The old farmhouse is habitable again, and we reconstructed the calf barn to accommodate more private rooms. Both buildings were reconstructed with materials suitable for humans and the environment.

At this point, 20 adults and 11 children between 2 and 69 years old and from eastern and western Germany live together in our communal home. We share the housework and our money and are there for each other by trying to solve problems together.

We are planning to reconstruct the former cow barn in order to build a bakery with a wood-burning stove and a large communal room for seminars, meetings, children's activities, and more. So far, our large barn has been serving as a meeting place in the summertime.

Our projects and household needs are paid for out of a common purse, to which everybody contributes half of their individual income.

We try to live in an ecologically responsible way and hope to do our part in keeping the Earth a hospitable place in times to come. In our educational programs, we try to pass on the experiences we have had with each other and our lifestyle to others; we also make use of knowledge and abilities gathered before our time together.

The legal body responsible for our educational work is the nonprofit association OekoLeA—Verein für Bildung und Kultur, Oekologie and Gesundheit e.V. Everybody who is interested in what we are doing or would like to support our work can join this association and become a sponsor. [May99]

OLYMPIA HOUSING COLLECTIVE

**129 Percival St NW
Olympia WA 98502**

**360-352-2401
tescstudentcoop@hotmail.com
OHCollective@hotmail.com**

Began Sep99 | Pop. 30 | Forming
Diet: Vegetarian | Urban

The Olympia Housing Collective was founded in the summer of 1999 by a group of students from the Evergreen State College. We currently occupy five houses with a membership of 30. We operate on a consensus decision-making system and emphasize a diet of locally produced organic food. We eat and live together. We aim to provide affordable housing in a self-manag-

Listings

ing, nonhierarchical environment and are open to students as well as all people. We are working toward ownership of our own houses. The Olympia Housing Collective supports helping out other cool organizations and individuals. [Oct99, sase requested, email preferred]

ONE SPIRIT FREE CATHOLIC COMMUNITY

13419 Cavalier Woods Dr
Clifton VA 20124

703-818-8080
jimhburch@aol.com

Began 1998 | Pop. 80 | Spiritual

We meet weekly for upbeat, relevant, spiritual services and other times socially. We seek the "experience" of God, rather than the lessons "about" God. We are ecumenical: everybody of any religion is welcome. Communion is open to all. We stretch theology and seek to make the wonderful teachings of Christ come from behind the encrustations of the ages to a relevant and vibrant joy today. Married men and women may be invited to ordination. The biblical Gospel message (which is not "literal" or "inerrant") is enhanced by continued revelation of God, who is among us and speaks today through such voices as Teilhard de Chardin, Neale Donald Walsch, Matthew Fox, Desmond Tutu, Deepak Chopra, Nelson Mandela, etc. Members are members by saying so, and they give if and what time, money, or effort they wish, knowing that their presence is our mutual greatest gift to each other. We judge no one by what they have done or are doing now, recognizing that God loves us all equally and unequivocally ... And so, can we do less? [Aug99]

ONE WORLD FAMILY COMMUNE

535 Spencer St
Santa Rosa CA 95404

707-527-8380
owfc@sonic.net
http://www.galactic.org/

Began 1967 | Pop. 9
Diet: Vegan | Urban | Spiritual

(Also known as Universal Industrial Church.) There are seven of us in the One World Family Commune who came together 30 years ago when we recognized the truth of the messages coming through Allen Michael from Galactica. Beginning in San Francisco, we operated our natural-food restaurant in Mill Valley, Berkeley, Sacramento, and Stockton. We published *Cosmic Cookery* and four books of channelings coming through Allen Michael, and as Starmast Publications and Productions we produce videos shown on public-access TV in Santa Rosa, Sacramento, Berkeley, Palo Alto, Los Angeles, Malibu, Denver, and Washington, DC.

We recognize usury money, money with interest attached, to be a manifestation of satanic power (negated energies) and the reason there are war, crime, disease, and poverty on this planet. Allen Michael is a high galactic being in a body at this "time of the end" to channel the plan, the worldwide work stoppage/karma yoga exercise and 30/30 plan to end the money system and begin the world-sharing society of God consciousness. We are autonomous self-government, led by wisdom in our decisions by consensus. We share our energies in providing for our daily needs, communications, and producing videos. As the energies rise, we anticipate the opportunity to demonstrate, on a large scale, living according to

natural law in an environment that includes our many "schools of experiences" for people to experience the magic of sharing and forgiveness. [Dec98, no openings]

ONGOING COHOUSING COMMUNITY

1905 NE Going St
Portland OR 97211
stevea@pacifier.com

Began 1991 | Pop. 19
Diet: Vegetarian | Urban

This retrofit cooperative urban block has been operating as an intentional cohousing community for over eight years. Currently there are 15 adults and 4 children under the age of six in seven households.

Although from the outside the community looks like any typical inner-city neighborhood, upon closer examination there are shared resources; shared yards, gardens, and children's play area; regularly scheduled meal sharing; ecological site improvements; and an extended-family environment including various life celebrations. Many cohousing members are active in environmental or social-justice work and/or involved in various artistic endeavors. There are often shared housing situations available and sometimes houses for sale on the adjoining block. [Jul99, cc, sase required]

ORCA LANDING

731 N 96th St
Seattle WA 98103

206-789-2540, 206-789-2878
orcaland@halcyon.com

Began 1990 | Pop. 6
Diet: Omnivore | Urban

Orca Landing is an urban cooperative in Seattle, Washington. We've been in our current location since 1990. Composed of six adults and two children, with a third on the way, we operate by consensus even though one of us actually owns the property. We have been busy enlarging our home, researching land trusts, and investing in our relationships as we grow a neotribal extended family.

As a community we've chosen not to embrace any specific political, environmental, or religious causes but to encourage individuals to pursue their own paths. There is, for example, a variety of spiritual beliefs in our household. In lieu of any official

Key to bracketed text: cc = cannot commit to prompt correspondance, sase = self-addressed stamped envelope

overriding agenda, all of us on different levels are involved in networking with our neighbors and various local organizations, including Northwest Intentional Communities Association (NICA). We are interested in fostering communication across whatever divides people from one another. Most of us, for example, have been through Landmark Education's Curriculum for Living, including the Forum. We use the distinctions of the Landmark Forum to empower the dynamic community conversation we live in as we focus on what's possible. While we are not egalitarian, we practice voluntary simplicity, enjoy the arts and music and other creative pursuits, and share a love of outdoor adventure and wilderness. [Mar99, sase requested]

OSHO MEVLANA

Osho Mevlana
Lot 26, Bilin Rd
Myocum NSW 2482
AUSTRALIA

0266 844 096
mitra@earth.path.net
http://www.ozi.con/mevlana/

Began 1996
Diet: Vegetarian | Rural | Spiritual

Osho Mevlana is an open residential community that has been created as an integrated experiment in living, inspired by the vision of Osho. The community welcomes people from any background or walk of life.

We are joined together by a common desire to wake up and create the space in which an Osho Buddhafield can happen, to promote personal growth and creative expression.

We do this by sharing ownership of common areas for meditations, meals, workshops, healing, visitors, etc. We also aim to create viable businesses and jobs, either linked to the meditation center or otherwise.

We own individual houses and respect individual privacy. The residents are varied in nationality, age, and occupation; some work in the center, while others earn a living outside. We are trying to provide a variety of housing options and costs. Some residents are shareholders; others rent.

We are rural, in rolling hills near Bryon Bay but just 10 minutes from town, beaches, and several other communities. The nature on the property of Osho Mevlana itself is abundant and typical of Byron Shire: hillside rain-forest pockets; large wetland forests;

koalas; wallabies; many different birds; and beautiful views. [Dec98]

OSHO MIASTO

I-53010 Frosini Siena
ITALY

0039-0577-960124

Began 1981 | Pop. 28 | Forming
Diet: Vegan | Rural | Spiritual

Osho Miasto is a Buddhafield, a group of friends who have gathered together with a common longing to provoke the divine that is the potential of all human beings. Meditation and love are the two themes that form the vision of the commune. This is inspired by the enlightened mystic Osho, who left the body in January 1990.

Our daily life is varied, consisting of various meditations both passive and active, traditional and modern. The work that is undertaken is also considered meditation, and there is a large therapy and meditation program of workshops, courses, and trainings. Therapy is seen as a preparation for meditation.

Miasto is set on a hilltop deep in the Tuscan countryside. The buildings, some dating from the fifteenth century, are made from beautiful local stone and blend harmoniously with the vast surrounding forests and fields. [Jul99, no openings]

OSTERWEIL COOPERATIVE

338 E Jefferson
Ann Arbor MI 48104

734-996-5956, 734-996-5957

Began 1946 | Pop. 13
Diet: Omnivore | Urban

Osterweil Co-op is a member of the Inter-Cooperative Council (ICC). It is geared toward providing affordable housing to students who attend colleges and universities in the area.

We are primarily a vegetarian house, though we do serve meat and nonveggie dishes. Meals are made by the members five nights a week.

Members share rooms with like-sexed members. We have five double rooms and three singles. Rooms are distributed on a seniority list determined by the number of semesters a person has lived in Osterweil.

The Osterweil house is a quaint three-story brick-and-stucco building that dates back to post-World War II. It is located

only two minutes from the University of Michigan.

Members are expected to give five or six hours of their time a week back to the house in the form of officer positions and other house works. [Jan99, cc, no openings]

OTAMATEA ECO-VILLAGE

Oneriri Rd
Kaiwaka RD2
NEW ZEALAND

+64-9-431 29 21, +64-9-431 22 31
hiepe_drueckler@clear.net.nz
otamatea@clear.net.nz

Began Jan99 | Pop. 27 | Forming
Diet: Omnivore | Rural

Vision Statement:
Otamatea Eco-village:
Will practice permaculture in a spirit of cooperation, mutual support, and respect for one another and the land.

Will preserve and enhance the native ecosystems on the land and sea around us.

Will create fertile, holistically integrated agricultural systems and a village culture that abundantly provides our community's needs for healthy living at all levels: physical, social, emotional, intellectual, and spiritual.

Will do this sustainably, ethically, and with beauty and creative variety.

Will be a positive part of the wider New Zealand society, especially as a model of sustainability and biodiversity.

Will be part of the wider global culture evolution, giving and receiving knowledge, wisdom, inspiration, and love. [Sep99]

OTHONA COMMUNITY, THE

East Hall Farm
East End Rd
Bradwell-On-Sea
Essex CM0 7PN, England
UNITED KINGDOM

+44 01621 776564
kate.mulkern@unisys.com
http://www.nodeknot.demon.co.uk/
othona.htm

Began 1946 | Pop. 600
Diet: Omnivore | Rural | Spiritual

(Also known as East Hall Farm.) The Othona Community is an ecumenical Christian community founded in 1946 by an Anglican clergyman, Rev. Norman Motley. Now a registered charity, we have a lifestyle based on nondogmatic Christianity. Who comes? People of all faiths (and none), of all ages, of all backgrounds, and from all over the world—anyone who values a sense of community—come for breaks ranging from a few days to several weeks. Where is it ? Othona has centers in Essex and Dorset, run by a small "core" community. What do we do? We aim to grow together through the following means.

Work: Everyone shares chores such as washing up, and there are extra tasks for willing hands.

Worship: Our twice-daily services are taken by volunteers, so each service is different—maybe traditional, Celtic, silent, incorporating drama, or a children's service.

Study: Many weeks have a speaker/facilitator. Past study themes have included diverse topics such as Celtic Christianity, letters of St. Paul, art in nature, massage, and retreat breaks. Some weeks are especially aimed at children, often incorporating drama and music.

Play: Both our centers are in the countryside by the sea, so swimming and walking are popular. There is no TV at Othona, so entertainment, like the cooking, is always homemade! [Jan98, cc]

OUR ECOVILLAGE

Box 530
Shawnigan Lake BC V0R 2W0
CANADA

250-743-3002
our@pacificcoast.net

Began 1990 | Pop. 10 | Re-Forming
Diet: Vegetarian | Rural | Spiritual

Our Ecovillage is a sustainable land-stewardship community that endeavors to foster the interconnectedness between all things. Support of individual, family, intentional community, and wider community. Appropriate/green building, permaculture, deep-ecology, social-justice, and child/youth focus. All this on a beautiful, private, farm-based setting complete with farm animals, a lake, and eagles! We are *intercultural, interfaith, and intergenerational.* [Mar99, sase requested]

OWEN HOUSE

1017 Oakland
Ann Arbor MI 48104
http://www.umich.edu/~umicc/

Owen houses 24 people in three singles,

nine doubles, and one spacious triple. Our boarders come from Stevens and the neighborhood. We boast a nicely inviting fireplace, a state-of-the-art VCR, a piano and an organ, a spacious bike shed and a freshly refurnished porch with an elegant porch swing.

We eat meat sometimes but always have vegetarian alternatives. All in all, Owen has been and continues to be a great house. [Oct99]

OWL FARM

c/o Oregon Women's Land Trust
PO Box 1692
Roseburg OR 97470

OWL Farm, a beautiful 150 acres of meadows and forests, has long been a sanctuary for lesbians, other women, and children, and we welcome you to enjoy her beauty. At this time, OWL Farm is in transition. We are no longer "open women's land," but we are committed to making the land available to women as visitors and/or for a short-term stay. As well, we envision the creation of an intentional community on the land and welcome proposals from groups of women interested in becoming our caretaking collective. Please write for guidelines. Potential visitors need to be prepared to be totally self-sufficient. Again, write for information and directions. Women only, please. [sase requested]

PADANARAM SETTLEMENT

Attn: Rachel Summerton
RR 1 Box 478
Williams IN 47470

812-388-5599, 812-388-5571
padanarm@tima.com
http://www.kiva.net/~padanarm/

Began 1966 | Pop. 200
Diet: Omnivore | Rural | Spiritual

(Also known as God's Valley.) Padanaram Settlement is a utopian community established in 1966 for the purpose of building a microcosm city of kingdomism, the future religious and political (polit theo) style of living to be practiced in the millennium. Small kinglets will have their own busi-

nesses, schools, and farmlands and will be autonomous yet joined together in a network of communities that will encompass the globe. This is called the ICU (International Communal Utopia). We live together on 3,000 acres in southern Indiana. We have woods, streams, organically certified farmland for produce and herbs. We have orchards and cattle. Our five principles: As you would that men do unto you, do unto them. Hold all things in common. From he that has much, much is required. Distribution to each according to the need. He that won't work, neither shall he eat. We believe in whosoever will, and thus we have open conventions the first weekend in June and mid-October. We also have an open house one Sunday in October. Our newsletter, *Millennial Chronicles,* tells of our daily life and our view of the future. Wisdom is our leader, truth our guide. We have books and articles about our village. We prefer visitors to come to conventions or in summer months since we don't have formal sleeping rooms. Contact person: Rachel Summerton. [Jan99]

PAGAN ISLAND COMMUNITY (PIC)

703 S Norwood Ave
Tulsa OK 74112
WaterSpryt@aol.com
http://members.aol.com/WaterSpryt/

Began 1997 | Pop. 36 | Forming
Diet: No red meat | Rural | Spiritual

Pagan Island Community (PIC) is a growing group of Earth-centered families, working toward forming our dream village in the tropics. We will live by sustainable farming and fishing in a rural setting. We want to raise our kids in peace, health, and simplicity. We seek new members who can help our effort succeed. People do not have to be wealthy to join us, as long they can provide essentials for themselves and any dependents.

We are not a traditional commune. We will have our own homes and possessions but work together on a communal farm and share a town center. We will form our community guidelines and deal with problems in an open egalitarian forum, reaching decisions by consensus.

We seek an island or large tract with fertile soil and a strong ecosystem where we may live lightly, gently finding our place in the existing food chain. Our family is headed down to Costa Rica in September of

Key to bracketed text: cc = cannot commit to prompt correspondance, sase = self-addressed stamped envelope

1999 to scout out possible community sites for our project. We prize diverse, creative, freethinkers who will make our village strong and viable. If you wish to join our e-mail list, please e-mail me at WaterSpryt@aol.com.

Blessed be! —Meli Chang-Turpen, moderator of the PIC list. [Sep99, sase required]

PALMGROVE COMMUNITY FARMS

PO Box 455
Utu-Abak Abak AKS
NIGERIA

085-501022, 085-203080

Began 1990 | Pop. 270 | Rural/Urban

In the fall of 1989 a group of Nigerians concerned about the needs of our people wrote asking to become part of the Hutterian Brethren Church. Two of their leaders visited Crystal Spring Colony in Manitoba, Canada, staying for two months to experience the life of a Christian community. Before they went to Canada in 1989, Inno Idiong, one of today's Palmgrove leaders, started a communal group made up of young people in 1987 and conscienctized them toward community-oriented projects as a substitute for poverty and other social ills.

While in Canada, the two Nigerians discovered that the Hutterites have successfully established for about 450 years what they are trying to do in Nigeria. So they asked the Hutterites to come to Nigeria and help establish a similar community without destroying the African cultural values.

Our daily lives together start with morning prayers three times a week, from 5:30 a.m. to 6:00 a.m. Then work starts with the sunrise at 7:00 a.m., followed by a bowl of porridge. Thereafter, sisters help to clean up after communal meals; the brothers and young people go back to work. Break before noon for lunch; after lunch some take a rest for one hour and 30 minutes, optionally; others can do personal things. Return to work at 2:00 p.m. and stop for dinner at 6:00 p.m.; dinner comes up at 7:00 p.m., and young people can play at the interval. This seems to be the circle except for Saturdays and Sundays.

In spite of the Christian-based communal influence on our lives, we still cherish our African traditional values, such as our extended family status, and our social system is protected. Despite our tremendous exposure to new roles like living a shared life with strangers, we still stay African, though not without strong Christian ideals and daily calling to love one another. Our projects are still ongoing and challenging, especially the school-building projects. The Hutterites are assisting us to build a school for about 600 children, not only for our kids but for the kids from the larger communities. [Jun99, sase required]

PANGAIA

RR 2 Box 3311
Pahoa HI 96778
pangaia@secalarm.com
http://www.rawtimes.com/
   pangaia.html

Began 1992 | Pop. 5 | Re-Forming
Diet: Omnivore | Rural | Spiritual

Pangaia is a 10-year-old permaculture experiment and community with a focus on growing and eating raw foods and recreating extended family. Our vision is of living sustainably with the land with as many folks as the aina (land) can manage. We are open to anyone that shares this vision and also resonates with the folks already here. Our strongest influences of the past have been the ideas of instinctive nutrition (raw-food nutrition), permaculture, communal living experiences and experimentation, open and honest communication, coparenting, and most recently the theories of Viktor Shauberger regarding nature, i.e., water, soil, trees, and natural Earth energies like biomagnetism and levitation. We strongly encourage anyone interested in Pangaia and/or nature and its preservation to read the book *Living Energies*, by Callum Coats, or any other books written about the life and work of Viktor Shauberger. Also, if anyone is presently familiar with the Shauberger concepts, we invite you to contact us and share experiences. Working together daily with the land and eating from the trees instead of the refrigerator are our lifestyle. We have coined the word "farm-nerd" to represent ourselves. If this sounds like your idea of fun, then come join us. Aloha from all of us at Pangaia! [Aug99, sase requested]

Trying to run a meeting?

FIC has some tools you need—the best books around on consensus facilitation.

http://consensusbooks.ic.org/

PANTERRA

8579 Hardscrabble Rd
Westfield NY 14787

716-326-3993, 716-326-3833

Began 1992 | Pop. 2 | Re-Forming
Diet: Vegetarian | Rural | Spiritual

Panterra is a community dedicated to personal enrichment. Currently, we use our relationships with ourselves, with others, and with all aspects of living to evaluate and foster personal change and understanding. Our hope is to create an environment where each person may achieve some degree of personal enrichment with support from the community.

We conduct classes and workshops designed to enhance self-esteem and creativity. Although we are primarily a community of two, we have had individuals stay for periods of time with set purposes. We are willing to share ideas and resources with others to encourage self-empowerment and community improvement.

In part, our intention is to reduce suffering where and when we can. We do not claim to have answers, but we do offer possibilities. We do not declare universal truths, but we do advance the search for personal current truth and its understanding. We honor the story of individuals and avoid adherence to dogmatic forms. Artistic and creative expression are actively supported, but we reserve the right to exclude expressions of violence within the community. [May99, cc, sase requested]

PARADISE GARDENS

PO Box 584
Hilo Hawai'i
Hawaiian Islands (96721)

808-933-9517
paradisegardens@hotmail.com
paradise@hialoha.net
http://www.angelfire.com/
   pq/paradisegardens/

Began 1990 | Pop. 2 | Forming
Diet: Vegan | Rural | Spiritual

The purpose of the Paradise Restoration Project is to restore the Earth to its paradisial state by creating and maintaining permanent Paradise Gardens sanctuaries worldwide. We are starting locally, on the big island of Hawaii. We know that a fruitarian diet is the most ideal diet, and the paradisian way of life is necessary for us all

Additions and corrections: Email: directory@ic.org, Web: http://directory.ic.org/, Mail: RR 1 Box 156-D, Rutledge MO 63563, USA.

to live as nature intended and in the very best of health.

We live by the principle that "money" is only good for helping to achieve our goals until "money" isn't needed at all. We do no "business," have no employees or positions, and do not engage in any sort of commercial activity. We support only Earth-friendly existing "businesses," until "businesses" are not needed at all because we have all learned to share the Earth and our possessions.

We realize that this takes full dedication to our goals and requires full, equal participation of all involved; therefore a unanimous Consensus Council exists for all important decision making.

We would love to have the first free festival as soon as possible and also envision having paradise festivals, where well-known and unknown performers and presenters get together for an entire week or two and have the greatest not-for-profit festivals ever, for the most centrally important cause possible today. [Oct99, sase required]

PARKER STREET COOPERATIVE, INC.

**2335-41 Parker St
Berkeley CA 94704**

**510-548-6608
slrcnorwood@igc.org**

Began 1987 | Diet: Omnivore | Urban

We are a limited-equity housing cooperative (LEHC) of 34 adults and 3 children in 24 mostly one-bedroom units in two three-story buildings near the University of California, Berkeley. As yet we have no shared kitchen and dining area, but each fourth floor has a large common room with laundry facilities and a large deck that overlooks the bay. Outside, ivy and asphalt are giving way to garden plots with edible plants, flowers, grape and kiwi vines, and 10 fruit trees.

We hold a potluck supper/business meeting and several committee meetings each month. The mention of "piano" or "cat" is guaranteed to generate controversy. Self-managed, we are getting better at consensus decision making. Five renters from our pre-cooperative days still live here, and not all members participate—both situations pose challenges.

When a vacancy occurs, we try to select people who want to get involved. The state law for an LEHC limits the selling price for a unit when the owner moves out, which

keeps our housing affordable. Our units are now well below market rate for the San Francisco Bay area. We welcome visitors to our monthly potluck meetings but ask that you contact a member first. [Nov98, cc, sase requested, no openings]

PARNASSUS RISING

**PO Box 33681
Phoenix AZ 85067**

Began 1990 | Pop. 4 | Forming
Diet: No red meat | Rural/Urban

Parnassus Rising (Reborn Commies ha ha! Acts 2:44, 45; and Acts 4:32–35) projects communitarian intentional family growing into intentional community seeking alternative sexual, religious, economic, political orientation, and privacy rights with nonpolitically Korrect human rights; not consensus; prefer Americans who have put their lives on the line for US freedoms against guns.

We seek people like ourselves: sexually/politically liberated; no cowed, guilt-ridden, or white-male bashers; skilled, knowledgeable, communicative, hardworking, adventurous, literate, clean of STDs/HIV I and II (willing to get tests regularly); no smoking (anything); no dope (anything); no boozing (abuse of any sort of alcoholic beverage); no compulsive gamblers; no fascists, left or right; ultimately to share true inventions and innovations and the benefits of noncompetitive businesses and build the humanist city, Parnassus. If willing to relocate and you have the ability to work outside for a short time, send recent resume in cursive/longhand. [Jan99, sase required]

PATHFINDER FELLOWSHIP

**25 Sheffield Terrace
London W8 7NQ, England
UNITED KINGDOM**

**0171 727 5586
Barbara@bickerstethhouse.demon.co.uk**

Began 1922 | Pop. 17
Diet: Omnivore | Urban | Spiritual

(Also known as Bickersteth House.) We are a small Anglican Christian community. Our purpose is Christian education for young people. We live together much like a large family, sharing meals as well as cooking and other household chores. Monday night is community night. We

have a chapel service before our usual evening meal and a house meeting afterward. We also often have outside speakers or study and discussion time.

This is a place where we hope to grow in our Christian faith, where we try to love God and to love each other. [Mar99, cc, sase requested, no openings]

PEACE FARM

**HC 2 Box 25
Panhandle TX 79068**

**806-335-1715
pfarm@earthlink.com**

Began 1986 | Pop. 1
Diet: Vegetarian | Rural

The Peace Farm is a 20-acre farm located across from the rail exit of the nuclear train at Pantex—the United States' nuclear-weapons assembly plant. The Peace Farm's mission is to create an environment for peace through peaceful means, to assert that peace can exist only where there is justice, and to develop an ecological model for non-violent social change. Subscriptions are $5/year for Peace Farm's bimonthly newsletter, the *Advocate*. [Nov98]

PEOPLE HOUSE

**3035 W 25th Ave
Denver CO 80211**

303-480-5130, 303-237-5049

Began 1974 | Re-Forming
Urban | Spiritual

People House spiritual community is a non-profit, nonsectarian organization dedicated to fostering awareness and a healthy way of life in individuals, families, and groups through fellowship, education, facilitation, and leadership training.

"We are not a house of religion, but a home for the spirit." We have been in existence for 25 years and are now embarking on an adventure of building our own intentional community. We believe, in order to keep such a community alive and vibrant, it must have a catalytic agent around which it is formed. Ours is one of service, so we are building a center of renewal for all people to come aside from the day-to-day humdrum world and take the time to renew their spirit. An interfaith community built on a concept of universal love, a unity for all.

We already have a nucleus of devoted ministers, teachers, counselors, and leaders, along

---

Key to bracketed text: cc = cannot commit to prompt correspondance, sase = self-addressed stamped envelope

with many good programs available to the public. We will provide space for other leaders in body work, healing arts, and the performing arts. We intend to provide a space for all to grow in the path of life each is on.

The community when finally finished will consist of cohousing units and separate clustered homes plus the buildings for the center activities including retreats and workshops. [Mar99, cc]

PEOPLE OF THE LIVING GOD

Rt 2 Box 423
McMinnville TN 37110
931-692-3236, 931-692-3730
POTLG@BLOMAND.NET
http://www.people-livingGod.org/

Began 1935 | Pop. 63
Diet: Omnivore | Urban | Spiritual

(Also known as Homeland Acres.) People of the Living God see community as the most viable answer to the Sermon on the Mount and a direct follow-up of the early church as recorded in Acts 2:44–46. We are Sabatarians. We publish a free monthly newsletter—*Testimony of Truth*. Send name and address to be put on the mailing list. [Jan99, cc]

PHANTO BOLO

PO Box 594
Cripple Creek CO 80813
dharmagic@hotmail.com

Began 1993 | Pop. 8 | Forming
Diet: No red meat | Rural | Spiritual

We WIBOME (Walking in Balance on Mother Earth) like to call ourselves the smallest and least-structured intentional community in North America. A few good neighbors occupy about 80 acres on a rural ranch at 9,700 feet, in view of Pikes Peak. An extended family of over 200 gathers here on this sacred land to celebrate our love for Mother Earth. Sweat lodges, wheels, potlucks, and joyful visits happen year-round. Phanto Bolo has no leaders and no rules, save one: the law of love. The community, though still growing, will remain small. The individual residents who form our nucleus are slowly getting established, but resources are limited. We give what we can, hosting frequent visitors and sharing. Anyone wishing to visit Phanto Bolo should contact us at least one month in advance.

We welcome correspondence and inquiries. [Oct99, sase requested]

PHOENIX CO-OP, THE

636 Langdon St
Madison WI 53703
608-256-1770, 608-256-3131

Began 1996 | Pop. 25 | Forming
Diet: Omnivore | Rural

The Phoenix Co-op is right across the street from the Memorial Library of the University of Wisconsin campus. The spacious mansion houses about 30 members. The house is beautified by decorative faces, a spiral staircase, and large fireplaces. The food co-op is designed for both meat eaters and vegetarians. Phoenix provides a relaxed environment for members to share their outside interests. It uses a modified-consensus decision-making process. [Jan99]

PHOENIX COMMUNITY

Colorado USA
dreamcd@USA.net
http://www.dreamcd.com/

Began 1983 | Pop. 3
Diet: Omnivore | Urban | Spiritual

Phoenix is an upscale urban Colorado group marriage of two women (46 and 59) and one man (58), based on intense love and on life-long healing, growth, and transformation. All three of us are marriage and family therapists (imagine three therapists living happily together!). Our vital shared focus is that we personally explore the awesome phenomena, processes, and energies of transpersonal realms of consciousness, together. This leads us to transcendent love, and often to grace, beyond all that most people believe is possible. Our vision is that the transpersonal offers rapid human evolution for the global future, and we explore that in our field: psychology and healing.

When we visualize who might join us, we see a man or possibly a couple (since we need gender balance we cannot add another woman next), age 48 to 59 (between our ages), who thrives on extremely deep and intense intimacy and intense personal growth and is therefore successful in life and shares our interests. We're nonsmokers, moderately health oriented, highly heterosexual, and fidelitous to each other. To visit, please e-mail us at dreamcd@USA.net and

tell us about yourself, your vision for relationship, and your major interests. [Oct99]

PIÑON ECOVILLAGE

PO Box 911
Santa Fe NM 87504
505-988-5261, 505-660-8835
pinon@ic.org
sean@ic.org

Began Jun99 | Pop. 2 | Forming
Diet: Vegetarian | Rural

We are a forming community committed to building a diverse egalitarian society that embraces ecological sustainability, nonviolence, feminism, multiculturalism, and caring about each other. We value energy spent on improving interpersonal communication and deepening our connections to each other and the environment around us. Our approach to health is holistic, and we seek to integrate many healing traditions into our everyday lives. We have no common spiritual belief, but we support each other in following our own paths. The voice of every member is valued, and decisions at Piñon are made by consensus. At Piñon we share income, labor, and resources. Each member works an average of 35 hours per week on income-producing work, gardening, cooking, building, creative projects, and various household tasks. In return, the community provides members with food, shelter, clothing, health care, and other needs and amenities.

Piñon members have lived in income-sharing communities and have been active in cooperative living and alternative economic structures for many years. Currently, we are active in the Federation of Egalitarian Communities (FEC), the Fellowship for Intentional Community (FIC), and the Queer In Community (QIC) network. We are engaged with the greater world around us: locally, nationally, and globally. We support members in political activism and volunteer work that embodies our community values. Community income currently comes from a nonprofit mail-order business and FIC work. One of us is a student of Acupuncture and Oriental Medicine who will begin practicing in 2002.

We are seeking land in the mountains of New Mexico, and hope to begin building in 2000. Eventually, we expect to become a small ecovillage of 25 to 200. Our size will depend on what is sustainable for the site we find. We welcome new members at any stage of our forming, and also encourage dialogue with those who want to be involved in ways other than full membership. [Oct99]

PIONEER COOPERATIVE

340 Parkway Circle
Davis CA 95616

Pop. 10 | Re-Forming
Diet: Omnivore | Urban

Pioneer Cooperative is located on the University of California, Davis, campus. It is one of two small living organizations created by Davis Campus Cooperatives. Ten students reside in each 10-bedroom, four-bathroom house. Students cooperate in everyday living situations, class studies, excursions, etc. Members also take part in cooking common meals and in cooperative chores. The Davis Campus Cooperatives provide friendly family environments for daily student life. [Feb99, cc]

PIONEER VALLEY COHOUSING

120 Pulpit Hill Rd
Amherst MA 01002

413-549-5799
marykraus@cohousing.com

Began 1994 | Pop. 90 | Rural

(Also known as Cherry Hill Cohousing.) The Pioneer Valley Cohousing Group has created a style of housing that encourages a strong sense of community, supports our need for privacy, makes life affordable, and provides a secure and enriched setting for children and adults. We have a place where people know their neighbors in a meaningful way, a neighborhood where different traditions and values are respected and where we can all have a sense of security and belonging.

Our group purchased a 25-acre meadow site in north Amherst where we built 32 units and a large common house, moving in June–September 1994. Our 7 acres contain a clustered mix of single, duplex, and triplex buildings. While residents own their own homes, they also own a share of the com-

mon house for dining and other community activities. Optional dinners several nights a week, gardens, play and work spaces, hiking trails, and other shared amenities chosen by residents have social and economic advantages. The common house includes a large kitchen/dining hall, children's playrooms, guest rooms, laundry facilities, library, and recycling center.

The community is a short walk from a municipal lake; a recreation park with tennis, swimming, and playing fields; a small shopping center; a library; the university; and public transportation. [Aug99, sase requested]

PLANTS FOR A FUTURE

The Field
Penpol
Lostwithiel
Cornwall PL22 0NG, England
UNITED KINGDOM

+44 1208 873554
pfaf@scs.leeds.ac.uk
http://www.scs.leeds.ac.uk/pfaf/

Began 1986 | Pop. 5
Diet: Vegan | Rural

Plants for a Future is a resource center for rare and unusual plants, particularly those that have edible, medicinal, or other uses. We practice vegan-organic permaculture with emphasis on creating an ecologically sustainable environment and the use of perennial plants.

We have two pieces of land, in Devon and Cornwall, where we demonstrate our agricultural principles and carry out research into interesting plants.
We are in the process of constructing an ecovillage.

The project consists of a registered charity and a workers cooperative. Many volunteers also help in the project. [Jan99]

PLEASANT HILL EZ COHOUSING

Lisa Ln
Pleasant Hill CA 94523

925-228-1310
goehringhunn@gowebway.com
dancerbarb@aol.com
http://www.members.ad.com/
  dancerbarb/

Began 2001 | Forming | Urban

We are a suburban cohousing group build-

Key to bracketed text: cc = cannot commit to prompt correspondance, sase = self-addressed stamped envelope

ing a community on 2.2 acres of suburban land in the San Francisco Bay area. We are working together to design our site with 32–38 self-sufficient townhouse-style units along with a common house (kitchen/dining room, workshop, laundry, playroom), gardens, and perhaps a pool. We plan to compost, recycle, and incorporate sustainable technology into our site design. We are an intergenerational group desiring to live in harmony with each other and the larger community and nature. We're hoping to move in to our new home in 2001 and until then continue to share resources and good times as we build our own little neighborhood. [Sep99, sase requested]

PLOW CREEK FELLOWSHIP

**19183 Plow Creek Rd
Tiskilwa IL 61368**

**815-646-4851, 815-646-6600
mstahnke@juno.com**

Began 1971 | Pop. 36 | Re-Forming
Diet: Omnivore | Rural | Spiritual

We are an intentional Christian community, associated with the Mennonite Church. Located in rural Illinois, we are part of Shalom Mission Communities, with involvement especially in Central America. We welcome those who acknowledge Jesus as Lord of their lives and wish to share in our life together as a part of discipleship. Values of mutual respect, justice, compassion for the poor, fidelity in marriage, and pacifism form the core of our life together. Hospitality and being connected with other cultures through personal relationships are also important in our shared life. Some of our members work at a variety of jobs in the larger community, while others help in the farming, growing fruits and vegetables using methods that are environmentally friendly.

For further information, please contact Louise Stahnke at the fellowship address. [Sep99]

POD OF DOLPHINS

**187 Dolphin Ln NE
Check VA 24072**

**540-651-4314
dolphins@swva.net**

Began 1996 | Pop. 5 | Forming
Diet: Omnivore | Rural | Spiritual

Our community is a polyfidelity family of three adults and two children. Joining our

family is not required to join the community. We are Earth-centered spiritual seekers, working on personal growth. Decisions are made by consensus. We all work or go to school off the property. We garden organically and raise milk goats. We have started a community room, pantry, and space for solar equipment and hope to build a home. We are looking at cooperative land ownership of this 7 1/2 acres plus any future land purchases. [Mar99, sase requested]

POTASH HILL COMMUNITY

**9 Frazier Ln
Cummington MA 01026**

**413-634-0181
bigwheel@massed.net**

Began 1995 | Pop. 15 | Rural

On 115 acres of woods and pastures in western Massachusetts, 25 miles west of Northhampton, a five-college town. Thirteen privately owned 2- to 5-acre lots ranging from $23,000–$30,000 surrounded by a 60-acre land trust. Community sauna, garden, and community building. Six households established. Our fundamental principle is to establish and uphold harmony, cooperation, creativity, and reciprocity of support. We value personal autonomy, relationships, business, the arts, natural healing, education, celebration, and fun. We foresee a community of independent thinkers with initiative to take responsibility for shaping their lives and their community. [Oct99, sase requested]

PRIORITIES INSTITUTE, THE

**PO Box 89
Pine CO 80470**

**303-838-8105, 303-838-8105 fax
mail@priorities.org
http://www.priorities.org/**

Began 1998 | Pop. 2 | Forming
Diet: Omnivore | Rural | Spiritual

(Also known as Crescent Moon Lodge.) Fun, intellectual family has a unique, 3,000-square-foot lodge on 11 gorgeous acres, 7,500 feet up, on Buffalo Creek, completely surrounded by Pike National Forest, 60 miles southwest of Denver. Spectacular mountain biking and hiking, wildflowers, wildlife, views, incredible music collection, some instruments for merrymaking. We're off-grid, solar powered, and on-line. We run an educational nonprofit (and focus on

moral evolution, current events, governmental structure, and car-free city designs; contact for free newsletter: *Livable Cities*). We create models for autoless, livable cities for up to 90,000 people. We'll give free labor to design cohousing for select groups: contact us. Ideally, we'd love to have investors to create a cohousing complex on property and make our lodge the common house. Our roads aren't plowed in winter, and it's a one-to two-hour drive to professional employment. At the moment the property is for sale. If it sells we would want to join a community, preferably an Ithaca-ecovillage-type development out west. We're not egalitarian, vegetarian, New Age yuppies, or biblical, but we are tolerant. We love reading, designing sustainable communities, well-behaved pets and kids, research and writing, visiting hip communities, educational programs, homeschooling, history, gardening, light partying, controlled drinking, silly humor, tasty foods, lotsa' friends, meeting interesting folks, music, living in the here and now while reflecting on the past and planning a better future. [Aug99]

PRO-FEM

**Tom Newman
Silver City NM
tan@pobox.com
http://www.profem.com/**

Began 1999 | Forming
Diet: Omnivore | Rural | Spiritual

Men and women are different in essential ways. Men and women are not interchangeable. Men's and women's biology causes them to have different goals and abilities. Men protect women from the man's world. Women help men discover the attractions of family life and the home. Many women want to be taken care of and protected by their husband or lover. Many people believe their desire to be taken care of is a sign of either weakness or mental illness. It is neither. This desire is an aspect of femininity. These women are feminine women. Pro-fem believes in equal rights and equal opportunity for women. But Pro-fem also believes that if a woman decides she'd rather focus on her femininity—as a wife and mother or as a caregiver, for instance—than on her masculinity—as a competitor in the business world, for instance—her decision should be respected and honored. To disparage her decision is to disparage femininity. Modern Western societies have lost their respect for femininity. Pro-fem exists to help feminine women by promoting respect for femininity. The Pro-fem community offers women an environment in which their femininity is honored, respected, and celebrated and offers men an environment in which their responsible leadership is essential. [Jul99]

PROJEKT EULENSPIEGEL

Zum Eulenspiegel - Modell Wasserburg eV
Dorfstr 25
D-88142 Wasserburg/Boder
GERMANY
08382-887875, 08382-89056 fax

Began 1976 | Diet: Omnivore | Rural

We are a community that has been living and working together in Wasserburg at the Lake of Constance since 1976. We are running a self-governed and ecologically oriented restaurant. It is our goal to run an ecologically sound business.

We are not guided by a dogma—except that everybody is equal at our place. The means of production are owned by the "Modell Wesserburg." All important decisions are carried by everybody. The daily decisions required in the kitchen and service area are made by some that were selected to do so. They either make these decisions alone or in consultation.

The nonprofit organization Modell Wasserburg is the owner of the building and the legal body responsible for the entire project. This organization also supports the Jedermensch-verlag (our own publishing house) that publishes a quarterly journal— the *Jedermensch*—and writings of Peter Schilinski, one of the founders of the project. We have a public roundtable discussion every Tuesday at 8 p.m. Apart from that, the Modell Wasserburg Inc. also supports local and not-so-local social and political activities in various ways.

Our project grew out of an anthroposophist orientation, and some of us are still involved in this. We are, however, open to everybody. [Apr99]

PROWOKULTA

Frankfurt
GERMANY
info@prowokulta.org
http://www.prowokulta.org/

Began 1995 | Pop. 27 | Urban

ProWoKultA is a community in Frankfurt, Germany of about 25 people between 20 and 32 years old, plus two babies. Since 1995, we have been using 11 of 18 apartments in an apartment building in a suburb, and have about 400 square meters of additional shared space in this building for all kinds of activities. [Nov99]

PROYECTO ECO-VILLAS - ASOCIACIÓN GAIA

Oficina de Gaia
Almafuerte 1732
San Martìn (CP 1650)
Buenos Aires
ARGENTINA

54 02 227 15 552 554
54 01 4 755 6240
54 01 4 752 2197 fax
gaia@wamani.apc.org
http://www.gaia.org/

Began 1996 | Diet: Vegetarian | Rural

Translation: We are a pioneering, changing group and in constant growth ... We have not yet fully become a community, but we share communitarian life with the stable residents, the visitors, the participants in courses, and the volunteers that arrive from remote places ... Two people (Silvia and Gustavo) are those that maintain the vision, being the guardians from the beginning of the project ... We are open to receiving new stable members with common commitment and vision; we also like visitors. We are enthusiastic about the work; we have done much in just a short time, and we have enjoyed the transformation process, for both the place and ourselves. We put much emphasis on education, sharing with others all tools and information that we possess. We have worked like a center of inspiration and diffusion of ecovillages and permaculture in the southern region. We enjoy our place here in La Paz, the deep contact with nature, and dance ... We have lived a life of voluntary simplicity. We feel that's appropriate when offering sustainable models to a social economy so impoverished as Argentina. [Feb99]

PRUDENCE CRANDALL HOUSE

438 66th St
Oakland CA 94609

510-652-7600
abarnard@stmarys-ca.edu

Began 1972 | Pop. 8
Diet: Omnivore | Urban

(Also known as Alcatraz - 66th St CoHousing.) We aren't sure how we will create a cohousing community, but we choose to not be consumed by meetings to work it out.

Our cohousing community is growing one unit at a time, in existing housing like N Street cohousing community in Davis, California. Most cohousing in the United States requires lots of up-front effort, is new construction, is highly structured organizationally, is as expensive as traditional housing, and is composed primarily of traditional nuclear families. In contrast we are evolving organically by adding existing neighboring houses one unit at a time, in a "moderately priced" neighborhood. Each household decides what and how to contribute to our abundant existing resources, which helps to minimize meetings. Brief, daily, informal exchanges develop our sense of community, such as eating and doing projects together and picking up stuff for each other when shopping.

We began by simply tearing down the fences between yards and sharing some meals. We share tools and skills such as computing, gardening, house and garden layout, and woodworking. We aim to share more: fun times, meditation, vegetable gardens, guest rooms, bicycle storage, children's play space, books, etc. [Dec98, sase required]

PUMPKIN HOLLOW COMMUNITY

1467 Pumpkin Hollow Rd
Liberty TN 37095

615-536-5022
sunfrogj@hotmail.com

Began 1996 | Pop. 6 | Forming
Diet: Omnivore | Rural

Founded in 1996, Pumpkin Hollow Community shares 120 beautiful acres in the hills of middle Tennessee. Our diverse cooperative is part of a loose local milieu that includes various other communes and lots of friendly neighbors. We embrace erotic and ethnic diversity in our plans to grow from

Key to bracketed text: cc = cannot commit to prompt correspondance, sase = self-addressed stamped envelope

our current crew of five adults and three kids. We love animals, trees, Earth, sex, home brew, homemade stuff, beauty, creativity, and each other.

We experiment with ways of living and healing. Interests include homeschooling/deschooling, organic gardening, writing poems, building homes, cultivating herbs, creating cottage industries, scavenging stuff, composting shit, creating art, making music, dancing by the fire, cooking vegetarian feasts, partying with our friends, wearing fabulous drag, worshiping the Earth, and living freely and peacefully.

We share expenses but not incomes, mix work with play, use consensus decision making at family meetings, and love living together (most of the time). We want to grow, and we need people to join us. We seek gardeners, builders, carpenters, artists, writers, many genders, cooks, parents and people who like kids, dreamers, and doers. Write us to arrange a visit. [Feb99, cc, sase requested]

PUMPKIN HOLLOW FARM

1184 Route 11
Craryville NY 12521

518-325-3583
pumpkin@taconic.net
http://www.theosophical.org/
   pumpkin.html

Began 1937
Diet: Vegetarian | Rural | Spiritual

Pumpkin Hollow Farm is a community in a rural retreat environment that seeks to live out the objectives of the worldwide Theosophical Society. We are committed to fellowship and service as well as the investigation of the natural laws that govern life. We offer opportunities for self-discovery, meditation, healing, and connecting with nature. [Dec98]

PURPLE ROSE

1531 Fulton St
San Francisco CA 94117

Began 1978 | Pop. 10
Diet: Vegetarian | Urban

Purple Rose is an active collective household. We take our collectivity seriously—but we also enjoy our playtime together and the closeness that the whole experience brings about.

Collectively owning our old Victorian

house means freedom from landlord-imposed restrictions but also means more responsibility for maintenance. (Two previous housemates are on the title as a matter of form, but they do not "own" the house.)

Most evenings we share family-style dinners, which are primarily vegetarian. We also value being very open and direct—talking a lot with each other in a very personal way, about very personal things. Some of this happens at our weekly house meetings.

Presently we have 10 members who can only be classified politically as independents—though we lean toward working for a better life for all people, not just a favored few. We are avid recyclers, do our best to maintain the planet, and use organic products when feasible. We feel we are working for the future in the present time. [Jul99, cc, sase requested, no openings]

QUARRIES, THE

8970 Schuyler Rd
Schuyler VA 22969

804-831-1020, 804-831-1021 fax
quarries@aol.com
http://www.thequarries.com/

Began 1999 | Pop. 2 | Forming | Rural
Practicing the principles of responsible environmental design, building, and progressive community development. Wooded homesites, southern exposures, recreational/sculptural quarries, nature trails, wildlife sanctuary, and "aviary" community building. Home design standards for energy efficiency and healthy, sustainable materials selections. Promotion of live/work opportunities. Community sharing of sensitive areas of land, including quarries, active beaver ponds, and long loop trails. Sanctuaries for animals and birds. [Nov99]

QUARRY HILL

606 Fiske Rd #23
Rochester VT 05767

802-767-3902
ladybell@sover.net

Began 1960 | Diet: Vegetarian | Rural
(Also known as Vermont Creative Center.)
Quarry Hill, Vermont's oldest and largest

alternative community, was founded in 1946 as an artists' retreat. Quarry Hill has been a haven for creative and open-minded people for 45 years. During the 1960s and 1970s we experienced a surge in population and became a closely knit community, though not a planned, "intentional" one. Among the few rules: absolutely no violence toward children. We run a small private school. Folks generally make their own expenses, though members help each other out as necessary. Families typically eat on their own, with occasional potlucks.

We are always happy to meet energetic, nondogmatic, helpful people! We are going through many changes and welcome everyone. Visitors are welcome! We have a small dormitory. Bring tents for summer camping (the best season for visits). Please write or call before planning a visit and ask for our brochure. Small financial contribution requested or work exchange if broke. [Aug99, sase required]

QUMBYA COOPERATIVE

5130 S University Ave
Chicago IL 60615

773-667-8105, 773-667-5100
e-tulbert@uchicago.edu
http://http.bsd.uchicago.edu/
~h-blair/qumbya.html

Began 1991 | Pop. 34
Diet: Vegetarian | Urban

(Also known as Haymarket House and Bowers House.) We're a group of students, artists, community organizers, and others who share food, fun, and friendship in our two old houses. We cook vegetarian/vegan homemade food and dine together most nights. Members participate by cooking (once every few weeks), by doing a chore (from shopping for organic produce to vacuuming), and by coming to weekly meetings. We also work on the house together, doing minor maintenance with our own people power.

Our houses are great for people new to the area—or anyone sick of the apartment blues. We are a diverse community accepting of many different lifestyles. It's a terrific situation for those seeking community, a chance to gain new skills and to share with others. We are in Chicago, near the U of Chicago, and close to the downtown loop.

If you're interested, give a call or write e-mail. We'd love to have you over for dinner! [Jan99]

RACHANA COMMUNITY

Redmond WA

425-868-4159, 425-836-0505
nwavatar@earthlink.net

Began 1992 | Pop. 6
Diet: No red meat | Rural/Urban | Spiritual

(Also known as Osho Rachana Longhouse.) Rachana is a spiritually based intentional community of diverse individuals committed to healthy, conscience living. We are a community where the diversity and uniqueness of each member are honored and respected at all times. At Rachana, our commitment to one another is to have a community that works for everyone with no one left out. We are a community that holds the point of view that we create and are responsible for our own reality.

The Rachana Community occupies 15 pristine acres of land in Happy Valley just a four-mile drive from Redmond, Washington. We enjoy a 7,000-square-foot community center with an indoor swimming pool, a hot tub, a TV/VCR viewing room, and facilities for many other related activities. We are surrounded by a greenbelt of evergreen trees and vegetation providing complete privacy for the rustic cabins and shelters occupied by our members and guests. Our land contains a wildlife sanctuary for many species of birds and animals with a small private lake and nature trails to explore. In the summer months we have camping, sunbathing, and recreational facilities available to our members and guests. [Nov98, cc]

RAINBOW FAMILY GATHERINGS

rob@welcomehome.org
http://www.welcomehome.org/

Began 1972
Diet: Vegetarian | Rural | Spiritual

Some say we're the largest nonorganization of nonmembers in the world. We have no leaders and no organization. To be honest, the Rainbow Family means different things to different people. I think it's safe to say we're into intentional-community building, nonviolence, and alternative lifestyles. We also believe that peace and love are a great thing and there isn't enough of that in this world. Many of our traditions are based on Native American traditions, and we have a strong orientation to take care of the Earth. We gather in the national forest yearly to pray for peace on this planet. [Jan99]

RAINBOW HEARTH SANCTUARY

HCR5 Box 836
1445 Waterway Ln
Burnet TX 78611

512-756-7878 (Lodge), 512-756-7833 (Office)
demeter@tstar.net
http://www.pro-view.net/retreat.htm

Pop. 6 | Diet: No red meat | Rural

Rainbow Hearth is an ecospiritual center based on permaculture, interspecies communication, music, arts, and life skills to stay healthy, viable, and in balance with the Earth. Our commitment is to live with dignity, comfort, purpose, delight, and integrity and in heart space.

Rainbow Hearth's 7 1/2 acres rise from lakeshore to 180 feet above the lake through woods, organic gardens, orchards, and meadows. Our 30-acre neighborhood of private landholders is bordered by enormous ranches recognized as critical for water quality and wildlife habitat. A 900-acre state park is nearby.

Members and neighbors are self-employed in teaching, holistic health, writing, entertainment, landscaping, building, and business consulting. We combine simple lifestyles with high-tech capabilities. The neighborhood children are wise to the ways of nature, and they roam freely and safely.

Interested persons may rent available rooms or houses or purchase lots in the immediate neighborhood. Rainbow Hearth offers a few rooms, cottages, and select camp and RV sites.

The Whole Works! Institute—a nonprofit corporation—sponsors an Earth-keeper internship program of particular interest to persons committed to exploring powerful and effective alternatives to mainstream living options. Spiritual and physical regeneration retreats are available. Inquiries welcome. [Oct99, sase required]

RAINBOW HOUSE

1115 Tennessee St
Lawrence KS 66044

785-842-0381

Began 1977 | Pop. 9
Diet: Omnivore | Urban

The Rainbow House is a cooperative consisting of 10 women and men who are interested in using creative ideas to maintain a peaceful and enjoyable living situation. We share the responsibilities of the house's operation—from housework to decision making on house policy. There is no manager, and no leader. We are a group of equals working for ourselves and for each other.

We have a great old house in Lawrence, Kansas, which has a solar greenhouse and a huge organic garden plot. Everyone at the house has their own room; we share a living room, a dining room, a kitchen, bathrooms, and a laundry. Although we require group interaction to function, the house is large enough to afford each person the privacy they need.

House members devote some time each week to the house's operation. This includes a weekly house meeting, some housework, and an occasional fix-up project. We feel that the time spent is well worth the benefits of living in such a fun and enjoyable place. [Nov98]

RAINBOW PEACE CARAVAN

Somewhere in South America
lioraadler@aol.com
http://www.photoamazonica.com/arcoiris/index.html

Began 1996
Diet: No red meat | Rural/Urban

We are an international group of artists and ecologists traveling for the last three years from Mexico to Tierra de Fuego, South America, in our own converted buses. By networking with indigenous, ecological, and alternative groups we create bridges and plant seeds. Multimedia theater, workshops and courses (especially permaculture, natural-buildings construction, and ecovillage design), conferences, audiovisuals, bioregional gatherings, and ceremonial villages are the means by which we promote our message of peace, hope, unity, and harmony with la Madre Tierra. We are a mobile ecovillage training center, bringing practical solutions to people interested in creating more sustainable lives. We learn, teach,

Key to bracketed text: cc = cannot commit to prompt correspondance, sase = self-addressed stamped envelope

motivate, share, and inspire. We live simply, communally, and joyfully. We expect this project to grow and to continue for several more years. [May99]

RAINBOW VALLEY

PO Box 108
Takaka
NEW ZEALAND
035257000, 035258209
035257484 fax
robert.jenkin@xtra.co.nz

Began 1974 | Diet: Omnivore | Rural

(Also known as Te Anatoki.) A community of individuals. Our 100 hectares is an open valley between forest-covered hills. The Anatoki River leads up to wilderness and down to the wider community of Golden Bay. Community is first and foremost about people, not land. The people cooperate and share in different ways and at different levels. Differences are respected. Communication is recognized as vital. We want the community to be an environment that encourages cooperative work in all its forms, self-expression, and self exploration.

We aim to follow the path of nonviolence (physical and emotional) in conflict resolution. Affairs pertaining to the whole community are resolved through meetings, with consensus always the aim. A company structure represents us legally, in which all members are entitled to equal shares. Children play an important part in our community, helping us achieve a sense of extended family. Our community house has a vital role as the heart place, channeling communication, social life, and community spirit. The farming/gardening/conserving of communal land is a strong focus, while various arts and crafts manifest another dimension. All residents are responsible for their own income. Produce is sold for agreed purposes or is shared. Visitors are welcome when there is space. [Oct99]

RAINBOW VALLEY AGRICULTURAL COOPERATIVE (RVAC)

Rt 2 Box 28
Sanger TX 76266
940-458-0337, 940-365-2004

Began 1978 | Pop. 32
Diet: Omnivore | Rural

We are a close-knit community on 220 acres of rolling prairie and wooded stream bottoms. Individuals construct their own off-the-grid houses, roads, and water systems. Organic. No pesticides, herbicides, hunting, trapping, or fishing. Restricted tree and branch cutting. Abundant wildlife. Very beautiful 120-acre mostly wooded community parkland borders most homesites. Meetings monthly. Elections for president, vice president, treasurer, and secretary are yearly. Three years left on property note. Community well and waterlines. [Feb99, sase requested]

RAPHA COMMUNITY

c/o Julia Ketcham
1420 Salt Springs Rd
Syracuse NY 13214
315-449-9627
jsketcha@mailbox.syr.edu

Began 1971 | Pop. 41
Urban | Spiritual

Rapha (from the Hebrew word for healing) began in the late 1960s as a small ecumenical house church. We are nonresidential with shared volunteer rotating leadership and make decisions by consensus. We are incorporated as a nonprofit tax-exempt service organization. We are committed to each other to be a caring extended family as we make the spiritual journey together. This sacred work has led us from our Judeo-Christian beginnings, to increasing openness to all spiritual paths, to a planetary consciousness.

We live out our vision by trying to be honest and faithful with each other and by trying to learn healthy conflict resolution and forgiveness when we fail each other. We weep and we celebrate together. We try to evoke in each other true calling by worshiping together; by going on weekend retreats; by shared meals, recreation, service projects, and study. We meet once a month for worship and divide into small groups called cells that usually meet every two weeks. Recent cells are dream interpretation, massage, quilt making, parenting, and retirement issues. [Oct99, cc, sase requested]

RAT & TAT FAMILIEN-GEMEINSCHAFT

Haus Benediktus
A-3710 Frauendorf 76
AUSTRIA
0663/9223711, WIEN/4935055

Began 1996 | Pop. 13 | Forming
Rural/Urban | Spiritual

Self-sufficient family-like community, principles of the first Christians, lifestyle similar to Oneida, farming with "lost crops of the Incas," interested in international-contact conflict solving by humanistic therapy combined with prayer. Different houses come with different density of sharing connected in a public association to advise one another and the helpless. [Mar99]

RAVEN ROCKS

Southeastern Ohio

Began 1970 | Pop. 11 | Rural

Raven Rocks, established in 1970, is a small rural project in the northern edge of Ohio Appalachia. It is a community of purpose, brought together and held together by common values and goals that have found focus in the effort to pay for, restore, and set aside for permanent preservation more than 1,000 acres of hill and ravine lands. The original environmental concern— to rescue the property from strip mining for coal—has grown to include a variety of member-financed projects, including several structures above and underground, that utilize a wide range of conservation techniques and solar strategies. The larger of two underground buildings was designed for public demonstration and will incorporate seven solar strategies in one structure. Also part of this demonstration will be a biointensive garden. All agricultural projects—including our Christmas-tree operation, grass-fed cattle, and gardens at all the homes—have been organic since the initial purchase. Most of our acreage has been set aside for natural restoration of the hardwood forest native to the area. The entire property, including the homes and other improvements, is designed as permanent preserve and hence not available for sale or development.

Ten of 11 current members are from the original group of 19. Members earn their own livings, then volunteer the time required (about 7,000 hours annually) to raise Christmas trees that pay for the land

Listings

and to do the work of the corporation, which was set up as legal owner.

Education—or reeducation, for those of us who are adults—has been a fundamental interest of this group. Most of our efforts, therefore, have an educational intent—whether to educate ourselves or others. We are striving to get more of our multifaceted public statement and demonstration in place and fear that the effort could be jeopardized by too much premature publicity and traffic. Hence, for the immediate future we are withholding phone number and information about location.

REBA PLACE FELLOWSHIP

PO Box 6575
Evanston IL 60202

847-328-6066, 847-475-8715
847-328-8431 fax
Reba_Place@juno.com

Began 1957 | Pop. 50
Urban | Spiritual

Reba Place Fellowship began in 1957 in what has become an ethnically diverse neighborhood in south Evanston. Its forty-some members and children now live in large multifamily homes and apartment buildings in Evanston and in Rogers Park, in north Chicago. Reba sponsors affordable housing for many low-income families. Fellowship members work in shared community ministries and in "outside" earning jobs, mostly in the service professions.

Reba Place Fellowship's long-term commitment to its local neighborhoods has encouraged the formation of two congregations and given life to a couple of cooperative "villages" within the city. In recent years Reba has worked to review its structures, to become a more reconciling and empowering

presence within its racially diverse neighborhoods. After 42 years of community experience, Reba is still under construction. Interns and visitors welcome. [Aug99, sase requested]

REEVIS MOUNTAIN SCHOOL OF SELF-RELIANCE

HC2 Box 1534
Roosevelt AZ 85545

520-467-2675

Began 1980 | Pop. 4 | Re-Forming
Diet: Omnivore | Rural | Spiritual

We are a spiritually oriented, self-reliant, wholesome natural-foods farm family. Our vision is to raise awareness of our eternal divinity by living what we love and seeking truth each day.

Our 12-acre homesite is a remote, high-desert, riparian valley in the Superstitian Wilderness. Access is an 8-mile hike or a 4 x 4 drive to highway; 10 miles to the nearest "outside" socializing/telephone opportunity.

Our lifestyle is rustic and junk-food- and media-free. We began as a New Age community focused on self-sufficiency and survival skills. Today we're a family/sanctuary, an organic farm, and a classroom. Funding sources: class fees, donations, an herbal remedies mail-order business.

We accept a small number of students for 30 days of "learning by doing" and a $350.00 tuition. This fee and work exchange provide room and board, a peaceful, healing environment, and a mentor who has enriched the lives of many. Longer-term residency is open to those who complete their 30 days stay harmoniously. We do not accept children/pets. Opportunities for outside employment are nil as our access road

makes commuting a real challenge. [Jan99, sase required]

RENAISSANCE CO-OP

1520 Gilbert Ct
Ann Arbor MI 48105
http://www.umich.edu/~umicc/

Pop. 66

Renaissance shares the same building as O'Keeffe co-op on the University of Michigan north campus. Living up to its name, the co-op is comprised of a diverse range of people across all continents who share an equally wide range of interests. Numerous foreign languages are spoken, and rarely does one not get exposed to new and interesting cultures.

The house is predominantly occupied by graduate students. A quiet setting amenable to the studious, Renaissance is an ideal place for the academic. However, not to be outdone by its central-campus cousins, the co-op also offers many social activities that range from wild parties to ice-cream socials to football in the yard. Hey, we have to let loose, too.

Every year at Renaissance brings in new faces, new cultures, new friends. The one constant at the house is the friendliness, the fun, and a commitment to make the cooperative environment work. Call us to arrange to come over for dinner and check out our house! [Oct99]

RENAISSANCE VILLAGE

PO Box 1086
Penn Valley CA 95946

Began Sep99 | Pop. 2 | Forming
Diet: Vegetarian | Rural | Spiritual

(Also known as Ananda Dhiira.) Renaissance Village is a community forming in the Sierra Nevada foothills. On 20 acres of land, we are creating a self-sufficient, sustainable community with spiritual and moral values as its foundation.

We are in the process of creating a retreat site and an organic farm. Later on we hope to encompass other projects, such as a holistic healing center, progressive schools, literacy programs, ecological regeneration, and even a bakery!

Our community is a place for people awakening to social and spiritual awareness. It is a catalyst for total individual and collective transformation on all levels—physical,

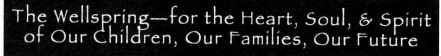

Key to bracketed text: cc = cannot commit to prompt correspondance, sase = self-addressed stamped envelope

mental, and spiritual. It is also a place of spiritual renewal, offering practical ways to reintegrate ourselves through eating a wholesome, organically grown vegetarian diet and regularly practicing Ashtanga yoga and meditation.

Renaissance Village exists within the larger framework of Ananda Marga, an international, progressive, social-service organization with branches in 160 countries. It is one of the few global organizations of Third World origin to render voluntary social service and disaster relief. Ananda Marga's social programs include disaster relief, inexpensive or free schools, children's homes, medical clinics, refugee help, and multipurpose development projects that help people help themselves. [Oct99, sase requested]

RIDGE HOUSE CO-OP

2420 Ridge Rd
Berkeley CA 94709

510-548-9722

We are a cooperative that houses students, primarily students attending the University of California, Berkeley. Our vision is to give students an opportunity to work together and live together in a harmonic and peaceful environment. [Jan98, sase required]

RIO BONITO - BELIZE

16401 Stone Jug Rd
Sutter Creek CA 95685

209-296-7157
StoneJug@hotmail.com

Began 1982 | Pop. 7 | Forming
Diet: No red meat | Rural

(Also known as Las Palmas.) We are an organic, natural-living retreat in two locations, one in Belize, Central America, and the other in California in the Sierra Mountains east of Sacramento. Some of us go back and forth part of the year, and others stay mainly in one of the two locations.

We farm in both locations and have other home-based businesses. We live a simple, peaceful life, and we especially love the tropical lifestyle in Belize. Our vision is to have two fully functioning communities in both locations. In order for that to happen, we need more people of like mind, more positive energy, and more money. Please write or phone if you are interested in knowing more. [Sep99, sase requested]

RIPARIA

PO Box 4812
Chico CA 95927

530-895-8786
RTrau77613@aol.com

Began 1987 | Pop. 25
Diet: Vegetarian | Rural

Riparia is an intentional community on 12 acres. Riparia has nine homes, a year-round creek, organic gardens, and orchards. There are 25 people presently living in our community. We have a good mix of ages with both young people and elders.

We interact with the greater Chico area, including sponsoring fund-raisers and other events at Riparia to benefit local organizations. Our focus is right livelihood and working on environmental, peace, and social-justice issues. We are learning to live cooperatively yet retaining a strong commitment to individuality. [Oct99, sase requested, no openings]

RIVER CITY HOUSING COLLECTIVE

200 S Summit St
Iowa City IA 52240

319-337-5260, 319-337-8445

Began 1977 | Pop. 29
Diet: Vegetarian | Urban

(Also known as Summit House, Anomy House.) Our collective currently consists of two large houses close enough to walk to the university or downtown. We own both houses, and we are going to buy another. We each pay a share slightly below the average cost to rent in the area but we are requiring each member to work a minimum of 16 hours a month for the collective. This work includes cooking, shopping, maintenance, management, meetings, and committees such as newsletter, education/cultures, membership, work credit, recycling, and food club. We especially need individuals skilled in plumbing, electrical, and carpentry. We also appreciate skills such as cooking/baking, music, and teaching.

This is a consensus community, so we are learning about tolerance, teamwork, real-estate management, and group process. We interview people who want to live here as a group, usually over dinner, and then make a group decision on membership/boarding privileges.

If you live here you must like children,

pets, and composting. Success is a process, not a destination.

We need hardworking, friendly people who appreciate diversity. [Apr99, sase requested]

RIVER FARM COMMUNITY LAND TRUST

3231 Hillside Rd
Deming WA 98244

360-592-5222

Pop. 26 | Diet: Omnivore | Rural

We live in the Pacific Cascadia bioregion in the northwest corner of the United States and are one of the five communities in the Evergreen Land Trust. Eighteen adults and nine children live here, and there is some yearly turnover.

Our community is maintaining protected wildlife areas, practicing organic ecologically sensitive farming, and acting as an educational source for the community and each other. Our farm is a mixture of forest, gardens, and fields. We also have sensitive areas of marsh and streams, a good-size river, and mountainside. We value independence and practical homesteading. We practice consensus decision making. We work to improve our communication skills and to widen our views. We are open to written correspondence and endeavor to network with similar folks.

We are active in our local watershed and actively practice sustainable forestry.

Please, mail inquiries only. [Jan99, cc, sase requested, no openings]

RIVER HAYVEN ECO-VILLAGE AND TUBING SOCIETY

N-9562 County Rd G
Colfax WI 54730

715-632-2529
sjfreund@win.bright.net
http://riverhayven.gq.nu/

Began 1992 | Pop. 11 | Re-Forming
Diet: Omnivore | Rural

(Also known as Hay River or Riverside.) We see our village as a home and/or recreation area for people who seek the companionship and support of others who regard the Earth and all life on it as sacred. Our commonality lies in our reverence and interdependence with nature and Mother Earth. We embrace concepts of immanent divinity and emergent evolution. We see ourselves as actively involved in helping save the present world from social and ecological ruin as well as working to actualize a visionary future. We envision our roots deep in the Earth and the past, with our branches reaching toward the stars and the future. We will relate to each other as a tribe, with interconnecting clans and families, bound together by our common love and reverence for our home, the living Earth.

Our land is varied, with rolling hills covered by oak woods, white pine, jack pine, maple, and reemerging prairie. We have a mile and a half of frontage on the river that includes several acres of ponds and floodplain. Eagles, otter, deer, beaver, and turkey are a few of the animals abundant on this land.

Our community is organized as a cooperative, and we have memberships available for residential living and/or recreation. Our membership fees vary according to the use level desired. [Aug99, sase required]

RIVERDALE COHOUSING

Attn: K Chung
c/o 164 Cambridge Ave
Toronto Ontario M4K 2L9
CANADA

416-461-6461, 416-535-3430
416-462-0133 fax
dbuck@yorku.ca
ajamieson@cbrc.com

Began Jun99 | Pop. 60 | Forming
Diet: Omnivore | Urban | Spiritual

(Also known as Womyn's Intentional Community Assoc.) Urban retrofit, creating a village within the city. Many people have put years of work into building the foundations for this group, which came together in early 1998 to become Riverdale Cohousing.

In 1999, members of the group purchased 3 properties in close proximity, which have become home to 6 households. Other properties will be added through purchase or rental, and interested neighbours will be invited to join us.

We are developing a participatory community where people know their neighbours, and where young and old live and play together - sharing community meals, planting a garden, conserving the environment, and providing safe outdoor areas for children and adults. We participate in activities and decision-making that affect our neighbourhood and local government. [Sep99, cc, sase required]

RIVERSIDE COMMUNITY

RD 2
Upper Moutere
Nelson
NEW ZEALAND

03-5267805, 03-5267033 x44
chris@riverside.org.nz

Began 1941 | Pop. 34
Diet: Omnivore | Rural

Riverside is a 58-year-old intentional community near Nelson, New Zealand. Based on humanitarian/Christian, pacifist, socialist principles; these determine our organization and structures. Our legal structure is a charitable trust that owns all land, buildings, vehicles, etc., and donates surplus to help others.

We support ourselves from the 500-acre farm of dairy cows, apple orchards, and forestry. Some members work outside the community. We practice income sharing. All farm income, salaries from outside jobs, or state benefits are pooled, and members receive a graded allowance according to family size.

Decisions are made by consensus at the weekly meeting. We have no leaders. We are pacifist. We work with nonviolence, justice, and equality to build peace. We have not a defined spiritual path; members make their own.

We have 20 adult members and 14 children plus 19 people who rent houses and are not committed members. Membership is not restricted, and some assistance is given to those who leave. We live in family units within the community family; ages range from 0 to 87. With our hardworking rural lifestyle, we celebrate six seasonal festivals to bring our spirit and our Earth together in ourselves. Visitors welcome; please write first. [May99, cc]

ROSEWIND COHOUSING

c/o Lynn Nadeau Secretary
3221 Haines St
Port Townsend WA 98368

360-379-3835 fax
olyhost@olypen.com,
welcome@olympus.net
http://olypen.com/sstowell/rosewind/

Began 1997 | Pop. 40 | Forming
Diet: Omnivore | Urban

RoseWind Cohousing is a community of people who want to know and care about their neighbors. We want to form social connections that will make our daily lives better and more meaningful. We would like to live a little more lightly on the land by sharing, by preserving green space, and by practicing a little sustainable agriculture within our small-town community. We want to live and learn together. We want to work and play together. We want to learn to function as a group that is respectful of individuals, using consensus to make decisions and set policies.

We have designed a neighborhood that includes a car-free central commons, which our landscape committee is helping us develop into a productive and beautiful green space. Our privately owned lots show our individuality in the diversity of building styles. Our common house is still in the design stage, but we currently hold weekly

Key to bracketed text: cc = cannot commit to prompt correspondance, sase = self-addressed stamped envelope

potlucks, a monthly meeting, and special events in a wonderful space lent to us by a member of the community. We have been lucky enough to annex a special, small piece of land designated as a wildlife sanctuary, where birds and wildlife are more protected from domestic pets and tall trees create a haven.

We struggle with the daily realities of group decision making and human conflict, and through it all we maintain our loving connections with one another. [Jan99, sase requested]

ROSNEATH FARM ECO-VILLAGE

McLachlan Rd
PO Box 250
Dunsborough WA 6281
AUSTRALIA

(+61) 041-231-8385

Began 1994 | Pop. 6 | Forming
Urban

Our village project is just over three hours drive south of Perth. Visiting is by appointment only.

We will sell 71 strata title lots. Instead of dividing the land up into 2-hectare bush blocks like almost everyone else, we propose to have an average lot size of under 2,000 square meters—half an acre—so we can preserve about 60 hectares of forest and streams and 60 hectares of farming land. We have started converting the land from conventional cattle grazing to intensive, organic, permaculture-guided, autonomous microenterprises. Read this again slowly! By autonomous we mean that individuals or families will run their own farming operation, be it beekeeping, wine making, marron farming, orchards, or vegetable gardens. They will negotiate leases of land and facilities from the body corporate.

Rezoning has been achieved for the residences, the farming activities, and two special development nodes. Tourism activities will be in 4 hectares in the northwest corner, with lots of buffers to protect privacy. The village center on the east side will cater to residents. There we will build a laundry, a store, an office, a library, a computer room, workshops, a freezer room, meeting rooms, guest houses, etc. We aim to provide a wide range of facilities so well that people feel no need to duplicate these in their homes. [Nov98, cc, sase required]

ROSY BRANCH FARM

328 Stone Mountain Rd
Black Mountain NC 28711

Began 1987 | Pop. 23
Diet: Omnivore | Rural

Rosy Branch Farm is a neoindigenous forest community with an interest in ancient cultures and permaculture. Begun in 1985, we originally came together through a meditation group with ecological and spiritual interests. We currently have eight families living on the land (50 acres). We are not actively seeking new members, but we're into cooperation and sharing information—including labor exchange, trading visits, etc.

Economically each family is fairly independent, though we're developing right livelihood at the community level. We have created a nonprofit project called Good Medicine that works to raise awareness of the large population of Mayan people in Guatemala and Mexico. We believe that indigenous values are valuable to the Earth—there's a lot for our culture to learn about living within the limits of our resources. We arrange periodic trips to their region, help the weavers sell their goods. Community and cooperation are very helpful in pursuing this work. [Apr99, no openings]

ROWE CAMP & CONFERENCE CENTER

King's Highway Rd
Rowe MA 01367

413-339-4954
413-339-5728 fax
Retreat@RoweCenter.org
http://www.RoweCenter.org/

Began 1973 | Pop. 12
Diet: Omnivore | Rural

Rowe Camp and Conference Center is located in the beautiful Berkshires, three miles from Vermont. Since 1924 we have run a small creative summer camp for teenagers. In 1974, our conference center was founded. We offer weekends and week-long retreats for adults and families on a wide variety of religious, political, psychological, and health issues.

Our work-study program is a chance for people who want to slow down, take stock, explore new directions, engage in creative and meaningful work, and be a part of a value-based, supportive community. Work-study participants work 33 hours a week in

exchange for room, board, and the opportunity to participate in many of our programs. The stay lasts anywhere from six weeks to a year, and work is arranged by matching your skills and preferences with Rowe's needs, which may include housekeeping, maintaining our buildings and grounds, office work, and more. Our cooking internship is an opportunity to learn vegetarian cooking and bread baking from our wonderful cooks.

The study portion is self-directed and includes personal study, group work, attendance at conferences, individual meetings with an adviser, the experience of living in community, and the opportunity to practice new skills.

Rowe Camp and Conference Center balances a respect for the integrity and freedom of each person with the needs of the community and the organization. We are dedicated to fostering a new society that can nurture the best in each of us, reward idealism and caring, and expand hope and vision. [Sep99, no openings]

RUTH'S HOUSE

321 N Thayer St
Ann Arbor MI 48104

734-665-0320, 734-665-6216

Pop. 12 | Diet: Omnivore | Urban

Ruth's is a small student cooperative house of 11 rooms housing 12 people in Ann Arbor. [Jan99, cc, sase requested, no openings]

SACRED MOUNTAIN RANCH

Central Eastern Arizona
le@cybertrails.com
http://www.cybertrails.com/
~le/ranch.html

Began Nov98 | Pop. 4 | Forming
Diet: No red meat

Located in the White Mountains of Arizona on 20 acres of pines in a mild climate. Would you like to wake up to birds singing, listen to coyotes howling at night, and stumble across awesome elk during the day?

Who are we? We are David and Jan Lerner, planning a community to be run by consensus of all its members.

Additions and corrections: Email: directory@ic.org, Web: http://directory.ic.org/, Mail: RR 1 Box 156-D, Rutledge MO 63563, USA.

These are the basic ideas that we plan to build the community around:

• We consider spiritual transformation our primary motivation in life (no, we don't mean religion; no, we don't all follow a certain path). People who will join us have an intuitive understanding of the unity of all life, will know that love is our empowerment and is who and what we are, and will recognize the divine, nonphysical essence of each individual.

• At least parts of the area will be clothing optional, particularly around the hot tub. We practice radical honesty, and all close interactions have a sacred quality.

• We are health oriented and will add a retreat center for those among us who wish to teach a new vision of health and spirituality.

We are already off the grid, having a solar well with a 3,000-gallon storage tank and a three-bedroom house, solar powered and attached to a septic tank. All electricity is from solar panels and a wind generator. Internet access is by cellular phone, or we may rent a small office in town. Price estimates for rental or buy-in will be given on request. [Dec98]

SACRED OAK COMMUNITY, THE

129 Warren Rd
Selma OR 97538

541-597-2461
sacredagreement@hotmail.com

Began Jun99 | Pop. 4 | Forming
Diet: Vegan | Rural

We are a vegan, organic, toward self-sustainable, clothing-optional community in southern Oregon, looking for potential leaders and members, people passionate about a whole new way of life. We share food, utilities, rent, and work equally and practice consensus decision making, complete honesty, and the expression of vulnerability. Freedom of expression, creative, emotional, sexual, spiritual, etc., as weird and different as it may be, is welcome and warmly encouraged. People on an intense spiritual path, people who seek to be naked and open with their body and emotions, creative artists, healers, and simply sensitive individuals looking for a safe environment are all welcome. Nonviolence, respect of others' privacy, nonwastefulness, and truth telling are a must. Please, no recreational drugs, alcohol, or smoking. We have a large, rustic

country house, two beautiful ponds, five acres of meadows and woods, an organic garden, and space for RVs and tipis. We are a healing-arts center, an educational facility for self-sustainable skills and other workshops, and the principal office of a nonprofit corporation.

Please tell us about yourself, your passions and dreams, and if we all feel a connection, we'll invite you over for a couple of days, then take it from there. [Sep99]

SAINTS' CHRISTIAN RETREAT, THE

759 NE 72nd St
Trenton MO 64683

660-673-6760, 660-673-6860

Began 1996 | Pop. 8 | Re-Forming
Diet: Omnivore | Rural | Spiritual

The Saints' Christian Retreat is a community for Christians who desire to live in close connection with other saints. Through fellowship, Bible study, worship, and sharing of resources the spiritual and natural needs of each member are ministered to. The community hopes to become a vital part of spreading the Gospel through distribution

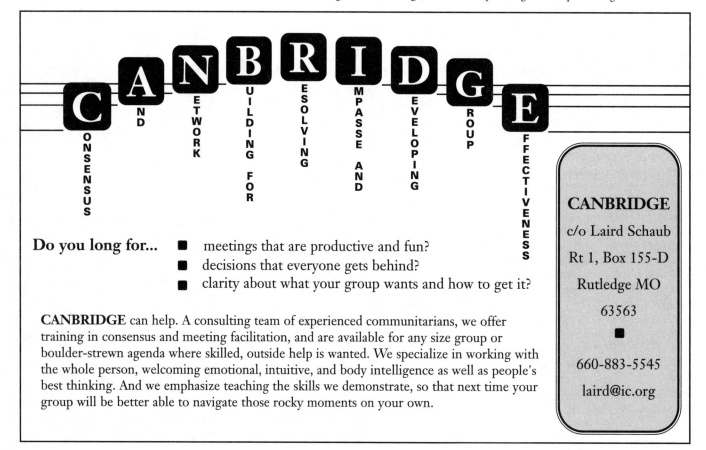

CANBRIDGE

C ONSENSUS
AN D
N ETWORK
B UILDING
FOR
R ESOLVING
I MPASSE AND
D EVELOPING
G ROUP
E FFECTIVENESS

Do you long for...
■ meetings that are productive and fun?
■ decisions that everyone gets behind?
■ clarity about what your group wants and how to get it?

CANBRIDGE can help. A consulting team of experienced communitarians, we offer training in consensus and meeting facilitation, and are available for any size group or boulder-strewn agenda where skilled, outside help is wanted. We specialize in working with the whole person, welcoming emotional, intuitive, and body intelligence as well as people's best thinking. And we emphasize teaching the skills we demonstrate, so that next time your group will be better able to navigate those rocky moments on your own.

CANBRIDGE
c/o Laird Schaub
Rt 1, Box 155-D
Rutledge MO
63563
■
660-883-5545
laird@ic.org

Key to bracketed text: cc = cannot commit to prompt correspondance, sase = self-addressed stamped envelope

of printed literature, through a radio broadcast, and by daily precept and example. As God prospers the work, the group plans to meet the natural needs as well as the spiritual for those in distress. [Jan99]

SAINTS FRANCIS & THERESE CATHOLIC WORKER HOUSE

**52 Mason St
Worcester MA 01610**

508-753-3588, 508-753-3089

Began 1986 | Pop. 9
Diet: Vegetarian | Urban | Spiritual

We are a lay Catholic community living in voluntary poverty, holding our goods in common, attempting to offer hospitality to homeless men and women and to work for peace and justice, in the spirit of Christ, the early church, and the saints. We pray together somewhat irregularly and publish a newspaper called the *Catholic Radical* six times a year.

We work to promote a consistent ethic of life that opposes war, the death penalty, euthanasia, and abortion. We sponsor many demonstrations and work for peace on various international campaigns in war zones and areas of conflict. We are not government funded and draw on anarchist roots. [Nov98]

SALAMANDER SPRINGS

**PO Box 531
Haddock GA 31033**

**912-952-3544
bobburns61@yahoo.com,
    eric@ttrout.ecology.uga.edu
http:///www.gnat.net/
    ~goshawk/sal.htm**

Began 1998 | Pop. 7 | Forming
Diet: No red meat | Rural

Salamander Springs is an ecovillage/intentional community in formation on 50 acres of recovering clear-cut land in central Georgia. Our visions are to practice a sustainable and restorative human presence on this damaged land and to witness to the possibility of cooperation between people and the land, resulting in better health for both. Organic gardening, permaculture, alternative building, alternative-energy sources, recycling and salvage, land-based income sources, homeschooling, and celebrations are among our projects developing from this vision. [Dec98]

SALT CREEK INTENTIONAL COMMUNITY

**585 Wasankari Rd
Port Angeles WA 98363**

**360-928-3022
thenwhat@olypen.com**

Pop. 4 | Forming | Rural

Our intention as a forming community is to live peacefully, lovingly, simply, and efficiently with as little impact on the land as possible. We intend to save as much of our land as possible in its natural, wooded, riparian, wetland, and agricultural state. We intend to form a community-supported organic farm. We encourage qualities such as a adaptability and diversity. [Oct99]

SAN MATEO COOPERATIVE COMMUNITY

**3329 Los Prados St
San Mateo CA 94403**

**650-547-7155
sanda@bigfoot.com
http://www.wordrunner.com/
    sanda/smcc.htm**

Began 1998 | Pop. 9 | Re-Forming
Diet: Omnivore | Urban | Spiritual

We are forming a small urban intentional community facing a lagoon between San Mateo and Foster City. We purchased a four-unit building and expect to purchase a second soon. We have planted fruit trees and are developing organic gardens. We are seeking other "families" to co-own and/or rent in some form of a cooperative—something between intentional community and cohousing. We are creating community with a local neighborhood group. The location is wonderful: lots of birds, sunrise over the water, nearby biking/walking path, park with playground, tennis/basketball courts, and city amenities of proximity to freeway and public transportation, etc.

Values we would like to see "grow" on this site can be summed up in the concept of sustainable development: growing some of our own food; supporting local organic farmers in farmers' markets or in a community-supported agriculture (CSA); reducing, reusing, recycling; avoiding buying food and other items that contribute to the destruction of local economies and the environment. We want to share time in the garden and at the dinner table with the people we live with as well as other activities. We seek open communication and a deep expression

of feelings. We expect those wishing to join us to have a commitment to these values and goals as well. [Sep99, sase required]

SANDHILL FARM

**Route 1 Box 155-CD
Rutledge MO 63563**

**660-883-5543, 660-883-5545 fax
sandhill@ic.org**

Began 1974 | Pop. 8
Diet: Omnivore | Rural

We are a supportive family of friends (six adults, two children) farming communally on 135 acres in rural northeast Missouri. We grow our food through organic and biodynamic methods and share income, meals, vehicles, and other resources. The land includes gardens, orchards, woods, hayfields, cropland, and pasture. Our income is derived from foods we produce (sorghum, tempeh, honey, garlic, mustard, and horseradish) and from individuals pursuing personal interests—administrative work for the Fellowship for Intentional Community, process consulting, and organic-farm inspection. We like to keep our lifestyle simple and healthy. While we do raise animals for meat and serve meat on occasion, we have a primarily vegetarian diet. Vegans can also easily be accomodated as long as they are comfortable living in an environment that supports animal husbandry on a small scale.

We tend to work hard, especially during the growing season, and get satisfaction from providing for ourselves as much as we can while maintaining close ties to neighbors, communities, friends, and family. Regular celebrations and social occasions, including weekly dinners with Dancing Rabbit, are important to us. Sandhill is active in the communities and organic movements.

Equality of opportunity, nonviolence, and honesty are core values. We hold meetings once or twice a week and make decisions by consensus. We value communication and support and expect one another to be available for feedback about what we say or do as a member of the group. We are open to new members, including children, as housing allows. Our long-range vision is to grow to 12 adults plus kids. Children here are educated both on and off the farm in the environment that suits them best. We strive to maintain a multigenerational balance and are open and supportive toward alternative relationships. A visit for up to one week can

Listings

be arranged most times of the year. Please write and introduce yourself. Extra hands are appreciated during our growing season, especially the sorghum harvest (September–October). [Oct99, sase requested]

SANTA ROSA CREEK COMMONS

887 Sonoma Ave #0
Santa Rosa CA 95404

707-523-0626

Began 1982 | Pop. 39 | Urban

A limited-equity housing co-op for all ages located on two acres in downtown Santa Rosa, 60 miles north of San Francisco. We have 27 units of 0 to 3 bedrooms, a community room, laundry, garden, and wooded creek.

We wish to live cooperatively, resolve conflicts peacefully. Issues are decided by consensus. Every adult is on the board of directors. All are asked to work at least eight hours per month, being on two committees and taking part in monthly cleanups. We manage and maintain the property, with help of the resident maintenance manager. Units may not be used to generate income traffic. We have a monthly potluck, holiday events, a singing group, autobiographies, etc.

Members buy shares, the price based on size of unit ($9,000 to $16,000), and pay monthly charges of $475 to $800. Ten units are for those eligible for low-income housing assistance. (State qualification is processed by the commons.) These shares are $750 to $2,500, and monthly charge is 25 percent of income plus 10 percent of assets over $5,000.

For all applicants, the process of getting on our waiting list includes several interviews, taking part in an event, and attending a board and a committee meeting. We encourage families with children to apply. [Dec98]

SASSAFRAS RIDGE FARM

C/O Buck Route Box 350
Hinton WV 25951
farmhouse@inetone.net

Began 1972 | Pop. 28
Rural | Spiritual

Sasssafaras Ridge Farm, founded in 1972 by three young adults sharing an old shack, has evolved. Our intentional neighborhood, with boundaries greatly expanded by friends' purchases of adjacent farms and forest, grew from 240 to over 400 acres. Ten households shelter one to five people each (children included) in solo, partner, and nuclear family. Households are economically autonomous and privately owned. Half the land and most farm equipment are owned by several partners.

We join in preparation and celebration of Earth holidays with the broader community, with religious freedom. We share and center in and by a half-acre pond.

The mountainous, wooded farm includes 20 acres of hay, 40 of pasture, creeks, and two ponds. A clean canoeable river, kayaking, and white-water rafting are near.

Activities include gardening, animal care, fence, firewood, and construction. Equal access and responsibility are fundamental to our cooperative intent.

Within Sassafras, one household is willing to trade two- to five-days room and vegetarian meals for labor. Written prearrangements required. No space offered for new residents! [Nov98, sase required, no openings]

SBSHC: SANTA BARBARA STUDENT HOUSING COOPERATIVE

6503 Madrid Rd Suite J
Isla Vista CA 93117

805-685-6964, 805-685-0898 fax
sbshc@sb.net

Began 1977 | Pop. 71
Diet: Omnivore | Urban

The Santa Barbara Student Housing Cooperative (SBSHC) provides students democratic control; community ownership; safe, inexpensive housing; and greater social interaction. A wide range of students from a variety of backgrounds and countries is attracted to our student housing co-ops. We own three group houses and one apartment building located near the University of California, Santa Barbara, campus.

SBSHC has an open membership policy. Not only do we not discriminate in any way, but we actively encourage diversity among our groups in order to stimulate education and awareness.

Members must attend house meetings two to three times per academic quarter and complete at least five hours of co-op work duties per quarter, in addition to normal house chores and maintenance. Members own and operate the co-op. Rent charges reflect the costs of running and maintaining the co-ops. No profits are made; income goes toward paying off loans as well as paying staff salaries, with surplus earnings being reinvested in the buildings, the residents, and further co-op expansion. A portion of the budget is assigned to member-education programs and workshops.

SBSHC is committed to environmentally responsible living. We are also affiliated with the North American Students of Cooperative Organization (NASCO). [Nov98]

SEADS OF TRUTH, INC.

PO Box 192
Harrington ME 04643

207-483-9763
SEADS @nemaine.com

Began 1980 | Pop. 3 | Forming
Diet: Omnivore | Rural

Solar Energy Awareness and Demonstration Seminars is a not-for-profit group establishing a self-sufficient alternative-energy community and seminar center on 60 acres in rural Maine. We hold solar workshops on a wide range of topics, including photovoltaic-

Key to bracketed text: cc = cannot commit to prompt correspondance, sase = self-addressed stamped envelope

panel construction, hydroponic-grow systems, and lifestyle counseling. We are using a community-land-trust model and stress voluntary cooperation and mutual aid—working with others, using group consensus and sharing. We promote and participate in peace activism and activities, stressing a renewable-energy future. After a provisional period, families will have an opportunity for individual, limited-equity home ownership on common land. Members will share responsibilities and benefits of operating the solar-powered seminar center and traveler hostel in our common building, in operation for 18 years. Greenhouse, gardens, and independent solar-electric utility are our step toward self-sufficiency as well as world peace. We are still in the formative stages and need "real" people and families to continue the process into the twenty-first century. Please write or e-mail. [Dec98, cc, sase requested]

SEATTLE'S INTENTIONAL COMMUNITY PROGRAM

4540 15th Ave NE
Seattle WA 98105

206-524-7301 #214
susanf@upc.org

Began 1992 | Pop. 17
Diet: Omnivore | Urban | Spiritual

Our hope is to provide an urban discipleship experience in Christian intentional community for young adults: to train them to be the next generation of church leadership, who will choose a biblical lifestyle that embraces incarnational ministry to and with the urban poor.

House members commit to one year in covenant community in the inner city of Seattle. They each volunteer with an established ministry to street youth, at-risk children, refugees, or inner-city churches. In addition to the 10 hours per week of volunteering, the house members work a regular job and are expected to eat together, worship together once a week within the house, maintain a close tie to their church community, and meet as a house weekly with a facilitator. This person mediates conflict, facilitates discussions, and provides information about urban/community issues.

Most of our members are recent college graduates who are discerning a call into missionary work. Intentional community helps provide a place of support and challenge. Members can renew their covenant for a

second year, and many opt to remain in community long term. We have had over 90 people participate in the program, many forming communities in other cities. [Oct99, no openings]

SEEKERS AND SETTLERS

9023 Warbler Dr
Tallahassee FL 32310

850-421-0068, 850-421-1151 fax
parico@supernet.net
**http://members.tripod.com/
    ~kidnez/index.html**

Began 1998 | Pop. 4 | Forming
Diet: Vegetarian | Rural

A community *free* of dogma and social constraints!

On 2 1/2 acres of wooded land, with a large house and gardens and trails, Seekers and Settlers is still *forming*. We are an organic group that changes with the folks who are flowing in and out.

Paula opened her land and house to the experiment: "*One* of my ideas for community is *Wanderers and Settlers:* a base for those who want to travel but who also want a *home* where they can recenter and refresh themselves. I want to be free to travel myself, knowing that all will be cared for by those who are the current *settlers*."

Nez, formerly of Zendik Farm, has shared in the experiment for the past year: "We are forming a community of ideas based on experience, integrating what works and discarding what doesn't, providing for and taking care of each other, to create a place we can call *home*. Our ideas are different, but our *ideals* are the same. We all want a pleasurable, unrestricted *life*. We let each other go about it and help each other do it. True community."

Looking for those who love and respect nature, we welcome visits by anyone serious about living in community who think this might be the one. Since we are still "forming," we want folks who have financial resources and who can do the work.

Check our Web site for updates. [Aug99, cc, email preferred]

SENECA FALLS CO-OP

2309 Nueces
Austin TX 78705

512-472-2052

Newly remodeled, Seneca is designed for

graduate and upper-division students and offers a studious and responsible, yet relaxed, atmosphere. With 19 members and many single rooms available, the house strikes a balance between community and personal space. The co-op strives to be health and environment conscious. Primarily vegetarian food is served, but some accommodations are made for meat eaters. Senecans welcome cats in individuals' rooms; dogs must be approved by a house vote. Smoking is limited to private rooms.

Acceptance of nonstudents and lower-division students is by a vote of house members. [Feb99, cc, sase required]

SHADY GROVE

c/o Liza Gabriel Ravenhart
P O Box 688
Penngrove CA 94951
Liza@sacredsexuality.org
MonkeyO@aol.com
http://mythicimages.com/

Began 1996 | Pop. 8
Diet: Omnivore | Rural/Urban | Spiritual

(Also known as The Ravenhart Family.) Shady Grove is named for the oak and redwood trees that shade the fenced half-acre courtyard between our four buildings in the rural/suburban north San Francisco Bay Area. We are eight polyamorous, bisexual, and straight adults living together in a loosely structured extended family. We share a hot tub. We each have private space. Our few meetings are by consensus. We have chickens and grow some of our food. Most of us are Pagan and many belong to The Church of All Worlds. Many of us lead workshops and write articles on Paganism, polyamory, the awakening Earth, and related topics. Five of us comprise the Ravenhart Family. The Ravenharts founded Shady Grove and operate their own home-based business that creates and distributes beautiful figurines of gods and goddesses: TheaGenesis, LLC (The Mythic Images Collection). The most popular goddess figurine we sell symbolizes our strongest common value. She is Called The Millennial Gaia, an intricately worked figure of a pregnant woman with the Earth as her belly, representing the Earth as vibrant, conscious, alive, and sacred. She is our hope for the future. [Oct99, sase required, email preferred]

SHAMBALLA

**c/o PO Box 10
Bellingen 2454
AUSTRALIA**

**02 6655 1367, 02 6655 1826
tazo007@hotmail.com**

Began 1973 | Rural

We all appreciate the beauty of where we live. We mostly live quite separately. We have meetings to organize roads and sporadic working bees for privet removal, etc. [Mar99]

SHANNON FARM COMMUNITY

**274 Shannon Farm Ln
Afton VA 22920**

**804-361-1417, 804-361-1180
http://www.ic.org/shannonfarm/**

Began 1973 | Pop. 89
Diet: Omnivore | Rural

Shannon is a cooperative intentional community, home to over 60 adults who range in age from the 20s to the 60s and over 20 children from infants to teenagers. Together, we share 520 acres of mountain forests, pastures, and river-bottom hayfields at the base of the Blue Ridge Mountains, located 27 miles west of Charlottesville.

The purpose of Shannon Farm is to be a residential intentional community where people share land, encourage member-managed agriculture and businesses, and support cooperative and harmonious living situations here and in the larger world.

No overall belief system, other than a commitment to cooperative living, has defined our community since moving onto the land in 1974. Different lifestyles coexist readily at Shannon, and we seek new members of diverse races, ages, financial resources, and adult sexual orientations. Our spiritual values are based on concern about each other's well-being, ecological land stewardship, and respect for the right of each member to express their own beliefs about the nature of reality. While committed to our intentional community, we remain connected to the wider society through jobs, friendships, and individual interests.

The land and all buildings are owned by the community as a private, nonspeculative land-and-housing trust. Shannon members finance their personal homes and own long-term leases that may be transferred to other members at a fixed maximum price. So far,

we have built 30 homes for families and individuals, three group houses, and several small cabins. Shannon homes are grouped in eight clusters, one of which is exclusively solar powered. There are farm buildings, a 3-acre lake, and other recreational facilities by the river. A cabinet-shop complex has been developed, with sites available for more small industry.

Shannon Farm Community is financed by monthly membership dues—7 percent of personal income after taxes. There is no joining fee; but personal assets are necessary to finance house construction or purchase one of the few leaseholds that occasionally become available. Expectations of members include participation in physical, organizational, or social work; monthly dues payment; and involvement in community events.

Over half of us commute to work. We support ourselves by cabinet making, construction, teaching, nursing, physical therapy, massage, counseling, health research, auto mechanics, computer programming and training, administration, retail sales, insurance services, technical writing, and artwork.

People who wish to explore Shannon may start by visiting on monthly meeting day, usually held on the first Saturday of each month. Members are responsible for their own housing, which is often off the land at first. Shannon does not operate a central kitchen or offer apprenticeships. So, with many of us maintaining full-time jobs, we are not set up for long initial visits. However, we are open to new people and welcome those who share a commitment to the values of our community—those who want to help build Shannon and the global intentional-communities movement.

For more information or to schedule a visit, please write to our visitor coordinator. [Sep99, sase requested]

SHARING COMMUNITY

**24370 Brown Rd
South Bloomingville OH 43152,
740-332-0205
sf@bright.net
deye@bright.net**

Began 1999 | Pop. 4 | Forming
Diet: Omnivore | Rural

Sharing Community is a rural intentional community located 60 miles southeast of Columbus, Ohio, in the foothills of the

Appalachian Mountains. Our immediate area includes numerous artisans and fun-loving, educated households. We are located less than one hour from the university town of Athens, Ohio, and near several towns where employment is available. The community is composed of 60 acres of wooded hillsides and rolling meadows with abundant wildlife. Currently we are two households, with the expectation of adding additional, compatible members.

Goals: stewardship of the land and the environment; sustainable lifestyles; consensus-based decision making; respect for individual diversity; caring for fellow members; and charitable works. Members live in individual energy-efficient houses. Members are expected to follow a healthy lifestyle, excluding use of drugs or excessive alcohol. Members are self-supporting; no employment is available at the community at this time.

We consider ourselves to be self-aware, lifelong learners who are seeking the best ways to live out our values. We are seeking other thoughtful, fun-loving individuals and families to explore ways to share simpler, cooperative, sustainable lifestyles in a rural setting. Families with children are especially encouraged to apply. Applications to: Sharing Community, 24370 Brown Road, South Bloomingville, OH 43152. [Feb99]

SHARINGWOOD

**22125 E Lost Lake Rd
Snohomish WA 98296**

**360-668-1439, 360-668-2487
sharingwood@yahoo.com
http://sharingwood.addr.com/**

Began 1990 | Pop. 85
Diet: Omnivore | Rural/Urban

We live on 39 forested acres in south Snohomish County, about 25 miles northeast from Seattle. Sharingwood is a lot-development model, where members buy lots and build their own homes to meet individual budgets and tastes.

We use a variety of decision-making approaches, although consensus is the goal on most issues. We use a decision board to empower small groups to make specific decisions that do not really require the input of the entire membership.

In addition to a monthly meeting, we have found that sharing circles can play an important role in nurturing a deeper sense of trust within the community. Here, members find an opportunity to come together and share honestly and openly in a safe space.

Initiated by individuals, people do things together like homeschooling, yoga, meditation, sharing resources, organic gardening, work parties, hot tub, food co-op, campfires, playfield, concerts, children's activities, sign language.

The "enchanting" nature of the native forests and the many trails that surround the community define a village-like setting. Wilderness to some, sanctuary to others, for most it offers a comforting contrast to our workaday world. [Apr99, no openings]

SHEPHERD'S GATE COMMUNITY

1654 Humboldt St
Denver CO 80218

303-830-8045

Began 1991 | Pop. 9
Urban | Spiritual

Shepherd's Gate is a diverse religious community devoted to support of each other, the neighborhood, and society. We offer hospitality and lodging to those in need of short-term housing. [Mar99]

SHEPHERDSFIELD

777 Shepherdsfield Rd
Fulton MO 65251

573-642-1439

Began 1979 | Pop. 29
Diet: Omnivore | Rural

Shepherdsfield is a Christian fellowship that tries to live as the early Christians did and as recorded in the Acts of the Apostles, including the "sharing of all things in common." We have accepted Jesus Christ as the way, the truth, and the life. Through him we have found answers to the many questions that arise in trying to live together and in reaching out to others.

We presently have about 100 souls associated with our community. We are located in a farming area within driving distance of Columbia and Jefferson City, Missouri. We earn our living through an organic bakery; a wallpapering, window-washing, and painting company; several cottage industries; and some printing and publishing. We have a large ministry that reaches over the world in studies of Scripture and principles of life. We operate our own school for our children

and take seriously the task of raising children in an environment of "purity and childlikeness."

Our desire has been to show others that Christianity is not limited to the institutional forms that have so disenchanted many people and led them to reject the claims of our master, Jesus of Nazareth. We would not want to mislead anyone by claiming our life is a utopia that requires little or no effort for the individual. Quite the contrary, true peace and brotherhood can only be accomplished when the utmost of diligence is applied in living out and promoting the necessary qualities. That requires struggle in order for the goodness of God to be "fleshed out" in us. However, we find great joy in living for him in the present and seeing ourselves and others changed from day to day.

If you would like to visit us, please write or call in advance. We have varying lengths of visitation before a person may apply to become a novice, which can eventually lead to becoming a member. [Jan99, sase requested]

SHERWOOD CO-OP

4746 18th Ave NE
Seattle WA 98105

206-524-1958, 206-522-7872

Began 1930s | Pop. 13
Diet: Vegetarian | Urban

The Sherwood Co-op was started in the thirties by University of Washington students. At its high point, it was made up of five member-owned houses. Presently, we are 13 co-ed, mostly students from accredited schools all over Seattle, living in one 13-bedroom house in the university district of Seattle. Our work-share system includes regular dinners, cleaning of the kitchen, weekly chores, and capital repairs of the house. We buy the bulk of our food collectively. We generally eat vegan meals at house dinners, buy dairy and eggs as a group, and infrequently eat meat. We continue to consider/seek ways to own our property again. We are members of North American Students of Cooperation (NASCO).

Our mission is to provide low-cost housing for students, so that students can focus on their studies and contribute to their community and have more time to be creative in life. We emphasize sustainable living and introducing cooperative living as a lifestyle

choice beyond school. [Oct99, cc, sase required]

SHILOAH VALLEY COMMUNITY

EskDale Center
1100 Circle Drive
EskDale UT 84728

435-855-2471, 435-855-2474

Began 1955 | Pop. 59
Diet: Omnivore | Rural | Spiritual

Shiloah Valley Community is a Christian community with a strong identification with Israel, particularly the tribe of Levi. Education and music are emphasized in the private K–12 school. The religious organization behind the community is the Order of Aaron. We view ourselves as a ministry, not a denomination. We welcome all Christians and desire to work with any Christians seeking reconciliation within the body of Christ. We have similarities with Anabaptist communities, charismatic Christians, and messianic Jews. We observe the Israelite feasts of Passover, Shavuot, and Sukkot. Economically we function as a common fund. We love to have visitors at almost any time. Our primary support comes from a 200-cow dairy and a large farm, but we have many other economic pursuits. We are active in the larger community, holding annual July Fourth and Christmas celebrations for all in the valley. [Nov98, sase requested]

SHILOH COMMUNITY

PO Box 97
Sulphur Springs AR 72768
501-298-3299, 501-298-3297

The Shiloh Community founded by E. Crosby Monroe in southwestern New York in 1942 actively followed a communal way of life since its inception. The underlying focus is developing Christian spiritual growth, both as individuals and as a community, and living lives in a way that reflects this priority. This focus has evolved independent of any specific religious affiliation and might be most accurately described as esoteric Christianity. (This implies going beyond first-order Christianity. Hebrews 6:1, 2.) Rev. Monroe died in 1961.

In this self-supporting community, a progression of occupations followed: general farming, dairy farming, meat processing, flour milling, retail baking, then wholesale

Additions and corrections: Email: directory@ic.org, Web: http://directory.ic.org/, Mail: RR 1 Box 156-D, Rutledge MO 63563, USA.

baking and distribution. By the mid-1960s the need for an improved setting for the family and businesses occurred. In 1968 a grand hotel was acquired in the beautiful Arkansas Ozarks, which now serves as the community's central facility (including offices, bakery, health-food store, cafeteria, and retirement wing for the elderly). Another community-owned business is the Shiloh Christian Retreat Center. The Shiloh bakery uses whole-grain flours and natural sweeteners and oils in the manufacturing of Shiloh Farms bread.

At this stage of the community's development, many of the members are senior citizens, respected elders who continue to be actively involved in daily community life to the extent that they are able. However running the businesses is very demanding. The community would like to attract some younger families to take on some of the responsibilities (and satisfactions). A very comfortable, supportive, and safe community environment for raising a family has been created. There is a hope to attract others who appreciate the community's commitment to the deeper Christian values that make this lifestyle possible.

A word about the "conservative" nature found at the Shiloh Community. Newcomers often arrive with inspired visions and enthusiastic energy for implementing new ideas, then find themselves frustrated by the unwillingness of the "old-timers" to jump on the bandwagon. Creativity and enthusiasm are valued but need to be balanced by maturity and commitment. Essentially, it may take a while to prove one's self, moving forward one step at a time. Because of the before-mentioned focus of our community we do not accept persons with "antigovernment" philosophies. The expression of true Christian

---

loves, patience, and hard work are the assets most likely to win our confidence.

SHIM GUM DO ZEN SWORD CENTER

**203 Chestnut Hill Ave
Boston MA 02135**

**617-787-1506
simgumdo@tiac.net
http://ShimGumDo.org/**

Began 1976 | Pop. 106
Diet: Omnivore | Rural | Spiritual

American Buddhist Shim Gum Do Association, Inc., is the main teaching center of the Zen martial art called shim gum do, which means "mind sword path." The founding master of shim gum do is enlightened Zen master Chang Sik Kim. Master Kim began his formal training at the Hwa Gye Temple of the Chyoge order of Zen Buddhism in Korea at the age of 13. At the age of 21, Master Kim underwent a 100-day retreat. During this time he discovered shim gum do, and he attained enlightenment. Shim gum do is an enlightenment way, the goal being to attain clear mind, clear thinking, and clear action. Students have the opportunity to study directly under shim gum do's founding master. We offer ongoing classes in shim gum do and in meditation. We also have a residential program for those who are interested in a more intensive study of shim gum do and traditional Zen practices. [Jan99]

SHIVALILA

**PO Box 1966
Pahoa HI 96778**

**808-965-9371
shivalila@aol.com**

Began 1994 | Pop. 16
Diet: Omnivore | Rural

(Also known as Kauihelani.) We are a multicultural community, spanning wide diversities of ethnic and class backgrounds. Most simply put, this community is about mothers and babies. We put ourselves in service to the mother/child bond, acknowledging it as the very foundation of culture. We parent each other's children as our own, and both men and women take active part as primary nurturers of children. We don't have a lot of rules. We've found four basic agreements to be most useful in guiding us. These are open and honest communication; nonvio-

---

lence; renunciation of ownership on all levels (from material possessions to lovers and children); and tantra, which includes identification with nature and babies. We steward 47 acres in the midst of Hawaii's beautiful rain forest. We sleep together in one longhouse and function through our days as a unit, making most decisions cooperatively. The flow of life varies among activities including farming, building, playing with and homeschooling children, swimming, sign-language classes (one of our members is deaf), art, music, and dance. Regular, spontaneous satsanghs (truth-telling gatherings) are the arena in which we address emotional material. Frequently, these discussions revolve around the issues of competition, jealousy, power, and control. We do not shy away from confrontation, which we have found to be a potent and effective tool toward transformation. This is not a place for the weakhearted or those who wish to play it nice. We do find resolution, however, through this sometimes painful process of self-exposure, and in five years have emerged as a cohesive, bonded clan. We enjoy each other's company and are poised for the gradual growth and expansion of this way of life. [Aug99, cc, sase requested]

SHORT MOUNTAIN SANCTUARY, INC.

**247 Sanctuary Ln
Liberty TN 37095**

615-563-4397

Began 1981 | Pop. 18
Diet: Omnivore | Rural

Short Mountain Sanctuary (SMS) is a collective providing queer safe space. We strive to live lightly on the land and to maintain an environment that is open, free, and stimulating to each person's growth and creativity. We make decisions by consensus. Life here is simple and rustic. We drink springwater, use an outhouse, and heat with wood. What electricity we have we collect from the sun. The heart of the community is an antebellum log cabin that serves as kitchen, dining, library, and common space. Residents live in a variety of homebuilt one- to five-person dwellings. We grow much of our food, herbs, and dazzling flowers. Goats supply us with milk and chickens with eggs. We publish *RFD: A Country Journal for Queer Folk Everywhere* and host two faerie gatherings a year (May and October). Since SMS started in 1981 we have become a magnet for

---

Key to bracketed text: cc = cannot commit to prompt correspondance, sase = self-addressed stamped envelope

queers and the people who love us who wish to live rurally with a sense of community. Three new intentional communities have formed nearby: Ida, Sun Valley, and Pumpkin Hollow, and a growing group of friends lives independently in the surrounding countryside. As an extended community we share resources, party, and help each other out. We are a sanctuary and welcome visitors anytime. [Nov98, cc, sase requested]

SICHLASSENFALLEN

1139 N 21st St
Milwaukee WI 53233

414-933-2063

Began 1965 | Pop. 6
Diet: Omnivore | Urban

Since our founding 34 years ago, Sichlassenfallen has continued a commitment to community service, equality, peace, and living with the environment. New members and past members add a continuing richness to our community's central values and lifestyle.

We are part of a large housing co-op actively involved with area issues. Decisions are made by consensus, with majority rule if necessary, and we share expenses, chores, and responsibilities. Individual efforts are supported, and freedom of thought and choice is valued.

While we are a stable community, we seek new members occasionally, so please contact us if you are relocating in our area. We enjoy contact and visitors from other communities, and we have a large Victorian home located near the downtown area. Please contact us in advance. [Dec98]

SIMEON CENTER

Route 23
Claverack, Columbia County NY

518-325-3648, 518-672-7901
518-672-0181 fax
brucefrishkoff@usa.net
ttc14365@taconic.net

Began 1993 | Diet: Omnivore | Rural

(Also known as Columbia County Cohousing.) We are a forming cohousing community in Columbia County, New York, two miles from the Taconic Parkway between Hudson and Hillsdale. The place is open and wooded land with a beautiful lake and Catskill views. We plan up to 21 households for families, couples, and individuals.

Our goals: Return to a neighborhood lifestyle; all ages—babies to 101 (wheelchair accessible); social and cultural opportunities, chamber music, folk dancing, film nights, discussion groups; reduced living costs through shared facilities, library, playrooms, laundry, studios, gardens, shops. Call us for more information. [Jan99]

SIMON COMMUNITY, THE

PO Box 1187
London NWS 4HW, England
UNITED KINGDOM

0171-485-6639

Began 1963
Diet: Omnivore | Rural/Urban

The Simon Community is a community of volunteers and ex-homeless people attempting to care and campaign for London's homeless. The community caters to those for whom no other adequate provision exists, for whatever reason. This includes providing an emergency night shelter, three residential houses (one a farm), and extensive outreach work.

Anyone spoken to on the streets is considered a member of Simon, however briefly. The community is nonrehabilitative in that we accept that for some people rough sleeping is a valid lifestyle and would not pressure anyone to change this. However, we do our best to provide access to all possible services (e.g., detox) when requested.

The community is run on a group-based structure, with consensus decisions at all levels. The community is a registered charity but does not accept any government funding, as this allows us to remain independent in our policies. Voluntary workers live in a community project, are allowed one day off per week, receive 26 pounds a week and commit themselves to a period of at least three months. [Jan99, cc]

SIRIUS

72 Baker Rd
Shutesbury MA 01072

413-259-1251
sirius@siriuscommunity.org
http://www.siriuscommunity.org/

Began 1979 | Pop. 38
Diet: Vegetarian | Rural | Spiritual

Sirius is an educational, spiritual community founded in 1978 by former members of the Findhorn Community in Scotland. It is one

part of an expanding network of light, working to increase the consciousness of the Earth's inhabitants.

Sirius is a demonstration center for a community way of life based on principles of respect for the individual, cooperation with nature and all life, and living our lives with spiritual integrity that recognizes we are all in a process of growth with every experience in our life offering valuable lessons. We honor the highest truths common to all religions, and our ecumenical approach is a source of inspiration for visitors and members. Meditation and attunement are central to our life together.

Sirius also demonstrates ecological ways of living, including organic pest-free food production, solar and environmentally friendly building practices, recycling of "waste" materials, using composting toilets, and living a more nonpolluting, less consumptive lifestyle. Healing of the planet is of primary importance to us, and we are members of the Global Ecovillage Network and are the northeast office of the Ecovillage Network of the Americas. [Nov98]

Additions and corrections: Email: directory@ic.org, Web: http://directory.ic.org/, Mail: RR 1 Box 156-D, Rutledge MO 63563, USA.

SIVANANDA ASHRAM YOGA RANCH COLONY

PO Box 195
Budd Rd
Woodbourne NY 12788

914-436-6492
YogaRanch@sivananda.org
http://www.sivananda.org/ranch.html

Began 1974 | Pop. 11
Diet: Vegetarian | Rural | Spiritual

The Sivananda Ashram Yoga Ranch, founded in 1974 by Indian yoga master, Swami Vishnu- Devananda, on 77 acres of Catskill wood, is part of an international organization of yoga schools and retreats. We are an intentional community that both teaches and practices a spiritual lifestyle of self-mastery of body and mind, selfless service, devotion, and philosophy. Residents participate in daily meditation, prayer, and study; yoga asana classes, service, and vegetarian meals. The ashram also serves the community by holding workshops covering a variety of holistic practices, classical Indian and western music concerts and dance performances, and spiritual rituals such as sweat lodges and Hindu pujas. A sauna and swimming pond are also available. Our meals are wholly vegetarian. We grow much of our food in our organic garden and greenhouse. Most purchased food is also organic. The ashram serves guests year-round. The community welcomes serious aspirants to participate in our work-study program and possibly stay on as staff. A four-week residential yoga teachers' training course is offered each September. The ashram is a nonprofit spiritual/educational corporation run and maintained by an all-volunteer staff, work-study residents, and other helpers. [Oct99]

SKUNK VALLEY COMMUNITY FARM

c/o Jay Robinson
1423 - 168th Ave
Ackworth IA 50001

515-961-9791
robinj@storm.simpson.edu

Began 1999 | Pop. 2 | Forming
Diet: Vegan | Rural

We are a community in formation, looking to come together over the next six years. We are an intentional community of longer- and shorter-term residents who seek to live in harmony with the land and each other. We

have three main foci: (1) a spiritual/mental/physical retreat center for small groups and individuals; (2) a natural preserve of wooded and prairie areas; and (3) a community-supported agriculture (CSA) farm providing food for a wider membership.

At the time of the publication of this directory, we are seeking like-minded individuals to join in this vision and to help in the formation of the community and the building of the overall project. We are located 30 miles from Des Moines and from Ames. Please be in touch if you have any possible leadings in this direction. Thank you! [Aug99]

SKY WOODS COSYNEGAL

PO Box 4176
Muskegon Hgts MI 49444

Began 1972 | Re-Forming
Diet: Omnivore | Rural/Urban

We believe the heart of our humanity is an essentially social nature whose fullest realization is one with the destiny of community. We believe that global survival depends on compassionate commitment of all our resources to create a truly advanced social and ecological awareness. We must replace competition and aggression with mature skills of cooperation and humanization.

We are a holistic and politically conscious community that has existed for over 15 years. We seek out the wisdom of the ages and other cultures, using a lifelong learning process to evolve an ever-more-harmonious and accountable lifestyle. Community has given us the high privilege of real-life participation in mutual self-creation.

We think we have made credible advances over sexism, ageism, racism, and possessiveness toward material resources or others. Those advances have been based on rational self-criticism; democratic consensus/majority decision making; full-disclosure relationships; ample group communication and expression; collective sharing and control of all socially significant material resources; and a firm rejection of one of the last strongholds of the competitive mentality—preferential monogamy or possessive relationships. Our exhilaration and sustaining ideal is a fully egalitarian community.

Some of us have already committed ourselves to a lifetime together. We have a few acres of beautiful wooded hill country on the shore of the inland sea, a small organic farm, a home, and several cottage industries.

We produce some arts and crafts and are deeply into alternative energy, holistic health, nutrition, organic gardening, and orcharding.

We welcome visitors but request that arrangements be made in advance. [Dec98]

SKYHOUSE COMMUNITY

1-2K Dancing Rabbit Ln
Rutledge MO 63563

660-883-5511
skyhouse@ic.org

http://www.dancingrabbit.org/

Began 1995 | Pop. 6
Diet: Vegetarian | Rural

As part of the Dancing Rabbit Ecovillage (see separate listing), Skyhouse strives to be a model of ecological living. We are an income-sharing community, and our money and resources are held in common. Members do a variety of tasks, and new folks are plugged in to existing projects and businesses or can bring jobs and ideas with them. We are committed to nonviolence, egalitarianism, and the breakdown of culturally constructed gender roles. We meet as a group to make decisions by consensus, resolve conflicts, and help each other work through life's challenges.

On a summer evening you might find us coming together after a hard day's work. Some folks come in from the gardens, while others have been building our straw-bale homes, doing computer work, or preparing for an upcoming alternative-energy workshop. Members, interns, and visitors gather at the community table in the open-air kitchen, while the day's cooks put finishing touches on dinner at the wood-burning stove. After a delicious meal offering bread and tofu (made from scratch), homegrown veggies, and home-brewed beer, folks gather for a sing-along or sit and joke about the day's events. The end of the day brings another brilliant sunset shining its golden light over the nearby pond and far-off rolling hills.

Does this sound too good to be true? Arrange a visit to see for yourself. We are actively seeking new members, so come add your unique perspective and energetic pioneering spirit to our tight-knit group. Help make our ecovillage grow! [Apr99, sase requested]

Key to bracketed text: cc = cannot commit to prompt correspondance, sase = self-addressed stamped envelope

SKYROS HOLISTIC HOLIDAYS

92 Prince of Wales Rd
London NWS 3NE, England
UNITED KINGDOM

171-267-4424, 171-284-3065
skyros@easynet.co.uk
www.skyros.com/

Began 1979
Diet: No red meat | Rural/Urban

Founded in 1979 by Dina Glouberman and Yannis Andricopoulos, Skyros was Europe's first alternative holiday center. It has pioneered the holistic approach to life and created a community experience that is now used as a model throughout the world. With two centers in Greece and one in the Caribbean, Skyros continues to be innovative, personal, and exciting.

The Skyros approach is inspired by classical Greece and brings together feelings and intellect, the physical and spiritual, individuality and community. Years after a Skyros holiday, participants still call it "the best holiday I ever had" or "a turning point in my life." The easygoing and genuine atmosphere of camaraderie and mutual encouragement allows people to relax and enjoy themselves more than they thought possible. It is also the ideal environment for expansion, creativity, and challenge. Courses are taught by a team of more than 100 facilitators, many of whom have an international reputation and all of whom are outstanding and committed teachers. [Mar98]

SOCIETY FOR THE PROMOTION OF CREATIVE INTERCHANGE

rayanderson@hotmail.com

Began 1987 | Pop. 2 | Forming
Diet: Vegan | Urban | Spiritual

We are looking for potential members only among people who have these two qualifications:

1. They hunger and thirst to be known and valued as persons, as centers of independent judgment in relation to the possible courses of action arising out of immediate face-to-face situations. Far too often they experience themselves as valued only as they suppress their own original thoughts and feelings, put on a mask, and conform to other people's purposes and expectations.

2. They are willing to seriously consider and possibly adopt a whole new way of life, if it is one that can truly provide both for a profound sense of belonging and for being cherished as a person.

If this describes you, please contact us at via email. [Aug99]

SOJOURNER TRUTH HOUSE

1507 Washtenau
Ann Arbor MI 48104

734-998-0712
sojo.truth@umich.edu

Pop. 50 | Diet: Omnivore | Urban

We are a friendly, nonsmoking house that generally attracts a diverse mix of graduate, international, and undergraduate students. Truth House is located close to the University of Michigan campus. We have lots of fun (when we're not hard at work), and we've even got a couple of pets! We look forward to meeting you—drop by for dinner; it is always at six p.m.! [Jan99, sase requested]

SOLTERRA

98 Solterra Way
Durham NC 27705

919-403-7028, 919-490-9047 fax
GJKrass@Juno.com

Began 1998 | Pop. 80
Diet: Omnivore | Rural/Urban

Solterra is a passive-solar cohousing community nestled in a semirural area but close to the amenities of several major universities, including Duke and the University of North Carolina, Chapel Hill. Our 20 acres are open and wooded, and the single-family homes and sites are privately owned. Each home is car accessible. Members share ownership in the common lands, paths, play spaces, roads, and common gardens. One side of our property abuts forestland owned by Duke. We enjoy Durham city services and close-by excellent public and private schools. Our eclectic members come from every part of the country and range in age from 0 to 110. Our interests are broad, and our consensus form of management includes committees to oversee all phases of the development and social life of Solterra. Right now, our major project is the planning and building of the common house. Currently, we share meals weekly. When weather permits, we use the little common house, a wonderful shed near the adult-friendly tree house. Eating styles vary, from meat eaters to macrobiotics, and our common meals reflect these tastes. There are 15 resident families; we'll have 40 when Solterra is built out. All except one of our lots has been sold. We also have a few resale lots, and we're actively seeking new members, adults and children. We welcome visitors; just let us know when you can come. [Sep99]

SONG OF THE MORNING

9607 Sturgeon Valley Rd
Vanderbilt MI 49795

517-983-4107
guestsrv@goldenlotus.org

Began 1971 | Pop. 9
Diet: Vegetarian | Rural | Spiritual

(Also known as Golden Lotus, Inc.) Song of the Morning Yoga Retreat Center in scenic northern Michigan draws visitors from across the country as well as from Canada, Australia, and Europe. Most come to attend events, but some come just for spiritual R&R.

For 28 years our focus has been to help people commune with their inner presence

Additions and corrections: Email: directory@ic.org, Web: http://directory.ic.org/, Mail: RR 1 Box 156-D, Rutledge MO 63563, USA.

through yogic meditation. Our spiritual director, Bob Raymer, is a direct disciple of Paramahansa Yogananda. He has also been with other great spiritual teachers such as Swami Ramdas, Sai Baba, Ananda Moyi Ma, Ammachi, and Baba Muktananda. Bob's comforting presence and wise guidance are reassuring and inspiring to those seeking the truth of their being.

Our year-round events include meditation retreats, Clear Light healing retreats, cross-country ski weekends, vegetarian-cooking classes, and music retreats. Ongoing services include Sunday service and evening meditation. Our own Golden Heart Players Chanting Band enhances the remarkable spiritual energy generated here.

Our friendly staff puts guests at ease. A limited number of rooms are available; delicious vegetarian meals are included in the reasonable lodging rates. Our 800 acres feature a lake, a river, and easy walking trails to shrines of the masters. [Oct99]

SONGAIA

22421 39th Ave SE
Bothell WA 98021

425-486-2035
http://home.sprynet.com/
sprgnet/rachelb/

Began 1987 | Pop. 19
Diet: No red meat | Rural/Urban

Songaia is a semirural cohousing community located on 11 acres of wooded hillside and pastures. Our plans call for 13 homes ranging in size from one to three bedrooms, arranged around a green village commons. Members share the use of all the grounds, including garden, greenhouse, orchard, and forest. The common house contains the dining/meeting room, laundry, food co-op, and guest rooms. Shared evening meals are prepared in our large kitchen with fresh organic produce from our land.

Songaia has been an ongoing residential community for more than 10 years. We value simplicity and cooperation and have chosen an Earth-conscious, sustainable lifestyle. Life at Songaia is active: members gather frequently for singing, work parties, celebrations, and social activities. Small working subgroups oversee the ongoing tasks of managing the property, organizing community events, and nurturing our children. We aim to create a strong network of diverse friends and caring neighbors, a safe supportive environment where children,

elders, and families of all types can live lightly on the land. [Jan99]

SONOMA COUNTY COHOUSING

2341 Creekwood Court
Santa Rosa CA 95409

707-570-1834
gsyphers@xenergy.com
eris@wco.com
http://www.wco.com/
~eris/socoho.html

Began 1998 | Pop. 15 | Forming
(Also known as Windsor Cohousing.) We are a group of families working to create a cohousing community in Sonoma County, California. We are currently looking for land in the Cotati area, and we are seeking new members. We are not organized around any particular religious, political, or lifestyle issue—what we share is our intention to create a neighborhood that by its physical design and social structure facilitates community. Our community will house 20–30 families in townhouse-style units, owned by individual families; common space will include a kitchen, a dining room, a garden, children's play areas, a hot tub, a workshop, etc. Community dinners and workdays will be a part of our lives. All of our decisions are made by consensus. [May99, sase requested]

SOUTHEASTERN MICHIGAN ECO-COMMUNITY

PO Box 4101
Ann Arbor MI 48106

734-428-9249
semeco@ic.org
http://www.ic.org/semeco/

Began 1999 | Forming
We are a group of individuals, couples, and families with children creating an eco-community. We are evolving toward an ecologically sustainable culture through community. We share a whole-systems approach, including interest in permaculture, renewable energy, ecological/organic gardening or farming, and natural medicine. We strive to be caring and supportive of one another and work to get along with each other in our daily lives and through a basically consensus model of decision making. We have a vision of one urban and one rural site in the greater Ann Arbor area of

Michigan that will be mutually supportive and will have homes available at low to moderate cost.

We recognize the diversity in nature and society as essential to the health of an ecosystem and strive to model diversity in our community. We value children and their learning as a part of our community commitment. We are forming a tapestry of interconnections within the community, including common spaces for meals and celebrations, a garden or farm, and other ways of sharing our resources. We will create other common spaces, each providing different amenities, balanced by private personal spaces that reflect their inhabitants' choices. Some of us want to earn our income within the community through cottage industries, and some of us plan to create a teaching center on issues related to sustainability and community.

We welcome new participants who share similar values in our community development. [Aug99, sase required]

SOUTHERN CASSADAGA SPIRITUALIST CAMP

PO Box 319
Cassadaga FL 32706

904-426-3171

Began 1894 | Rural | Spiritual
Designated as a historic district on the National Register of Historic Places, the Southern Cassadaga Spiritualist Camp Meeting Association is a unique religious community founded in 1894. We are located on a 55-acre tract of land, off I-4, midway between Daytona Beach and Orlando, Florida. While members may own the homes they live in, the association retains ownership of the land and offers lifetime leases. We also own and manage two apartment buildings.

The purpose of our community is to promote the understanding of the religion, science, and philosophy of spiritualism and to offer a nurturing environment for like-minded people. We have ongoing educational programs for those wishing to develop their mediumship and/or healing abilities, and we also offer ministerial courses. A number of mediums, healers, and ministers live and work on the grounds. Our unique offerings attract many visitors to our church services, our spiritual/metaphysical bookstore, and our counselors. Seminars and workshops are also offered frequently, and

Key to bracketed text: cc = cannot commit to prompt correspondance, sase = self-addressed stamped envelope

the public is invited to attend all activities. Please write for our Annual Program, enclosing $1 to cover shipping and handling. [Aug99]

SOUTHERN OREGON WOMEN'S NETWORK

2000 King Mountain Trail
Sunny Valley OR 97497

Began 1972 | Pop. 72 | Forming
Diet: Omnivore | Rural/Urban | Spiritual

Our origins in the 1970s were rural, feminist, and lesbian, developing our creative and survival skills. Now in towns and on land near the I-5 freeway in the southern half of Oregon, we welcome newcomers. Three area newsletters give information on activities and opportunities. Many groups have met regularly for 10–15 years, offering friendship, growth, and strong support. [Jan99, sase requested]

SOUTHWEST SUFI COMMUNITY (SSC)

PO Box 373
Silver City NM 88062
MorningGlory@oro.net
http://www.teleport.com/
~Ruhaniat/SSC.html

Began 1993 | Pop. 75
Diet: Vegetarian | Rural | Spiritual

The Southwest Sufi Community (SSC), located near Silver City, New Mexico, is first and foremost a spiritually oriented community, promoting understanding of the Sufi message but also open to students of other inclusive spiritual paths. We learn through experience and eat, dance, and pray together. The community, begun in June 1995, is establishing a retreat center, a nature preserve, and a residential village on 1,900 acres along Bear Creek.

People interested in residency at the Southwest Sufi Community should be pioneering, financially stable, and in good health. People in their 20s and 30s are especially welcome. The SSC is located in a poor county with low employment prospects. Since the land is remote from town, it is not practical to commute. People should expect to support themselves in creative ways independent of the community.

The best way to get to know the community is to attend a weeklong camp (usually in April, June, or October). The day rate is

$33/day or $231/week and up and includes camping, vegetarian meals, classes, and hands-on land projects. We accept visitors at other times, usually on weekends. Please write or e-mail before planning a visit and tell us you saw this listing in the *Communities Directory*. [Sep99]

SOWING CIRCLE

15290 Coleman Valley Rd
Occidental CA 95465

707-874-1557
http://www.oaec.org/

Began 1994 | Pop. 19
Diet: Vegetarian | Rural

(Also known as Occidental Arts and Ecology Center.) Sowing Circle is an intentional community set on 80 acres outside Occidental in Sonoma County, California. The land was formerly the home of the Farallones Institute (1974–1990), which educated thousands of people about appropriate technologies and biointensive organic

gardening. In 1994, Sowing Circle created the Occidental Arts and Ecology Center (OAEC), a nonprofit organization, to expand upon the Farallones Institute's good work.

OAEC offers residential workshops in permaculture, forming intentional communities, organic gardening and seed saving, "corporations and democracy," the fine arts, starting school gardens, and horticultural therapy. Call for a catalogue of programs.

While Sowing Circle and OAEC are two distinct legal and financial entities, we share the responsibilities of communal living, including cooking, cleaning, gardening, and facility maintenance. We are committed to exploring new approaches to sustainability, both in terms of low-impact living and of community building. We seek to help reverse current social and economic patterns that create hyperindividualism, consumerism, and alienation from nature. We strive to create a practice of right livelihood. [Dec98, cc, no openings]

Additions and corrections: Email: directory@ic.org, Web: http://directory.ic.org/, Mail: RR 1 Box 156-D, Rutledge MO 63563, USA.

SPADEFOOT

503 E University Blvd
Tucson AZ 85705

520-882-7079

Began 1995 | Pop. 20
Diet: Vegetarian | Urban

(Also known as University Community Housing Project.) Spadefoot is a Rochdale-principles-based, North American Students of Cooperation (NASCO)-affiliated, non-profit corporation. All full members are board members. We're leaderless and founderless. We're a diverse mix of yuppies and hippies, some young and old. Economic savings are distributed evenly. There is no seniority or probationary period. No dues to pay. We've been liberating through low-cost living for three years and may soon buy the house. When this happens, costs should fall 25 percent.

Full members pay $320–$450/month. Associates pay $100. These prices include all meals (six), food, utilities, phone, laundry, voice mail, garden, and computers. Associates sleep out.

Half the house is committed to the long term, but we also appreciate the variety and cost savings that the more transitory half provides. We serve as a staging area for the communities movement in Tucson, as we are forced to turn people away for lack of space. This is especially true for men, as we enforce a 40 percent minimum female policy. We can help anyone who shows up.

Say no to ritualistic, autocratic, and hypocritical "leaders." Call Elliott Kelly, at 520-882-7079. [Nov98, sase required]

SPARROW HAWK VILLAGE

Community Association
12 Summit Ridge Drive
Tahlequah OK 74464

918-458-0063, 918-453-9097
alreetz@tah-usa.net
stede@ipa.net

Began 1981 | Pop. 84
Diet: Omnivore | Rural | Spiritual

Sparrow Hawk Village, an intentional spiritual community, was established in 1981. We are nestled among 440 acres of gently rolling Ozark forest filled with abundant wildlife and natural, serene beauty. Organic community gardens, orchards, horse pastures, hiking trails, springs, a waterfall, and over a mile of river frontage, bordered by 700 acres of primitive state forest, significantly add to our quality of life.

Sparrow Hawk Village is open to members of all faiths. While many villagers are esoteric Christian, we are blessed with members of various western and eastern practices, which creates a diverse spiritual experience. Our residents are involved in the healing arts, music, counseling, dowsing, aura photography, teaching, meditating, spiritual dance, and esoteric studies. This is a place of growth. Energy vortexes here accelerate personal and interpersonal evolution.

Many of our residents are creatively self-employed, while others have jobs in the nearby town, where there are ever-increasing employment opportunities. Some work as nurses, teachers, healers, and artisans. Several residents have begun a Waldorf-school initiative so that we will soon have a school in the village.

Village life is enriched by a constant stream of international guests and students who participate in classes and workshops offered by accredited programs of Sancta Sophia Seminary. The campus includes a beautiful church, an esoteric library, a bookstore, a gift shop, a Wellness Center, and administrative offices. Daily meditations, Sunday services, and other spiritually oriented gatherings are available at the church and in village homes. Many villagers participate in a weekly meditation for world peace.

We are currently building our community center, which will serve as a hub for community activities and programs for all ages created to enhance the values of unity, love, peace, and community building. As we strive for higher levels of awareness we create an evolving wheel of light that is a work of sacred art, through the expression of itself.

Sparrow Hawk Village is located at the end of a county road 5 miles off Oklahoma State Scenic Highway 10 and approximately 11 miles from Tahlequah, Oklahoma, capital of the Cherokee Nation and location of Northeastern State University. We invite you to visit, study, or live in Sparrow Hawk Village. If you are interested in visiting, guest rooms and a campground are available for a nominal fee. Reservations are recommended. For those interested in living here, there are homes and homesites for sale and a few rentals. [Sep99, cc, sase requested]

Key to bracketed text: cc = cannot commit to prompt correspondance, sase = self-addressed stamped envelope

SPHERE OF LIGHT

PO Box 188
Morristown NJ 07960
http://www.SphereOfLight.com/
village/

Began 1998 | Pop. 4 | Forming
Diet: Vegan | Rural/Urban | Spiritual

The Sphere of Light Community is here to
be a center of peace, love, and positivity for
all of creation.

World transformation via inspiration!

Think loving, healthy, spiritually fun relations with others. A place where we live to
serve humanity in this great awakening of
life!

We are simply one part of the coming
wave of love and light that is building to
revitalize and replenish our beautiful world.

We are here to cocreate a place for people
to support and be supported in their spiritual growth and evolution.

Being, yoga, meditation, music, singing,
drumming, fasting, laughing, dancing, playing, breathing, and ommmmmmm.

"Love in every breath, joy in every action!"
[Sep99]

SPIRAL GARDEN

Paula Arico - Seekers & Settlers
9023 Warbler Drive
Tallahassee FL 32310

850-421-0068
parico@supernet.net
dougalderson@earthlink.net

Began 1980 | Pop. 35 | Diet: Omnivore
Spiral Garden began around 1980 when a
group of friends purchased a chunk of land
south of Tallahassee and divided it up
among themselves with the idea of creating
a loose-knit community. Others joined by
purchasing adjoining lots as they became
available, and this process continues today.

We are more of an intentional neighborhood of families and individuals who get
together for potlucks, birthdays, saunas,
swimming, and special occasions. There is
one household, headed by Paula Arico, that
is more communally oriented and is open to
visitors and long-term guests. There are a
trail that runs through the community and a
message board. We are accepting and tolerant of one another, and we enjoy a love for
the outdoors and nature. We tend to be natural foods oriented and adhere to ecological
principles, although we have no steadfast
rules or guidelines. Some of the individual

households are unique, such as a three-story
yurt on a sinkhole.

Most people work in various jobs and
professions in Tallahassee. We have an
annual community weekend where different
members teach a course or share a skill or
hobby with other members. In warm
months, folks often swim in a nearby sinkhole or at the famous Wakulla Springs
(about six miles away). Gardening seems to
be a common endeavor. While some in the
community dream of creating a community
center and more of an intentional community with a common spiritual focus, most
seem satisfied with the more informal community or neighborhood that has evolved.
[Aug99, sase requested]

SPIRAL WIMMIN'S LAND TRUST

HC 72 Box 94A
Monticello KY 42633
maryspiral@juno.com

Began 1979 | Pop. 5
Diet: Omnivore | Rural | Spiritual

Spiral is located on 300 acres in the hills
between Lake Cumberland and the Daniel
Boone National Forest. One of our purposes
is to provide space for lesbians to learn nontraditional skills and to develop lesbian
intentional community that strives for self-
sufficiency and cooperation.

There are two houses, six cabins, a campground, and two barns. Visitors and campers
are welcome. Camping is primitive; fee is
$5–$7 per night, with work exchange available. We are looking for community members and supportive members. Wimmin
interested in community membership par-
take in our resident-exploring-membership
program.

Apprentices are encouraged to apply to
Blue Skink Farm, our new cottage industry.
The farm grows organic fruits, vegetables,
and flowers for a CSA (community shared
agriculture) and a market garden. Through
the apprenticeship, wimmin will be exposed
to organic production of vegetables, fruits,
flowers, irrigation construction, maintenance and repair of machinery, CSA operation, processing produce, etc.

If you would like to visit us, let us know a
little about yourself, when you would like to
visit, and how long you would like to stay.
Write, phone, or e-mail. [Sep99, sase
required]

SPIRIT JOURNEY

PO Box 614
Ashland OR 97520
aliciab@jeffnet.org

Began Nov99 | Pop. 3 | Forming
Diet: Omnivore | Rural | Spiritual

Spirit Journey is a small forming community
on a farm that is becoming more sustainable, near Ashland, Oregon. Our vision is to
live simply with animals, plants, and humans
while providing a safe space for folks to
remember who they are through music,
dance, healing, and ceremony. At present,
we offer a public gathering on the second
Wednesday evening of each month at 7:30
pm, entitled Singing and Dancing Your
Prayers—we envision more such gather-
ings/concerts/playshops. On our 1.5 acres,
we have fruit trees, an organic herb and vegetable garden, a greenhouse, a medicine
wheel meditation garden, a sacred sauna,
and a ceremonial fire pit. We welcome men
and children, though at present we are three
women with horses, llamas, dogs, cats, and
ducks. [Oct99, cc, sase requested]

SPRINGTREE COMMUNITY

Rt 2 Box 536
Scottsville VA 24590

804-286-3466

Began 1972 | Pop. 6
Diet: No red meat | Rural

We are three married midage couples. Our
commune (established in 1971) is on 120
rural acres. We share income, eat meals
together, organize work by preference.
We are eclectic, independent, and frugal.
While we are aging, this is not a retirement
community (!). Our group goals are often
expressed through work—gardening,
orcharding, and tree planting; keeping
chickens; maintaining our two houses. We
support ourselves with income from outside
jobs.

We intend to remain a small, close group.
We strive to keep the community flexible in
meeting our changing needs for stability and
adventure, individual activity, and group
cohesiveness. We value commitment and
compatibility.

Visitors are welcome by prior arrangement. In season, we can have apprentices for
one to six months learning and practicing
ecological gardening, community, and coun-
try-living skills. For more information, write

Listings

and tell us about yourself. [Nov98, sase requested, no openings]

SRI AUROBINDO SADHANA PEETHAM

2621 W Hwy 12
Lodi CA 95242

209-339-3710x5, 209-339-1342x5
sasp@lodinet.com

Began 1993 | Pop. 4
Diet: Vegetarian | Rural | Spiritual

(Also known as Atmaniketan Ashram.) Sri Aurobindo Sadhana Peetham is a small ashram for the practice of Sri Aurobindo's integral yoga. We provide residential facilities and work activities as a field for the Sadhana (spiritual practice). The basic needs of the members are provided for, and the collective work supports the financial expenses of the ashram. The rules of the Sri Aurobindo Ashram in Pondicherry, India: No drugs/alcohol, no smoking, no sex, and no politics are followed here, and an atmosphere is attempted to be cultivated and maintained that honors and reflects the divine presence. Collective meditations are held daily, as well as a weekly study group and monthly retreats that are attended by friends and visitors from the outlying community. A vegetarian diet is observed. No member plays the role of the spiritual leader of the ashram. The cultivation of the inner guru and reliance on the divine force of Sri Aurobindo and mother's presence and teachings are the guiding principle. Practical direction of the day-to-day operations is overseen by a board of directors. Sri Aurobindo Sadhana Peetham is registered as a nonprofit religious corporation. Our main purpose is to provide a collective environment for one-pointed concentration on the Sadhana. [Jan99]

ST FRANCIS CATHOLIC WORKER

9631 Peppertree Rd
Spotsylvania VA 22553

540-972-3218

Began 1979 | Pop. 2 | Rural | Spiritual
A Catholic Worker community shares faith and duties involved in running a spiritual-retreat ministry for our sisters and brothers who are very poor or homeless. [Feb99]

ST FRANCIS CATHOLIC WORKER

4652 N Kenmore
Chicago IL 60640

773-561-5073

Began 1974 | Pop. 15
Diet: Omnivore | Urban

We're a bunch of organic-goat-cheese-eating, bicycle-riding, recycling, composting, anarchal pacifists sharing our home with people who have lost theirs. We try to live simply, but it's hard when we dumpster Chicago's finest.

We align ourselves with various struggles for social justice on a local, national, and global level. Our neighborhood is ethnically, economically, and psychologically diverse, and we're just four blocks from Lake Michigan.

Our house started 25 years ago in the Catholic Worker tradition, but followers of any, all, or none of the above religions are welcomed. Members of the decision-making community, i.e., "workers," generally work outside the house part-time and are around the house at other times to do hospitality, collect food and stuff, fix things, etc. Visitors are always welcome. [Feb99, cc]

ST JOHN'S ORDER

642 Myrtle Ave
South San Francisco CA 94080

Began 1970 | Pop. 4 | Re-Forming
Diet: Vegetarian | Urban | Spiritual

(Also known as Kailas Shugendo, Shugen Church.) St. John's Order is a religious community founded in the late 1960s by Bishop Dr. Ajari Pemchekov. He descended from the Russian Lamaist tradition and Russian Old Believers of Siberia, a unique place where various religious traditions lived side by side in harmony, i.e., Christianity, Buddhism, and Shamism.

Dr. Ajari was a charismatic man of profound religious experience, wisdom, and vision. He sought to plant the seeds of esoteric dharma in the West, reconciling those teachings with people's Christian background. He assimilated and synthesized teachings of Christianity with those of Tibet and Japan through his own spiritual practice. He brought religious students together to live in a community where we could study and pursue religious teachings.

Tibetan teachings are readily available here in the West, as is orthodox Christianity, but Japanese esotericism has rarely been taught. We provide a unique opportunity to study all three. Daily practice consists of meditation, chanting, and liturgical and devotional worship. Meditation and liturgical rites are open to the public.

Two sisters of the order, longtime members of the community, provide leadership and continue to hand down teachings to others. Community members help maintain the residence, feed the homeless, visit the sick, participate in devotional worship, and receive spiritual training.

We are vegetarian and do not allow smoking, alcohol, or drugs on the premises.

We welcome new members to share the joys of spiritual communal life, learning how to love and help others. [Feb99]

ST JOSEPH THE WORKER HOUSE AND FARM

122 Johnson Rd
Foster RI 02825

401-392-1358

Began 1997 | Pop. 3
Diet: Omnivore | Rural | Spiritual

We are a family-based Catholic Worker community who live on a five-acre farm. We use our two spare bedrooms to offer hospitality to those in need, particularly women in crisis pregnancy situations.

We have sheep, goats, chickens, and a very large garden. We donate all our extra food to shelters and soup kitchens.

We pray the Liturgy of the Hours, go to daily mass, and pray the rosary daily.

We welcome volunteers to visit our farm. [Feb99]

ST JUDE CATHOLIC WORKER HOUSE COMMUNITY

317 S Randolph St
PO Box 1612
Champaign IL 61824

217-355-9774

Began 1980 | Pop. 3 | Forming
Urban | Spiritual

St. Jude Catholic Worker House, a house of hospitality for single women and families, has a noon soup kitchen open to anyone in need seven days a week. Live-in volunteer community practices works of mercy by serving the poor by managing the house of hospitality. Weekly roundtable discussion on

---

Key to bracketed text: cc = cannot commit to prompt correspondance, sase = self-addressed stamped envelope

practical aspects of managing the house, application to faith, social justice, etc.

Volunteers other than live-ins coordinate soup kitchen and help with other household tasks. Prefer applicants who have some experience ministering to the poor, one+ year commitment, and a desire to put Gospel values into practice through ministry to the poor. Room and board, small monthly stipend provided. Send inquiries to the address listed. [Sep99]

ST MARTIN DE PORRES CATHOLIC WORKER (CT)

26 Clark St
Hartford CT 06120

860-724-7066
cdoucot@erols.com

Began 1993 | Pop. 6
Diet: Omnivore | Urban | Spiritual

(Also known as Hartford Catholic Worker.) St. Martin's core community is a young couple with two pre–grade-school-age boys and two adult men. There is no boss. Our common work includes: Monday: food co-op; Tuesday: housecleaning; Wednesday: furniture pantry; Thursday: furniture gathering; Saturday: children's work. Ongoing work includes newsletter, peace work, wood gathering for heat, activities with neighborhood children. During the summer we host a summer camp. Much of our time is unstructured. We usually eat dinners together, and we try to pray together each evening. [Sep99]

STARLAND

56925 Yucca Trail #355
Yucca Valley CA 92284

760-364-1029, 760-364-2069
starland69@aol.com
http://www.communityvisions.org/STARLAND/

Began 1997 | Pop. 6 | Forming
Diet: Omnivore | Rural/Urban | Spiritual

Starland is a retreat facility open to spiritual, cultural, recreational, sexual, social, or other groups as a location for gatherings, retreats, or workshops. Our lifestyle is based on erotic spirituality, polysexuality, and polyamory and is clothing optional. We seek individuals who share our vision and want to be involved, as a full- or part-time resident, in the development and operation of Starland.

The complex includes communal meeting and dining spaces; group and individual residence accommodations; a variety of spaces for relaxation and recreation, including a spa and several gardens. There is potential for ample expansion of amenities.

We are located on a beautiful 10-acre promontory with panoramic views and adjacent to hundreds of acres of undeveloped desert, mountain, canyon, and forest areas. Our high-desert location enjoys clean air and mild four-seasons climate. We also have independent houses in the nearby village.

Our umbrella organization, Community Visions, Inc., runs retreats and operates special-interest clubs with members who visit Starland. We would love to hear from anyone who is interested in joining us as well as from members of similar groups. [Sep99, sase requested]

STARSEED COMMUNITY

672 Chapel Rd
Savoy MA 01256

413-743-0417

Began 1987 | Pop. 5 | Forming
Diet: Vegetarian | Rural | Spiritual

Starseed is a healing sanctuary, holistic retreat center, and interfaith spiritual community located in a beautiful, rural, mountain area. Our intention is to nurture a loving self-sufficient community and to maintain a sacred sanctuary and retreat space for people to come for healing and transformation.

Our membership presently consists of our nuclear family residing on the land and supporting members living in surrounding towns. We are calling other kindred spirits to live on the land with us as cocreators of this sacred space.

We are interested in growing organic foods and medicinal herbs, flower gardens, forestry, music, art, woodworking, ecology, alternative structures, all forms of personal and planetary healing, and spiritual development.

Our vision is to have some land in a trust, the main buildings collectively owned or established nonprofit, and some house lots privately owned. We are looking for financial partners as well as active working partners to live on the land with us. We especially welcome healers, gardeners, carpenters, artists, and those with business skills. We see our resident core nucleus as small—8–10 people plus children. We wel-

come all races, nationalities, and ages. [Sep99, cc, sase requested]

STEPPING STONES HOUSING CO-OPERATIVE

154 Stiby Rd
Yeovil BA21 3ER, England
UNITED KINGDOM

+44 0870 733 2538
sasandalex@gn.apc.org
http://www.gn.apc.org/ss/

Began 1997 | Pop. 20 | Forming
Diet: Vegan | Rural

Stepping Stones is a housing cooperative seeking to purchase a small farm in western England or the Welsh borders. Our aim is to provide affordable housing for our members, cooperative employment in a range of small-scale enterprises for the local community, and a safe habitat for wildlife on the land. We see the work of Stepping Stones as part of the wider movement for a just and ecological society. As a member of Radical Routes, we are opposed to hierarchy and committed to equal opportunities. We operate according to international cooperative principles. [Dec98, sase requested, no openings]

STEVENS HOUSE

816 South Forest
Ann Arbor MI 48104

734-996-5980, 734-996-5981

Began 1943 | Pop. 20
Diet: Omnivore | Urban

A.K. Stevens House is primarily for college students, although others are welcome by house vote. Most of our members attend either the University of Michigan, Eastern Michigan University, or Washtenaw Community College. We are situated close to the U of M's central campus.

Amenities include living room; house stereo, CD and tape players; study room; porch swing; piano; fireplace; bike port; and parking for 8–10 cars. We do not have a TV by choice. Instead of watching TV, we hang out on the porch or in the living room, read the *New York Times*, or make beer runs to the local convenience store.

We have 10 women and 10 men, but this can also change by house vote. All house decisions are made by consensus unless we consent otherwise. Visitors and guests are welcome with house approval. Since our

Listings

kitchen is tiny, we eat our dinners at one of the other nearby student housing cooperatives. If you have any questions, please feel free to call or stop by. [Feb99]

STEWART LITTLE CO-OP

211 Stewart Ave
Ithaca NY 14850

607-273-1983
stewart_little@cornell.edu
http://members.xoom.com/stewart_l/

Began 1978 | Pop. 14
Diet: Vegetarian | Urban

We are a cooperative of 14 people aged in our 20s and 30s. Our community consists of people from different ethnic backgrounds and sexual orientations, reflecting the character of this small upstate New York university town. We usually try to maintain an even gender ratio. Our house is an old, somewhat run down, but beautiful Victorian mansion, located on a hill between downtown Ithaca and Cornell University. Many of us have some link with Cornell University as graduate students or workers.

We share all food (vegetarian) and eat together every evening. Dinner is cooked by one member in rotation, and shopping and cleaning are also shared. Each member has a specific responsibility within the house such as accounting, composting, recycling, dealing with membership applications, or managing the kitchen.

The spirit of our community is evident in our energetic conversations and social gatherings. "Stewart Little Cooperative, population 14, a good place to live." [Apr99, cc, sase requested]

STIFTELSEN STJÄRNSUND

Bruksallen 16
S-77071 St Järnsund
SWEDEN

+46-225-80001, +46-225-80301 fax
info@frid.nu
http://frid.nu/

Began 1984
Diet: No red meat | Rural | Spiritual

Stiftelsen Stjärnsund is a center for spiritual development and for bringing a holistic view of life into reality. We who work at the foundation believe that the increasing consciousness of us all will bring new patterns of society, where spiritual values can be integrated with culture and science. Stiftelsen Stjärnsund was founded in 1984, and the initiative to begin was inspired by the Findhorn Foundation in Scotland. The foundation is a nonprofit organization and is completely independent of political and religious organizations. We have no leader, either spiritual or worldly, but all activity occurs in cooperation and through personal responsibility.

Our course center is a large red-painted timber building from the 1890s. There is accommodation for 25 overnight guests. We have two large course rooms, a dining room, a well-equipped kitchen, a library, a meditation room, and a boutique. For those interested in music there is a grand piano.

The foundation also owns five houses, built around 1915, where most of those who work in the foundation live. There are greenhouses and a garden using organic cultivation methods for our own needs. [May99]

STILL WATER SABBATICAL

PO Box 598
Plains MT 59859

406-826-5934
pln5576@montana.com

Began 1994 | Pop. 15
Diet: Omnivore | Rural | Spiritual

We are an unincorporated association, legally structured on a nonprofit, religious basis. Our statement of faith and brochure are available on request. We stress a need for open, healthy, productive discussion and the avoidance of dogma.

During the past eight years we have worked toward developing reliable funding sources; we prefer not to rely on donations and cannot guarantee deductibility. Our facility consists of our homes, a small research library, and a shop located on 40 acres. The site is operated as a homestead.

On-site members, the board, and off-site voting members are required to commit to our statement of faith and the goals and ideals of Sabbatical. We welcome the input, visits, and support of others; our mailing list already includes people in this category.

Our library resources are available by correspondence or visitation. Due to the size of our current staff, please be patient with our response time. Currently, we have limited

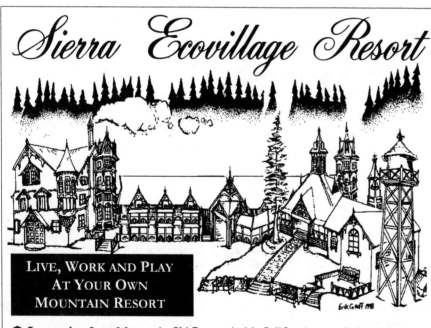
Key to bracketed text: cc = cannot commit to prompt correspondance, sase = self-addressed stamped envelope

lodging and therefore must insist that we be contacted before you visit our area. [Oct99, sase requested]

STONE GRAIL THEATRE COMMUNITY

PO Box 441
Alexander NC 28701
http://www.angelfire.com/
or/stonegrail/

Began 1998 | Forming
Diet: No red meat | Rural | Spiritual

We are a newly founding, vision-based group of artists, artisans, healers, farmers, and teachers, centered around Stone Grail Theatre. We value nonviolence; consensus decision making; a strong desire for personal growth and self-responsibility; respect for each other, for the Earth, and for all life living upon the Earth; beauty and simplicity; the creative imagination; the ability to see the higher self and unique gifts of each individual; and reverence for the creative spirit that speaks to and through each of us. We envision arts and crafts studios, single and multifamily houses, a biodynamic farm, a central mostly vegetarian kitchen, a Waldorf-style school, perhaps an animal sanctuary, and other enterprises. We seek creative, compassionate, courageous individuals of all ages with a strong spiritual center; self-respect and respect for others; and an ability to listen, learn, and grow, wishing to live a highly creative and spiritual life with *other authentic* selves. We are going to look for and buy land in the beautiful Blue Ridge Mountains near Asheville, North Carolina. Look for our new address and more information on the community and the theater on our Web site. Stone Grail Theatre works with mythology and the mysteries. [Aug99, sase requested]

STONE SOUP CO-OP

4637 N Ashland
Chicago IL 60640

773-561-5131

Began 1997 | Pop. 18
Diet: Vegetarian | Urban

Stone Soup is an urban intentional community dedicated to joy and justice. Our members are organizers, teachers, social workers, students, artists, and others doing creative work for social change. We support each other's commitment to social justice with a caring, creative, and fun living environment.

Stone Soup is located in Chicago's uptown neighborhood, in a former church convent that we rent from the Catholic Church. We are not religiously affiliated. Members have outside jobs and pay a flat fee to the co-op each month. Communal dinners are held five nights a week, including a weekly Tuesday potluck that is open to the public (please call ahead). Although we are currently at our membership capacity, we accommodate some short-term visitors who make arrangements in advance. [Sep99, no openings]

STORYBOOK GLEN

PO Box 95
Pettigrew AZ 72752

501-677-2679, 501-677-3070
501-677-2679 fax
scriss8581@aol.com
artcetra@aol.com
http://www.storybookglen.com/

Began 1998 | Pop. 8 | Forming
Diet: No red meat | Rural | Spiritual

A forming community that began as a family and will strive to always be an extended family. Our mission statement is: "To dwell in community as accepting, respecting kindred and to offer a Godly service of hope and encouragement by showing a better way of life."

We live on forested land, garden organically, and homeschool. We intend to beautifully landscape cleared property in flowers and herbs, trails, paths, vistas, and views offering a tranquil harmony and moving visual experience. This will be used in a dried-flower business and as the setting for family getaways, retreats, and youth camps, where team building, cooperative initiatives, activities, craft classes, and seasonal celebrations will take place.

Housing will be alternative type for both community members and guests.

Already much of this is in place, but we are still forming. We are not ready for new members.

We try to walk with the spirit. We believe God is real and to be godly we must be real too. To us *real* translates as our service: recreational exploration of authentic living. [Aug99]

STRANGERS & GUESTS CATHOLIC WORKER COMMUNITY

108 Hillcrest Drive
Maloy IA 50836

Began 1986 | Pop. 4
Diet: Omnivore | Rural | Spiritual

Small community in very rural southwest Iowa in Catholic Worker personalist tradition; 12+ years. Organic garden, dairy goats, ecumenical Scripture study, handweaving rag rugs. Our family has been here since 1986. Other folks have come and joined us for varied length of stay for many reasons. We are glad to welcome visitors/guests and/or apprentices. We find common ground with others in our area. Active in peace issues regionally and try to involve also in local issues and needs, i.e., effects of corporation agriculture. Food buying co-op. Running water. No TV. We try to bring awareness of national and international issues to this area. Simple lifestyle. Working a variety of part-time jobs for cash. [Aug99]

STUDENT HERITAGE HOUSES

2222 Pearl St
Austin TX 78705

512-476-2667, 512-476-5336
512-476-5578 fax
utwc@yahoo.com

Began 1936 | Pop. 196 | Re-Forming
Urban

(Also known as UT Women's Cooperatives.) Student Heritage Houses has been providing affordable student housing since 1936. We feature a democratically controlled home environment, and the benefits of shared economic resources that enable a high comfort level. Our mission is to make housing around the University of Texas campus affordable, thus making education more accessible. [Nov99]

Additions and corrections: Email: directory@ic.org, Web: http://directory.ic.org/, Mail: RR 1 Box 156-D, Rutledge MO 63563, USA.

Listings

STUDENTS COOPERATIVE ASSOCIATION

**1648 Alder
Eugene OR 97401**

**541-683-1112
asuosch@gladstone.uoregon.edu
http://gladstone.uoregon.edu/
~asuosch/sca.html**

Began 1937 | Pop. 60
Diet: Omnivore | Urban

The Students' Cooperative Association is a student-owned and student-operated housing organization in Eugene, Oregon. Our primary purpose is to provide cooperative, affordable housing to college students. We achieve this by buying our food in bulk and cooking our own meals, as well as doing most of the maintenance and all of the general cleaning.

The co-ops strive to foster diversity as well as create a strong sense of community. The members run the houses, so there is no landlord making a profit from your home. This also means the members have the responsibility to keep food on the table and the house in order. [Jan99]

SU CASA CATHOLIC WORKER COMMUNITY

**5045 S Laflin
Chicago IL 60609**

**773-376-9263
danieldlp@aol.com**

Began 1990 | Pop. 11
Diet: Omnivore | Urban | Spiritual

(Also known as Central American Martyrs Center.) Su Casa provides a healing and safe environment for homeless Latino families who need food, shelter, and a link to needed services to prepare them for interdependent living. Through our Sunday soup kitchen, neighborhood garden, playground, and activities, we have grown to know our Hispanic and African-American neighbors and partner with them in making the neighborhood a better place to live.

We engage our public in the social-justice issues related to our work through our bimonthly newsletter, staff presentation, and Plunge Group live-in experiences. Following the Catholic Worker tradition, staff are committed to living a simple, nonviolent lifestyle, living with the poor, and fostering justice in our neighborhood and community. As community members, volunteers are expected to live the Catholic Worker lifestyle, serve as needed, and share themselves spiritually. [Jan99, sase requested]

SUMMIT AVENUE COOPERATIVE

**1820 Summit Ave
Madison WI 53705**

608-238-3441

Began 1970 | Pop. 18
Diet: No red meat | Urban

We are an 18-member, independent, self-sustaining housing cooperative on the near west side of Madison, Wisconsin. The co-op was formed in 1970 when we obtained ownership of a large, three-story house from an agricultural fraternity at the University of Wisconsin–Madison.

The membership has gone through many changes since then, but the goal has always been to provide affordable housing in a friendly, family-like community environment. Our current membership is very diverse (both students and professionals from all walks of life, ranging in age from 20 to 55), and we share no particular political or ideological bent. We all share the duties of running the house (from cooking to cleaning to keeping the books) through a five-hours-per-week work-job system.

The heart of our community life revolves around the delicious, vegetarian-option house meals served Sunday–Thursday at 6 p.m. We make decisions (usually by simple majority) at mandatory house meetings held every 2 1/2 weeks. Ad hoc committees are regularly created to handle specific projects such as financial planning or landscape planning.

What makes us so unique? We're a bunch of quirky, unrelated folks who manage to operate almost like a family and run a clean, friendly *home*. It works! [Mar99, cc]

SUN MEADOWS, INC.

**303 Bannon Creek Rd
Tonasket WA 98855**

509-486-4333

Began 1973 | Pop. 4 | Re-Forming
Diet: No red meat | Rural

Located in the foothills of the Cascade mountains in north-central Washington State, Sun Meadows Farms has the goal of being a self-sufficient community unrestricted by traditional roles.

Sun Meadows was incorporated as a nonprofit in 1974 and currently owns 40 acres of land with three houses. Members are responsible for their own finances, vehicles, and personal belongings. Sun Meadows is sustained by monthly dues in exchange for living in the homes owned and maintained by the corporation.

We have chosen to power our homes with alternative sources: solar, battery, and generated. Our water is pumped from a spring to a holding tank and gravity-fed to the houses. Our rural county has limited professional income opportunities, and the farm has the potential to support agriculturally based cottage industries.

We are open to people of vision who deliberately choose to be part of an intentional community and are capable of living harmoniously with others and tolerant of people's personal philosophies, intent, and personality.

We strive on an individual and community level to be ecologically conservative, realizing we are sustained on a delicately balanced ecosystem. We focus on education and practicing homesteading skills such as carpentry, animal husbandry, organic gardening, food preservation, and mechanics.

Over the past 25 years, Sun Meadows has hosted hundreds of people from all walks of life, each staying from a day to many years. With minimal infrastructure, Sun Meadows is the vision and the action of people who are participating at the given moment. [Nov98, sase requested]

SUNFLOWER COOPERATIVE

**1122 S 3rd St
Austin TX 78704**

Began 1980 | Pop. 7
Diet: Vegetarian | Urban

A small urban community cooperative practicing personal growth, vegetarianism, and conflict resolution through open communication and mediation. We operate by consensus and by shared labor and resources. [Aug99, sase requested]

Key to bracketed text: cc = cannot commit to prompt correspondance, sase = self-addressed stamped envelope

SUNNYSIDE FARM CHRISTIAN COMMUNITY

**9101 Holiness Highway
Mokane MO 65059**

573-676-5609

Began 1992
Diet: Omnivore | Rural | Spiritual

We believe the faithful followers of the Lord Jesus Christ will soon endure a "great tribulation" of 3 1/2 years followed by his glorious Second Coming. We are seeking to unite with other followers in these last days to prepare to meet him. We are endeavoring to restore the pure Christianity practiced by the early church as described in the Holy Bible. "Not forsaking the assembling of ourselves together, as the manner of some is, but exhorting one another: and so much the more, as ye see the day approaching" (Hebrews 10:25). Our understanding of Holy Scriptures is very similar to the United Pentecostal Church International, although we have never had any ties with this organization. Acts 2:38, "Repent and be baptized in the name of the Lord Jesus Christ and ye shall receive the gift of the Holy Ghost," is understood to be God's plan of salvation. Our living quarters are a single 12-bedroom house located in a secluded rural setting surrounded by 500 wooded acres (can't see the smoke from the nearest neighbor's chimney; accessible only by boat during high water). The King James Bible is our rule book. We have no gurus. Marriage or celibacy is required. We eat healthy and kosher. We

maintain political neutrality. We welcome gentle spirits who are not easily offended (Psalm 119:165). [Jan99, sase requested]

SUNRISE FARM COMMUNITY

**W Tree
Victoria 3885
AUSTRALIA**

03-5155-0336, 03-5152-0276

Began 1978 | Pop. 28
Diet: No red meat | Rural

We have just celebrated our twentieth year. We are 22 members with shares in 600 acres of undulating land, a creek through the middle, and many dams. Each has rights to a house site of 5 acres on a 99-year continuum lease plus shares the rest of the land. We are allowing the bush trees to regenerate. We are land for wildlife. We have horses, few sheep, goats, fowl. We have chestnut and fruit orchards, plus each member has own garden.

We run our own food co-op on a honor scheme; try to have the best of food. We are not into drugs or alcohol. Great primary school bus past our door, but it is not good that the secondary school is 140 miles away. We do have homes for sale (plus a share). At any one time only half of our members live on our farm. Each member pays $200 each year into our farm fund account, so cheap beautiful place to live. [Jan99, sase required]

SUNRISE RANCH

**5569 No County Rd 29
Loveland CO 80538**

**970-679-4200, 970-679-4251
http://www.emissaries.org/**

Began 1946 | Pop. 98
Diet: Omnivore | Rural | Spiritual

Sunrise Ranch is a 55-year-old Emissary community located about 10 miles west of Loveland, Colorado, a little over an hour north of Denver. The Emissaries (Also known as Emissaries of Divine Light) are a worldwide spiritual organization dedicated to the spiritual regeneration of humankind. The demonstration of practical spirituality in each aspect of living is one of the Emissaries' main concerns.

Sunrise Ranch has about 100 residents, 85 adults and 15 children. The community has weekly worship services, an elected community council, weekly community meetings, organic gardens and farming operations, and a retreat and conference business handling groups up to 300.

Slightly over half the residents either work outside the community or have their own businesses on the property. Resident employees handle gardening and landscaping, childcare and elder care, property maintenance, administrative functions, and the retreat business. All community members are required to contribute some time to community tasks.

The economic, governmental, and managerial systems are always in a process of

Additions and corrections: Email: directory@ic.org, Web: http://directory.ic.org/, Mail: RR 1 Box 156-D, Rutledge MO 63563, USA.

change and transformation. While external changes have their ebb and flow, there is a firm commitment to our spiritual heritage and a strong, focused intent on the radiant expression of the divine.

Becoming a community member involves several stages ranging from a few days' visit to longer stays. We welcome visitors. We ask that you please call before arriving. Overnight rates are currently $50 per night, $40 double occupancy, meals included. Some work-share arrangements are available from time to time. [Mar99]

SUNWARD COHOUSING

424 Little Lake Dr
Ann Arbor MI 48103

734-214-5560
info@sunward.org
http://www.sunward.org/

Began 1998 | Pop. 85
Diet: Omnivore | Rural/Urban

Sunward Cohousing offers its residents the benefits of a traditional village—a friendly and safe community with a sense of extended family and the opportunity to share resources. Construction of 40 privately owned townhouses and a common house with extensive shared facilities was completed in 1998. Buildings are enhanced by natural lighting and energy-efficient materials. Housing is clustered on a portion of our 20-acre site to enhance human relationships and preserve green space, including woods, ponds, prairie, and gardens.

We are a diverse group of people, but we share a common commitment to the process of developing and maintaining our community, using consensus decision making. Occasional openings via purchase, rental, or home share. [Sep99]

SUNWISE CO-OP

2535 Westerness Dr
Davis CA 95616

530-753-7657

Began 1978 | Pop. 9
Diet: Vegetarian | Urban

We are a large house in an urban setting. We are simply working, studying, and living here. We garden, share many meals, and have weekly meetings. Our house is passive solar; we are environmentally conscientious, buy organic, and don't bring meat into the house. Our focus is on sharing, mutual respect, consensus decision making, and having fun! [Jan99]

SUSAN B. ANTHONY WOMEN'S LAND TRUST (SUBAMUH)

PO Box 5853
Athens OH 45701

740-448-6424, 740-448-7242
ad965@seorf.ohiou.edu
http://www.netins.net/
showcase/kaytsine/subamub.htm

Began 1981 | Pop. 6
Diet: Omnivore | Rural

(Also known as Memorial UnRest Home.) We are a community of five women residents and one child living in three dwellings—feminist, ecologically attuned, politically active. We share 150 acres 10 miles from Athens, Ohio, home of Ohio University (20,000 students) and Hocking Technical College (4,000 students). Inquiries, visitors, and exploring members welcome.

Major decisions are made by consensus of residents and a nine-member board. We seek a balance between individual freedom and the welfare of the community. We have

safe, congenial, inexpensive living space. After a one-year provisional membership, women can build a home, bring a mobile home, convert an outbuilding, or share space. The terrain is rugged—accessibility is problematic.

Susan B. Anthony Women's Land Trust is a nonprofit, tax-exempt women's outdoor education center. We host workshops on topics such as racism, nature and the arts, and practical skills for women. We have a campground for individuals and groups by advance reservation only. We are active in the women's community, which includes a women's center, a monthly newsletter, quarterly coffeehouses, a NOW (National Organization for Women) chapter, a university women's studies program, and a women's chorus. A farmer's market, public radio, worker-owned businesses, and many alternative projects enhance this scenic area in the Appalachian foothills. [Sep99]

SVANHOLM

Svanholm Allé 2
DK-4050 Skibby
DENMARK

47566670, 47566607 fax
http://www.ecovillages.org/
denmark/svanholm/

Began 1978 | Diet: Omnivore | Rural
The Svanholm Community consists of about 70 adults and 40 children aged from 0 to 80. We own an estate with 625 acres of farmland and 408 acres of park and woodlands.

When we bought the property in 1978 we wanted to live in a production collective based on shared work, shared economy, and shared decision making. We wanted *whole* lives, with influence on our work and daily living, and a place where our children would thrive with animals and fresh air. We live in smaller groups in some 12 different houses on and around the old estate, and these are the centers of daily social life.

Most of us work at home in one of the production areas or service areas; some 20 people have jobs outside the community. Our main production is organic farming.

We pool all income in a common fund, and we each receive a monthly allowance for clothes, amusements, etc.

Our decision-making authority is the weekly communal meeting, where we do not vote but discuss our way to agreement.

Working visitors are occasionally welcome (mostly around harvest) but—unfortu-

Sunward Cohousing

Occasional opportunities for home sharing, rental, and purchase

Ann Arbor, MI   www.sunward.org   734.214.5560

Key to bracketed text: cc = cannot commit to prompt correspondance, sase = self-addressed stamped envelope

nately—only if they are European Union citizens. This is because of working-permit regulations. [Mar99]

SWEETWATER COMMUNITY LAND TRUST

**2435 Sweetwater Ln
Mansfield MO 65704**

**417-741-7363, 417-741-6630
jcutler@concentric.net**

Began 1984 | Pop. 19
Diet: Omnivore | Rural

We have 480 acres of rural land; 60 acres is farmable, the rest is hilly/wooded. Land is owned and managed by the trust, which gives 99-year leases for 10-acre home sites. Buildings, tools, vehicles, businesses, etc., are privately owned; individuals and families manage their own finances. We function as a "neighborhood" where members regulate their own community involvement (from totally private to cooperative housing, gardens, businesses, etc.). Sharing and mutual support are common. We manage Sweetwater by informal discussion and consensus and by cooperative arrangements among equals. Our focus is land stewardship and environmental quality, optimizing human well-being and relationships ("sustainable culture"). We are nondiscriminatory. [Nov98, cc, sase required]

SYLVIRON COOPERATIVE

**4771 Rolland Rd
Blanchard MI 49310**

**517-561-5037, 517-561-5193 fax
jwelty@power-net.net**

Began 1995 | Pop. 56 | Forming | Rural
We pattern our community after the one described in the novel *Sylviron* (copy available for $8). We believe in freedom and in neighborliness. We are a cooperative resort and business incubator, with permanent housing. [Sep99]

SYNERGY HOUSE

**Attn: RA or Managing Staff
550 San Juan
Stanford CA 94305**

Began 1972 | Pop. 45 | Re-Forming
Diet: Vegan | Urban

Synergy is a cooperative house at Stanford University. We are officially vegetarian, try

to buy socially responsible products, and make house decisions by consensus. We value community and give lots of hugs.

Many Synners are active in campus activism, working on campaigns for environmental justice, lesbian/gay/bisexual/transgender issues, and other projects. We have a small vegetable garden, keep a house journal, and bake fresh bread nightly. On campus we have a bit of a hippie reputation, and rumors circulate about naked bread baking in our kitchen. True? Come visit!

Residents do weekly clean-and-cook jobs, plus there are quarterly house, bathroom, and kitchen clean crews and a yearly compost duty. Our house is full of creative, high-energy students—lots of art, music, and exploration go on in our beautiful house on the hill. We throw large parties for Halloween, Valentine's Day, and Beltane every year. I think many Synners would agree that the experience of living here is fun, challenging, and teaches us much about ourselves and the environment and community to which we belong. [Jan99, cc, sase requested, no openings]

TACOMA CATHOLIC WORKER

**1417 So G St
Tacoma WA 98405**

253-572-6582

Began 1989 | Pop. 12
Diet: Omnivore | Urban | Spiritual

(Also known as Guadalupe House & Gardens.) The Tacoma Catholic Worker provides transitional housing for single homeless adults. We live with the 5–10 guests we serve. People on the street can take showers, use our bathroom and phone, and get mail. We try to help find shelter, drug-treatment, or mental-health services. We accept no grants or government money; funds are donated.

Spring 1999 will see 9–10 Catholic Workers. Each receives a (tiny) $40/month stipend. The underfunded Washington State health plan may someday cover us too. Staff gather at morning meeting/prayer and occasional retreats. We work on political issues that impact the poor and publish a newsletter noted among Catholic Workers for occasional humor.

Each Tuesday, people of all walks of life share a meal and liturgy in our living room. This is usually Catholic mass-ish, with women or men leading. We make no spiritual requirements on guests.

We helped start a four-acre organic garden on nearby empty lots. A visitor commented that our poor neighborhood feels like a "village." How will gentrification affect it? We are working to sustain our diverse community, starting in our houses and gardens (with many hands and hearts) and growing.

"Women and accordion players get special preference—not a quota, just a goal." [Dec98, cc]

TAIZÉ COMMUNITY

**F-71250 Taizé
FRANCE**

**(0033) 385 50 30 30
(0033) 385 50 30 02
(0033) 385 50 30 15 fax
community@taize.fr
meetings@taize.fr
http://www.taize.fr/**

Began 1940 | Rural | Spiritual
The Taizé Community is an ecumenical Christian monastic community based in the small village of Taizé in eastern France. A hundred brothers from over 25 different countries bring together the gifts of the Roman Catholic, Anglican, Lutheran, and Reformed traditions to live a sign of reconciliation among Christians and in the entire human family in what they describe as a "parable of community." The community is self-supporting, living by the work of its members. For over 30 years now tens of thousands of visitors, mainly young adults between 18 and 30, have been coming to Taizé annually to share the life of the community for a week of worship, Bible study, work, and discussion. The songs of Taizé and its meditative yet simple prayer style have inspired churches throughout the world. The community has no wish to create a movement centered on itself but instead encourages people to return to their local situations to be creators of trust and reconciliation there. [Mar99]

TAKOMA VILLAGE COHOUSING

**c/o Eco Housing Corp
7768 Woodmont Ave Suite 200
Bethesda MD 20814**

**301-654-0058
zabaldo@earthlink.net
http://www.home.earthlink.net/
~takomavillag/**

Began 2000 | Pop. 46 | Forming
Diet: Omnivore | Urban

Takoma Village is the first urban cohousing community in the greater metro Washington, DC, area. It's the first urban project in the mid-Atlantic states and one of only three on the eastern seaboard. Forty-three units plus the common house. One and a half blocks from mass transit. We are using many energy-efficient systems, green tech, and green materials. We have nine units left and are excited about the possibility of having more families among our membership.

Although we are fully subscribed, households do move from time to time. If you are interested in living in our community, please call us about our waiting list. We are always delighted to meet new friends. [Oct99]

TALKING CEDARS

**Box 372
Tofino BC V0R 2Z0
CANADA**

**250-726-8330, 250-753-5767
kadesh@bc.sympatico.ca
gdauncey@islandnet.com
http://www.earthfuture.com/tofino/**

Forming | Rural/Urban | Spiritual
(Also known as Crow Circle Collective.) Talking Cedars is an ecovillage that is being planned in 17 acres of old-growth forest, two miles south of Tofino, close to the Pacific Ocean on the west coast of Vancouver Island, Canada. Coho salmon spawn in a protected creek in the forest.

Since 1988, young people from around the world have camped on the property. A development plan is now being created to create a cohousing-style ecovillage for 100 people (48 units of housing), combined with a retreat center, allowing the residents to offer year-round workshops and retreats. We hope construction will begin in 2000, with occupancy beginning in the fall. Prices will probably range from $130,000 to $250,000 Canadian.

Tofino is surrounded by the beauty of Clayoquot Sound, a place of incomparable forest and ocean beauty, visited by many people who come in search of peace, nature, and tranquility. The ecovillage will be a clustered pedestrian community with passive-solar houses built from environmentally sound materials.

The project is being designed by a team that does not include future residents, so this is an unusual situation where the future residents will have a wide-open canvas to define the nature of the community and its activities. [Aug99, sase required]

TAMERA - CENTER FOR HUMANE ECOLOGY

**Monte do Cerro
P-7630 Colos
PORTUGAL**

**+351-283-635306
+351-283-635374 fax
tamera@mail.telepac.pt
http://www.ecovillages.org/
portugal/tamera/**

Began 1995
Diet: Vegetarian | Rural | Spiritual

Tamera is a project for a future worth living. The project sees itself as a base for global peace work. The research work deals with new ways of healing humans and nature. The aim is to develop a cultural model of a nonviolent lifestyle for a couple of hundred people and the implementation of a "healing biotope." A "healing biotope" is a life community of people, animals, and plants whose life forces complement each other and are no longer blocked by each other through violence and fear. Between people the character of Tamera is guided honesty in relationships, truth in love, and transparency in the community and above all taking on one's own responsibility and thus steering free of leadership cults. Currently 30 staff members live and work at Tamera, but during each summer there are many guests who like to help building up the project. A youth project and the "youth school for global learning" are just starting. New ideas for professions and new commitments in political and humanitarian fields can be found here and on travels to other continents and cultures. Tamera is looking for support and cooperation with other committed peace workers and future-orientated communities. Our main "meeting point" for contact and

network is the annual summer camp. [Oct99]

TANGUY HOMESTEADS

**c/o June Doxtad
19 Twin Pine Way
Glen Mills PA 19342**

**610-399-0931, 610-399-6724
giftbags@erols.com**

Began 1945 | Pop. 93 | Rural

(Also known as Fellowship Cooperative Homesteads.) Tanguy Homesteads began in 1945 when six families bought a 100-acre farm for low-cost housing, cooperatively owned, open to all races and religions. We now have 38 families, varying in race, political perspective, religion, and job skills. Each member family owns a home on 2 acres, plus shares in Tanguy and the community center, ballfield, pond, and woods.

Tanguy is guided by a set of bylaws, but change is a source of constant renewal. Each resident adult is expected to attend our monthly membership meetings and serve on at least one committee, where most work is done. Committees include Activities, Community Building, Land, Pond, Finance, Homestead, New Members, Publications, and Tractor. Members elect new officers and the board of directors each year.

In the monthly meetings we make decisions as a community. No votes are taken ordinarily; decisions are reached through "substantial agreement." Workdays are important in getting many projects completed. Celebrations, holidays, an annual camping trip, ball games, fishing contests, singing, dances, and weekly potlucks all contribute to our community spirit.

We have a monthly assessment ($40), used to maintain road, building, and pond; to pay taxes and insurance; and to support activities. Prospective members are encouraged to attend meetings and community events to learn about Tanguy. [Jan99, sase requested]

TAOWORKS VILLAGE

**920-208-7874
taoworks@taoworks.org
http://www.taoworks.org/**

Began 1996
Diet: Omnivore | Spiritual

TaoWorks Village is an Internet Taoist community. The Web server is our real estate,

Key to bracketed text: *cc = cannot commit to prompt correspondance, sase = self-addressed stamped envelope*

and hypertext links our roads. Businesses and individuals reside in our community by having their Web pages hosted at our Web site. For those residents with their own home page or Web site hosted someplace else, we create a page in our village and link it to their main Web site.

We provide public services such as a library, newspaper, and town hall to keep the village running smoothly, and we promote the Taoist philosophy in daily life. One of our projects is a mailing list called the daily verse. It is e-mailed daily and provides residents and others with a bit of inspirational philosophy taken from Taoist and many other sources. Please visit our peaceful and friendly village often, as new residents and services are constantly being added. [Oct99, cc]

TEKIAH COMMUNITY

439 Valley Dr NW
Floyd VA 24091

540-745-5835
tekiah@hemphammocks.com
http://www.thefec.org/
   brochure/tekiah.htm
http://www.hemphammocks.com/

Began 1991 | Pop. 3 | Re-Forming
Diet: Omnivore | Rural

(Also known as Institute for Sustainable Living.) Tekiah Community is a small income-sharing group within the broader base of Abundant Dawn Community.

Some of our core values include clear and ongoing communication; ecological responsibility; growing organic food; consensus process; emotional as well as physical/economic connections of respect and trust; and being of service to self, life, and others.

As we get settled on Abundant Dawn Land (90 acres in the bend of a river near Floyd, Virginia), we are developing a land plan, establishing garden spaces, building structures, and much, much more.

We are also nurturing our new cottage industry— producing hemp hammocks and hemp bags. Other work we do includes agricultural research and working at a local CSA (community-supported agriculture) farm.

We are looking for others who want to share their lives with us. Because we value each new member finding income-producing work that has heart for them, we require they support themselves during the provisional membership period. This can be accomplished by a financial contribution or

a commitment of work in a Tekiah business. [Sep99, cc, sase requested, email preferred]

TEN STONES COMMUNITY

802-425-4937
Edorah@aol.com

Began 1994 | Pop. 44
Diet: No red meat | Rural

Ten Stones is an intentional community designed, organized, and developed by its 13 member families. It embraces 88 acres of woodland, meadow, and agricultural land and 13 clustered, privately owned, half-acre homesites. We have no common creed other than a desire to live cooperatively, ecologically, and economically. Our community features a constructed wetland for wastewater treatment, five straw-bale homes, and an organic subscription garden (CSA). We are currently designing a common house in which we will eat, celebrate, meditate, and work together. We enjoy sharing resources, caring for each other's children, and designing rituals to mark important events in our lives. Our community also enjoys assisting others—individuals, study groups, and other intentional communities—in learning to build community for themselves. Ten Stones is full and while we are happy to give tours and share information, we cannot accommodate long-term visitors. [Nov98, cc, sase required, no openings]

TERAMO TEXAS

Box 542205
Houston TX 77254

512-455-3668, 713-691-4340
mail@teramotexas.com
http://www.teramotexas.com/

Began Jan99 | Pop. 17 | Forming
Diet: No red meat | Rural/Urban

Might as well have a grand vision, so ours is to build a new city and have fun doing it.

Our goal is to create the most pleasant, least expensive place to live but with a real futuristic layout.

It would be perfect for the mobility challenged.

See our Web site. [Jan99]

TERRA NOVA COMMUNITY

1404 Gary St
Columbia MO 65203

573-443-5253
terranovacommunity@juno.com

Began 1995 | Pop. 4
Diet: Omnivore | Urban

We're a close-knit group of friends whose vision includes surrounding ourselves with even more friends, either in our own household or in houses that border our 1.5 acres. As these come up for sale, we hope people with similar values will buy them. In the common green space, we've planted fruit and nut trees and are slowly developing a wooded area, a wildflower meadow, and a large garden with part set aside for use by others. Our location in town makes it easy to walk, bike, or bus, minimizing our auto use.

Our household (five or six people) is a mix of income sharers and expense sharers living in two small houses. We emphasize urban sustainability, lower-impact consumption, communication, and working through personal differences. We come together daily for the evening meal and twice weekly for meetings. Important decisions are made by consensus. We value learning about ourselves and each other and are creating deep friendships. Neighboring households that associate with us would be compatible but have their own personalities.

Our wider circle of friends includes a collective and a budding cohousing group. Columbia itself has a lot to offer, with two colleges and a university and the attendant theater, concerts, and lectures. There are active groups working for peace, justice, the environment, and gay issues. A farmers' market is close by. Please contact us for more information or to arrange a visit. [Sep99, sase requested]

THREE SPRINGS COMMUNITY LAND TRUST

59820 Italian Bar Rd
North Fork CA 93643
farm@sierratel.com

Began 1996 | Pop. 7
Diet: Vegetarian | Rural

Three Springs is an environmentally oriented, consensus-based community founded in 1993. We presently have 7 members with plans for 12–14 adults. Our primary focus is to share our land and strive to create healthy relationships with each other and all living things around us. We are excited about the communities movement and what it can do in a positive way for people and the Earth. As we gain experience, we hope to share information and resources to help others.

We are located in the foothills of the Sierra Nevadas, 45 miles northeast of Fresno and 30 miles southeast of Yosemite National Park. Our 160 acres is an idyllic, peaceful, rural setting with a diversity of native plants and animals. A year-round creek with waterfalls, swimming holes, and rock formations runs through our land, and thousands of acres of national forest are adjacent to us. We have recently created Three Springs Community Land Trust to protect our land and share common ownership. We also plan to put a conservation easement on the property with environmental guidelines and zoned areas for community living.

We currently have a community-supported agriculture (CSA) garden project and plans for other cottage enterprises and a nonprofit educational organization. We believe in living lightly on the land, which we define as sustenance (growing and harvesting much of our own food), shelter (working with environmentally oriented architecture), social and spiritual (developing and nurturing healthy relationships). Please feel free to write. [Sep99, sase requested]

TIBETAN BUDDHIST LEARNING CENTER

93 Angen Rd
Washington NJ 07882

908-689-6080

Began 1958

(Also known as Lamaist Buddhist Monastery of America.) The Tibetan Buddhist Learning Center (TBLC), Labsum Shedrub Ling, was founded through the great efforts of Geshe Wangyal, a Kalmyk-Mongolian lama who received his Buddhist training in Kalmykia and in Tibet. The center was founded in 1958. Over the years, Geshe-la took on Western students who had developed an interest in learning about Tibetan Buddhism. Before Geshe-la passed away on January 30, 1983, he appointed Joshua W. C. Cutler as director of the activities of the center. In the following year, His Holiness the Fourteenth Dalai Lama of Tibet, always revered by Geshe-la as the spiritual head of the center, advised that the English name be

changed to the Tibetan Buddhist Learning Center to clearly reflect that its main activity is teaching Tibetan Buddhism.

In summer, winter, and spring, TBLC gives weekend seminars intended as intensive instructions on specific topics for beginners and advanced students alike. Our primary aim: to develop a Buddhism that is culturally American and, at its heart, not different from the Buddhism that traveled from India through Tibet to TBLC's Tibetan monk-scholars and students in the United States.

TBLC also has a limited number of resident students who study Tibetan language and Buddhist philosophy for extended periods of time. Living in this Buddhist contemplative community gives them a unique opportunity to apply the Buddhist teachings in a practical way. [Aug99]

TOLSTOY FARM

32320 Mill Canyon Rd N
Davenport WA 99122
bright@famrc.org

Began 1963 | Pop. 48
Diet: Omnivore | Rural

(Also known as Mill Canyon Benevolent Society.) We are a decentralized rural community sharing 240 acres of canyon land in eastern Washington. The two main parcels are nonprofit corporations with dweller-owned homes, some on and some off the grid. Five adjoining parcels are owned by alumni.

We are 50 people whose lifestyles and interests are varied, from seasonal laborers and weekenders to rural commuters to primitivists who rarely leave the canyon; from high-tech to no-tech; from carnies to vegans.

Our differing pursuits include growing organic food to eat and sell, self-sufficiency, potlucks, carpentry, quilting, computers, cooking, massage, herbs, mycology, art, seed saving, nature loving, volleyball, brewing, crafts, parenting, flowers, orchards, reading, relaxing, rebellion, rituals, music, and compost.

Farm-grown veggies sell in Spokane and through community-supported agricultures (CSAs). A limited number of apprenticeships are available yearly. Occasional openings occur when a member sells. Buyers must be approved through consensus meetings. We have one general meeting a year and weekly potlucks. We associate and/or dissociate with each other freely. In reference to our

typical shortcomings, one member notes, "We are a microcosm of the outside world." Those wishing information should write or e-mail and inspire us to respond. [Feb99, cc, sase requested, no openings]

TOMORROW'S BREAD TODAY

301 E 26th
Houston TX 77008

281-481-1496
Don@tbt.org
http://www.tbt.org/

Began 1998 | Pop. 8 | Forming
Diet: Omnivore | Rural/Urban | Spiritual

(Also known as The Order of Love, Peace, Truth, Tolerance, and Cooperation.) We have been given the opportunity and the means to help people live their lives more abundantly through sharing their works, their goods, their suffering, and their loves. We want to humbly follow our bliss and change the world so that sorrow is replaced by joy. We think that many others have done this and are doing this better than we can do it. We like what Dorothy Day said and did, and we like what the Bruderhof Communities say and do. Reading about them and watching their efforts help us do our work. [Jan99]

TONANTZIN LAND INSTITUTE

Jorge Garcia
Program Director
PO Box 7889 Old Town Station
Alburquerque NM 87194

505-277-5465, 505-277-0804
505-277-2986 fax
tonantzi@unm.edu
atila@unm.edu
http://www.tonantzin.org/

Began 1982 | Rural | Spiritual

Nuestra comunidad esta basada en una zona semi-urbana con grandes conexiones con areas rurales. Nos unen ceremonias y compromisos comunales que definen de cada uno de los componenetes. Los que la componemos, en su mayoria, somos indigenas de varias etnias. Tenemos Xichanos, Dines, Apaches, Mexicanos indigenas, y miembros de otras tribus norte americanas. Nuestra vision se centra en el bien comunal. A la par con Tonantzin Land Institute, trabajamos en programas que esperamos estipulen un crecimiento economico el cual nos lleve a tener una control sobre lo que hacemos.

Key to bracketed text: cc = cannot commit to prompt correspondance, sase = self-addressed stamped envelope

Our community is in a semiurban zone with great connections to rural areas. We have community ceremonies and commitments originated by individual members. Our membership is made up of several indigenous ethnic groups. We have Chicanos, Dines, Apaches, Mexican Indians, and members of other North American tribes. Our vision is centered in the community good. Along with the Tonantzin Land Institute we work in programs that allow local control and stimulate economic growth so as to have greater control of what we do. [Jul99]

TORIC

PO Box 93-5055
Margate FL 33093
954-772-8970

Began 1992 | Pop. 3 | Forming | Urban
We believe in independence fostered by the security we have through trusting, caring, and sharing with each other.

TORIC is an acronym for Trust Openness Respect Interdependence Commitment.

We live the TORIC ideals. [Nov98, sase requested]

TORONTO CATHOLIC WORKER

5 Close Ave
Toronto Ontario M6K 2V2
CANADA
416-516-8198

Began 1990 | Pop. 18
Diet: Omnivore | Urban | Spiritual

We are a 9-year-old community located in the west end of Toronto. We live in seven adjoining households (some houses, some apartments) with a total of about 30 people, aged 2–60+. Two houses are large "houses of hospitality" where people who need a supportive home, often temporarily, live with people who have made a long-term full-time commitment to the community. The other five households are smaller, and most people in them are doing various kinds of studies or work—some of them also offer hospitality on a smaller scale.

The 60-year-old Catholic Worker tradition in which we try to live, and believe we can best live out in community, is one of prayer, hospitality, simplicity, nonviolent resistance to oppression, and clarification of thought. Our collective activities include

weekly worship, gardening, publication of a paper, protest, lots of formal and informal discussions, coffeehouses, and retreats. We also support each other in our individual pursuits and struggles.

Our common liturgy is Christian, but our individual beliefs are diverse. Gays and lesbians are integral to our community. We are exploring farming. We welcome visitors (please call if overnight), inquiries, or mustard-seed requests. [Feb99]

TOWN HEAD COLLECTIVE (THC)

Townhead Cottages
Dunford Bridge
Sheffield S36 4TG, England
UNITED KINGDOM

Began 1994 | Diet: Vegetarian | Rural

Our community consists of a group of people committed to environmental sustainability, anarchy, and dogs. We have found a base in some abandoned buildings, the sad relics of a failed housing co-op. All our electricity is generated from the wind, sun, and water: we compost our shit and reclaim building materials and food.

Our structure consists of friends, getting on with things, and liking each other. We are not open to new members, as we believe that if you want to live in a community you should seek out like-minded people and set up your own. Squat the lot. [Feb99, no openings]

TRES PLACITAS DEL RIO

1706/1710 W Alameda
Santa Fe NM 87501
505-820-7458, 505-820-2499

Began 1996 | Pop. 16 | Forming
Diet: Omnivore | Rural/Urban

Tres Placitas Del Rio is a small-scale cohousing community. We live in an urban neighborhood with a rural feel along a tree-lined river. As of 1/99 we are 11 adults and 5 children in five households ages 0–87. A maximum of 11 houses plus community structures is anticipated on 2.5 acres around a large open space. Pattern language, permaculture, and each member's uniqueness shape and enrich our community. Homes are owner designed and sometimes owner built. We love children, animals, gardens, and creativity. An attitude of resource consciousness and land stewardship is fostered.

We operate by consensus and are striving to find the balance between community life and personal freedom. Our relationships are based on mutual respect between committed, caring, creative, and responsible individuals of all ages. We tend to engage actively in the social and political issues of our larger community and the planet. We are (extra)ordinary people from varied backgrounds living life in community without pretense. Tres Placitas is a strong base for a healthy life—a place to settle in and call it home. [Jan99, sase required]

TRIBE, THE

PO Box 845
Paulden AZ 86334
tribe@lankaster.com

Began 1993 | Pop. 13
Diet: No red meat | Rural | Spiritual

With spring we are regenerated and made new, returning to our small core. Still embracing big ideas, still structuring our life beneath the model of our ideal society. We strongly believe in grand changes ahead and in nonviolent, nonjudging, positive thoughts. The spirit and science of the cosmic dance mold our perceptions. Ideas in harmony with the symbols of our current age insure us. This is our call to the few who will live and cocreate changes with us; we feel your presence on the horizon, growing closer with each day. Room here for a yurt, an RV, and/or a small cob house or two. Children to companion with ours are ideal but, please, no public schooling. [Nov98, sase requested]

TRILLIUM COMMUNITY LAND TRUST

PO Box 1330
Jacksonville OR 97530
trillium@mind.net

Began 1976 | Pop. 2 | Re-Forming
Rural | Spiritual

We are an intentional community ecovillage hosting an educational, cultural, spiritual, arts, and retreat center deep in the Siskiyou Mountains of southwest Oregon. [Sep99]

Additions and corrections: Email: directory@ic.org, Web: http://directory.ic.org/, Mail: RR 1 Box 156-D, Rutledge MO 63563, USA.

TROUBADOUR MÄRCHENZENTRUM

Bretthorst Str 140
D-32602 Vlotho
GERMANY

05733-10801, 05733-180873 fax

Began 1983 | Forming
Diet: VegetarianSpiritual

One year full of new experiences at Troubadour. Who is this for? For professional people who wish to create a new life for themselves. For young people who wish to orient themselves in the world of work.

The Märchenzentrum ("fairy-tale center") Troubadour is offering its knowledge and ability to people who wish to actively participate for one year in a group-living and group-working community. For all of 12 years now, Troubadour has realized its extraordinary goal of giving a social, cultural, and therapeutic impulse while being economically independent of subsidies. Troubadour is now offering a 1-year work experience for all those interested in gaining life-oriented and sound experiences.

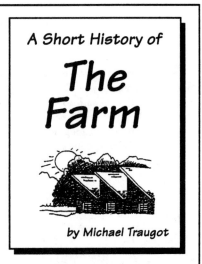

In the technical area: working with computers (Apple Macintosh), layout of journals, word processing, printing, mail order, production of a magazine, organization, advertisement, handicrafts, and garden work.

In the social area: living in a community with children.

In the therapeutic area: getting to know the Lichttaetigkeit ("light work") and the inner path through the seven Ur-Märchenstufen ("ancient steps of fairy tales").

Conditions: During the first month we will get to know each other. The guest pays 17 German marks per day for food and accommodation. During the second and third trial months, food and accommodation are free for the guest.

Interested? Then call us. Troubadour Märchenzentrum Inc. (Karlheinz Schudt). [Sep99]

TRUTH CONSCIOUSNESS SACRED MOUNTAIN ASHRAM

Sacred Mountain Ashram
10668 Gold Hill Rd
Boulder CO 80302

Desert Ashram
3403 W Sweetwater Dr
Tucson AZ 85745

303-447-1637/459-3538
520-743-0384

Began 1974
Diet: Vegetarian | Rural | Spiritual

(Also known as Desert Ashram.) Founded in 1974 by Prabhushri Swami Amar Jyoti, Truth Consciousness maintains ashrams and centers for sadhaks (seekers) devoted to spiritual awakening. The centers are universal and nondenominational, providing a setting for disciples and devotees to grow spiritually under the direct guidance of the master. Some reside at the ashrams, while others live in the mainstream community.

The major program is biweekly satsang (literally, communion with Truth) by Prabhushri Swamiji, which is open to all seekers. Satsang is preceded by chanting and followed by silent meditation. Other programs include aarati (worship), meditation, retreats, karma yoga (voluntary service), and study. Every facet of life is seen as part of spiritual practice.

Truth Consciousness publishes books and audio discourses by the master, chanting tapes, and a thrice-yearly spiritual journal,

Light of Consciousness. While there is no fee for any programs other than retreats, donations are always welcome. Truth Consciousness is a nonprofit, tax-exempt organization. Inquiries may be directed to either ashram. [Jan99, sase requested]

TUI LAND TRUST

RD 1 Wainui Bay
Takaka
NEW ZEALAND

03 525 9654
kayawayne@goldenbay.net.co.nz

Began 1983 | Pop. 47
Diet: Vegetarian | Rural

The Tui Community is situated in Wainui Bay, adjacent to Abel Tasman National Park in Golden Bay, Aotearoa, New Zealand. The primary objective of the community is to live close to the land and to create an environment supportive of families and personal growth. We promote growth and education in many areas, including healing, counseling, and permaculture. As a community living together, we are seeking wholeness through fulfilling relationships with ourselves, others, and the planet. We have no specific common religious or political creed or spiritual leader. Our teachers are all around and within us. Children are regarded as communal as well as parental responsibility. Our group has had long-term involvement with human potential and communication development. We come together for our daily lunch; our weekly business meetings; and for such events as meditations, sharings, for creative expression, healing, and personal growth, celebrations, working bees, and "Tukis" (a way of deep and open communication adopted and adapted from the Maori culture). We welcome visitors who are genuine in their interest to participate in community life. [Nov99]

TULLSTUGAN KOLLEKTIVHUS

c/o Ann Mari Engel
Dorjgrand 4
S-116 68 Stockholm
SWEDEN

+46-8-6423233, +46-8-6423233 fax
annmari.engel@iti.a.se
ann-mari.engel@pol.stockholm.se

Began 1993 | Diet: Omnivore | Urban
The Tullstugan unit is based on the Swedish "self-work model" of collective housing (as

distinct from the classical collective-housing unit, which was based on services through employed staff). This means that cooking in the central kitchen is compulsory and a pre-condition for getting an apartment in the unit. The two main ideas are to provide for a basic sense of community and to facilitate everyday life by collectivizing at least some evening meals a week. The most frequent Swedish model is based on a municipal-housing company initiating a building project and then inviting interested people to move in after application. Apartments are thus rented to people who do not know each other in advance. New applicants can be rejected (by the community) only on the basis of not appearing to be serious about compulsory work and not fitting into the desired family structure (usually a desire for mixture of households). This means that no ownership rights have to be paid and that collective housing is accessible also to low-income people (although in our unit the rents are fairly high). In the Swedish context, cooperative ownership takes the form of condominiums, which means that apartments can be sold at market prices, which in turn has proved to be detrimental to the community. [May99]

TURTLEDOVE POND

9274 Whippoorwill Trail
Jupiter FL 33478

561-746-5624 fax
turtledovepond@webtv.net

Forming | Rural | Spiritual

Turtledove Pond Co-op Community forming for spiritually sensitive, vegetarian healing artists, singers, dancers, and musicians to work and play creatively, meditatively, harmoniously together on 2 1/2 sacred acres of blissfully serene and secluded tropical-rain-forest paradise/wildlife sanctuary in Jupiter, Florida. One overriding goal: to be in a state of inner peace always in the here and now, sharing fun and the fruits of our loving labor with the world community through high-quality published books, audio- and video-tapes, concerts, workshops, and retreats.

We especially welcome high-spirited, conscious, audio-video maestros and positive people of all ages to coproduce original, inspirational, intergenerational, interfaith musicals.

No cigarettes, addicts, cults, or negatory scenarios, please.

Fax resume and brief statement of personal/artistic goals. [Aug99, sase requested]

TURTLES ISLAND

Box 394
Hicks Hill Rd
Stanfordville NY 12581

518-398-1388, 518-398-1337

Began 1964 | Pop. 6 | Re-Forming
Rural/Urban

We are a "1960s" community, re-forming as an ecobuilding, housing community. Members solicited. We are located in a mountainous part of the Hudson Valley on 72 acres unsuited for agriculture but suitable for gardening.

We offer primitive housing, and we have sites available for your building.

In return we request that new members care passionately about some ecological project and that you (they) translate that caring into action while you live here.

Weekly meetings by consensus. Daily meals in common. Simple living encouraged. [Jan99, cc, sase requested]

TWELVE TRIBES (NETWORK)

888-893-5838
http://www.twelvetribes.com/

Began 1972 | Diet: Omnivore | Spiritual

The Twelve Tribes of Israel.

We are a tribal people. The folk that you will meet in the communities listed below are part of a tribespeople. Our life is expressed through living together in community. We love working with each other on our farms and in our cottage industries; doing folk dances and playing music; building; teaching our children at home; and caring for one another. Our desire is to live as naturally as possible by being close to Creation and to people. Our vision: not a lifestyle, but the forming of a *new* nation—the twelve-tribed nation of Israel. We want to be restored back to what we were created to be.

Tribe actually means groups of families who live together in clans, united through a common ancestor. We believe in the God of Israel and follow in the steps of a man who had faith, who burned with a passion for something more than what he saw existing in the world around him. He walked away from the confined, leveled mentality of the society in which he lived, in the hope of

finding a new beginning. He looked forward to the start of a new nation of people who were connected to their Creator and to one another. His name was Abraham. Most people know him as the founder of the nation of Israel. If you were to read the Bible you would discover that the entire book speaks continually about *tribes*. The God of Abraham has always had a desire to be accurately represented by a united, tribal people who express His very character and nature to the world. Through their oneness of heart and purpose, this tribal nation would prove His existence, manifesting the love and unity of a people connected to Him.

As the stars of the sky, and as the sand which is on the seashore, God promised to multiply his seed and make a great nation out of him (Genesis 22:16-18). Our Creator was faithful. Abraham fathered Isaac, and from Isaac came a son named Jacob (whose name was later changed to *Israel*). From Jacob came 12 sons who became the tribes that housed the descendants of Abraham. Thus Abraham found the *new beginning* he longed for—the twelve-tribed nation of Israel.

Each tribe was made up of clans and each clan was made up of families. Those families were made up of husbands and wives who desired to rule over their households and raise their children in the way of their God. The tribal life that grew out of these families was the *corporate life* that our Creator desired for man to have from the very beginning. He wanted a people who would be joined together for a common purpose, who would live at peace with one another, and in absolute unity.

However, this unity and peace didn't last long. Like every other nation that has been on this Earth, it ended up broken and divided. Thousands of years after God had spoken to Abraham, another man walked the earth with the same heart and desire as Abraham. He, too, longed for that twelve-tribed nation to fulfill all that it was meant to. His name was Yahshua, the Messiah. You might have heard of Him as *Jesus*, but we call Him by His Hebrew name. His name means *Yahweh's Salvation*. He had the power to save men from their sins and to remedy the very things that caused them to be separated and divided from one another. He spoke a clear message as He walked the Earth. This message called people out of the *evil* society they were a part of, compelling them to leave their *old* life and sins behind them, and to become part of a whole *new* social order within community. Yahshua saw

Additions and corrections: Email: directory@ic.org, Web: http://directory.ic.org/, Mail: RR 1 Box 156-D, Rutledge MO 63563, USA.

that *natural* Israel was not fit to represent God to the world, nor could they maintain unity among themselves. He recognized the need for a *spiritual* twelve-tribed Israel to emerge.

He spoke the same message to all men because He knew in the heart of every person there was *common ground.* No matter what religion you are a part of, what country or social class or period of history you live in, or whether you are a man, a woman, or a child, the common ground among us all is *the conscience.* Our Creator gave everyone a conscience, the instinctive knowledge of right and wrong. In that knowledge we know that a loving Creator *does* exist and that we owe our very life to Him. We understand that there is an inward law that governs our behavior. This inner law is meant to be an expression of everything that is good. It is meant to be immovable and unchanging like the stars of the heavens in order to *keep us on course.* The more a person silences that voice within him, the more evil he becomes and the more guilt he accumulates. No matter how you try to cover it all up—therapy courses, philosophies, and positive affirmations—nothing really erases the guilt. You end up deceiving yourself into thinking you're a good person, especially when you compare your life to others' lives which seem more evil than yours. Yet, deep down inside, your conscience knows everything you've ever done (no matter what you do to try to hide it). Religions and philosophies can mask it over or put a nice veneer on it, but the grass roots reality is: your guilt remains.

The faith we live by has caused us to leave everything behind—our possessions, our ambitions, our relationships, yes, even our own lives—in order to follow Yahshua and participate in the forming of this new nation. Those who are a part of this new society have given up their self-satisfied, self-seeking pursuits and have entered into a tribal life of caring for others, sharing what they have, and loving one another more than they love themselves. Ahh...true freedom!

Can you picture how life would be if we all had this kind of love? We would all care for each other and truly appreciate one another deeply. There would be no wars or violence to plague mankind ever again. We would all live in peace and harmony and this would only be the beginning. Your imagination can fill in the rest. For those of us already gathered, we no longer need to just

imagine. We listened to the voice of hope and saw the condition of our dirty conscience. We saw our need for *forgiveness.* Now we stand together with others who saw their same need and as a people we are experiencing the reality of what we once only dreamed of. It's the new land where people from every nation—the rich and poor, male and female—can live together in complete peace and trust for one another. Yahshua called this life we have in common *the light of the world.* It is the witness of His kingdom. It stands in bold contrast to the darkness of the world's societies.

We are so thankful that we can share with you the longing of our Creator's heart: a nation of twelve tribes living together in unity. He is the Creator of the universe, the same One who created the radiance of the sun and the wing of a butterfly, who washed the sky blue and put music in the heart of a bird, the One who gave us the freedom to be in love with one another and live in unity…Who would have thought that this God was the God of Tribes? [Feb99]

TWELVE TRIBES COMMUNAUTÉ DE SUS

F-64190 Sus-Navarenx
FRANCE

33 05 59 66 14 28
33 05 59 66 20 34 fax

Began 1983 | Pop. 116
Diet: Omnivore | Rural | Spiritual

Near the southern border of France, in view of the Pyrenees Mountains, is the small village of Sus. Here, you may often see flocks of sheep with their shepherds, but since 1983 there is also a flock of a different kind … Yes, here in Sus dwells a flock of 140 people from many backgrounds and nations who have been gathered together in the hope of demonstrating the life of love and peace that the Son of God came to establish on Earth. No longer lonely and alienated from one another in this society that holds up independence and materialism as its supreme god, this little flock has become a tribe who works at different crafts and lives a simple life together, sharing all things in common just like the first disciples of Yahshua. Our community is made up of families with many children and single people who are living in two big houses on the same property. We earn our living making shoes, clothing, furniture and selling them at different markets and fairs in the whole of

France. But besides running our businesses, our everyday life contains much activity: cooking, shopping, cleaning, and fixing houses and vehicles. However, all that would be in vain if our children would not take on our hearts and follow in our footsteps. Indeed, we take to heart what God wanted for Abraham when he commanded Abraham to teach his children in the way of Yahweh. Therefore, the parents teach their own children with the help of some friends who are gifted as teachers. They work together and help each other to raise children who will do what is right and just. We also do our best to include our children in our daily social life.

We are open to hearing from you by phone or letter, and we also invite people to come visit us. Our doors and our hearts are open to you, so please come for a day or to stay … [Feb99]

TWELVE TRIBES COMMUNIDAD DE QUATRO BARRAS

CP 122
83425 Quatro Barras Parana
BRAZIL

(41) 967-0098

Began 1997 | Pop. 40
Diet: Omnivore | Rural | Spiritual

The community in Quatro Barras began in 1997 when the community in Londrina, Parana, overflowed into the Curitiba area and into two small rural properties near the Baitaca Mountain. We now live a very simple "down-to-earth" lifestyle, taking the bread, beeswax candles, and leather goods we make at home to the large markets in the metropolis of Curitiba. We are a small community of about 40 men, women, and children, cut out of the multifaceted Brazilian society, who have given themselves to their Creator and a common life of love and sharing of all things. The beans and rice we grow and harvest are what you will find on our tables; and the humble, rustic homes we live in are open to all who have a heart for the same love we have found in our Maker, Yahshua, and each other. We consider the life we live very normal, and those willing to participate with a whole heart are welcome. [Feb99]

TWELVE TRIBES COMMUNIDAD DE SAN SEBASTIAN

Paseo de Ulia 375
ES-20013 San Sebastian
SPAIN

Began 1994 | Pop. 71
Diet: Omnivore | Urban | Spiritual

We started living in the community in San Sebastian in 1994 when a wonderful couple opened up their home to us in Monte Ulia. Then the life of love and unity lived by the disciples of Yahshua, the Messiah, began to blossom here. We earn our living from working at our natural-beeswax candle shop, which is our main industry. We bake whole-wheat bread in a firewood oven as well. These two products are mainly sold at the many craft fairs that there are in Spain. We are about 30 people living in a house placed at the top of a hill with a nice view of the ocean on one side and the city of San Sebastian surrounded by green hills on the other. Our door is open for people who look for true life and friendship. [Feb99]

TWELVE TRIBES COMMUNIDAD EN BUENOS AIRES

Batallon Norte y Mansilla
1748 Las Malvinas /
General Rodriguez
Provincia de Buenos Aires
ARGENTINA

54 (237) 484-3409

Began 1997 | Pop. 22
Diet: Omnivore | Rural | Spiritual

Our community here in Argentina began in 1997. We are a small community of about 20 people. Our community is located in a semirural environment, near the capital, Buenos Aires. Our main occupations are organic gardening, whole-wheat-bread making, and the development of alternative-energy methods. We travel frequently to different parts of the country, selling whole-sale natural foods and the products we make in our cottage industries at crafts fairs. Our life together in community is a simple expression of the love we have for one another. The deep personal relationships we have with each other are being built daily through our common life in the community. Our community and our common life together are based on our obedience to the simple, clear teachings of our master, Yahshua, the Son of God. Our lives and relationships are being restored daily

through our life of love. We invite and welcome all who are interested in our life and our community to come and visit. Our homes and our hearts are open to you. [Feb99]

TWELVE TRIBES COMMUNIDADE DE LONDRINA

Rua Jayme Americano 420
Jardim California
Londrina Parana 86040-030
BRAZIL

(43) 339-2228, (043) 337-4562
(within Brazil)

Began 1992 | Pop. 44
Diet: Omnivore | Urban | Spiritual

The community in Londrina began in 1992 when we traveled down from the north of Brazil to the fertile south, where we would also have easier access to other countries in South America.

We now consist of several families and single people, about 40 in all, living a simple life of caring in a "typical" middle-sized Brazilian city. We make and sell our 100 percent whole-wheat bread and baked goods and handmade beeswax candles to support ourselves and as a way to meet anyone who may be interested in searching for their Creator with all their heart, learning to please him in every way by the strength that he himself supplies. The only proof of the reality of having a personal relationship with our invisible Creator is a tangible life of love, without hypocrisy, expressed to his highest creation—the people with whom we live and whom we meet each day. We know by experience that this cannot be done simply by trying in our own strength and are very grateful that we are being shown the way to really live with a pure heart. We warmly invite you to visit us or contact us. [Feb99]

TWELVE TRIBES COMMUNITY AT STENTWOOD FARMS

Stentwood Farm
Dunkeswell (Near Honiton)
Devon EX14 ORW, England
UNITED KINGDOM

(44) 1823 681155

Began 1997 | Pop. 25
Diet: Omnivore | Urban | Spiritual

Since 1997 we have lived as a small commu-

nity in the east of Devon on a little farm that needs a lot of restoration, just like our lives. We are here as a little light in the darkness, just beginning to shine here in Britain, a demonstration of God's kingdom on the Earth where human relationships are truly being restored. Living as one big family, we are learning to trust one another and be vulnerable, to share our hearts with one another and be personal. This is salvation to those of us who grew up in such a closed and hostile society as Britain. We are being healed of our hardness, learning to judge ourselves, and beginning to come back to being like we were created to be, to bear the likeness of our loving Creator, to love like he loves.

There are about five families and several single people here, always busy fixing the house, or working in our little candle business, or getting on with the daily privileges around the house. You might meet us at one of the markets in the local towns around here or in the summertime at music festivals with our big mobile café, called Common Ground, where we go looking to meet any others who are longing for a new, clean life free from compromise.

Please call, write, or feel free to visit. [Feb99]

TWELVE TRIBES COMMUNITY IN BELLOWS FALLS

Basin Farm
PO Box 108
Bellows Falls VT 05101

802-463-3230

Began 1984 | Pop. 115
Diet: Omnivore | Rural/Urban | Spiritual

From nearby Fall Mountain overlooking Bellows Falls it's not hard to spot our farm—two green patches stitched together by a silver river onto the sleeve of town. We began as a small community in neighboring Westminster Station in 1984. Since then we have grown to about 115 people, a modest farm, two additional houses, and a rustic wholesome-foods café. For many of us would-be farmers the hard work and ups and downs of organic agriculture have been full of surprises. Who knows what growing echinacea and infusing honey may hold in store? We hope that many people from all ages, religions, and backgrounds will come visit us. Our focus is our love for our God and our master, Yahshua, and caring for the people who will live for him. [Feb99]

Key to bracketed text: cc = cannot commit to prompt correspondance, sase = self-addressed stamped envelope

TWELVE TRIBES COMMUNITY IN BOSTON

92 Melville Ave
Dorchester MA 02124

617-436-6114

Began 1981 | Pop. 35
Diet: Omnivore | Urban | Spiritual

Isn't there a place where men, women, and children dwell in harmony? Isn't there a place where the barriers of race, social class, and gender are broken down? Our community in Boston has realized such a life since it began in 1981. We are a people devoted to one another because we are devoted to the one who made us. We are a community of roughly 50 people that includes married couples as well as single men and women. Together we run the Common Ground Café and Common Sense Store, which we have maintained for nearly five years. We are looking toward development of a wholesome-food market. We also operate a small carpentry/odd-jobs business. We love to serve others from the fruits of the spirit we have received—love, joy, peace, patience, kindness … We value human life as the most precious expression of our God's character. Through his love we are being restored to love. What else could we do but give our lives back to him by laying down our lives for one another, seeing to it that there are no needy among us. We love meeting new people with whom we can share our life. We live to see this life of love fill the whole Earth. [Feb99]

TWELVE TRIBES COMMUNITY IN CAMBRIDGE

41 North Union St
Cambridge NY 12816

518-677-5880

Began 1997 | Pop. 72
Diet: Omnivore | Rural | Spiritual

We are a people who have fallen in love with one another because we have fallen in love with the one who is love … Yahshua, the Son of God. His love is contagious. When we heard the news of what he did, how he lived and died for us, it made us want to respond. We see that devoting our lives to him and his people is the only appropriate response for what he did. We live together as a community of believers following his words and teachings daily. We are a part of a larger group of people, a nation, the Twelve Tribes. Our community in Cambridge, New

York, is a farming community established in 1997. It is nestled in the rolling hills of the upper Hudson River Valley. It is called the Common Sense Farm, and here we support ourselves with a cottage industry that makes wholesome and practical personal-care products. This keeps our developing farm from coming under economic pressure to produce more than what is normal and healthy—protecting our land and animals. We are young and old, families and single people, coming from different backgrounds, but we all have the same desire, and that is to love one another supremely, just as Yahshua loved us—caring for each other and giving up our time, our space, our belongings, even our own personal goals and ambitions. Whatever it will take to see his kingdom of peace and justice established here on Earth, now. Each new day is another opportunity to learn how to do this in our relationships with one another because that is where it all starts anyway, isn't it?

Please come visit us any time. You do not need to fill out an application. You do not need any money. Call, or write us a letter, or just drop in. [Feb99]

TWELVE TRIBES COMMUNITY IN COLORADO SPRINGS

5346 Constitution Ave
Colorado Springs CO 80915
719-573-1907

Pop. 20
Diet: Omnivore | Urban | Spiritual

The community in Colorado Springs is still in its early beginnings, so we are not fully settled at this address. We are searching for the right housing situation for our soon-to-be five families and several single men and women. Our men are working together in the building trades, and we live and share together as one extended family to love and care for one another just as the Son of God loved us in taking upon himself our iniquities in order that we might have life. In this, he has shown us a new way of relating to one another, bearing one another's burdens, establishing a new social life of true unity. He is the center of our life together, and we are always looking for those who want to follow him. We are here for any who are seeking a true alternative to the many Christian ministries headquartered here.

Our current address will always be able to be found in the "Where We Are" section of

our Web page: http://www.twelvetribes.com. Our God has always made a home for all the lonely no matter where we live. [Feb99]

TWELVE TRIBES COMMUNITY IN COXSACKIE

7 Ely St
Coxsackie NY 12051

518-731-2181

Began 1997 | Pop. 54
Diet: Omnivore | Urban | Spiritual

The community in Coxsackie began quite by "accident" when one day in the fall of 1997, one of our women set off in search of a laundromat in which to dry her clothes. As she drove through the sleepy lower village she was taken by the beautiful, old, and quite unused buildings nestled together on the Hudson River. One building in particular, the Dolan Block, caught her eye. This derelict but once-famous opera house stood empty and forlorn. She never did get her clothes dried down here in lower Coxsackie, but she hurried to tell her husband of the building and its wonderful restoration potential. Knowing how much our Creator loves restoration, we purchased the building. Before long a few families moved into the lower village to begin the restoration of this and another empty building close by. Now these buildings hold our Common Sense store and our print shop and are a hub of activity as we serve the other Twelve Tribes communities with their printing needs. Everything from literature about our wonderful life in Messiah to labels for our cottage-industry products is printed here. There is also a thriving woodshop in which skilled craftsmen and their apprentices transform old, reclaimed wood into beautiful, practical furniture. We are a growing community of 60 or so people dwelling together in several households and sharing all things in common right in the midst of the older, historic part of the village. It is because of the love and forgiveness of Yahshua, the Son of God, that we have chosen to devote our lives to each other and to our Creator. We desire to obey and keep his commandments as we learn to love deeply and from the heart. We warmly invite others to come see and enter into this new social order with us and put an end to the alienation and strife that have plagued human relationships over the centuries. Restoration is a wonderful process! [Feb99]

TWELVE TRIBES COMMUNITY IN HAMBURG

2051 North Creek Rd
Lake View NY 14085

716-627-2098

Began 1993 | Pop. 72
Diet: Omnivore | Urban | Spiritual

The community in Hamburg began in 1993 in East Aurora, New York, with a construction crew and a very small household of 15–20 people. We have moved a few times since then and have opened a bakery, an iron forge, and a copper-lamp shop. As the early church did, our life centers around our master, Yahshua, as we devote our lives to him and to each other daily. We all live together and share all things in common just as the disciples our master gathered did after he rose victoriously over death.

Our industries allow us to work alongside our children and each other. This also allows us to be visible to all those who live around us as people come into our bakery and we go to craft shows to display our products. We are now approximately 60 people in two households and are always looking for ways to share with others the life that we have in our master, Yahshua. Most of us were searching for meaning to life and for real love that allows us to lay down our lives every day for our brothers and sisters. We are really thankful for the way our master searched us out and led us into the path of someone who had already been immersed in this life. We know there are many other people out there with the same heart as ours, and we are always looking to share what we have found with them. This is a way of life that does away with loneliness and separation, a true unity of heart and mind. One heart, one mind, one way, the way of Yahshua. We live a simple, normal life and wholeheartedly welcome visitors, be it for a day or to stay. [Feb99]

TWELVE TRIBES COMMUNITY IN HYANNIS

14 Main St
Hyannis MA 02601

508-790-1620

Began 1991 | Pop. 55
Diet: Omnivore | Urban | Spiritual

We've been together here on the Cape, in Hyannis, Massachusetts, since 1991 and number about 50 people. We live in households where we share the responsibilities and needs of the day, and we also run the Common Ground Café on Main Street, where we serve delicious, wholesome food. Hyannis is famous for tourism and thus is a good location to meet people from all over the world. We are nothing fancy or showy but a humble people who depend on our God. He is the God of Abraham, Isaac, and Jacob. Once we were not a people, lost and alienated, but now he has gathered us together into his family, where we are set free to love the way he loves. Because of the power of true forgiveness we live a life in harmony with one another. We have given up everything to follow him. He is our master. His name is Yahshua. With all our hearts we want to do our part to see his kingdom and his justice established on the Earth. [Feb99]

TWELVE TRIBES COMMUNITY IN ISLAND POND

PO Box 449
Mountain St
Island Pond VT 05846

802-723-9708

Began 1978 | Pop. 51
Diet: Omnivore | Urban | Spiritual

The Community in Island Pond began in 1978. Eventually we grew to 14 houses and over 300 people. We decided to spread out and not just keep growing here in Island Pond. So over a period of time members were sent to different localities in New England and throughout the world to continue the life they had lived here. Presently we are two houses and about 40 people ages ranging up to 82 years old. Island Pond is a little town nestled in a small valley surrounded by the beautiful green mountains of Vermont. Our main house is an old three-story railroad hotel that sits picturesquely on a hill overlooking the town and the peaceful little lake with an island in the center of it. We have a small business where we work together selling shoes and clothing. The primary purpose of our store is to create an environment where people can come and taste the love, the warmth, and the care of our master, Yahshua, by the way we serve them and by the way we relate to one another. We began our shop through a burden of one of our members that we would be able to have access to quality shoes, socks, and clothing. This has blossomed into a lovely rustic store where people from all over New England come to shop.

The purpose of our presence here in Island Pond is to be a witness of the love and character of Yahshua the Messiah (Jesus Christ of the Scriptures) by being of one heart and mind, working together to accomplish his will on this Earth. We live as one big family, sharing everything in common. We work for the common good rather than a paycheck. We submit to one another because the love of God has been poured into our hearts. We have abandoned our lives, as commanded in the Scriptures (our possessions, opinions, preferences, and independence), to do the will of God. We are not perfect, but we are growing in love for one another and Yahshua, who is the center of our life. Our doors are open 24 hours a day, and we invite you to come and visit us. [Feb99]

TWELVE TRIBES COMMUNITY IN LANCASTER

12 High St
Lancaster NH 03584

603-788-4376

Began 1988 | Pop. 35
Diet: Omnivore | Urban | Spiritual

The community in Lancaster began in 1988 when a small group of us had vision to restore an old, fire-damaged building down on Main Street. Amazingly, restoration has been coming to this building just as it has been in our lives as we've given ourselves to sharing a common life of love and unity— devoted to one another and to our Creator. At this time there are about 35 of us living and working together. Every morning and evening we gather together to sing, dance, and share from the overflow of our hearts the thanksgiving we have for the one we believe made it possible for us to have this rich, full life together: our master, Yahshua the Messiah.

We own and operate a shoe-and-clothing store in our building and also have a general contracting business, as we look forward to completing our building by adding a café that will be called the Common Ground and will adjoin the shoe store, where we can all work together, providing a place for others to come and meet us on "common ground." Our desire is for people to see a true demonstration of those who live and work together in unity as a result of the forgiveness they've received from Yahshua ... the ultimate restoration! Our hope is to share our life with anyone who also seeks this

Key to bracketed text: cc = cannot commit to prompt correspondance, sase = self-addressed stamped envelope

same unity through a good conscience and belief in Yahshua—the Son of God. [Feb99]

TWELVE TRIBES COMMUNITY IN OAK HILL

Oak Hill Plantation
Route 81 Box 81A
Oak Hill NY 12460

518-239-8148

Began 1997 | Pop. 77
Diet: Omnivore | Rural | Spiritual

Oak Hill Plantation is a 100-acre farm that forms the nucleus of the community in Oak Hill. In the fall of 1997 a couple of families moved here with the vision of raising children in a normal, healthy environment. We wanted our children to be able to work hard and be connected to the land like human beings were intended to from the beginning. An organic garden and a small collection of cows, goats, and chickens provide the catalyst for teaching our children respect for every living thing our Creator made. We have grown quickly, now numbering more than 80, inhabiting three houses on the farm property and spilling over into others in the village. We are currently building a new house on the farm, as well as erecting a large workshop where we can work near our families and make the components for post-and-beam houses. In the near future we plan to build a lodge for year-round festivals and celebrations, all part of the rich life we receive when we forsake our self-centered existence to live for others like our master, Yahshua, did. [Feb99]

TWELVE TRIBES COMMUNITY IN PALENVILLE

The Pine Grove
Rte 23A
Palenville NY 12463

518-678-2206

Began 1996 | Pop. 88
Diet: Omnivore | Rural | Spiritual

At the foot of the Kaaterskill Clove in the Catskill Mountains of New York is the small village of Palenville. Our community started here in the spring of 1996 with the purchase of a former resort hotel known as the Pine Grove. It had been operated as a summer resort until the early 1970s, after which it fell into disuse and disrepair, which we are now in the process of restoring. We are establishing a small cottage industry making natural-beeswax candles. We love cottage industry because it enables us to work alongside one another and our children, building each other up in the daily circumstances of our life together as we build a new social order. Just as the property we are living on is being restored, so is every aspect of our lives: social, emotional, mental, physical, and spiritual. As the disciples of Yahshua ha Mashiach (Jesus Christ) we have left an abnormal society based on self-concern, and we are learning to live as he did: a life of sacrificial love for others. We have responded to his love for us by coming into obedience to him and laying down our lives as servants to each other by the grace a true relationship with him supplies.

If a society based on self-denying love and sharing sounds normal to you please call, write, or visit us. [Feb99]

TWELVE TRIBES COMMUNITY IN RUTLAND

24 Cottage St
Rutland VT 05701

802-773-0160

Began 1993 | Pop. 67
Diet: Omnivore | Urban | Spiritual

The sun coming up over the Green Mountains finds us already hard at work in our households here in Rutland, Vermont, at the base of Killington Mountain. The community here was started in 1993 with a few families. Now we are about 70 people. We have a cottage industry where we work together called Common Sense Natural Soap and Bodycare. We make bar and liquid soaps and shampoos, along with salves and skin oils. The work is simple, enabling all ages to work together. It also gives a chance for new disciples and visitors to come and join right in. A great thing about our cottage industry is that our children can work with us at meaningful tasks that teach them responsibility and give them dignity. This is in coordination with their homeschooling, apprenticeship training.

None of us deliberately set out to live in community. We heard a message that could free us of the guilt we acquired living selfishly in the world. The Son of God, Yahshua (or commonly known as Jesus), lived a life free of sin and guilt and offered himself as an example for us to follow. He laid his own life down to reconnect us to God. He gave us his spirit to deliver us from anger, greed, selfishness, fear, loneliness, and every other thing that would cause human beings to be alienated from God and each other. As a result of his example, we desired to live like he did, being together, loving others, sacrificing careers, possessions, relationships that kept us alone in the world, without God, and separated from the covenants of promise found in the Bible. Living together is a natural outcome of obeying his words and following his examples. We love visitors. We welcome you to visit our homes or soap shop. [Feb99]

TWELVE TRIBES COMMUNITY IN SYDNEY

1375 Remembrance Drive
Picton NSW 2571
AUSTRALIA

(02) 46 772 668

Began 1995 | Pop. 60
Diet: Omnivore | Urban | Spiritual

"Peppercorn Creek Farm" is located just over the Razorback Ranges, an hour south of Sydney in a rural town called Picton. At first, we lived in the large city of Sydney, but it was our desire to find a place in the country, a lifestyle more conducive to raising our children. In 1995, we met a man with a 21-acre farm an hour outside of Sydney who changed his life and gifted us his farm. On that farm we now have sheep, chickens, and the beginnings of an organic garden. We are in the process of building accommodations for the 60 people in our community, which include 14 children. We live a simple life, working hard on our farm and in our trades, like painting and decorating, landscaping, plumbing, and carpentry. We have just begun our first cottage industries of natural-beeswax-candle making and pottery. We also take our portable wooden café to different festivals and events throughout Sydney as well as nationwide. It is called the Common Ground Café.

The life we live in community is not something new—it is actually something very old. Our life is spoken of in the Bible in Acts 2:44,45 and 4:32. It says that all those who believed "were together" and shared everything in common. We are convicted to return to the original pattern of the church, which was in community. Their lives together, as extended families, demonstrated the life and power of Messiah through their unity and love for one another. There is always someone at home. Please come and visit us anytime. [Feb99]

Additions and corrections: Email: directory@ic.org, Web: http://directory.ic.org/, Mail: RR 1 Box 156-D, Rutledge MO 63563, USA.

TWELVE TRIBES COMMUNITY IN THE LAKE OF THE OZARKS

PO Box 1906
Warsaw MO 65355

660-438-4481

Began 1998 | Pop. 53
Diet: Omnivore | Urban | Spiritual

The community here began in the summer of 1998 when we purchased a historic hotel on Main Street in the village of Warsaw. Warsaw is located on the Lake of the Ozarks in central Missouri. We built a small café in the lower level, called the Underground Railway, that we operate for the sake of reaching out to the lonely. We have open-forum meetings every Tuesday night at 7:30 to discuss the deep issues that affect every one of us. We are building a wholesome-food store and a larger café on the main floor. We also live upstairs in the hotel and in other buildings in town. We are in the process of moving our beeswax-candle industry and pottery shop here from our community in St. Joseph, Missouri. At present we are approximately 50 people—several families and single people. We have devoted our lives to bringing God's kingdom of love to the Earth. We gather morning and evening to share our hearts and sing and worship Yahshua, God's own Son, who died to set us free from sin and death. It is only by the grace of his spirit dwelling in our hearts that we can love one another and forgive each other and remain together. We are being restored together to the image of our Creator as we grow in his love. The good fruit of love and unity in a people who dwell together in peace will be the living witness that God really did send his Son and that he loves us (John 17:20–23). We welcome visitors and would be happy to correspond with those who are interested in our life. [Feb99]

TWELVE TRIBES COMMUNITY IN WEST PALM BEACH

Jog Run Farm
6311 Wallis Rd
West Palm Beach FL 33413

561-697-9448

Began 1995 | Pop. 55
Diet: Omnivore | Urban | Spiritual

The people of the Twelve Tribes have come to dwell on this 5-acre farm here on the western edge of West Palm Beach in south Florida. A woman from this area opened up her home in 1995 to share it with others who have the same heart she did—to give everything to the God who created us. Here on this small piece of property about 40 of us live and work each day. We have some farm animals that our children love caring for. We are also experimenting with growing vegetables organically and working to restore the land to a fruitful state. Besides the work we do here on the property, we have a crew of men who run a tree-care industry and a stump-grinding business. This industry supports us year-round and gives us opportunity to meet many people. We also have a nice wooden cart we take out to craft fairs on which we sell beeswax candles that we have decorated with natural pressed flowers.

Here you will find the same life and the same message found at any of the Twelve Tribes communities, a people who are forgiven and are learning to love as we have been loved by our master, Yahshua the Messiah. If you desire a life of self-sacrificing love that truly satisfies beyond all selfish pursuits, then come and see what you were created for. We hope to meet you soon! [Feb99]

TWELVE TRIBES COMMUNITY IN WINNIPEG

89 East Gate Drive
Winnipeg Manitoba R3C 2C2
CANADA

204-786-8787

Began 1983 | Pop. 87
Diet: Omnivore | Rural/Urban | Spiritual

The community in Winnipeg was established in 1993 after relocating from Nova Scotia, where we began in 1983. We now own three homes in an area called Armstrong Point, where we are surrounded by a beautiful river on two sides. There are more than 120 of us including children. We operate a café called Common Ground, a shoe-repair shop where we specialize in the fabrication of custom-made moccasins and sandals, a beeswax-candle shop, and a small machine shop.

We are the first of many communities that will be gathered in different localities across Canada. Through our common life together, we are learning how people from different backgrounds and cultures can actually live together in perfect unity. The faith we live by was perfectly expressed by our master, Yahshua, the Messiah. We believe in him, and it is his spirit that is living in our midst that teaches us to overcome our own selfish ways and to love and forgive each other.

We have a hope that does not disappoint because we are part of a new holy nation, the restored twelve tribes of spiritual Israel that will usher in the rule of Messiah on the Earth, the true New Age.

You can visit us any time. Our homes are always open for visitors, whether it is for a day or forever. [Feb99]

TWELVE TRIBES GEMEINSCHAFT IN OBERBRONNEN

Wirtsgasse 3
D-73495 Stodtlen-Oberbronnen
GERMANY

49-7964-1550

Began 1995 | Pop. 40
Diet: Omnivore | Urban | Spiritual

Our community consists of about 40 people. Since Oberbronnen is tucked away in the rural hills of southern Germany it is not easily found. However, those who seek a way out of the "normal" life in society and hope for a new pure beginning find their way to the little village of Oberbronnen. We have been here since 1995.

We do not have a complicated philosophy or a lifestyle dominated by religious rituals, but rather we lead a simple life of learning to love and care for each other in a practical way, just like the early disciples of Yahshua did. We make our living by selling natural clothing at markets. We try to be as self-sufficient as possible, so our days are filled with cooking, sewing, working in the vegetable field, etc. You might meet us at some market in southern Germany, singing in the streets, at music festivals or other events. But if you'd like to get to know our life, we would surely love to have you come by any time for as long as you wish. [Feb99]

TWELVE TRIBES GEMEINSCHAFT IN PENNINGBUTTEL

Unter den Linden 15
D-27711 Osterholz-Scharmbeck
GERMANY

04791-89657

Pop. 36
Diet: Omnivore | Urban | Spiritual

In the outskirts of Bremen, up in northern Germany, in the small village of Pennigbuttel there is a small community of a different kind. We are several families with lots of wonderful children living in a large, old farmhouse. We have lived here for five years and operate a small odd-job business. We grow some of our own produce, and we have two small home industries, where we produce natural clothing and beautiful beeswax candles. Although we have come from many backgrounds, as disciples of Yahshua we have come to know the roots and the true meaning of life. Being part of the communities of the Twelve Tribes, we are restoring the age-old foundations, treasuring each other, sharing what we have, and establishing a new social order where everyone is motivated by genuine love toward each other. You are heartily welcome to come for a day or to stay. [Feb99]

TWIN OAKS COMMUNITY

138-D Twin Oaks Rd
Louisa VA 23093

540-894-5126
twinoaks@ic.org
http://www.twinoaks.org/

Began 1967 | Pop. 90
Diet: Omnivore | Rural

Twin Oaks is an ecovillage of 100 people living on 450 acres of farmland and forestland in rural Virginia. The ecovillage was founded in 1967, and our lifestyle reflects our values of egalitarianism, ecology, and nonviolence. We welcome scheduled visitors throughout the year.

We are economically self-sufficient and income sharing. Our hammocks and chairs business generates most of our income; indexing books and making tofu provide most of the rest. These businesses provide about one-third of our work; the balance goes into a variety of tasks that benefit our quality of life—including organic gardening, milking cows, equipment and building maintenance, office work, and much more. Our work schedules are very flexible.

Twin Oaks has developed an elaborate community culture. Our everyday lives include many recreational activities—social and support groups, performances, music, games, dance, and art. Our culture values tolerance of diversity and sustainable living. We share our vehicles, we build our own buildings, and we have little internal use of money.

Some of us work actively for peace and justice, ecology, and feminism. Each summer we host a women's gathering. We also host a communities conference every fall, open to experienced communards, those seeking community, and forming communities.

We offer a three-hour tour on many Saturday afternoons; please call during business hours to reserve a tour. Our three-week visitor program is a prerequisite for membership and must be arranged by letter or e-mail well in advance of the proposed stay. Information about visiting is available on our Web site or by mail. For information about books and newsletters written about Twin Oaks, contact Community Bookshelf (see ad on inside back cover). [Nov98]

TWO ACRE WOOD COHOUSING

656 Robinson Rd
Sebastopol CA 95472

707-829-7950
robbinps@aol.com

Began May99 | Pop. 35 | Forming
Diet: Omnivore | Urban

(Also known as Jewell Hill Cohousing.) Two Acre Wood Cohousing is a community in the traditional cohousing mold. We are generally all politically progressive and environmentally conscious and interested in learning to live together in a supportive, loving community with lots of room for individual differences. We have no official philosophy.

We will be moving into the newly built neighborhood in the spring of 1999. We will be maintaining a list of people who might be interested in purchasing a unit should one become available. There may also be some rental opportunities. [Nov98, sase requested, no openings]

TWO PIERS HOUSING CO-OPERATIVE

c/o Tony Cook
120 Eastern Toad
Brighton
E Sussex BN2 2AJ, England
UNITED KINGDOM

01273 739779
twopiers@co-op.org
twopiers@easynet.co.uk
http://www.co-op.org/

Began 1976 | Urban

We are a cooperative, open to anyone willing to accept the responsibilities of member-ship. Responsibilities are based upon the efficient management of our housing in accordance with the mutual benefits of the community. We impose no restrictive rules/codes/ideologies/belief systems at all upon ourselves other than the obvious liberating ones of respect for one another and the environment, paying one's fair share of the costs, and the development and maintenance of collective responsibility. Our structure is as close to a direct democracy as one can find anywhere on the planet. We are active in the support and promotion of co-ops, including the initiating and setting up of the national housing-cooperative representative body. We have recently completed the electronic networking of all our properties with Apple Macintoshes and are presently working toward the greening of our properties. [Jan99]

Additions and corrections: Email: directory@ic.org, Web: http://directory.ic.org/, Mail: RR 1 Box 156-D, Rutledge MO 63563, USA.

Listings

UDGAARDEN

Udgaarden 24
DK - 8471 Sabro
DENMARK

+45 86 94 96 18, +45 86 94 91 17
+45 86 12 77 41 fax
Udgaarden@lading.dk
kaj.larsen@adr.dk
http://www.ecovillages.org/
denmark/udgaardenilading/

Began 1985 | Diet: Omnivore | Rural

The Udgaarden was created with intentions of making a practical and social society with special attention to environmental and ecological values.

Our ecological farm, run by ourselves, supplies all beef, pork, mutton, and eggs and nearly all vegetables.

We are neither socialist nor religious by conviction. We are ordinary people avoiding any tendencies toward fundamentalism, be it political, religious, spiritual, sexist, or other. The whiskey we drink is not ecological, but we occasionally drink organic beer or wine, when we come across it.

All grownups have full-time jobs outside the commune. All work—farming and keeping the buildings and everything in order—is done voluntarily. Everyone does the work that interests them the most. This has worked OK for eight years.

In the common house, hot evening meals are served on workdays.

Our houses are low-energy houses, and our heat supply is CO2 neutral: solar panels and a wood-pellet burner. Roof rainwater is filtered and used for toilets and the common laundry.

We are open to visitors who make arrangements in advance. Major groups will be charged 300 dkr./$50. We cannot offer stay or work. [May99]

IC Web Site

Intentional Communities on the Web
Make your home on the Web with us.

www.ic.org

UFA-FABRIK KOMMUNE

Viktoriastraße 10-18
D-12105 Berlin - Süd
GERMANY

049-0-30-755-03-0
049-0-30-755-03-116
049-0-30-755-03-117 fax
info@ufafabrik.de
sigrid.niemer@ufafabrik.de
http://www.ufafabrik.de/

Began 1976 | Diet: Omnivore | Urban

In the summer of 1979, over 100 people took over the desolate grounds of the former UFA-Film studios, creating a comprehensive work and living project for innovative social, cultural, and ecological lifestyles. We now have 50 resident members (ages 1 month to 90 years) and about 120 employees. Our four-acre site, leased from the city, includes a bakery, an organic market, an international café, two large theaters, a cultural center, and an animal farm. We host a wide variety of classes, a free school, a circus school, Germany's number one samba band, an ongoing ecology exhibition, and an International Theatre Festival in alternate summers.

The urban village of 16,000 square meters (approximately four acres) is divided into various areas. The spirit of enterprise you can discover here encourages people's involvement and has inspired many to take chances in their lives. [Mar99]

UNION ACRES INTENTIONAL COMMUNITY

990 Heartwood Way
Whittier NC 28789

828-497-4111
lachristie@earthlink.net

Began Dec89 | Pop. 42 | Re-Forming
Diet: Vegetarian | Rural | Spiritual

Founded in 1989 in the gorgeous mountains of western North Carolina, Union Acres is one hour west of Asheville on 80 acres of views and streams—24 residential lots potentially and 7 acres of common land. Based on Earth stewardship and simplicity with consensus decision making and community service. Our stated purpose is to live as neighbors in peace, harmony, and ecological balance with respect to one another and all life.

Our members are diverse in backgrounds, ages, occupations, and interests. Homes include straw bale, passive and active solar, and solar earth berm. Eclectic spirituality such as Native American ritual, seasonal observations of Equinox, Solstice, Maypole, Christmas, Sukkot (harvest) are expressed.

We are family oriented with 20 adults and 11 children. Interests and activities include food co-op, gardening, potlucks, homesteading, and homeschooling. Many members horseback ride, kayak and canoe, contradance, and pursue plans to develop a nearby retreat center.

We seek people who will actively participate in community life through work and play. Visitors need to call before coming. Arrangements can be made by e-mailing Annie at lachristie@earthlink.net or calling 828-497-4111. There are homes and wooded lots for sale now. Send $5 for detailed brochure to: Union Acres, 654 Heartwood Way, Whittier, NC 28789, or call 828-497-2869 or 828-497-4964. [Sep99, sase requested]

UNITY KITCHEN COMMUNITY OF THE CATHOLIC WORKER

PO Box 650
Syracuse NY 13201

315-478-5552, 315-475-6761

Began 1970 | Pop. 4
Urban | Spiritual

Unity Kitchen Community of the Catholic Worker is a small Catholic community that submits to the teaching authority of the Roman Catholic Church and uses only valid worship forms.

We witness to the unity and sanctity of human life and to the value and dignity of every person from the conception to natural death, which means we speak against all abortion, euthanasia, capital punishment, war making, and oppression of the powerless. We express our witness through our newsletter, the *Unity Grapevine*, through Good Friday Way of the Cross, through public-speaking engagements, and through our dinner hospitality for the poor.

We offer a family-style dinner to 24 registered guests (same guests at every dinner). It is a gracious, peaceful, dignifying sit-down dinner in a beautiful setting. Each table of 6 is served by a nonpoor volunteer who also sits and shares in the dinner and fellowship. We are currently open Monday and Wednesday for dinner and Sunday for Mass and refreshments. Room and board are provided for workers and stipend of $10 weekly and a day off a week. [Jan99]

Key to bracketed text: cc = cannot commit to prompt correspondance, sase = self-addressed stamped envelope

UNIVERSAL RESIDENTIAL PURE COMMUNES RESOURCE MANAV KENDRA SANT MAT KINDLY INTERNATIONAL NETWORK DIVINE

PO Box 1086
Ben Lomond CA 95005

831-425-3334, 888-681-9791
URPCRMKSMKIND@ic.org
brotherlittlestar@yahoo.com
http://profiles.yahoo.com/
URPCRMKSMKIND/

Began 1984 | Forming | Diet: Vegan
URPCRMKSMKIND is a resource/networking center for people wishing to form/co-create and/or seek/join intentional communities that are strictly to be for folks who enjoy living the following simply high minimum standard of pure 'n' healthy lifestyle: Bee-Vegan (no meat, fish, fowl, eggs, dairy) and "straight-edge"/nontoxic/ vital 'n' clear natural high way (NA/NS/ND = no alcohol, no smoking, no drugs); and this all includes the rare but wonderfully excellent requirement of no pets/domestic animals! Our name is Universal Residential Pure Communes Resource Manav Kendra Sant Mat Kindly International Network Divine. Anyone who wants to sincerely know the reasons why may simply contact us, preferably if convincing you of the correctness of this wisdom will result in you wanting to join this all-important global movement! We will assist present and future communities who sincerely want to upgrade their lifestyle as their practical sensibilities and evolution of consciousness catch up with their purported ideals! We welcome all sorts of assistance from any-/everyone! Please contact us for further information and/or to help in any/every way! Earnestly, your friends with Love in True Knowledge 'n' Wisdom! [Apr99, cc, sase requested]

UNIVERSITY STUDENTS' COOPERATIVE ASSOCIATION

2424 Ridge Rd
Berkeley CA 94709

510-848-1936
housing@usca.org
http://www.usca.org/

Began 1933 | Pop. 1250
Diet: Omnivore | Urban

The University Students' Cooperative Association (USCA) is the largest student housing cooperative in North America, housing over 1,200 people. Although a private nonprofit corporation, the USCA works in cooperation with the University of California to provide housing for its students.

About 900 of the USCA's members live in room-and-board houses scattered around the Berkeley campus, including 17 large houses that each function as a separate cooperative household with elected managers for room assignment, work organization (housekeeping, food service, etc.), and maintenance. A central support staff of about 25 nonmembers provides technical information to members as well as oversees day-to-day administration (such as house-keeping applications and organizational financing). We also provide warehousing and support services to individual house food programs. [Nov98]

UNKNOWN TRUTH FELLOWSHIP WORKERS - ATLANTIS

342 Garnet Lake Rd
Warrensburg NY 12885

518-623-2831
http://www.albany.net/
~cjones/atlantis/

Began 1943 | Pop. 1 | Forming
Rural | Spiritual

Unknown Truth Fellowship Workers believe in the true religion now as well as seek it. Vibes come from it directing us. We are celibate as "the Kingdom is unmarried, man left wives, I am the resurrection." We ally with such communes as Yahwehists, Shakers, serpent-handling Pentecostals, Cave Saints, Waldenses, Native Americans, naturalists, UFOs, etc. We eat kosher and organic. In seeking truth much is yet to be learned. Weider exercise, outdoor living, shamanism, genetic structuring, astrology, archaeology, gold mining, rock hounding, crafts, herbs, much more. We also have a writing ministry.

Yahwehists teach that the name Christ Jesus comes from Greek manuscripts XEs-sex equal to 666. Millions of close encounters say that there is no Creator and that the Savior was a charlatan. A few books we recommend are *Subliminal Seduction*, by Key, *The Sacred Mushroom and the Cross*, by Allegro, *Foxfire 7*, and *Gnostics*—Inner Light Publications, Box 753, New Brunswick, NJ 08903.

Funds permitting, we hope to purchase land for our commune and truth research center. The good old revival spirit will prevail. Our library of 5,000 volumes is available to members. We mail out the book *Snake Handlers*, illustrated by Carden and Pelton, for $5 and also distribute other literature. Member of MENSA, the high-IQ society. The True Unknown religion has led us to the lost island of Atlantis. Picture of carved stones and story of find is $10. Charles Berlitz says that Atlantis discovered will bring world peace through acceptance of an older culture. All queries answered. [Nov98, sase required]

UTOPIAGGIA

I-05010 Montegabbione (Tr)
ITALY

X39-076387020
klschibel@tin.it

Began 1975 | Pop. 19
Diet: Omnivore | Rural

We are an anarchic humanitarian commune living as ecologically as possible with the land. The community started in lower Bavaria in 1975 and moved to central Italy in 1982. Many of the founding members came out of the movement of the 1960s. There are 20 adults and 10 adolescents and children living in three houses on 100 hectares of hills, the Land. A large flock of sheep provides the basis for commercial cheese production. We keep horses and poultry, and among the activities we are engaged in, there are pottery and other handicrafts as well as language courses (Italian, German, English). There are openings for new members. Visitors are always welcome but should write first. [May99]

VAIL HOUSE

602 Lawrence
Ann Arbor MI 48104

Began 1960

Vail Cooperative House has great historical significance. The building proper was con-

Additions and corrections: Email: directory@ic.org, Web: http://directory.ic.org/, Mail: RR 1 Box 156-D, Rutledge MO 63563, USA.

structed in 1853 and has been recognized by the Ann Arbor Historical Commission; one of the pillars on the front porch bears a plaque that identifies it as the Hubbell Gregory House. Gregory was the original owner of the house, and his descendants lived here until 1914. Then it was the residence of the family of Horace Prettyman, who owned the Ann Arbor Press. In 1960 it was purchased by the Inter-Cooperative Council (ICC) and opened as a women's housing cooperative in the fall of 1961. In addition to being one of the oldest houses in Ann Arbor, Vail House also boasts a magnificent oak tree in its front yard that has been estimated to be over 200 years old!

Vail Cooperative House was named for Stefan T. Vail, who was an ICC member and president in the mid-1950s. He was a brilliant student of economics and helped to devise the financial structure of the ICC before leaving Ann Arbor to teach economics at Harvard. Sadly, Stefan Vail was killed in Greece in 1958 when he was visiting his family. Soon after, the ICC board of directors voted to name the next house they purchased after Vail, in recognition of his contributions to the organization.

Today, Vail Cooperative House has retained much of its original wood flooring, paneling, and trim while adding modern conveniences. The house contains a TV, a VCR, a piano, five bathrooms, laundry facilities, and a modernized kitchen, with a beautiful mural in the dining room. Outside, we have a huge backyard with a volleyball net, a basketball hoop and backboard, and a bike shed.

Most importantly, living at Vail House will give you the opportunity to meet new people who reside at Vail, Linder, and Ruth's houses and even make lasting friendships. Together, we will make Vail our home. We will have the opportunity to make improvements, take care of what others have left for us, and make sure that the house is left in better condition than when we found it. By working cooperatively, you can make the years you spend at Vail some of the best of your life. [Oct99]

Join the FIC!

and support projects like the *Directory* and *Communities* magazine.

To become a member, use the form on page 456, or call 800-995-8342.

VALE INC, THE

PO Box 207
Yellow Springs OH 45387
937-767-1461, 937-767-1511

Began 1960 | Pop. 40
Diet: Omnivore | Rural

The Vale of five families was incorporated in 1960. About 1980 we decided to turn its 40 acres over to Community Service, Inc., to be held in trust. Seventeen of its wooded acres are in easement, never to be built upon. Five younger families with small children have joined in the last 15 years. Each family lives in its own home, and all but one earns its livelihood outside the Vale. We manage the land (woods and common play area), utilities, and half a mile of lane together. Prospective members need to live here at least one year before applying for membership. At the moment we have no openings for renting or for building.

Business is decided by consensus. Business meetings are usually every other month. We have seasonal get-togethers in opposite months. [Nov98, sase requested, no openings]

VALLEY OF LIGHT

Box 34
Deer AR 72628
501-575-0567
sotardragon@juno.com

Pop. 8 | Re-Forming
Diet: Vegetarian | Rural/Urban

Valley of Light is a spiritually oriented community whose emphasis is on self-realization and self-sufficiency, located on 49 acres in a secluded valley. Projected land use includes separate areas for community activity, residences, and cropland/pasture.

Goals: Create a time/space where the self-realization of each member is fully supported and nurtured. Live in harmony with each other and nature. Share spiritual life together. Flow with universal energy so all actions are appropriate. Become self-sufficient so that conditions "outside" have little effect on the community.

Notes: The community is egalitarian. The structure consists of goals, membership rights, and agreements. There is a three-month to one-year trial membership period (by consensus). The diet is basically vegetarian. Planned: homeschooling, cottage industries, separate sleeping quarters for each family: all other facilities are communal. There is a membership fee, and a permanent

member may "purchase" a 99-year lease on a 1-acre parcel. The valley is a "multispiritual path" community, open to all people regardless of age, sex, race, or ideology, according to consensus of current members. [Jan99, sase requested]

VALSØLILLEGÅRD

Knud Lavardsvej 94
DK-4174 Jystrup
DENMARK

Began 1982 | Pop. 36
Diet: Omnivore | Rural

We are mainly living in separate families—two families share their everyday life—one lives single. We all are nuclear families. You also may say it is a community of couples with children. The many children make it attractive to families. The indoor and outdoor facilities make it great for children, but when they grow older it is a hassle because of the 4-kilometer transport to the village, 12 kilometers to town, to friends, and arrangements.

We all work out of the house. One couple grows vegetables and meat (organic) for self-support and makes some extra money that way, besides their jobs in town.

We live so far out that we consider ourselves dependent on cars. [May99, cc, no openings]

VARSITY HOUSE

119 NW 9th St
Corvallis OR 97330
541-758-7216

Pop. 49 | Diet: Omnivore | Urban
Varsity House is a Christian cooperative house for young men attending Oregon State University or Linn-Benton Community College. [May99, sase requested]

VILLAGE IN THE CITY

c/o Felix
712 Pennsylvania Ave
St Louis MO 63130
314-726-0650, 314-863-3138
events@sprintmail.com
felix@wueconc.wustl. edu

Pop. 15 | Forming | Urban
"Community of the future with roots in the past" is the vision of Village in the City,

---

Key to bracketed text: cc = cannot commit to prompt correspondance, sase = self-addressed stamped envelope

based on the cohousing model, in St. Louis, Missouri. Now in the planning stage, we invite you to join us in building an urban condominium community that strikes a balance between privacy and community.

Village in the City will be planned and run by its residents. Private, completely independent living units will be arranged around a multipurpose common house including mailbox center, dining/kitchen area for shared meals as desired, sitting area, play areas for children and adults, laundry, workshop, and other features to be decided. The physical design of our space will promote informal interactions.

Ours is a family-oriented, intergenerational approach where residents actively cooperate to foster the well-being of children and adults. Beyond our cohousing community, we are also concerned with issues in the wider community and expect to cooperate with our neighbors to address these issues.

We value the intact urban neighborhoods of earlier years and believe we can help rebuild urban community with multiple diversity. Our preferred location is one that will offer access to shops, restaurants, cultural resources, library, metrolink, and Forest Park. New construction or renovation will be used. [Sep99, sasc requested]

VILLAGE OF HARMONY

221 Jurado Ave
Bosque NM 87006
villageofharmony@juno.com

Began 1995 | Pop. 8 | Forming
Diet: Vegan | Rural

We are a small community formed in 1995. Our focus is love, peace, harmony, seeking joy in all aspects of life. Village of Harmony is located on a desert mesa surrounded by mountains, approximately five miles east of the Rio Grande River and a wetlands preserve. The weather is mild, sunny with low humidity. We build alternative houses, use solar electricity, and grow food year-round. We have no mortgages, no bills, and work part-time jobs. We are accepting memberships (no drugs, booze, or firearms) and can help others find inexpensive building lots and achieve self-sufficiency. Write for other information and directions. [Sep99, sasc requested]

VINE AND FIG TREE

11076 County Rd 267
Lanett AL 36863

334-499-2380, 334-499-2444
vineyfig@mindspring.com

Began 1986 | Pop. 8
Diet: Omnivore | Rural

Vine and Fig Tree, established in 1986, is presently six adults and two small children. We are serious organic gardeners, share many meals, share costs on a variable basis, and try to make decisions by consensus.

"Vine and Fig Tree where all shall live in peace and be unafraid" is a vision and challenge for us to grow in loving nonviolence among ourselves and with all of creation.

Some actively participate in voter registration, war-tax resistance, and actions to close the Army's School of the Americas. Our main activist work is in bringing an end to the death penalty; two of us cochair Project Hope to Abolish the Death Penalty, founded by inmates on Alabama's Death Row.

An occasional gathering place for small groups, Vine and Fig Tree needs help with getting facilities to host larger events. We still dream of creating a land-based economy and envision the creation of a diverse, open, and enriching homeschool experience for our children.

In addition to our gardens, we tend a flock of very happy chickens.

We have fruit trees, berries, and a new muscadine "vineyard." We currently have two small, cozy cabins open for visitors. Please send us a letter if you are interested. We are open to new members. [Sep99, sasc requested]

VIVEKANANDA MONASTERY AND RETREAT CENTER

6723 122nd Ave
Fennville MI 49408

616-543-4545

Began 1960 | Pop. 7
Diet: Vegetarian | Rural | Spiritual

(Also known as Vedanta Monastery.) Vivekananda Monastery is just two things. First, it's an ashram. Second, it's an educational institution dedicating to teaching what an ashram is all about: inner development aimed at discovering the Divine, within and without. [Nov98, sasc requested]

VIVEKANANDA VEDANTA SOCIETY

54235 S Hyde Park Blvd
Chicago IL 60615

773-363-0027
chivedanta@aol.com

Began 1967 | Pop. 11
Diet: Vegetarian | Rural/Urban | Spiritual

The Vivekananda Vedanta Society of Chicago is a branch of the Ramakrishna math and mission with headquarters in Belur Math, India. The Ramakrishna math and mission, which is dedicated to the twin ideals of realizing God within and serving God in man, has 135 centers throughout the world, of which 12 are in the United States. The society maintains a temple and monastery in Chicago and a monastery with retreat facilities in Ganges, Michigan. Both centers maintain bookshops and libraries of books on eastern and western spirituality. Ganges also has a museum of Indian culture. [Nov98]

WAHOO!

4510 NE Holman St
Portland OR 97218
WahooCommunity@hotmail.com
http://www.WahooCommunity.com/

Began 1998 | Pop. 9 | Forming
Diet: Omnivore

WAHOO! A celebration of life, love, and abundance! Our motto: love—art—food!

WAHOO! is in the beginning stages of forming. We currently have 8 members and foresee 8–12 more people joining in the fun. We are in the initial process of looking for land. Our ideal site will be located on large acreage in the Pacific northwest, accessible to an urban area. Homes will be privately owned on community-owned land. We will utilize a variety of ecological technologies to create buildings that demonstrate a respect for the land. A retreat center is planned where we will hold workshops of various types, including permaculture, Earth-based philosophy, and various healing arts. We will also have an art center to facilitate our creative inspirations.

We envision homes with a private feel, yet a short walk to the community's center. We value sharing labor, laughs, and love. We

Additions and corrections: Email: directory@ic.org, Web: http://directory.ic.org/, Mail: RR 1 Box 156-D, Rutledge MO 63563, USA.

participate in the raising of our food, improvements to our land, weekly shared meals, and loving assistance with the raising of each other's children.

WAHOO! is committed to sustainability in all areas of our lives: ecologically, spiritually, psychologically, and financially. We pursue our Earth connection through permaculture, wild crafting, and appropriate use of technology. We enrich our spirituality through respect and support for a variety of spiritual practices, through gardening, and through humor. We sustain ourselves psychologically through the use of art, music, community activities, and a commitment to open communication. We develop financially through cottage industries on our land, as well as work opportunities off-site.

We welcome your inquiries! For current information, please visit our Web site, or write to us. [May99, sase requested]

WAITAKERE ECO-NEIGHBOURHOOD COHOUSING PROJECT

PO Box 44 137
Point Chevalier
Auckland
NEW ZEALAND

+649 378 9230
ecohousing@xtra.co.nz
http://www.cohousing.pl.net/

Began 1995 | Urban

We are a group of people currently living in regular nuclear households, with a vision of establishing a cohousing neighborhood that will serve as a model of a socially and environmentally sustainable community.

We intend to acquire sufficient land within Waitakere City to develop a 25–30 dwelling ecohousing neighborhood based on the cohousing model that is proving so successful in Scandinavia and the United States. Developed and managed by the residents themselves, cohousing combines the autonomy of private dwellings with the advantages of community living. Each household has a private, self-contained residence but also shares extensive common facilities with the larger group, arranged and designed to encourage a strong sense of community.

In addition to modeling social sustainability, the neighborhood will be designed to the highest practical standards of environmentally sustainable human settlement, including the layout and design of neighborhood and buildings, choice of materials, landscaping, and services. [Jan99]

WALKER CREEK FARM

1802 Peter Burns Rd
Mt Vernon WA 98273

360-422-8915, 360-422-5709

Began 1975 | Pop. 17
Diet: Omnivore | Rural

The 24-year-old Walker Creek community retains about half of its 20 acres in woodland and protects a salmon-spawning creek. The rest of the land includes private gardens and homes and communal roads, trails, lawns, orchards, and play equipment. Each home contains an independent family, extended family, or individual. The adult population, usually about 10 people, meets monthly to share a meal and reach consensus on issues facing the community. At this time, there is no room for new members and no winterized guest facility, but we are in the process of converting a barn into a community center/guest house. [Nov98, cc, sase required, no openings]

WALNUT HOUSE COOPERATIVE

1740 Walnut St
Berkeley CA 94709

510-549-3140

Began 1981 | Pop. 25 | Urban

We are a nonprofit housing co-op located near the University of California, Berkeley, campus. Members occupy a 22-unit, three-story apartment building. We provide well-maintained, affordable housing in a friendly community atmosphere. Members are asked to contribute eight hours of work per month in addition to their monthly assessment. [Jan99, sase required, no openings]

WATERMARGIN COOPERATIVE

103 McGraw Pl
Ithaca NY 14850

607-272-9441

Began 1948 | Pop. 23
Diet: Omnivore | Rural/Urban

Begun in 1948 as a radical student experiment in interracial living, Watermargin today is less politically charged but continues to educate its members, all Cornell students, about community living with members of diverse backgrounds. Many house members are very politically or socially active and bring very different perspectives to our nightly dinners together. Watermargin often sponsors speakers or events open to the Cornell community that address a variety of social issues, in keeping with the house motto, All People Are Family. [Jan99, no openings]

WATERSMEET HOMES

S93 W27685
Edgewood Ave
Mukwonago WI 53149

414-363-2810

Forming | Rural/Urban | Spiritual

Watersmeet Eco Village—a life of respect to/with all living resources. ("Eco" means "economical/ecological.")

A neighborhood teeming with energy from both external and internal forces. Incorporating all human, plant, animal, mineral, and spiritual entities in a harmonious environment. Establishing the balance of humanity with nature. Within the laws of God. Available by fall of 2001 will be 132 owner-occupied condominiums for both singles and families situated on 110 acres of river and bike-trail frontage. An organic farm will be interlacing the open space, providing a sustainable/nutritional food source for its shareholders. Adjoining these units will be a retreat center with conference halls, pool, health spa, church, dining facilities, and golf course. Watersmeet is located 30 minutes from downtown Milwaukee. All buildings will be designed 100 percent handicap accessible and certifiable under the American Lung Association's Healthy House Program. Holistic living for a whole community. [Nov98, sase requested]

WÄXTHUSET VÄDDÖ

Fjäll 6908
S-76040 Väddö
SWEDEN

46-175-31290, 46-175-31097
46-175-31617 fax
toomas.tuulse@waxthuset.se
lena.kristina@waxthuset.se

Began 1979 | Pop. 19
Diet: Vegetarian | Rural | Spiritual

(Also known as Life University.) We call our place the "House for Growth," as we get together to practice living in truth, simplic-

---

Key to bracketed text: cc = cannot commit to prompt correspondance, sase = self-addressed stamped envelope

ity, and love. We meet every morning and share how we feel and what we are going to do during the day. We receive people for rehabilitation, and that is our main income. We work a lot with music, art, and singing and have massage, yoga, and body work as part of our healing. Our farm is on an island, Vaddo, in the beautiful archipelago northeast of Stockholm, the capital of Sweden. Here we want to build a "university for life"—heal with growing natural food; build our houses from the lumber in the forest; be ecological; use wind power, solar energy, etc. Real life for real people that want to remember God and set a new standard for what is a sustainable society. The earth is rich, well balanced without having been artificially treated. We have several little houses spread out where we do our work. We have a growth center for courses and an international group of people living with us for various lengths of time. There is a network of people around our community relating in cultural activities. We want to start a society school. We invite people to come and give their creativity, love, and healing power. [Jul99]

WE'MOON LAND

PO Box 1395-CD
Estacada OR 97023

503-630-3628
wemoon@teleport.com
http://www.teleport.com/~wemoon/

Began 1973 | Pop. 12 | Re-Forming
Diet: Vegetarian | Rural | Spiritual

We'Moon Land is an intergenerational wimmin's land-based intentional community located on 52 acres, 35 miles from Portland, 5 miles from Estacada. The land has been held by and for womyn since 1973 (formerly known as Who Farm and We'Moon Healing Ground). We are a thriving community of 9–13 womyn (mostly lesbian) and girl children ranging in age from 4 to 56. We are creating a healthy spirit reality in harmony with Earth and ourselves. We are evolving our structure from sole ownership 'moonaged' by a resident collective to becoming a federal tax-exempt nonprofit 501(c)3 who will hold title to the land. We use consensus to make decisions and are committed to having clear communication—we have feelings/clearing meetings to resolve conflict when necessary.

We're striving toward getting off the grid, using permaculture and alternative building technologies, and growing more of our own food—our land is Oregon Tilth certified organic. We intend to support more home-based businesses—we currently are home to Mother Tongue Ink, publisher of We'Moon calendar, which currently provides livelihood for several members.

We are not seeking new residents, and we welcome womyn, girl children, and boy children under age seven to visit. Write for further information. [Dec98, cc, sase requested, no openings]

WELLSPRING

PO Box 72
Newburg WI 53060

414-675-6755

Began 1988 | Pop. 4
Diet: Vegetarian | Rural | Spiritual

Wellspring's residential community is integrally connected to the garden program March thru November. Members from the larger community support Wellspring and its educational programs: wellness education, the arts, ecology and gardening, and personal-growth retreats. The retreat and conference center is open to the public as are its bed-and-breakfast and international hostel.

Local families subscribe to 25 weeks of organic produce each season. Volunteers help the community with the work. There are plans to acquire an adjacent field for expanded orchards, gardens, and vineyards with acreage set aside for a cohousing intentional neighborhood. Another five families are needed to realize this dream.

Wellspring is an easy driving distance from Milwaukee yet is surrounded by nearly 1,000 acres of green space, a nature center, and country landscape. River frontage, meadows, woods, and a restored prairie enhance the natural beauty of Wellspring. [Feb99, cc, sase requested]

WESTSIDE VEGETARIAN COMMUNITY

12479 Walsh Ave
Los Angeles CA 90066
fsotcher@aol.com

Began 1993 | Pop. 8
Diet: Vegetarian | Urban

We hold the belief that healthy vegetarians can live a quality life together. A big part of living harmoniously is a deep appreciation for the gifts, talents, and differences of each person. We believe in solving problems by encouraging open discussion of differences between individuals or by using procedures that involve house meetings held on an as-needed basis.

All residents are expected to respect the rights of others to live in a harmonious and positive environment. Individuals are not to impose their values on others. Manipulation is inappropriate. Residents are expected to remain stable mentally, physically, and financially. [Nov98, cc]

WESTWOOD COHOUSING

43 Vermont Ct
Asheville NC 28806

828-281-3253, 828-250-0433 fax
probbinswestwood@mindspring.com
http://westwoodcoho.home.
mindspring.com/westwood.html

Began 1998 | Urban

Westwood Cohousing Association is an intentional community in Asheville, North Carolina, nestled in a wooded setting with 24 clustered dwellings and a common house in the center of the community. The buildings have a central heat and hot-water system with solar collectors on the common-house roof and radiant floor heating, and landscaping according to permaculture principles.

The community infrastructure has been completed since the summer of 1998, and everyone has moved in and is working together to create a pleasant living space and community. Dinners are held twice a week in the common house, with everyone participating in their creation. Work days are more infrequent, but with everyone helping, a lot gets done! [Dec98, cc, sase required]

WEYST, THE

Pater Petrusstraat 21
NL-5423 SV Handel
THE NETHERLANDS
(0) 492-322509

Began 1984 | Pop. 5 | Rural | Spiritual
(Affiliated with Gandhian Ark.) The Weyst is located in a former Franciscan monastery. Based on service, nonviolence. Organic garden, meditation room. Peace and cultural group center. Volunteers welcome in exchange for board and lodging. Social workplace for Dutch government "alternative

punishment" instead of prison. Vegetarian, no smoking. Write in advance. [May99]

WHITE BUFFALO FARM

1675-4110 Olde River Rd
Paonia CO 81428

970-527-3041
WLtalmage@mail.tds.net

Began 1975 | Pop. 14
Diet: Omnivore | Rural | Spiritual

White Buffalo Farm is an intentional Fifth World community dedicated to the manifestation of a higher spiritual vibration of love-light-wisdom on Mother Earth.

The community expresses itself spiritually in drum circles, dream circles, sweat lodge, vision quest, and Fifth-World rituals and ceremonies that enhance our connectedness to Mother Earth and all the planetary kingdoms.

We are dedicated to creating sanctuary from the main culture while working in spiritual service to raise Mother Earth. We are dedicated to enlightening ourselves, the larger circle of humankind, and protecting Mother Earth from our ignorance. [Sep99, sase requested]

WHITEHALL CO-OP

2500 Nueces
Austin TX 78705

512-472-3329, 512-472-7382

Began 1949 | Pop. 13
Diet: Vegetarian | Urban

Founded August 6, 1949, Whitehall Co-op is Texas's oldest housing cooperative. The 13-member household includes a variety of ages and occupations, and everyone contributes equally to monetary costs and household labor. Whitehall is a nonsexist, nonracist, noncompetitive living environment. All decisions are made by consensus.

Our goals include obtaining intimate, meaningful tribal/familial bonds, emotional support, and spontaneous and planned creation and play. We are learning proper use of resources, noncompetitiveness, and communication skills. We want to be a part of a significant, nonexploitive socioeconomic movement.

The household is vegetarian, though fish meals are occasionally prepared. No smoking of any sort is allowed in Whitehall. All members have individual rooms with semi-private bathrooms. Whitehall was the first Texas recipient of funds from the National

Co-op Bank (Washington, DC) in 1979 for use in construction of a professional-grade kitchen. [Nov98, sase required, no openings]

WHOLE HEALTH FOUNDATION

1760 Lake Drive
Cardiff CA 92007

760-753-0321, 760-633-1061 fax
trust@sd.znet.com

Began 1972 | Pop. 12
Diet: Vegetarian | Urban

Whole Health Foundation is a holistic residential opportunity, one mile from the Pacific Ocean in southern California, 20 miles north of San Diego. We are all non-smokers and mostly vegetarian with occasional seafood or poultry preparation. We share a 13-bedroom eight-bath home with a year-round edible organic garden, outdoor solar shower, Jacuzzi, sauna, laundry, both filtered and distilled drinking water, whole-house filtration for ideal shower and bathing water, air purifier for kitchen and common areas to create negative ions and low-level ozone to eliminate airborne material, Norwalk juicer, electric wheatgrass juicer, and food dehydrator. No meat preparation, drugs, or alcohol abuse are permitted. We offer community-making workshops and residential fasting and rejuvenation programs for between $450 and $295 per week, depending on the level of supervision. Short-term visitors are welcome with prior notice for $50 per day and/or work in the organic garden. Longer-term residential housing is available from $450 to $550 per month. This opportunity is available to provide optimum health support for established vegetarians and others who want to live full-time in a holistic-health-community setting. Most residents have stayed for several years and some for only a few months. Contact William Polowniak the above address. For information and personal reply send $5. [Jan99]

WHOLE VILLAGE KING

225 King Summit
King Ontario L7B 1A3
CANADA

416-364-2036, 905-833-2813 fax
joinus@wholevillage.org
http://www.wholevillage.org/

Began 1995 | Pop. 82 | Forming
Diet: Omnivore | Rural

Whole Village King (WVK) has acquired a

tract of land in King Township, north of Toronto, with three major objectives:
  • to create an intentional community of up to 30 families, based on principles of cohousing;
  • to operate a biodynamic farm as an integral part of the community;
  • to achieve these goals consistent with principles of sustainable land stewardship.

Our intention is to create an ecologically sustainable and environmentally sensitive community. We propose to protect and enhance the natural habitat through a system of land stewardship embracing the unique geographical, historical, cultural, and biological attributes of the land.

Whole Village King is a solution for two difficult problems: the steady loss of farmland to urbanization and the devastating effects of low commodity prices on farmers and the rural communities that they belong to. Through a comprehensive conservation agreement, all of the WVK property, except for the compact housing cluster, will be preserved forever as farmland, managed forest, or natural areas. Each member family will be included in their community supported agriculture venture, where the farmers growing food for WVK on the land will be guaranteed a living wage and the respect and support they deserve. [Sep99]

WHOLELIFE HOUSING

Box 524
918 16th Ave NW
Calgary Alberta T2M 0K3
CANADA

403-276-4296
wholelife@home.com

Began 1995 | Pop. 41 | Forming | Urban

WholeLife Housing is actively planning the creation of an inner-city cohousing development of 24–26 units in Calgary, Alberta, Canada. We are a diverse group, consisting of singles, couples, and families ranging in age from 2 to 74. Of the 40 people in our 14 current households, 16 are children.

According to our vision statement, we are creating an affordable community that celebrates the potential of cooperation. We want to live in a place where our actions can reflect our commitment to each other and to social and environmental responsibility.

We consider ourselves an energetic, capable, and varied group that values diversity and community involvement. We do not share any particular ideology beyond the

Key to bracketed text: cc = cannot commit to prompt correspondance, sase = self-addressed stamped envelope

belief that living more closely with our neighbors will enrich our lives. [Sep99]

WILD IRIS RANCH

Box 42
Jenner CA 95450

707-632-5458
marwiz@thegrid.net

Began 1992 | Pop. 4 | Forming
Diet: Vegetarian | Rural

Wild Iris (Also known as Rejenneration) is forming on five knoll-top acres with stunning ocean and mountain views in an ecologically diverse canyon on the wild and beautiful Sonoma coast less than two hours from San Francisco. Current plans include three buildings in which to live and work, two of which have been built (as well as an orchard and a garden and infrastructure.) We are looking for more partners who share our values of simplicity; Earth stewardship; respect for diversity; hard work; healthy balanced lifestyle; emotional and fiscal stability to buy into the land and to help build and then live in the largest dwelling. Process and details will be clarified as a core group evolves, therefore our chart information roughly represents where we are going. We have a long-term goal of becoming a sanctuary for our urban-dwelling friends so that they can regenerate their personal spirit and connection with the planet. Please write or e-mail us, including a brief personal history, to obtain current information. If you include a phone number, we may call. We do not accept drop-in visitors. [Dec98, cc, sase required]

WILLIAM STRINGFELLOW CATHOLIC WORKER

2130 N Linn St
Peoria IL 61604

309-681-9892, 309-686-2887

Began Nov98 | Pop. 3 | Re-Forming
Diet: Vegan | Urban | Spiritual

(Also known as Peoria Catholic Worker.) The Catholic Worker has been in existence for many years. Since our previous house burned down several years ago, we have concentrated on serving public meals every Sunday. We recently bought a house and are in the process of getting it ready for hospitality. We also plan to start a community garden. Our main goal is to try to live up to the ideals of the Sermon on the Mount.

Besides doing charitable work, we are also involved in various justice and peace work, concentrating on ending militarism.

We eventually plan to offer hospitality and are thinking of offering hospitality to families of Pekin federal prisoners.

We all have jobs outside the house so that we can pay for food, utilities, and the mortgage. All of us are involved in peace and justice issues. [Mar99, cc]

WINDSONG COHOUSING

20543 - 96th Ave #27
Langley BC V1M 3W3
CANADA

604-882-5337
acarpent@direct.ca
http://www.cohousing.ca/
cohsng4/windsong/

Windsong is a cohousing community consisting of 34 homes and a 5,500-square-foot common house on a six-acre site in Langley, British Columbia, Canada. The common house will have many amenities, such as space to share the occasional evening meal, childcare, teen center, shared office space, guest rooms, craft room, workshop, and future expansion space. Our homes are clustered on two acres of the site with four acres preserved as a nature preserve. Windsong is modeled from the Danish experience, which has reached a third level of success, which is a pedestrian-oriented community with a glassed-in pedestrian street. This model allows for year-round interaction between neighbors, which is more effective in sustaining a sense of community. Windsong will also have organic-garden allotments. Windsong is within easy bus and sky-train connection to Vancouver. Windsong is close to schools and parks and a 15-minute walk to the village center. There are good views of the mountains north of the site. A mixed community of families, singles, seniors with a diversity of income levels. An ideal place to live! For more information contact Alan Carpenter.

WINDSPIRIT COMMUNITY

2300 Dripping Springs Rd
Winkelman AZ 85292

Began 1995 | Pop. 24
Diet: Vegetarian | Rural | Spiritual

In 1995 we purchased 16 acres of the former Christmas Star land. Our many fruit trees

and gardens continue to be cared for organically on this desert oasis. All land is held in common, with each member having their unofficial site on which to pursue their visions.

We are creating a low-impact, ecofriendly, sustainable coalition of souls healing and growing as individuals and as a community. Nature is our teacher as we listen to the voices of plants, stones, and stars. Each day brings new opportunities to cast the ego aside and separate the action from the person in order to work toward our common good as caretakers of this planet in transition, and to further explore our true individual roles as sacred players in this ever-beautiful and often absurd cosmic theater of life. We sing and play together, and many of us are involved in such areas as jewelry, dance, painting, stained glass, and more. The products of our creativity contribute to our existence, yet many also work in the world as necessary, while being conscious of the dominant dysfunctional system as little as possible. Visitors are welcome with advance notice. Practical (building, etc.) and/or spiritual skills welcome. [Oct98, sase requested]

WINDTREE RANCH

RR 2 Box 1
Douglas AZ 85607
windtreeranch@theriver.com
http://www.Windtree.org/

Began 1997 | Pop. 12 | Forming
Diet: Vegan | Rural | Spiritual

(Also known as Summerland Monastery, Inc., ATC.) Building ecosustainable lifestyles; delicious, colorful vegan meals of organically grown fruits and veggies we grow, prepared in our straw-bale hall; weaving recycled treasures into gnomelike homes made from paper and stone; snuggled into majestic red-rock mountains with breathtaking views and abundant wildlife: cougar, wolf, fox, deer, and bird sanctuary. Developing spiritual peace through connecting with Mother Earth in daily activities: construction, gardening, and other right-livelihood undertakings. We love and emotionally support each other's joys, gifts, and sorrows by following a path of tolerance and acceptance of personal choices. By willingly sharing finances, knowledge, and labor within a barter system we work to sustain this non-profit-oriented, non-ownership-oriented lifestyle for generations to come. By example we teach those children who share this sacred space with us. We live each day with the ever-present goal of ecosustainable, off-grid freedom from consumerist lifestyles as our way of quietly preparing for the Earth changes in a positive, cooperative, enlightening chance for us to heal ourselves physically, emotionally, and spiritually while our Mother Earth heals herself. We welcome like-minded healthy, whole, happy people to join us. [Sep99, sase required]

WINDWALKER FARM

1981 Indiana Rd
Ottawa KS 66067

785-746-8885
windwalker@computer-services.com

Began 1994 | Pop. 6 | Forming
Diet: Vegetarian | Rural

Windwalker Farm is located 5 miles southwest of Ottawa, Kansas, which is also 40 miles from Lawrence, Kansas, and 50 minutes from Kansas City. We live on 100 certified organic acres, including cropland, pasture, woods, and 6 acres of ponds. At Windwalker Farm we are committed to a community where good food and health are a right for all; education and work are productive and joyful; knowledge and natural resources are shared by all; an emphasis is placed on our connections with other people and the Earth; all living things enjoy peace, harmony, and freedom. Although we are in the forming stages of our community, we are striving for a community that fully demonstrates "living lightly on the land." We share as our vision a spiritual-based, integrated system for personal and community growth. Our core values include engaging in voluntary simplicity; becoming native to place; being responsible stewards; living in harmony; good food and good health; providing lifelong education to all, shared by all (we also embrace the unschooling concept); becoming self sufficient and sustainable; providing a nurturing, loving environment for child raising; and sharing an Earth-honoring spirituality while recognizing everyone's unique spiritual path. We have a certified permaculture instructor among our members. We are completing our first passive-solar, straw-bale house, which will be off the grid. [Oct99, sase required]

WINDWARD

55 Windward Ln
Klickitat WA 98628

509-369-2000
windward@gorge.net
http://www.windward.org/

Began 1980 | Pop. 12
Diet: Omnivore | Rural

Windward is about sustainable, self-reliant living that combines stewardship, entrepreneurial skills, and artistic expression. It's a pursuit of independent projects within a framework of cooperative association and mutual support.

Our fiber sheep and dairy goats set the rhythm of an intellectually dynamic and physically active life. On our 111-acre site, we're interweaving the skills of the past with appropriate technology to create a hands-on, back-to-basics way to practice right livelihood.

Our criteria: (1) we have to be better off with you than without you; (2) say what you mean and mean what you say; and (3) take it seriously or take it somewhere else.

If you can handle that, please visit our Web site. If you like what you see, the next step would be to write a letter introducing yourself to windward@gorge.net. [Sep99]

WINSLOW COHOUSING

353 Wallace Way NE
Bainbridge Island WA 98110

206-780-1323, 206-780-1323 fax
http://www.winslowcohousing.org/

Began 1992 | Pop. 81
Diet: Omnivore | Rural/Urban

Winslow Cohousing is located on Bainbridge Island in Puget Sound, 35 minutes west of downtown Seattle by Washington State ferry. Escorted tours are often available at 10:15 a.m. on Saturdays. Call 206-780-1323 to confirm time and dates. Or send $3 for information package and plans.

We are organized as a stock cooperative with 30 dwelling units and a common house on 6 acres with woods and gardens, within walking/biking distance of schools, shops, library, medical. Unit types range from studios to four bedrooms. All units are self-sufficient, with kitchens, dining areas, living rooms, bedrooms, and bathrooms. The group formed in 1989, started construction in 1991, and moved in early in 1992.

We are a caring, supportive, consensus-based community, trying to live lightly on the land, valuing sustainability, frugality, and our meals together five nights a week. [Sep99]

WISCOY VALLEY LAND COOPERATIVE

Rt 3 Box 163
Winona MN 55987

507-452-4990

Began 1975 | Pop. 34 | Rural

We are a land cooperative of around 25 adults and several children living on 356 acres in southeast Minnesota.

We share the land in common, but housing, incomes, diet, schooling, etc., are individual's responsibility.

We have very little turnover at our land co-op and find replacements by word of mouth. [Mar99, sase requested, no openings]

WISE WOMAN CENTER / LAUGHING ROCK FARM

PO Box 64
Woodstock NY 12498

914-246-8081

Began 1984 | Pop. 9 | Forming
Diet: Omnivore | Rural | Spiritual

(Also known as Rowdybush Farm.) Goddesses, goats, and green witches gather at the Wise Woman Center to reweave the healing cloak of the ancients. Community members of Laughing Rock Farm prepare organic wild-food meals including fresh goat cheeses for the guests, who come to study herbal medicine with Susun S Weed and spirit healing with Vicki Noble, Z Budapest, Whitefeather, and many others. Community members have time to attend all workshops and weekday goat walks plus plant talks with Weed. There is an emphasis on the Green Nations: herb gardens and herbal remedies for people and animals—we have goats, geese, rabbits, cats, ducks—and herbal wild-food good cooking. We forage for mushrooms in our rocky magical forest where fairies play with us, the turtles swim with us in the river and ponds, and the owl's cry soothes our hearts. Life in our community is based on speaking your truth every morning at talking stick. We seek to love all parts of ourselves compassionately. Personal time is encouraged—women are paid a day's wage to take a "moon day" once a month. Personal responsibility is absolutely required of all members, as is participation in simple ceremonies celebrating life and the seasons. Our days and nights are rich with experience and learning. [Nov98, cc]

Key to bracketed text: cc = cannot commit to prompt correspondance, sase = self-addressed stamped envelope

WOMAN'S WORLD

PO Box 655
Madisonville LA 70447

504-892-0765, 941-567-2026
shewolfww@aol.com

Began 1993 | Pop. 3 | Forming
Diet: Vegetarian | Rural

Woman's World is a forming lesbian village with individual homes intended. Our common grounds will cover 20 acres of our 115-acre property with the rest private deeded plots. We welcome lesbians of all ages, visitors, apprentices, and "trial" members.

This land lends itself to crop production, animal raising, and cottage industries. Solar power and water collection are feasible along with conventional utilities. We operate a small, rugged campground without modern facilities, which allows visitors to tent, truck, and RV camp while seeking community. We intend to live lightly on the land, provide a haven for women, and eventually build a retirement and assisted-living facility. We are currently seeking only lesbian adults with personal resources sufficient to be totally responsible for their needs; women capable of building (or hiring built) shelters of any kind. Jobs are plentiful in the area. We have mild winters, hot summers, and delightful springs and falls. Right now pioneers are most likely to enjoy this community as it begins its building processes. The land is secure, and the current residents have been in the area establishing good relationships. Land costs are reasonable for private ownership, and utilities are affordable. General cost of living is reasonable, and the soil is fertile for growing food. Arranged visits are required. [Jul99, sase requested]

WOMANSHARE

PO Box 681
Grants Pass OR 97526

541-862-2807

WomanShare is a home and small family of lesbians in southern Oregon. We have been a vital participant in the women's land movement since 1974, offering workshops, apprenticeships, celebrations, and community gatherings. We welcome all women visitors.

Each woman who lives at WomanShare has her own cabin, and we have a cabin for visitors. Cabins are small women-built living spaces with wood stoves and electricity. The communal main house is open to all. We have some shared meals, daily chores, and

seasonal work projects. Visitor participation is always greatly appreciated. WomanShare has a garden, bath house, and composting toilet.

We ask for a sliding-scale donation of $15–$35 per woman per night (or take $5 off for one hour of work donation). Lodging will be in a private cabin. Bring food, bedding, and flashlight. When you call WomanShare for a reservation, we will send you a map to find us.

Periodically, we are open for new members or extended visits and retreats. If you are interested, please call or write. [sase requested]

WOMEN'S ART COLONY AT MILLETT FARM

20 Old Overlook Rd
Poughkeepsie NY 12603

914-473-9267, 212-473-2546

Began 1998 | Diet: Omnivore | Rural
(Also known as The Farm.) The Women's Art Colony at Millett Farm summer residence for women artists and writers. Work exchange half day for studio space. Food contribution $80/week. Private rooms, darkroom, silk-screen studio, woodworking studio with machine tools. Swimming pond, 40 acres of woods. Residents learn building, mechanical, and tree farming skills. Communal dining—chef cooks meals; communal readings and studio visits. Purpose is empowerment and growth of women artists in supportive and beautiful environment. Orientation is feminist and progressive politics but tolerant and individualistic. Founder Kate Millett together with friends. Ten residents each summer. The farm has hundreds of members— past residents, friends, and supporters. The year 1999 marks its twentieth year of existence and its tenth year as a self-sufficient, self-supporting community for women artists. [Jan99, sase requested]

WOODBURN HILL FARM

27290 Woodburn Hill Rd
Mechanicsville MD 20659

301-884-5616

Began 1975 | Pop. 13
Diet: Omnivore | Rural

Woodburn Hill Farm was founded on a formerly Amish farm in 1975. After 13 years of communal sharing of meals, work, childcare, and expenses, in 1988 we turned to a co-op model with family units more independent.

At present, we're struggling with our definition of community.

The place is owned by our corporation of 28 shareholders, a multiracial group, all connected with the farm over the years. Decisions are made by consensus. Residents can be shareholders or not, but both types pay rent to the corporation to cover expenses. There are currently 10 adults and 3 children on 128 acres. We have one main house with common areas and three living spaces; three separate family houses; two trailers; assorted barns; and a new modular house with four living spaces, a large meeting room, and a geothermal heat pump. The rest of our heat is mostly wood stoves. We work locally in education, the arts, helping professions, and organic agriculture.

We try to "live lightly" here: gardening organically, recycling, composting. We tend toward vegetarian and are loosely committed to holistic health and nonsexist working. All adult residents share in the upkeep, with seasonal workdays and rotating chore sign-ups.

We are looking for creative, stable people who value cooperative living, ecological and social justice, spirituality, and celebrations.

Those interested should contact us in advance of a visit. [Nov98, sase requested]

Additions and corrections: Email: directory@ic.org, Web: http://directory.ic.org/, Mail: RR 1 Box 156-D, Rutledge MO 63563, USA.

Listings

WYGELIA

2919 Monocacy Bottom Rd
Adamstown MD 21710

301-831-8280
wygelia@erols.com

Began 1985 | Pop. 3 | Forming
Diet: Omnivore | Rural

(Also known as The Ditmans, JLD Associates). We are a group of three adults, two living on the land and one in Canada. We have 65 acres of hilly wooded land 40 miles from Washington, DC, and 6 miles from Frederick, Maryland. We represent a broad spectrum of training and skills, including fabric arts, upholstery, foundry, engineering, blacksmithing, welding, woodworking, and more. We have a large and well-equipped shop space. We have a large house with space for two to six more members and land for one more house within present zoning rules.

We are committed to empowering creativity and self-expression, to open communication, to personal growth, and to not keeping resentments.

We share our income, space, labor, meals, good thinking, and music. We are a haven for arts/craft and high-tech people who seek a secluded, extended-family type of home. We operate businesses from the land, and off-site income-earning opportunities exist within easy driving distance.

We seek new members; we welcome visitors. Please call in advance, no drop-ins. [Sep99, sase requested]

YAHARA LINDEN GATHERING

2117 Linden Ave
Madison WI 53704

608-249-4474, 608-249-4131

Began 1977 | Pop. 6
Diet: Omnivore | Urban

Yahara Linden Gathering is a housing cooperative in Madison, Wisconsin. Currently six adults live in a 100-year-old house in a mixed neighborhood near bus lines and bike paths.

We are committed to making the house a welcoming home. We have a garden, a cat, and a dog. We eat mostly organic food with an emphasis on locally grown or produced.

We are working-class folks with many interests, and we welcome open-minded diversity. [Feb99, sase requested, no openings]

YAMAGISHI-KAI

Gip Code 519-1424
555 Kawahigashi Iga-cho
Ayama-gun Mie prefecture
JAPAN

+81 595-45-4594
kai_kouhoubu@yamagishi.or.jp
http://www.yamagishi.or.jp/
environment/index.html

Began 1958 | Pop. 4000
Diet: No red meat | Rural/Urban

Yamagishism Life Jikkenchi has been built, with the hope that all people will be able to live happily and peacefully, and all healthy both materially and mentally. We believe that creating such a happy society is not beyond imagination, but that it is quite possible with certain concrete ideas, methods, and practices.

In this village, no one is struggling over his rights or duties. Clothing, food, and housing are all free. No chief, no managers—no orders, no controls. It's a village worth living a true life in. We villagers learn the real essense of nature and human beings by growing vegetables or taking care of animals and noticing the true way of living. And through this village life, we develop our sociality to live as a one-body society, and now we are enjoying the benefits of living together in plenitude. In this village, everyone can live a true and healthy life based on the most ordinary and the most prosperous life of human beings. One-body management with one wallet.

There are 24 Yamagishi villages in Japan and one in each of the following countries: Brazil, Thailand, Switzerland, Germany, and Korea. Together we have 4,000 people. [May99]

YESSS COMMUNITY

344 Indiana Ave
Venice CA 90291

310-399-0032, 310-664-1907

Began 1991 | Pop. 65 | Forming
Diet: No red meat | Urban | Spiritual

(Also known as Positive Living Center.) A Free Spirit spiritual community near the beach in Venice. Seek positive, healthy people. Semivegi, no drugs. Equal opportunities of helping community growth to everyone.

Meditation and yoga center, three homes, 20 bedrooms. An ashram for self-growth, no master but you who are also the student. Expansion oriented. Home of the largest public free-speech display in the world on the Venice Boardwalk every weekend. Developed by community founder Arhata, aka Erik Olson, ex–Wall Street account executive. Also a healing center under direction of Ki Steelman, Reiki master. [Jan99]

YOGAVILLE - SATCHIDANANDA ASHRAM

Buckingham VA 23921
cyi@yogaville.org
http://www.yogaville.org/

Began 1980 | Pop. 223
Diet: Vegetarian | Rural | Spiritual

Satchidananda Ashram—Yogaville is a spiritual center where people of diverse faiths come together to practice the principles of Integral Yoga, as taught by Sri Swami Satchidananda (Also referred to as Sri Gurudev.) We are situated on 1,000 acres of woodland along the James River at the foothills of the Blue Ridge Mountains in Buckingham, Virginia.

We conduct seminars, workshops, and retreats in various aspects of yoga, as well as teacher-training certification courses. We also have a school for young children from ages 6 to 12. In addition, we offer a summer Indian dance camp, room for private retreats, special women's retreats, cardiac-yoga teacher training, and much more. [May99]

YOGODA COMMUNITY PROJECT

8217 Ardleigh St
Philadelphia PA 19118

215-753-7058
yogoda@wj.net
http://www.wj.net/yogoda/

Began Feb99 | Pop. 2 | Forming
Diet: Vegetarian | Rural | Spiritual

Yogoda Community Project is a group of individuals dedicated to creating a spiritual community based upon the teachings of Paramahansa Yogananda. Company is stronger than willpower. Our goal is to create an environment that will be conducive to spiritual growth, a community whose goal is God-communion. The uplifting influence of spiritual companions is an invaluable help along the path to the infinite.

A daily routine of meditation will be the backbone of living at Yogoda, along with plain living and high thinking. Service to God, guru, and each other will be our standard way of living.

Key to bracketed text: cc = cannot commit to prompt correspondance, sase = self-addressed stamped envelope

Currently, Yogoda has some members living cooperatively in Philadelphia, Pennsylvania, as a stepping stone to forming our eventual rural community. Fully realized, Yogoda will be a community of around 30 residents. We have an e-mail discussion list. We are looking to join forces with other devotees. If you are interested in being part of Yogoda, please write, call, or e-mail us to get more information.

Yogoda is not formally affiliated with Self-Realization Fellowship or Yogoda Satsanga Society of India. [Mar99, sase requested]

YOHANA

"Locations forming in Santa Barbara CA and Hilo Hawaii"
yourespecial@hotmail.com

Began 1998 | Pop. 3 | Forming
Diet: Vegan | Rural/Urban

We are a forming young-adult-oriented community with two locations, one in Santa Barbara, California, and another in Hilo, Hawaii. Our interests would include personal growth, pursuit of knowledge, health, recreation, entertainment, music, lifestyles, arts, and culture. We are not into drugs, alcohol, tobacco, or specific religious beliefs.

The name Yohana is temporary. [Oct99]

YONDERFAMILY HOUSING AND LAND TRUST INC.

Rt 2 Box 108
Jeffersonville GA 31044
912-945-6078, 877-945-6078

Began 1967
Diet: Omnivore | Rural | Spiritual

Yonderfamily began in 1967 as a bus caravan of young hippies traveling across country seeking adventure. A sign was put in the destination window above the driver saying, Yonder. Yonder was where we were headed, and it first became the name of the caravan, then became the name of the family and eventually my own name. Our family consisted of anyone who was on the bus.

We supported ourselves by farm labor and forest work planting trees, etc. As time went on and children were born on the bus, our priorities changed to seeking land and community. Many attempts to be welcome home somewhere ended in dissolution, arrest, or having to leave to avoid a bad trip, child-welfare harassment, or hostility from local inhabitants, and we were on the road again.

In 1988 I bought a farm in middle Georgia, and we are still there raising hippies and planting trees. All you have to do to be here is show up. To stay you must help with whatever we are doing, fit in, and don't eat shit and bother people. Rent is $20 per week or labor trade. Also there is community or forest work for cash, and there are plenty of organic gardening and building going on. We also occasionally host gatherings, councils, and other events and hope to have a concert here soon. You may visit anytime. —Abe Yondananda. [Jan99, cc, sase requested]

YORK CENTER COMMUNITY CO-OPERATIVE, INC.

800 E 13th St
Lombard IL 60148

Began 1947 | Pop. 200

The York Center Community, Inc., is a 50+-year-old housing cooperative consisting of 79 individual homes, each on up to one acre of land in the suburban (DuPage County) Chicago area. The housing cooperative was founded upon Rochdale principles, which include a nondiscriminatory clause, a rarity in the 1940s! Historically, it was a catalyst for President Truman's executive order outlawing discriminatory practices in Federal Housing Administration (FHA) financing. Its structure has been upheld by the Illinois Supreme Court (1960). In terms of demographics and lifestyles, it generally reflects those of the middle-class suburban United States but with a professional population a bit skewed toward, not limited to, human-service professions. We value people of goodwill who wish to become a part of our community. [Sep99]

ZACCHAEUS HOUSE

89 Pine St
Binghampton NY 13901
607-773-0246

Began 1973 | Pop. 10
Diet: Omnivore | Rural/Urban

The Catholic Worker Movement, founded by Dorothy Day and Peter Maurin in 1933, is grounded in a firm belief in the God-given dignity of every human person. Today over 140 Catholic Worker communities remain committed to nonviolence, voluntary poverty, prayer, and hospitality for the homeless, exiled, hungry, and foresaken. Catholic Workers continue to protest injustice, war, racism, and violence of all forms. [Apr99, no openings]

ZEGG - CENTER FOR EXPERIMENTAL CULTURAL DESIGN

Rosa-Luxemburg Str 89
D-14806 Belzig
GERMANY
+49.033841.59510
+49.033841.59530
+49.033841.59512 fax
infopost@zegg.dinoco.de
zeggpol@zegg.dinoco.de
http://www.mir.org/zegg/

Began 1978 | Diet: Vegetarian | Rural

ZEGG is an international meeting point for questions of a future worth living. It is a study center for cooperation with nature, for questions of autonomy and survival, for new solutions in love, and for the creation of a network for a humane world. ZEGG experiments in community as a model for life and a building ground for a concrete utopia to establish a world free of fear, violence, and sexual repression.

In order to increase communication among each other the ZEGG community uses a ritual of the "forum." This creates the necessary transparency and trust for living together. In the past it turned out to be an essential practice that effectively helped the group to sail through every internal crisis.

ZEGG residents live together in small households of different sizes. Each person is responsible for their financial situation.

There are some companies on the compound, active in ecotechnology or in serving areas. Some of the members are employed at these companies or at ZEGG Limited.

For various areas of responsibility there are committees, such as conferences and seminars, childcare, finances, property, social issues. Important decisions are prepared in these committees and then presented to the plenary, where they are decided by all members by consensus. [Jan99]

Additions and corrections: Email: directory@ic.org, Web: http://directory.ic.org/, Mail: RR 1 Box 156-D, Rutledge MO 63563, USA.

ZEN BUDDHIST TEMPLE

1214 Packard
Ann Arbor MI 48104

734-761-6520, 734-995-0435 fax
buddhaa2@cyberspace.org

Began 1970 | Urban | Spiritual

We are an urban sangha (community) where members of any religion may practice Zen meditation. Our practice is based on the lineage of the Korean Buddhist Chogye order. We offer meditation courses, retreats, yoga classes, right-livelihood business workshops, lectures, a yearly peace camp, and special services in addition to our two public services every Sunday.

We also have a dharma worker's program and a three-year seminary program. We occasionally accept resident visitors by arrangement. Physical work is part of Zen training, and our active sangha members get together for gardening, temple maintenance, lawn care, our annual Great Green Recycling Yard Sale, our Big Buddha's Birthday Celebration, and so on.

All are welcome to call or write for further information. [Aug99]

ZENDIK FARM ARTS FOUNDATION

229 Regan Jackson Rd
Mill Spring NC 28756

828-625-9020, 828-625-8280
mail@zendik.org
http://www.zendik.org/

Began 1969 | Pop. 60
Diet: Omnivore | Rural | Spiritual

Zendik Farm is a cooperative community of artists, activists, and organic farmers committed to the survival of the human species through the practice of the Earth-saving philosophy known as Ecolibrium. Founded 30 years ago, we are a working model of a sustainable society based on honesty, cooperation, creativity, and universal responsibility.

We have recently moved and are restoring a beautiful old farm outside of Asheville, NC. We practice organic farming, dance, mechanics, music, eco-architecture, video, theater, animal care, natural healing, and other art forms.

We survive financially from donations brought in by our apprenticeship program, music CDs, and quarterly magazine—the largest underground magazine in the country. We run cable access TV shows in cities around the world. We believe that ecology is the only true religion, truth the only valid pursuit, and cooperation the only workable social ideal.

Zendik Farm offers long and short apprenticeships. Call for details. Send $3–$5 for a copy of *Zendik Farm Magazine*. [Oct99, cc, sase requested]

ZENTRUM WALDEGG — INTERNATIONAL COURSE AND COMMUNITY CENTER

CH-3823 Wengen
SWITZERLAND

0041(0)33.855 44 22
0041(0)33.855 44 22 fax

Began 1989 | Diet: No red meat
Our Vision:

An experimental community where people can learn to balance their four dimensional health needs and integrate these needs into their personal growth, evolution, and everyday life.

A place to live from the heart, to create, to relate, to be alive, and to experience a sustainable quality of life. A space where clear communication, mutual trust, freedom of choice, and service are valued.

A lively experiential and educational course and community center where people from around the world exchange and practice evolutionary health concepts of rejuvenation, longevity, agelessness, and immortality. [May99]

ZEPHYR

180 Zephyr Circle
Floyd VA 24091

Began 1981 | Pop. 19 | Rural

We are an intentional neighborhood in the Blue Ridge Mountains. We are full and are not accepting new members. Potential visitors please contact by mail only. We require advance notice.

ZEPHYR VALLEY COMMUNITY CO-OP

Rt 1 Box 121
Rushford MN 55971

Began 1995 | Pop. 21
Diet: Omnivore | Rural

Zephyr Valley Community Co-op was established so that we could house ourselves in a rural community. We bought our farm in 1994.

Our land is a 550-acre farm in southeastern Minnesota. It spans a wide range of ecosystems: wetland, river bottom, cropland, woodland, prairie, pond, and ridge.

The current members share some values that have guided us as we have begun our endeavor. We hope to live lightly on the land and use its resources with care. We encourage diversity. We participate in the wider rural neighborhood.

Our membership includes nine adults and eight kids. We have a musician, a nurse, a forester, an artist, a soap maker, an organic farmer, a student, and more. Our kids are great!

Our official structure follows: The co-op owns the land. Dwellings are privately built and owned by members. Members may use the land for private business ventures by paying a user fee. We use consensus for making decisions about the land. Lifestyle, spirituality, etc., are private matters. We share community meal once a week and often gather informally.

To join, one must become a trial member first. Members make a capital investment, and we all pay a monthly fee for ongoing expenses. [Mar99, sase requested]

ZIM ZAM VEGAN COMMUNITY

362 London Rd
Asheville NC 28803

828-277-0758
ab414@seorf.ohiou.edu
http://seorf.ohiou.edu/~ab414/

Began 1996 | Pop. 2 | Forming
Diet: Vegan | Urban

Imagine with us ...

You lie on a hemp hammock eating grapes from the arbor above. You're grateful for the privacy trees create on a mere acre of land. Estara calls your name. "Over here," you answer. "Could you please go to the co-op and get some quinoa and lentils? We need them for the dinner." She brushes past the cherry dogwood and picks a kiwi from the vine. "No problem," you respond. She hands you cloth bags and house shopping money. "Can I go too?" asks four-year old Amy from a nearby tree fort. "Both her moms consent," assures Estara. "Love to have you along, Amy." Still you linger, watching squirrels chase each other through the chestnut trees, appreciating this small wildlife haven, free from cats, dogs, or other owned animals. On the way you stop at the composting toilet and praise Amy as she washes her hands unasked

---

Key to bracketed text: cc = cannot commit to prompt correspondance, sase = self-addressed stamped envelope

Twin Oaks Community

twinoaks@ic.org
www.twinoaks.org
138-D Twin Oaks Road
Louisa, VA 23093
(540) 894-5126

Twin Oaks is an ecovillage of 100 people living on 450 acres of farm and forest land in rural Virginia. Founded in 1967, our lifestyle reflects our values of egalitarianism, ecology and non-violence. We welcome scheduled visitors throughout the year.

We are economically self-sufficient and income-sharing. Our hammocks, book indexing, and tofu businesses provide about one third of our work; the balance goes into tasks that benefit our quality of life–including organic gardening, carpentry/construction, milking cows, office work, and much more. Our work schedules are very flexible.

Our culture values tolerance of diversity and sustainable living. We share our vehicles, build our own buildings and grow our own food.

Twin Oaks has an elaborate community culture. Our everyday lives include social and support groups, music, dance, and art. Some of us work actively for peace and justice, ecology and feminism. Each summer we host a Women's Gathering and Communities Conference, inviting women, community seekers, and experienced communards to our home.

We invite you to visit or tour Twin Oaks. For more information, please contact us or visit our website.

Looking for the perfect gift?

(or just thinking about taking a short vacation in your own backyard?)

You can do both and support the communites movement at the same time with a TWIN OAKS HAMMOCK or CHAIR

We've been handcrafting fine outdoor furniture since 1967.

Check out our website at www.twinoakstore.com or call us at 540-894-5125

from the roof water catchment. At the pond you pause to spot one of the croaking frogs you hear. Then, holding Amy's hand, you cross the street to the bus stop, where you accept, instead, a ride from one of your friendly neighbors. We're currently two on an acre of lawnscape in a farm-style house, three miles from downtown. We've vision and determination. Come imagine with us. Create the transformation. [Dec98, sase requested]

ZION

980 Lola Whitten Rd
Selmer TN 38375

901-645-8036, 901-645-6678
901-935-2720 fax
shammahbn@yahoo.com
http://www.bethelsprings.com/

Began 1996 | Pop. 216
Diet: Omnivore | Rural | Spiritual

(Also known as Kingdom of Yah in Bethel Springs, Tsion Hadashah.) We believe the kingdom of God has not been seen on the Earth, except in short glimpses, since the demise of the early church. We believe that Yahweh, God of Israel, is now restoring that kingdom. We believe this not because we predicted it or read it but because we are watching him do what we dared not expect.

Yahweh's kingdom, which he has always called Zion, is where brothers dwell together in unity and where the blessing, everlasting life, is commanded by God. It is marked by total surrender to his will, and it is opposed, by its very nature, to every other way, life, and kingdom that exist.

We reject earthly weapons and leave politics to God himself. Our weapons are not earthly, but they are mighty through God, and they transform men and overcome every obstacle in our path. We don't vote, and we don't fight with guns or our hands; we pray.

We follow the spirit of God, and we believe that it is the spirit of God we follow because what results is the fulfillment of the Scriptures and matches what is found in the Bible. [Jul99]

ZION UCC INTENTIONAL COMMUNITY, THE

435-437 First St
Henderson KY 42420

502-826-0605, 502-826-0281
zion@zioncommunity.org
http://www.zioncommunity.org/

Began 1992 | Pop. 60 | Forming
Diet: Omnivore | Urban | Spiritual

The Zion UCC Intentional Community is located in Henderson, Kentucky, and is related to the United Church of Christ (UCC). The Zion Community includes both a UCC congregation of more than 200 members and an intentional covenant community of approximately 60. Zion UCC, organized in 1871, was once a dying church, when in 1992, it was reconstituted and revisioned as an intentional community.

The Zion Community places particular emphasis on intentional relationships with God and one another, community prayer, common meals, living joyfully, welcoming strangers, consensus-styled decision making, and shared responsibility. The community is located in an urban-related suburb of Evansville, Indiana.

Covenant members are engaged in a discernment process each July through October, when members reflect upon, write, and present their own covenant statements to live and work in community. Although members live in their own housing, a particular emphasis is placed on living in the immediate neighborhood, even though many members live a considerable distance from the community's center.

The Paff Haus is the community's meetinghouse. It is a peace-and-justice community center that is home to numerous organizations, services, and projects. Members maintain a community garden, a literary journal called Out of Line, a parish nursing program, an HIV/AIDS ministry, and many special outreach programs to the poor and marginalized. Peace with Justice Week: A National Gathering of Peace and Justice Activists is held each October and brings together some 400 activists, artists, musicians, writers, and religious leaders from across the country. [Feb99]

ZUNI MOUNTAIN SANCTUARY

PO Box 636
Ramah NM 87321

505-783-4002
dbalsam@prodigy.com
http://www.geocities.com/
westhollwood/heights/53471/

Began 1995 | Pop. 8 | Forming
Diet: Vegetarian | Rural | Spiritual

We are a gender-inclusive Radical Faerie Sanctuary on 315 acres in a four-season mountain climate, striving to create an Earth-oriented rural permaculture community to support our individual and collective spiritual and creative growth. We share our community space on an ongoing basis (our gates remain open) and through seasonal gatherings. As a step toward economic self-sufficiency, we operate Oso Notch Pottery. We invite all people of different philosophies, religions, and worldviews to join in our commitment to live in love, harmony, and respect for each other and the Earth for the work and play we call stewardship of the land. Our newsletter comes out four times a year. We recognize changes in lunar and solar phases and invite other queer folk to join us in that celebration. We welcome faggots, dykes, and breeders! [Nov98, sase requested, no openings]

Jillian Downey

About the Resources

In this section we list organizations whose work might be helpful to people who are active in the communities movement or are interested in community. We aimed for broader umbrella organizations and networks rather than those that were very specialized or local in scope. Our reasoning was that the umbrella organizations and networks will be good sources of information and referrals within their subject areas, with more complete and timely information on their niches than we could hope to compile ourselves.

We've organized the resources into categories. If you know the subject area you need information in, go to the subject category and browse. The categories are as follows:

- Agriculture
- Arts/Media/Culture
- Business/Trade/Commerce
- Community Structures/Land Trusts
- Ecology/Permaculture
- Education/Youth
- Energy/Technology/Science
- Food (Vegetarian/Organic/Preserving)
- Health/Personal Growth/Travel
- Housing/Construction
- Networking
- Research
- Spirituality/Religion

If you know the name of the resource you're looking for, simply use the alphabetical index on the next page to find its page number.

In addition, there is an expanded Resources list on the Web at http://directory.ic.org/ We are relying on readers and site users to provide us with suggestions of new resources and updated information on the current list—please stop by, or drop us an email at directory@ic.org. If you prefer to use regular mail, there is a form at the back of the book for *Communities Directory Additions and Corrections.* Please fill it out and send to the address indicated. Thanks for your help!

Resources, Alphabetical List

We invite you to assist us with additions and corrections. Updated information will be available on the Web at http://directory.ic.org/

Ⓖ

Agriculture

AGROECOLOGY PROGRAM UCSC

**University of California
Santa Cruz CA 95064**

**831-459-4140, 831-459-2799 Fax
http://zzyx.ucsc.edu/casfs/**

The Center for Agroecology and Sustainable Food Systems (the Center) is a research and education group at the University of California, Santa Cruz (UCSC). The Center's goal is to research, develop, and advance sustainable food and agricultural systems that are environmentally sound, economically viable, socially responsible, nonexploitative, and that serve as a foundation for future generations. Beyond the campus, we collaborate with nongovernmental organizations (NGOs), growers, community members, visiting students and researchers, and state and federal agencies, including the UC Cooperative Extension and the US Department of Agriculture. On the UCSC campus, the Center operates the four-acre Alan Chadwick garden and the 25-acre farm. Both sites are managed using organic production methods, and serve as research and training facilities for students, staff, and faculty. The public is welcome to visit both facilities.

AMERICAN COMMUNITY GARDENING ASSOCIATION (ACGA)

**100 N 20th St 5th Fl
Philadelphia PA 19103**

**215-988-8785, 215-988-8810 Fax
sallymcc@libertynet.org
smccabe@pennhort.org
http://communitygarden.org/**

The American Community Gardening Association (ACGA) is a national nonprofit membership organization of professionals, volunteers, and supporters of community greening in urban and rural communities, and promotes the growth of community gardening.

APPROPRIATE TECHNOLOGY TRANSFER FOR RURAL AREAS (ATTRA)

**Box 3657
Fayetteville AR 72702**

**800-346-9140
http://www.attra.org/**

Appropriate Technology Transfer for Rural Areas (ATTRA) is the national sustainable farming information center operated by the private nonprofit National Center for Appropriate Technology (NCAT). ATTRA provides technical assistance to farmers, extension agents, market gardeners, agricultural researchers, and other agricultural professionals in all 50 states.

BIODYNAMIC FARMING AND GARDENING ASSOCIATION (BDA)

**PO Box 29135
San Francisco CA 94129**

**415-561-7797, 415-561-7796 Fax
biodynamic@aol.com
http://www.biodynamics.com/**

Founded in 1938 to advance the practices and principles of biodynamic agriculture, the Association advocates an ecological, no-synthetic, sustainable approach to agriculture. In addition to publishing books and the bimonthly magazine *BIO-DYNAMICS*, they support regionally based programs of research, training, conferences, field days, and workshops.

CENTER FOR RURAL AFFAIRS

**PO Box 406
Walthill NE 68067**

**402-846-5428, 402-846-5420 Fax
info@cfra.org
http://www.cfra.org/**

Committed to building communities that stand for social justice, economic opportunity, and stewardship, it is a private, nonprofit organization sponsoring a diverse program for agriculture and rural communities. It engages in research, education, advocacy, and service work, and publishes the free monthly Center for Rural Affairs newsletter, as well as books, research reports, and special reports.

ORGANIC MATERIALS REVIEW INSTITUTE (OMRI)

**PO Box 11558
Eugene OR 97440**

**541-343-7600, 541-343-8971 Fax
info@omri.org
http://www.omri.org/**

The Organic Materials Review Institute (OMRI) is a 501(c)3 nonprofit organization created to benefit the organic community and the general public. Its primary mission is to publish and disseminate generic and specific (brand name) lists of materials allowed and prohibited for use in the production, processing, and handling of organic food and fiber. OMRI also conducts scientific research and education on the use of materials by the organic industry.

RODALE INSTITUTE

**611 Siegfriedale Rd
Kutztown PA 19530**

610-683-1400

Making the vital connection between healthy soil and healthy people has been the central thrust of Rodale Institute for more than three generations. The first task was finding agricultural solutions to major health and environmental problems. The second was proving that they worked. The third is now sharing them with the world.

Throughout the half-century since J. I. Rodale bought a Pennsylvania farm to test his radical yet timeless ideas, the first and second tasks have largely been completed. The third has become Rodale Institute's unswerving mission.

The labels for Rodale-style farming have changed over time—from organic to low-input to sustainable to regenerative—but the intent is unchanged: to provide more healthful food by creating and maintaining healthy soil.

Today's Rodale Institute is dedicated to worldwide communication of the soil-food-health connection, to lending strength and unity to the voices demanding change. It's a crucial act, an investment in life itself for ourselves and our children.

Additions and corrections: Email: directory@ic.org, Web: http://directory.ic.org/, Mail: RR 1 Box 156-D, Rutledge MO 63563, USA.

(...Agriculture, continued)

SEED SAVERS EXCHANGE (SSE)

**3076 N Winn Rd
Decorah IA 52101**

319-382-5990, 319-382-5872 Fax

Seed Savers Exchange (SSE) is a non-profit organization dedicated to the preservation of heirloom vegetables and fruits. SSE's members receive three publications each year, containing articles about historic gardening, Heritage Farm's projects, heirloom plant profiles, Plant Finder service, and more. *Seed Savers Yearbook* offers access to 11,000 rare varieties offered by SSE's members. Many are true heirlooms brought to North America when gardeners and farmers immigrated. SSE's annual yearbooks are by far the best access to heirloom varieties in the world. Membership fees provide vital support for SSE's genetic preservation projects at Heritage Farm, where 18,000 heirloom vegetable varieties are being maintained.

WILLING WORKERS ON ORGANIC FARMS (WWOOF)

**RR 2 S18 C9
Nelson BC V1L-5P5
Canada**

**250-354-4417, 250-354-4417
wwoofcan@uniserve.com
http://www.members.tripod.com/
~wwoof/**

Willing Workers on Organic Farms (WWOOF) offers placements on 400 organic farms all across Canada, and about 20 in the United States. (WWOOF has "expanded" into the United States, since there is no official US WWOOF.) Volunteers (WWOOFers) help for four to six hours per day in exchange for accommodation, meals, and an interesting experience. Members receive the descriptive catalog from which they can choose the farm they would like to contact and help.

⑥

Arts/Culture/Media

ALLIANCE OF ARTISTS' COMMUNITIES

**2311 E Burnside
Portland OR 97214**

**503-797-6988, 503-797-9560 Fax
aac@teleport.com
http://www.artistcommunities.org/**

The Alliance of Artists' Communities is a national service organization that supports the field of artists' communities and residency programs. It does this by encouraging collaboration among members of the field, providing leadership on field issues, setting professional standards, raising the visibility of artists' communities, and promoting philanthropy in the field.

Artists' communities are professionally run organizations that provide time, space, and support for artists' creative research and risk-taking in environments rich in stimulation and fellowship. Whether they are located in pastoral settings or in the middle of urban warehouse districts, artists' communities have been founded on the principle that through the arts, culture flourishes and society's dreams are realized.

ALTERNATIVE PRESS CENTER

**PO Box 33109
1443 Gorsuch Ave
Baltimore MD 21218**

**410-243-2471
altpress@altpress.org
http://www.altpress.org/**

We have published the *Alternative Press Index* (API) since 1969. It is the most complete index available for periodicals that chronicle social change in the United States and around the world. Published quarterly with annual cumulation in print as well as in CD-ROM and Web versions, the API is a comprehensive guide to 280 alternative, progressive, and radical journals, magazines, and newspapers. 20,000 articles are indexed each year. Selected abstracts from research journals are reprinted in the annual cumulation as well as in the CD-ROM and Web versions.

The Alternative Press Center also co-publishes with the Independent Press Association a directory of 328 periodicals called *Annotations: a Guide to the Independent Critical Press.* The APC operates a library of socialist, feminist, ecological, antiracist, and anarchist materials in Baltimore.

COMMUNITY BOOKSHELF

**RR 1 Box 156-D
Rutledge MO 63563**

**800-995-8342, 660-883-5545
660-883-5545 Fax
bookshelf@ic.org
http://bookshelf.ic.org/**

Community Bookshelf is a mail-order bookselling business run by the Fellowship for Intentional Community, publishers of this directory. It offers a wide selection of books on community, co-ops, and other aspects of alternative living and politics. Write, email, or call for a free catalog! (See ad on inside back cover.) Open Monday through Friday, 9:00 am to 5:00 pm US Central time.

INDEPENDENT MEDIA INSTITUTE (IMI)

**77 Federal St 2nd Fl
San Francisco CA 94107**

**415-284-1420, 415-284-1414 Fax
thausman@iaj.xo.com
http://www.independentmedia.org/**

The Independent Media Institute (IMI) is a nonprofit organization dedicated to strengthening and supporting independent and alternative journalism, and to improving the public's access to independent information sources. We believe that democracy is enhanced, and public debate broadened, as more voices are heard and points of view made available.

INSTITUTE FOR GLOBAL COMMUNICATIONS (IGC)

**PO Box 29904
San Francisco CA 94129**

**415-561-6100, 415-561-6101 Fax
http://www.igc.org/**

The Institute for Global Communications (IGC) is a nonprofit organization that provides alternative sources of informa-

We invite you to assist us with additions and corrections. Updated information will be available on the Web at http://directory.ic.org/

tion as well as online access and comprehensive Internet services for progressive individuals and organizations. Bringing Internet tools and online services to organizations and activists, with plans for the future to address the changes in the ways people access and use the Internet, we will provide flexible online collaboration tools and act as a clearinghouse for technological advancements. Our goal is to be the gateway for progressive Internet users.

MACROCOSM USA, INC.

PO Box 969
Cambria CA 93428

805-927-2515
brockway@macronet.org
http://www.macronet.org/macronet/

Macrocosm USA, Inc., a 501(c)3, is a nonprofit, tax-exempt, educational clearinghouse for progressives. Its purpose is to compile and edit materials into utilitarian formats such as handbooks, databases, a databank, and newsletters. The organization maintains a database of over 6,000 organizations, periodicals, publishers and businesses, media contacts, and other resource guides.

Macrocosm USA strives to present solutions and holistic approaches to urgent social and environmental problems and to provide materials to aid in understanding the social and environmental sciences. As an electronic networking hub, it will endeavor to become a vital international network of people, projects, and organizations. A small staff and interns will be necessary to ensure the continuation of its efforts. Tax-deductible contributions and memberships are welcome. Macrocosm USA has relied on no grant monies. It seeks to work with individuals and organizations who desire to reduce duplication and merge efforts. Perhaps by reducing redundancy we may, with many hands, make light work—as well as save time and money in the face of dwindling resources.

NATIONAL FEDERATION OF COMMUNITY BROADCASTERS (NFCB)

Fort Mason Center Bldg D
San Francisco CA 94123

415-771-1160
http://www.nfcb.org/memapp.html

The National Federation of Community Broadcasters (NFCB) is a national membership organization of community-oriented, noncommercial radio stations. Large and small, rural and urban, eclectic and targeted toward specific communities, the member stations are distinguished by their commitment to localism and to community participation and support.

SING OUT!

PO Box 5253
Bethlehem PA 18015

888-SING-OUT
info@singout.org
http://www.singout.org/

Since May of 1950, *Sing Out!* has been sharing songs and information about folk music. Each issue, of approximately 200 pages, includes complete lead sheets for 20 or more traditional and contemporary folk songs, plus feature articles and interviews, instrumental teach-ins, tons of recording and book reviews, the most comprehensive and up-to-date folk festival and camp listing anywhere, plus regular columns on the folk process, songwriting, storytelling, and folk dance. It also maintains a folk music "resource center," including thousands of items (recordings, photos, books, periodicals, and much more) available to its members.

Business/Commerce/ Trade

CENTER FOR A NEW AMERICAN DREAM

6930 Carroll Ave Suite 900
Takoma Park MD 20912

301-891-ENUF (3683)
301-891-3684 Fax
newdream@newdream.org
http://www.newdream.org/

The Center for a New American Dream is a not-for-profit membership-based organization dedicated to reducing and shifting North American consumption while fostering opportunities for people to lead more secure and fulfilling lives. The organization helps individuals, communities, and businesses establish sustainable practices that will ensure a healthy planet for future generations.

The Center was founded in 1997 with the recognition that the recent, highly materialistic definition of the American dream is undermining our families, communities, and the natural world. The Center serves as a hub for numerous local and national organizations promoting cultural, behavioral, industrial, and spiritual changes that are vital to reclaiming a healthy American dream. It distributes educational materials and conducts campaigns to help individuals make constructive changes within their homes, schools, workplaces, and communities.

CO-OP AMERICA

1612 K St NW Suite 600
Washington DC 20006

800-58-GREEN, 202-872-5307
202-331-8166 Fax
info@coopamerica.org
http://www.coopamerica.org/

Co-op America, a national nonprofit organization founded in 1982, provides the economic strategies, organizing power, and practical tools for businesses and individuals to address today's social and environmental problems. While many environmental organizations choose to fight important political and legal battles, Co-op America is the leading force

(...Business/Commerce/Trade, continued)

in educating and empowering our nation's people and businesses to make significant improvements through the economic system.

Our programs: (1) Green Business Program—starts and supports small socially and environmentally responsible businesses. (2) Consumer Education and Empowerment Program—helps people use their purchasing and investing power to create a more just and sustainable future. (3) Corporate Responsibility Program—encourages corporations to become socially and environmentally responsible; provides information about boycotts and shareholder resolutions against irresponsible companies. (4) Sustainable Living Program—provides information about practical measures people can take to make their personal, community, and work lives more meaningful and sustainable.

Our publications: (1) *Co-op America's National Green Pages*™—the largest annual directory of America's leading socially and environmentally responsible businesses. (2) *Co-op America Quarterly*—the nationally acclaimed magazine with information on how consumer power can produce progressive social change for the environment, housing, work, food, and other concerns. (3) *Boycott Action News*—up-to-date information on new and ongoing boycotts, published quarterly within our magazine. (4) *Financial Planning Handbook for Responsible Investors*—helps people make financial decisions that are both "values-added" and meet personal financial needs and goals. (5) *Co-op America Connections*—covers the latest information on how socially responsible businesses are responding to today's intensely competitive marketplace. In addition to these publications, we offer travel, long-distance phone, and credit card services from socially responsible companies.

CO-OP RESOURCE CENTER

1442-A Walnut St #415
Berkeley CA 94709

530-753-2667, 916-944-7935 Fax
Murnighan@aol.com

The Co-op Resource Center publishes a comprehensive catalog of over 240 books, videos, and other informational items about cooperatives. Representing the cooperative efforts of 17 organizations, the catalog is intended to provide access to knowledge and analysis about cooperatives.

COMMUNITY ECO-DESIGN NETWORK (CEN)

3137 Chicago Ave S
Minneapolis MN 55407

612-722-3260, 612-823-3964 Fax
erichart@mtn.org
http://www.cedn.org/

The Community Eco-Design Network (CEN) is a network of people, organizations, and businesses interested in ecological design and construction. We specialize in bringing together these groups to build innovative structures that showcase ecological design.

CEN was founded in 1995 as a non-profit organization committed to the research and implementation of sustainable technology for the built environment. Our goal is to help assist in the transition from a petrochemical-based technology and economy to a biostrategic-based technology and economy. Our focus is on projects that are neighborhood-sized in scale and are building a sustainable economic base.

E. F. SCHUMACHER SOCIETY

140 Jug End Rd
Great Barrington MA 01230

413-528-1737
efssociety@aol.com
http://www.schumachersociety.org/

The E. F. Schumacher Society was founded in 1980. The Society promotes the ideas inherent in the decentralist tradition and implements them in practical programs for local economic self-reliance.

The organization's purpose is as follows. (1) Initiate model grassroots programs for community renewal. (2) Gather a body of information to support the practical work. (3) Organize conferences and lectures to create fellowship, celebrate achievements, and provide a forum for continuing discussion. (4) Publish the results of these activities to educate a growing audience.

The Society's regional programs in microlending, community land trusts, local currencies, and consumer-supported farming have been replicated in small communities and urban neighborhoods throughout North America, and also in places as distant as Lake Baikal in Siberia. The E. F. Schumacher Library houses an 8,000-volume collection devoted to the study of human-scale institutions, mutual aid, respect for the land, and community renewal. The collection is computer-catalogued, and its index is accessible over the Internet.

Taken together, the programs of the Society present an integrated vision that can lead to a sustainable, decentralized "economy of permanence" that nurtures the Earth and its inhabitants.

INSTITUTE FOR SOCIAL INNOVATIONS

20 Heber Rd
London NW2 6AA
UK

+44 (0)181-208-2853
+44 (0)181-452-6434 Fax
rhino@dial.pipex.com
http://www.globalideasbank.org/

Is yours a new, imaginative, and feasible idea or project for improving the quality of life? If so (or if you know of such a scheme, or have a newspaper cutting about a likely project), please submit it, in less than 1,000 words, to the Institute's online Global Ideas Bank. This is accessed over a million times a year at present and already contains several thousand best ideas submitted by members of the public worldwide. Readers can vote on the ideas.

The Global Ideas Bank offers a total of 1,000 pounds (UK sterling) in awards (annually, with a deadline of June 1st) for the best nontechnological ideas or projects sent in. The Institute for Social Inventions, a nonprofit organization, also runs social invention workshops in schools, has a network of 400 members and subscribers around the world, and is a

We invite you to assist us with additions and corrections. Updated information will be available on the Web at http://directory.ic.org/

founding member of the European Social Innovations Exchange.

INTERNATIONAL CO-OPERATIVES ALLIANCE (ICA)

15 route des Morillons
1218 Grand-Saconnex
Geneva
Switzerland

(+41) 022-929-88-88
(+41) 022-798-41-22 Fax
ca@coop.org
http://www.coop.org/

The International Co-operatives Alliance (ICA) is an international nongovernmental organization that unites, represents, and serves cooperatives worldwide. ICA provides information from all continents on the cooperative movement in different economic sectors: agriculture, banking, credit, consumer, energy, fisheries, housing, insurance, workers, tourism, and health care, as well as links to other sites and issues of interest to cooperators.

NATIONAL COOPERATIVE BANK (NCB)

1401 Eye St NW Suite 700
Washington DC 20005

202-336-7700
http://www.cooperative.org/
http://www.ncb.com/

National Cooperative Bank (NCB), together with its development arm, NCB Development Corporation, provides a broad array of financial products and services, guided by cooperative principles, to commercial and real estate ventures throughout the United States. These ventures include traditional cooperatives such as retailer-owned grocery wholesale cooperatives, franchisee-owned purchasing cooperatives, and market-rate housing cooperatives. NCB was chartered by Congress in 1978. In 1981, NCB was restructured as a privately held financial institution, owned by its borrowers.

NATIONAL COOPERATIVE BUSINESS ASSOCIATION (NCBA)

1401 New York Ave NW
Suite 1100
Washington DC 20005
ncba@ncba.org
http://www.cooperative.org/
intro.cfm

The National Cooperative Business Association (NCBA) is a national cross-industry membership and trade association representing cooperatives of over 100 million US residents and 47,000 businesses ranging in size from small buying clubs to businesses included in the Fortune 500. We support cooperatives worldwide through training and technical assistance publications and programs.

RUDOLF STEINER FOUNDATION

Presidio Bldg 1002B
PO Box 29915
San Francisco CA 94129

415-561-3900, 415-561-3919 Fax
mail@rsfoundation.org
http://www.rsfoundation.org/
core.html

Since 1984, the Rudolf Steiner Foundation has been a progressive financial service organization supporting social and environmental change—particularly the kinds of change inspired by Rudolf Steiner, best known as the founder of Waldorf education and biodynamic farming. Our basic work is to connect philanthropists and investors with worthy projects in need of grants or loans.

Rudolf Steiner addressed the soul and spiritual poverty that modern humanity had fallen into by challenging it to rise above materialism and to accept responsibility for the disadvantaged, the developing capacities of children, a life-sustaining Earth, and the universe. He worked for the basic human principles of freedom in cultural affairs, equality in political affairs, and interdependence in a sustainable economy.

The Rudolf Steiner Foundation supports initiatives that are in accord with Rudolf Steiner's life mission for the self-development of each individual and the advancement of human freedom. The areas in which the Foundation supports research and activities include, but are not limited to: education and the arts; science and caring for the Earth; social responsibility and mutual support; medical and religious renewal; and associative economic relationships.

SOCIAL INVESTMENT FORUM

1612 K St NW Suite 650
Washington DC 20006

202-872-5319, 202-822-8471 Fax
info@socialinvest.org
http://www.socialinvest.org/

Our savings and investments can help create a better world! Our new guide gives you hands-on advice and information to help you put your dollars to work to build healthy communities, promote economic equity, and foster a clean environment. Use this dynamic resource guide to discover up-to-date return and performance information on a range of socially responsible investment options. Be sure to consult a financial advisor before investing.

SUPPORT CENTER FOR NONPROFIT MANAGEMENT

706 Mission St 5th Fl
San Francisco CA 94103

415-541-9000, 415-541-7708 Fax
ontap@ontap.org
http://www.supportcenter.org/sf/

With offices in San Francisco and San Jose, the Support Center is a consulting and training organization with a regional focus and a national reach. Through consulting, workshops, publications, and special management programs, we seek to help nonprofits use the best management tools and concepts to help them best serve their communities.

SUSTAINABLE BUSINESS.COM

231 W Pulaski Rd
Huntington Station NY 11746

516-423-3277, 516-423-4725 Fax
rfried@bccom.com
http://www.sustainablebusiness.com/

Sustainable Business.com is the center for environment and business on the Web, providing news, resources, insight, and inspiration to accelerate momentum toward a green economy.

(...Business/Commerce/Trade, continued)

It watches businesses, evaluates changes, and recommends sustainable businesses and jobs. It features a monthly online magazine that culls news, articles, and columns from over 35 leading sustainable business trade publications and individuals. Also, it helps green businesses find the resources they need to grow and helps investors find promising opportunities. Businesses can post listings as well as browse "Capital Available" solicitations.

UNIVERSITY OF WISCONSIN CENTER FOR COOPERATIVES (UWCC)

230 Taylor Hall 427 Lorch St
Madison WI 53706

608-262-3981, 608-262-3251 Fax
reynolds@aae.wisc.edu
http://www.wisc.edu/uwcc/

The University of Wisconsin Center for Cooperatives (UWCC) studies and promotes cooperative action as a means of meeting people's economic and social needs. It develops, promotes, and coordinates educational programs, technical assistance, and research on the cooperative form of business.

UPSTART SERVICES WORKERS CO-OPERATIVE

154 Stiby Rd
Yeovil BA21 3ER
UK

+0870-733-2538
sasandalex@gn.apc.org
http://www.gn.apc.org/ss/upstart/

Our goal is the growth of ecologically sustainable cooperatives committed to networking and mutual aid. We contribute to this process by providing comprehensive training and support services. We hope to work with groups and individuals wanting to set up new cooperatives, and to help turn their dreams into reality.

Our aims are as follows: to provide training and support in all areas of cooperative working, including finance, effective organization, economic viability, and group and individual skills; to provide

comprehensive training for new co-ops, including ongoing support once established; to provide affordable services, through economic risk-sharing and deferred payment; to train co-ops wherever possible to be self-reliant; to provide an effective and professional service; to educate people in the need for cooperative social change; to research and publish relevant information and advice; to network with other organizations involved in co-op support; to aid the personal development of our members and share skills; and to provide sustainable paid employment for our members.

Community Structures/Land Trusts

FOUNDATION FOR COMMUNITY ENCOURAGEMENT (FCE)

PO Box 17210
Seattle WA 98107

888-784-9001, 206-784-9077 Fax
inquire@fce-community.org
http://www.fce-community.org/

The Foundation for Community Encouragement (FCE), a nonprofit, educational foundation, teaches the principles and values of community to individuals, groups, and organizations.

It has grown dramatically since 1984. More than 375 workshops, conferences, seminars, and speaking engagements have been conducted for thousands of participants in the United States, Canada, the United Kingdom, and Australia. The focus of these events has been to teach groups how to achieve a sense of community or collective spirit and how, as a community, to identify a common purpose and accomplish agreed-upon goals.

FCE has a national office in Seattle, Washington, and has 76 facilitators—professionals in a wide range of occupations, who live in many parts of the United States and Canada, and who have been trained to work with groups and lead the community-building process. Facilitators and clients are carefully matched.

INSTITUTE FOR COMMUNITY ECONOMICS (ICE)

57 School St
Springfield MA 01105

iceconomic@aol.com

The Institute for Community Economics (ICE) is a national nonprofit organization that provides technical and financial assistance to community-based organizations working to produce and preserve affordable housing, land, jobs, and social services in communities where they are most needed. Our primary mission is to give communities the practical tools and skills for regaining control over their land in order to ensure its appropriate development and economically just allocation.

Our principal program for preserving affordable housing and farmland is the development of community land trusts (CLTs), a model that we developed in 1967. We are the primary provider of technical assistance for developing CLTs in the United States, and currently coordinate a national network of over 90 CLTs operating in both urban and rural communities in 23 states. We also operate a revolving loan fund, which accepts loans from socially concerned individual and institutional lenders, and directs low-cost lending capital primarily to nonprofit community groups that provide affordable housing. The fund often provides the critical initial funding for startup projects, money that enables them to develop a track record and approach conventional lenders. Write or call for free information about our programs.

INSTITUTE FOR CULTURAL AFFAIRS (ICA)

Rue Amédée Lynen 8
B-1210 Brussels
Belgium

(32) (0)2 219 00 87
icab@linkline.be
http://www.icaworld.org/

The Institute for Cultural Affairs (ICA) is a worldwide, private, nonprofit organization. Our aim is to develop and implement methods of individual, community, and organizational development. Our programs are highly participatory in nature and are often conducted in collaboration with other organizations, be they public, private, voluntary, or local

We invite you to assist us with additions and corrections. Updated information will be available on the Web at http://directory.ic.org/

community groups.

ICA activities include community meeting facilitation, educational research and training, organizational transformation, youth and women's programs, sustainable rural development symposia and projects, leadership training, personal development workshops, strategic planning seminars, conference facilitation, documentation, and evaluation. We have offices in 32 countries.

LAND TRUST ALLIANCE (LTA)

1319 F St NW Suite 501
Washington DC 20004

202-638-4725, 202-638-4730 Fax
http://www.lta.org/

The Land Trust Alliance (LTA) was formed in 1982 by four of the nation's leading land trusts to increase the effectiveness of the many diverse, independent, and geographically widespread land trusts. LTA has become the umbrella group for the land trust movement.

The Alliance not only provides a broad range of services from insurance to training aimed at helping to strengthen individual land trusts, but also acts as the voice for land trusts in Washington DC. The Alliance focuses on public policy issues of direct interest to land trusts, playing both an educational and an advocacy role.

The Alliance also publishes *Exchange*, the only professional journal for land trusts, and serves as an information source about land trusts for journalists and the public. With Hastings College of the Law in San Francisco, the Alliance established in 1990 the Land Conservation Law Institute to provide legal information to land trusts and attorneys. The Alliance also organizes the national land trust rally every 18 months, now the largest land conservation conference in North America.

TRUST FOR PUBLIC LAND (TPL)

116 New Montgomery St 4th Fl
San Francisco CA 94105

800-714-LAND, 415-495-4014
http://www.igc.apc.org/tpl/

Founded in 1973, the Trust for Public Land (TPL) works to conserve land for people. Working with citizens' groups and public agencies, TPL helps communities protect land for the public to enjoy as parks, open space, community gardens, recreation areas, and places important to the United States' cultural and historic heritage.

⑥

Ecology/ Permaculture

CENTRAL ROCKY MOUNTAIN PERMACULTURE INSTITUTE (CRMPI)

PO Box 631
Basalt CO 81621

970-927-4158
permacul@rof.net
http://www.permaculture.net/ Colorado/

Central Rocky Mountain Permaculture Institute (CRMPI), located at 7,000 feet in the Colorado Rockies, and founded by Jerome Osentowski in 1987, features an integrated forest-garden landscape of greenhouses, terraced beds, diverse plant species, and orchards. With only 100 frost-free days and 14 inches of rainfall annually, Jerome has created a hands-on demonstration site of remarkable fertility, diversity, and abundance—a mountain-top "Shangri-La" of innovative permaculture design.

CRMPI sponsors a variety of educational programs locally and internationally, and internship programs, courses, and weekend workshops. Our two main workshops of the year are our five-week intensive course as well as our 13TH annual two-week live-in permaculture design course—both feature nationally known instructors. We also offer consulting services for permaculture design, greenhouse design, and ecological golf-course design. Our Director, Jerome Osentowski, is available to make presentations or teach workshops at other locations.

Our other activities include a five-year-old demonstration farm in Nicaragua as well as our new Permaculture Afloat program in the Bahamas.

CULTURE'S EDGE

1025 Camp Elliott Rd
Black Mountain NC 28711
culturesedge@earthaven.org
http://www.earthaven.org/culture/ edge.htm

Culture's Edge is a not-for-profit charitable corporation dedicated to supporting, demonstrating, and catalyzing the development of healthy, sustainable, and regenerative culture. At the core of this mission is the creation of responsible relationships within and among the human and natural communities through research, education, and application of appropriate traditional and innovative tools, skills, and practices.

ECOLOGICAL SOCIETY OF AMERICA (ESA)

2010 Massachusetts Ave NW
Suite 400
Washington DC 20036

202-833-8773, 202-833-8775 Fax
esahq@esa.org
http://esa.sdsc.edu/

The Ecological Society of America (ESA) is a nonpartisan, nonprofit organization of scientists founded in 1915 to stimulate sound ecological research, clarify and communicate the science of ecology, and promote the responsible application of ecological knowledge to public issues.

ECOVILLAGE TRAINING CENTER (ETC)

PO Box 90
Summertown TN 38483

931-964-4324, 931-964-2200 Fax
ecovillage@thefarm.org
http://www.thefarm.org/etc/

The Ecovillage Training Center (ETC) assists transition toward a sustainable society through instruction in meeting basic needs for food, shelter, energy, gainful employment, and community.

ETC offers an immersion experience in sustainable living: courses and workshops, internships, and special demonstrations in green lifestyles. Set amongst The Farm community's 1,700 acres of woods and meadows, the ETC is a living laboratory with a mandate to increase biodiversity. Sustainable technologies and principles

(...Ecology/Permaculture, continued)

surround you as you study and work throughout the training center—its inn, organic garden, forests, swales, and ponds—in a permaculture consciousness, within an outstanding networking community of students and teachers.

ETC has hosted permaculture courses, courses in installing solar electricity and water heating, and yurt, cob, roundpole, and strawbale construction, a midwifery conference, a children's camp, and ongoing demonstrations in alternative energy, hybrid vehicles, and organic gardening. We inaugurated a student exchange program with Israeli kibbutz and a social justice program for training disadvantaged populations.

INSTITUTE FOR DEEP ECOLOGY

PO Box 1050
Occidental CA 95465

707-874-2347, 707-874-2367 Fax
ide@igc.org

A nonprofit corporation that promotes ecological values and actions through workshops, publications, and support networks.

PERMACULTURE ASSOCIATION OF BRITAIN

+44 (0)1654 712188
office@permaculture.org.uk
http://www.permaculture.org.uk/

The Association is an educational charity run by its members and helps people use permaculture in their everyday lives to improve their quality of life and the environment around them. It supports individuals, projects, and groups working with permaculture in Britain by: running a national office providing information and support; running a membership scheme to inform, support, and network between permaculture activists and groups in Britain; supporting the development of permaculture education; organizing national and local events, including the Annual Convergence, the largest permaculture gathering in Britain; networking nationally and internationally; providing information to its members, the media, and the wider public; seeking funding to research and develop permaculture projects; and working to make permaculture accessible to all people in Britain.

PERMACULTURE DRYLANDS INSTITUTE (PDI)

PO Box 156
Santa Fe NM 85704

505-983-0663
http://www.permaculture.net/PDI/

Permaculture Drylands Institute (PDI) is a nonprofit educational organization founded in 1986 to promote permaculture as a way of living and working in arid regions throughout the world. Established activities of the Institute and its graduates include: education, publications, demonstration projects, site-assessment, design consultation, and technical assistance.

Over 3,500 people have received training in permaculture principles and techniques from PDI and its graduates. The Institute has graduated more than 1,000 people from its eight-day basic permaculture design course, and its 60-hour advanced design course. Many more have been reached through various workshops. PDI has also offered programs through schools, at elementary through college levels.

PLANET DRUM FOUNDATION

PO Box 31251
Shasta Bioregion
San Francisco CA 94131

415-285-6556, 415-285-6563 Fax
planetdrum@igc.org
http://www.planetdrum.org/

Planet Drum was founded in 1973 to provide an effective grassroots approach to ecology that emphasizes sustainability, community self-determination, and regional self-reliance. In association with community activists and ecologists, Planet Drum developed the concept of a bioregion: a distinct area with coherent and interconnected plant and animal communities and natural systems, often defined by a watershed. A bioregion is a whole "life-place" with unique requirements for human inhabitation that are necessary if that bioregion is not to be disrupted and injured. Through its projects, publications, speakers, and workshops, Planet Drum helps start new bioregional groups and encourages local organizations and individuals to find ways to live within the natural confines of bioregions.

URBAN ECOLOGY

405 14th St Suite 900
Oakland CA 94612

510-251-6330, 510-251-2117 Fax
urbanecology@urbanecology.org
http://www.urbanecology.org/

Urban Ecology is a membership organization dedicated to building ecologically and socially healthy cities. Our mission is to develop and communicate innovative alternatives to the ways we build, making it possible for humanity to live in an ecologically sustainable manner that permits all people—and all species—the opportunity and fullness of life.

We work to create ecological cities by following these principles: Revise land-use priorities to create compact, diverse, green, safe, pleasant, and vital mixed-use communities near transit nodes and other transportation facilities. Revise transportation priorities to favor foot, bicycle, cart, and transit over autos, and to emphasize "access by proximity." Restore damaged urban environments, especially creeks, shorelines, ridgelines, and wetlands. Create decent, affordable, safe, convenient, and racially and economically mixed housing. Nurture social justice and create improved opportunities for women, people of color, and the disabled. Support local agriculture, urban greening projects, and community gardening. Promote recycling, innovative appropriate technology, and resource conservation while reducing pollution and hazardous wastes. Work with businesses to support ecologically sound economic activity while discouraging pollution, waste, and the use and production of hazardous materials. Promote voluntary simplicity and discourage excessive consumption of material goods. Increase awareness of the local environment and bioregion through local activist and educational projects that increase public awareness of ecological sustainability issues.

We invite you to assist us with additions and corrections. Updated information will be available on the Web at http://directory.ic.org/

Education/Youth

ALTERNATIVE EDUCATION RESOURCE ORGANIZATION (AERO)

417 Roslyn Rd
Roslyn Heights NY 11577

800-769-4171, 516-621-2195
516-625-3257 Fax
JerryAERO@aol.com
http://www.edrev.org/

The Alternative Education Resource Organization (AERO) is a nonprofit organization sponsored by the School of Living. AERO helps people who want to change education into a more empowering and holistic form. It helps individuals and groups of people who want to start new community schools, both public and private, or change existing schools. AERO provides information to people interested in homeschooling their children, or in finding private or public alternative schools. It helped develop *The Handbook of Alternative Education* and *The Almanac of Education Choices*, which list thousands of alternative schools and homeschool resources, and it publishes a magazine, *Education Revolution* (formerly *AERO-Gramme*).

CO-OPS 4 KIDS

http://www.coop.org/menu/kidsite.html

A service on the Web offered by the International Co-operatives Alliance (ICA). Cooperative businesses are democratically controlled by the people that use and operate them. Cooperation means people working together to meet their common needs according to the cooperative principles. There are different kinds of co-ops in almost every country, and probably some in your own community. Kids can get involved in co-ops by becoming members, co-op leaders, and supporters of cooperative ideals. Co-ops have values that kids share: they care about the environment, education, fairness, and building communities.

NATIONAL ASSOC. FOR LEGAL SUPPORT OF ALTERNATIVE SCHOOLS (NALSAS)

PO Box 2823
Santa Fe NM 87504

505-471-6928, 505-474-3220 Fax

The National Association for Legal Support of Alternative Schools (NALSAS) is a national information and legal service center designed to research, coordinate, and support legal actions involving nonpublic educational alternatives. We challenge compulsory attendance laws as violative of First Amendment rights and state provisions for noncompulsory learning arrangements (such as homeschooling).

NATIONAL COALITION OF ALTERNATIVE COMMUNITY SCHOOLS

1266 Rosewood Unit 1
Ann Arbor MI 48104

734-668-9171
djjv66e@prodigy.com

We are an organization of individuals, families, groups, and private schools who are united in their desire to create a new structure for education that is committed to creating an egalitarian society, by actively working against racism, sexism, ageism, and all forms of social, political, and economic oppression through participant control. Students, parents, and staff are empowered to create and implement their own learning programs. We publish a newsletter, and a directory of alternative schools and resources, with more than 400 listings in 47 states and 18 countries. We hold a national conference each spring, and various regional conferences as well.

NATIONAL HOME SCHOOL ASSOCIATION (NHA)

PO Box 290
Hartland MI 48353

513-772-9580

The National Home School Association (NHA) exists to advocate individual choice and freedom in education, to serve families who choose to homeschool, and to inform the general public about home education.

NEW HORIZONS FOR LEARNING (NHL)

PO Box 15329
Seattle WA 98115

206-547-7936
building@newhorizons.org
http://www.newhorizons.org/

New Horizons for Learning (NHL) is an independent, international, nonprofit network of people supporting an expanded vision of learning that identifies and fosters the fullest development of human capacities. We offer resources for learning organizations, and translate research and theory into workable solutions. We have constructed the Building (our Web site project) to provide information about people who are making a difference, environments that support teaching and learning, and guides to promising, research-supported resources of all kinds.

Our activities include publishing materials, producing conferences, consulting, and collaborating on projects and programs. Since we began the network in 1980, we've met many terrific people who share the conviction that everyone can learn more efficiently, and that learning is a lifelong process. Their support, volunteer work, and input keeps the network fresh and in touch with the best ideas in the world.

YOUTH FOR ENVIRONMENTAL SANITY (YES!)

420 Bronco Rd
Soquel CA 95073

877-293-7226, 831-462-6970 Fax
camps@yesworld.org
http://www.yesworld.org/

Youth for Environmental Sanity (YES!) was founded in 1990 by 16-year-old Ocean Robbins and 19-year-old Ryan Eliason. Since then, YES! has become one of the most successful youth-run environmental organizations in the world.

YES!'s national speaking and workshop tour has given inspirational presentations for 590,000 students in thousands of high school assemblies and college venues. By 1999, YES! had held 43 one-, two-, and three-week-long summer camps in seven countries. YES! Action Camps inform, inspire, and empower youth ages 15 to 25+ to take positive action for healthy people and a healthy planet. YES!'s 1996

(...Education/Youth, continued)

World Youth Leadership Camp brought together 40 of the world's most outstanding young environmental leaders from 20 countries for a week of networking, skills sharing, and community building.

Energy/Technology/ Science

AMERICAN HYDROGEN ASSOCIATION (AHA)

1739 W 7th Ave
Mesa AZ 85202

480-827-7915, 480-967-6601 Fax
aha@getnet.com
http://www.clean-air.org/

The purpose of the American Hydrogen Association (AHA) is to facilitate achievements of prosperity without pollution and to close the information gap among researchers, industry, and the public, drawing on worldwide developments concerning hydrogen, solar, wind, hydro, ocean, and biomass resource materials, energy conversion, wealth-addition economics, and the environment.

The goal of AHA is to stimulate interest and help establish the renewable hydrogen energy economy by the year 2010. To achieve this goal, the American Hydrogen Association is working in cooperation with governmental organizations, environmental groups and industry, communities, and schools to promote understanding of hydrogen technology, and help create a marketplace for pollution-free hydrogen energy.

AMERICAN SOLAR ENERGY SOCIETY (ASES)

2400 Central Ave #B-1
Boulder CO 80301

303-443-3130, 303-443-3212 Fax
ases@ases.org
http://www.ases.org/solar/

The American Solar Energy Society (ASES) is a national organization dedi-

cated to advancing the use of solar energy for the benefit of US citizens and the global environment. ASES promotes the widespread near-term and long-term use of solar energy.

AMERICAN WIND ENERGY ASSOCIATION (AWEA)

122 C St NW 4th Fl
Washington DC 20001

202-383-2500, 202-383-2505 Fax
windmail@awea.org
http://www.awea.org/

The American Wind Energy Association (AWEA) promotes wind energy as a clean source of electricity for consumers around the world. The Association provides up-to-date information on: wind-energy projects operating worldwide, new projects in various stages of development, companies working in the wind-energy field, trade associations, wind-energy advocates, technology development, and policy developments related to wind and other renewable energy development. In addition, AWEA represents hundreds of wind-energy advocates from around the world.

CENTER FOR RENEWABLE ENERGY AND SUSTAINABLE TECHNOLOGY (CREST)

1624 Franklin St #1000
Oakland CA 94612

510-588-5600, 202-530-2202
510-588-5609 Fax
http://solstice.crest.org/

The Center for Renewable Energy and Sustainable Technology (CREST) was formed in 1993, and produces educational multimedia CD-ROMs and operates Solstice, an Internet information service for the sustainable energy field. CREST has offices in both Washington, DC and Oakland, California.

CENTER OF EXCELLENCE FOR SUSTAINABLE DEVELOPMENT

1617 Cole Blvd
Golden CO 80401

800-363-3732, 303-275-4830 Fax
sustainable.development@hq.doe.gov
http://www.sustainable.doe.gov/

The US Department of Energy's (DOE's) Center of Excellence for Sustainable Development provides a variety of assistance to communities. Much of the information that can help your community develop more sustainably is available in the resource database and the articles and ordinances that are accessible from our home page on the Web. We also are developing programs to provide personalized technical assistance to communities. The types of assistance we can provide communities include the following: (1) helping people identify public and private sources of technical and financial assistance to carry out their individual program; (2) providing people with information about the public participation processes other communities have found work best in planning and implementing sustainable development; and (3) developing a menu of energy efficiency and renewable energy programs that fit the unique needs of each community.

CENTRE FOR ALTERNATIVE TECHNOLOGIES (CAT)

Machynlleth
Powys SY20 9AZ
UK

+44 (0)1654-702400
+44 (0)1654-702782 Fax
help@catinfo.demon.co.uk
http://www.cat.org.uk/

The Center for Alternative Technologies (CAT) is an educational charity striving to achieve the best cooperation among the natural, technological, and human worlds. We test, live with, and display strategies and tools for doing this. We are working for a sustainable future!

CAT is concerned with the search for globally sustainable, whole and ecologically sound technologies and ways of life. Within this search, the role of CAT is to explore and demonstrate a wide range of alternatives, communicating to other people the options for achieving positive change in their own lives.

We invite you to assist us with additions and corrections. Updated information will be available on the Web at http://directory.ic.org/

This communication involves three actions: inspiring—instilling the desire to change by practical example; informing—feeding the desire to change by providing the most appropriate information; and enabling—providing effective and continuing support to put the change into practice.

CAT has a holistic approach to its work, integrating ideas and practice relating to land use, shelter, energy conservation and use, diet and health, waste management, and recycling. Through its resident community and work organization, CAT is also committed to the implementation of cooperative principles and best achievable environmental practices.

INSTITUTE FOR LOCAL SELF-RELIANCE

2425 18th St NW
Washington DC 20009

202-232-4108

The Institute for Local Self-Reliance is a nonprofit research organization that promotes the development of healthy local economies through proper use of local resources and the use of environmentally sound technologies. We work with local governments, community groups, and businesses to achieve locally managed, sustainable economic development. Our research currently focuses on innovative and affordable alternatives to petroleum-based plastics, state-of-the-art scrap-based manufacturing operations, and the best recycling programs and technologies. We offer technical assistance in both rural and urban regions throughout the United States. Write to us for a list of publications.

INTERNATIONAL NETWORK FOR SUSTAINABLE ENERGY (INFORSE)

PO Box 2059
1013 Copenhagen
Denmark

+45 3312 1307, +45 3312 1308
inforse@inforse.dk
http://www.inforse.dk/

The International Network for Sustainable Energy (INFORSE) is a network of more than 170 nongovernmental organizations (NGOs) worldwide, many of which are umbrella organizations. All of these organizations work to promote sustainable energy and social development. In addition to the preparation of specific programs and projects, INFORSE is active in the exchange of information and awareness campaigns. It provides a meeting place for organizations working at all levels and is in regular contact with United Nations agencies, multilateral development banks, and other international bodies active in the energy field. Regional INFORSE coordinators meet once a year to plan global activities.

NATIONAL CENTER FOR APPROPRIATE TECHNOLOGY (NCAT)

3040 Continental Dr
Butte MT 59702

406-494-4572, 406-494-2905 Fax
info@ncat.org
http://www.ncat.org/

The National Center for Appropriate Technology (NCAT), established as a nonprofit corporation in 1976, works to find solutions that use local resources to address problems that face all US residents, especially society's most disadvantaged citizens. Through more than 20 years of service, NCAT's work has grown from addressing the immediate energy needs of low-income people to promoting a wide array of sustainable technologies and technology transfer, including nationally recognized work in energy and resource efficiency and sustainable agriculture.

NCAT has helped individuals, communities, government agencies, nonprofits, and others with appropriate technology and sustainable development issues by providing the expertise for a broad range of programs and projects.

NATIONAL RENEWABLE ENERGY LABORATORY (NREL)

http://www.nrel.gov/

The National Renewable Energy Laboratory's (NREL's) mission is to lead the nation toward a sustainable energy future by developing renewable energy technologies, improving energy efficiency, advancing related science and engineering, and facilitating commercialization.

NREL is a national laboratory owned by the US Department of Energy and managed by Midwest Research Institute, Battelle Memorial Institute, and Bechtel National, Inc. Almost 50 areas of scientific investigation include energy and efficiency, photovoltaics, wind energy, biomass-derived fuels and chemicals, energy-efficient buildings, advanced vehicles, solar manufacturing, industrial processes, solar thermal systems, hydrogen fuel cells, superconductivity, and geothermal and waste-to-energy technologies.

RENEW AMERICA

1200 18th St NW Suite 1100
Washington DC 20036

202-721-1545, 202-467-5780 Fax
renewamerica@counterpart.org
http://www.crest.org/
renew_america/

Renew America coordinates a network of community and environmental groups, businesses, government leaders, and civic activists to exchange ideas and expertise for improving the environment. By finding and promoting programs that work, we help to inspire communities and businesses to meet today's environmental challenges. Renew America's Environmental Success Index chronicles more than 1,400 effective environmental programs nationwide that measurably protect, restore, or enhance the environment. When individuals or organizations face a specific environmental problem, they can learn how projects in the Index address similar issues. The ongoing search for environmental programs reaches out to local and national organizations, corporate executives, educational institutions, and all levels of government. Programs in the Index meet tough standards for program effectiveness, natural resource conservation, economic progress, and human development.

Additions and corrections: Email: directory@ic.org, Web: http://directory.ic.org/, Mail: RR 1 Box 156-D, Rutledge MO 63563, USA.

*(...Energy/Technology/
Science, continued)*

ROCKY MOUNTAIN INSTITUTE (RMI)

**1739 Snowmass Creek Rd
Old Snowmass CO 81654**

**970-927-3851, 970-927-3420 Fax
rjacobs@rmi.org
http://www.rmi.org/**

Rocky Mountain Institute (RMI) is an independent, nonprofit research and educational foundation with a vision across boundaries. Seeking ideas that transcend ideology, and harnessing the problem-solving power of free-market economics, RMI's mission is to foster the efficient and sustainable use of resources as a path to global security.

Established in 1982 by resource analysts Hunter and Amory Lovins, research is focused in seven interrelated areas: energy, transportation, green real estate development, climate change, water, economic renewal, and corporate sustainability.

Working mainly in the United States, but with a global perspective, Rocky Mountain Institute devises new solutions to old problems—or, better yet, new ways to avoid problems altogether.

RMI's headquarters, located at 7,100 feet in Old Snowmass, Colorado, is a working example of resource efficiency and renewable energy in harmony with people and the environment. Since 1984, more than 40,000 visitors have toured the building to learn about its energy- and water-saving features.

SOLAR COOKERS INTERNATIONAL (SCI)

**1919 21st St Suite 101
Sacramento CA 95814**

916-455-4499, 916-455-4498 Fax

Solar Cookers International (SCI), an educational, nonprofit organization, was formed in 1987 by a group of educators and skilled solar cooks. It is led by a volunteer board of directors. There are hundreds of volunteers worldwide teaching solar cooking in their own communities.

To reach the millions in need, SCI acts as an international clearinghouse of solar cooker information. By providing a range of information services like educational materials and teaching tools, research, training, and communication networks among solar cooking groups, SCI empowers many others worldwide.

UNION OF CONCERNED SCIENTISTS (UCS)

**Two Brattle Square
Cambridge MA 02238**

**617-547-5552, 617-864-9405 Fax
ucs@ucsusa.org
http://www.ucsusa.org/**

The Union of Concerned Scientists (UCS) works to improve the environment in ways that preserve our health, protect our safety, and enhance the quality of life in our communities. We work to ensure that all people have clean air and energy, as well as safe and sufficient food. We strive for a future that is free from the threats of global warming and nuclear war, and a planet that supports a rich abundance of life. In short, UCS seeks a great change in humankind's stewardship of the Earth.

By forging a partnership between scientists and concerned citizens, UCS is uniquely able to secure the changes in governmental policy, corporate behavior, and people's actions needed to achieve these goals.

We combine rigorous scientific analysis, innovative policy development, and tenacious citizen advocacy to make positive, tangible improvements in people's lives. UCS works for change globally, nationally, and in communities throughout the United States.

WORLD FUTURE SOCIETY

**7910 Woodmont Ave #450
Bethesda MD 20814**

**301-656-8274, 301-951-0394 Fax
wfsinfo@wfs.org
http://www.wfs.org/**

The World Future Society is an association of people interested in how social and technological developments are shaping the future. The Society was founded in 1966, and is chartered as a nonprofit educational and scientific organization. We strive to serve as a neutral clearinghouse for ideas about the future—including forecasts, recommendations, and alternative scenarios. Membership is open to anyone who would like to know more about what the future will hold. We presently have 30,000 members in more than 80 countries, and over 100 local chapters worldwide. Annual dues include a subscription to our bimonthly magazine, *The Futurist*.

⑥

Food (Vegetarian, Organic, Preserving)

CANADIAN AND UNITED STATES FOOD CO-OP DIRECTORY

**PO Box 2600 Station A
Springfield Ave
Champaign IL 61825**

**217-352-3347
jbarclay@prairienet.org.
http://www.prairienet.org/
co-op/directory/**

A cooperative or co-op is an organization owned and controlled democratically by its members. There are over 300 food cooperatives in the United States. Our directory focuses on food co-ops in the United States and Canada, but the worldwide cooperative movement has over 700 million members in agricultural, banking, credit and savings, energy, industry, insurance, fishery, tourism, housing, and many other types of cooperatives. Co-ops give consumers and workers control over the places we bank, shop, work, and live in order to improve the quality of our lives.

INTERNATIONAL VEGETARIAN UNION

**c/o Parkdale Dunham Rd
Altrincham WA14 4QG Cheshire
UK**

http://www.ivu.org/

The International Vegetarian Union is a nonprofit organization with membership open to any vegetarian society subscribing to the vegetarian ethic whose executive authority is vested in vegetarians. Associate membership is open to any organization that is in sympathy with animal welfare, humanitarian, health, or similar relevant objectives.

We invite you to assist us with additions and corrections. Updated information will be available on the Web at http://directory.ic.org/

Resources

NORTH AMERICAN VEGETARIAN SOCIETY (NAVS)

PO Box 72
Dolgeville NY 13329

518-568-7970, 518-568-7979 Fax

The North American Vegetarian Society (NAVS) is a nonprofit educational organization dedicated to the vegetarian way of life. We organize and sponsor annual vegetarian conferences, including two world events. NAVS works year-round to provide factual information to its members, the public, local groups, interested organizations, and the media. Our educational efforts include: publishing *Vegetarian Voice*, our quarterly newsmagazine; sponsoring both regional and national conferences; distributing books and other educational materials by mail and at local and national events; and responding to inquiries from all sectors of society.

NAVS has instituted a local-chapter program to further broaden vegetarian outreach. As originator and organizer of the annual celebration of World Vegetarian Day (October 1), NAVS seeks to promote the joy, compassion, and life-enhancing possibilities of vegetarianism.

PRESERVING FOOD SAFELY

http://www.msue.msu.edu/msue/ imp/mod01/master01.html

A full text database on the Web on canning, freezing, and drying of food. Based on the US Department of Agriculture's *Complete Guide to Home Canning*. (Last full revision in September of 1994.)

VEGANS IN COMMUNITY

veganboi@aol.com
http://www.ic.org/vegan/

While most intentional communities are not vegan or vegetarian, many do accommodate vegans in their midst to varying degrees. This is not true of all communities, however; a few make no provisions at all for vegans, and as a consequence, vegans don't join. If you're an individual looking for a community, this Web page can help you get a vegan's-eye view of how vegan-friendly a given community is. This Web page is effective only to the extent that vegans living in community actually list themselves on it as contacts. If

you're a vegan living in community, please make sure that at least one vegan from your community is listed. That puts you in touch with vegans in other communities as well as potential visitors and members who are vegan.

VEGETARIAN RESOURCE GROUP (VRG)

PO Box 1463
Baltimore MD 21203

410-366-8343
vrg@vrg.org
http://www.vrg.org/

The Vegetarian Resource Group (VRG) is a nonprofit organization dedicated to educating the public on vegetarianism and the interrelated issues of health, nutrition, ecology, ethics, and world hunger. In addition to publishing the *Vegetarian Journal*, VRG produces and sells cookbooks, other books, pamphlets, and article reprints.

Health/Personal Growth/Travel

ALTERNATIVE MEDICINE HOMEPAGE

Charles B Wessel
MLS Falk Library
of the Health Sciences
University of Pittsburgh
Pittsburgh PA 15261

cbw+@pitt.edu
http://www.pitt.edu/~cbw/altm.html

Alternative Medicine Homepage is a jump station for sources of information on unconventional, unorthodox, unproven or alternative, complementary, innovative, integrative therapies. Alternative therapies include, but are not limited to, the following disciplines: folk medicine, herbal medicine, diet fads, homeopathy, faith healing, new age healing, chiropractic, acupuncture, naturopathy, massage, and music therapy. The Alternative Medicine Homepage provides links to Internet information sources and does not replace care by a qualified health practitioner.

AMERICAN FIELD SERVICE INTERCULTURAL PROGRAMS (AFS)

310 SW Fourth Ave
Info Center Suite 630
Portland OR 97204

800-AFS-INFO, 503-241-1653 Fax
afsinfo@afs.org
http://www.afs.org/usa/

American Field Service Intercultural Programs (AFS) is an international, not-for-profit, nongovernmental organization that promotes intercultural learning through worldwide exchange programs for students, teachers, adults, and families. Since its founding, AFS has been a people-to-people movement that transcends national, social, political, and religious barriers. We have a long-held commitment to socioeconomic diversity and are the only major citizen exchange organization in the United States that actively recruits minority, handicapped, and underprivileged teenagers, often with no expense to these participants. Participants in AFS programs gain a more profound cultural understanding of other societies, which is essential to the achievement of social justice and lasting peace in a world of diversity.

CHEMICAL INJURY INFORMATION NETWORK (CIIN)

PO Box 301
White Sulphur Springs MT 59645

406-547-2255, 406-547-2455 Fax
http://ciin.org/

The Chemical Injury Information Network (CIIN) is a tax-exempt, nonprofit, charitable support and advocacy organization run by the chemically injured for the benefit of the chemically injured. It focuses primarily on education, credible research into Multiple Chemical Sensitivities (MCS), and the empowerment of the chemically injured.

CIIN provides its members: (1) expert witness/doctor referrals; (2) attorney referrals; (3) a list of organization(s) in the state where the member resides; (4) a list of CIIN members for the state where the member resides; (5) referrals to experts in the fields of electromagnetic fields (EMFs), less-toxic pesticide and weed control, etc.; (6) peer counseling;

*(...Health/Personal Growth/
Travel, continued)*

(7) CIIN's monthly newsletter, *Our Toxic Times;* (8) materials for educational events, such as Earth Day booths; and (9) resource materials.

DISABILITIES INFORMATION RESOURCES (DINF)

**7 Belmont Circle
Trenton NJ 08618**

**609-984-8044, 609-984-8048 Fax
ingram@prodworks.com
http://www.dinf.org/**

Disabilities Information Resources (DINF) has been set up to collect information on disabilities and disabilities-related subjects and make it available through the Web.

The information will be accessible to anyone, but special attention will be paid by DINF to reach out to third-world countries where the world majority of people with disability live and information may not be currently available or easily accessible. The information may be in text, image, audio, multimedia, or combined formats. The information will be accessible directly via standard Web browsers, nonvisual browsers, and by users calling into the servers and using the telephone as a Web browser. It is fundamental to the DINF projects that all information provided will be fully accessible to all the potential user communities.

GROWING PLACE

**http://ourworld.compuserve.com/
homepages/growingplace/**

A partial directory on the Web, of centers, workshops, and organizations devoted to personal growth and intentional community. Looking for ways to grow, meet new people, and have new experiences? Looking for an offbeat lifestyle, or new ways of relating? Would you like to be a different kind of person than you are now? Growing Place is the place to start.

HOSPITALITY EXCHANGE

**PO Box 561
Lewistown MT 59457**

**406-538-8770
hospitalityex@hotmail.com
http://www.goldray.com/hospitality/**

The Hospitality Exchange is a traveler's directory of friendly, travel-loving people who offer each other the gift of hospitality in their homes. Members like to travel, be hosted by other members, and, in turn, host traveling members themselves. Each *Directory* contains listings of the membership. Each listing provides details on that member's interests and the hospitality they can provide.

HOSTELLING INTERNATIONAL—AMERICAN YOUTH HOSTELS (HI-AYH)

**PO Box 37613
Washington DC 20013**

**202-783-6161, 202-783-6171 Fax
hiayhserv@hiayh.org
http://www.hiayh.org/**

Hostelling International—American Youth Hostels (HI-AYH), a nonprofit organization, promotes international understanding through its network of hostels and educational and recreational travel programs. Hostels are inexpensive, dormitory-style accommodations for travelers of all ages. The HI-AYH network includes 140 hostels nationwide in major cities and beautiful natural settings. Most hostels have rooms available for couples, families, and large groups. HI-AYH is the US affiliate of the International Youth Hostel Federation, which maintains 4,500 hostels in 70 countries.

LA LECHE LEAGUE INTERNATIONAL

**1400 N Meacham Rd
Schaumburg IL 60173**

**847-519-7730
http://www.lalecheleague.org/**

La Leche League International is an international, nonprofit, nonsectarian organization dedicated to providing education, information, support, and encouragement to women who want to breast feed. All breast-feeding mothers, as well as future breast-feeding mothers, are welcome to come to our meetings or call our Leaders for breast-feeding help. We also provide health-care professionals with continuing education opportunities and the latest research on lactation management.

MIDWIVES' ALLIANCE OF NORTH AMERICA (MANA)

**5462 Madison St
Hilliard OH 43026**

**888-923-MANA [6262]
http://www.mana.org/**

The Midwives' Alliance of North America (MANA) is an organization of North American midwives and their advocates. MANA's central mission is to promote midwifery as a quality health-care option for North American families.

MANA-Canada, Box 26141 RPO, Sherbrook Winnipeg, Manitoba Canada R3C 4K9.

NATIONAL CENTER FOR COMPLEMENTARY AND ALTERNATIVE MEDICINE (NCCAM)

**PO Box 8218
Silver Spring MD 20907**

**888-644-6226, 301-495-4957 Fax
http://nccam.nih.gov/**

The US National Institute of Health's (NIH's) National Center for Complementary and Alternative Medicine (NCCAM) conducts and supports basic and applied research and training, and disseminates information on complementary and alternative medicine to practitioners and the public.

NATIONAL WOMEN'S HEALTH RESOURCE CENTER INC. (NWHRC)

**120 Albany St Suite 820
New Brunswick NJ 08901**

**877-98-NWHRC [986-9472]
732-828-8575
http://www.healthywomen.org/**

It can be tough to find reliable medical data and credible answers to health questions. That's why we're here, the National Women's Health Resource Center (NWHRC), the national clearinghouse for information and resources about

---

We invite you to assist us with additions and corrections. Updated information will be available on the Web at http://directory.ic.org/

women's health. Our primary goal is to educate health-care consumers and empower them to make intelligent decisions. We do this by providing women with easy-to-understand and easy-to-reach information and services.

SACRED SPACE INSTITUTE

PO Box 4322-C
San Rafael CA 94913
pad@well.com
http://www.lovewithoutlimits.com/

The Sacred Space Institute grew out of an erotic affinity group of intimate peers with the common goal of supporting each other's spiritual evolution. Our intention is to create a context in which the arts of whole-systems healing, sacred sexuality, and new-paradigm relating can be taught, developed, applied, given professional legitimacy, and disseminated to a wide international public. We offer workshops on polyamory, new-paradigm relating, and sacred sexuality in many cities in the United States and abroad. We are also available to coach individuals, couples, and families in person or by phone. We've been doing this work since 1984—let our experience serve you!

SIMPLE LIVING NETWORK

PO Box 233
Trout Lake WA 98650

509-395-2323, 509-395-2128 Fax
slnet@slnet.com
http://www.simpleliving.net/

The Simple Living Network provides tools for those who are serious about learning to live a more conscious, simple, healthy, and Earth-friendly lifestyle.

Although it may seem strange that something called "The Simple Living Network" has a Web site and mail-order catalog, the reality is that this is the most effective, efficient, and simple way we have found to introduce hundreds of thousands of people around the world to the many simplicity resources available. This is also the most Earth-friendly method—no paper, no printing, and no postage or shipping of expensive newsletters and catalogs.

Housing/ Construction

CENTER FOR RESOURCEFUL BUILDING TECHNOLOGY (CRBT)

PO Box 100
Missoula MT 59806
crbt@montana.com
http://www.montana.com/CRBT/

The Center for Resourceful Building Technology (CRBT) is a nonprofit corporation dedicated to promoting environmentally responsible practices in construction. Its mission is to serve as both catalyst and facilitator in encouraging building technologies that realize a sustainable and efficient use of resources. Through research, education, and demonstration, CRBT promotes resource efficiency in building design, materials selection, and construction practices.

FEDERATION OF HOUSING COLLECTIVES (FOHCOL)

Claisebrook Lotteries House
31-33 Moore St
East Perth WA 6005
Australia

+61(08) 9325 8333
+61(08) 9325 8113 Fax
fohcol@vianet.net.au
http://www.vianet.net.au/~fohcol/

The Federation of Housing Collectives (FOHCOL) is the representative body for housing cooperatives in western Australia. It is a not-for-profit organization.

HABITAT FOR HUMANITY

121 Habitat St
Americus GA 31709

912-924-6935, 912-924-6541 Fax
public_info@habitat.org
http://www.habitat.org/

Habitat For Humanity is an ecumenical, grassroots, Christian ministry with the goal of eliminating poverty housing. There are over 1100 affiliated projects in the United States, and 164 projects in 35 other countries. Funding comes from individuals, churches, corporations, foundations, and other organizations that are moved by concern and compassion to help those in need. Mortgage payments are put into a local "Fund for Humanity" and recycled to build new houses. No government funds are used for construction, though grants are accepted for land acquisition and infrastructure costs. Habitat operates with a core group of paid clerical and support staff, but relies primarily on volunteer labor. Each affiliated project is run by a local board.

NATIONAL ASSOCIATION OF HOUSING COOPERATIVES (NAHC)

1614 King St
Alexandria VA 22314

703-549-5201
coophousing@usa.net
http://www.coophousing.org/

National Association of Housing Cooperatives (NAHC) is a nonprofit national federation of housing co-ops, professionals, organizations, and individuals promoting the interests of co-op housing communities. We provide technical assistance and training to housing co-op boards and members to help them improve the operation of their co-op.

RADICAL ROUTES

c/o Cornerstone Resource Centre
16 Sholebroke Ave
Leeds LS7 3HB
UK

(+44) 113-262-9365
cornerstone@gn.apc.org
http://www.radicalroutes.org.uk/

Radical Routes is a UK-wide secondary cooperative whose members are small independent workers' or housing co-ops. Each in its own way is working for a socially just and ecologically sustainable society. Our central aim is to empower people to take control of and responsibility for their own lives, especially in the areas of work, housing, and education.

We act as a mutual aid network for our members and associates, providing help and information on both the technical and practical aspects of setting up and running small democratic co-ops. There is a strong emphasis on participation, soli-

(...Housing/Construction, continued)

darity, and personal support. We are a network of friends, not a bureaucratic hierarchy, and hope to remain that way as we grow and develop a more local regional structure.

We are a recognized Promoting Body for Housing Co-operatives and so are able to offer a relatively cheap registration service. This is handled by one of our members, Catalyst Collective Ltd., and is available to any potential co-op, not just prospective members of Radical Routes.

We also operate an ethical investment scheme providing a loan fund for our members. Most commonly we make top-up loans for the purchase of property, with Triodos Bank, The Ecology Building Society, or ICOF acting as the main lender. Although Radical Routes might only provide 20 to 30 percent of the purchase price, this contribution is often essential for the project to go ahead.

SUSTAINABLE BUILDING SOURCEBOOK

Austin TX
billc@greenbuilder.com
http://www.greenbuilder.com/
sourcebook/contents.html

Our Green Building Program information is disseminated with little extra effort and no extra expense on the Web, and builders and homeowners have easy access to detailed guidelines and resources on topics that can otherwise be hard to find. Categories include: Sustainable Sources, Sustainable Sources Bookstore, Directory of Green Building Professionals, Sustainable Building Calendar, and Green Building Conferences.

Networking

CANADIAN COHOUSING NETWORK (CCN)

#24 - 20543 96th Ave
Langley BC V1M 3W3
Canada

604-888-1158, 604-882-9331 Fax
http://www.cohousing.ca/

The Canadian Cohousing Network (CCN) is a registered nonprofit organization that promotes the creation of cohousing communities as a model for sustainable development by raising public awareness about cohousing and by bringing people together to form communities. CCN links individuals and cohousing groups together to share resources and make the process of creating a community easier, more economical, and fun!

CO-OP RESOURCES AND SERVICES PROJECT (CRSP)

3551 White House Pl
Los Angeles CA 90004

213-738-1254, 213-386-8873 Fax
crsp@ic.org
http://www.ic.org/laev/

Co-op Resources and Services Project (CRSP), a nonprofit tax-exempt organization founded in 1980, is committed to small urban ecological cooperative communities. Our primary project is the Los Angeles Eco-Village. We provide public tours, a lending library of publications and videos, slide show presentations, public speakers, technical assistance for developing urban sustainable neighborhoods, and workshops on sustainable urban community development. CRSP also provides an ecological revolving loan fund (ELF) for those interested in making socially and environmentally responsible loans.

COHOUSING NETWORK (TCN)

PO Box 2584
Berkeley CA 94702

303-584-3237
http://www.cohousing.org/

The Cohousing Network (TCN) is a

nonprofit educational corporation established in 1997. Throughout North America, TCN promotes and encourages the cohousing concept. TCN supports both individuals and groups in creating and maintaining communities, and provides networking opportunities for those interested in cohousing.

We serve: (1) seekers of cohousing communities, (2) communities in development stages, (3) completed communities, and (4) government agencies and businesses who deal with cohousing communities.

Cohousing communities are small-scale neighborhoods that provide a new kind of balance between personal privacy and living among neighbors who know and care about each other. They often include a multigenerational mix of singles, couples, families with children, and elders. Individual homes are self-sufficient with complete kitchens, etc., but enjoy convenient access to shared space, including a "common house" with enhanced facilities such as a large dining room, children's play room, workshops. Neighbors often take turns cooking meals for their neighbors, and sharing in community responsibilities.

COMMUNITY LANDS ACCESS NETWORK INC. (CLAN)

306 Smith St
Collingwood VIC 3066
Australia

61-3-9419-6980
61-3-9416-2081 Fax
fp@wild.net.au
http://www.green.net.au/clan/

We are Community Lands Access Network Inc. (CLAN), a nonprofit association and environmental group networking individuals and groups with resources for present and future communities. CLAN is also buying multiple lands nationwide across Australia that are open to anyone artistically, socially, ecologically, or spiritually sustainable to work or live on the land.

If someone wants to set up: alternative schools, cooperative businesses, communities, conservation and wildlife reserves/regenerated bush land, ecovillages, health and spiritual sanctuaries, or organic/permaculture farms, CLAN wants to help out.

Send for info, join a work group at your local branch or over the email system, donate ideas, goods, or money toward projects or properties, and help manifest dreams into reality. Also: PO Box 2189, Fitzroy-BC VIC 3065 Australia

COMMUNITY-SEEKERS' NETWORK OF NEW ENGLAND

PO Box 2743
Cambridge MA 02238

781-784-4297
DonBr@att.net

We are a regional network for joining and starting intentional communities, and for learning about issues that are relevant to the communities movement as a whole. We have established or are in the process of creating the following: meetings, dinners, group trips to established communities, a newsletter with a many-to-many/open letters forum, and a catalogue of vision statements by individuals, core groups, and communities that are reforming. We welcome inquiries from outside our region.

ECOVILLAGE NETWORK OF THE AMERICAS (ENA)

PO Box 90
Summertown TN 38483

931-964-3992, 931-964-2200 Fax
ecovillage@thefarm.org
http://www.gaia.org/

The Ecovillage Network of the Americas (ENA) is a public policy research, education, and networking project operated by subsistence workers and volunteers. Our focus is the need of future generations for a safe and healthy planet to inhabit.

We aim to create and present to the world outstanding examples of what it means in live in harmony with nature in a sustainable way. We promote and facilitate communities—whether rural or urban—which develop and implement technologies and practices such that human activities are harmlessly integrated into the natural world in a way that is supportive of healthy human development and can be successfully continued into the indefinite future.

The purposes and objectives of the Ecovillage Network of the Americas are as follows: (1) to support and nurture the integrity, sustainability, and evolution of ecovillages within the Americas; (2) to facilitate the creation of new ecovillages; (3) to foster and facilitate cooperation and diverse exchange among ecovillages in the Americas; (4) to proactively represent ecovillages in the forum of public discourse, before the governments of their respective nations, and in international councils; (5) to support participants of the ecovillage movement in their personal growth and professional integrity; (6) to explore and create innovative and sustainable forms of organization; (7) to promote the research, development, and use of appropriate technologies; and (8) to encourage the experience, understanding, and knowledge of ways of living in harmony with each other and the Earth. (See also Global Ecovillage Network.)

ENVIROLINK

5808 Forbes Ave 2nd Fl
Pittsburgh PA 15217

412-420-6400 ask for EnviroLink
412-420-6404 Fax
support@envirolink.org
http://www.envirolink.org/

EnviroLink is a nonprofit organization, a grassroots online community that unites hundreds of organizations and volunteers around the world with millions of people in more than 150 countries. It is a very useful tool for finding a wide variety of environmental information, from updated endangered species lists to groups in your area doing work for environmental change.

FEDERATION OF EGALITARIAN COMMUNITIES (FEC)

c/o East Wind Community
HC-3 Box 3370-D
Tecumseh MO 65760

417-679-4682
fec@ic.org
http://www.thefec.org/

The Federation of Egalitarian Communities (FEC), established in 1976, is a network of North American intentional communities. Each FEC community embraces four principle values: income sharing, egalitarianism, nonviolence, and cooperation. Our communities hold their land, labor, and other resources in common, and are committed to equality, ecology, and participatory government. There are six full member communities and six communities-in-dialogue, ranging in size from homesteads to small villages. Three have been in existence for at least 20 years, two others for 15 years.

We encourage social and labor exchanges among member communities, the pooling of resources, and support of community-owned and community-operated industries. We value cooperation above competition, and the creation of a healthy, supportive environment above materialistic gain—how we do things is as important as what we do. Delegates from each community meet at least once a year in open meetings to discuss issues and make decisions about inter-community programs.

FEDERATION OF SOUTHERN COOPERATIVES / LAND ASSISTANCE FUND (FSC/LAF)

2769 Church St
East Point GA 30344

404-765-0991, 404-765-9678 Fax

Since 1967, the Federation of Southern Cooperatives (FSC) has been the primary focal point for the rural cooperative movement among southern black and poor white farmers and rural residents. The Land Assistance Fund (LAF) was formed in 1971 to help black land owners across the south purchase "primary agriculture" land, and to retain property threatened by creditors, tax collectors, and unscrupulous land dealers. The FSC/LAF represents the merged program and shared history of both groups.

Building on the work of the Civil Rights movement, the Federation has organized a community-based cooperative economic development movement among 30,000 low-income families working in over 100 rural communities in 11 southern states. It provides services, resources, technical assistance, and advocacy to its membership of cooperatives and credit unions and their individual member families. Individual and family memberships are available and can be paid in installments.

(...Networking, continued)

FELLOWSHIP FOR INTENTIONAL COMMUNITY (FIC)

**RR 1 Box 156-D
Rutledge MO 63563**

**660-883-5545, 660-883-5545 Fax
fic@ic.org
http://www.ic.org/**

The Fellowship for Intentional Community (FIC) is interested in helping people looking for more community in their lives. Building on its roots in the intentional communities movement, the FIC offers a wide range of services, including publications, referrals, and events.

FIC has four primary missions: (1) to openly provide accurate and comprehensive information about living in intentional communities; (2) to promote dialogue, understanding, and cooperation among existing communities and related organizations; (3) to make the realities, options, and lessons of intentional communities readily accessible to the wider culture; and (4) to provide moral, financial, and technical support to forming and established communities in need.

Intentional communities have existed for many centuries as places where people build alternatives to meet their needs. Although there are thousands of intentional communities in existence today, and many others in the formative stages, most people are unaware of them or the roots from which they spring. The Fellowship is increasing public awareness about what intentional communities are offering, both for those who want to join them and for those who are inspired by their example of living cooperatively.

FIC publishes this *Communities Directory* and the quarterly *Communities* magazine. The organization comes together twice a year to make decisions by consensus, everyone is welcome to attend. In addition, periodic Art of Community conferences are held around the country. We are a membership-supported organization—membership benefits include announcements of our twice yearly meetings, our newsletter, and entry to becoming a member of the Sunrise Credit Union. See the Appendix for information on how to join the FIC.

GLOBAL ECOVILLAGE NETWORK (GEN)

**Gaia Villages
Copenhagen
Denmark
http://www.gaia.org/**

Human settlements are in crisis in both the north and the south, but for different reasons. In a larger sense, the human settlements crisis is part of the greater issue of a planet experiencing the limits to growth. There is a growing consensus that we have to learn to live sustainably if we are to survive as a species.

The Global Ecovillage Network (GEN) was founded in 1994 to assist in the following areas: supporting the development of sustainable human settlements, assisting in the exchange of information amongst the settlements, and making information widely available about ecovillage concepts and demonstration sites.

Three GEN regions cover the globe. Contact the secretariat in your region.

GEN Oceania and Asia, contact: Max O. Lindegger, email: ecosol@peg.apc.org

GEN Europe, contact: Lucilla Borio, email: info@gen-europe.org

Ecovillage Network of the Americas (ENA), contact: Albert Bates, email: ecovillage@thefarm.org

NATIVEWEB

http://www.nativeweb.org/

Indexed and searchable database contains hundreds of links concerning Native, Aboriginal, and Indigenous internet resources on all seven continents. Also includes a resource center and a community center.

NEIGHBORNETS NETWORK

**206-721-0217
habib@thegarden.net
http://www.neighbornets.org/**

"Neighbornets" is a new name for an intentional community of people who live in the same general neighborhood who choose to form closer bonds with one another. In many cases, these people will be acquaintances who wish to deepen their friendship. The form and organizational structure (if any) of neighbornets may vary widely but they are always based on sharing, for example: sharing time with one another; sharing resources; sharing labor; and sharing preparation for possible emergencies.

Neighbornets provide the benefits of community-based sharing for today's urban and suburban lifestyles. Furthermore, neighbornets are intentional communities, and share in the base of experience of residential intentional communities such as cohousing. This experience includes important techniques applicable to any type of community, such as consensus-based decision making.

What makes neighbornets different from other intentional communities is that, while the members live in the same "part of town," they do not need to live in the same building, next door to each other, or even on the same block. Neighbornets are *not* intended to necessarily involve everybody in a specific neighborhood. Instead, they are intended to be self-selected groupings of people who choose to spend time with one another and share resources.

NORTH AMERICAN STUDENTS OF COOPERATION (NASCO)

**PO Box 7715
Ann Arbor MI 48107**

**734-663-0889, 734-663-5072 Fax
NASCO@umich.edu
http://www.umich.edu/~nasco/**

The North American Students of Cooperation (NASCO) is a federation of student cooperatives in the United States and Canada. NASCO's mission is to strengthen existing cooperatives and expand the student co-op movement by providing resources, assisting development, and encouraging the active participation of student co-ops in the North American cooperative sector.

As an association of campus cooperatives, NASCO provides student cooperatives with operational assistance, encourages the development of new student cooperatives, and serves as an advocate for student cooperatives. NASCO teaches leadership skills, provides information, and serves as the central link facilitating the fruition of the Rochdale vision in the student sector. By strengthening the student co-op movement, we believe we can strengthen the future of cooperatives generally.

We invite you to assist us with additions and corrections. Updated information will be available on the Web at http://directory.ic.org/

West coast office:
PO Box 12816, Berkeley CA 94712, 510-848-2667
Canadian office:
415 Yonge St Suite 601, Toronto Ontario M5B 2E7 Canada, 416-348-9666 x26

NORTHWEST INTENTIONAL COMMUNITIES ASSOCIATION (NICA)

22110 E Lost Lake Rd
Snohomish WA 98296
Floriferous@msn.com
http://www.infoteam.com/
nonprofit/nica/

Our mission: to coordinate the exchange of information and resources among intentional communities in the US northwest; facilitate communication and networking among local, regional, and national intentional communities organizations; ascertain and promote intentional community's aims and values that contribute most to community sustainability; foster and assist the study of and education on all major elements of intentional communities; and assist organizing and financing efforts of and for intentional communities.

For the last five years we have published *Community Resources*, a small newsletter. We include information from our gatherings, resources such as books, Web sites, etc., and also list communities with openings and people looking for communities.

In the spring and summer we organize communities gatherings; intimate social networking events that are hosted by northwest intentional communities. The gatherings provide opportunities for communities to meet each other, talk about similarities and differences, and share our community experiences and learnings with each other. The gatherings are not designed to be promotional or seeker events, although a small number of community seekers typically attend. Starting in 1998, we began to sponsor intentional community promotional events such as booths at home shows and fairs, and a monthly potluck in Seattle.

Our Intentional Community Resources pages on the Web contain a comprehensive collection of online and offline information about all aspects of intentional communities.

OREGON WOMON'S LAND TRUST (OWLT)

PO Box 1692
Roseburg OR 97470

Oregon Womon's Land Trust (OWLT), founded in 1975 by northwest lesbian feminists, is a nonprofit, tax-exempt corporation. We hold title to OWL Farm (see community listing), one of the first wimmin's lands to be developed in the 1970s. We are committed to providing womyn with access to land and land wisdom.

Our mission includes intentions to make land resources available to lesbians and other womyn who would not otherwise have access, to provide education in self-sufficiency and country life skills, to develop womyn's community on land, and to preserve land as a sacred heritage. We anticipate that other lesbian/wimmin's lands may eventually come under OWLT's ownership umbrella, with continued independence for each land group. Write for more information about OWLT and/or about wimmin's lands in Oregon.

PAN COMMUNITY COUNCIL

PO Box 102
Nimbin NSW 2480
Australia
simonclo@nor.com.au
http://www.nor.com.au/users/
pancom/

Pan Community Council (PanCom) was formed in 1987 with the primary aims of promoting social interactions among communities; assisting with dealings with councils and government bodies; fostering sustainable economic initiatives; and protecting the environment.

PanCom represents intentional communities mainly in the northeast corner of the state of New South Wales. There are approximately 100 such communities in this area and they are very diverse in structure and activities. However, it is fair to say that most communities are committed to living in a low-cost way that minimizes their impact on the environment. Many people in communities have built their own houses and grow a proportion of their own food.

PanCom produces a newsletter, holds community meetings, lobbies the govern-

ment and its departments, and issues media statements on policy matters.

PEREGRINE FOUNDATION

PO Box 460141
San Francisco CA 94146

415-821-2090
http://www.perefound.org/
MOST newsletter:
http://www.ic.org/morningstar/

The Peregrine Foundation is a charitable, educational public foundation created in 1992 to assist families and individuals living in or exiting from experimental social groups. Its newsletters and books inform the public-at-large about the structure and ideologies of various religious sects, communes, and intentional communities.

In 1989, a modest two-page *KIT Round-Robin* newsletter was sent to 30 names, all formerly of a high-demand religious sect known variously as the Bruderhof, the Society of Brothers, or the Hutterian Brethren East. Within a year it expanded to 18,000 words, mailed each month to over 350 addresses. Two years later the all-volunteer staff created the Peregrine Foundation as the parent organization and started the Carrier Pigeon Press to publish book-length memoirs and a series titled "Women from Utopia." Other projects followed, including annual conferences in Massachusetts and the United Kingdom, a BBS for email contacts, and ongoing searches for other "graduates" and survivors. Subscriptions available for the *KIT* Bruderhof newsletter and the *MOST* newsletter (for alumni of the Morning Star and Wheeler's Ranch "open land" communities). Write for a brochure or a free issue.

QUEER IN COMMUNITY (QIC)

RD 1 Box 149
Pitman PA 17964

717-425-2548
qic@ic.org
http://www.ic.org/qic/

The network is formed of individuals who identify themselves as queer or queer-positive, who either live in intentional community or would like to, and affiliated queer and queer-positive communities. By queer-positive, we mean welcoming with open arms, embracing the queerness of

Resources

(...Networking, continued)

queer members and friends, and considering a queer life path to be a positive thing!

Community living can provide a supportive environment for queer people in a homophobic world. The communities in our network actively welcome the diversity of lesbians, gay men, bisexuals, and transgendered people. We also include communities that center specifically around gay and lesbian issues, such as faery land and womyn's land.

SUSTAINABLE COMMUNITIES NETWORK

info@sustainable.org
http://www.sustainable.org/

The Sustainable Communities Network is for those who want to help make their communities more livable. We hope to increase the visibility of what has worked for other communities, and to promote a lively exchange of information to help create community sustainability in both urban and rural areas.

In many communities—large and small, rural and urban—issues are being addressed in an interconnected manner. They are demonstrating how innovative strategies can produce communities that are more environmentally sound, economically prosperous, and socially equitable. Learn about principles of sustainability and visioning processes and how they can help guide community initiatives. Find out how $mart Growth can guide planning in neighborhoods and regions and what tools are available to help. Locate your local community network and civic engagement opportunities. Then tell us what other resources you need to help make your community more sustainable.

VAKGROEP

Lauwerecht 55
3515 GN Utrecht
Netherlands

+31-30-272-1660
amf@amf.xs4all.nl

The Vakgroep is a federation of approximately 10 small businesses, five voluntary projects, and 15 housing cooperatives. Most of the projects are based in Utrecht in the Netherlands, although there are projects in several other Dutch cities, and rural projects in Lorraine, France.

What the projects have in common is that they are all run on a collective basis—there are no bosses. The Vakgroep was started in 1974 as a think tank (de Keerkring—Tropic of Capricorn) and has developed various structures through which the projects support each other by means of mutual aid.

These include: (1) Kollektieve Kas—a collective fund into which member projects pay contributions, which provides financial support both inside and outside the federation; (2) a housing group (that helps housing projects); (3) Komma—a communications and publicity group; and (4) the Ana Maria Fonds—an ethical investment fund, which is being extended into a collection of funds for the financial support of social and political projects.

Within the network there is a consultancy and advice partnership, de Verandering ("Change"), which provides advice and support to social and political projects in the Netherlands and elsewhere, sometimes on a "no cure no pay" basis. This is often carried out in conjunction with other businesses in the network. Voluntary projects include a puppet theatre and artists' studios.

The Vakgroep is part of an international network of similar federations, which includes Verband, a sister federation in Nijmegen, Netherlands; three federations in Germany (RGW-Berlin, VERbunt, and WIBeN); and Radical Routes, a federation in Britain.

VILLAGE EARTH PROJECT

Engineering Research Center
Colorado State University
Room W-109
Fort Collins CO 80523

970-491-5754
alberts@engr.colostate.edu
http://www.villageearth.org/

The goal of the Village Earth Project and the Consortium for Sustainable Village-Based Development (CSVBD) is to join together with other nongovernmental organizations (NGOs) and individuals to help connect rural villages (two-thirds of the world's population) to global resources—including energy resources, information resources, hard and soft appropriate technologies, social resources, and financial resources—for self-reliant, sustainable, village-based development.

Village Earth is a program for the new millennium. It is based on evidence that lack of access to proper resources is the block to building a better life and that poverty is a symptom rather than the cause. Village Earth joins the forces of individuals and organizations, using the unique gifts of each to provide access to essential resources and to provide training to villages across the globe. Village Earth empowers people to achieve and sustain their hopes and dreams through their own efforts and actions.

WOMEN'S ENVIRONMENT AND DEVELOPMENT ORGANIZATION (WEDO)

355 Lexington Ave 3rd Fl
New York NY 10017

212-973-0325, 212-973-0335 Fax
wedo@igc.org
http://www.wedo.org/frmain.htm

Women's Environment and Development Organization (WEDO) is an international advocacy network actively working to transform society to achieve a healthy and peaceful planet. We work for social, political, economic, and environmental justice for all, through the empowerment of women, in all their diversity, and their equal participation with men in decision making, from grassroots to global arenas. WEDO supports the politics of diversity and inclusion. It seeks to cross-fertilize and connect various movements to build a strong, unified movement for social change in the next century by emphasizing democratic values, pluralism and diversity, good governance, and greater accountability by all public institutions and decision makers.

We invite you to assist us with additions and corrections. Updated information will be available on the Web at http://directory.ic.org/

⑥
Research

CENTER FOR COMMUNAL STUDIES (CCS)

8600 University Blvd
University of Southern Indiana
Evansville IN 47712

812-464-1727, 812-464-1960 Fax

Center for Communal Studies (CCS) serves as an international clearinghouse for community information. CCS is a research facility with a communal database and an archival collection of manuscripts, photographs, recordings, publications, and artifacts from 130 historic and nearly 550 contemporary intentional communities. CCS sponsors conferences, seminars, classes, speakers, publications, small research grants, and related educational projects. We welcome inquires, program suggestions, and materials for the Center archives.

COMMUNAL STUDIES ASSOCIATION (CSA)

PO Box 122
Amana IA 52203

319-622-6446
csa@netins.net, csa@ic.org
http://www.ic.org/csa/

The Communal Studies Association (CSA) was founded in 1975 as the National Historic Communal Studies Association. In 1990, the name was changed to reflect its expanding interest in contemporary intentional communities. The CSA is proud of its diverse membership, which includes university faculty, staff of historic communal sites, members of intentional communities, and others with an interest in communal studies.

Each year in late September or early October, the CSA holds a conference. The location of the conference is usually at a restored historic communal site, and past locations have been the Shaker communities of Pleasant Hill, Hancock, and Mount Lebanon, and the Harmonist sites of New Harmony and Old Economy. Our conferences feature presentations of formal papers, panel discussions, and tours of historic and contemporary communities.

The CSA publishes an annual journal, *Communal Societies*, and a semiannual newsletter. The journal includes articles and book reviews, written by academics, communitarians, and preservationists. The CSA newsletter provides a calendar of events, book announcements, and information on our upcoming conferences and activities. Both publications are sent to all members of the CSA. The CSA also publishes a brochure of historical communal sites around the United States.

The mission of the CSA is as follows: to encourage and facilitate the preservation, restoration, and public interpretation of America's historic communal sites; to provide a forum for the study of communal societies, past and present; and to communicate to the general public the successful ideas from, and lessons learned by, communal societies.

DATACENTER

1904 Franklin St Suite 900
Oakland CA 94612

510-835-4692, 510-835-3017 Fax
datacenter@datacenter.org
http://www.igc.org/datacenter/

The DataCenter is an independent nonprofit research center. We are celebrating two decades of providing strategic research and documentation services.

Information is a powerful tool for change. The DataCenter develops original sources and adds value to existing information sources by conducting targeted research and analysis, publishing, accessing progressive publications, and training community-based organizations in the use of information technology.

We support domestic and international progressive organizing, advocacy, policy development, and broad-based educational efforts. Those we serve include community organizations, policy institutes, socially responsible investing companies, libraries, media, journalists, and organizations located internationally.

EMPOWERMENT RESOURCES

PO Box 3190
Silver Springs MD 20918

301-408-2041, 301-445-6095 Fax
empower@EmpowermentResources.com
http://www.EmpowermentResources.com/

Empowerment Resources is your Internet guide to empowerment and the green movement. This Web site serves as an information source for individuals, activists, businesses, nonprofits, other organizations, and the media. Knowledge is power. Empower the people.

ENVIRONMENTAL DEFENSE FUND

New York NY 10010
Bill_Pease@edf.org
http://www.scorecard.org/

Our Scorecard on the Web features a "type in your zip code" approach to finding local information about US environmental conditions and problems. The site's interactive maps let you click down to a local neighborhood in a second or two. The goal is to make the local environment as easy to check on as the local weather.

The first kind of local environmental information to appear on Scorecard covered releases of toxic chemicals from industrial facilities, together with the health effects of the animal waste from pigs, cattle, sheep, etc., county by county and, in some regions, farm by farm. We then added information about local environmental priorities, showing what expert panels have identified as the top environmental problems in particular states and regions, wherever such studies have been completed.

INTENTIONAL COMMUNITY RESOURCE PAGE

http://www.infoteam.com/nonprofit/nica/resource.html

A Web site maintained by the Northwest Intentional Communities Association (NICA), this site provides information on the following categories: Getting Started—first steps for starting a community, creating a vision statement, samples; Group Process Resources—meetings, decision making, conflict-resolution

Resources

(...Research, continued)

papers, Web sites, books, and articles; Locating a Site—locating and purchasing land; Legal Resources—lawyers, bylaws, legal documents, ownership forms; Designing Your Community—group design process, site, unit, and common-house design; Dealing With Money—working with banks, affordability; Building Your Community—dealing with contractors and construction, alternative building sources and information; Recruitment and Marketing—finding the people, selling your stuff; General Resources—books, articles, Web sites, papers, theses, videos about intentional communities; and Cohousing Resources—books, articles, Web sites, papers, and theses specific to cohousing.

INTERNATIONAL COMMUNAL STUDIES ASSOCIATION (ICSA)

Yad Tabenkin
Ramat Efal 52960
Israel

+972-3-5301217, +972-3-5301227
+972-3-5346376 Fax
yadtab@inter.net.il
http://www.ic.org/icsa/

The International Communal Studies Association (ICSA) was formed to provide a common framework for a scholarly exchange of information on communes throughout the world. The organization is multidisciplinary and strives for international representation among its members. It also engages in the following activities. (1) It functions as a clearing-house for research projects, encourages comparative studies, and maintains a list of communal organizations and individuals active in communal and kibbutz research. (2) International conferences are held every few years and are organized in the host country by ICSA members. (3) The ICSA publishes a biannual *Bulletin* that supplies scholars with useful basic material of an interdisciplinary character. The *Bulletin* is not intended as a comprehensive catalog, but we hope that members will supply us with the widest range of information on their studies and activities.

POLITICAL RESOURCES, INC.

PO Box 3177
Burlington VT 05401

800-423-2677, 802-660-2869
(802)864-9502 Fax
info@politicalresources.com
http://www.PoliticalResources.com/

Political Resources, Inc. publishes the *Political Resource Directory*, markets and brokers direct mail lists, and maintains a Web site (Political Resources Online). The *Political Resource Directory* is the most complete and comprehensive guide to over 3,000 consultants and political professionals working in the industry. We are the official directory for the American Association of Political Consultants. Our online *Directory* lists the company locations and specializations of our entire database. The directory can be searched based on specialization (e.g., pollsters, fundraising, strategy, yard signs, printers, and 20 other categories).

RELIGIOUS MOVEMENTS HOMEPAGE

**http://cti.itc.virginia.edu/~jkh8x/
soc257/home.html**

This site seeks to provide a foundation for understanding how religious groups emerge, grow, stagnate, reinvigorate themselves, and sometimes die. It also seeks to promote understanding of religion more broadly without preference for or against any particular religious group.

SOCIETY FOR UTOPIAN STUDIES (SUS)

English Department
University of Maine
Orono ME 04469

207-581-3809
naomi_jacobs@umit.maine.edu
http://www.utoronto.ca/utopia/

Founded in 1975, the Society for Utopian Studies (SUS) is an international, interdisciplinary association devoted to the study of utopianism in all its forms, with a particular emphasis on literary and experimental utopias. Although many members are involved in activism or intentional living, the Society's purpose is scholarly inquiry, rather than the pursuit of utopian projects.

Scholars representing a wide variety of disciplines are active in the association and approach utopian studies from such diverse backgrounds as American Studies, Architecture, the Arts, Classics, Cultural Studies, Economics, Engineering, Environmental Studies, Gender Studies, History, Languages and Literature, Philosophy, Political Science, Psychology, Sociology, and Urban Planning. The Society publishes the journal *Utopian Studies* and a newsletter, *Utopus Discovered*, which contains information about upcoming conferences and workshops, and a bibliography of recent publications in the field.

The Society's annual meetings provide an ideal venue for intellectual interchange in a cooperative, noncompetitive, congenial, and convivial environment. Membership in the Society includes announcements regarding the annual meeting, *Utopian Studies*, and *Utopus Discovered*.

TRANSACTION NET: COMPLEMENTARY COMMUNITY CURRENCY SYSTEMS

zisk@well.com
**http://www.transaction.net/money/
community/**

A local exchange trading system (LETS) is a brilliant way to exchange goods and services. Using an internal local currency saves cash and builds strong links in local communities.

No central authority is required to guarantee the currency and manage its supply—LETS is backed by goods and services, and is created as mutual credit. Given that there is no interest on LETS currency, the built-in incentive to discount the future found in national currencies is reduced, but not reversed.

LETS money is created as mutual credit—each transaction is recorded as a corresponding credit and debit in the two participants' accounts. The quantity of currency issued is thus automatically sufficient and (unlike fiat money) does not depend on the judgment and effort of a central authority.

We invite you to assist us with additions and corrections. Updated information will be available on the Web at http://directory.ic.org/

WORLDWATCH INSTITUTE

1776 Massachusetts Ave NW
Washington DC 20036

202-452-1999, 202-296-7365 Fax
worldwatch@worldwatch.org
http://www.worldwatch.org/

Worldwatch Institute is a nonprofit public policy research organization dedicated to informing policy makers and the public about emerging global problems and trends and the complex links between the world economy and its environmental support systems.

Spirituality/Religion

CATHOLIC WORKER HOME PAGE (CWHP)

5236 N 5th St
Arlington VA 22203
agf@cais.com
http://www.catholicworker.org/

The Catholic Worker (CW) movement, founded by Dorothy Day and Peter Maurin in 1933, is grounded in a firm belief in the God-given dignity of every human person. Today, over 140 Catholic Worker communities remain committed to nonviolence, voluntary poverty, prayer, and hospitality for the homeless, exiled, hungry, and forsaken. Catholic Workers continue to protest injustice, war, racism, and violence of all forms. The Catholic Worker Home Page (CWHP) provides basic reference information about Dorothy Day and the Catholic Worker movement. It features biographies and writings of Dorothy Day, Peter Maurin, and Ammon Hennacy, a bibliography on the CW movement, a directory of CW houses, and links to major CW archival collections and other Web sites of interest to Catholic Workers.

The CWHP is always looking for ideas and submissions. Specifically: poems, ads from CW houses seeking volunteers, product and ordering information from CW houses with cottage industries, ideas for additional topics you want to see covered on the Web site, information and excerpts from books pertinent to the

movement. Also, we want to know about new CW houses or those which have closed.

CIRCLE NETWORK

PO Box 219
Mt Horeb WI 53572

608-924-2216
circle@mhtc.net
http://www.circlesanctuary.org/

Circle Network is an international referral and information exchange network coordinated by Circle Sanctuary and founded in 1977 by Selena Fox. Circle Network includes communities, centers, festivals, networks, Web site resources, other groups, and individuals involved with one or more aspects of Nature Spirituality, such as Wiccan paths, Druidism, Animism, Goddess spirituality, Shamanism, Contemporary Paganism, Celtic spirituality, and Pantheism. Circle Network helps those attuned to the spiritual dimensions of Nature connect with each other. Circle Network is linked through a variety of networking periodicals, including the quarterly *CIRCLE* magazine (formerly known as *Circle Network News*) and the annual *Circle Guide to Pagan Groups*.

Within Circle Network is a special network, the Lady Liberty League, which offers referral networking assistance to Pagans and other Nature folk who are experiencing discrimination and/or harassment due to their spiritual orientation. A quarterly report with news of new and existing cases is published in-print in *CIRCLE* magazine and on-line at the Lady Liberty League Web site.

Circle Network membership is open to Nature folk who practice one or more forms of Nature spirituality that honors Nature and has a code of ethics that promotes well-being for self, others, and the planet. There is no fee to become part of Circle Network. Donations are appreciated and tax deductible in the United States. A free brochure with more information about Circle Network and other aspects of Circle Sanctuary's work is available upon request.

EARTHSPIRIT

PO Box 723
Williamsburg MA 01096
earthspirit@earthspirit.com
http://www.earthspirit.com/info.html

EarthSpirit is a nonprofit organization providing services to a nationwide network of Pagans and others following an Earth-centered spiritual path. Based in the Boston area, our membership extends across the United States, and also to several other countries.

FAITH AND SOCIAL JUSTICE

universalist@hotmail.com
http://www.geocities.com/
CapitolHill/1764/

This Web page is dedicated to providing resources, links, and articles for people of faith who are concerned about social justice issues. With the war on the poor going full speed in the 1990s; with the scapegoating of immigrants, the poor, and gay and lesbians; with the attacks on worker rights, working conditions, and wages; and with oppression, war-making, and hunger across the globe; we need now more than ever a faith-based response for those who do care about economic justice, environmental stewardship, peacemaking, and concern for human rights for all.

HUTTERIAN BRETHREN

http://hutterianbrethren.com/

The Hutterian Brethren in North America Web page is a useful informational tool. Hutterites are a religious group begun in the 1530s. They live communally in rural North America. Learn about their unique lifestyle, religion, customs, traditions, and history. Discover how Hutterian Brethren in North America earn their living, what they do in their leisure time, and what their schools are like.

JEWISH COMMUNITY ONLINE

JewishComm@aol.com
http://www.jewish.com/

Links to Jewish information on the Web. This page is updated monthly.

Additions and corrections: Email: directory@ic.org, Web: http://directory.ic.org/, Mail: RR 1 Box 156-D, Rutledge MO 63563, USA.

(...Spirituality/Religion, continued)

NETWORK OF SHARED-LIVING CHRISTIAN COMMUNITIES (NSLCC)

604-984-9539
ca@helix.net
http://www.freeyellow.com/
   members4/zealous/ncc.htm

The Network of Shared-Living Christian Communities (NSLCC) exists to be a support network to strengthen and encourage Christians and Christian groups who desire to be in shared-living communities. These communities exist to fulfill the great commission of their Lord and Savior Jesus Christ—to make disciples of all nations.

NORTH AMERICAN COALITION FOR CHRISTIANITY AND ECOLOGY (NACCE)

PO Box 40011
St Paul MN 55104

651-698-0349
eudyson@worldnet.att.net
http://www.nacce.org/

The North American Coalition for Christianity and Ecology (NACCE) is an ecumenical, voluntary, tax-exempt organization designed to do the following: address effectively our continuing destruction of the Earth; teach reverence for God's creation, with the understanding that humans are not separate from the natural world; bring Christians into a loving relationship with the Earth; facilitate the formation of regional Earth-keeping ministries; provide information and resources for study of issues in the context of biblical theology and contemporary science; and to promote church partnerships with other organizations concerned with ecology and social justice.

ORDER OF SAINT BENEDICT

osb@www2.csbsju.edu
http://www.osb.org/

The Order of Saint Benedict has an extensive Web site featuring the following. International email directories; a geographic index of Order of Saint Benedict international institutions; retreat centers;

Saints of the Order Academic Resources; the American Benedictine Academy; the American Benedictine Review; Anglican Benedictines, Cistercians, and Trappists; the Alliance for International Monasticism; Monastic Interreligious Dialogue; academic institutions; schools; resources; the Association of Benedictine Campus Ministers; the Association of Benedictine Colleges and Universities; Monastic Studies; periodicals and serials; The American Benedictine Review; Saints in Benedictine Martyrology; the Alliance for International Monasticism; and International Benedictines for Peace.

QUAKER RESOURCES ON THE WEB

wsamuel@cpcug.org
http://cpcug.org/user/wsamuel/
   quaker.html

The Quaker (Religious Society of Friends) Resources on the Web site is an extensive collection of Quaker-related information and links.

SHAMBHALA INTERNATIONAL

1084 Tower Rd
Halifax Nova Scotia B3H 2Y5
Canada

902-425-4275, 902-423-2750
info@shambhala.org
http://www.shambhala.org/

Shambhala International is a worldwide network of meditation centers providing instruction, classes, and programs, founded by Chögyam Trungpa Rinpoche, a master of the Shambhala and Tibetan Buddhist traditions.

Meditation in the Shambhala tradition uncovers a natural sense of goodness, fearlessness, and humor, a way of personal warriorship, and a vision of enlightened society. The Gates to Shambhala are the various ways to being awake in the world, through Shambhala Training, Buddhist awareness practice, and contemplative arts.

SISTERSITE

http://www.geocities.com/Wellesley/
   1114/index.html

SisterSite is a cyberplace for religious

women and their friends. SisterSite's purpose is to serve as a clearinghouse for information on women's religious congregations, the history of religious life, and the contemporary concerns of women in church and society. While its content and focus is primarily Catholic, it also hopes to serve the needs of those in other religious traditions. SisterSite welcomes an eclectic range both of topics and of subscribers—including married and single (as well as vowed and ordained) women and men from many Christian (and other) denominations. There is also is an internet discussion group founded in 1994 and sponsored by Sister-L, that currently has about 900 subscribers and is devoted to the history and contemporary concerns of women religious. SisterSite reflects this diversity, as well as an ongoing openness to new directions it may find itself taking in the future.

For now, SisterSite sees its mission as twofold. The first is to serve as a central clearinghouse for links to relevant Web sites—including the largest possible list of home pages for congregations of nuns and sisters, as well as those for individual sisters and other participants in Sister-L, and some of their ministries (including colleges, hospitals, and other institutions and efforts under the sponsorship of congregations). Additionally, there will be links to sites that contribute to broader insight and action on behalf of women's concerns, social justice, and ministry. Other "link lists" will connect SisterSite users to sites focusing on publishing and scholarship relevant to these purposes in fields such as theology, Women's Studies, and history. And because sisters work collaboratively with others, including other religious, there will be links to men's congregations, particularly those who foster greater participation of all people in church and society. Second, SisterSite provides a place where new scholarship and creative efforts relating to religious life can be made widely available, and a forum where such efforts can be fostered and advanced.

We invite you to assist us with additions and corrections. Updated information will be available on the Web at http://directory.ic.org/

SOJOURNERS

2401 15th St NW
Washington DC 20009

800-714-7474, 202-328-8842,
202-328-8757
sojourners@sojourners.com
http://www.sojourners.com/

Rooted in the solid ground of prophetic biblical tradition, Sojourners is a progressive Christian voice that preaches not political correctness, but rather compassion, community, and commitment. We invite you to explore the intersection of faith, politics, and culture. With an extensive and easy to use link section, we are a clearinghouse for both classical and progressive Christian-related resources.

THE BUDDHIST RESOURCE FILE

aming@ccbs.edu.tw
http://ccbs.ntu.edu.tw/BRF/
bibliography.html

An immense list of resources on Buddhist activities and literature. It provides an index that facilitates access to different Buddhist associations, centers, texts, and more. Explore the different schools of Buddhism from this resourceful site.

WATER

8035 13th St
Silver Spring MD 20910

301-589-2509, 301-589-3150
water@hers.com
http://www.his.com/~mhunt/

WATER is a feminist educational center, a network of justice-seeking people that began in 1983 as a response to the need for serious theological, ethical, and liturgical development for and by women. We work locally, nationally, and internationally doing programs, projects, publications, workshops, retreats, counseling, and liturgical planning, and have helped thousands of people to be a part of an inclusive church and society. *WATERwheel* is our newsletter published quarterly by WATER. Complimentary copies are available on request for conferences, seminars, classes, or discussion groups.

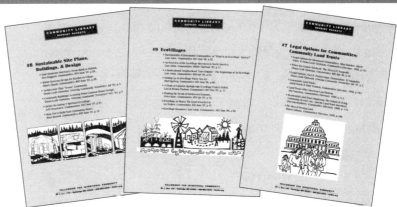
Resources

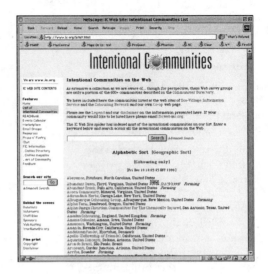

Jillian Downey

About the Recommended Reading List

New for this edition, the annotated Recommended Reading List is our first effort at compiling a list of texts (and there are also a few videos), with descriptions, that we thought might be of interest to *Directory* readers.

We organized the books by subject rather than alphabetically, in the following categories:

- Agriculture and Gardening
- Bibliography
- Building and Architecture
- Children and Parenting
- Community Issues
- Decision Making, Politics, and Legal
- Directory and Reference
- Economics and Labor
- Health, Healing, and Relationships
- History
- Indigenous People and Diversity
- Play and Celebration
- Social Theory
- Spirituality and Religion
- Sustainability and the Environment
- Utopian Fiction
- Women in Community

We know it's not an exhaustive list—there are lots of wonderful books out there. That's why we hope to develop this list much further on the Web. Please check out the Web version at http://directory.ic.org/ and feel free to email directory@ic.org with your suggestions for additional titles.

We collected the titles and their descriptions from a number of sources, including: *Communities* magazine book reviews; Community Bookshelf's catalog; people who responded to our call for suggestions of their favorite community-related books; individuals' Web sites that had book information; and publishers' Web sites that had book reviews or promotional materials.

If you are interested in reading any of these books, and your local library or independent bookstore does not have them, we have some suggestions of likely sources.

- **Community Bookshelf** is a great place to start your search; find the book you want and support the communities movement at the same time. Go to http://bookshelf.ic.org/ or contact FIC, RR 1 Box 156-D, Rutledge MO 63563, USA. Tel: 800-995-8342 (660-883-5545) Email: fic@ic.org
- There are a number of Web sites that have compiled large amounts of information on used, rare, and out-of-print titles, with searching and online ordering capabilities. They include: BookFinder (http://www.bookfinder.com), Advanced Book Exchange (http://www.abebooks.com/), and Bibliofind (http://www.bibliofind.com/).

Agriculture and Gardening

Color Handbook of Garden Insects
Anna Carr, 1979, Rodale Press, 245 pp
This full-color field guide enables identification of common insects that may be inhabiting your orchard or vegetable garden. Most common North American species of predators, pests, and pollinators are included with information on feeding habits, life cycles, and host plants.

Country Women: A Handbook for the New Farmer
Sherry Thomas, Jeanne Tetrault, 1976, Anchor Books, 320 pp
Country Women is a practical guide for women (though just as practical for men) on how to buy land, dig a well, grow vegetables organically, deliver a goat, buy a stove, and build a fence at the least possible expense and with minimum reliance on outside and professional help.

Encyclopedia of Country Living
Carla Emery, 1994 (9th edition), Sasquatch Books, 858 pp
This is a huge compendium of valuable information on every homesteading skill and activity you can imagine, including numerous old-fashioned recipes.

Energy-Efficient and Environmental Landscaping
Anne Simon Moffat, Marc Schiler and the staff of Green Living, 1994, Appropriate Solutions Press, 230 pp
This is a comprehensive guide to environmental landscaping, including: how to use native plants, composting, natural lawn care, xeriscaping (low water use), and moneysaving ideas on the kinds of plants/trees to use around a house and where to locate them.

Farms of Tomorrow Revisited: Community Supported Farms, Farm Supported Communities
Steven McFadden and Trauger M. Groh, 1998, Bio-Dynamic Farming and Gardening Assoc., 312 pp
In this book, the authors give practical examples and information that will be of service to growers and shareholders alike without losing sight of the heart and excitement that makes CSA central to the renewal of agriculture.

Five Acres and Independence: A Handbook for Small Farm Management
Maurice Grenville Kains and J. E. Oldfield, 1978, Dover Publications, 397 pp
A classic text covering all of the areas of the small farm, this book provides good advice about everything from where to put your buildings to what to put in them, as well as information about plants, animals, and capital expenses.

Forest Farming
J. Sholto Douglas and Robert A. de J. Hart, 1976, Watkins, 197 pp
In *Forest Farming*, the authors explain the use of forest and tree crops to increase food production and industrial development without doing environmental harm.

How to Make It on the Land
Ray Cohan, 1972, Prentice-Hall, Inc., 219 pp
This farming source book gives advice and information on how to live in the country, especially for the unskilled city dweller. It guides you step-by-step toward total pastoral independence.

Knott's Handbook for Vegetable Growers
Oscar A. Lorenz and Donald N. Maynard, 1988, John Wiley and Sons (3rd edition), 456 pp
A complete reference on growing vegetable crops, this book covers all aspects, from preparing soil to harvesting and storage. It is not based on organic techniques, but will be useful to anyone producing significant quantities of their own food or growing for market.

New Organic Grower: A Master's Manual of Tools and Techniques for the Home and Market Gardener, The
Eliot Coleman, 1995, Chelsea Green Publishing, 304 pp
Intended for the serious gardener or small-scale market farmer, this book describes practical and sustainable ways of growing organic vegetables, with detailed coverage of scale and capital, marketing, livestock, the winter garden, soil fertility, weeds, and many other topics.

Putting Food By
Janet Greene, Ruth Hertzberg and Beatrice Vaughan, 1988, Penguin, 420 pp
This compendium of food preservation techniques includes information on the best methods for canning, freezing, pickling, and drying, and a short chapter on root cellaring.

Root Cellaring
Mike and Nancy Bubel, 1979, Rodale Press, 297 pp
The Bubels fully describe this low-tech method of food preservation and storage in their book, from which crops and varieties to plant through harvest and preparation. They include information on the food values of various crops and the many types of root cellar designs.

Small-Scale Grain Raising
Gene Logsdon, 1977, Rodale Press, 305 pp
A complete guide to growing grains and dried beans for home consumption, this book discusses each crop in detail, including varieties, growing methods, quantities used per person, and uses of by-products like straw and chaff.

Stocking Up
Organic Gardening and Farming, editors, 1977, Rodale Press, 532 pp
A classic text on how to preserve food naturally, this book covers vegetables and fruits, dairy products, meat, and fish. Techniques include canning, drying, and smoking as well as storing dry goods such as grains, beans, and nuts.

We invite you to assist us with additions and corrections. Updated information will be available on the Web at http://directory.ic.org/

Bibliography

Alternative Lifestyles
Jefferson P. Selth, 1986, Greenwood Publishing Group
This bibliography describes 36 special collections in the United States, which include both published and unpublished research materials in the fields of intentional communities (communes), nudism, sexual behavior, and sexual freedom.

American Communes, 1860–1960: A Bibliography (Sects and Cults in America Bibliographical Guides, Vol. 13)
Timothy Miller, 1990, Garland Publishing
Books, articles, theses, dissertations, and some manuscripts are covered in this book on communes after 1860, including later communes that are the direct offspring of their predecessors.

American Communes to 1860: A Bibliography (Bibliographies on Sects and Cults in America Series, Vol. 12)
Phillip N. Dare, 1990, Garland Publishing
Nearly 50 collective settlements are represented in this bibliography by the nearly 2,000 references to articles, dissertations, monographs, bibliographies, and to primary archival material if accessible.

Community Tools: Resources on Communitarian Values and History and for Community Design, Management and Education
Allen Butcher, 1995, Fourth World Services, 43 pp
This is a thorough listing of books, articles, conferences, classes, and workshops. The author also analyzes and categorizes communities.

Building and Architecture

Build It With Bales
Matts Myhrman and S. O. MacDonald, 1997, Out on Bale (2nd version), 143 pp
This user-friendly book offers step-by-step instruction on building a straw-bale house, including choosing the right bales, site selection, preliminary conceptual design, foundations, stacking, moisture protection strategies, and more.

Ceramic Houses and Earth Architecture: How to Build Your Own
Nader Khalili, 1996, Cal-Earth Press
Khalili has written a step-by-step guide, with experiential advice, technical guidance, and encouragement. To the author, earth houses are the obvious response to the 21st century housing shortages, deforestation, and the energy crunch.

Cob Builders Handbook: You Can Hand-Sculpt Your Own Home, The
Becky Bee, 1998, Chelsea Green Publishing Co., 173 pp
From advice on "snuggling" foundation rocks together to practical explanations of creating the right mix, in this handbook the author really shows that she knows how to work with earth. Sculpt, have fun, get dirty, and still create something useful.

Cobber's Companion: How to Build Your Own Earthen Home, The
Michael Smith, 1997, Cob Cottage Company, 117 pp
Cob walls provide thermal mass (which stores and radiates heat) but not insulation. This book was written for more technically and structurally minded builders than *The Cob Builders Handbook*.

Cohousing: A Contemporary Approach to Housing Ourselves
Kathryn McCamant and Charles Durrett, 1994, Ten Speed Press (2nd edition), 288 pp
For the beginner, this revised edition defines cohousing and makes it possible to visualize this type of community. For those who know what cohousing is, it gives step-by-step information on how to make a cohousing community a reality.

CoHousing Handbook: Building a Place for Community, The
Chris Hanson, 1996, Hartley and Marks, 278 pp
This is a practical guidebook offering detailed advice on creating a successful cohousing project, with chapters on everything from forming a core group to designing and constructing buildings.

Community Design Primer
Randolph T. Hester, Jr., 1990, Ridge Times Press, 116 pp
Although this book was written for professionals who design recreation areas, open spaces, neighborhoods, and public or communal housing, others can also benefit from its good ideas. Experiential exercises on values are included, to help the reader recognize unquestioned assumptions or subconscious beliefs about what works well or looks good. This can help group members be less dogmatic and more open to the "group wisdom."

Cottage Water Systems
Max Burns, 1995, Cottage Life Books, 160 pp
Cottage Water Systems is an excellent resource for those with rural independent water systems. Springs, wells, cisterns, pumps, plumbing, purification, composting toilets, privies, septic systems, and winter water problems are covered.

Designing and Building a Solar House
Donald Watson, 1977, Garden Way Publishing, 281 pp
The author, an architect who has been a designer or consultant on over 80 solar homes, describes both passive and active solar heating and cooling systems in this work, and illustrates them with over 400 photos.

Booklist

Additions and corrections: Email: directory@ic.org, Web: http://directory.ic.org/, Mail: RR 1 Box 156-D, Rutledge MO 63563, USA.

(...Building and Architecture, continued)

Earth Sheltered Community Design

Underground Space Center, University of Minnesota, 1981, Van Nostrand Reinhold, 270 pp

With a focus on energy-efficient residential development, the design aspects examined here include: site selection, topography, soil data, orientation, climate, roads, utilities, site design, density, and marketability.

Eco-Building Schools: Alternative Educational Resources in Environmentally Sensitive Design and Building

Sandra Leibowitz, 1996, Ecological Design Institute, 20 pp

This is a useful booklet for anyone seeking to learn environmentally sound building and design: strawbale, cob, adobe, timber framing, ceramic domes, geodesic domes, passive solar design, photovoltaics/wind generators/micro-hydro systems, permaculture, constructed wetlands, low fuel and solar cook stoves, and more. It includes 36 different schools and programs.

Ecological Design

Sim Van Der Ryn and Stuart Cowan, 1995, Island Press, 200 pp

This book presents a vision of how the living world and the human world can be rejoined by taking ecology as the basis for design—adapting and integrating human design with natural processes.

Energy-Efficient Houses

Fine Homebuilding, Great Houses Series, 1993, The Taunton Press, 159 pp

A beautifully illustrated look at a variety of existing energy-efficient homes, this book includes descriptions of many passive heating and cooling designs, and also has details on super insulation, sun spaces, and more active systems.

From the Ground Up

John N. Cole and Charles Wing, 1976, Little, Brown and Company, 244 pp

Cole and Wing have put together a compendium of insights, information, and illustrations designed to provide you with what you need to know to plan, design, site, and build your own postindustrial home.

Home Water Supply, The

Stu Campbell, 1983, Storey Communications, Inc., 236 pp

A guide for how to find, filter, store, and conserve water, this book gives thorough coverage of water systems from source to end use, including average consumption per person and how to repair the various parts of any system.

Independent Home, The

Michael Potts, 1993, Chelsea Green Publishing, 300 pp

Not primarily a how-to manual, this is a definitive book on getting off the grid that includes a variety of techniques and many ideas from personal stories of people who are not plugged in to their local power system.

Low-Cost, Energy-Efficient Shelter for the Owner and Builder

Eugene Eccli, editor, 1976, Rodale Press, 408 pp

This is a collection of articles from a variety of architects and engineers on renovation, recycling, use of on-site resources, and solar design, that includes everything from simple winterizing projects to complete design and construction.

Natural Solar Architecture, A Passive Primer

David Wright, 1978, Van Nostrand Reinhold, 250 pp

A solid foundation on which to plan a passive solar structure is provided in this book. The concepts of solar design are presented in a very folksy but thorough way to help architectural professionals and laypeople alike.

Owner Built Home, The

Ken Kern, 1975, Charles Scribner's Sons, 374 pp

This book includes many practical tips and specific ideas to assist the owner/builder. Suggestions include: pay as you go, supply your own labor, use native materials, and do your own design and plan.

Passive Solar Construction Handbook, The

Steven Winter Associates, Inc., 1983, Rodale Press, 328 pp

Hundreds of illustrated and labeled building details and construction notes are included in this handbook, which is primarily for residential construction, both new and retrofit. Systems presented include the following: direct gain, thermal storage wall, attached sun space, and convective loop.

Passive Solar Design Handbook

US Department of Energy, 1984, Van Nostrand Reinhold Company, 750 pp

This is a definitive guide to passive solar design that was originally published by the US Department of Energy, and provides essential theory, analysis, and implementation of nonmechanical systems for harnessing solar energy.

Passive Solar Homes

US Department of Housing and Urban Development, 1982, Facts on File, 284 pp

Detailed illustrations, descriptions, and plans are given here, along with designs for different climatic conditions, help on choosing and developing your site, and information on planning, orienting, and insulating your home.

Pattern Language, A

Christopher Alexander, Sara Ishikawa, and Murray Silverstein, 1977, Oxford University Press, 1171 pp

Extraordinarily thorough and accessible, this book has become a bible for home builders, contractors, and developers who care about creating healthy, high-level design.

Primer on Sustainable Building, A

Dianna Lopez Barnett and William D. Browning, 1995, Rocky Mountain Institute, 138 pp

Written for architects, developers, general contractors, landscapers, and home owners, this book demonstrates how a holistic approach to design can result in a building even better than the sum of its parts.

We invite you to assist us with additions and corrections. Updated information will be available on the Web at http://directory.ic.org/

Rebuilding Community in America: Housing for Ecological Living, Personal Empowerment, and the New Extended Family
Ken Norwood and Kathleen Smith, 1995, Shared Living Resource Center, 406 pp
Full of resources for planning, organizing, and designing rural and urban sustainable communities, this book puts its emphasis on community as a housing alternative, and includes architectural renderings, floor plans of shared housing designs, and site plans.

Self-Sufficient House, The
Frank Coffee, 1981, Holt, Rinehart and Winston, 213 pp
Coffee's book describes things you can do and items you can purchase to make yourself more independent of outside systems. Areas covered include: water, waste water, heating, cooling, and electricity generation.

Shelter Sketchbook: Timeless Building Solutions, A
John S. Taylor, 1997, Chelsea Green Publishing, 157 pp
This book features detailed drawings of windows, doors, floors, roofs, house plans, and heating and cooling systems from more than 600 simple, practical structures, from turn-of-the-century straw bale barns in Nebraska to 1000-year-old earth-sheltered homes in China.

Simply Build Green
John Talbot, 1993, Findhorn Press, 220 pp
A comprehensive collection of advice for building ecologically friendly homes, this book provides information on: roofing materials, floor products, and wall types, plus a background on and comparisons of the most commonly used alternative building materials.

Slate Roof Bible, The
Joseph Jenkins, 1997, Jenkins Publishing, 287 pp
This book is a comprehensive step-by-step guide to making and repairing slate roofs, with hundreds of photos and drawings, tables, maps, and graphs. Everything you need to know to install and maintain a stone roof is included.

Solar Architecture
Greg Franta and Kenneth Oson, 1978, Ann Arbor Science Publishers, Inc., 330 pp
Collected from the proceedings of the Ann Arbor Forum of 1977, the techniques, methods, and materials used in energy-conscious design and construction concepts are covered here—techniques that should deliver the best results at the lowest cost.

Solar Energy Handbook
Dr. Jan F. Kreider and Dr. Frank Kreith, 1981, McGraw-Hill Book Company, 1120 pp
Highly technical, this book covers the history of solar energy use, methods for producing heat from sunlight, solar conversion systems, high-temperature solar installations, advanced and indirect systems, and legal, economic, and social considerations.

Solar Houses
Louis Gropp, 1978, Pantheon Books, 160 pp
Both active and passive solar designs are explored in this well-illustrated book, which also includes information on manufactured solar homes and 48 energy-saving designs. Plans are available by mail.

Straw Bale House Book, The
Athena Swentzell Steen, Bill Steen, David Bainbridge and David Eisenberg, 1994, Chelsea Green Publishing, 336 pp
This guide to building living structures with straw bales covers the following: benefits of building with straw bales; safety concerns; building codes; insurance; and techniques for building walls, windows, doors, foundations, roofs, floors, and plastering the straw walls.

Superinsulated Home Book, The
J. D. Ned Nisson and Gautam Dutt, 1985, John Wiley and Sons, 316 pp
This thorough description of the design and construction of super insulated houses also includes discussions of air tightness, controlled ventilation, and passive solar features. Additionally, it is a good resource for lists of various materials, their r-values, and where they can be acquired.

Timeless Way of Building
Christopher Alexander, 1979, Oxford University Press
All the great principles have one thing in common—they are simple. After one realizes such a simple but profound principle, one cannot stop wondering how one survived without its knowledge. *Timeless Way of Building* is about a common language that can be shared to build artifacts that are alive, and stresses that a design should always concentrate on the "whole" and not on assembling parts.

Children and Parenting

Almanac of Education Choices, The
Jerry Mintz, 1996
The first comprehensive directory of educational alternatives in the United States and Canada, this collection of educational alternatives will communicate to the public the broad scope and availability of this movement, as well as foster communication and networking within it. Available from the author, tel: 800-769-4171.

Children in Community
The Society of Brothers (Bruderhof), 1974, The Plough Press, 170 pp
The authors describe here the child-rearing and child-educating philosophy of the Bruderhof communities, and attempt to give a sense of what it's like to grow up there.

Common Vision: Parenting and Educating for Wholeness, The
David Marshak, 1997, Peter Lang Publishing, 246 pp
Common Vision compares descriptions of and recommendations for how to enhance child development by three eminent spiritual teachers: Rudolf Steiner, Sri Aurobindo, and Inayat Khan.

Booklist

Additions and corrections: Email: directory@ic.org, Web: http://directory.ic.org/, Mail: RR 1 Box 156-D, Rutledge MO 63563, USA.

(...Children and Parenting, continued)

Dumbing Us Down: The Hidden Curriculum of Compulsory Schooling

John Taylor Gatto, 1992, 104 pp

The author, a former teacher, shares his views here about some of the debilitating affects of current US educational system and explains why less schooling would benefit children and society.

Everyone Wins! Cooperative Games and Activities

Sambhava and Jasette Luvmour, 1990, New Society Publishers, 100 pp

Over 150 cooperative games and activities are shared here. Designed to foster team cooperation rather than competitive opposition, these games are an excellent reference for teachers, families, or any group of people, young or old.

Geography of Childhood: Why Children Need Wild Places, The

Gary Paul Nabhan and Stephen Trimble, 1994, Beacon Press, 184 pp

In this unique collaboration, naturalists Gary Nabhan and Stephen Trimble investigate how children come to care deeply about the natural world.

Home School Source Book, The

Donn Reed, 1994, Brook Farm Books, 298 pp

Reed's source book lists more than 2000 books and related materials, with an emphasis on liberal arts global education from birth to adulthood. Ideas, curricula, publications, software, support groups, and legal responsibilities are covered, and it includes essays and commentary.

How to Talk So Kids Will Listen and Listen So Kids Will Talk

Adele Faber, Elaine Mazlish, and Kimberly Ann Coe, 1995, Avon Books, 242 pp

A communication tool kit based on a series of workshops, this book provides a step-by-step approach to improving relationships. The "Reminder" pages, helpful cartoon illustrations, and excellent exercises will improve your ability as a parent to talk and problem solve with your children.

Kids Can Cook

Dorothy R. Bates, 1987, Book Publishing Company, 119 pp

These recipes highlight healthful foods kids like to eat and cook themselves. The instructions are presented simply and clearly and are suitable for youngsters 10 and older.

Making Sense of the Media: A Handbook of Popular Education Techniques

Eleonora Castano Ferreira and João Castano Ferreira, 1997, Monthly Review Press, 123 pp

This is a handbook for teaching critical analysis of the mass media that is written in an articulate, lively, clear, and richly illustrated format. Its lessons empower students by developing their ability to understand and analyze messages found in advertising, political campaigns, television news, sitcoms, and melodramas.

Moon Over Crete, The

Jyotsna Sreenivasan, 1994, Smooth Stone Press, 128 pp

A great example of empowering and thoughtful fiction for kids, this is the historically-accurate story of an 11-year-old girl who time travels back to ancient Crete, a place where women are recognized as the equals of men.

Raising Peaceful Children in a Violent World

Nancy Lee Cecil, 1995, Innisfree Press, 253 pp

This practical guidebook for parents and teachers who wish to create a safe, peaceful environment for children offers tips on how to respond in potentially violent situations, on discipline strategies, and on family activities that promote peace.

Resolving Family and Other Conflicts: Everybody Wins

Mendel Lieberman and Marion Hardie, 1981, Unity Press, 222 pp

In this book, the authors share how to fight fairly, reconcile sexual differences and value conflicts, deal with compulsive behavior, and handle problems that arise between parents and children.

Sharing Nature With Children

Joseph Cornell, 1983, Dawn Publications, 143 pp

Sharing Nature With Children describes Cornell's philosophy of outdoor education and gives instructions for parents and teachers about playing outdoor education games that work.

Watermelons, Not War: A Support Book for Parenting in the Nuclear Age

Kate Cloud, 1984, New Society Publishers, 157 pp

Cloud's book offers a compassionate approach to the difficult task of raising well-informed, secure kids in a world of nuclear power and nuclear weapons.

When Sons and Daughters Choose Alternative Lifestyles

Mariana Caplan, 1996, Hohm Press, 230 pp

Written for the relatives and friends of the person who has made unexpected choices by pursuing an unorthodox lifestyle, practicing a nonmainstream spiritual practice, or living in an intentional community, this book provides dozens of brief, first-person anecdotes from families and adult children alike.

Who Speaks for Wolf: A Native American Learning Story

Paula Underwood, 1991, Tribe of Two Press, 51 pp

Praised by the US Department of Education and the Texas Council on the Humanities, this modern classic is used in classrooms throughout the nation.

We invite you to assist us with additions and corrections. Updated information will be available on the Web at http://directory.ic.org/

Community Issues

At One With All Life: A Personal Journey in Gaian Communities
Judith L. Boice, 1990, Findhorn Press, 287 pp
In this work, the author shares travels to the Bear tribe, to Findhorn in Scotland, to Auroville in India, and to the Australian desert in search of Earth-centered leaderless groups.

Cooperative Housing Compendium: Resources for Collaborative Living
Lottie Cohen and Lois Arkin, 1993, Co-op Resources and Services Project, 190 pp
This book covers all the building blocks of putting together a community, be it a small shared living space or an entire ecovillage. Topics include: legal issues, community structure, land development, resources, and financing.

Coops, Communes and Collectives
John Case and Rosemary Taylor (Rosabeth Moss Kanter), 1979, Pantheon
This is an edited volume with two main sections—one of communal case studies and the other of explorations of various issues involved in community living.

Creating Community Anywhere: Finding Support and Connection in a Fragmented World
Carolyn R. Shaffer and Kristin Anundsen, 1993, Jeremy P. Tarcher/Putnam/Perigee Books, 334 pp
The authors explain in this book how to create community spirit without having to move to community, through living, working, playing, and sharing together. They discuss how to develop support groups, social clubs, ritual groups, neighborhood associations, electronic networks, workplace teams, and spiritual communities.

Eco-Villages and Sustainable Communities
Diane and Bob Gilman, 1991, Context Institute, 213 pp
Offering excellent suggestions for starting new communities, this book is primarily about ecovillages—what they are, why we need them, and how to create them.

Findhorn Community: Creating a Human Identity for the 21st Century, The
Carol Riddell, 1991, Findhorn Press, 290 pp
Riddell has written a chronicle of the past, present, and future of one of the world's most renowned "new age" communities.

Guidebook for Intentional Communities
Griscom Morgan, editor, 1988, 41 pp
Revised from "An Intentional Community Handbook," this is a wonderfully eclectic collection of essays and personal observations on community life.

Seeds of Tomorrow: New Age Communities That Work
Cris and Oliver Popenoe, 1984, Harper and Row, Inc., 289 pp
This book surveys and analyzes a range of communities, examining their origins, the principles and beliefs that motivate them, their administrative structures, business and financial resources, as well as obstacles faced and methods for overcoming them.

Shared Visions, Shared Lives: Communal Living Around the Globe
Bill Metcalf, editor, 1996, Findhorn Press, 192 pp
In this work, Metcalf has put together very frank and personal cross-cultural accounts of what it's like to live communally today; to be born and reared, to have children, and to face death within a communal living situation.

Utopia 101: Intentional Communities...the Cooperative Quest to Build a Better World
Geoph Kozeny, 2000, Community Catalyst Project (CCP), Video
Geoph Kozeny, a core staff member for the first two editions of the *Communities Directory*, has spent nearly three years creating this documentary about intentional communities. Now you can see how 18 communities look "up close," while you listen to community members, in their own words, tell stories about their communities, including their candid thoughts on what has worked and what hasn't. More than two hours of information and inspiration!

Ways We Live: Exploring Community
Susan Berlin, 1997, New Society Publishers, 170 pp
In this work, Berlin makes the connection between available time and the strength of community; if our identity is tied up with the constant search for money or prestige, then there's not a lot of time or energy left over for people. It includes stories from community gardens in inner cities to grassroots map making inspiring a sense of place.

"We're in Charge" CoHousing Communities of Older People in the Netherlands: Lessons for Britain?
M. Breton, 1998, Policy Press—Bristol England, 88 pp
A valuable resource for local authorities, housing, community care agencies, community groups, older people's groups, policy makers, and academics, this book provides important information for older people thinking about future options.

Decision Making, Politics and Legal

Builders of the Dawn: Community Lifestyles in a Changing World
Corrinne McLaughlin and Gordon Davidson, 1985, Stillpoint Publishing, 372 pp
McLaughlin and Davidon's book offers workable guidelines for those interested in building tomorrow's communities, and covers such topics as: self-reliance and healing, relationships, patterns of governance, leadership, and diversity of economic systems.

Booklist

(...Decision Making, Politics and Legal, continued)

Building United Judgment: A Handbook for Consensus Decision Making
Michel Avery, et al, 1981, Fellowship for Intentional Community, 124 pp
Originally published by the Center for Conflict Resolution, and now published by the FIC, this classic handbook provides a review of methods that can make a group's efforts work well, including communication skills, working with emotions, conflict and problem solving, and more.

Community, Inc.
Allen Butcher, 1992, self-published monograph, 19 pp
Legal incorporation options for intentional communities are laid out here. Specific information is included for each option, with examples of communities using those legal forms, and comments on their experiences with those structures.

Community Land Trust Handbook, The
Institute for Community Economics, 1982, Rodale Press, 230 pp
This handbook suggests financial and legal steps to protect forest and farm land, redevelop run-down urban neighborhoods, and encourage the construction of low-income housing.

Creating Harmony: Conflict Resolution in Community
Hildur Jackson, editor, 1999, Gaia Trust/Permanent Publications, 288 pp
This book is full of original ideas and inspiration. Contributors from all over the world share their experience in setting up communities, forming proactive groups, and pioneering new techniques.

Creating Successful Communities, A Guidebook to Growth Management Strategies
Michael A. Mantell, Stephen F. Harper, and Luther Propst, 1989, Island Press, 230 pp
Developed for civic activists, policy makers, and planners, this book gives practical guidelines for developing workable action plans for restoring distinctiveness and livability to communities, and provides strategies for effective participation in growth-management decision making.

Democracy in Small Groups: Participation, Decision Making and Communication
John Gastil, 1993, New Society Publishers, 211 pp
Gastil's book explores the dynamics of the following: practicing democracy; the relationship between speaking rights and listening responsibilities; full access to information; agenda setting; surveys on consensus; majority rule; proportional outcomes; and ways to practice democracy in personal, family, and neighborhood life.

Facilitator's Guide to Participatory Decision-Making
Sam Kaner, 1996, New Society Publishers, 255 pp
In this work, Kaner provides helpful hints for group leaders, the dynamics and processes of decision making, group process skills, agenda design, discussion techniques, and more.

Getting to Yes: Negotiating Agreement Without Giving In
Roger Fisher and William Ury, 1981, Penguin, 161 pp
Getting to Yes is a step-by-step guide to mutually acceptable problem solving in difficult situations. It's about getting your principles straight, using them, and what to do in difficult real-world situations.

Grassroots and Nonprofit Leadership: A Guide to Organizations in Changing Times
Berit Lakey, George Lakey, Rod Napier, and Janice Robinson, 1995, New Society Publishers, 215 pp
A collection of ideas for making your grassroots organization better through improved direction, leadership, and balance, this book weaves together theory, experience, and context to help leaders deal creatively and concretely with the full range of community organizational issues.

Great Meetings! How to Facilitate Like a Pro
Dee Kelsey and Pam Plumb, 1997, Hanson Park Press, 173 pp
This is a user-friendly resource book designed to help meeting leaders, facilitators, and participants understand the important steps for planning and facilitating a great meeting.

How to Make Meetings Work
Michael Doyle and David Straus, 1993, Berkeley Publishing Group, 301 pp
Tested on more than 10,000 participants, the Interaction Method of conducting meetings demonstrates how time and people can be better used in meetings, and is proven to increase productivity by up to 15 percent.

Insight and Action: How to Discover and Support a Life of Integrity and Commitment to Change
Tova Green, Peter Woodrow, with Fran Peavey, 1994, New Society Publishers, 160 pp
Three valuable processes for overcoming periods of doubt, indecision, and discouragement are presented here. Section 1: Support Groups, Section II: Clearness for Individual Decision Making, Section III: Strategic Questioning.

Leadership for Change: Toward a Feminist Model
Bruce Kokopeli and George Lakey, New Society Publishers, 32 pp
A concise overview of the strategies used to break free of patriarchal patterns and behaviors, this short book empowers groups seeking both personal and political change.

Making Meetings Work: A Guide for Leaders and Group Members
Leland P. Bradford, 1976, Pfeiffer and Co.
This is a classic, still-valuable book for group-centered leadership, especially chapter three, "Clues to Group Dysfunction."

Making Things Happen: How to Be an Effective Volunteer
Joan Wolfe and Peter A. A. Berle, 1991, Island Press, 226 pp
Volunteerism is the backbone of the environmental movement. Unfortunately, many volunteers are not as effective as they could be because they must perform jobs for which they have little or no training. *Making Things Happen* teaches volunteers the basic skills they need to make a stronger impact.

We invite you to assist us with additions and corrections. Updated information will be available on the Web at http://directory.ic.org/

Manual for Group Facilitators, A

Brian Auvine, et al, 1978 (original), Fellowship for Intentional Community, 89 pp
Originally published by the Center for Conflict Resolution, and now published by the FIC, this manual is a straightforward and comprehensive guide to a very important community skill. Topics include the following: sample agendas, how to get a meeting started and on the right track, group process, communication, dynamics, conflict in groups, crisis intervention, and creative problem solving.

Model for Nonviolent Communication, A

Marshall B. Rosenberg, 1983, 36 pp
This is an examination of the clear and concise use of language as a means of peaceful and cooperative problem solving.

Nonviolent Communication: A Language of Compassion

Marshall Rosenberg, 1998, Center for Nonviolent Communication
This is a complete, step-by-step guide to the nonviolent communication method, with plenty of examples and exercises.

On Conflict and Consensus: A Handbook on Formal Consensus

CT Butler and Amy Rothstein, 1987, Food Not Bombs Publishing, 63 pp
CT Butler, a political activist and consensus trainer, developed the Formal Consensus process as a more structured method for refining a proposal and handling objections to it than the more common Quaker-derived consensus method.

On Creating a Community: A Guide for Organizations, Personal Productivity and International Peace

William Polowniak, 1994, Quantun Publishers, 262 pp
This is a helpful guidebook for understanding the process of building community. Introducing the "Trust Level Theory," the author gives practical advice on dealing with defense mechanisms, on the obstacles to expect and how to overcome them, and on problems with leadership.

Planning A Meeting

Center for Alternatives, Center for Alternatives, Berkeley CA
This book demonstrates how to plan an effective meeting and create an agenda, and dramatizes a "before" picture of a haphazard, conflict-laden meeting, and an "after" picture of a productive facilitated meeting.

Resolving Conflicts With Others and Within Yourself

Gini Graham Scott, 1990, New Harbingers Publications
Rob Sandelin recommends this book as "a detailed, step-by-step practical guide to identifying causes of conflict, with tools and techniques for working through conflicts, and good case histories."

Skilled Facilitator: Practical Wisdom for Developing Effective Groups, The

Roger Schwarz, 1994, Jossey-Bass Inc., 336 pp
In his book, Schwarz shows what makes a group effective and how a facilitator can improve group effectiveness by identifying patterns of behavior that are getting in the way, helping the group stick to a few critical ground rules, and encouraging them to deal more openly with conflict.

Spiritual Politics: Changing the World From the Inside Out

Corinne McLaughlin and Gordon Davidson, 1994, Ballantine, 475 pp
The book begins with the premise that politics really has to do with the bringing together of our best resources in the name of governance and service. Vital ideas are shared, about how our lives and actions are inextricably linked to all things, and how we can and must use this understanding to change the way politics are played.

Directory and Reference

Appropriate Technology Microfiche Library

1993, Appropriate Technology Project
This microfiche collection is a comprehensive resource that contains the complete text of over 1,000 useful appropriate technology books from around the world.

Appropriate Technology Sourcebook

Ken Darrow, Mike Saxenian, et al, 1993, Appropriate Technology Project, 800 pp
This is a bibliography of over 1,000 documents and books that provide solutions to our everyday needs, with sections on food production, water supply, small-scale energy generation, tools and human-powered machines, health care, and more.

Co-ops from A to Z: NASCO's 1996 Guide to Campus Co-ops

North American Students of Cooperation, 1996, NASCO, 60 pp
NASCO is an association of campus cooperatives in Canada and the United States, providing student cooperatives with operational assistance, encouraging the development of new student cooperatives, and serving as an advocate for student cooperatives. Their *Guide* lists names and contact information for all their member co-ops.

Diggers and Dreamers

Edited by Sarah Bunker, Chris Coates, David Hodgson and Jonathan How, 2000, Diggers and Dreamers Publications, 216 pp
This is the well-known British communities directory with many international contacts and resources. Half the book is a selection of wide-ranging articles, the other half is a directory listing UK communities, with an additional overseas section.

Directory of Wimmin's Lands

Shewolf, 1999 (3rd edition), Shewolf, 64 pp
This directory contains the philosophies and contacts for 75 wimmin's settlements and gathering places in the United States and Canada. Please note that it is available only from the editor and will be mailed to women only. To order by mail: Royal T., 2013 Rue Royal, New Orleans LA 70116, USA. Within the United States send money order for $13.00, international send $15.00. Email: Wimminland@aol.com

Booklist

(...Directory and Reference, continued)

Encyclopedia of American Communes, 1663–1963

Foster Stockwell, 1999, McFarland and Co, Inc, Publishers, 280 pp
Stockwell's book details the over 500 communes established in America from 1663 to 1963. Entries include the name of the commune, the years it operated, the community's leaders, a brief history, a discussion of extant buildings or artifacts, and sources for further study.

Eurotopia: Leben in Gemeinschaft

2000, Eurotopia, 262 pp
Eurotopia is a directory of German intentional communities, written in German. *Eurotopia*, Rosa-Luxenburg-Str. 89, D-14806 Belzig, Germany. Tel/fax: 033841-595-40.

GEN Directory of Eco-villages in Europe, The

Babro Grindheim and Declan Kennedy, editors, 1998, Global Eco-village Network (GEN) - Europe, 184 pp
This directory lists ecovillages from Russia to Turkey, covering community histories, present situations, and plans for the future. It provides complete contact information and European resource centers. An updated directory will be printed in 2000.

Guide to Community-Based Sustainable Groups and Centres, A

1991, Global Village Action Network, 135 pp
This book includes descriptions and contact information for over 100 self-help and resource groups in 37 countries.

Macrocosm, USA

Sandi Brockway, editor, 1993, Macrocosm, USA, Inc., 464 pp
A compilation of information for progressive political activists, Brockway's book contains reprinted articles from a range of leftist, peace, environmental, feminist, and other journals, as well as extensive listings of organizations, periodicals, books, publishers, and other resources.

Public Works

Walter Szykitka, editor, 1974, Links Books, 1023 pp
Most of the material in this "handbook for self-reliant living" is from the public domain, especially government publications. Topics include: first aid, wilderness survival, child care, food, tools, how to interact with governments or lawyers, transportation, and communication.

Sanctuaries: A Guide to Lodgings, Monasteries, Abbeys, and Retreats

Jack Kelly and Marcia Kelly, 1996, Bell Tower, 336 pp
This guidebook lists over 1,200 retreats, in every state of the union, where it is possible to find refuge, peace, and refreshment.

Transformative Adventures, Vacations & Retreats: An International Directory of 300+ Host Organizations

John Benson, 1994, New Millennium Publishing, 304 pp
In his book, Benson lists 305 organizations that host more than 3,000 opportunities for transformative experience, ranging from weekend getaways to multi-month community sojourns.

Whole Heaven Catalog: A Resource Guide to Products, Services, Arts, Crafts, and Festivals of Religious, Spiritual, and Cooperative Communities

Marcia M. Kelly and Jack Kelly, 1998, Random House, 336 pp
The Kellys have collected listings for products and services from over 250 religious, spiritual, and cooperative communities to create this book. Listings include caramels from the Catholic Trapistine sisters in Dubuque, Iowa, and bicycle trailers from Cerro Gordo Community in Cottage Grove, Oregon.

Woman's Source Book: Tools for Connecting the Community of Women, The

Ilene Rosoff, editor, 1996, Celestial Arts
This amazing collection of articles, books, Web sites, CD-ROM, media, and resource listings is a resource for everything and anything you might need in life—much like *The Whole Earth Catalog*, with a focus on women's needs and issues. It is very contemporary, without neglecting classic sources.

Economics and Labor

Best Investment: Land in a Loving Community, The

David Felder, 1982, Wellington Press, 164 pp
A straightforward introduction on how great it is to live in a land co-op and how cheap it is to live simply, this book covers the advantages and disadvantages of land trusts: utopianism, buying land, voluntary simplicity, construction, farming barter, community dynamics.

Building Sustainable Communities: Tools and Concepts for Self-Reliant Economic Change

C. George Benello, Robert S. Swann, Shann Turnbull, and Ward Morehouse, 1997, Bootstrap Press
This book covers alternative economics, including alternative currencies, land trusts, land banks, workplace democratization, and banking systems, and provides tools and concepts for self-reliant economic change.

Classifications of Communitarianism: Sharing, Privacy and the Ownership and Control of Wealth

Allen Butcher, 1992, Fourth World Services, 37 pp
In this short work, the author defines communities on continua based on levels of sharing, privacy, and the ownership and control of wealth.

Country Dreams: Your Guide to Saving Time and Money, While Still Getting What You Want and Need in Country Property!

Alan Schabilion, 1991, Misty Mountain Press, 150 pp
This book covers the whys and hows of buying country property. It will help prospective buyers evaluate land and buildings and make decisions, and will guide them through negotiations and financing.

We invite you to assist us with additions and corrections. Updated information will be available on the Web at http://directory.ic.org/

Creating Alternative Futures: The End of Economics
Hazel Henderson, 1978, Perigee Books, 418 pp
This book is made up of Hazel Henderson's collected writings, with a forward by E. F. Schumacher. She writes about recycling, economic growth, resource limitations, and the means to move our society toward more democratic, egalitarian ideals.

Down to Earth: Toward a Philosophy of Nonviolent Living
John Nolt, 1995, Earth Knows Publications, 224 pp
In his book, Nolt advocates a "steady-state" economy. "The free market exists to maximize satisfaction of human desire. But it does so by providing incentive to produce goods for which there is an immediate desire. The free market maximizes satisfaction of desires only for the present generation."

End of Affluence, The
Paul R. Ehrlich, 1974, Ballantine Books, 301 pp
Ehrlich predicts in his book a growing defection from the American Way of Consumption—a movement whose leadership will not come from our established institutions, business corporations, or government, but from ourselves.

Every Willing Hand
Bryan Beaorse, 1979, Hu Press, 98 pp
Beaorse explains here how we can save our society and the world with an economic policy based on providing well-paid jobs for all. Teacher of Sufism to many, he brought together science and spirituality in his own being.

How to Live on Nothing
Joan Ranson Shortney, 1961, Pocket Books, 336 pp
A practical guide for simple living based on personal experience, this book shares 1,000 and more ways to use wit and imagination to live very well on very little.

How to Survive Without a Salary
Charles Long, 1996, Warwick, 208 pp
Long has written a point-by-point guide to embracing a practical and fulfilling "conserver" lifestyle; he explains how to get along with less and hang on to what you have. He covers saving, budgeting, bartering, income options, buying alternatives, and much more.

Invested in the Common Good
Susan Meeker-Lowry, 1995, New Society Publishers, 258 pp
A practical antidote to economic uncertainty and globalization, this book provides suggestions about how to invest our money, time, and skills to create vibrant, homegrown economies inoculated against large corporations and rooted in local ecosystems and cultures.

Mortgage Free!
Rob Roy, 1998, Chelsea Green Publishing, 368 pp
This is a banker's worst nightmare—a working blueprint for building and owning your own home and land, free and clear. It outlines detailed strategies for raising and saving money, buying property, and designing shrewdly.

New Money for Healthy Communities
Thomas H. Greco, Jr., 1994, 201 pp
An introduction to alternative monetary systems, Greco's book provides the history and philosophy behind them, as well as a useful how-to section. Wealth is skills, expertise, willingness to trade, and good faith of people in a community.

Paradigms in Progress: Live Beyond Economics
Hazel Henderson, 1991, Berrett-Koehler, 293 pp
In her book, Henderson explains changes in society that are occurring globally, and proposes new, more workable, approaches to old economic, social, and political problems.

Small is Beautiful: Economics as if People Mattered
E. F. Schumacher, 1973, Harper and Row, 305 pp
The author documents here the current use of resources—the questions of size, production, land, and energy, and discusses alternatives for the greater good, such as humanistic technology, socialism, and new patterns of ownership. It is a primer for the transformation of industrialization.

Stories of Renewal: Community Building and the Future of Urban America (a Report from the Rockefeller Foundation)
Joan Walsh, 1997
Walsh's book is a clearly written and succinct overview report of mainstream, urban, mostly foundation-supported, comprehensive community development projects of recent years. It can be read online at http://www.ncbn.org/

Their Own Idea: Lessons from Workers' Cooperatives
Malcolm Harper, 1992, Intermediate Technology Publications, 145 pp
Harper's economic survey of contemporary worker-owned producer cooperatives contains useful insights into why some cooperatives have succeeded, and why they have not succeeded more often.

Time-Based Economics: A Community Building Dynamic
Allen Butcher, 1997, 41 pp
This work discusses economic forms that present alternatives to a monetary-based economy, including both contemporary and historical systems. It is particularly relevant to those developing intentional communities.

Voluntary Simplicity
Duane Elgin, 1993, Will Morrow and Co., Inc., 245 pp
In *Voluntary Simplicity*, the author illuminates patterns of changes that an increasing number of Americans are making in their everyday lives. By embracing, either partially or totally, the tenets of voluntary simplicity, frugal consumption, ecological awareness, and personal growth, people can change their lives and the world.

We Own It
Honingsberg, Kamaroff, and Beatty, 1982, Bell Springs Publishing, 165 pp
This book covers starting and managing cooperatives and employee-owned ventures. It provides thorough information on a variety of choices for the legal structure of your venture, and includes sample bylaws and articles of incorporation.

Booklist

Additions and corrections: Email: directory@ic.org, Web: http://directory.ic.org/, Mail: RR 1 Box 156-D, Rutledge MO 63563, USA.

(...Economics and Labor, continued)

When Workers Decide: Workplace Democracy Takes Root in America
Len Krimerman and Frank Lindenfeld, editors, 1992, 298 pp
Full of testimonies, examples, analysis, and resources, this book will help everyone interested in finding viable alternatives to corporate capitalism.

Who's Counting? Marilyn Waring on Sex, Lies and Global Economics
Terre Nash, Bullfrog Films, Video
This is a film about the global reality of simpler cooperative living as seen through the eyes of a feisty feminist author, goat farmer, and ex-member of the New Zealand parliament. It is a devastating critique of mainstream economics and the public assumptions that support it.

Your Money or Your Life
Joe Dominguez and Vicki Robin, 1992, Penguin Books, 350 pp
This book spells out a plan to financial independence—working long enough doing something aligned with your values to save enough money to invest and live modestly on the interest. It also shows how to identify attitudes toward money, live simply, and create a plan to generate financial independence over a period of years.

Health, Healing, and Relationships

Chemical Exposures: Low Levels and High Stakes
A. Ashford and C. Miller, 1998, John Wiley and Sons (2nd edition)
If you would like to learn more about Multiple Chemical Sensitivities and related disorders (such as Sick Building Syndrome) this is a very useful text.

Circles of Strength: Community Alternatives to Alienation
Helen Forsey, 1992, New Society Publishers, 144 pp
Forsey has put together a collection of essays and interviews highlighting the healing potential of community, with contributions from Sonia Johnson, Marge Piercy, Laird Sandhill, and Margo Adair.

Conscious Loving: The Journey to Co-Commitment
Gay and Kathlyn Hendricks, 1990, Bantam
Conscious Loving offers clear and powerful suggestions for improving relationships, including the three most important keys to enduring love and intimacy: feel all your feelings, tell the microscopic truth, and keep your agreements. These basic skills can be used for improving all of our connections to others.

Dealing Creatively With Death: A Manual of Death Education and Simple Burial
Ernest Morgan, 1998, Barclay House Books, 163 pp
Morgan's small encyclopedia covers practical solutions to all death-related issues, such as youth suicide, hospice care, living wills, the right to die, simple burials, anatomical gifts, and death ceremonies.

He includes lists of resources, support groups, hospice organizations, and organ banks.

Eight Essential Traits of Couples Who Thrive, The
Susan Page, 1997, Dell, 288 pp
Formerly titled "Now That I'm Married, Why Isn't Everything Perfect?". The author of this book draws on more than 20 years of couples' counseling experience.

Gesundheit!
Patch Adams, 1998, Healing Arts Press, 208 pp
Nurtured by the generosity and idealism of its supporters, the Gesundheit Institute is giving shape to the dream of building a free, full-scale hospital and health care community that will be open to anyone from anywhere.

History of Psychiatry: From the Era of the Asylum to the Age of Prozac, A
Edward Shorter, 1997, John Wiley and Sons Inc.
A champion of psychiatry, in this work the author gives more of the nitty gritty about who tried what, when, with what results.

Love and Survival: The Scientific Basis for the Healing Power of Intimacy
Dean Ornish, M.D., 1998, Harper Collins, 260 pp
The author, a respected cardiologist and research scientist, demonstrated scientifically that heart disease could be reversed through a rigorous combination of medical treatment and lifestyle changes, including diet, yoga, exercise, and meditation. In this work, he shows that the better the quality of your relationships, the bigger the boost they give to your health.

Methods Work . . . If You Do, The
Cornucopia, 1980, Living Love Publishing, 104 pp
In this book, the residents of Cornucopia demonstrate how to heal negative and addictive programming by handling addictions, pinpointing the center of consciousness, focusing, exploring insights, and understanding the Twelve Pathways. It is specially designed for groups.

New Farm Vegetarian Cookbook, The
Dorothy R. Bates and Louise Hagler, editors, 1988, The Book Publishing Co., 224 pp
This is a revised edition of a fine vegan cookbook, that includes many recipes for tofu, tempeh, and gluten as protein sources, along with plenty of good desserts and a unique section on vegetarian baby nutrition.

Recovery From Schizophrenia: Psychiatry and Political Economy
Richard Warner, 1994, Routledge
This book was written with a lay audience in mind. Sections on labor demonstrate surprising ties between economic boom times and the prevalence of mental illness, and especially interesting are the chapters on schizophrenia in the third world and on antipsychotic drugs.

We invite you to assist us with additions and corrections. Updated information will be available on the Web at http://directory.ic.org/

Secrets of Natural Healing With Food

Nancy Appleton, Ph.D., 1995, Sterling Publications, 183 pp
Homeostasis or balanced body chemistry is the key to health. Dr. Appleton shows here what you do that upsets your body chemistry and what you can do to regain and maintain it.

Spiritual Midwifery

Ina May Gaskin, 1990, Book Publishing Company, 480 pp
This book presents the insights and experience developed by midwives at The Farm. The first half offers brief "amazing birth tales," allowing us to briefly step in as quiet witnesses to this crucial and dramatic moment in people's lives. The second half provides detailed, straightforward, accurate, and readable information on pregnancy and birth.

Staying Well in a Toxic World: Understanding Environmental Illness, Multiple Chemical Sensitivity, Chemical Injury, and Sick Building Syndrome

L. Lawson, 1994, Lynnword Press, Chicago
This book is filled with practical information about the little understood illnesses caused by exposures to modern chemicals, and reveals how the toxicity of common chemicals in products as diverse as carpeting, computers, and cosmetics affects our health. Available from Lynnword@aol.com.

Tofu Tollbooth: A Guide to Natural Food Stores and Eating Spots With Lots of Other Cool Stops Along the Way, The

Elizabeth Zipern and Dar Williams, 1999, Ceres Press/Ardwork Press
This is a book by and for travelers that helps you stay healthy at home and on the road. It is a treasure trove of natural and organic food stores and other great places to stop, eat, and take a breather in the 48 contiguous states.

Untouched: The Need for Genuine Affection in an Impersonal World

Mariana Caplan, 1998, Hohm Press, 384 pp
This uncompromising and inspiring work exposes the personal and social consequences of decreased physical affection. It offers positive solutions for countering the effects of growing depersonalization in our times.

History

Almost One Hundred Years of Togetherness

Saadia Gelb, 1996, Shmuel Press, 160 pp
This work offers tidbits and anecdotes to provide an insightful sampling of kibbutz life, past and present. Many of the experiences will ring true to North American communitarians, such as cultural clashes between those from different backgrounds, thankless administrative jobs, and distrust of "outside" experts.

America's Communal Utopias

Donald Pitzer, editor, 1997, University of North Carolina Press, 592 pp
For those interested in the American communal past (which has many lessons of value to contemporary communitarians, who really don't have to be reinventing the wheel as often as they do), this is an excellent overview of it all.

Arthur Morgan Remembered: An American Saga

Ernest Morgan, 1991, Community Service, Inc., 120 pp
American renaissance man Arthur Morgan was a renowned engineer and innovator; a pioneer of new, more cooperative forms of social organization; and an advocate of the "small community." Influencing Ghandi with his writings on education, he was the inspiration for and a consultant to newly independent India's new rural university system.

Celery Wine

Elaine Sundancer, 1973, Community Publications Cooperative
Celery Wine is a charming, idiosyncratic account of life on a country commune of the 1960s era.

Cities on a Hill: A Journey Through Contemporary American Cultures

Frances Fitzgerald, 1981, Simon and Schuster, Inc., 290 pp
In *Cities on a Hill*, Fitzgerald examines four radically different communities: a fundamentalist church, a guru-inspired commune, a Sunbelt retirement community, and a gay activist community—all embodying the visionary drive to shake the past and build anew.

Collected Leaves of Twin Oaks (Vol. 2), The

Various authors, Twin Oaks Community (vol. 2), 92 pp
This is a collection of issue numbers 16 through 30, from 1972–74, of the Twin Oaks newsletter. It includes an index and is spiral bound.

Communes and the Green Vision: Counterculture, Lifestyle, and the New Age

David Pepper, 1991, 243 pp
This is an in-depth study of English communes and their prospects for improving the world.

Communes, USA: A Personal Tour

Richard Fairfield, 1971, Penguin Books, Inc., 400 pp
Fairfield documents his journey through the commune movement of the late 1960s and early '70s in this book, from conventional farm settlements to the most radical experiments within the then-budding counterculture.

Communistic Societies of the United States, from Personal Visit and Observation, The

Charles Nordhoff, 1966 (original 1875), Dover Publications, 439 pp
In his book, Nordhoff details the history, religious or other guiding philosophy, social habits, customs, business, vignettes, interviews, food, clothing, buildings, everyday conversations, and intellectual and aesthetic aspirations within each of the 14 societies described.

Community in the Lord

Paul Hinnebusch, 1975, Ave Maria Press, 240 pp
Hinnebusch writes out of his experience in the charismatic Community of God's Delight in Dallas, Texas. "We have tried to

(...History, continued)

include those elements which we think are integral to every Christian community."

Community Is Possible: Repairing America's Roots

Harry Boyte, 1984, Harper and Row, 233 pp

In this volume, Boyte documents the story of social activism and empowerment in the United States from the Transcendentalists of the early 19TH century to the Civil Rights movement and beyond, and looks at how these movements can be translated into a modern context.

Community of the Future and the Future of Community, The

Arthur E. Morgan, 1957, Community Services Inc., 166 pp

Morgan believed that the small community needed to be affirmed at a time when the nation was rushing headlong to bigness, and wrote this treatise on the concept of community. Morgan was one of the principal leaders of the intentional communities movement of the mid-20th century.

Community: The Story of Riverside

Lynn Rain, 1991, Riverside Trust Board, 217 pp

Rain has written the history of a New Zealand community founded in 1941 as a Christian pacifist haven dedicated to peace and social justice.

Creation of Feminist Consciousness (Vol. 2), The

Gerda Lerner, 1993, Oxford University Press (vol.2), 416 pp

From the middle ages (the seventh century) to the 1870s, this book on historic women's writings on sexism and social evolution covers the social and cultural elements that made a feminist consciousness possible.

Creation of Patriarchy (Vol. 1), The

Gerda Lerner, 1986, Oxford University Press (vol. 1), 303 pp

From Mesopotamian cultures to 400 BCE, this volume covers the history of gender roles in societies and cultures, and gives a detailed understanding of the emergence of misogyny and the climate for the creation of patriarchy.

Encyclopedia of American Communes, 1663–1963

Foster Stockwell, 1998, McFarland and Co., Inc., 280 pp

This encyclopedia gives details on the over 500 communes established in the United States from 1663 to 1963. Entries include the name of the commune, the years it operated, the community's leaders, a brief history, a discussion of extant buildings or artifacts, and sources for further study. The groups are cooperative, collective, experimental, socialistic, and sometimes religious.

Findhorn Foundation: Straight From the Heart

Sam O'Brien, producer/director, 1995, Sam and Assoc. Production, Video

Through the voices and images of its people, captured on film, the story of building community is told: working with people, education, ecological building, environmental work, global networking, and infusing everyday life with spiritual values.

Follow the Dirt Road

Monique Gauthier, 1992, Video

This film is an introduction to intentional communities in the '90s. It follows community living through interviews with residents of Twin Oaks, East Wind, Lama Foundation, and more, and answers such questions as: What are they like? Why do people choose to live in them? What can we learn from them? The video can be purchased from: 207 Evergreen Court, Landenberg PA 19350, USA, tel: 610-274-2402, email: monique@ic.org

From Utopian Dreaming to Communal Reality: Cooperative Lifestyles in Australia

Bill Metcalf, editor, 1995, University of New South Wales Press, 198 pp

This is a book of transformations, written by the "elders" of the Australian communities movement. It contains founders' descriptions of 10 widely different Australian communities, plus chapters on the rich history of intentional communities in Australia.

Getting Back Together

Robert Houriet, 1971, Coward, McCann and George Heagan, Inc., 412 pp

This is Houriet's account of his travels to many of the communes that arose during the late 1960s and early '70s. Transcribed from his diary, it is very personal and digs into the goings-on within the first "hippie communes" of the United States.

Goodenough Story, a Goodenough Life: An Experiment in Community Formation and Self-Governance, A

Goodenough Community, 1993, Goodenough Community, 173 pp

The following is a quote from the Covenant of the Goodenough Community: "We, the Goodenough Community, create a culture that enables human growth. Through our relationships, we develop and heal ourselves and each other, allowing spirit to emerge, thus freeing our creativity and vitality to serve the good of all."

Hutterian Brethren: The Agricultural Economy and Social Organization of a Communal People

John W. Bennet, 1967, Stanford University Press, 298 pp

The author explains here how one group of typical colonists found their land, established their economy, and worked out relations with the local inhabitants, and why the Hutterites have been so successful.

Hutterite Society

John A. Hostetler, 1997, Johns Hopkins University Press, 403 pp

The Hutterites have been living communally for nearly 500 years, and they are thriving today, so they must be doing something right. Hostetler tells their story.

Hutterites in North America, The

John A. Hostetler and Gertrude Enders Huntington, 1980, Holt, Rinehart and Winston, Inc., 141 pp

This is a study of the Hutterites from an anthropological and sociological perspective. Detailed day-to-day living patterns follow the course of a Hutterite child from birth to death, describing each stage of socialization and acculturation.

We invite you to assist us with additions and corrections. Updated information will be available on the Web at http://directory.ic.org/

In the Company of Others: Making Community in the Modern World

Claude Whitmyer, editor, 1993, Jeremy P. Tarcher, Inc., 272 pp
A collection of some of the best articles and stories on community from the past 50 years, these essays offer practical advice about communication, authority, and decision making, and profile successful communities of all kinds.

Inside a People's Commune

Chu Li and Tien Chieh-Yun, 1974, Foreign Languages Press, 212 pp
An insider's look at Chiliying, a Chinese commune of the 1970s, this book helps readers understand better the character, functions, and advantages of these social collectives, many of which are now defunct due to the intrusion of capitalism.

Is It Utopia Yet? An Insider's View of Twin Oaks Community in Its 26th Year

Kat Kincade, 1994, Twin Oaks Publishing, 320 pp
A first-hand account of Twin Oaks' development and community building, this book includes descriptions of conflict and leadership questions in this egalitarian community, and many cartoons by Jonathan Roth.

Joyful Community, The

Benjamin Zablocki, 1971, Penguin Books Inc., 362 pp
Zablocki's story of the Bruderhof, an experiment in Christian communal living, highlights their everyday life and relation to humankind's undying quest for brotherhood.

Koinonia Remembered, The First Fifty Years

Kay N. Weiner, editor, 1992, Koinonia, 222 pp
Koinonia is a Christian community in Georgia focused especially on the ideas of farming and care of the soil, civil rights, nonviolent direct action, shared social ethics, and simple living.

Living the Dream: A Documentary Study of Twin Oaks Community, 1979–83

Ingrid Komar, 1989, Twin Oaks Community, 408 pp
Written in cooperation with the members of Twin Oaks, this book covers everything from decision making and economics to interpersonal relationships.

Love in the Mortar Joints: The Story of Habitat for Humanity

Millard Fuller and Diane Scott, 1980, New Win Publishing, 190 pp
This is an inspiring account of the formative years of this world-renowned center for nonprofit housing.

Magic of Findhorn, The

Paul Hawken, 1975, Bantam Books, 343 pp
This is Hawken's account of the legendary community where he lived for a year: how it began, who lived there at the time, and what it means to the troubled world outside.

Mary's City of David: A Pictorial History of the Israelite House of David as Reorganized by Mary Purnell

R. James Taylor, 1996, Mary's City of David, 182 pp
Taylor's book includes 250 vintage photos with text telling the story of a radical Christian community founded in 1903. For 25 years the community thrived ahead of its time, opening a vegetarian restaurant and honoring women with a strong voice in decision making.

Memoirs of Peasant Tolstoyans in Soviet Russia

William Edgerton, translator, 1993, Indiana University Press, 294 pp
Around 1900, rural communities influenced by Leo Tolstoy's ideas on personal and social renewal flourished in Russia and eastern Europe. Eventually Soviet policy forced the communities to move to western Siberia, and as members refused to take part in policies that they disagreed with, most of the adult members were interred in forced labor camps. Much of this material was written in secret and hidden from the authorities.

New Harmony Movement, The

George B. Lockwood, 1971, Dover Publications, 404 pp
Lockwood has written a historical view of the town of New Harmony, a utopia founded by Robert Owen in 1824. He describes their education system, the role of women, contemporary reports about the colony, and the causes for its eventual disintegration.

New World Utopias: A Photographic History of the Search for Community

Paul Kagan, 1975, Penguin Books, Inc., 191 pp
A photographic survey of communal life in the American West from 1870 to the present, this book includes discoveries from ruins of vanished communities, present-day ruins of once thriving communities, and current communities, and covers the political, religious, and occult.

People Called the Shakers: A Search for the Perfect Society, The

Edward Deming Andrews, 1953, Dover Publications, Inc., 351 pp
The book opens with the Shaker contribution to the history of US social experimentation, and follows with the origin of the movement in 18th-century England, immigration to New England, early experiments in communism, expansion to the American West, and then the decline after the Civil War.

Quest for Utopia in Twentieth Century America; Vol. 1: 1900–60, The

Timothy Miller, 1998, Syracuse University Press (vol. 1), 254 pp
This is the first volume of a two-volume study of intentional communities in the United States during the 20th century. Miller belies the assertion that the period was virtually devoid of communes. After reviewing older groups that were operating until the early 1900s, he provides a decade-by-decade account of dozens of new groups up to the outbreak of hippyism.

Search for Community, The

George Melnyk, 1985, Black Rose Books, 170 pp
A scholarly work on the worldwide co-op movement and its prospects for creating equality and meaning, Melnyk's book studies the achievements and failures of a wide variety of cooperative living arrangements, with a view to extracting features that would best meet the needs of a developing modern Western community.

Booklist

(...History, continued)

Shaker Experience in America: A History of the United Society of Believers, The
Stephen J. Stein, 1994, Yale University Press, 576 pp
This is a general history of the Shakers, from their origins in 18TH-century England to the present day. Stein draws on written and oral testimony by Shakers over the past two centuries, and offers a full and often revisionist account of the movement.

Short History of the Farm, A
Michael Traugot, 1994, Book Publishing Co., 80 pp
The author of this work was one of the founding members of this legendary "hippie" commune in rural Tennessee. This overview covers the following: the Monday Night Class, the caravan odyssey, their rapid population growth, natural childbirth, *Spiritual Midwifery*, agricultural ventures, the Plenty Foundation, and much more.

Special Love/Special Sex
Robert S. Fogerty, editor, 1994, Syracuse University Press, 231 pp
This work presents the journal of a young member of the Oneida community, written in 1876 and 1877, annotated by the editor. The diary describes a young man's joy and despair in his love relationship with another member.

Story of ZEGG, The
Fritz Leonard, 1992, Center for Experimental Cultural Design, Video
This film is an exploration of the German community of ZEGG, a successful community of 100 people living, working, loving, laughing, and learning together, struggling toward a single goal—the creation of a world without fear or violence.

Total Loss Farm: A Year in the Life
Raymond Mungo, 1971, Bantam Books
Mungo was perhaps the best writer of the many who lived communally in the 1960s; his books are wonderfully sweet and charming.

Voices From the Farm
Rupert Fike, editor, 1998, Book Publishing Co., 162 pp
This is a history of this famous community from its beginnings in San Francisco to modern-day reality, told through humorous, sincere anecdotes by the people who were there.

Walden Two Experiment: The First Five Years of Twin Oaks Community, A
Kat Kincade, 1973, Quill, 271 pp
Written by one of the founders of the community, this book follows the trials and joys of the first five years of an attempt to bring the ideas in B. F. Skinner's book *Walden Two* to life.

We Build the Road as We Travel
Ron Morrison, 1991, Essential Book Publishers, 276 pp
Morrison's book shares the story of the successful Mondragon cooperatives in Spain.

Indigenous Peoples & Diversity

Breaking Old Patterns, Weaving New Ties: Alliance Building
Margo Adair and Sharon Howell, 1992, Tools for Change, 30 pp
In this work, the authors offer deeply thoughtful, compassionate advice about how to stop (largely unconscious) destructive attitudes and behaviors, become helpful and effective allies with people of color and other groups, and build a truly multicultural and multiracial society.

Cotton Patch Evidence: The Story of Clarence Jordan and the Koinonia Farm Experiment (1942-1970), The
Dallas Lee, 1971, Harper and Row, 240 pp
An interracial community in the deep south, Koinonia still thrives.

Cultural Etiquette: A Guide for the Well-Intentioned
Amoja Three Rivers, 1991, Market Wimmin, 38 pp
This is a short, concise, straight-ahead set of guidelines, written with humor and wry understanding, that can be immediately used to undo the habits of unconscious racist remarks and actions.

Fantasies of the Master Race
Ward Churchill, 1992, City Lights Books, 304 pp
This collection of essays looks at representations of Native Americans in literature and film, delineating a history of cultural propaganda that has served to support the continued colonization of Native America.

From a Native Daughter: Colonialism and Sovereignty in Hawaii
Haunani Kay Trask, 1993, University of Hawaii Press, 301 pp
From a Native Daugher is about colonialism and the push for sovereignty in native Hawaii.

Homophobia: A Weapon of Sexism
Suzanne Pharr, 1997, Chardon Press/ Woman's Project, 91 pp.
The first book of its kind on the subject of homophobia and sexism, this is a great primer for understanding common elements of oppression used by sexism, racism, homophobia, and heterosexism to keep people oppressed. It is essential reading for those whose lives and organizations are affected by homophobia and for those who seek to understand this sometimes subtle form of oppression and inequality.

Indians Are Us?
Ward Churchill, 1994, Common Courage Press, 382 pp
This is a book of essays on the commercialization of Native American cultures and the threat to indigenous struggles for sovereignty and freedom.

Unequal Sisters: A Multicultural Reader in U.S. Women's History
Ellen Carol DuBois and Vicki L. Ruiz, editors, 1994, Routledge, 473 pp
This is a book of essays illustrating the diversity and difficulties in minority US women's lives.

We invite you to assist us with additions and corrections. Updated information will be available on the Web at http://directory.ic.org/

Uprooting Racism: How White People Can Work for Racial Justice
Paul Kivel, 1995, New Society Publishers, 243 pp
Through a series of short sections, Kivel lays bare the underlying dynamics of systematized, entrenched racism, and advises how white people can intervene strategically to stop it, personally and institutionally.

View From the Shore
Northeast Quarterly, 1990, Akwe Kon Press, 107 pp
This is a collection of Native American perspectives on the Quincentenary.

Rise Up Singing
Peter Blood-Patterson, editor, 1988, Sing Out! Publications, 288 pp
Guitar chords and words for 1200 songs, arranged alphabetically within chapter groupings ("lullabies," "love songs," etc.), are provided in this wonderful spiral-bound book. From ballads to the Beatles, Bob Dylan to Broadway, here are the words to the songs you love.

To Celebrate: Reshaping Holidays and Rites of Passage
Alternatives, 1987, Alternatives, 224 pp
This is a guide to noncommercialized observance of many traditional holidays and celebrations, with an emphasis on personalized social involvement.

Play and Celebration

100 Graces: Mealtime Blessings
Marcia and Jack Kelly, 1992, Harmony Books (Crown Publishers), 111 pp
"Saying grace" is a tradition found in every culture. Ways of giving thanks from a wide variety of traditions—Buddhist, Christian, Jewish, Hindu, Islamic, and Native American, are covered in *100 Graces.*

Circle of Song: Songs, Chants, and Dances for Ritual and Celebration
Kate Marks, 1994, Full Circle Press, 278 pp
This is a ceremonial resource book, ideal for community celebrations and rituals, and especially for Earth-based ritual and workshops. It features words and music for 300 Pagan, Native American, African, Christian, Jewish, and Hindu songs.

Heavenly Feasts: Memorable Meals From Monasteries, Abbeys, and Retreats
Marcia Kelly, 1997, Harmony Books (Crown Publishers), 192 pp
Favorite holiday and special-occasion recipes of religious communities are shared here, including feasts for both meat-eaters and vegetarians.

Playfair: Everybody's Guide to Noncompetitive Play
Matt Weinstein and Joel Goodman, 1980, 250 pp
A fun, all-ages approach to free-spirited frolic and camaraderie, this is a book of noncompetitive games, for parties, meetings, or whatever.

Rainbow Spirit: From the Heart of the Fire
Conscious Wave, 1998, Conscious Wave, Inc., Video, 120 minutes
A staged-yet-authentic performance of traditional and original Rainbow Family songs and chants that have inspired many at Rainbow Family gathering for over 25 years, this film is a prayer for peace among all nations; hope for the future; and love and respect for our creator, Mother Earth, and all our relations.

Social Theory

Burning All Illusions: A Guide to Personal and Political Freedom
David Edwards, 1996, South End Press, 246 pp
To change ourselves and society we need to remove the limits on what we think possible. We need to question the assumptions behind those limits. The author makes the case here that we are not as free as we believe and explains that our thinking is conditioned in ways of which we are largely unaware.

Cities of Light: A Plan for This Age
J. Donald Waters, 1987, Crystal Clarity Publishing, 129 pp
The author describes here practical solutions to some of the most common problems of life, which were worked out in living situations by people dedicated to self-improvement.

Community and Growth
Jean Vanier, translated by Ann Shearer, 1989, Paulist Press, 350 pp
Written by the founder of the L'Arche International Federation of communities, this inspirational Christian work concerns love, healing, service, family, and community. It addresses the problem of increasing alienation, isolation, and loneliness in our modern technological world.

Different Drum: Community-Making and Peace, The
M. Scott Peck, 1988, Simon and Schuster, 336 pp
In *The Road Less Traveled,* M. Scott Peck took readers on a personal journey of psychological and spiritual development. In *The Different Drum,* he takes the next step—to the larger experience of living and working in community.

Dynamic Utopia
Robert C. Schehr, editor, 1998, Bergin and Garvey
Dynamic Utopia articulates a significant theoretical alternative to contemporary social movement theory. It applies chaos theory, and is in opposition to the linear conceptualizations of movement (birth, growth, and decay) that are characteristic of classical and most contemporary social movement theory.

Additions and corrections: Email: directory@ic.org, Web: http://directory.ic.org/, Mail: RR 1 Box 156-D, Rutledge MO 63563, USA.

Booklist

(...Social Theory, continued)

Greening of America, The
Charles Reich, 1970, Bantam Books, 433 pp
This is a 1960s manifesto of the emerging new culture, based on the values of ecology, nonviolence, and social and economic equality.

In the Absence of the Sacred: The Failure of Technology & the Survival of the Indian Nations
Jerry Mander, 1991; Sierra Club Books, 446 pp
A thorough examination of society's reliance on gadgetry at the expense of deeper connections to our environment, this book is a heartfelt plea to rethink the industrial world's rush to oblivion through its pursuit of technology.

Kibbutz, Venture in Utopia
Melford E. Spiro, 1955, Harvard University Press
This is an anthropological study of an Israeli kibbutz that raises broad questions about the nature and limits of cooperative societies.

Manufacturing Consent: Noam Chomsky and the Media
Mark Achbar and Peter Wintonick, What's Left, Video
Chomsky is a renowned linguistics professor who researches all sides of domestic and international news through various foreign news services. He incisively criticizes economic, political, and social structures, particularly in the United States, and this film is a classic in media and cultural criticism.

Marx–Engels Reader, The
Robert Tucker, Ph.D., editor, 1978, W. W. Norton and Co., 786 pp
This volume shows the chronological development of the two great thinkers; selections covered range from history, society, and economics, to politics, philosophy, and the strategy and tactics of social evolution.

New Covenant With Nature: Notes on the End of Civilization and the Renewal of Culture, A
Richard Heinberg, 1996, Quest Books, 219 pp
A radical and thought-provoking book, it addresses such vital questions as: "Has modern civilisation really improved human life?"; "Is money evil?"; "Is government necessary?"; and "What can we each do to renew our connection with all that is wild, generative, and free?" We must begin by rethinking the society from the ground up.

Planethood: The Key to Your Future
Benjamin Ferencz and Ken Keyes, Jr., 1991, Love Line Books, 196 pp
Planethood explains how the problem of extinction by nuclear war or environmental ruin can be solved, by replacing the law of force with the force of law, thereby creating prosperity and rescuing the environment.

Principles of Cellularism
Adrian Aguirre, 1990, 78 pp
This book shares a model for community by a member of Krutsio in Baja California, Mexico.

Simplicity: Notes, Stories and Exercises for Developing Unimaginable Wealth
Mark A. Burch, 1995, New Society Publishers, 130 pp
The author offers here "a serious process of self-exploration and growth in mindfulness." Simplicity is not false asceticism, involuntary destitution, or naive back-to-the-land movements. "Simplicity is joyous; poverty is not." He investigates what simplicity is in relation to yourself, others, the Earth, and spirituality.

Utopias: The American Experience
Gairdner B. Moment and Otto F. Kraushaar, editors, 1980, The Scarecrow Press, Inc., 251 pp
Utopias is a collection of essays based on a lecture series on American utopias sponsored by Goucher College and Johns Hopkins University, in which both modern and historical communities are described and analyzed.

Spirituality and Religion

Bones and Ash
Ma Jaya Sati Bhagavati, 1995, Jaya Press, 147 pp
"Ma" is a highly unlikely Indian-style guru—a former rollerblading Jewish artist from Brooklyn whose religious journey began with a vision of Christ in her living room, and continued with a pilgrimage to India and spiritual study with Neem Karoli Baba. Originally a private journal, it was turned into a book of some 109 poems.

Book of Enlightened Masters: Western Teachers in Eastern Traditions, The
Andrew Rawlinson, 1997, Open Court, 650 pp
Altering the dialogue about Eastern spirituality in the West, this book displays for the first time the dimensions of this spiritual phenomenon.

Chasm of Fire: A Woman's Experience With the Teachings of a Sufi Master
Irina Tweedie, 1993, Element (reissue)
Irina Tweedie awakened to a religious and spiritual quest that took her to India, where she found a Sufi teacher who was to revolutionize her life. This book was written from the diary she kept while under his tutelage.

Cutting Through Spiritual Materialism
Chogyam Trungpa, 1987, Shambhala, 250 pp
This is a clear and eloquent transmission of how the mind works. Chogyam Trungpa, often referred to as one of the few Asian, Buddhist lamas who truly understands the Western mind, here transcends East and West by addressing, simply and eloquently, the processes of the mind and ego.

We invite you to assist us with additions and corrections. Updated information will be available on the Web at http://directory.ic.org/

Dreaming the Dark: Magic, Sex, and Politics
Starhawk, 1982, Beacon Press, 242 pp
In her work, Starhawk brings her mystic gifts to the burning social concerns of the day. Through understanding energy, we can create immanence to replace a tradition of power over others.

Fire, Salt, And Peace: Intentional Christian Communities Alive In North America
David Janzen, 1996, Paralepsis Books, 207 pp
Christian communities are one of the largest components of the intentional communities movement, and in this book Janzen has provided the most complete recent survey of them.

Guru Papers: Masks of Authoritarian Power, The
Joel Kramer and Diana Alstad, 1993, Frog, Ltd./North Atlantic Books, 385 pp
Spiritual leaders, generically termed "gurus," are authoritarian when they expect to be obeyed without question, and either punish or refuse to deal with those who do not. However, as the authors carefully distinguish here, authority based on a leadership role, or even on special spiritual knowledge, does not have to be authoritarian.

Life Together
Dietrich Bonhoeffer, 1954, Harper Collins, 122 pp
An influential book in the Christian intentional communities movement, this is a spiritual treatise on community from a deeply pious point of view, written by a Lutheran pastor who was imprisoned and eventually died in a Nazi concentration camp.

Living Together Alone: The New American Monasteries
Charles A. Fracchia, 1979, Harper and Row, 186 pp
This book is a first-hand report on the worlds of prayer, meditation, and simple work and the deeply felt need to hammer out alone, yet in the midst of other seekers, a vision of life's purpose. The author chronicles visits to monastic communities, talks to leaders and members, and shows what they believe and how they live.

Needs of a New Age Community
John G. Bennett, 1977, Coombe Springs Press, 99 pp
This is a compilation of talks by Bennett, founder and spiritual teacher of Sherbourne House, a community in England. He helped people see for themselves the practical core of the spiritual path and avoid the twin evils of doubt and philosophizing.

Paradise Found: Beautiful Retreats and Sanctuaries
Stanley Young and Melba Levick, 1995, Chronicle Books, 131 pp
This book covers a broad range of retreats, from healing centers to Christian abbeys and Buddhist temples. Each retreat is profiled, with information on customs, types of food served, accommodations, and suggestions for making the most of a visit.

Reflections on Living: 30 Years in a Spiritual Community
Sara Cryer, 1998, Crystal Clarity Publishers, 304 pp
Filled with inspiring first-hand accounts of life in a spiritual intentional community, this book takes the great wave of Eastern thought that has permeated our culture and puts it into practical everyday reality.

Sacred Tree, The
The Four Worlds Development Project, 1984, Lotus Light Publications, 87 pp
The Sacred Tree is a guidebook for Native American spirituality. Through the guidance of the tribal elders, native values and traditions are being taught as the primary key to unlocking the force that will move Native peoples on the path of their own development.

Soul of the Indian: An Interpretation, The
Charles A. Eastman (Ohiyesa), 1980, University of Nebraska Press, 170 pp
This is a historical depiction of Native American spirituality, first published in 1911 by the grandson of a Sioux chief. This knowledge was passed down from antiquity by tribal elders, and preserved here for all who don't have the benefit of the heritage of old wisdom of the tribes.

Spiritual Legacy of the American Indian, The
Joseph Epes Brown, 1964, Crossroad Publishing Company, 34 pp
In his Pendle Hill Pamphlet that throws light on Native American religions, Brown highlights the pervasiveness of religion in every aspect of Native American life and culture.

Strange Gods: The Great American Cult Scare
David G. Bromley and Anson D. Shupe, Jr., 1981, Beacon Press, 249 pp
The authors here insist, on the basis of hard data, that much of the 1970s-era controversy over "cults" was a hoax, and after an in-depth study of several new religions, they conclude that the most practical, insightful way to understand the controversy is to see it as a conflict of interest. In a conflict of interest two parties desire very different outcomes in the same situation, but one gains only at the expense of the other.

Sustainability and the Environment

Back to Basics
Readers Digest Editoral, 1997, Readers Digest, 456 pp
This book is packed with hundreds of projects and illustrated step-by-step sequences to help you learn to live more self-sufficiently, with sections on shelter, alternative energy sources, growing and preserving food, home crafts, and even recreation. It includes over 2,000 photos, diagrams and drawings.

Beyond the Limits
Donella H. Meadows, Dennis L. Meadows, and Jorgen Randers, 1992, Chelsea Green Publishing, 300 pp
The authors have been studying and computer modeling the growth of human population and use of resources, and have reached the conclusion that human use of essential resources has surpassed sustainable rates. In their book they predict the consquences of this and suggest what needs to be altered to avoid such consequences.

Additions and corrections: Email: directory@ic.org, Web: http://directory.ic.org/, Mail: RR 1 Box 156-D, Rutledge MO 63563, USA.

Booklist

(...Sustainability and the Environment, continued)

Capturing Heat: Five Earth-Friendly Cooking Technologies and How to Build Them

Dean Still and Jim Kness, 1996, Aprovecho Research Center, 34 pp

Aprovecho Research Center has been pioneering energy-efficient and nonpolluting technologies since 1981. This book shares several techniques, including solar cookers, hay box "slow cookers," and the rocket stove. Designs are detailed and easy-to-follow using inexpensive materials.

Common Groundwork: A Practical Guide to Protecting Rural and Urban Land

Institute for Environmental Education, editor, 1993, 207 pp

Common Groundwork is a handbook for making land-use decisions.

Defending the Earth: A Dialogue Between Murray Bookchin and Dave Foreman

Steve Chase, editor, 1991, South End Press, 147 pp

In this book, eco-philosopher Murray Bookchin and Earth First cofounder Dave Foreman seek common ground and explore their differing, though often overlapping, perspectives on the following: environmental ethics, social justice, nature philosophy, and the best strategies for radical ecological activism.

Earth User's Guide to Permaculture

Rosemary Morrow, 1998, Kangaroo Press (Simon and Schuster - Australia), 152 pp

This user-friendly book is an informative and practical guide to permaculture. By working through a series of practical exercises and following real-life examples, you will learn how to design a permaculture system on your land. Whether you own an inner-city balcony, a garden in the suburbs, or a farm in the country, you will find this book a useful guide to developing a more sustainable lifestyle.

Eco-City Dimensions: Healthy Communities, Healthy Planet

Mark Roseland, editor, 1997, New Society Publishers, 211 pp

In this collection of 18 essays, writers from the United States, Canada, northern Europe, Australia, and New Zealand put forth their visions of healthy cities, designed for people instead of cars, with sustainable economies and affordable housing.

Eco-Villages and Sustainable Communities: Models for 21st Century Living

Jillian Conrad and Drew Withington, editors, 1996, Findhorn Press, 100 pp

The proceedings of a conference held at Findhorn, this is a series of essays (speeches and workshop sessions) from the activists who are currently working in the field of sustainability.

Ecological Democracy

Roy Morrison, 1995, South End Press, 279 pp

In this book, the author maps a course for transforming our industrial society into a revitalized, participatory, and ecologically respectful democracy.

Energy-Efficient Community Planning

James Ridgeway, JG Press, 221 pp

In his book, Ridgeway describes energy programs in a variety of US cities, and covers conservation programs, food policy, energy audit programs, and recycling.

Futures by Design: The Practice of Ecological Planning (The New Catalyst Bioregional)

edited by Doug Aberley, 1994, New Society Publishers, 214 pp

This book "... offers a smorgasbord of ideas for turning our deteriorated relationship with the Earth into one of harmony. Essays on: creation of whole systems, sustainable cities, wildlife and human impact ... inspiring and optimistic."

Gaviotas: A Village to Reinvent the World

Alan Weisman, 1998, Chelsea Green Publishing, 232 pp

In *Gaviotas*, Weisman tells the story of a Colombian community developing its own sustainable technologies as well as an evolving environmental ethic. The United Nations has called Gaviotas "a model for the developing world."

Humanure Handbook: A Guide to Composting Human Manure, The

J. C. Jenkins, 1994, Jenkins Publishing, 198 pp

This work covers systems from simple low-tech composting to high-end composting toilets, septic systems, and other wastewater treatment. It gives thorough biological analyses of what goes into and comes out of human waste, and facts on how human waste can be broken down into safe, pathogen-free garden gold.

Introduction to Permaculture

Bill Mollison and Reny Mia Slay, 1999, Tagari Publications, Tyalgum Australia, 216 pp

This is a hands-on guide to basic elements of permaculture concepts and designing sustainable human settlements, with clear text and illustrations covering the following: philosophy, land use, microclimate, annual and perennial plants, animals, soils, water management, and human needs woven into intricately connected productive communities.

Least Toxic Home Pest Control

Dan Stein, 1991, Book Publishing Company, 112 pp

The secret to controlling pests without insecticides is outsmarting them! This book is honest, friendly, humorous, concise, practical, and environmentally sensitive.

Living Lightly: Travels in Post-Consumer Society

Walter Schwarz and Dorothy Schwarz, 1999, Jon Carpenter Publishing, 400 pp

This is an account of the authors' travels across four continents among people "living lightly" on the Earth—more self-reliant, more neighborly, more in tune with their environment, and less stressed than the majority who strive for success in the consumer economy.

Living With the Land: Communities Restoring the Earth

Christine Meyer and Faith Moosang, editors, 1992, New Society Publishers, 131 pp

Meyer and Moosang have put together a lively collection of inspiring, first-hand accounts of communities from around the world tak-

We invite you to assist us with additions and corrections. Updated information will be available on the Web at http://directory.ic.org/

ing charge of their destinies by taking back their land and waters and using them in ecologically and economically sustainable ways.

Manual of Practical Homesteading, The

John Vivian, 1975, Rodale Press, 340 pp
As much as it can be written instead of experienced, this book provides information on the skills necessary to live a highly independent, self-reliant life. It focuses on food production, from gardening and orchards to raising livestock.

Our Ecological Footprint: Reducing Human Impact on the Earth

Mathis Wackernagel and William Rees, 1996, New Society Publishers, 160 pp
This important book presents a way to assess humanity's impact on the Earth and to help understand the challenges and strategies involved in achieving true sustainability in the future. It presents a powerful tool for measuring and visualizing the resources required to sustain households, communities, regions, and nations.

Overshoot

William R. Catton, 1982, University of Illinois Press, 298 pp
This book clearly sets forth many of the principles of current ecological and environmental thought. Analysis of current actions that need change are presented in detail, and possible future directions and solutions are described.

Permaculture: A Designer's Manual

Bill Mollison, 1997, Ten Speed Press, 576 pp
The groundwork philosophy of permaculture is laid first, and this book moves from there to the practical business of actual design. The emphasis is on letting various plant and animal species work together as much as possible, to form a basically self-sustaining system from which people can reap a continual harvest, not only of food, but of interest and self-respect.

Rays of Hope: The Transition to a Post-Petroleum World

Denis Hayes, 1977, W. W. Norton and Co., 240 pp
Hayes has written about the present dependence on fossil fuels for food, transportation, heating, and even economic growth, and offers alternatives through the use of wind, water, sun, plants, and even waste.

Renewables Are Ready: People Creating Renewable Energy Solutions

Nancy Cole and PJ Skerrett, 1995, Chelsea Green Publishing, 240 pp
Aimed primarily toward communities and groups rather than individuals, this is a comprehensive network of articles and information about renewable energy projects now in progress throughout the United States. A variety of photovoltaic, wind generator, and micro-hydropower projects are discussed.

Sustainable Cities: Concepts and Strategies for Eco-City Development

Bob Walter, editor, 1992, Eco-Home Media, 354 pp
Sustainable Cities is "a comprehensive collection of essays from experts in every facet of the subject, from water management and xeriscaping to waste management and transportation."

Sustainable Communities: A New Design Synthesis for Cities, Suburbs, and Towns

Sim Van Der Ryn and Peter Calthorpe, 1986, Sierra Club Books, 238 pp
Descriptions of existing communities are used to illustrate the concepts expressed here, and although the focus is on buildings and energy systems, this book also contains a good chapter on sustainable food systems and transportation.

Village Wisdom: Future Cities

Richard Register and Brady Peeks, editors, 1997, EcoCity Builders, 227 pp
This book is made up of the proceedings of the Third International Ecocity and Ecovillage Conference held in Senegal in 1996. It offers solutions and innovative ideas from around the world, and symbolizes cooperation between diverse cultures, between city and village, between the progress of technology and the wisdom of traditions.

Utopian Fiction

1984

George Orwell, 1949 (original), The New American Library, Inc., 267 pp
Orwell's classic dystopian novel satirizes totalitarianism and unthinking devotion to the "organization."

Dispossessed: An Ambiguous Utopia, The

Ursula K. LeGuin, 1994, Harper
LeGuin's story deals with the possibility of creating a functional anarchistic society, and the problems linked with doing so.

Ecotopia

Ernest Callenbach, 1975, Bantam Books, 213 pp
The premise of this work is that the northwestern portion of the United States secedes in 1980. The book takes place in 1999, when a reporter is allowed to visit the isolated area to report on the progress of this social experiment. It provides hopeful clues on how we might change our systems to become more in balance with nature.

Erewhon

Samuel Butler, 1872 (original), various, 192 pp
Erewhon is a 19TH-century satire attacking many aspects of Victorian society, including the Church, the Universities, and family life in general.

Fifth Sacred Thing

Starhawk, 1994, Bantam Books, 496 pp
An unforgettable epic, *Fifth Sacred Thing* brilliantly dramatizes the choices we must make in order to insure the survival of our selves, our society, and our planet.

Booklist

(...Utopian Fiction, continued)

He, She, and It
Marge Piercy, 1997, Ballantine Books
This is an unforgettable feminist dystopian work and a haunting vision of the future America.

Herland
Charlotte Perkins Gilman, 1979, Pantheon Books, 146 pp
Written in 1915, this feminist utopian novel is both humorous and compelling. Three American male explorers discover an all-female society somewhere in unknown parts of the world.

Island
Aldous Huxley, 1962, Harper and Row, 335 pp
Island is a utopian novel to counterpoint Huxley's better known dystopia *Brave New World*. The same mechanisms which horrify us in *Brave New World* are used by the described island nation to promote a heaven on Earth.

Looking Backward
Edward Bellamy, 1888 (original), various, 351 pp
Bellamy tells the story here of a man put to sleep in 1887 who awakens in 2000—a "perfect society" from the perspective of a 19TH-century American humanitarian.

Stranger in a Strange Land
Robert Heinlein, 1995, Ace Books, 438 pp
Winner of the 1962 Hugo Award, this novel focuses on the character of Valentine Michael Smith, born during, and the only survivor of, the first manned mission to Mars. Raised by Martians and coming back to Earth as a true innocent, he ultimately confronts the fate reserved for all messiahs. The original manuscript had 50,000 words cut, and they have been reinstated for the 1995 edition.

Utopia
Sir Thomas Moore, 1516 (original), various, 127 pp
Originally written in Latin as an ironic commentary on the social order in Elizabethan England, Moore's descriptions of an ideal society are still relevant today. The word "utopia" was coined by Moore from Greek words meaning "no place."

Walden Two
B. F. Skinner, 1948, Macmillan, 320 pp
This is Skinner's fictional description of a modern utopia, as proposed by a behavioral psychologist.

Woman on the Edge of Time
Marge Piercy, 1997, Ballantine Books
This novel tells the story of one woman's time travels from a present-day psychiatric ward to a nonsexist, communal country in the future where people's survival is ensured based on need, not money. A sense of freedom, choice, and safety are part of the future world; the present day is the complete opposite.

Women in Community

Counting Ourselves In: A Women's Community Economic Development Handbook
WomenFutures, 1993, Women Futures, 56 pp
This is a basic, practical, and encouraging guide for women getting involved in the broad area of community economic development. It includes suggestions for workshops to help women get community economic development projects started, with mostly Canadian resources and examples.

Feminism
Miriam Schneir, 1994, Random House, 374 pp
Feminism covers the essential historical writings from 18TH-century rebels to World War II.

Feminism in Our Time
Miriam Schneir, 1994, Random House, 488 pp
Feminism in Our Time covers the essential writings from Simone de Beauvior to young feminists of the 1990s. It is well balanced for a historical perspective.

Healing the Wounds: The Promise of Ecofeminism
Judith Plant, editor, 1989, 262 pp
Challenging and profound, this collection of essays, interviews, and poetry explores the central role of women in altering our current destructive social course. Contributors include: Starhawk, Joanna Macy, Margot Adler, and Ursula K. LeGuin.

On the Wild Side: Meetings With Remarkable Women
Marigold Fine and Shana Ross, Sowing Circle Productions, Video
A fast-moving, energetic piece, this film encourages women and girls to step outside of old, limiting ideals and cultural restrictions into renewed power and freedom through singing, dancing, drumming, creativity, connection with nature, and wisdom.

Women in the Kibbutz
Lionel Tiger and Joseph Shepher, 1975, Harcourt, Brace and Jovanovich, 334 pp
Based on the lives of 34,000 kibbutz dwellers, this sociological study covers sexual ideologies, child rearing, money, and more, though the examination of the lives of three generations of kibbutz women.

Women, Race and Class
Angela Y. Davis, 1981, Random House, 244 pp
Davis's book is one of the first and most important works on the interrelatedness of sexism, racism, and classism.

Hoping to acquire one of these books or videos? Please check with Community Bookshelf first—find the book you want and support the FIC at the same time. Go to http://bookshelf.ic.org/ or contact FIC, RR 1 Box 156-D, Rutledge MO 63563, USA. Tel: 800-995-8342 (660-883-5545), email: fic@ic.org

We invite you to assist us with additions and corrections. Updated information will be available on the Web at http://directory.ic.org/

Jillian Downey

About the Appendix

The Appendix, coming last but certainly not least, contains elements (such as the Indexes) that can greatly enhance your use of this book, and also provides information about other products and services that will likely be of interest to *Directory* readers. In addition, don't miss the tear-out cards at the back— send in the *Directory Updates* card to receive your annual packet of corrections and revisions to the community data in this book.

Appendix

Additional Community Information and Feedback

CREATING THIS DIRECTORY was a collaborative effort, and the interactive process does not stop with your getting this book. You may need information you haven't found in the *Directory*, or you may have news about communities or resources that we don't. Either way, we want to be in touch with you, to strengthen everyone's knowledge. Feedback can be a two-way street and we welcome traffic in both directions.

How We Can Help You

What If the Contact Information Is Incorrect?

If, for instance, a listed phone number is disconnected (don't overlook the possibility that the area code has been changed!), or a letter to a listed address is returned as undeliverable, please get in touch with us. We may have new information, or know where to get it.

What If You Don't Find What You're Looking For?

Our first suggestion is to revisit "How to Use This Directory" on page 5, to see if you've tried every avenue available to you in this book. If you still can't find what you want, you can contact us with your specific request. Maybe you're looking for a community with characteristics not covered in the Cross-Reference Chart or Index. Maybe you want to know if there are additional communities or resources fitting your interests that haven't been listed. We'll do what we can. There may be a charge for this service, depending on the nature of the request, and whether or not we can help. If there is a charge, we'll discuss this with you before proceeding.

What If You Want Additional Background Information About a Listed Community?

To start, consider asking the community directly for more information. Additionally, the Fellowship keeps extensive files and may be able to help in two ways. First, we may be able to tell you some of the community's history in the movement.

Second, as will be explained in more detail just below, we maintain a Feedback File about every community for which we receive complaints that don't get amicably resolved. For the cost of $1 per community, we will tell you if there is a Feedback File on that community, and, if there is, we'll send you a summary of all complaints and community responses. Payment for this service must accompany each request.

How You Can Help Us

Use the Additions and Corrections Form

Please use this form, on page 456, to inform us of incorrect listing information, or any information about unlisted communities and resources you think belong in this book. If the form is missing, send your news to the address at the bottom of the next page.

Fill Out the Directory Evaluation Survey

This survey starts on page 428; please take a few moments to let us know how useful the *Directory* has been for you, and your ideas about how it could be improved. We're always trying to make it better, and we need your input to do the best possible job.

Let Us Know If You Have Complaints About a Listed Group

If through direct contact you discover a significant difference between a community or resource's self-description and reality, we want to know about it. Please notify us at the address at the bottom of the next page. First, we may be able to offer an innocent explanation for the discrepancy. Second, we may be able to facilitate an agreeable resolution to any dispute or complaint. Third, we will maintain a Feedback

Jillian Downey

File on any community about which there are unresolved difficulties.

FIC's Community Feedback Files

Here's how the Feedback Files work. If you send us a complaint about a community, we'll first contact you to make sure we understand all the details, and the history of what you've done to inform the community and resolve any differences directly. Possibly we can explain things in a way that will satisfy some of your concerns. However, where this doesn't satisfy, we'll contact the community and get their input on the matter. To the extent that differences are settled to the satisfaction of all, great. Where disagreement persists, we'll open a Feedback File on the community, which includes the comments of all concerned.

We will not publicize that we have a file on any specific community, only that we maintain files in general. For a fee of $1 per community, we will let people know whether there is a file on that group, and, if there is, provide a summary of the comments from all parties. We will not supply the names and addresses of people registering complaints unless they give express permission to do so. To request Feedback File summaries for listed communities, send a list of the groups you want to know about—plus a dollar for each

name on the list—to the address at the bottom of the page. We'll send you what we have.

The Fellowship has thought long and hard on the best way to handle critical feedback about intentional communities, and the Feedback Files are our current best thinking on how to engage in this thorny area. On the one hand, we are concerned with seekers getting access to full information about communities. On the other, we are concerned with protecting community reputations from rash attacks. Honest misunderstandings can explain a lot, and we are reluctant to record criticisms and pass them along until we are satisfied they are substantial and unresolvable. Let us hear how well this meets your needs!

Directory Feedback
RR 1 Box 156-D
Rutledge MO 63563 USA
Tel/Fax: 660-883-5545
Email: fic@ic.org

Directory Evaluation Form

E INVITE YOU TO TAKE A FEW MINUTES to fill out and send in this survey, telling us your thoughts on what worked well for you and how the *Directory* can be improved. Please photocopy this page, and mail with any additional pages of comments to the address at the bottom. Or see us at http://directory.ic.org/

About You

1. Age
○ under 20   ○ 20–24   ○ 25–29   ○ 30–39
○ 40–49   ○ 50–59   ○ 60–69   ○ 70+

2. Community Living (*please pick one*)
○ I've never lived in a community.
○ I used to live in a community, but don't now.
○ I live in a community.

About Us: Evaluating the *Directory*

The space may not be adequate, so don't be shy about attaching extra sheets. For each numbered question below, please circle your best choice.

	Importance to you	Ease of Use
	trivial ... crucial!	hard ... easy!
3. Articles	1 2 3 4 5	1 2 3 4 5
4. Maps	1 2 3 4 5	1 2 3 4 5
5. Cross-Reference Chart	1 2 3 4 5	1 2 3 4 5
6. Community Listings	1 2 3 4 5	1 2 3 4 5
7. Resource Listings	1 2 3 4 5	1 2 3 4 5
8. Book List	1 2 3 4 5	1 2 3 4 5
9. Indexes	1 2 3 4 5	1 2 3 4 5

Feature Articles
10. Breadth of topics covered
TERRIBLE   WEAK   ADEQUATE   GOOD   EXCELLENT

11. Relevance of articles to your interests
TERRIBLE   WEAK   ADEQUATE   GOOD   EXCELLENT

Suggestions for improving:

Missing topics you would have liked covered:

Maps
Suggestions for improving layout and presentation:

Cross-Reference Chart
12. Relevance of catgories to your interests
TERRIBLE   WEAK   ADEQUATE   GOOD   EXCELLENT

Suggestions for improving:

Categories to add, drop, or do differently:

Community Listings
Suggestions for improving:

Resource Listings
Suggestions for improving:

Missing resources you would have liked covered:

Recommended Reading List
Suggestions for improving:

Missing books you would have liked covered:

Indexes
13. Breadth of Community Listings keyword index
TERRIBLE   WEAK   ADEQUATE   GOOD   EXCELLENT

14. Usefulness of Article index
TERRIBLE   WEAK   ADEQUATE   GOOD   EXCELLENT

Suggestions for improving either index:

Miscellaneous
15. Overall layout of the *Directory*
TERRIBLE   WEAK   ADEQUATE   GOOD   EXCELLENT

16. Operating instructions
TERRIBLE   WEAK   ADEQUATE   GOOD   EXCELLENT

17. Value for price paid
TERRIBLE   WEAK   ADEQUATE   GOOD   EXCELLENT

18. Usefulness of display ads
TERRIBLE   WEAK   ADEQUATE   GOOD   EXCELLENT

Thanks for filling out the form! Please mail to:
Directory Evaluation, RR 1 Box 156-D, Rutledge MO 63563, USA

List of Advertisers

You will find a wide selection of quality community-related opportunities, organizations, products, and services offered in the display ads in the *Directory;* we hope they will be useful to you. All but five of the ads are placed in the Community Listings section. Where applicable, we tried to place community products and services next to the community that they are associated with.

An Introduction to the Index Section
Article Index and the Community Listings Keyword Index

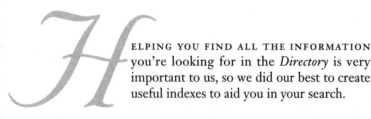

HELPING YOU FIND ALL THE INFORMATION you're looking for in the *Directory* is very important to us, so we did our best to create useful indexes to aid you in your search.

Article Index

The article index is a full back-of-the-book index of the 33 articles that make up the first section of the *Directory*.

Community Listings Keyword Index

The Community Listings Keyword Index, though by no means exhaustive, is a vital tool for rooting out some of the information packed between the covers of this book. To get the most out of your *Directory*, use this index in conjunction with the Maps and the Cross-Reference Chart.

This index is based on the listing each group provided about itself. If a community is not indexed under a particular keyword, that does not necessarily mean that the group does not practice or pursue that particular value—it may mean only that *they did not mention that aspect in their description.*

We tried to index groups based on the areas of focus they offer our readers, and on those recurring questions we hear from people searching for their ideal community.

We chose not to index many of the values or daily practices of community life that got covered in the Cross-Reference Chart. For example, if you wish to know if a group shares all its income and assets, look in the Chart and not here. Other values, such as "nonviolence" and "voluntary simplicity," are not covered in the Chart, yet were frequently mentioned in community descriptions—so we tried to cover those in the Community Listings Keyword Index.

Realizing that vocational considerations often play a major role in community searches, we also indexed many common community businesses. To the extent possible, we indexed such endeavors as restaurants, woodworking shops, conference centers, etc. For the same reason, we've also indexed certain spiritual paths—such as Catholic Workers, Zen Buddhists, Hutterian Brethren, Quakers, etc.

Some communities included in the Community Listings do not appear in the Community Listings Keyword Index even once. Most of those submitted very brief, sketchy descriptions that did not mention any of the specific practices or resources that we indexed.

The names used in the Community Listings Keyword Index may look strange at first glance. In the interest of conserving space, we have used shortened index names. This could be the first word of a group's full name, or the entire name if it's not more than about a dozen letters long. More often it's a shorthand blending of words and abbreviations—each is unique and (hopefully) easily identifiable. A cross-reference is provided in the Chart where both the full name and the short name appear together.

Both of the indexes were prepared by Twin Oaks Indexing, a professional book indexing business of Twin Oaks Community in Virginia.

While we hope you find the *Directory* comprehensive and easy to use, we invite your ideas for improving future editions. Send us your comments and suggestions, using the form on page 428, and leads to groups you think should be included, using the form on page 456.

In our *Directory* survey we asked the following question:

"It can be very difficult placing communities into categories, and yet for some communities this is straightforward and informative. Not all communities will fit but if you have some clarity, please pick only one category:"

420 (58%) answered... here's how they fell out:

    104 (25%) cooperative house
     71 (17%) ecovillage
     69 (16%) cohousing
     55 (13%) intentional neighborhood
     47 (11%) commune
     40 (10%) land trust/coop
     34 (8%) ashram/monastery/temple

Article Index

Community Listings Keyword Index

Note: This index was created from the actual words used in each community's listing, with the exception of the asterisked (*) categories, which were compiled from the answers to a question on our survey. Categories in italic refer the reader on to other related categories.

TibetanBuddh, TruthConsc, VivekanandaM, VivekanandaV, Yogaville, YogodaCmty, ZenBuddhist, ZuniMountain.

ASHRAMS
KashiAshram, MaYogaShakti, MolloyAshram, Sivananda, SriAurobindo, TruthConsc, VivekanandaM, YesssCmty, Yogaville.
SEE ALSO: Monasteries

AUDIO/VIDEO
AquarianRes, OneWorldFam, Turtledove, Yogaville, ZendikFarm.

AUSTRALIA
BackyardTech, CascadeCoho, Cennednyss, Co-ordCo-op, CrossroadsMe, CrystalWater, Gabalah, JesusChrist, MolloyAshram, MtMurrindal, OshoMevlana, RoseneathFarm, Shamballa, SunriseFarm, 12CmtySydney.

AUSTRIA
RatandTat.

AYURVEDA
Atmasantulan.

BAKERIES
Arcosanti, Downeast, HeartwoodCom, Innisfree, ShilohCommun, 12CmtyBuenos, 12CmtyHambur, 12CmtyLondri, 12CmtyQuatro, 12CmtySanSeb, UFA-Fabrik.

BANDS
See Music Concerts

BARTER
DancingRabbt, DaytonHouse, DunmireHollo, WindTreeRnch.

BED-AND-BREAKFAST/GUEST HOUSE
AcmeArtists, Kanatsiohare, Lebensgarten, MonteVuala, NewVrindaban, Wellspring.

BEHAVIORAL PSYCHOLOGY
LosHorcones.
SEE ALSO: Walden Two

BELGIUM
LaVieilleVoi.

BELIZE
RioBonito.

BICYCLES
BearCreek, GreenHouseCo.

BIODIVERSITY
AtlantiRis, EcoVilLoudou, OtamateaEcoV.
SEE ALSO: Diversity, Ecology, Environment

BIODYNAMICS
AbundantFree, CamphillClan, CamphillKimb, CamphillMinn, CamphillMour, CamphillNA, CamphillNewt, CamphillPenn, CamphillSolt, EdenRanch, EsseneSkoola, FellowshipCo, LofstedtFarm, Montclaire, SandhillFarm, WholeVillage.
SEE ALSO: Anthroposophy, Steiner

BIRTHING
FarmThe.

BISEXUALITY
HeiWa, IntlPuppydog, Martha'sHous, Nasalam, ShadyGrove, SynergyHouse.

BLACKSMITHING
AtlantisRis, BearCreek, Wygelia.
SEE ALSO: Metal Shops

BOOKS—MAILORDER
CrystalWater, LIFE, TwinOaks, UnknownTruth.

BOOKSTORES
AlphaFarm, Arcobaleno, BearCreek, CoraniHousin, DancingRabbt, MountMadonna, SouthernCass, SparrowHawk, Turtledove, VivekanandaV.

BRAZIL
LothlorienBR, 12CmtyLondri, 12CmtyQuatro.

BRUDERHOF
TomorrowsBrd.
SEE ALSO: Hutterian Brethren

BUDDHAFIELD
OshoMevlana, OshoMiasto.

BUDDHISM
Hesbjerg, LosangDragpa, ShimGumDoZen, TibetanBuddh, ZenBuddhist.
SEE ALSO: Zen

BUILDING CONSTRUCTION
AbundantDawn, ConcordOasis, DancingWater, Edges.

BUILDING RENOVATION/ RECYCLING
FreetheLand, Gwerin, MariposaGrov, MarshCommons, MaxWoodInst, NewJerusalem, 12CmtyCrox, 12CmtyLancas, 12CmtyPalen.

BUILDING TECHNOLOGY
AlchemyFarm, AwaawaroaBay, ClareHouse, ComGround-ON, CommRetreat, CrystalWater, DayspringCir, DragonBelly, LightFreedom, LostValley, Quarries, Sirius, TakomaVil, VillageHarmon.
SEE ALSO: Architecture, Earthships, Ferro-cement, Passive Solar

CAFES
See Restaurants

CAMPGROUNDS
DeHobbitstcc, Dragonfly, Ganas, HuntingtnOWL, LothlorienIN, RachanaCmty, Skyros, SparrowHawk, SpiralWimmin, SusanBAnthon, Woman'sWorld.

CAMPHILL
See Anthroposophy, Steiner

CAMPS—FAMILY
Iona, SouthwestSuf, Tamera.

CAMPS—KIDS
FranciscanWo, LosHorcones, RoweCamp, StMartinCW.

CAMPS—WOMEN
CampSister.
SEE ALSO: Gatherings—Women

CANADA
AAAAforTLC, ComGround-ON, DownieStreet, Edenvale, GandhiFarm, LeNovalis, LofstedtFarm, LothlorienON, MaisonEmmanu, MiddleRoad, Morninglory, MorningStarR, MulveyCreek, NorthernSun, OurEcovillag, Riverdale, WholeLife, WholeVillage, WindsongCoho, 12CmtyWinnip.

CANDLE MAKING
DeHobbitstee, IsleofErraid, 12CmtyLakeOz, 12CmtyLondri, 12CmtyPalen, 12CmtyPennin, 12CmtyQuatro, 12CmtySanSeb, 12CmtyStentw, 12CmtySydney, 12CmtyWestPa, 12CmtyWinnip.

Note: This index was created from the actual words used in each community's listing, with the exception of the asterisked (*) categories, which were compiled from the answers to a question on our survey. Categories in italic refer the reader on to other related categories.

Index

PiñonEcovil, PurpleRose, RainbowValNZ, Shivalila, TuiLandTrust, Wygelia, ZEGG. SEE ALSO: Personal Growth, Relationships

COMMUNITY BUILDING
Breitenbush, DownieStreet, Goodenough, Grimstone, Iona, LamaFdtn, OjaiFdtn, RainbowFam, TenStones, WholeHealth.

COMMUNITY IN ISLAND POND
See Twelve Tribes

COMMUNITY NETWORKING
(North America)
ComingHome, DolphinCmty, DunmireHollo, EcoVilEmerg, Huehuecoyotl, JesuitVolNW, Kidstown, LittleFlower, MonktonWyld, MountainHome, MountMadonna, OrcaLanding, Padanaram, PiñonEcovil, PlowCreek, RainbowPeace, RiverFarm, SandhillFarm, Sichlassenfa, SouthernOreg, Spadefoot, HutterBreth, Tamera, ThreeSprings, TruthConsc, TwinOaks, TwoPiers, UniversitSCA, UnknownTruth.

COMMUNITY NETWORKS, INTER-NATIONAL
See International Networks

COMMUNITY ORGANIZING
Ness, SusanBAnthon.
SEE ALSO: Activism, Neighborhood Organizing, Peace & Justice

COMMUNITY SERVICE
See Service-Oriented Communities

COMMUNITY-SUPPORTED AGRICULTURE
See CSAs

COMPOSTING
CactusRose, PumpkinHolTN, RiverCity, WoodburnHill.

COMPOSTING TOILETS
AgapeMA, BeechHill, CrossroadsMe, DancingBones, DayspringCir, Earthworm, Edges, LongBranch, Malu'AinaCen, Sirius, ZimZamVegan.

COMPUTER LITERACY
LeNovalis.

COMPUTER PUBLISHING
See Desktop Publishing

CONCERTS
See Music Concerts

CONFERENCE CENTERS
Breitenbush, Edenvale, FarmThe, Ganas, Heathcote, HighWind, Kalani, Kanatsiohare, LostValley, MountMadonna, RoweCamp, SunriseRanch, TwinOaks, Wellspring, ZEGG.
SEE ALSO: Workshop Centers

CONFLICT RESOLUTION
ComingHome, CreeksideVA, DapalaFarm, DeHobbitstee, Ganas.
SEE ALSO: Facilitation

CONSCIENTIOUS OBJECTORS
See Antimilitary, War-Tax Resistance

CONSCIOUSNESS
Auroville, CircleDivine, DawningStar, Findhorn, FridemStift, HarbinHotSpr, HighWind, LamaFdtn, NewLand, OneWorldFam, RaphaCmty, Sirius, TruthConsc, UniversalRes.

CONSENSUS DECISION MAKING
AlphaFarm.

CONSERVATION
Cennednyss, Co-ordCo-op, ComGround-AL, EcoCityProj, WholeVillage.
SEE ALSO: Composting, Energy Conservation, Environment, Recycling

COOPERATION
EarthArtVill, EastWind, EcoVilLoudou, EternalCause, Folkhaven, HorizonsEcoV, KibbutzLotan, KibbutzMvmt, KibbutzNeoS, Adidam, SkyWoodsCos, Songaia.

COOPERATIVE HOUSE CATE-GORY *
AshramCmty, BealHouse, BeaverLodge, BlackWalnut, BoschCoop, BowerHouse, BrightMorn, Brigid, BrownAssoc, BuckmanHall, CactusRose, CampNewHope, CampSister, CasaAmistad, ChesterCreek, ChickenShack, CoLibriUrban, CollegiatLiv, CooperStreet, CoraniHousin, Covenental, DenverCW, DenverSpace, Downeast, DownieStreet, Du-má, East-West, ElderWood, ElsworthCoop, EmmaGoldman, EnchantedGar, EternalCause, FairviewHous, FerencyCo-op, FriendsCo-op, GoodrichFarm, GreenHouseCo,

GreenhouseWA, GregoryHouse, HawkCircle, Headlands, Heartsong, HeiWa, Henderson, Hillegass, HouseofPeace, ICC-Austin, KarenHouseCW, KingmanHall, LeNovalis, LeeAbbeyAsto, LivingROCK, LothlorienWI, MadisonCC, MadisonSt, MarathonCoop, Martha'sHous, Masala, MichiganSoc, Mørdrupgård, Nakamura, NewCommunity, Niche/Tucson, NinthStreet, OaklandEliz, OfekShalom, OlympiaHous, OrcaLanding, Osterweil, PhoenixCoop, PioneerCoop, PurpleRose, QumbyaCoop, RainbowHouse, RiverCity, Ruth'sHouse, SBSHC, Shepherd'sGa, SherwoodCoop, Sichlassenfa, SojournerTru, Spadefoot, SpiritJourne, StFranCW-IL, StevensHouse, StewartLittl, StoneSoup, StudentsCoOR, SuCasaCW, SummitAvenue, Sunflower, Sunnyside, SunwiseCoop, SynergyHouse, UniversitSCA, VarsityHouse, Watermargin, Whitehall, WholeHealth, WildIrisRnch, WilliamStrCW, WiseWomanCtr, YaharaLinden, ZimZamVegan.

COOPERATIVES
See Housing Co-ops, Student Co-ops, Urban Cooperatives

COTTAGE INDUSTRIES
Adirondack, DapalaFarm, KommuneNiede, LamaFdtn, NewVrindaban, PumpkinHolTN, RioBonito, ShadyGrove, Shepherdsfie, SkyWoodsCos, SouthEMECO, Sunmeadow, Tekiah, 12CmtyBuenos, 12CmtyCambr, 12CmtyPalen, 12CmtyPennin, 12CmtyRutlan, 12CmtySydney, WAHOO!.
SEE ALSO: Art, Bakeries, Candle Making, Crafts, Dairies, Disabilities, Hammocks, Hospitality, Indexing, Metal Shops, Prayer Flags, Print Shops, Weaving

COUNCIL PROCESS
OjaiFdtn.
SEE ALSO: Group Process

COURSE IN MIRACLES
Appletree, LightFreedom.

CRAFTS
AcornCmty, BacktoLand, Birdsfoot, CamphillMour, CamphillPenn, CamphillUSA, DunmireHollo, FellowshipCo, Hermitage, Innisfree, Kanatsiohare, Lebensgarten, LightasColor,

Note: This index was created from the actual words used in each community's listing, with the exception of the asterisked (*) categories, which were compiled from the answers to a question on our survey. Categories in italic refer the reader on to other related categories.

CREATIVITY

AcmeArtists, EarthHeartCe, FullMoonRisi, GandhiFarm, GlenIvy, Goodenough, Heartsong, KibbutzNeoS, Panterra, QuarryHill, SacredOak, Skyros, SocietyCreat, StoneGrail, Wäxthuset, WindSpirit, Wygelia

CSAs (COMMUNITY-SUPPORTED AGRICULTURE)

AcornCmty, DapalaFarm, HighWind, Hundredfold, LofstedtFarm, NewEnviron, SaltCreek, SanMateoCoop, SkunkValley, SpiralWimmin, Tekiah, TenStones, ThreeSprings, TolstoyFarm, Wellspring, WholeVillage.

CULTURE

Aleskam, DeltaInfinit, Goodenough.

DAIRIES

PodofDolphin, Riverside, ShiloahVal, Utopiaggia, Windward.

DANCE

Atlantis, DancingBones, DreamingLiz, Ida, SparrowHawk, Turtledove, ZendikFarm.

DEATH ROW

See Prisoners

DECISION MAKING

See Consensus, Facilitation, Group Process

DENMARK

Hertha, Hesbjerg, Mørdrupgård, Svanholm, Udgaarden, Valsølillegå.

DESKTOP PUBLISHING

HighWind, Märchenzentr.

DIET

See Nutrition & Diet

DIRECT ACTION

See Antimilitary, Activism

DISABILITIES

CamphillAssoc, CamphillClan, CamphillKim, CamphillMinn, CamphillMour, CamphillNA, CamphillNewt, CamphillSolt, CamphillSpec, CamphillTrif, CamphillUSA, CasaMariaCW, ColibriUrban, Edenvale, FellowshipCo, FranciscanWo, Gwerin, Innisfree, L'ArcheErie, L'ArcheHome, LIFE, L'ArcheMobil, MaisonEmmanu.

DISARMAMENT

See Antimilitary, Nuclear Disarmament

DISASTER RELIEF

RenaissanceV.

DIVERSITY

AbundantDawn, AwaawaroaBay, BeechHill, Brigid, ChristineCtr, CielCoho, Columbanus, ComGround-AL, ComingHome, CommonPlace, Cooperstreet, DancingRabbt, DayspringCir, DebsHouse, DreamtimeVil, Du-má, EastLake, EastWind, EdenRanch, Edges, EnoCommons, FairOaksCoho, FriendsCo-op, Heathcote, Hillegass, HoldenVil, LosAngEcoV, Meadowdance, PumpkinHolTN, QumbyaCoop, RachanaCmty, SaltCreek, ShannonFarm, SouthEMECO, SummitAvenue, TanguyHomest, TwinOaks, VillageInThe, WholeLife, ZephyrValley.
SEE ALSO: Multicultural, Multigenerational, Multilingual

DRAFT RESISTANCE

See Antimilitary, Peace & Justice

DRAMA

See Theater

DRUG ABUSE

See Recovery

EARTH-BASED SPIRITUALITY

Blackberry, ComGround-ON, Earthseed, EmeraldEarth, HiddenValley, OakGroveFdtn, PaganIsland, PodofDolphin, RiverHayven, WAHOO!, WhiteBuffalo, Windwalker.
SEE ALSO: Native American, Pagan, Shamanism

EASTERN SPIRITUALITY

See Buddhism, Hare Krishna, Sufi, Yoga, Zen

ECOLOGICAL SUSTAINABILITY

BeaconHillWA, ComingHome, DancingRabbt, EcoVilEmerg, FloweringDes, FormingCmty, Fruitvale, Heathcote, Hesbjerg, Intersection, KynHearth, PiñonEcovil, SouthEMECO, TownHead.

ECOLOGY

Aleskam, Atlantis, BeaverLodge, Celo, ChacraMilla, Cornerstone, Downeast, Du-má, Earthworm, EastWind, FloweringDes, FullMoonRisi, JupiterHollo, KibbutzLotan, SusanBAnthon, TwinOaks, Utopiaggia, ZendikFarm.
SEE ALSO: Environment, Ecovillages

ECONOMIC DEVELOPMENT

Meadowdance.
SEE ALSO: Sustainable Economics

ECO-TOURISM

Aleskam, Kalani

ECOVILLAGE CATEGORY *

AbundantDawn, Aerious, AquariusNat, Auroville, BacktoLand, Bethlehem, CarpenterVil, CerroGordo, ComGround-ON, CrystalWater, DancingRabbt, DeltaInfinit, DomeCountry, DragonBelly, EarthArtVill, EcoCityProj, EcoVilCohoNY, EcoVilEmerg, EcoVilLoudou, EdenRanch, GandhiFarm, GardenoVegan, Gesundheit!, GlobalVillag, GoldenEagle, GreaterWorld, Hertha, HighFlowing, HorizonsEcoV, JohnTLyleCtr, Kalani, KynHeartH, LocustGrove, LongBranch, LostValley, LothlorienIN, LoveIsrael, Meadowdance, MolinoCreek, Monadnock, Moonshadow, MorningStarR, MountainHome, NaturesSpiri, NorthernSun, OhioBioEnvi, OtamateaEcoV, OurEcovillag, Padanaram, PaganIsland, PiñonEcovil, Quarries, RainbowHeart, ReevisMtn, RenaissanceV, RioBonito, RiverHayven, SalamanderSp, SEADSofTruth, SouthEMECO, SphereLight, SylvironCoop, TeramoTexas, TrilliumCLT, TurtlesIsl, ValleyLight, WAHOO!, Watersmeet, WindTreeRnch, Windward, Yohana.

ECOVILLAGES

Aleskam, AquariusNat, AwaawaroaBay, ComGround-ON, CrystalWaters, DancingBones, DancingRabbt, DolphinCmty, DomeCountry, DreamtimeVil, EcoVilLaHerm, EcoVilLoudou, EdenRanch, Findhorn, HighFlowing, HorizonsEcoV, Huehuecoyotl, JohnTLyleCtr, KynHearth, LaSendaEcoV, LosAngEcoV, Monadnock, Montclaire, NamastéGreen,

---

MichiganWomy, Niederkaufun, Nishnajida, StrangersCW, 12CmtyBuenos, 12CmtydeSus, 12CmtyHambur, 12CmtyQuatro, Utopiaggia, WindSpirit.
SEE ALSO: Arts & Crafts, Candle Making

OtamateaEcoV, OurEcovillag, PiñonEcovil, PlantFuture, ProyectoEcoV, RiverHayven, RoseneathFarm, SalamanderSp, Sirius, SkyHouse, SouthEMECO, TwinOaks, Watersmeet.

EDUCATION

CentreforAlt, ChacraMilla, Columbanus, ComGround-VA, DapalaFarm, ElSemillero, FloweringDes, FullMoonRisi, GlobalVillag, Goodenough, HighWind, LearnersTrek, LongBranch, LostValley, Malu'AinaCen, MonktonWyld, Moonshadow, NewLand, OekoLeA-Ulos, Pathfinder, RavenRocks, SunMeadows, Utopiaggia.
SEE ALSO: Homeschooling, Schools, or specific topics

EGALITARIAN

AcornCmty, Ainaola, BeaconHillWA, Blackberry, CantineIsld, ComingHome, GAIACmty, JollyRancher, LosHorcones, LothlorienWI, PaganIsland, SkyHouse, SkyWoodsCos, TwinOaks, ValleyLight.
SEE ALSO: Equality

ELDERLY/SENIORS

FellowshipCo, JesusPeople, ShilohCommun.

EMISSARIES

Edenvale, GlenIvy, OakwoodFarm, SunriseRanch.

ENERGY ALTERNATIVES

AwaawaroaBay, BacktoLand, Breitenbush, CarpenterVil, ComGround-AL, DancingRabbt, DunmireHollo, Edges, GlobalVillag, GoldenEagle, HiddenValley, LightFreedom, LothlorienIN, GardenSpirit, MolinoCreek, NorthernSun, RainbowValTX, SalamanderSp, SunMeadow, TownHead, 12CmtyBuenos, Udgaarden.
SEE ALSO: Hydroelectric Power, Solar Energy

ENERGY EFFICIENCY

BeaverLodge, CentreforAlt, Chickenshack, CircleSpring, ColumbiaCoho, DapalaFarm, EarthArtVill, EcoVilCohoNY, HawkCircle, Highline, JumpingOffCLT, Quarries, SunwardCoho, TakomaVil.

ENGLAND

AshramCmty, BarnThe, BeechHill, BirchwdHall, CamphillPenn,

CoraniHousin, Cornerstone, Earthworm, Frankleigh, GrailCmty, Grimstone, Gwerin, LeeAbbeyAsto, LittleGrove, LosangDragpa, LowerShaw, MonktonWyld, NewCreation, OthonaCmty, Pathfinder, PlantsFuture, SimonCmty, Skyros, SteppingSton, TownHead, 12CmtyStentw, TwoPiers.
SEE ALSO: Northern Ireland, Scotland, United Kingdom, Wales

ENTERTAINMENT

See Audio/Video, Clowning, Music Concerts, Theater

ENVIRONMENT

Aleskam, Birdsfoot, Blackberry, BreadandRose, CielCoho, CircleDivine, ColibriUrban, ColumbiaCoho, ConcordOasis, CooperStreet, CreeksideVA, CwrtyCylchau, EastLake, ElSemillero, FinneyFarm, Folkhavcn, GAIACmty, GlobalVillag, LichenCo-op, LongBranch, Sweetwater.
SEE ALSO: Bioregionalism, Conservation, Ecology, Ecological Sustainability, Energy Alternatives, Forestry, Greens, Nature Preserves, Nuclear Power Opposition, Permaculture, Recycling, Restoration, Stewardship, Sustainable Agriculture, Wildlife Sanctuaries

ENVIRONMENTAL ILLNESS

See Chemical Sensitivity

EQUALITY

Du-má, KibbutzLotan, KibbutzTamuz, Moonshadow, RainbowHouse, Riverside, SandhillFarm, Sichlassenfa.
SEE ALSO: Egalitarian, Human Rights, Peace & Justice

ESOTERIC CHRISTIANITY

AshramCmty, FatherDivine, LoveIsrael, NewCreation, OthonaCmty, PeopleLiving, RaphaCmty, ShiloahVal, ShilohCommun, SparrowHawk, Sunnyside, Zion.
SEE ALSO: Twelve Tribes

ESPAÑOL

See Spanish-Speaking

ESPERANTO

NewHumanity.

ESSENE

EnchantedGar, EsseneCoop, EsseneSkoola.

ETHNO-ECOTOURISM

Aleskam.

EXTENDED FAMILY

HouseofPeace, Huehuecoyotl, LakeVillage, LIFE, NewJerusalem, Nomadelfia, OrcaLanding, Palmgrove, Pangaia, PhantoBolo, Storybook, Wygelia, 12CmtyColo, 12CmtyIsland.
SEE ALSO: Tribal

FACILITATION

AlphaFarm.

FAERIE

See Gay, Radical Faeries

FAMILY HOUSEHOLDS

AshlandVine, BrynGweled, Celo, DunmireHollo, JollyRancher, JulianWoods, JupiterHollo, KibbutzMvmt, LaVieilleVoi, MaatDompin, Riverside, RosyBranch, TenStones, TuliLandTrust.

FEEDBACK

Ganas.
SEE ALSO: Communication—Interpersonal

FEMINISM

AcornCmty, BirchwdHall, CactusRose, GreenhouseWA, LothlorienWI, Martha'sHous, MonteVuala, PiñonEcovil, SusanBAnthon, TwinOaks, Woman'sArt.
SEE ALSO: Equality, Lesbian, Women

FERRO-CEMENT

Adirondack.

FESTIVALS

LothlorienIN, LowerShaw, MichiganWomy, ParadiseGard, 12CmtyOakHill.
SEE ALSO: Celebrations, Gatherings

FINDHORN-INSPIRED COMMUNITIES

Stiftelsen, IsleofErraid, LightasColor, LothlorienBR, Sirius.

FOOD—PRODUCERS

Aprovecho, CamphillClan, CarpenterVil, KibbutzNeoS, SandhillFarm, TolstoyFarm.
SEE ALSO: Aquaculture, CSAs, Dairies, Herbs, Hydroponics, Maple Sugaring, Orchards, Organic Farming, Organic Gardening, Soy Products, Vineyards

Note: This index was created from the actual words used in each community's listing, with the exception of the asterisked (*) categories, which were compiled from the answers to a question on our survey. Categories in italic refer the reader on to other related categories.

FOOD—STORES
Ananda, Arcobaleno, AshramCmty, CamphillNewt, NewVrindaban, ShilohCommun.

FORESTRY
Aprovecho, AtlanticRis, CerroGordo, CrystalWaters, FoxHousing, RiverFarm, Riverside, Yonderfamily.

FRANCE
CommdeLArche, CommdePain, TaizéCmty, 12CmtydeSus.

FRANCISCAN
FranciscanWo.

FURNITURE
Ganas, HighWind, ShannonFarm, 12CmtyCrox, 12CmtydeSus.

FUTURE
AquarianRes.

GAMES
See Play

GARDENING
CircleSpring, DaytonHouse, Edges, GrailCmty, Huehuecoyotl, IsleofErraid, JulianWoods, LandSteward, Laurieston, SpiralGarden, Springtree, StJosephCW, TurtleIsl.
SEE ALSO: Agriculture, Organic Gardening

GATHERINGS—MEN: RESOURCES
FaerieCamp, Nomenus, ShortMtn, ZuniMountain.

GATHERINGS—PUBLIC
Aerious, AnandaKanan, ChacraMilla, HighWind, JesusPeople, PhantoBolo, SpiritJourne, TaizéCmty, ZionUCC.

GATHERINGS—WOMEN
CampSister, HuntingtnOWL, MichiganWomy, TwinOaks, WomanShare.

GAY
BrightMorn, FaerieCamp, HeiWa, IntlPuppydog, LesbianGaySp, Martha'sHous, Nasalam, Nomenus, SynergyHouse, TorontoCW, ZuniMountain.
SEE ALSO: Lesbian, Queer-friendly, Radical Faeries

GERMANY
DolphinCmty, FreieChrist, Kana-Gemeins, Lebensgarten, Märchenzentr, Niederkaufun, OekoLeA-Ulos, ProjektEulen, ProWoKultA, UFA-Fabrik, 12CmtyOberbr, 12CmtyPennin.

GIBB, JACK
TorontoTori(N).

GODDESS FIGURINES
ShadyGrove.

GRAY WATER
See Water Treatment

GREECE
NewHumanity.

GREEN POLITICS
BirchwdHall, Cornerstone, GreenHouseCo, KarenHouseCW.
SEE ALSO: Neighborhood Organizing, Sustainable Economics

GROUP MARRIAGE
See Polyamory

GROUP PROCESS
AlphaFarm, Covenental, Ganas, Goodenough, OjaiFdtn.

GROWERS
See Food—Producers

HAMMOCKS
Dandelion, EastWind, Tekiah, TwinOaks.

HANDICAPPED
See Disabilities

HARE KRISHNA
NewGoloka, NewVrindavan.

HEALING CENTERS
Breitenbush, Gesundheit!, Hairakhandi, HeartwoodIns, SacredOak, Wäxthuset, WholeHealth, ZentrumWalde.

HEALTH & HEALING
Aerious, AquarianConc, AtlantisRis, Atmasantulan, BearCreek, EarthHeartCe, Earthseed, EcoVilLoudou, Hearthaven, Heartsong, Montclaire, PhoenixCmty, SouthernCass, Tamera.
SEE ALSO: Healing Centers, HIV Activism, New Age, Nutrition, Therapy

HERBALISM
Moonshadow, ReevisMtn, WiseWomanCtr.

HERBS
Adirondack, Birdsfoot, ReevisMtn.

HISTORIC SITES
BellnghmCoho, LinderHouse, SouthernCass, 12CmtyCrox, 12CmtyIsland, 12CmtyLakeOz.

HIV ACTIVISM
KashiAshram, ZionUCC.

HOLLAND
EmmausHaarz.
SEE ALSO: Netherlands

HOMELESSNESS
AgapeLayApos, BatonRougeCW, CasaMariaCW, CathWorkMD, CathWorkOH, ClareHouse, DorothyDayCW, EmmausCmty, EmmausHaarz, GreenHouseCo, JesusPeople, Kana-Gemeins, OaklandEliz, SaintsFranci, SimonCmty, StFranCW-VA, StJohnsOrder, SuCasaCW, TacomaCW, Zacchaeus.
SEE ALSO: Catholic Worker

HOMESCHOOLING
AcornCmty, BacktoLand, ComGround-VA, CommonPlace, FinneyFarm, HiddenValley, Morninglory, PumpkinHolTN, SalamanderSp, Shivalila, Storybook, 12CmtyRutlan.

HOMESTEADING
Aerious, Ainaola, ComGround-VA, CommonPlace, FormingCmty, Homestead, Morninglory, Ness, O'BrienLake, RiverFarm, StillWater, SunMeadows.

HOSPITALITY
BatonRougeCW, BreadandRose, CasaMariaCW, ClareHouse, Columbanus, DenverCW, DorothyDayCW, EmmausCmty, FranciscanWo, GreenhouseCo, Hearthaven, KarenHouseCW, LIFE, SaintsFranci, Shepherd'sGa, StFranCW-IL, StJudeCW, TorontoCW, UnityKitchen, WilliamStrCW.
SEE ALSO: Bed & Breakfast/Guest House, Campgrounds

HOSPITALS
See Healing Centers

Index

HOSTEL
Wellspring.

HOT SPRINGS
Breitenbush, HarbinHotSpr.

HOUSING ASSOCIATION
Gwerin.
SEE ALSO: Affordable/Low-Cost Housing, Cohousing

HOUSING CO-OPS
BirchwdHall, ColibriUrban, Cornerstone, DebsHouse, Earthworm, East-West, FoxHousing, Fruitvale, GreenHouseCo, MadisonCC, MarathonCoop, Martha'sHous, Masala, RainbowHouse, Sichlassenfa, SteppingSton, StewartLittl, SummitAvenue, TwoPiers, WalnutHouse, Whitehall, YaharaLinden, YorkCenter.

HUMAN POTENTIAL
TuliLandTrust.
SEE ALSO: Personal Growth

HUMAN RIGHTS
Cennednyss, ColibriUrban, Kidstown.
SEE ALSO: Civil Rights, Elderly, Gay, Homelessness, Lesbian, Multicultural, Native American, Peace & Justice

HUMAN UNITY
Auroville.

HUTTERIAN BRETHREN
Palmgrove, HutterBreth.
SEE ALSO: Bruderhof

HYDROELECTRIC POWER
BacktoLand, Breitenbush, EarthHeartCe, Laurieston.

HYDROPONICS
AquariusNat, SEADSofTruth.
SEE ALSO: Aquaculture

INDEXING
TwinOaks.

INDIA
Atmasantulan, Auroville.

INDIGENOUS PEOPLES
Aleskam, RosyBranch, Tonantzin.
SEE ALSO: Native Americans, Third World

INTENTIONAL NEIGHBORHOOD CATEGORY *
AshlandVine, AssocEarth, AtlantisRisi, Bali, BrynGweled, CamphillTrif, CedarHollow, DawningStar, ElohimCity, FinneyFarm, Folkhaven, FunFamily, Goodenough, GreeningLife, HarbinHotSpr, HighWind, HolyCity, JupiterHollo, LIFE, LightasColor, LightFreedom, MaisonEmmanu, MichiganWomy, Monan'sRill, Morninglory, NewJerusalem, NoahProject, O'BrienLake, OakwoodFarm, PeopleLiving, PhantoBolo, PotashHill, Pro-Fem, QuarryHill, Riparia, SaintsChrist, SanMateoCoop, Sassafras, SeattleIntl, ShadyGrove, SparrowHawk, SpiralGarden, StillWater, StoneGrail, TaoWorksVil, TorontoCW, TribeThe, UnionAcres, ValeThe, VillageHarmo, Wellspring, Woman'sWorld, ZephyrFloyd, ZephyrValley, ZionUCC.

INTERFAITH
LamaFdtn, PeopleHouse, StarseedCmty, TaizéCmty.

INTERGENERATIONAL
Covenental, PleasantHill, We'MoonLand.
SEE ALSO: Multigenerational

INTERNATIONAL COMPOSITION
CamphillClan, CamphillPenn, Huehuecoyotl, JonahHouse, KibbutzKetur, LakeVillage, O'KeefeCoop, TaizéCmty, 12CmtydeSus, Wäxthuset, ZentrumWalde.

INTERNATIONAL NETWORKS
Adidam, Ananda, CamphilAssoc, Damanhur, FarmThe, Findhorn, KadeshBiyqah, Kana-Gemeins, KibbutzMvmt, L'ArcheErie, Maharishi, MaYogaShakti, NewCreation, NewGoloka, NewHumanity, RenaissanceV, Sivananda, 12CmtyNet, VivekanandaV, Yamagishi, Yogaville.

INTERNET
LearnersTrek, TaoWorksVil.

INTERNSHIPS
AgapeMA, Ananda, Arcosanti, Birdsfoot, CampSister, CircleSpring, DancingRabbt, EmeraldEarth, HealingGrace, Kindness, LandSteward, LongBranch, LosAngEcoV, LostValley, RainbowHeart, RebaPlace, RoweCamp, SkyHouse.

SEE ALSO: Apprentice, Residency, Volunteers, Work-Study Programs

INTERSPECIES COMMUNICATION
RainbowHeart.

ISRAEL
NeveShalom.
SEE ALSO: Kibbutzim

ITALY
Arcobaleno, Damanhur, Hairakhandi, Nomadelfia, Utopiaggia.

JAPAN
Ittoen, Yamagishi.

JEWISH
AAAAforTLC, BeisAharon, NeveShalom, OfekShalom.
SEE ALSO: Israel, Kibbutzim

JOBS
See Right Livelihood

JOURNALS
See Magazines, Publications

JUSTICE
See Human Rights, Peace & Justice

KIBBUTZIM
KibbutzKetur, KibbutzLotan, KibbutzMvmt, KibbutzNeoS, KibbutzTamuz.

LAND CO-OPS
Adirondack, AshlandVine, AtlantisRis, BlueHeron, BlueMoonCoop, BrynGweled, Celo, CerroGordo, Co-ordCo-op, CommonPlace, CrystalWater, DancingWater, Dandelion, DragonBelly, DunmireHollo, Edges, FarValley, GoodrichFarm, GreaterWorld, GreeningLife, HawkCircle, Headlands, LothlorienON, Miccosukee, Monan'sRill, MtMurrindal, MulveyCreek, NewLand, NorthernSun, PhantoBolo, PodofDolphin, PumpkinHolTN, QuarryHill, RainbowValTX, RenaissanceV, Riverside, RosyBranch, Sassafras, ShannonFarm, StarseedCmty, TanguyHomest, UnionAcres, Windward, WiscoyValley, WoodburnHill, ZephyrValley.

LAND RESTORATION
See Restoration (Environment)

Note: This index was created from the actual words used in each community's listing, with the exception of the asterisked (*) categories, which were compiled from the answers to a question on our survey. Categories in italic refer the reader on to other related categories.

LANDSCAPING
AquarianConc, CwrtyCylchau, 12CmtyWestPa.

LAND TRUST / CO-OP CATEGORY *
AbundantFree, Aprovecho, BearCreek, Birdsfoot, BlueHeron, BlueMoonCoop, ComGround-VA, CommonPlace, DancingWater, DapalaFarm, EarthRe-Leaf, Edges, ElSemillero, FairviewCoop, FarmThe, HillTopFarm, HuntingtnOWL, JulianWoods, JumpOffCLT, LakeVillage, LandSteward, LichenCo-op, LifeCenter, LofstedtFarm, LothlorienON, MaatDompin, Miccosukee, MtMurrindal, MulveyCreek, NorthMount, RainbowValTX, RiverFarm, SantaRosa, SpiralWimmin, SusanBAnthon, TuiLandTrust, WalkerCreek, WindSpirit, Windwalker, WiscoyValley.

LAND TRUSTS
BearCreek, ComGround-AL, Comground-VA, ComingHome, DancingBones, DapalaFarm, EarthRe-Leaf, EmeraldEarth, GingerRidge, Greenwood, Heathcote, HiddenValley, HuntingtnOWL, JulianWoods, JumpOffCLT, LichenCo-op, LofstedtFarm, NamastéGreen, Ness, Niche/Tucson, NorthMount, OwlFarm, PotashHill, Sweetwater, ThreeSprings, TrilliumCLT, TuliLandTrust, ValeThe, Yonderfamily.

LANGUAGE
See Spanish-Speaking, Esperanto, Multilingual

LEFT POLITICS
BlueHeron.
SEE ALSO: Activism

LESBIAN
ChesterCreek, HeiWa, HuntingtnOWL, LesbianGaySp, Martha'sHous, Nasalam, OwlFarm, SpiralWimmin, SynergyHouse, TorontoCW, We'MoonLand, Woman'sWorld, WomanShare, ZuniMountain.
SEE ALSO: Human Rights, Women

LIBERTARIANISM
AtlantisRis, Huehuecoyotl.

LIBRARY
BackyardTech, EnchantedGar, NewHumanity, SparrowHawk, StillWater, UnknownTruth, VivekanandaV.

LIGHT CENTERS
DawningStar, EternalCause, Heartlight, HighFlowing, Ittoen, LightasColor, MethowCenter, SphereLight.
SEE ALSO: Emissaries, Findhorn-Inspired, New Age

LIMITED EQUITY CO-OPS
AcmeArtists, NinthStreet, ParkerStreet, SantaRosa, SEADSofTruth.

LOCAL SELF-RELIANCE
See Self-Sufficiency, Sustainable Economics

LOT-DEVELOPMENT MODEL
Sharingwood.

LOW-INCOME HOUSING
See Affordable/Low-Cost Housing

LUTHERAN
HoldenVil.

MAGAZINES/JOURNALS
AgapeTN, JesusPeople, KibbutzMvmt, LostValley, Märchenzentr, MadreGrande, GardenSpirit, MountainHome, ShortMtn, TruthConsc, ZendikFarm, ZionUCC.
SEE ALSO: Newsletters

MAIL-ORDER PRODUCTS
DolphinCmty, LightasColor, PiñonEcovil, ReevisMtn.
SEE ALSO: Books—Mailorder

MAPLE SUGARING
BlueMoonCoop.

MASSAGE
Atmasantulan, HarbinHotSpr.

MAYAN
HighFlowing, RosyBranch.

MEDIA
DreamtimeVil, GlobalVillag, KibbutzNeotS, Moonshadow, RainbowPeace.
SEE ALSO: Audio/Video

MEDIATION
See Conflict Resolution, Facilitation

MEDIEVALISTS
CrossroadsMe.

MEDITATION
Ananda, AnandaKanan, Arcobaleno, Atmasantulan, BarnThe, Heartlight, IsleofErraid, LosangDragpa, Maharishi, MolloyAshram, NaturesSpiri, NewGoloka, OjaiFdtn, OshoMevlana, OshoMiasto, RenaissanceV, ShimGunDoZen, Sirius, Sivananda, SongMorning, SparrowHawk, YesssCmty, YogodaCmty, ZenBuddhist.
SEE ALSO: Buddhism, Yoga, Zen

MEN
See Gatherings—Men, Gay, Radical Faeries

MENNONITE
PlowCreek.

MENTAL DISABILITIES
See Disabilities

MENTORING
Heartsong, Magic.

METAL SHOPS
Niederkaufun, 12CmtyHambur.
SEE ALSO: Blacksmithing

METAPHYSICS
SouthernCass.
SEE ALSO: Consciousness, Spirituality

MEXICO
EcoVilLaHerm, Huehuecoyotl, LosHorcones.
SEE ALSO: Spanish-Speaking

MIDWIFERY
FarmThe.

MILITARY RESISTANCE
See Antimilitary, Nuclear Disarmament, Peace & Justice, War Tax Resistance

MINORITIES
See Human Rights, Multicultural

MOBILE ECOVILLAGE
RainbowPeace.

MONASTERIES
AbbeyGenesee, ChristHills, CorpusChrist, Hesbjerg, MadreGrande, Nahziryah, TaizéCmty, VivekanandaV.

MULTICULTURAL
AcornCmty, CielCoho, HiddenValley, LeeAbbeyAsto, PiñonEcovil, Shivalila.

MULTIGENERATIONAL
BellnghmCoho, EcoVilCohoNY, FairviewHous, WholeLife.
SEE ALSO: Intergenerational

MULTILINGUAL
ChacraMilla, DeRegenboog, LeNovalis, O'KeefeCoop, Utopiaggia.
SEE ALSO: Spanish-Speaking

MULTIRACIAL
BatonRougeCW, Covenental, EmmausCmty, RebaPlace, WoodburnHill.

MUSEUMS
See Historic Sites

MUSIC
Atlantis, DunmireHollo, FairviewHous, FellowshipCo, HighFlowing, Ida, LothlorienIN, Meadowdance, Morninglory, Songaia, SparrowHawk, SynergyHouse, Turtledove, ZendikFarm.

MUSIC CONCERTS
AquarianConc, JesusPeople, LothlorienWI, MichiganWomy, SongMorning, Turtledove, UFA-Fabrik.

NATIVE AMERICAN
DolphinCmty, GoldenEagle, Kanatsiohare, LocustGrove, Nishnajida, OakGroveFdtn, RainbowFam.
SEE ALSO: Earth-based Spirituality, Indigenous Peoples, Shamanism, Sweat Lodges

NATURE SANCTUARIES
BearCreek, EarthRe-Leaf, HealingGrace, LothlorienIN, Miccosukee, RavenRocks, RoseneathFarm, Sivananda, SouthwestSuf.
SEE ALSO: Wildlife Sanctuaries

NEIGHBORHOOD ORGANIZING
BoschCoop, LowerShaw, MaxWoodInst, RebaPlace.

NEIGHBORHOOD OUTREACH
AquarianConc, CactusRose, CasaAmistad, EastLake, Gwerin, Headlands, LeeAbbeyAsto, LosAngEcoV, Riverdale, SpiralGarden, VillageInThe, ZephyrValley.

NETHERLANDS
DeHobbitstee, EmmausHaarz, Landelijike, WeystThe.

NETWORKS
See Community Building, Community Networks, International Networks

NEW AGE
Arcobaleno.
SEE ALSO: Health & Healing, Light Centers, Spirituality

NEW SOCIAL ORDER IN MESSIAH
See Twelve Tribes

NEWSLETTERS (ABOUT COMMUNITIES)
Headlands, HeartwoodCom, KarenHouseCW, NewEnviron, Padanaram, PeaceFarm, SainstFranci, SouthernOreg, SuCasaCW, SusanBAnthon, TacomaCW, TwinOaks, UnityKitchen, ZuniMountain.

NEW ZEALAND
AwaawaroaBay, CreeksideNZ, HeartwoodCom, OtamateaEcoV, Riverside, TuiLandTrust, WaitakereEco.

NICARAGUA
JubileePartn.

NIGERIA
Palmgrove.

NONHIERARCHICAL GOVERNMENT
CardiffPlace, GandhiFarm, OlympiaHous, Steppingston.
SEE ALSO: Antimilitary, Peace & Justice

NONPROFIT
AlphaOmega, Arcosanti, BacktoLand, CerroGordo, ChristineCtr, CoLibriUrban, EcoCityProj, EmeraldEarth, FaerieCamp, FridemStift, Goodenough, HeartwoodCom, Hermitage, Innisfree, LandSteward, Lebensgarten, LifeCenter, LostValley, Magic.Inc, Malu'AinaCen, Moonshadow, NaturesSpiri, OekoLeA-Ulos, PeopleHouse, Priorities, ProjektEulen, RainbowHeart, RaphaCmty, RosyBranch, SacredOak, SEADSofTruth, Sivananda, SowingCircle, Spadefoot, StillWater, SusanBAnthon, TruthConsc.

NONRESIDENTIAL COMMUNITIES
RaphaCmty.

NONVIOLENCE
AgapeMA, BeaconHillWA, Blackberry, CasaMariaCW, CathWorkOH, ComingHome, CommdeLArche, DeRegenboog, EarthRe-Leaf, EastWind, EmmausCmty, FairviewCoop, FranciscanWo, Hearthaven, HillTopFarm, HouseofPeace, KarenHouseCW, KashiAshram, LittleFlower, Malu'AinaCen, PiñonEcovil, RainbowFam, Riverside, SacredOak, SandhillFarm, SkyHouse, StoneGrail, SuCasaCW, Tamera, TorontoCW, Tribe.The, TwinOaks, VineandFig, WeystThe, Zacchaeus.
SEE ALSO: Antimilitary, Catholic Worker, Civil Disobedience

NORTHERN IRELAND
CamphillClan, CamphillMour, Columbanus.

NUCLEAR DISARMAMENT
LittleFlower.
SEE ALSO: Peace & Justice, Antimilitary

NUDIST
See Clothing-Optional/Textile-Free

NUTRITION & DIET
BearCreek, DragonBelly, ParadiseGard, WholeHealth.
SEE ALSO: Raw Foods, Vegan, Vegetarian

ORCHARDS
Amata, BacktoLand, BeechHill, Cennednyss, DunmireHollo, EarthRe-Leaf, FairOaksCoho, FinneyFarm, GreeningLife, Heathcote, LightFreedom, LosHorcones, MtMurrindal, Padanaram, Riparia, Riverside, SandhillFarm, SkyWoodsCos, Songaia, SparrowHawk, Springtree, SunriseFarm.

ORGANIC FARMING
Atlantis, Birdsfoot, Cennednyss, CerroGordo, DeHobbitstee, DragonBelly, EarthRe-Leaf, EcoCityProj, EcoVilCohoNY, Edenvale, EnchantedGar, EsseneSkoola, GingerRidge, GoodrichFarm, GreeningLife, Kanatsiohare, KibbutzNeoS, KitezhChildr, MolinoCreek, Padanaram, PlowCreek, RavenRocks, ReevisMtn, RenaissanceV, RiverFarm, ShiloahVal, SkyWoodsCos,

Note: This index was created from the actual words used in each community's listing, with the exception of the asterisked (*) categories, which were compiled from the answers to a question on our survey. Categories in italic refer the reader on to other related categories.

Svanholm, 12CmtyBellow, Udgaarden, Watersmeet, ZendikFarm.

ORGANIC GARDENING

Downeast, Dragonfly, DunmireHollo, EastLake, ElSemillero, FairOaksCoho, FinneyFarm, FoxHousing, FridemStift, FriendsCo-op, GlobalVillag, GreenhouseWA, Guayrapá, Heathcote, HiddenValley, HighHorizons, JollyRancher, KarenHouseCW, KommuneNiede, LightFreedom, LosAngEcoV, LothlorienIN, LostValley, GardenSpirit, MadisonSt, MadreGrande, Morninglory, Nahziryah, PumpkinHolTN, RainbowHeart, RainbowHouse, Riparia, SalamanderSp, SanMateoCoop, Sirius, Sivananda, Songaia, SowingCircle, SparrowHawk, SpiritJourne, Storybook, StrangersCW, SunriseRanch, TacomaCW, Tekiah, 12CmtyBuenos, 12CmtyOakHill, TwinOaks, VineandFig, WeystThe, WholeHealth, WoodburnHill, Yonderfamily.
SEE ALSO: Biodynamics, Gardening, Permaculture, Seeds

PACIFISM
See Peace & Justice, Antimilitary, Nonviolence

PAGAN
COMNGround, Glendower, PaganIsland, ShadyGrove.
SEE ALSO: Earth-based Spirituality, Shamanism

PALESTINIAN
NeveShalom.

PARANORMAL PHENOMENA
See Metaphysics, UFOs

PARENTING SKILLS
Hillegass.

PASSIVE SOLAR BUILDINGS
LaSendaEcoV, SunwiseCoop, Windwalker.
SEE ALSO: Building Technology, Underground Buildings.

PEACE
BreadandRose, DunmireHollo, GlobalVillag, Hesbjerg, JonahHouse, JubileePartn, LosHorcones, Maharishi, PlowCreek, Sichlassenfa, StrangersCW, Tamera, WeystThe.

PEACE & JUSTICE
BeaconHillWA, Blackberry, BoschCoop, CactusRose, CathWorkMD, Cennednyss, CommunityHos, DeRegenboog, EmeraldEarth, Fruitvale, HeiWa, Iona, JesuitVolNW, JubileePartn, KarenHouseCW, Malu'AinaCen, MountainHome, PeaceFarm, Riparia, Riverside, SaintsFranci, StFranCW-IL, StJudeCW, SuCasaCW, TwinOaks, WilliamStrCW, ZionUCC.
SEE ALSO: Activism, Catholic Worker, Human Rights, Prisoners, Refugees, Social Change, Third World

PEER COUNSELING
BrightMorn, CominHome, Du-má, HiddenValley.

PERFORMING ARTS
See Dance, Music Concerts, Theater

PERMACULTURE
Ainaola, BarkingFrogs, CarpenterVil, CaveCreek, CedarHollow, ComGround-ON, CoraniHousin, Cornerstone, CrossroadsMe, CrystalWaters, DancingWater, DreamtimeVil, Earthaven, EarthRe-Leaf, Earthworm, EcoCityProj, EcoVilCohoNY, EdenRanch, Edges, FairviewCoop, FloweringDes, GandhiFarm, GreaterWorld, Greenwood, Heathcote, HighHorizons, LostValley, OjaiFdtn, Pangaia, PlantsFuture, ProyectoEcoV, RainbowHeart, RoseneathFarm, RosyBranch, SalamanderSp, TresPlacitas, WAHOO!, We'MoonLand, ZuniMountain.
SEE ALSO: Sustainable Agriculture

PERSONAL GROWTH
AcornCmty, BacktoLand, BrightMorn, ChacraMilla, DeHobbitstee, Du-má, ElSemillero, EnchantedGar, FairviewCoop, GlenIvy, Goodenough, Guayrapá, Heartsong, HeiWa, LearnersTrek, LichenCo-op, LostValley, MariposaGrp, Montclaire, MorningStarR, OshoMevlana, Panterra, PhoenixCmty, PodofDolphin, StoneGrail, TuliLandTrust, Wellspring, Wygelia, Yohana, ZentrumWalde.
SEE ALSO: Communication—Interpersonal, Consciousness, Human Potential, Relationship Skills, Spiritual Education, Therapy, Vision Quests

PERSONAL HYGIENE PRODUCTS
12CmtyCambr, 12CmtyRutlan.

PHOTOVOLTAICS
See Solar Energy

PLANNED NEIGHBORHOODS
See Cohousing, Ecovillages

PLAY
Brigid, ComGround-VA, Gesundheit!, Whitehall.

POLAND
AssocEarth

POLITICAL ACTIVISM
See Activism, Green Politics, Left Politics, Nuclear Disarmament, Peace & Justice

POLITICS
See Anarchism, Feminism, Green Politics, Left Politics, Libertarianism, Radical Faeries

POLYAMORY
COMNGround, Glendower, HillTopFarm, KynHearth, PhoenixCmty, PodofDolphin, ShadyGrove, Starland

PORTUGAL
Tamera.

POVERTY
See Antipoverty, Homelessness

PRAYER FLAGS
LamaFdtn.

PRESERVATION
See Conservation

PRINT SHOPS
12CmtyCrox.

PRISONERS
CathWorkMD, CathWorkOH, Kindness, LittleFlower, VineandFig.

PSYCHOLOGY
DaytonHouse, PhoenixCmty.
SEE ALSO: Behavioral Psychology, Group Process, Therapy

PUBLICATIONS
See Magazines/Journals, Newsletters, and specific subjects

PUBLISHING
AquarianConc, AshramCmty, FarmThe, FunFamily, Iona, KadeshBiyqah, Kindness, LocustGrove, Magic.Inc, MaxWoodInst,

MountainHome, Nahziryah, NewEnviron, OakGroveFdtn, OneWorlFam, ProjektEulen, Shepherdsfie, ShortMtn, TruthConsc, We'MoonLand.
SEE ALSO: Desktop Publishing

QUAKER
AshlandVine, BrightMorn, CasaAmistad.

QUEER-FRIENDLY
BlackElk, BoschCoop, CactusRose, ComGround-ON, Hermitage, Ida, LothlorienWI, ShannonFarm, ShortMtn, ZuniMountain.
SEE ALSO: Gay, Lesbian

RACIAL JUSTICE
BatonRougeCW.
SEE ALSO: Multiracial, Peace & Justice

RADICAL FAERIES
FaerieCamp, Nomenus, ShortMtn, ZuniMountain.
SEE ALSO: Gay

RAINBOW FAMILY
RainbowFam.

RAPE COUNSELING
See Shelters—Women

RAW FOODS
Ainaola, EarthRe-Leaf, Pangaia.

RECOVERY
CampNewHope, CasaMariaCW, FreieChrist, HumanityRis, MountainHome, Wäxthuset.

RECREATION
See Games, Play

RECYCLING
BeechHill, BlueHeron, CrossroadsMe, Downeast, Du-má, EcoCityProj, Greenwood, HawkCircle, KynHearth, PurpleRose, SalamanderSp, Sirius, WoodburnHill.
SEE ALSO: Composting, Conservation, Environment

RECYCLING—BUILDINGS
MaxWoodInst.
SEE ALSO: Building Renovation

RECYCLING—THRIFT STORES
AgapeLayApos, BearCreek, Ganas.

REEVALUATION COUNSELING
See Peer Counseling

REFERRALS
See Community Networks, Networking

REFUGEES
FreieChrist, JubileePartn, KarenHouseCW, NewJerusalem, RenaissanceV, SeattleIntl.

RELATIONSHIPS
See Communication—Interpersonal, Polyamory, Sexuality

RELATIONSHIP SKILLS
Ganas, LosHorcones, SkywoodsCos.

RELIGIOUS ORIENTATION
See Spiritual Orientation.

RESIDENCY PROGRAMS
AlphaFarm, Arcosanti, LowerShaw, ReevisMtn, SouthwestSuf, SpiralWimmin, TidetanBuddh, WholeHealth.
SEE ALSO: Apprentice, Internships, Volunteers, Work-Study Programs

RESISTANCE COMMUNITY
See Catholic Worker

RESOURCE CONSERVATION
See Conservation

RESTAURANTS
AlphaFarm, Ananda, Arcobaleno, Arcosanti, CommunityHos, CamphillNewt, NewVrindaban, OneWorldFam, ProjektEulen, ShilohCommun, 12CmtyBellow, 12CmtyBoston, 12CmtyHyan, 12CmtyLakeOz, 12CmtyLancas, 12CmtyStentw, 12CmtyWinnip, UFA-Fabrik.

RESTORATION (ENVIRONMENT)
CedarHollow, CircleSpring, GreaterWorld, OhioBio-Envi.

RETIREMENT
See Elderly/Seniors

RETREAT CENTERS
AbbeyGenesee, Aerious, Ananda, AnandaKanan, BarnThe, Breitenbush, CampSister, ChacraMilla, ChristineCtr, ComGround-ON, CommRetreat CorpusChrist, DawningStar, Edenvale, Edges, HarbinHotSpr, Hermitage,

HighWind, Kalani, LocustGrove, LostValley, MolloyAshram, Nahziryah, NewHumanity, Nomenus, OjaiFdtn, PumpkinHolNY, RainbowHeart, RenaissanceV, RoweCamp, SacredMtn, SaintsChrist, ShilohCommun, SkunkValley, SongMorning, SouthwestSuf, Starland, StFranCW-VA, SunriseRanch, TorontoCW, TrilliumCLT, TruthConsc, Turtledove, VivekanandaM, VivekanandaV, WAHOO!, Watersmeet, Yogaville, ZenBuddhist.

RIGHT LIVELIHOOD
KibbutzLotan, SowingCircle, WindTreeRnch, Windward.

RITUALS
Arcobaleno, DancingBones, Du-má, Earthseed, EmeraldEarth, EnchantedGar, FullMoonRisi, Greenwood, KashiAshram, WhiteBuffalo.
SEE ALSO: Celebrations, Gatherings

ROLLING THUNDER
GoldenEagle.

RURAL LIVING SKILLS
See Homesteading

RURAL/URBAN SISTER COMMUNITIES
CooperStreet, Ganas, MariposaGrov, MountMadonna, WildIrisRnch.

RUSSIA
Aleskam, KitezhChildr.

RUSSIAN ORTHODOX
AgapeTN.

SANCTUARIES, ENVIRONMENTAL
See Nature Sanctuaries, Wildlife Sanctuaries

SANCTUARY MOVEMENT
See Human Rights, Refugees

SANITATION
See Water Treatment

SAWMILLING
Dragonfly, Padanaram.

SCHOOLS—ADULT EDUCATION
FarmThe, ReevisMtn.

Note: This index was created from the actual words used in each community's listing, with the exception of the asterisked (*) categories, which were compiled from the answers to a question on our survey. Categories in italic refer the reader on to other related categories.

SCHOOLS—CHILDREN
Ananda, AquarianConc, BeisAharon, Birdsfoot, CamphillSpec, FarmThe, FranciscanWo, Heartlight, Kanatsiohare, KashiAshram, LosHorcones, MountMadonna, Padanaram, Palmgrove, QuarryHill, Shepherdsfie, ShiloahVal, UFA-Fabrik, Yogaville.
SEE ALSO: Homeschooling, Waldorf

SCOTLAND
CamphillNewt, Findhorn, Iona, IsleofErraid, KitezhChild, Laurieston.
SEE ALSO: United Kingdom

SEEDS/SEEDLINGS
Atlantis, DownieStreet, SowingCircle.

SELF-REALIZATION
HeartwoodIns, ValleyLight.
SEE ALSO: Human Potential, Personal Growth

SELF-SUFFICIENCY
BarnThe, ColibriUrban, ComingHome, CommonPlace, DapalaFarm, EarthRe-Leaf, ElderWood, ElohimCity, EmmausCmty, FarValley, Folkhaven, FormingCmty, Gabalah, GandhiFarm, GardenoVegan, GoldenEagle, Greenwood, Hairakhandi, HiddenValley, HighFlowing, JollyRancher, JumpingOffCLT, KadeshBiyqah, LaSendaEcoV, Lindsbergs, LocustGrove, LosHorcones, LothlorienIN, Moonshadow, MulveyCreek, OwlFarm, RatandTat, ReevisMtn, SEADSofTruth, SpiralWimmin, StarseedCmty, SunMeadows, TolstoyFarm, 12CmtyOberbr, ValleyLight, Windwalker.

SEMINARIES
SparrowHawk, ZenBuddhist.

SENIOR CITIZENS
See Elderly/Seniors

SERVICE-ORIENTED COMMUNITIES
Ananda, Atmasantulan, CamphilAssoc, CamphillNA, CommduPain, DenverCW, DolphinCmty, Innisfree, Intersection, Ittoen, JesusPeople, JubileePartn, KashiAshram, Kindness, Magic.Inc, MountMadonna, RaphaCmty, RenaissanceV, Sichlassenfa, WeystThe.
SEE ALSO: Catholic Worker

SEVENTH-DAY ADVENTIST
Sunnyside

SEWAGE
See Water Treatment

SEXUALITY
Ainaola, Family.The, Nasalam, PumpkinHolTN.
SEE ALSO: Bisexual, Gay, Lesbian, Polyamory, Relationship Skills

SHAMANISM
HighFlowing, HumanityRis, LightasColor.
SEE ALSO: Native American, Earth-Based Spirituality, Pagan

SHELTERS
See Homelessness

SHELTERS—WOMEN
CasaMariaCW, KarenHouseCW, OaklandEliz, StJosephCW.

SIMPLE LIVING
AgapeMA, BlueMoonCoop, BreadandRose, CedarHollow, Columbanus, CommundeLArche, CommunityHou, DeHobbitstee, EarthArtVill, EcoVilLoudou, ElSemillero, GandhiFarm, GentleWorld, IsleofErraid, Ittoen, JesuitVolNW, JupiterHollo, LightMorning, Malu'AinaCen, MolloyAshram, MulveyCreek, NorthernSun, SandhillFarm, ShortMtn, Songaia, StFranCW-IL, StoneGrail, StrangersCW, SuCasaCW, TorontoCW, TurtleIsl, 12CmtyQuatro, UnionAcres.
SEE ALSO: Voluntary Simplicity

SMALL BUSINESS
See Cottage Industry

SNAKE HANDLERS
UnknownTruth.

SOCIAL CHANGE
BeaconHillWA, BrightMorn, Celo, ComGround-AL, CommRetreat, Du-má, EmmausCmty, MariposaGrov, Montclaire, Moonshadow, PeaceFarm, StoneSoup.
SEE ALSO: Human Rights, Peace & Justice, Prisoners

SOLAR POWER
AgapeMA, AlchemyFarm, AquariusNat, AtlantisRis, BacktoLand, BackyardTech, BlueMoonCoop, CaveCreek, CerroGordo, CircleSpring, Edges, Homestead, JohnTLyleCtr, KynHearth, Malu'AinaCen, Morninglory, MountainHome, Priorities, RavenRocks, SacredMtn, SEADSofTruth, ShortMtn, Sirius, Solterra, Udgaarden, UnionAcres, VillageHarmon, Westwood.
SEE ALSO: Energy Alternatives, Passive Solar

SOUP KITCHENS
See Homelessness

SOY PRODUCTS
FarmThe, TwinOaks.

SPAIN
ElBloque, ElSemillero, Guayrapá, 12CmtySanSeb.

SPANISH-SPEAKING/ESPAÑOL
ChacraMilla, GlobalVillag, Niche/Tucson, Tonantzin.
SEE ALSO: Argentina, Mexico, Nicaragua, Colombia

SPECIAL NEEDS
See Disabilities

SPIRITUAL
Kindness, UnionAcres.

SPIRITUAL CENTERS
See Ashrams, Monasteries, Self-Realization, Seminaries

SPIRITUAL EDUCATION
Ananda, AquarianConc, Arcobaleno, ChristineCtr, Findhorn, LamaFdtn, MorningStarR, SacredMtn, ShimGumDoZen, SouthernCass, StarseedCmty, TibetanBuddh, TruthConsc, VivekanandaM, YesssCmty, YogodaCmty, ZenBuddhist.

SPIRITUAL ORIENTATION
See Christian, Earth-Based Spirituality, Eastern Spirituality, Jewish, Theosophy

SQUATTERS
FreetheLand, TownHead.

STEINER, RUDOLF
CamphillKimb, CamphillMinn, CamphillMour, CamphillNewt, CamphillSolt, CamphillSpec, CamphillTrif, FellowshipCo, MaisonEmmanu.
SEE ALSO: Anthroposophy, Biodynamics, Camphill, Waldorf

STEWARDSHIP

Aerious, BlueMoonCoop, Breitenbush, CircleDivine, CommonPlace, DancingRabbt, EarthArtVill, FairviewCoop, GlobalVillag, HeartwoodIns, JupiterHollo, LamaFdtn, LandSteward, Ness, OakwoodFarm, OjaiFdtn, ShannonFarm, SharingCmty, Sweetwater, TresPlacitas, UnionAcres, WholeVillage, WildIrisRnch, ZuniMountain.
SEE ALSO: Land Trusts, Sustainability, Nature Preserves, Wildlife Sanctuaries

STRAW-BALE BUILDINGS

AgapeMA, CaveCreek, CircleSpring, ConcordOasis, DancingRabbt, DawningStar, HighFlowing, SkyHouse, TenStones, UnionAcres, WindTreeRnch, Windwalker.

STUDENT CO-OPS

StevensHouse, BealHouse, BowerHouse, BrownAssoc, BuckmanHall, CollegiatLiv, ElsworthCoop, FerencyCo-op, GlenwoodCoop, GregoryHouse, Henderson, Homestead, ICC-AnnArbor, ICC-Austin, JointHouse, KingHouse, KingmanHall, LesterHouse, LinderHouse, LivingROCK, LutherBuchel, ManzanitaVil, MichiganSoc, Minnie'sCoop, Nakamura, NewCommunity, O'KeefeCoop, OfekShalom, Osterweil, OwenHouse, PhoenixCoop, PioneerCoop, RenaissanceC, RidgeHouse, Ruth'sHouse, SBSHC, SenecaFalls, SherwoodCoop, SojournerTru, Spadefoot, StudentHerit, StudentsCoOR, SynergyHouse, UniversitSCA, VailHouse, VarsityHouse, Watermargin.

STUDY PROGRAMS
See Work-Study, Schools—Adult

SUBSTANCE ABUSE
See Recovery

SUFI
Abode, Anaami, SouthwestSuf.

SUSTAINABILITY

Ainaola, BackyardTech, CentreforAlt, Chickenshack, ComGround-ON, EarthArtVil, EarthHeartCe, EastBayCoho, EastWind, EcoCityProj, EdenRanch, EmeraldEarth, FairviewCoop, FarmThe, FullMoonRisi, HeiWa, KynHearth, Meadowdance, Monadnock, Montclaire, OakGroveFdtn, SowingCircle, TerraNova, WAHOO!, WaitakereEco.
SEE ALSO: Ecological Sustainability, Ecovillages

SUSTAINABLE AGRICULTURE

AbunDawn, AlchemyFarm, AtlantisRis, CedarHollow, CircleSpring, HighFlowing, JohnTLyleCtr, JumpingOffCLT, PaganIsland, RosewindCoho.
SEE ALSO: Agriculture, Biodynamics, Bioregionalism, Food—Producers, Greens, Organic Farming, Organic Gardening, Permaculture

SUSTAINABLE DEVELOPMENT
Aleskam, AssocEarth, SanMateoCoop.

SUSTAINABLE ECONOMICS
GAIACmty.
SEE ALSO: Bioregionalism, Cooperation

SUSTAINABLE LIVING

Birdsfoot, ColibriUrban, Damanhur, EastBayCoho, EmeraldEarth, EsseneCoop, HighWind, JumpingOffCLT, LakeVillage, MorningStarR, SharingCmty, Songaia.

SWEAT LODGES
Nishnajida, PhantoBolo, Songaia.

SWEDEN
Stiftelsen, KadeshBiyqah, Lindsbergs, Tulstugan.

SWITZERLAND
ZentrumWalde.

TANTRIC
Nasalam.

TAOIST
TaoWorksVil.

TECHNOLOGY
See Alternative/Appropriate Technology, Building Technology

TELEVISION/CABLE ACCESS
ZendikFarm.

TEXTILE-FREE
AquariusNat.
SEE ALSO: Clothing-Optional

THEATER
AquarianConc, Atlantis, Ida, RainbowPeace, StoneGrail, UFA-Fabrik.

THEOSOPHY
PumpkinHolNY.

THERAPY

BurchHouse, CamphillClan, CamphillTrif, Goodenough, HumanityRis, Lebensgarten, LothlorienBR, OshoMiasto.
SEE ALSO: Feedback, Disabilities, Human Potential, Massage, Peer Counseling, Personal Growth, Recovery

THIRD WORLD
EmmausHaarz, RenaissanceV.

TIBETAN BUDDHISM
See Buddhism

TRANSFORMATION
See Light Centers, New Age, Self-Realization

TREES
See Forestry, Orchards

TRIBAL

Ainaola, Atlantis, Folkhaven, HealingGrace, HighFlowing, Nasalam, RiverHayven, Tonantzin, Tribe.The.
SEE ALSO: Extended Family

TWELVE-STEP PROGRAMS
See Recovery

TWELVE TRIBES

12CmtyBellow, 12CmtyBoston, 12CmtyBuenos, 12CmtyCambr, 12CmtyCrox, 12CmtydeSus, 12CmtyHambur, 12CmtyHyan, 12CmtyIsland, 12CmtyLakeOz, 12CmtyLancas, 12CmtyLondri, 12CmtyNet, 12CmtyOahHill, 12CmtyOberbr, 12CmtyPalen, 12CmtyPennin, 12CmtyQuatro, 12CmtyRutlan, 12CmtySanSeb, 12CmtyStentw, 12CmtySydney, 12CmtyWestPa, 12CmtyWinnip.

UFOS
MethowCenter.

UNDERGROUND BUILDINGS
RavenRocks.
SEE ALSO: Passive Solar Buildings

UNITED KINGDOM
AshramCmty, BarnThe, BeechHill, BeisAharon, BirchwdHall, CamphillClan, CamphillMour, CamphillNewt, CamphillPenn, CentreforAlt,

Note: *This index was created from the actual words used in each community's listing, with the exception of the asterisked (*) categories, which were compiled from the answers to a question on our survey. Categories in italic refer the reader on to other related categories.*

Index

Communities Magazine Back Issues

FROM 1972 TO THE PRESENT, *Communities* magazine has consistently offered excellent information, stories, and community wisdom to the movement. Here is a list of all those back issues, which the Fellowship for Intentional Community is proud to make available. Single issues are $6 each; double issues count as two.

Communitas #1*: A New Community Journal; Virginia communities; Philadelphia Life Center; Alpha Farm. (Jul '72)

Communitas #2*: Country life; conferences; Meadowlark therapeutic community; School of Living; Mulberry Farm; Arthur Morgan. (Sep '72)

#1 Directory '72: Membership selection, Camphill Village; Twin Oaks; women and communal societies. (Dec '72)

#2 Law, Communes, Land Trusts: Rural poverty; Open Gate; Papaya; Changes Therapeutic Community. (Feb '73)

#3 Community Market Development: Ananda; economic Clearinghouse. (Spr '73)

#4 Schools and Community: The Vale School; The Farm; community heritage. (Sum '73)

#5 Personal Change/Social Change: Community culture; Boston co-op houses; group relationships. (Oct '73)

#6 Overseas Community: May Valley Co-op; Christian communes; back-to-the-land. (Jan '74)

#7 1974 Directory: Women in community; Prisoners' struggles; People of Color and community. (Mar '74)

#8 Individuality and Intimacy: Jealousy, open relationships, couples, singles; Christian homesteading. (May '74)

#9 Children in Community: Iris Mountain; Twin Oaks; Ananda; children's books. (Jul '74)

#10 Work: Labor credit systems; Times Change process. (Nov '74)

#11 Land Reform: Ownership and use; planning; living on the land; Paolo Soleri; energy. (Dec '74)

#12 Directory '75: Karum; networking; building new society. (Jan '75)

#13 Spiritual Life in Community: Christian, ashrams, secular, atheist, ritual; composting. (Mar '75)

#14 Therapy: encounter groups; spiritual therapy; overcoming jealousy; The Farm. (May '75)

#15 Research and Education in Community: Survival schools; martial arts; Paolo Soleri interview. (Jul '75)

#16 Planning: Ecology and economics; short and long-range contingencies; why plan? land use; alternative energy. (Sep '75)

#17 Family, Sex, and Marriage: Gay relationships; gender roles; childrearing; spiritual marriage; German communes. (Nov '75)

#18 Directory '76: Government; Twin Oaks; Project Artaud; East Wind. (Jan '76)

#19 Urban Communities: New Haven; Twin Cities; Phil. Life Ctr; take back the night; structure and decision making. (Mar '76)

#20 Middle Class Communes: How to start; interpersonal skills; teenagers in communes; sharing housework. (May '76)

#21 Kibbutzim: Local relations; Ananda Co-op Village; social planning; food co-ops. (Jul '76)

#22 Networking in the Ozarks: Kibbutz family; norms vs. rules; community market; Findhorn. (Sep '76)

#23 Women and Work in the Kibbutz: Rainbow Family; leaving community; Project America. (Nov '76)

#24 Building Community: Physical design; culture; decentralized politics; Directory '77; Another Place Farm. (Jan '77)

#25 Don't Start a Commune in 1977: … join an existing one instead; Neighborhood Planning Council in DC; first FEC assembly, international communities. (Mar '77)

#26 Rebuilding the City: Urban co-ops: Austin, NY, DC, Greenbriar Community. (May '77)

#27 Movement for a New Society: Social class; long-range planning; older women; Plowshare Community. (Jul '77)

#28 Seabrook: A political community; middle-aged men in community; ex-Twin Oakers. (Sep '77)

#29 Democratic Management: Consensus; leadership; group consciousness; The Ark. (Nov '77)

#30 Directory '78: School of Living and Deep Run Farm; financing; Roger Ulrich interview. (Jan '78)

#31 Learning in Community: Teaching and learning for all ages; spiritual abortion. (Mar '78)

#32 Future of Community: FEC; Cerro Gordo; Karass; The Community Soap Factory. (May '78)

#33 A Woman's Issue: Mothers and daughters; Virginia Blaisdell interview; feminism in MNS; nontraditional work. (Jul '78)

#34 West Coast Communal Movement: Hoedads, Alpha Farm, co-op grocery, salvage biz, other activities in CA and OR. (Sep '78)

#35 Consumer Co-op Bank: Income and resource sharing; Utopian heritage. (Nov '78)

#36 Kerista: British Columbia; Circle of Gold. (Jan '79)

#37/38 Guide to Cooperative Alternatives: Double issue on community participation, social change, well-being, appropriate technology, networking; *Directory of Intentional Communities*; resource listings. $15, 184 pgs. (Sum '79)

*Communitas was a predecessor to *Communities* that ran for two issues.

#39 Federation Women: The Hutterites; travel ashram community; Healing Waters; Industrial Co-op Assoc. (Aug '79)

#40 Worker-Owned Businesses: Community development; urban ecology; feminist credit union; trusteeship. (Oct '79)

#41 Relationships: Friendships, family, sexuality; Renaissance Community. (Dec '79)

#42 Regionalism—The Southeast: Another Place; Co-op Anti-nuke; community resources. (Feb '80)

#43 Health and Well-Being: Massage; setting up a tofu kitchen; feminist retreat; radical psychiatry; cmty health clinic. (Apr '80)

#44 Consumer Cooperative Alliance: Housing; food; arts; energy. (Jun '80)

#45 Art Collectives: Freestate Anti-nuke; Rainbow Family; women in Oregon communities. (Oct '80)

#46 Directory '81: Culture; pregnancy; econ.; potlatch. (Dec '80)

#47 Stories: Cmty organizing; economics and work; culture. (Feb '81)

#48 Communities Around the World: Cuba, China, Israel, India, Spain, El Salvador, England. (Apr '81)

#49 Tempeh Production: Overcoming masculine oppression; social change; credit unions; insurance. (Jun '81)

#50 Dying: Hospice, grieving, death in community, rituals, practical guide to home death. (Oct '81)

#51 Political Paradigms for the '80s. (Dec '81)

#52 Barter Network: Santa Cruz Women's Health Collective; worker-owned businesses. (Feb '82)

#53 Spiritual Communities: Lama, Sirius, The Farm, Renaissance, Abode of the Message, Shambhala. (Apr '82)

#54 Peace: Bright Morning Star interview; social activism; community land trust; Meg Christian; kibbutz. (Jun '82)

#55 Building Economic Democracy: Co-op Bank; legal network; worker buyout; unions. (Oct '82)

#56 10th Anniversary Issue and Directory '83: best of *Communities*. (Dec '82)

#57 Women in Business: Feminist therapy; Audubon Expedition; Women's Resource Distribution Company; science fiction; peace movement. (Feb '83)

#58 Co-op America Debut: Catalog; Sisterfire; Consumer Co-op Bank. (Apr '83)

#59 Computers: Arab/Jewish settlement; holistic living; growing pains. (Jul '83)

#60 Gatherings '83: Michigan public schools; Solidarity. (Oct '83)

#61 Parenting, Childcare, and Education: Co-op housing; Syracuse Cultural Workers; planning. (Win '84)

#62 Progressive Economics and Politics: Co-op housing; new ideas for your community and kibbutz society. (Spr '84)

#63 Living in Community: Stelle, Emissaries of Divine Light; peace efforts in Nicaragua; women's peace camp; democratic management. (Sum '84)

#64 Social Notes: The Great Alternative Life Group; old folks in a future world; case against consensus; kibbutz and educ. (Fall '84)

#65 Greenham Women's Peace Camp: The Farm; educ. for cooperation; justice in India; spiritual fraud; Jubilee Partners. (Win '84)

#66 Directory '85/'86: Builders of the Dawn; Rainbow Gathering. (Spr '85)

#67 Technology in Community: Sunrise Ranch, Ponderosa Village, Windstar. (Sum '85)

#68 Historic Communal Societies: Shakers; Harmony; Zoar; Amana; Icarians, Fourierists, and Llano. (Fall '85)

#69 South Africa: Appropriate technology for developing countries; community homes for the mentally disabled; Windstar Foundation. (Win '86)

#70 San Francisco Bay Area: Co-ops, clinics, housing, the Cheeseboard Collective. (Spr '86)

#71/72 Model Communities: Past, present, future; historic future cities; Kerista: polyfidelity. (Sum/Fall '86)

#73 FEC—10 Years: Social, gender, political, organizational issues. (Win '87)

#74 Urban Middle-Class Communes: Sirius; Clairemont Project; Ozark Regional Land trust; Aprovecho and End of the Road; alternative special education; Findhorn. (Sum '87)

#75 Planetization: Gaian politics, faith for the planetary age, Green mvmnt, eco-feminism, deep ecology, Christian stewardship. (Sum '88)

#76 Education in Community: Cooperative alternative education, Twin Oaks, Stelle, Mt. Madonna School, Centrepoint, Camphill Villages, The Farm School. (Spr '90)

#77/78 1990–91 Directory of Intentional Communities: All feature articles in first edition of *Directory*. 129 pgs. (Nov '90)

#79 We're Back(!): FIC Highlights; Directory update. (Win '93)

#80/81 Vision and Leadership: Buddhist community, What happened to Kerista?, the URI split up, Sunflower House, Co-op America, collaborative decision making. (Spr/Sum '93)

#82 Women in Community: Women at Twin Oaks, The Farm; Women in Bruderhof, Hutterite, Shaker, Oneidan communities; Maggie Kuhn. (Spr '94)

#83 Celebration of Community: Highlights of the Aug '93 gathering: Kirkpatrick Sale/Bioregionalism, Dorothy Maclean/ Findhorn, Corinne McLaughlin/leadership, Gordon Davidson/spiritual economics, Noel Brown/environment; founders panels. (Sum '94)

#84 Growing Up in Community: Idyllic, nurturing, humorous, confusing, and frightening aspects of community childhood—in commune, kibbutz, The Farm, Christian, Bruderhof, activist, and secular egalitarian communities. (Fall '94)

#85 What We Have Learned: The Transition at King View Farm, Co-op Wars; A Closer Look into "Cults." (Win '94)

#86 Nurturing Our Potential: "We Have to Keep Growing?", Toward Gender Harmony, Conflict, Multiple Parenting. (Spr '95)

#87 Love, Romance and Sex: Community Ideals and Personal Loves; Re-Sacralizing Marriage; ZEGG; Healing from Abuse in Community; Spiritual Growth and Multiple Relationships. (Sum '95)

#88 Intentional Communities and "Cults": What Really Happened at Waco?; Religious Intolerance; Deprogramming Our Members. (Fall '95)

#89 Growing Older in Community: Choosing to Age in Community; Supporting the Aging Process in Community; Listening to the Wisdom of Our Elders; Stephen Gaskin on Rocinante; "Benevolent Dictators" in Community? (Win '95)

#90 Diversity, Homogeneity in Community: Are We Keeping Culturally Diverse People Out?; A Multicultural Neighborhood; Hidden Selectors; Cultural Etiquette; Racism and Denial. (Spr '96)

#91 Ecovillages: What Is an Ecovillage? Setting Up an Ecovillage Where You Are; Planning and Zoning—Encouraging News; Ecovillages in Ithaca, Israel, Canada, Scotland, Senegal. (Sum '96)

#92 Christian Communities Then and Now: A Shiloh Sister's Story; Southern Hospitality, "Cotton Patch" Style; Where Have All the (Seventies) Communities Gone?; Authority and Submission in Christian Communities. (Fall '96)

#93 Celebrating Arts and Creativity: And the Tree of Life Rises; Let's Dance!; Flowering of Art at East Blair; Chaos, Control, and the Courage to Create; Community as Performance Art. (Win '96)

#94 Making a Living: Boss? What Boss?; Profit is Not a Dirty Word; Creating Value-Added Products; Making It On Our Own; Work and Commitment in Two Communities; Telecommuting; Making a Living or Making a Life. (Spr '97)

#95 Sustainable Building and Design: Building with Nature, Earth, Magic; How Not to Build Your Community Home; Whole-Systems Design for Earthaven Village; Recycling Old Buildings. (Sum '97)

#96 Breaking Bread in Community: Food Fight!; Dinners at the Sharingwood Cafe; Wildcrafting in Our Yard; Growing Your Own and Selling It, Too; Dining in Cohousing. (Fall '97)

#97 25th Anniversary Issue!: Lessons from the Communes; The Way We Were; Communities Movement Today; The "Shadow Side" of Community; 25 Years of *Communities*. (Win '97)

#98 Values, Vision, and Money: Manifesting Our Dreams; Money as "Shadow" Issue at Findhorn; Identity and Money at Shenoa; Social Class and Money; How Much is Enough?; Confronting the Petty Tyrant; Mega-Bucks Money Pressures in Community? (Spr '98)

#99 Sustainable Communities: Living the Permaculture Dream; Building Design That Fosters Community; What Does Your Land Say?; Building with Mud!; Salvaging Building Materials; What is Bau-Biologie and How Can You Use It?; Using the Internet to Find Your Community. (Sum '98)

#100 Political Activism in Community: Risking Jail; Agents of Goodwill; Health Care as Politics in Ecuador; Community Living as a Political Act; An Ecovillage on Erin's Isle. (Fall '98)

#101 Communities, the Millennium, and Y2K: The Year 2000: Social Chaos or Social Transformation; How Communities are Preparing; How I "Got It" About Y2K; Patch Adams on the Movie "Patch Adams" (Win '98)

#102 Health and Healing: Patch Adams on Health and Healing; Is Community Good for Your Health?; Staying Healthy in Community; When Your Community is Criticized on National TV? (Spr '99)

#103 Walden Two Communities: Where Are They Now? Science of Behavior, Sí!; Growing Up at Los Horcones; Path with a Behaviorist Heart; Damanhur: "Magical Mystery Tour" (Sum '99)

#104 Conflict and Connection: Living "Naka-Ima" at Lost Valley; Assessing Community Well-Being; About Open-Hearted Listening; Working with Difficult Meeting Behaviors; Nonviolent Communication: Transforming Conflict and Enhancing Connection. (Fall '99)

#105 Transition and Change: Death and Rebirth at Skywoods; The Many Lives of Hof Marienhöhe; Hard Fall to Accountability; Community Life in the 21st Century; Finding New Members. (Win '99)

#106 Cohousing Communities: Building a Green Community on a Budget; Reinvigorating Urban Neighborhoods; Building Community and Land Development-Incompatible Worlds?; Ten Principles for Cohousing Construction Management; The Cohousing Network; Sunday at Duwamish Cohousing. (Spr '00)

Communities Magazine Back Issue Order Form

Some back issues are out of print and available only as photocopies. Double issues count as two. All prices include shipping. (Orders from outside the US please add 10 percent.)

1 issue: $6

Multiple Copy Discounts
2–4 issues: $5 each
5–9 issues: $4.50 each
10–19 issues: $4 each
20 or more issues: $3.50 each

Complete Set of Back Issues
Includes both in-print and photocopied issues: $350

For more information, use the address or phone number at right, email us at fic@ic.org, or view our Web site at http://www.ic.org/

○ Individual Back Issues: Please send issue #s_____
for a total of _____ magazines. Cost (see Multiple Copy Discounts) $_____

○ Complete Set: All in-print and photocopied back issues: $350 $_____

Total amount (payable in US funds to *Communities*) $_____

(International orders add 10 percent for additional postage) $_____

Total enclosed/charged $_____

○ Charge Visa/MC/Disc # _____ Exp Date _____

○ Please do not share my name with like-minded organizations.

_____
NAME   EMAIL   PHONE DAY/EVENINGS

http://
_____
COMMUNITY/ORGANIZATION NAME (IF APPLICABLE)   WEB ADDRESS

_____
STREET   CITY/TOWN

_____
STATE/PROVINCE   ZIP/POSTAL CODE   COUNTRY   TODAY'S DATE

Please clip or photocopy and mail to: *Communities*, RR 1 Box 156-D, Rutledge MO 63563, USA. Or, call 800-995-8342 (660-883-5545), or email fic@ic.org

FIC Workshop Audio Tapes

E'VE PICKED OUT SOME FAVORITE AUDIO tapes of workshops, panels, forums, and keynote speeches from Fellowship for Intentional Community events and made them available. Don't miss what our experienced speakers had to say. Please circle the ones you want, and fill out the form below. Tapes cost $8.50 each, which includes postage for US orders, and every sixth tape is free.

Tapes From the 1993 Celebration of Community

C93-1   Health and Community Panel
C93-2   Challenges Facing the Communities Movement; *Caroline Estes.* Bioregionalism, Community, and the Future; *Kirkpatrick Sale*
C93-4   Founders Panel: Small, Rural Communities
C93-14   Founders Panel: Urban Communities
C93-15   Children in Community and Their Education; *Daniel Greenberg*
C93-17   Urban Ecovillage Process: Retrofitting for Sustainability; *Lois Arkin*
C93-20   The Post-Community Experience: Life After the Dream; *Joe Peterson*
C93-21   Children Who Grew Up in Community (adult discussion); *Susan Davenport-Moore*
C93-25   Polyfidelity Panel
C93-26   Founders Panel: Large, Spiritual Communities
C93-31   Introduction to Consensus; *Laird Schaub*
C93-35   Land Trust for Community; *Dan Questenberry*
C93-40   Founders Panel: Large, Rural Communities
C93-45   Introduction to Facilitation; *Laird Schaub*
C93-46   How to Love More Successfully: Polyfidelity; *Ryam Nearing*
C93-55   Everything You Wanted to Know about Starting Community; *Stephan Brown*
C93-57   Class Issues and Community Living; *Allen Hancock and Dawn Lamp*
C93-78   Prescription for Happiness—Love, Friendship, Community; *Patch Adams*
C93-78   The Future of Communities; *Corinne McLaughlin*

C93-97   Green Dollars: Setting Up and Running a Local Trade/Barter System; *Tony Hansen*

Tapes From Art of Community Conferences

069903   Affordable and Energy Efficient Design Features for Homes; *Roger Hadley*
069906   Rebuilding Communities: The Asset Approach; *John Kretzmann*
069909   Meetings that Inspire!; *Paul DeLapa*
069914   Resident Controlled Affordable Housing; *Hank Obermayer*
069918   Sustainable Communities in Urban Neighborhoods; *Arkin, Obermayer, Elizabeth*
069928   Building Better Communication Skills; *Betty Didcoct*
119703   Finding Your Community: An Art or a Science?; *Geoph Kozeny*
119704   Manifesting Our Dreams: The Process of Visionary Development; *Jeff Grossberg*
119705   Raising and Educating Children in Community; *Lerman, Klaif, Morris*
119706   Conflict: Fight or Flight or Opportunity: Attacking the Issue, Not Each Other; *Laird Schaub*
119708   Six "Ingredients" for Forming Communities That Help Reduce Conflict Down the Road; *Diana Christian*
119709   Building a Business While Building Community; *Arkin, Baker, Becker, Wallace*
119711   Where We Are on the Long and Winding Road: Visioning and Planning in Communities (2 tape set); *Jeff Grossberg*
119713   Legal Options for Communities; *Butcher, Hollis, Sirna*
119714   We Tried Consensus and Got Stuck: Now What?; *Caroline Estes, Laird Schaub*
119812   Consensus: Decisions That Bring People Together; *Caroline Estes*
119821   Cohousing Communities: North American Examples; *Kathryn McCamant*
119824   So You Want To Be in Business? The Nuts and Bolts of Getting It Going and Getting It Right; *Terry O'Keefe*
119834   Spirituality as a Foundation for Community; *Dr. Mary Curran*
119835   Advanced Consensus; *Caroline Estes*

Please photocopy this page and return with credit card information or a check or money order in US dollars to: FIC, RR 1 Box 156-D, Rutledge MO 63563, USA. Or, call 800-995-8342 (660-883-5545), or email fic@ic.org

Charge Visa/MC/Disc_____   Exp Date _____

❑ Please do not share my name with like-minded organizations.

NAME

COMMUNITY/ORGANIZATION NAME (IF APPLICABLE)

STREET

STATE/PROVINCE   ZIP/POSTAL CODE   COUNTRY

EMAIL

http://
WEB ADDRESS

CITY/TOWN

PHONE DAY/EVENINGS

TODAY'S DATE

Please send the circled tapes.
Every sixth tape is free.

_____ # of tapes

x $8.50, for a total of $_____

_____ # of free tapes $_____0_____
(International orders add
10% for postage) $_____

Total enclosed/charged $_____

Shipping charges for US orders already included.

Key to FIC Publications and Products

*T*HIS BOOK IS FULL OF OFFERINGS from the Fellowship for Intentional Community (FIC), and we provide this handy summary for all the FIC publications and products, letting you know how to order and where to find additional information in the *Directory*. All prices include shipping and are payable in US dollars. Costs for shipping via surface mail to addresses outside the United States are shown in parentheses.

Where to Contact

Communities
138-D Twin Oaks Rd
Louisa VA 23093 USA

Tel: 800-462-8240
(540-894-5798)

Email: order@ic.org
*Order on the Web via our
secure server*—
http://www.ic.org/

๏ *Communities Directory,* order additional copies for $34 ($38) each; quantity discounts available. See order form on page 456.

๏ *Communities* **magazine subscription,** $20 ($24) for a one-year individual subscription (four issues), $6 ($7) for a sample issue. See colored order card at the back of the book.

๏ *Visions of Utopia: Intentional Communities ... Cooperative Experiments to Build a Better World* $38 ($40). A full-length color video on community. Over two years in the making, it's an FIC/Community Catalyst Project joint venture, available in June 2000. See colored order card at the back of the book.

๏ *Communities Directory Update*—annual supplements of *Directory* additions and changes. One copy is free when you return the colored card at the back of the book, otherwise $5 ($8) one-time fee for every *Update* published for this edition. Also note that listings updates are summarized quarterly in *Communities* magazine.

๏ *Communities* **magazine back issues,** $6 ($7) each, quantity discounts available. See the complete list of back issues plus an order form, starting on page 450.

๏ *Building United Judgment,* a classic introduction to secular consensus, now published by FIC, $19 ($21).

๏ *A Manual for Group Facilitation,* another group process classic, laying out the fundamentals of whole-person facilitation—a must for those learning consensus. Now published by FIC, $19 ($21).

๏ **Community Bookshelf** is the FICs mail-order book business. (See ad on inside back cover.) It specializes in titles on community and sustainable living. Contact us for the most recent catalog, or visit http://bookshelf.ic.org/

๏ **Workshop audio tapes** from the 1993 Celebration of Community and the FICs Art of Community conferences. $8.50 each; quantity discounts available. See order form on previous page.

๏ *Community Library Reprint Packets* offer compilations (22–32 pages) of the best articles from various FIC publications on specific topics, such as *Finding Your Community Home* and *Leadership and Decision Making.* Call or write to request a complete listing and order form, or see ad on page 401.

๏ **FIC T-shirts,** 100 percent cotton, available in S, M, L, and XL sizes, $14 ($16). FIC logo T-shirt *(pictured at right)* available in the following colors: green logo on natural shirt, white logo on purple shirt, white logo on black shirt. Art of Community logo T-shirt *(not pictured)* available as black logo on white, red, and tie-dyed shirts.

FIC
RR 1 Box 156-D
Rutledge MO 63563 USA

Tel: 800-995-8342
(660-883-5545)

Email: fic@ic.org

FIC Membership, Events, and Movement Services

IN ADDITION TO ITS PUBLICATIONS AND PRODUCTS, the Fellowship for Intentional Community (FIC) produces events and provides the variety of services listed below. We invite readers inspired by our work to build a more cooperative world to consider supporting us as FIC members. Dues and donations—which are tax deductible—make up an important part of our budget, enabling us to carry out our ambitious programs.

FIC Membership

⚘ When you become an **FIC member,** your dues directly support the work of the organization. In return, you receive the following benefits: (1) the opportunity to join the Sunrise Credit Union, the only credit union operating within an intentional community (see ad on page 343); (2) discounts on selected FIC products, on advertising in *Communities* magazine, and on registration for FIC's Art of Community conferences; (3) invitations to our semi-annual organizational meetings; and (4) our periodic newsletter. Joining the Fellowship strengthens the whole communities movement. See the membership form on page 456.

FIC Events

⚘ Since 1997, the FIC has been hosting regional weekend conferences called the **Art of Community.** They are excellent opportunities to learn about and experience community—and a chance for some unparalleled networking. Contact us for information on when and where the next event will be, or see http://www.ic.org/.

⚘ FIC has created a model for bringing people together to talk about community—in whatever way that touches their lives. This is our **Community Dialog** project and we've prepared a packet of materials for hosting a discussion in your home or organization. It's fun and easy! Ask us for a packet.

⚘ Every six months, the FIC board and all those involved in the work of the organization gather for a four-day **organizational meeting,** in rotating locations across the continent and hosted by intentional communities. Meetings operate by consensus with opportunities for input from everyone in the room. Newcomers are always welcome. Contact us for information about the next meeting.

FIC Services, Updates, Referrals, and Feedback

⚘ The **FIC Loan Fund** has money for communities wishing to start or improve community businesses.

⚘ FIC is glad to receive **Additions and Corrections** to information in the *Communities Directory.* There is a form on page 456 for your convenience.

⚘ FIC maintains a **Database** of intentional communities, with more information than we can print in this book. Contact us for customized search requests; there may be a charge for this service, depending on the time needed to fulfill the request.

⚘ Visit the **Intentional Communities Web site** for a wealth of information on community, and links to individual community Web sites. http://www.ic.org/.

⚘ The FIC keeps **Feedback Files** on communities—if we've received any unresolved critical feedback on a community, we'll hold it in a file along with that community's response. For $1/community we'll send a summary of what we have. See page 427 for details.

Where to Contact

FIC
RR 1 Box 156-D
Rutledge MO 63563 USA

Tel: 660-883-5545

Email: fic@ic.org

Fellowship for Intentional Community Membership

Yes, I wish to join the Fellowship!

❏ New member ❏ Renewal

❏ Individual ❏ $30 basic ❏ $15 low-income

❏ Community ❏ $40 for 1–9 members ❏ $75 for 10–40 ❏ $100 for over 40

❏ Organization $50

❏ Donor ❏ Supporting $100 ❏ Sustaining $250 ❏ Sponsoring $500

❏ Check enclosed. ❏ Charge Visa/MC/Disc #_____

❏ Please do not share my name with like-minded organizations. Exp Date: _____

NAME OF INDIVIDUAL/CONTACT PERSON	EMAIL	PHONE DAY/EVENINGS

http://

COMMUNITY/ORGANIZATION NAME (IF APPLICABLE)	WEB ADDRESS	

STREET	CITY/TOWN

STATE/PROVINCE	ZIP/POSTAL CODE	COUNTRY	TODAY'S DATE	3.1

You can support the work of the FIC by becoming a **member**. In addition to a warm, fuzzy feeling, benefits include: eligibility to join the Sunrise Credit Union; discounts on FIC products, on *Communities* magazine advertising, and on registration to FIC Art of Community events; invitations to our semi-annual organizational meetings; and our periodic newsletter. Please photocopy this form, and mail with credit card information or payment to: FIC Membership, RR 1 Box 156-D, Rutledge MO 63563, USA. Or, email fic@ic.org, or call 660-883-5545. As a 501(c)3 organization, donations beyond basic membership are tax deductible. Thanks very much!

Communities Directory Additions and Corrections

Check all that apply: ❏ Community ❏ Resource ❏ Book/Video ❏ Correction ❏ Addition

http://

COMMUNITY/RESOURCE/BOOK TITLE	WEB ADDRESS	

CONTACT PERSON	EMAIL	PHONE DAY/EVENINGS

STREET	CITY/TOWN

STATE/PROVINCE	ZIP/POSTAL CODE	COUNTRY

YOUR NAME	EMAIL	PHONE DAY/EVENINGS

STREET	CITY/TOWN

STATE/PROVINCE	ZIP/POSTAL CODE	COUNTRY	TODAY'S DATE

3.1

Please use this form to let us know of any listings missing from this book, or contact information that is not accurate. The communities movement changes fast, and you can help us keep up. Send the names and addresses of any new communities or resources, old ones you know of that are not listed, or suggestions of titles to be added to our booklist. Also, if you discover any errors in what we have printed, such as disconnected phone numbers or closed PO Boxes, be sure to let us know that, too. Please photocopy this form, and mail to: Directory Changes, RR 1 Box 156-D, Rutledge MO 63563, USA. Or email them in, to fic@ic.org, or call 660-883-5545. Thanks!

Communities Directory Order Form

Number of *Directories*:_____ Total amount enclosed/charged: $_____

❏ Check enclosed.

❏ Charge my Visa/MC/Disc #_____

❏ Please do not share my name with like-minded organizations. Exp Date:_____

NAME	EMAIL	PHONE DAY/EVENINGS

http://

COMMUNITY/ORGANIZATION NAME (IF APPLICABLE)	WEB ADDRESS	

STREET	CITY/TOWN

STATE/PROVINCE	ZIP/POSTAL CODE	COUNTRY	TODAY'S DATE

3.1

Help us get the word out about communities—buy additional copies of the Directory for yourself or for your friends!
Price per single copy, shipping included (prices for shipping via surface mail to addresses outside the US in parentheses): $34 ($38) for individuals, $44 ($48) for institutions. All prices in US dollars.
Quantity Discounts
1-2 copies no discount, 3–4 copies 20% off, 5-9 copies 30% off, 10+ copies 40% off.
Call or email for a quote on shipping. Please mail this form with credit card information or payment to Directory, 138-D Twin Oaks Rd, Louisa VA 23093, USA. Or, email order@ic.org, call 800-462-8240, or order on our secure Web server, http://www.ic.org/